American River College Library
4700 College Oak Drive
Sacramento, CA 95841

The SAGE Handbook of
Social Work

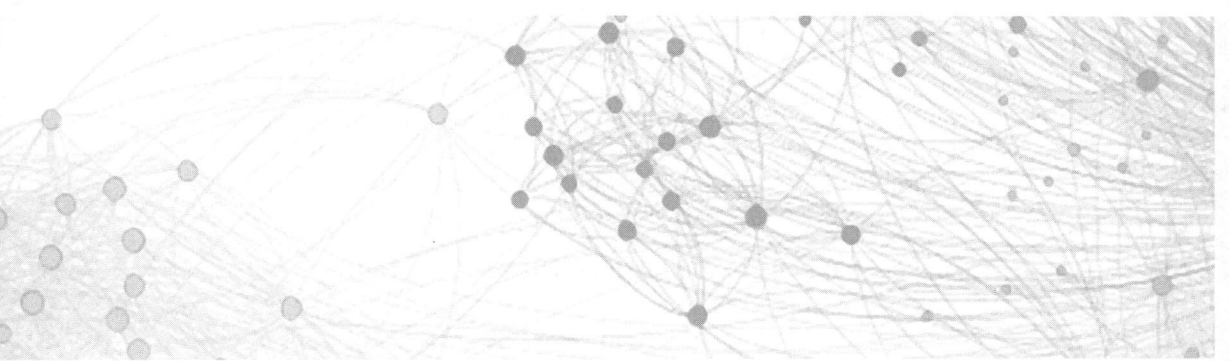

SAGE has been part of the global academic community since 1965, supporting high quality research and learning that transforms society and our understanding of individuals, groups, and cultures. SAGE is the independent, innovative, natural home for authors, editors and societies who share our commitment and passion for the social sciences.

Find out more at: **www.sagepublications.com**

The SAGE Handbook of
Social Work

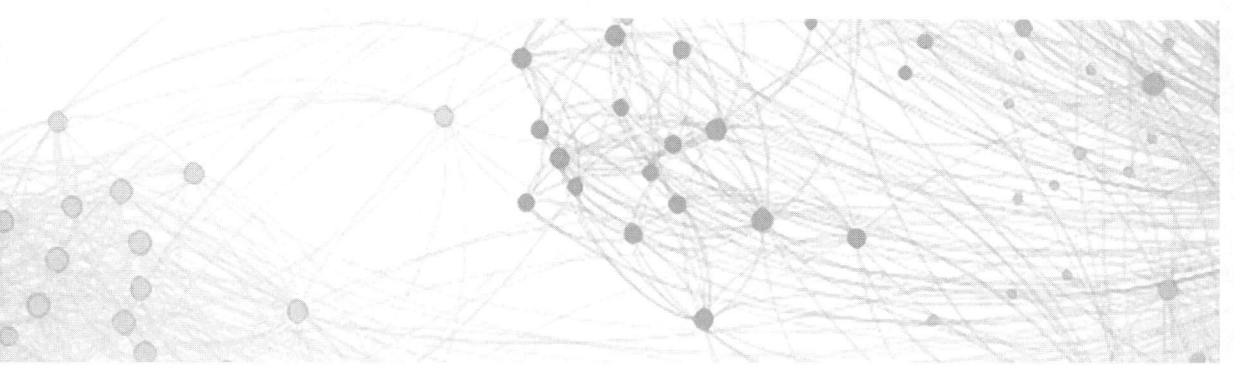

Edited by
Mel Gray, James Midgley and Stephen A. Webb

Los Angeles | London | New Delhi
Singapore | Washington DC

Introduction © Mel Gray, James Midgley and Stephen A. Webb 2012

Chapter 1 © David G. Gil 2012	Chapter 24 © Richard Hugman 2012
Chapter 2 © Mimi Abramovitz 2012	Chapter 25 © Daniel Gredig, Ian Shaw and Peter Sommerfeld 2012
Chapter 3 © Robert P. Fairbanks II 2012	Chapter 26 © Bruce A. Thyer 2012
Chapter 4 © Sanford Schram 2012	Chapter 27 © Brian J. Taylor 2012
Chapter 5 © Mary Daly 2012	Chapter 28 © Donald Forrester 2012
Chapter 6 © James Midgley 2012	Chapter 29 © Deborah K. Padgett 2012
Chapter 7 © Pamela Trevithick 2012	Chapter 30 © Mark Baldwin 2012
Chapter 8 © Gordon Jack 2012	Chapter 31 © Elaine Sharland 2012
Chapter 9 © Eileen Gambrill 2012	Chapter 32 © Stan Houston 2012
Chapter 10 © Jacqueline Corcoran 2012	Chapter 33 © Barbara Fawcett 2012
Chapter 11 © W. Patrick Sullivan 2012	Chapter 34 © Nancy R. Hooyman 2012
Chapter 12 © Karen Healy 2012	Chapter 35 © Romel W. Mackelprang 2012
Chapter 13 © Paula Doherty and Sue White 2012	Chapter 36 © Doreen Elliott and Uma A. Segal 2012
Chapter 14 © Eileen Munro 2012	Chapter 37 © Holly Matto 2012
Chapter 15 © Marlene G. Cooper and Joan Lesser 2012	Chapter 38 © Nicola Carr 2012
Chapter 16 © Barry Cournoyer 2012	Chapter 39 © Steven Walker 2012
Chapter 17 © Karen S. Haynes 2012	Chapter 40 © Paul Michael Garrett 2012
Chapter 18 © Keith Popple 2012	Chapter 41 © David Stoesz and Howard Karger 2012
Chapter 19 © Frederic Reamer 2012	Chapter 42 © Imogen Taylor 2012
Chapter 20 © Donna McAuliffe 2012	Chapter 43 © Thomas Ley 2012
Chapter 21 © Lena Dominelli 2012	Chapter 44 © Peter Beresford 2012
Chapter 22 © Brid Featherstone and Kate Morris 2012	Chapter 45 © Narda Razack 2012
Chapter 23 © Purnima Sundar, John Sylvestre and Amandeep Bassi 2012	Chapter 46 © Kwaku Osei-Hwedie and Morena J. Rankopo 2012
	Chapter 47 © Iain Ferguson 2012

First published 2012

Apart from any fair dealing for the purposes of research or private study, or criticism or review, as permitted under the Copyright, Designs and Patents Act, 1988, this publication may be reproduced, stored or transmitted in any form, or by any means, only with the prior permission in writing of the publishers, or in the case of reprographic reproduction, in accordance with the terms of licences issued by the Copyright Licensing Agency. Enquiries concerning reproduction outside those terms should be sent to the publishers.

SAGE Publications Ltd
1 Oliver's Yard
55 City Road
London EC1Y 1SP

SAGE Publications Inc.
2455 Teller Road
Thousand Oaks, California 91320

SAGE Publications India Pvt Ltd
B 1/I 1 Mohan Cooperative Industrial Area
Mathura Road
New Delhi 110 044

SAGE Publications Asia-Pacific Pte Ltd
3 Church Street
#10-04 Samsung Hub
Singapore 049483

Library of Congress Control Number: 2011938033

British Library Cataloguing in Publication data
A catalogue record for this book is available from the British Library

ISBN 978-1-84920-751-5

Typeset by Cenveo Publisher Services
Printed by MPG Books Group, Bodmin, Cornwall
Printed on paper from sustainable resources

Contents

	List of Editors and Contributors	ix
	INTRODUCTION *Mel Gray, James Midgley, and Stephen A. Webb*	1
	SECTION 1 WELFARE, SOCIAL POLICY, AND SOCIAL WORK	**15**
1	Social Work, Social Policy, and Welfarism *David G. Gil*	19
2	Theorising the Neoliberal Welfare State for Social Work *Mimi Abramovitz*	33
3	New Modalities of Welfare Governance *Robert P. Fairbanks II*	51
4	Welfare Professionals and Street-Level Bureaucrats *Sanford F. Schram*	67
5	Gender and Welfare *Mary Daly*	81
6	Welfare and Social Development *James Midgley*	94
	SECTION 2 SOCIAL WORK PERSPECTIVES	**109**
7	Practice Perspectives *Pamela Trevithick*	113
8	Ecological Perspective *Gordon Jack*	129
9	Behavioural Perspectives *Eileen Gambrill*	143

10	Family Perspectives *Jacqueline Corcoran*	161
11	Strengths Perspective *W. Patrick Sullivan*	176
12	Critical Perspectives *Karen Healy*	191

SECTION 3   SOCIAL WORK PRACTICE — 207

13	Knowledge for Reflexive Practice *Paula Doherty and Sue White*	211
14	Risk Assessment and Decision Making *Eileen Munro*	224
15	Integrative Psychotherapy *Marlene Cooper and Joan Lesser*	236
16	Crisis Intervention *Barry R. Cournoyer*	248
17	Empowering and Transformative Practice *Karen S. Haynes*	264
18	Community Practice *Keith Popple*	279

SECTION 4   SOCIAL WORK VALUES AND ETHICS — 295

19	Codes of Ethics *Frederic G. Reamer*	299
20	Ethical Decision Making *Donna McAuliffe*	316
21	Anti-Oppressive Practice *Lena Dominelli*	328
22	Feminist Ethics of Care *Brid Featherstone and Kate Morris*	341
23	Diversity and Social Work Practice *Purnima Sundar, John Sylvestre, and Amandeep Bassi*	355
24	Human Rights and Social Justice *Richard Hugman*	372

SECTION 5 SOCIAL WORK RESEARCH   **387**

25 Mapping the Social Work Research Agenda   391
    Daniel Gredig, Ian Shaw, and Peter Sommerfeld

26 Evidence-Based Practice and Social Work   408
    Bruce A. Thyer

27 Intervention Research   424
    Brian J. Taylor

28 Evaluation Research   440
    Donald Forrester

29 Qualitative Social Work Research   454
    Deborah K. Padgett

30 Participatory Action Research   467
    Mark Baldwin

31 Systematic Review   482
    Elaine Sharland

SECTION 6 SOCIAL WORK IN CONTEXT   **499**

32 Child and Family Social Work   503
    Stan Houston

33 Mental Health   515
    Barbara Fawcett

34 Older People   531
    Nancy R. Hooyman

35 Disability   547
    Romel W. Mackelprang

36 Immigrants and Refugees   564
    Doreen Elliott and Uma A. Segal

37 Drug and Alcohol Interventions   579
    Holly Matto

38 Criminal and Juvenile Justice   597
    Nicola Carr

39 Family Support Services   613
    Steven Walker

SECTION 7 FUTURE CHALLENGES FOR SOCIAL WORK   627

40 The Future(s) of Social Work   631
    Paul Michael Garrett

41 Social Work Education   646
    David Stoesz and Howard Karger

42 Interprofessional Practice   660
    Imogen Taylor

43 New Technologies for Practice   677
    Thomas Ley

44 Service-User Involvement   693
    Peter Beresford

45 International Social Work   707
    Narda Razack

46 Social Work in 'Developing' Countries   723
    Kwaku Osei-Hwedie and Morena J. Rankopo

47 The Politics of Social Work   740
    Iain Ferguson

    Index   755

List of Editors and Contributors

EDITORS

Mel Gray is Professor of Social Work and Research Professor in the Research Institute for Social Inclusion and Wellbeing, University of Newcastle, New South Wales, Australia. She has published extensively on social work and social development. Recent books include *Indigenous Social Work around the World* (with Coates & Yellow Bird, Ashgate 2008), *Social Work Theories and Methods* (with Webb, Sage 2008), *Evidence-based Social Work* (with Plath & Webb, Routledge 2009), *Ethics and Value Perspectives in Social Work* (with Webb, Palgrave 2010), *International Social Work* – 4 vols (with Webb, Sage 2010), *Environmental Social Work* (with Coates & Hetherington, Routledge 2012), *Decolonizing Social Work* (with Coates, Hetherington, & Yellow Bird, Ashgate 2012), *Social Work Theories and Methods* (2nd ed., with Webb, Sage 2012), and *New Politics of Critical Social Work* (with Webb, 2012 Palgrave). Mel is Associate Editor of the *International Journal of Social Welfare*.

James Midgley is Harry and Riva Specht Professor of Public Social Services at the School of Social Welfare University of California, Berkeley, USA. He has published widely on issues of social development, international social welfare, and social policy. Among his most recent books are *Social Security, the Economy and Development* (editor with Kwong-leung Tang, Palgrave 2008), *The Handbook of Social Policy* (editor with Michelle Livermore, Sage 2009), *Social Work and Social Development* (editor with Amy Conley, Oxford University Press 2010), *Grassroots Social Security in Asia* (editor with Mitsuhiko Hosaka, Routledge 2011), and *Colonialism and Welfare: Social Policy and the British Imperial Legacy* (editor with David Piachaud, Edward Elgar 2011). He is a Fellow of the American Academy of Social Work and Social Welfare and an Honorary Professor at the Hong Kong Polytechnic University, Nihon Fukishi University in Japan, the University of Johannesburg, South Africa, and Sun Yat-sen University in China.

Stephen A. Webb is Professor of Human Sciences and Director of the Research Institute for Social Inclusion and Wellbeing at the University of Newcastle in New South Wales, Australia and Visiting Professorial Fellow at University of Sussex, UK. His research focuses on theoretical approaches to social work drawing on contemporary social theory, evidence-based practice and social work ethics and values. He is author of several books including most recently *Social Work in a Risk Society* (Palgrave 2006), *Social Work Theories and Methods* (with Gray, Sage 2008) and *Evidence-based Social Work* (with Gray & Plath, Routledge 2009). He is co-editor (with Gray) of Sage's four-volume *International Social Work* (2009), which includes a selection of seminal social work texts, and *Ethics and Value Perspectives in Social Work* (with Gray, Palgrave 2009). Most recently, he has completed the second edition of *Social

Work Theories and Methods (with Gray, Sage) and *New Politics of Critical Social Work* (with Gray, Palgrave). In 2010 and 2012, he served on the Australian Research Council, Excellence in Research for Australia (ERA) panel member for the field of social work. His *British Journal of Social Work* article on evidence-based practice is the world's highest cited social work publication and ranked as the most influential journal article in the discipline over the past decade (Hodge et.al, 2011).

ASSOCIATE EDITORS

Lena Dominelli, Chair in Applied Social Sciences and Associate Director at the Institute of Hazards, Risk and Resilience Research at Durham University, has two major research projects on environmental issues and climate change and has a wealth of experience as an educator, researcher and practitioner. She has published widely, including several classics that have been translated into other languages. Her most recent books are: *Introducing Social Work; Social Work in a Globalising World*; and *Green Social Work*. A leading figure in social work education internationally, Lena was elected President of the International Association of Schools of Social Work from 1996–2004, chairs its Committees on Disaster Interventions and Climate Change and attended the UNFCCC discussions in Cancun and Durban. Lena has received various honours for her work.

Robert P. Fairbanks II, Assistant Professor at the School of Social Service Administration, University of Chicago, USA, has published works on welfare state theory, critical social policy analysis, and critical ethnography in the neoliberal city. His research focuses on ways in which informal poverty survival mechanisms articulate with the restructuring of the contemporary welfare state and political economy of cities. His most recent book *How it Works: Recovering Citizens in Post-Welfare Philadelphia* (University of Chicago Press 2009), is an ethnographic study examining how unlicensed, unregulated drug and alcohol recovery houses operate as street-level anti-poverty strategies and mechanisms of governmentality in postindustrial Philadelphia.

Paul Michael Garrett is the Director of Social Work at the National University of Ireland in Galway. He is the author of three books critically examining social work and social policy relating to children and families: *Remaking Social Work with Children and Families* (2003), *Social Work with Irish Children and Families in Britain* (2004), and *'Transforming' Children's Services?* (2009). His work has appeared in academic journals across a range of disciplines and he has presented papers at a number of international conferences. He is a member of the editorial boards of *Critical Social Policy* (where he is Editor of the Reviews Section) and the *European Journal of Social Work*.

Stan Houston qualified as a social worker in 1981. He then spent the following 16 years practising in a range of child and family social work settings in Belfast, Northern Ireland. In 1997, he entered higher education. Since then, his interests have focused on the application of critical social theory and moral philosophy to social work practice and research, particularly in the field of child welfare.

Brian J. Taylor (Ph.D.) is Senior Lecturer in Social Work at the University of Ulster in Northern Ireland. He previously spent 12 years as a social work practitioner and manager, and 15 years in social work training and organisation development in health and social care organisations. He has lead role at the University for social work research and for the development of post-qualifying education in social work. His main research and teaching interests are in research methods, decision making, assessment, risk, evidence-based practice, quality improvement, and interprofessional working.

Pamela Trevithick is Visiting Professor in Social Work at Buckinghamshire New University, UK, and author of the international bestselling text *Social Work Skills and Knowledge: A Practice Handbook* (Open University Press 2012) – a groundbreaking book translated into five languages: Chinese, Japanese, Swedish, Spanish, and Korean. She is the Chair of GAPS, a membership organisation established in 1984 to promote relationship-based approaches, and psychodynamic and systemic thinking in social work (gaps.org.uk). She is also a member of SWAN (Social Work Action Network), the former co-editor of the journal *Groupwork*, and a member of two other editorial boards – the *Journal of Social Work Practice* and *Communities, Children and Families Australia*.

Sue White is Professor of Social Work (Children and Families) at the University of Birmingham, UK. Her research focuses primarily on professional decision making in child welfare. She conducted two influential UK Research Council funded studies: on electronic information-sharing in multidisciplinary child welfare practice and the impact of performance management and the Integrated Children's System. She served on the Social Work Task Force and the Reference Group for the Munro Review of Child Protection in England. She is a member of the Social Work Reform Board, Chair of the Association of Professors of Social Work, and Editor in Chief of *Child and Family Social Work*.

CONTRIBUTORS

Mimi Abramovitz (DSW, Columbia University School of Social Work) is The Bertha Capen Reynolds Professor of Social Policy at The Silberman School of Social Work at Hunter School and The Graduate Center, CUNY, USA. She is also a member of the Consortial Faculty at the Murphy Institute for Worker Education and Labor Studies, CUNY. Widely published in the area of women, poverty, and the welfare state, she is the author of *Regulating the Lives of Women: Social Welfare Policy from Colonial Times to the Present*, the award-winning *Under Attack, Fighting Back: Women and Welfare in the US*, and co-author of *The Dynamics of Social Welfare Policy*, and *Taxes are a Women's Issue: Reframing the Debate*. She is currently writing *Gender Obligations: The History of Low-Income Women's Activism since 1900*.

Mark Baldwin, Senior Lecturer in Social Work at the University of Bath in the UK, teaches social work with adults, community profiling, and 'race' and racism to undergraduates, and participatory research methods to postgraduates. His research interests fall within a participatory methodology and have focused upon the empowerment of people with learning difficulties and the facilitation of workers in health and social work as they struggle to maintain professional knowledge and values in the face of managerialism. Mark is a member of the radical campaigning social work network SWAN (Social Work Action Network) and is on the SWAN National Committee. He contributed a chapter to the recent publication edited by Michael Lavalette, *Radical Social Work Today: Social Work at the Crossroads* (The Policy Press 2011).

Amandeep Bassi is a Ph.D. candidate in experimental psychology at University of Ottawa, Canada. She holds a Bachelor of Arts Honours degree in Psychology from Kwantlen Polytechnic University. Her research interest is aligned within the field of community psychology and lies specifically with the exploration of best practices in delivering supportive housing programmes. She has had direct experience of working with the community through a multi-agency evaluation of supportive housing in Ottawa, Ontario.

Peter Beresford OBE is Professor of Social Policy and Director of the Centre for Citizen Participation at Brunel University, UK. He is also Chair of Shaping Our Lives, the national service user and disabled people's organisation and network, and a long-term user of mental health services. He has a long-standing involvement in issues of participation and empowerment as a writer, researcher, educator, and campaigner. He is Visiting Professor at Edge Hill University, Liverpool, and a Trustee of the National Skills Academy for Social Care.

Nicola Carr is a Lecturer in the School of Sociology, Social Policy and Social Work at Queen's University, Belfast, Northern Ireland, where she teaches on social work in the criminal justice system. She is a trained practitioner and has previously worked as a Probation Officer in the UK. She has conducted a range of research with adults and young people involved in both criminal justice and child protection systems. She is currently undertaking a qualitative longitudinal study of young people leaving custody.

Jacqueline Corcoran (Ph.D.) is Professor at Virginia Commonwealth University, USA, where she teaches direct practice, human behaviour, and research. Her speciality areas are systematic review methodology, strengths-based models, and mental health. She has published over 50 articles and book chapters and 11 textbooks in social work, the most recent of which is *Child and Adolescent Mental Health* (2010 Oxford). and two forthcoming books from Oxford, *Research in Social Work* and *Helping Skills in Social Work* (see http://www.jacquelinecorcoran.com/).

Barry R. Cournoyer is a licensed clinical social worker and Professor of Social Work in Indianapolis, Indiana, USA. During his more than 30 years with the Indiana University School of Social Work, he has served as Associated Dean for Quality Improvement and Editor of the journal *Advances in Social Work*. He has published numerous journal articles, book chapters, and conference papers and authored or co-authored several books, including: *The Social Work Portfolio: Planning, Assessing, and Documenting Lifelong Learning in a Dynamic Profession* (2002), *The Evidence-Based Social Work Skills Book* (2004), *Social Work Processes* (7th ed., 2005), and *The Social Work Skills Workbook* (6th ed., 2011).

Mary Daly is Professor of Sociology at the School of Sociology, Social Policy and Social Work at Queen's University, Belfast, Northern Ireland. Among the fields on which she has published are poverty, welfare, gender, family, and the labour market. Much of her work is comparative, in a European and international context, and she is especially interested in matters to do with how policies in different European countries relate to gender and families. Her latest book, published by Polity in 2011, is entitled *Welfare*.

Paula Doherty qualified as a social worker in 2008 and is currently a doctoral student at the University of Lancaster, UK, working on an ethnographic study of decision making in child protection where cases are deemed to be on the 'edge of care proceedings'. Her interests include professional judgement and decision making in child welfare, and conversation and discourse analysis.

Doreen Elliott (Ph.D.) is a Professor of Social Work and Distinguished Teaching Professor at the University of Texas, Arlington, USA. She has published widely on international social work and social development. As well as numerous journal articles and chapters, she has published 11 books, including three international handbooks on social welfare, social work education, and social work theory and practice co-edited with Nazneen S. Mayadas and Thomas D. Watts. Most recently she has published *Immigration Worldwide* (2010) co-edited with Uma A. Segal and Nazneen S. Mayadas and *Refugees Worldwide* (2012), a four-volume series co-edited with Uma Segal.

Barbara Fawcett is Professor of Social Work and Policy Studies in the Faculty of Education and Social Work at the University of Sydney, Australia. Previously she was Head of the Department of Applied Social Science and Humanities at the University of Bradford, UK, where she is now Honorary Research Professor. Prior to entering the University of Bradford, she spent 13 years in the field. Her research interests focus on mental health, disability, women and violence, participative action research and postmodern feminism. She has written numerous books and articles and concentrates particularly on the inter-relationships between theoretical perspectives, policy, and practice.

Brid Featherstone is Professor of Social Care at the Open University, UK. She has worked as a social worker in the field of child welfare and has a particular interest in applying feminist theory to child welfare policies and practices. She is a founder member of the international network on gender and child welfare. Recent publications include *Working with Men in Health and Social Care* (with Scourfield & Rivett, Sage 2009) and *Contemporary Fathering* (The Policy Press 2009).

Iain Ferguson is a Senior Lecturer in Social Work in the Department of Applied Social Sciences at the University of Stirling, Scotland, and also a Research Fellow at the University of the Witwatersrand, South Africa. He is the author of a number of books and articles, including *Reclaiming Social Work: Challenging Neo-Liberalism and Promoting Social Justice* (Sage 2008) and *Radical Social Work in Practice* (with Rona Woodward, Policy Press, 2009). He is one of the authors of the *Manifesto for Social Work and Social Justice* (www.socialworkfuture.org) and a member of the Steering Committee of the Social Work Action Network.

Donald Forrester is Professor of Social Work Research at the University of Bedfordshire, UK, where he is Director of the Tilda Goldberg Research Centre. Professor Forrester worked for 10 years in child and family social work, before moving into research. His research interests have been driven by his practice concerns around what works for whom and how difficult assessment decisions are made. Over the last 10 years he has led a large number of research projects with funding in excess of £2 million using methodologies ranging from biographical and narrative approaches through to randomised controlled trials and quasi-experimental studies.

Eileen Gambrill is the Hutto Patterson Professor of Child and Family Studies at the School of Social Welfare, University of California at Berkeley, USA, where she teaches both research and practice. Her research interests include professional decision making, evidence-informed practice and the role of critical thinking within this, propaganda in the helping professions and its harmful effects, and the ethics of helping. Recent publications include *Critical Thinking in Clinical Practice: Improving the Quality of Judgements and Decisions* (3rd ed., John Wiley & Sons), *Social Work Practice: A Critical Thinker's Guide* (3rd ed., Oxford), *Critical Thinking for Helping Professionals: A Skills-based Workbook* (3rd ed.,with Len Gibbs, Oxford), *Propaganda in the Helping Professions* (Oxford 2012).

David Gil was born in 1924 in Vienna, Austria, and was forced to leave his home and family following the German occupation in 1938. He worked on farms in Sweden and Palestine, and in social services in Palestine, Israel, and the USA. He earned a doctorate in social welfare at the University of Pennsylvania. He has taught at the Heller School for Social Policy and

Management, Brandeis University from 1964 until 2011. His publications include *Violence against Children*, *Unravelling Social Policy*, *The Challenge of Social Equality*, *Beyond the Jungle*, *Confronting Injustice and Oppression* and over 50 essays in professional journals.

Daniel Gredig is Professor and Dean of Master-Studies in Social Work at the University of Applied Sciences Northwestern Switzerland, School of Social Work. He was trained in social work at the University of Fribourg (Switzerland) and at the Freie Universität Berlin (Germany). He received his Ph.D. from the University of Zurich. His research and publications of the last years have focused on the history of social work, research-based intervention development and innovation in social work, HIV prevention, HIV protective behaviour and social services for people living with HIV and AIDS.

Karen S. Haynes, President of California State University San Marcos, USA since 2004, was previously President of the University of Houston-Victoria for 8.5 years and Dean of the Graduate School of Social Work for ten years. Dr Haynes has moved from social worker to social transformer, long championing higher education as an engine of individual opportunity and regional vitality. Under her leadership, the university has won acclaim for excellence in 21st-century learning, educational access, and diversity, and for institutional accountability and community engagement. She has authored numerous articles on political social work and co-authored the landmark text, *Affecting Change: Social Workers in the Political Arena.*

Karen Healy is Professor of Social Work at The University of Queensland, Brisbane, Australia. She has written extensively on social work theory and practice. Her research interests include constructive critical practice, particularly in work with vulnerable children and young people, and their families, international comparison of child welfare systems, and professional identities and workforce development in social work and human services. Her current research projects include family participation in child welfare practice, analysis of family support and crisis interventions with homeless families, and best practice in professional support and development of newly qualified social workers.

Nancy Hooyman, Dean Emeritus at the University of Washington, School of Social Work, USA, holds the Hooyman Professorship of Gerontology. Nationally recognised for her scholarship in ageing and multigenerational policy, gender inequities in family caregiving, and feminist gerontology, she has published ten books and more than 130 articles and chapters on gerontological issues. She is Co-Principal Investigator of the Council on Social Work Education's National Center for Gerontological Social Work Education. A Fellow in the Gerontological Society of America, she received the Significant Lifetime Achievement in Social Work Education Award from the Council on Social Work Education in 2009.

Richard Hugman is Professor of Social Work at the University of New South Wales, Sydney, Australia. Formerly a social work practitioner, he has since taught and researched in universities in Australia and the UK. His recent work has focused on ethics (*New Approaches in Ethics for the Caring Professions*, Palgrave 2005) and international social work (*Understanding International Social Work: A Critical Analysis*, Palgrave 2010). He is Chair of the International Federation of Social Workers' permanent committee on ethics and acted as a consultant for UNICEF Vietnam to advise the Vietnam Government on the establishment of professional social work there.

Gordon Jack is Professor of Social Work at Northumbria University, UK. He worked for 15 years as a practitioner and manager in local authority children's services in the north of

England before taking up his first academic post at Exeter University in 1991. He moved to Durham University as Reader in Social Work in 1996 and took up his current post in 2011. His main research interests lie in the fields of social ecology, social policy, and child well-being. Most recently, he has investigated the influence of children's attachments to the places in which they have grown up on their identity, sense of security and belonging, with a particular focus on promoting the place attachments of children in care.

Howard Karger is Professor and Head of the School of Social Work and Human Services, University of Queensland, Australia. A two-time Senior Fulbright Fellow, he has published widely in national and international journals. His books include: *Shortchanged: Life and Debt in the Fringe Economy* (winner 2006 Independent Publishers Award in Investment/Finance/ Economics); *American Social Welfare Policy* (with D. Stoesz); *The Politics of Child Abuse and Neglect in America* (with D. Stoesz & L. Costin); *Social Work and Community in a Private World* (with R. Fisher); and *A Dream Deferred: How Social Work Education Lost Its Way and What Can Be Done* (with D. Stoesz & T. Carrilio).

Joan Granucci Lesser (Ph.D.) is founder and practising clinician with The Pioneer Valley Professionals, a multidisciplinary clinical practice in Holyoke, Massachussetts, USA. She is also Adjunct Associate Professor at Smith College School for Social Work, where she was former full-time faculty and Chair of Social Work Practice. Her most recent books include *Human Behavior and the Social Environment: Theory and Practice* (2nd ed. with D.S. Pope) and *Clinical Social Work Practice: An Integrated Approach* (4th ed. with M. Cooper). Her interests include multicultural clinical practice, research, and education; neurological disorders in children and adolescents; and the treatment of trauma.

Thomas Ley graduated in social pedagogy in Mainz, Germany. He spent 2005–2008 on a scholarship of the graduate programme 'Youth Welfare in Transition' funded by the German Research Foundation, located at Bielefeld University and 2009–2010 as a scientific assistant at the Center of Social Service Studies, Faculty of Educational Science, Bielefeld University. Currently, he is working in an EU research project 'Workable – Making Capabilities Work' at the Bielefeld Center for Education and Capability Research at Bielefeld University. His fields of interests include information technologies in social work, youth welfare research, residential care (as well from a historical perspective), and qualitative research in social work.

Romel W. Mackelprang is the Director of the Center for Disability Studies and Universal Access at Eastern Washington University, USA, where he has been a Social Work Professor since 1987. He has been involved in the disability rights movement and in independent living for more than three decades. His research and multiple publications apply a human rights approach to disability and have included spinal cord injury, brain injury, HIV and AIDS, and developmental disability. He recently initiated research in six African countries on the impacts of donated wheelchairs on people's lives in developing countries.

Holly C. Matto (MSW, Ph.D.) is Associate Professor in the College of Health and Human Services Department of Social Work at George Mason University in Fairfax, Virginia, USA. Prior to that Dr Matto was at VCU School of Social Work for ten years where she taught theories of human behaviour, direct practice, and research methods in the master's and doctoral programme. Her social work practice experience and current research interests are in substance abuse assessment and treatment innovations with adolescents and adults. She is currently conducting research that uses neuroimaging technology to examine brain change associated with behavioural health interventions for substance-dependent adults.

Donna McAuliffe is an Associate Professor in the School of Human Services and Social Work, Griffith University, Queensland, Australia. She has a diverse social work practice background and has worked in academia for the past 12 years, developing her specialisation in the field of professional ethics. She is the Convenor of the National Ethics Group for the Australian Association of Social Workers, and led the 2010 review of the AASW Code of Ethics. She regularly provides continuing professional education on ethical decision making for practitioners and managers in community and government organisations.

Kate Morris, Associate Professor in the Centre for Social Work, University of Nottingham, UK, is currently exploring the involvement of families in the reviews of cases when a child has died or suffered serious injury as a result of abuse and is leading an exploratory study of the lived experiences of families with multiple and complex needs. This builds on her previous work for the UK government as part of the 'Think Family' policy stream, and her work internationally reviewing the evidence concerned with the impact and effect of family decision making in care and protection.

Eileen Munro is Professor of Social Policy at the London School of Economics, UK. She was a social worker for many years before taking up an academic career. She has studied philosophy, in particular the philosophy of science, and this has fuelled her interest in the reasoning skills needed in social work. Her current research interests are in how best to combine intuitive and analytic reasoning in risk assessment and decision making in child protection. She is also studying the role of the wider organisational system in promoting or hindering good critical thinking.

Kwaku Osei-Hwedie (Ph.D.) is Professor of Social Work and Dean, School of Governance and Leadership at the Ghana Institute of Management and Public Administration. He has taught social work in the USA, and previously was head of department in the Universities of Zambia and Botswana, respectively. He has published extensively on social work and social development focusing on culturally relevant social work practice and education. His latest publications include *The Politics of Socio-Economic Development in Southern Africa* (with B.Z. Osei-Hwedie, GIMPA Press, Accra 2010) and *HIV/AIDS and Social Welfare: Issues in Prevention, Management and Care* (with B.Z. Osei-Hwedie & M.J. Rankopo, GIMPA Press, Accra 2010).

Deborah Padgett, Professor at New York University's Silver School of Social Work, USA, is an anthropologist and public health researcher. She has published extensively on health and mental health needs and service use of homeless adults and women at risk of breast cancer. She is the editor or author of four books including *Qualitative Methods in Social Work Research* (2008). Principal investigator on two R01 grants funded by the National Institute of Mental Health, Dr Padgett is currently leading a qualitative study examining housing and recovery among formerly homeless adults.

Keith Popple is Professor and Head of Social Work at London South Bank University, UK. Previously a field worker in social services, he has written widely about the relationship between 'community' and social work. He is joint author with Paul Stepney of *Social Work and the Community: A Critical Context for Practice* (Palgrave 2008) and a member of the Editorial

Boards of the *British Journal of Social Work*, and the *Community Development Journal*. The second edition of his well-received text *Analysing Community Work: Its Theory and Practice* (Open University Press) is due for publication in 2012.

Morena J. Rankopo (Ph.D.), Senior Lecturer and former MSW coordinator in the Department of Social Work, University of Botswana, has published on community development, gender mainstreaming in social work education, volunteerism and HIV and AIDS, community- and home-based care in HIV and AIDS, and culturally relevant social work practice and education. He is currently involved in training law enforcement officers on policing anti-gender-based violence in Botswana. His latest publication is *HIV/AIDS and Social Welfare: Issues in Prevention, Management and Care* (with B.Z. Osei-Hwedie & K. Osei-Hwedie, GIMPA Press, Accra 2010).

Narda Razack (Ph.D.) is Associate Dean, External, in the Faculty of Liberal Arts and Professional Studies and Associate Professor in the School of Social Work at York University in Canada. She co-edited the journal *Social Justice: A Journal of Crime, Conflict and World Order* and is currently involved in two funded research projects: *Assets Coming Together for Youth: Linking Research, Policy and Action for Positive Youth Development* and *Social Work in Nigeria*. She has published and continues to research in the areas of critical race and spatial and postcolonial theory focusing on North–South relations, globalisation, and critical international social work.

Frederic Reamer is Professor in the School of Social Work, Rhode Island College, Providence, Rhode Island, USA. Reamer is the author of *Social Work Values and Ethics*, *The Social Work Ethics Casebook*, *Ethical Standards in Social Work*, *The Philosophical Foundations of Social Work*, *The Social Work Ethics Audit*, *Social Work Malpractice and Liability*, *Heinous Crime*, and *Criminal Lessons*, among others. He is the author of chapters on professional ethics in the *Encyclopaedia of Social Work*, *Encyclopaedia of Bioethics*, and *Encyclopaedia of Applied Ethics*. Reamer chaired the committee that wrote the current NASW Code of Ethics.

Sanford Schram teaches social theory and policy in the Graduate School of Social Work and Social Research at Bryn Mawr College, USA. His publications include the award-winning *Words of Welfare: The Poverty of Social Science and the Social Science of Poverty* (1995), *Change Research: A Case Study of Housing Advocacy and Social Work Research* (2011) (with Corey Shdaimah and Roland Stahl), and *Disciplining the Poor: Neoliberal Paternalism and the Persistent Power of Race* (with Joe Soss and Richard C. Fording, 2011). Schram has published many articles and book chapters, including pieces in *Political Theory*, the *American Sociological Review*, *Polity*, the *American Political Science Review*, and the *American Journal of Political Science*.

Uma A. Segal (Ph.D.) is Professor and Director of the baccalaureate programme in the School of Social Work at the University of Missouri, St Louis, USA. Her areas of research interest and publication are immigrant and refugee concerns, Asian American acculturation, and cross-national issues in family violence. In 2004, Dr Segal was appointed Editor-in-Chief of the *Journal of Immigrant and Refugee Studies* and has moved toward making it a premier journal on international and interdisciplinary studies in migration. She is co-editor, with Doreen Elliott and Nazneen Mayadas, of Immigration worldwide (Oxford University Press, 2010) and, with Doreen Elliott, of Refugees worldwide (Praeger Publishers, 2012), and author of A framework for immigration: Asians in the United States (Columbia University Press, 2002).

Elaine Sharland is Senior Lecturer in Social Work and Social Care at the University of Sussex, UK. Her primary research interests are in social work and social care knowledge production and exchange, interdisciplinary research and capacity development, and young people and risk. She has a particular interest in the development of social work research and review methodologies, and is Director of the Sussex Registered Provider of Knowledge Reviews for the Social Care Institute for Excellence, England. During 2008–2010, she acted as Strategic Advisor for Social Work and Social Care Research to the UK Economic and Social Research Council.

Ian Shaw is Professor of Social Work in the Department of Social Policy and Social work at the University of York, UK, and Professor of Social Work. He co-founded the journal *Qualitative Social Work*, and the *European Conference for Social Work Research*. Much of his work is on the borders and research and practice, and sociology and social work, and is often informed by an interest in qualitative methodology. His recent work includes the *Sage Handbook of Social Work Research* a radical reworking of his *Evaluating in Practice* and *Practice and Research* (both Ashgate). His current research includes the historical relationship between social work and sociology, especially in the USA and Europe.

Peter Sommerfeld is Professor of Social Work at the University of Applied Sciences Northwestern Switzerland, School of Social Work. Recent research has been completed in the fields of probation services, psychiatry, and occupational social work. He has mostly published in German on a broad variety of themes, including social work research, professionalism, adventure pedagogy, social work and psychiatry, and social work and urban development. In English he has published on evidence-based social work. He teaches theories of social work and general systems theory. He is co-president of the Swiss Society for Social Work.

David Stoesz is Professor of Social Policy at Virginia Commonwealth University, USA, and Executive Director of Policy America, a nonprofit committed to innovations in social policy. His books include *American Social Welfare Policy* (with Howard Karger), *A Poverty of Imagination: Bootstrap Capitalism Sequel to Welfare Reform*, and *Quixote's Ghost: The Right, the* Liberati*, and the Future of Social Policy*, which won the 2006 Pro Humanitate Literary Award. His most recent book, *A Dream Deferred: How Social Work Education Lost Its Way and What Can Be Done* (with Howard Karger & Terry Carrilio) critiques the social work accreditation monopoly in the USA.

Patrick Sullivan serves as Professor at the Indiana University School of Social Work, USA. He also served as Director of the Indiana Division of Mental Health and Addiction from 1994 to 1998. While earning a Ph.D. at the University of Kansas, Sullivan helped develop the strengths model of social work practice, and has extended the model in mental health and addictions treatment. He received the Distinguished Hoosier Award from Governor Frank O'Bannon in 1997 and earned the Sagamore of the Wabash, Indiana's highest civilian award from Governor Joseph Kernan in 2004 for his work in mental health and addictions.

Purnima Sundar is Manager of Evaluation Support at the Ontario Centre of Excellence for Child and Youth Mental Health at the Children's Hospital of Eastern Ontario, Canada. Purnima works with child and youth mental health organisations to support the use of evidence-informed practice to improve mental health outcomes for children, youth, and families. She has over 12 years of experience doing community-based, participatory action research and programme evaluation in the areas of youth and mental health, and diversity and multiculturalism. Her research interests include working to understand how social workers can provide culturally appropriate mental health services to ethnoracially diverse families.

John Sylvestre is an Associate Professor in the School of Psychology, and a Senior Researcher at the Centre for Research on Educational and Community Services, at the University of Ottawa, Canada. He is currently Senior Editor of the *Canadian Journal of Community Mental Health*. He has many years of experience conducting research and programme evaluations of various aspects of local and provincial community mental health systems in Canada, including housing for people with serious mental illness, crisis intervention, and court outreach programmes.

Imogen Taylor is Professor of Social Work, University of Sussex, UK, moving there in 2001 from University of Bristol, School for Policy Studies where she worked for 10 years. She obtained her MSW at the University of Toronto, working in mental health before joining the Faculty of Social Work there. She was Co-Director of UK Higher Education Academy Social Policy and Social Work Subject Centre for five years and was awarded a National Teaching Fellowship in 2003. Her research is primarily in pedagogy for the professions. She joined the UK Social Policy and Social Work Research Excellence Framework Panel in 2011.

Bruce A. Thyer (Ph.D., LCSW) is Professor and former Dean, School of Social Work, Florida State University, USA, and before that, Distinguished Research Professor of Social Work, University of Georgia. He has authored or edited over 25 books in the fields of social work, psychology, and behaviour analysis, as well as more than 250 articles and 60 book chapters. His research interests are in the areas of evaluation research, evidence-based practice, clinical social work, applied behaviour analysis, and social work theory. He is the founding and current editor of *Research on Social Work Practice*, now in its 22nd year of publication.

Steven Walker trained in social policy and social work at the London School of Economics, UK, and worked in the field for 15 years in child protection, family support, and child and adolescent mental health services. His 15-year academic career includes undergraduate and postgraduate social work teaching, the development of an interprofessional child and adolescent mental health programme, and research into family support services, disability equality, children's rights, and the mental health of young soldiers.

Introduction

Mel Gray, James Midgley, and Stephen A. Webb

Welcome to the stimulating and engaging world of social work. The contexts for social work are often complex, usually demanding, and always challenging. Social workers today need to be knowledgeable, reflective, ethical, accountable, and professionally competent. As agents of change they are often involved in transformative roles that impact both socially and economically on service users. Most importantly, perhaps, social workers often take an ethical stance in defence of certain human rights, issues of social justice, and antidiscriminatory practice. The themes and content of social work knowledge are equally broad, diverse, and contestable.

The SAGE Handbook of Social Work is a one-stop reference work that captures and presents contemporary material in a comprehensive international collection. It is the world's first major reference work in the field with such a generic focus. It aims to provide a definitive benchmark by addressing new developments alongside more traditional ones in social work. This *Handbook* is a vital compendium that any researcher, student, practitioner, or policy maker can pick up and use for a number of different topics related to social work. It provides an authoritative guide to the theory, method, and values of the profession and pays close attention to the primary debates of today impacting on social work. Indeed, the uniqueness of this large volume is not only that it serves as a major reference work for students and practitioners but that it also provides the most comprehensive and authoritative survey of contemporary social work.

This international reference work is partly occasioned by the significant increase of worldwide interest in social work, leading some to consider that it has now reached global proportions. Increasingly, the social work knowledge base is drawing on international experience, through access to the variety of overseas research and practice examples. The movement towards developing a profession more confidently grounded in research has been one of the most significant international trends in social work during the past decade (Beddoe, 2011). It is also suggested that the problems experienced by service users are caused as much by global as by national forces, and local problems cannot be understood without reference to global economic, political, and cultural circumstances (Ife, 2000). This has led some to try to develop a common base of global social work practice. The volume is also occasioned by the growing awareness that very significant changes have taken place in social work in recent years. The net effect of new knowledge, policy, and rapid legislative changes in social work, coupled with shifting values around social justice, inclusion, and cultural recognition has been the proliferation of new approaches in social work. Social work has evolved greatly as both a field of professional practice and an academic discipline since its inception in the late 19th century. In addition, social work has had to confront new challenges from changing policy agendas, transitions in welfare, the shift of interest towards service-user involvement, the rise of evidence-based practice, the advent of globalisation and neoliberal politics, and the 'professionalisation' of frontline practice by a range of risk performance and regulatory regimes. It has done this while retaining a core set of values focusing on social justice, anti-oppressive practice, and the ethics of recognition. One of the distinctive features of social work is its continuing adherence to a set of progressive social values and ethical principles.

In undertaking this ambitious project, three leading international figures in social work, Mel Gray, James Midgley, and Stephen A. Webb were selected as editors to bring together the foremost international exponents of the different strands that contribute towards the makeup of modern social work. The editors were greatly assisted by a carefully selected group of associate editors, namely, Robert Fairbanks II (Section 1), Pamela Trevithick (Section 2), Sue White (Section 3), Lena Dominelli (Section 4), Brian Taylor (Section 5), Stan Houston (Section 6), and Paul Michael Garrett (Section 7). Each of these assistant editors provided essential expert evaluations of each chapter providing feedback to the editors on individual contributions. Drawn from an international field of excellence, the contributors were commissioned to use the most up-to-date research available to provide a critical, international analysis of their area of expertise. The result is this essential resource collection that not only reflects upon the condition of social work today but also looks to future developments.

Social work research and practice have changed enormously over the last 40 years or so, with the values, knowledge base and language constantly evolving. While this emerging diversity of practice approaches appears quite striking, there continues to be something of a 'mainstream' even though it is navigated by fewer than before.

Internationally, social work has grown in stature and influence, making important contributions to the social sciences. Social work holds special research promise because it explicitly attempts to cut across diverse social, cultural, economic, and political dimensions. Within the contemporary situation, social work also addresses many of the pressing problems facing people across the globe. In some key respects, social work is more than a field of interventions or set of ideas. It is, in effect, a response to and possible solution for the maladies of a postmodern world and hence, by implication, an ethical stance in contemporary societies. Perhaps this is a consequence of the fact that the emergence of social work in many countries has been explicitly tied to forms of political activism and community engagement. To a great extent, the pathways and procedures for developing social work follow not only from attention to a particular subject matter, modes of intervention, or theoretical perspective but also to a set of moral commitments. This *Handbook* seeks to identify the dimensions of social work and its varied effects, to discuss social work in relation to its intellectual history, its varying definitions and roles, its current affiliations and leanings and diverse objects of intervention, and its possible futures. The uniqueness and originality of contemporary social work is reflected in the sections into which the chapters have been grouped. These important dimensions were identified by carefully gathering together some of the most highly cited, influential, and seminal authors in social work as well as several new authors making promising contributions. This then is a presentation of international researchers' significant and original contribution to the field of social work today. In bringing together highly influential authors, and a range of contemporary concepts, methods and values, it is our intention that this major international reference in social work will be a valuable addition to students, researchers, practitioners, policy makers, government and nongovernment organisations, and specialists and nonspecialists in the fields of social work, human services, welfare, social pedagogy, community work, and social development. It is hoped that the reader will find *The SAGE Handbook of Social Work* a state-of-the art guide and invaluable reference work on the contemporary scene in social work as it is practised in diverse geopolitical contexts around the world.

NATURE AND ROLE OF SOCIAL WORK

Over recent years there has been extensive work from professional associations, key stakeholder organisations, researchers, and service-user groups in trying to identify the nature and role of social work. For example, a number of core principles have been identified as underpinning social work:

- it is a problem-solving activity;
- the focus is on the whole of a person's or family's life, their social support network, their neighbourhood, and community;
- the value system is based on human and civil rights;
- the social model is the framework for practice;
- social workers work with individuals, families, groups, or communities to define together the outcomes they are seeking;
- the process and the relationship are a core part of the service and can represent a service in itself;
- the purpose of social work is to increase the life chances and opportunities of people using services by building on their strengths, expertise, and experience to maximise their capacities (Brand et al., 2005, pp. 2–3).

It is generally agreed that any adequate understanding of the role of social work must take account of the interlocking nature of values, principles, and tasks. It is also recognised that, in order for social work to have legitimacy and currency, it has to have a balance between essential rules, principles, and professional expertise. However, as previously noted, it has proved enormously difficult to reach agreement about the nature and role of social work in modern societies (Gray & Webb, 2010). Indeed, the above core principles are partial and likely to provoke criticisms about various emphases, use of language, and coverage. For instance, some would strongly contest the claim that the value system is based on human and civil rights, arguing instead that these are just one small component of the core values (Webb, 2009). Establishing just what legitimate role social workers play will always be problematic in the absence of an agreed basis for the development of the 'profession' of social work. As long ago as 1915, Abraham Flexner (2001) raised the thorny question of whether social work constituted a profession in the strict sense of the term:

> Consideration of the objects of social work leads to the same conclusion. I have made the point that all the established and recognized professions have definite and specific ends: medicine, law, architecture, engineering – one can draw a clear line of demarcation about their respective fields. This is not true of social work. It appears not so much a definite field as an aspect of work in many fields. An aspect of medicine belongs to social work, as do certain aspects of law, education, architecture, etc (Flexner, 2001, p. 161).

Social work's disparate nature and loose boundaries have long plagued attempts to consolidate it as an enclosed configuration with a specific professional identity. However, though the roles attributed to social workers have changed and continue to be subject to review, the values and principles on which social work is based have remained relatively constant. Nevertheless, debate about the function and purpose of social work remains healthily contestable. As Askeland and Payne (2001) suggested: 'Social work has always been subject to competing claims of definition and practice, as social workers, politicians, service users and policy makers have struggled to lay claims on what social work is, and what it might be' (p. 14). This has much to do with the diverse and multidisciplinary nature of its concepts, methods, and values as well as it regional specificities and local determinations. It also has to do with debates, disputes, and sometimes irreconcilable tensions within the field of social work and beyond. So how one might one make sense of the nature and role of social work? As a professional field of intervention, it is characterised by specific forms of knowledge and method, and exhibits an internal logic which helps to define its main parameters. Indeed, the chapters in this volume provide a systematic resource to the leading perspectives and trends in social work. As discussed below, social work is not conceived as belonging to any one discipline, since the very nature of social issues stretch and form across the social sciences. However, in surveying the language, knowledge, research, purpose, professional affiliations, roles, practice interventions, and mandatory responsibilities, it might be asked whether it is possible to identify a particular logic or root rationality that finds a complex meaning in social work and moves it beyond its simple manifestation: Is there a single line of meaning or an essential rationality that structures the nature of social work? Put another way, is there a meta-rationality at work in all forms and aspects of social work that structures it to mesh in a particular way? It is possible to ask what is the underlying presuppositional logic that typically characterises social work? Through the important new texts gathered together in this volume, it is possible to discern an underlying logic to social work that is understandable as a sort of glue which holds it together. What is being sought here is structural similarity across fields in social work. There is a level of integration which underpins social work such that its constituting formative rationality can be accurately identified. There is a peculiar knot that social work posits between a two-level structure: a logic of regulation and a logic of security that when read dialectically shows the relation is part of a larger move in which each term is inscribed reciprocally in the logic of the other. The launching pad for this reflection concerns the principles on which social work is founded. The underlying logic of regulation and security explains the essential rationality of social work. As a result, all transformation in the internal mechanisms and function of social work should be understood as an inter-related process between the twin logics of security and regulation. These are, in fact, coterminous with the rationality of social work.

This Weberian reading of social work maintains that it is best explained both developmentally and functionally as part of the wider historical rationalisation of modernity. With this caricature, it is plain to see social work as a significant feature in the project of modernity. If this analysis is correct in identifying and isolating the twin logics of regulation and security as doubly constitutive of social work, the knot that binds them points towards a Weberian *theory of rationality*. In this way, it is possible to trace the interpretive key in the field of social work that is inscribed at the intersection of two linked logics, constituting its overarching rationality. The task of explication is to account for and outline the conditions that structure the action-orienting logic of regulation and security in social work as they conform to the ordering of rationality in modern societies. Broadly, along foundationalist lines, it is easy to see how these two logics conform to Max Weber's distinction between instrumental and substantive rationality. Weber reconstituted rationality by introducing a social dimension and developing sophisticated distinctions between different kinds of rationality. They hinge on differences in the relationships among values, goals, beliefs, and action. One such distinction is in the relationship between means and ends, which differentiates formal or instrumental rationality from substantive rationality. Weber defined instrumental and substantive rationality as a logical relationship between means and ends based on assessing the impacts of projected actions. The former is means–end driven, calculating, self-interested, predictive, and regulative, with the latter focusing on broader expressive values, affects, and meanings. While instrumental rationality is limited to means, taking ends as given, substantive rationality includes 'the actor's own rationally pursued and calculated ends' (Weber, 1922, p. 12). This sort of rationality does not lend itself to procedure, or rigid or scripted methods. It is a moral–practical rationality, whereby an action is oriented towards understanding, while the former is a calculating rationality (Habermas, 1984). Social work is determined, on the one hand, by an instrumental rationality, as complicit in calculating and regulatory practice and, on the other, by a substantive rationality, in security, affect, and safety, through dialogic and expressive face-to-face work (Webb, 2006).

Logic of regulation

The rationality of regulation is constitutive of modern social work and an increasingly pervasive aspect in its reach and depth of influence. As a mode of ordering, it is frequently achieved by legal rules, procedures, policy guidelines, and regulatory mandates that are likely to be backed by behavioural sanctions and standards. Hood et al. (2001) explain that successful regulatory regimes must possess three linked components to be effective: information gathering, standard setting, and behaviour modification. These activities sit at the centre of many of social work's tasks. Indeed, regulation penetrates all aspects of social work whereby professional interventions are increasingly controlled, monitored, and audited. In many respects, these are risk-management systems that focus on the requirement of regulatory objectives, records of compliance, the quality of performance management systems, and their capacity to comply. To regulate is to govern and control through a set of rule-bound actions or procedures, which adjust behaviour in respect of some time or quantity to some prescribed standards. This is often referred to as the normative function of social work. As a form of determinate judgement, the logic of regulation monitors specific targets, measures their performance, and tries to adjust their behaviour. For regulation to work successfully, it requires benchmarks and rules to be standardised and repeated in achieving the same results. Regulation is one important way in which risks are managed, with systems-based risk management as a form of self-regulation. With this trend, the introduction of more external regulatory processes can be seen in the mixture of competitive, quality assurance, performance management, and bureaucratic processes. The predominant regulatory tendencies that underlie social work are mirrored in many of the most notable features of the last two decades, that is, the prominence given to regulation as a technique of governance and the rise of a 'new regulatory state', especially in Western democracies. With this shift, marketised public policies are given prominence with the regulatory state acting essentially as a controlling form of governance over people's lives. These trends are evident in Part 1, where the impacts of neoliberalism on frontline social work practice become abundantly evident.

Logic of security

The second rationality underlying social work is the logic of security. Drawing on the work of Francois Ewald (1991), significant shifts in the relation between welfare and social work can be identified, not only in terms of the maintenance of social order and national productivity but also as a mode of protection based on the creation of security and safety for vulnerable citizens. To be secure is to be free from fear, harm, apprehension, contamination, or doubt. How safe is safe enough is a crucial question for social workers in their work with children and vulnerable adults. The focus is not on closed circuits of control and regulation, but on calculations of the possible and probable in terms of an individual or community's protection from harm. In this sense, the concrete experience of security in the daily lives of people is crucial. It is within these parameters that the significance of face-to-face relationships in social work becomes most apparent. These involve relationship building and maintenance, shared meanings and empathy, and establishing trust, reciprocity, and confidence between practitioner and client. This might be expressed as the 'we-relationship' between social worker and client that takes places in a shared spatio-temporal domain. Only in face-to-face encounters is the other person – the social worker or client – apprehended as uniquely individual within a particular situation. The essence of the face-to-face encounter is simultaneity – the recognition of getting or coming together – to build relationships for change or continuity. This is often referred to as intersubjectivity, understood as a fundamental category within the social worker–client dynamic, the foundation for relationship building at the core of direct work with clients. Therefore, the rationality of security can be stretched to include safety, vulnerability, coping strategies, social support, and care and protection. Expert mediating systems, such as social work, are crucially caught up within the logic of security with 'we-relationships', trust, and empathy as key markers of direct work (Webb, 2006). Social work acts as a kind of social guardian that is forward looking as well as providential in protecting against risk and harm.

In summary, it is contended that an essential rationality of modern social work is to be found as it is ambivalently configured through the twin logics of regulation and security, which work in and through one another. On the one hand, the interplay between the two logics shows how risk regulation has come to dominate social work while, on the other, an increased sensitivity to security, trust, and vulnerability also significantly shapes the contours of social work. This results in the development of expert forms of protection with social work increasingly acting as an immunisation function in modern societies.

FUNCTIONS OF SOCIAL WORK

Having identified the twin logics constituting social work, the discussion now turns to the way they are historically shaped and determined, that is, how they manifest as 'social work in action' and are conveyed as a field of interventions forming part of the State apparatus within modern societies. What are the underlying components of social work as a materiality, as series of material practices that legitimate its place and function within the contemporary landscape? In a sense, the function of social work is primarily an exercise in immunising those sectors of society that are most vulnerable and disadvantaged. In this way it is possible to uncover the 'functional imperatives' that provide a useful description of the targets towards which social work orientates or aims its operations under specific conditions. Social work is composed of functions – discourses, practices, or effects – which produce a designated or latent consequence in a given social context with immunity as its central, overarching function.

Immunity is both a legal and a medical term that implies the negative protection of an agent who, for purposes of that protection, ceases to be bound to certain obligations. This is the dimension at which human life is inscribed, constituted, recognised, and defined within a given sociopolitical order. Modernity witnessed the entrance of human life into the domain of national politics as an object of care (Bazzicalupo, 2006). Thus it is possible to conceive social work's function as a protective, safety regime keenly involved in the governance of human vulnerability within the State apparatus. The institutions of the State are all premised on the idea of the need to protect humans from the excesses of capitalist greed and social exclusion. The administration of poor relief in late-Victorian charity organisation was emblematic of this original immunity impulse at work. Developing this historical lineage, Abbott (1988) located the construction of personal problems to the rising concern with social order in the last quarter of the 19th century. This is exactly the same period in which social work emerged on the modern landscape as charity work. He identified the professionally defined epidemic of 'nerves' – bad nerves and nerves ailments – as central to the need for intervention in personal affairs during this period. Psychiatry emerged later in the 1920s and psychoanalysis in the 1930s. Abbott (1988) noted, by 'the 1930s, a firm subjective structure was created that would not require serious attention until the renewed competition of psychology and social work forced a rebiologizing of personal problems in the 1970s' (p. 303). Nevertheless, social work was heavily dependent on psychiatry for its increased professional status and legitimacy:

> Social workers were finding individual approaches to personal problems far more congenial than the social diagnosis approach bequeathed on them by Mary Richmond. The individual approaches, which they borrowed directly from psychiatry offered therapeutic answers that casework did not (Abbott, 1988, p. 302).

Abbott (1988) showed how the normalising role of social work increasingly individualised personal problems by borrowing heavily from the more authoritative field of psychiatry:

> How much more attractive to deal with the individual or family as a self-enclosed unit to be adjusted to society, rather than society to it [and] . . . Psychiatric social work flourished during the twenties, becoming the most prestigious of the social work specialities (Abbott, 1988, p. 303).

Social work takes place in this paradoxical movement of separating or dividing life from itself in order to protect it (Giorgi & Pinkus, 2006). It provides a shelter of immunity from the excesses of politics and economics but, in turn, demands a regulative and legal role in the governance of vulnerability and need. It is for this reason that the juridico-moral character of the service user is so critical for social work in attempting to install its normative regime. In immunising the service user against risk, social work temporarily breaks the circuit of social production placing the social worker and service user outside of it. The immunity dispositif might be seen at work most acutely in social work's preoccupation with risk, where it is increasingly cast as a part of a risk-management regime. It is as if, rather than adjusting the level of protection to the effective nature of the risk, what is adjusted is the perception of the risk to the growing demand for protection, which is to say risk is artificially created in order to control it, as insurance companies routinely do (Esposito, 2008). Thus social work as a State apparatus continuously performs the reciprocal strengthening between risk, protection, and insurance. This preoccupation with self-protection as immunity is distinctive in characterising the nature of social work. From this point of view, the immunity function is more than a defensive apparatus superimposed on the individual or community, but a core internal mechanism for social work practice. The normative immunising character of social work is an *ethos* of governance from the inside, by the inside: As a core component of social work's internal architecture, the system of immunity must also simultaneously immunise itself from those given care and protection under its auspices. It is best to think of this as a form of autoimmunity. It is under these conditions that expert systems, such as evidence-based practice, risk management, and new communication technologies for casework emerge. Their purpose is precisely to formally 'bracket off' the service user within a regime of professionalised expertise. Care technologies, like evidence-based practice, help procure social work's very own immunity defence against the increasing demands of the reflexive service user.

It is, however, the societal immunisation function of social work that most clearly situates its location within the regulative and security logic of modernity. This line of thought is indebted to the work of Roberto Esposito who pursued this project in *Communitas* (2010) and *Immunitas* (2011), where he developed the argument that the modern subject or self, with all of its civil and political rights, emerges as an attempt to attain immunity from the contagion of that which is extra-individual, namely, the possibility of radical community. For Esposito, immunity conceptually allows us to envisage a common ground for practices of protection, such as epidemiology, the hygienic movement in urban design and education, and eugenics. It has a very similar meaning to the logic of security discussed above. Indeed, the novelty of Esposito's project resides in his characterisation of the convergence of the legal and biomedical fields in configuring the twin logics of security and regulation discussed above. From plastic bicycle helmets, the refrigeration of food, unemployment benefits, and immigration laws to US post-9/11 states of emergency, immunity functions are to be found everywhere. With the latter it is precisely the ordinary laws that are being used exceptionally in order to re-establish the conditions of their normal application. Such is the case of the Immigration Law after the enactment of the US Patriot Act. By stretching Esposito's theorising of modernity as a series of complex, biopolitical processes of immunisation, social work can be located as the fold that, in some way, separates community from itself, sheltering it from the often unbearable excess of politics and economics. Social work's biopolitics cannot be separated from the political economy of life. It is thus inscribed at the tangential line where law and the conditions of life intersect. Life and law emerge as the two constitutive elements of social work in action, in its material practice. Perhaps it is for this very reason that there are such huge public and media outcries at the death of children under the care of social workers. With child deaths, law and life are abruptly confronted in the most shocking way. In providing immunitary declension from the excesses of politics and economics, social work is literally given the power to preserve life, social life. As part of the State apparatus of governing vulnerability, it is a negative form of the protection of life. It saves, secures, insures, and preserves the individual, family, or community to which it pertains. Enacting the immunity logic in social work is two-fold: real and symbolic, and constitutional and normative. Here immunisation as a normalising process is most apparent: as a praxis, which regularises while containing, and secures while engineering. It controls, regulates, prohibits, and disciplines lifestyles by winning the cooperation of those who are being controlled with all attracted by a biopolitical project to which they cannot say no (Bazzicalupo, 2006). This allows a further step in tracking the developmental nature of social work in relation to modernity. Modernity typically refers to the post-traditional period, which is marked by the move from feudalism towards capitalism, industrialisation, secularisation, rationalisation, and the nation-state. Conceptually, modernity relates to the modern era. In this historical task, social work can be coupled to modernist regimes and institutions, as it constitutes a particular articulation or tonality of modernity, one that ultimately coincides with politics, economics, and a culturally conditioned morality (Webb, 2007). The immunity function of social work drives its governance role in a historically determined grid relating to the unfolding logics of security and regulation as part of the project of modernity and its adjunct capitalist-state formation. It is this situatedness of social work to which the next section turns.

SITUATING SOCIAL WORK

In recent years, various fields within social work have been subject to a number of major government reviews, public inquiries, special commissions, and in-depth policy analyses. These have helped identify, appraise, and synthesise important aspects of social work in context. In some important respects, these sorts of analyses help attenuate the immediate and most pressing issues faced by social workers while, at the same time, provide an independent and objective assessment. One such review undertaken in England is Eileen Munro's (see Chapter 14) independent review of child protection which began in June 2010. It makes some very far-reaching and sweeping recommendations for improving this area of social service practice. It is one of the most comprehensive, sophisticated, and analytically refined reviews ever undertaken in the area of child protection. Munro (2011) recommended, for example:

> the Government revise statutory, multi-agency guidance to remove unnecessary or unhelpful prescription and focus only on essential rules for effective multi-agency working and on the principles that underpin good practice. For example, the prescribed timescales for social work assessments should be removed, since they distort practice (Munro, 2011, p. 7).

The Munro Review clearly identifies problems with the deeply embedded 'tick box' culture in social work agencies. Munro (2011) argues:

> The demands of bureaucracy have reduced their capacity to work directly with children, young people and families. Services have become so standardised that they do not provide the required range of responses to the variety of need that is presented (Munro, 2011, pp. 6–7).

Most strikingly, the review recommends 'a radical reduction in the amount of central prescription to help professionals move from a compliance culture to a learning culture, where they have more freedom to use their expertise in assessing need and providing the right help' (Munro, 2011, p. 7).

These high levels of prescription have, according to the Munro Review (2011), 'also hampered the profession's ability to take responsibility for developing its own knowledge and skills' (p. 8). Public sector services in all developed economies have been continually subject to new demands for accountability and transparency, leading to the creation of complex audit systems. This is often referred to as the impact of public sector 'managerialism' on social work. Munro (2004) has consistently drawn attention to the negative effects of an auditing culture arguing that social work presents particular challenges because of the nature of its knowledge base:

> Improvement in services to users cannot be achieved just by managerial changes but requires rigorous research to increase our understanding of what works. The process of making social work 'auditable' is in danger of being destructive, creating a simplistic description of practice and focusing on achieving service outputs with little attention to user outcomes (Munro, 2004, p. 1075).

One common characteristic of all attempts to define the nature and role of the profession is an explicit acknowledgement of the inter-relationship between social work and the context in which its tasks of regulation, risk management, and protection are carried out. Social work is inevitably shaped by the changing policy, legislative, and political contexts in which it operates. Perhaps owing to the persistence of its core values and progressive ethical principles, social work has consistently sought to locate itself within socially liberal as opposed to socially authoritarian positions. As an established professional discipline, it has a distinctive part to play in protecting and securing the well-being of children, adults, families, and communities. Social work makes a particular contribution in situations where there are high levels of complexity, uncertainty, vulnerability, conflicts of interest, and risk. It is always situated on the moving border between process and event, between the real and the possible. This border, this limit, or frontline is the site of intervention. The task of social work is inherently interventionist, located as it is within a wide range of contexts and geographies. How these shape the function and purpose of social work is critical to understanding its changing dimensions. Crucially, the tasks relate to the way in which social work is caught up in winds of change and determined by shifting political ideology, economy, public attitudes, and government policy. The impact of the Global Economic Crisis and economic recession is likely to have profound and long-lasting effects on social work. Public spending austerity cuts are taking place across the globe, with Europe hit particularly hard in countries like Britain, Italy, Portugal, Greece, Spain, and Ireland. This is most dramatically shown in the huge public sector cuts in Britain announced by the Liberal–Conservative Coalition Government. These cuts began to bite in April 2011 with thousands of publicly funded services across Britain being lost, with devastating consequences. At the time of writing, the aftermath of the London Riots in predominantly ethnically Black areas of Tottenham and Hackney are being diagnosed against a backdrop in which youth offending teams and outreach services are being cut by 30% in the very same inner city areas (*Guardian*, 25 March 2011). In the context of the riots and the British government's 'Big Society' agenda, some of these decisions are most perplexing. Many of the organisations that will close down are small community groups or local charities previously supported by central or local government grants to provide important neighbourhood services for the mentally ill, disabled, older, and young people:

> The cuts affect a wide spectrum of projects: youth offending teams will shrink, probation staff numbers will dwindle, refugee advice centres will halve in size, Sure Start services will disappear, domestic violence centres will have to restrict the number of people they can help, HIV-prevention schemes will end (*Guardian*, 25 March 2011).

Social work is at the hard end of neoliberalism and the transformation of society into an 'enterprise society' based on the market, competition, inequality, and the privilege of the individual. As Venn and Terranova (2009) state: 'The core strategies of individualization, insecuritization and depoliticization are used as part of neoliberal social policy to undermine the principles and practices of mutualization, solidarity and redistribution that the Welfare State had promoted' (p. 9). The strategic aim of neoliberal politics is the restoration of the power of capital to determine the distribution of wealth and establish the enterprise as the single dominant form. This requires that it target society – and by implication social work – as a whole for a fundamental reconstruction, putting in place new mechanisms to control, regulate, and govern individual conduct (see Chapters 3 and 4). Increasingly, social workers are required by the apparatus of the State to perform a central role in controlling individual conduct or the 'enterprise of self' (McNay, 2009). A critical question remains in lieu of these dramatic effects on social work. How does it fashion a new political imaginary from fragmentary, diffuse, and often antagonistic practitioners and clients, who may be united in principle against the exigencies of neoliberalism and capitalism but diverge in practice, in terms of the sites, strategies, and specific natures of their own oppression? Exposing social work activity to a critical stance enables the exploration of relations of power and forms of domination. It also involves identifying how commitments to integrated models of social justice and core progressive principles such as empowerment and anti-oppressive practice can be attained. Some have argued that there is a necessity to recast Critical Social Work drawing on recent post-Marxist approaches, such as the writings of Alain Badiou and Slajov Zizek, and in mobilising social work as vehicle of social justice (Gilbert & Powell, 2010; Webb, 2011).

TERRITORIES AND BOUNDARIES OF SOCIAL WORK

In the long struggle for demarcation, the tasks and roles of social work, the relation to other professions, and the links between them change continually. As already seen, in situating social work these changes often arise because of things external to the profession: technology, politics, and other social forces, divide tasks and reconfigure them. It is, however, difficult to evaluate the external effects on social work without first examining its own internal dynamics and the relation it has to nearby social science disciplines. If assessment, intervention, and case management are important aspects of professional practice, this work is closely tied to a system of knowledge that formalises the skills on which this work proceeds. Like other professions, such as teaching and nursing, professional knowledge in use is significant for social work because application is its main purpose. Gambrill (2000) identified the importance of connecting knowledge with doing, suggesting that critical thinking is an important component of the ethical problem-solving process and of understanding practitioner decisions and the interventions they provide. Social work, as a practical endeavour, requires knowledge beyond theory alone (Larrison, 2009). The knowledge base must also connect to what social workers do. However, social work develops abstract, conceptual, and formal knowledge, such as research on organisations, policy analysis, methods of intervention, and ethical principles. Abbott (1995) conceived of the professions as living in an ecology in which there were professions and turfs, and a social and cultural mapping – the mapping of jurisdiction – between those professions and turfs. If the notion of boundaries is a most fertile thinking tool for understanding social work, it is, in part, because it captures a fundamental social process, that of the relationality between professions, institutions, and locations. Abbott (1995) came to regard social work's jurisdiction as a contested turf war, with its functions emerging as a continuous process of conflict and change. Professions like social work, teaching, psychology, and nursing compete with one another for jurisdictional monopolies, and for the legitimacy of their claimed expertise, thereby constituting a constantly changing system of professions. In mapping the territory constituting professional social work, Abbott (1995) developed the notion of enclosure to demonstrate the way in which it was shaped by conflicts at its boundaries, rather than internal mechanisms of purpose and function. He showed how social work's enclosure was continually contested by psychologists and psychiatrists in child guidance clinics in the USA. In a highly original analysis, Abbott (1995) examined future prospects for social work in the face of interprofessional turf wars and its dependence on the State and associated nongovernmental agency funding.

According to Abbott (1995), the dependence on government funding, along with the dispossessed low status of many of its clients, put social work in a precarious position. Altruism does not sell in the contemporary neoliberal political climate.

In part, a related issue at stake here is the view that social work's jurisdictional problem is that it has never developed a distinctive, widely shared, research paradigm. Social work has constantly and consistently been dogged with the enduring problem of generating an identity as a specialist discipline. In some important ways, *Handbooks* such as this neatly rebut this longstanding view that social work has not been able to develop a distinctive knowledge base.

Research increasingly demonstrates the changing relationship between social work and the growing interdisciplinary area of applied social studies known as a form of knowledge production referred to by Gibbons et al. (1994) as 'Mode 2' in contradistinction to discipline-based Mode 1 knowledge development. Mode 2, as practical and user driven, is becoming the preferred form of government knowledge in contemporary audit cultures (Gray & Schubert, 2011). It is apparent that, while disciplines such as sociology and economics 'export' concepts, methodologies, and personnel, social work is very much an 'importer', since it lacks the internal disciplinary integrity of other 'exporter' disciplines, such as economics, political science, and anthropology (Abbott, 1988; Holmwood, 2010). In this respect, social work researchers and practitioners *are* successful 'adapters', and what they adapt shapes the discipline. In spite of attempts in the UK and USA to ratchet up the quality of social work research, the consequence is an increasingly blurred distinction between social work as a discipline and the interdisciplinary area of applied social studies with a potential loss of disciplinary and, indeed, professional identity (Gibbs, 2001; Sharland, 2011). It may well be the case that this loss of professional identity in social work – and the blurring, for example, with social care and human services – is associated with a reduced ability to reproduce a critical sensibility within social work and makes it docile to the impacts and constraints of audit culture with its flexible adaptation of interdisciplinary knowledge. On top of this is social work's vulnerability to external pressures and inability to constantly demonstrate its relevance to professional practice. These pressures come from left-wing social movements as well as from regulative state authorities and right-wing neoliberal critics. These external pressures inevitably contribute to internal disagreement, but social work has been at war with itself at least since the 1960s.

Shulman (2004) argued that professional pedagogy is compromised when all the dimensions of practice – the intellectual, technical, and moral – are out of balance. In some respects, social work has encouraged a standoff between more technical forms of 'research for practice' and speculative theoretical concerns, which means it often finds it difficult to offer more sustained, methodological elaboration or intellectual advance. This tension has especially been amplified by the changing and expansive repertoire of practice learning options of professional training courses, with the increasing emphasis on certain anodyne notions of 'practice competencies'. Social work is constantly searching for its own professional knowledge jurisdiction and defending its professional boundaries. This involves the profession in complex processes of competition with rivals, and searches for particular kinds of niche expertise (Abbott, 1988). The legitimating force of 'scientific knowledge' is arguably one of the reasons why it was so quick and canny to grab hold of the coat tails of medicine's evidence-based practice regime.

In line with other social science disciplines, over the past decade, there has been a determined push to move social work outside of the boundaries of the nation-state as its implicit unit of intervention and source of funding to a much broader field. In some quarters, this has invoked notions of global social work and transnational joined-up practice and the development of what can be called a 'cosmopolitan social work'. To speak of a cosmopolitan social work in this context means broadening the horizon to include a variety of Western and non-Western cultural modernities. The conceptual challenge for an expansive cosmopolitan social work is to identify the patterns of variation, their origin, and ethical consequences across a range of cultures and geographies (Beck & Grande, 2010; Held, 2004). Two editors of this *Handbook*, Mel Gray and James Midgley, have made significant contributions to this emergent cosmopolitan social work agenda. They have shown how it is impossible to talk meaningfully about methodological cosmopolitanism without pulling down the walls of Eurocentrism. They have shown how social work needs to open up perspectives on to the world beyond Europe, on to the entanglements of histories of colonisation, racial domination, and indigenous practices as well as on to border-transcending dynamics, dependencies, interdependencies, and intermingling of modernities at different stages of development. This requires a shift away from thinking about social work in the *singular*: social work neither national nor global but social work absolutely understood in universal terms, whereas thinking about social work in the *plural* refers to the very different paths and contexts of social processes. This is no longer sufficient, if it ever was. It inevitably leads to the category error of implicitly applying conclusions drawn from *one* form of social work to social work in general, which then becomes a universal frame of reference (Gray, 2005; Gray & Fook, 2004). This is not to suggest that universal principles for social work are impossible but rather to criticise the hegemonic short circuit from *one* form of social work to a social work in general. The two leading international professional bodies, the *International Federation of Social Workers* and the *International Association of Social Workers*, would do well to heed the significant criticism raised against their universalising agenda. This defective mode might be called the self-provincialisation

Esposito, R. (2008). *Bios: Biopolitics and philosophy*. Minneapolis, MN: University of Minnesota Press.

Esposito, R. (2010). *Communitas: The origin and destiny of community*. Stanford, CA: Stanford University Press.

Esposito, R. (2011). *Immunitas: The protection and negation of life*. Cambridge: Polity Press.

Ewald, F. (1991). Insurance and risk. In G. Burchell, Gordon, C., & Miller, P. (eds), *The Foucault effect: Studies in governmentality*. Chicago, IL: University of Chicago Press, pp.197–210.

Flexner, A. (2001). Is social work a profession? *Research on Social Work Practice*, *11*, 152–165.

Gambrill, E. (2000). The role of critical thinking in evidence-based social work. In P. Allen-Meares & Garvin, C.D. (eds) *Handbook of direct practice*. Thousand Oaks, CA: Sage, pp. 43–64.

Gibbons, M., Limoges, C., Nowotny, H., Schwartzman, S., Scott, P., & Trow, M. (1994). *The new production of knowledge: The dynamics of science and research in contemporary societies*. London: Sage.

Gibbs, A. (2001). The changing nature and context of social work research. *British Journal of Social Work*, *31*(5), 687–704.

Gilbert, T., & Powell, J.L. (2010). Power and social work in the United Kingdom: A Foucauldian excursion. *Journal of Social Work*, *10*(1), 3–22.

Giorgi, G., & Pinkus, K. (2006). Zones of exception: Biopolitical territories in the neoliberal era. *Diacritics*, *36*(2), 99–108.

Gray, M. (2005). Dilemmas of international social work: Paradoxical processes in indigenisation, imperialism and universalism. *International Journal of Social Welfare*, *14*(2), 230–237.

Gray, M., & Fook, J. (2004). The quest for a universal social work: Some issues and implications, *Social Work Education*, *23*(5), 625–644.

Gray, M., & Schubert, L. (2011). Sustainable social work: Modelling knowledge production, transfer and evidence-based practice. *International Journal of Social Welfare*. Article first published online: 16 May 2011 doi: 10.1111/j.1468-2397.2011.00802.x.

Gray, M., & Webb, S.A. (eds) (2010). *International social work*, vol.1. London: Sage Library of Social Welfare.

Habermas, J. (1984). *Theory of communicative action: vol 1*. Boston: Beacon Press.

Held, D. (2004). *Global covenant: The social democratic alternative to the Washington Consensus*. Cambridge: Polity Press.

Holmwood, J. (2010). Sociology's misfortune: Disciplines, interdisciplinarity and the impact of audit culture. *British Journal of Sociology*, *61*(4), 639–658.

Hood, C., Rothstein, H., & Baldwin, R. (2001). *The government of risk: Understanding risk regulation regimes*. New York: Oxford University Press.

Ife, J. (2000). Localized needs and a globalized economy: Bridging the gap with social work practice. Social Work and Globalisation. *Special Issue of Canadian Social Work*, *2*(1), 50–64.

Larrison, T.E. (2009). *Capturing the space in-between: Understanding the relevance of professional 'use of self' for social work education through hermeneutic phenomenology*. Dissertation submitted for degree of Doctor of Philosophy, University of Illinois at Urbana-Champaign. http://gradworks.umi.com/3363133.pdf.

McNay, L. (2009). Self as enterprise: Dilemmas of control and resistance in Foucault's *The Birth of Biopolitics*'. *Theory, Culture and Society*, *26*(6), 55–77.

Munro, E. (2004). The impact of audit on social work practice. *British Journal of Social Work*, *34*(8), 1075–1095.

Munro, E. (2011). *The Munro Review of Child Protection: A child-centred system*. London: UK Department of Education. Retrieved on 8 September 2011 from http://www.education.gov.uk/munroreview/downloads/8875_DfE_Munro_Report_TAGGED.pdf

Sharland, E. (2011). All together now? Building disciplinary and inter-disciplinary research capacity in social work and social care. *British Journal of Social Work*, 1–19 doi:10.1093/bjsw/bcr061.

Shulman, L.S. (2004). *The wisdom of practice: Essays on teaching, learning, and learning to teach*. San Francisco, CA: Jossey-Bass.

Venn, C., & Terranova, T. (2009). Thinking after Michel Foucault. *Theory, Culture and Society*, *26*(1), 1–11.

Webb, S.A. (2006). *Social work in a risk society*. London: Palgrave.

Webb, S.A. (2007). The comfort of strangers: The emergence of social work in late Victorian England (Part One). *European Journal of Social Work*, *10*(1), 39–54.

Webb, S.A. (2009). Against difference and diversity in social work: The case of human rights. *International Journal of Social Welfare*, *18*(2), 307–316.

Webb, S.A. (2011). (Re)Assembling the Left: The politics of redistribution and recognition in social work. *British Journal of Social Work*, *40*(8), 2364–2379.

Weber, M. (1922). *Economy and society*. Berkeley, CA: University of California Press.

SECTION 1

Welfare, Social Policy, and Social Work

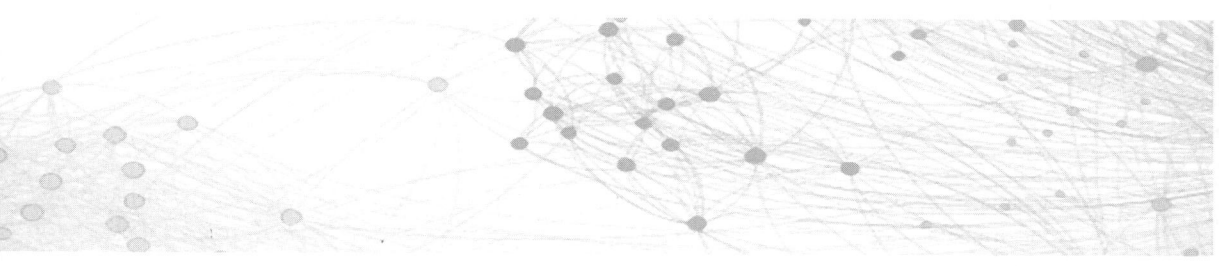

INTRODUCTION

Section 1 on welfare, social policy, and social work examines welfare theory and its various approaches, including issues relating to the transformation of welfare and the nature and influence of social policy. The contemporary welfare state debate revolves around changing definitions of and ideas about welfare, the changing institutions responsible for its delivery, the implementation of welfare legislation and policy, and the practices in and through which welfare is delivered, today often referred to as welfare governance. There seems to be some agreement that claims as to the dismantling of the welfare state and the welfare state crisis is overstated. What functions does social work play as a functionary of welfare in regulating the poor? Arguably both relief practices and labour laws have the same general purpose, 'to augment the regulation of labor by compensating for the vagaries and weaknesses of control based largely on market incentives' (Piven & Cloward, 2010, p. 167). This section provides a fresh and contemporary examination of the role of social work as part of relief in a transformed welfare state. Relief – or welfare more broadly – gives government a large and important role in the market-oriented capitalist system and becomes a central political issue within an electoral system on which government depends for its continued power. Here a key focus is on the changing forms of welfare governance as they impact on social policy and social work.

In the opening chapter, Chapter 1 on social policy and welfarism, David Gil places human needs as central to our understanding of social work practice in contemporary social welfare services as he attempts to unravel the origins, functions, and dynamics of social and global injustice and their manifestations in socially constructed 'ill-fare'. Individual and social development and well-being depend crucially on the role of welfare services – and social work practice – in alleviating the destructive symptoms of social and global injustice.

In 'theorising welfare' in Chapter 2, Mimi Abramowitz discusses the rise of neoliberalism and its impact on the United States welfare state, the well-being of families, the delivery of human services, and social work. She argues that both the rise of the welfare state and the subsequent neoliberal effort to dismantle it were not accidental or simply political. Rather, they represent contrasting governmental responses to the two major economic crises of the 20th century: the Great Depression and economic recession in the mid-1970s. In charting the collapse of the US middle class and the transfer of wealth to the already wealthy, she points out that the Global Economic Crisis is not just another financial downturn, but that the USA could be facing a systemic crisis of capitalism that is only resolved through major restructuring of the political economy. The chapter examines the dynamics of these shifts and the way in which neoliberalism has placed the well-being of families, effective human services, and social work values in jeopardy.

In Chapter 3, Robert Fairbanks examines how the transformation from a Keynesian–Fordist welfare state to a post-Keynesian – 'post-welfare' – regime of capitalist accumulation articulates with the proliferation of (potentially) novel forms of welfare governance in the complex and contradictory post-welfare moment. Though there is some general consensus on the extent to which neoliberalism is characterised by – and indeed perhaps even makes a virtue of – unevenness across institutional, economic, and political contexts, there are still important disagreements about its historical significance for the question of welfare governance and social regulation. Fairbanks traces the concept of regulation from its Victorian-era antecedents in civil society, to its national form in the welfarist era and its market form in the post-welfare era to delineate the analytical traditions of political economy and governmentality in welfare state theory. He provides a framework for historically and geographically contingent analysis and criticism of contemporary welfare state transformation. He illustrates the ways in which variant welfare state forms – neoliberal, neocorporatist, neostatist, and neocommunitarian – have evolved from institutional legacies, the balance of political forces, and the changing economic and political conjunctures in which different strategies are pursued.

Sanford Schram revisits Mark Lipsky's pathbreaking ideas about 'welfare professionals and street-level bureaucrats' in Chapter 4 showing how work on the frontlines of welfare bureaucracies has been changing, often quite dramatically, and how workers' discretion in the current era is, as in the past, often regarded as part of the problem, while also seen as necessary to accomplish public policy goals. He focuses on the changing environment in which these enduring challenges occur; the changed nature of frontline worker discretion in an era of auditing systems that facilitate greater surveillance of worker actions; and the changing nature of welfare organisations, now often contract agencies, with their own hiring standards, procedures, and performance pressures related to contract renewal. Even under these flexible, short term labour hiring regimes highlights how workers still need to have discretion in order to perform their jobs effectively. Since their discretion is frequently treated as problematic, it is still constrained by various management stratagems, if in new ways. Lastly, he highlights how the issue of frontline discretion is affected by the shift to 'a neoliberal–paternalist regime' of poverty governance in which the challenge is finding the right balance between managerial control and frontline discretion.

In Chapter 5, Mary Daly skilfully elaborates on the relationship between gender and welfare in contemporary societies. Both concepts are problematised, especially from the perspective of social change. Gender equality as an idea and political goal is subjected to critical scrutiny. Welfare, too, is a rather problematic concept, not least because in it are lodged complex issues about the well-being of individuals *vis-à-vis* that of collectivities, such as families and communities. The chapter focuses on key questions centring on how the relationship between gender and welfare is to be understood, especially in the context of changing gender roles and relations, and politics and policies instituted to address gender inequalities. The chapter engages with the mobilization of a progressive agenda for gender relations as it looks towards the future. Issues of individual autonomy arise as do matters of family, care, and equality.

In Chapter 6 on 'welfare and social development', James Midgley discusses the influential theory of social development, which builds on ideas of social and human capital in its aim to end the bifurcation of social welfare and economic development. Social development sees social policy as productivist and investment oriented and aims to foster a new conception of redistribution as social investment to harness the power of economic growth for social ends and to invest in people and enhance their capacity to participate in the productive economy. Midgley discusses ways in which social development works: through increasing the cost effectiveness of social welfare; enhancing human capital investments; promoting social capital formation; developing individual and community assets; facilitating economic participation through productive employment and self-employment; removing barriers to economic participation; and creating a social climate conducive to development. He argues that by enhancing social rights and promoting social justice, social development offers a new institutional policy alternative to social policy today.

REFERENCE

Piven, F.F., & Cloward, R. (2010). Relief, labour and civil disorder: An overview. In M. Gray & Webb, S.A. (eds). *International social work,* vol. 1. London: Sage.

Social Work, Social Policy, and Welfarism

David G. Gil

Social work and welfarism evolved as societal responses to systemic social injustice and social-structural 'ill-fare'. To understand social work and welfarism, one has, therefore, to unravel the origins, functions, and dynamics of social and global injustice and social ill-fare. To do so, this chapter examines the following:

1. human needs as a frame of reference for individual and social development, well-being, and social and global justice;
2. meanings of social and global justice;
3. socially just communities and human nature;
4. universal dimensions of social policy systems;
5. emergence and spread of social injustice through coercive, undemocratic processes from local to global levels: oppression, domination, and exploitation;
6. economic systems, social justice, and social injustice;
7. welfarism and social work; and
8. social justice model of social work.

HUMAN NEEDS, INDIVIDUAL AND SOCIAL DEVELOPMENT, WELL-BEING, AND SOCIAL JUSTICE

Like all living beings, humans tend to grow and develop spontaneously, and to 'fare well' when they can meet universal, intrinsic needs in their natural and socially evolved environments. When a seed is put into the ground, the sun shines, the rains fall, and there are appropriate nutrients in the soil, the seed will unfold its innate potential spontaneously and become the plant it is inherently capable of becoming. Analogously, human beings whose real needs can be met in their natural and social environments will spontaneously unfold their rich potential and will become what they are inherently capable of becoming. And entire human societies evolving in environments conducive to the realisation of the innate needs, capabilities and potential of all their members will become fully developed, rich societies. Hence, it is necessary to identify the universal, intrinsic needs of the human species as a frame of reference for environments conducive to the full realisation of these needs and for the well-being or 'well-faring' of entire societies. Many scholars who have studied human needs tend to agree on the following set of inter-related needs (Fromm, 1955; Gil, 1973; Maslow, 1970).

1   *Biological–material needs*: Stable provision of biological necessities; sexual satisfaction; and regular access to life-sustaining and enhancing goods and services, the types, quantity, and quality of which vary among different cultures and over time.
2   *Social–psychological needs*: Stable, meaningful social relations and a sense of belonging to a community, involving mutual respect, acceptance, affirmation, care and love, and opportunities for self-discovery and for the emergence of a positive self-identity.
3   *Productive–creative needs*: Meaningful participation, in accordance with one's innate capacities and stage of development, in the productive activities of one's community and society.
4   *Security needs*: A sense of trust and security emerging from the experience of steady fulfillment of one's biological–material, social–psychological, and productive–creative needs.
5   *Self-actualisation needs*: Becoming what one is innately capable of becoming through creative productivity and self-expression.
6   *Spiritual needs*: Discovering and giving coherence to one's existence in relation to people, nature, and the world along known, unknown, and ultimately unknowable dimensions.

The way these inter-related human needs are expressed tends to change over time in different social contexts. Their substance and dynamics are, however, constant and universal. Human survival, development, and physical, emotional, and social health and well-being depend always on adequate levels of fulfillment of these basic human needs.

People's subjective perceptions of their needs and interests result not only from becoming conscious of their basic, innate needs, but also from socialisation in particular societies with unique ways of life and socially constructed definitions of needs and interests. People's actual perceptions of their needs and interests may, therefore, correspond to, overlap with, substitute for, or conflict with their basic needs and real interests. When perceived needs and interests do not overlap sufficiently with people's basic needs and interests, socially defined substitutes (e.g., material wealth) may be realised, while basic needs (e.g., meaningful human relations) remain unfulfilled. Whether people correctly perceive their basic needs and interests, and can actually satisfy them in everyday life, depends on their natural environment and their socially evolved ways of life (i.e., the organisational systems of their societies). When these systems are just they are conducive to everyone's need fulfillment. When they are unjust, fulfillment of real needs is unlikely.

MEANINGS OF SOCIAL AND GLOBAL JUSTICE

Many advocates of social justice do not specify their understanding of this concept. However, such specification is necessary for deliberations of strategies toward the realisation of social justice from local to global levels. This chapter, therefore, sketches an understanding of social justice on three related levels: individual human relations; social institutions and values; and global human relations (Gil, 2004).

Socially just human relations require equal acknowledgement and treatment of everyone as autonomous, authentic subjects with equal rights and responsibilities, rather than as objects to be used and exploited as is typically done in unjust human relations of the prevailing capitalist economic culture. This conception of social justice was foreshadowed in biblical and gospel sources, as illustrated by sayings such as 'Love thy neighbour as thyself'. Similar ideas of social justice can be found in the Koran and in sacred scriptures of Buddhists, Hindus, Confucians, and other Asian, African, and (native) American traditions.

On the level of social institutions and values, social justice means socially established living conditions and ways of life conducive to the fulfillment of everyone's intrinsic needs and the realisation of everyone's innate potential, from local to global levels. Socially just societies, whenever and wherever they existed throughout history, have been egalitarian, structurally nonviolent, and genuinely democratic (Kanter, 1972; Kropotkin, 1956). 'Egalitarian' as used here is not a mathematical but a social–philosophical notion (Tawney, 1931). It means all people have equal rights, responsibilities, and opportunities in all spheres of life, including control of resources; organisation of work; distribution of goods, services, and rights; governance; and social reproduction. 'Equality' does not mean everything is divided and distributed in identical shares but distributions are geared thoughtfully to individual differences and everyone's needs are acknowledged equally.

Socially just societies do not require 'structural violence' by the state, as socially unjust societies do (Gil, 1996) and they tend to practice genuine, rather than merely ritualistic, 'ballot-box' democracy. In the context of social, economic, and political equality of socially just societies, no individuals, groups, or social classes can monopolise power over other people and the state by using accumulated wealth to influence the outcome of elections as is usually done in unjust societies.

Values are guidelines which people evolved in the course of social evolution to differentiate behaviours whose outcomes they valued and which they, therefore, considered worthy of repetition, from behaviours whose outcomes they disliked and which they, therefore, believed should be avoided. The frame of reference for what is good and valued, and what is evil and not valued, are the real and perceived needs and interests of those who judge behavioural outcomes, usually dominant groups of societies (Gil, 1992).

Table 1.1 Value dimensions

Just societies	Unjust societies
Equality	Inequality
Liberty	Domination and exploitation
Individuality	Selfishness and individualism
Collectivity orientation and mutualism	Disregard for community
Cooperation	Competition

Table 1.1 shows the value dimensions differentiating socially just from socially unjust societies.

Social justice on a scale of global human relations implies a vision of over six billion fully developed people living in fully developed communities and societies. This vision involves extending just individual relations to all of the world's people and extending the institutional context of social justice from local and national to global levels. This vision implies also a peaceful world without structural violence by states and without counter-violence by individuals and groups, including the type of counter-violence labelled 'terrorism'.

The institutional requirements of global justice would have to be met by sharing the aggregate of productive resources, knowledge, work, goods, and services of the global community in ways conducive to meeting everyone's intrinsic needs and realising everyone's innate capacities. People everywhere would thus have equal social, economic, and political rights, responsibilities, and opportunities, and no one would be dominated and exploited by others.

Contrary to intuitive assumptions and fears, redistribution of resources, knowledge, work, goods, and services in accordance with principles of global justice would not cause declines in the quality of life of currently privileged people and nations. For global wealth is not a fixed, zero-sum quantity and quality but could be enhanced both quantitatively and qualitatively as the productive potential of currently underdeveloped people and countries is liberated. The quality of life for all would actually be enriched immensely when people everywhere are free to develop their innate capacities and entitled to use necessary productive resources and accumulated knowledge and skills in meaningful productive endeavours. The 'real' wealth of humankind is, after all, not the aggregate of privately controlled capital, but the aggregate of realised human potential and of knowledge and skills generated since early stages of social evolution.

SOCIALLY JUST COMMUNITIES AND HUMAN NATURE

Contrary to widely held, taken-for-granted beliefs, oppression and social injustice are not inevitable characteristics of human life. The study of social evolution reveals these practices did not become firmly established in human societies until some ten thousand years ago, following the discovery, development, and spread of agriculture, animal husbandry, and crafts gradually resulting in a relatively stable economic surplus.

Before sketching the attributes of early, socially just human communities, some observations on human nature seem necessary. While destructive tendencies are, indeed, intrinsic to human nature, this does not mean relating and interacting destructively is ever inevitable, rather than merely possible. Humans, by their nature, can relate and interact destructively, as well as constructively, but neither mode of relations and interactions is ever inevitable. Constructive modes of relations and interactions are as intrinsic to human nature as destructive ones, and are, therefore, equally possible. There is as much evidence for constructive human relations and interactions throughout social evolution, as there is of destructive ones. An important question to ask is, therefore, what forces determine when humans relate and interact in accordance with their destructive and constructive potential, respectively. The logical answer to this question seems to be socially evolved and maintained conditions of life influence people's choices of specific behavioural tendencies from the broad range of possible constructive and destructive behaviours intrinsic to human nature.

For many millennia, from the emergence of the human species in Africa until the 'agricultural revolution', people tended to live in small, isolated nomadic communities subsisting by gathering, fishing, and hunting. The internal organisation of these early societies was usually based on egalitarian, cooperative, and communal principles, reflective of constructive human potential, and did not involve systemic oppression, exploitation, and injustice, reflective of destructive human potential.

People's resources during these early stages of social evolution consisted of human capacities, their accumulated experiences and orally transmitted knowledge and traditions, and the natural wealth of the territories they inhabited. Stewardship over these resources was exercised collectively toward the goal of meeting everyone's survival needs. Work roles were barely differentiated, as nearly everyone had to participate in securing the basic necessities for survival. Whatever division of work did emerge tended to be based on age, sex, physical conditions, and individual capacities, but not, as during later stages of social evolution, on discriminatory social criteria, such as tribe, race, religion, caste, or class.

Exchanges of work products and the distribution of goods and services tended to be balanced and egalitarian (i.e., nonexploitative). In the course of their lives, most people contributed to and received from aggregate social production about as much as others. Social, civil, and political rights and responsibilities also tended to be shared equally and linked to age, sex, and capacities. People enjoyed roughly equal liberties and were subject to roughly equal constraints concerning work and reproduction.

These essentially egalitarian modes of resource stewardship, exchange and distribution, governance, socialisation, and reproduction seem to have required little coercion beyond childrearing and conformity-inducing public opinion. For under conditions prevailing in these early societies, people seem to have been self-motivated as their work was typically linked directly to their real interests and the satisfaction of their basic needs.

Levels of conflict within societies seem to have been relatively low during the early stages of evolution, as everyone's needs were deemed equally important, and were met accordingly, subject to limits set by the resources and the collective productivity of societies. Also, since the gathering, hunting, and fishing mode of production necessitated nearly everyone's participation to assure provisions of basic needs, few opportunities existed for the emergence of crafts and the generation of a stable economic surplus – the disposition and appropriation of which became a potential source of conflicts during later stages of social evolution.

Apart from their egalitarian, cooperative, and communal value premises, the ways of life of early human societies were not conducive to establishing systems of economic exploitation such as slavery, serfdom, and exploitative wage labour. Their simple technologies, typically, did not enable people to produce, in the course of their lives, significantly more than they consumed for their subsistence. They were, therefore, unable to generate an economic surplus for appropriation and exploitation by others, the material basis and precondition for the emergence of systems of oppression.

The intention is not to idealise the ways of life of early human societies or to advocate returning to that primeval stage of social evolution in order to overcome oppression and social injustice in contemporary societies. It is also not to suggest human relations were then free from oppressive tendencies, especially in relations between men and women, older and younger persons, and members of societies and strangers they encountered. Relations between different societies were not always peaceful then.

However, from what has been learned by anthropology, archaeology, and history about this very long, pre-agricultural and preliterate period of human evolution, oppression, and social injustice in relation to the key institutions of social life, as perpetrated routinely by many societies over the past ten millennia, were not institutionalised policies and practices. It is, therefore, possible to derive important insights from the values and ways of life of early human communities and thus enhance people's ability to overcome oppression and injustice in contemporary societies.

While the gradual emergence and institutionalisation of domination, exploitation, and social injustice were widespread consequences of the agricultural revolution, not all societies with developed agriculture evolved systems of oppression and structured social injustice. Some societies used the economic surplus resulting from their increased productivity toward enhancing the quality of life for all their members and they continued to manage resources, organise work and production, and exchange and distribute goods in accordance with egalitarian, cooperative, and communal values. Illustrations of this tendency have been identified by anthropologists and historians among native peoples in the Americas, Africa, and elsewhere. Many of these native societies preserved essentially nonoppressive and socially just ways of life until, and often beyond, the violent conquests of their lands by colonising European empires (Farb, 1968; Zinn, 1995).

UNIVERSAL DIMENSIONS OF SOCIAL POLICY SYSTEMS

Whether life in societies is shaped by values of social justice or social injustice, and whether people 'fare-well' or 'fare-ill' depends mainly on their social policy systems. Social policies are human-evolved rules for actions, interactions, and social relations in any human group. They are rooted in basic and perceived human needs (Gil, 1992). Humans must generate and transmit to their offspring rules for ways of social life because the human species is genetically less programmed than other species entering life with genetically transmitted programmes for their existence. Programmes for human ways of life are transmitted largely through cultural rather than genetic processes. Social policies, at any time and place, operate through the following essential, universal institutional processes or variables and their manifold interactions:

1. development, management, and conservation of natural and human-created resources;
2. organisation of work and production of life-sustaining and life-enhancing, concrete and non-concrete, goods and services;
3. exchange and distribution of life-sustaining and life-enhancing goods and services, and of social, civil, and political rights and responsibilities;
4. governance; and
5. reproduction, socialisation, and social control.

Through the specific operations and interactions of these essential institutional processes or variables, social policies shape the following linked outcome variables of ways of life:

1. circumstances of living of individuals, groups, and classes;
2. relative power of individuals, groups, and classes;
3. nature and quality of human relations among individuals, groups, and classes; and
4. overall quality of life in society.

The ways in which the five operating variables of social policy systems function in different societies are evolved, and are subject to change, by people's choices, actions, and interactions in the course of their history. The mode of functioning of these operating variables determines whether the outcome variables will be socially just or unjust. The particular manner of functioning of the operating variables is shaped and constrained by the dominant values of given societies. These value dimensions were identified above in relation to social justice. As the evolution of social policies is motivated by the drive to meet human needs, a suitable criterion for evaluating specific policies, and entire policy systems, is the extent to which these needs can actually be met or to which the ways of life of given societies conform to the principles and requirements of social justice.

EMERGENCE AND SPREAD OF SOCIAL INJUSTICE THROUGH COERCIVE, UNDEMOCRATIC PROCESSES FROM LOCAL TO GLOBAL LEVELS: OPPRESSION, DOMINATION, AND EXPLOITATION

Oppression means relations of domination and exploitation between individuals, social groups, and entire peoples, resulting in systemic social injustice, manifested in multidimensional, socially structured inequalities. Oppression and social injustice did not come about voluntarily following the development and spread of agriculture, but through coercive, undemocratic processes. Two related types of establishing domination, exploitation, and social injustice may be distinguished:

1. exploiting strangers (i.e., other societies and their people and resources);
2. exploiting fellow citizens within societies.

Oppressing and exploiting strangers

When accelerating population increases in pre-agricultural, nomadic tribes unsettled a relatively stable balance between their needs and their natural environments and caused scarcities of food and other needed resources, they tended to invade settlements of peasant communities, who had preceded them in developing agriculture, in order to appropriate their crops. Such invasions were the beginnings of warfare aimed at gaining resources. Invasions of peasant communities around harvest times led eventually to their coercive enslavement by marauding nomads, who had become accustomed to securing their food by appropriating the fruits of other people's work and by forcing them to continue raising crops and routinely turn over much of their products to the invaders as tribute, in acknowledgement of submission.

With time social, psychological, and ideological dimensions evolved around the economic roots of oppressive, exploitative relations. The prestige of farming work performed by the enslaved people declined relative to the prestige of activities engaged in by the dominant people (i.e., military and governance functions, regardless of the objective importance of the work and functions). Perceptions of the relative prestige of different work, and of the status of the workers, became internalised into the consciousness of everyone involved in oppressive, exploitative relations and became the core of discriminatory practices and ideologies concerning different occupations, social groups, castes, classes, and peoples. Phenomena such as social caste and class structures, occupational hierarchies, sexism, racism, ethnocentrism, and so forth, are contemporary manifestations of these ancient tendencies.

Dominating other societies in order to exploit their resources, the potential of their people to work, and their human-created goods and services, as was done on relatively small scales by marauding nomadic tribes, has gradually become the model for establishing colonies and empires during antiquity, the Middle Ages, and modern times. Details have varied from case to case, but institutional practices have remained essentially the same throughout the history of conquest and colonialism, and so have the social, psychological, and ideological dimensions, as well as the secular and religious justifications for oppression, exploitation, social and global injustice, and discrimination (Frank, 1978; Magdoff, 1969).

Exploiting and oppressing fellow citizens

Oppression and injustice emerged following the spreading of agriculture within many, but not all, societies as a possible consequence of occupational, social, and spatial differentiations. Whether or not these differentiations resulted in oppressive relations and socially unjust conditions seems to have depended largely on the terms of exchange evolving between peasants in rural communities and people pursuing newly emerging crafts and other occupations and roles, mainly in urban centres. If exchanges were fairly balanced in terms of human and material resources invested in specific products and services, then relations between a society's peasantry and social groups pursuing other occupations, and living mainly in cities, could evolve along voluntary, noncoercive, nonoppressive, and synergetic patterns with everyone benefiting equally (Maslow et al., 1970). If, on the other hand, exchanges were imbalanced (i.e., unjust), establishment and maintenance of such conditions typically required physical and ideological coercion (i.e., oppression and societal violence). In these situations, urban dwellers were bent upon exploiting the peasantry, and gradually also each other, as occupational specialisations and social differentiations multiplied, and as each occupational and social group or class tried to appropriate as much as possible of the aggregate economic surplus by struggling for privileged shares of available goods and services.

Unjust and oppressive societies based on coercively maintained exploitative exchanges among people and classes engaging in different occupations, performing different social roles, and enjoying different levels of rights, responsibilities, and liberty, were not as stable and resistant to change as pre-agricultural, egalitarian, cooperative, and communal societies. They were changing continuously as a result of gradually intensifying competition and conflicts among individuals and social and occupational groups, who gained control over different shares of resources and roles in the work system, and who consequently were able to command different shares in the distribution of goods and services, and civil and political rights and power.

During early stages of the emergence of unjust and oppressive relations, following the establishment of societies based on agriculture and crafts, the egalitarian, cooperative, and communal values, ideology, and consciousness of pre-agricultural societies were gradually transformed into their opposites. These value changes toward inequality, competition, and selfishness were conducive to the ongoing development and stabilisation of occupationally, spatially, and socially fragmented and stratified societies. Once inequalities concerning resources, social and occupational roles, goods, services, and rights were established in a society, they tended to be perpetuated, since individuals and groups who controlled larger shares of resources and access to preferred work were in advantageous positions to assure continuation of these privileges, and even to increase them. Also emerging legal and political institutions tended to reflect prevailing societal inequalities and differences of power among competing interest groups and classes and were, therefore, unlikely to upset a temporary equilibrium among them.

The processes, dynamics, and logic of conflict and competition within societies originated apparently in minor initial inequalities in exchanges among individuals and occupational and social groups, which barely required coercion. However, the emerging tendency to legitimate, institutionalise, and increase initial minimal inequalities did require coercion. This resulted usually in resistance from victimised groups, to which privileged groups reacted with intensified coercion. The vicious circle of domination and exploitation, resistance and repression intensified with time, as people tended to focus on, and to react to, the latest violent stage in the cycle, but usually did not trace the sources of their destructive interactions. They lacked, therefore, insights to reverse their course and to move in alternative, constructive, nonexploitative directions.

The tendency for inequalities to intensify in societies, once initiated on a small scale, has important implications for social workers and others who advocate reductions rather than elimination of inequalities. As long as inequalities, at any level, are considered legitimate and are being enforced by governments, competitive interactions focused on restructuring inequalities tend to continue among individuals, social groups, and classes, and a genuine sense of community and solidarity is unlikely to evolve.

One reason for the constant intensification of coercion in unjust and oppressive societies was the motivation of people to work declined in proportion to the increase in exploitation. Work discipline had, therefore, to be assured by ever more overt and covert coercion. Hypocritical expectations concerning a work ethic became typical elements of socialisation and of religions and ideologies which interpreted and justified unequal conditions of life and work. In turn, socialisation and indoctrination had to be routinely backed up by elaborate systems of submission-inducing rewards and sanctions, and by a system of social control, involving open and secret police and military forces, the instruments of legitimate violence within inegalitarian societies, and among societies of unjust and exploitative global systems.

The long history of the origins and development of oppression and injustice within and among societies over the past ten thousand years is essentially a series of variations on the theme of coercively initiated and maintained exploitative modes of resource control, work and production, exchange and distribution, and governance and socialisation. This history is a tragic one indeed. The mere mention of coercive work systems, such as ancient and recent slavery, feudal serfdom, and early and contemporary industrial and agricultural exploitative wage labour, brings to mind images of toiling people, transformed, not by their own choice, into dehumanised factors of production, dominated and exploited by tyrants and slave masters, absolute rulers and aristocrats, and individual and corporate, capitalist employers. Such work systems could never have been established and perpetuated without massive coercion and violence in the form of civil and foreign wars, genocide, murder, torture, imprisonment, starvation, destitution, discrimination, unemployment, and the ever-present threat of these and other oppressive measures (Hunt & Sherman, 1986; Pope John Paul II, 1982; Tucker, 1978).

ECONOMIC SYSTEMS, SOCIAL JUSTICE, AND SOCIAL INJUSTICE

Economic practices and ideologies tend to be shaped by the dominant values of their societies. When these values stress equality, liberty, cooperation, sharing, and community, as was the case in early, socially just, nomadic societies, economic practices are geared to the fulfillment of everyone's real needs, and people are not dominated and exploited by others. On the other hand, when dominant values of societies stress inequality, selfishness, individualism, and competition, as is the case in socially unjust, feudal and capitalist societies, the main goal of economic practices is not to meet everyone's real needs, but to materially enrich dominant social classes and individual and corporate entrepreneurs. People working under feudalism and in capitalist enterprises are, therefore, usually dominated and exploited. The intensity of domination and exploitation tends to vary with time, place, and type of enterprise. It is also influenced, to some degree, by public policies and the relative political power of landlords, entrepreneurs, and workers and their unions. However, in spite of these variations, feudal and capitalist economic systems cannot function unless working people are dominated by, and dependent on, landlords and entrepreneurs, and unless adequate profits are generated through exploitation. Feudal and capitalist economic systems are, therefore, by definition, incompatible with social justice and freedom, and with genuine democracy.

WELFARISM AND SOCIAL WORK

Merriam Webster's Collegiate Dictionary (10th edition) defines 'welfarism' as 'the complex of policies, attitudes, and beliefs associated with the welfare state'. It defines 'social work' as 'any of various professional activities and methods concretely concerned with providing social services and esp. with the investigation, treatment, and material aid of the economically underprivileged and socially maladjusted'. As suggested at the outset, social work and welfarism evolved as societal responses to systemic social injustice and its manifestations as social-structural ill-fare. The roots and functions of welfarism and social work are complex. They involve a sense of guilt by privileged segments of societies concerning socially structured, multiple inequalities benefiting them and a corresponding ancient sense of human siblinghood and solidarity, acknowledged by religious teachings and social philosophy. They also involve efforts to maintain the status quo of social injustice and defend it against social change movements. Finally, they involve appeals to self-interest of citizens as well as overt and covert measures to control dominated and exploited social groups in order to assure their submission to prevailing systems of work, production, and distribution of goods, services, and civil and political rights.

The scope, contents, and quality of welfarism and social work in different societies tended to vary over time in relation to changes in economic realities and the political philosophy of governments. Regardless of these changes, welfarism and social work aimed usually to alleviate destructive consequences and symptoms of social and global injustice. They were never intended to eliminate social-structural ill-fare and its roots in the very fabric of unjust societies and cultures. While the roots of social injustice and ill-fare cannot be eliminated as long as capitalist economic systems and corresponding cultural tendencies prevail, welfarism and social work could be enhanced significantly in the context of now prevailing realities. Evidence for this can be found in the scope and quality of social provisions and welfare services in many capitalist countries in Europe and elsewhere. By using revenues from progressive tax systems, adequate healthcare, childcare, education, housing, social security, and income security could be assured to everyone. Poverty and unemployment could be reduced by public work programmes and by redistributing work. Such redistribution could be accomplished by reducing the length of work days through legally established, flexible limits. Finally, a public system of children's allowances and caretaker wages for childcare, care of the sick and elderly by parents and relatives could be established to spread work and income in addition to providing emotional benefits (Gil, 1992).

SOCIAL JUSTICE MODEL OF SOCIAL WORK

Can social workers, while helping people deal with diverse social problems in prevailing realities, act also as agents of fundamental social change, aimed at overcoming injustice and oppression? There are no easy answers to this question, but growing numbers of social workers in the USA and elsewhere think a social change or 'radical orientation' could be integrated into everyday practice (Bailey & Brake, 1975; Galper, 1980; Gil, 1976, 1987, 1998; Reynolds, 1986). Doing so could eventually resolve contradictions between the conventional tendency of social work and welfarism to help people adjust to the status quo of domination and exploitation, and the ethical imperative to confront injustice and oppression.

To transcend conventional social work practice and function as agents of social change, social workers require theoretical and philosophical perspectives and practice principles different from those now prominent in the profession. They also require an attitude of experimentation and critical consciousness toward their practice, and they need to help one another to evaluate it, and to deal constructively with resistance from administrators, supervisors, and colleagues in organisations practising along conventional lines. Support-and-study groups of radical social workers and networks of such groups could facilitate mutual help among practitioners who feel often isolated in their places of work. Radical social work is based on Marxist assumptions discussed earlier in this chapter concerning human nature and human needs; individual and political struggles for social justice and social development; social evolution, social policies, and social values; human relations to the natural and cultural environment; and the meanings of social and global justice (see Chapter 47). It involves the following practice principles discussed below:

1   rejecting political neutrality;
2   rejecting value neutrality;
3   transcending technical or professional approaches;
4   facilitating critical consciousness through dialogue;
5   advocating human rights;
6   confronting obstacles to needs fulfillment;
7   gaining insight into personal oppression;
8   prefiguring future possibilities; and
9   spreading critical consciousness and building social movements.

Rejecting political neutrality

Radical practice ought to contribute consciously to political struggles for social justice and human liberation. This principle differs from the conventional view that mixing politics and practice is unethical and unprofessional and practice ought, therefore, to be politically neutral. Many social workers view politics as a domain apart from practice, and tend to consider it a private affair, to be engaged in only away from their practice settings. However, political neutrality is an illusion since social work practice usually has political roots and consequences, regardless of the intentions and consciousness of practitioners. Political neutrality would require practitioners neither to support nor challenge the societal status quo. Yet, not challenging an existing social order means actually supporting it tacitly rather than being neutral toward it. Hence neutrality in itself is a political act for it transforms practice into a subtle tool for supporting the status quo, while preventing it from becoming a tool for challenging it. Political support for the status quo, rather than neutrality is also implicit in the view of many social workers that people's problems are due mainly to individual shortcomings, as well as in practice approaches based on this view, which support adaptation to prevailing social realities. Since political consequences of social work practice seem thus unavoidable, though practitioners may not be aware of them, the view mixing politics and practice is unethical and unprofessional seems invalid. It would, therefore, be more appropriate in ethical terms, to replace unintended, covert political aspects of practice with consciously chosen, overt ones, and to hold social workers accountable for their political choices and for the consequences of these choices. An appropriate political choice for radical social workers would be a commitment to social justice and human liberation.

Rejecting value neutrality

Just as radical practice cannot be politically neutral, it also cannot be value free for social work practice either reflects and upholds the dominant values of society, or rejects and replaces them. Radical social workers would therefore have to reject the notion of value-free practice. They would consciously have to choose values opposed to those shaping existing, unjust, and oppressive institutions. The core values of radical social work would, therefore, have to be equality, liberty, cooperation, and affirmation of community in pursuit of individual and social development. People would have to be considered equal in worth and dignity, in spite of individual and cultural differences, and they would have to have equal rights, responsibilities, and constraints in all spheres of life, and be free from domination and exploitation (Tawney, 1931). These values seem crucial for radical practice since the problems people bring to social workers tend to result, directly or indirectly, from societal dynamics shaped by values of inequality, selfishness, competition, domination and exploitation.

Transcending technical or professional approaches

Radical social workers need to transcend technical or professional approaches, fragmented by fields of service, and concerned mainly with relieving symptoms and facilitating coping under prevailing social conditions. While these are valid and important short-range objectives, they do not confront the roots of social problems in the fabric of society. Social problems are usually not isolated fragments to be overcome by 'professional and technical fixes' but symptoms of the totality of particular ways of life. Radical social workers need to help people trace the links between their particular problems and the dynamics of their ways of life, and to support them in confronting the problems at their roots.

Facilitating critical consciousness through dialogue

An appropriate medium for radical social work practice, regardless of function, level, and setting, is an emancipating dialogical process. Such a process involves sensitive exploration of problems, as experienced and perceived by people; supportive measures designed to ameliorate these problems; and help with unraveling links between the perceived problems and their societal roots and dynamics (Freire, 1970). Emancipating dialogue is also intended to facilitate insights into human nature, into the shaping of social realities by people, and into people's capacities to change and reshape these realities. It also aims to help people affirm their worth, dignity, rights, and potential collective power, and to support them in the pursuit of fundamental solutions to their problems, through involvement in social movements that struggle against injustice and oppression. Dialogical process must never deteriorate into indoctrination, for its ultimate aim is to facilitate emergence of critical consciousness through sensitive, supportive, liberating, nonauthoritarian, and nonhierarchic relationships.

Advocating human rights

Another important principle of radical practice is advocacy, aimed at assuring the exercise of all rights to which people are entitled under prevailing policies. However, these policies do not grant adequate rights for they have shaped the very conditions under which people's problems have emerged and continue to be regenerated. Advocacy by radical social workers would therefore have to transcend demands for implementing existing rights. It would have to present demands for equal rights, responsibilities, constraints, and opportunities, and would have to challenge policy proposals which tend to be mere variations on ancient themes of inequality, domination, and exploitation.

Confronting obstacles to needs fulfillment

Radical social workers consider the fulfillment of common human needs and the development of people's innate capacities the goal of just and free societies. They would have to facilitate, therefore, insights into obstacles to need fulfillment and human development in 'violent' social structures, such as coercively established and maintained, exploiting and alienating modes of work and systems of rights distribution. Based on these insights, they would have to advocate transformation and redesign of prevailing systems of work and rights distribution, in ways conducive to unobstructed human development (Gil, 1996).

Gaining insight into personal oppression

Radical social workers would need to explore whether, in the prevailing social realities, they too may be unable to actualise their innate potential; whether their individual development may also be inhibited; and whether they too may be victims of dominating and exploiting, social, economic, and political dynamics, though in different forms, and to a lesser extent the people they serve. They may realise through such explorations they too have a personal stake in human liberation and social equality, and they would have to identify with oppressed people, including the ones they serve, and join their struggles and movements, rather than identify with dominant classes and their institutions, values, and policies. Furthermore, they may conclude they would have to transcend prevailing formal divisions between themselves and the people they serve, divisions reflective of conventional concepts of professionalism and expertise, according to which education, competence and skills entitle people to privilege, authority, and higher social status.

Prefiguring future possibilities

Radical social work would have to involve efforts to transform the style and quality of practice relations and administration in social services from vertical, authoritarian, nonegalitarian patterns toward horizontal, participatory-democratic, egalitarian ones, as far as this is possible in prevailing realities. Every space within existing settings, which radical practitioners can influence, could be transformed to reflect alternative possible human relations. In this way, elements of alternative realities, or prefigurations of future possibilities, could be created experimentally, within existing service organisations, by and for the providers and users of the services. Unions and support-and-study groups of social workers could incorporate elements of such prefigurations and could link up with local and translocal networks of social movements for human liberation. Undoubtedly, such efforts and experiments are difficult to carry out. They are likely to involve risks, resistance, and conflicts, since they test and try to expand the limits of what is possible within prevailing realities. Such testing and expansion of limits are, however, essential aspects of liberation processes (Gorz, 1967).

Spreading critical consciousness and building social movements

Finally, radical social workers would need to initiate dialogues with colleagues concerning workplace, practice, and social justice issues, in order to spread critical consciousness concerning these matters. They would also have to organise unions and support-and-study groups at their workplaces and participate in social and political action and movement building within and beyond their local communities.

EPILOGUE

Can the vision of social and global justice that motivates the practice of radical social workers be realised and replace the status quo of structural ill-fare and welfarism? While the current tendencies of the human species seem to move mainly in the opposite direction toward perpetuation and intensification of violence-enforced injustice, from local to global levels, there are no reasons, in theory, to doubt people can reverse this current suicidal course. Such a reversal would, however, require massive, multigenerational, revolutionary efforts by nonviolent social movements to spread critical consciousness and evolve alternative patterns of social institutions, shaped by values of equality, liberty, sharing, and cooperation.

Rather than becoming paralysed by negative scenarios predicted by analysts, social justice activists, including social workers committed to their ethical mandate, need to intensify their struggles against the causes of injustice and oppression in order to increase the probability of avoiding the self-destruction of the human species. Antonio Gramsci's (in Hoare & Smith, 1971) answer to the existential dilemma, while jailed under fascism in Italy for his commitment to social justice and human equality, seems as sound a guide to present global realities, as it was in his time: what is needed is *pessimism of the mind, optimism of the will*.

REFERENCES

Bailey, R., & Brake, M. (eds) (1975). *Radical social work*. London: Edward Arnold.
Farb, P. (1968). *Man's rise to civilization*. New York: Avon Books.
Frank, A.G. (1978). *World accumulation 1492–1789*. New York: Monthly Review.
Freire, P. (1970). *Pedagogy of the oppressed*. New York: Herder and Herder.
Fromm, E. (1955). *The sane society*. Greenwich, CT: Fawcett.
Galper, J. (1980). *Social work practice: A radical approach*. Englewood Cliffs, NJ: Prentice Hall.
Gil, D.G. (1973). *Unravelling social policy*. Cambridge, MA: Schenkman.
Gil, D.G. (1976). *The challenge of social equality*. Cambridge, MA: Schenkman.
Gil, D.G. (1987). Human services and human liberation: Notes on practice and education. *Journal of Teaching in Social Work, 1*(2), 155–165.
Gil, D.G. (1992). *Unravelling social policy* (5th ed.). Rochester, VT: Schenkman.
Gil, D.G. (1996). Preventing violence in a structurally violent society: Mission impossible. *American Journal of Orthopsychiatry, 66*(1), 77–84.
Gil, D.G. (1998). *Confronting injustice and oppression*. New York: Columbia University Press.

Gil, D.G. (2004). *Perspectives on social justice. Reflections*, *10*(4), 32–39.

Gorz, A. (1967). *Strategy for labor.* Boston: Beacon Press.

Hoare, Q., & Smith, G.N. (eds) (1971). *Selections from the prison notebooks of Antonio Gramsci.* New York: International Publishers.

Hunt, E.K., & Sherman, H.J. (1986). *Economics.* New York: Harper and Row.

Kanter, R.M. (1972). *Communes: Creating and managing the collective life.* New York: Harper and Row.

Kropotkin, P. (1956). *Mutual aid.* Boston, MA: Porter Sargent.

Magdoff, H. (1969). *The age of imperialism.* New York: Monthly Review.

Maslow, A.H. (1970). *Motivation and personality.* New York: Harper and Row.

Maslow, A.H., Honigmann, J.J., & Mead, M. (1970). Synergy: Some notes of Ruth Benedict. *American Anthropologist*, *72*(2), 320–333.

Pope John Paul II (1982). *On human work: Laborem exercens.* Boston, MA: Daughters of St Paul.

Reynolds, B.C. (1986). in Freedberg, S. (1986). Religion, profession, and politics: Bertha Capen Reynolds' challenge to social work. *Smith College Studies in Social Work*, *56*(2), 95–110.

Tawney, R.H. (1931). *Equality.* London: George Allen and Unwin.

Tucker, R. (ed.) (1978). *The Marx-Engels reader* (2nd ed.). New York: W.W. Norton.

Zinn, H. (1995). *A people's history of the United States.* New York: Harper and Row.

Theorising the Neoliberal Welfare State for Social Work

Mimi Abramovitz

Neoliberalism is not a familiar term in the USA where the word 'liberal' refers to a political, not an economic theory. Yet under the name of 'Reaganomics' or 'supply-side economics', neoliberalism has shaped US social policy, the delivery of social services, and social work practice since the mid-1970s when the US economy plunged into a serious economic crisis. Neoliberal economic theory of the welfare state differs sharply from the New Deal/Great Society tradition in democratic politics, commonly referred to as 'liberal' in the USA. It represents a modern version of standard *laissez-faire* doctrine guiding the US economy prior to the Great Depression. It argues for market rules to govern societies in the belief the advancement of human well-being depends on the liberation of individual initiative within an institutional framework based on free markets, free trade, and private property rights and in which the government's main role is to create the conditions for profitable market activity and then to step back (Harvey, 2005). Endorsing market dynamics, neoliberalism's core principles include freedom (from external coercion), individualism (the unfettered pursuit of self-interest), and restricted state action. The theory limits state intervention to ensure free competition, maintain law and order, enforce contracts, and protect private property and national defence. Fundamentally hostile to social welfare programmes, it begrudgingly tolerates temporary and emergency government intervention in this arena (Mullaly, 2007).

The neoliberal conceptualisation contrasts sharply with liberal political theory guiding the development of the welfare state after World War II in the USA, Britain, Western Europe, and Scandinavia. While also pro-market, liberal political theory called for government to mediate the excesses of the market by ensuring a minimum level of well-being (Mullaly, 2007; Wilensky & Lebeaux, 1958). British sociologist T.H. Marshall (1992) added that governments should provide a minimum standard of income, nutrition, health, housing, and education to every citizen as a right, and not as charity. Historically, he noted modern governments began to address the social right (to income and economic support) in the 20th century in response to problems created by industrialisation. This generally followed the granting of civil rights (to free speech and a fair trial) in the 18th century and political rights (to vote or hold office) in the 19th century (see Chapter 24).

The 20th century social rights approximate those outlined in the Universal Declaration of Human Rights (1948) and were often implemented in response to pressure from social movements. Esping-Andersen's (1990) analysis of welfare state regimes included three ideal welfare state types whose social and economic rights varied with how the nation organised the relationship between the state, the market, and the individual, and included the liberal or Keynesian welfare state (as found in the USA and UK), the conservative-corporatist welfare state (e.g., Germany), and the social-democratic welfare state (e.g., Sweden and Denmark). In the USA, conservatives are sceptical of the state intervention favoured by liberals within the Keynesian welfare state.

Neoliberal theory became dominant in the USA in the mid-1970s and extended the definition of the market from a simple system of exchange to include all processes of voluntary agreement among persons. Its policies are most often associated with the structural adjustment programmes administered by several international bodies, including the World Bank, the International Monetary Fund, and the World Trade Organisation. However, during the last three decades, neoliberalism also gained considerable traction in the USA, Canada, Britain, and Western Europe where its antistate approach influenced welfare state policies, albeit at varying paces and in different ways.

Seeing market-driven economic growth as a better alternative than the Keynesian welfare state, supporters defend neoliberal policies with two main arguments: (i) there is no alternative to the market economy, and (ii) a rising tide lifts all boats. The first view popularised by Margaret Thatcher, conservative British Prime Minister (1975–1990), holds to avoid disaster, societies have no choice but to uphold free markets, free trade, and globalisation. The second argument implies the benefits of business-friendly neoliberalism will automatically trickle down to the average person. During the last three decades, neoliberalism trumped many of the ideas and policies introduced by the New Deal coalition and its – liberal-progressive – tradition in democratic politics, As a result, neoliberal assumptions became embedded in 'common sense', for example, the taken-for-granted consciousness of large numbers of people, including those whose interests may not be served by its policies. Social work critics, among others, say its 'survival of the fittest' approach to civic life transformed social welfare policy in ways that conflict with social work values and ethics (Dominelli, 1999; Garrett, 2010).

THE WELFARE STATE AND 20TH CENTURY ECONOMIC CRISES

Traditional liberal political theory supporting an expanded welfare state has guided US social welfare policy since the 1930s when the collapse of the economy led to the birth of the welfare state. However, a second major crisis in the mid-1970s gave rise to the neoliberal paradigm. Yet neither the rise of the US welfare state in the 1930s nor the neoliberal paradigm surfacing in the mid-1970s was accidental. The Social Structures of Accumulation (SSA) theory suggests these developments are best understood as part of a broader response to the two major economic crises of the 20th century (McDonnough et al., 2010). In both, the 1930s and the mid-1970s, the SSA or the institutional arrangements creating the conditions for profits and growth during the prior 50 years faltered. They no longer worked for the powers-that-be in business and government called who then for their 'reform'. The resolution of each crisis followed considerable political conflict eventually forcing a major reorganisation of the prevailing SSA (Bowles et al., 1986; Lippit, 2010; Kotz, 2003a, 2003b; McDonough et al., 2010).

First economic crisis: advent of the New Deal

The two major economic crises erupting in the USA during the 20th century elicited dramatically different responses from business and government. The stock market crash of 1929 made it clear that the *laissez-faire* SSA powering economic growth since the 1890s no longer worked. The 1930s elite blamed their economic woes on the failure of the market and, however unwillingly, called upon the federal government to enact policies to promote economic growth and mute the period's mounting unrest. Faced with extreme hardship, the poor, working, and middle classes also took to the streets. They too demanded a new and stronger government response.

After considerable political struggle over the character of the next SSA, Washington responded with the New Deal ushering in a major restructuring of the political economy. Among many other changes, two new institutional arrangements legitimised the emergent SSA. The Supreme Court declared the constitutionality of federal responsibility for the general welfare. Second, officialdom, that is, the national political and economic elites, accepted the economic theory of John Maynard Keynes calling for greater government spending to increase aggregate demand and otherwise stimulate economic growth (Bowles et al., 1986). The New Deal helped business, banks, farmers, workers, and some (mostly white) families get back on their feet. (The law excluded Black domestic and farm workers for years to come.) Despite this spending, it took the stimulus of war production to produce a full economic recovery (Bernstein, 1960).

The New Deal represented a new SSA based on *expanding the role of the state* and *redistributing income downward*. Newly created institutional arrangements contributed to these goals: (i) the highly progressive income tax code (i.e., 25 brackets, a tax rate of 94% on the top bracket, and high corporate taxation; and (ii) the 1935 Social Security Act that transferred social welfare responsibility from the states to the federal government and created an entitlement to income support – some 50 years after most other industrial nations had invested in social welfare (Abramovitz, 1996). From 1945 to 1975, the US welfare state grew in response to population growth, the emergence of new needs, increased revenues, greater administrative capacity – and the victories of the increasingly militant social movements demanding a larger share of the economic pie.

Impact of the New Deal: enhanced social, economic, and political functions

Some say the New Deal SSA helped to 'save capitalism from itself' by carrying out a complex set of social, economic, and political functions. The *social functions* of the welfare state ensure the well-being of the individuals and families. Following the New Deal and World War II, rising tax revenues enabled the government to provide a minimum level of income below which no one was expected to live, especially not the white middle class. Revenues rose from 16.5% of gross domestic product (GDP) (1947) to a peak of 19.7% (1969) and spending on human resources increased from 3.5% of GDP (1947) to a high of 11.7% (1976) (The White House, 2010a). The programmes helped families to function more fully and effectively by compensating millions of people for income lost due to old age, illness, disability, joblessness, and absence of parental support. They also provided an array of health, education, housing, employment, and social services.

The resulting redistribution of resources downward reduced poverty and inequality. The percentage of the population living in poverty fell sharply from 22.4% (1959) to 11.1% (1973) (US Census Bureau, 2010a). The inequality gap also narrowed. The share of the national income held by the top 20% of earners fell from 42.7% (1949) to 40.5% (1968). Meanwhile, the share held by the bottom 20% rose from 4.5% (1949) to a high 5.8% (1974) (US Census Bureau, 2003). Black median income rose from 51% of white median income (1947) to a high of 61% (1972) (Working Group on Extreme Inequality, 2009). However, in exchange for greater economic security, welfare state rules and regulations forced many recipients to comply with white middle-class work and family norms or risk penalties for departing from these prescribed roles.

The economic functions of the welfare state that helped to create the conditions for profitable economic activity are less widely recognised than its antipoverty role. Indeed, this multifaceted institution secured at least some corporate support because government assistance served business by helping families to: (i) increase their purchasing power, which ensured the daily consumption of goods and services produced by business and industry; (ii) raise children to fulfil proper adult work and family roles, which supplied business with a healthy, educated, and socialised workforce; and (iii) provide care to those too old, young, or ill to support themselves, activities which were typically carried out by women's unpaid labour in the home (Abramovitz, 1992a) (see Chapter 5). Government benefits also (iv) supplemented wages allowing employers to pay less; and (v) quieted the social unrest produced by market inequality. More generally, cash assistance (vi) mediated the tension arising when the conditions promoting profitable production (e.g., low wages and high unemployment) simultaneously undercut the capacity of families to carry out their socially assigned, caretaking tasks on which profits also depend.

The postwar progressive tax code and the expanded welfare state helped to fuel economic growth. The real GDP increased an average of 3.99% a year from 1947 to 1973 due to welfare state spending but also pent up war demand, technological advances, the Cold War arms race, and US control of world markets, among other historical factors (Measuring Worth, n.d.). Since wages rose in tandem with increased productivity, workers reaped a fair share of the economic pie their efforts helped to expand (Bernstein & Allegretto, 2007).

The *political functions* of the welfare state include promoting political stability. The redistribution of income downward and the expansion of the welfare state eased discontent among the disadvantaged, legitimised 'the system' as fair, and otherwise contributed to electoral calm and business profits. Indeed access to benefits mediated two key contradictions: (i) the conflict between the above-noted requirements of economic production and family well-being; and (ii) the conflict between the democratic promise of equal opportunity for all and market-based inequalities. Further, New Deal labour legislation, especially The Wagner Act (1935) and the Taft Hartley Act (1947), articulated an informal set of mutual expectations or labour 'accords' in which unions exchanged higher wages and better working conditions for longer contracts, and fewer and less militant strikes (e.g., the reduced turmoil) sought by US corporations. The resulting stability smoothed the way for higher profits, improved wages, better working conditions (Lippit, 2010; McDonough et al., 2010; Neumann & Rissman, 1984), and the growth of union membership peaking in the mid-1950s with the merger of the American Federation of Labor (AFL) and the Congress of Industrial Organization (CIO). In the 1960s, business and government entered into similar race and gender accords in which the civil rights and women's liberation movements exchanged an improved standard of living for less political conflict (Abramovitz, 1992b). The expanded welfare state helped to raise the standard of living for many, if not all, US households, especially the white middle class. The real minimum wage (in 2006 US$) increased from $2.82 an hour (1948) to a high of $7.17 (1968) and real private sector wages grew from $7.86 per hour (in 1982 US$) in 1964 to a high of $8.99 (1976). Median family income more than doubled from $20,102 (1947) to $40,656 (1977) (Economic Policy Institute, 2007; US Census Bureau, 1998). As a result, from 1947 to 1973 real median income and productivity grew hand-in-hand increasing by 103.9%

and 103.7%, respectively (Mishel et al., 2007). Overall employee compensation rose from 52% of the national income (1947) to over 60% (1970) and pre-tax corporate profits fell from a high of 11% (1951) to low of 8% (1975) and 6% (1980) (Aron-Dine & Shapiro, 2007).

Second economic crisis: crisis of capital accumulation

The second economic crisis surfaced in the mid-1970s as structural shifts in the domestic and global economies undermined the effectiveness of the postwar SSA. Third World revolutions (e.g., Vietnam and others), loss of easy access to cheap raw materials abroad, reduced world power, mounting economic competition from Germany and Japan, and greater business costs at home signalled the end of postwar prosperity. The resulting higher prices, rising interest rates, mounting national debt, limited savings, and constricted corporate investment set off a crisis of profitability (Weisskopf, 1981).

By the mid-1970s, the economic elite began to blame these threats to their power and profits on the New Deal and War on Poverty. The welfare state – already an easy target owing to ongoing racism and hostility to the poor – became the poster child for the neoliberal attack on 'big government' for several reasons (Harvey, 2005): (i) business and government who previously supported social programmes, however halting, were now blamed for rising investment costs on increased social welfare spending and 'excessive taxation'; (ii) globalisation reduced the reliance of US firms on their workers which lessened their need for social programmes to foster productivity and weakened trade unions which alleviated corporate worries about labour unrest (Amott, 1993); and, finally, (iii) the expanded welfare state unexpectedly emboldened social movements which undercut rather than promoted political stability. Like a strike fund, access to cash benefits operated as an economic backup to reduce worker's fears of unemployment and make it possible for women to challenge male domination and for persons of colour to challenge white supremacy and otherwise helped to tilt the balance of power towards those with less.

NEOLIBERAL RESPONSE: U-TURN IN PUBLIC POLICY

Neoliberalism, the dominant response to the second economic crisis of the 20th century, surfaced in the USA in the mid-1970s, when President Carter campaigned for the Democratic Party's nomination on an anti-Washington platform (Bresler, 2008). Best known as 'Reaganomics' or 'supply-side economics', neoliberalism was launched in full by the Reagan Administration and pursued in varying degrees by every US administration since then. Seeking to restore the primacy of the market and undo both the New Deal and the Great Society programmes, it rewrote the rules governing the relationship between business, individuals, and the state. The new SSA sparked a U-turn in public policy calling for downsizing the state and redistributing income upwards.

The now familiar SSA or institutional arrangements put in place to achieve these ends included: (i) tax cuts for wealthy individuals and firms eviscerating the progressive tax code; (ii) privatisation or shifting social welfare responsibility from the federal government to the private sector viewed as more efficient and effective; and (iii) devolution or shifting social welfare responsibility from the federal government to the states and, in some cases, municipalities. The strategy also favoured (iv) deregulation reducing federal oversight of business, banks, and labour markets and weakened consumer and environmental protections; (v) lowering labour costs; and (vi) weakening the influence of social movements best positioned to resist this austerity programme. At the same time, the New Right that gained ground in the early 1980s stood for (vii) restoring patriarchal 'family values', and (viii) a colour-blind social order to undo the gains of the women's liberation and civil rights movements.

IMPACT OF NEOLIBERALISM: DIMINISHED SOCIAL, ECONOMIC, AND POLITICAL FUNCTIONS OF THE WELFARE STATE

By the mid-1970s, the neoliberal strategy geared to downsizing the welfare state and redistributing income upwards began to take its toll. To paraphrase former US President Bill Clinton (1996), the era of big government was over. The strategy was grounded in tax and spending cuts. In 1981, newly elected President Reagan declared 'The taxing power of Government must be used to provide revenues for legitimate Government purposes ... It must not be used to regulate the economy or bring about social change' (Weisman, 1981, p. 1). The number of tax brackets dropped from 16 (1980) to four (1988) (Reagan) and three (1991) (Bush I). They inched up to five (Clinton) and six (Bush II) where they stood in 2010. Reagan also dropped the tax rate on the top bracket from 50% (1982) to 28% (1988), the lowest rate since 1920 (Tax Policy Center, n.d.a). The rate rose to 39% (Clinton) and fell to 35% (Bush). The corporate income tax rate dropped to a low of 34% (1988) and 35% today (Tax Policy Center, n.d.b). Still somewhat graduated, the US tax code became considerably less progressive than in the past.

Revenues helping to cover the cost of government during the postwar years fell from 19.7% of the GDP (1969) to 14.8% (2009) – the lowest level since 1951 (The White House, 2010a). Despite population growth, rising prices, new unmet needs, and other demands on the welfare state, spending on human resources fell from 11.7% of GDP (1976) to 11.4% (2000), which was less than what was spent in 1995. Eventually, ever-rising healthcare costs (not necessarily improved access or quality) and the economic crisis forced spending to a new high of 15.1% (2009) (The White House, 2010b). To counter this growth, the supply-siders insisted on more tax cuts ignoring that economic growth during a tax hike period (1993–2001) had exceeded that of two tax cut periods (1981–1993 and 2001–2007) (Ettlinger & Irons, 2008); and that from 2001 to 2007 entitlements accounted for 10% of the deficit compared to 48% for tax cuts (Center on Budget and Policy Priorities, 2008).

This ongoing retrenchment undercut *the social functions* of the welfare state, especially its capacity to support family functioning and community well-being. Many readers will know 'welfare reform' stripped the programme – then known as Aid to Families with Dependent Children (AFDC) – of its status as an entitlement programme. However, neoliberalism did not spare the Unemployment Insurance or Social Security programmes serving the middle class as well as the poor. Instead, new policies restricted access to all three entitlement programmes, reduced the number of eligible recipients, and lowered the benefit amounts (The White House, 2010c). The preference for privatisation intensified the use of the Earned Income tax credits and other asset-building strategies over direct government payment of benefits (Abramovitz, 2001; Brooks, 2008; Garrett, 2010). The still unsuccessful drive to replace Social Security with private Individual Retirement Accounts falls into this category.

With the deterioration of the welfare state's social functions, poverty rose and the inequality gap widened. In contrast to declining poverty during the postwar period, with neoliberalism the rate jumped from a low of 11.1% (1973) to a high of 15.3% (1983). It fell temporarily during the economic boom of the late 1990s, but after 2000 the rate began to climb again reaching over 14% in 2009 – an increase of four million from 2008 and the highest percentage in 15 years (see Table 2.1). More than 25% of Blacks and just under 25% of all Latinos lived in poverty in 2009 (US Census Bureau, 2010a). Without

Table 2.1   Poverty rates by selected years

Year	Poverty rate (%)
1960	22.2
1973	11.1
1983	15.2 (peak)
1990	13.5
1993	15.1
1995	13.8
2000	11.3 (low)
2005	12.6
2007	12.5
2008	13.2
2009	14.3

extended unemployment insurance benefits, the number would have increased by an additional 3.3 million people (Sherman et al., 2010).

The cumulative economic costs of childhood poverty have been estimated to be about $500 billion per year, or about 4% of GDP (Irons, 2009). Poverty also negatively affects educational achievement, cognitive development, and emotional and behavioural outcomes, all of which can have lasting consequences for children and adults.

Neoliberal policies converted the inequality gap into a chasm. Over the last 30 years, the top 1% of the country has received 36% of all household income gain. The share of national income held by the top fifth of earners (which had fallen during the postwar years) rose from 42.6% (1968) to 50.3% (2009), the highest share on record. At the same time, the share of the bottom fifth fell from a high of 4.3% (1974) to a low of 3.4% (2009). The share of the middle fifth fell from a high of 17.6% (1968) to 14.7% (2009) (US Census Bureau, 2010c).

The ratio of the top 1% of earners more than doubled from 9.4-to-1 to 19.9-to-1 between 1979 and 2006. Similarly, the after-tax income of the top 1% of US households jumped from $360,000 (1979) to $1.3 million (2009), while the much lower after-tax income of the middle 20% of households barely changed, moving from $34,000 to $50,000. That is, the after-tax income of the top 1% grew by 281% from 1979 to 2007 compared to 95% for the top fifth, 25% for the middle fifth, and 16% for the lowest group (see Figures 2.1 and 2.2).

Wealth disparities also grew. By 2004 the top 1% of the US households owned about

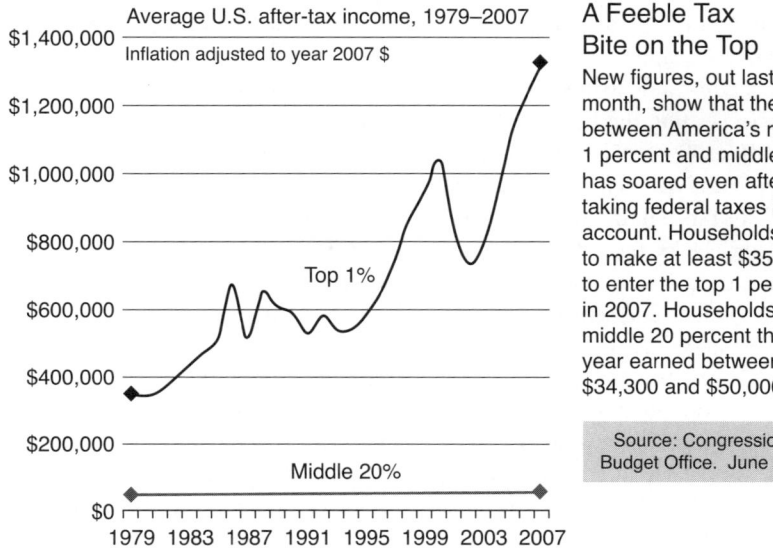

Figure 2.1   Average US after-tax income (1979–2007). (Source: Sherman & Stone, 2010)

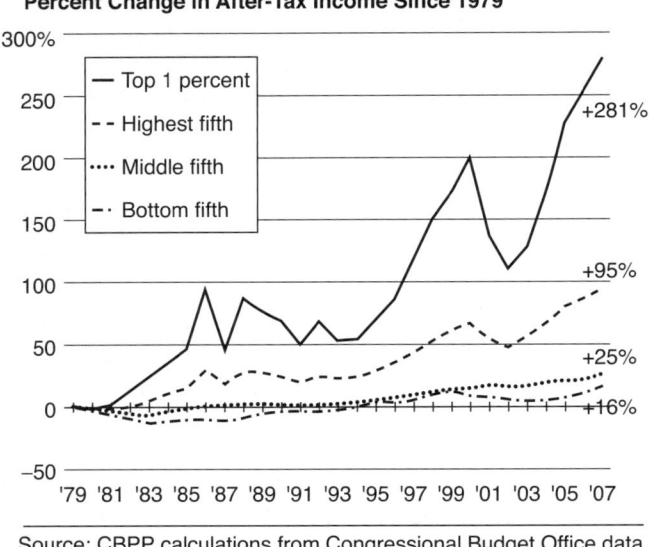

Figure 2.2 Incomes at the top dwarf those of low- and middle-income households. (Source: Sherman & Stone, 2010)

one-third of all the net worth (wealth minus debts), the top 20% controlled 85%, while the bottom 80% had only 15% (Magdoff & Yates, 2009). The top of 1% of the nation acquired much more of the nation's increased wealth than did the bottom 60% (Alter, 2010). The always wide racial disparities grew wider. After increasing from 51% of white median income in 1947 to a high of 61% in 1972, Black median income fell to about 52% in 1992 and then (reflecting the booming nineties) rose to 60% (1999) only to fall to 58% (2006). In 2009 White (non-Hispanic) earners comprised 80% of those in the top fifth compared to 5.7% for Blacks, 6.6% for Hispanics (of any race), and 6.3% for Asians. Blacks and Latinos were underrepresented at the top and overrepresented in the lowest two-fifths of earners (US Census Bureau, 2010d).

These patterns combined with globalisation reduced corporate interest in *the economic functions* of the welfare state they had previously relied on to create the conditions for profitable economic activity. With the fall of the Berlin Wall and the marketisation of China, US corporations found new consumers in Eastern Europe and Asia. This diminished their interest in supporting a welfare state to increase household purchasing power. Similarly, globalisation lessened corporate need for a welfare state that supplied them with healthy, educated, and properly socialised workers. Instead, US firms stepped up their efforts to lower labour costs (Greenhouse, 1983) by exporting production overseas, weakening unions, and shrinking the welfare state.

Deindustrialisation at home and outsourcing production abroad lowered labour costs by draining the US economy of 'good' jobs. After replacing highly paid unionised jobs in manufacturing with low-paid, non-unionised service jobs at home, business and industry searched for cheap labour abroad – aided by neoliberal free trade policies. They also weakened the influence of labour unions. In the early 1980s, President Reagan famously broke the federal air traffic controller's strike, in turn, empowering employers to launch a major assault on the rest of organised labour. Around that time, a Ford Foundation labour specialist observed 'Private and public employers will probably become more adamant in resisting union demands ...

Companies that have had antiunion ideas on their mind are going to be encouraged to act' (Serrin, 1981, n.p.). Reagan's public opposition to affirmative action and abortion similarly signalled permission to also attack civil rights and women's movement gains. Faced with massive job losses and corporate assault, union membership fell from a peak of 35% of the civilian labour force (1955) to 20% (1983) to a low of 13.1% (2006) (US Department of Labor, 2010a), with less fall off in the public than private sector (US Department of Labor, 2010b). Finally, by reducing access to cash benefits retrenchment increased the supply of workers looking for low paid jobs, forced workers and unions to moderate their wage demands, weakened the hard-won bargaining power of social movements – all of which pressed wages down. Labour costs fell. As noted earlier, from 1948 to 1970 the share of national income going to wages and salaries *rose* from 55.6% to 59.3%. However, with the advent of neoliberalism, the share of national income going to wages *fell* from the 1970 high to a new low of 51.6% (2006) – lower than in 1929 (Aron-Dine & Shapiro, 2007). According to the 2009 US Census (2010b), median incomes were 5% lower in 2009 than in 1999. Unlike the war years, when wages grew in tandem with productivity, wage growth has lagged far behind since the mid-1970s (Mishel et al., 2009; see Table 2.2).

Harvard economist Lawrence Katz told *The New York Times*, 'This is the first time in memory that an entire decade has produced essentially no economic growth for the typical American household' (cited in Herbert, 2010, p. A7). Not surprisingly, economic insecurity intensified. Based on its new Economic Security Index and mirroring the U-turn in public policy detailed here, the Rockefeller Foundation found, over the past 40 years, the share of (North) Americans experiencing economic insecurity rose substantially. The Index counts anyone as economically insecure if their income dropped 25% or more in one year and they did not have the financial resources to offset the loss. Using Census data in 2007 (before the recent meltdown), approximately 46 million Americans fell into this group, up from 28 million in 1985. In the past, economic security fluctuated with economic ups and downs but with neoliberalism it rose in both bad and in improved times (Hacker et al., 2010). This pattern mirrored labour market trends. During the seven recessions from 1948 to 1980 it took an average of 9–12 months for employment to reach pre-recession peaks. In the wake of the 1990 recession it took 23 months and 39 months after the 2001 downturn (Bivens & Shierholz, 2010). Not surprisingly, public opinion polls continue to report (North) Americans were highly worried about their job and financial situation (Gallup.com, 2010).

Alan Greenspan (1997), former chair of the US Federal Reserve Board and neoliberal champion, explained how business benefited from workers' economic insecurity when he observed a 'heightened sense of job insecurity . . . helps to subdue wage gains . . .'. Indeed, as economic insecurity mounted, the share of national income going to wages fell, while that going to profits rose from a low of 8% (1973) to an all-time high of 13.8% (2006). From 2001 to 2007, despite sluggish economic growth, corporate profits rose on average 10.8% per year compared to 7.4% for other comparable postwar periods (Aron-Dine et al., 2008). Perhaps this is why in 2005, when asked to choose between a union and no representation, 53% of non-unionised workers chose a union, up from 32% in 1990s and 30% in the 1980s. In the 1990s, 90% of unionised workers said they would vote for their union in a new election. Many other workers sought representation through

Table 2.2 Changes in productivity and wages (1947–2007)

Year	Change in productivity	Changes in real average wages
1947–1967	–	2.3%
1967–1973	2.5%	1.8%
1973–1979	1.2%	0.0%
1979–1989	1.4%	−0.6%
1989–2000	1.9%	0.6%
2000–2007	2.6%	0.4%

on-the-job worker committees (Freeman, 2007). With this, membership in public and private sector unions rose from 2006 to 2008, but fell slightly during the recession due to less employment (US Department of Labor, 2010a, 2010b).

Neoliberalism paradoxically undercut *the political functions* of the postwar welfare state, which business had relied on to avert or subdue unrest or otherwise foster political stability. Instead, neoliberal welfare state policies risked generating political instability. Cutting taxes and spending have yielded more unmet needs, higher poverty, falling wages, and greater inequality – four well-known ways to provoke political unrest. As early as 1998, the author of a Morgan Stanley economic report stated:

> With worker rewards (compensation) lagging worker contributions (productivity) since the early 1980s, I have argued that it was only a matter of time before a politically-inspired backlash would occur that would shift the pendulum of economic power from capital (shareholders) back to workers. While it hasn't happened yet, there is no reason to believe that such a reflex action won't occur at some point in the not-so-distant future (Editors, 2004, p. 4).

Although progressive workers, students, and welfare state clients are less likely to take to the streets than their European counterparts when confronted with a falling standard of living, the powers-that-be continue to worry mounting inequality and unabated economic insecurity risk political instability. In April 2000, William R. Cline, a trade expert at the Institute of International Finance told *Business Week*: 'What worries many people about globalisation [strongly linked to neoliberalism] is that the U.S. does little to help those who lose out. You want to make sure that the benefits of trade are fairly shared' (in Bernstein, 2000). Former Federal Reserve Chairman Alan Greenspan stated

> an increased concentration of income . . . is not the type of thing which a democratic society, a capitalist democratic society can really accept without addressing . . . because excluding significant parts of the population from the fruits of economic growth risks a backlash that can threaten prosperity' (in Altman et al., 2006, p. 18).

Writing in *The New York Times*, Peter Goodman (2007) noted 'unease with market forces can be heard ... [t]he invisible hand is being asked to account for what it has wrought' (n.p.). It is unlikely these observers had in mind the current group producing the most active social and political disruption in the USA – the far right Tea Party.

IMPLICATIONS FOR SOCIAL WORK

The postwar welfare state attempted to mediate the contradictions between the requirements of economic production (e.g., low wages and high unemployment) and the basis of family well-being (e.g., high wages and low unemployment) with some success. However, as antigovernment neoliberal policies took hold, they intensified the contradiction between aiding profits or meeting people's needs, and led to more health and social problems. Given social work's location at the juncture of the individual and society, the profession once again faced picking up the slack in a context of declining resources which often led to an exacerbation of its more punitive and controlling functions. Neoliberalism's call for downsizing the state never extended to all programmes. As Harvey (2005) and Navarro (2007) point out, neoliberal practice often differed from neoliberal theory. Despite its call for a smaller state, neoliberalism actually expanded state activities when it came to defence, national security, corporate welfare, and overall surveillance as well as the growth of prisons, the greater use of welfare-to-work programmes, strict sentencing laws, zero tolerance policing, the policing of public schools, among many other punitive, controlling or intrusive practices and policies. Social workers increasingly employed in such settings, often find themselves, knowingly or unknowingly, helping to carry out the neoliberal agenda.

Neoliberalism generated great economic hardship as more and more poor and working-class families earned too little or lacked cash benefits they needed to buy food, housing, health services, and childcare (Boushey et al., 2001). In 2003, 47% of poor families and 16% of nonpoor families experienced at least one hardship: overcrowded housing, food insecurity, or lack of medical care, with greater hardship rates among families of colour. In 2005, 16 million poor households paid more of their income in rent than the federally defined affordability standard or lived in overcrowded or substandard housing. Food hardship rose nationally from 16.3% of households in the first quarter of 2008 to 19.5% in the fourth quarter of 2008. In 2009 it hovered between 17.9% and 18.8% (Food Research Action Center, 2010).

In 2007 more than 40 million adults skipped some healthcare due to lack of money (e.g., medical, dental, mental health, and prescription drugs; Center on Budget and Policy Priorities, 2007). As private coverage declined, the share of uninsured persons rose from 15.4% (2008) to 16.7% (2009) – or 50.7 million – the largest single-year increase on record since 1987 (US Census Bureau, 2010b). In 2010 'hardship withdrawals' from 401(k) pension plans soared to their the highest level in 10 years, jumping from 45,000 in 2009 to 62,000 in 2010 – even though this action risked penalties and or less future retirement income. Nearly 40% of black workers and almost a third of Hispanic workers borrowed from these accounts compared to just 20% of White workers (Smith, 2010; Toplansky, 2010).

Social workers deal with social as well as economic problems. Wilkinson and Pickett (2009) examined more than 20 rich nations and found a linear relationship between an inequality gap and the presence of health and social problems. The nations with the largest inequality gap also had lower life expectancy, higher infant mortality, more mental illness and obesity, higher rates of teen births, school dropouts, murder, and less upward mobility. The researchers reported the USA had the largest inequality gap in the world and the inequality gap predicted the level of a country's health and social problems more accurately than its poverty rate. Similarly, among the 50 US states, those with the greatest inequality gap also had higher rates of health and social problems.

At the same time that poverty, hardship, and social problems increased, social services lost ground or became more punitive. The neoliberal retrenchment brought lower benefits and more restrictive eligibility requirements, but also renewed emphasis on self-help, deterrence, stiff work requirements, stigmatisation of single motherhood, penalties and sanctions for minor missteps, and the victim-blaming assumption something was wrong with clients rather than something had happened to them.

Neoliberalism's emphasis on devolution and privatisation further subjected social services to the logic of the market that undercut the quality of services provided. Services turned over to local communities suffered local racial bias or a lack of matching with federal funds or both. Privatisation created incentives for governments to purchase services from private not-for-profit but also from private for-profit social agencies. It also led agencies to adopt business management models (e.g., fees for services, and hiring low-paid and less skilled staff) stressing efficiency, productivity, and cost savings over quality care and furthered the commodification of interpersonal relationships embodied in caring work (Abramovitz, 1986, 1998, 2005; Dominelli, 1999; Ferguson, 2004; Garrett, 2010; see Chapter 22).

In a study of the impact of the neoliberal welfare reform on social services in New York City, Abramovitz (2005) found social service workers were doing more with less. They reported running up hill just to fix the problems retrenchment had created for their clients and felt less effective, had less control over their work, and experienced troublesome ethical dilemmas leading to significant stress and burnout. Agency directors who adopted compensatory strategies to make up for lost funds sadly described them as 'mission drift'.

Neoliberalism also intensified the welfare state's capacity to regulate behaviour. According to Schram et al., (2008), neoliberal governments increasingly govern poverty using new forms of the old emphasis on social control. This included a return to paternalist and custodial approaches emphasising directive, supervisory, and punitive policy tools and preference for decentralised systems to discipline subordinated populations for failure to integrate themselves into low-wage labour markets and or to follow heterosexual marriage norms – all of which falls heaviest on persons of colour (see Chapter 4). In *Regulating the Lives of Women*, Abramovitz (1996) concluded neoliberalism's new rules and regulations penalised those viewed as departing from prescribed work and family roles and otherwise engaged in 'irresponsible behaviour'. The latter included abortion, single motherhood, and same-sex marriage, among other personal choices. The neoliberal emphasis on individual choice also dismisses the reality of institutional racism and sexism and claims concerns about such oppression lack merit. Creating the semblance of colour and gender blindness allows the problems to go unaddressed (Roberts & Mahtani, 2010). This makes it harder for social workers to recognise the injuries of class, race, and gender and to rigorously engage in anti-oppressive practice (see Chapter 21). Similarly, an increased emphasis on narrow definitions of 'what works' leads social work to emphasise individual and behavioural change, to think of the change as a technical matter, to downplay its causes, and to pay less attention to the social determinants of health and social problems.

Finally, increased reliance of private charitable giving – another component of neoliberal privatisation – enlarged the 'charitable divide'. As the income of the top 10% of earners increased, they contributed more to the arts, cultural organisations, and universities. Meanwhile nonprofit agencies found it harder to attract large charitable donations, and the income and contributions from their regular but less affluent donors dwindled – even while the sagging economy increased the demand for services (Marx, 2010).

Social workers, among many others, ask how it is that 'the people' were convinced to accept a U-turn in public policy undermining their well-being and self-interest. 'The people' are not stupid but were poorly informed – or misinformed – by the war of ideas waged by neoliberalism's proponents. With considerable help from the media, well-paid lobbyists and wealthy contributors fueled an ideological campaign using rhetoric hypocritically arguing against big government while supporting policies benefiting the elite (Domhoff, 1990; George, 1999, Navarro, 2007). Their campaign played to four prevailing 'panics': (i) the economic panic among the anxious middle class suffering falling wages and disappearing jobs; (ii) the political panic among business and government leaders who feared the disaffected might rise up and blame them for the nation's mounting social and economic problems; (iii) the racial panic among White people which surfaced as persons of colour and immigrants began to institutionalise their hard-won gains; and (iv) the moral panic induced by changes in women's role and family structures advancing women's and gay rights.

CONCLUSION: FUTURE OF NEOLIBERALISM

Proponents of neoliberalism promised their pro-market, antistate strategy would trickle down to the average person. Although wealthy individuals and large corporations benefited from the upward redistribution of income, wealth, and profits, the failure of the promised economic growth to materialise contributed to the first economic crisis of the 21st century, popularly known as the Great Recession. Indeed, economic growth during the demonised 'big government' era outdid that during the celebrated neoliberal period. From 1947 to 1973, GDP growth averaged just less than 4% per annum (Measuring Worth, n.d.). But by the mid-1970s, the historic events and public policies motoring this sturdy growth lost steam. Advocates of neoliberalism stepped in with tax and spending cuts and other policies increasing profits and wealth but failed to generate growth (Measuring Worth, n.d.). From 1979 to 2007, the average annual growth rate fell to 2.96%. The 2.6% annual growth rate (2000–2007) was the weakest or near weakest since World War II (Aron-Dine et al., 2008). From 2007 to 2009, GDP growth averaged minus 1.01% (Measuring Worth, n.d.). The prolonged economic stagnation, in turn, provoked the credit and housing asset bubbles temporarily obscuring the underlying problem (Foster & Magdoff, 2008). By 2007, household debt had reached 100% of the GDP, financial business debt totalled 116%, and US debt amounted to 350% (Magdoff & Yates, 2009). This 'financialisation' kept the economy going until the bubble burst and brought growth to a virtual standstill.

Ominous signs prior to the 2008 meltdown led some neoliberal moderates to question the continued demonisation of government, the impact of mounting inequality, and the political consequences of the inequality gap. As far back as 2004, Orszag (2004) – then Brookings Institute economist – observed the deficit-financed tax cuts were unlikely to have significant positive effects on economic growth in the long term, and might well reduce it. In 2006 a Report by the Brooking Institute's Hamilton Project directed by Robert. E. Rubin, Clinton's Treasury Secretary and Obama's economic advisor, concluded 'getting government out of the way' is fundamentally misguided since sound government policy is essential to maximising long-term (economic) growth. The Report recommended greater government investment in both human capital and opportunities (Altman et al., 2006, p. 18). To ensure the productivity of workers and advance the USA's 'promise of opportunity, prosperity and growth', the Report called for government-supported access to financial assistance, educational training opportunities, and basic healthcare. It added market forces 'must be supported and supplemented by an effective public role, one in which government ensure[d] that the rules of the game [we]re fair, transparent, and binding for all parties' (Altman et al., 2006, p.14).

During the 2008 presidential primaries, conservative *New York Times* columnist David Brooks (2008) wrote: 'Supply Side Economics had a good run', adding today's 'Republicans [must] envision a different role for government than the 1980's Republicans' because workers 'want a government that is on their side'. Brooks recommended child tax credits to reduce stress on young families, universal healthcare, a tuition tax credit to help with education, and wage subsidies for laid-off workers forced to take low-paying jobs. Despite their differences, both Brooks and the Hamilton Project agreed the neoliberal tax cuts and hostility to government had become counterproductive. Both implicitly acknowledged the need for government to play a role in fostering family well-being, profitable economic growth, and political stability. In contrast, the recent US Tea Party movement favours shrinking the size of the state if not bringing the government down completely.

Others worry neoliberal inequality increases the vulnerability of the wider economic system. Their data show a major economic crisis followed each time the share of income controlled by the top 1% (and top 10%) peaked. In 1928, after 50 years of *laissez-faire* economic policy, the top 1% of US households claimed a record 23.9% of the pre-tax national income, the largest share since 1913. The following year the stock market crashed, leading to the Great Depression. In 2007, after almost 40 years of neoliberal *laissez-faire* policies, the top 1% of US households again claimed a record high 23.5% of the pre-tax national income, the highest share since 1928. In 2008, the US stock market crashed, leading to the Great Recession (Story, 2010). While the relationship between inequality and economic crises continues to be debated, one researcher suggested inequality might have 'pushed people at the bottom of the ladder toward choices that put the financial system at risk' and 'putting too much power in the hands of Wall Street titans enables them to promote policies that benefit them but that could put the system in jeopardy' (Story, 2010).

In 2006, Janet L. Yellen, President and CEO of the Federal Reserve Bank of San Francisco, declared 'there are signs that rising inequality is . . . impairing social cohesion, and could, ultimately, undermine American democracy'. Supreme Court Justice Louis Brandeis (1856–1941) summed the problem up many years ago when he said: 'We can have democracy in this county or we can have great wealth concentrated in the hands a few but we cannot have both' (cited in Collins & Yeskel, 2005, p. 13).

The collapse of the US middle class and the huge transfer of wealth to the already wealthy might be the biggest domestic story of our time. According to Kotz (2009), rather than just another financial downturn, the USA could be facing a systemic crisis of capitalism that would only be resolved through major restructuring of the political economy. The middle ground, if one ever existed, is fast receding. As with the prior economic crisis, the answer depends on the outcome of the political struggle, which social workers downplay or ignore at their own risk. If they become silent, tolerate, or promote actions violating humane practices, they implicitly align themselves with the neoliberal standards that violate the social justice underpinnings of social work.

Some people think taking a stand politicises a previously neutral, objective, and apolitical profession. Yet social work has always been political in that it deals either with the shaping of human consciousness or the allocation of resources. Since social workers cannot avoid the political, it is far better to address these issues explicitly than to pretend they do not exist. The history of the profession suggests activism on behalf of social work values offers a more ethical and effective option than calls for social work to avoid the political. Without such political struggles over the years, neither social work nor society would have changed for the better (see Chapter 17).

REFERENCES

Abramovitz, M. (1986). Privatizing the welfare state: A review. *Social Work, 31*(4), 257–264.

Abramovitz, M. (1992a). Poor women in a bind: Social reproduction without social supports. *Affilia: Journal of Women and Social Work, 7*(2), 3–44.

Abramovitz, M. (1992b). The Reagan legacy: Undoing class, race, and gender accords. *Journal of Sociology and Social Welfare, 19*(1), 91–110.

Abramovitz, M. (1996). *Regulating the lives of women: Social welfare policy from colonial times to the present.* Boston, MA: South End Press.

Abramovitz, M. (1998). The perils of privatization. *Ms Magazine*, January, p. 29.

Abramovitz, M. (2001). Everyone is still on welfare: The role of redistribution in social policy. *Social Work, 46*(4), 297–308.

Abramovitz, M. (2005). The largely untold story of welfare reform and the human services, *Social Work, 50*(2), 175–186.

Alter, J. (2010). The state of liberalism, *The New York Times. Book Review.* October 21, p. 1–14.

Altman, R.C., Brodoff, J.E., Orszag, P.R., & Rubin, R.R. (2006). *The Hamilton Project: An economic strategy for advancing opportunity, prosperity and growth.* The Brookings Institution. Retrieved June 18, 2010 from www.brookings.edu/es/hamilton/THP_Strategy.pdf

Amott, T. (1993). *Caught in the crisis.* New York: Monthly Review Press.

Aron-Dine, A., & Shapiro, I. (2007). *Share of national income going to wages and salaries at record low in 2006.* Center on Budget and Policy Priorities. Retrieved July 28, 2010 from http://www.cbpp.org/cms/?fa=view&id=634

Aron-Dine, A., Kogan, R., & Stone, C. (2008). *How robust was the 2001–2007 economic expansion?* Center on Budget and Policy Priorities. Retrieved July 28, 2010 from http://www.cbpp.org/cms/?fa=view&id=575\

Bernstein, A. (2000). Backlash: Behind the anxiety over globalization. *Business Week Online*. Retrieved July 25, 2010 from www.businessweek.com/2000/00_17/b3678001.htm

Bernstein, I. (1960). *The lean years: The history of the American worker, 1920–1933*. Boston, MA: Houghton Mifflin Co.

Bernstein, M.J., & Allegretto, S. (2007). *The state of working America, 2006–2007*. Economic Policy Institute. Ithaca, NY: Cornell University Press, pp. 45–46.

Bivens, J., & Shierholz, H.H. (2010). *For job seekers, no recovery in sight: Why prospects for job growth and unemployment remain dim*. Economic Policy Institute. Briefing Paper #259. Retrieved August 22, 2010 from http://www.epi.org/publications/entry/bp259/

Boushey, H.G., Gunderson, C., Brocht J., & Bernstein, J. (2001). *Hardships in America. The real story of working families*. Washington, DC: Economic Policy Institute.

Bowles, S.M., Gordon. D., & Weisskopf, T. (1986). Power and profits: The social structures of accumulation and the profitability of the post war economy. *Review of Radical Political Economics, 18*(1&2) 132–167.

Bresler, R.J. (2008). Liberalism's third act? *USA Today* (society for the advancement of education). Retrieved July 28, 2010 from http://findarticles.com/p/articles/mi_m1272/is_2752_316/ai_n24258648/?tag=content;col1

Brooks, D. (2008). Middle class capitalists. *New York Times*. Retrieved July 30, 2010 from http://www.nytimes.com/2008/01/11/opinion/11brooks.html?scp=7&sq=brooks+david&st=nyt

Center on Budget and Policy Priorities (CBPP) (2007). *Poverty and hardship affect tens of millions of Americans*. Retrieved July 18, 2010 from www.cbpp.org/12-20-07pov.htm#_edn5.

Center on Budget and Policy Priorities (CBPP) (2008). *Myth #1: Tax cuts 'pay for themselves'*. Retrieved July 29, 2010 from http://www.cbpp.org/cms/?fa=view&id=692#m1

Clinton, W. (1996). *State of the Union Address U.S. Capitol*. Washington, DC: January 23. Retrieved August 2, 2010 from http://clinton4.nara.gov/WH/New/other/sotu.html

Collins, C., & Yeskel, F. (2005). *Economic apartheid in America*. New York: The New Press.

Domhoff, W. (1990). *The power elite and the state*. New York: Aldine.

Dominelli, L. (1999). Neo-liberalism, social exclusion and welfare clients in a global economy. *International Journal of Social Welfare, 8*(1), 14–22.

Economic Policy Institute (2007). *Issue guide, minimum wage Table 4: The real value of the minimum wage, 1947–2006*. Retrieved July 20, 2009 from http://www.epi.org/issueguides/minwage/table4.pdf

Editors (2004). The stagnation of employment. *Monthly Review*, April, pp. 3–17.

Esping-Andersen, G. (1990). *The three worlds of welfare capitalism*. Princeton, NJ: Princeton University Press.

Ettlinger, M., & Irons, J. (2008). *Take a walk on the supply side: Tax cuts on profits, savings, and the wealthy fail to spur economic growth*. Center for American Progress and the Economic Policy Institute. Retrieved July 30, 2010 from http://www.americanprogress.org/issues/2008/09/pdf/supply_side.pdf

Ferguson, I. (2004). Neoliberalism, the third way, social work: The UK experience. *Social Work and Society, 2*(1), 1–9. Retrieved October 10, 2010 from http://www.socwork.net/2004/1/articles/425

Food Research Action Center (2010). *New data reveal extent of hunger in every corner of the U.S.* Retrieved August 12, 2010 from http://frac.org/Press_Release/food_hardship_report_jan2010.htm

Foster, J.B., & Magdoff, F. (2008). Financial explosion and stagnation: Back to the real economy. *Monthly Review, 60*(7), 1–29.

Freeman, R. (2007). *Do workers still want union: More than ever*. Economic Policy Institute. Briefing Paper #182, February 22. Retrieved September 18, 2010 from http://www.sharedprosperity.org/bp182.html

Gallup.com (2010). *Polls business and economy: About 40% of Americans worrying about money*. Retrieved August 19, 2010 from www.gallup.com/tag/Business%2band%2bEconomy.aspx

Garrett, P.M. (2010). Examining the 'conservative revolution': Neoliberalism and social work education. *Social Work Education, 29*(4), 340–355.

George, S. (1999). A short history of neoliberalism. *Conference on Economic Sovereignty in a Globalizing World*. March 24–26. Retrieved June 10, 2010 from http://www.globalexchange.org/campaigns/econ101/neoliberalism.html

Goodman, P.S. (2007). The free market: A false idol after all. *The New York Times*, 30 December. Retrieved July 9, 2010 from http://www.nytimes.com/2007/12/30/weekinreview/30goodman.html?_r=1&scp=1&sq= T e+free+market%3A+A+False+Idol&st=nyt

Greenhouse, S. (1983). The corporate assault on wages. *New York Times*. Retrieved August 13, 2010 from http://www.nytimes.com/1983/10/09/business/the-corporate-assault-wages.html?scp=18&sq=employer+wage+reductions&st=nyt

Greenspan, A. (1997). *Testimony before the Committee on Banking, Housing, and Urban Affairs.*, US Senate, July 22. Retrieved July 18, 2010 from file:///Info%20&%20data%20on%20Issues/Labor%20Market%20Issues%20/%20Greenspan%20-Job%20insecurity–%20July%2022,%201997.webarchivei

Hacker, J., Huber, G., Rehm. P., Schlesinger, M., & Valletta, R. (2010). *Economic security at risk: Findings from the economic security index.* New York: Rockefeller Foundation.

Harvey, D. (2005). *A brief history of neoliberalism.* New York: Oxford University Press.

Herbert, B. (2010). Two different worlds. *New York Times*, p. A7.

Irons, J.S. (2009). *Economic scarring: The long-term impacts of the recession.* Economic Policy Institute. Briefing Paper #343. Retrieved August 15, 2010 from http://www.epi.org/publications/entry/bp243/

Kotz, D. (2003a). Neoliberalism and the SSA theory of long run capital accumulation. Paper presented at the *Allied Social Science Associations Convention*, Washington, DC.

Kotz, D. (2003b). Neoliberalism and the US expansion of the 1990s. *Monthly Review*, *54*(11), 15–33.

Kotz, D. (2009). The financial and economic crisis of 2008: A systemic crisis of neoliberal capitalism. Paper prepared for a panel on *The Global Financial Crisis: Heterodox Perspective* at the Annual Convention of the Allied Social Science Association, San Francisco, CA.

Lippit, V.C. (2010). Social structures of accumulation theory. In D. Kotz, McDonough, T., & Reich, M. (eds), *Contemporary capitalism and its crises.* New York: Cambridge University Press, pp. 45–71.

Magdoff, F., & Yates, M.C. (2009). *The ABCs of the economic crisis.* New York: Monthly Review Press.

Marshall, T.H. (1992). Citizenship and social class. In T.H. Marshall & Bottomore, T. (eds), *Citizen and social class and other essays.* London: Pluto Press, pp. 8–17.

Marx, J.D. (2010). Commentary. Deregulating social welfare. *Social Work*, *55*(4), 371.

McDonough, T., Reich, M., & Kotz, D. (2010). Introduction: Social structure of accumulation theory. In T. McDonough, Reich, M., & Kotz, D. (eds), *Contemporary capitalism and its crises.* New York: Cambridge University Press, pp. 1–22.

Measuring Worth (n.d.). *Annualized growth rate of various historical economic crises.* US GDP (real). Retrieved August 20, 2010 from http://www.measuringworth.com/

Mishel, L. (2008). *Income inequality continues staggering 25-year growth trend.* Economic Policy Institute. June 18. Retrieved August 25, 2010 from http://www.epi.org/economic_snapshots/entry/webfeatures_snapshots_20080618/

Mishel, L., Bernstein, J., &. Allegretto, S. (2007). *The state of working America 2006–2007.* Economic Policy Institute. Ithaca, NY: Cornell University Press, pp. 45–46.

Mishel, L., Bernstein, J., & Shierholz, H. (2009). *The state of working America 2008/2009.* Economic Policy Institute T.3.4: Trends in average wages and average hours, 1967–2006 (2007 dollars). New York: ILR Press.

Mullaly, B. (2007). *The new structural social work* (3rd ed.). New York: Oxford University Press.

Navarro, V. (2007). Neoliberalism as class ideology: Or the political causes of the growth of inequalities. International. *Journal of Health Services*, *37*(1), 47–62.

Neumann, G.R., & Rissman, E.R. (1984). Where have all the union members gone? *Journal of Labor Economics*, *2*(2), 175–192.

Orszag, P. (2004). *The budget deficit: Does it matter?* Speech before the City Club of Cleveland, Retrieved July 16, 2010 from www.brookings.edu/views/speeches/20040716orszag.pdf

Roberts, D.J., & Mahtani, M. (2010) Neoliberalizing race, racing neoliberalism: Placing 'race' in neoliberal discourses. *Antipode*, *42*(2), 248–257.

Schram, S.F., Fording R., & Soss, J. (2008). Neo-liberal poverty governance: Race, place and the punitive turn in US welfare policy. C*ambridge Journal of Regions, Economy and Society*, *1*, pp. 17–36.

Serrin, W. (1981). Reagan's stance on PATCO causes union anxiety. *The New York Times.* Retrieved August 2, 2010 from http://www.nytimes.com/1981/10/21/us/reagan-stance-on-patco-causes-unions-anxiety.html?scp=11&sq=Reagan+air+traffic+controllers+strike&st=nyt

Sherman, A., & Stone, C. (2010). *Income gaps between very rich and everyone else more than tripled in last three decades.* Center on Budget and Policy Priorities (CBPP). Retrieved December 17, 2010 from http://www.cbpp.org/cms/?fa=view&id=3220

Sherman, A., Trisi, D., Greenstein, R., & Broaddus, M. (2010). *Census data show large jump in poverty and the ranks of the uninsured in 2009.* Center on Budget and Policy Priorities. Retrieved October 1, 2010 from http://www.cbpp.org/cms/index.cfm?fa=view&id=3294

Smith, A. (2010). *401K withdrawal spike*. CNNMoney.com. Retrieved September 21, 2010 from http://money.cnn.com/2010/08/20/news/economy/fidelity_401k_withdrawal/index.htm

Story, L. (2010). Income inequality and financial crises. *The New York Times*, 21 August. Retrieved August 26, 2010 from http://www.nytimes.com/2010/08/22/weekinreview/22story.html?scp=1&sq=Story%2C+Louise+Slicing+Pie&st=nyt

Tax Policy Center (n.d.a). *Historical individual tax parameters*. Retrieved July 22, 2010 from http://www.taxpolicycenter.org/taxfacts/displayafact.cfm?Docid=543

Tax Policy Center (n.d.b). *Historical corporate tax parameters*. Retrieved July 22, 2010 from http://www.taxpolicycenter.org/taxfacts/displayafact.cfm?Docid=65

Toplansky, E.F. (2010). Disturbing trend and worse to come. *American Thinker*. Retrieved September 30, 2010 from http://www.americanthinker.com/blog/2010/08/disturbing_trend_and_worse_to.html

United Nations (1948). *Universal Declaration of Human Rights*. Retrieved November 25, 2011 from http://www.un.org/en/documents/udhr/

US Census Bureau (1998). *Measuring 50 years of economic change, P60-203*. Table 2.1 Retrieved September 15 from www.census.gov/prod/3/98pubs/p60-203.pdf

US Census Bureau (2003). *Share of aggregate income received by each fifth and top 5 percent of families: 1947 to 2001*. Statistical Abstract of the United States, No HS.-26. Retrieved September 15 from http://www.census.gov/statab/hist/HS-26.pdf

US Census Bureau (2010a). *Poverty data historical tables*. T.2. Poverty status of people by family relationship, race and Hispanic origin, 1959–2009. Retrieved September 15, 2010 from http://www.census.gov/hhes/www/poverty/data/historical/people.html

US Census Bureau (2010b). *Income, poverty and health insurance coverage in the United States, 2009 (P60-238)*. Retrieved September 15, 2010 from http://www.census.gov/hhes/www/income/income.html

US Census Bureau (2010c). *Income, poverty and health insurance coverage in the United States, 2009 (P60-238)*.Table H-2. Retrieved September 20, 2010 from http://www.census.gov/hhes/www/income/data/historical/inequality/index.html

US Census Bureau (2010d). *Current population survey social and economic supplement. Table HINC-05*. Retrieved September 25, 2010 from http://www.census.gov/hhes/www/cpstables/032010/hhinc/new05_000.htm

US Department of Labor, Bureau of Labor Statistics (2010a). *Table 1. Union affiliation of employed wages and salary workers by selected characteristics*. Retrieved September 15, 2010 from http://www.bls.gov/cps/cpslutabs.htm

US Department of Labor, Bureau of Labor Statistics (2010b). *Table 3. Union affiliation of employed wages and salary workers by occupation and industry*. Retrieved August 19, 2010 from http://www.bls.gov/cps/cpslutabs.htm

Weisman S.R. (1981). Intentionally or not, tax policy is a social policy. *New York Times*, August 2. Retrieved August 14, 2010 from http://www.nytimes.com/1981/08/02/weekinreview/intentionally-or-not-tax-policy-is-a-social-policy.html

Weisskopf, T. (1981). The current economic crisis in historical perspective. *Socialist Review*, *57*, pp. 9–54.

White House (The) (2010a). Office of Management and Budget. *President's budget historical tables*. Table 1.3. Summary of receipts, outlays, and surpluses or deficits (–) in current dollars, constant (FY 2005) dollars, and as percentages of GDP, 1940–2015. Retrieved July 3, 2010 from http://www.whitehouse.gov/omb/budget/Historicals

White House (The) (2010b). Office of Management and Budget. *President's budget historical tables*. Table 3.1. Outlays for Superfunctions and function, 1940–2105. Retrieved July 3, 2010 from http://www.whitehouse.gov/omb/budget/Historicals/

White House (The) (2010c) Office of Management and Budget. President's budget historical tables. Table 1.3. *Summary of receipts, outlays, and surpluses or deficits (–) in current dollars, constant (fy 2005) dollars, and as percentages of GDP, 1940-2015*. Retrieved July 3, 2010 from http://www.whitehouse.gov/omb/budget/Historicals

Wilensky, H.L., & Lebeaux, C.N. (1958). *Industrial society and social welfare: The impact of industrialization on the supply and organization of social welfare services in the United States*. New York: Russell Sage Foundation.

Wilkinson, R., & Pickett, K. (2009). *The spirit level: Why greater equality makes societies stronger*. New York: Bloomsbury Press.

Working Group on Extreme Inequality (2009). *Racial dimensions of inequality racial wealth divide: Median family income by race, 1947.* Retrieved September 7, 2010 from http://extremeinequality.org/?page_id=23

Yellen, J. (2006). Speech to the Center for the Study of Democracy 2006–2007. *Economics of Governance Lecture*, University of California, Irvine. Retrieved August 22, 2010 from http://www.frbsf.org/news/speeches/2006/1106.html

New Modalities of Welfare Governance

Robert P. Fairbanks II

Ample debate has transpired about the ways in which the transformation from a Keynesian/Fordist welfare state to a post-Keynesian, 'post-welfare' regime of capitalist accumulation has produced new (i.e., historically novel) modalities of welfare governance. A central analytical objective of this chapter is to consider how one might go about the task of discerning the extent to which continuity versus rupture is sought in the shifting regulatory principles of contemporary welfare policy and practice. Late 20th century claims as to the subjugation of the political to the economic and the declining significance of national sovereignty producing a wholesale root-and-branch realignment of welfare states are now subject to criticism, qualification, and revision. It is perhaps more prudent for welfare critics to consider how the institutionally inherited landscapes of welfarism continue to *matter* in contemporary welfare state restructure. Vestigial welfare forms fundamentally slow the rate of change (Polanyi, 2001), producing chronic unevenness and partiality as stubborn path dependencies yield hybrid modalities of governance. It behooves social workers then to challenge the hegemony of neoliberal roll-out narratives by focusing on the complex and contradictory regulatory climate of the post-welfare moment. Moreover, if neoliberalism is characterised by – and even makes a virtue of – unevenness and variegation across institutional, economic, and political contexts (Brenner et al., 2010), then certainly there are important – and importantly elusive – variations and problematics still to be considered. The point here is not to simply uncover variation for variation's sake. Rather, social workers are still at pains to answer: what is the historical significance of variegated neoliberal regulation *vis-à-vis* the question of welfare governance?

By and large, this question will be bracketed in order to create a framework for evaluating continuity versus rupture in contemporary welfare arrangements. The chapter explores, selectively, the extant literature preoccupied with historical transformations in the *regulatory functions* of relief and security. Welfare theorists have taken up the question of regulation from varying philosophical and theoretical positions, and at different points in time: from its Poor Law foundations to its Victorian era antecedents in civil society to its national (Keynesian, Fordist, New Deal/Great Society) form in the welfarist era and its market form in the post-welfare (neoliberal, post-Keynesian, post-Fordist, advanced liberal) era (see Chapter 2). By tracing the concept of regulation through key welfare state theorists, such as Karl Polanyi, Francis Fox Piven and Richard Cloward, Jamie Peck, Bob Jessop, Gosta Esping-Anderson, and Michel Foucault, the chapter reviews a profoundly interdisciplinary and critically important literature for students of welfare and social work. Its primary objectives are to: (i) distil and delineate the analytical tradition of political economy for welfare state theory in order to (ii) suggest how an appreciation of the history and philosophy of regulatory principles is crucial for scholarly criticism and empirical analysis of contemporary welfare state transformation. Such an approach, informed by the long view in welfare state regulation theory, illustrates the ways in which variegated welfare state forms – neoliberal, neocorporatist, neostatist, and neocommunitarian – evolve from institutional legacies, the balance of political forces, and the changing economic and political conjunctures in which social service imperatives take hold.

REGULATION IN THE ABSTRACT: THE TIMEPIECE METAPHOR

In his 2001 book *The Price of Citizenship*: *Redefining the American Welfare State*, Michael Katz invokes the metaphor of the timepiece to reflect upon the regulatory idiosyncrasies of the US welfare state:

> The American welfare state resembles a massive watch that fails to keep very accurate time. Some of its components are rusty and outmoded; others poorly designed; some work very well. They were fabricated by different craftsmen who usually did not consult with one another; they interact imperfectly; and at times they work at cross purposes (Katz, 2001, p.10).

The metaphor of the timepiece is a useful way to ascertain, provisionally at least, the significance of regulation in modalities of welfare governance. Speaking of regulation in the context of welfare most often evokes thoughts of social control theories or neo-Marxian theories on regulating the labour supply. Increasingly, however, considerable thought has been given to the realm of self-regulation as a crucial component of empowerment, capabilities, or strengths-based approaches in social work practice (Gray, 2011). Others have conceived of civil society, self-governance, participation, and voluntarism as essential regulatory components of democratic liberalism and associationalism. In all cases, the timepiece metaphor is useful as it begins to capture the complexity and nuance, the emancipatory and coercive elements of regulation in social welfare.

To push the point further, Albert Hirschman illustrates how foundational political economists, such as Sir James Steuart, have similarly employed the metaphor of the 'watch mechanism' to describe the significance of regulatory precision in the liberal economy of 18th-century Britain (Hirschman, 1977, as cited by Gordon, 1991). As Colin Gordon (1991) notes (quoting Steuart directly), Steuart likens the 'modern economy' to the watch mechanism in two key respects:

> On the one hand, the watch is so delicate that it is immediately destroyed if ... touched by any but the gentlest hand; on the other hand, these same watches are continually going wrong; sometimes the spring is found too weak, at other times too strong for the machine ... and the workman's hand becomes necessary to set it right (Gordon, 1991, p.17).

Steuart argued that arbitrary, careless, or excessive handling of the watch's jewel movements was not only inelegant but more importantly imprudent in the art of governance. Frequent corrective interventions were paramount, to be sure, but only if performed by the 'expert and solicitous statesman' in possession of a light hand, an order of skill worthy of the most discerning craftsman. Certainly, as Gordon (1991) writes, several of Steuart's leading contemporaries were much less charitable in their assessment of the skilled statesmen. Adam Smith, for example, struck a much more begrudging tone in his call to set a 'limit on the ineptitude' of the state's regulatory hand, as opposed to augmenting or stylising governmental expertise. But the metaphorical associations in question – too much or too little, enabled or curtailed, administered or distributed, centripetal or centrifugal – provide a compelling inroad to the question of regulation in welfare state theory.

This chapter argues that regulation is omnipresent in all matters of reflection and normative thought for social policy and practice (see p. 5 of Editors introduction on 'the logic of regulation'). It also argues that the regulatory antecedents of contemporary welfare governance dilemmas derive from earlier philosophical debates concerning poverty, pauperism, security, and the proper relationship between states, markets, and civil society more broadly. All of these concepts are immanent to the principle of *laissez-faire* from classical economics, perhaps the most 'celebrated slogan-formula' in the history of liberal thought (Gordon, 1991). Far from an absence of government *per se*, for Foucault *laissez-faire* is none other than a *method of government*; or more provocatively, a way of acting or not acting. *Laissez-faire* thus implies an injunction 'not to impede the course of things, but to ensure the play of natural and necessary modes of regulation, to make regulations which permit natural regulation to operate' (Foucault, 1978, cited in Gordon, 1991, p. 17).

Foucault's treatment of *laissez-faire* opens us up to activist forms of statecraft that require a steady hand, not only for corrective intervention, but also for measures of calculated indifference or disaffection (non-action or non-intervention). *Laissez-faire* is a strategy not strictly for disciplining or prohibiting, but more importantly of organising to allow for movement, precisely by 'getting the components of reality to work in relation to each other, thanks to and through a series of analyses and specific arrangements' (Foucault, 2007, lecture 18 January 1978, p. 47). These measures produce powerful regulatory effects in their own right. When considering the imperatives of precision in *laissez-faire* doctrine, one begins to see a similar vision of the skilled watchmender engaged in the art of government. Further exploration of the significance for social work is warranted at the outset.

FOUNDATIONAL BEGINNINGS: EHRENREICH'S ALTRUISTIC IMAGINATION

Questions of regulation have long been at the centre of philosophical debates on the role of social work and social policy in economic liberalism. It is in this sense John Ehrenreich (1985) contended the birth of social work is explained by its function as a major *transmitter* of ideology. His seminal text, *The Altruistic Imagination*, focuses on the rise of social movements, the drive for professional status among social workers, and the changing needs of business to regulate markets and the workforce across the 20th century. For Ehrenreich (1985), the origins of US social policy and social work lie in progressivism, which originated in response to the chaos of the new industrial order. The reorganisation of the working class under industrialism fragmented the labour process with the radical isolation of work life from home life. In the process, indigenous networks of support and mutual aid were disrupted, and central aspects of immigrant and working-class cultures destroyed. The replacement of local mutual aid networks by mass culture, via the development of a mass consumer market defined by individual, privatised consumption of commodities, introduced persistent threats of anomie throughout the late 19th century and well into the 20th (Ehrenreich, 1985).

The shaking up and recasting of class interests under an industrialised economy was critical to the origins of the progressive movement. Key to this was a new understanding of the link between the state of the poor and the good of the whole, as Ehrenreich (1985:24) notes:

> For change to occur, it was necessary for the middle and upper classes to recognize the crisis in the lives of the immigrants and the poor as a crisis for 'society,' that is, for themselves. Only then were (progressives) goaded into action (p. 24).

At the turn of the century, economic surplus was collected and concentrated in private foundations and the public sector, and made available increasingly for use in new fields of social intervention, statecraft, and political development. Ehrenreich traces the conditions of possibility for progressivism to an unprecedented capacity for long-term economic and social planning. With the need for a supportive infrastructure and a grid for the emergent national economy, local political strongholds – municipal machines – were usurped and a new wave of reform took hold (Katz, 1996). New forms of statecraft produced new administrative techniques, geared to build, rebuild, and fine tune political institutions. The overall objective was to rationalise production in order to create a stabilised, efficient, and self-reproducing order (Ehrenreich, 1985).

As Ehrenreich (1985) notes, the politically and economically motivated penetration of working-class and immigrant community life was an essential part of the story, but there was more at stake than simply crude (and increasingly outmoded) forms of disciplinary or repressive force. The historical timeframe of Ehrenreich's (1985) work coincides with the advent and invention of *the social* as a strategy to enumerate the poor as a site worthy of scientific analysis. The linkage of the social to the political introduced social techniques of government (e.g., social work) enabling experts to treat one segment of the population as a problem while gesturing toward the mutual interests uniting all parts of 'society as a whole' (Cruikshank, 1999; Foucault, 1991). Through a reconstitution of the political at the level of the social, a full compendium of thoughts and actions were made possible, including new forms of professional expertise geared to address a diverse set of categorical and highly specialised problems. The social sciences – themselves enabled by the historical condition of liberalism, which designated their object – provided a way of representing (via mapping procedures, such as statistics) the autonomous dynamics of society. The purpose was to modernise disciplinary knowledge so as to assess objects of regulation as sites of intervention or non-intervention, ultimately in accordance with the imperatives of modern welfare governance (Barry et al., 1996).

In time, the *conduct* of individual members of society became the object of philanthropic, hygienic, and medical programmes. The social itself became increasingly traversed by innumerable interventions from missionaries to schools, 'friendly' home visiting, and public health regimes. As this broad array of assemblages took shape, rather maladroitly, into the public–private semi-welfare state, their myriad interventions took diverse technical forms – determined in part by the class status of their targeted population (Rose, 1990). In this respect, as Ehrenreich (1985) argues, the origins of US social policy are located in the efforts to produce a more socially integrated, enlightened, modernised, and properly regulated working class. The progressive goal was not to overthrow but to modify capitalism by organising for movement and circulation – of commodities, political forms of capital, and demographic flows. In short, a more elegant, *regulated* functionality was achieved through welfare governance, thereby enabling a national economy to operate with greater precision and efficiency. Statecraft could no longer rely on primitive work tests and poorhouses alone. The regulatory skill of the watchmender and the art of modern governance were essential.

The *Altruistic Imagination* is a foundational text for matters concerning the regulatory functions of welfare. Ehrenreich (1985) chronicled the long-standing polar tension between social reform and individual change in social work and social policy. As evidenced by the age-old debate: do we explain human misery in terms of the social environment, or rather on the basis of character flaws? Ehrenreich (1985) argues what is important 'is not so much which position is right, but rather why does each appear so persuasive at different historical moments' (p. 12). For Ehrenreich (1985), regardless of timeframe, the persistent dialectical tension between 'inner and outer' is interesting not simply because of its centrality in academic and professional debates, but more so because the tension is built into the very architecture, or edifice of social policy and practice as a *condition of its possibility*. In other words, political economic conditions and their imperatives breathe life into the very act of trying to change either the individual or their social realities. This fundamental tension acts as a mainspring of regulatory precision in the watch mechanism of welfare governance. By extension, the tension itself must be considered as the fount and matrix of welfare governance under economic liberalism and its successor arrangement, neoliberalism. Indeed, juxtaposing structure and agency is precisely how neoliberalism works.

The forgoing sections analyse the significance of the regulatory question for social policy and practice by considering the analytical traditions of historical institutionalism, state regulation theory, and governmentality. Carefully deliberating the works of key thinkers in each camp equips social workers to discern the regulatory stakes of key economic principles in social welfare arrangements. An exploration such as this must begin with the masterwork of Karl Polanyi, undertaken in what follows.

POLANYI'S *GREAT TRANSFORMATION*: TOWNSEND, SPEENHAMLAND, AND THE DOUBLE MOVEMENT

The study of Speenhamland is the study of 19th century civilization ... our social consciousness is cast in its mold (Polanyi, 2001, p. 87).

According to Karl Polanyi (2001), market liberalism was born out of a philosophical penchant for nonbureaucratic methods. It evolved into a veritable faith in man's secular salvation via the self-regulating market, or *laissez-faire*. Polanyi (2001) turned the notion of *laissez-faire* on its head, however, with his concept of the *double movement*. Produced in the clash of the organising principles of economic liberalism and social protection, the double movement produced 'deep-seated institutional strain' that ultimately shaped the contours of 19th-century social history.

Polanyi (2001) insisted that disembedding the economy from social relationships and political institutions necessarily entails an ongoing role for the state in managing and regulating the 'fictitious commodities' of land, labour, and money. By illustrating how the role of the state is to be found, empirically, in welfare measures seeking to alter, regulate, or slow the rate of change, Polanyi's study gave birth to a long analytical tradition in regulation theory and political economy. For Polanyi, *the fountainhead* – or 'fount and matrix' of 19th-century civilisation is the self-regulating market, which gives rise to a very specific configuration of the social and a very violent set of originating forces to political economy for welfare scholars. The central intervention lies in his argument that liberal thinkers, however, have misread the history of the industrial revolution by over-privileging the free market. For Polanyi, the misreading in question relates to the critical importance of poverty and welfare regulation as central drivers of 19th-century enlightenment thought. It is in this spirit that he offers a meta-analytical claim about the significance of poverty and relief practices for 19th-century governance:

> The problem of poverty centered around two closely related subjects: pauperism and political economy. Though we will deal with their impact on modern consciousness separately, they formed part of one indivisible whole: the discovery of society (Polanyi, 2001, p. 108).

Polanyi (2001) discusses the crucial shift in reflections on pauperism between 1780 and 1800, from Adam Smith's *Wealth of Nations* to Townsend's *Dissertation on the Poor Laws*. The transitional period in question marked an interregnum between an age dominated by the inventors of state (More and Machiavelli, Luther, and Calvin) to an age in which thinkers from Hegel to Ricardo to Malthus discovered the existence of a society not subject to the laws of the state, but rather one that subjected the state to its own laws. Questions of modern welfare governance are all here. From Smith's humanist thesis on the wealth of nations as depending crucially upon a balance of power between material wealth and government policy in safety in security, to Bentham's utilitarian schema to derive surplus from the labour of paupers, to Owen's syndicalist visions for worker cooperatives and Colleges of Industry (Polanyi, 2001).

For our purposes, the most important point is the matter of pauperism and its regulatory imperatives under economic liberalism. Deliberations on pauperism deeply influenced a century and a half of Enlightenment thought. This truism places the question of social welfare squarely within the traditions of political economy, philosophy, and modern governance. Two substantive case analyses from the *Great Transformation* illustrate this with exceptional clarity. First, Polanyi analyses Townsend's *Dissertation on the Poor Laws*. This rather obscure study produced a new starting point for political science by injecting naturalism into matters concerning the proper size and scale of the state. Perhaps originating the economic parlour game of 'Crusoe Economics', Townsend wrote of an island in the Pacific Ocean populated by goats and dogs (goats stocked by the English for future food supply in colonialist exploits; dogs landed by the Spanish as a counter strategy to kill said food supply). In Townsend's treatise, which would set the tone of 19th-century economic thought, the fortuitous – if mythical – experiment revealed how balance was restored in nature. By way of a most seductive lapse into naturalism, Townsend deduced that 'it is the quantity of food which regulates the number of the human species' (in Polanyi, 2001, p. 118). None other than Malthus and Darwin followed on from the 'maxims which Townsend deduced from goats and dogs', the substance of which was applied – at Townsend's behest – to the reform of the Poor Law. In essence, Townsend argued men are only in need of their natural entitlement to their own hunger, which will impel them to work and to labour in a 'peaceable' way. Any added layers of political provision or coercion are, therefore, not only superfluous, but by extension even *unjust* since paternalistic impulses actually create an aporia to the motivating force of hunger. In this conception, the pangs of hunger – natural incentives – become the fount and matrix of the self-regulating market and the foundation of freedom in a liberal polity. As summarised by Polanyi (2001):

> Hobbes had argued the need for a despot because men were like beasts; Townsend insisted that they were *actually* beasts and that, precisely for that reason, only a minimum of government was required (p. 119; emphasis in original).

It was from this premise, Polanyi (2001) argues, that free society came to be imagined as comprising 'two races: property owners and laborers. The number of the latter was limited by the amount of food; and as long as property was safe, hunger would drive them to work' (p. 120). This new foundation of 19th-century thought accorded with the emerging market system and its transformations in private property, regimes of accumulation, and social modes of regulation. The insoluble problem of poverty, Polanyi

(2001) states, forced the likes of Malthus, Ricardo, and Burke to endorse Townsend's lapse into naturalism and, therefore, to shift the locus of regulatory intervention and its principles from the sovereign body politic to the laws of population and the administrative problems of pauperism. Put simply, Townsend's solution for reform lay in the abolition of the Elizabethan Poor Law statutes such that labour could find its natural price in the market. In Polanyi's (2001) final assessment, 'it was from the island of goats and dogs that Victorian England drew its sentimental education' (p. 123).

The second site of analysis for Polanyi (2001) is the subject of the Speenhamland laws, implemented on a national scale – although locally administered – in England from 1795 to 1834. The Speenhamland Law antedates capitalism, or perhaps better stated, slowed the rate of change toward market liberalism by preventing the creation of a labour market proper in England. The Speenhamland law provided the 'right to live' through the guarantee of a subsistence wage, scaled to the fluctuating prices of bread, via public relief subsidies or 'aid in wages'. It proclaimed 'no man should starve, as the parish would enable him to subsist however little he earned' (Polanyi, 2001, p. 104). As Polanyi (2001) argues, the results of Speenhamland were 'ghastly': protecting rural England and the labouring population against 'the full force of the market mechanism' would eventually '[eat] into the marrow of society' (p. 106).

The reasons for this are complex, but infinitely significant. The Speenhamland Law stood as an obstacle to the new capitalist economy, as paternalistic regulation prevented workers from taking their place in the free market. Labour was commodified long after land and capital, effectively resulting in its pauperisation. In essence, 'workers were forced to sell their labor, but deprived its market value ... a class of employers was born, but no corresponding class of employees' (Polanyi, 2001, p. 84). Under aid in wages, there were few incentives to work efficiently or effectively with a guaranteed right to life. The self-respect of the common man sank to the low point where he preferred relief to wages, and employers also had a bottomless capacity to depress the price of labour given its public subsidisation. In time employers would realise pauperised labour was insidiously destructive to their own interests as well. The central contradiction lay in the miraculous growth in early 19th century production in England, accompanied by near starvation of the masses.

The case of Speenhamland embodies and reveals the rationalities and postulates of thought underlying the regulatory principles of welfare governance still to this day. The foundational and durable significance of Speenhamland rests, Polanyi (2001) notes, in the protracted effects of the allowance system that made it possible to explain the human and social degradation of early capitalism. Regulatory attempts to slow the rate of change had injured those who were meant to be protected. For Polanyi (2001), the historical consequences of this experiment were critical to the subsequent state-building projects of 19th-century *laissez-faire* doctrine: 'The laws governing (market liberalism) had asserted themselves and manifested their radical antagonism to the principle of paternalism' (p. 84). The impossibility of a capitalist order with a public wage system had become clear: human labour had to become fully commodified.

The advent of the market wage system required a withdrawal of the 'right to live', or the legal claim to subsistence, which, in turn, led to the Reform Bill of 1832 and Poor Law Reform of 1834. These two enactments are commonly regarded as the starting point of modern capitalism. Poor Law Reform outlawed and abolished outdoor relief, and with it the right to live as an obstruction to the labour market. To be sure, severe suffering followed with the rupturing transformations of a primitively competitive labour market. But the repeal finally cleared the way for proletarianisation. By 1870s, the labouring poor eventually formed trade unions for protection and brought on a labour market proper in the process. The self-protection of society eventually took shape in the factory laws and social welfare legislation that joined the industrial working class movement (Polanyi, 2001).

The Speenhamland Law illustrates Polanyi's thesis of the double movement. Protective measures originating in vestigial political forms reacted against the forces of commodification in land and labour in order to slow the rate of change. But perhaps more importantly, the study of Speenhamland is significant for its lasting influence on 19th-century thought. Under the auspices of the Speenhamland experiment, as well as its abolishment, 'a world was uncovered the very existence of which had not been suspected, that of the laws governing complex *society*' (Polanyi, 2001, p. 88). It is here that Polanyi locates the origins of political economy in matters of welfare governance, the study of the economic affairs of the state in relation to men in their collective well-being.

HISTORICAL INSTITUTIONALISM: PIVEN AND CLOWARD, AND ESPING-ANDERSEN

While Polanyi's historical focus was the 19th century, several scholars have extended his analysis by showing how greater reliance on the self-regulating market increasingly dictates and shapes the parameters of regulation in late 20th-century capitalism. Whether speaking of 'advanced marginality' (Wacquant) or 'bare life' (Agamben), the ratcheting down of social protections and the escalation of risk and vulnerability are posited as adjuncts to contemporary market liberalisation and – at least in Wacquant's case – as a measure of both state withdrawal and the ascendancy of the 'carceral-assistential' state. Polanyi's work has influenced several welfare scholars, from Titmuss to Beveridge, David Harvey to Jacob Hacker. Two other notables are discussed at length in this section.

First, in their classic 1971 text *Regulating the Poor: The Functions of Public Welfare*, Francis Fox Piven and Richard Cloward revolutionised disciplinary thought on the institutional functions of relief. In the opening of their pivotal text, they argued the economic and political functions of relief had not been appropriately theorised under the auspices of historical analysis. Indeed, they quipped:

> much of the literature on relief – whether the arid moralisms and pieties of the nineteenth-century writers or the ostensibly 'value-neutral' analyses of the twentieth-century professionals and technicians – merely serves to obscure the central role of relief (Piven & Cloward, 1993, p. xviii).

Since its inception in the English Poor Laws, the authors contended, the classical function of relief was to maintain civil disorder and enforce work. More specifically, *expansive* relief practices were designed to mute civil disorder, while *restrictive* relief practices were designed to reinforce work norms (Piven & Cloward, 1993).

The premises of political economy are essential to their analysis. If all human societies must compel their members to work, then there are great stakes involved in understanding how, why, and where – in states, markets, or civil society – governing bodies must administer regulatory intervention. Capitalist arrangements create unique challenges in this regard, precisely because capitalism 'relies on the market – the promise of financial rewards and penalties – to motivate men and women and hold them to their occupational tasks' (Piven & Cloward, 1993, p. 4). This basic premise holds durable implications. Capitalism is marked by continuous changes in labour needs, making chronic change and fluctuation an essential feature of capitalist arrangements. Labour roles can, therefore, never be assigned by tradition, nor can they be lodged in bureaucracy or centralised in government. Depression and rapid modernisation are periodic features of capitalism, and unemployment is always present (Piven & Cloward, 1993).

As Piven and Cloward (1993) show, when the market changes drastically, market incentives are not powerful or fast enough in their own right to recalibrate workers to new modes of production. The consequences are significant for the maintenance of social order, as mass unemployment severs 'workers from the institutions through which they are regulated and controlled'. Therefore, 'because the market is unable to control men's behavior, at least for a time, a surrogate system of control must be evolved, at least for a time' (Piven & Cloward, 1993, p. 7). That system is relief. Its chief institutional function is to restore work roles and to regulate marginal labour.

Gosta Esping-Andersen's (1990) seminal text, *The Three Worlds of Welfare Capitalism*, adds a great deal of analytical nuance to the table. Following Polanyi's line, Esping-Andersen (1990) begins with the premise 'the main springs of modern social policy lie in the process by which human needs and labor power become commodities and hence, our well-being came to depend on our relation to the cash nexus' (p. 35). With this process, and with the 'withering away of "pre-commodified" social protection' (p. 35), that is, the shift from the church, the family, or the Lord to the *labour contract* as the lynchpin of survival, the nature of social policy transformed. For Esping-Andersen (1990), a primary function of contemporary social policy entails 'stripping society of the institutional layers that guaranteed social protection outside of the labor contract' (p. 21). Here is where Polanyi's notion of the *double movement re-emerges*. As labour is unable to withhold itself for long without recourse to alternative means of subsistence outside of the cash nexus, the politics of commodifying workers is bound to produce its opposite in the regulatory forces of *decommodification*: whether in the form of social welfare policy, social democracy, or collective action.

For Esping-Andersen (1990), the variability of welfare state evolution reflects competing responses to pressures for decommodification. The important question for welfare state analysis is not merely spending allotments, but rather the extent to which policies are: (i) emancipatory, (i.e., they provide an exit or legitimate exemption from either the cash nexus or statist power); and (ii) legitimising or delegitimising of markets or states (i.e., do policies contradict or aid markets, either by crowding out the state by making the market work, or crowding out the market via state building projects). In each dimension, the welfare state is a stratifying institution and an active force in the ordering of social relations. In the classic frame of political science, the welfare state is a regulatory agent that dictates who gets what, how, when, why, and under what conditions.

Esping-Andersen's (1990) central analytical shift, from the blackbox of expenditures to the regulatory mechanisms of welfare states, produces his well known welfare state typologies. First, the *liberal welfare state*: characteristically means tested, with modest universal transfers and market differentiated welfare. Here the state encourages the market either passively (via regulatory principles of stigma and less eligibility) or actively (by subsidising private welfare schemes). The archetypes are the USA, Canada, and Australia. Second, the *corporatist/statist welfare tradition*: a characteristically conservative legacy updated to cater to the new class structure via rights granted by the state edifice on basis of class, status, patronage, and loyalty to central authority. The archetypes are Germany, Austria, Italy, and France. Third, the *social democratic welfare states*: a mix of highly decommodifying and universalistic programmes nonetheless tailored to differentiated expectations. The socialist democratic welfare state crowds out the private market and constructs universal solidarity in favour of the welfare state (Esping-Andersen, 1990).

Esping-Andersen's (1990) typologies show the full stakes of regulatory principles in welfare state political development. Liberal states work through the market, by creating the conditions under which markets function as the pre-eminent sphere for distribution of goods and services. Corporatist logics of loyalty and patronage subjugate the market to vestigial political authority. Democratic socialist states use the state mechanism to crowd out markets and produce levels of security to enable the individual to thrive. Clearly visible here is that attention to regulatory principles and their stratifying effects are critical for students of the welfare state.

STATE REGULATION THEORY

Piven and Cloward's (1993) and Esping-Andersen's (1990) foundational theses have been indispensable for more than one generation of welfare scholars. But a closer look at other key texts suggests how many different directions the concept of regulation can take us, and how much more sophisticated the study of regulation can and, indeed, has become in explaining the transformation of the welfare state. Regulation theorists have been at the forefront of the endeavour to map welfare state restructuring, from its postwar New Deal/Great Society form to its post-1970 development in accordance with the political economic imperatives of globalisation. Chief among the state regulation theorists studying the welfare state is Bob Jessop (1994), who has theorised the movement from Fordism to post-Fordism as a complex and inter-related set of changes in the labour process and the overall dynamic of macroeconomic growth. It also involves changes in the *social mode* of economic regulation, which guides and governs the prevailing mode of growth in the overall character of the political and social order associated with it. With this in mind, Jessop's key argument is that the state has undergone a restructuring and reorientation in two key respects: (i) there is a fundamental shift from the Keynesian welfare state appropriate to the Fordist mode of growth to a Schumpeterian workfare state more suited in form and function to an emerging post-Fordism; and (ii) there is also a tendential 'hollowing out' of the national state, with state capacities new and old alike, being reorganised (Jessop, 1994).

As David Harvey notes, 'Fordism depended on a distinctive type of labour process – characterised by mass production of consumer durables based on moving assembly line techniques operated by a semi-skilled labour-force – and a relatively stable mode of virtuous economic growth in relatively closed economies' (Harvey, 1989).

It also entailed a social mode of economic regulation (Harvey, 1989; Jessop, 1994). The key features included union recognition, monetary policy oriented to securing effective aggregate demand, approximation of full employment, and indexation of welfare benefits financed through progressive taxation (Jessop, 1994). The turn to post-Fordism, on the other hand, involves a decidedly less stable mode of macroeconomic growth based on the dominance of a flexible and permanently innovative pattern of accumulation (Harvey, 1989). The social mode of economic regulation involves supply-side innovation and flexibility in each main area of regulation, with polarised wage relations recomposed so the rising incomes of core workers are no longer linked to either the incomes of other workers, or to the economically inactive (Jessop, 1994). Politically, new forms of state intervention respond to fiscal crisis by starving the welfare state and growing the private sector. The state also attacks what David Harvey (1989) calls 'rigidities' and dysfunctions in bureaucratic administration, planning, and unionisation. At the time of Jessop's writing, the mode of what he terms 'societalization', or the social mode of regulation, remained unsettled, at least when compared to the relatively homogenous suburbanised consciousness that led to the creation of the white middle class in postwar Keynesianism (via the US Federal Housing Administration (FHA) and the US Veterans' Administration (GI Bill); see Jackson, 1985).

For Jessop (1994), a key component of this historical shift is the advent of *The Schumpeterian Workfare State*, which holds definitive objectives in economic and social reproduction to: (i) promote product, process, organisational, and market innovation in open economies in order to strengthen the competitiveness of the national economy by intervening on the supply side; and (ii) subordinate social policy to the needs of labour market flexibility or the constraints of international competition, or both. Workfare thus becomes an integral mechanism of the Schumpeterian Workfare State in that it effectively resolves the crises borne out of the Keynesian welfare state and helps to consolidate the emerging dynamic of a post-Fordist accumulation regime (Jessop, 1994). What is interesting here is that the state is clearly not simply retrenched but rather takes on a form that 'is structurally congruent and functionally adequate' (Jessop, 1994, p. 265) in the realms of innovation, competitiveness, and the restructuring and reorientation of social reproduction pace the imperatives of flexism. There is also a move to subordinate the welfare state to market forces and devolve problems too large in scale for the Federal government to state, urban, or local units. Thus neoliberal forms in the USA – as opposed to neocorporatist and neostatist elsewhere – require strong state action during transition in order to restructure markets – and to create them aggressively where none existed – leading to a 'hollowing out' and reconstruction rather than simply a demise per se (Jessop, 1994).

The debates on neoliberalism and post-Fordism have been rampant since the 1980s and the welfare state occupies a central place within them. To cite another key example, in Loïc Wacquant's (2009) highly anticipated book *Punishing the Poor: The Neoliberal Government of Social Insecurity*, he elaborates a trenchant diagnosis of the punitive policy turn taken by advanced societies following the US-led model of deregulation and welfare retrenchment. Wacquant (2009) articulates a new form of government, responding not to rising criminality but rather to a rising wave of *social insecurity* that has effectively relinked social welfare and penal policies to restore their original mission at the birth of capitalism. Western society has witnessed a colonisation of the welfare sector via state projects wedding restrictive workfare and expansive prisonfare policies for the purposes of normalising, supervising, and neutralising the destitute and disruptive factions of the postindustrial proletariat (or urban *precariat*) (Wacquant, 2009). The late 20th-century penalisation of poverty, Wacquant contends, has proven to be a protean vector for state projects charged with the task of ordering social insecurity.

Following Bourdieu, Wacquant attempts to sketch the dynamic recomposition of the bureaucratic field. Reversing the late 19th-century bifurcation of labour and crime policy, a conjuncture has been reached in which 'the misery of American welfare and the grandeur of American prisonfare at century's end are two sides of the same political coin' (Wacquant, 2009, p. 292). The management of advanced marginality requires ambidextrous innovations in contemporary statecraft, forged by the authoritarian right hand and 'assistential' left hand of the state. For Wacquant, this entails undermining whatever antagonisms may have once existed between the right hand of market authoritarianism and the left hand of social work, social welfare, and street-level bureaucratic institutions (see Chapter 4). The two hands now operate in tandem, almost seamlessly, to 'execute a tight grip on postindustrial dilemmas of labor market flexibilization and advanced social marginality' (Peck, 2010, p. 105).

As a partial corrective to Wacquant's relatively monolithic carceral–assistential state, Neil Brenner, Jamie Peck, and Nik Theodore have shown convincingly neoliberalism does not pulsate out from a single control centre or heartland, nor can it be adequately theorised in the type of ambient complex Wacquant sketches so provocatively. The story of neoliberalisation is not one of a fully formed, coherently functioning regime-like state, but rather one of a 'relationally constituted' and highly variegated transformational process unfolding across 'multiple sites and spaces of 'co-formation' (Peck et al., 2010, p. 106). The problematic of variegation must be central to any adequate account of regulatory restructure, as '"the project" of neoliberalization can only be understood as a politically (re)constructed, non-linear, and indeed *mongrel* phenomenon' (Peck et al., 2010, p. 105). The methodological implications of these statements demand a rethinking of contemporary welfare analysis.

Recent crises in political economic arrangements have important implications for social policy and social service provision across the globe, as emergent forms of subjectivity and regulation are co-constituted against a backdrop of welfare state transformation. The now widespread assumption of an emerging *post-welfarism*, a radically transformed, but nonetheless still actually existing welfarism, illustrates the stakes of these forms quite powerfully at the onset of the 21st century. At the forefront of the debates are differing viewpoints on regulation, emerging from two analytical camps occupying similar historical timelines though nonetheless growing up in relative isolation from one another. Taken in turn, state regulation theorists have assumed a prominent role in mapping the modalities, prototypes, and zigzagging pathways of regulatory transfer. For these scholars, particularly the critical geographers among them (*critical theory of scale*), the local exigencies of institutionally inherited landscapes are the key to understanding – in sufficiently spatial terms – the inherently uneven rescaling and activation tendencies of regulatory change. This has led to considerations of a 'careful mapping of emergent state forms' and welfare resettlements that are decidedly 'post-Keynesian' in form and function. Processes of de- or re-regulation, neoliberal 'hollowing out', and de- or re-territorialisation have been essential in understanding how macroeconomic steering (i.e., capital accumulation and its associated regulatory problems in welfare arrangements) is always articulated in territory and place. The political–economic interpretation has clearly shown that Keynesian doctrine, formally designed to stabilise the postwar economy through a mix of welfare statism, rising standards of living, control over wages, and a relatively reformist state, has given way to political economic regimes more suited in form and function to an 'ambient neoliberalism', to borrow Loïc Wacquant's phrase.

Scholars in the governmentality camp have re-theorised the concept of regulation at the level of conduct and the production of ethical subjectivity. Equally important to modes of *regulation* and *accumulation*, these theorists contend, are the rationalisation processes facilitating state restructurings at the level of subjectivity and rationality: the unsystematic meanings and experiences that manifest as the *instrument and effect* of contemporary state restructuring: *political rationalities*. Governmentality theorists focus in particular on contemporary discursive regularities and the patterns of social practices designed and deployed – in accordance with new political and economic imperatives – to reconfigure pre-existing relationships between citizens and states. In order to flesh out the specifics of the ethical sphere of regulation sufficiently, the chapter now turns to a review of the governmentality literature in its final section.

GOVERNMENTALITY

Michel Foucault focused meticulously on temporal movements. Much of his work focused on the replacement of a sovereign society by a disciplinary society – from the Prince to the Juridical subject/contract law; to the subsequent replacement of a disciplinary society by a society of government. As Gordon (1991) notes, Foucault's complex analyses of governance stretch across four central historical domains: (i) antiquity – notably Greek philosophy's concern with the nature of government as a form of pastoral power; (ii) early modern Europe – doctrines of government associated with the idea of reason of state and the police state, or *Cameralism*; (iii) 18th- and 19th-century liberalism (Foucault here develops his conception of the art of government in relation to political economy, *laissez-faire*, progress, and security); and (iv) postwar forms (1945–1980) of neoliberal thought.

The critical domains to this chapter are clearly the third and the fourth. Foucault's insights in these periods are important in matters of social welfare for several reasons discussed below, but at the outset it is also important to highlight how his work revolutionised the analysis of power. For one, Foucault insisted on analysing the microphysics of power in practices, rather than in state institutions per se. He also moved scholarly discussions of power well beyond what he considered to be the traps of structuralism: its endless search for the sovereign and the headquarters or origin of power; and its dualistic insistence on conceptualising power as either repressive or emancipatory. For Foucault, rather:

> power is only power (rather than violence or force) when addressed to individuals who are free to act in one way or another ... (power) acts upon and through an open set of practical and ethical possibilities; it is never a fixed and closed regime, but rather an endless and open strategic game (Gordon, 1991, p. 5).

What becomes critical, for Foucault, is how liberalism itself provides an endlessly reflexive penchant for critique of the state and an ever-shifting set of limits and possibilities for regulatory intervention. Foucault's move then, is not so much 'to expose the inveterate contradictions of liberalism', 'but to rather to expose liberalism itself as a prodigiously fertile problematic, a continuing vector of political invention' (Gordon, 1991, p. 18).

Herein lies the theoretical originality, and regulatory vehemence, of liberalism. It abandons the relatively fixed configurations of power associated with sovereignty in order to accommodate the necessary dynamism for making and remaking strategic *social* modalities of statecraft. So long as the exercise of power was conceived as an exercise of the sovereign, the art of government could not be developed, as the end of sovereignty was simply submission to sovereignty (Foucault, 1991; Gordon, 1991). With the emergence of *population* and *the social*, the common good becomes the end of sovereignty. Multiform tactics emanating from the welfare state are the means. This movement brings about the emergence of *population* as datum – as the growth of wealth and demography unblocks the art of government from the sovereign, the juridical, and the family – as a field of intervention and a regulatory objective of governmental techniques (Foucault, 1991).

Foucault described governmentality as follows: (i) the ensemble formed by the institutions, analyses, procedures, and calculations allowing the exercise of a very specific and complex form of power on its target *population*; *political economy* as its principle form of knowledge; and *security* – read welfare – as its essential technical means; (ii) the tendency which over time has led steadily towards the pre-eminence over all other forms – sovereignty and discipline – of this type of power which may be termed government – resulting in the formation of a whole series of governmental apparatuses and a whole complex of knowledges operating in the social; and (iii) the process of governmentalisation, from the state of justice of the middle ages to the art of government. The tactics of government make possible the continual definition and redefinition of what is within the competence of the state and what is not. The state, as such, can only be understood in its survival and its limits on the basis of the general tactics of governmentality (Foucault, 1991).

Foucault's concept of governmentality has produced new understandings of the reciprocal construction of welfare subjectivities within the context of global and local economic transformations. What is at stake is the prospect of producing analytical inroads not only to the immanently human configurations playing out in response to the economic transformations of late capitalism but also to the many ways in which these transformations actively have reshaped both subjectivity *and* the regulatory strategies of state and local governance. By the latter is meant the many informal assemblages of collective responsibility and self-help operating in the tradition of voluntarism in the post-welfare age. While apparently decoupled from the state apparatus at first glance, myriad configurations of the shadow welfare state have emerged to forge inscrutably complex partnerships with state systems – primarily in response to devolutionary trends in the neoliberal era.

Foucault's insights prompt welfare theorists to conceptualise social configurations of civil society, voluntarism, and self-help not as self-regulating, autonomous spheres, but rather as technologies intimately coupled with the actions and interests of the state. It should be noted such a conceptualisation stands in stark contrast to the stated claims of politicians and scholars, many of whom have emerged in recent years to lament a certain 'decline in civil society' (see, e.g., Robert Putnam's [2001] *Bowling Alone*). In the imaginary of a growing number of policy pundits and think-tank provocateurs, this 'crisis' of civil society can be linked to myriad social ills, including increases in crime and addiction; reduced confidence in government and electoral processes; and a general civic malaise, apathy, and abdication of responsibility (Hyatt, 2001). As a panacea to this erosion of good citizenship, notions such as voluntarism, service, and self-help have been dusted off in attempts to resuscitate a declining yet venerable civil society, which has always stood as the preferred alternative to state action – posited historically as an 'unequivocal good in American political culture that distrusts government and exalts the individual' (Katz, 2001, p. 165). Civil society has been deployed as a mediating structure between markets and states, thus enabling a certain extension of democracy through the creation of dense networks of individual relationships, which in turn create the relays and bonds essential for civic engagement and effective democratic governance (Cruikshank, 1999; Katz, 2001).

With Foucault's insights, regulatory forms of welfare governance are conceivable as actually *enacting and activating* power, operating *through* rather than despite the value systems and civil liberties of poor subjects. As opposed to notions of state retrenchment, retreat, or withdrawal, understanding is engendered of the ways in which the state *extends* its power within the context of neoliberal economics; that is, the ways in which governments under pressure from the global economy redistribute the disciplines of the competitive world market throughout the interstices of the social body (Gordon, 1991). This is not to diminish an analytical agenda focused on the withdrawal of public services, but rather to supplement these discussions by emphasising the simple fact that the state has not ceased all involvement. Conversely, by operating through civil society, the state has reinvented its role by occupying various knowledge systems of welfare governance, typically characterised by notions of participation, empowerment, self-esteem, and self-help.

CONCLUSION

This chapter has considered the question of regulation throughout the history and philosophy of the welfare state. By reviewing seminal texts from Ehrenreich, Polanyi, Piven and Cloward, Esping-Anderson, Jessop, and Foucault, it has revealed the many ways in which the concept of regulation – from the political economic as well as the post-structuralist tradition – is an essential heuristic for scholars of social work and social welfare. While the literature explored in this chapter belies easy summarisation, there are three central analytical threads crucial for inquiry into contemporary – or new – modalities of welfare governance. First, as the great thinker Polanyi has shown, the chapter has argued social welfare policy and practice must always be considered based on its relationship to the changing conditions of political economy. Cycles of welfare reform always operate in an historical conjuncture, and can only be properly discerned when equipped with an epistemology of the shifting relationships between markets, states, and civil society. As the work of Ehrenreich, Piven and Cloward, and Esping-Andersen reveals, social welfare policy and practice must always be analysed against the forces of history and its shifting regulatory configurations. Secondly, the shift from a Keynesian to a neoliberal economy has provoked radical unevenness and variegation in contemporary regulation that can only be mapped under the auspices of the state regulation theoretical tradition. As the work of Jessop reveals, each historical regime of accumulation entails its own forms of social regulation, and its own form of *homo economicus*. One cannot begin to gauge properly the artful gestures of regulatory imperatives in the global era without proper attention to the shifting relationships comprising any political economy, and the waning of the nation state prompts a definitive need for the insights of these thinkers. Finally, the work of Michel Foucault leads to an incorporation of the realm of ethical subjectivity in any analysis of welfare regulation. Without proper attention to the shifting relationships between citizen and state, as well as the myriad realms within which the state is activating novel forms of regulatory power in the contemporary age, new modalities of welfare governance can hardly begin to be understood. The analytical tradition of regulation in welfare governance is clearly robust and essential for students of social work and social welfare. Only by way of an interdisciplinary approach bringing together the core insights of traditions ranging from historical institutionalism to state regulation theory to governmentality can social workers begin to ascertain the complex and highly nuanced hand of the watchmender as it operates in time and space.

REFERENCES

Barry, A., Osbourne, T., & Rose, N. (eds) (1996). *Foucault and political reason: Liberalism, neoliberalism, and rationalities of government.* Chicago, IL: University of Chicago Press.

Brenner, N., Peck, J., & Theodore, N. (2010). Variegated neoliberalization: Geographies, modalities, pathways. *Global Networks 10*(2), 182–222.

Cruikshank, B. (1999). *The will to empower: Democratic citizens and other subjects.* Chicago, IL: Cornell University Press.

Ehrenreich, J. (1985). *The altruistic imagination: A history of social work and social policy in the United States.* Ithaca, NY: Cornell University Press.

Esping-Andersen, G. (1990). *The three worlds of welfare capitalism.* Princeton, NJ: Princeton University Press.

Foucault, M. (1991). Governmentality. In G. Burchell, Gordon, C., & Miller, P. (eds), *The Foucault effect: Studies in governmentality: with two lectures by and an interview with Michel Foucault.* Chicago, IL: University of Chicago Press, pp. 87–104.

Foucault, M. (2007). *Security, territory, population: Lectures at the College de France.* Basingstoke: Palgrave.

Gray, M. (2011). Back to basics: A critique of the strengths perspective in social work. *Families in Society: The Journal of Contemporary Social Services, 92*(1), 5–11.

Gordon, C. (1991). Governmental rationality: An introduction. In G. Burchell, Gordon, C., & Miller, P. (eds), *The Foucault effect: Studies in governmentality: with two lectures by and an interview with Michel Foucault.* Chicago, IL: University of Chicago Press.

Harvey, D. (1989). *The condition of postmodernity: An enquiry into the origins of cultural change.* Oxford: Blackwell Publishers.

Hirschman, A. (1977). *The passions and the interests: Political arguments for capitalism before its triumph.* Princeton, NJ: Princeton Univesity Press.

Hyatt, S.B. (2001). From citizen to volunteer: Neoliberal governance and the erasure of poverty. In J. Goode & Maskovsky, J. (eds), *New poverty studies: The ethnography of power, politics, and impoverished people in the United States.* New York: New York University Press, pp. 435–469.

Jackson, K. (1985). *Crabgrass frontier: The suburbanization of the United States.* Oxford: Oxford University Press.

Jessop, B. (1994). Post-Fordism and the State. In A. Amin (ed.), *Post-Fordism: A reader.* Oxford: Blackwell, pp. 251–279.

Katz, M.B. (1996). *In the shadow of the poorhouse: A social history of welfare in America.* New York: Basic Books.

Katz, M. (2001). *The price of citizenship: Redefining the American welfare state.* New York: Metropolitan Press.

Peck, J. (2010). Zombie neoliberalism and the ambidextrous state. *Theoretical Criminology, 14*(104), 104–110.

Peck, J., Theodore, N., & Brenner, N. (2010). Postneoliberalism and its malcontents. *Antipode, 41,* 94–116.

Piven, F.F., & Cloward, R.A. (1993). *Regulating the poor: The functions of public welfare.* New York: Vintage Books.

Polanyi, K. (2001). *The great transformation: the political and economic origins of our time,* (2nd ed.). Boston, MA: Beacon Press.

Putnam, R. (2001). *Bowling alone: The collapse and revival of American community.* New York: Simon and Schuster.

Rose, N. (1990). *Governing the soul: The shaping of the private self.* London: Routledge.

Wacquant, L.J.D. (2009). *Punishing the poor: The neoliberal government of social insecurity.* Durham, NC: Duke University Press.

4

Welfare Professionals and Street-Level Bureaucrats

Sanford F. Schram

Welfare governance is undergoing a transformation in advanced capitalist societies, where a neoliberal–paternalist regime of poverty management is emerging. Since the era of Reagan and Thatcher, the economistic ideology of neoliberalism has merged with a new paternalism creating a focus on disciplining the poor to become market compliant (Soss et al., 2011). Across advanced political economies, there is growing pressure to move beyond the Keynesian redistributive welfare state toward a disciplinary post-Keynesian regime of poverty management informed by these neoliberal and paternalist ideologies (Ferguson, 2007; Harris, 2002). As a result, the dream of ending poverty in the name of bringing social justice to the poor is replaced with the more functionalist goal of managing poverty to contain its deleterious effects on society and the economy.

Neoliberalism is best understood as a re-envisioning of the relationship of the state to the market, granting greater leeway to markets to operate without government restrictions, while marketising state programmes so they themselves operate in market-compliant ways to get clients to do the same (Brown, 2003). Related to this, the central assumption of the current push for more paternalist social welfare policies is that the state must accept responsibility for 'telling the poor what to do' so *clients*, just as much as the *programmes*, adhere to the strictures of economic rationality (Mead, 1998). Neoliberal organisational reforms under welfare include devolution, contracting with private provider agencies, and performance management systems to ensure accountability by these contracting agencies in meeting their quotas of moving recipients from welfare to work as quickly as possible. Paternalist policy tools for achieving the goals of welfare reform include time limits, work requirements, and sanctions or financial penalties for failure to comply with welfare-to-work programme rules.

The combining of neoliberalism and paternalism to restructure welfare policy has been successful in varying degrees in different ways in diverse countries around the world, but perhaps nowhere has it been more successful than in the USA (DuBois, 2010;

Peck & Theodore, 2010; Wacquant, 2009). In the last two decades, this transformed context has effected dramatic changes in the implementation of welfare policy in the USA, including significant changes in the role of frontline workers who administer welfare programmes. This chapter applies Michael Lipsky's (1983) highly influential theory regarding the uses of discretion by street-level bureaucrats to understand the changing role of welfare case managers in implementing welfare policy today. Since the passage of the Personal Responsibility and Work Opportunity Reconciliation Act of 1996, welfare – specifically the policy focusing primarily on aiding single mothers with young children – has shifted from largely being a cash assistance programme to focusing on moving recipients from welfare to work as quickly as possible. As a result, the role of case managers in implementing this policy has changed and so has their ability to exercise discretion to work with clients effectively. This chapter focuses on how this transformed context has affected the discretionary practices of frontline welfare-to-work case managers.

There are good reasons to rely on Lipsky's theory of street-level bureaucracy to understand the changes affecting frontline social welfare professionals. Given the often ambiguous goals associated with their work in the unavoidably amorphous area of social welfare programming, and the less-than-ideal work conditions stemming from lack of public support and inadequate funding, welfare professionals ineliminably have latitude in implementing the rules and regulations of public welfare systems and often, of necessity, must use this discretion to establish shortcuts and simplifications so they can better cope with their responsibilities. Yet, in the process, policy gets made in the interface between worker and client, for better or worse.

This chapter seeks to demonstrate the focus on case manager discretion is still as appropriate as ever. Yet, the substantive issues regarding the ends toward which discretion is now directed are, at times, quite different than before. The chapter highlights the changing environment affecting enduring challenges concerning the discretion of welfare professionals, with a particular focus on the changed substantive nature of frontline worker discretion in an era of neoliberal paternalism. Today, different types of workers in different types of agencies are doing very different types of work on the frontline of welfare bureaucracies. This chapter concentrates on welfare-to-work case managers and how they still need to have discretion in order to perform their jobs effectively but their discretion is frequently treated as problematic and, therefore, constrained by various management stratagem, if in new ways. The dynamic between caseworker discretion and management control has morphed with a new performance-management environment of surveillance for enforcing market-compliant behaviour on agencies and clients alike. The chapter assesses the implications of this new environment of surveillance on the ability of case managers to use discretion to improve client outcomes. After tracing the changes of welfare case management up to the current period, the chapter examines the changed role of case managers today, the effects of the changed environment on their discretion, and the implications for clients. The chapter concludes by discussing how we should not want fully to circumscribe the discretion of frontline welfare workers, even as we criticise the way they use it. The challenge is finding the right balance regarding this enduring issue, recognising it is now occurring in a transformed organisational environment. The chapter ends with consideration of how case managers should respond to the new realities of poverty governance.

WELFARE CASE MANAGEMENT IN HISTORICAL PERSPECTIVE

The role of case managers in implementing welfare policy has varied over time. In the late 19th century, friendly visitors of the local chapters of the Charitable Organization Society (COS) made house visits to promote moral uplift geared to 'improving the poor' (Katz, 1997). State Mothers' Pensions programmes following in the early 20th century also involved case management focused on providing aid only to 'worthy parents' who could ensure a 'suitable home' for their children (Moehling, 2004). Professionalising efforts were noticeable with attempts to systematise case management by leaders of the COS movement, such as Mary Richmond, who codified the basic precepts of casework as a 'therapeutic model of professional service' (Axinn & Levin, 1997, p. 149). With the Great Depression, the federal government began to be involved when the Social Security Act of 1935 initiated what became the Aid to Families with Dependent Children (AFDC) programme. The Social Security Act structured AFDC as a federal programme relying on states to comply with basic rules to receive federal funding. States retained discretion in setting benefits and prescribing some programme rules, whose application would inevitably vary given the role of case managers in determining which applicants qualified for what benefits (Gordon, 1994). Case managers in many states could deny eligibility to applicants by invoking unfit parent, 'suitable-home' or 'man-in-the-house' rules when there was reason to suspect the mother had given birth to children out of wedlock or was currently in a relationship with a male who was not the father of the children. Sometimes simply being an African-American single mother was enough of a reason to deem an applicant disqualified for public assistance (Reese, 2005).

Right into the 1960s, most case managers for public assistance were not professional social workers, that is, they most often did not possess a Master's degree in social work (Steiner, 1971). Instead, social workers with a Master's degree were increasingly moving into working in other fields of social work, often in the private sector, and a growing proportion worked as therapists and counsellors treating clients for various behavioural health issues (Dill, 2001).

By the late 1960s, the leaders of the major social work professional organisations, including most especially the National Association of Social Workers, were advocating to separate the income determination from social service provision responsibilities of case managers, in part so working with public assistance clients would be more attractive to social work professionals. Determining eligibility for cash assistance was the less attractive side of the case manager's responsibilities and often extended beyond making initial judgements about the character of applicants as much as their needs. Even less attractive to social welfare professionals interested in helping clients overcome adversity was the fact the income determination side also included monitoring and surveillance of recipients after they had begun to receive cash payments to make sure they remained in compliance with expectations concerning their family and work life. Removing clients from the rolls for failure to report earnings or because they had a man in the house living with them made case managers out to be more like police officers than professional social workers trained to help people overcome their barriers to achieve self-sufficiency.

The separation of income and services was finally achieved with federal amendments to the Social Security Act in 1972 (Diller, 2000). Welfare rights litigation had played its role in finally bringing this separation into being (Davis, 1995). In response to a series of US Supreme Court decisions handed down in the late 1960s and early 1970s, states were under increased pressure to determine eligibility in a more standardised and routinised way in order to reduce the chances case managers were using subjective judgements, including most especially racial prejudices, about the character of applicants to decide who would receive cash benefits. In addition to the litigation's effect in easing access to public assistance, mobilisation by the welfare rights movement, spearheaded by the National Welfare Rights Organization, had produced an unprecedented rise in the number of AFDC recipients (Kornbluh, 2007). As a result, the caseloads for frontline public assistance workers mushroomed, making the idea of providing individualised case management services to each client simply unrealistic. Therefore, in addition to the pressure from the leading social work professional associations, welfare rights litigation and welfare rights organisations were contributing to make the idea of separating services from income increasingly attractive.

Yet, in most states, the separation of income and services led to case managers being shunted over into working in child welfare units focused on deciding whether children should be left with their parents or removed from the home and placed elsewhere, most often in a fostercare arrangement (Coleman, 1998). This work was quite different. While it increasingly involved a similar population as the families cycled through the public assistance system, it involved a more intense focus on child protective services. It was also highly investigative in nature and not the service alternative many professionals had hoped would come into public assistance. Hence it did not provide the opportunity to do supportive professional work with low-income families as advocated by the major professionals associations in the late 1960s. The ideal of professionalised social service provision in the public assistance system seemed to be infinitely deferred.

The Social Services Block Grant legislation in 1974 capped funding but allowed states to provide a variety of social services, creating opportunities for more professionals to be involved in social services related to aiding public assistance clients in addressing their issues to achieve self-sufficiency (Derthick, 1975). Yet, more and more financially strapped social welfare departments were increasingly turning to contracting with non-profits and other providers for a full gamut of social services from job training to child care to addictions treatment (Smith & Lipsky, 1993). The contracting system provided a financial safety valve: services could be purchased at lower costs because contract providers did not have to meet civil service requirements and could often substitute a professionalised workforce for a deskilled staff who might be supervised by a professional. Such models proliferated across service domains from the 1970s onwards, further complicating the efforts to professionalise service provision to low-income public assistance families.

Another complicating development was the growing focus on welfare-to-work as the main site for social service programming related to public assistance clients (Dill, 2001). The growing backlash against welfare associated with growing concern about increased numbers of families receiving cash assistance led to more efforts to focus social service programming on welfare-to-work services as part of a broader fight to reduce welfare dependency (Handler & Hasenfeld, 1991). States came under increasing pressure to reduce errors in eligibility determination and turned to practices of 'bureaucratic disentitlement', whereby potentially eligible clients were denied access to assistance (Lipsky, 1984), In spite of the focus on reducing welfare dependency, legislative initiatives to promote more programming around welfare-to-work failed to produce reductions in the caseload from the 1970s into the early 1990s. The major piece of legislation to fall under suspicion in this regard was the Family Support Act of 1998. The long night of gridlock over welfare reform persisted in part due to this failure to reduce the rolls and helped usher in a growing impatience fuelling support for more dramatic reform of welfare policy. The failure of employment services to reduce the rolls suggested to some policy makers that supportive services to promote employability were not what was needed. The leading critic was Lawrence Mead (1992) who argued forcefully that supported work programmes and long-term training did not evaluate as well as programmes focused on placing recipients in jobs as quickly as possible. This perspective gained ascendancy in Congress as Republicans rode to power in the 1994 mid-term elections with a 'Contract with America' promising, among other changes, welfare reform. The call for a more dramatic approach to moving recipients off welfare and into jobs reached a crescendo. After two vetoes from President Bill Clinton, who himself had campaigned for the presidency by promising to 'end welfare as we know it', agreement was reached and the gridlock over welfare reform was broken (Weaver, 2000). The Personal Responsibility and Work Opportunity Reconciliation Act of 1996 ushered in a new era of get-tough welfare policy including with it a new role for case management. Case management became once again central to working with welfare recipients, if not in the ways that the leaders of the social work profession had wanted.

NEW WELFARE CASE MANAGEMENT

Case management returned to cash assistance where eligibility determination had been routinised. Case management returned to centre stage with welfare reform but it was within a transformed context giving case managers a very different role. Welfare reform reflected the shift to a neoliberal–paternalist regime of poverty governance promoting a disciplinary approach to managing the problems of poverty. Welfare became less of a programme dispensing assistance and more a behavioural modification programme focused on getting recipients to change their work and family habits so that they and their families could live without welfare and rely solely on paid employment (Schram, 2006). The 1996 legislation abolished AFDC and replaced it with the block grant programme Temporary Assistance for Needy Families (TANF). The law imposed time limits and work requirements, and emphasised the use of sanctions (financial penalties for failure to comply with programme rules). It gave states options about imposing stricter time limits and work requirements and allowed states to impose other restrictions, such as a family cap on family benefits regardless of family size or additional children born to a mother receiving assistance. The TANF block grant could be used by states for things other than cash assistance. Within five years of the law being enacted, more than half the TANF block grant was going for services rather than cash (Allard, 2009).

Case management under welfare reform unavoidably followed the neoliberal–paternalist logic of the 1996 policy (see Soss et al., 2011). The law called for case managers to be involved actively in ensuring recipients took the necessary steps to move from welfare to work as quickly as possible. The central way in which case managers were to be involved in overseeing clients as they moved from welfare to work was by working with recipients to ensure they were completing what the law called their Individual Responsibility Plans (IRPs). The law required each TANF applicant approved for assistance to sign an IRP, which essentially involved promising to take a series of steps designed to facilitate movement from welfare to work. The steps involved typically included taking classes, completing job searches, and even working a required number of hours all focused on improving employability. Failure to complete required activities in the time allowed, at the times designated, and for the required amounts of time resulted in a sanction being imposed. States could vary their IRPs, even calling them by other names, such as 'contracts of mutual responsibility', implying not just the client but also the case manager, the agency, and the state were agreeing to hold up their end of the bargain to support the client in making the transition to relying on paid employment. Yet, across all states, case managers came to be centrally involved with clients through the IRP. Case managers introduced clients to the IRP, monitored client progress in completing the IRP, and imposed sanctions when compliance was not achieved.

The case manager had become a job coach with enforcement responsibilities. While there were supposed to be counselling and mentoring roles for the new frontline welfare bureaucrats, this has not really materialised. In-depth studies of case management under the neoliberal–paternalist regime associated with welfare reform indicate case managers are, perhaps even more than as in the 1950s, more cops than counsellors, as studies in a number of states have demonstrated (Morgen, et al., 2010; Ridzi, 2009; Soss et al., 2011; Watkins-Hayes, 2009). Case managers are mostly involved in enforcement of IRPs and the process of sanctioning when clients fail to adhere to their plans.

NEW PUBLIC MANAGEMENT: THE CONDITIONS FOR PERFORMANCE ANXIETY

The practices associated with the new welfare case management are not only affected by changes in policy but also the organisational innovations for implementing the policy. According to Soss et al. (2011) under welfare reform, an elongated neoliberal–paternalist organisational structure has evolved to implement the new approach to managing welfare clients. The new welfare case managers work at the bottom of a disciplinary chain enforced by performance standards.

Consistent with the marketising logic of neoliberal–paternalism, welfare provision in the USA has been restructured, root and branch, to conform to the 'new public management' – a reform movement seeking 'to replace traditional rule-based, authority-driven processes with market-based, competition-driven tactics' (Kettl, 2005, p. 3). Thus, welfare policy authority has been dispersed to a wide variety of locales and actors through devolution and privatisation (Gainsborough, 2003). At the same time, new systems of performance-based competition and management have been used to discipline the use of discretion by lower level actors in this more decentralised policy environment (Schram et al., 2008). The new organisational forms create a more flexible, decentralised system allowing aid recipients to be disciplined according to local conditions and needs but, at the same time, pressuring local providers in a variety of ways to bring their practices into line with centralised programme goals. While discretion of frontline workers persists in this transformed system, it is very much funnelled through the narrow channel of trying to meet performance quotas for moving recipients off welfare and into jobs.

The national government has quotas the states are expected to meet in moving recipients from welfare to work. States often have similar goals that counties or regional workforce boards must meet. In turn, private provider agencies very often administer performance contracts with their own quotas that must be met if those contracts are to be renewed. This performance pressure is inevitably passed to frontline workers who are increasingly monitored, often electronically, to ensure their decisions regarding clients translate into contract agencies meeting their performance goals.

Indeed, the new welfare system is perhaps best understood as a decentralised chain of disciplinary relationships running from the federal government to states, to local regional boards, to contracted service providers, to frontline workers and, ultimately, to welfare clients. At each point in this cascade, benchmarks for outcomes are established and monitored, and managerial techniques, incentives, and penalties are used to discipline actors below. Thus, state officials exercise freedom of choice when it comes to policy means, but they must choose from a subject position tied to federal funding streams and their goals. Local officials are encouraged to innovate as they compete for contracts and bonuses, but their creative energies are channelled by the relentless pressures of performance systems rewarding only the mandated programme goals. In this disciplinary chain, case managers are given discretion to allocate benefits, services, and penalties, but their choices are monitored and constrained because they must remain focused on moving recipients from welfare to work. TANF clients sign IRPs as free market actors entering a contractual exchange of benefits for work activities, but their freedom is little more than the opportunity to succeed or fail in complying with these mandated programme requirements (see Soss et al., 2011).

Examining the whole chain of governance at once, it quickly becomes apparent welfare reform is not just about bringing market discipline to clients. It is equally about imposing market discipline on welfare provision itself. The new tools of governance (Bevir, 2007), such as performance systems, are instruments for a deeper project of governmentality (Foucault, 1991), designed to produce self-disciplining governing authorities by cultivating appropriate 'governing mentalities' (Campbell, 2000). In significant respects, this shift in poverty governance preceded welfare reform, gathering momentum during the presidencies of Ronald Reagan and George Herbert Walker Bush, and emerging in full form during the early 1990s in the movement to 'reinvent government' (Osborne & Gaebler, 1992). Today, with the 'new public management' firmly entrenched, the personnel of the welfare system are subjected to a neoliberal disciplinary regime so they will ensure clients of the welfare system are subjected to the same.

By extending the reach of government via contractual relationships with community-based organisations, the new system of governance enables the power of the state to grow even as the public sector itself shrinks. Deploying market mythologies, the new public management promises contracted local actors will be freed to go their own ways and then, later, will be judged by their performance and given the information they need to improve. The reality, however, involves a more complex interplay of structure and agency (Moynihan, 2008). The focusing effects of outcome benchmarks, the pressures of competition, the prospects of incurring rewards or penalties, and the awareness one is being closely monitored are features of performance management doing more than just making agents accountable. These pressure points associated with the 'new public management' reconstitute agency culture. Under this system, local providers learn quickly they must make active use of disciplinary tools in handling clients if they are to achieve programme goals and maintain profitability. Within this 'business model' approach to managing welfare, clients and administrators alike must work within the ascendant understanding of market logic, responding to incentives and penalties, and behaving in ways conforming to corresponding market pressures.

FROM 'SOCIAL WORK' TO THE 'BUSINESS MODEL': THE NEW ORGANISATIONAL CULTURE

The new welfare case management operates in a transformed organisational culture. One way to characterise this change is a shift from 'social work' to the 'business model'. This is how case managers in Florida consistently called the shift when interviewed (see Soss et al., 2011). Like many dichotomies, this one is used to sharpen up differences for purposes of making a distinction perhaps more clear in theory than it actually is in practice. Yet, there is good reason to think across the country case managers recruited to the new system have been socialised to see this distinction. 'Social work' represents the bad old days when welfare policy coddled recipients and did not expect much from them, with the result being growing rolls and problems of long-term dependency. The 'business model' represents a new day where agencies are run like businesses, where case managers instruct clients in the ways of the world of work, and where clients are expected to act like employers by being punctual, completing their assigned tasks, and receiving compensation only to the extent they bank the billable hours. In Florida, the linguistic markings of case managers and clients alike highlight the business model orientation. Case managers are called 'career counsellors' who are helping clients get occupational careers and clients are themselves called 'candidates', as in job candidates who are ready, willing, and able to work.

Yet, the pervasiveness of performance management standards is the main way in which the business model permeates the consciousness of welfare-to-work case managers. In poverty governance today, performance systems standards are everywhere, with national government setting standards for states, states setting standards for localities, localities setting standards for contract agencies, and agencies setting standards for case managers who, in turn, discipline clients to get them to meet their own performance standards, especially in terms of working enough hours to fulfil work requirements and continue to receive benefits.

'New public management' advocates for performance management systems often talk of it as an administratively neutral technique. At the same time, however, performance systems are shrouded by free-market images of autonomy, innovation, and efficiency. Performance systems are championed as creating a more decentralised, flexible, and efficient but still accountable system of governance. These systems, however, are rarely seen or investigated as disciplinary regimes.

Soss et al. (2011) find performance measurement has had a profound effect on the organisational culture of the local welfare bureaucracy. This study features interviews with case managers revealing tremendous pressure to meet performance benchmarks, which has likely led to a strong emphasis on sanctions, i.e., financial penalties, as a tool for regulating client behaviour. In addition, the evidence suggests this emphasis on discipline may have come at the expense of client needs, and has likely led to an exacerbation of race and class disparities in sanctioning and client well-being. In other words, performance systems discipline frontline officials just as surely as sanctions discipline clients. Indeed, the technologies of discipline governing actors on the two sides of the welfare case manager's desk have strong parallels. Both rest on incentives for right behaviour and penalties for noncompliance; both aim to reshape the motivations of targets so they will pursue preferred ends as self-regulating subjects; and neither controls behaviour completely enough to forestall subversion. Just as welfare clients resist and evade the supervisory regimes of welfare-to-work programmes (Gilliom, 2001), so too do service providers subvert the goals of performance management at the frontlines of welfare reform. As Michel Foucault (1980) notes, this ubiquity of resistance should not be confused with a weakness of disciplinary power. To the contrary, performance pressures have profound effects on consciousness and behaviour at the frontlines of welfare reform, and these effects matter greatly for remaining focused on enforcing discipline in the new welfare-to-work regime. Just as earlier case managers used their discretion to cope with their responsibilities, there is good reason to think the new case managers use discretion at their disposal to cope with the performance pressures associated with the new system.

THE RECOVERY MODEL COMES TO WELFARE: THE NEW STAFFING PATTERN

The ability of the new case managers to use discretion is further complicated by changes in staffing. The practices of frontline welfare case managers today not only reflect the new policy orientation toward public assistance and the new organisational context for implementing that policy, they also reflect the changing composition of the case management workforce. There is growing evidence the new case managers disproportionately comprise former recipients (see Ridzi, 2009; Soss et al., 2011; Watkins-Hayes, 2009). There are a variety of reasons for this development. Contract agencies need not meet civil service requirements and can hire more cheaply to staff a deskilled kind of case management largely involving monitoring client adherence to welfare-to-work contracts. A relevant and less costly pool of qualified workers are former recipients who know the system and can show current recipients the ropes they must hold on to in order to make their way to the next level and off welfare into the world of work.

A second factor arguably is as welfare dependency came to be seen as analogous to being treated like other dependencies, including chemical dependencies, then it becomes more plausible for there to be the importation of a recovery model where those who have overcome their addiction can show others how to do the same. With the shift to a more decentralised, privatised system of provision, local welfare-to-work contract agencies have been able to deskill welfare-to-work case management further than previously; to forego relying on civil servants, social workers, and other professionals; and to hire former welfare recipients as a low-cost, if more community based, cadre of workers. While this may often be a simple cost-saving measure made available by the shift toward reliance on local private contract agencies, it is also entirely consistent with the recovery model philosophy, both in its spiritual and clinical dimensions. These former recipients are commonly referred to in the literature as 'success stories' (Cherry, 2007; Schram & Soss, 2001). Yet, Frank Ridzi (2009), in his ethnography of one county's welfare office, chooses another more prismatic metaphor to characterise these former recipients who provide role models for current recipients. Ridzi (2009) draws on Pierre Bourdieu to label the former recipient case managers as 'oblates'. Bourdieu (2005) notes, originally, 'oblate' was a term referring in the Catholic Church to the lay children recruited for the priesthood, and then turns the phrase to the more generalised problem of recruiting and educating the workers who staff the bureaucracy.

The Oblate, Success Story, and Former Recipient can put a more friendly face on the welfare bureaucracy when it becomes a local contract agency staffed by folks from the community. Yet, relying on oblates to fill case management positions can work in more insidious ways producing what Cathy Cohen (1999) has called 'advanced marginalization', where some members of a marginalised group gain access to upward mobility by taking on positions responsible for monitoring and disciplining other members of that marginalised group. The friendly face of the oblate may mask the disciplinary nature of neoliberal–paternalist poverty management. It can also turn local, insider information back against the welfare population as when oblates use their community status to report and punish behaviour based on their subjective judgements about what is going on locally, say regarding who is taking welfare and why. While some oblates can use their insider status to be more sympathetic to clients, others can use it as a way to treat recipients more suspiciously.

DISCRETION AND NEW WELFARE CASE MANAGEMENT

Much of what has been discussed in the foregoing is entirely consistent with Michael Lipsky's (1983) influential theory regarding the discretion of frontline street-level bureaucrats, such as welfare case managers. Case management has returned to cash assistance where eligibility determination had been routinised. Today's welfare case managers, as frontline workers of a new sort, whether they are from the community or not, still exercise significant discretion in interpreting program rules and applying penalties (Lipsky, 1983). Their decisions, however, are mostly limited now to conditioning the extent to which discipline is imposed on clients, particularly via the sanctioning process, which has come to be central to moving recipients from welfare to work under the welfare reform.

Case manager discretion today mostly matters in decisions regarding which clients will be punished when for failure to adhere strictly to the requirements they must meet. Case managers are responsible for assessing client needs and capabilities. They identify which clients should be relieved of certain work requirements or not. In doing so, the case manager establishes specific parameters for particular clients. Ultimately, these parameters matter most for deciding whether to initiate sanction procedures in response to an infraction and whether the circumstances of the infraction justify a 'good cause' exception to the rules. 'Good cause' exemptions for having to meet welfare-to-work requirements in the new US system can vary by state, but, at a minimum, according to national policy, include considerations about the availability of childcare. Most states also grant good cause exemptions when a recipient is ill or incapacitated, is caring for an incapacitated family member, or lacks transportation. States can add other exemptions as well but most states stick to these basic exemptions. In addition, there is often local variation as to how strictly good cause exemptions are enforced, especially regarding what documentation is required, such as a doctor's note to prove illness as a reason for missing appointments or failing to reach the number of required hours of work or participation in work-related activities. Case workers in this context get to exercise discretion in how strictly they enforce these requirements for gaining a good cause exemption.

While this is a limited form of discretion that does not go beyond deciding whether or not to impose a sanction, it is still discretion nonetheless, and this discretion shares much in common with case management discretion that came before it and is prevalent in other areas of social provision (Soss et al., 2011). The exercise of this sort of discretion by case managers is enhanced by the relative ineffectiveness of traditional monitoring strategies. As was the case under the prior welfare regimes and in other areas of social provision, case management rarely operates under the direct watch of supervisors (Prottas, 1979). Further, of necessity, case managers tend to process cases at rates making continual consultation impractical (Maynard-Moody & Musheno, 2003). While general rules do place broad limits on case managers, they cannot be designed to cover all conceivable situations. Finally, welfare-to-work clients occupy a dependent position in a relationship defined by unequal control of power resources (Hasenfeld, 1985). Under the TANF programme clients have lost entitlement status as well as some formal rights of appeal – developments that seem likely to have further weakened clients' abilities to impose limits on caseworker discretion (Mink, 1998).

Recognising the weakness of these constraints, most observers agree 'discretion is inevitable' in street-level work (Maynard-Moody & Musheno, 2003, p. 329), and may be influenced by two sets of factors. On the one hand, the personal values of frontline workers are likely to play a significant role in the many choices and decisions they make during the implementation process. However, the exercise of discretion, as has already been suggested, may also be influenced by values and incentives reflected in the organisational culture (Ridzi, 2009). In short, the imposition of discipline by case managers can be understood, not just as events happening to some clients more than others (as in most of the current literature). For instance, some clients may be more likely to be sanctioned because of personal characteristics, such as laziness or lack of willingness to commit to the strictures of the welfare-to-work regime. Yet, other clients may get sanctioned because caseworkers confront intense performance pressures and simply lack the time to deal with those clients fairly.

This conclusion has important implications for rethinking case management discretion in the current era. Images of uncontrolled case managers acting on personal whim have been a staple of anxieties regarding welfare reform, even from its inception. Critics on the right have worried that liberal or lazy frontline workers might not really implement the demanding new procedures of welfare-to-work programmes. Critics on the left have worried that expanded programme requirements and tough punitive tools would give case managers *carte blanche* to treat clients in arbitrary and unjust ways. Field studies of implementation have, at times, inadvertently reinforced these anxieties by making it clear frontline discretion is endemic, cannot be eradicated by supervision or procedure, and functions to rewrite policy on the ground as street-level bureaucrats select, interpret, and adapt the broad rules they inherit. The evidence presented in this chapter suggests neither position is accurate.

At one level, the analysis provided here does not contradict the studies following up on Lipsky's original analysis (Brodkin, 1997; Maynard-Moody & Musheno, 2003). Rather, it underscores the perils of taking this lesson from the literature while failing to appreciate what leading scholars have equally emphasised: the organisational forces shaping worker autonomy and channelling behaviour at the frontlines. It is important to remember Lipsky (1983) argued the fact frontline workers are weakly constrained by rules does not mean they are free to act as they wish. As others have since reminded us, case managers' uses of discretion are not '*ad hoc*, unsystematic, or incomprehensible' (Feldman, 1992, p. 163), nor are they mere reflections of individual preference and decision making (Baumgartner, 1992; Mashaw, 1983). Indeed, a central point of the literature on street-level bureaucracy has always been organisational routines, tools, norms, incentives, information systems, and categories of understanding function as mechanisms of social control shaping the use of discretion in predictable ways.

Yet, the analysis of the new frontline welfare bureaucrats presented here also underscores the limits of discretion in the work lives of local programme managers and caseworkers. The discretion possessed by welfare case managers today is *broad*, in the sense they are authorised to make a wide variety of decisions affecting the client. But case manager discretion does not run very *deep* if by 'deep' one means an individual liberty to treat clients as one would like or in ways to provide alternative means to help recipients achieve self-sufficiency. Discretion today is as thin as the services available to help clients escape poverty. Instead, the thin discretion remaining is largely the discretion to grant exemptions or impose penalties. Today welfare case managers are under tremendous performance pressure and have strong incentives to attend to this pressure. The computer key strokes needed to initiate action, by design, ensure their uses of discretion will be tracked in the information system and, partly as a result, case managers make their choices as actors who know they are being observed and evaluated. Welfare reform has initiated a tougher regime of social control even if this new system is often administered by former recipients from the community. Yet, this new regime is not just tougher for welfare clients. It is also tougher for the employees who serve as their caseworkers. The organisational regime today, arguably more than in the past, conditions the expectations case managers have about how to treat their clients. Today, new forms of performance pressures associated with electronic systems monitoring caseworkers as much as the clients focus case managers' energies to discipline recipients. We should not expect otherwise, if for no other reason than case managers' uses of discretion today, as in the past, are conditioned by the tools they have at their disposal, the policy goals they are expected to help achieve, and the specific objectives their agencies set out for them to realise. These tools today are largely limited to imposing discipline.

It is true a substantial amount of discretion remains at the frontlines of welfare administration. Yet, it is the policy and organisational context that affects how that discretion is used. Today, that discretion is largely given over to coping with intense performance pressures to move recipients from welfare to work as quickly as possible. There are limited, but real, opportunities for case managers to use discretion to counteract the pressure to be focused on disciplining clients. Soss et al. (2011) find examples of these opportunities when it is reported case managers shift burdens on to themselves in an effort to protect clients. Yet, we also find it in instances when case managers act on their personal frustrations by sanctioning in cases where they otherwise would not, and who use threats and impositions of sanctions as a way to exert greater control over client behaviour.

A closer look at these examples also serves to underscore what Lipsky (1983) taught when he first articulated his theory of street-level bureaucracy: *the dependence of individual agency on organisational forces*. While Foucault (1980) emphasised how disciplinary power instigates its own resistance, he also saw how it shaped the terrain that resistance must traverse. For instance, case managers who want to help their clients maintain their access to assistance today have few options but try to bring client behaviour into line with the organisational imperatives they confront, they are acting in precisely the ways that Lipsky (1983) emphasised in explaining how bureaucratic processes give rise to discretionary practices of rationing, silencing, and disentitlement. Going with the flow, case managers today most often must rely on disciplinary practices, such as sanctioning, in order to get clients where they need to be if they are to survive in the changed organisational climate. There may be 'burden-shifting' case managers who choose to protect their clients and swim against the organisational tide, but their small numbers and their stories testify to the difficulty of doing so, the personal costs involved, and the forces arrayed against maintaining such a strategy over the long haul.

CONCLUSION

Today, welfare-to-work programmes have become central to administering public assistance benefits to low-income parents with children. In most cases, these families are headed largely by single mothers. Welfare case management in these programmes takes place in a policy and organisational environment transformed by the shift to a neoliberal–paternalist approach to poverty management prominently featuring disciplinary practices enforcing quotas for moving recipients from welfare to work as quickly as possible. The value of this approach for clients remains suspect, given most recipients end up in low-wage jobs and do not really rise much above that over time (Collins & Mayer, 2010). Forcing people into low-wage jobs hardly seems like the kind of thing professional social workers are keen to undertake. However, there is no need for them to worry since most of the case management positions in the transformed welfare system are deskilled, low-paying jobs with minimal qualification requirements. In fact, these positions are often filled by former welfare recipients.

Welfare case management today continues to prove 'discretion is inevitable' (Maynard-Moody & Musheno, 2003). Case management has returned to cash assistance where eligibility determination had been routinised. However, that discretion today operates in a transformed policy and organisational context conditioning case management to be focused on imposing discipline as part of the process of moving recipients from welfare to work. This reduced menu for making discretionary decisions poses real challenges for case managers interested in still doing traditional client-centred 'social work' in an era of the 'business model'. While changes in the policy and organisational context are necessary perhaps to the point of moving beyond a focus on the greatly restricted TANF programme, case managers can still seek to innovate on behalf of their clients in their uses of discretion. Collaborating with other case managers probably occurs regularly. However, such sharing of information and mutual learning can be magnified through concerted collective efforts. If they try, case managers can still be 'guerrillas in the bureaucracy' (Needleman & Needleman, 1974) who work to change the system from within. Antonio Gramsci (1971) famously distinguished the 'war of position' (changing the internal culture through rethinking accepted practice) with the 'war of maneuver' (armed insurrection). Neoliberal–paternalism right now requires a war of position.

REFERENCES

Allard, S. (2009). *Out of reach: Place, poverty, and the new American welfare state*. New Haven, CT: Yale University Press.

Axinn, J., & Levin, H. (1997). *Social welfare: A history of the American response to need*. New York: Allyn & Bacon.

Baumgartner, M. (1992). The myth of discretion. In K. Hawkins (ed.), *The uses of discretion*. Oxford: Clarendon Press, pp. 129–162.

Bevir, M. (ed.) (2007). *The encyclopedia of governance* (Vol. I and II). London: Sage.

Bourdieu, P. (2005). From the king's house to the reason of the state: A model of the genesis of the bureaucratic field. In L. Wacquant (ed.). *Pierre Bourdieu and democratic politics*. London: Polity Press, pp. 29–54.

Brodkin, E. (1997). Inside the welfare contract. *Social Service Review, 71*, 1–33.

Brown, W. (2003). Neo-liberalism and the end of liberal democracy. *Theory and Event, 7*. Available at http://muse.jhu.edu/journals/theory_and_event/

Campbell, N. (2000). *Using women: Gender, drug policy, and social justice*. New York: Routledge.

Cherry, R. (2007). *Welfare transformed*. New York: Oxford University Press.

Coleman, D. (1998). *Training workers for welfare reform: An agenda for social work*. Berkeley, CA: UD Data, University of California.

Cohen, C. (1999). *The boundaries of blackness: AIDS and the breakdown of black politics*. Chicago, IL: University of Chicago Press.

Collins, J., & Mayer, J. (2010). *Both hands tied: Welfare reform and the race to the bottom of the low-wage labor market*. Chicago, IL: University of Chicago Press.

Davis, M. (1995). *Brutal need: Lawyers and the welfare rights movement, 1960-1973*. New Haven, CT: Yale University Press.

Derthick, M. (1975). *Uncontrollable spending for social services grants*. Washington, DC: Brookings.

Dill, A. (2001). *Managing to care: Case management and service system reform*. New York: Aldine.

Diller, M. (2000). The revolution in welfare administration: Rules, discretion, and entrepreneurial government. *New York University Law Review, 75*, 1121–1220.

DuBois, V. (2010). *The bureaucrat and the poor: Encounters in French welfare offices*. London: Ashgate.

Feldman, M. (1992). Social limits to discretion: An organizational view. In K. Hawkins (ed.), *The uses of discretion*. Oxford: Clarendon Press, pp. 163–184.

Ferguson, I. (2007). *Reclaiming social work: Challenging neo-liberalism and promoting social justice*. Newbury Park, CA: Sage.

Foucault, M. (1980). Power and strategies. In C. Gordon (ed.), *Power/knowledge: Selected interviews and other writings, 1972–1977*. Brighton: Harvester Press, pp. 134–145.

Foucault, M. (1991). Governmentality. Trans. R. Braidotti and revised by C. Gordon. In G. Burchell, Gordon, C., & Miller, P. (eds), *The Foucault effect: Studies in governmentality*. Chicago, IL: University of Chicago Press, pp. 87–104.

Gainsborough, J. (2003). To devolve or not to devolve? Welfare reform in the states. *Policy Studies Journal, 31*, 603–623.

Gilliom, J. (2001). *Overseers of the poor: Resistance, surveillance, and the limits of privacy*. Chicago, IL: University of Chicago Press.

Gordon, L. (1994). *Pitied but not entitled: Single mothers and the history of welfare 1890–1935*. New York: The Free Press.

Gramsci, A. (1971). *Selections from the prison notebooks* (Q. Hoare & G. Nowell-Smith, eds. & trans.). New York: International Publishers.

Handler, J., & Hasenfeld, Y. (1991). *The moral construction of poverty*. Newbury Park, CA: Sage.

Harris, J. (2002). *The social work business*. New York: Routledge.

Hasenfeld, Y. (1985). Citizens' encounters with welfare state bureaucracies. *Social Service Review, 59*, 622–635.

Katz, M. (1997). *Improving poor people: The welfare state, the 'underclass,' and urban schools as history*. Princeton, NJ: Princeton University Press.

Kettl, D. (2005). *The global public management revolution: A report on the transformation of governance*. Washington, DC: Brookings Institution.

Kornbluh, F. (2007). *The battle for welfare rights: Politics and poverty in modern America*. Philadelphia, PA: University of Pennsylvania Press.

Lipsky, M. (1983). *Street-level bureaucracy: Dilemmas of the individual in public services*. New York: Russell Sage Foundation.

Lipsky, M. (1984). Bureaucratic disentitlement in social welfare programs. *Social Service Review, 58,* 1–17.

Mashaw, J. (1983). *Bureaucratic justice*. New Haven, CT: Yale University Press.

Maynard-Moody, S., & Musheno, M. (2003). *Cops, teachers, counselors: Stories from the front lines of public service*. Ann Arbor, MI: University of Michigan Press.

Mead, L. (1992). *The new politics of poverty: The nonworking poor in America*. New York: Basic Books.

Mead, L. (1998). Telling the poor what to do. *The Public Interest, 132,* 97–112.

Mink, G. (1998). *Welfare's end*. Ithaca, NY: Cornell University Press.

Moehling, C. (2004). *Mothers' pension legislation and the cross-state variation in welfare generosity*. Unpublished paper.

Morgen, S., Acker, J., & Weigt, J. (2010). *Stretched thin: Poor families, welfare work, and welfare reform*. Ithaca, NY: Cornell University Press.

Moynihan, D. (2008). *The dynamics of performance management: Constructing information and reform*. Washington, DC: Georgetown University Press.

Needleman, M., & Needleman, C. (1974). *Guerrillas in the bureaucracy*. New York: John Wiley.

Osborne, D., & Gaebler, T. (1992). *Reinventing government: How the entrepreneurial spirit is transforming the public sector*. Reading, MA: Addison Wesley.

Peck, J., & Theodore, N. (2010). Recombinant workfare, across Americas: Transnationalizing 'fast' welfare policy. *Geoforum, 41*(2), 169–174.

Prottas, J. (1979). *People processing: The street-level bureaucrat in public bureaucracies*. Lexington, MA: Lexington Books.

Reese, E. (2005). *Backlash against welfare mothers: Then and now*. Berkeley, CA: University of California Press.

Ridzi, F. (2009). *Selling welfare reform: Work-first and the new common sense of employment*. New York: New York University Press.

Schram, S.F. (2006). *Welfare discipline: Discourse, governance, and globalization*. Philadelphia, PA: Temple University Press.

Schram, S.F., & Soss, J. (2001). Success stories: Welfare reform, policy discourse, and the politics of research. *The Annals of the American Academy of Political and Social Science, 557,* 49–65.

Schram, S.F., Fording, R.C., & Soss, J. (2008). Neoliberal poverty governance: Race, place and the punitive turn in U.S. welfare policy. *Cambridge Journal of Regions, Economy and Society, 1,* 1–20.

Smith, S., & Lipsky, M. (1993). *Nonprofits for hire: The welfare state in the age of contracting*. Cambridge, MA: Harvard University Press.

Soss, J., Fording, R.C., & Schram, S.F. (2011). *Disciplining the poor: Neoliberal paternalism and the persistent power of race*. Chicago, IL: University of Chicago Press.

Steiner, G. (1971). *The state of welfare*. Washington, DC: The Brookings Institution.

Wacquant, L. (2009). *Punishing the poor: The neoliberal government of social insecurity*. Durham, NC: Duke University Press.

Watkins-Hayes, C. (2009). *The new welfare bureaucrats: Situated bureaucrats and entanglements of race, class, and welfare*. Chicago, IL: University of Chicago Press.

Weaver, R.K. (2000). *Ending welfare as we know it*. Washington, DC: Brookings Institution Press.

5

Gender and Welfare

Mary Daly

This chapter's focus is the relationship between gender and welfare, especially in the context of social and political change. It is both conceptual and empirical in orientation, with two main aims. The first is to identify the constituent elements of both concepts and to consider how one can relate them in a way that does justice to the complexities involved and the insights of the growing body of knowledge about each. Both are relatively problematic concepts, not least because in them are lodged complex philosophical questions about the well-being of individuals *vis-à-vis* that of collectivities, such as families and the wider community. From the point of view of the chapter, the key questions centre on how one should think of welfare and well-being from a perspective informed by gender. It is suggested care is an essential part of the intellectual framework. The second aim of the chapter is to apply a critical gender lens to social policy and especially to think through the reforms that are being made and those that should be made.

The chapter is organised as follows. The first two sections discuss the concepts of gender and welfare in turn. In the former case, the intent is to offer a clear and sufficiently complex conceptualisation of gender; in the latter, the goal is to introduce different ways of conceptualising and understanding welfare. The third section introduces the concept of care as a lens through which to view and understand how welfare and gender are interconnected. The fourth section examines some of the most recent changes in welfare state programmes (focusing mainly on Europe) to see how welfare, gender, and care are actually being reconfigured. The fifth and final section of the chapter engages with the matter of a progressive agenda for gender relations as we look towards the future.

GENDER

Gender has been defined and conceptualised in a range of ways. In the most limited definition, gender may be understood as a classificatory concept to categorise the differences between individual women and men. Such a definition tends to work to a dichotomous logic. It is, therefore, difficult to extend it beyond a description of sexual difference, rooted in biology. Neither a dichotomous categorisation nor a biological understanding of gender helps much in the way of analysing gender as part of society. For this purpose, one must treat gender as a social practice, following Connell (1987). As such, gender is continually created and reconstituted by the activities of women and men as well as by social institutions, such as the family, the welfare state, the educational system, and the labour market. A notion of gender as social practice moves one away from thinking about it as fixed and incorporates the agency of individuals, collectivities, and institutions in supporting or resisting existing norms and power relations. It injects a dynamic element into the concept and creates that the expectation contesting notions of gender, arising from the interests of different social actors, provide a motor for social change. The term gender relations is preferred to gender since gender is seen, not as a dichotomous categorisation but as sets of norms and relations embedded within social structure and social action. Mary Daly and Katherine Rake (2003) defined gender relations as a composite of three elements: *resources*, *social roles*, and *power relations*.

Resources refer to goods and capacities at one's disposal. They both express and influence lifestyle, social status, and well-being in fundamental ways. Their distribution is frequently contested – indeed the welfare state was introduced to effect a more equal distribution of resources. When viewed from a gender perspective, time and opportunities have to be set alongside the more common understanding of resources as money or financial assets. A gender analysis also suggests the combination of resources matters and individuals require quite specific combinations of resources depending on their circumstances. For example, to take up employment a mother requires somebody to substitute for her time as well as a wage level making it worth her while to be in paid work given the 'costs' involved for her.

Social roles are the second element of gender relations. They refer to the extent to which norms and behaviours are regular and patterned for women and men. Parental and family roles are the most obvious examples of how social norms prescribe particular behaviours for women and men. For individuals, roles provide a set of guidelines about how to behave as well as conferring and affirming aspects of identity; at a more macro-level they act as stabilising mechanisms. Welfare states help to determine the form and meaning of social roles by, for example, treating men as the providers for their families. Practices related to welfare states, including the agency of social workers, also affect the choice of roles available to people, not least because they help to set up the rewards and penalties attaching to particular roles. Their effect on social roles is therefore an important aspect of the agency of welfare states.

There are close links between roles and power relations, the third component of gender relations. Indeed, power relations derive from and are closely associated with roles as well as other social phenomena. A focus on power relations serves to open up our analyses to the possibility the welfare state affects the power resources of individual women and men, and their distribution between them as (part of) social groups. The relative power of different groups (and interests) may be mirrored and expressed in the activity of the welfare state. The transfer of resources, via taxation and social security, is obviously important here. There is a more subtle power relation operating as well, however, in which the welfare state mediates between interests and, where contests arise, acts as an arbiter and judge. For example, deciding on the circumstances deemed to merit support from the state involves a selection process. Additionally, casting policies – and thereby setting up a form of competition between the claims of different groups or sets of activities – in particular modes serves to constrain the ways in which issues and contested claims are dealt with.

WELFARE

Welfare is the second major concept in this chapter. In discussing it, the author wishes to differentiate welfare from the welfare state (discussed later). Welfare is an ideal, albeit a highly contested one. Some of the key issues involved question whether welfare is a process or an end state, whether it is relative or absolute in the sense of relating to a basic set of needs that are part of the human condition, and the extent to which public resources should be expended to increase welfare and well-being. In regard to the latter, the welfare state in highly-developed countries is, in any way, the institution most concerned with collective welfare. It shares this space with the family though, and also to varying degrees within and across countries the community and voluntary sector and even the market. Hence, it is important not to elide welfare and the welfare state.

While it is used quite loosely in popular discourse, in academic scholarship the concept of welfare has very particular origins. Its history in the social sciences lies in three particular sets of scholarship: neoclassical economics, political philosophy, and social work and social policy (Daly, 2011). It is worth taking a moment to outline how each frames the concept of welfare.

In neoclassical economics, welfare refers to the utilities or pleasure generated by market-based exchanges. This perspective views welfare primarily in material terms and identifies the main sources and determinants of welfare as generated by market exchanges or through the provision of a limited range of public goods. People get satisfaction (welfare) from exchanging the resources they have through market-based transactions with others. In philosophy and political science, welfare is developed as a contested ethical principle and a goal of political organisation. Here, welfare is situated within a range of beliefs about the appropriate moral and political order in society and the appropriate distribution of resources. Welfare is seen to be inextricably bound up with discussions relating to such ethical principles as equality, justice, freedom, and rights and whether and how welfare as a goal of political life is to be realised in public institutions and political practice. The social disciplines locate welfare in the need for and achievement of organised forms of social support and intervention, particularly in response to perceived individual need and 'social problems'. Their interest in welfare directs them especially (but not by any means exclusively) to a subsection of the population – those who cannot provide for themselves, the 'needy' sectors of society. Welfare in a social vein is intimately connected, then, with societal ends and functioning, especially in terms of the measures to be taken to address such phenomena as poverty, unemployment, ill-health, and social inequality.

Viewed in the round, welfare's original meanings are strong on material resources and the institutions and practices governing access to resources and social aid. Key elements of what might be called the classical conception of welfare tap into the nature of social divisions and their consequences as well as opposing philosophical and political positions on how to address these and other 'social problems'. There is very little in this that sees welfare as gendered though. To the extent recognition of structured social division – conceived in terms of resources, roles, or power – exists, it is social class inequalities that have received the lion's share of attention. However, there is a whole body of new scholarship on well-being that might be a more fruitful place to look for insights about welfare, broadly conceived.

What is being referred to here is the work on subjective well-being, a topic which has had a meteoric rise over the last decades. While space does not allow for consideration of the vast scholarship on this, noteworthy are the two main conceptual approaches to subjective well-being – the Benthamite subjective–hedonic individualistic perspective and the Aristotelian objective–eudaimonic–relational approach (Bruni & Porta, 2005). The assessment of people's subjective well-being typically ranges over three components: life satisfaction, presence of positive mood, and the absence of negative mood (Diener, 1984). This kind of work taps into people's emotional state and aspects of their psychological well-being, such as feeling satisfied, being healthy, showing an interest in other people, having a sense of life achievement, and being in control (Hills & Argyle, 2002; Searle, 2008). Happiness, especially, has come to the fore as a leading concept in the field. In fact, happiness research is claimed by some to be fast becoming a 'new science' (see Layard (2005) and the World Database on Happiness at: http://www.eur.nl/fsw/research/happiness). In this perspective, levels of individual happiness or emotional state are taken as a key indicator of quality of life and well-being. This has led to calls to make happiness the avowed goal of policy (Layard, 2005).

The concept of well-being has a more general application also as a description of the state of individuals' life situation or 'being' (McGillivray, 2007). Here it shades into an approach linking people's subjective well-being with their objective circumstances. The interest in connecting people's assessment of their mental state with the resources and experiences they have available has led to an extensive literature across a range of disciplines (Searle, 2008). This dual focus is part of the appeal of the concept of well-being. Another perceived strength is the concept's sense of multidimensionality – it typically incorporates physical well-being, material well-being, social well-being, and psychological well-being (Felce & Perry, 1995). In essence, work on a more general concept of well-being is pushing the concept towards agency and a greater recognition of people's embeddedness in relations and contexts.

A further very influential conceptualisation of well-being is that which follows from the work of economist Amartya Sen (1984, 1999, *inter alia*). His is a normative theory which is centred round the question of what makes a good life for a human being. He concludes it is their capabilities – the freedom they have to achieve what is valuable and important to them (see Chapters 1 and 24). For Sen, therefore, well-being is to be assessed in terms of people's capability to engage in valuable activities or acts and to reach valuable states of being, functionings. It is not resources or command over commodities per se that matter in determining quality of life or even justice. Rather, Sen suggests a change of paradigm: from commodities to capabilities and from goods to what they allow people to obtain and do. Opportunities are more important for him than resources or goods, which are means rather than ends. While it is obvious his perspective invests hugely in agency, it also has a sense of state or condition – the former relates to 'doings' and the latter to 'beings'. Both doing and being are connected in the concept of 'functionings' (the illustrative examples of which include healthfulness, longevity, and literacy). The critical element, though, is capabilities. It is these that confer the freedom or opportunity to achieve certain preferred lifestyles. People (should) have capability sets – resources to achieve whatever it is they value. Well-being in Sen's view, then, is determined both by one's set of capabilities and set of functionings. Sen adopts an expansive conception of what is valuable in human life, rather than specifying desired outcomes. He, therefore, does not subscribe to the view there are universal basic needs. He has, though, focused attention on what he calls 'basic capabilities' (escaping morbidity and mortality, for example), although he has never provided an indication of a range of appropriate functionings or capabilities. Martha Nussbaum (2000) used Sen's approach to devise a list of essential capabilities to live at a minimum decent level with dignity (see Chapter 24) but, among other things, the concept of capabilities remains difficult to operationalise and interpret. In policy-making circles, for example, it has often been interpreted as human capital rather than human capabilities (Dean, 2010).

Taking an overview, the turn to well-being and capabilities provides a welcome corrective to some of the classic understandings of welfare in several respects. For example, it shifts the focus away from what people buy and consume to their feelings and subjective responses to their situation. Moreover, the newer work resists taking income or other aspects of people's 'external' lives as proxies for their well-being and is inclusive of life spheres beyond the market. Above all though, the approach valorises people's assessments of their situation, challenging the tendency for researchers and experts to 'know' without consulting people. That said, the focus on subjective well-being has particularities which, in certain circumstances, may turn out to be weaknesses. First, the scholarship is part of a move to a greater interest than heretofore in individual processes and people's emotional life. The happiness approach, in particular, runs the risk of prioritising short-term, pleasure-seeking activity and is relatively insensitive to the context in which the emotion is experienced (Wilkinson, 2007). Misgivings must also be lodged about the assumption our behaviour is guided by our own pleasure or sense of fulfilment. Even Sen's work has an ideal of people as autonomous agents and it has little sense either of the social nature of well-being or the structural impediments perpetuating social divisions. The well-being and capabilities approaches are popular because they pick up on and advance the movement to a new paradigm in the social sciences – one oriented to agency as against structure and individual as against group or collectivity.

The work on welfare and well-being has not been a particularly gender-oriented scholarship, although some work has been done on Sen's capability perspective from a gender focus (Lewis & Giullari, 2005; Robeyns, 2007). In the next section, the perspective of care is outlined along with some of the relevant literature which shapes understanding of the complexities of welfare or well-being from a gender perspective. Using care as a focus takes scholarship away from an individualistic focus and towards an appreciation of deeply embedded gender relations.

CARE

Care is a word in widespread usage but it has rather different meanings. Daly and Lewis (2000) defined it to refer to the activities and relations involved in meeting the physical and emotional needs of dependent adults and children, and the normative, economic, and social frameworks within which these are distributed and carried out. As a concept, care has origins in two literatures. In the first, it is elaborated as a vital domain of life and human activity frequently hidden or overlooked, but a profound part of human life and welfare. The second treats care as an issue for public policy and intervention, in a body of work examining the growth and expansion of services and benefits oriented to the personal care of children and adults who cannot provide for their own needs. The first literature is of greater interest in this section as the next section of the chapter considers public policies around care.

Care has been most developed in feminist work. These theorists of care have elaborated and used the concept to reveal and characterise the particularity of relations and practices associated with giving or receiving care from another person. Here the concept has a number of histories. One impulse to scholarship, initially anyway, was to reveal a hidden, undervalued and taken-for-granted aspect of women's lives. Care was conceived mainly as (oppressed) labour in this early work (Williams, 2002). The focus was on 'informal care' and the conditions under which the activities involved were carried out, in particular their unpaid and familialised nature. Care as a gendered phenomenon is an enduring focus in the literature. This abiding interest led to work on both the material and moral conditions surrounding caregiving and care-receiving. It also revealed the relational features of care, especially its nonstrategic character. The most sociological literature draws out the societal settlements associated with care – such as the gender division of labour, the concertation between the market, state and family in how the relevant activities are framed and organised – and the meanings of care for women and for their identity. Over time this literature has built up a body of work emphasising the uniqueness and complexity of care, as a relationship, a set of activities, an orientation or way of being, and a domain of social life. Both the positive and negative aspects of care are drawn out, the latter especially in terms of the imposition of an obligation to care, the hard work involved and the frequently disadvantageous conditions in which care is carried out. Care as a moral perspective or orientation has received a lot of theoretical attention also. One strong strand of work, which elaborates caregiving as an ethical practice and contrasts it with other principles, such as justice, has especially helped to lay bare and critique the value choices and orientations underlying social and other forms of policy (Hankivsky, 2004). It also reveals how the scale of values is biased towards men and male activities (see Chapter 22).

The concept of care extends the meaning of welfare or well-being in a number of ways. In the first instance, it shows how people's welfare hinges critically on the kinds of care they receive when they need it, both physical care, and emotional sustenance and support. This is the accustomed meaning of care – servicing the needs not just of the young, those who are ill, and elderly people and others who cannot take care of themselves, but also those who are able-bodied. Welfare in this view is the meeting of needs – it normalises the situation in which all people have needs. But there is a broader set of dimensions to care as well. As an ethical practice, care requires from the caregiver the characteristics of attentiveness, responsibility, competence, and responsiveness (Held, 2005; Tronto, 1993). To recognise this sense in which care extends understanding of welfare requires movement beyond a perspective viewing care as confined to the settings and relationships connoting need, obligation, and dependency. Seen in broader terms, a focus on care emphasises the relational foundations of all social life. There is no place here for solo individuals. Rather, key elements of people's welfare inhere in their relations with others and the reciprocity around responses to need and the receipt of recognition and value for who people are. No metric prevails. This extension of the meaning of welfare views care not in terms of meeting need but as an orientation towards both self and others. Among other things, care shifts the focus from general rules to actual relations of mutual responsibility and contributes to the development of a set of moral principles focusing on actual relationships rather than general or abstract relations (Gilligan, 1982; Tronto, 1987). The idea of caring about is important here also: caring about the environment, the welfare of animals, or some political cause, for instance. It also involves taking responsibility (Sevenhuijsen, 1998; Tronto, 1993). The reference is not just to how people respond to the needs of intimates but also how they view strangers and intimates alike. To be able to recognise this may require them to change their understanding of how they function and, instead of seeing themselves as independent, view themselves and those around them as interdependent and vulnerable (even when able-bodied).

The next sections of the chapter move from theoretical considerations to relevant policy applications of this framework. The idea is to see, first of all, how welfare state reform is proceeding (in Europe mainly) and, secondly, to engage in a thought exercise around a progressive agenda from the perspective of gender, welfare, and care.

BROAD OVERVIEW OF WELFARE STATES' APPROACH TO GENDER, WELFARE, AND CARE

It is uncontroversial to say there is a restructuring of social policy going on in Europe and the developed welfare states generally. In this, gender equality has fallen from view.

In Europe gender equality was a big story in the 1980s and 1990s – national governments and the European Union (EU) undertook wide-ranging reforms in their social and employment policies so as to reduce gender discrimination and eliminate barriers and impediments for women's employment. There was a concern about each of the three dimensions of gender relations identified as constitutive of gender in the opening section of this chapter: resources, roles, and power relations. Now, while there is still some concern with gender-related roles and resources, they are not leading reform and power relations seem to have fallen from view. Rather, reform is driven more by the search after a set of general individualised objectives around self-sufficiency, human capital, and economic functioning. The focus on activation – enabling or compelling people to be active for the purposes of employment and self-sufficiency – is widely acknowledged as a leading policy idea(l) and objective. But aspects of family life are central to the reforms as well – in fact one could say *the focus has shifted from gender to family*. This is to be seen in the bundle of issue animating policy reform across countries which focus on family relations and family functioning in quite fundamental ways. They mirror closely the concerns of the EU and the Organisation for Economic Cooperation and Development (OECD; Lewis, 2006; Mahon, 2006). The new social policy consensus typically legitimates state activity and social and economic reorganisation along the following lines:

- encouraging, if not compelling, employment, for benefit claimants, 'workless households', and women;
- providing for the education and/or care of young children;
- balancing work and family life;
- targeting men's behaviour as fathers;
- providing financial assistance for families with care tasks and obligations.

The 'passive' welfare state, which confers benefits by status, entitlement, and/or need, was seen to be 'unfit for purpose' in a knowledge-driven, competitive global economy. The more legitimate function of social security in such altered conditions should be to enable people to be employed and self-sufficient, especially those at the lower end of the income and skills' continuum. When pressed into service as a social policy agenda, this makes for increasing conditionality to the receipt of benefits, a greater role for social security and taxation in subsidising low-waged employment, and a closer relationship between benefit receipt and training and work-motivational provision. 'Workless households' – defined without any reference to care – are problematised as an anomaly in this scenario and so policy seeks to change the work ethic and labour market-related practice in such households. Everyone who is not in the labour market is subject to scrutiny, including those who have caring-related obligations. Lone mothers, for example, have been singled out for measures incentivising or compelling their employment (especially in The Netherlands, Ireland, and the UK). The low levels of employment among mothers more generally also became a concern: non-employed mothers are represented as an underutilised source of labour, and by implication a 'cost' on the public purse and a 'burden' on male wages.

A second notable policy focus is the education and care of young children. In the last ten years or so, states in Western Europe have taken much greater interest in educational provision for young children (those aged between 0 and 3 years) and have tried to change the ideologies around the rearing of young children, especially in facilitating nonparental care of young children. While not quite pushing an open door, this draws on the roots of some European welfare states. Indeed, out-of-home provision for young children was a hallmark of the Scandinavian welfare states, for example, and France and Belgium, to a lesser extent. There is wide consensus today on the need for educational development of Europe's young children. Hence, there is a Europe-wide trend towards pre-schooling of young children. But this is nowhere being developed under the aegis of educational policy alone. Rather, it is refracted through a number of policy lenses and objectives, with concerns around family stability and functioning and women's and men's labour supply overlaid upon or interlinking with more long-standing concerns around child well-being and pedagogical performance.

Balancing work and family life, 'reconciliation' as it is known, has become an important objective in its own right in Europe, without having much pre-history as a concept in European social policies. Promoted strongly by the EU as a means of gender equality, it may serve a number of masters, including gender equality, quality of life, efficiency of work organisation, and employment flexibility (Lewis, 2006; Stratigaki, 2004). In terms of a policy programme, it has overseen especially the extension of parenting-related leaves (maternity, paternity, and parental) and also some flexibilisation of the organisation of employment to accommodate the schedules and exigencies of childrearing and family life more broadly. It is now commonplace in Europe for working parents, fathers as well as mothers, to be able to avail of some period of paid leave from employment, which recognises their caring-related obligations and for them to be in a position to seek to vary their times of employment on child-related grounds. In effect, giving care as a parent is legitimated as a basis of entitlement to 'caring time' sponsored by the state (and employers, to a lesser extent). These moves also signify the development of parenting policies in Europe under the auspices of the welfare state. Lister et al. (2007) say the trend is towards longer periods of leave and less gender-segregated leave arrangements (see also Bettio & Plantenga, 2004; Morgan, 2009). While enabling people to be out of employment might seem at odds with the activation and self-sufficiency orientation of policy reform, the fact both are concurrent emphases of policy betokens complexity. It should be kept in mind the work–family balance perspective may not be attributable solely to better accommodating the needs of the marketplace or to gender. Rather, family life, its existence and its quality, and the role of family as a social institution, also proffer an underlying policy rationale.

Men's behaviour as fathers is also a focus of policy interest. Starting in Norway in 1993, the 'daddy quota' – whereby a proportion of the parental leave is designated for the father and is lost to the family if he does not take it – is proving influential across Western Europe. The aim of this and paternity leaves, which are directed towards fathers only, is to encourage fathers' involvement in the early life of their young children. While it has a number of roots, including some in father–child bonding, it also has purchase on gender equality. It draws from a problematisation of the unequal distribution of family-related tasks between women and men as one of the sources of women's disadvantage, and a barrier to greater female employment. However, a gender sameness perspective dominates here, whereby the role envisaged for both genders contains elements of worker and carer, and a carer role (albeit limited) for men. Countries vary, however, in the extent to which change in fathers' behaviours is targeted as norm or practice. In most countries, the measures could be said to be symbolic – many of the parental and paternal leaves are unpaid or paid at a flat-rate for example, a very low-grade incentive. The Scandinavian countries constitute the opposing pole of high-grade incentivising. In Sweden, for example, a gender equality bonus exists for children born after July 1, 2008: mothers and fathers who take an equal number of days will receive the maximum bonus possible, provided the other parent is in employment when the leave is taken.

A further notable propensity of policy today is a readiness to assist and subsidise the family with care-related tasks and or expenses. Europe has long made payments to families rearing children. Most commonly known as child or family benefits, these payments were, in origin, subventions to the family man to help with the costs associated with children (Gauthier, 1996; Montanari, 2000). They were often paid through the wage packet. As they became generalised in Europe, they retained their core purpose of assisting families financially and hence effecting some form of horizontal redistribution or 'justice' between families with children and those without. Because they were sometimes paid to the mother as the caring parent (e.g., in the UK and Ireland), they had some care and gender connotations but they were nowhere introduced for the purpose of financially compensating the caring parent. The new care-related subsidies and payments, which have taken root in Europe in the last decade or so, are very different in being care-oriented (in the sense they seek to compensate financially for involvement in care and also are underlaid by a value position on what constitutes appropriate care). If child benefits could be said to be about valuing family and family relationships, the new payments for childcare are more instrumentally oriented towards organising childcare so that it (i) is 'shared' and (ii) does not interfere too much with mothers' capacity for employment. They represent at base a commodification of care (Knijn & Ostner, 2002; Ungerson, 1997).

Overall, in regard to care a (particular type of) redistributive paradigm is at play (Sevenhuijsen, 2002). Care-related tasks become a focus of redistribution, at two levels: (i) at the micro-level between women and men via the paternity and parental leaves; and (ii) at a more macro-level via the increasing state, market, and community sector involvement in childcare and other forms of service provision. In none of this is gender equality a strong principle.

TOWARDS A PROGRESSIVE POLICY AGENDA

One of the main messages of a critical analysis of reforms is that gender needs to be an explicit focus of policies. Moreover, for the purposes of policy, gender needs to be conceived in the complex manner set out in the first part of this article: resources, roles, and power relations. Furthermore, care needs to be included as a central component of welfare.

How much the state should provide for the welfare of individuals and families is an open and difficult question. In these neoliberal times, arguments against an interventionist approach are easily marshalled. If individuals and families were left to their own devices, they might be better able to weather whatever storms they encountered. Interventionist policies may also be charged with social engineering. However, counter arguments are also compelling, not least the claim that the development of a gender and family or care policy is integral to the future of developed market societies given the need to find a balance between economic and social objectives. In any case, intervention is already under way. A widespread element of the reform constellation today is its strong moral and normative undertones, not just in terms of increased state purview and regulation of behaviours heretofore considered 'private' but also in prosecuting distinctions between good and bad, deserving and undeserving, and troubled and troublesome (Tisdall, 2006).

A first key element is the activities and relations involved in care as it applies not just to children but also to elderly and other family members. Considering them as 'care' confirms the activities and relations involved as holistic, recognising that they extend right across the life span and know no real boundaries between home and elsewhere. Giving greater recognition and value to caring should have a firm place in a progressive agenda. How to actually achieve this is remarkably difficult, however. A number of steps are suggested.

In the first instance, care should be viewed as a need and a responsibility potentially affecting all individuals, and many institutions. Hence it requires interventions at different levels, from individuals, through households, civil society, state, and market (Pascall & Lewis, 2004). There should be no monopoly of care, either within or outside the family, and social policy should actively seek to redistribute care – in much the same way as income redistribution is accepted as a legitimate social goal. Of course, caregiving has to be resourced – for this purpose, the concept or idea of 'care capital' might be a useful frame. Giving payments for care is one way – these already have what seems like a firm place in social policy provision, in Europe anyway. But such payments will work only if set at a sufficiently high rate – too low payments run the risk of ghettoising the activity and confirming it as a low-wage, low-skill, and low-status activity. In addition, low payments act against gender equality, incentivising women but not men to undertake caring activities. But, on their own, payments are an insufficient response – recognising the value of unpaid work extends beyond remunerating it. A second element of valuing care relates to rights. The duty elements of care are more familiar to us but actually rights are vital to good-quality caregiving and receiving. A movement towards granting home carers pensions and other entitlements serves to strengthen the rights basis of care (see Chapter 24). Equally, granting rights around access and quality to those who are at the receiving end of care, such as children or older people, is important. A third essential element is services. A whole range of health and personal social services is required. A fourth element is time. This is actually the root resource conferred by employment leave, along with income replacement. The Netherlands has recently gone one step beyond employment leave, introducing a scheme whereby Dutch workers can trade time for money by building up a time and income bank, resourced from part of their normal wages and salary and unused leave time, which can later be used for goals such as more income, daycare for children, or reduced hours of work (Knijn, 2008). The Dutch government is also making a deliberate attempt to redistribute the existing volume of both paid and unpaid work by actively improving the quality of part-time work. While the fruits of these measures is awaited, at the present time the division of paid and unpaid work continues to have a strong gender cast in the Netherlands (Knijn, 2008).

Focusing on the dynamics and quality of care might also serve to address some of the complex moral issues involved in the domain of family, especially as they relate to interpersonal relations. Policy often either ignores or misunderstands felt obligations and responsibilities among kin. One compelling insight of research is, for women, the relationship between employment and family is an active one in the sense of being a site of fine-graded decision making and careful reasoning, in which morality plays a large role (Barlow et al., 2002). For example, research on mothers in the UK shows them typically trying to find employment 'fitting' around the family (Brannen et al., 2004). It is now known there is some trade-off for women (e.g., between work *or* family) in all social policy systems in Europe (Daly, 2000). The scale of the trade-off matters as does its sign (e.g., a negative trade-off between women's labour supply and fertility is commonplace in Europe). Even the Scandinavian countries are discovering gender equality is more intractable than was assumed. Datta Gupta et al. (2006) identify the emergence of a new male breadwinner society in these countries whereby mothers self-select into relatively low-paid jobs in the public sector, where it is easier to combine a career with family responsibilities, while men tend to locate themselves in the private sector. The results of this and other research raises doubts about potential 'boomerang effects' of policies on women's position in the labour market (Datta Gupta et al., 2006). In effect, gender equality is something of a moving target in that measures intended to alleviate it once in place appear to encounter, or even lead to, new 'glass ceilings'.

There are certainly real limits to gender equality understood in the sameness model – mainly because it leaves underlying structures and stereotypes unchanged and fails adequately to meet people's wish to be involved closely in the care of their close relatives and intimates. Policy has to be held to a higher standard than this. As Nancy Fraser (1994) has said, the goal is not to make men and women identical to each other, but rather to promote a universal caregiver model, whereby care is shared, not just between women and men, but also among the state, employers, and companies, and the voluntary sector and community at large. It is necessary to cleave to employment and career as a goal for the majority of women. This does not necessarily mean depriving women of the choice to rear families or to care for their ill or elderly relatives themselves, but it does mean extending that choice in a real way to men as well.

These are two essential conditions of gender equality at the present time: that it be the norm for women to be employed and that it equally be the norm for men to undertake caring-related activities. This, in turn, and the latter especially, leads to a third condition: better sharing of unpaid work. The movement of women into the labour force has not resulted in a significantly improved sharing of home-based work between women and men: the average woman does between two and three times the amount of unpaid work carried out by men (Gershuny, 2000). The present arrangement works only because it rests on a gender division of opportunities and costs. This, the failed revolution, has to be within the policy radar as well. Paternity leave, as it exists in most countries, is not especially oriented to overturning this source of inequality. Usually of short duration and restricted to the period around the child's birth, it is oriented more to the father–child relationship than to mother–father sharing. It is a step in the right direction, however. The conditions attaching are as always crucial. Experience to date suggests two lessons: men will, or can afford, to take paternal or parental leave only when it has a high wage replacement ratio; and services to supplement and, at times, replace parental activities are crucial.

When it comes to unpaid work, the appropriate response is not to mandate for equal sharing in *strictu sensu* – parents with task charts ticking off 'who does what' – but rather to place greater value in and on the sphere of care and associated activity. In the spirit of the measures outlined above, it means treating home and work as interconnected. Pascall and Lewis (2004) speak of a logic of gender equality in care work, income, time, and voice, as well as in paid employment. Glucksmann's (2005) concept of the total social organisation of labour is also relevant here. With this approach, she has in mind the manner in which all the labour in a society is divided up and allocated to different structures, institutions, activities, and people. In practice, this kind of approach means developing an entire environment favouring more equal sharing between men and women across spheres and resources: in paid work, care work, income, time, and voice. It is important to think through the desired end when it comes to better sharing between women and men – better sharing of what? Housework? Childrearing?

The approach taken to children and young people is especially important in all of this. While children have been made a prime consideration in the contemporary policy constellation, the extent to which policy targets a good childhood is limited. For Lister (2008), such a policy for children *qua* children means focusing on two inter-related elements: their well-being and their citizenship. Taking a citizen perspective allows policy makers to have a guiding framework which rests on children's membership of society, and in that context their rights, their responsibilities, their status, respect, and their level of recognition *vis-à-vis* other sectors of the population (Lister, 2007). The family life of children and young people has to be a consistent priority. Overall, a progressive agenda around gender, welfare, and care means being open to change on many fronts and mindful of the need to protect individual welfare. It also means balancing this with exigencies and concerns about collective well-being and equality between women and men understood in the broad way developed in this chapter.

REFERENCES

Barlow, A., Duncan, S., & James, G. (2002). New Labour, the rationality mistake and family policy in Britain. In A. Carling, Duncan, S., & Edwards, R. (eds), *Analysing families: Morality and rationality in policy and practice*. London: Routledge.

Bettio, F., & Plantenga, J. (2004). Comparing care regimes in Europe. *Feminist Economics, 10*(1), 85–113.

Brannen, J., Moss, P., & Mooney, A. (2004). *Working and caring over the twentieth century: Change and continuity in four-generation families*. London: Palgrave.

Bruni, L., & Porta, P.L. (eds) (2005). *Economics and happiness: Framing the analysis*. Oxford: Oxford University Press.

Connell, R.W. (1987). *Gender and power*. Stanford, CA: Stanford University Press.

Daly, M. (2000). A fine balance women's labour market participation in international comparison. In F. Scharpf & Schmidt, V.E. (eds), *Welfare and work in the open economy*, Vol II, *Diverse responses to common challenges*. Oxford: Oxford University Press, pp. 467–510.

Daly, M. (2011). *Welfare*. Cambridge: Polity Press.

Daly, M., & Lewis, J. (2000). The concept of social care and the analysis of contemporary welfare states, *British Journal of Sociology, 51*(2), 281–298.

Daly, M., & Rake, K. (2003). *Gender and the welfare state: Care, work and welfare in Europe and the USA*. Cambridge: Polity Press.

Datta Gupta, N., Smith, N., & Verner, M. (2006). *Child care and parental leave in the Nordic countries: A model to aspire to?* Bonn: IZA Discussion Paper no. 2014.

Dean, H. (2010). *Understanding human need social issues, policy and practice*. Bristol: Policy Press.

Diener, E. (1984). Subjective well-being, *Psychological Bulletin, 95*, 542–575.

Felce, D., & Perry, J. (1995). Quality of life: Its definition and measurement, *Research in Developmental Disabilities, 16*(1), 51–74.

Fraser, N. (1994). After the family wage: Gender equity and the welfare state, *Political Theory, 22*(4), 591–668.

Gauthier, A.H. (1996). *The state and the family*. Oxford: Clarendon Press.

Gershuny, J. (2000). *Changing times: Work and leisure in post-industrial society*. New York: Oxford University Press.

Gilligan, C. (1982). *In a different voice*. Cambridge, MA: Harvard University Press.

Glucksmann, M. (2005). Shifting boundaries and interconnections: Extending the 'total social organisation of labour'. In L. Pettinger, Parry, J., Taylor, R., & Glucksmann, M. (eds), *A new sociology of work?* Oxford: Blackwell, pp. 19–36.

Hankivsky, O. (2004). *Social policy and the ethic of care*. Vancouver, BC: UBC Press.

Held, V. (2005). *The ethics of care: Personal, political, and global*. New York: Oxford University Press.

Hills, P., & Argyle, M. (2002). The Oxford Happiness Questionnaire: A compact scale for the measurement of psychological well-being. *Personality and Individual Difference, 33*(7), 1073–1082.

Knijn, T. (2008). Private responsibility and some support: Family policies in The Netherlands. In I. Ostner, & Schmitt, C. (eds), *Family policies in the context of family change The Nordic countries in comparative perspective*. Wiesbaden: VS Verlag fuer Sozialwissenschaften, pp.155–173.

Knijn, T., & Ostner, I. (2002). Commodification and decommodification. In B. Hobson, Lewis, J., & Siim, B. (eds), *Contested concepts in gender and social politics*. Cheltenham: Edward Elgar, pp. 141–169.

Layard, R. (2005). *Happiness lessons from a new science*. New York: The Penguin Press.

Lewis, J. (2006). Work/family reconciliation, equal opportunities and social policies: the interpretation of policy trajectories at the EU level and the meaning of gender equality. *Journal of European Public Policy, 13*(3), 420–437.

Lewis, J., & Giullari, S. (2005). The adult worker model family, gender equality and care: The search for new policy principles and the possibilities and problems of a capabilities approach. *Economy and Society, 34*(1), 76–104.

Lister, R. (2007). Why citizenship: Where, when and how children? *Theoretical Inquires in Law, 8*(2), 693–718.

Lister R. (2008). Investing in children and childhood: A new welfare policy paradigm and its implications. In A. Leira & Saraceno, C. (eds), *Childhood, changing contexts*. Bingley: Emerald, JAI Press, pp. 383–408.

Lister, R., Williams, F., Antonnen, A., Bussemaker, J., Gerhard, U., Heinen, J., Johansson, S., Leira, A., Siim, B., & Tobbio, C. with Gavanas, A. (2007). *Gendering citizenship in Western Europe: New challenges for citizenship research in a cross-national context*. Bristol: Policy Press.

Mahon, R. (2006). The OECD and the work/family reconciliation agenda: Competing frames. In J. Lewis (ed.), *Children, changing families and welfare states*. Cheltenham: Edward Elgar, pp. 173–197.

McGillivray, M. (2007). Human well-being: Issues, concepts and measures. In McGillivray, M. (ed.), *Human well-being concept and measurement*. Basingstoke: Palgrave, pp. 1–22.

Montanari, I. (2000). From family wage to marriage subsidy and child benefits: Controversy and consensus in the development of family support. *Journal of European Social Policy*, *10*(4), 307–333.

Morgan, K.J. (2009). Caring time policies in Western Europe: Trends and implications. *Comparative European Politics*, *7*(1), 37–55.

Nussbaum, M. (2000). *Women and human development: The capabilities approach*. Cambridge: Cambridge University Press.

Pascall, G., & Lewis, J. (2004). Emerging gender regimes and policies for gender equality in a wider Europe. *Journal of Social Policy*, *33*(3), 373–394.

Robeyns, I. (2007). When will society be gender just? In J. Browne (ed.), *The future of gender*. Cambridge: Cambridge University Press, pp. 54–74.

Searle, B. (2008). *Well-being*. Bristol: Policy Press.

Sen, A. (1984). *Resources, values and development*. Oxford: Basil Blackwell.

Sen, A. (1999). *Development as freedom*. New York: Knopf.

Sevenhuijsen, S. (1998). *Citizenship and the ethics of care Feminist considerations on justice, morality and politics*. London: Routledge.

Sevenhuijsen, S. (2002). Normative concepts in Dutch policies on work and care. In S. Bashevkin (ed.), *Women's work is never done: Comparative studies in care-giving, employment, and social policy reform*. New York: Routledge, pp. 15–37.

Stratigaki, M. (2004). The cooptation of gender concepts in EU policies: The case of 'reconciliation of work and family'. *Social Politics*, *11*(1), 30–56.

Tisdall, E.K.M. (2006). Antisocial behaviour legislation meets children's services: Challenging perspectives on children, parents and the state. *Critical Social Policy*, *26*(1), 101–120.

Tronto, J.C. (1987). Beyond gender difference to a theory of care. *Signs*, *12*(4), 644–663.

Tronto, J.C. (1993). *Moral boundaries. A political argument for an ethic of care*. London: Routledge.

Ungerson, C. (1997). Social politics and the commodification of care. *Social Politics*, *4*(3), 362–381.

Wilkinson, W. (2007). *In pursuit of happiness research: Is it reliable? What does it imply for policy?* Washington, DC: Cato Institute Policy Analysis, No 590.

Williams, F. (2002). In and beyond New Labour: Towards a new political ethics of care. *Critical Social Policy*, *21*(4), 467–493.

6

Welfare and Social Development

James Midgley

The belief that social welfare (or social well-being as the term is now more widely known) can be achieved through a progressive development process rooted in economic growth is widely accepted in the developing countries of the Global South. It has also gained support in Western, industrialised nations where economic growth is now given higher priority in economic policy than ever before. However, it is widely recognised that economic growth of itself does not result in improvements in welfare for the population as a whole. Although growth has brought about historically unprecedented improvements in standards of living, poverty and deprivation persist. This is the case in both the developing and Western countries. In the developing countries, economic growth has indeed created employment and raised incomes but many millions of people continue to live on the margins of survival. While some enjoy the benefits of growth, the majority – and specially the population in the rural areas – continues to struggle to make ends meet much as they have done for centuries. In the cities, shanty towns housing millions of poor people proliferate while high-rise office buildings, glitzy shopping centres, and suburban neighbourhoods catering for the wealthy and the growing middle class expand. In the Western countries, living standards have reached previously unimaginable levels but poverty has not been eradicated. The paradox of poverty and deprivation in the midst of economic growth reveals the distorted nature of the development process and is a key challenge social development seeks to address.

As the problem of unequal and distorted development has been recognised, the narrow economism of conventional development thinking has been questioned and a more holistic and egalitarian view emphasising the social dimensions of development has gained acceptance. Advocates of this approach argue the 'social aspects' of development should be given priority, and economic growth should be specifically focused on alleviating poverty, improving health, nutrition, and education, and raising standards of living for all. By directing economic growth towards social ends, they contend the problems of poverty, deprivation, and inequality can be addressed. In this context the term 'social development' has gained support over the years. However, as is shown, these ideas are not universally accepted and numerous criticisms of the social development approach have been made.

This chapter discusses the social development approach. It traces its history, identifies its key features, and discusses the theoretical principles informing social development practice. Three strategic approaches which draw on normative theories and shape social development interventions are then discussed. They are the individualist enterprise strategy, the populist community strategy, and the collectivist statist strategy. Social development interventions include policies, programmes, and projects seeking to improve peoples' material well-being through investing in capabilities and enhancing participation in the productive economy. A number of interventions of this kind are described. The chapter concludes with a brief comment on social development's prospects and limitations.

HISTORICAL EVOLUTION OF SOCIAL DEVELOPMENT

Although the term social development was only popularised in the 1950s and 1960s, it has far older roots reflecting a preoccupation in many cultures with notions of change and progress. As Nisbet (1980) has shown, social thinkers have pondered the nature and causes of change since the time of the ancient civilisations. However, ancient social thought generally favoured cyclical explanations. Progressive theories involving a linear process of steady improvements only became popular after the 17th century when European thinkers became aware of the material prosperity and intellectual progress of their own time. Many progressive theories attributed the causes of change to impersonal social and economic forces, but some recognised the role of human agency as a primary cause of change.

In the 19th century, the biological notion of evolution was employed by social thinkers to suggest societies are propelled to higher levels of complexity and sophistication by similar evolutionary social forces. Evolutionary ideas were also used to: (i) legitimate European imperialism, which it was believed, would promote progressive change among the peoples of the colonies who were said to be at a 'lower stage' of evolutionary development; and (ii) justify limited state intervention contending government policies designed to direct the process of change would have disastrous long-term consequences. This argument was eventually challenged by social liberals and social democrats who argued the widespread conditions of poverty and deprivation associated with rapid industrialisation and urbanisation in the Western countries could best be addressed through state intervention. As Western governments introduced social reforms, the term 'social evolution' was gradually replaced by 'social development'.

Interventionist ideas found expression in economic planning, and particularly in Soviet centralised planning and Keynesian demand-management economics in the 1930s. Interventionism also found expression in social policy, particularly in the New Deal in the USA and in the adoption in Britain of Beveridge's proposals for a centrally directed and comprehensive system of state social services. Full employment was given high priority and the need for investments in education and housing, as well and as income protection, was stressed. The view social and economic policies should be closely integrated was generally accepted although, as Midgley (1999) suggests, it was subsequently abandoned by many social policy scholars.

At this time, the nationalist movements campaigning for independence from European imperial rule also embraced interventionism. After independence, economic planning was widely adopted, but many governments prioritised economic growth over social welfare believing growth would increase wage employment and raise standards of living. Because economic growth was given high priority, the social service provisions introduced during the colonial era were often condemned for impeding economic development (Livingston, 1969). Colonial welfare officials in West Africa responded to this criticism by introducing mass literacy campaigns as well as a variety of community-based infrastructural and productive economic projects. In the 1950s, the term community development was adopted to connote these activities and, in time, it was augmented by the broader term social development. Similar community-based activities were introduced throughout the Global South largely through the efforts of the United Nations, which became a major proponent of social development.

The United Nations and other international agencies diffused social development around the world. The organisation actively encouraged the expansion of community development but, in the 1960s, the community development approach was augmented by national social planning. This new emphasis led many governments to formulate development plans paying greater attention to the social aspects of development and plans adopted not only set economic growth targets but also expanded health, education, and the social services, and addressed the problem of poverty (Hall & Midgley, 2004). Other international agencies, such as the International Labour Organization (ILO) and the United Nations Children's Fund (UNICEF), supported this initiative as did the World Bank under the presidency of Robert McNamara which now placed greater emphasis on poverty alleviation. Subsequently, feminists such as Boserup (1970) and Rogers (1980) campaigned for a greater focus on the gender dimensions of development, and growing concern about the environmental impact of economic growth policies resulted in the adoption of the formulation in the 1980s of the sustainable development approach by the Bruntland Commission (1987).

These events fostered a broader, holistic conception of development that transcended the narrow economic focus of conventional development policy and gave greater emphasis to social, environmental, gender, and other interventions. However, in the 1970s, the role of the state was increasingly questioned. Community activists point to authoritarianism and corruption in the governments of many developing countries arguing, therefore, that poverty eradication would only be achieved by actively promoting peoples' participation in development, particularly at the local level. Similarly, women activists urged that steps be taken to foster the full participation of women in development programmes and projects. Women's associations, particularly at the grassroots level would, it was argued, make a more significant contribution to social development than government agencies. A similar emphasis was placed on promoting sustainable development projects at the local level.

Another challenge came from market liberals who claimed government planning, heavy taxation, and bureaucratic regulation had stifled economic growth. This problem could be addressed by retrenching the state, promoting entrepreneurship, creating vibrant markets, and opening national economies to international trade. By adopting market-friendly policies, businesses would flourish, employment opportunities would expand, and incomes would rise. The Reagan administration in the USA and the Thatcher government in Britain actively promoted these ideas, which now featured prominently in their aid policies. The International Monetary Fund and the World Bank also embraced this approach and aggressively used their lending policies to promote marketisation. Since many developing countries had become indebted through excessive borrowing, aid was usually provided on condition debtor nations adopted market liberal structural adjustment programmes.

In the 1990s, following the collapse of the Soviet Union, increased global trade, and economic liberalisation, the adoption of market liberalism resulted in the retrenchment of government social development programmes in many countries. Market liberalism also exerted a growing influence on social development and interventions such as microenterprise gained popularity. In addition, reflecting the populist emphasis on community participation, nongovernmental organisations began to play a much more important role in social development. As Lewis and Kanji (2009) reveal, international donors increasingly bypassed governments and directly funded these organisations. The imposition of structural adjustment programmes further enfeebled the government's role. Government social service budgets were cut, user fees were imposed, and social programmes retrenched.

Although by the 1990s it seemed the statist approach to social welfare had been undermined, the United Nations countered by convening the World Summit on Social Development in Copenhagen in 1995. The Summit was attended by many international leaders who agreed on a set of social development targets enshrined in the *Copenhagen Declaration* (United Nations, 1996). Five years later, at a special session of the United Nations General Assembly, the organisation's member states adopted the Millennium Development Goals, which redefined the targets of the *Copenhagen Declaration*, and specifically proposed to halve the incidence of global poverty by 2015 (United Nations, 2005). A number of other targets related to nutrition, the status of women, and maternal and child health were also adopted. Although progress has been uneven, a meeting of the United Nations in September 2010 to assess the situation concluded, despite the negative impact of the global recession, the incidence of absolute poverty had declined in many parts of the world and progress had also been made on the implementation of the other goals. In addition, the Millennium initiative has been characterised by an unusually high degree of international support and a renewed commitment to social development.

FEATURES AND PRINCIPLES OF SOCIAL DEVELOPMENT

The field of social development is characterised by diverse conceptual ideas and practical approaches, which complicates the task of formulating a widely accepted standard definition. Consequently, the term is often used loosely to connote the 'social aspects' of development or to refer to community-based development or gender projects. Unfortunately, the lack of a standard definition has created much confusion. The problem has been exacerbated by the frequent expression of excessively rhetorical and hortatory sentiments linking social development to various commendable ideals but failing to specify what social development involves in practical terms. In addition, various scholars writing about social development have employed different disciplinary preferences to emphasise its diverse aspects. In sociology, for example, the term has been used in a very abstract way to connote processes of societal change (Chodak, 1973). In development studies, it is loosely associated with community-based projects, while in economics it has been linked to development planning, employment creation, and raising incomes (United Nations, 1971). Some economists, such as Birdsall (1993) of the World Bank, believe there is no difference between economic and social development and Friedman (1989) agrees, arguing social development goals can best be achieved through economic liberalisation. On the other hand, many social work and social policy scholars contend economic and social development are distinctive spheres of activity which should be harmonised within a broad, multifaceted development process.

Social workers have been actively involved in promoting social development since the 1970s when a group of social work educators in the USA founded the International Consortium for Social Development. They included scholars who had migrated to the USA from developing countries, such as India and Sri Lanka. Midgley (2010) believes they were among the first to formulate a working definition of social development and to identify its key principles. Paiva's (1977) formative definition, which was published in a leading North American social welfare journal, viewed social development as the 'capacity of people to work continuously for their own and society's welfare' (p. 332). Pandey (1981) defined social development in more practical terms as a process resulting in the 'improvement of the quality of life of people ... a more equitable distribution of resources ... and special measures that will enable marginal groups and communities to move into the mainstream' (p. 33). This definition is in many respects similar to the ideals expressed in the *Copenhagen Declaration* some 15 years later. At this time, Midgley (1995) defined social development as 'a process of planned social change designed to promote the well-being of the population as a whole in conjunction with a dynamic process of economic development' (p. 25). Subsequent definitions by social work scholars, such as Miah (2008), have extended this definition to place greater emphasis on microfinance, microenterprise, and community- and market-based activities. Although originating in social work, these definitions are multidisciplinary and invoke a wider political economy approach to the field.

Social development principles

Among the principles of the social development approach identified by social work and social policy writers are the notions of process, change, intervention, and universalism. These principles reflect different normative and ideological perspectives and reveal the underlying ideological struggles characterising efforts to achieve social development goals. As suggested earlier, the notion of progressive social change is a key principle of social development. Social development advocates reject static or conservative views condoning prevailing social conditions or concluding nothing can be done to improve human welfare. They take an optimistic view believing change is possible and social problems, such as poverty, social deprivation, ill-health, illiteracy, inadequate shelter, inequality, exploitation, and injustice, can be addressed. While this view has been criticised as idealistic and even utopian, they contend social development policies and programmes have brought about significant improvements in many parts of the world and further improvements are possible.

The importance of the concept of progressive social change in social development reflects the notion of social development as an evolving process. Social development advocates make the obvious point social change is not instantaneous but evolves over time, and involves different agents and the allocation of resources and political commitment. Social development may, therefore, be contrasted with other approaches such as charitable giving or social service delivery which do not emphasise the need for an ongoing, progressive process of change.

The notion of process in social development also reflects the broader, multifaceted concept of development mentioned earlier and the interdependence of the economic, social, gender, political, and ecological dimensions of the development process. Social development advocates insist these different dimensions are effectively linked in development policies, programmes, and projects. This idea finds expression in three axioms, which first require the harmonisation of different components of the development process and the adoption of organisational arrangements for achieving this. Although conventional social policy thinking has drawn a sharp distinction between economic and social interventions, contending these are separate domains, social development writers urge the introduction of formal arrangements effectively integrating economic and social policymaking.

A second axiom is economic development policies should be 'people-centred' and sustainable, and promote the well-being of the population as a whole by addressing the distortions of development. This has been a recurrent theme in social development writing for many years and its advocates have included notable scholars, such as Myrdal (1970), Seers (1969), and Sen (1985, 1999).

People-centred development requires economic development policies actively promoting economic participation through creating remunerative employment, raising incomes, investing in education and skills, and ensuring economic growth improves the standards of living of the population as a whole.

A third axiom is social policies, programmes, and projects should enhance participation of needy people in the productive economy through social investments. Interventions, for example, mobilising human and social capital, creating employment opportunities, promoting microenterprises, encouraging asset accumulation, and removing barriers to economic participation are given high priority. These *productivist* investments, as they are also known, promote material well-being by enhancing capabilities and fostering economic participation. In addition, they contribute positively to development. Although often targeted at poor families and those who are traditionally served by the welfare system, they have universal relevance. The goal of promoting social welfare through *productivist* interventions is arguably social development's most distinctive feature.

The principle of agency or intervention is another key principle in social development. Proponents of social development believe the process of progressive social change does not occur spontaneously or haphazardly, or because of innate social and economic forces, but rather because of the efforts of human beings, organisations, and governments committed to improving social conditions. Different agents, they point out, contribute to the social development process. They include households and families, community-based civil society associations, and faith-based organisations among others. The state is another vitally important agent for promoting social change. However, there are strong disagreements about the role of these different agents and particularly the contribution of the state, which, as was noted earlier, has now been widely denigrated.

There has been a tendency to privilege one of these agents in social development thinking but some scholars, such as Midgley (1995), contend that they can all be effectively utilised within the context of a wider, pluralistic conception of state-directed intervention. Although his proposal for 'managed pluralism' may appear to offer a viable compromise, partisan preferences persist. Of course, the limitations of state intervention must be recognised. Obviously, weak, corrupt, and authoritarian governments are unlikely to foster progressive social change. On the other hand, not all governments fall into this category and, despite numerous challenges, the power and resources of the state have been harnessed to promote social development.

As is shown below, the social development process is informed by different normative theories that inspire different strategies and interventions, but it also reflects a preference for pragmatic, incremental experimentation. Social development's pragmatism reveals an historic association with the progressive reformism of social liberalism and democratic socialism, but community and social activism is an integral part of social development thinking. The role of activism has recently been reaffirmed in projects involving poor women, ethnic and linguistic minorities, and the poorest sections of the community.

Universalism is another key principle of social development. Social development transcends a narrow focus on the most needy and vulnerable groups and seeks instead to promote the well-being of the population as a whole. However, this does not preclude a concern with needy and exploited people and communities. Social development policies and programmes are often targeted on poor people living in rural communities and urban informal settlements, or on women, tribal minorities, and nomadic communities, but these 'pro-poor' interventions operate within a universalistic set of programmes and policies that benefit the rest of the population as well.

Finally, attempts to conceptualise social developments have been concerned with goals. As noted in the introduction to this chapter, social development is committed to enhancing the well-being of populations by addressing the ubiquitous problem of distorted development and responding to the problems of poverty, widespread deprivation, and inequality. In addition to these practical goals, social development effort is also concerned with creating opportunities and fostering equality and with achieving social rights and social justice.

SOCIAL DEVELOPMENT STRATEGIES AND INTERVENTIONS

Because social development is primarily focused on the tasks of alleviating poverty, meeting social needs, and addressing social problems, it is understandable that practical interventions rather than abstract concepts and theories have been emphasised in the social development literature. A large number of interventions that range from local community development projects to national social planning have been adopted by social development practitioners. As mentioned earlier, social development practice relies on various agents who play an active role in implementing these interventions. They include households, community development workers, non-profit organisations, and government agencies.

Social development interventions also reflect the influence of wider, ideologically motivated strategies that shape specific interventions and the activities of different agents. Three strategies – the individualist enterprise strategy, the populist community strategy and the collectivist statist strategy – can be identified. Strategies are different from interventions in that they are major normative approaches while interventions are specific policies, projects, and programmes. For example, microcredit and microenterprise interventions reflect a wider strategy of assisting individuals and households to launch small businesses that operate on the economic market. On the other hand, a cash transfer, minimum wage mandate, or a food subsidy provided by government reflects the statist strategy. Similarly, an intervention that mobilises local village people to construct a clinic reflects the populist community strategy. Of course, different strategic approaches and interventions can be combined. Indeed, many social development programmes and projects mingle local community effort with state-funded projects as well as market-based economic activities. In these cases, different strategies intermix in a complex way to inform specific social development interventions. However, as the microenterprise example given earlier suggests, it is usually possible to detect a preponderant influence of one strategy in any particular intervention. To better understand how social development interventions are configured, the normative dimensions of different strategies as well as the role of different agents should be clarified.

Normative preferences and social development strategies

Tracing social development's intellectual heritage, Midgley (2003) believes that efforts to promote social development have been inspired by three major normative traditions all of which reflect a Western, modernist legacy in which notions of progress and intervention are emphasised. As suggested earlier, these normative perspectives are overtly ideological but are nevertheless tempered by a pragmatic tendency among social development practitioners to incrementally implement different policies, programmes, and projects.

The individualist enterprise strategy reflects the recent ascendancy of market liberal ideas in social development, which stress the role of rational individuals and households in utilising capabilities and resources to maximise their own welfare. Advocates of this approach argue that social development should support their actions through interventions such as microfinance and microenterprise development and individual asset accumulation. In addition to interventions of this kind, there has been a growing interest in risk management interventions. In 2001, the World Bank adopted what was described as a social risk management framework that would assist vulnerable households to respond to adversity (Holzmann & Kozel, 2007). Another development is the idea of integrating the poor more effectively into market activities. Prahalad (2005) believes that this can be achieved by marketing and franchising goods and services in poor communities. These activities will not only address the poverty problem but, he contends, reveal the fortune that can be made at the bottom of the pyramid. Stoesz (2000) takes a similar view arguing that poverty can be effectively addressed by promoting 'bootstrap capitalism' among the poor.

The individualist enterprise strategy requires that individuals and households function rationally and autonomously. It is in this regard that some social development writers, such as Paiva (1977), originally placed emphasis on interventions that strengthen people's capacity to promote their own well-being. These ideas are compatible with the capabilities approach popularised by Sen (1985, 1999), and with notions of strengths and empowerment that pervade much social development writing today (Midgley, 2010). The individualist enterprise strategy is also dependent on a wider capitalist culture that facilitates autonomous rational action. A good deal of social development writing since the 1980s has been critical of the prevalence of collectivist statism, which, it is believed, impedes economic growth and social progress. In the late 1980s, de Soto (1989) railed against the state corporatist traditions of Latin American countries that, he claimed, stifled informal sector entrepreneurship and impeded development. The World Bank (2001) took up the theme, urging the adoption of 'market friendly' development strategies. The diffusion of markets through economic globalisation has also been welcomed as a way of fostering an enterprise culture on a worldwide scale.

A second social development strategy, which is informed by populist ideology, contends that social development goals can best be met through communities and associations that collaboratively engage in projects and programmes to raise standards of living. Unlike the individualist, enterprise approach, which privileges the role of individuals and households in social development, the community approach stresses the need for cooperative action by community members acting under the leadership of elected community councils or civic associations. This strategy encourages a variety of associations to engage in social development and it emphasises the role of social movements in bringing about social change. In addition to formal non-governmental organisations, grassroots women's groups, local faith-based organisations, and mutual aid associations are encouraged to participate in social development.

Democratic participation, shared governance, and collective ownership are key elements of the populist, community strategy. Members express their views and participate actively in the decision-making process and they freely give their time to implement social development projects. Even though funds may be obtained from external sources, projects are owned by the community as a whole. Collaboration, democratic participation, and joint ownership are believed to be an important mechanism for community empowerment and for fostering social solidarity. Empowerment is also associated with activism, and, in many cases, advocates of the populist approach are enthusiastic proponents of community action directed at both external and local elites. Activism also characterises many women's groups, as well as associations representing ethnic or tribal minorities, and this often involves vigorous opposition against discrimination, exploitation, and oppression. These activities are bolstered by the activism of progressive social movements.

The role of government in social development is emphasised in the collectivist, statist strategy. Advocates of this approach believe that the state has the resources and authority to promote social development, particularly when mobilised by democratic and socially committed governments that represent the interest of their citizens. Governments, it is argued, are uniquely placed to take a holistic view and to formulate and implement development policies and programmes at the national level. They can mobilise substantial administrative expertise as well as legislation, regulation, and budgetary allocations to achieve this goal. National policies not only benefit the population as a whole, but also can be directed towards needy and vulnerable groups. The problems of exploitation and discrimination can also be addressed through government policies. The statist approach reflects technocratic ideas that posit the need for skilled policy makers, planners, and administrators as well as local practitioners who utilise their expertise to promote participation in social development activities.

State-managed social development endeavours have been actively supported by international aid, technical assistance, and the other activities of development organisations and donor governments. Although national governments usually assume overall responsibility for social development, intergovernmental collaboration has also played a major role. Treaties, conventions, and international gatherings, such as the World Social Summit of 1995 and the Millennium Summit of 2000, have all fostered a statist approach to social development on a global scale.

The collectivist, statist strategy is inspired by socialist ideology, which contends that the state is a large collective, owned by its citizens who are served by politicians, as well as planners and administrators. Accountability is achieved through democratic elections, lobbying, and media and other mechanisms that give voice to popular opinion. These processes are bolstered by laws, judicial mechanisms, and enforceable human and social rights. The notion of rights has become increasingly important in social development thinking in recent years (Midgley, 2007; Molyneux & Lazar, 2003; Moser & Norton, 2001) and a good deal of international effort has been devoted to promoting a rights-based development approach. Effectively implementing a rights-based development approach requires that the state not only enforces but also promotes these rights.

These different strategies are often viewed as incompatible and even antagonistic but they all have positive features that can be effectively combined within a wider pluralistic system managed by the state. As noted earlier, the concept of managed pluralism forms an integral part of what Midgley (1995) called the institutional approach to social development. This approach creates a broader framework in which the contribution of different normative perspectives and different agents is recognised and utilised.

SOCIAL DEVELOPMENT INTERVENTIONS

A number of policies, programmes, and projects that reflect wider social development principles and normative preferences have been implemented over the years. These have been well documented by social development writers (Midgley, 1999; Midgley & Sherraden, 2009; Midgley & Tang, 2001) and are not discussed in any detail here. As noted at the beginning of this chapter, these interventions include human and social capital investments, the accumulation of individual and community assets, the creation of employment and self-employment opportunities, the extension of social protection, the removal of barriers to economic participation, and the promotion of cost-effective programmes and projects. A large number of different programmes and projects, which have an explicit social investment function, can be categorised under these interventions.

Human capital investments provide the knowledge, skills, and capabilities people need to participate effectively in the productive economy. The need for knowledge and skills is being emphasised all over the world today, and many governments are committed to improving educational opportunities. Emphasis is also being placed on childcare, pre-school education, literacy training, job skilling and re-skilling, and lifelong learning. Most people, including poor people, recognise the importance of education and will often make a major sacrifice to send their children to school. The willingness of poor families to invest in education should be supported fully by governments, and the cost they incur should be minimised. It is in this regard that human capital investments can effectively mobilise and balance the resources of individual households, communities, and the state. Although social development practitioners emphasise the need for educational interventions, human capital development is also promoted through good nutrition and healthcare programmes. Human capital investments bring positive benefits not only to individuals and but also to society as a whole, and they should, as Schultz (1981) argued many years ago, be given high priority.

Social capital refers to investments that strengthen social networks and participation in community activities. Social capital is also mobilised by a variety of civil society associations. The creation of social capital fosters cooperation and solidarity and, as Putnam and his coworkers (1993) demonstrated, it also promotes economic development and raises standards of living. Accordingly, community-level development projects that integrate social and economic activities have been emphasised. Participation in civic activities is also given high priority. The concepts of empowerment and activism have also played a major role in this approach, and through active participation, people have been encouraged to take control of their own affairs and resist exploitation and oppression. The mobilisation of social capital not only gives expression to the populist community strategy, but also involves external resources provided by the state. This is been an integral part of community development programmes in the Global South for many years.

The promotion of wage employment has been a primary goal of economic development efforts since the 1950s, and it is equally important in social development, but here the focus is on poor people and those with special needs. Social development advocates believe that governments should play a major role in promoting employment opportunities for these groups. They should also support community and business enterprises that foster this goal. They believe that beneficial partnerships between the state, communities, and commercial enterprises can be forged, and they recommend that incentives should be offered to both private enterprises and community-based cooperatives to stimulate wage employment. Although cooperatives that create employment are not as popular as before, they have a major role to play and deserve support. State-funded community works projects, which have been used for many years to alleviate poverty, should also be strengthened. In addition to these interventions, the need for adequate wages, safe and healthy working conditions, and the creation of decent work opportunities must also be prioritised.

In view of the challenges facing employment creation in many parts of the world, the role of self-employment has been recognised by social development writers and practitioners who now believe that microenterprises funded through small loans can contribute to raising the incomes of poor families. Spurred by the success of the Grameen Bank and similar initiatives, and the popularisation of market liberal ideas, microenterprise initiatives have proliferated. Although the claims of microenterprise advocates are often overly optimistic and should be tempered by the recognition that this approach is only likely to benefit some low-income people, it has made a contribution to social development by facilitating informal sector activities, raising the incomes of some low-income families and, to some degree, empower women (Midgley, 2008; Remenyi & Quinones, 2000). On the other hand, a number of highly critical accounts of the expansions of microfinance programmes in the developing world, and particularly of the way microfinance has been decoupled from microenterprise, have recently been published (Bateman, 2010; Roy, 2010).

Asset development programmes have also become popular in recent years. Asset development involves the accumulation of financial assets by individuals and households as well the creation of community-owned assets, such as schools, clinics, clean water supplies, and feeder roads. This latter goal has long been an integral part of community development in the Global South and remains an integral component of community-based social development around the world today (Kretzman & McKnight, 1993; Mathie & Cunningham, 2008; Moser & Dani, 2008). The accumulation of financial assets has been promoted through the creation of child savings accounts in some Western countries and through matched savings accounts, known as Individual Development Accounts or IDAs. Invented by Sherraden (1991), these accounts have been established in the USA and in some other countries as well. Matches are provided by nongovernmental organisations, foundations, and governments, and create an incentive for poor families to save. Although studies have shown that the amounts saved are not significant, they increase the credit worthiness of poor families, provide access to banks, and have positive psychological and social effects (Schreiner & Sherraden, 2007).

Although social protection programmes have not been a major part of social development in the past, the investment implications of income transfers are being recognised and more widely used. For example, the conditional cash transfer programmes introduced in Mexico and Brazil in the 1990s (Fiszbein & Schady, 2009) are being adopted elsewhere. These programmes have been accompanied by the expansion of 'unconditional' income transfers by some governments, particularly in Southern Africa, which believe that flexible means-tested and universal pensions, child allowances, and other income transfer programmes targeted at poor families contribute positively to development. It has been shown that injecting cash into the household budgets of poor families increases their consumption and demand for goods and services, results in the creation of small household enterprises, and promotes school attendance, all of which have positive implications for development. A number of African governments have expanded means-tested social protection programmes of this kind in recent years (Ellis et al., 2009; Patel & Trieghaardt, 2008).

Recognising that there are many barriers that prevent the participation of poor people in development, policies that facilitate participation have been advocated by many social development scholars and practitioners. These barriers include discriminatory practices against women, minorities, people with disabilities, and the elderly, among others. Removing barriers of this kind requires an active role for the state in enacting and enforcing nondiscriminatory legislation and affirmative action programmes. It also requires that governments address institutionalised inequalities, and strengthen opportunities for people to recognise their potential. In addition, participation in the economy requires that issues of peace and justice be addressed. Social development goals are unlikely to be realised in societies where violence is commonplace and where entrenched elites perpetuate their privileges and impede the efforts of the majority to improve their standards of living. In these cases, activism can contribute to the election of governments that serve the interests of their citizens. As was suggested earlier in this chapter, social development ideals are best implemented in peaceful and just societies characterised by democratic participation and a commitment to human rights.

Finally, social development's proponents are today more cognisant of the need to evaluate interventions and ensure that they are cost effective. As pressures on social expenditures have increased, the need to ensure that social development projects and programmes do in fact meet their stated objectives is more widely accepted. Today, various technologies ranging from cost–benefit analysis to outcome evaluation are more widely used and, in addition, a more generalised evidence-based approach to social development practice has also become popular. It is likely that cost effectiveness will become an increasingly important principle in social development practice in the future.

CONCLUSION: LIMITATIONS AND PROSPECTS OF SOCIAL DEVELOPMENT

As will be recognized, social development is not a highly systematic or coherent approach to social welfare. Instead, it is comprised of different programmes and projects that have been implemented in an incremental and unmethodical way. The problem is compounded by the influence of disparate normative ideas which propose that quite different interventions be adopted to achieve social development goals. Although some social development scholars have attempted to formulate a coherent conceptual basis for social development practice, their efforts have not been very successful with the result that social development is open to the criticism that it hardly comprises a methodical or effective approach in the field of social welfare.

Nevertheless, this chapter has shown that social development thinking is characterised by basic assumptions and principles. It is these that are often singled out for critical comment by scholars of quite different normative proclivities. For example, social development's commitment to progressive social change through human agency has been challenged by postmodernists as well as Marxists. Postmodernists reject social development's faith in progress, while Marxists question the possibility of achieving significant social change within the framework of a capitalist society. Radical populists take a similar position contending that it is only through popular social movements and a vigorous commitment to challenging entrenched power structures that meaningful change can be brought about.

These criticisms reflect a preference for very different normative approaches and it is perhaps paradoxical that all of these different ideological influences have found expression in social development. For example, radical populism has exerted considerable influence, but it is juxtaposed against the socialist insistence that the state under democratic control is best able to achieve social development goals. This premise is, in turn, vigorously rejected by market liberals who believe that improvements in standards of living can best be achieved through enterprise and participation in the market economy. This has created tensions within social development as advocates of different perspectives have insisted on the validity of their own approaches. In addition, the social development field as a whole has sometimes been equated with a particular perspective so that it has been attacked for being excessively statist or romantically populist or committed to market liberalism. This latter criticism has been more frequently voiced in recent times as market liberal ideas have exerted growing influence in social development. For example, the use of microfinance and microenterprise in social development has become so popular that the legitimate criticisms levied against this approach are sometimes viewed as an indictment of social development as a whole.

Social development's association with economic development is often the subject of critical comment even though this criticism is often uninformed. Although social development's link with economic development is premised on a people-centred approach, which requires that the benefits of economic growth be redistributed to enhance the welfare of the population as a whole, the very mention of the phrase 'economic growth' suggests to some that social development is little more than a form of neoliberalism and an apology for unrestrained, predatory capitalism. Another criticism comes from social workers who are committed to a helping approach involving the altruistic transfer of services and resources to those in need. They are appalled by the notions of social investment and economic participation even though social work has a long-standing commitment to restorative interventions. Similarly, populist radicals often claim that their own challenge to entrenched power structures is a more effective way of bringing about change than social development's pragmatic approach. This criticism ignores the historic role of activism in social development, and again fails to recognise that different perspectives can be harmonised to achieve desirable goals. Another criticism comes from advocates of a green, steady-state economy, who challenge the view that economic growth is an effective way of achieving improvements in standards of living. In view of the negative effects of consumerism and the environmental damage caused by rapid economic growth in many parts of the world, this is a legitimate concern which is only partially addressed by social development's commitment to sustainability.

Many social development advocates are not indifferent to these and other critiques, and some have attempted to respond to them by refocusing interventions in ways that address the field's deficiencies. Nevertheless, they do believe that the strategies and interventions discussed earlier can bring about progressive social change and improvements in social welfare. But they do not deny that there are formidable obstacles to achieving social development goals. Economic volatility and global recession, climatic adversity, wars and domestic conflicts, and entrenched power structures continue to impede the goal of addressing the distortions that characterise much development effort. Nevertheless, they are committed to implementing social development interventions in conjunction with sustainable economic development policies and programmes that raise standards of living and promote the well-being of all. They are also persuaded that despite major challenges and obstacles, much has been achieved.

As noted earlier, the meeting at the United Nations in September 2010 to review progress in achieving the Millennium Development Goals confirmed this opinion. However, it was also recognised that much more needs to be done. Although the achievement of social well-being for the world's peoples will require a major political commitment, enhanced international cooperation, the mobilisation of additional resources, and the adoption of global redistributive policies, the social development approach nevertheless has a major role to play. Hopefully, this role will be strengthened in the coming years.

REFERENCES

Bateman, M. (2010). *Why doesn't microfinance work: The destructive rise of local neoloiberalism.* New York: Zed Books.

Birdsall, N. (1993). *Social development is economic development.* Washington, DC: World Bank.

Boserup, E. (1970). *Women's role in economic development.* London: Allen and Unwin.

Bruntland Commission (World Commission on Environment and Development). (1987). *Our common future: From one earth to one world.* Geneva: United Nations.

Chodak, S. (1973). *Societal development: Five approaches with conclusions from comparative analysis.* New York: Oxford University Press.

de Soto, H. (1989). *The other path: The invisible revolution in the Third World.* New York: Harper and Row.

Ellis, F., Devereux, S., & White, P. (2009). *Social protection in Africa.* Northampton, MA: Edward Elgar.

Fiszbein, R., & Schady, N. (2009). *Condition cash transfers: Reducing present and future poverty.* Washington, DC: World Bank.

Friedman, M. (1989). Using the market for social development. *The CATO Journal, 8*(3), 567–579.

Hall, A., & Midgley, J. (2004). *Social policy for development.* Thousand Oaks, CA: Sage.

Holzmann, R., & Kozel, V. (2007). The role of social risk management in development: A World Bank view. *IDS Bulletin, 38*(3), 8–13.

Kretzman, J., & McKnight, J. (1993). *Building communities from the inside out: A path toward finding and mobilizing a community's assets*. Evanston, IL: Institute for Policy Research, Northwest University.

Lewis, D., & Kanji, N. (2009). *Non-governmental organizations and development*. New York: Routledge.

Livingston, A. (1969). *Social policy in developing countries*. London: Routledge and Kegan Paul.

Mathie, A., & Cunningham, G. (2008). *From clients to citizens: Communities changing the course of their own development*. Rugby, Warwickshire: Intermediate Technology Publications.

Miah, M.R. (2008). Social development. In L. Davis & Mizrahi, T., et al. (eds), *Encyclopedia of Social Work* (20th ed.). New York: Oxford University Press, pp. 38–41.

Midgley, J. (1995). *Social development: The developmental perspective in social welfare*. Thousand Oaks, CA: Sage.

Midgley, J. (1999). Growth, redistribution and welfare: Towards social investment. *Social Service Review, 77*(1), 3–21.

Midgley, J. (2003). Social development: The intellectual heritage. *Journal of International Development, 15*(7), 831–844.

Midgley, J. (2007). Development, social development and human rights. In E. Reichert (ed.), *Challenges in human rights: A social work perspective*. New York: Columbia University Press, pp. 97–121.

Midgley, J. (2008). Microenterprise, global poverty and social development. *International Social Work, 51*(4), 1–13.

Midgley, J. (2010). The theory of developmental social work. In J. Midgey & Conley, A. (eds), *Social work and social development: Theories and skills for developmental social work*. New York: Oxford New University Press, pp. 3–28.

Midgley, J., & Sherraden, M. (2009). The social development perspective in social policy. In J. Midgley & Livermore, M. (eds), *Handbook of social policy* (2nd ed.). Thousand Oaks, CA: Sage, pp. 263–278.

Midgley, J., & Tang, K.L. (2001). Social policy, economic growth and developmental welfare. *International Journal of Social Welfare, 10*(4), 242–250.

Molyneux, M., & Lazar, S. (2003). *Doing the rights thing: Rights-based development and Latin American NGOs*. London: ITDC Publishing.

Moser, C., & Dani, A.A. (eds), (2008). *Assets, livelihoods, and social policy*. Washington, DC: The World Bank.

Moser, C., & Norton, A. (2001). *To claim our rights: Livelihood, security, human rights and sustainable development*. London: Overseas Development Institute.

Myrdal, G. (1970). *The challenge of world poverty*. Harmondsworth, Penguin Books.

Nisbet, R. (1980). *History of the idea of progress*. New York: Basic Books.

Paiva, F.J.X. (1977). A conception of social development. *Social Service Review, 51*(2), 327–336.

Pandey, R. (1981). Strategies for social development: An analytical approach. In J. Jones & Pandey, R. (eds), *Social development: Conceptual, methodological and policy issues*. New York: St Martin's Press, pp. 33–49.

Patel, L., & Trieghaardt, J. (2008). South Africa: Social security, poverty and development. In J. Midgley & Tang, K.L. (eds), *Social security, the economy and development*. New York: Palgrave, pp. 85–109.

Prahalad, C.K. (2005). *The fortune at the bottom of the pyramid: Eradicating poverty through profits*. Upper Saddle River, NJ: Wharton School Publishing.

Putnam, R.D. with Leonardi, R., & Nanetti, R.Y. (1993). *Making democracy work: Civic traditions in modern Italy*. Princeton, NJ: Princeton University Press.

Remenyi, J., & Quinones, B. (eds), (2000). *Microfinance and poverty alleviation: Case studies from Asia and the Pacific*. New York: Pinter.

Rogers, B. (1980). *The domestication of women: Discrimination in developing countries*. London: Tavistock.

Roy, A. (2010). *Poverty capital: Microfinance and the making of development*. New York: Routledge.

Schreiner, M., & Sherraden, M. (2007). *Can the poor save? Saving and asset building in individual development accounts*. New Brunswick, NJ: Transaction.

Schultz, T.W. (1981). *Investing in people*. Berkeley, CA: University of California Press.

Seers, D. (1969). The meaning of development. *International Development Review, 11*(4), 1–6.

Sen, A. (1985). *Commodities and capabilities*. Amsterdam: North-Holland.

Sen, A. (1999). *Development as Freedom*. New York: Knopf.

Sherraden, M. (1991). *Assets and the poor: A new American welfare policy*. Armonk, NY: M.E. Sharpe.

Stoesz, D. (2000). *Poverty of imagination: Bootstrap capitalism, sequel to welfare reform*. Madison, WI: University of Wisconsin Press.

United Nations (1971). Social policy and planning in national development. *International Social Development Review, 3*, 4–15.

United Nations (1996). *Report of the World Summit for Social Development: Copenhagen, 6–12 March 1995*. New York: United Nations.

United Nations (2005). *Investing in development: A practical plan to achieve the millennium development goals*. New York: United Nations.

World Bank (2001). *World Development Report, 2000/2001: Attacking poverty*. Washington, DC: World Bank.

SECTION 2
Social Work Perspectives

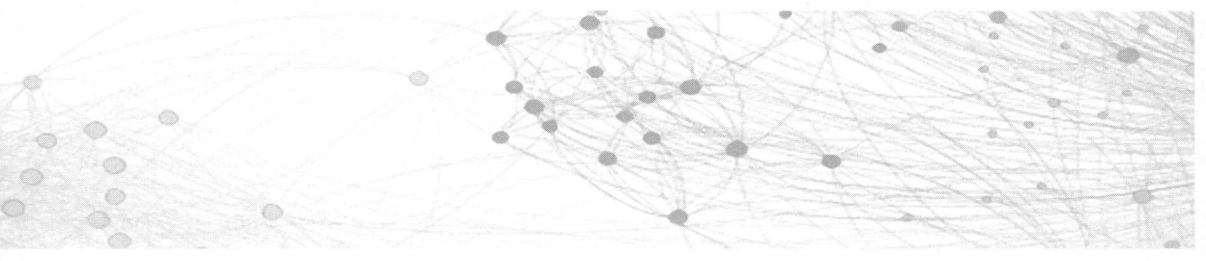

INTRODUCTION

Section 2 on social work perspectives provides an overview of key perspectives that have been formed within social work and shows how these have been adopted and critiqued by social workers. The chapters in this section cover a range of practice theories and approaches to direct work, within a social work frame of reference and a professional value base. A perspective is a way of looking at the world or a type of reasoning about how to approach a problem. When considering the concept of perspective, C. Wright Mills is often cited with his *Sociological Imagination* describing a sociological mindset that is being able to connect individual experiences to societal relationships. The 'social perspective' is a way of looking at the complex dimensions of society. It sees society as something over and above the people who are living in that society. In social work, perspectives are derived from complex theoretical and methodological frameworks used to analyse and explain areas of intervention. Coverage of a range of perspectives will assist students and practitioners in developing a framework for integrating theory and methods to different practice contexts. Adopting a particular perspective or combination of perspectives is often dependent on the client group and type of social service provision offered. Arguably, assessment, planning, and intervention should be guided by explicit perspectives.

In providing material that forges a connection between social work and methodologically driven and conceptual approaches, this section is important for readers in making sense of the various frameworks informing the implementation of social work interventions. It will help readers map a set of influences and trajectories, particularly in relation to different ideological and normative perspectives, by running them between or across one another. This helps to establish key links and to identify relationships for or against different standpoints and the way in which these have been translated into various fields of practice.

In Chapter 7, Pamela Trevithick introduces social work practice as a highly skilled activity that calls for an extensive knowledge base, a professional education, and well-honed intellectual ability. Through presentation of a practice example, Trevithick describes the use of her Knowledge and Skills Practice Framework systematically to structure and inform the interventions used in terms of three knowledge domains: theoretical, factual, and practice knowledge. A particular feature of this framework is its location of service users' knowledge within the same framework as that of social workers and other professionals who draw upon a diverse range of 'practice perspectives', as this section shows.

In Chapter 8, Gordon Jack elaborates the 'ecosystems perspective' still dominant in social work today, and explains the way that ecological theory has been applied to human development, helping social workers to understand the ways in which children and adults both shape and are shaped by their environments. These shaping processes take place through interactions between safety and risk factors in different spheres of life. Using examples from work with children and families, the implications of an ecological perspective for the development of holistic and anti-oppressive forms of social work practice are critically examined. Jack highlights the central importance of developing a culture of listening to the personal experiences of the children and adults with whom social work engages. This means promoting access to sources of support, especially through informal social networks and building the capacity of different communities to meet the needs of their members.

Chapter 9 turns attention to behavioural perspectives, first introduced to social work by Edwin J. Thomas (1967), to meet the growing demand for empirically based practice. Eileen Gambrill discusses the hallmarks of behavioural perspectives; common misconceptions; varieties of behavioural practice and related theory (e.g., applied behavioural analysis and cognitive-behavioural methods); and variants of behavioural social work found in a range of individual, family, group, and community contexts of practice (e.g., health, mental health, and schools). Adherents of behavioural social work claim that this perspective offers empirically tested, strengths-oriented, client-centred, environmentally based social work interventions. It is argued that these serve the key objectives of social work practice better than any other existing methodology.

In Chapter 10, Jacqueline Corcoran discusses the centrality of the family in social work. Based on her extensive research on family interventions, she reviews current knowledge in this field of social work practice and provides a critical review of effective family-based interventions drawing out the significant differences between family-based and individually based interventions. Family systems models, solution-focused therapy, behavioural family therapy, and multicomponent models are critically discussed. She examines the nature of effective family-based interventions in light of recent innovations in evidence-based practice and research in family therapy.

In Chapter 11, Patrick Sullivan examines the strengths perspective that refocused therapeutic thought, which was predominantly grounded in problems, symptoms, and deficiencies to a strengths-based, solution-oriented approach. He argues that a problem-deficit orientation poses barriers for clients, including the individualisation of problems, the victimisation of clients, and the pathologisation of their situations. The strengths perspective builds upon earlier ecosystems approaches and the ecological understanding of the person-in-environment broadening the focus from individuals to families and communities. Sullivan examines the historical development of the strengths perspective (and model for practice), its applications in mental health practice and extension into other fields of practice, and fidelity, reinventions, and extension in clinical practice, as well as the developing research agenda to refine and shape strengths-based practice models.

In Chapter 12, Karen Healy develops an analysis of critical perspectives in social work that seek to examine the structural causes of social problems and the ways in which they marginalise and oppress people. Calling for transformatory or emancipatory forms of social work practice, they challenge the individual level focus of conventional social work approaches by engaging in a historical and critical analysis. This draws on important concepts, such as emancipation and social justice thus confronting dominant socio-economic arrangements associated with patriarchal capitalism, colonialism, racism, heterosexism, ableism, and ageism. Healy shows how, in interrogating the social environment, several elements emerge which can be thought of as 'key' conceptual features of critical social work: (i) problematisation of dominant social and economic structures through adoption of a 'conflict' or 'change' perspective; (ii) a focus on multiple, intersecting forms of oppression produced and reinforced by structures; (iii) concentration on the dialectical nature of the interaction between individuals and macro-level structures; and (iv) dominant discourses which construct and entrench particular explanations and interpretations of social problems and people's experience of them. She demonstrates how critical perspectives can be effectively used for social work interventions and their congruence with core social work values.

7

Practice Perspectives

Pamela Trevithick

This chapter highlights how different practice perspectives reflect the way in which social workers think about and interpret events, and the actions they take in practice. It begins with a brief account of why a focus on *practice perspectives* is important and illustrates this through the lens of a *knowledge and skills framework* designed to integrate theory and practice (see Figure 7.1). This framework emphasises three identifiable perspectives in any practice encounter, namely, the perspective of the practitioner, services user, and agency, all of which are influenced, in different ways, by the legislative and policy agenda of the government of the day and dominant ideology. The chapter focuses on key developments in recent years in child protection in England and draws on a case example to indicate how these different practice perspectives shape the assessment process, decision making, and action in social work (see also Chapter 14).

THE IMPORTANCE OF PRACTICE PERSPECTIVES IN SOCIAL WORK

In their broadest use, *perspectives* cover whole areas of human experience. They are shaped by the assumptions and interpretations social workers make about the world and what it means to be human – how people come to be who they are and the factors influencing their development:

> A perspective is a way of seeing the world that is influenced by one's angle or particular point of view. Often our perspectives are shaped by a variety of theories ... which come to colour the way we think about the people, situations, events and problems we deal with in social work (Gray, 2010, p. 97).

All human beings make assumptions in order to classify phenomena and to find meaning. However, an important influence on thought, feeling, and action is ideology, which describes a set of ideas, beliefs, or assumptions purporting 'to form a comprehensive vision of the truth' (Gray & Webb, 2009, p. 85) or to assert what is 'real' or 'true' in a given situation. It is a concept with 'a close connection with power, since ideological systems serve to legitimate the differential power held by groups' (Giddens, 2001, p. 691).

In relation to the practice perspectives adopted in social work, these too are underpinned by a number of assumptions influencing social workers' observations and beliefs about people and how they should respond to the situations they encounter. Various social work approaches to working with people are based on a number of assumptions and perspectives about human beings and human behaviour, although these may not always be made explicit. These perspectives inform differing perceptions and interpretations of personal and social problems, and the factors giving rise to particular dilemmas as to how social workers might work effectively with others to bring about the kind of change needed or desired. A social work approach or perspective 'should include ... evidence about the nature of effective working relationships, and methods to use within these relationships to promote change' (Munro, 2011a, p. 12). However, making assumptions explicit can be a difficult undertaking when they lie beyond our immediate awareness – unnamed and, therefore, unowned. For this reason, considerable importance is given to critical thinking, critical reflection, and reflexivity as a way to recognise the assumptions social workers make and their impact on their practice (see Chapter 13). In this chapter, a knowledge and skills framework is used to identify, organise, and integrate the growing number of theories and perspectives in social work.

A KNOWLEDGE AND SKILLS FRAMEWORK INTEGRATING THEORY AND PRACTICE

The following account describes how knowledge and skills are categorised in this chapter, as shown in Figure 7.1. This conceptualisation builds on several important publications on this subject (Connolly, 2007; Drury Hudson, 1997; Osmond, 2005; Pawson et al., 2003) but categorises similar themes differently, in terms of three domains: *theoretical*, *factual*, and *practice knowledge*. A case example illustrates the relevance of this framework in practice, and how knowledge and skills might be used to inform analysis, decision making, and action (for further coverage, see Trevithick, 2008, 2012). There is an ongoing lack of clarity about what constitutes the knowledge and skills base of social work, with 'no universally accepted idea of valid knowledge, skills or expertise for social workers' (Scottish Executive, 2005, p. 2).

The integration of knowledge and skills in Figure 7.1 provides a users' map of the knowledge base for professional social work practice. Because of the importance of critical thinking and analysis (Gibbs & Gambrill, 1996) and critical reflection, or reflexivity (Sheppard, 1998) in social work (see also Chapter 13), these activities form part of the social work practice perspectives and approaches that most social workers use to intervene in the lives of others. The first two knowledge domains – *theoretical* and *factual knowledge* – focus on *knowing that* (Ryle, 1949) and concern knowledge creation and acquisition. The third domain of *practice knowledge* comprises the skills and interventions used by practitioners in translating theoretical and factual knowledge into practice. Historically, the main skills or interventions used in social work have been grouped under the heading *communication skills* (Koprowska, 2010; Lishman, 2009). However, communication skills are important to all social work interventions and include verbal and nonverbal and recording and report-writing skills. As such, 'interpersonal [communication] skills, grounded in theory and knowledge, are at the heart of the [social work] enterprise' (Stevenson, 2005, p. 581).

A central feature of the practice knowledge domain is practitioners' self-presentation as 'professional social workers', including how they use self-knowledge and intuition (Munro, 2011a, 2011b) or tacit knowledge (Polanyi, 1967) to inform their communications and interventions with clients. Practitioners use their skills – and *interventions* – while drawing on their *theoretical*, *factual*, and *practical knowledge*, and adapting these to fit the practice context and needs of service users. An important aspect of practice knowledge is the knowledge service

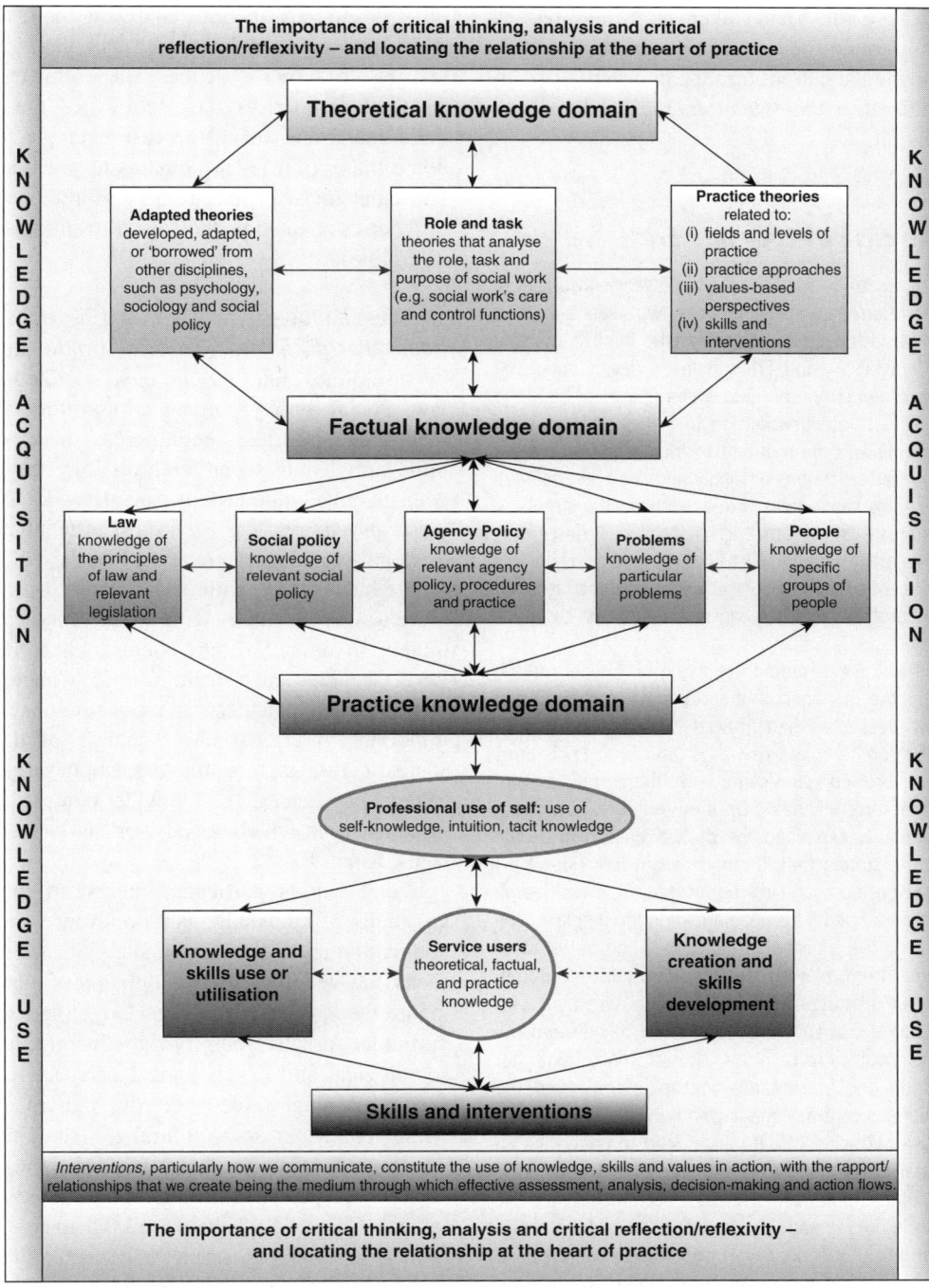

Figure 7.1 A knowledge and skills framework integrating theory and practice in social work.

users, carers, and other interested parties bring to the social work encounter – and this knowledge can, in turn, be conceptualised in terms of its *theoretical*, *factual*, and *practice* content.

The case of Lucy and Eric

Lucy, aged 19, and Eric, her three-year-old son, were first referred to social services two years ago by a health visitor concerned about the family's housing circumstances and Eric's delayed development. At the time, Lucy and Eric were living in bed and breakfast accommodation which they had to vacate from nine in the morning to four in the afternoon. Lucy had no friends or family and she and Eric were forced to spend long periods walking the streets or sitting in cafes, with Eric having very little contact with other children. Re-housing and a children's day centre (nursery) place were recommended and allocated later in the year, whereupon the case was closed.

The case resumed following a phone referral from the manager of the children's centre. Earlier that week staff had noticed two large bruises on Eric's forehead and two days later both Eric's arms were bruised, consistent with finger marks from being 'forcefully held'. On these two occasions, Lucy voluntarily explained the bruises on arrival at the centre, stating that Eric had caught one side of his head on the corner of the kitchen table and, as he tumbled, had hit his head again on the fireplace. She noticed the bruising to his arms when he returned home from playing outside with older children. Eric's explanation was he had been 'wrestling with big boys' but Lucy was too scared to question the boys involved in case this 'caused trouble' with her neighbours. In response to the referral from the children's centre Manager, and given Eric's age and these two incidents, it was agreed to undertake an initial assessment. This was completed within the stipulated timescale with the recommendation Eric should not be made the subject of a Child Protection Plan but that further work should be undertaken to gain a clearer picture of Lucy's situation and care of Eric.

Theoretical knowledge domain

The theoretical knowledge domain (see Figure 7.2) comprises three categories: theories 'borrowed', adapted, and developed from other disciplines; theories analysing the task and purpose of social work; and theories relating to direct practice. The following account summarises the features of these three categories, using the case example to relate these knowledge domains to practice. Particular focus is placed on the importance of theories adapted or 'borrowed' from other disciplines.

Theories 'borrowed', adapted, and developed from other disciplines Theories originating in disciplines like psychology, sociology, law, social policy, organisational theory, medicine, politics, economics, history, philosophy, and social anthropology have been openly embraced by social work. Of these, psychology has been most influential, especially in Western contexts, like the USA (see Chapter 15), with social work being increasingly located within the medical model. In other Western contexts, like the UK, Canada, and Australia (see Chapter 12), sociological perspectives have been important to critical understanding of the sociostructural factors affecting people's day-to-day experiences, and the wider context or system within which social work is located (see Chapter 8).

Social work's particular interest in this vast body of knowledge is its relevance and application to direct practice situations. This focus has led to the development of new theories and sources of knowledge, and in particular practice approaches integrating sociological and psychological perspectives and combining a focus on the individual within the wider sociocultural milieu. This whole-person approach is found in most social work perspectives, including the ecological (Chapter 8), behavioural (Chapter 9), family (Chapter 10), strengths (Chapter 11), and critical (Chapter 12) perspectives. The *person-in-situation* focus has a long history in *social casework* (Gitterman & Germaine, 2008; Hollis, 1964) and is also embedded in newer *constructive* (Parton & O'Byrne, 2000), *structural* (Mullaly, 2007), and *radical* social work approaches (see Chapter 47).

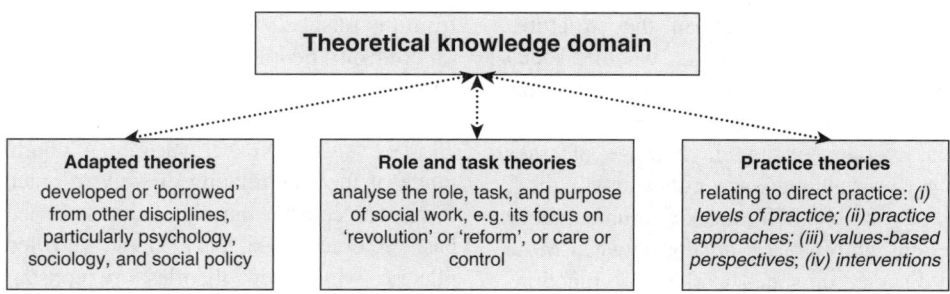

Figure 7.2 Theoretical knowledge domain.

Each perspective places emphasis on different dimensions of social work practice (Ruch et al., 2010; Trevithick, 2003), as indicated in relation to the case example:

Psychology, the most 'borrowed' discipline, offers insights into biological, behavioural, cognitive, humanistic, psychodynamic, and cross-cultural dimensions (Hockenbury & Hockenbury, 2006). From a biological perspective, this might lead the social worker to explore issues relating to Lucy and Eric's physical health, particularly whether Eric's physical and emotional development is age appropriate. A cognitive perspective might focus on Lucy's thoughts, feelings, and beliefs, particularly her perception of events leading to Eric's injuries and the extent to which she considered Eric to be at risk. A behavioural perspective might focus on Eric's behaviour – both at home and at nursery school – while a humanistic perspective could throw light on how Lucy makes sense of the world and the meaning she gives to her experiences. A psychodynamic perspective might focus on the quality of the relationship between Eric and Lucy, or how to contain Lucy's anxieties about issues causing her concern. A cross-cultural or historical perspective could lead to an understanding of the cultural norms Lucy has learnt from her own upbringing, particularly her experiences of being parented and how these might influence her current behaviour and relationship with Eric.

Other theoretical perspectives, such as a sociological perspective, could help illuminate the factors shaping Lucy and Eric's everyday experiences and outlook on life. In this area or particular community, social class is likely to be important, and evident in Lucy's and Eric's outlook and expectations, and how they are seen and treated by others. Similarly, Lucy's gender and age is likely to be a focus of concern and possible hostility, depending on how single parents or 'teenage' mothers are perceived within Lucy's social world. Contemporary social policy relating to Lucy's entitlement to child and housing benefits, income support, and daycare provision are highly relevant. These policy decisions could be viewed from a political perspective, which, in turn, could be linked to economic or organisational theory or economics in relation to the impact of New Public Management (NPM) – or managerialism – on service provision. A medical policy perspective would focus on Lucy and Eric's access to medical care and the extent to which health inequalities impacted on their everyday lives (Marmot, 2010).

Clearly, numerous perspectives contribute to the understanding the social worker could develop about Lucy and Eric's situation. Social workers tend to take a broad or holistic social perspective, taking different dimensions into account, leading to a better understanding, and the chance to work in more effective, collaborative, and creative ways. However, the importance of being tentative in the hypotheses put forward, and supporting these with evidence, including 'disconfirming' evidence' (Taylor & White, 2006, p. 939), is essential to avoid a 'blinkered' or biased understanding. On the other hand, however, there are organisational and policy constraints governing the possible course of action open to the social worker in this situation – regardless of professional stipulations of the role, task, or purpose of social work to which the discussion now turns.

Theories analysing the role, task, and purpose of social work Theories analysing the role, task, and purpose of social work in society broadly question whether the profession should transform or reform the structures impinging on clients, that is, whether social workers should pursue social causes or carry out essential social functions (Howe, 2009). Social workers engage in a range of tasks and perform maintenance, controlling, caring, therapeutic or helping, or emancipatory functions with tension arising between those who disagree on social work's core functions (Dominelli, 2009; Howe, 1994). This has been variously expressed as the conflict between whether social work is essentially a rational–technical activity associated with new managerialism enforcing rules and regulations and conforming to organisational and policy standards or whether it is a value-based practical–moral activity with an emancipatory mission (Parton, 2000).

It could be argued the role and task of social work in the UK has not moved on significantly since this subject was covered in the Seebohm Report (1968) and Barclay Report (1982). Interestingly, both focused on the extent to which the burden of bureaucracy hindered the provision of quality services and whether social work should be providing generalist or specialist services. Since then, the role of social workers has once again fallen under the spotlight following public inquiries into the non-accidental death of children (Blewett et al., 2007; General Social Care Council, 2008; Laming, 2003, 2009; Munro, 2011b). How social workers interpret their role is largely dependent on agency policy and the context within which the work is located, as well as the perspective adopted by individual social workers, but this too is often mediated by the extent to which professional discretion is encouraged or inhibited (Munro, 2010).

A statutory social worker in child protection might consider Eric's bruises and Lucy's care warranted further investigation (control), whereas a social worker employed in a voluntary agency might consider it appropriate to focus on Lucy's living situation and support network (care) (see Chapter 39). Both would be concerned about Lucy's ability to care for Eric given incidents arising from his unsupervised play and her capacity to confront people and protect Eric from harm.

Theories relating to direct practice A complex range of theories relating directly to practice forms an 'eclectic but significant knowledge base' (Gould, 2006, p. 121) or 'knowledge pile' to which new theories are constantly being added with few ever being deducted. In the UK, there has been little attempt to order or categorise the vast range of theories informing social work, hence Trevithick's knowledge framework herein presented. It is not surprising then that social workers can find it hard to articulate and specify 'which theories, if any, they are using' (Munro, 1998, p. 102). This difficulty is compounded by the absence of a consistent use of practice terms, despite more recent texts including glossaries of key terms (Chenoweth & McAuliffe, 2008; Gray & Webb, 2009; Wilson et al., 2008). A different, ongoing difficulty arises because social work skills and interventions have not yet become the focus of research, although there is evidence of a growing interest in this area (Fraser et al., 2009; Rothman, 2003) in light of the increasing push towards evidence-based practice (see Chapter 26). Trevithick categorises direct practice theories as follows.

1. *Fields and levels of practice* covering the micro-, meso- or mezzo-, and macro-level: work with individuals (including counselling) and with families (including family therapy) at the micro level; work with groups (groupwork) and organisations at the meso-level; and work with communities (including community development) and social policy at the macro-level (see Chapter 8).
2. *Practice approaches* draw on a coherent and identifiable body of theory applied and adapted in a systematic way in response to the situation encountered and the context for the work. The approaches most often covered in social work publications include person or client centred; behavioural cognitive or cognitive behavioural; task centred; psychodynamic or psychosocial; strengths based; solution focused; and ecological and systems – ecosystems – approaches (see Howe, 2009; and the chapters included in this section).

3 *Values-based perspectives* often attempt to mediate the impact of disadvantage or discrimination in some way. The perspectives most commonly adopted in social work include anti-oppressive, antidiscriminatory, and empowerment perspectives; feminist and radical or activist perspectives and those focusing on promoting or advocating for the rights of disabled people, children and young people, and Black and minority groups (Gray & Webb, 2009).

4 *Skills and interventions* generally indicate a range of generalist and specialist skills and interventions. A *skill* is an action with a specific goal. It can be learnt, involves actions performed in sequence, and can be organised in ways involving economy of effort, evaluated in terms of its relevance and effectiveness. *Generalist skills* (sometimes referred to as *generic skills*) indicate the ability to apply basic knowledge and skills across a wide range of contexts involving individual, group, family, and community needs (Trevithick, 2011). They have the advantage of being more transferable than many specialist skills, and are often the foundation on which specialist skills are developed. *Specialist skills* indicate superior knowledge leading to the ability to use advanced skills and specialist types of intervention when working with specific client groups, problem areas, settings, or contexts. These additional skills are most often acquired through further training in a particular theory or practice approach, for example, in cognitive behavioural approaches (see Chapter 9) and family interventions (see Chapter 10) – and consolidated through extensive practice experience and ongoing supervision.

If skills were defined in terms of what might be learnt, then interventions would describe how learning might be translated into practice, drawing on evidence to support their use in particular situations. *Interventions* constitute knowledge, skills, and values in action and are designed to influence – or to alter – a particular situation, course of events or thoughts, feelings, and behaviours. Knowledge and values are highlighted in this definition, together with the importance of taking into account practitioner expertise, client values and preferences, the context of practice, and the importance of practitioners being open to change when intervening in the lives of other people.

To gather a clearer picture of the situation and Lucy's care of Eric, the social worker would use a range of generalist, information-gathering skills, such as observation, listening, and questioning, while drawing on relevant theories and research in order to interpret, analyse, and make sense of the information gathered. Questions can easily be interpreted as judgemental or critical – such as those touching on sensitive issues relating to Lucy's care of Eric – need to be communicated with skill and compassionate concern (Broadhurst et al., 2010). The ability to establish an honest and purposeful relationship with Lucy is more likely to lead to a more open and frank exchange and also lessen the likelihood of defences (a psychoanalytic concept) being triggered and vital information being withheld.

This situation also calls for the use of intuitive reasoning, as well as a sound knowledge and skills base. The complex nature of the interaction between social workers and service users is indicated in the following important quote from Munro (2011a):

> When social workers are talking to a child and family in their home, they are drawing on several sources of information and making swift decisions and changes as the interview progresses. Their conscious mind is paying attention to the purpose of their visit; at an intuitive level they are forming a picture of the child and family and sensing the dynamics in the room, noting evidence of anger, confusion, or anxiety. This feeds into their conscious awareness and helps shape the way the interview progresses. Their own emotional reaction is one source of information; the despair, for example, that some parents feel evokes an empathic response in others. It will be argued that previous reforms have concentrated too much on the explicit, logical aspects of reasoning and this has contributed to a skewed management framework that undervalues intuitive reasoning and emotions and thus fails to give appropriate support to those aspects (Munro, 2011a, p. 35).

This section has reviewed the theoretical knowledge domain in terms of three types of theories: those adapted from other disciplines; concerning the role, task, and purpose of social work; and relating to direct social work practice. The extent to which social workers' interventions are knowledge based, or research or evidence based, is controversial (see research section). In Trevithick's conceptualisation, research is not considered to be a source of knowledge in its own right but a method by which knowledge can be acquired and updated (Trevithick, 2008). In the same way, theories need to be updated constantly – confirmed, revised, or refuted – in light of new sources of information, often drawing on research findings, but these findings are of limited value unless they are brought 'alive' through interpretation and analysis and related to contemporary practice concerns. This can, in turn, lead to the development of new theories, practice approaches, skills, and interventions.

Factual knowledge domain

As shown in Figure 7.3, common terms used to describe factual knowledge include research findings, data, statistics, figures, and records, all of which are likely to reflect a particular theoretical perspective. Factual knowledge is important in social work in five distinct but overlapping areas: (i) law and legislation; (ii) social policy; (iii) agency policy, procedures, and systems; (iv) information relating to particular problems; and (v) information relating to specific groups of people.

Law or legislation It is essential for social workers to have a general awareness of relevant key legislation but the sheer volume of legislation passed in recent years has made it difficult to keep abreast of changes introduced. For example, 30 Acts were passed by the UK Labour Government directly impacting on social work practice between 1997 and 2007 (Brammer, 2007).

If, at some point, there were sufficient evidence to suggest Eric had suffered – or would be likely to suffer – significant harm, then an investigation would be carried out under Section 47 of the Children Act 1989. Or, if Eric's development was later found to fall within the category of a 'child in need', that is, unlikely to progress in terms of health or development without the provision of services, then support services could be provided under Section 17 of the Children Act 1989. In relation to most local authorities in the UK, children are unlikely to access a service if they are not designated a 'child in need' but where the threshold lies in terms of service provision tends to be based on the discretion of the local authority.

Social policy The policy frameworks and government priorities relating to resource provision and operational requirements in relation to housing, employment, social security, healthcare, education, and personal services are collectively referred to as social policy (Spicker, 1995). Alongside the weight of legislative changes, from 1997 the New Labour Party introduced a 'plethora of policy initiatives' designed to reform and 'modernize' the welfare state (Piachaud & Sutherland, 2001).

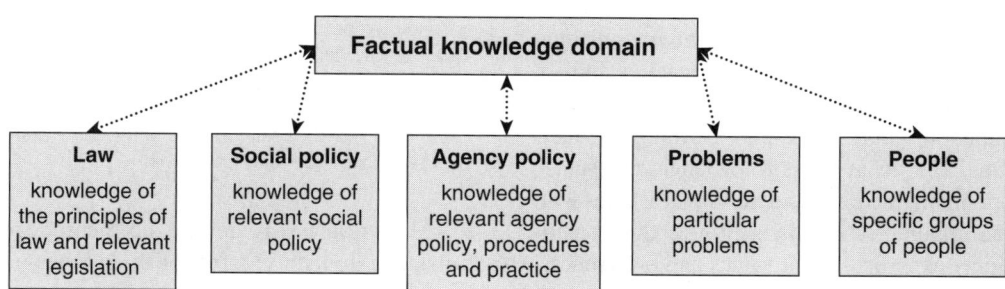

Figure 7.3   Factual knowledge domain.

In relation to Eric and Lucy, their housing needs were addressed when they were first referred for social work support two years earlier and Eric's developmental needs were being monitored partly by the local children's day centre. However, living on welfare benefits set below the poverty line is likely to be stressful for Lucy as an unsupported single parent. One possible source of support Lucy might request could involve help with employment options. Also, strategies to address her social isolation could have a positive impact on Lucy's and Eric's well-being and quality of life.

Agency policy, procedures, and practices In support of legislation and social policy requirements, the government devises codes, duties, guidance, regulations, and powers that outline the expectations placed on local authorities (Brammer, 2007; Brayne & Carr, 2008). These are translated into policies, procedures, and practice guidelines relating to service provision and include stipulations local authorities place on services 'outsourced' to the private, voluntary, and independent sector. This covers a vast number of agencies. For example, there are 150 local councils in England which, Jones (2008) argues, constitutes a 'wasteful arrangement', leading to serious inconsistencies in the way local authorities use their discretionary powers to 'determine who gets help'. Similar variations are evident in the nonstatutory sector where in 2006, there were roughly 500,000 non-profit organisations, including 190,000 charities in England and Wales alone (Miliband, 2006), making it difficult for social workers to keep up-to-date with locally applicable services. Given the different ways agencies organise services, it is important for social workers to be familiar with key legislation and social policy requirements underpinning agency policies and procedures mindful of the competing pressures leading local authorities to 'dislodge practice from its lawful base' (Braye et al., 2007, p. 323). For this reason, adhering to agency policies and procedures should not be seen to replace knowledge-based decision making, or practitioner autonomy based on lawful and ethical principles and social work's Code of Practice.

The extent to which it might be possible to work with Lucy and Eric from a particular perspective, such as relationship-based approach, would depend partly on the practice approach promoted within a particular agency and also the practice orientation, knowledge, and skills that individual social workers might bring to the work. Other variations might be found in the different ways agencies respond to government requirements, particularly those tied to targets and indicators (Social Work Task Force, 2009a, 2009b) and also the priority given to eliciting the views of service users and carers, including children and young people. The impact on agency's priorities when faced with increasingly limited resources and funding should not be forgotten.

Specific social problems Another area of factual knowledge focuses on social problems, such as alcohol and substance abuse (see Chapter 37); child abuse and neglect (see Chapter 32); family violence, mental illness (see Chapter 33), juvenile and criminal justice (see Chapter 38), asylum seekers and refugees (see Chapter 36), and older people (see Chapter 34). There is a strong overlap between certain social problems and particular groups of people. For example, statistics indicate that working-class people are more vulnerable to mental illness than their middle-class counterparts – a situation that highlights the impact of social factors and one that calls for intervention at a structural level (Rogers & Pilgrim, 2010).

A line of enquiry to be followed in relation to Lucy could focus on her social isolation and poverty. For example, putting her in touch with other young mothers who were struggling to rear young children, or to live on state benefits, could help to break down feelings of isolation and act as a source of social support strongly associated with 'psychological well-being' (Jack, 2000, p. 707). Similarly, finding employment could not only mean more income but also ensure Lucy was in contact with other people, which could enhance her self-esteem and self-confidence (Sheppard, 1994). These suggestions could only be taken forward with Lucy's full consent, but her social isolation, low self-confidence, and fear of retaliation could help to explain her reluctance to question the boys who were said to have bruised Eric's arms.

Particular groups of people This area of factual knowledge may be ordered in terms of people's class, race, gender, age, disability, sexual orientation, culture, ethnicity, and religious beliefs. Statistics on people most likely to be in contact with social workers provide a stark reminder of income and health inequalities. For example, in 2009, an estimated 13.4 million people in the UK (22%) – almost a quarter of the population – were income poor (Joseph Rowntree Foundation, 2009). Yet in terms of income, the average wealth of the richest 10% of the UK population was estimated to be over £853,000 per annum – 100 times higher than the poorest 10%, whose income was estimated to be £8800 or less (Hills et al., 2010a). Roughly 80–90% of service users are on a state benefit, including means-tested payments (Walker & Walker, 2009) and most benefits fall below the 'poverty line' (MacInnes et al., 2010). The impact of long-term poverty is compounded by other inequalities in the area of health, education, housing, employment, and life chances. This often leads to the social exclusion of people in poverty from decision-making processes – and discrimination tends to be more profound for women, people with disabilities, and people from ethnic minority groups (Marmot Review, 2010).

As a young woman, Lucy could be subjected to discrimination because of her age and also because she is an unsupported single parent, living in poverty. This can lead to a situation where some health professionals might feel judgemental and unsympathetic to the difficulties she faces, perhaps unaware of their potentially discriminatory stance. Some North American studies have indicated a link between poverty and child neglect (McSherry, 2004), while other authors stress the importance of social factors – or 'social evils' – giving rise to parental neglect (Stevenson, 1998). From a different perspective, Sheppard (1994) notes a link between depression and working-class mothers, and how this can lead to childcare problems which, when severe, could place a child at risk. These points are hypothetical and further evidence would be needed to assess their relevance to Lucy's situation.

This section has described five areas of factual knowledge: law or legislation; social policy; agency policy and procedures; knowledge of social problems, and knowledge of particular groups of people. It has emphasised the need to update, revise, and refute knowledge constantly, and take account of new sources of information and research findings before relating them to practice concerns to ensure an ongoing dialogue between theory and practice. In this task, it is important to recognise the factual knowledge service users bring to their work – their knowledge of how *legislation* operates, the *policy* decisions impacting on the services they receive, and how different *agencies* interpret policy requirements. Service users also have their own understanding of their *problems*, and how certain problems are manifest in relation to certain *groups of people*.

Practice knowledge domain
The practice knowledge domain is focused on how knowledge and skills are applied in practice, particularly how different areas of theoretical and factual knowledge are used to inform the intervention process (see Figure 7.4).

As outlined earlier, theoretical and factual knowledge concern knowledge acquisition – or *knowing that* – whereas practice knowledge focuses on *knowing how* (Ryle, 1949), namely, what social workers *actually do* in practice. The knowledge used in practice can derive from four key sources: (i) personal learning (life experience); (ii) formal teaching and learning; (iii) practice experience; and (iv) focused reading or research findings. These sources are important because the way in which knowledge is acquired influences

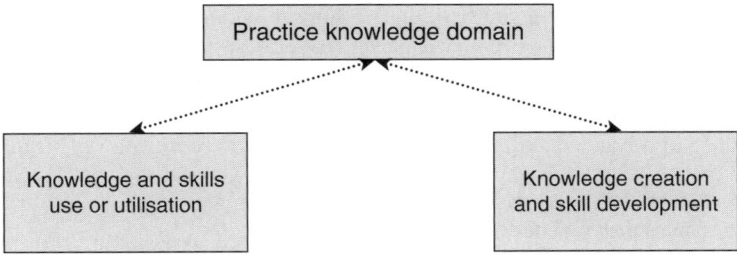

Figure 7.4 Practice knowledge domain.

how it is used. For example, rote or didactic instruction might lead to 'surface' learning with students having little comprehension of the meaning or significance of the knowledge gained (Howe, 1996). Didactic, 'talk-and-chalk' learning needs to be complemented by experiential forms of learning promoting reflexivity, critical thinking, and critical reflection (Lam, 2009; Sheppard & Ryan, 2003; Taylor & White, 2006). Dreyfus and Dreyfus (1986) conceptualised skill acquisition in terms of five stages where the student moves from novice, to *advanced beginner*, *competent* practitioner, *proficient* practitioner, and finally *expert* or *virtuoso*.

Knowledge and skills use or utilisation In social work, knowledge is often judged in terms of its utility, 'practice validity' (Sheppard, 1998, p. 763), or 'fit for use' (Pawson et al., 2003, p. 39). Relevance and accessibility are highly valued. However, often there is a gap between the 'producers' (academics and researchers) and 'users' (practitioners) of knowledge. This division is discernible in the 'specialised language' (Eraut, 1994, p. 30) used in academic circles – declarative, procedural, and product knowledge – which do not form part of the lexicon of terms used by social workers in their everyday practice. For some, this calls for a 'radical reform of the way' knowledge is produced (Marsh & Fisher, 2008, p. 975) by conducting research relating directly to practice concerns; involving practitioners in research; and ensuring research is solution focused. It is unlikely this division will be bridged unless a clinical grade is introduced into social work, similar to that in medicine, where academics are paid at a higher grade for working in practice contexts.

This division between the 'producers' and 'users' of knowledge has led some academics to suggest social workers may not be drawing on knowledge to inform their practice while others have argued theory and practice are being synthesised by practitioners but not in ways clearly evident in terms of producing 'a good verbal description' (Schön, 1983, p. 31) of what they do. This view is indicated in a research study which suggested that 'knowing' could sometimes be communicated in less formal ways and 'expressed via examples, stories, metaphor, as well as understandings that resembled existing *theoretical knowledge* or that which had been reformulated and synthesized in practice' (Osmond & O'Connor, 2004, p. 677). Similarly, Bogo (2006) writes in terms of practitioners' knowledge being 'incorporated to create an intricate, complex, multilayered knowledge framework and practice model' (p. 15). Given the wide variation in how agencies and practitioners interpret their role, this is an area where a major, comparative, in-depth research study is needed if we are to understand in greater detail the factors informing practitioners' analysis, reflection, decision making, action, and the extent to which these actions could be considered beneficial and effective for service users. A feature of this research needs to include coverage of the type and quality of the interventions used. Most social work interventions will be generalist in character but the use of generalist skills and interventions can indicate the presence of advanced skills.

When working with children, such as Eric, where there are concerns about their well-being and safety, it is important to note 'competing ideas about risk to children and the best ways of addressing these' (Parton 2010, p. 2). The concept of risk could involve a concern about 'significant harm' or about broader issues relating to Eric's overall development, such as those embodied in Every Child Matters (Department for Education and Skills, 2003, p. 6). Of central importance is Lucy's perspective on and perception of events, particularly how she views her relationship and care of Eric and the involvement of social workers in her life. An important aspect involves exploring the extent to which Lucy is able to 'use social work help' (Munro, 1998, p. 93).

Knowledge creation and skills development In social work, the 'interpretive use of an idea in a new context is in itself a minor act of knowledge creation' (Eraut, 1994, p. 54). This creative activity involves adapting and synthesising knowledge about skills and interventions in innovative and imaginative ways, uniquely suited to the situation and individuals involved. Social workers generate new knowledge through practice by experimenting and problem solving, especially in relation to ways in which professional standards, government legislation, social policy, or agency protocols affect service users. Frontline social workers have vital information to influence policy and change agency practice. Practitioner-generated (Cha, et al., 2006) or craft knowledge (Eraut, 1994) is more commonly described as practice wisdom (Sheppard, 1995).

This creative and 'intuitive use of self' (England, 1986, p. 32) links to the concept of emotional intelligence (Goleman, 1996) and the ability to fine tune body language, choice of words, and the tone, speed, and timing of social work communication in ways to encourage, as much as possible, an open, honest, and meaningful dialogue with service users. Some understanding thus acquired may lie beyond social workers' awareness, and may be described in terms of the psychoanalytic concepts of transference and counter-transference (Koprowska, 2010; Lishman, 2009) or as *tacit knowledge* – a term coined by Polanyi (1967) to imply it is possible for human beings to know – or to infer – more than they can sometimes say or identify. For Dreyfus and Dreyfus (1986), tacit knowledge and intuition are features of 'expert knowledge' (p. 124). However, it is important to view these intuitive hunches as hypotheses – as an awareness of physical, emotional, and intellectual reactions needs to be clarified and rigorously tested against other sources of information before being acted upon.

The ability to understand the relationship between the various factors impacting on Lucy and Eric and the extent to which these need to be reinforced, influenced, or changed call for all sources of knowledge to be used creatively. This includes drawing on the knowledge Lucy brings to the encounter, for example, the explanations she uses to understand her life and to assess Eric's needs and development (*theoretical knowledge*), her understanding of the financial support she is entitled to receive in relation to housing and welfare benefits (*factual* knowledge) and her understanding of the role played by social workers, health visitors, and other health and welfare professionals (*practice knowledge*). In addition to these more tangible and explicit forms of knowledge, other less explicit forms of knowledge can be used to illuminate the social worker's understanding of Lucy's situation. These could be thought to dwell in the realm of the feelings or emotions communicated – the feelings the social worker senses when Lucy and Eric communicate, the quality of their rapport and relationship, the extent to which they see other people, including professionals, as a potential threat or resource, the moods the social worker picks up and the feelings she communicates. Accessing these feelings involves her self-knowledge and ability to use her intuition and tacit knowledge thoughtfully and sensitively. It also involves adapting and transferring what she knows – or assumes she knows – using her own self-knowledge or practice wisdom (Sheppard, 1995) as a reference point.

One of the most important sites for skills development is direct practice (Eraut, 2008). However, there is a dearth of social work research studies analysing the range and quality of practitioners' interpersonal or communication skills, and the kind of knowledge used to inform the chosen intervention (Richards et al., 2005; Trevithick, 2008). An example of the kind of research needed in this area can be found in the work of Forrester et al. (2008), which examined the communication skills employed by childcare practitioners, using an actor to play the part of the parent. The findings of the 24 taped interviews undertaken gave cause for concern:

> There is a sense in which communication skills are often taken for granted within social work: like the air we breathe, they provide an invisible but essential context for everything that we do. Yet the findings suggest that often social workers are not communicating well with parents. The implications for training, professional supervision and research are profound (Forrester et al., 2008, p. 50).

The extent to which social workers have the opportunity to develop their practice skills in key areas has not been a central feature of continuing professional development and is a area of practice warranting much greater emphasis. An interesting research study could link the conceptualisation of *novice*, *advanced beginner*, *competent*, *proficient*, and *expert* (Dreyfus & Dreyfus, 1986) to the skills acquired on social work training courses and used by social workers in the situations they encounter in direct practice.

CONCLUSION

Social work is – and has to be – a knowledgeable and skilled activity. This chapter has drawn a 'users' map' indicating the extensive knowledge and skills base of social work. A central feature of the framework is the *theoretical*, *factual*, and *practice* domains highlighting the knowledge all parties bring to the encounter, particularly social workers and service users; the knowledge essential and central to informing social workers' assessment and analysis of the client's situation; the decisions they make; the actions they take; and the interventions they use. Social work practice is much more than the different forms of knowledge the social worker uses. Equally important are the relationships social workers build, how they communicate, and the values they embrace. This chapter ends with a diagram depicting the diverse and overlapping features of the framework herein presented (see Figure 7.5).

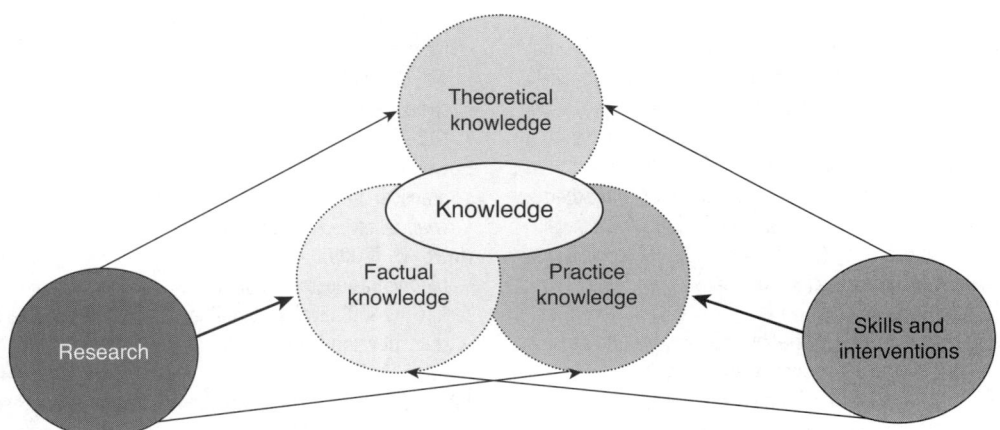

Figure 7.5 Diverse forms of knowledge for practice.

REFERENCES

Barclay Report (1982). *Social workers: Their roles and task*. London: Bedford Square Press.

Blewett, J., Lewis, J., & Tunstill, J. (2007). *The changing roles and tasks of social work: A literature informed discussion paper*. London: General Social Care Council.

Bogo, M. (2006). Social work practice: *Concepts, processes, and interviewing*. Chichester: Columbia University Press.

Brammer, A. (2007). *Social work law* (2nd ed.). Harlow: Pearson Education.

Braye, S., Preston-Shoot, M., & Thorpe, A. (2007). Beyond the classroom: Learning social work law in practice. *Journal of Social Work, 7*, 322–340.

Brayne, H., & Carr, H. (2008). *Law for social workers* (10th ed.). Oxford: Oxford University Press.

Broadhurst, K., Hall, C., Wastell, D., White, S., & Pithouse, A. (2010). Risk, instrumentalism and the humane project in social work: Identifying the informal logics of risk management in children's statutory services. *British Journal of Social Work, 40*, 1046–1064.

Cha, T., Kuo, E., & March, J. (2006). Useful knowledge for social work practice. *Social Work & Society, 4*(1). Retrieved June 26, 2011 from http://www.socwork.net/2006/1/debate/chakuomarch

Chenoweth, L., & McAuliffe, D. (2008). *The road to social work and human service practice* (2nd ed.). Victoria: Thompson.

Connolly, M. (2007). Practice frameworks, conceptual maps to guide interventions in child welfare. *British Journal of Social Work, 37*, 825–837.

Department for Education and Skills (2003). *Every child matters* (Cmnd 5860). London: The Stationery Office.

Dominelli, L. (2009). Anti-oppressive practices: The challenges for the 21st century. In R. Adams, Dominelli, L., & Payne, M. (eds), *Social work: Themes, issues and critical debates* (3rd ed.). Basingstoke: Palgrave.

Dreyfus, H.L., & Dreyfus, S.E. (1986). *Mind over machine: The power of human intuition and expertise in the era of the computer*. Oxford: Basil Blackwell.

Drury Hudson, J. (1997). A model of professional knowledge for social work. *Australian Social Work, 50*(3), 35–44.

England, H. (1986). *Social work as art: Making sense of good practice*. London: Allen & Unwin.

Eraut, M. (1994). *Developing professional knowledge and competence*. London: Falmer Press.

Eraut, M. (2008). *How professionals learn through work*. Unpublished paper from SCEPTrE, University of Sussex.

Forrester, D., Kershaw, S., Moss, H., & Hughes, L. (2008). Communication skills in child protection: How do social workers talk to parents? *Child and Family Social Work, 13*, 41–51.

Fraser, M.W., Richman, J.M., Galisnsky, M.J., & Day, S.H. (2009). *Intervention research: Developing social programs*. Oxford: Oxford University Press.

General Social Care Council (2008). *Social work at its best: A statement of social work roles and tasks for the 21st century*. London: GSCC.

Gibbs, L., & Gambrill, E. (1996). *Critical thinking for social workers: Exercises for the helping profession*. Thousand Oaks, CA: Pine Forge Press.

Giddens, A. (2001). *Sociology* (4th ed.). Cambridge: Polity Press.

Gitterman, C.B., & Germain, A. (2008). *The life model of social work practice: Advances in theory and practice* (3rd ed.). Chichester, NH: Columbia University Press.

Goleman, D. (1996). *Emotional intelligence: Why it can matter more than IQ*. London: Bloomsbury.

Gould, N. (2006). An inclusive approach to knowledge for mental health social work practice and policy. *British Journal of Social Work, 36*, 109–125.

Gray, M. (2010). Theories of social work practice. In L. Nicholas, Rautenbach, J., & Maistry, M. (eds), *Introduction to social work*. Cape Town: Juta.

Gray, M., & Webb, S.A. (eds) (2009). *Social work theories and methods*. London: Sage.

Hills, J., Brewer, M., Jenkins, S., Lister, R., Lupton, R., Machin, S., Mills, C., Modood, T., Rees, T., & Riddel, S. (2010). *An anatomy of economic inequality in the UK: Summary*. Report of the National Equality Panel. London: Government Equalities Office.

Hockenbury, D.H., & Hockenbury, S.E. (2006). *Psychology* (4th ed.). New York: Worth.

Hollis, F. (1964). *Casework: A psychosocial therapy*. New York: Random House.

Howe, D. (1994). Modernity, post modernity and social work. *British Journal of Social Work, 24*, 513–532.

Howe, D. (1996). Surface and depth in social-work practice. In N. Parton (ed.), *Social theory, social change and social work*. London: Routledge.

Howe, D. (2009). *A brief introduction to social work theory*. Basingstoke: Palgrave.

Jack, G. (2000). Ecological influences on parenting and child development. *British Journal of Social Work, 30*, 703–720.

Jones, R. (2008). The sixth giant: We need another giant step to tackle care and support, *The Guardian*, Wednesday October 1, 2008.

Joseph Rowntree Foundation (2009). *Monitoring poverty and social exclusion*. Retrieved September 9,

2010 from http://www.jrf.org.uk/publications/monitoring-poverty-2009

Koprowska, J. (2010). *Communication and interpersonal skills in social work* (3rd ed.). Exeter: Learning Matters.

Lam, D.O. (2009). Impact of problem-based learning on social work students: Growth and limits. *British Journal of Social Work, 39*, 1499–1517.

Laming, H. (2003). *The Victoria Climbié Inquiry Report.* Cm. 5370. London: The Stationery Office.

Laming, H. (2009). *The protection of children in England: A progress report.* London: TSO. Retrieved June 14, 2010 from http://publications.everychildmatters.gov.uk/eOrderingDownload/HC-330.pdf

Lishman, J. (2009). *Communication in social work* (2nd ed.). Basingstoke: Palgrave.

MacInnes, T., Kenway, P., & Parekh, A. (2009). *Monitoring poverty and social exclusion 2009.* York: Joseph Rowntree Foundation.

Marmot Review (2009). *Fair society, healthy lives: The Marmot review.* Retrieved September 1, 2010 from http://www.marmot-review.org.uk

Marsh, P., & Fisher, M. (2008). The development of problem-solving knowledge for social care practice. *British Journal of Social Work, 38*, 971–987.

McSherry, D. (2004). Which came first, the chicken or the egg? Examining the relationship between child neglect and poverty. *British Journal of Social Work, 34*, 727–733.

Miliband, D. (2006). Speech to the National Council for Voluntary Organisations' Annual Conference, *The Guardian*, February 21, 2006.

Mullaly, B. (2007). *The new structural social work* (3rd ed.). Oxford: Oxford University Press.

Munro, E. (1998). Improving social workers' knowledge base in child protection work', *British Journal of Social Work, 28*, 89–105.

Munro, E. (2010). *The Munro Review of Child Protection. Part One: A systems analysis.* Retrieved November 19, 2010 from http://www.education.gov.uk/munroreview/downloads/TheMunroReviewofChildProtection-Part%20one.pdf

Munro, E. (2011a). *The Munro review of child protection interim report: The child's journey.* 2010. Retrieved February 19, 2011 from http://www.education.gov.uk/publications/standard/publicationDetail/Page1/DFE-00010-2011

Munro, E. (2011b). *Munro review of child protection, final report: A child-centred system.* London: Department for Education.

Osmond, J. (2005). The knowledge spectrum: A framework for teaching knowledge and its use in social work practice. *British Journal of Social Work, 35*, 881–900.

Osmond, J., & O'Connor, I. (2004). Formalizing the unformalized: Practitioners' communication of knowledge in practice. *British Journal of Social Work, 34*, 677–692.

Palmer, G. (2010). *Relative poverty, absolute poverty and social exclusion.* Retrieved September 17, 2010 from JRF Poverty Site: http://www.poverty.org.uk/summary/social%20exclusion.shtml

Parton, N. (2000). Some thoughts on the relationship between theory and practice in and for social work. *British Journal of Social Work, 30*, 449–463.

Parton, N. (2010). Child protection and safeguarding in England: Changing and competing conceptions of risk and their implications for social work. *British Journal of Social Work*, Advance Access published December 10, 2010, 10.1093/bjsw/bcq119.

Parton, N., & O'Byrne, P. (2000). *Constructive social work: Towards a new practice.* Basingstoke: Palgrave.

Pawson, R., Boaz, A., Grayson, L., Long, A., & Barnes, C. (2003). *Types and quality of knowledge in social care.* SCIE Knowledge Review 7. Bristol: Policy Press.

Piachaud, D., & Sutherland, H. (2001). Child poverty in Britain and the New Labour Government. *Journal Social Policy, 30*(1), 95–118.

Polanyi, M. (1967). *The tacit dimension.* London, Routledge and Kegan Paul.

Richards, S., Ruch, G. & Trevithick, P. (2005). Communication skills training for practice, the ethical dilemma for social work education. *Social Work Education, 24*(4), 409–417.

Rogers, A., & Pilgrim, D. (2010). *A sociology of mental health and illness* (4th ed.). Buckingham: Open University Press.

Rothman, D. (2003). Intervention research. In R.L. Edwards (ed.), *Encyclopedia of Social Work* (19th ed.). vol. 1. Washington, DC: National Association of Social Workers, pp. 323–334.

Ruch, G., Turney, D., & Ward, A. (eds) (2010). *Relationship-based social work: Getting to the heart of practice.* London: Jessica Kingsley.

Ryle, G. (1949). *The concept of mind.* Chicago, IL: The University of Chicago Press.

Schön, D. (1983). *The reflective practitioner: How professionals think in action.* New York: Basic Books.

Scottish Executive (2005). *The role of the social worker in the 21st century: A literature review.* Edinburgh: Scottish Executive Education Department.

Seebohm Report (1968). *Report of the Committee on Local Authority and Allied Personal Social Services* (Cmnd 3703). London: HMSO.

Sheppard, M. (1994). Childcare, social support and maternal depression: A review and application of findings. *British Journal of Social Work, 24,* 287–310.

Sheppard, M. (1995). Social work, social science and practice wisdom. *British Journal of Social Work, 25,* 33–51.

Sheppard, M. (1998). 'Practice validity, reflexivity and knowledge for social work', *British Journal of Social Work, 28,* 763–781.

Sheppard, M., & Ryan, K. (2003). Practitioners as rule using analysts: A further development of process knowledge in social work. *British Journal of Social Work, 33,* 157–176.

Social Work Task Force (SWTF) (2009a). *Facing up to the task: The interim report of the Social Work Task Force. July 2009.* Retrieved December 5, 2009 from http://publications.education.gov.uk/default.aspx?PageFunction=productdetails&PageMode=publications&ProductId=DCSF-00752-2009&

Social Work Task Force (SWTF) (2009b). *Building a safe, confident future: The final report of the Social Work Task Force.* Retrieved February 4, 2010 from http://education.gov.uk/publications/standard/publicationDetail/page1/DFE-00601-2010

Spicker, P. (1995). *Social policy: Themes and approaches.* Hemel Hempstead: Prentice Hall/Harvester Wheatsheaf.

Stevenson, O. (1998). *Neglected children and their families.* Oxford: Blackwell.

Stevenson, O. (2005). Genericism and specialization: The story since 1970. *British Journal of Social Work, 35,* 569–586.

Taylor, C., & White, S. (2006). Knowledge and reasoning in social work, educating for humane judgement. *British Journal of Social Work, 36,* 937–954.

Trevithick, P. (2003). Effective relationship-based practice: A theoretical exploration. *Journal of Social Work Practice,* 17(2), 173–186.

Trevithick, P. (2008). Revisiting the knowledge base of social work: A framework for practice. *British Journal of Social Work, 38,* 1212–1237.

Trevithick, P. (2011). The generalist versus specialist debate in social work education in the UK. In J. Lishman (ed.), *Research highlights in social work.* London: Jessica Kingsley.

Trevithick, P. (2012). *Social work skills: A practice handbook* (3rd ed.), Maidenhead: Open University Press.

Walker, C., & Walker, A. (2009). Social policy and social work. In R. Adams, Dominelli, L., & Payne, M. (eds), *Social work: Themes, issues and critical debates* (3rd ed.). Basingstoke: Palgrave.

Wilson, K., Ruch, G., Lymbery, M., & Cooper, A. (2008). *Social work: An introduction to contemporary practice.* Harlow: Pearson Education.

8

Ecological Perspective

Gordon Jack

Social workers routinely find themselves in situations in which the needs of individuals, groups, or communities experiencing problems need to be assessed in order to determine the services or interventions that will help to safeguard them from harm and promote their well-being. Even in apparently straightforward cases, the social worker can be faced with a bewildering range of information that quickly becomes overwhelming without the help of some sort of organising framework. Ecological theory provides the basis for what is probably the most widely used organising framework in social work today.

In its broadest sense, the term 'ecology' refers to the study of the relationships between living organisms and their environments. Within this paradigm, the earth is understood to comprise a number of systems and subsystems, involving plants, animals, humans, and their physical surroundings, which are involved in constant processes of mutual interaction, with changes in one system often affecting others and vice versa. The developmental psychologist, Urie Bronfenbrenner, is usually credited as the first person to apply ecological thinking specifically to the social sphere of human development, although as he himself acknowledged (Bronfenbrenner, 1979), the ideas upon which his work was founded were far from new, drawing particularly on the formula developed by his former teacher that behaviour is a function of person and environment interactions (Lewin, 1936).

In what follows, the organising framework provided by social ecological theory is explained, including consideration of some of the most important ways in which people both shape and are shaped by their immediate and wider environments. Using examples primarily concerning parenting and the development of children, the implications of an ecological perspective for holistic, anti-oppressive social work practice are considered. The central importance of developing an understanding of the personal experiences and views of the people with whom social workers engage is highlighted, together with the benefits of promoting their access to informal sources of support, and of building the capacity of communities to meet the needs of their members.

BRONFENBRENNER'S ECOLOGY OF HUMAN DEVELOPMENT

Within an ecological perspective, developmental outcomes are understood to be dependent on the interplay between strengths and vulnerabilities in the various settings within which people live their lives, including their families, friendship networks, school or work situations, neighbourhoods, and the wider communities of interest and the society to which they belong. Bronfenbrenner (1979) emphasised the dynamic and reciprocal nature of these processes, noting they involve

> the progressive, mutual accommodation between an active, growing human being and the changing properties of the immediate settings in which the developing person lives, as this process is affected by relations between these settings, and by larger contexts in which the settings are embedded (p. 21).

These settings can be represented as a nested arrangement of concentric structures, each contained within the next, rather like a set of Russian dolls, with the individual positioned at the centre, surrounded by what are known as the micro-, meso-, exo-, and macro-systems (see Figure 8.1). Micro-systems involve the pattern of activities, roles, and interpersonal relations experienced by the developing person in a given setting, while the meso-system describes the inter-relations among two or more settings in which the developing person actively participates. Moving outwards, the exo-system involves one or more settings that do not involve the developing person as an active participant, but in which events occur that affect (or are affected by) what happens in the settings containing the developing person, and the macro-system consists of the influences of the subcultures and the culture as a whole to which the individual belongs, along with any belief systems or ideology underpinning them (Bronfenbrenner, 1979). A fifth layer, the chrono-system, was subsequently added to the model to take account of changes in the external environment over time (Bronfenbrenner, 1986).

The ecological approach, therefore, makes it clear that individuals and their environments can never be understood separately from one another, always viewing development in its context, with the properties of the person and the environment, the structure of environmental settings, and the processes taking place within and between them all viewed as interdependent (Bronfenbrenner, 1979). Bronfenbrenner's theory also emphasises the importance of adopting a phenomenological perspective, in which an individual's subjective experiences and perceptions are considered to be essential in developing an accurate picture of their lives.

One of the reasons ecological theory is so useful for social work practice is that it provides a holistic organising framework within which to locate all of the different elements of people's lives and the connections between them. This serves to remind social workers that the problems they encounter, rather than having a single cause, are more likely to be the product of combinations of factors at multiple levels of influence, with small changes in one or more key factors having the potential to generate significant influences on a problem over time (Glass & McAtee, 2006). It also helps social workers and other health and welfare practitioners to see what is and is not within the scope of individuals, families, or communities to control, pointing the way towards what are likely to be the most appropriate and effective forms of intervention (Lounsbury & Mitchell, 2009).

ECOLOGICAL FRAMEWORKS FOR WORK WITH CHILDREN AND FAMILIES

The central importance of an ecological perspective for social work practice is nowhere more evident than in the large number of

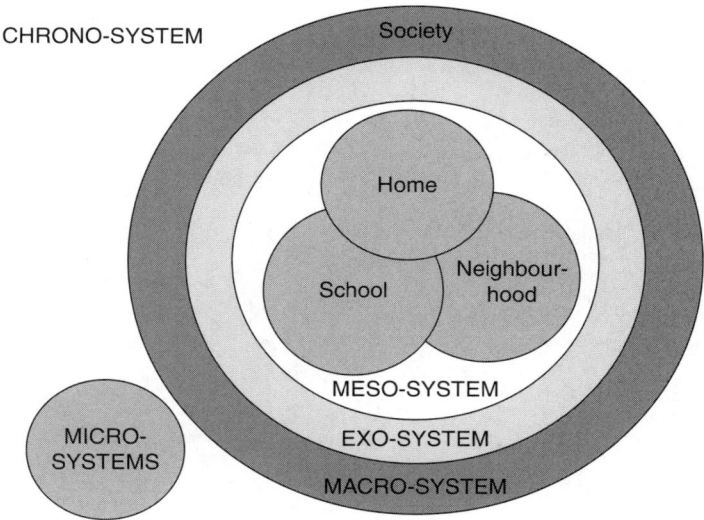

Figure 8.1 The ecology of human development (adapted from Bronfenbrenner, 1979).

ecologically oriented frameworks for assessing the development and well-being of children and their families that have been developed around the world in recent years (e.g., Bradshaw & Richardson, 2009; Fattore et al., 2009; Green et al., 2009). For example, in 2000 the UK government introduced a framework for the assessment of 'children in need', which was explicitly based on ecological theory (Department of Health, Department for Education and Employment and Home Office, 2000). Rather than using Bronfenbrenner's concentric circles, the factors to be taken into consideration were arranged along the three sides of a triangle, representing, respectively: children's developmental needs; parental capacity; and wider family and environment (as illustrated in Figure 8.2). In order to ensure the interactive principles of ecological theory are translated into practice, the forms for recording assessments within this model require consideration of each element of children's developmental needs in relation to each element of parenting capacity, with the results of this analysis then considered in relation to the wider family and environmental circumstances.

While the UK framework has attracted criticism for reinforcing the tendency of social work agencies to focus more attention on the influence of factors *within* the family than on the influence of *external* factors (Calder & Hackett, 2004; Jack & Gill, 2003), there is little doubt it has promoted a more holistic approach to the assessment of children's needs. However, evidence about the implementation of assessment frameworks such as this indicates analysis of the information gathered, particularly the systems-oriented analysis which is a central component of ecological theory, is not well developed (e.g., Cleaver & Walker, 2004). While this may partly be explained by the tight timescales within which assessments often have to be completed, it is also attributable to limited knowledge of the social ecological research base amongst social workers. In order to address this deficit, the ecologically oriented research evidence in relation to two of the most important areas for social work practice with children and families – parenting behaviour and child maltreatment – is now considered.

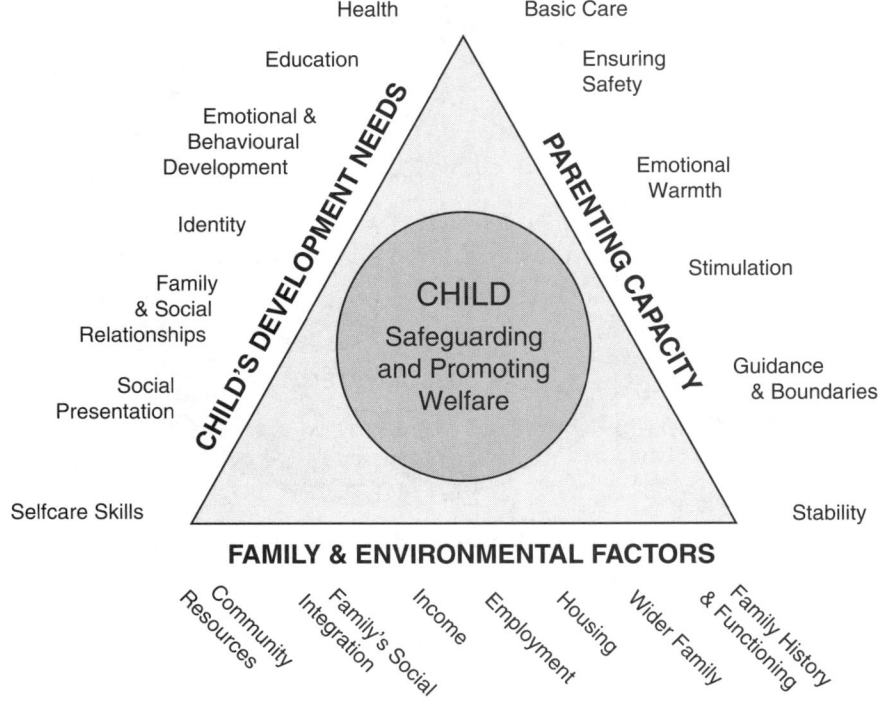

Figure 8.2 An ecological assessment framework (adapted from Department of Health, Department for Education and Employments and Home Office, 2000).

ECOLOGICAL DETERMINANTS OF PARENTING BEHAVIOUR AND CHILD MALTREATMENT

Based on the original ecological model developed by Bronfenbrenner, and subsequent comprehensive reviews of the research (e.g., Belsky & Jaffee, 2006; Cicchetti & Valentino, 2006), it is now well established that outcomes for children depend upon interactions between the child's own characteristics, such as their temperament, the characteristics of their parents, such as their personality, developmental history, adult relationships and psychological well-being, and contextual factors, such as the qualities of the local neighbourhood.

Mechanisms of influence

The interactions involved in these ecological processes are governed by a number of potential mechanisms of influence (Luster & Okagaki, 1993). The first and perhaps most obvious is a *cumulative* mechanism, whereby different factors at individual, family, and community levels of influence serve to reinforce each other. This mechanism is evident in the many research studies which reveal the way a single risk factor, such as history of parental depression or family poverty, increases the likelihood of child maltreatment occurring to only a limited extent, whereas the risk increases considerably if these factors exist in combination (Garmezy, 1994; Rutter, 1979). Alternatively, moderating or mediating mechanisms might be in operation, where the effects of one factor on another depend upon the characteristics of a third factor. For example, the existence of a supportive relationship with a spouse has been shown to *moderate* the otherwise negative influence of a parent's adverse family background on their capacity to provide satisfactory parenting themselves (e.g., Quinton et al., 1984). And, while the greatest risks of child maltreatment in the UK have been found to be associated with socioeconomic deprivation and the various characteristics of the parents, the effects of these parental background factors are largely *mediated* through their influence on socioeconomic factors (Sidebotham et al., 2006).

Two further potential mechanisms touch on Bronfenbrenner's chrono-system. The first involves the *selection* processes that operate when the characteristics of a person at one point in time influence the context in which their parenting takes place at a later point in time. This is illustrated by a series of research studies with neglectful mothers carried out in the USA (Polansky et al., 1985). In a comparison with a sample of non-neglectful mothers from similar socioeconomic backgrounds, the researchers found the negative personality traits that had characterised the neglectful mothers since their schooldays (often as a result of rejection or abusive treatment from their own parents) subsequently limited their personal and neighbourhood support networks, causing problems when they became parents. The final mechanism discussed here (although this by no means exhausts all of the possibilities) concerns the *developmental pathways* that tend to link one context to the next, as illustrated by the extensive international health inequalities literature, which shows that persistent or repeated disadvantages experienced in childhood are likely to lead to disadvantaged circumstances in adulthood, with negative consequences for health (e.g., Blaxter, 1990; Davey Smith, 2003; Graham, 2000; Shaw et al., 1999).

An example of social ecological research into child maltreatment

The importance of an ecological perspective for social work practice is well illustrated by series of studies undertaken by James Garbarino and his colleagues in different areas of the USA, designed to explore the influence of community-level factors on child maltreatment. The first thing this body of work demonstrates is the way a number of inter-related socioeconomic and demographic factors, including community level measures of poverty, unemployment, overcrowding, ethnic background, household composition, educational attainment, and length of residence accounted for the majority of the variance between the officially recorded rates of child maltreatment in different areas (Garbarino & Croucher, 1978; Garbarino & Kostelny, 1992).

However, in order to investigate what accounted for the remainder of the variance, Garbarino and his colleagues had to supplement their quantitative data with the subjective views of residents and community leaders in neighbourhoods with either higher or lower than predicted rates of child maltreatment for their level of disadvantage. In the first of these studies, comparing two socioeconomically and demographically matched areas, families living in the 'high-risk' area reported a lack of mutually supportive relationships and informal social networks in their neighbourhood, largely due to fears of either being exploited by others or of being a burden on them, which compounded their own problems. This contrasted with the families living in the 'low-risk' area who reported more frequent involvement in a range of supportive neighbourhood interactions, which included keeping an eye on children playing in the neighbourhood, intervening if children's safety was threatened, and offering help with childcare. The researchers concluded the high-risk area needed outside intervention to increase its capacity to fend for itself and to strengthen individual families (Garbarino & Sherman, 1980).

The second study took this aspect of the analysis a stage further by charting the recorded and predicted child maltreatment rates of four matched areas between 1980 and 1986 (Garbarino & Kostelny, 1992). Two of these areas ('North' and 'West'), which had similar levels of recorded child maltreatment at the start of the study, changed markedly over the next six years. 'North', which started as an area with reported rates of child maltreatment slightly lower than predicted by its socioeconomic and demographic profile, became a much higher risk area during this period, whilst 'West' moved in the opposite direction, starting out as a higher risk area than 'North', but becoming a much lower-risk area by the end of the study period. Interviews with community leaders revealed that between 1980 and 1986 'North' was perceived to have become a more unstable area, with limited levels of community participation and informal interactions between neighbours, whilst 'West' had developed stronger formal and informal support systems, becoming what was described as a 'poor but decent place to live'. Similar findings about the influence of what is usually called 'social capital', which refers to the connections among individuals, including social networks and the norms of reciprocity and trust arising from them (see, e.g., Putnam, 2000), on rates of officially recorded child maltreatment and other social problems such as violent crime have been reported from other parts of North America and the rest of the world, including Australia and the UK (Barnes, 2007; Coulton et al., 1995; Sampson et al., 1997; Vinson et al., 1996). It is this combination of quantitative and qualitative methods of analysis, based on information about the impact of factors at different levels of influence, which points the way toward the main components of ecological social work practice.

DEVELOPING ECOLOGICAL SOCIAL WORK PRACTICE

From what has been discussed so far, it is clear social workers wishing to develop ecological practice (Gill & Jack, 2007) will be concerned with the way in which factors at different levels of influence in people's lives help to shape (as well as being shaped by) their behaviour and the environments in which they live. Unfortunately, while ecologically oriented assessment frameworks are now well established in many parts of the world, organisational priorities for service provision and the allocation of resources still tend to place more emphasis on the influence of factors *within* families and households in shaping behaviour than on factors *outside* these settings. If social workers are not alive to this tendency, it is all too easy to practice in ways that uncritically accept a rather narrow focus on what happens within households, with inadequate account taken of the way in which structural inequalities in society influence people's behaviour and well-being. If practice fails fully to recognise the extent to which people's backgrounds, personal characteristics, family circumstances, and opportunities in life are all influenced by the community and society contexts within which they live their lives, it runs the risk of reinforcing the very disadvantages and oppression it ought to be challenging (Thompson, 2006). In order to promote the development of holistic, anti-oppressive ways of working fully taking into account all of the factors influencing people's behaviour and circumstances, three essential components of ecological practice are now discussed.

Creating a culture of listening to adults and children

As has already been noted, the ecological perspective places an emphasis on phenomenology, with an individual's own perceptions about their circumstances forming a central feature of assessments of their needs and any subsequent action. A fundamental component of anti-oppressive social work practice is the ability to listen carefully to people talking about the problems they are experiencing in their lives. In describing their problems, most people will quite naturally present what is essentially an ecological picture of their lives, ranging over several issues at individual, family, community, and society levels of influence they think are significant, and identifying the connections between them. For example, a single parent mother involved with social workers because her teenage son is beyond her control and engaging in criminal behaviour might talk about the way her history of abuse and depression, difficult relationship with her ex-partner, and limited wider family support all make daily life very hard for her, particularly in the context of her low income (with little prospect of paid employment) and overcrowded housing in a deprived local neighbourhood. Unfortunately, it is all too easy for practitioners faced with this complex array of inter-related issues to exercise a form of selective hearing, perhaps unconsciously, which reflects the requirements, procedures, and service arrangements of their employing organisations rather than the capturing the full reality of people's lives (Gill & Jack, 2007). In the UK, for example, where income maintenance and housing issues have traditionally been the responsibility of other professionals, assessments undertaken by social workers have tended to underplay the significance of these issues in the lives of the people with whom they are working, leading to accusations of what has been called 'poverty blindness' (see, e.g., Becker, 1997; Clark & Davis, 1997; Dowling, 1999; Packman, 1986).

What is required for anti-oppressive practice, therefore, is an approach that is based on knowledge about the full range of social ecological influences on people's behaviour and circumstances, and which places value on listening to and acknowledging people's own perceptions about their lives, no matter what the requirements and expectations of the organisations employing social workers. While assessments of need must always include information from a range of other sources, it is only by listening to (and recording) the views and perceptions of the people directly involved that a full ecological understanding of the problems they are facing, and the connections they make between them, can be developed (Gill & Jack, 2007).

Promoting informal social networks

The second component of ecological practice being considered here is based on the recognition that informal personal relationships which provide individuals with support are beneficial for their health and well-being (e.g., Blaxter, 1990; Gottlieb, 1981; Holt-Lunstad et al., 2010; Wills, 1985). Empirical studies of the influence of personal networks of support on individual health and illness, which began to emerge in North America in the 1970s, demonstrated that strengthening personal social support could help to prevent illness and protect individuals from the effects of crises in their lives (Cassell, 1976; Cobb, 1976). Later studies highlighted the need to disaggregate different aspects of social support, including the size, density, and structure of relationship networks, as well as the qualities and availability of relationships at different times and in a variety of situations (Sarason et al., 1990). For example, various studies highlighted the way personal networks of relationships can be sources of stress and danger, as well as of support and safety (Dunst et al., 1997; Gibbons, 1990; Korbin, 1989), including a study of lone mothers living in North America that found criticism within their support networks increased the levels of stress they experienced, resulting in less sensitive parenting and greater risk to their children (Moncher, 1995).

The most important functions of social support are generally understood to be the provision of information and advice, practical help, and emotional support (Cochran & Brassard, 1979; Crockenberg, 1988; Cutrona & Russell, 1990). Emotional support, for example, has been shown to be beneficial in protecting against the potentially harmful effects of stress on the personal health and well-being of people of all ages (Brown & Harris, 1978; Brown et al., 1986; Cohen & Wills, 1985; Kessler & McLeod, 1985). Conversely, social isolation has been found to increase the risk of poorer health and child neglect (Belsky, 1984; Thompson, 1995).

Social support can be provided by a wide range of different people, including partners, relatives, friends, neighbours, work colleagues, and lay and professional helpers. Importantly for the development of ecological social work practice, different types and levels of support are typically provided by different network members, with that provided by adult partners and close relatives generally being the most significant, followed by support provided by extended kin and friends, then neighbours, and finally professionals (Bronfenbrenner, 1986; Gibbons, 1990; Gill et al., 2000). This means attempts by social workers to provide help and support to individuals and families are more likely to be effective if they focus on strengthening the natural helping networks of those with whom they are working. Where this is not possible or sufficient, it is helpful if more formal, professionally organised support services can replicate the features making informal support more effective and acceptable to most people (Ghate & Hazel, 2002). These include choice about whether or not to accept help in the first place, as well as some control over the nature of the support provided, and opportunities to reciprocate any support accepted, either at the time or at some future date (Beckman, 1991; Trivette et al., 1997).

There are a number of well-established methods for assessing personal social support networks. Probably the best known and most widely used is the eco-map (Hartman, 1978), an example of which is shown in Figure 8.3, with the key person or family situated in the centre and significant people and systems in their life arranged around them, and the nature of the relationships involved indicated by their position on the diagram and the types of connecting lines used, often with the addition of arrows and written comments.

Eco-maps provide a very effective tool for aiding communication with people across a wide range of ages and capacities, helping to visually identify some of the strengths and weaknesses that exist within a person's social network which discussion alone is unlikely to reveal. Because an eco-map is capable of presenting a lot of information on a single sheet of paper, it also helps people to develop a more holistic understanding of their circumstances at a particular point in time, as well as focusing attention on the interface between themselves and the significant people and systems in their lives, indicating where specific interventions may need to be the targeted. Completed at different times or focusing on different stages, eco-maps also allow for changes in a person's life to be assessed. For example, they were used by a social worker in a medical rehabilitation setting to help patients (and their families) portray their world before their accident or illness, and the changes they envisaged would occur in their lives following their discharge from hospital. This

> helped them to mourn interests and activities that would have to be relinquished and also to recognise sources of support and gratification that would continue to be available. The mapping encouraged anticipatory planning and preparation for a new life, consideration of appropriate replacements for lost activities, and possible new resources to be tapped, all of which could expand [their] horizons (Hartman, 1978, p. 474).

Other approaches to representing social networks have been used in social work (see, e.g., Hill, 2002), including the 'social network map' devised by Tracey and Whittaker (1990). This collates written information about the most important members of a person's social network, identifying their relationship to the subject (e.g., household or extended family member, work, school or other friend, neighbour, organisational contact, or professional), and rating the qualities of each relationship

ECOLOGICAL PERSPECTIVE 137

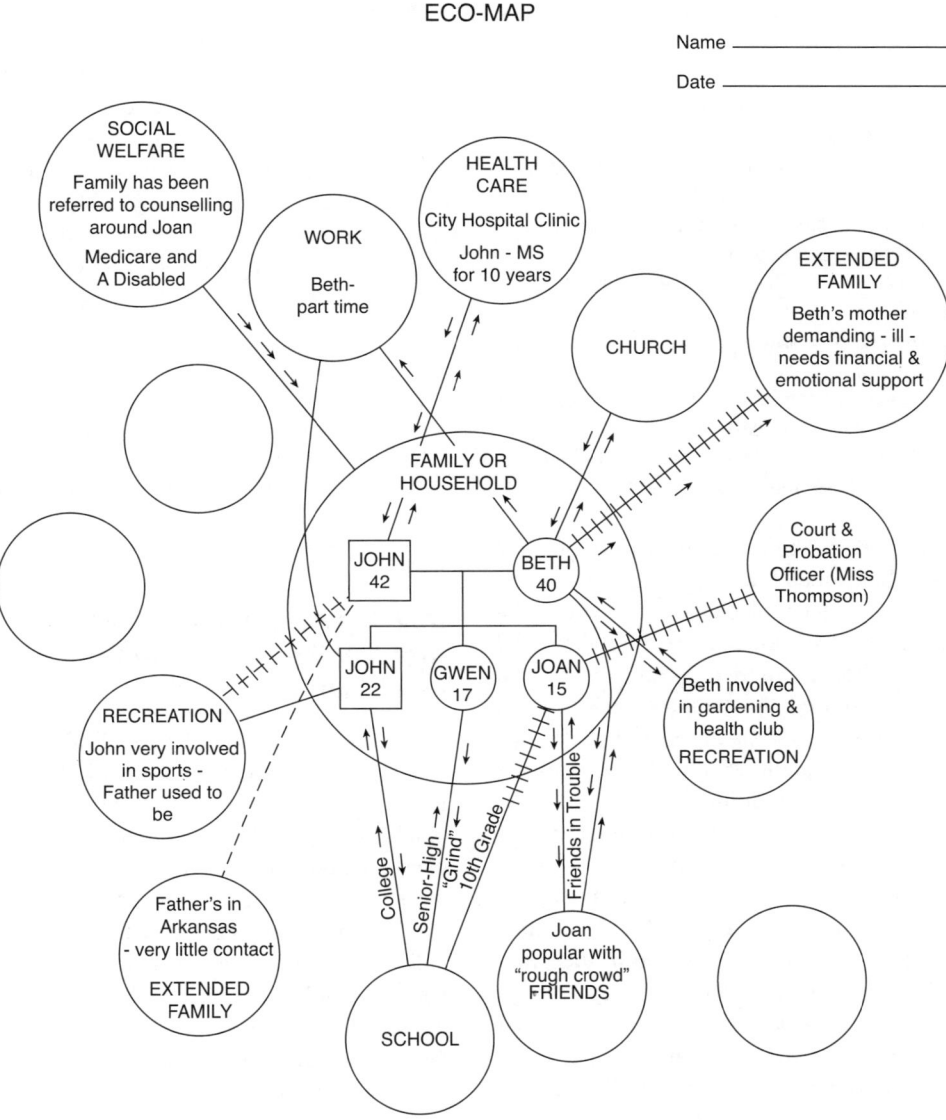

Figure 8.3 An eco-map (adapted from Warren, 1993)

on a number of different dimensions, such as:

- concrete support provided (1 = rarely; 2 = sometimes; 3 = frequently);
- emotional support provided (1 = rarely; 2 = sometimes; 3 = frequently);
- information/advice provided (1 = rarely; 2 = sometimes; 3 = frequently);
- critical (1 = rarely; 2 = sometimes; 3 = frequently);
- closeness (1 = not close; 2 = quite close; 3 = very close);
- frequency of contact (1 = less than once/year; 2 = monthly; 3 = at least weekly);
- duration of relationship (1 = less than 1 year; 2 = 1–5 years; 3 = more than 5 years).

Once again, the aim is to help the people with whom social workers are engaged to develop a better understanding of where the strengths and weaknesses within their social networks lie, and to identify any actions that may be required to strengthen their social support resources. Tracey (1990) used this approach to examine the social support resources of 45 families in the USA who were 'at-risk of disruption through out of home placement' of one or more of their children. She found these families could not be classified as socially isolated, as they named an average of 19 people in their network, although the ratio of friends to relatives in their networks was lower than that found in the general population. This meant they were often dependent for help on a limited number of relatives who could not necessarily be relied upon to provide support. This is evident in the fact only 8% of respondents said there was anyone within their households who provided them with support. More widely, 12% of network members were rated as 'almost always critical', with nearly two-thirds reporting they had at least one critical network member with whom they were in daily contact.

A number of implications for practice were identified in this study, including the potential benefits of helping family members to make and maintain new friendships, and interventions designed specifically to reduce conflict in relationships. In addition, the study found reciprocity in relationships was positively associated with practical help – the more respondents were able to provide help to others, the more likely they were to perceive similar support was available to them. So, services enabling people to give as well as receive help may enhance access to social support resources. Tracey (1990) concluded:

> Efforts may be needed to assist families in creating or developing a supportive social network and to enable families to make use of available resources. Such interventions may ultimately allow practitioners to incorporate social and environmental factors more effectively in their work with at-risk families (p. 256).

Developing the capacity of disadvantaged communities to meet their own needs

The final component of ecological practice considered here concerns the capacity of different communities, whether based on geographical boundaries or common interests, to meet the needs of their members. The aim of this strand of ecological practice, like the other two strands already considered, is to promote holistic and empowering ways of working, as far as possible, taking as their starting point the self-defined needs and aspirations of different individuals and groups, with the aim of building on their existing strengths.

In considering how to build community capacity, it is important at the outset to recognise communities are complex, often heterogeneous social entities, consisting of a range of people with different backgrounds, identities, needs and interests (Hoggett, 1997). Given this complexity, it is important for practitioners to develop a good level of knowledge about the socioeconomic circumstances and demographics of the different communities with which they are working, and an ecological understanding of the way in which they function, including the normal patterns of social interaction and any tensions existing between different individuals and groups. This requires the development and maintenance of reliable and up-to-date community profiles, incorporating information from a variety of quantitative and qualitative sources, including the perceptions of local residents (and others) about the communities to which they belong (for examples, see Green, 2000; Hawtin et al., 1994; Murtagh, 1999).

The value of community profiling for ecological social work practice is illustrated in a study undertaken by the UK children's charity, Barnardo's, which aimed to increase the capacity of a disadvantaged community in the South West region of England producing high levels of child welfare referrals to local agencies to provide a safer environment for the children and young people who lived there (Gill et al., 2000). The traditional approach to such welfare concerns in the UK is to allocate individual social workers to the families deemed to be in the greatest need, with the caseworker having statutory responsibility for the protection of children, including making arrangements for the provision of any family support services that may be required. Barnardo's were interested in the impact community factors were having on families living in this area, which had very few community-based family support services.

The community profile developed in this project included socioeconomic, demographic, and child welfare data about the area, as well as data from interviews with a sample of parents with young children about their existing sources of support and the difficulties they faced. The interviews revealed, despite high levels of divorce, separation, and lone parenthood, most families living in this area had strong extended family support networks. They had regular contact with their own parents (particularly their mothers) and other relatives, many of whom lived nearby, engaging with them in a wide range of reciprocal exchanges of support. However, a smaller group of families who were identified as having significant problems, lacked support from their extended families, often as a consequence of frequent moves of home.

In identifying both the strong kin-based support networks of the majority of families with young children living in this area, and a more vulnerable group of families lacking adequate support, the community profile developed by Barnardo's provided the basis for social work staff to facilitate the development of a range of largely informal support services for parents, including parent and toddler groups and adult education programmes, which increased the opportunities for groups of adults and children to meet together, thereby providing each other with a degree of mutual support and enhancing the capacity of this high-risk area to promote the well-being of parents and children. Many other examples of similar approaches to extending the capacity of local communities to meet the needs of their members, including not only parents and their children, but also a wide range of adults with different support needs, can be found in the social work literature (see, e.g., Jack & Jack, 2000; Nelson & Baldwin, 2004; Newton, 1992; Wright, 2004).

CONCLUSION

The ecological perspective discussed in this chapter provides an important organising framework for social work practice that is increasingly being used around the world. Ecological theory helps social workers to understand the way in which all of the different elements of people's lives, at individual, family, neighbourhood, and society levels of influence, interact together to shape their behaviour and circumstances. In combination with a systems-oriented approach to the analysis of the information collected and an emphasis on the importance of phenomenology, seeing people's lives and problems from their own point of view, the ecological perspective provides the basis for the development of holistic, anti-oppressive social work practice.

However, in order to translate the potential of the ecological perspective successfully into everyday practice, social workers need to ensure they are familiar not only with the ecological model itself, but also with the research evidence which identifies the most significant factors operating in relation to the individuals, groups or communities with whom they are working, as well as the wider cultural, economic and political contexts within which that work is taking place. While it has only been possible to consider a small amount of the available research evidence here, together with the general messages for practice that it highlights, many of the other chapters in this volume should help practitioners working in a range of settings and with a variety of people to develop knowledge of the research which is most relevant to their own area of practice.

REFERENCES

Barnes, J. (2007). *Down our way: The relevance of neighbourhoods for parenting and child development.* Chichester: John Wiley and Sons.

Becker, S. (1997). *Responding to poverty: The politics of cash and care.* Harlow: Addison Wesley Longman.

Beckman, P.J. (1991). Comparison of mothers' and fathers' perceptions of the effect of young children with and without disabilities. *American Journal of Mental Retardation, 95,* 585–595.

Belsky, J. (1984). The determinants of parenting, *Child Development, 55,* 83–96.

Belsky, J., & Jaffee, S.R. (2006). The multiple determinants of parenting. In D. Cicchetti & Cohen, D.J. (eds), *Developmental psychopathology* (Vol. 3)*: Risk, disorder and adaptation.* Hoboken, NJ: John Wiley and Sons, pp. 38–85.

Blaxter, M. (1990). *Health and lifestyles.* London: Routledge.

Bradshaw, J., & Richardson, D. (2009). An index of child well-being in Europe. *Child Indicators Research, 2,* 319–351.

Bronfenbrenner, U. (1979). *The ecology of human development: Experiments by nature and design.* Cambridge, MA: Harvard University Press.

Bronfenbrenner, U. (1986). Recent advances in research on the ecology of human development. In R.K. Silbereisen, Eyferth, K., & Rudinger, G. (eds), *Development as action in context: Problem behavior and normal youth development.* New York: Springer-Verlag, pp. 287–309.

Brown, G.W., & Harris, T. (1978). *Social origins of depression: A study of psychiatric disorder in women.* London: Tavistock.

Brown, G.W., Andrews, B., Harris, T.O., Adler, Z., & Bridge, I. (1986). Social support, self esteem and depression. *Psychological Medicine, 16,* 813–831.

Cassell, J. (1976). Psychosocial processes and stress: Theoretical formulations. *International Journal of Health Services, 4,* 471–482.

Calder, M.C., & Hackett, S. (eds) (2004). *Assessment in child care: Using and developing frameworks for practice.* Lyme Regis: Russell House.

Cicchetti, D., & Valentino, K. (2006). An ecological–transactional perspective on child maltreatment: Failure of the average expectable environment and its influence on child development. In D. Cicchetti & Cohen, D.J. (eds), *Developmental psychopathology* (Vol. 3)*: Risk, disorder and adaptation.* Hoboken, NJ: John Wiley and Sons, pp. 129–201.

Clark, B., & Davis, A. (1997). When money's too tight to mention. *Professional Social Work*, March, 12–13.

Cleaver, H., & Walker, S., with Meadows, P. (2004). *Assessing children's needs and circumstances: The impact of the assessment framework.* London: Jessica Kingsley.

Cobb, S. (1976). Social support as a moderator of life stress. *Psychosomatic Medicine, 38,* 300–314.

Cochran, M.M., & Brassard, J.A. (1979). Child development and personal social networks. *Child Development, 50,* 601–615.

Cohen, S., & Wills, T.A. (1985). Stress, social support and the buffering hypothesis, *Psychological Review, 98,* 310–357.

Coulton, C.J., Korbin, J.E., Su, M., & Chow, J. (1995). Community level factors and child maltreatment rates. *Child Development, 66,* 1262–1276.

Crockenberg, S. (1988). Social support and parenting. In H. Fitzgerald, Lester, B., & Yogman, M. (eds), *Theory and research in behavioural paediatrics* (Vol. 4). New York: Plenum, pp. 67–92.

Cutrona, C. E., & Russell, D. (1990). Type of social support and specific stress: Toward a theory of optimal matching. In I.G. Sarason, Sarason, B.R. & Pierce, G.R. (eds), *Social Support: An interactional view.* New York: Wiley, pp. 319–366.

Davey Smith, G. (2003). *Health inequalities: Lifecourse approaches.* Bristol: The Policy Press.

Department of Health, Department for Education and Employment, and Home Office (2000) *Framework for the Assessment of Children in Need and their Families.* London: The Stationery Office.

Dowling, M. (1999). *Social work and poverty: Attitudes and actions.* Aldershot: Ashgate.

Dunst, C.J., Trivette, C.M., & Jodry, W. (1997). Influences of social support on children with disabilities and their families. In M.J. Guralnick (ed.), *The effectiveness of early intervention.* Baltimore, MA: Paul H. Brookes, pp. 499–522.

Fattore, T., Mason, J., & Watson, E. (2009). When children are asked about their well-being: Towards a framework for guiding policy. *Child Indicators Research, 2,* 57–77.

Garbarino, J., & Croucher, A. (1978). Defining the community context for parent–child relations: The correlates of child maltreatment. *Child Development, 49,* 604–616.

Garbarino, J., & Kostelny, K. (1992). Child maltreatment as a community problem. *Child Abuse & Neglect, 16,* 455–464.

Garbarino, J., & Sherman, D. (1980). High-risk neighborhoods and high-risk families: The human ecology of child maltreatment. *Child Development, 51,* 188–198.

Garmezy, N. (1994). Reflections and commentary on risk, resilience and development. In R.J. Haggerty, Sherrod, L.R., Garmezy, N., & Rutter, M. (eds), *Stress, risk and resilience in children and adolescents.* Cambridge: Cambridge University Press, pp. 1–18.

Ghate, D., & Hazel, N. (2002). *Parenting in poor environments: stress, support and coping.* London: Jessica Kingsley.

Gibbons, J. (1990). *Family support and prevention: Studies in local areas.* London: HMSO.

Gill, O., Tanner, C., & Bland, L. (2000). *Family support: Strengths and pressures in a high-risk neighbourhood.* Barkingside: Barnardo's.

Gill, O., & Jack, G. (2007). *The child and family in context: Developing ecological practice in disadvantaged communities.* Lyme Regis: Russell House.

Glass, T.A., & McAtee, M.J. (2006). Behavioral science at the crossroads in public health: Extending horizons, envisioning the future. *Social Science and Medicine, 62,* 1650–1671.

Gottlieb, B.H. (1981). Social networks and social support in community mental health. In B.H. Gottlieb (ed.), *Social networks and social support.* Beverley Hills, CA: Sage, pp. 11–42.

Graham, H. (2000). *Understanding health inequalities.* Buckingham: Open University Press.

Green, R. (2000). Applying a community needs profiling approach to tackling service user poverty. *British Journal of Social Work, 30,* 287–303.

Greene, S., Williams, J., Doyle, E., Harris, E., McCrory, C., Murray, A., Quail, A., Swords, L., Thornton, M., Layte, R., O'Dowd, T., & Whelan, C.T. (2009). *Growing up in Ireland – National longitudinal study of children: Review of the literature pertaining to the 9-year cohort.* Dublin: The Stationery Office.

Hartman, A. (1978). Diagrammatic assessment of family relationships. *Social Casework, 59,* 465–476.

Hawtin, M., Hughes, G., & Percy-Smith, J. (1994). *Community profiling: Auditing social needs.* Buckingham: Open University Press.

Hill, M. (2002). Network assessments and diagrams: A flexible friend for social work practice and education. *Journal of Social Work, 2,* 233–254.

Hoggett, P. (1997). *Contested communities: Experiences, struggles, policies.* Bristol: The Policy Press.

Holt-Lunstad, J., Smith, T.B., & Layton, J.B. (2010). Social relationships and mortality risk: A meta-analytic review. *PLoS Medicine, 7,* 1–20.

Jack, G., & Gill, O. (2003). *The missing side of the triangle: Assessing the importance of family and environmental factors in the lives of children.* Barkingside: Barnardo's.

Jack G., & Gill, O. (2010). The role of communities in safeguarding children and young people. *Child Abuse Review, 19,* 82–96.

Jack, G., & Jack, D. (2000). Ecological social work: The application of a systems model of development in context. In P. Stepney & Ford, D. (eds), *Social work models, methods and theories: A framework for practice.* Lyme Regis: Russell House, pp. 93–104.

Kessler, R.C., & McLeod, J.D. (1985). Social support and mental health in community samples. In S. Cohen & Syme, S.L. (eds), *Social support and health.* Orlando, FL: Academic Press.

Korbin, J.E. (1989). Fatal maltreatment by mothers: A proposed framework. *Child Abuse and Neglect, 13,* 481–489.

Lewin, K. (1936). *Principles of topological psychology.* New York: McGraw-Hill.

Lounsbury, D.W., & Mitchell, S.G. (2009). Introduction to special issue on social ecological approaches to community health research and action. *American Journal of Community Psychology, 44,* 213–220.

Luster, T., & Okagaki, L. (1993). Multiple influences on parenting: Ecological and life-course perspectives. In T. Luster & Okagaki, L. (eds), *Parenting: An ecological perspective.* Hillsdale, NJ: Lawrence Erlbaum Associates, pp. 227–250.

Moncher, F. (1995). Social isolation and child abuse risk. *Families in Society: The Journal of Contemporary Social Services, 76*(3), 421–431.

Murtagh, B. (1999). Listening to communities: Locality research and planning. *Urban Studies, 36,* 1181–1193.

Nelson, S., & Baldwin, N. (2004). The Craigmillar project: Neighbourhood mapping to improve children's safety from sexual crime. *Child Abuse Review, 13*, 415–425.

Newton, J. (1992). *Preventing mental illness in practice*. London: Routledge.

Packman, J., with Randall, J., & Jacques, N. (1986). *Who needs care? Social work decisions about children*. Oxford: Blackwell.

Polansky, N.A., Gaudin, J.M., Ammons, P.W., & Davis, K.B. (1985). The psychological ecology of the neglectful mother. *Child Abuse and Neglect, 9*, 265–275.

Putnam, R.D. (2000). *Bowling alone: The collapse and revival of American community*. New York: Touchstone.

Quinton, D., Rutter, M., & Liddle, C. (1984). Institutional rearing, parenting difficulties and marital support. *Psychological Medicine, 14*, 107–124.

Rutter, M. (1979). Protective factors in children's responses to stress and disadvantage. In M.W. Kent & Rolf, J.E. (eds), *Primary prevention of psychopathology* (Vol. 3). Hanover, NH: University Press of New England, pp. 49–74.

Sampson, R.J., Raudenbush, S.W., & Earls, F. (1997). Neighbourhoods and violent crime: A multi-level study of collective efficacy. *Science, 277*, 1–7.

Sarason, B.R., Sarason, I.G., & Pierce, G.R. (eds), *Social support: An interactional view*. New York: Wiley.

Shaw, M., Dorling, D., Gordon, D., & Davey Smith, G. (1999). *The widening gap: Health inequalities and policy in Britain*. Bristol: The Policy Press.

Sidebotham, P, Heron, J., & the ALSPAC Study Team (2006). Child maltreatment in the 'children of the nineties': A cohort study of risk factors. *Child Abuse and Neglect, 30*, 497–522.

Thompson, N. (2006). *Anti-discriminatory practice* (4th ed.). Basingstoke: Palgrave.

Thompson, R.A. (1995). *Preventing child maltreatment through social support*. Thousand Oaks, CA: Sage.

Tracey, E.M. (1990). Identifying social support resources of at-risk families. *Social Work, 35*, 252–258.

Tracey, E.M., & Whittaker, J.K. (1990). The social network map: Assessing social support in clinical practice. *Families in Society: The Journal of Contemporary Social Services, 71*, 461–470.

Trivette, C.M., Dunst, C.J., & Deal, A. (1997). Resource-based approach to early intervention. In S.K. Thurman, Cornwell, J.R., & Gottwald, S.R. (eds), *Contexts of early intervention: Systems and settings*. Baltimore, MA: Paul H. Brookes, pp. 73–92.

Vinson, T., Baldry, W., & Hargreaves, J. (1996). Neighbourhoods, networks and child abuse. *British Journal of Social Work, 26*, 523–543.

Warren, C. (1993). *Family centres and the Children Act 1989: A training and development handbook*. Arundel: Tarrant Publishing Ltd.

Wills, T.A. (1985). Supportive functions of interpersonal relationships. In S. Cohen & Syme, S.L. (eds), *Social support and health*. Orlando, FL: Academic Press, pp. 61–82.

Wright, S. (2004). Child protection in the community. *Child Abuse Review, 13*, 384–398.

9

Behavioural Perspectives

Eileen Gambrill

Behavioural perspectives have captured the attention of social work practitioners and scholars in many countries. Behavioural methods were first introduced into social work in the 1960s at the University of Michigan by Edwin Thomas, who arranged a symposium that resulted in the publication of *The Socio-Behavioural Approach and Applications to Social Work* (Thomas, 1967). Research grants he received in those early years provided an opportunity to design behavioural practice guidelines for use in open practice settings (e.g., Gambrill et al., 1971; Thomas & Walter, 1973).

HALLMARKS OF BEHAVIOURAL PRACTICE

Hallmarks of a behavioural approach are compatible with historical interests of the profession such as drawing on empirical research to inform decisions, attending to environmental as well as psychological factors, 'starting where the client is' (conducting an individualised assessment), and building on personal and environmental resources (a strength-based, constructional approach; see Chapter 11). Although there are different 'kinds' of behavioural intervention, all share certain characteristics (see Table 9.1). If they do not, they drift away from what would accurately be called behavioural.

All emphasise the central importance of operant and respondent learning, for example, in understanding diverse cultural practices. Cognitivism (a sole focus on thoughts as the cause of behavior with little attention to environmental circumstances) is rejected. In behavioural views, actions, thoughts, and feelings are considered to be largely a function of learning histories, both past and present. Behaviour is considered to be influenced by the interaction between the kinds of learning experiences we have, as well as our genetic endowment, including different arousal thresholds. Biochemical and genetic influences are assumed to play a role; however, their interaction with learning variables is emphasised. For example, genetic differences in arousal thresholds affect the likelihood of developing anxiety reactions as does the availability of alternative repertoires that compete with anxiety-eliciting cues. Varied social histories result in a wide range

Table 9.1 Indicators of behavioural practice

A. What will be found

1. A focus on achieving hoped-for outcomes of concern to clients and significant others.
2. Translation of complaints into specific behaviours (including thoughts and feelings) that if altered would remove complaints. This may involve behaviour of significant others including staff in residential settings, parents, supervisors.
3. Use of empirical data regarding basic behavioural principles and related learning theory to guide assessment and intervention.
4. A constructional approach in which client assets and local resources are identified that can be put to good use in attaining desired outcomes including available skills and reinforcer profiles.
5. Descriptive analysis of concerns and related circumstances based on observation in real-life circumstances when feasible and relevant (i.e., clear description of related behaviours, setting events, antecedents, and consequences) including positive alternatives to undesired behaviours.
6. Functional analysis: Identification of factors that influence behaviours of concern by rearranging environmental factors and observing the effects.
7. Involvement of significant others who interact with clients and influence their behaviour.
8. Selection of intervention programmes based on what research suggests is effective and what clients find acceptable.
9. Ongoing evaluation of progress using both subjective and objective measures; comparison of data gathered during intervention with baseline data when feasible.
10. Clear description of assessment, intervention, and evaluation methods.
11. A concern for social validity; outcomes attained are valued by clients and significant others; procedures used are acceptable to clients.
12. Planning for generalization and maintenance of positive gains.

B. What will not be found

1. Appeals to thoughts or feelings as the causes of behaviour.
2. Appeals to personality dispositions as causes of behaviour.
3. Reliance on diagnostic labels; they provide neither information about problem-related causes nor guidelines for selecting plans.
4. Reliance on self-report alone for assessment and evaluation.
5. Vague statements of hoped-for outcomes, problems, and progress indicators.
6. Claims of success based on questionable criteria such as testimonials, and anecdotal experience.

of behaviour as illustrated in anthropological research. In addition, there are unique 'biological boundaries' on learning in different species and unique physiological influences on individuals. Research in both applied and laboratory settings has repeatedly demonstrated that it is possible to have reliable influence over behaviour by systematically varying environmental antecedents and consequences. It is this research that has yielded the principles of behaviour that describe relationships between behaviour and the environment.

All behavioural practice models share a commitment to a scientific approach to understanding behaviour in which procedures are clearly described, testable theories are preferred, and accuracy is tested by gaining feedback about outcomes. The contextual focus inherent in a behavioural perspective requires involvement of significant others – those who interact with and influence clients. The behavioural model, especially applied behaviour analysis, can be viewed as a consultation model in which professionals often help mediators, such as parents, teachers, or staff, to acquire valuable skills for interacting with their 'significant others' (e.g., children or residents). This consultant model emphasises the importance of domain-specific knowledge and skills, and the value of forming a collaborative working relationship (e.g., see Bergan & Kratochwill, 1990).

Rejection of special causative factors related to troubled or troubling behaviours and feelings

In the behavioural model, unlike the psychiatric model of behaviour (see Chapter 33), no sharp distinction is made concerning the causes of behaviour labelled as normal and behaviour labelled as abnormal ('disordered' or deviant). All behaviour is assumed to be influenced by the same principles of behaviour, even those that seem unusual. Behaviour viewed as deviant or 'disordered' typically serves adaptive functions, although at a high cost. Unique learning histories, involving both respondent and operant learning, create unique meanings for events (cueing and reinforcing influences for each individual). However, only when related contingencies (relationship between behaviours and their antecedents consequences) are clarified may the functions of behaviour become apparent. Behaviour always 'makes sense' in this manner.

Antecedents acquire influence over behaviour by virtue of their relation to the consequences of behaviour. Individual variations occur in response to different life experiences that, in turn, result in different kinds and degrees of vulnerability and resilience. A contextual view highlights the importance of understanding a person's 'environment' and related risks, challenges, and opportunities. Aggressive behaviours may occur because a child has not acquired effective social skills. Environmental contingencies are often 'hidden'. They are often not obvious, but must be discovered by observation. They are less vivid compared with our thoughts and feelings, which, because of this vividness, we often (mistakenly) assume, cause our behaviour.

Emphasis on the role of learning in developing and maintaining behaviour, rejection of a 'disease model' regarding troubled or troubling behavior including substance use (e.g., Heyman, 2009; see Chapter 37), decreases the likelihood of imposing negative labels on clients that provide little, if any, guidelines for removing complaints and that are stigmatising in the bargain. Indeed, it is ironic that social workers have embraced a psychiatric model to such a degree in the USA, given the historic attention to environmental influences related to concerns such as poverty and its consequences. For example, a review of class syllabi in psychopathology courses in social work programmes in the USA revealed an emphasis on a psychiatric framing of problems (LaCasse & Gomory, 2003).

Behaviour is of interest

Behaviour and the translation of concerns into behaviours that, if changed, would achieve hoped-for outcomes is the central subject matter of applied behaviour analysis. Behaviour refers to what people do, not to what they say they do (Baer et al., 1968, 1987). Cognitive behavioural therapists attend to covert behaviours (thoughts such as unrealistic expectations) as well as to overt behaviours of concern and related circumstances.

A preference for observation and testing assumptions

There is a preference for exploring the accuracy of beliefs by critically testing assumptions. Hunches are checked by identifying, via and/or self-monitoring observation, what behaviours (public or private) seem to be related to concerns (a descriptive analysis) and, based on this descriptive analysis, varying specific events and reviewing the results (conducting a functional analysis). Relevant interactions, for example, between parents and children, or staff and residents are observed in real-life settings (when feasible and possible) by clients or trained observers. There is an extensive literature describing the use of observation of interaction patterns, for example, between children and their teachers and parents, children and their peers, and staff and residents in residential settings.

Focus on current concerns and related antecedents and consequences

There is an interest in the relationship between current behaviour and related antecedents and consequences, as well as past patterns. Past learning experiences are assumed to be reflected in current behaviour. Joseph Wolpe (1990) applied principles of learning to the treatment of anxiety, using gradual exposure to feared events or objects to decrease fear. Anxiety was viewed as a learned reaction. Different people have different learning histories and arousal thresholds. Cultural values and related contingencies encourage particular reactions. Contingencies are associations between behaviour and what happens right after (consequences) and right before (antecedents) behaviour. Contingency management involves rearranging consequences and antecedents related to behaviours of concern to attain valued outcomes.

Selection of assessment and intervention methods is informed by related research

Practice is informed by empirical research both in applied and in laboratory settings that describes associations between behaviour and related factors. In areas in which research is sparse, behavioural principles and related theory are used to guide decisions. Behavioural principles describe different kinds of contingencies and their effects (e.g., positive and negative reinforcement) and factors that influence them, such as scheduling and contrast effects (e.g., Alberto & Troutman, 2008; Cooper et al., 2007; Martin & Pear, 2010; Sundel & Sundel, 2005). Replication is required to determine whether relationships found hold up on further intervention. If research demonstrates that observation of behaviour in the natural environment offers valuable information that complements and corrects impressions given by self-reports, then this kind of data will also be gathered if feasible and ethical. If the literature shows that one kind of intervention is more effective than another, then within ethical and practice limits, this is recommended.

Assessment and intervention are individualised

Each individual has a unique learning history as well as unique genetic and physiological differences. It is assumed that factors related to concerns can only be identified through an individualised, contextual assessment. This is the case whether the client is an individual, family, group, organisation, or community. A behavioural analysis includes a description of behaviours of concern as well as evidence that specific antecedents and consequences affect them. It requires a clear description of hoped-for outcomes as well as the behaviours needed to attain them, and description of the 'entering repertoires' of involved individuals (skills they already possess).

There is a review of both personal and environmental factors that may influence concerns and options. Possible influences include public policies and related legislation, other people's actions, the physical environment (e.g., community, neighbourhood, and classroom characteristics), tasks and materials, physiological changes, thoughts, arousal thresholds, and developmental factors. Contingencies on many levels, including political, economic, and social practices and policies, affect behaviour and options for change (Lamal,

1991; Lattal & Chase, 2010; Mattaini, 1993a).

A range of assessment methods is used as relevant and feasible, including self-report in the interview, role playing, observation in real-life settings, physiological measures, and self-monitoring (clients keep track of behaviours, thoughts, feelings, or outcomes in real-life settings). Because one method may not be accurate, multiple methods are used. Labelling is not of interest. Incentives are selected based on what is effective for each individual. Important distinctions include: (i) form and function; (ii) lack of motivation and lack of valuable behaviours; and (iii) response inhibition (e.g., high anxiety) and lack of needed skills. Overlooking these distinctions may result in selection of ineffective plans. The form of behaviour (its topography) does not indicate its function (why the behaviour occurs). Identical forms of behaviour may be maintained by very different contingencies. Just as the same behaviour may have different functions, different behaviours may have identical functions. Another important distinction is between lack of motivation and lack of needed behaviours. If a desired behaviour does not occur, its absence may point to either a lack of behaviour or lack of effective contingencies (a motivational concern).

A focus on outcomes that are important to client and significant others

Focus is on attaining outcomes that are clinically and socially significant: Do outcomes attained make a positive difference in the lives of clients? Do they result in positive gains in the future? The opinions of clients and significant others are sought to assess the social validity of outcomes (Schwartz & Baer, 1991). Attention to social as well as personal outcomes is a hallmark of applied behaviour analysis in which there is an emphasis on the social validity of procedures used, as well as effects (i.e., significant others as well as clients must be satisfied with results achieved if outcomes are judged a success). Clients are encouraged to involve significant others and to pursue changes that all parties value.

Clear description of concerns and hoped-for outcomes

Problems are translated into behaviours that would solve problems if changed. Because objectives are clearly stated, clients are in a better position to evaluate the success of services offered. Concerns differ in the complexity and variety of outcomes that must be achieved to resolve them. Some require changes in different behaviours in a variety of settings.

A close relationship between assessment and intervention

Attention to individual differences encourages a close link between assessment and intervention. Intervention methods are selected based on an individualised assessment. These are uniquely tailored to the particular circumstance of each client.

There is an educational and skill-building aim

Behavioural practice involves a constructional approach (e.g., see Gambrill, 2006; Schwartz & Goldiamond, 1975). There is an emphasis on helping clients to acquire the knowledge and skills needed to remove complaints and to achieve hoped-for outcomes. For example, in social skills training, clients acquire more effective interpersonal skills that benefit both themselves as well as others. Behavioural social workers draw on client assets, involve significant others, and search for neighbourhood and community resources that facilitate change.

Clear description of procedures

There is an emphasis on clear description of assessment and intervention methods. This fulfills one of the conditions for informed consent. Clear description makes it possible to gather data about the effects of methods. Differential reinforcement is often used in which desired behaviour is positively reinforced and undesired behaviour is no longer reinforced. Punishment is avoided because of both ethical and practical reasons (e.g., it is not effective in increasing and maintaining desired alternative behaviours).

Careful tracking of progress

There is a concern for collecting both subjective (client reports) as well as objective data regarding the effects of intervention (e.g., does a parent provide more positive feedback to her child and fewer punishing events?). For example, the frequency, magnitude, or duration of behaviours of concern before intervention (baseline) is compared with the frequency, magnitude, or duration during change efforts. Single-case designs are used to track progress so that timely decisions can be made depending on degree of progress (e.g., Bloom et al., 2009; Kazi, 1998). Data concerning progress provides feedback for both clients and social workers as to what is working (or not) and to what degree.

Planning for generalisation and maintenance

Behavioural practice involves planning for the generalisation and durability of change in real-life settings both during assessment (e.g., involving significant others) as well as intervention (fading out any artificial procedures). For example, if family members are partially responsible for maintaining the troubling behaviour of a relative, their involvement in assessment and intervention is more likely to result in the maintenance of positive outcomes (e.g., see Pinkston & Linsk, 1984). Behavioural practice also involves planning for the generalisation of effects to other situations, behaviours, or both.

A concern with ethical issues

Many characteristics of behavioural practice are directly related to ethical practice: selecting procedures based on the empirical literature as well as acceptability to clients, building on client assets, increasing clients' options through increasing their skills and knowledge, clearly identifying desired outcomes, carefully tracking progress, avoiding punishment, clearly describing procedures, and pursuing outcomes that help clients and significant others to improve the quality of their lives (see, e.g., Van Houten et al., 1988). Effective parent training programmes involve parents and are designed to increase positive parenting skills (e.g., Barth et al., 2009). Consideration of ethical concerns requires a review of outcomes pursued in terms of unfair pressures on clients and significant others as well as avoidance of negative labels, including psychiatric diagnoses that reflect the consensus of professionals based on changing values.

VARIETIES OF BEHAVIOURAL PRACTICE, THEORY, AND PHILOSOPHY

Variations in behavioural views, such as cognitive behavioural and radical behavioural, reflect different assumptions about the causes of behaviour and what intervention should focus on (thoughts and or environmental factors), and different preferred methodologies (the study of group differences, or the intensive study of individuals). However, all emphasise the role of environmental contingencies (associations between behaviour and related antecedents, and consequences and recurrent patterns over time) and options for change via rearranging such contingencies.

Radical behaviourism

Radical behaviourism is the philosophy related to applied behaviour analysis, as well as a theoretical account of behaviour some believe to be thoughtful and comprehensive (e.g., see Lattel & Chase, 2010; Rachlin, 1991; Skinner, 1974; Thyer, 1999). The role of selection by consequences is emphasized (Skinner, 1981). The belief in a 'science of behaviour' is a basic premise of radical behaviourism (i.e., the belief that behaviour is knowable and that knowledge can be discovered through empirical inquiry). It is not claimed that a radical behavioural perspective is the only scientific psychology. However, it is argued that this and related scientific approaches are most likely to yield knowledge about behaviour and how it can be altered, compared to other approaches.

Radical behaviourism is perhaps more misunderstood and misrepresented, and attracts more objections than any other perspective in psychology (Thyer, 2005; see misconceptions and myths later). Radical behaviourism does not embrace associationism, operationism, positivism, or environmental determinism. It is not assumed that contingencies determine behavior. To so assign such causal power is labelled 'radical environmentalism' and radical behaviourism does not advocate radical environmentalism. Radical behaviourism is so named because it represented a radical break with earlier forms such as John Watson's methodological behaviourism. Not only are private events such as thoughts and feelings not dismissed, they are viewed as behaviours that themselves require an explanation (traced to their environmental, evolutionary, and or physiological origins). They are assumed to have the same functions as public (observable) events (see, e.g., Skinner's [1974] discussion of the self as well as Diller & Lattal, 2008; Hayes et al., 2001). The advantage of viewing thoughts and feelings as behaviours is that they cannot as readily be inaccurately presumed to be the sole cause of behaviour; they themselves are behaviours in need of explanation.

Applied behaviour analysis

Applied behaviour analysis involves the application of findings from the experimental analysis of behaviour to outcomes of importance to individuals, families, groups, communities, and policy decisions at state and federal levels. It involves the systematic investigation of variables that influence behaviour (Baer et al., 1968, 1987). Such analysis is contextual. It calls for identification of the contingencies (associations between behaviours and related antecedents and consequences) that influence behaviours of concern at multiple system levels. Central to applied behaviour analysis is rearranging contingencies. This requires information about what these contingencies are. Such information may be gathered in a variety of ways, including reports in interviews and observation in real-life situations.

Causes of behaviour are sought in the relationships between behaviour and environmental events, not in the feelings and thoughts that are considered to be collateral effects or byproducts of these contingencies (Skinner, 1969, 1974). In everyday life we often attribute behaviour to feelings. Such accounts are incomplete. They are partial. Feelings and thoughts are vivid, thus readily available to assume as causes of behaviour. In contrast, environmental circumstances are often less vivid, and so easily overlooked, especially by professionals who rely on clients' self-report in interviews. So too is our past history (biographies that shaped our behaviour) typically less vivid, unless focused on as in certain kinds of therapy. This encourages confusion between feeling free and being free. As Skinner (1971) suggests, simply because you feel free does not mean you are uninfluenced by your environments.

Behaviour analysis emphasises the importance of a functional assessment of behaviour in which environmental factors related to behaviours of interest are identified through rearranging contingencies (altering what happens before and after behaviour). This is preceded by a descriptive analysis based on data collection in real-life situations when relevant and feasible. Private events (e.g., thoughts and feelings) as well as public events are assumed to be subject to environmental influence. Although behavioural principles are clearly spelled out, their application to real-life concerns is often complex, requiring conceptual understanding as well as technical knowledge (e.g. see Layng, 2009). Consider also Heyman's (2009) analysis of addiction. He notes the different effects of short- and long-term consequences in 'choice' behaviour (to drink or not) in his critique of the disease model of substance misuse. Gambling behaviour is maintained by a schedule of reinforcement that produces a high rate of behaviour and is difficult to extinguish.

Applied refers to the extent to which a behaviour is socially important. Behaviour refers to what people do. The social validity of outcomes is emphasised; behaviours focused on must have immediate importance to involved individuals. Thus, significant others, such as teachers, parents, or residential staff, are included in assessing the value of changes that occur. The social validity of procedures is emphasised; procedures used must be acceptable to clients and significant others. Real rather than conceptual influence is of interest. The latter refers to writing theoretical descriptions, that is, behaviour must change, not just what involved parties say has changed. The effects of altering a given variable are tracked on an ongoing basis.

Analytic requires 'a believable demonstration of the events that can be responsible for the occurrence or nonoccurrence of that behaviour' (Baer et al., 1968, p. 94) – a demonstration of experimental control by altering presumed causes:

> The analytic challenges for anyone who deserves to be called an 'applied behavior analyst' are: (a) to restate the complained-of problem in behavioural terms; (b) to change the behaviors indicated by that restatement; and then (c) to see whether changing them has decreased the complaining response (Baer, 1982, p. 284).

Procedures used should be clearly described so that others can replicate them and the conceptual analysis should be consistent with behavioural principles. The analysis of behaviour has been achieved when one can exercise influence over it. Another characteristic of this framework is a concern with generalisation and maintenance. Is a desired behaviour change durable; is it maintained over time? Does it occur in other environments and involve other individuals not focused on?

Applied behaviour analysts have taken a leading role in developing and evaluating programmes of benefit to a wide range of clients, including students at all levels of education, people with developmental and physical disabilities, people with chronic pain, pre-delinquents, those involved in the criminal justice system, the unemployed, the elderly, clients who misuse drugs and alcohol, the depressed, parents, and children, and clients alleged to have severe 'mental disorders' (e.g., see Briggs & Rzepnicki, 2004: Hawken & Johnston, 2008). Operant theory and related methods have contributed important principles and guidance to social work and other helping professions such as use of positive reinforcement and avoidance of punishment when possible as a way to alter behaviour, given its many limitations. There is an extensive behavioural literature in the area of health (behavioural medicine), organisational change, and school wide positive behavioural support systems (Sailor et al., 2009; Scott et al., 2008; Sugai & Horner, 2005). It has been applied to community concerns such as helping residents to decrease their utility bills (e.g., see review in Mattaini, 1993a).

A radical behavioural view is inherently political. It emphasises the mutual influence of people and their environments. This contextual view encourages us to dig beneath the surface of slogans such as 'empowerment' and 'social justice' to determine what they mean – do hoped-for outcomes occur? A behavioural analysis reveals rather than hides contexts including discriminatory arrest patterns involving young African-American men for small amounts of marijuana and imprisoning them encouraged by the 'war on drugs' in the USA (Alexander, 2010). Examination of 'meta-contingencies' reveals political, legal, economic, and social incentives and related values that create and maintain social and personal problems (e.g., see Lamal, 1991). Our environments are interlinked at multiple levels, each of which hold certain risks and provide certain opportunities. The knowledge, skills, and values we develop and the environments we create are related to the risks and opportunities we confront, which are influenced by environmental contingencies.

Our experiences create changes in the brain, which, in turn, influence our moods and behaviour. Change on one level may create opportunities and risks on another. If it is not possible to create desired changes on one level, it may be possible on another. Recognising the connections between economic, political, and social influences (including cultural differences) and personal characteristics (choices we make) can help us to avoid oversimplified causal views that focus only on interiors (psychological and biological characteristics of individuals), ignoring environmental influences, such as discriminatory practices and policies. Focusing on interiors such as thoughts and brain diseases allows the creators of influential contingencies to remain unknown while blaming the less powerful.

Skinner suggested that the only way to exert counter-control regarding controlling policies and practice was to understand how we are controlled. Only in this way may sources of discrimination and oppression be identified. If I can convince you that your problems are due to a brain disease or to your feelings and thoughts, you are not likely to look around and examine your environments to explore related factors [see, e.g., Ehrenreich's (2009) critique of positive psychology]. Consider who benefits and who loses from focusing on altering self-esteem of children in classrooms when change is needed in the design of school contingency systems (e.g., Sugai & Horner, 2005).

Cognitive behavioural methods

Cognitive behavioural methods focus on altering thoughts such as rules and expectations as well as overt behaviours presumed to be related to complaints. An analysis of both cognitive and environmental variables related to problems is conducted to prepare a case formulation. Cognitive variables are assumed to play an important mediating role. Various conceptions of thought processes include conditioning (e.g., thoughts reflect learning experiences and function as cues and consequences), information processing (e.g., focus is on encoding, decoding what is perceived), and constructive narrative (we construct our own realities and representations of the world). Each conception may suggest a somewhat (or very) different focus. Here too, an individual assessment and careful evaluation of progress is considered important as is the testing of assumptions. Behavioural methods such as social skills training and exposure to feared situations accompany cognitive methods as relevant, thus the name cognitive behavioural therapy.

Thoughts are addressed, both as events to be influenced (such as a high frequency of negative self-statements) and as cues and consequences that influence behaviours and feelings. Techniques are aimed directly at altering cognitions including schema (internal models of self or the world presumed to be involved in perceiving, coding, and recalling information) and unrealistic expectations (everyone must like me). It is assumed that we present an important part of our environment via our expectations, goals, and standards. Social learning theory involves an information-processing view in which verbal and classical conditioning, social influence, and incentive effects are addressed in cognitive terms. The importance of vicarious learning experiences via observation of others is emphasised.

Thoughts are considered to play an important role in the complex processes that affect attention and in the degree to which different kinds of interventions are effective in altering 'self-efficacy'. It is assumed that efficacy expectations develop through learning experience. Thus, both social learning theory and radical behaviourism stress the role of learning. Emotional reactions are altered through respondent conditioning (altering the relationship between stimulus events). Here too, learning principles are appealed to. In cognitive behavioural programmes designed to decrease social anxiety, participants learn to identify anxiety-provoking thoughts (e.g., 'I'll faint' or 'I'll look like a fool') and to focus on functional tasks. In addition, exposure to feared situations is arranged. Other commonly used behavioural methods include activity scheduling (for depression), graded task assignments, behavioural rehearsal, and relaxation training. Cognitive behavioural methods have been promoted by the government in the UK as 'evidence-based' interventions.

Over the past few years, acceptance and commitment therapy (ACT), guided by relational frame theory (RFT) has gained in popularity. ACT makes use of acceptance and mindfulness interventions as well as commitment and behaviour change strategies (e.g., see Hayes & Strosahl, 2010). RFT concerns the way in which language affects our lives and involves us in futile efforts (e.g., Hayes et al., 2001). The Association for Contextual Behavioural Science was initiated to create a new form of behaviour analysis. The later term was not used because of misunderstandings of behaviour analysis according to the creators of the organisation. This new form pays key attention to language and cognition drawing on research related to RFT. It is argued that one should be familiar with behavioural principles to comprehend both ACT and RFT. These developments are sometimes referred to as 'third-generation behaviour therapy' (see Hayes et al., 2004). Functional analytic psychotherapy focuses on the therapeutic relationship (e.g., see Kohlenberg et al., 1996, 2006). Dialectical behaviour therapy draws on both cognitive and behavioural principles and methods as well as Buddhist ideas of acceptance and commitment (Linehan, 1993).

MYTHS AND MISCONCEPTIONS ABOUT CONTINGENCY MANAGEMENT

Misconceptions and misinformation about behavioural approaches have hindered use of valuable theory and methods. Distorted descriptions of behavioural approaches are common, especially radical behaviourism (Thyer, 2005). Acquiring an accurate understanding of related theory and research requires deep reading and an accurate understanding of what science is and what it is not.

Altering contingencies dehumanises people

For both practical and ethical reasons, goals pursued should be selected by clients and significant others and a collaborative working relationship should be established that emphasises client involvement in making decisions. A contextual assessment in which relevant environmental contingencies are explored decreases the likelihood of 'victim blaming' – viewing clients as the cause of problems. Helping clients acquire positive behaviour change skills increases their influence over their environments in ways that maximise positive consequences.

Contingencies are all powerful

Often it is not an easy matter to change someone's behaviour without his or her awareness. If we do not want our behaviour altered, it is unlikely that others can do so unless they have access to influential contingencies. Genetic differences in arousal thresholds, as well as other biological factors, also influence behaviour.

Underlying causes are not addressed

In contrast to the belief that contingencies are all powerful is the belief that they have little or no influence and, that if we focus on them, we ignore underlying causes such as feelings and thoughts. Behaviour, feelings, and thoughts are influenced by environmental contingencies. Thousands of studies both in laboratory and applied settings have demonstrated the effects of consequences on behaviour, thoughts, and feelings. This does not imply radical environmentalism (the belief that our behaviour is determined by environmental events); many other influences come into play. Any approach, including contingency analysis, can be carried out in an ineffective manner in which key contingencies are ignored (e.g., Kunkel, 1970). A contextual analysis of both self-presented and environmental contingencies is required to describe concerns and identify promising options clearly. Such an analysis and accompanied related plans minimise the likelihood of unwanted negative effects due to an incomplete assessment.

Thoughts and feelings are not considered

Thoughts and feelings provide clues about contingencies (e.g., our experiences with certain individuals) and cognitive behavioural programmes focus directly on altering them (e.g., increasing helpful self-statements). They are integrally involved in 'rule-governed' behaviour (verbal description of contingencies that may or may not reflect those in real life). However, focusing solely on thoughts and feelings (as in 'He hit her because he was angry') provides *incomplete* accounts. For example, we do not know the antecedents to 'anger' or the consequences of related behaviours such as hitting that may maintain them. Nor do we know what repertoires may be missing (e.g., effective conflict resolution skills) that may be integral to the persistence of disliked behaviours such as aggression.

Individual differences are ignored

Attention to individual differences is a hallmark of contingency analysis. Individuals, families, groups, organisations, and communities differ in their reinforcer and punisher profiles (what is valued and what is disliked) and related contingencies. Only if the unique value of different consequences to different individuals, groups, organisations, or communities is understood can successful programmes be implemented. For a classic example of the failure of economic development programmes due to lack of attention to cultural differences, see Kunkel (1970). Each individual has a unique learning history moulded by his or her culture as well as by genetic and physiological differences. Individual learning histories create unique 'meanings' of events for each individual, group, organisation, or community. Cultures differ in their reinforcer profile.

The helper–client relationship is unimportant

Warmth, respect, and empathy contribute to mutual understanding and a collaborative working relationship as shown by the extensive literature in this area. However, the relationship is not viewed as the only or even key source of change. Candid recognition of the social influence effects in the helping process decreases the likelihood that they will be used (knowingly or not) in unethical and ineffective ways.

People learn how to manipulate each other

Manipulation refers to influencing others in an unfair or fraudulent way for one's own profit (*Webster's New World Collegiate Dictionary*, 1988). Helping clients attain outcomes they value in a context of informed consent is hardly manipulative. Helping clients to acquire effective behaviour change skills increases their influence over their environments (a large part of which may be provided by other people), but it does not teach them to manipulate this environment in an insidious or unfair way. So, too, with social skills training in which clients acquire more effective relationships skills that offer benefits both to themselves and to others.

Control is imposed where none exists

This incorrect belief overlooks sources of influence already present. People have been trying to change other people's behaviour throughout the centuries. Many people either do not possess or do not use positive change skills, and rely instead on negative methods such as criticism, nagging, and hitting. Much unhappiness and misery results. Problems are often aggravated by use of punitive methods. Not only may this be ineffective, it creates bad feelings as well as counteraggression. Both punishing and nonreinforcing environments contribute to burnout among helpers and are related to problems such as depression and anxiety. Just because pre-existing contingencies are not 'planned', does not mean they are without influence. Viewing people as totally free contributes to misplaced blame on families and individuals for problems such as poverty, discrimination and oppression; political and economic causes are overlooked. Denying the influence of environmental contingencies no more negates their effects than would the law of gravity be suspended if we did not believe it. However, denial of such influence does permit those in privileged positions to blame poverty, discrimination, and oppression on those who experience them.

Contingencies that already exist are more natural

It is sometimes said that the contingencies that already exist are 'more natural', meaning that no one has arranged them to attain given ends and that they do more good than harm. Actually, many contingencies are deliberately arranged by, for example, governmental agencies. The public relations and advertising industries are in business to influence our behaviour and to make a profit in doing so. Ethical problems cannot be avoided by refusing to recognise influence and its consequences. The question is: 'Who benefits and who loses from ignorance about influential contingencies?' If knowledge about and skill in altering real-life contingencies provide freedom from unwanted influence, isn't this a benefit rather than a harm?

I'm already doing it

One way to discount something new is to say: 'I already know that'; 'I already do it'. We rearrange contingencies every day. This does not mean we do so in a systematic way in pursuit of specific outcomes. It is the systematic nature of and a completeness with which contingencies are analysed and altered in relation to specific objectives together with the ongoing monitoring of progress that are key to success. Occasional unevaluated use of positive incentives to change vaguely or even well-defined behaviours is not likely to be successful, or success will be less than would be possible. Mallott (1994) suggests that we often resort to unconscious motivational explanations to understand why we and others do not follow through with actions that correspond with our values because of limited understanding of the causes of poor self-management (e.g., Watson & Tharp, 2007).

Extrinsic reinforcers undermine intrinsic ones

Some people argue that using reinforcement to alter behaviour (e.g., to increase study behaviour) undermines the intrinsic reinforcing value of behaviours. In fact, external reinforcers that are not functionally superfluous can be used to increase intrinsic motivation. Research in a number of areas illustrates the key role of corrective feedback in learning. External reinforcers should not be introduced when intrinsic ones are present unless the latter result in injury to self or others; contrived reinforcers should only be used when natural consequences are not feasible. New repertoires are made functional by arranging natural reinforcing consequences. If it is necessary to introduce artificial reinforcers, such as token or points, plans are made for their removal so that behaviour is maintained in real-life circumstances.

Rearranging contingencies takes little skill

There are a relatively small number of key concepts related to rearranging contingencies; however, their application in real life is often complex. Unless this is understood, a focus on rearranging contingencies may seem simple-minded. A contingency analysis requires an understanding of basic behavioural principles as well as a variety of assessment skills such as observation of interaction patterns. A contextual analysis may reveal the need to address complex social contingencies, such as the behaviour of local school boards, school principles, and school teachers as reflected in school-wide positive behaviour support systems (Sugai & Horner, 2005). Rearranging contingencies in a way that maximises the likelihood of attaining outcomes that clients value requires knowledge and skill. For example, there are different schedules of reinforcement that affect behaviour in different ways (e.g., rate of behaviour and resistance to extinction). Without a firm grasp of this knowledge, opportunities to help clients enhance the qualities of their lives may be lost because concerns are misunderstood. Both knowledge and accompanying procedural skills are needed to translate concerns into relevant behaviours, to discover maintaining conditions, and to select and implement effective plans. Behavioural cusps can be taken advantage of (Bosch & Fuqua, 2001) as well as scheduling effects.

Contingency management is only useful at the individual level

Understanding and rearranging contingencies are key aspects of helping clients at all system levels including the community (Jaime, et al., 2007). This is required to discover misapplied and unapplied contingencies related to situations of concern. Arranging management systems in service agencies that ensure high-quality services is of concern, not only to professionals, but to clients as well. Quality performance can be encouraged by identifying clear standards, arranging needed training and feedback, and involving all staff in setting standards and selecting feedback methods (LaVigna et al., 1994). Contingency analysis is also useful at the cultural level to explore how contingencies at different levels (individual, family, group, organisation, community, and policy) influence behaviours of interest (Kunkel, 1970).

SOCIAL WORK AND BEHAVIOURAL PERSPECTIVES

The social work contribution to behavioural practice is many faceted. One consists of using behavioural methods with new clients and problems or in new settings. For example, social workers have been in the forefront of applying behavioural methods to work with elderly clients and their caregivers (Pinkston & Linsk, 1984), and children and families (e.g., Dangel & Polster, 1984); couples (Stuart, 1980), unwanted pregnancies (Gilchrist et al., 1985), spouse battering (Edelson & Tolman, 1992), and work with groups (Rose, 1989; Tolman & Rose, 1990); for a more detailed discussion of earlier contributions, see Gambrill (1995). A second kind of contribution involves replicating behavioural procedures with similar clients or concerns or in similar settings. A third involves the creation and evaluation of new intervention programmes drawing on behavioural research and theory such as Edwin Thomas's unilateral family therapy with the spouses of alcoholics (Thomas et al., 1987).

Behaviourally oriented social workers have conducted clinical research with a wide range of clients, including parents and children (Smagner & Sullivan, 2005), people labelled schizophrenic (Wong et al., 2004); antisocial youth (e.g., Fraser et al., 2004), concerns of the elderly (e.g., Pinkston & Linsk, 1984), clients with obsessive compulsive behaviour (Steketee & Frost, 2006). Social workers have prepared books suggesting the value of behavioural theory and methods in social work. Examples are Corcoran (2005), Gambrill (2012a), Mattaini and Thyer (1996), Ronen and Freeman (2007), Sheldon and MacDonald (2008) and Wodarski (2009). Social workers have prepared reviews and books for use by all helping professionals. Recent examples include MacDonald (2001) and Sheldon (2010). They have encouraged use of single-case evaluations and suggested innovative uses of graphics designed to enhance practice effectiveness (Mattaini, 1993b).

The vision that some had in the 1960s of the future role of behavioural methods in social work has been realised only in part. It would be a safe bet to estimate that most social workers do not use behavioural methods in a way that maximises their potential to help clients. In some ways we have moved backwards. In the late 1960s, the University of Michigan, School of Social Work required all master's degree students to take a course in basic behavioural principles. (An advanced course was added at students' request.) To my knowledge no school of social work now does so. Few, if any, bachelor's or master's degree programmes in social work provide a deep understanding of related theory and empirical research coupled with working knowledge and skill in their effective applications. Applied behaviour analysis and the science and philosophy on which it is based have not been as popular among social workers as cognitive behavioural methods. Many embrace cognitive behavioural methods with a distinct preference for the cognitive over the behavioural. Some descriptions and applications border on cognitivism (see earlier discussion). The lure of cognitivism is strong and compatible with the popularity of mentalistic terms (Moore, 2001).

There has been a piecemeal use of behavioural methods that may confuse people about what behavioural practice is and dilute success. For example, in *Task Strategies*, William Reid (1992) rechristened scores of behavioural methods as 'task strategies' and separated practice recommendations from their conceptual origins (Gambrill, 1994). Thyer (2005) suggests that principles and practices are borrowed without attributing them to their origins, 'creating neologisms in order to gain the appearance of creating something new' (p. 331).

A number of factors continue to limit the extent to which social workers use behavioural methods, including lack of training and resources required to implement effective programmes. Obstacles include service systems which do not permit time for functional behavioural assessments and systematic intervention. Social workers often use individually focused methods with clients who have been harmed by discriminatory practices and policies. Such work is vital, but so is altering the harmful contingencies responsible for injustices. The behavioural perspective, especially radical behaviourism, calls for a contextual analysis in which influential contingency systems are examined on many levels. Such probing may be actively avoided by interested parties. The contextual analysis integral to applied behavioural analysis that is so compatible with social work's historical concern with the role of environmental factors and social reform is at odds with a 'band-aid' approach to 'pursuit of' hoped-for outcomes. Looking widely does not fit with the residual social service systems in which the searchlight is narrowly focused on client's thoughts and brains. Looking widely reveals influential practices and policies that are far beyond a focus on the individual.

Disagreements about the criteria that should be used to decide what knowledge is and how to get it interfere with critically testing claims of effectiveness. Misunderstanding of science (what it is and what it is not) is a key obstacle (Phillips, 2000). A behavioural perspective is at odds with the medicalisation of deviance that advances apace in the helping professions (Conrad, 2007; Gambrill, 2012b; Moynihan & Cassels, 2005; Szasz, 2007). It does not fit with the juggernaut of biological psychiatry with its focus on alleged 'brain disorders' and use of medication. It does not fit with the 'addiction industry' (e.g., Heyman, 2009).

THE FUTURE

Great strides have been made in the behavioural field at large in many areas, including behavioural medicine, developmental disabilities, anxiety and depression, individuals with severe 'mental illness,' parent–child interaction, delinquency, quality of educational settings and prevention including work in the community (e.g., Scott et al., 2008; Sugai & Horner, 2005), prevention (e.g., Hawkins & Johnston, 2008) and work in the community (e.g., Hawkins et al., 2010). Behavioural views comprise many of the ingredients in modular intervention programmes (e.g., Chorpita et al., 2005; Nakamura & Chorpita, 2004). Conceptual and methodological developments, such as taking advantage of momentum effects and behavioural cusps, illustrate promising options (e.g., Bosch & Fuqua, 2001; Pelaez et al., 2008).

The increasing call for accountability on the part of funding sources and consumer interest groups should encourage use of behavioural methods with demonstrated value in helping clients. The behavioural perspective shares with the philosophy of evidence-informed practice and policy, a concern to take advantage of research findings that can benefit clients within a collaborative relationship in which clients and significant others are involved as informed participants. It is not, contrary to what some claim, one of the origins of evidence-based practice. As with understanding any theory, deep rather than superficial reading is needed to understand and accurately represent it.

REFERENCES

Alberto, P.A., & Troutman, A.C. (2008). *Applied behavior analysis for teachers* (8th ed.). Upper Saddle River, NJ: Merrill/Prentice Hall.

Alexander, M. (2010). *The new Jim Crow: Mass incarceration in the age of color blindness.* New York: The New Press.

Baer, D.M. (1982). Applied behavior analysis. In G.T Wilson & Franks, C.F. (eds), *Contemporary behavior therapy: Conceptual and empirical foundations.* New York: Guilford, pp. 277–309.

Baer, D.M., Wolf, M.M., & Risley, T.R. (1968). Some current dimensions of applied behavior analysis. *Journal of Applied Behavior Analysis*, 1, 91–97.

Baer, D.M., Wolf, M.M., & Risley, T.R. (1987). Some still current dimensions of applied behavior analysis. *Journal of Behavior Analysis*, 20, 313–327.

Bandura, A. (1986). *Social foundations of thought and action.* Englewood Cliffs, NJ: Prentice Hall.

Barth, R.P., Landsverk, J., Chamberlain, P., Reid, J.B., Rolls, J. A., Hurlburt, M.S., et al. (2009). Parent-training programs in child welfare services: Planning for a more evidence-based approach to serving biological parents. *Research on Social Work Practice, 15*(5), 353–371.

Bergan, J.R., & Kratochwill, T.R. (1990). *Behavioural consultation in therapy.* New York: Plenum.

Bloom, M., Fischer, J., & Orme, J.G. (2009). *Evaluating practice: Guidelines for the accountable professional* (4th ed.). Boston: Allyn & Bacon.

Bosch, S., & Fuqua, R.W. (2001). Behavioural cusps: A model for selecting target behaviors. *Journal of Applied Behavior Analysis, 34*, 123–125.

Boerke, K.W., & Reitman, D. (2011). Token economies. In W.W. Fisher, C.C. Piazza & H.S. Roane (eds) (2011), *Handbook of Applied Behavior Analysis.* New York: Guilford.

Briggs, H.E., & Rzepnicki, T. (eds) (2004). *Using evidence in social work practice: Behavioural perspectives.* Chicago, IL: Lyceum.

Chorpita, B.F., Daleiden, E., & Weisz, J.R. (2005). Modularity in the design and application of therapeutic interventions. *Applied and Preventive Psychology, 11*, 141–156.

Conrad, P. (2007). *The medicalization of society: On the transformation of human conditions into treatment disorders.* Baltimore, MD: John Hopkins University Press.

Cooper, J., Heron, T., & Heward, W. (2007). *Applied behavior analysis.* Upper Saddle River, NJ: Prentice Hall.

Corcoran, J. (2005). *Cognitive-behavioural methods: A workbook for social workers.* New York: Oxford.

Dangel, R.F., & Polster, R.A. (1984). *Parent training: Foundations of research and practice.* New York: Guilford.

Diller, J.W., & Lattal, K.A. (2008). Radical behaviorism and Buddhism: Complementarities and conflicts. *Behavior Analyst, 31*, 163–177.

Edelson, J.L., & Tolman, R.M. (1992). *Intervention for men who batter: An ecological approach.* Newbury Park: Sage.

Ehrenreich, B. (2009). *Bright sided: How positive thinking is undermining America.* New York: Metropolitan Books.

Fraser, M.W., Day, S.H., Galinsky, M.J., Hodges, V.G., & Smokowski, P.R. (2004). Conduct problems and peer rejection in childhood: A randomized trial of the Making Choices and Strong Families programs. *Research on Social Work Practice, 14*, 313–324.

Gambrill, E. (1994). What's in a name? Task-centered, empirical and behavioural practice. *Social Service Review, 12*, 578–599.

Gambrill, E. (1995). Behavioural social work: Past, present, and future. *Research on Social Work Practice, 5*, 480–484.

Gambrill, E. (2012a). *Social work practice: A critical thinker's guide* (3rd ed.). New York: Oxford University Press.

Gambrill, E. (2012b). *Propaganda in the helping professions.* New York: Oxford University Press.

Gambrill, E.D., Thomas, E.J., & Carter, R.D. (1971). Procedure for socio-behavioural practice in open settings. *Social Work, 16*, 51–62.

Gilchrist, L.D., Schinke, S.P., & Blythe, B. (1985). Preventing unwanted adolescent pregnancies. In L.D. Gilchrist & Schinke, S.P. (eds), *Preventing social health problems through life skills training.* Seattle, WA: Center for Social Welfare Research, University of Washington, pp. 55–62.

Gilchrist, L.D., Schinke, S.P., & Maxwell, J.S. (1987). Life skills counseling for preventing problems in adolescence. *Journal of Social Service Research, 10*, 73–84.

Goldiamond, I. (1974). Toward a constructional approach to social problems: Ethical and constitutional issues raised by applied behavior analysis. *Behaviorism, 2*, 1–84.

Goldiamond, I. (1984). Training parent trainers and ethicists in nonlinear analysis of behavior. In R.F. Dangel & R.A. Polster, (eds), *Parent training: Foundations of research and practice*, pp. 504–546. New York: Guilford.

Granvold, D.K. (1994). *Cognitive and behavioural treatment: Methods and applications.* Pacific Grove, CA: Brooks/Cole.

Hawkins, J.D., Shapiro, V.B., Fagan, A.A. (2010). Disseminating effective community prevention practices: Opportunities for social work education. *Research on Social Work Practice, 20*(5), 518–527.

Hayes, S.C., Barnes-Holmes, D., & Roche, B. (2001). *Relational frame theory: A post-Skinnerian account of human language and cognition.* New York: Kluwer, Academic/Plenum Publishers.

Hayes, S.C., Follette, V.M., & Linehan, M.M. (eds) (2004). *Mindfulness and acceptance: Expanding the cognitive-behavioural tradition.* New York: Guilford Press.

Hayes, S.C., & Strosahl, K.D. (2010). *A practical guide for acceptance and commitment therapy.* New York: Springer, Inc.

Hawken, L.S. & Johnston, S.J. (2008). Preventing severe problem behavior in young children: The behavior education program. *Journal of Early and Intensive Behavior Intervention, 4*(3), 599–613.

Heyman, G.M. (2009). *Addiction: A disorder of choice.* Cambridge, MA: Harvard University Press.

Jaime, L., Milford, J.L., & Smith, J.E. (2007). Community reinforcement and the dissemination of evidence-based practice: Implications for public policy.

International Journal of Behavioral Consultation and Therapy, 3(1), 77–87.

Kazi, M. (1998). Single case evaluation by social workers. Aldershot: Ashgate.

Kohlenberg, B.S., Tsai, M., & Kohlenberg, R. (2006). Functional analytic therapy and the treatment of complex post traumatic stress disorder. In V.M. Follette & Ruzek, J.I. (eds), Cognitive-behavioural therapies for trauma. New York: Guilford.

Kohlenberg, R. J., Tsai, M., & Kohlenberg, B.S. (1996). Functional analysis in behavior therapy. In M. Hersen, Eisler, R M., & Miller, P.M. (eds), Progress in behavior modification. Newbury Park, CA: Sage, pp. 1–24.

Kunkel, J. (1970). Social and economic growth: A behavioural perspective of social change. New York: Oxford University Press.

LaCasse, J.R., & Gomory, T. (2003). Is graduate social work education promoting a critical approach to mental health practice? Journal of Social Work Education, 39, 383–408.

Lamal, P.A. (eds) (1991). Behavioural analysis of societies and cultural practices. Washington, DC: Hemisphere Press.

Lattal, K.A., & Chase, P.N. (2010). Behavior therapy and philosophy. New York: Plenum Press.

LaVigna, G.W., Willis, T.J., Shaull, J.E, Abedi, M., & Sweitzer, M. (l994). The periodic service review: A total quality assurance system for human services and education. Baltimore, MD: Paul H. Brookes.

Layng, T.V.J. (2009). The search for effective clinical behavior analysis: the nonlinear thinking of Israel Goldiamond. The Behavior Analyst, 32, 163–184.

Linehan, M.M. (1993). Cognitive-behavioural treatment of borderline personality disorder. New York: Guilford.

MacDonald, G. (2001). Effective interventions for child abuse and neglect: An evidence-based approach to evaluating and planning interventions. Chichester: John Wiley.

Mallott, R.W. (1994). Rule governed behavior, self-management & performance management. Kalamazoo, MI: Western Michigan University, Department of Psychology.

Martin, G.L., & Pear, J. (2010). Behavior modification: What it is and how to do it (9th ed.). Upper Saddle River, NJ: Prentice-Hall.

Mattaini, M.A. (1993a). Behavior analysis and community practice: A review. Research on Social Work Practice, 3, 420–447.

Mattaini, M. (1993b). More than a thousand words: Graphics for clinical practice. Washington, DC: National Association of Social Workers.

Mattaini, M.A., & Thyer, B.A. (eds) (1996). Finding solutions to social problems: Behavioural strategies for change. Washington, DC: American Psychological Association.

Moore, J. (2001). On psychological terms that appeal to the mental. Behavior and Philosophy, 29, 167–186.

Moynihan, R., & Cassels, A. (2005). Selling sickness: How the world's biggest pharmaceutical companies are turning us all into patients. New York: Nation Books.

Nakamura, B.J., & Chorpita, B.F. (2004). A brief report on modular cognitive behavior therapy. Emotional and Behavioural Disorders in Youth, 4, 39–41.

Pelaez, M., Gewirtz, J.L., & Wong, S.E. (2008). A critique of stage theories of human development. In B. Thyer (vol. ed.). Comprehensive handbook of social work and social welfare. Vol. 2. New York: Sage, pp. 503–518.

Phillips, D.C. (2000). The social scientist's bestiary: A guide to fabled threats to, and defenses of, naturalistic social science (2nd ed.). New York: Pergamon.

Pinkston, E.M., & Linsk, N.L. (1984). Care of the elderly: A family approach. New York: Pergamon.

Rachlin, H. (1991). Introduction to modern behaviorism (3rd ed.). New York: W.H. Freeman.

Reid, W.I. (1992). Task strategies: An empirical approach to clinical social work. New York: Columbia University Press.

Ronen, T., & Freeman, A. (2007). Cognitive-behavior therapy: Research and practice in clinical social work practice. New York: Springer.

Rose, S.D. (1989). Working with adults in groups: A cognitive behavioural approach. San Francisco: Jossey-Bass.

Sailor, W., Dunlap, G., Sugai, G., & Horner, R. (eds.) Handbook of Positive Behavior support. New York: Springer.

Scott, T.M., Gagnon, J.C., & Nelson, C.M. (2008). School-wide systems of positive behavior support: A framework for reducing school crime and violence. Journal of Behavior Analysis of Offender and victim: Treatment and Prevention, 1(3), 259–272.

Schwartz, A., & Goldiamond, I. (1975). Social casework: A behavioural approach. New York: Columbia University Press.

Schwartz, I.S., & Baer, D.M. (1991). Social validity assessments: Is current practice state of the art? Journal of Applied Behavior Analysis, 24, 189–204.

Sheldon, B. (2010). Cognitive-behavioural therapy: Research and practice in health and social care (2nd ed.). Abingdon: Routledge.

Sheldon, B., & MacDonald, G. (2008). *The textbook of social work*. London: Routledge.

Shibano, M. (2007). Behavioural family treatment in Japan: Design and development of a parent training program. In H.E. Briggs & Rzepnicki, T. (eds), *Using evidence in social work practice: Behavioural perspectives*. Chicago, IL: Lyceum, pp. 145–159.

Skinner, B.F. (1969). *Contingencies of reinforcement: A theoretical analysis*. New York: Appleton-Century-Crofts.

Skinner, B.F. (1971). *Beyond freedom & dignity*. New York: Knopf.

Skinner, B.F. (1974). *About behaviorism*. New York: Alfred A. Knopf.

Skinner, B.F. (1981). *Selection by consequences. Science*, 213, 501–504.

Smagner, J.P., & Sullivan, M.H. (2005). Investigating the effectiveness of behavioural parent training with involuntary clients. *Research on Social Work Practice*, 15, 431–439.

Steketee, G., & Frost, R.O. (2006). *Compulsive hoarding and acquiring: Therapist guide*. New York: Oxford.

Stuart, R.B. (1980). *Helping couples change: A social learning approach to marital therapy*. New York: Guilford.

Sugai, G., & Horner, R.H. (2005). Schoolwide positive behaviour supports: Achieving and sustaining effective learning environments for all students. In W.L. Hewards, Heron, T.E., Neef, N.A. et al. (eds), *Focus on behavior analysis in education: Achievement, challenges, and opportunities*. Pearson: Merrill Prentice Hall.

Sundel, M., & Sundel, S.S. (2005). *Behavioural change in the human services: Behavioural and cognitive principles and applications* (5th ed.). Newbury Park: Sage.

Szasz, T. (2007). *The medicalization of every day life: Selected essays*. New York: Syracuse University Press.

Thomas, E.J. (ed.). (1967). *The socio-behavioural approach and applications to social work*. New York: Council on Social Work Education.

Thomas, E.J., Santas, C., Bronson, D., & Oyserman, D. (1987). Unilateral family therapy with the spouses of alcoholics. *Journal of Social Service Research*, 10, 145–162.

Thomas, E.J., & Walter, C.L. (1973). Guidelines for behavioural practice in the open community agency: Procedure and evaluation. *Behaviour Research and Therapy*, 11, 193–205.

Thyer, B.A. (ed.). (1999). *The philosophical legacy of behaviorism*. Dordrecht: Kluwer Academic.

Thyer, B.A. (2005). The misfortune of behavioural social work: Misprized, misread and misconstrued. In S.A. Kirk (ed.), *Mental disorders in the social environment: Critical perspectives*. New York: Columbia University Press, pp. 330–343.

Tolman, R.M., & Rose, S.D. (1990). Teaching clients to cope with stress: The effectiveness of structured group stress management training. *Journal of Social Service Research*, 30, 45–66.

Van Houten, R., Axelrod, S., Bailey, J.S., Favell, J.E., Foxx, R.M., Iwata, B.A., & Lovaas, O. (1988). Position statement on a client's right to effective behavioural treatment. *Journal of Applied Behavior Analysis*, 21, 381–384.

Watson, D.L., & Tharp, R.G. (2006). *Self-directed behavior* (9th ed.). Belmont, CA: Thomson/Wadsworth.

Webster's New World Dictionary (1988). New York: Simon & Schuster.

Wodarski, J. (2009). *Behavioural medicine: A social worker's guide*. New York: Routledge.

Wolpe, J. (1990). *The practice of behavior therapy*. Elmsford, NY: Pergamon.

Wong, S.E., Wilder, D.A., Schock, K., & Cray, C. (2004). Behavioural interventions for serious and persistent mental disorders. In Briggs, H.E., & Rzepnicki, T. (eds), *Using evidence in social work practice: Behavioural perspectives*. Chicago, IL: Lyceum, pp. 210–230.

10

Family Perspectives

Jacqueline Corcoran

In the US National Association of Social Workers' (NASW) Code of Ethics, the importance of human relationships is emphasised as a core value of the profession (NASW, 1999). Social workers not only provide a relationship to clients, they also work to build and enhance the naturally existing relationships in clients' lives. Therefore, work with families must be a centrepiece of social work practice.

Family social work is informed by diverse perspectives influencing the types of therapeutic models used. For example, from an ecological systems perspective, it is defined as work 'with any part of the family system … where membership in the family is a concern, or where the family or some part of the family system is the target for change' (Yanca & Johnson, 2008; see Chapter 8). However, a specialised literature has not developed within the field of family social work practice with the notable exception of Hartman and Laird (1983) in the early 1980s. Nichols (2009) is one of the few in the family therapy field acknowledging the contribution of social work to the development of family therapy (Wood, 2001). Indeed, 'the core paradigm of social work – treating the person-in-the-environment – anticipated family therapy's ecological approach long before systems theory was introduced' (Nichols, 2009, p. 13).

Wood (2001) traces the origins of social work with families to well before the turn of the 19th century in both the UK and the USA with the Charities Organisation Societies movement and 'friendly visiting'. Settlement homes were also formed, and from these dual influences, professional social work developed. Therefore, social workers and their predecessors have a long history of work with families pre-dating the development of 'family therapy' by about 50 years. Wood (2001) suggests social work was not given due credit for its influence on family therapy because of the field's gender status – social workers were mainly female – and the field's lack of professional power – social work grew out of practical helping rather than academia and, therefore, writing and publication of professional ideas was downplayed.

Wood (2001) also points out social workers worked with Nathan Ackerman, the psychiatrist who is viewed as the originator of family therapy, but were not given credit for the formulation of their ideas. Ackerman et al., (1961) did acknowledge '[s]ince the beginning of the profession, social workers have been concerned with the family, both as the critical social unit and as the focus of intervention' (as cited in Nichols, 2009, p. 13). Additionally, social workers, such as Virginia Satir, who were part of the new family therapy movement did not discuss the influence of social work on their family work and seemed to distance themselves from the profession in order to retain status among the psychiatrists who dominated this developing field (Wood, 2001).

Social work has contributed both to the fundamental importance of work with families and to the use of systems theory in family, although the family therapy field has formulated the techniques giving rise to change in working with family systems. Social work, in contrast, has tended to avoid offering techniques and strategies to work with families, focusing instead on the need for a holistic understanding of the client, the family, and the environmental context (Wood, 2001). However, practitioners often want to understand the techniques enabling them to improve family functioning, which are derived from various perspectives on family functioning. These include family therapy, informed by systems theory, and behavioural (or cognitive behavioural) family therapy, informed by behavioural perspectives (see Chapter 9), which will be presented in this chapter as well as the evidence of their application to child problems. Prevention approaches using family support are discussed, mostly from the UK perspective, in Chapter 39.

This chapter centres on the US perspective, although it is broadened by presentation of the evidence basis of family interventions from the standpoint of systematic reviews, when available, from the Campbell Collaboration and the Cochrane Collaboration. Both of these organisations require that studies must be drawn from worldwide sources and not limited to English-language documents. Therefore, the generalisability of their findings to other countries is made more valid.

In this chapter, when systematic reviews and meta-analyses are lacking, family models are evaluated for their evidence basis through the standpoint of the American Psychological Association (APA) Division 12 Task Force Criteria for *empirically supported treatment* (Chambless & Hollon, 1998; see Appendix). In addition to quantitative evidence, the perceptions of family members in the process of undergoing family therapy are also described, typically through the findings of qualitative research (see Chapter 29). First, however, a case study is presented and discussed, following the presentation of each type of family intervention model.

THE CASE OF KELLY

Kelly is a 13-year-old, Caucasian female, who is currently detained at the county juvenile detention centre for violating the conditions of probation by continuing to run away from home. Kelly stated she does not get along with her stepfather (he has been in her life for two years) and has a conflicted relationship with her mother, yet, she enjoys a close relationship with her sister (age 14). Kelly's parents agree her stepfather is strict and inflexible about rules while her mother gets in the middle of conflicts between her husband and her daughters. Kelly's mother and stepfather claim their relationship is 'alright', but the arguments over discipline and the behaviour of Kelly, in particular, exact a toll.

Kelly's father works in retail, and her mother said she quit her job as a secretary when she was diagnosed with breast cancer. According to her parents, Kelly was an honour roll student and a member of the safety patrol and the school choir until her behaviour changed drastically about a year ago.

In the past year, Kelly has refused to obey her parents' rules and has run away from home over a dozen times. She often stays out late at night and refuses to tell her parents where she is going or with whom. She often misses school when on the run, and her grades have suffered significantly. Kelly admitted to hanging out with males who were in their twenties, including known gang members, but denied personal membership in any gang. She admitted to engaging in sexual activity with at least ten male partners in the past several months. On at least two occasions she had sex with male strangers in laundromats for $5 because she was trying to save up enough money to move to another state.

Kelly's parents reported any time she does not get her way she throws temper tantrums and threatens to run away. They stated she went from being a sweet, loving child to being disrespectful and unmanageable. Kelly's acting out seemed to start when her older sister disclosed to her mother that their biological father sexually molested her. Kelly denies she witnessed the sexual abuse or that she was sexually abused herself. After the sexual abuse disclosure, Kelly's mother was diagnosed with breast cancer. Kelly has shared some concern about this, stating 'I don't want my mom to die'.

Kelly said she had started using various substances about a year ago. Marijuana is her drug of choice, but she also uses alcohol to excess. She admitted to dextromethorphan (DXM) use beginning this past year. DXM is the active ingredient found in many over-the-counter cough and cold medications producing hallucinogen and stimulant effects in high doses. Seven months ago, because of her running away and substance use, Kelly was placed in a county shelter care residential facility. While there, staff reportedly took her to the hospital after she ingested ten tablets of DXM.

Both parents deny her stepfather has a problem with alcohol. However, Kelly's mother said Kelly's biological father was an 'alcoholic', and it was one of the reasons she left him, along with his sporadic employment. Kelly has not had contact with her father since the divorce three years ago.

Kelly believes her problems will be solved when she and her sister are able to get along with their mother and stepfather. Kelly does not wish to return home until her relationship with her parents improves and they no longer see the need to criticise her and yell at her.

FAMILY SYSTEMS PERSPECTIVES

Because of the development of ecological systems theory as a way to reconcile the split in social work between 'micro' and 'macro' practice in the 1970s (Wood, 1961), social workers will already be familiar with many of the concepts from the ecological systems approach underlying family therapy, including *circular causality* – symptoms do not stem from linear causes, i.e., one person's problems, but emerge from family interaction patterns (Aponte, 2002; Minuchin, 1974) and *homeostasis* (Jackson, 1965) – symptoms arise and resistance to change occurs because of the nature of systems to remain in a status quo position.

Over the years, various therapeutic models have emerged from family systems perspectives (Nichols, 2009). In the 1960s, the communications model started the movement (Watzlawick et al., 1967). In the 1970s, structural family therapy predominated (Minuchin, 1974), and in the 1980s strategic therapy held sway (Haley, 1991; Palazzoli & Boscolo, 1990; Watzlawich et al., 1974).

Despite its long-standing influence, there is a dearth of well-controlled studies testing family systems models. One problem to which family systems has been applied, albeit with modifications, involves eating disorders, namely, anorexia nervosa (AN), which is characterised by disturbances in a person's eating behaviours and perceptions of body weight and shape (APA, 2000). Influenced by Minuchin's pathbreaking family systems therapy (Minuchin et al., 1978), which predominantly dealt with AN, the Maudsley model was developed by Dare and Eisler at London's Maudsley Hospital in the 1980s with the main aim of getting the parents to unite to stand up to an externalised illness and re-feed their adolescent until a healthy weight was resumed (Lock et al., 2001). Family treatment may include therapeutic techniques from traditional family therapy or other schools of psychotherapy so in this way departs from family systems therapy.

Two randomised studies compared the Maudsley model to individual therapy (i.e., psychodynamically oriented individual therapy; Lock et al., 2010; Robin et al., 1999) and eclectic individual therapy (Russell et al., 1987). Keel and Haedt (2008) concluded from an APA Task Force 12 review that the Maudsley model was probably efficacious for AN.

The Maudsley model has influenced other family interventions for adolescents and young adults with AN (Ball & Mitchell, 2004; Robin et al., 1994) and bulimia nervosa

(Le Grange et al., 2007; Schmidt et al., 2007), but in these, family therapy has not established itself as more helpful than individual therapy (Schmidt et al., 2007) or even supportive therapy (Le Grange et al., 2007).

To echo these findings, a systematic review was conducted of randomised, controlled trials of family therapy for AN (Fisher et al., 2010). Based on 13 studies, there was some evidence family therapy may be more effective than treatment as usual but not other psychotherapies for remission from AN: 'There were no differences in relapse rates, symptom scores, weight measures, or the number of drop outs between those treated with family therapy versus any other comparison group' (Fisher et al., 2010, p. 2).

A qualitative study looked at how adolescent clients with eating disorders and their parents viewed family therapy. The adolescents saw the need for family therapy but were not as keen as their parents about it. The teens described the conjoint family work as 'challenging' and 'often unhelpful' (Roots et al., 2009, p. 335). The views among parents were that siblings were not well-included in the treatment. The researchers of the qualitative study were pleased families did not find themselves feeling blamed for their child's eating disorder and advocated for the provision of parental support groups (without the adolescent being present).

Another qualitative study centred on parental reactions to the Maudsley model of family therapy specifically (Rhodes et al., 2009). Parents described many benefits of the model. They liked the fact that it gave them permission to be strict with their daughters about getting them to eat. They also appreciated the aspect of externalising the eating disorder, or separating the eating disorder from their child. Further, they benefited from the therapists' stance of bolstering the authority of parents to work together to surmount the eating disorder. Single parents particularly enjoyed the aspect of being able to share their parenting and divorce challenges with a caring person. Only one couple found treatment unhelpful, and three other parents, while 'generally positive, were critical of the therapist's insistence all family members should attend each appointment' (Rhodes et al., 2009, p. 190).

Systemic family therapy has also been tested for depression. In a randomised, controlled trial, Brent et al. (1996) compared systemic family therapy, with cognitive behavioural therapy (CBT) and nondirective supportive therapy. At the end of treatment, all conditions produced improvements in psychological adjustment and suicidality, although remission was more common in the CBT group (60%) than in either the family therapy or nonsupportive therapy. At two-year follow-up, different conditions affected different areas of functioning (Kolko et al., 2000). Not surprisingly, given its emphasis on family relationships, family therapy positively influenced family conflict and parent–child relationship problems. But interestingly, both supportive therapy and CBT significantly reduced anxiety over the family therapy group.

Finally, for Latino adolescents (mainly Cuban-American) with substance abuse, brief strategic–structural therapy has been developed (Szapocznik et al., 2003). Based on an APA Division 12 Task Force review, brief strategic–structural therapy has been classified as 'probably efficacious' for Latino youth (Huey & Polo, 2008).

Hence, from these two examples, despite its long history and the fact family systems perspectives continue to influence clinical practice in community settings, little research has been conducted through the years on this type of family intervention. Those child problems that have been studied, including eating disorders, depression, and substance abuse, overall show that family systems therapy has not established itself as superior to individual therapies, but more research is clearly needed.

In applying family systems therapy to the case of Kelly above, structural family therapy was the specific model selected for illustration. In addition to the typical constructs of systems, structural family therapy emphasises the importance of a hierarchical structure to the family, which means interaction patterns are indicative of an organisational system in which parents hold authority over their children. The main assumption of the structural approach, therefore, is families present to treatment with symptoms because of a problematic structure (Minuchin, 1974). In this light, Kelly's problems – her running away, angry outbursts, substance abuse, and prostitution – are seen as the result of a maladaptive structure in which parents are not in charge of the problem. Families are vulnerable when negotiating a particular life stage (in Kelly's case, the family is newly part of the adolescent stage) or when stressors pile up (disclosure of sexual abuse by Kelly's sister, mother's diagnosis of breast cancer) and the family is unable to manage (Minuchin et al., 1967, 1978). In such cases, the family is not flexibly able to adapt their interaction patterns to changed circumstances, and symptoms such as Kelly's may result.

The central goal of structural family therapy becomes the creation of a well-functioning structure. Stepfamilies introduce challenges to the family structure since biological parents still comprise the parental subsystem. Unfortunately, owing to the biological father's abandonment, alcoholism, and now the sexual abuse disclosure, he is unable to play a role in that subsystem. The stepfather is to play only a supporting role to the biological parent (Kelly's mother). The complaint is he is overly strict and Kelly's mother is lenient. The therapist's job will be to direct *enactments*, working with interactions in the session, so a new pattern is formed (Aponte, 2002; Minuchin, 1974), one in which Kelly's mother plays the central authoritarian role and the stepfather only acts to bolster, rather than subvert, her authority. In this way, the problems of the asymptomatic child, Kelly, should be resolved.

In the research, family systems therapy has not been established as more effective than other approaches, but the field could benefit from more study as research is scant. As will be seen in a later section, family systems therapy has played a role in the development of multidimensional models, especially for adolescent behaviour problems and substance abuse, as well as constructivist approaches, such as narrative therapy and solution-focused therapy.

SOLUTION-FOCUSED FAMILY THERAPY

Evolving from family systems therapy, but adding to it the influence of constructivism, newer family therapies have evolved, namely narrative and solution-focused family therapies. Wood (2001) notes narrative family therapy, with its emphasis on 'restory-ing' clients' lives (White, 2007), may also hearken back to early social work. In the first social work textbook, *Social Diagnosis*, Mary Richmond (1917) described the necessity of understanding the client's 'story'. Additionally, some brands of narrative family therapy focus on a social justice context for clients' problems; this echoes long-term social work values and traditions (Wood, 2001).

A greater emphasis in this chapter is solution-focused therapy developed by deShazer, Berg, and colleagues (Berg, 1994; Berg & Miller, 1992; Cade & O'Hanlon, 1993; de Shazer et al., 1986; O'Hanlon & Weiner-Davis, 1989). Note again, as with the development of family systems therapy, social workers, namely, Insoo Kim Berg, Peter De Jong, Michelle Weiner-Davis, and Wallace Gingerich, were critical to the formulation of solution-focused therapy. However, they did not describe social work as an influence and associated themselves with the family therapy field instead.

Solution-focused therapy shares with family systems a focus on the contextual nature of behaviour and the idea about change being instigated at any point in a system as change reverberates throughout a system (de Shazer et al., 1986). The constructivist influence – claiming knowledge about reality is constructed from social interactions – is seen in solution-focused therapy in the way language and questioning is used to influence the way clients view their problems, the potential for solutions, and the expectancy for change (Berg & De Jong, 1996).

Solution-focused therapy emphasises the strengths people bring and how these can be applied to the change process. Clients are assumed to have the capability to solve their own problems through resources found by eliciting and exploring times when the problem does not exert its negative influence and or when the client has managed the problem more successfully. Rather than focusing on the past and the history of the problem, using solution-focused therapy, the attention orients on a future without the problem as a way to build vision, hope, and motivation for the client.

Four group-design (experimental or quasi-experimental) studies have been conducted on solution-focused therapy with families (Corcoran, 2000; Eakes, et al., 1997; Ingersoll-Dayton et al., 1999; Zimmerman et al., 1996). In a review of solution-focused therapy treatment outcome studies (Corcoran & Pillai, 2009), effect sizes of studies were provided. The effect sizes for the family intervention studies ranged considerably – from medium effects (Zimmerman et al., 1996) to low (Eakes et al., 1997) to negligible (Corcoran, 2000; Ingersoll-Dayton et al., 1999). Effect sizes were unable to be synthesised because of differing outcomes among studies. Because of these ranges in effect sizes, at this point it is difficult to ascertain the effectiveness of solution-focused therapy with families.

In solution-focused family therapy, goals and solutions are formulated by clients. Therefore, Kelly's goal about getting along with her mother and stepfather and improving the relationship with them will be seen as a valid starting point for the work. The practitioner may work on helping the family envision a problem-free future to see their way out of present problematic circumstances. An example of future-oriented questioning would be: What will it look like when Kelly is clean and living at home and the problem is solved? What will she and her family members be doing and saying? These types of questions bypass a problem-saturated present and get members to think in a more flexible way about when the problem is resolved. Relationship questions and asking clients to report from the perspective of other family members (e.g., 'Tori what will your mom say needs to happen so you and your parents would get along better?' or 'How might that be helpful?') help with clarity of goals, enact the systemic orientation, and emphasise the circular nature of interaction patterns. One of the main interventions in solution-focused therapy is exception-finding, discovering times when the problem was better (or not as bad) and enlarging upon these 'exceptions to the problem' by the following types of questions: 'When does Kelly stay home, mind her parents, and discuss issues without arguments?' 'What is going on then?' 'Who is there?' 'What are she and her family members doing and saying during those times?' 'How does she make this happen?' These types of interventions and sample questions help empower the family to come to their own ideas about what will be helpful for them in resolving the situation with Kelly and to take small steps toward their goals, which are assumed to spiral into further positive change.

BEHAVIOURAL FAMILY THERAPY

Behavioural family therapy is generally referred to as parent training. Behaviour theory as applied to child behaviour problems postulates both parent and child engage in coercive cycles, which typically begin with the parent issuing a directive to the child. The child then responds in a coercive manner through noncompliance, whining, or yelling. At that point, the parent may withdraw the command, which acts to reinforce a child's disobedient behaviour negatively. Negative reinforcement is defined as the termination of an aversive event; in this case, if a parental command is withdrawn, the child's noncompliance is increased. The parent may also be negatively reinforced for coercive behaviour. If, following noncompliance, the parent escalates the command (raises the voice, uses physical aggression), the child may obey, which reinforces the parent's use of these aversive tactics. According to the principles of operant conditioning, positive reinforcement also plays a role in that parents attend to child deviant rather than pro-social behaviours, which increases the likelihood of future deviant behaviour.

In parent training programmes, behavioural principles are applied to increase a child's positive behaviours and decrease negative behaviours. Desirable and appropriate child behaviours are encouraged through the use of positive reinforcement techniques such as attention, praise, token economies, and privileges. Undesirable behaviours are decreased through ignoring and punishment, such as time-out from reinforcement. Parents are taught these tactics through the use of didactic presentations, modelling, role-plays, and homework assignments.

The research treatment for antisocial behaviour and attention deficit hyperactivity disorder (ADHD) has been dominated by parent training, and the available systematic reviews and meta-analyses for these problems are now reviewed. For child behavioural problems, which are also referred to as aggression, antisocial, anger, and conduct problems, two reviews are of relevance: a meta-analysis on parent training programmes for child aggression ($N = 30$ studies; McCart et al., 2006); and a systematic review of the parenting programmes for children with conduct problems (Dretzke et al., 2009; $N = 24$ randomised, controlled trials). Taken together, the quantitative reviews of the parent training literature indicate these programmes are effective for positively influencing child behaviour at a small to medium effect.

In the area of ADHD, a meta-analysis was conducted of treatments ($N = 16$ studies) in which parents were involved in the intervention (Corcoran & Dattalo, 2006). The studies, all using parent training, had a low to moderate effect on ADHD and externalising symptoms. It must be recognised some of the control conditions involved viable treatments, such as medication and child treatment; therefore, the fact parent-involved treatment produced overall gains above and beyond these control treatments is noteworthy. Parent-involved treatment had an even higher effect on child internalising symptoms and family functioning than on externalising and ADHD symptoms.

Further, the Multi-Modal Treatment Study (MTA) of Children with Attention-deficit/Hyperactivity Disorder Cooperative Group Study, the largest randomised, controlled trial study to date on the treatment of youth ADHD ($N = 579$), has been undertaken, comparing the differential effectiveness of medication, behaviour therapy, combined treatment, compared to a community control condition. At 14-month post-test, the combined treatment (medication and behaviour therapy) performed better than behaviour therapy alone in terms of reduction in ADHD symptoms, but not in a statistically significant way from medication alone (Swanson et al., 2008). Children in the combination group were taking a 20% lower dose than those in the medication group. This suggests the addition of behaviour therapy allowed children to take a lower dose and still have the same benefits (Swanson et al., 2008). At 36-month follow-up, any advantages of medication had disappeared. There was a protective effect for behaviour therapy against early substance use. Weight and height were diminished in children now ages 11–13 years who had taken medication. The findings from the MTA study do not provide clear guidelines on treatment. Indeed, authors of the MTA study disagree among themselves about appropriate treatment and whether behavioural treatment, medication, or a combined approach should be offered (Vedantam, 2009).

If parent training were the method of family treatment chosen for Kelly and her family, the parents (Kelly's mother and stepfather) might be the focus of the intervention, at least initially. Specific and concrete goals would be formulated at the outset starting with a couple of the following behaviours of Kelly's they would likely want to change, such as increasing the number of abstinent days; practising safe sex; communicating feelings rather than acting them out; and reducing running away and tantrums. Parents would be taught how to reinforce Kelly's compliance through positive reinforcement (praise and privileges) and punishing misbehaviour through the taking away of privileges. Education on these techniques would be provided, as well as role-playing opportunities, so parents could practise the needed skills.

COMBINED FAMILY MODELS

An evolving trend, particularly with antisocial problems in adolescents is the design of multidimensional models including behavioural therapy and family systems techniques. These include multisystemic treatment, treatment fostercare, functional family therapy, multidimensional family therapy, and family behavioural treatment (for coverage of generalist family social work, see Chapter 32, and for family support models, see Chapter 39).

Multisystemic treatment

Henggeler and colleagues (e.g., Henggeler & Lee, 2003) have created a model emphasising the multiple systems impacting on the development of delinquency. Bronfenbrenner's (1979) theory of the social–ecological model of development postulates the systems surrounding individuals influence their behaviour in both direct and indirect ways. The micro-systems (the most direct systems impacting on the child, such as immediate and extended family) and meso-systems (more distal influences the child and his or her micro-systems are embedded within, such as the school or neighbourhood) impact the child and are impacted by the child in a systemic fashion. Systems affecting and affected by delinquent behaviour include the child's own intrapersonal system (i.e., cognitive ability, social skills), the parent–child system, the family system, the school system (interactions with teachers), and the child–peer system (e.g., Henggeler, 1991).

Although multisystemic treatment (MST) has been touted as an evidence-based model by many sources, including federal entities, such as the National Institute on Drug Abuse, National Institute on Mental Health, Surgeon General's Office, Center for Substance Abuse Prevention, the Office of Juvenile Justice and Delinquency Prevention, and the Substance Abuse and Mental Health Services Administration (see Littell, 2005), the systematic review of eight studies indicated that, of several outcomes measures – arrests and time incarcerated, teen adjustment, parent adjustment, and pro-social involvement – none was significantly improved with MST compared to control (Littell et al., 2005). Furthermore, treatment and control conditions (usual services or individual therapy) were not always comparable, despite claims of randomisation to conditions in studies. This might have biased the findings toward the treatment group.

When applied to the case of Kelly, MST might include parent training and structural family therapy. The practitioner might also work with other systems besides the family, including the individual system (Kelly's sexual risk behaviours and substance abuse triggers and coping); the parent system (Kelly's mother's adjustment to the breast cancer diagnosis and her other daughter's sexual abuse, specifically); and the couple system (Kelly's mother and stepfather admit to having problems due to the stress of

Kelly's behaviour). In MST, the social worker would work intensively with the family in order to address the multiple issues influencing the various systems levels and their functioning.

Treatment fostercare

Treatment fostercare programmes serve children and youth who are at risk for being placed in institutional or other restrictive, non-home settings due to their emotional, behavioural, medical, or developmental problems. Often these children face a series of progressively more restrictive placements. One type of treatment fostercare, multidimensional treatment fostercare (MTFC; Chamberlain & Smith, 2003), is targeted specifically for youth with severe and chronic delinquent behaviour. MTFC is a community-based programme originally developed as an alternative to institutional-, residential-, and group-care placements. Youth are placed one per foster home for 6–9 months and given intensive support and treatment in the foster-home setting. The foster parents receive a 20-hour pre-service training conducted by experienced foster parents and learn to implement a daily token reinforcement system involving frequent positive reinforcement, and clear and consistent limits. During treatment, the foster parents report point levels on the token reinforcement system by daily telephone calls to programme supervisors, and they meet weekly with supervisors for support and supervision (Eyberg et al., 2008).

Youth in MTFC meet at least weekly with individual therapists who provide support and advocacy, and work with the youth on problem-solving skills, anger expression, social skills development, and educational or vocational planning. They also meet once or twice a week (2–6 hours per week) with behavioural support specialists trained in applied behaviour analysis who focus on teaching and reinforcing pro-social behaviours during intensive one-on-one interactions in the community (e.g., restaurants and sports teams). Finally, youth have regular appointments with a consulting psychiatrist for medication management. At the same time, youth are in MTFC treatment, the biological parents (or other aftercare resource) receive intensive parent management training designed to assist in the reintegration of youth back into their homes and communities after treatment.

A recent Cochrane Collaboration review on treatment fostercare located only five studies meeting the inclusion criteria (Macdonald & Turner, 2008). Although results favoured treatment, fostercare studies typically did not assess similar outcome measures; quantitative synthesis, therefore, was difficult. The authors concluded treatment fostercare may be a successful alternative to more costly higher levels of care, such as residential treatment, and may help young people avoid some of the deleterious outcomes for children with compulsive disorder (Macdonald & Turner, 2008). However, the authors also warn the evidence is not as robust as the claims that have been made, as there have been many published articles touting its effectiveness.

Functional family therapy

Alexander and Parsons (1982) developed functional family therapy in which systems, cognitive, and behavioural theories are integrated. Juvenile offending and other clinical problems are conceptualised from the standpoint of the functions they serve for the family system as well as for individual family members (Alexander & Parsons, 1982). Behaviour is viewed in the context of family relationships in which the individual may be attempting to achieve greater closeness, greater separation, or some balance between the two in the relationship. For example, behaviour problems may unite parents around their child's difficult behaviour; alternatively, conduct problems may be the child's attempt to signal the family is too restrictive. Because maladaptive processes within the family develop in lieu of more direct means of fulfilling these functions, the goal of functional family therapy is to alter interaction and communication patterns so more adaptive functioning is experienced. As well as communication patterns of the family, coercive interactions between parent and child are also targets for functional family intervention (Alexander & Parsons, 1982).

Currently, a systematic review is being conducted on functional family therapy (FFT; see Littell et al., 2008), but results are not yet available. Recently, FFT has been tested in a community setting against probation services for youth with behavioural problems and did not perform more favourably (Sexton & Turner, 2010). However, high practitioner adherence to treatment fidelity was associated with better outcomes for FFT, suggesting FFT 'must be delivered in a clinically specific and precise manner to produce positive outcomes' (Sexton & Turner, 2010, p. 346).

Multidimensional family therapy

Multidimensional family therapy (MDFT) is a multicomponent intervention targeting individual, peer, school, and family risk factors associated with adolescent substance abuse (Liddle et al., 2001). The *individual adolescent domain involves* engaging teens in treatment and building communication skills, social competence, and alternatives to substance use. The *parent domain* engages parents in therapy, increases their behavioural and emotional involvement with the adolescents, and improves parental monitoring and limit setting. The *family interactional domain* focuses on decreasing conflict and improving emotional attachments, patterns of communication, and problem-solving techniques using multiparticipant family sessions. The *extrafamilial domain* fosters family competency and collaborative involvement within all social systems in which the teen participates (e.g., school, juvenile justice, recreational; Liddle et al., 2009). The therapist meets with the adolescent, parents, or in conjoint sessions as needed. MDFT can be delivered from one to three times per week over the course of 3–6 months depending on the treatment setting – office-based, in-home, outpatient, day treatment, residential treatment – and the severity of adolescent problems and family functioning. Regardless of the version, therapists work simultaneously in four interdependent treatment domains according to the particular risk and protection profile of the adolescent and family.

Three randomised, controlled trials have been conducted with one under way. In the initial study, MDFT was compared to adolescent group therapy and multifamily educational intervention Liddle et al., 2001). Results indicated improvement among youths in all three treatments, with MDFT showing superior improvement overall. MDFT has been compared to cognitive behavioural treatment both in group (Liddle et al., 2004, 2009) and individual formats (Liddle et al., 2008). CBT – either individually or group – and MDFT both produced improvements. In Liddle et al. (2008), few differences between conditions were found, although substance use problem severity was reduced more for the MDFT condition. For Liddle et al. (2009), at 12 months, MDFT showed superior outcomes at 12-month follow-up on substance use and delinquency. Currently, a cross-national, randomised, controlled study (in Belgium, France, Germany, the Netherlands, and Switzerland) is under way (Rigter et al., 2010).

Family behavioural treatment

Family behavioural treatment, offered for adolescents with conduct problems and drug use (Donohue & Azrin, 2001; Donohue et al., 2009), has been categorized as a multidimensional model because of the many targets of intervention (Waldron & Turner, 2008).

The initial process involves an assessment to identify the factors contributing to the reinforcement of substance use, such as cognitive, verbal, social, and family concerns. These targets are analysed and processed with the family, which may include siblings and peers, and a set of strategies is chosen to meet the individual needs of the client. Youth are taught strategies to avoid and manage triggers. Behavioural interventions with the parents include contracting to supervise the child's therapeutic homework tasks and providing rewards for child activities incompatible with drug use, including cooperation with monitoring. Treatment usually involves 16–20 sessions ranging in time from 1 to 2 hours and spread out over as long as a one-year period.

Because behavioural family therapy has not been subject to a systematic review or meta-analysis, only the results of the APA Division 12 Task Force Criteria according to Waldron and Turner (2008) will be reported here. Behavioural family therapy was categorised as a 'probably efficacious' approach for adolescent substance abuse based on two randomised trials in terms of reduction in substance use and improvements in psychological adjustment and academic performance (Azrin et al., 1994a, 1994b, 2001).

CONCLUSION

This chapter has discussed the intervention models developed from the family perspective and has applied an evidence basis of these models to child problems. Most of these models are enacted by clinical practitioners rather than as a part of other social work roles, although some of the problems presented herein, such as substance abuse and behavioural problems, are those commonly seen in settings in which social workers are employed. Family interventions are also applied in community settings, although this practice context is understudied (Weisz et al., 2005). As outlined by Wood (2001), family social work has not developed its own literature, despite the first social work journal being *The Family* (now *Families in Society*). Writings in this area (e.g., Yanca & Johnson, 2008) have tended to describe in general terms how to approach work with families but has lacked the level of prescription needed for research. However, family interventions have the advantage of being ecologically valid in that they address the environment of the child and, therefore, are consistent not only with ethical values of helping clients improve their relationships, but also the 'historic and defining feature of social work [which] is the profession's focus on individual wellbeing in a social context' (Preamble, NASW Code of Ethics).

REFERENCES

Ackerman, N., Beatman, F., & Sherman, S. (eds) (1961). *Exploring the base for family therapy.* New York: Family Services Association of America.

Alexander, J., & Parsons, B.V. (1982). *Functional family therapy.* Monterey, CA: Brooks-Cole.

American Psychiatric Association (APA). (2000) *Diagnostic and Statistical Manual of Mental Disorders* (4th ed.). Text Revision. Washington, DC.

Aponte, H. (2002). Spirituality: The heart of therapy. *Journal of Family Psychotherapy, 13*, 13–26.

Azrin, N.H., Donohue, B., Besalel, V.A., Kogan, E.S., & Acierno, R. (1994a). Youth drug abuse treatment: A controlled outcome study. *Journal of Child and Adolescent Substance Abuse, 3,* 1–16.

Azrin, N.H., McMahon, P., Besalel, V.A., Donohue, B.C., Acierno, R., & Kogan, E.S. (1994b). Behavior therapy for drug abuse: A controlled outcome study. *Behavior Research and Therapy, 32,* 857–866.

Azrin, N.H., Donohue, B., Teichner, G.A., Crum, T., Howell, J., & DeCato, L.A. (2001). A controlled evaluation and description of individual-cognitive problem solving and family behavior therapies in dually-diagnosed conduct disordered and substance-dependent youth. *Journal of Child and Adolescent Substance Abuse, 11*(1), 1–43.

Ball, J., & Mitchell, P. (2004). A randomized controlled study of cognitive behavior therapy and behavioral family therapy for anorexia nervosa patients. *Eating disorders, 12(4)*, 303–314.

Berg, I.K. (1994). *Family-based services: A solution-focused approach*. New York: W.W. Norton & Company, Inc.

Berg, I.K., & De Jong, P. (1996). Solution-building conversations: Co-constructing a sense of competence with clients. *Families in Society, 77*, 376–391.

Berg, I.K., & Miller, S. (1992). *Working with the problem drinker*. New York: W.W. Norton & Company, Inc.

Brent, D., Roth, C., Holder, D., & Kolko, D. (1996). Psychosocial interventions for treating adolescent suicidal depression: A comparison of three psychosocial interventions. *Psychosocial treatments for child and adolescent disorders: Empirically based strategies for clinical practice*. Washington, DC US: American Psychological Association (pp. 187–206).

Bronfenbrenner, U. (1979). *The ecology of human development*. Cambridge, MA: Harvard University Press.

Cade, B., & O'Hanlon, W.H. (1993). *A brief guide to brief therapy*. New York: W.W. Norton & Company, Inc.

Chamberlain, P., & Smith, D.K. (2003). Antisocial behavior in children and adolescents: The Oregon Multidimensional Treatment Foster Care model. In A.E. Kazdin & Weisz, J.R. (eds), *Evidence-based psychotherapies for children and adolescents*. New York: Guilford Press, pp. 282–300.

Chambless, D.L., & Hollon, S.D. (1998). Defining empirically supported therapies. *Journal of Consulting and Clinical Psychology, 66*, 7–18.

Corcoran, J. (2000). *Evidence-based social work practice with families: A lifespan approach*. New York: Springer Publishing.

Corcoran, J., & Dattalo, P. (2006). Parent involvement in treatment for ADHD: A meta-analysis of the published studies. *Research in Social Work Practice*.

Corcoran, J., & Pillai, V. (2009). A review of the research on solution-focused therapy. *British Journal of Social Work, 39*, 234–242.

de Shazer, S., Berg, I.K., Lipchick, E., Nunnally, E., Molnar, A., Gingerich, W., & Weiner-Davis, M. (1986). Brief therapy: Focused solution development. *Family Process, 25*, 207–221.

Donohue, B., & Azrin, N. (2001). Family behavior therapy. In E.F. Wagner & H.B. Waldron (Eds.), *Innovations in adolescent substance abuse interventions* (pp. 205–227). Amsterdam: Pergamon/Elsevier Science.

Donohue, B., Azrin, N., Allen, D., Romero, V., Hill, H., Tracy, K., Lapota, H., Gorney, S., Abdel-Al, R., Caldas, D., Herdzik, K., Bradshaw, K., Valdez, R., & Van Hasselt, V. (2009). Family behavior therapy for substance abuse and other associated problems: A review of its intervention components and applicability. *Behavior Modification, 33*, 495–519.

Dretzke, J., Davenport, C., Frew, E., Barlow, J., Stewart-Brown, S., Bayliss, S., Taylor, R., Sandercock, J., & Hyde, C. (2009). The clinical effectiveness of different parenting programmes for children with conduct problems: A systematic review of randomized controlled trials. *Child and Adolescent Psychiatry and Mental Health, 3 (7)*. Doi: 10.1186/1753-2000-3-7.

Eakes, G., Walsh, S., Markowski, M., Cain, H., & Swanson, M. (1997). Family centered brief solution-focused therapy with chronic schizophrenia: A pilot study. *Journal of Family Therapy, 19*, 145–158.

Eyberg, S.M., Nelson, M.M., & Boggs, S.R. (2008). Evidence-based psychosocial treatments for children and adolescents with disruptive behavior. *Journal of Clinical Child and Adolescent Psychology, 37(1)*, 215–237.

Fisher, C., Hetrick, S., & Rushford, N. (2010). Family therapy for anorexia nervosa. *Cochrane Database of Systematic Reviews*, Issue 4. Art No.: CD004780.

Haley, J. (1991). *Problem-solving therapy* (2nd ed.). Hoboken, NJ: Jossey-Bass.

Hartman, A., & Laird, J. (1983). *Family centred social work practice*. New York: The Free Press.

Henggeler, S.W. (1991). Multidimensional causal models of delinquent behavior and their implications for treatment. In R. Cohen & Siegel, A.W. (eds), *Context and development*. Hillsdale, NJ: Erlbaum, pp. 211–231.

Henggeler, S.W., & Lee, T. (2003). Multisystemic treatment of serious clinical problems. In A.E. Kazdin & Weisz, J.R. (eds), *Evidence-based psychotherapies for children and adolescents*. New York: Guilford Press, pp. 301–322.

Huey, S.J., Jr, & Polo, A.J. (2008). Evidence-based psychosocial treatments for ethnic minority youth. *Journal of Clinical Child and Adolescent Psychology, 37(1)*, 262–301.

Ingersoll-Dayton, B., Schroepfer, T., Pryce, J., & Waarala, C. (2003). Enhancing relationships in nursing homes through empowerment. *Social Work, 48(3)*, 420–424.

Jackson, D. (1965). The study of the family. *Family Process, 4(1)*, 1.

Keel, P., & Haedt, A. (2008). Evidence-based psychosocial treatments for eating problems and eating disorders. *Journal of Clinical Child & Adolescent Psychology, 37(1)*, 39–61.

Kolko, D.J., Brent, D.A., Baugher, M., Bridge, J., & Birmaher, B. (2000). Cognitive and family therapies for adolescent depression: Treatment specificity, medication, and moderation. *Journal of Consulting and Clinical Psychology, 68,* 303–314.

Le Grange, D., Crosby, R.D., Rathouz, P.J., & Leventhal, B.L. (2007). A randomized controlled comparison of family-based treatment and supportive psychotherapy for adolescent bulimia nervosa. *Archives of General Psychiatry, 64(9),* 1049–1056.

Liddle, H.A., Dakof, G.A., Diamond, G.S., Parker, G.S., Barrett, K., & Tejeda, M. (2001). Multidimensional family therapy for adolescent substance abuse: Results of a randomized clinical trial. *American Journal of Drug and Alcohol Abuse, 27,* 651–687.

Liddle, H., Rowe, C., Dakof, G., Henderson, C., & Greenbaum, P. (2009). Multidimensional family therapy for young adolescent substance abuse: Twelve-month outcomes of a randomized controlled trial. *Journal of Consulting and Clinical Psychology, 77,* 12–25.

Liddle, H.A., Rowe, C.L., Dakof, G.A., Ungaro, R.A., & Henderson, C.E. (2004). Early intervention for adolescent substance abuse: Pretreatment to posttreatment outcomes of a randomized clinical trial comparing multidimensional family therapy and peer group treatment. *Journal of Psychoactive Drugs, 36,* 49–63.

Littell, J.H. (2005). Lessons from a systematic review of effects of multisystemic therapy. *Children and Youth Services Review, 27*(4), 445–463.

Littell, J.H., Corcoran, J., & Pillai, V. (2008). *Systematic reviews and meta-analysis.* New York: Oxford University Press.

Littell, J.H., Popa, M., & Forsythe, B. (2005). Multisystemic therapy for social, emotional, and behavioral problems in youth aged 10–17. Retrieved on January 8, 2009 from http://www.campbellcollaboration.org/campbell_library/index.php

Lock, J., Le Grange, D., Agras, W.S., & Dare, C. (2001). *Treatment manual for anorexia nervosa: A family-based approach.* New York: Guilford Press.

Lock, J., Le Grange, D., Agras, W.S., Moye, A., Bryson, S., & Jo, B. (2010). Randomized clinical trial comparing family-based treatment with adolescent-focused individual therapy for adolescents with anorexia nervosa. *Archives of General Psychiatry, 67,* 1025–1032.

McCart, M.R., Priester, P.E., Davies, W.H., & Azen, R. (2006). Differential effectiveness of behavioral parent-braining and cognitive-behavioral therapy for antisocial youth: A meta-analysis. *Journal of Abnormal Child Psychology, 34,* 527–543.

Macdonald, G., & Turner, W. (2008). Treatment foster care for improving outcomes in children and young people. *Cochrane Database of Systematic Reviews,* Issue 1, CD005649.

Minuchin, S. (1974). *Families and family therapy.* Cambridge, MA: Harvard University Press.

Munchin, S., Montalvo, B., Guerney, B.G., Jr., Rosman, B.L., & Schumer, F. (1967). *Families of the slums: An exploration of their structure and treatment.* New York: Basic Books.

Minuchin, S., Rosman, B.L., & Baker, L. (1978). *Psychosomatic families: Anorexia in context.* Cambridge, MA: Harvard University Press.

National Association of Social Workers (1999). *Code of Ethics.* Washington DC: NASW. http://www.naswdc.org/pubs/code/code.asp

Nichols, M. (2009). *The lost art of listening: how learning to listen can improve relationships.* New York: The Guilford Press.

Palazzoli, M.S., & Boscolo, B. (1990). *Paradox and counterparadox: A new model in the therapy of the family in schizophrenic transaction.* NY: Jason Aronson.

Rhodes, P., Brown, J., & Madden, S. (2009). The Maudsley model of family-based treatment for anorexia nervosa: A qualitative evaluation of parent-to-parent consultation. *Journal of Marital and Family Therapy, 35,* 181–192.

Richmond, M.E. (1917). *Social diagnosis.* New York: Russell Sage Foundation.

Rigter, H., Pelc, I., Tossmann, P., Phan, O., Grichting, E., Hendriks, V., & Rowe, C. (2010). INCANT: A transnational randomized trial of multidimensional family therapy versus treatment as usual for adolescents with cannabis use disorder. *BioMed Central Psychiatry, 10,* 38.

Robin, A.L., Siegel, P.T., Koepke, T., Moye, A.W., & Tice, S. (1994). Family therapy versus individual therapy for adolescent females with anorexia nervosa. *Developmental and Behavioral Pediatrics, 15(2),* 111–116.

Robin, A.L., Seigel, P.T., Moye, A.W., Gilroy, M., Barker, D.A., & Sikand, A. (1999). A controlled comparison of family versus individual therapy for adolescents with anorexia nervosa. *Journal of the American Academy of Child and Adolescent Psychiatry, 38,* 1482–1489.

Roots, P., Rowlands, L., & Gowers, S. (2009). User satisfaction with services in a randomized controlled trial of adolescent anorexia nervosa. *European Eating Disorders Review, 17,* 331–337.

Russell, G.F., Szmukler, G.I., Dare, C., & Eisler, I. (1987). An evaluation of family therapy in anorexia nervosa and bulimia nervosa. *Archives of General Psychiatry, 44*(12), 1047–1056.

Schmidt, U., Lee, S., Beecham, J., Perkins, S., Treasure, J., Yi, I., Winn, S., Robinson, P., Murphy, R., Keville, S., Johnson-Sabine, E., Jenkins, M., Frost, S., Dodge, L.,

Berelowitz, M., & Eisler, I. (2007). A randomized controlled trial of family therapy and cognitive behavior therapy guided self-care for adolescents with bulimia nervosa and related disorders. *American Journal of Psychiatry, 164*(4), 591–598.

Sexton, T., & Turner, C.W. (2010). The effectiveness of functional family therapy for youth with behavioural problems in a community practice setting. *Journal of Family Psychology, 24*, 339–348.

Swanson, J., Arnold, L., Kraemer, H., Hechtman, L., Molina, B., Hinshaw, S., et al. (2008). Evidence, interpretation, and qualification from multiple reports of long-term outcomes in the multimodal treatment study of children with ADHD (MTA): Part I: Executive summary. *Journal of Attention Disorders, 12*(1), 4–14.

Szapocznik, J., Hervis, O.E., & Schwartz, S.J. (2003). *Brief strategic family therapy for adolescent drug abuse* (NIDA Therapy Manuals Series, NIH Publication 03-4751). Rockville, MD: National Institute on Drug Abuse.

Vedantam, S. (2009). *Debate over drugs for ADHD reignites.* Retrieved on March 27, 2009 from http://www.washingtonpost.com/wp-dyn/content/article/2009/3/26

Waldron, H.B., & Turner, C.W. (2008). Evidence based psychosocial treatments for adolescent substance abuse. *Journal of Clinical Child & Adolescent Psychology, 37*(1), 238–261.

Watzlawick, P., Beavin Bavelas, J., & Jackson, D.D. (1967). *Pragmatics of human communication. a study of interactional patterns, pathologies and paradoxes.* New York: W.W. Norton & Company.

Watzlawick, P., Weakland, H.J., & Fisch, R. (1974). *Change.* New York: Norton.

Weakland, J.H. (1974). Brief therapy: focused problem resolution. *Family Process, 13*(2), 141–168.

Weisz, J., Sandler, L., Durlak, J., & Anton, B. (2005). Promoting and protecting youth mental health through evidence-based prevention and treatment. *American Psychologist, 60*, 628–648.

White, M. (2007). *Maps of narrative practice.* New York: W.W. Norton.

Wood, A. (2001). The origins of family systems work: Social workers' contributions to the development of family theory and practice. *Australian Social Work, 5*, 15–29.

Wood, B. (1961). *The making of the good neighbor policy.* New York: Columbia University Press.

Yanca, S., & Johnson, L. (2008). *Generalist social work practice with families.* Boston, MA: Pearson.

Zimmerman, T.S., Jacobsen, R.B., MacIntyre, M., & Watson, C. (1996). Solution focused parenting groups: An empirical study. *Journal of Systemic Therapies, 15*(4), 12–25.

APPENDIX: STANDARDS OF EVIDENCE APPRAISAL

Systematic reviews and meta-analyses

A *systematic review* aims comprehensively to locate and synthesise the research bearing on a particular question, using organised, transparent, and replicable procedures at each step in the process (Littell et al., 2008; see Chapter 31). *Meta-analysis* is a set of statistical methods for combining quantitative results from multiple studies to produce an overall summary of empirical knowledge on a given topic. Whenever possible, Cochrane Collaboration systematic reviews are presented. The Cochrane Collaboration is an international, nonprofit organisation devoted to high-calibre systematic reviews on health and mental health care (see www.cochrane.org).

AMERICAN PSYCHOLOGICAL ASSOCIATION (APA) DIVISION 12 TASK FORCE CRITERIA

In the APA Division 2 Task Force Criteria for *empirically supported treatment* (Chambless & Hollon, 1998), 'well-established' and 'probably efficacious', 'possibly efficacious', and 'experimental' treatments have been delineated. For 'well-established treatments', at least two group-design experiments, conducted by independent investigatory teams, show statistically significantly findings over medication, psychosocial placebo, or another treatment. Alternatively, the treatment may be equivalent to an already established treatment in experiments with statistical power being sufficient to detect moderate differences. Furthermore, treatment is manualised and targeted for a specified problem, and outcome measures are reliable and valid. Appropriate data analysis is also used. For treatments defined as 'probably efficacious', at least two studies must show the intervention to be more effective than no-treatment control. For 'possibly efficacious', at least one study must indicate that a treatment is superior in the absence of conflicting evidence.

REFERENCES

Fisher, C., Hetrick, S., & Rushford, N. (2010). Family therapy for anorexia nervosa. *Cochrane Database of Systematic Reviews*, Issue 4. Art No.: CD004780.

11

Strengths Perspective

W. Patrick Sullivan

The emergence of the strengths perspective, as it has been articulated in contemporary social work, was a function of chance, the result of the convergence of several key personalities at the University of Kansas School Social Welfare in the early 1980s. It began when Ronna Chamberlain, who had extensive experience serving individuals with serious and persistent mental illnesses, enrolled in the Ph.D. programme. As fate would have it, she was assigned to work with Charlie Rapp who would serve as her faculty mentor. Before entering academia, Rapp had gained a reputation in child welfare circles in Illinois for his optimism in the face of seemingly hopeless situations, and his persistent advocacy on behalf of children and families in need. Although Rapp and Chamberlain came from different practice backgrounds, the duo found more similarities than differences when reviewing their work history. Their previous experiences, and the practice wisdom they shared, guided the development of a pilot case management project subsequently launched at a local community mental health centre. This pilot programme, initially identified as the 'resource acquisition model', was refined and shaped by succeeding replications and ultimately became widely known as the strengths model.

There were those who quickly grasped the significance of a method predicated, not on disease or pathology, but rather on psychosocial strengths. By extension, it was also recognised the utility of this model went well beyond the narrow confines of case management and mental health services. As a cadre of interested parties began to dig beneath the surface, they were encouraged when the early returns on the intervention were positive. What made this a particularly heady time was a prevailing sense the bedrock principles and philosophy which sustained the model could stimulate a significant paradigm shift in social work practice as a whole. As these ideas and results were shared beyond the School of Social Welfare, a group of like-minded educators, researchers, and practitioners were invited to participate in a small conference in Lawrence, Kansas, and from there, the strengths perspective was born (Modrcin et al., 1985; Rapp, 1992; Rapp & Chamberlain, 1985; Rapp & Goscha, 2006; Rapp & Wintersteen, 1989; Weick et al., 1989). However, it was popularised by, and spread widely mainly due to the collection edited by Dennis Saleebey (1992), then Professor of Social Work at the University of Kansas.

Like all new ideas, this unconventional method initially engendered some stout resistance, but a renewed focus on strengths also had appeal. The basic tenets of the strengths perspective resonated with fundamental social work values, and offered a humanistic approach to services focusing initially on some of the most vulnerable and stigmatised groups (Rapp, 1992; Weick et al., 1989). It was also evident the conceptual framework serving to brace the original case management model was portable in a wide variety of settings and fields of practice. Not surprisingly, as time has marched on, various aspects of the strengths model have been borrowed, reshaped, and reinvented, in part *because* it is heavily grounded by values and inherently malleable concepts. As research on the diffusion of innovations indicates, modifications in all new products or ideas can be expected. While such revisions can be fruitful, there is always concern such alterations may be too extreme and deviate significantly from the original intent and thrust of the invention (Rogers, 2003). This caution may be relevant here, particularly as selective components of the strengths model have been incorporated in the narrowest of clinical packages. Additionally, there is always the fear that innovations may be embraced too enthusiastically, and in the nearly three decades since its introduction, there are basic assumptions and practice behaviours germane to the strengths model still demanding greater scrutiny.

This chapter provides a historical overview of strengths-based practice with an emphasis on the primary assumptions and principles traditionally guiding practical applications. It outlines the basic practice framework and, while the lion's share of attention is devoted to behavioural healthcare, other areas where the model has been broadly adopted are also acknowledged. Finally, the general efficacy of strengths-based interventions is explored and an agenda for future research presented.

A HISTORICAL OVERVIEW

The first days

In 1982, armed with a $10,000 grant and a group of social work students completing their field work, Rapp and Chamberlain were prepared to test the viability of their shared vision in an initial case management project. During the planning phase, the team developed a list of desirable client outcomes to shape the day-by-day work of these new case managers, and subsequently serve as the standards by which success could be measured. This list of outcomes included vocational activity of some kind, independent living, developing friendships, and positive use of leisure time. Today, these would be viewed as relatively standard goals. However, context is an important consideration here, because at that juncture the most common set of proposed outcomes for treatment of serious mental illness would include items such as compliance with medications and appointments, improved hygiene, symptom management, and perhaps a reduction in inpatient care. While it would be unfair to suggest there was a complete absence of interest in an enhanced set of outcome goals, more often than not these goals were truncated in predictable ways. Thus, the housing goal was for a service recipient to move to a group home, and a vocational goal meant work in a sheltered setting or a mental health sponsored work team such as a landscaping or cleaning crew. So what perplexed Rapp, Chamberlain and others who had joined them, was how existing case management models could possibly address the list of goals they had developed. Their scepticism was based on the fact that the predominate service strategy in vogue at the time, often referred to as brokering, consisted of linking consumers to a standard set of specialised mental health services and ancillary programmes. In essence, the existing models could not deliver more ambitious outcomes in an appreciable manner because the very blueprint of these programmes reflected a more conservative set of expectations for recipients of care. So if the Kansas team had hopes of reaching higher, the only realistic path available to them was to try something radically different.

Key assumptions and principles of the strengths model

By 1982, the world of mental health care was in flux. Owing to humanistic, fiscal, and legal considerations, the hospital was no longer the primary locus of care, prompting an urgent need to develop and implement efficacious community-based programmes. In addition, it was now abundantly clear that the full range of goals needed to ensure community tenure could rarely be attained via an exclusive clinical approach. It was also painfully obvious that social forces, particularly stigma and a lack of real-world opportunities, only added to the challenges individuals faced in their quest to become legitimate actors in daily social processes. So what could be done to increase the community tenure and quality of life of those facing among the most vexing of challenges? It was here Rapp drew upon his previous experience with William Davidson in child welfare, and saw the utility of two key assumptions guiding his work in this field (Davidson & Rapp, 1976). In time, these assumptions would prove to be the lodestars shaping the development of a fresh approach to case management. The first assumption posits behaviour is, in part, a function of the resources available to people. The second key assumption claims society, at least in word and theory, values equal access to available resources. Operationalising these assumptions in professional practice, as detailed below, put the resource acquisition model of case management firmly within the classic, but now oft-neglected boundaries of social work practice, in particular, the long-standing focus on the person-in-environment and the historical commitment to social advocacy (Wintersteen, 1986). As Salebeey (2006) suggests, 'Operating from a strengths perspective is good, basic, social work practice. There is nothing here that is not coincidental with the core of values that energizes and drives the profession' (p. 78).

These assumptions are simple enough to grasp, so it is easy to ponder them, nod in agreement, or even quibble a bit on the margins. However, the ramifications of truly bringing these ideas alive can alter the scope of social work practice dramatically. Imagine a practice environment where you could begin with a blank sheet of paper, a world where nothing is considered out of bounds or deemed unrealistic. In this scenario one could envision surrounding a vulnerable individual with every conceivable support needed to ensure success. Doing this exercise, at least occasionally, is vital given the many seemingly intractable situations social workers confront. Its power lies in the ability to unlock a level of creative thinking so routinely stifled in the daily grind of work. Consider the most serious forms of mental illness, conditions for which we still have more questions than answers. There may be general agreement that psychotropic medications are an essential ingredient to a care plan, yet even here medications are a type of support, not a cure. Many aspects of behavioural healthcare can be considered in a like fashion. Important services are offered to help people surmount the impact of a primary process, but unfortunately, these interventions only help people travel half the distance they need to cover. For example, alcohol and drug treatment can help people get a loose grip on troubling substance use, but in the absence of work, positive relationships, and healthy use of leisure time, how long will the effects of treatment last? To be truly impactful, service packages must do more. A narrow focus on deficits shrinks the horizon and restricts the vision of the helper, and even the recipient, about what is possible and what the person can be. The strengths model aims to strike all such tethers by looking far beyond the immediate problem.

Since the strengths model of case management was introduced, a new generation of community-based programmes has emerged placing the importance of supports front and centre in the planning process (see Drake & Bond, 2008; Leff et al., 2009). Here, when clients fail to reach their goals or backslide, the first impulse is to examine how available supports can be altered or buttressed, rather than simply accepting the disappointing outcome as a confirmation of the diagnosis. Reality can be a harsh master, and certainly time constraints, money, caseload size, and a host of significant obstacles are present in contemporary human services. In the face of these impediments, the idealised world portrayed above will likely never exist. However, this nod to pragmatism does not negate the central claims of the strengths model nor what may be truly possible for the people served. It is merely a commentary on the current state of social services.

Trying a fresh approach, the strengths model of case management places a high premium on creativity, and eschews unimaginative programming and interventions resulting in cookie-cutter care plans ignoring individual uniqueness and paying little heed to the goals and aspirations of recipients or service users. The basic framework of the strengths model of case management is relatively easy to describe. In simple terms, case managers first engage recipients in the completion of a strengths-based assessment. This assessment is designed to identify consumer strengths in a wide array of life domains, such as health, vocational and educational activity, living arrangements, and social supports, with an emphasis on current and past activities that can be beneficial in the pursuit of individually tailored goals. The goals that follow are generally proactive and behavioural – meaning rooted in tangible outcomes. Drawing from the first assumption, the general intent is to consider what social resources can aid consumers in their quest. From there, the worker and recipient work side by side to develop an action plan detailing the necessary steps to secure these resources. Almost by definition, and particularly given the challenges presented by serious and persistent mental illnesses, executing this role requires staff to be out of the office and on the streets. Also germane to this role, as foreshadowed by the second key assumption, is advocacy – often needed to help others, particularly those who serve as formal or informal gatekeepers to resources, overcome their fear of people with mental illnesses, and more forcefully executed when recipients face blatant discrimination.

The success of the initial project captured the fancy of many (Rapp & Wintersteen, 1989). So, as additional case management projects were initiated across Kansas, and as requests for training arrived from other parts of the nation, there were opportunities to gain a better understanding of what seemed to drive effective services. Over time, a host of key principles were developed – principles which have remained remarkably stable over time. Some of these guiding principles were specific to case management. Those that are broader in scope are described below.

The first principle suggests *persons with psychiatric challenges can 'recover, reclaim, and transform their lives'* (Rapp & Goscha, 2006, p. 55, emphasis added). By simply replacing the term psychiatric challenges with a range of human conditions and situations, the usefulness and appropriateness of this guideline for social work practice is obvious. More than anything, this principle focuses on the attitude and beliefs of the helper, and argues a hopeful and optimistic posture is called for, even more so when the struggles that the recipients of care face, are daunting. While it can be suggested that this viewpoint has always been required for effective social work practice, when first offered, this upbeat stance challenged prevailing attitudes about individuals who faced conditions like schizophrenia. The term 'chronically mentally ill', the blanket label then in vogue to describe people with the most serious forms of mental illness, reflected shared assumptions about the life chances of many who had spent years under psychiatric care. Indeed, it would take time before the term recovery became a common feature of the lexicon in mental health, and to have discussed this concept with regards to this population then – and in some circles now – was considered naïve at best. What is particularly troublesome is how such pessimism can pervade the hearts, minds, and outlook of even the best helpers and negatively impact the organisational culture of social services. Deegan (1990), writing from her experience as a recipient of service, has suggested professional helpers, in attitude and deed, often practise in a manner that is dehumanising and depersonalising. While adopting these attitudes can serve as a self-preservation strategy for those on the frontlines, the impact on recipients can be profound. In fact, Deegan (1990) poignantly referred to this phenomenon as spirit breaking.

Optimism, it was believed, could be contagious, but beyond this, the first principle also presaged another crucial conviction of strengths-based practice. The second key principle argues all people have innate strengths and abilities that, even if now dormant, can ultimately be activated to promote positive growth. Professional helpers in mental health spend countless hours learning the language and the discernment skills that are part and parcel of the process of differential diagnosis and assessment. Once the issue has been identified and named, all efforts are extended to address and hopefully ameliorate the problem. While this model can produce wonderful results, it too has limitations. There is no Diagnostic and Statistical Manual for strengths, and nor should there be. Diagnostic categories represent an attempt to develop useful categories to identify various human conditions and problems. The attempt is to capture in a name what seems to be common among a wide group of people. Strengths are idiosyncratic, and while as a guide, assessment tools can help practitioners search for these strengths categorically (interpersonal skills, social supports, attitudes, aptitudes, physical skills, and so on), no simple overarching term can be coined that would be innately useful to the helping enterprise.

The strengths perspective challenges helpers to view situations from an entirely different lens – and it is a proposition proving to be a stumbling block for some (Blundo, 2001). If traditional models of care follow an inherent logic, the same is true for strengths-based work. To this end, the first task is to identify individual strengths and abilities, which, while occasionally challenging, is relatively straightforward. It is the next logical step that distinguishes this model from prevailing practice in mental health and other similar fields. The second principle states *interventions and care plans should build from, amplify, and enhance individual strengths*. When faithfully executed, everything the practitioner does – engagement, assessment, care planning, thus all phases of direct practice – must be animated by this principle. This can be done. In the early years of this work, to the amazement of many, the diagnosis of the consumers was never revealed to case managers. The task at hand was to truly hone in on the individual's interests and abilities – past, present, and future – and to develop a list of goals they, not the programme staff, were interested in pursuing. In essence, the quest was to see the person behind the diagnosis. As the strengths model became more prominent and popular in social work, it became commonplace to see *some* components of strengths-based work embraced, but leave important vestiges of the traditional paradigm firmly in place. As an example, today it is not unusual to find a section on client strengths included on standard assessment forms, but with the end product and the intent of the exercise unchanged. Here, strengths have been indentified, which is admirable, but in essence they are deemed simply an afterthought, certainly not viewed as the centrepiece from which work proceeds. Needless to say, this falls far short of demonstrating fidelity to the strengths model (Blundo, 2001; Graybeal, 2001).

A cautionary note is needed here. Then, and now, there is no attempt to deny people have serious problems or the difficulties they face are not real. People come to human service organisations looking for help, or at the very least because they are concerned about others. To that end, there are a host of specialised services and treatments already poised to deal with these very maladies and, predictably, some are more successful than others. The intent of strengths-informed work is not to traverse old ground, but to stimulate client growth and change from a different direction. The overriding belief is all people who are successful have been adroit at recognising and building on their strengths and securing the resources they need to maximise their life chances and overall satisfaction (Rapp & Goscha, 2006). While the people commonly served by social workers may have had more difficulty following this blueprint, conceptually they are no different. Everything that happens in strengths-based practice flows from this perspective. The focus is on producing tangible outcomes in a wide range of life domains. The power of the model, as described more fully below, lies in its practicality. However, it is always important to remain clear on the scope of the intervention. Therefore, there are no claims strengths-based case management or other variations on this theme can cure mental illness or substance abuse problems, or topple the structural inequalities that lead to poverty and differential rates of disease and illness.

Consistent with first of the two fundamental assumptions noted above, the third enduring principle *underscores the importance of social resources to the well-being of people, and argues, contrary to popular opinion, such resources are omnipresent in the communities where we work and live* (see Sullivan, 1992). This stance is counterintuitive, at least from the perspective of most in the human services where bemoaning the lack of resources is a daily occurrence. So how could it be suggested social resources abound? The simple answer lies in the way resources are conceived from a strengths perspective. Here, the power of using the common resources available to all people is touted, and there is a genuine effort to refrain from the use of specialised services, particularly those designed to serve as a social prosthesis for consumers of services. Simply put, it is believed every human need does not need to be matched with a corresponding social programme. Furthermore, while specialised resources are generally scarce, usually expensive, and often stigmatising, from a strengths point of view naturally occurring resources are nearly limitless. Here the practitioner looks for a home not a bed or placement, activities of daily living is not something addressed in an educational group, but something learned in the real world every day, and the goal is for people to find work at a real job not in a shelter. When work is in full swing, the professional should always ponder what person, group, business, church, or organisation can replace the functions they provide or are provided by the host agency. The quest is always to search for your replacement. Similar to the caveat above, it would be foolhardy to suggest there are not cases when specialised resources are needed. The contention is they should be used as a last resort, and for a very select group of individuals.

Two key principles of the strengths model pay special attention to the relationship between the professional and the recipient of services. The first deems the relationship is 'primary and essential' (Rapp & Goscha, 2006, p. 64). On the face of it, this would seem to be self-evident, but there are a range of reasons why it is important to restate this here. The nature of strengths-based work, particularly case management, is easily misunderstood. By spending time in the community, working on daily living issues, and tracking down resources, it is easy to dismiss this role as a mere paraprofessional function. Nothing could be farther from the truth. The savvy case manager is a skilful helper using every therapeutic tool at his or her disposal, is an expert in community resources, entitlement rules, effective advocacy, and functions flawlessly in a multidisciplinary team. In this role, the professional must also work with recipients to identify and exploit their strengths and abilities.

In the early days, this style of practice was confusing, perplexing, and even considered outrageous to veteran professionals who were used to help being offered at arm's length. Concerns were raised about boundary issues specifically where it was felt clients would misconstrue the nature of the relationship. Interestingly, in the initial pilot project concerns were quickly raised when it became apparent consumers were calling case managers when they were in crisis and need – not the primary therapist. As time passed, it became clear the relationship was strengthened as a result of the simple acts of assistance and words of encouragement case managers offered. Help cleaning an apartment, assistance cooking a meal, a joke told in the park, or a simple call when times were difficult, were the items highlighted by recipients as keys to the relationship, and even turning points in their recovery process (see Sullivan, 1994).

One subtle but critical belief inherent to the strengths models is that the keys to recovery are not credited to the specialised knowledge of professionals, but are vested in the individual. Thus, from the beginning mutuality has been underscored, and, as another key principle asserted, the recipient was to be viewed as the director of the overall process (Rapp & Goscha, 2006). It would be too strong to contend this was a complete break from the traditions of therapeutic relationships, but it remained a striking point of departure when used with individuals viewed as significantly compromised. What does this mean in actual practice? How common elements of the helping process are illuminated by a strengths orientation is detailed below.

KEY ELEMENTS OF THE STRENGTHS-BASED HELPING PROCESS

The strengths assessment

While completing an assessments is a standard feature of most helping endeavours, it is often treated as a required activity, necessary for reimbursement, and as a tool used to zero in on a problem definition or diagnosis. In practice, once the target issue has been identified and an initial care plan has been established, the utility of the assessment as a useful tool often diminishes appreciably. The strengths assessment, as a process and as a product, has some distinct attributes reflecting the organic nature of the actual document and the specific nature of strengths-based practice.

Portrayed as a temporal sequence, the assessment is usually conceived as the step preceding the phase of actual helping and, in fact, the admonition to refrain from intervening prematurely has been a mantra imparted to neophytes for decades. In the most benign situations, the assessment interview can be akin to a standard intake procedure conducted in most medical settings. At worst, the experience can be painful, requiring people to repeat troubling episodes in their personal history, recount areas of personal failing or inadequacy, and, in general, expose those aspects of their lives that are, at the very least, embarrassing. Blundo (2006) notes, when practitioners proceed down this path:

> What we usually see as most provocative are the 'problems' apparent in the story being told. We look for what is going wrong, symptoms, failings, underlying pathologies, and the history of the problem to substantiate these early assumptions that are being constructed into a mental picture of our client. It's the client's faults and weaknesses that we key in on as most significant in our listening. In many ways we are rewriting or translating the story told by the client into our own professional language, a language largely made up of concepts having to do with problems, pathology, deficits, and failings to which we will apply some form of intervention (p. 26).

What's worse, when the participant has been struggling with a persistent condition, or requires assistance from a wide range of caregivers, it is a near certainty they have been asked to complete a similar exercise multiple times.

From the moment the first strengths-based case management projects commenced, it was recognised the process of assessment was not just a precursor to the helping process, but rather an important intervention in itself. One of the key tasks in working with those who face the greatest challenges, and who have been the most compromised by illness, trauma, or other life circumstances, is to work with them to uncover, reveal, and recognise individual strengths and strengths in the world around them. Strengths can be as easily overlooked by the recipient of care as by the professional entrusted to serve them. This task is not merely restricted to the current snapshot of the world as it is, but should include a life review identifying past passions, interests, involvements, and accomplishments. In general, completing a strengths assessment requires a conversation, marked by the use of non-threatening probes and simple open-ended questions. In the optimum situation, the professional is not a slave to a checklist, but rather takes his or her cues from the service recipient by exploring some areas in depth and leaving others for a different time. Saleebey (2006) offers some important keys to stimulating the conversation, particularly when the consumer's world view is saturated with problems:

> First, it is incumbent on the practitioner to provide the words and images of strength, wholeness, and capacity where they may be lacking. Second, it is important for the practitioner to be an affirmative mirror, beaming back to the client a reflection of that person's positive attributes, accomplishments, skills, and talents. Last, it is wise to carefully lay out with an individual what may be possible in his or her life – big or small things, it doesn't matter. And all of this must ring true to the person and be grounded in the dailiness of life (p. 89).

Certainly there is a desire to cover all key life domains when completing an assessment, but the process is nearly as important as the final product. Oftentimes, as noted above, the goal is to energise the recipient, to shine light on things consumers enjoy or have enjoyed, and to particularly underscore those periods of time, no matter how far in the past, when things were going better. It is indeed about strengths, and as a result, in the best of outcomes the interaction breeds hope, enthusiasm, and optimism.

Nonetheless, it is also important to realise people generally present – or are coerced – for care in times when they feel overwhelmed and are suffering from immense grief and pain. The identification of strengths, abilities, accomplishments, and possibilities may be a roadmap out of their current plight, but skilful professionals have a feel for the right time to move the conversation from problems to possible solutions. Offering a clinical perspective, Rashid and Ostermann (2009) argue:

> Deficit-oriented models of assessment ... paint an incomplete picture of the client, reducing clarity, information, and completeness. Clinical assessment should be a hybrid endeavor: exploring strengths as well as weaknesses. The focus of assessment should be collecting not only stories of unmet needs but also tales of fulfillment. Assessment should explore not just conflicts but also compromises, transgressions as well as acts of compassion, selfishness of others, but also genuine actions of sharing, grudges as well as expressions of gratitude, and episodes of vengeance as well as instances of forgiveness. It is about exploring in an authentic way hubris as well as humanity, haste as well as self-restraint, hate as well as love, pain of trauma as well as growth from it (p. 490).

What makes strengths assessments different is that they are designed to be fluid documents. As the relationship proceeds and comfort levels rise, more information is obtained. Perhaps a consumer reveals past activities or interests, or even important people in their life with whom they would like to reconnect. Thus, instead of simply becoming another client file stuffed in a drawer or stored in a computer, this assessment is constantly updated and referred to. In actual practice, discussions about possible goals and activities can occur seamlessly as the assessment is completed. If a past activity is referenced, the alert professional explores any current interest in this endeavour. If a recipient acknowledges an unmet goal or a fleeting aspiration, the conversation shifts to a consideration of what obstacles must be removed or steps taken to move forward again.

Because the assessment and goal-setting process are consanguineous in this model, and consistent with the basic guiding assumptions, good strengths assessments direct attention outside the person and consider what external resources exist to support the goals outlined by recipients (Sullivan & Rapp, 2006). There are a number of strengths assessments to choose from, and while there are variations among them, the importance of active listening and learning from consumers is a consistent theme, and in each case strengths discovery is not seen as a secondary activity nor are the areas of strength ignored as the work proceeds (Anderson et al., 2009; Graybeal, 2001; McQuaide & Ehrenreich, 1997; Rapp & Goscha, 2006).

Goal and case planning

Good case plans flow naturally from the assessment process, and if the identification of strengths has been the centrepiece of this activity, it stands to reason these are the building blocks for the work to follow. Given the broadband nature of individual strengths, there are a myriad of ways such assets can be brought into play in any therapeutic situation. So conceived, a focus on individual strengths in clinical settings can place the model alongside many person-centred therapy and enrichment models that came before. Yet, consistent with the foundations of social work practice – and the historical assumptions and traditions that shaped this model – strengths-informed work is firmly rooted in the person-in-environment perspective (see Chapter 8). While an understanding of the interplay of forces ranging from the emotions and cognitions of the individual, to the most dramatic events in the social environment can be helpful in understanding pathology and dysfunction, strengths-based work strives to identify and build from the healthy and sustaining forces alive inside and outside the recipient of care (Sullivan, 1992; Sullivan & Rapp, 2006). When the work truly commences, the focus remains squarely on the here-and-now, with goal and case plans designed to attain the real-world goals recipients identify as meaningful to them.

While perhaps surprising, the strengths model of case management, and other related interventions, have been particularly popular in services focused on some of the most vulnerable in society – those with severe and persistent mental illnesses, children with serious emotional challenges, individuals struggling with alcohol and substance misuse, persons involved with the criminal justice system, and the poor (see Saleebey, 2009). There are a number of expressions used to describe the plight of those who fall into the above categories, with negative terms, such as disaffiliated, disenfranchised, and discarded top on the list. Taken as a group, each of these descriptors portrays those who routinely reside on the margins of society, and who are often called clients in human service agencies.

Drawing from ecological principles, Taylor (1997) suggests such persons occupy an entrapped social niche. These niches, he argues, are highly stigmatised, and the people who occupy them commonly lack the skills, resources, and the support needed to escape. Sadly, these same people often become defined by the niche they occupy and the labels assigned to them (e.g., alcoholic, schizophrenic, and ex-con) reflect social disapproval. It is not surprising many bound by this situation can only find comfort when they associate with others in common straits. The opposite condition – and one highly desired by most people – is to inhabit an enriched niche, a place where one possesses all the tools and opportunities necessary to enjoy a satisfying life replete with all the benefits of authentic membership in society. While the concept of the social niche may be abstract, one way to characterise the goal of much strengths-based practice, particularly with the most vulnerable, is as an attempt to help people escape niche entrapment (Sullivan & Rapp, 2009). At times, the focus is on the skills and abilities the person needs to accomplish their stated goals. At other moments, the target of an intervention is to increase the available opportunities in the surrounding world. In practice, this may require directly confronting barriers to full social participation unjustly erected via stigma, law, policy, and fear. At stake is social integration, a key consideration for many served by social workers. Social integration has physical, emotional, sociological, and psychological components, and it is marked by having a place and a stake in life. Ware et al. (2007) discuss this goal in light of Nobel Prize-winning economist Amartya Sen's capabilities model (see Chapters 1, 24, and 41). Capability involves a:

> Degree of human agency – what people can actually do and be in everyday life. What people can do and be is in turn contingent on having competencies and opportunities. Opportunities are provided by social environments. To ensure capability, social circumstances must offer opportunities for individual competency to be developed and exercised. To define social integration, we borrow from the capabilities approach its emphasis on agency, its developmental perspective, its recognition that individual development is contingent on supportive social environments, and its core concepts of competency and opportunity in delineating the process through which social integration develops (Ware et al., 2007, p. 470).

Strengths-based practice is difficult to capture in a manual, because, executed faithfully, a high level of creativity is required to develop individualised case plans. While the consumer remains the ultimate director of the process, professional partners can help translate the overall goal of the consumer into a working plan. Successful plans, it is posited, draw heavily from the inventory of individual and environmental strengths identified in the assessment. Staying within an ecological framework, the overall goal is to help recipients find the perfect niche, and as a marker of overall social integration, the outcome is a function of both an individual and social processes (Sullivan & Rapp, 2009). A perfect niche is found, according to Rapp and Goscha (2006), when 'the requirements and needs of the setting are perfectly matched with the desires, talents, and even idiosyncrasies of the person' (p. 168).

Ironically, deficits – or pathology-focused interventions and strengths-based models are, in many ways, mirror images of each other. Both consider how individual and environmental factors influence behaviour, and consider the types of modifications needed to promote the health and well-being or recipients of care. At issue is what side of the equation one wants to emphasise. Consider the following case.

Dave Darland, a 42-year-old man diagnosed with schizophrenia, has been hospitalised seven times since his 19th birthday, and was most recently discharged two years ago. In the past year, his condition has deteriorated significantly. While he lives in his own run-down apartment, of late he has had tremendous difficulty keeping the premises clean, he has also neglected his personal care, and his bizarre behaviour, which includes yelling in responses to imaginary threats, has caused his neighbours much concern. However, there have been periods over the past decade where Dave has done fairly well. For a short time, he attended a voluntary drop-in centre sponsored by the local mental health centre, and, because he was an outstanding high school athlete, there was a time when he participated in pick-up basketball games in the neighbourhood. He has obtained a number of jobs with the help of a case manager, but he has rarely lasted in these positions for more than a few months in part because he fails to take his medications and ultimately refuses to leave his home.

The deficits presented in this case are many, and veteran helpers will see hundreds of cases like this over the course of their career. From a standard approach, there are many ways to proceed. The first order of business is to consider a return to inpatient care, and beyond this, ascertain where the demands of independent living are just too great. Personal care is certainly an issue, beginning with medication compliance, and moving forward toward grooming and other matters of personal hygiene. Groups covering these very topics are routinely offered by the mental health centre. Rest assured, all of these interventions have been tried before and, while there always seems to be improvement for the short-run, unfortunately, Dave seems locked in a viscous cycle generally ending with another inpatient stay or, at least, a return to congregate living.

The traditional manner to intervene in this situation should be familiar to those who have worked in the field. Let's look at this case from a different angle.

Dave was assigned a new case manager who began by completing a strengths assessment. Not surprisingly, Dave's athletic success was discussed, but also emphasised were those periods when things went well. Dave reported things became difficult for him when he moved into his new apartment, in part because he was no longer able to catch a bus to the drop-in centre. He admitted he tended to have more trouble on the days where he had little to do, and said, while it was good to work, he really didn't like landscaping and janitorial work and these were the opportunities regularly presented to him. He said he really missed the drop-in centre and he genuinely liked getting out and just shooting baskets from time to time. As the case manager probed deeper, Dave reiterated he really wanted to return to the drop-in centre to see some old friends, and he would like to find a job that interested him.

A key phase in strengths-based work has been the use of behaviourally anchored goals. These goals become a part of a written contract between the recipient and professional, and are tailored to the specific situation of each person. As a general rule, professionals work with consumers to establish an initial goal has a high likelihood of accomplishment. This first taste of success helps build consumer confidence and enthusiasm, and can also place the working relationship on solid footing. All consumer goals, no matter how apparently outlandish, can be broken down into concrete, measurable, and achievable steps (see Rapp & Goscha, 2006). It is essential consumers are placed in the lead in this phase of helping. Even in those cases where they are unable to decisively state their ultimate desires with conviction, they must constantly be encouraged to make their wishes known. This is a crucial issue, as much of what is deemed consumer noncompliance is actually a passive statement of disinterest.

A subtle example of this can be found in the case example offered above. The consumer expresses an interest in some form of work, but had little interest in the past jobs obtained for him.

> As the relationship developed, the case manager learned just how much Dave knew about basketball and how passionate he was about the sport. Until a new living situation could be arranged on a local bus line, the case manager, with Dave's permission, contacted a consumer who attended the drop-in centre and who expressed a willingness to give Dave a ride several times a week. Once the transportation situation was resolved, Dave began attending the drop-in centre, rekindling old relationships and quickly made new friends. As his job interests were explored in greater depth, the case manager asked Dave if he would have any desire to get involved with the local semi-pro basketball team. He quickly agreed. As the case manger and Dave considered the requirements of a new position, Dave admitted he must pay greater attention to his appearance and, at one point, the case manager accompanied him to a local Goodwill shop where he acquired some suitable new work clothes. Soon, with the support of the case manager, Dave was able to volunteer as an usher at the basketball games and, as he demonstrated he was a dependable worker, he was eventually hired as a ticket-taker. Because the job was so important to him, staff noted he rarely missed appointments, and issues with medication compliance reduced dramatically.

In both scenarios, supports are offered. From a deficits perspective, Dave's personal challenges and liabilities, coupled with an environment presenting demands he could not match, meant he was, for the moment, unable to function independently. In the second scenario, there is also a desire to provide the consumer with the supports he needs. Here the focus is on individual and environmental strengths. It began with an assessment of interests, aspirations, and those areas of life Dave enjoyed and were viewed as meaningful. Significantly, one perspective understood Dave's behaviour in terms of illness and pathology, and also saw the social environment as toxic and overwhelming for him. In the second scenario, the case mangers considered what natural resources could be used in order to provide the supports and opportunities Dave needed to retain a chance to live as independently as possible. Indeed, when individual interests and strengths are matched with opportunities in the world at large, there is a chance for people to find their perfect niche.

Effectiveness of the strengths model

The use of strengths-based approaches in human services is ubiquitous, but it is unusual to find well-articulated and all-encompassing models lending themselves easily to direct scrutiny. In practice, professionals may include strengths in formal assessments and ensure various interviews and therapeutic sessions thereafter make room for a discussion and use of individual strengths. At the macro-level, one can find models of community development stressing the importance of identifying and building on neighbourhood and local strengths and assets, as opposed to the common tendency to focus exclusively on needs and problems (Kretzmann & McKnight, 1993). Yet, in reality, the popularity of strengths-based methods has been based as much on faith, values, and the conviction of adherents, as it has on strong empirical research. In part, this is because a focus on strengths, as offered in the examples above, is often merely one part of an overall package of services, and there has been scant interest in teasing out the independent contribution of this single component of care.

Of all existing examples of strengths-based work, case management services have been studied the most because the model is well articulated and thus is well positioned to be examined closely (see Rapp & Goscha, 2006). While small in number, several early studies indicated strengths-based case management made a difference in the lives of consumers facing serious mental illnesses, and the excitement about these early returns led to the proliferation of the model across the nation and world. Reviewing the first series of projects faithfully implementing the model in mental health services, Rapp and Wintersteen (1989) found high levels of individual goal attainment across key life domains in areas such as independent living, vocational and educational status, social support, and health. They also found evidence that case management reduced the use of psychiatric hospitalisation. These findings and more were also confirmed in subsequent studies. Stannard (1999) found consumers served in the strengths model of case management showed general improvement across most life domains, but made statistically significant gains in overall quality of life and in vocational and educational outcomes when compared to those served in a generalist case management programme. Macias et al. (1994) found use of the strengths model resulted in reduced levels of symptomatology, greater sense of overall well-being, and an improved performance in daily living. Interestingly, these authors also note these improvements were also reported by family members, which, in turn, reduced their level of overall burden. In a subsequent study, Macias et al. (1997), found use of the strengths model resulted in significant improvements in three targeted areas, increasing recipient's income (generally achieved by helping individuals obtain available benefits), social support, and maintaining overall physical health. In addition, primary therapists of these same consumers reported there was improvement in psychiatric symptomatology in comparison to the study's control group. In a more recent work, Barry et al. (2003) studied the impact of a strengths model versus assertive community treatment, a model of care long accepted as efficacious. In this study, both models reduced the use of inpatient care, but the strengths model was more effective at reducing overall consumer symptomatology.

The strengths model of case management has proven to be successful in substance abuse treatment as demonstrated by the pioneering work of the late Harvey Siegal and Richard Rapp at Wright State University. In a series of initial studies, case management proved to be an effective method to improve treatment retention, a key outcome in this field (Rapp et al., 1998; Siegal et al., 1996; Siegal et al., 2002). Research also demonstrated the goal-setting method used in the strengths model could be employed effectively in substance abuse treatment (Rapp, 2006), and also enhanced employment outcomes and involvement with the criminal justice system (Rapp et al., 1998, Siegal et al., 1996). Recent work in this field has focused on the critical role of linkages to other aspects of healthcare, in particular HIV and AIDS care (Rapp & Lane, 2009).

It is clear many of the underlying assumptions of the strengths model remain relatively untested, including some key features of the model viewed as particularly important (Gray, 2011). However, Kishthardt (1993), in an ethnographic study, confirms consumers find completing the strengths assessment to be beneficial, as well as the process of goal and case planning. Brun and Rapp (2001) note the importance of the relationship between consumer and case manager as reported by those in substance abuse treatment, but offer an important caveat with regards to the focus on strengths within the context of care. Based on their research, it seems many consumers are pleased and surprised to be asked about interests and aspirations, and enjoyed reviewing those moments in life where they had experienced success in particular. However, consumers also reported it was important to take time and reflect on and discuss the problems they had faced, leading Brun and Rapp (2001) to argue some balance should be maintained in this phase of helping.

Finally, a study implementing the strengths model with youth facing significant emotional and behavioural issues offered an observation with possible wide-ranging implications. In this study, Cox (2006) underscored the important role of the therapist's acceptance of the strengths approach and suggested the helpers prevailing attitude might well impact on the effectiveness of subsequent services. More specifically, Cox observed the data generated by a strengths assessment could be useful but the utility of these data was tempered by the professional's belief that the information was noteworthy. Certainly more work remains to be done as many elements of the strengths model should be placed more closely under the microscope. Because the strengths model so closely matches fundamental social work values and resonates with a humanistic impulse germane to the field, there is a tendency, at times, to trumpet the promise of the model too loudly, and to oversell the overall impact of the method in the face of the significant individual and social challenges professionals confront each day (Gray, 2011). Case management, for example, is a useful intervention with wide utility in human services. However, case managers are also commonly at the bottom of the organisational chart, and rarely have the level of clout needed to repair systems in disarray. Heroic efforts by professionals and consumers alike should not provide licence to overlook basic areas of social injustice, inequitable resource allocation, and abuses of civil rights still abounding (see Gray, 2011; and Chapter 4 in this volume). Nonetheless, as demonstrated here, the strengths model has been an important addition to social work practice as reflected in its widespread adoption over the past quarter-century and because it appears to have made a significant difference in the life of many consumers of service.

REFERENCES

Anderson, K., Cowger, C., & Snively, C. (2009). Assessing strengths: Identifying acts of resistance to violence and oppression. In D. Saleebey (ed.), *The strengths perspective in social work practice* (5th ed.). Boston, MA: Pearson Education, Inc., pp. 181–200.

Barry, K., Zeber, J., Blow, F., & Valenstein, M. (2003). Effect of strengths model versus assertive community treatment model on participant outcomes and utilization: Two-year follow-up. *Psychiatric Rehabilitation Journal, 26*(3), 268–277.

Blundo, R. (2001). Learning strengths-based practice: Challenging our personal and professional frames. *Families in Society, 82*(3), 296–304.

Blundo, R. (2006). Shifting our habits of mind: Learning to practice from a strengths perspective. In D. Saleebey (ed.), *The strengths perspective in social work practice* (4th ed.). Boston: Pearson Education Inc., pp. 25–45.

Brun, C., & Rapp, R. (2001). Strengths-based case management: Individuals' perspectives on strengths and their case manager relationship. *Social Work, 46*(3), 278–288.

Cox, K. (2006). Investigating the impact of strengths-based assessment on youth with emotional or behavioral disorders. *Journal of Child and Family Studies, 15*(3), 287–301.

Davidson, W., & Rapp, C.A. (1976). Child advocacy in the justice system. *Social Work, 21*(3), 225–232.

Deegan, P. (1990). Spirit breaking: When the helping professions hurt. *Humanistic Psychology, 18*(3), 301–313.

Drake, R., & Bond, G. (2008). The future of supported employment for people with severe mental illness. *Psychiatric Rehabilitation Journal, 31*(4), 367–376.

Gray, M. (2011). Back to basics: A critique of the strengths perspective in social work. *Families in Society: The Journal of Contemporary Social Services, 92*(1), 5–11.

Graybeal, C. (2001). Strengths-based social work assessment: Transforming the dominant paradigm. *Families in Society: The Journal of Contemporary Social Services, 82*(3), 233–242.

Kishthardt, W. (1993). An empowerment agenda for case management research: Evaluating the strengths model from the consumers' perspective. In M. Harris & Bergman, H. (eds), *Case management: Theory and practice*. Washington, DC: American Psychiatric Association, pp. 165–182.

Kretzmann, J.P. & McKnight, J.L. (1993). *Building communities from the inside out: Toward finding and mobilizing a community's assets*. Evanston, IL: Northwestern University, Center for Urban Affairs and Policy Research.

Leff, H.S., Chow, C., Pepin, R., Conley, J., Allen, I.E., & Seaman, C. (2009). Does one size fit all? What we can and can't learn from a meta-analysis of housing models for persons with mental illness. *Psychiatric Services, 60*(4), 473–482.

Macias, C., Farley, O.W., Jackson, R., & Kinney, R. (1997). Case management in the context of capitation financing: An evaluation of the strengths model. *Administration and Policy in Mental Health, 24*(6), 535–543.

Macias, C., Kinney, R., Farley, O.W., Jackson, R., & Vos, B. (1994). The role of case management within a community support system: Partnership with psychosocial rehabilitation. *Community Mental Health Journal, 30*(4), 323–339.

McQuaide, S., & Ehrenreich, J. (1997). Assessing client strengths. *Families in Society: The Journal of Contemporary Social Services, 78*(2), 201–212.

Modrcin, M., Rapp, C.A., & Chamberlain, R. (1985). *Case management with psychiatrically disabled individuals: Curriculum and training program*. Unpublished manuscript. Lawrence: University of Kansas, School of Social Welfare.

Rapp, C.A. (1992). The strengths perspective of case management with persons suffering from severe mental illness. In D. Saleebey (ed.), *The strengths perspective in social work practice*. New York: Longman, pp. 45–58.

Rapp, C.A., & Chamberlain, R. (1985). Case management services for the chronically mentally ill. *Social Work, 30*(5), 417–422.

Rapp, C.A., & Goscha, R. (2006). *The strengths model: Case management with people with psychiatric disabilities* (2nd ed.). New York: Oxford University Press.

Rapp, C.A., & Wintersteen, R. (1989). The strengths model of case management: Results from twelve demonstrations. *Journal of Psychosocial Rehabilitation, 13*(1), 23–32.

Rapp, R. (2006). Strengths-based case management: Enhancing treatment for persons with substance abuse problems. In D. Saleebey (ed.), *The strengths perspective in social work practice* (4th ed.). Boston, MA: Allyn & Bacon, pp. 128–147.

Rapp, R., & Lane, D.T. (2009). Implementation of brief strengths-based case management: An evidence-based intervention for improving linkage with care. In D. Saleebey (ed.), *The strengths perspective in social work practice* (5th ed.). Boston, MA: Pearson Education, Inc, pp. 146–160.

Rapp, R., Siegal, H., & Saha, P. (1998). Predicting postprimary treatment services and drug use outcome: A multivariate analysis. *American Journal of Drug and Alcohol Abuse, 24*(4), 603–615.

Rashid, T., & Ostermann, R. (2009). Strength-based assessment in clinical practice. *Journal of Clinical Psychology: In Session, 65*(5), 488–498.

Rogers, E. (2003). *Diffusion of innovations* (5th ed.). New York: The Free Press.

Saleebey, D. (1992). (ed.) *The strengths perspective in social work practice*. New York: Longman.

Saleebey, D. (2006). The strengths approach to practice. In D. Saleebey (ed.), *The strengths perspective in social work practice* (4th ed.). Boston, MA: Pearson Education, Inc., pp. 77–92.

Saleebey, D. (2009). *The strengths perspective in social work practice* (5th ed.). Boston, MA: Pearson Education, Inc.

Siegal, H., Fisher, J., Rapp, R., Kelliher, C., Wagner, J., O'Brien, W., & Cole, P. (1996). Enhancing substance abuse treatment with case management: Its impact on employment. *Journal of Substance Abuse Treatment, 13*, 93–98.

Siegal, H., Li, L., & Rapp, R. (2002). Case management as a therapeutic enhancement: Impact on post-treatment criminality. *Journal of Addictive Diseases, 21*, 37–46.

Stannard, R. (1999). The effect of training in a strengths model of case management on client outcomes in a community mental health center. *Community Mental Health Journal, 35*(2), 169–179.

Sullivan, W.P. (1992). Reconsidering the environment as a helping resource. In D. Saleebey (ed.), *The strengths perspective in social work practice*. New York: Longman, pp. 148–157.

Sullivan, W.P. (1994). A long and winding road: The process of recovery from severe mental illness. *Innovations and Research, 3*(3), 19–27.

Sullivan, W.P., & Rapp, C.A. (2006). Honoring philosophical traditions: The strengths model and the social environment. In D. Saleebey (ed.), *The strengths perspective in social work practice* (4th ed.). Boston, MA: Pearson Education, Inc., pp. 261–278.

Sullivan, W.P., & Rapp, C.A. (2009). Honoring philosophical traditions: The strengths model and the social environment. In D. Saleebey (ed.), *The strengths perspective in social work practice* (5th ed.). Boston, MA: Pearson Education, Inc., pp. 220–239.

Taylor, J. (1997). Niches and practice: Extending the ecological perspective. In D. Saleebey (ed.), *The strengths perspective in social work practice* (2nd ed.). New York: Longman, pp. 217–227.

Ware, N., Hopper, K., Tugenberg, T., Dickey, B., & Fisher, D. (2007). Connectedness and citizenship: Redefining social integration. *Psychiatric Services, 58*(4), 469–474.

Weick, A., Rapp, C.A., Sullivan, W.P., & Kisthardt, W. (1989). A strengths perspective for social work practice. *Social Work, 34*(4), 350–354.

Wintersteen, R.T. (1986). Rehabilitating the chronically mentally ill: Social work's claim to leadership. *Social Work, 31*(5), 332–337.

12

Critical Perspectives

Karen Healy

The chapter begins with an outline of critical perspectives on social work practice and presents a definition of critical social work, the purpose of which is to orient the reader to the practical and philosophical influences of critical perspectives on social work writing and practice. Thereafter, an historical overview of the influence of critical perspectives begins with a definition of critical perspectives, which is drawn primarily from modernist critical traditions, such as those associated with critical social science. The ways in which these critical perspectives are reflected in the work of critical social work are discussed starting with the work of Jane Addams and the Hull House Movement. Thereafter, the way in which a range of critical social work authors in the 20th and 21st centuries brought critical perspectives to bear in aligning social work with visions of progressive social transformation is outlined and contemporary links between critical social work practice and progressive social movements are discussed. The influence of postmodern and post-structural theories on critical social work is considered. A case example is provided to illustrate the importance of critical perspectives to social work, the development of the critical tradition, and the influence of postmodern critical perspectives. Contemporary challenges to critical perspectives in social work are also considered, focusing primarily on the influence of new public management philosophies on opportunities to apply critical traditions in practice.

CRITICAL PERSPECTIVES IN SOCIAL WORK

Over the past decade, there has emerged a growing body of work on critical perspectives in, rather than on, social work practice (Allan et al., 2009; Fook, 2002; Fook & Gardner, 2007; Healy, 2000, 2009; Jones et al., 2008;). While, it is argued, the profession has a long tradition of critical writing about social work practice, what is distinctive and interesting about this emerging body of critical social work is its constructive focus. These are forms of critical social work writing seeking to articulate how social workers can use, and build, critical practice in the diverse contexts of social work. Of particular interest is the growing body of writing showing how to practise critically in contexts of practice more accurately characterised as largely or primarily sites of social control (H. Ferguson, 2008; Healy, 1998, 2000; O'Gara, 2008), particularly sites of statutory social work practice, such as child protection, mental health, and correctional services. This recent body of critical social work writing has emerged against a backdrop of the deepening challenges posed by neoliberalism and new public management on many of the institutional contexts of social work practice (Healy, 2009; McDonald, 2006).

WHAT IS CRITICAL SOCIAL WORK?

Critical social workers are committed to achieving social justice through social work practice. In some ways, this commitment is unremarkable in so far as social justice is recognised as a core value of social work practice by the International Federation of Social Workers and also in the ethical codes of many professional social workers' associations throughout the world (Banks, 2006). What is distinctive to critical social work are the practice principles through which the profession's commitment to social justice is realised. As Healy (2000) defined it, critical social workers emphasise the following.

- A commitment to standing alongside oppressed and excluded individuals and communities (Leonard, 1994).
- Dialogical relationships between social workers and service users or community members.
- Recognition of the profoundly influential role of social, economic, and political systems in shaping individual and community experiences and opportunities, and the relationships between service providers and users (Leonard, 1995).
- A commitment to the transformation of the processes and structures perpetuating domination and exploitation both at the level of human service provision and in the broader society.

There are a wide variety of critical forms of social work. These include structural, radical, feminist, anti-oppressive, and post-structural forms of social work practice (Hick & Pozutto, 2005). Critical social workers see social work practice as a site of social oppression and, potentially, of social transformation. While critical social workers recognise social workers' involvement in oppressive social practices, they also consider that social workers have the capacity to contribute to a more inclusive, equitable, and just society. Critical social workers seek to achieve the values of respect, inclusion, and equality within the context of their relationships with service users, but also seek to contribute to changes at other levels of service and social systems. For example, critical social workers support movements to build the capacity of service users to challenge the dominance of human service professionals so as to create a space in which service users can have genuine influence on the definition of service need and provision. Critical social workers also seek to challenge discriminatory attitudes, such as sexist, racist, and disabilist views contributing to the vulnerability and marginalisation of people with whom they work.

Early beginnings

The critical tradition has a long history in social work. This history is often dated back to the Settlement Movement in the USA, which emerged in the late 19th century and, in particular, to the work of Jane Addams, the pioneering community worker and peace activist who won the Noble Prize for Peace in 1931 (Healy, 2000; Johnson, 2004). The Settlement Movement emerged as an alternative to the individualistic helping ethos dominating the Charitable Organisational Societies prominent at this time (Fisher, 2005). Members of the Settlement House Movement adopted a multidimensional approach to social transformation as, according to Berry (cited in Fisher, 2005), 'aiding individuals, building community, and changing society were all integral parts of the community organization practice pyramid' (p. 39).

While the Settlement Movement was influential in the emerging field of social work in the first decades of the 20th century, its influence declined in the post-World War I period. In the following four decades, critical social work ideas continued to be espoused and developed in the work of individual critical thinkers, such as Bertha Capen Reynolds (1963). However, during this period, psychodynamic perspectives dominated the social work profession and there was little evidence of a critical social work movement (Healy, 2005; Reisch & Andrews, 2002; Rojek et al., 1988).

In the 1960s and 1970s, a significant and internally diverse critical social work practice movement emerged, supported by the new social movements and a proliferation of critical social science literature at the time. This resurgent critical social work movement was united in its opposition to the individualist ethos that had dominated professional social work over the preceding four decades (Rojek et al., 1988). However, the critical social work movement was internally divided by the various and divergent analyses of social oppression and strategies for social change. A variety of strands of critical social work emerged, including radical social work, inspired by Marxist critiques of the welfare state, and feminist and antiracist social work. Substantial divisions were evident within the critical social work canon. For example, feminist social workers critiqued the gender blindness of radical social work (Hanmer, 1977) and antiracist social workers raised concerns about inadequate attention to racial and ethnic equality in various critical social work traditions.

From the late 1970s, critical social workers were involved in developing critical theories for practice that were responsive to a variety of forms of oppression including, but not limited to, class oppression. Canadian social workers coined the term 'structural social work' as a distinctive approach to critical practice that recognised class and a variety of identity-based forms of oppression (Moreau, 1990; see also Carniol, 1992; Mullaly, 1993).

In the UK, the term 'anti-oppressive' practice was used increasingly to refer to forms of social work practice seeking to understand and eliminate diverse forms of social oppression (Dalrymple & Burke, 1995, see Chapter 21).

Early theoretical influences

Initially, critical social work philosophies emerging in the 1960s drew extensively on the work of Karl Marx (Healy, 2000). Indeed, the influence of Marxist philosophy on critical social science and critical social work practice has been profound. The radical social movement from this time drew from Marxist philosophy the notion that the structures and processes of capitalist society had disempowering effects for vulnerable individuals and communities (Bolger et al., 1981). According to Marx (1972), all people, but particularly the proletariat and other disadvantaged groups, were de-powered by the capitalist mode of production as they were no longer able to recognise themselves as active creators of the society in which they lived. The Marxist notion of false consciousness or the idea people develop a false understanding of the social order as an unchangeable reality, was, and continues to be, an important idea for critical social workers (Bishop, 2002; Corrigan & Leonard, 1978; Fook, 1993; Moreau, 1990). Another influential Marxist idea in modernist approaches to critical social work is the notion society can be understood as a social totality in which two opposites exist, namely, the bourgeoisie and the proletariat or 'oppressor and oppressed' (Marx & Engels, 1972, p. 336). In understanding the world as comprising opposing forces, the critical social worker seeks to encourage the oppressed to act collectively to achieve a more equitable distribution of society's resources (Moreau, 1979, 1990).

Beyond Marxism, there are a variety of bodies of critical social theory for social workers to draw on. However, social workers have not drawn upon all forms of modern critical theory coming to prominence in the post-1960s period. There is, for example, only a small body of social work literature engaging with the Frankfurt School, particularly Jürgen Habermas, to critique the operation of social service systems in late-modern capitalism (Houston, 2009). A key reason for this limited engagement by social work theorists – and their failure to include critical social work theories in the tradition of the Frankfurt School – is the lack of obvious relevance of this School to social work. Although Habermas (1998) shares with social workers a central concern with democratic communication, his work is so reliant on specialist philosophical terminology as to, ironically, render it inaccessible to many social workers, particularly those who lack a background in social philosophy. There seems to be little attempt by Habermas to bridge the distance between the specialist theoretical field he occupies and that of the caring occupations to which his ideas of communicative action might be applied, and there appear to be only a small group of social work authors willing to undertake this task (Gray & Lovat, 2007, 2008; Hayes & Houston, 2007; Houston, 2002, 2009; Lovat & Gray, 2008). A further barrier to social workers' engagement with the Frankfurt School is the lack of compelling evidence to suggest this School, even in the work of Habermas, has much to offer in building a constructive critical social work project. Undoubtedly, the work of Habermas and others within the Frankfurt School can provide critical insights into the limited capacities of social workers operating under conditions of late-modern capitalism to engage in democratic communication with service users (see Houston, 2002). Yet, even without referring to the insights of the Frankfurt School, many social work commentators recognise the new, and increasingly constrained, environments in which contemporary social work practice occurs (see Annison et al., 2008; Healy, 2009; McDonald, 2006). Perhaps, more pertinently, it is not clear what the Frankfurt School thinkers offer to the development of constructive critical practices in the face of these challenges. Given key thinkers within the Frankfurt School, such as Adorno and Horkeimer, became increasingly disillusioned with the potential for progressive social change in late-modern capitalist societies (Kellner, 1993), it is difficult to see how their writing might contribute to constructive critical social work practices.

Modernist critical social science theories

Of much greater influence on the development of critical social work, particularly post-1970, is a group of critical theories that can be banded together under the term 'modernist critical social science'. This variant of critical social theory reflects the Enlightenment belief that, through reason and action, people can fundamentally reorder their individual and collective life circumstances (Fay, 1987; Healy, 2000). While Marx remains an influential figure in modernist critical social science, critical social scientists do not prioritise capitalist processes of production as the underpinning cause of social oppression. Instead, modernist critical social science theorists recognise a wide variety of structural processes, such as those associated with patriarchy or colonialisation, as contributors to social oppression. Critical social work theorists have also been engaged with, and influenced by, the new social movements, such as the mental health survivors' movement (see Macfarlane, 2009). Diverse theoretical traditions and citizen-led movements have decentralised the place of capitalism and the class system in the critical social workers' analysis of social oppression and in their approaches to social transformation.

Notwithstanding the diversity of modernist critical social science theories, these approaches are characterised by shared theoretical assumptions (Fay, 1987). Healy (2000) saw several of these assumptions as especially relevant to critical social work practice as follows.

- *Society can be understood as totality.* An understanding of the social totality explains the nature of local social relations. For example, Marxists believe capitalist social processes shape social relationships at every level of society and modernist feminists argue patriarchy explains these relations.
- *Society comprises opposing forces and these forces are in conflict with one another.* It is widely agreed among those drawing on modernist critical social theory, these opposing forces are fundamentally unequal and relationships of oppression emerge as those with more power dominate the less powerful. Critical social science theories identify the conflicting interests of the oppressor and oppressed groups noting, unless intense pressure is applied, the oppressors will not forgo their privileged power and influence (Hoatson, 2003).
- *The development of critical consciousness is a necessary precursor to action.* Modern critical social science theorists and critical social workers emphasise that the oppressed have a false understanding, referred to as false consciousness, of the nature of the social order. False consciousness refers to an acceptance of dominant ideologies, or world views 'which service the interests of powerful groups' in society (Wearing, 1986, p. 34). Critical social workers contend these false beliefs cannot but be challenged so service users can more clearly recognise their capacities to act rationally and consciously in their own interests and in the interests of other oppressed people (Fook, 1993; see also Freire, 1997).
- The collective participation of the oppressed in the process of change: Critical social science theorists emphasise the needs for oppressed groups to act collectively in their shared interests. This notion of collective action is ubiquitous in the critical social work literature where it is emphasised the service users and communities working together can challenge entrenched interests, such as entrenched interest of professional groups in retaining their status and power.

The transformative nature of these ideas meant modernist forms of critical practice were, inevitably, in tension with the dominant ideas in many of the health and welfare institutions where social workers practised. However, from the 1990s onwards, the modernist foundations of critical social work were questioned from within, as some critical social workers began to engage with the challenges, and the opportunities, provided by postmodern and post-structural ideas.

Postmodern and post-structural theories

Postmodern and post-structural theories, hereafter referred to as post-theories, are widely debated among social workers and their relevance to critical social work is hotly contested. Post-theories challenge many of the core assumptions on which modernist social science theory, including critical social science theory, depend. Challenges to modernist notions of reason, power, progress, identity, and social totality have had profound implications for critical social work practice (H. Ferguson, 2008; Fook, 2002; Healy, 2000; Leonard, 1997).

Many critical social workers have been motivated to engage with post-theories because of the opportunities they provide to theorise how critical practice may be enacted in the diverse institutional sites of social work practice. Some critical social workers have turned to post-theories because of their dissatisfaction with the failure of modernist forms of critical social work to: (i) engage constructively with social work practice, especially in fields where social control is an ever-present and overt reality of practice; and (ii) acknowledge the power relations inherent in apparently liberatory forms of practice (Healy, 1998, 1999). Harry Ferguson (2008) captures this disillusion in his remark:

> Critical social work theory has too often remained at the level of negative critique, idealistically prescribing what should *not* be done, while the actual practicalities of what *can* and often *should* be done, and how is ignored or left at the level of aspiration. Thus it has largely avoided any encounter with best practice, leaving out how critical practice can be done well (p. 8).

There are several ways in which the negative critique that has dominated modernist critical social work is problematic. One is it has contributed little to understanding how social workers with a critical outlook can engage with those forms of service provision where the overt use of power is inevitable. While, for example, anti-oppressive practitioners have encouraged social workers to minimise their use of power, this falls short of helping critical workers to understand how they might constructively use the power they inevitably wield.

The negative critique of social workers' professional power has left social workers especially vulnerable to the inroads being made by new public management. Indeed, the extensive critique of social workers' involvement in social control activities, found within the critical literature (see Donzelot, 1997), coincides neatly with, and provides social workers with little defence against, the new public management agenda of deprofessionalising social work services (Healy, 2009). Given modernist critical social scientists and critical social workers have so problematised social workers' involvement in social control in fields such as child protection, mental health, and corrective services, it is difficult for them to defend social workers' involvement in these domains now that new public management philosophies threaten their continuing existence in them (Healy, 2009). If social workers are to retain, or even attain, their place in human services fields, where highly vulnerable services users are subject to statutory authority, they must be able to articulate not only their capacity to support and advocate, but also to wield the forms of authority and power inherent in these roles responsibly (Healy, 2010).

Since the 1990s, a significant body of work has emerged linking post-theories to critical social work (see H. Ferguson, 2008; Fook, 2002; Healy, 1999, 2000, 2005a, 2005b; Juhila, 2004; Leonard, 1997; O'Gara, 2008). Although some theorists challenge the relevance of post-theories to social work generally (Peile & McCouat, 1997) and to critical practice in particular (H. Ferguson, 2008; Gray & Webb, 2009), the large and expanding body of work incorporating postmodern and post-structural perspectives suggests many social work commentators hold a different view (see Fawcett, 2009).

There are several ways in which post-theories can be seen to support the continuing development of constructive critical social work practices. First, post-theories disrupt the view of power, including statutory authority, as a wholly negative force. In his writings on the genealogy of power, Foucault (1980, 1982) implores us to consider the ubiquitous nature of power, the way in which it can be experienced as productive, as well as oppressive, and how an inductive approach to power may show power to be more complex than revealed by an analysis of overarching social processes. This view of power is important for recognising the power inherent in all social work practice, and not only in those contexts where overt social control is enacted. This post-theoretical view of power also opens up possibilities for social workers to recognise the empowering, as well as the oppressive effects of statutory and professional power in practice (O'Gara, 2008).

Second, a focus on discourse, as proposed by post-theories, reveals the constitutive power of language in shaping what social work 'is' and possibilities for action. From a post-structural perspective, the entities of social work practice – the social worker, the service user, and the practice context – are spoken into being through discourse. Some critical social workers have drawn on the notion of the constitutive power of language to question the opposition between controlling and emancipatory forms of social work, found in modernist accounts of critical practice, and instead focus on how the identities and power relations inherent in social work practices are constituted within specific realms of social work practice (Healy, 1999, 2000; Jones & Spreadbury, 2008). From a post-theoretical perspective, there is no reality outside of discourse and so it follows there is no form of social work practice and no 'type' of social work practitioner, critical or otherwise, who is ever free of the systems of power in which they operate. Again this is a profound challenge to modernist critical discourse, which has portrayed critical social workers as 'disembodied and heroic actors who stand outside the systems of power and speak the truth to them' (Healy, 2000, p. 135).

The third reason is critical post-perspectives promote ethical practice in so far as social workers are required to interrogate the truth claims underpinning their practice. This is challenging to modernist critical social work since critical social science principles are held to present a true reflection of the world as it is. From a post-theory perspective, these principles need to be subjected to critical interrogation within specific contexts of practice and, from a Foucauldian perspective, the will to power, even within apparently liberatory practices, needs to be examined. Jan Fook (2002) has explored the relevance of critical reflection to interrogating the truth claims underpinning critical social work practices, such as critical consciousness-raising.

Some social work commentators contest the relevance of post perspectives for critical social work (I. Ferguson, 2008; Gray & Webb, 2009). This section concentrates on three of the objections raised by critical social workers working in the modernist critical traditions towards the inroads made by post-theories over the past two decades; see I. Ferguson (2008) for an extensive and articulate outline of objections to postmodernism from a Marxist-informed critical social work perspective. One concern posed by modernist critical social workers is post-theories threaten to further decentralise class as a key analytic concept in critical social work. In their critique of the influence of postmodernism on critical social work, Gray and Webb (2009) assert:

> Now class is seen as one, if particularly influential, variable among many. This displacement of class as a universal signifier of oppression permits Critical social work a retheorization in terms of alliances between relatively diffuse oppressed groups (p. 81).

Yet while post-theories challenge the central position in critical practice, it is clear this challenge was well under way even without the influence of post ideas. As pointed out earlier, critical practice has been challenged from both critical social theorists, such as feminist and antiracist commentators, and from new social movements, such as the disability rights and mental health survivors' movements, to recognise the diversity of oppressions to which service users are subject. It could be argued post-theories take the destabilisation of the modern critical social work project even further by not only destabilising class but also the idea of a fixed identity as a basis for critical practice. In contrast to modernist critical approaches, from a post-theoretical perspective, identity is viewed as fluid and unstable. Post-theories challenge social workers to analyse how particularly 'identities' interact with historical and local discursive practices in order to understand how power relations operate within a specific setting. This deconstructive approach to identity is profoundly threatening to modern critical social work theories, which have often depended on fixed identity categories, such as man or woman, middle class or working class, and able-bodied or disabled, as a basis for analysing oppression and for collective action. Yet, some critical social work commentators have argued the destabilisation of fixed identities has opened critical social work to recognise diversity among social workers and within and between oppressed groups, such as differences among women (Juhila, 2004).

Some commentators question the theoretical compatibility of modernist and postmodern or post-structural theoretical ideas as a basis for critical social work. Indeed, Gray and Webb (2009) argue critical social workers' attempts to combine modern critical theories, particularly Marxism, and post-theories, have contributed to a 'confused state of affairs' (p. 81). Yet, in many fields of social philosophy, from politics to feminism, and in the applied disciplines, such as education and social work, commentators have found the tensions between modern and postmodern ideas productive for interrogating the truth claims of their fields and disciplines (see Fook, 2002; Yeatman, 1994). Yeatman (1994) urges us not to miss the opportunities provided for emancipatory politics as she asserts:

> By entering into a deconstructive relationship to the modern emancipatory project ... postmodern politics can be seen to transform this project and, in this sense, to pursue it ... Postmodern emancipatory vision does not offer a utopian future, but works to develop contestatory political and public spaces, which open up in relation to existing systems of governance (p. ix).

Indeed, the very differences between modern and postmodern ideas provide opportunities for new ways of thinking and doing critical practice in a range of fields.

A further concern relates to post-theorists' view of language as constitutive. Poststructural theorists, in particular, contend language shapes what can be written, said, or even thought within a particular context (Healy, 2000). Some critical social workers argue this focus on language obscures the material realities, particularly those shaping service users' lives, and limits possibilities for change in the material conditions of the oppressed communities with whom social workers practice. Iain Ferguson (2008) argues:

> If there are only discourse and no material realities, then how can we hope, for example to establish a relationship between class and mental ill-health, or gender and depression, if the social 'facts' on which we rely to do so have no objective reality? (p. 110).

Many critical social workers would share Ferguson's (2008) concern that any dilution of the harrowing effects of material disadvantage among the service users and communities with whom social workers work is problematic. Yet this objection can be challenged on the grounds post-theorists do not argue there are no material realities, rather they propose that such realities can only be apprehended through language practices and these language practices constitute the material conditions people observe and experience. For example, most people would recognise that a phenomenon termed 'mental illness' exists but they would also recognise the meaning of mental illness – and the rights, capacities, and resources attributed to those experiencing mental illness – varies in different contexts, such as different geographical, historical, and institutional contexts. From a post-theoretical perspective, it is important to consider how the language practices, also known as discourses, operating in these contexts shape what can be said, thought, and felt about phenomena, such as mental illness within particular historical, geographical, and institutional locations (see Chapter 33).

Rather than an anathema to critical social work, the constitutive power of language is something most critical social workers, including many of those working within the modernist tradition, understand as they engage in struggles over language. For example, critical social work practice is replete with examples of social workers working alongside and on behalf of service users to contest narrow and stigmatising definitions of service users and their needs, and to replace such definitions with those recognising them as rights-bearing citizens and survivors. These language practices are vital to achieving change in the material conditions of service users (see Crossley & Crossley, 2001). In focusing on the constitutive power of language, post-theories challenge critical social workers not only to deny material conditions but also to interrogate critically how the language practices operating within a particular time and context shape key dimensions of practice, such as service users' and social workers' identities and the material effects of these language practices on the rights and resources available to people with these identities.

Let us turn to how critical social work approaches, informed by post-theories, can be applied to a practice example. The following case study is drawn from an example encountered in practice in which identifying details have been changed.

CASE STUDY: MANDY

Mandy is a 17-year-old young woman. Together with her partner, Justin, Mandy has a three-month-old son, Jack. Justin has been violent towards Mandy on several occasions, and today you are meeting with Mandy at the police station. You have been called in to the police station after Justin beat Mandy leaving her emotionally traumatised and with bruising to her eye and her upper arms. Justin has been detained under a domestic violence protection order though he is likely to be released on bail within 24 hours. Jack is currently at childcare and was not at home when Justin attacked Mandy. Both Mandy and Justin have disrupted family backgrounds. Mandy was placed in fostercare at 11 years of age because of severe physical and sexual abuse from her stepfather. Justin was placed in fostercare when he was an infant and had many changes of placement during his childhood, never really settling with any foster home. Mandy and Justin have been together for two years. Although shaken by what she has experienced, she wants to return home and to remain with Justin. Mandy says she does not want to cooperate with police investigation.

The main focus here is to consider how critical social workers, informed by both modernist critical social science and post-theories, might respond to this situation. From a post-theoretical perspective, the social worker would seek, first, to understand how her purpose is constructed through the discourses operating in the practice context. These discourses are likely to include institutional discourses, such as legal and policy discourses, which are likely to constitute her role as involving risk management, and professional social work discourse constituting her role through social work theories, such as systems and critical theories, and humanist values, such as self-determination and social justice.

In this case study, the social worker has been called into the police station. In critically analysing her purpose, she needs to understand 'who' called the worker in the matter and how the roles and responsibilities of the worker and the service user are constituted in this context. Consider, for example, the differences in how one's sense of purpose is constituted if one were called in as a child protection social worker compared to a domestic violence or family support worker. If, for example, the worker were a child protection officer, she would be compelled, under statutory law, to prioritise Jack's need for safety over other considerations, including Mandy's decisions about whether or not to return home. By contrast, as a domestic violence or family support worker, she would likely focus on Mandy's view of her situation and assist her to make a fully informed decision about her circumstance. In either context, she would be concerned with Mandy and Jack's safety but she would be likely to respond to them differently, in accordance with the discourses shaping her role and orientation to practice.

Let us assume that the worker is a child protection officer in this situation. From a modernist critical perspective, she would be critically aware of the social control dimensions of her role and the fact her very presence might be experienced as unhelpful and disempowering to Mandy as she makes decisions at this difficult and distressing time. From a modernist critical perspective, she would be alert to the indicators of social oppression in Mandy's story and, in particular, how matters of class, gender, and ethnicity might shape the options for action available to her. She would aim to raise Mandy's awareness she is not alone in her experiences and is not individually at fault. From a post-theoretical perspective, she would understand all accounts, including Mandy's account of her experience, are situated in time and place. She would aim to listen not only for what is present in the conversation but what and who is absent, and to the contradictions and tensions in Mandy's account. For example, she would recognise Mandy may have multiple and conflicting views of her situation of, for instance, both attachment and fear of her partner. She would seek to assist Mandy to articulate these tensions, such as possible tensions between being a young woman, a survivor of the 'care' system, a loving mother to Jack, and a partner to Justin, and assist her to explore how these different identities frame her decisions. From a post-theoretical perspective, she would be alert to missing perspectives, particularly Jack's perspective, as she listens to this account. She might ask Mandy to outline what she sees as Jack's views and interests, and what he might say about the decisions she is making, such as returning or leaving her home with Justin.

This review of critical practice attempts to show that critical social workers, whether in the modern or postmodern traditions, seek to understand social work practice within its societal and institutional contexts. Critical social work practice, informed by post-theories, departs from modernist approaches in several ways. One of the most important of these is in its focus on the constitutive power of language in shaping practice contexts and identities as workers as well as the identities of the service user. A post-theory account encourages social workers to recognise a number of discourses, which may contradict each other, are operating within their environment. The discourses may differently constitute their purpose and identity, and the tensions among these discourses may provide opportunities for them to work critically and creatively with service users. For example, in this case study, it would be professionally irresponsible, regardless of the social worker's role, to fail to assess the risks to Jack posed by the domestic violence to which he and Mandy are directly subject. Yet, this focus on risk need not entirely define the social work role, and the worker needs also to recognise other discourses shaping practice, such as the humanist values underpinning professional practice discourses encouraging her, for example, to recognise Mandy's capacities to protect and care for Jack. Another important way in which post-theories inform critical social work practice is through sensitising practitioners to the potentially silencing effects of critical truth claims. For example, while it is clear Mandy's vulnerability is influenced by her class and gender identities, the worker risks neglecting the ways in which Mandy has exercised power in her life, such as, for instance, in her decision to parent. A post-theoretical perspective encourages critical social workers to interrogate critically how the identity categories they apply to understand practice, such as categories associated with class, gender, and race, can lead them to ignore individual differences within those categories.

NEOLIBERALISM AND NEW PUBLIC MANAGEMENT: CAN CRITICAL PRACTICE SURVIVE?

While critical social workers have long debated the theoretical foundations of, and influences upon, their practice, what is new is the threat posed by neoliberalism and new public management for social work practice generally and critical social work in particular. For more than two decades, these philosophies have contributed to profound shifts in the organisational context of health and welfare services. A core idea of neoliberalism is the market is a central 'organising principles of social life' (Penna & O'Brien, 2009, p. 109). This idea is associated with a significant shift in the role of government from 'steering rather than rowing' as governments are repositioned as purchasers rather than providers of services (Osborne & Gaebler, 1993, p. 25; see Chapter 2).

The rise of neoliberalism has been accompanied by the growing dominance of new public management (NPM) in the organisation of health and welfare services. NPM is associated with an emphasis on administrative accountability, financial efficiency, and the management of risk in service provision. While critical social workers have always experienced tension between the institutional contexts of social work practice and their social change aspirations, the shift to NPM has narrowed the terrain for critical practice even further. NPM has contributed to a fragmentation of service provision and a reduction in the opportunities for social workers to practice in holistic, creative, and critical ways (Healy, 2009; McDonald, 2006).

Critical social workers need to understand the significance of neoliberalism and NPM for changing the conditions of health and welfare service provision. The idea, found in modernist critical social work that the critical practitioner can stand outside oppressive systems and speak truth to power, no longer makes sense if it ever did (Healy, 2000). Indeed, ironically, social workers are even threatened with exclusion from the very forms of practice they have critiqued, namely, those involving overt social control, as, it is argued by some proponents of NPM, social workers are insufficiently prepared for the risk-management aspects of contemporary human services work (Healy, 2009). One of the most pressing challenges for critical social workers today is to hold on to, and articulate, their capacity to work with the dualities of their role, which, in many contexts, involves both the management of risk and the provision of care. Critical social workers need both modernist critical social work and post-theoretical insights in order to enable them to theorise and practise the fluid and complex nature of social work identities and practices in the neoliberal welfare state. If they fail at this task, not only will the profession be seen as increasingly irrelevant to many areas of health and welfare provision, but also service users will be increasingly subject to policing-only approaches to human welfare provision.

STRENGTHS AND WEAKNESSES

This final section reviews the strengths and weaknesses of critical social work. While acknowledging the internal diversity of the critical social work tradition makes it difficult to comment in any general way on its possibilities and limitations, nonetheless, in a spirit of critical reflection, it is possible to show why some consider critical social work to be a project worth pursuing, while others question the viability or worth of this tradition.

One of the most compelling reasons for the continuing presence of a critical social work tradition is its emphasis on the societal, cultural, and institutional contexts of social work practice. Whether drawing on modern or postmodern theories, critical social workers analyse how societal and institutional arrangements shape, and constrain, social work practice and the possibilities available to service users. This emphasis on the broad contexts of practice requires social workers to shift their analysis and action beyond a focus on individual capacities and 'choices' to seeking to understand and change oppressive social conditions. Critical social workers enact a variety of strategies for achieving change in these conditions, including challenging stigmatising and oppressive definitions of service users' needs in policy and practice, through to facilitating collaborative forms of action to create change.

A second strength is the ethics of partnership and participation underpinning critical practice approaches. While the value of equality is accepted by social workers internationally as a core social work value (Banks, 2006), critical social workers interpret this value to require them to stand alongside oppressed citizens and facilitate their participation in creating change both at the level of service delivery and in the broader society. Critical social workers endorse the mantra of new social movements that, when it comes to working with service users, there should be 'nothing about us without us'. What this means is critical social workers seek to enable service users to articulate their capacities and needs on their own terms and to participate in changing service systems and society more generally so these needs are met.

A third strength of the critical tradition is these social workers have articulated a well-developed and diverse set of strategies for achieving social transformation through a wide variety of practice methods. Critical social workers have demonstrated how it is possible to incorporate critical perspectives in casework, family work, groupwork, and community, and policy practice (see Addams, 1961; Fook, 1993, 2002; Healy, 2000, 2005; Hoatson, 2003; Mullaly, 1993). Modernist critical social workers have emphasised the value of, and strategies for, collective action, while those drawing on postmodern ideas have also sensitised critical social workers to the tensions underlying collective identities. The emerging focus on strategies for, and debates about, best practice in critical social work is likely to further foster the capacities of critical social workers to incorporate the insights from critical social theory into the realities of social work practice (see Jones et al., 2008).

Yet, notwithstanding the strengths of the critical social work tradition, there are many weaknesses too. One weakness is the marginal status of critical social work within the social work profession and within many the contexts of social work practice. As a result of this marginal status, critical social workers are often in the position of advocating against accepted truths of the discipline or the context of practice but having little power to change the operations of these practice contexts. This outsider status can carry considerable professional and personal costs, especially for the newly qualified social worker, and, as a result, can be difficult to sustain.

The second weakness of the critical tradition is the lack of consensus about whether critical social work is, or should be, relevant to direct social work practice. This lack of consensus separates theory building in critical social work from other domains of social work theory. For example, ensuring practical relevance is a guiding principle in theory building in other domains of social work theory, such as the development of crisis intervention or systemic perspectives in social work (Healy, 2005a). This distrust of an aspiration to practical relevance in critical social work theorising has, in the words of McDonald (2006) contributed to the development of 'parallel universes, one occupied by critical (academic) social workers and occupied by practitioners in the field' (p. 183). Continuing debates about whether or not critical social work theory should be practically relevant seem to ignore the dramatic shifts in practice contexts over the past two decades due to the rise of NPM and neoliberalism and the consequent challenges to professional knowledge claims, and the increasing dominance of evidence-based practice. It is difficult to see how critical social work can survive as a viable mode of social work theory if social workers do not engage constructively with demands to articulate the practical relevance of the theories they espouse.

A third weakness of critical social work is its problematic fit with social work practice environments. The tensions between critical social work and the organisations of social work services have become pronounced as a result of the shift in the institutional contexts of social work practice. As McDonald (2009) observes, 'social workers are currently operating a human services environment which is at worst overtly hostile and at best indifferent to our endeavours as a collective group as well as to our core interests and objectives' (p. 244). Critical social work re-emerged in a period of growth in, and optimism, about the welfare state. As neoliberalism and NPM contribute to a reshaping of how health and welfare services are organised and delivered, the possibilities for a holistic practice orientated towards social transformation are greatly reduced. These changed circumstances do not necessarily mean modernist and postmodernist critical theories are irrelevant to critical practitioners, and indeed, it is contended, now more than ever, social workers need clarity about the principles and theoretical frames guiding their practice. However, if critical social work is to have any relevance to the new and emerging contexts of practice, critical social workers will need to identify the spaces in which critical practice is possible and develop relevant and workable strategies in these changed conditions. This requires a move beyond the critical social theories informing past practice to incorporating critical social theories focused on new and emerging social conditions. For example, the work of Bourdieu appears to provide new and exciting possibilities for interrogating the conditions of the present (see McDonald, 2006). Critical social workers also need to engage in research projects examining the possibilities and limits for constructive critical social work in the changed conditions of contemporary social work practice (see Allan et al., 2009; Jones et al., 2008).

CONCLUSION

This chapter has presented an overview of critical social work to show how critical social workers have made important contributions to social work theory and practice throughout the history of the profession. It has considered the debates about the influence of post-theories on critical social work theory and argued that these perspectives have been important in encouraging critical theorising in places where modernist critical social work has focused almost entirely on negative critiques of practice, such as the child protection agency and statutory mental health services. Finally, the recent and troubling shift in the context of health and welfare services was highlighted. There is no doubt critical social workers today face an increasingly constrained environment for continued involvement in transformative forms of practice. If social workers are to continue to develop the critical social work tradition, they will need the capacity to both understand and engage critically, and constructively, with these changed conditions. The rise of neoliberalism does not spell the end of critical social work but it does represent a new set of challenges for critical social workers. This chapter has shown there is much within social work's rich and diverse critical tradition to help guide the profession through the challenges it now faces.

REFERENCES

Addams, J. (1961). *Twenty years at hull-house.* New York: Signet, Macmillan.

Allan, J., Briskman, L., & Pease, B. (eds) (2009). *Critical social work: Theories and practices for a socially just world.* Sydney: Allen and Unwin.

Annison, J., Eadie, T., & Knight, C. (2008). People first: Probation officer perspectives on probation work. *Probation Journal: The Journal of Community and Criminal Justice, 55*(3), 259–271.

Banks, S. (2006). *Ethics and values in social work* (3rd ed.). Basingstoke: Palgrave.

Bishop, A. (2002). *Becoming an ally: Breaking the cycle of oppression.* Crows Nest: Allen and Unwin.

Bolger, S., Corrigan, P., Docking, J., & Frost, N. (1981). *Towards socialist welfare work.* London: The MacMillan Press.

Carniol, B. (1992). Structural social work: Maurice Moreau's challenge to social work practice. *Journal of Progressive Human Services, 3*(1), 1–20.

Corrigan, P., & Leonard, P. (1978). *Social work practice under capitalism: A Marxist approach.* London: Macmillan.

Crossley, M., & Crossley, N. (2001). 'Patient' voices, social movements and the habitus: How psychiatric survivors 'speak out'. *Social Science and Medicine, 52,* 1477–1489.

Dalrymple, J., & Burke, B. (1995). *Anti-oppressive practice: social care and the law.* Buckingham: Open University Press.

Donzelot, J. (1997). *The policing of families.* Baltimore, MD: Johns Hopkins University Press.

Fawcett, B. (2009). Postmodernism. In M. Gray & Webb, S. (eds), *Social work: theories and methods.* London: Sage, pp. 119–128.

Fay, B. (1987). *Critical social science: liberation and its limits.* Ithaca, NY: Cornell University Press.

Ferguson, H. (2008). Critical best practice: Critical perspectives. In K. Jones, Cooper, B., & Ferguson, H. (ed.), *Best practice in social work: Critical perspectives.* Basingstoke: Palgrave, pp. 15–37.

Ferguson, I. (2008). *Reclaiming social work: Challenging neo-liberalism and promoting social justice.* London: Sage.

Fisher, R. (2005). History, context, and emerging issues for community practice. In M. Weil (ed.), *The handbook of community practice.* Thousand Oaks, CA: Sage, pp. 34–58.

Fook, J. (1993). *Radical casework: A theory of practice.* St Leonards, Sydney: Allen and Unwin.

Fook, J. (2002). *Social work: Critical theory and practice.* London: Sage.

Fook, J., & Gardner, F. (2007). *Practising critical reflection: A resource handbook*. Maidenhead: Open University Press.

Foucault, M. (1980). Prison talk. In M. Morris & Patton, P. (eds), *Power/knowledge: Selected interviews and other writings 1972–1977*. New York: Pantheon Books, pp. 37–54.

Foucault, M. (1982). The subject and power. *Critical Inquiry, 8*, 777–795.

Freire, P. (1997). *Pedagogy of the oppressed*. New York: Continuum.

Gray, M., & Lovat, T. (2007). Horse and carriage: Why Habermas's discourse ethics gives virtue a *praxis* in social work. *Ethics and Social Welfare, 1*(3), 310–328.

Gray, M., & Lovat, T. (2008). Practical mysticism, Habermas and social work praxis. *Journal of Social Work, 8*(2), 149–163.

Gray, M., & Webb, S. (2009). Critical social work. In M. Gray & Webb, S. (eds), *Social work: Theories and method*. London: Sage, pp. 76–85.

Habermas, J. (1998). *On the pragmatics of communication*. Cambridge, MA: MIT Press.

Hanmer, J. (1977). Community action, women's aid and the women's liberation movement. In M. Mayo (ed.), *Women in the community*. London: Routledge and Kegan Paul, pp. 91–108.

Hayes, D., & Houston, S. (2007). 'Lifeworld', 'System' and Family Group Conferences: Habermas's contribution to discourse in child protection. *British Journal of Social Work, 37*(6), 987–1006.

Healy, K. (1998). Participation and child protection: the importance of context. *British Journal of Social Work, 28*, 897–914.

Healy, K. (1999). Power and activist social work. In B. Pease & Fook, J. (eds), *Transforming social work practice: Postmodern critical perspectives*. St Leonards, Sydney: Allen and Unwin, pp. 115–134.

Healy, K. (2000). *Social work practices: Contemporary perspectives on change*. London: Sage.

Healy, K. (2005a). *Social work theories in context: Creating frameworks for practice*. Basingstoke: Palgrave.

Healy, K. (2005b). Under reconstruction: renewing critical social work practices. In S. Hick, Fook, J., & Pozzuto, R. (eds), *Social work: A critical turn*. Toronto, ON: Thompson Educational Publishing, pp. 215–230.

Healy, K. (2009). A case of mistaken identity: The social welfare professions and new public management. *Journal of Sociology, 45*(4), 401–408.

Healy, K. (2010). Recognising and enabling social workers to promote child well-being and protection. *Australian Social Work, 63*(2), 141–144.

Hick, S., & Pozzuto, R. (2005). Introduction: towards "becoming" a critical social worker. In S. Hick, Fook, J., & Pozzuto, R. (eds), *Social work: A critical turn*. Toronto, ON: Thomson Educational Publishing, pp. ix–xviii.

Hoatson, L. (2003). The scope of community practice in the 21st century. In W. Weeks, Hoatson, L., & Dixon, J. (eds), *Community practices in Australia*. Melbourne: Pearson Education, pp. 23–32.

Houston, S. (2002). Re-thinking a systemic approach to child welfare: A critical response to the framework for the assessment of children in need and their families. *European Journal of Social Work, 5*(3), 301–312.

Houston, S. (2009). Jürgen Habermas. In M. Gray & Webb, S. (eds). *Social work: Theories and methods*. London: Sage, pp.13–22.

Johnson, A.K. (2004). Social work is standing on the legacy of Jane Addams: But are we sitting on the sidelines? *Social Work, 49*(2), 319–322.

Jones, K., Cooper, B., & Ferguson, H. (eds), *Best practice in social work: Critical perspectives*. Basingstoke: Palgrave.

Jones, K., & Spreadbury, K. (2008). Best practice in adult protection: Safety, choice and inclusion. In K. Jones, Cooper, B., & Ferguson, H. (eds). *Best practice in social work: Critical perspectives*. Basingstoke: Palgrave, pp. 55–68.

Juhila, K. (2004). Talking back to stigmatized identities: Negotiating culturally dominant categorizations in interviews with shelter residents. *Qualitative Social Work, 3*(3), 259–275.

Kellner, D. (1993). Critical theory today: Revisiting the classics. *Theory, Culture and Society, 10*, 43–60.

Leonard, P. (1994). Knowledge/power and postmodernism: Implications for the practice of a critical social work educatoin. *Canadian Social Work Review, 11*(1), 11–26.

Leonard, P. (1995). Postmodernism, socialism and social welfare. *Journal of Progressive Human Services, 6*(2), 3–19.

Leonard, P. (1997). *Postmodern welfare: Reconstructing an emancipatory project*. London: Sage.

Lovat, T., & Gray, M. (2008). Towards a proportionist social work ethics: A Habermasian perspective. *British Journal of Social Work, 38*, 1100–1114.

Macfarlane, S. (2009). Opening spaces for alternative understandings in mental health practice. In J. Allan, Briskman, L., & Pease, B. (eds), *Critical social work*. Sydney: Allen & Unwin, pp. 201–213.

Marx, K. (1972). Alienation and social classes. In R. C. Tucker (ed.). *The Marx-Engels reader*. New York: W.W. Norton, pp. 104–106.

Marx, K., & Engels, F. (1972). Manifesto of the Communist Party. In R.C. Tucker (ed.). *The Marx-Engels reader*. New York: W.W. Norton, pp. 331–362.

McDonald, C. (2006). *Challenging social work: The context of practice*. Basingstoke: Palgrave.

Moreau, M. (1979). A structural approach to social work practice. *Canadian Journal of Social Work Education, 5*(1), 78–94.

Moreau, M. (1990). Empowerment through advocacy and consciousness-raising: Implications of a structural approach to social work. *Journal of Sociology and Social Welfare, 17*(2), 53–67.

Mullaly, B. (1993). *Structural social work: Ideology, theory and practice*. Toronto, ON: McClelland and Stewart.

O'Gara, J. (2008). Best practice in emergency mental health social work: On using good judgment. In K. Jones, Cooper, B., & Ferguson, H. (eds), *Best practice in social work: Critical perspectives*. Basingstoke: Palgrave, pp. 213–234.

Osborne, D., & Gaebler, T. (1993). *Reinventing government: How the entrepreneurial spirit is transforming the public sector*. New York: Plume Books.

Peile, C., & McCouat, M. (1997). The rise of relativism: The future of theory and knowledge development in social work. *British Journal of Social Work, 27,* 343–360.

Penna, S., & O'Brien, M. (2009). Neoliberalism. In M. Gray & Webb, S. (eds), *Social work: Theories and methods*. London: Sage, pp. 109–118.

Reisch, M., & Andrews, J. (2002). *The road not taken: A history of radical social work in the United States*. New York: Brunner-Routledge.

Reynolds, B. (1963). *An unchartered journey: Fifty years of growth in social work*. New York: Citadel.

Rojek, C., Peacock, C., & Collins, S. (1988). *Social work and received Ideas*. London: Sage.

Wearing, B. (1986). Feminist theory and social work. In H. Marchant & Wearing, B. (eds), *Gender reclaimed: Women in social work*. Sydney: Hale and Iremonger, pp. 33–53.

Yeatman, A. (1994). *Postmodern revisionings of the political*. New York: Routledge.

SECTION 3

Social Work Practice

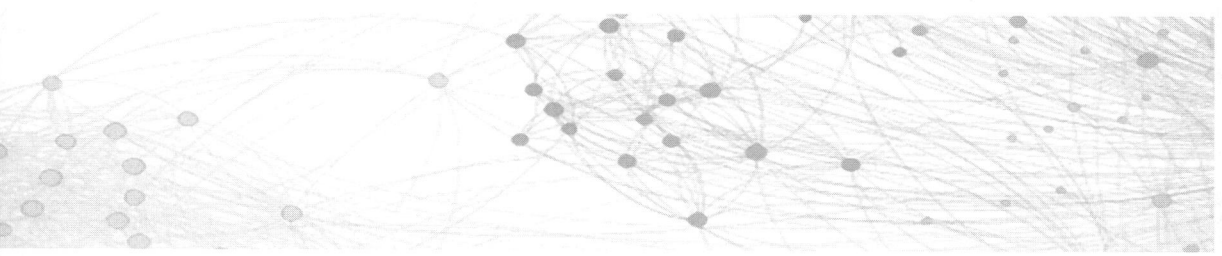

INTRODUCTION

In 1981, the National Association of Social Workers in the USA defined 'social work practice' as a professional endeavour, which aims to:

1. enhance the developmental, problem-solving, and coping capacities of people;
2. promote the effective and human operation of systems that provide resources and services to people;
3. link people with systems that provide them with resources, services, and opportunities; and
4. contribute to the development and improvement of social policy.

This broad definition of social work practice fails to attenuate the frame or sensibilities of practice-related issues as they are understood by students and practitioners. As mentioned in the Introduction, practice is always situated on the moving border between process and event, between the real and the possible. Generally speaking, social work is the nexus of 'arrays of activities' or practices that practitioners perform with greater or lesser commitment, dexterity, and skill. The term 'professional practice' tends to refer to where a student is required to extend knowledge and skills within a practical environment or 'practice setting'. Another frequently used term in social work is 'best practice', which is a technique or methodology that, through experience and research, has proven to lead reliably to a desired outcome. A commitment to using the best practices in any field is a commitment to using all the knowledge, methods, and skills at one's disposal to ensure success.

Social workers tend to agree there is no such thing as a coherent, unified 'practice theory', only a body of highly diverse processes, tasks, agendas, skills, and interventions that are loosely defined as a 'practice approach'. Fields or sites of intervention are specialist domains of practice – mental health, children and family work, disability and aged care, and so on – often exhibiting their own 'logic', specialities, processes, and priorities. Practitioners often rely on strategies which, even if they are not aimed at explicitly formulated goals, still turn out to be objectively adjusted to the situation. Action guided by a 'feel for the context' has all the appearances of the rational action but is just as likely to involve nuanced sensibilities and judgement. Dreyfus and Dreyfus's (1986) model of skill acquisition progressing from competency and proficiency to expertise helps capture the way practice is determined simultaneously by experience, context, and knowledge. This is sometimes called 'practice wisdom' relying on intuitive or professional judgement as a type of cognitive heuristic.

Section 3 concentrates on the important area of social work practice. The definition of social work practice is a contestable one but successive attempts to define it revisit a number of common components such that contemporary social work practice is seen to incorporate all of the following tasks: (i) direct intervention; (iii) risk assessment and decision making; (iii) advocacy; and (iv) community work. The notion of enabling, often achieved through negotiated change, is also linked closely with the theme of personal empowerment in social work. The degree to which the goals are identified by the individual or externally prescribed is debatable. Nevertheless, in this context, approaches like reflective practice and crisis interventions have become popular. From a different perspective, advocacy on behalf of or alongside the service user has also been seen as an important component of the role of a social worker. Some regard social work as a problem-solving activity that focuses on the whole of a person's or family's life, their social support network, their neighbourhood, and community. However, it is generally agreed that the process and the relationship form a core part of social work practice with service users and can represent the service in itself. This section, while not exhaustive, develops and identifies core elements of social work practice from a range of contexts, cases, and environments to give the reader a good understanding of different types of intervention.

In Chapter 13, Paula Doherty and Sue White carefully elucidate the current state of 'knowledge for practice' in social work and speculate on the consequences of various knowledge forms for practice. They address the uncertainties and contingencies of practice, and of the need for social workers to make more explicit use of formal knowledge to reduce this uncertainty. They argue that this focus on making certainty out of uncertainty glosses over the ways in which both knowledge and practice often propel practitioners towards early and certain judgements when a position of 'respectful uncertainty' might be more appropriate. In conclusion, they stress the need to recognise the ways in which both theory and popular knowledge is invoked to make unequivocal knowledge in case formulation and suggest ways in which students and social workers can be helped to remain in uncertainty and constantly interrogate their knowledge, case reasoning, and decision making.

In Chapter 14, Eileen Munro shows how, in recent decades, managing risk has become a major responsibility of social workers, risk both *to* service users (of being harmed) and *from* them (of causing harm). She highlights the complexity of predicting risk and the wisdom of hindsight, which leads to castigations for poor practice. In the debate between actuarial and intuitive approaches to risk assessment, Munro favours the reliability of the actuarial approach in making specific judgements about future risk. However, in the absence of conclusive research, professionals are entreated to treat risk assessments with caution and remain alert to evidence that challenges their assessment. To counter defensive practices in a risk-aversive society, Munro believes social workers need to develop a shared and deeper understanding of the process of assessing risk and of what counts as 'good enough' professional practice.

In Chapter 15, Marleen Cooper and Joan Lesser examine integrated psychotherapy, a multifaceted approach eminently well suited to direct social work practice. Its aim is to maximise a person's functioning in the intrapsychic, interpersonal, and sociopolitical spheres, and to facilitate wholeness by bringing together the affective, cognitive, behavioural, and physiological systems within a person. The chapter begins with an overview of integrative psychotherapy, examines common factors in psychotherapy, and then discusses several forms of psychotherapeutic integration, namely, technical, theoretical, and assimilative integration. Two of these approaches, technical and assimilative integration, are fully illustrated with case examples.

In Chapter 16, Barry Cournoyer's important contribution concentrates on short-term crisis intervention and trauma work seen as increasingly important in diverse social work practice contexts. He provides examples from practice to show how contemporary research on the impact of trauma informs effective evidence-based interventions for clients who have experienced extreme stress events, such as environmental disasters, violence toward individuals, and the onset of a life-threatening progressive illness, which trigger active crisis states. While some people adapt to the stressful circumstances and recover within days, others become traumatised so that the symptoms of distress continue at severe levels long after the life-threatening events have ended.

'All social work is political' begins Karen Haynes in Chapter 17, in discussing empowering, transformative modes of practice, and the growing need for social workers to affect social policy through political action. Haynes examines advocacy as the central mission of social work practice and means of empowering clients and the historic debate surrounding professionalism, social work's apolitical stance, and the distinguishing elements of empowerment practice. She argues that, as change agents and transformers, social workers have to engage in the political process and this includes advocacy and community-based practice.

In Chapter 18, Keith Popple locates community work in a theoretical approach that is mindful of the new European wave of radical ontologies of community as 'shared lack' and neoliberal individualism that has done so much damage to both individuals and communities. In advocating a transformative community practice, social work needs seriously to consider an approach to community practice that critiques and addresses structural inequalities, is critical aware of the problems inherent in the present delivery and management of social work, and has at core a compassion for those who have been damaged by a system that prioritises and sustains the unseemly and greedy pursuit of greater profit and power.

REFERENCE

Dreyfus, H.L., & Dreyfus, S.E. (1986). *Mind over machine: The power of human intuition and expertise in the age of the computer.* Oxford: Basil Blackwell.

13

Knowledge for Reflexive Practice

Paula Doherty and Sue White

The body map made at the time shows extensive bruising to his buttocks and other bruises to his face and chest, including the swelling to his forehead which had triggered the referral from the GP. There were also some minor scratches which Ms A said were caused by one of their two dogs. Child A was admitted for assessment ... A referral form was faxed to Haringey CYPS social workers the same day as the referral,

The Panel take the view that the threshold of concern in the child protection system at the time was too high. Both the hospital and the social work staff were too willing to believe the plausible accounts the mother was offering to explain child A's injuries. In the more holistic context of the case the explanations offered by Ms A should have been questioned. A different assessment of Ms A's parenting and her motivation to protect and care for her son should have been considered (Department for Education, 2010).

The quotations above are taken from the Serious Case Review (SCR) into the brutal killing of Peter Connelly (Baby P) in England in 2007. Peter was a toddler aged 17 months, who was subject to a child protection plan, supervised by the London Borough of Haringey Children and Young People's Service. The first extract refers to one of Peter's early referrals to hospital for investigation of his injuries, which occurred in December 2006, when he was nine months old and not independently mobile. He continued to sustain injuries, which the SCR panel reports with incredulity in the second extract. Peter died in August 2007. At the time of his death, he had multiple injuries, including eight broken ribs and a fracture of the thoraco-lumbar spine (a broken back). The case caused widespread moral outrage, a media witch-hunt against the social workers involved and a root and branch reform programme for social work in England. The full SCR was published on 26 October 2010. It provoked more speculation about how this could possibly have happened when Peter was known to agencies, regularly visited, frequently seen by health staff, including paediatricians, and had at least ten presentations at hospital, as well as periods as an inpatient. In her evidence to a House of Commons Select Committee given on 15 September 2010, Sharon Shoesmith, the former Director of Haringey Children and Young People's Service, who was sacked as a result of Peter's death, remarked:

I think one of the lasting issues of this case surrounds why all those professionals – police, doctors, consultants, nurses, health visitors and social workers – were caught in the trap of feeling that the mother was being genuine. Why did they not question that more? I think that has to be the overriding question ... I was in the room when the police officer came in and said that the mother had been charged with murder. Remember that no one was ever sentenced for murder, but I was in the room when that happened and those who knew Peter Connelly and the mother were completely taken aback and said, 'That couldn't possibly be the case. You must have it wrong: this couldn't be the case.' That was their reaction, having known this person (http://www.publications.parliament.uk/pa/cm201011/cmselect/cmeduc/465i/10091502.htm).

This chapter examines some aspects of reflexivity in social work and knowledge relating to professional decision making, which goes some way to explaining how such an event can take place, where apparently reasonable and benignly motivated staff make repeated errors in the attribution of cause and effect and fail to see what, with hindsight, was happening right under their noses. It argues attention to the interactional, social, and cultural contexts in which professional judgements take place is essential to open up the possibility for an ethical engagement with the moral nature of practice. An examination of the literature on human factors in decision making shows many of the errors of reasoning in the Peter Connelly case are not very surprising at all. But, there are no magic solutions to the fallibilities associated with human information processing and decision making. As this chapter shows, a rethinking of the kinds of knowledge and organisational environments needed for safer practice is urgently required.

For a variety of reasons, our intrinsic characteristics as human information processors operate as both friend and foe in social work decision making (White, 2009). At an individual level, people are equipped with an innate apparatus to assess their fellow human beings on an intuitive–emotional level, and alongside this, they have particular cognitive biases. The generation of hypotheses is affected by one's cognitive capacities in two principal ways: it is limited by what is *available* in memory and by 'psychological commitment' to the first hypothesis, which makes it more difficult subsequently to revise one's formulation (Dowie & Elstein, 1988, p. 19). This is confounded by the related tendency to seek out evidence to confirm a hypothesis, rather than searching for 'disconfirming' evidence. This is known as 'confirmation bias' (Wolf et al., 1985). Thus, once an interpretation of events has been settled on, practitioners tend to deviate little from their initial 'anchor' hypothesis (Kahneman et al., 1982).

It is crucial for the argument here to note, when social psychological and sociological dimensions, which generate powerfully normative cultural practices are added to the equation, a potent cocktail is created that can easily intoxicate practitioners with their own cherished convictions (Haidt, 2001; White, 2009), that is, socially dominant 'moral heuristics' (Sunstein, 2010), while barely being noticed by the interactants, can affect organisational and group decision making. It is common for generalised moral heuristics to be used in everyday human judgements. In many instances, according to Sunstein (2010), these work well, but they become problematic when 'generalizations are wrenched out of context and treated as freestanding or universal principles' (p. 4) and applied where they are *maybe* not applicable. The apparent universality of moral heuristics means rejection of them appears 'morally obtuse, possibly even monstrous' (Sunstein, 2010, p. 4). The illustrative example below is taken from recent ethnographic observations of decision making in a social work initial assessment team. The social worker (SW) explained to the researcher (R) there had been a recent referral about a volunteer in a youth centre who had entered into a sexual relationship with a young person attending the centre. The young person was 'looked after' by another local authority, in a residential establishment. [In the UK, the status being 'looked after' under the Children Act (1989) refers to all children accommodated by the local authority, either with parental agreement or on a court order.]

R: How old is [the young person]?
SW: 16, but he's [volunteer] in a position of trust ... there was a strategy discussion and it was no further action by the police!
R: right, so are you not happy with that decision then?
SW: No, he's breached his position of trust, even if [young person] is 16. I can't understand the decision ... it says here [reading from computer screen], *the Crown Prosecution Service have said that, [volunteer] was not, in a legal sense, as per the Act, in a position of trust, and hence we will not be proceeding.*

The Sexual Offences (Amendment) Act 2000 came into force on the 8 January 2001 in England, Scotland, and Wales, equalising the age of consent at 16, for gay men, lesbians, and heterosexuals. In the case above, the police had been requested by the youth centre's manager to be involved because of the volunteering aspect of the relationship. The Crown Prosecution Service (CPS) had deemed there had not been any criminal violation. The social worker disagreed with the decision made by the CPS not to take any criminal action against the volunteer and explained the local authority responsible for the young person would look into the matter further. This was a moral framing of the sexual relationship focused on the actions of the volunteer as violating a 'position of trust'. The potential for the social worker to construct the sexual relationship as consensual, or not harmful to the young person, was 'dwarfed by the violation of a trusting relationship' (Sunstein, 2010, p. 13) – a powerful cultural motif involving the act of 'betrayal'. An understanding of moral heuristics highlights the potential firing (and possibly misfiring) of widely held intuitions, which because of their cultural dominance (e.g., the 'monstrous' nature of a betrayal of trust; Sunstein, 2010, p. 4), do not get debated and their potentially questionable and ill-fitting properties are obscured.

Thus, professional activity can easily settle into what Argyris (1987) calls 'defensive routines' of locally normative, ritualised categorisations. What is more:

> To retain their power, defensive routines *must remain undiscussable*. Teams stay stuck in their defensive routines only when they pretend that they don't have any defensive routines, that everything is all right, and that they can say 'anything'. But how to make them discussable is a challenge (Senge, 1990, p. 255, original emphasis).

The challenge is to develop an orientation to both knowledge *use* and knowledge *making* (e.g., as it emerges in professional talk), which makes these defensive routines and moral heuristics 'discussable'. The chapter outlines some possibilities for nurturing this 'knowledge for reflexive practice', to render visible and contestable the social *work* in social work but first asks what assumptions have driven policy and practice change over recent years, arguably creating the conditions under which the retrospectively obvious errors in professional judgement revealed in the SCR into Peter Connelly's death could flourish?

ASSUMPTIONS ABOUT DECISION MAKING

Policy developments in the UK, but also across much of Europe, North America, Australia, and New Zealand, operate with an assumption organisational environments, and hence policy, should support and drive practitioners to travel as swiftly as possible, steering a steady course towards conditions of certainty. The world is out there, independent of the practitioner, and can become known through objective and dispassionate inquiry, observation, and crucially, multi-agency 'information sharing'. This:

> presupposes a universal, homogeneous and essential human nature that allows knowers to be substituted for one another ... Knowers are detached, neutral spectators, and the objects of knowledge are separate from them, inert items in the

observational knowledge-gathering process (Code, 1995, pp. 24–25).

Of course, this is a neat assumption for those designing policy. If social workers functioned as independent information processors, apprehending and appraising the world in its wondrous, abundant variety and all that was needed was vigilance, then surely, the more the merrier, many brains would make lighter work! Within this model, the work goes on inside the individual practitioner's head and is then communicated to other similarly independently thinking individuals, who, in turn observe, test, and appraise for themselves – what could be safer? Hence, for the last decade, there has been a raft of policy in the UK, particularly in England and Wales, aimed at facilitating information sharing:

> Improving outcomes for children and young people, so that every child achieves their potential, involves changes to culture and practice across the children's workforce ... Integrated working focuses on enabling and encouraging professionals to work together and to adopt common processes to deliver frontline services, coordinated and built around the needs of children and young people. (http://www.everychildmatters.gov.uk/delivering-services/integratedworking).

Working Together to Safeguard Children (Department for Education, 2010) maintains practitioners across a range of services and domains aim to *work together* to promote the health and well-being of children and protect them from significant harm. The premise behind such working is it will ensure a coming together of a range of specialisms to provide a holistic picture of a child's circumstances as the basis upon which practitioners should work. This chapter now goes on to argue this is a seriously flawed understanding of how human beings make decisions in many social situations.

DECISION MAKING AS A SOCIAL PROCESS

Making decisions in groups is part and parcel of social work. Some instances of group decision making are mandated and are implemented in response to what are seen to be fallibilities in individual decision making (Laming, 2003). However, judgements are also made in informal settings, such as supervision, or during serendipitous discussions with colleagues. The rationale for group decision making can be placed into three broad categories (see Davis, 1992).

1 The first is based on the premise that group decision making enhances individual decision making. This is said to increase the possibility of an appropriate response by reducing errors of judgement and, therefore, minimising the risk of bad decisions. It does so because of the interactions within a group and because a group has a wider range of knowledge upon which to draw. The main potential advantage, it is argued, is the coming together of a range of specialisms to counteract individual, potentially precipitous judgements and decisions. This has been the dominant understanding of the policy makers.
2 Group decision making is also said to increase the commitment to the decisions made because 'the work' has been agreed and not been imposed.
3 Risk is reduced because there are more people responsible for averting it.

The main thrust of the argument for group decision making, then, appears to be that discussion and debate (including conflict of opinion) will occur during decision-making activities and processes, allowing professionals to come to more nuanced decisions. However, the authors' own research carried out in children's services in the UK over a number of years shows debates in interprofessional fora, such as case conferences, are conspicuous by their absence (e.g., White, 2009; White & Stancombe, 2003; and Doherty's work in progress). The failure to reason in public rarely gets noticed in groups (Taleb, 2007), especially where it has become the norm in the group for certain members to speak and others not to do so. People rarely 'show their working' and seem not to notice when others similarly fail to do so. Free-thinking, individual brains seem strikingly predisposed to leading their owners passively down a particular primrose path. Maybe this is because the world, the families, their relationships, and their stories have been rightly appraised, accurately processed cognitively, and they are all correct? This is how it may routinely feel to the people involved in the discussions – these are, after all, defensive routines and thus are not noticed – but is such accuracy very likely considering how complex, ambiguous, and fragmented professionals' understandings of families can be (Munro, 2002)? The primrose path may be overgrown with very sharp thorns. So, how are these agreements so readily reached?

THE BYSTANDER EFFECT AND WORKING TOGETHER

The wider judgement and decision-making literature has been informative to social work. However, the bystander effect and diffusion of responsibility (e.g. Latané & Darley, 1976) seem to have been largely ignored. While subject to many nuances, these concepts, derived from social psychology, have utility for social work by providing a way of understanding the potential for inaction where it is maybe required. Very broadly these concepts suggest that where there are multiple potential 'helpers' and where there is no specific request made for help, there is the potential for no one to take action, others to be 'left to it', or for others to be perceived a closer to the problem in some way (c.f. Kogut & Beyth-Marom, 2008; Blair et al., 2005). Nelissen and Zeelenburg (2009) suggest that:

> The bystander effect shows that the presence of others diffuses personal responsibility (unpaginated)

The second SCR into the death of Peter Connelly illustrates the bystander effect at work in terms of reduced responsibility. The report states Peter was seen with Ms A (Peter's mother) by his general practitioner (GP) at the end of July 2007. The Executive Summary further tells us the GP had 'considerable misgivings about Peter's appearance and demeanour at that appointment'. The report then concludes this point by saying '[h]e [the GP] assumed that others would have similar concerns and would be in a better position to take action' (Paragraph 4.3.5, Haringey Local Safeguarding Children's Board, 2009). The following extract shows similar processes at work. It is taken from a transcribed meeting of professionals in an English local authority, collected during recent ethnographic research.

Extract 1

Health practitioner 1: I mean, we can stay involved with the core group. We will have nothing to report ... if we have no contact with the family and nothing to report at core group, do you still want us to come, or we still can, but I'm thinking about inefficiency in the system ...

Health practitioner 2: just to hear other people's news ...

Extract 2

Social worker: I know school aren't coming today, but she's rang and left a message this morning and she says that school is, they're doing really well at school aren't they ... OK, we'll give it a few more minutes and see if [name] turns up. If not, then.

Extract 3

Social worker: OK, I've spoken to [head teacher of school] and she said that she wasn't coming because they've only been in school two days but that he's [older child] has settled well. At the minute, you know. She'll give us more of an update.

The above extracts, one, as stated, from a meeting of professionals, and the other two from separate core group meetings, illustrate the importance of considering the bystander effect and its potential effect on decision making. The health practitioners in the first extract expressed that perhaps it was not necessary or beneficial for them to remain involved with the core group and they questioned what they could add to its decision-making remit given they were met with parental resistance to their involvement and did not feel best placed to be part of the core group. Similarly, the education professionals in the second two extracts do not feel they were in a position to take part in decision making as they had not seen the children in school due to the core group being scheduled for the start of term. What this means is, in all three examples, the group forum was reduced. In the third extract, attendance was reduced to just the social worker and the mother and, in the other core group, the input from education was reduced or simplified to a short report stating the child had settled in well. Education and health in these examples would not hear the input from other professionals or be able to discuss any questions from each other. It is a stilted and non-dialogical form of decision making. These professionals saw their input to the core group as resting on their domain specialisms. The invocation of domain-specific knowledge, or lack of it (it is nothing to do with me, I hardly know them) is another powerful ingredient in the process of carving certainty from uncertainty in professional practice.

DOMAIN KNOWLEDGE AND THE *AD HOCERY* OF DECISION MAKING

As can be seen in the above extracts, decision making in social work is dispersed over many sites and, potentially, in many places. At certain times and points, people from these domains come together to make decisions. By considering domain decision making, clues might be discerned about underlying processes and potential tensions where specialisms meet (Redelmeier & Tversky, 1992). This can be seen at work in the following extract between a children's services team manager, social worker, and legal representative providing legal advice to the local authority in a legal gateway meeting discussing whether or not the case should proceed to court for a care order in relation to the children of the family. The legal representative is providing his domain-specific knowledge and linking it to his expertise and know-how about the court system and, indeed, the individual judge in a particular court. The team manager talks about her own area of expertise and experience of finding alternatives for children to their present situation.

Legal representative: This file does not read well on paper. If we looked at matters objectively and going in front of [Family Proceedings Judge] at [place] then what would she make of this, then I think the answer is, she would be pretty unhappy …

Team manager: … I mean, you're right, it doesn't read well and there's a massive history to the family … I think the worry for me in this situation is, can we make a difference? If this case came into care, *are* we going to improve things? … I mean, let's face it none of these children are going for adoption. They're going to be subject to the fostering system … we've had two children of ours come into care recently, that through no fault of theirs or ours, they're onto their fourth placement.

Legal representative: mmm. When I said it doesn't read well, that's not to be interpreted by you as a barrister looking and criticising … that's not what's intended here because I can see … with the best will in the world, you're trying to work with keeping children at home. I'll just say and I'm throwing this into the air, is this better done down a legal route.

Legal representative [to social worker]: this [a case citation referred to earlier] is where the court of appeal has absolutely castigated social services … It went to the Court of Appeal and led to a consideration by the court of appeal of what was considered by them as good and bad social work practice. What the Court of Appeal are emphasising, and just to keep you guys safe and free from criticism in the future … My concern is that if this ultimately does lead to a court situation, then it just worries me that the way that you're talking is, to some extent … what worries me, as to potential exposure of you as a social work team … from a legal sense, my view [is], so that there's no criticism of you as a social work team.

Team manager: I can see where you're coming from [name] but I've got past the stage of. Where I'm not bothered about being criticised by the court … after 8 years [experience] … no child protection plan in the world is going to work if we don't try and address the mother's problems … We know it's going to meet threshold and we all know that any judge would have a moan about how longstanding a case it is … the question becomes one of not about thresholds, not about what judges or barristers are going to say but about whether we can, as practitioners, make these children's lives any better and that's still a question, that's still a debate that we're having.

Interactions here are organised by domain-specific knowledge and generate their own information (Atkinson, 1995; Mol, 2003) and judgements about the case. In this sense, the information is a decision that is re-transformed into information (Atkinson, 1995). The barrister has decided the case should go to court and his advice is to protect the local authority from criticism from the judge. His knowledge comes from his experience in court, his experience of the particular judge sitting in the court concerned, and his use of case law stating practitioners should be aware of the court's remit. These provide the basis of his talk. The decision made by the barrister is formed into information about the court and probable response from a particular judge. Case law is invoked to warrant this reading of the case and the risk the local authority will be rebuked by the judiciary. The team manager has judged the children should remain with their mother until therapeutic work is done with her and she is well placed to make this judgement given her experience as a practitioner and manager over 8 years, and her knowledge of alternatives forms of care for the children. The team manager states '... let's face it, none of these children are going for adoption. They're going to be subject to the fostering system ... we've had two [other] children [who are] onto their fourth placement'. Here the team manager is responding to the barrister's advice the case should go to court from the perspective of her domain-specific knowledge of fostering and the effects of multiple placements on children. The point is the decision frame shifted with the domain and rested on interactions between the barrister and the team manager. The team manager and the barrister – the more powerful professionals in this interaction – were each seeking to persuade the other of 'rightness' of each other's decision and alternative ideas and courses of action were discussed. There is, in some sense, argument and debate but the perspectives of the interactants solidify and polarise.

CONCURRENCE-SEEKING BEHAVIOUR AND CONSTRUCTIVE CONTROVERSY

Concurrence-seeking behaviour occurs in groups when members of a group inhibit discussion to avoid any disagreement or argument or to emphasise agreement. This means realistic appraisal of alternative ideas and courses of action do not occur. This closely resembles what Janis (1982) terms 'groupthink'. Groupthink occurs when group members involved in decision making do not voice their doubts and misgivings about what appears to be the consensus in a group in order to maintain group harmony, believing this is the right, moral, or correct thing to do. This preserves group agreement. Concurrence-seeking behaviour means a single person (or minority opinion) can perceive his or her own view(s) as idiosyncratic and thus, rather than being admonished by the group members, he or she relinquishes or does not state his or her opinions, and so concurs with the group. In both cases, decision making takes place in the context of cooperation and conflict avoidance.

In concurrence-seeking behaviour, disagreement, and any resultant debate, is suppressed due to individuals' apprehension about the group process and the prospect of disapprobation of their judgement or reasoning. This may be caused by some initial disagreement, which may be explicit, for example, by comments being disparaged, or implicit, for example, by not having comments acknowledged. The following is an extract from a core group. There were a number of professionals present at this meeting, including health, education, and children's services. The mother was also present. The social worker had been discussing points from the child protection plan and professionals were asked to make any comments they wished to make.

Health visitor: [directed towards the social worker] when I visited last I was a little bit concerned that they weren't having a proper breakfast that particular morning. (pause) [child] said, err. Do they get cereal before they go to school?

Mother: yeah they do. They eat well.
Health visitor: It was, err, yeah ... but according to [oldest child] they'd had crisps and biscuits, so maybe that's a one off [nervous laugh].
Social worker: OK, anything from school.
School nurse: No, no concern.
Social worker: Right. Last point I think, is home conditions.

The effect of concurrence-seeking behaviour is clearly visible in the above extract. Comments may be made, here in the form of a concern about what the children are being given to eat for breakfast, and may be silenced by way of 'no comment' made about them. The health visitor directs her talk to the social worker who, in return, makes no comment. There is a slight pause in the speech, indicating a response was expected. The health visitor then continues by directing her question to the mother *do they get cereal before they go to school*? The mother responds the children *do have breakfast and, in fact, eat well*. The social worker does not respond to the comments made by the health visitor or the mother, and moves on to the next point she wishes to raise. The health visitor's point is silenced and is not picked up by any other professionals. Tacitly, agreement is reached. The children eat appropriately and the health visitor thus relinquishes, or sets aside, the point she was making in relation to her concerns about nutrition in the face of others not expressing any similar concerns. It is an issue deemed to be resolved. The social worker, having not acknowledged the health visitor's concerns, does not overtly admonish, question, or, in any way, negate the health visitor and professional relations remain, *prima facie*, intact.

It is highly likely the failure to safeguard Peter Connelly was attributable to a combination of the bystander effect (somebody else will do it), domain-specific knowledge (the local authority lawyer had queried whether a court would grant an order, invoking their domain-specific knowledge), and the concurrence effect (everybody else believes the mother, I must be wrong). What does this tell us about organisational cultures in social work? How may we create agency environments which encourage debate and dialogue?

CREATING SAFER ORGANISATIONS

Lamentably, the widespread introduction of bureaucratised processes, in England in particular, has created organisational environments pushing social workers increasingly towards precipitous categorisations and hence have the effect of stifling debate (Broadhurst et al., 2009; Wastell et al., 2009; White et al., 2010). This tendency is exacerbated by the implementation of various electronic recording systems, which embed decisions in software, taking them out of the dialogical space, and rendering them immune from reflexive analysis.

In England, Professor Eileen Munro's (see Chapter 14) government review of child care practice aims to reduce bureaucracy and create systemic conditions more conducive to the complexities of the professional task. In her first report, she notes:

> It seems plausible at this stage of the review to conclude that the anxiety about managing uncertainty has supported the creation of a performance culture and regulatory regime which searches for compliance with process, finds the scrutiny of practice difficult, and is ultimately distanced from learning and reflective practice (Munro, 2010, p. 39).

Drawing on similar ideas derived from systems theory, Argyris and Schön (1996) famously have distinguished between single-loop and double-loop learning. These are related to Bateson's (1972) concepts of first- and second-order learning. In single-loop learning, actions are modified when achieved outcomes differ from those expected and valued within an organisation or culture. In double-loop learning, the actors question the very values and assumptions leading to the action being desirable in the first place. Thus, second-order or double-loop learning has transformative potential. When achieved, it helps us to 'see what we don't see' (Varela, 1992, p. 19) about our organisational and occupational *modi operandi*; but there are huge barriers to double-loop learning, such as the 'group think' effects discussed above.

There have been some attempts to theorise what characteristics an organisation should have and what activities it should promote to create the conditions for double-loop learning, that is, for the interrogation of its own cultures, values, and dominant knowledges. One product of this theorising is the notion of the 'learning organization' (Senge, 1990):

> At the heart of a learning organization is a shift of mind – from seeing ourselves as separate from the world to connected to the world, from seeing problems as caused by someone, or something "out there" to seeing how our actions create the problems we experience. A learning organization is a place where people are continually discovering how they create their reality. And how they can change it ... (pp. 12–13).

For social work, this has to involve the opening up of dialogical spaces and making debate 'business as usual'. In circumstances where different responses to the 'facts' are given and different experiences and perspectives are provided, the initial hypothesis is rendered uncertain. This might be termed a state of internal conflict or disequilibrium. At this point, the picture is made fuzzy and here there is the potential for group decision making to be meaningful and helpful. Practitioners are in a cognitive and emotional state, possibly making them receptive to new information and different 'versions' of the decision situation, and motivated to reach potentially more nuanced and sound decisions. For example, Smith et al., (1981) found individuals who expected debate were more accurate in understanding others' perspectives than were persons involved in concurrence-seeking discussions. Individuals in situations of debate and controversy are better able to take the opposing perspective than are individuals participating in situations where concurrence seeking was the tacitly accepted group norm (Johnson et al., 1985). So, concurrence-seeking behaviour can be counteracted by the promotion of debate, which increases peoples' awareness of issues outside of their own occupational group and domain-specific knowledge (Anspach, 1987). Used thus, group reasoning can be a positive force. Thus, we must seek to nurture organisational environments in which skilful participation in *constructive controversy* is encouraged (Johnson et al., 2000). Debate might be opened up with simple devices, such as gentle questioning of each other. The effect of such questioning and 'managing' of potential bystanding behaviour is observable in the extract below.

Health practitioner 1: If we have no contact with the family and nothing to report at core group, do you still want us to come or we still can err, but I'm thinking about inefficiency in the system.
Team manager child protection: I know, and we don't want to take your time unnecessarily.
Health practitioner 1: ... just to hear other people's news.
Social worker: If it would be good for you, and beneficial for you, if you're going to be coming back and doing individual work, then I would suggest that you still attend.
Health practitioner 2: Mmm, one of us could come.
Social worker: You will remain on the core group minutes and you will get the minutes. I don't know how much the minutes reflect, when you've read them and you've attended the meeting, whether you feel that they reflect what's happened in the meeting or an appraisal of what's happened in the meeting, there's more to them.
Health practitioner 1: Mmm, I suppose there's a lot more to those meetings. It's about the emotions and the sense of it.
Social worker: Yeahhh? That's okay then.

This was a meeting of the team manager, the social worker, and health professionals. The team manager had wanted this meeting as she said she felt certain professionals were failing to move on from their initial view the children should be removed from the care of their mother. In the meeting, the team manager explained she wanted the health practitioners to provide an opinion, stating their input had been helpful but largely descriptive. The team manager further explained she wanted to have an open and frank discussion. The health practitioners had been working with one of the children in the family and the mother. They had stopped working with the family, because the mother would not attend appointments and also because she was seen as circumventing the child having contact with them by cancelling appointments and such like. At the point of entering the talk, there was a discussion about whether or not it was worthwhile for the health professionals to continue to attend the core groups. They intimated, if they were not providing a service to anyone within the family (and they could be re-instructed at a later date if appropriate), then it was prudent for them to withdraw from the core group based on 'efficiency within the[ir] system'. The social worker then describes the disjuncture and loss of a more nuanced understanding of the children's situation, between attending a core group and receiving 'minutes' and suggests it would be fruitful for the health practitioners to continue to attend so they remain 'in tune' with the case. The health practitioners are persuaded by this and agree they should remain part of the decision-making group. This proved to be a potent moral position to invoke and, at the end of the meeting, the health professionals entered the next core group date into their diaries and were to agree between them which one would attend. The effects of the social worker gently questioning their withdrawal from the core group had the effect of drawing them back into the group and encouraging them to take a position on the decisions being made. If this kind of reflexive questioning approach is to be encouraged, ways must be found to give practitioners techniques for examining what they cannot see. How can these abilities be nurtured in qualifying and post-qualifying education?

BEING CONTROVERSIAL: CONSTRUCTIVE CONTROVERSY

Constructive controversy is a decision-making 'tool' or process borrowed from social psychology (Johnson et al., 1985, 2000) and has been explored in a variety of settings, including management decision making and high school education. It has considerable potential utility in social work settings. Its transfer into social work education and practice would ensure, from the outset, the ground was set for there to be an acknowledgement of the individual and social processes involved in 'case stories' and continued acceptance and working with, rather than *silencing* of, complexity and uncertainty. Constructive controversy opens up a dialogical space and renders silencing and concurrence seeking subject to question.

As shown above, moral heuristics can affect people's ability to see 'other views' ['the mother should (not) have done that, I would (not) have done that, why have they (not) done that']. There is the propensity for individuals to be anchored to their first hypothesis and for group decision making to be similarly slanted, potentially framed by a concurrence-seeking group moral heuristic, as Sharon Shoesmith stated in the Baby P Inquiry: '*Why did they [professionals] not question ... more?*' The constructive controversy literature contrasts the method and its utility with the disadvantages of concurrence-seeking behaviours. The dangers of concurrence seeking are, of course, that alternatives are closed off. Johnson and Johnson (2009) believe students are likely to experience uncertainty, cognitive conflict, disequilibrium, and epistemic curiosity about and towards the various constructions. Constructive controversy encourages that alternative constructions are laid out and rendered visible so, hopefully, more robust decision making takes place.

Constructive controversy in social work education: an exemplar

Each team is given a 'problem'. The 'problem' should be one that requires students to make and test at least one prediction and be realistically complex and relevant, and benefit from a group forum.

The first answer is prescribed to the team (e.g., is this a child protection case – yes or no). There is no consultation between teams at this stage. It may also mean that students will be formulating a case for which they do not agree and that more than one team has the same 'problem' and first answer.

Each team must prepare their analysis and decision – what knowledge or evidence has been used to formulate it and why?

Once positions are finalised the teams meet and present their analysis without interruption from the other team(s) who should make notes.

Then the teams then meet up and question each other: why do you think that, what is your knowledge base, and why is it not what I, they, or we analyse it a?.

The findings from each team are synthesised and agreement is reached about what is to be done and why.

As Varela (1992) notes:

most of our mental and active life is of the immediate coping variety, which is transparent, stable, and grounded in our personal histories. Because it is so immediate, not only do we not see it, we do not see that we do not see it, and this is why so few people have paid any intention to it ... Yet the question remains: how can this distinction between coping behaviours and abstract judgement, between situatedness and morality, be applied to the study of ethics and the notion of ethical experience? (p. 19).

In the domain of human relationships, professional talk centres not so much on uncertainty, but on complex characterisations. The popular nature of the ideas invoked apparently exempts practitioners from the imperative to justify their actions using formal knowledge. In the slippery world of relationships and interactions, professionals seem to suspend disbelief. For this reason, it is vital social workers learn to practise reflexively and interrogate their own 'case stories' as texts so as to understand the impact their own reasoning processes and the social factors discussed above have on their awareness of the needs of people who come to the attention of their services. This shifts the focus from knowledge use per se to the *knowledge-making* processes inherent in practice. As Goffman (1981) notes:

Everyone knows that when individuals in the presence of others respond to events, their glances, looks, and postural shifts carry all kinds of implication and meaning. When in these settings words are spoken, then tone of voice, manner of uptake, restarts and the variously positioned pauses similarly qualify ... Every adult is wonderfully accomplished in producing all of these effects, and wonderfully perceptive in catching their significance when performed by accessible others. Everywhere and constantly this gestural resource is employed, yet rarely itself is systematically examined ... So it remains to microanalysts of interaction to lumber in where the self-respecting decline to tread (pp. 1–2).

It is for social workers to become microanalysts for their own domains, but they need some skill to do this. It is hoped this chapter goes some way to providing a vocabulary and method through which an examination of the realm of the taken-for-granted can take place in everyday social work practice.

REFERENCES

Anspach, R. (1987). Prognostic conflict in life-and-death decisions: Organisation as an ecology of knowledge. *Journal of Health and Social Behaviour*, 28, 215–231.

Argyris, C. (1987). Reasoning, action strategies, and defensive routines: The case of OD practitioners. In R.A. Woodman & Pasmore, A.A. (eds), *Research in organisational change and development. Vol 1.* Greenwich, CT: JAI Press, pp. 89–128.

Argyris, C., & Schön, D. (1996). *Organizational learning II: Theory, method and practice*, Reading, MA: Addison Wesley.

Atkinson, P. (1995). *Medical talk and medical work: The liturgy of the clinic.* London: Sage.

Bateson, G. (1972). *Steps to an ecology of mind: Collected essays in anthropology, psychiatry, evolution, and epistemology.* Chicago, IL: University of Chicago Press.

Blair, C.A., Thompson, L.F., & Wuensch, K.L. (2005). Electronic helping behaviour: The virtual presence of others makes a difference. *Basic and Applied Social Psychology*, 27(2), 171–178.

Broadhurst, K., Wastell, D., White, S., Hall, C., Peckover, S., Thompson, K., Pithouse, A., & Davey, D. (advance access 2009). Performing 'Initial Assessment': Identifying the latent conditions for error at the front-door of local authority children's services.

British Journal of Social Work Advance Access, published online 18 January.

Code, L. (1995). *Rhetorical spaces*. New York: Routledge.

Davis, J.H. (1992). Some compelling intuitions about group consensus decisions, theoretical and empirical research, and interpersonal aggregation phenomena: Selected examples, 1950–1990. *Organizational Behavior and Human Decision Processes*, 52, 3–38.

Department for Children Schools and Families/Department for Education (UK). (2010). *Working Together to Safeguard Children: A guide to inter-agency working to safeguard and promote the welfare of children*. Retrieved November 11, 2010 from http://publications.education.gov.uk/default.aspx?PageFunction=productdetails&PageMode=publications&ProductId=DCSF-00305-2010&

Dowie, J., & Elstein, A. (eds). (1988). *Professional judgement: A reader in clinical decision making*. Cambridge, UK: Cambridge University Press.

Goffman, E. (1981). *Forms of talk*. Philadelphia, PA: University of Pennsylvania Press.

Haidt, J. (2001). The emotional dog and its rational tail: A social intuitionist approach to moral judgement. *Psychological Review*, 108(4), 814–834.

Haringey Local Safeguarding Children's Board (2009). *Executive summary second serious case review: Baby Peter*. Retrieved October 13, 2010 from http://www.haringeylscb.org/index/scr/haringeyscr.htm

Janis, I.L. (1982). *Groupthink: Psychological studies of policy decisions and fiascos* (2nd ed.), New York: Houghton Mifflin.

Johnson, D., & Johnson, R. (2009). Energizing learning: The instructional power of conflict. *Educational Researcher*, 38(1), 37–51.

Johnson, D.W., Johnson, R., Pierson, W., & Lyons, V. (1985). Controversy versus concurrence seeking in multi-grade and single-grade learning groups. *Journal of Research in Science Teaching*, 22(9), 835–848.

Johnson, D.W., Johnson, R., & Tjosvold, D. (2000). Constructive controversy: The value of intellectual opposition. In M. Deutsch & Coleman, P.T. (eds), *Handbook of conflict resolution: Theory and practice*. San Francisco, CA: Jossey-Bass Publishers, pp. 65–85.

Kahneman, D., Sloveic, P., & Tversky, A. (1982). *Judgement under uncertainty: Heuristics and biases*. New York: Cambridge University Press.

Kogut, T., & Beyth-Marom, R. (2008). Who helps more? How self-other discrepancies influence decisions in helping situations. *Judgment and Decision Making*, 3(8), 585–606.

Laming, Lord (2003). *The Victoria Climbié inquiry report of an inquiry by Lord Laming*, Retrieved October 5, 2010 from http://www.dh.gov.uk/en/Publicationsandstatistics/Publications/PublicationsPolicyAndGuidance/DH_4008654

Latanè, B., & Darley, J. (1976). Help in a crisis: Bystander response to an emergency. In J.W. Thibaut & Spence, J.T. (eds), *Contemporary topics in social psychology*. Morristown, NJ: General Learning Press. 309–332.

Kogut, T., & Beyth-Marom, R. (2008). Group inhibition of bystander intervention. *Journal of Personality and Social Psychology*, 10, 215–221.

Mol, A. (2003). *The body multiple: Ontology in medical practice*. Durham, NC: Duke University Press.

Munro, E. (2002). *Effective child protection*. London: Sage.

Munro, E. (2010). *Munro review of child protection – Part One: A systems analysis*. London: Department for Education. Retrieved January 2, 2011 from http://www.education.gov.uk/munroreview/downloads/TheMunroReviewofChildProtection-Part%20one.pdf

Nelissen, R.M.A., & Zeelenberg, M. (2009). Moral emotions as determinants of third-party punishment: Anger and guilt and the functions of altruistic sanctions. *Judgment and Decision making*, 4(7), 543–553.

Redelmeier, D.A., & Tversky, A. (1992). On the framing of multiple prospects. *Psychological Science*, 3, 191–193.

Senge, P.M. (1990). *The fifth discipline: The art and practice of the learning organization*. London: Century Business.

Smith, K., Johnson D. W., & Johnson, R. (1981). Can conflict be constructive? Controversy versus concurrence seeking in learning groups. *Journal of Educational Psychology*, 73, 651–663.

Sunstein, C.R. (2010). Moral heuristics and risk. In S. Roeser (ed.), Emotions and risky technologies. *The International Library of Ethics, Law and Technology*, 5(3), 231–244.

Taleb, N.N. (2007). *The black swan: The impact of the highly improbable*. New York, Random House.

Varela, F.J. (1992). *Ethical know-how: Action, wisdom and cognition*. Stanford, CA: Stanford University Press.

Wastell, D., White, S., Broadhurst, K., Hall, C., Peckover, S., & Pithouse, A. (2010). Children's services in the iron cage of performance management: Street level bureaucracy and the spectre of Švejkism. *International Journal of Social Welfare*, 19, 310–320.

White, S. (2009). Fabled uncertainty in social work: A coda to Spafford et al. *Journal of Social Work*, 9(2), 222–235.

White, S., & Stancombe, J. (2003). *Clinical judgement in the health and welfare professions: Extending the evidence base*. Maidenhead: Open University Press.

White, S., Wastell, D., Broadhurst, K., & Hall, C. (2010). When policy o'erleaps itself: The tragic tale of the Integrated Children's System. *Critical Social Policy, 30*, 405–429.

Wolf, F.M., Gruppen, L.D., & Billi, J.E. (1985). Differential diagnosis and competing hypotheses heuristic: A practical approach to judgement under uncertainty and Bayesian probability. *Journal of American Medical Association, 253*, 2858–2862.

14

Risk Assessment and Decision Making

Eileen Munro

Assessing and managing risk has become a major aspect of social work practice in recent decades. The risks social workers deal with are extremely varied and very important: Will these parents harm their children? Is the person with mental illness safe in the community? Can this disabled person live safely enough at home? There is considerable dispute about how best to manage risk and wide variations in practice. The opposing views are part of the wider dispute about the respective roles of intuitive understanding and formal knowledge in practice. At one extreme are those who argue clinical appraisal of risk is the best approach, while, at the other extreme, are those who contend such predictions should be made by using actuarial tools developed from empirical evidence about risk factors that leads to a score which then forms the basis for decisions on what action to take. There is also a continuum of views between these extremes, supporting some combination of both types of reasoning about risk.

The research on what happens in practice also presents a mixed picture. Actuarial tools have been adopted in some social work agencies but there is evidence of misuse by those practitioners who are sceptical of their value and who value clinical judgement more highly (English & Pecora, 1994; Gillingham & Bromfield, 2008). There is widespread use of some form of tool to assist social workers in assessing and managing risk, offering guidance on what information to collect and how to analyse it, though most are less automated than actuarial tools and often based on risk factors decided upon by a consensus of experienced workers rather than from empirical research.

'Risk' is an ambiguous term so its usage in this chapter requires definition before discussing it in more detail. Originally, it could refer to both good and bad outcomes (the risk – probability – of sun or rain tomorrow) but nowadays it is predominantly used to refer to undesirable outcomes. This is so in the social work literature and, therefore, how it is used here. However, it needs to be remembered that most risk assessments in social work require a balancing of the anticipated good and bad outcomes that may follow any course of action. Social workers rarely face a simple choice between a risky and safe path. Removing a child from an abusive home protects the child from some adverse outcomes, but also exposes them to new risks in fostercare and reduces their exposure to the positive elements of the birth family.

This chapter begins by discussing the rise of risk management in social work before addressing the conflicting views on how it can best be done. Research on human reasoning is drawn upon to identify the relative strengths and weaknesses of analytic and intuitive risk assessments. The role of risk assessment within the whole context of case management is then discussed. Social workers do not operate in a vacuum, but within a social and organisational context that influences how risk is managed. The pressures leading to defensive practice, with its adverse effects on service users, are examined before proposals are made for developing a better understanding of what is involved in risk management and of what can realistically be expected of social workers.

THE RISE OF RISK MANAGEMENT

Risk management has emerged as a social work responsibility since the 1970s not because of changes in the degree of uncertainty in the world but from changes in how societies view that uncertainty. The concept of the 'risk society' put forward by Beck (1992) and Giddens (1990) refers to the way in which societies have moved from a fatalistic acceptance of uncertainty to a concern that it can and should be managed. Luhmann (1992) argues that the change in language from uncertainty to risk brings with it a domain for decision making about the future and a responsibility for those decisions. Power (2007) points out:

> The phenomenon of 'risk' management of more and more aspects of social and organizational life reflects an increase in social *expectations* about the decidability and management of dangers and opportunities. More possible outcomes in the world are subject to demands for human decision and intervention, rather than being left in the hands of the gods (p.5).

In social work, this growing expectation that uncertainty can be managed by professionals has had a powerful influence on the development of all services, with increasing attention given to protecting people from future adverse events (Ferguson, 1997; Kemshall, 2002). In England, when the General Social Care Council was created in 2001, it chose as its slogan 'Protecting the public'. In many countries, child welfare services have been renamed child protection services. It has been cogently argued that there has been a significant shift in social work from a preoccupation with need to one with risk (Kemshall, 2002; Webb, 2006). The risks include both risks *to* and *from* service users. With children, the concern is typically with risk to them but, especially as they get older, there is growing concern about the risks they may pose from, for instance, anti-social or delinquent behaviour. For those suffering from mental health problems, there are risks both of self-harm and risk to others. Social workers also work with service users who choose to accept a level of risk because of the associated benefits. Older people, for example, may prefer to stay in their own homes despite some risks, rather than move into more protected accommodation. Deciding when to overrule someone's decision is a necessary though problematic task.

ANALYTIC VERSUS INTUITIVE RISK ASSESSMENT

While the language of risk management is relatively new in social work, social workers have long-standing responsibilities to make decisions about whether children are safe at home or whether people with mental illness need to be detained so some form of risk management took place. As risk language has become the more dominant way of discussing these decisions, researchers have studied how social workers are making them. The findings in US research were that the decisions were generally made in an unstructured and intuitive way, leading to poor accuracy and inconsistent practice ((English & Pecora, 1994; Wald & Woolverton, 1990). Since the 1980s, social work agencies in most developed countries have provided some guidance in the form of assessment tools for staff in dealing with risk decisions. The different designs of the tools, though, reflect the conflicting views on how risk can best be managed. These are based on different assumptions about what reasoning skills are relevant to the task: analytic or intuitive. Work in neurophysiology and neuropsychology has shown that humans have two ways of processing information and these lead to two ways of assessing risk and deciding how to manage it:

> Humans have two distinct minds within their brains: one intuitive and the other reflective. The intuitive mind is old, evolved early, and shares many of its features with animal cognition. It is the source of emotion and intuitions, and reflects both the habits acquired in our lifetime and the adaptive behaviours evolved by ancient ancestors. The reflective mind, by contrast, is recently evolved and distinctively human: it enables us to think in abstract and hypothetical ways about the world around us and to calculate the future consequences of our actions (Evans, 2010, book jacket).

In practice, most cognitive tasks involve some contribution from both our analytic and intuitive reasoning skills and, rather than viewing them as a dichotomy, it is more appropriate to think of a cognitive continuum, with different tasks using a different combination of each type (Hammond, 1996). This duality is reflected in the contrast between clinical and actuarial risk assessment, though neither is exclusively drawing on one type of reasoning. Clinical assessments do rely on an intuitive appraisal of the situation but can also be informed by research evidence on risk factors and probabilities. Actuarial risk assessment tools make extensive use of formal research to identify risk factors and formal probability theory to calculate their impact in a particular case. However, intuitive skills in relating to people are used to elicit the information needed when talking to service users. In discussing the comparative merits of clinical and actuarial risk assessment, this chapter does not ask 'which is best' but 'what are the strengths and weaknesses of each approach and in what contexts?' Intuition is sometimes presented as a mysterious or mystical process but its physical location and the features of the process are understood. It is only mysterious in the sense it is generally an unconscious process that occurs automatically in response to perceptions, integrating a wide range of data to produce a judgement in a relatively effortless way. Simon (1992) proposed the following definition of skilled intuition: 'the situation has provided a cue. This cue has given the expert access to information stored in memory, and the information provides the answer. Intuition is nothing more and nothing less than recognition' (Simon, 1992, p. 155). So, for example, the experienced social worker recognises that the atmosphere in a family is cold and critical on the basis of experience and the unconscious observation of a number of cues. Intuition need not remain unconscious but can be articulated to some degree, and this ability can be improved with practice. Supervision of casework typically involves helping practitioners draw out their reasoning so it can be reviewed.

Analytic thinking, in contrast, is conscious and controlled, using formal reasoning and explicit data and rules to deliberate and compute a conclusion. It is restricted by memory and processing capacity, time-consuming, and effortful. It develops with age and is vulnerable to the ageing process.

Two leading representatives of the two research traditions studying, respectively, analytic and intuitive reasoning are Daniel Kahneman (analytic) and Gary Klein (intuitive).

In 2009, they wrote a joint article exploring their differences and similarities (Kahneman & Klein, 2009). Although they began by expecting to disagree, they found considerable areas of agreement that led them to discuss the different circumstances under which the analytic or the intuitive approach might be most successful. Both agree some professionals' intuitive judgements are highly accurate and some are very flawed. Kahneman's work has focused on the errors and Klein's work on the successes:

> We found that the sharpest differences between the two of us were emotional rather than intellectual. Although DK is thrilled by the remarkable intuitive skills of experts that GK and others have described, he also takes considerable pleasure in demonstrations of human folly and in the comeuppance of overconfident pseudo-experts. For this part, GK recognizes that formal procedures and algorithms sometimes outdo human judgment, but he enjoys hearing about cases in which the bureaucratization of decision making fails (Kahneman & Klein, 2009, p. 518).

Klein is an exponent of *naturalistic decision making* and his work has studied professionals making risk assessments and decisions in real life. He has, for example, observed fire-fighters in action and then later discussed with them how they thought through their decisions (Klein, 2000). Like Simon (1992), he emphasises that intuition involves recognition, seeing a link between the current situation and previous ones. Expertise is developed as individuals meet varied scenarios and learn from experience, a process familiar to social workers. This 'recognition-primed decision model' has two components: decision makers size up the situation to recognise which course of action makes sense and they evaluate that course of action by imagining the future – what might happen if their assessment were correct. They then act but continue to keep a critical awareness on whether the situation is unfolding as they expected or whether they need to reappraise it:

> The power of intuition enables us to size up a situation quickly. The power of mental simulation lets us imagine how a course of action might be carried out. The power of metaphor lets us draw on our experience by suggesting parallels between the current situations and something else we have come across. The power of storytelling helps us consolidate our experiences to make them available in the future, either to ourselves or to others (Klein, 2000, p. 3).

Kahneman's work, on the other hand, was influenced by a seminal work by Paul Meehl (1954) who reviewed 20 studies comparing the accuracy of forecasts made by human judges (mostly clinical psychologists) and those predicted by simple statistical models. The forecasts related to a wide variety of outcomes, including academic success, patient relapse, and violence. Statistical predictions were more accurate than human predictions in almost every case. This finding has been repeated in subsequent comparisons too (Gilovich et al., 2008). Kahneman and his colleagues were inspired by this to embark on a programme of research on human intuitive reasoning that has identified a number of conditions under which intuitive judgements (Kahneman, Slovic & Tversky, 1982) are likely to depart from the laws of probability and be inaccurate. (For summaries, see Koehler & Harvey, 2007; Nisbett & Ross, 1980; Plous, 1993). This body of research lends weight to efforts in social work to devise actuarial methods of risk assessment and decision making.

The dual processing capacity of the brain means it is not a question of either/or in how we reason and the emerging evidence supports a view that the intuitive system that provides quick, holistic judgements is always in operation and these are then 'supplemented – or sometimes overridden – by the output of the more deliberate, serial and rule-based system' (Gilovich et al., 2008, p. 16). Kahneman was also motivated in undertaking this programme of research by his personal experience while working in the Psychological Research Unit of the Israel Defense Forces where one of his duties was to assess candidates for officer training. In an autobiography he wrote after winning the Nobel prize (Kahneman, 2003), he described the powerful sense of getting to know each candidate and his conviction that he could predict how well each would do in training. This sense of confidence in his judgement was not eroded by evidence later coming from the training school that showed his judgement was not good. He called this the 'illusion of validity' and it is a persistent problem in social work that intuitive judgements carry with them a strong sense of certainty that leads people to cling on to their judgements even when a growing body of evidence challenges them (Munro, 1999a). When this is combined with the earlier point that social workers cannot switch off their intuitive processing, then it suggests problems will emerge when using actuarial assessment tools. The analytic part of the brain will be working to one conclusion while the intuitive capacity may be throwing up another conclusion that comes with a strong sense of certainty. This may provide some explanation of why studies of actuarial tools in use find workers often override their conclusions or adapt the data to produce the conclusion they intuitively believe is correct (Gillingham, 2009; Lyle & Graham, 2000).

Kahneman and Klein, starting from their very different theoretical positions, were concerned to understand when each type of reasoning was most likely to produce the best results. Their analysis of their different approaches concluded that for expert intuition to be developed, two conditions must be satisfied:

> First, the environment must provide adequately valid cues to the nature of the situation. Secondly, people must have an opportunity to learn the valid cues ... Skilled intuitions will only develop in an environment of sufficient regularity, which provides valid cues to the situation (Kahneman & Klein, 2009, p. 520).

Applying this to social work, it raises questions about how much expertise can be developed intuitively in assessing the types of risk that are of social work concern. Are there sufficient regularities in the situation or is human behaviour in relation to risk scenarios of concern too complex? It can be argued this is a scenario where the individual will be poor at developing skill but where formal research will give more reliable conclusions. The range of service users seen by any one social worker is small. The feedback they receive about subsequent behaviour that provides a lesson on the accuracy of their risk assessments is likely to be delayed and incomplete, often biased towards hearing of incidents of adverse outcomes because they are more likely to be re-referred than cases with benign outcomes. This disheartening conclusion is supported by studies of intuitive risk assessments in child protection. One study found experience did not lead to any increased accuracy:

> Differences in ratings of the severity of risk for children involved in the child welfare system among less experienced and more experienced social workers are examined. Sixty-three social workers from a south western Ontario CAS participated: twenty-seven with less than three years of experience and thirty-six with more than three years of experience. Social workers read two scenarios and were asked to determine the extent of risk present to the child and indicate if that child should be taken into care. The findings indicate that social workers with different levels of experience do not differ in their perceptions of risk and in their decisions with regards to managing risk in the community. Increases in the number of children taken into care is not attributable to differential decision making based on experience (Sullivan et al., 2008, p. 699).

Another study of a consensus-based risk instrument found 'no predictive capacity for caseworkers subjective overall rating' [of risk] (Barberab et al., 2008, p. 173).

There are good reasons for expecting an actuarial approach to outperform intuitive judgements in assessing risk because the process involves two reasoning tasks that humans perform badly: identifying correlations between variables and computing the overall probability from a number of differently weighted variables. An actuarial tool is created by drawing on a wide sample of cases and data, using statistical significance tests that can identify even weakly valid cues, factors that are weakly correlated with adverse outcomes. These factors are then weighted and combined to construct an assessment tool which includes a predictive algorithm that computes the probabilities of the factors consistently, unlike human intuitive reasoning, and so produces above chance accuracy.

The statistical approach to analysing the data should also produce consistency in identifying risk factors. This has been shown not to be the case when constructing risk assessment tools by drawing on expert consensus of what factors are predictive of adverse outcomes. One comparative study of risk assessment tools in child welfare found no factors were common to all the risk models examined, and about 40% were only found in one model (Lyons et al.,1996). [See Gambrill and Shlonsky (2000) for a more detailed discussion of why social workers are prone to error in computing risk factors.]

THE ACCURACY OF RISK PREDICTION

The previous section has reached the conclusion that an actuarial approach is likely to achieve a higher level of accuracy than clinical judgements in predicting future adverse outcomes. However, one of the strengths of the actuarial approach is it encourages research to test the accuracy of risk predictions. When considering the types of risk predictions social workers are asked to make, the strongest message from research is they can achieve very limited accuracy, whatever type of reasoning they use. The issues that have received the most study are predicting maltreatment and predicting violence by people with mental illnesses.

In mental health, many actuarial tools have been developed and evaluated and the evidence shows they are far better than chance and clinical assessments (Buchanan, 2008). However, they still lead to a high rate of inaccuracy both in false positives (wrongly deeming someone at risk of being violent) and of false negatives (wrongly deeming someone nonviolent). Consequently, their use as a basis for clinical decision making is limited. A key clinical decision is whether to detain someone because he or she poses a sufficient risk to self or others. The question, therefore, is 'how many patients would need to be detained to prevent one incident of violence in the community?' The answer is complicated by the fact that the number of errors is related to the base rate of violence in the population. If detention of patients were based on such actuarial assessments, then Buchanan estimates that, to prevent moderate violence, ten patients would have to be detained to avoid one incident of violence. With the rarer severe violence, the number needed to be detained to prevent one incident rises to fifteen:

> At the rates seen in outpatient settings, current approaches, if used to screen and detain within hospitals those predicted to be violent, would result in the detention of many people to prevent each violent act. In these circumstances predictions of violence have to remain only some of the many considerations guiding clinical judgment. The relation between prevalence of violence and the number needed to detain means that this state of affairs is unlikely to change even if the psychometric qualities of prediction methods show further substantial improvement (Buchanan, 2008, p. 188).

Studies of actuarial instruments in child protection show a similar problem of high levels of inaccuracy, so that large numbers of children would need to be removed from their birth families to prevent one incidence of maltreatment. Since the accuracy relates to the base rate of the problem, instruments are more accurate when used on a population of families referred to child welfare services than on the general population. One calculation concluded, when used on child welfare referrals, a family who came out as positive for risk had a probability of 0.64 of being abusive but when used with the general population, a positive result meant a family had a 0.12 probability of being abusive (Munro, 2004).

It is unrealistic to expect this degree of fallibility to be reduced significantly by further research. The kind of adverse outcomes of concern to social workers arise from a complex interplay of social, psychological, and physical factors. Moreover, the simple view of causality as essentially linear (if A then B) is hard to sustain in light of the growing evidence on the complexity of the interactions between risk and resilience factors in producing problematic human behaviour (Bifulco, 2009; Farrington, 2006). In a complex world, predictions are necessarily of limited value because even small changes in the value of one variable can lead to large differences in outcome.

It must also be remembered that risk research of relevance to social work is typically dealing with behaviour that is at least socially undesirable if not criminal and many cases are therefore likely to be hidden. This creates problems for researchers in trying to identify a representative sample to study. In child welfare, studies typically look at known or alleged incidents of maltreatment but studies based on self-reports from victims old enough to participate report a far higher incidence. In a summary of such research, Gilbert et al. (2009) conclude that less than 10% of cases become known to official services. The findings also indicate that the sample of abusive families that become known to child protection services is *not* representative, with particularly serious biases on the factors of victim's age (with older children being under-recognised) and socioeconomic status (with families from low-income groups being over-represented). This limitation in our basic understanding of the incidence of adverse outcomes applies equally to both actuarial and intuitive methods of assessing risk.

The lessons to draw from these findings are: (i) in general, actuarial risk instruments outperform clinical judgement; and (ii) even their higher level of accuracy is very modest and this has implications for the confidence with which social workers act upon them. The problem for social workers is that they are usually faced with decisions that require decisive action. A conclusion phrased in the language of probabilities has to contribute to either/or decisions – either a patient is detained in hospital or released; either a child stays with the birth family or is removed. Risk management is difficult, both intellectually and emotionally.

THE ROLE OF RISK ASSESSMENT WITHIN CASE MANAGEMENT

A risk assessment deals, narrowly, with the probability of future adverse outcomes. It provides this one item of information and so is only a part of the total assessment that social workers need in working with any individual or family. A full assessment needs to identify and explore a wider range of social, psychological, and physical factors to construct a picture of service users' strengths and difficulties to inform case planning. The relationship between an assessment of risk and overall case management is one that has been much discussed (Rycus & Hughes, 2003; Shlonsky & Wagner, 2005).

Assessing risk, assessing need, and making decisions about how to help service users are separate cognitive tasks. Some agencies provide one assessment tool to cover both assessment tasks and these have been criticised for failing to acknowledge the differences between the two purposes: 'In such situations, neither standardized risk assessments nor in-depth formal assessments are effectively completed, and a preponderance of casework decisions may continue to be made largely on the basis of individual clinical judgment' (Rycus & Hughes, 2003, p. 13).

In England in the 1980s, the problem in child welfare was seen as inadequate risk assessments, leading to the introduction of government guidance on conducting them (Department of Health, 1988). By 2000, the problem was seen as social workers focusing too narrowly on risk and not undertaking a good enough assessment of need, leading to new guidance (Department of Health, 2000).

A risk assessment on its own has a limited role in case management. It focuses on risk factors that are often static, not dynamic in nature – age, gender, or ethnicity are not variables that social workers can help to alter. Even if the risk factors were dynamic, it could not straightforwardly be assumed that changing a risk factor will lead to a change in the incidence of the adverse outcome. Risk factors correlate with adverse outcomes but their causal connection is a separate research question. Furthermore, the focus on negative factors overlooks the strengths or resilience factors in the situation and these are equally important in planning how to respond.

Another area of discussion is about the repercussions of using assessment tools on the relationship with the service user. For those seeking to work *with* the individual or family, there is a concern that such tools lead to risk assessments being something done *to* rather than *with* service users and so are inconsistent with approaches that seek to empower them and involve them as 'equal partners in the process and outcomes of risk assessment and management, giving greater respect to the views, rights, and needs of offenders and accused persons as well as those suffering from mental health issues, disabilities or neglect' (Barry, 2007, p. 42). This issue seems to raise two different areas for discussion: gathering the required information and deciding how to use it in forming a plan of action. The assessment tool requires the social worker to collect a certain set of data and how this is done can vary. Some might choose to sit down and go through the form question by question; others might have a more open conversation in the course of which the data were gathered but also allows the services users' views to be fully expressed. In the area of *how* the findings are used to inform future case management, there is clearly scope for social workers to choose how much they share this decision with the service user and take account of their preferences, and willingness to take risks. When the risk is to the user himself or herself, then there is greater need to consider their preferences. When the risk is to others, the social worker has to give greater priority to the preferences of the possible victims.

UNREALISTIC EXPECTATIONS

Managing risk involves estimating the likelihood of adverse outcomes from the different options available and choosing the option that carries the lowest probability of harm, weighed against the benefits. It involves reducing risk but does not and cannot involve removing risk, since it involves fallible predictions about the future. Unfortunately, society has unrealistic expectations that lead to high levels of criticism when adverse outcomes arise, even when the professionals concerned made well-reasoned calculations of risk and chose the course of action that looked safest. The belief that risk is something that can be managed has heightened the level of liability and accountability of those charged with managing it. The risk society has a tendency to become the 'scapegoat society' (Beck, 1992).

In mental health work, for example, the biggest risk that patients pose is to themselves. In England and Wales, the National Confidential Inquiry into Suicides and Homicides (2010) reports that, in the period 1997 to 2006, the number of suicides among patients was 14,249 (26% of the general population suicide rate) and the number of homicides committed by people who had been known to mental health services in the previous 12 months was 589 (10% of the total homicide rate). However, the public are more aware of, and concerned about the latter and smaller risk that they pose to others, and this influences practice priorities (Taylor & Gunn, 1999). In child protection work, social workers face criticism if they underestimate risk to children and leave them in dangerous families but they also face criticism if the public see them as overestimating risk and removing children too readily (Myers, 1994; Parton, 2006).

The pressure from unrealistic expectations has created a new risk in social work of 'reputational risk' (Hood et al., 2001), of the worker or agency being blamed in the event of an adverse outcome. This can lead to defensive practice, where workers prefer the option that presents less risk of adverse outcomes without paying due attention to the adverse consequences linked to what appears to be the safer option chosen. So, for example, social workers may rush to remove a child from a foster home because of an allegation of poor behaviour by the foster carer without weighing up the risks to the child of being moved relative to the severity of the alleged misbehaviour. Defensive practice gives preference to avoiding the risks where the worker might be blamed over minimising the risks to the service user overall.

In child protection, this strategy has limited success because defensive practice leads to the removal of high numbers of children from their birth families and this, eventually, triggers a critical response from society (Munro, 1999b). This has led to considerable effort being made to improve risk management since this can reduce the overall number of errors of either kind (overestimating or underestimating risk). However, another organisational strategy is to seek to avoid blame by devising protocols for practice that set out what 'good practice' entails so that, if an adverse outcome occurs, workers and their managers can make the defence of 'due diligence' (Hood et al., 2001). This is reasonable if the protocol does indeed capture good practice but, in the complex area of child protection, no set of procedures captures the requisite variety needed to respond to the variety of family problems. Some scope for professional judgement is needed.

Efforts to find ways of managing risk in social work are spurred on both by the appropriate concern to minimise risk to service users and by the defensive concern to minimise risk to the agency or worker. A defensive culture can lead to agencies overvaluing the contribution that risk assessment tools can make to decisions on how to manage cases. Instead of recognising that they offer one piece of information, they can be used as the major determinant of case management. They offer an impersonal and transparent mechanism for assessing risk which can provide a defence of due diligence. At an individual level, they offer a comforting defence that the worker was just using the prescribed tool whereas defending a professional judgement is a much more personal matter.

CREATING A FAIR CULTURE FOR RISK MANAGEMENT

Defensive practice leads to poor decision making from the service users' point of view. Changing to a fair culture, however, is not an easy task in societies that are keen to find someone to blame (Douglas, 1992). Avoiding defensive practice requires understanding of the processes of risk assessment and decision making in conditions of uncertainty. It also requires a shared agreement on standards of good practice in reasoning about risk so individuals feel confident in their practice they will not be vilified in the event of an adverse outcome as long as they have acted to these standards.

The Association of Chief Police Officers in England has done valuable work in developing a set of principles that address both the cognitive and the psychological aspects of risk management. These were adapted to suit child protection (Munro, 2011) but could be extended to cover work in any high-risk area.

- *Principle 1*: The willingness to make decisions in conditions of uncertainty (i.e., risk taking) is a core professional requirement for all those working in child protection.
- *Principle 2:* Maintaining or achieving the safety, security and well-being of individuals and communities is a primary consideration in risk decision making.
- *Principle 3:* Risk taking involves judgement and balance, with decision makers required to consider the value and likelihood of the possible benefits of a particular decision against the seriousness and likelihood of the possible harms.

- *Principle 4:* Harm can never be totally prevented. Risk decisions should, therefore, be judged by the quality of the decision making, not by the outcome.
- *Principle 5:* Taking risk decisions, and reviewing others' risk decision making, is difficult so account should be taken of whether they involved dilemmas, emergencies, were part of a sequence of decisions or might appropriately be taken by other agencies. If the decision is shared, then the risk is shared too and the risk of error reduced.
- *Principle 6:* The standard expected and required of those working in child protection is that their risk decisions should be consistent with those that would have been made in the same circumstances by professionals of similar specialism or experience.
- *Principle 7:* Whether to record a decision is a risk decision in itself which should, to a large extent, be left to professional judgement. The decision whether or not to make a record, however, and the extent of that record, should be made after considering the likelihood of harm occurring and its seriousness.
- *Principle 8:* To reduce risk aversion and improve decision making, child protection needs a culture that learns from successes as well as failures. Good risk taking should be identified, celebrated, and shared in a regular review of significant events.
- *Principle 9:* Since good risk taking depends upon quality information, those working in child protection should work with partner agencies and others to share relevant information about people who pose a risk of harm to others or people who are vulnerable to the risk of being harmed.
- *Principle 10:* Those working in child protection who make decisions consistent with these principles should receive the encouragement, approval, and support of their organisation.

CONCLUSION

Assessing and managing a range of risks have become major responsibilities in social work. Society has come to believe that future adverse outcomes can be predicted and managed. Unfortunately, in practice, managing risk is often taken to mean eliminating it whereas reducing it is all that can reasonably be achieved. The problem is that society looks at the quality of risk assessments *after the adverse outcome has occurred*. With hindsight, the danger looks clear and so the professionals who failed to estimate it correctly are castigated for poor practice. For those having to make risk decisions with only foresight to help them, the world looks very different. The adverse outcome is only one of many possible ways that the future might unfold.

In the debate between actuarial and intuitive approaches to risk assessment, this chapter has come down in favour of the reliability of the actuarial approach in relation to the specific judgement about future risk. However, the research linked to this approach has highlighted the limited accuracy of either mechanism for predicting future adverse events. This reinforces the need for professionals to treat risk assessments with caution and to keep alert to evidence that challenges that assessment. It also illustrates how little professionals should rely on this one judgement in planning how to work with individuals or families. Broader assessments of needs and strengths are also needed to form a more rounded picture of functioning and to identify areas where change can be achieved.

The tendency of a risk society to become a scapegoating society has been well illustrated in social work where, in many countries, there are examples of media coverage of sad outcomes where social workers have been subjected to harsh criticism that has spilled over from the individuals concerned to harming the reputation and status of the profession in general (Social Work Task Force, 2009). In reaction to this, there is a tendency of agencies and individuals to resort to defensive practice, placing protection of self or agency above the protection of service users. To counter this, social workers need to develop a shared and deeper understanding of the process of assessing risk and of what counts as good enough professional practice. Only then, can the profession fight back against unrealistic demands from society to control the future.

REFERENCES

Barberab, J., Shlonsky, A., Black, T., Goodmand, D., & Trocme, N. (2008). Reliability and predictive validity of a consensus-based risk assessment tool. *Journal of Public Child Welfare*, 2(2), 173–195.

Barry, M. (2007). *Effective approaches to risk assessment in social work: An international literature review*. Edinburgh: Scottish Executive.

Beck, U. (1992). *Risk society*. London: Sage.

Bifulco, A. (2009). Risk and resilience in young Londoners. In D. Brom, Pat-Horenczyk, R. & Ford, J. (eds), *Treating traumatised children: Risk, resilience and recovery*. Hove: Routledge.

Buchanan, A. (2008). Risk of violence by psychiatric patients: Beyond the 'actuarial versus clinical' assessment debate. *Psychiatric Services*, 59, 184–190.

Department of Health (1988). *Protecting children: A guide for social workers undertaking a comprehensive assessment*. London: Department of Health.

Department of Health (2000). *Framework for the assessment of children in need and their families*. London: Department of Health.

Douglas, M. (1992). *Risk and blame: Essays in cultural theory*. London: Routledge.

English, D., & Pecora, P. (1994). Risk assessment as a practice method in child protective services. *Child Welfare*, 24(11), 451–473.

Evans, J. (2010). *Thinking twice: Two minds in one brain*. Oxford: Oxford University Press.

Farrington, D. (2006). *Childhood risk factors and risk-focused prevention*. London: Prime Minister's Strategy Unit.

Ferguson, H. (1997). Protecting children in new times: Child protection and the risk society. *Child & Family Social Work*, 2, 221–234.

Gambrill, E., & Shlonsky, A. (2000). Risk assessment in context. *Children and Youth Service Review*, 22(11/12), 813–837.

Giddens, A. (1990). *The consequences of modernity*. Cambridge: Polity Press.

Gilbert, R., Widom, C.S., Browne, K., Fergusson, D., Webb, E., & Janson, S. (2009). Burden and consequences of child maltreatment in high-income countries. *The Lancet*, 373, 68–81.

Gillingham, P. (2009). *The use of assessment tools in child protection: An ethnomethodological study*. Unpublished PhD Thesis. University of Melbourne. Retrieved from http://repository.unimelb.edu.au/10187/4337

Gillingham, P., & Bromfield, L. (2008). Child protection, risk assessment and blame ideology. *Children Australia*, 33(1), 18–24.

Gilovich, T., Griffin, D., & Kahneman, D. (eds) (2008). *Heuristics and biases: The psychology of intuitive judgment* (7th ed.). Cambridge: Cambridge University Press.

Hammond, K. (1996). *Human judgement and social policy*. Oxford: Oxford University Press.

Hood, C., Rothstein, H., & Baldwin, R. (2001). *The government of risk: Understanding risk regulation regimes*. Oxford: Oxford University Press.

Kahneman, D., Slovic, P., & Tversky, A. (eds) (1982). *Judgment under uncertainty: Heuristics and biases*. New York: Cambridge University Press.

Kahneman, D. (2003). Autobiography. In T. Frangsmyr (ed.), *Les Prix Nobel 2002*. Stockholm: Almqvist & Wiksell International.

Kahneman, D., & Klein, G. (2009). Conditions for intuitive expertise: A failure to disagree. *American Psychologist*, 64(6), 515–526.

Kemshall, H. (2002). *Risk, social policy and welfare*. Buckingham: Open University Press.

Klein, G. (2000). *Sources of power: How people make decisions*. Cambridge, MA: MIT Press.

Koehler, D., & Harvey, N. (eds) (2007). *Blackwell handbook of judgment and decision making*. Oxford: Blackwell Publishing.

Luhmann, N. (1992). *Risk: A sociological theory*. Berlin: de Gruyter.

Lyle, C., & Graham, E. (2000). Looks can be deceiving: Using a risk assessment instrument to evaluate the outcomes of child protection services. *Children and Youth Service Review*, 22, 935–949.

Lyons, P., Doueck, H.J., & Wodarski, J.S. (1996). Risk assessment for child protective services: A review of the empirical literature on instrument performance. *Social Work Research*, 20(3), 143–155.

Meehl, P. (1954). *Clinical vs statistical prediction: A theoretical analysis and a review of the evidence*. Minneapolis, MA: University of Minnesota Press.

Munro, E. (1999a). Common errors of reasoning in child protection. *Child Abuse and Neglect*, 23, 745–758.

Munro, E. (1999b). Protecting children in an anxious society. *Health, Risk and Society*, 1(1), 117–127.

Munro, E. (2004). A simpler way to understand the results of risk assessment instruments. *Children and Youth Service Review*, 26(9), 881–891.

Munro, E. (2011). *Munro review of child protection, final report: A child-centred system*. London: Department for Education.

Myers, J. (1994). *The backlash: Child protection under fire*. Thousand Oaks: Sage.

National Confidential Inquiry into Suicides and Homicides (2010). *Annual report, England and Wales*. Manchester: University of Manchester.

Nisbett, R., & Ross, L. (1980). *Human inference: Strategies and shortcomings of human judgment*. Englewood Cliffs, NJ: Prentice-Hall.

Parton, N. (2006). *Safeguarding childhood: Early intervention and surveillance in a late modern society*. Basingstoke: Palgrave Macmillan.

Plous, S. (1993). *The psychology of judgment and decision making*. New York: McGraw-Hill.

Power, M. (2007). *Organized uncertainty: Designing a world of risk management*. Oxford: Oxford University Press.

Rycus, J., & Hughes, R. (2003). *Issues in risk assessment in child protective services*. Columbus, OH: North American Resource Center for Child Welfare.

Shlonsky, A., & Wagner, D. (2005). The next step: Integrating actuarial risk assessment and clinical judgement into an evidence-based practice framework in CPS case management. *Children and Youth Service Review*, 27, 409–427

Simon, H. (1992). What is an explanation of behaviour? *Psychological Science, 3*, 150–161.

Social Work Task Force (2009). *Building a safe and confident future*. London: Department for Children, Schools and Families.

Sullivan, C., Whitehead, P., Leschied, A., Chiodo, D., & Hurley, D. (2008). Perception of risk among child protection workers. *Children and Youth Services Review, 30*, 699–704.

Taylor, P., & Gunn, J. (1999). Homicides by people with mental illness: myth and reality. *British Journal of Psychiatry, 174*, 9–14.

Wald, M.S., & Woolverton, M. (1990). Risk assessment: The emperor's new clothes? *Child Welfare, 119*(6), 483–499.

Webb, S.A. (2006). *Social work in a risk society*. Basingstoke: Palgrave.

15

Integrative Psychotherapy

Marlene Cooper and Joan Lesser

This chapter addresses a multifaceted approach used in clinically based social work practice referred to as integrative psychotherapy. While it largely concentrates on developments in the USA, the concept of integrative psychotherapy has international currency of relevance to social work underscored by university programmes across all continents. Its influence, for example, can be felt in the establishment of the European Association for Integrative Psychotherapy in 1993. In the USA, clinical social workers represent the largest group of behavioural health practitioners [National Association of Social Workers (NASW), 2005]. They provide more mental health services than professionals from all other disciplines combined (Drisko, 2004; O'Neill, 1999). Clinical social workers in the USA are often on the frontline, and are the first to diagnose and treat persons suffering from mental disorders and experiencing various emotional and behavioural disturbances. They are essential to community mental health centres, substance-abuse treatment and recovery programmes, hospitals and primary healthcare settings, child welfare agencies, ageing services, marital and family counselling, school settings, community services, and private practice settings, to name but a few. Direct practice with individuals, families, and groups requires that clinical social workers have knowledge of a wide range of theories of human behaviour, the social and cultural environment, psychosocial and personality development, and behaviour and cognition that aid in the assessment, diagnosis, and treatment of some of the most vulnerable members of society. While clinical social work's person-in-environment perspective provides a unique focus, 'a large percentage of these social work services consists of psychotherapy' (Drisko, 2004, p. 81).

The distinctive characteristic of integrative psychotherapy, discussed in this chapter, is its consideration of diverse theoretical views of human functioning before arriving at a treatment plan. Because of its diversity, integrative psychotherapy is eminently well suited to clinical social work practice. Its aim is to maximise a person's functioning in the intrapsychic, interpersonal, and sociopolitical spheres, and to facilitate wholeness by bringing together the affective, cognitive, behavioural, and physiological systems within a person. The chapter begins with an overview of integrative psychotherapy, examines common factors in psychotherapy, and then discusses several forms of psychotherapeutic integration, namely, technical, theoretical, and assimilative integration. Two of these approaches, technical and assimilative integration, are fully illustrated with case examples.

HISTORY OF INTEGRATIVE PSYCHOTHERAPY

Efforts at an integrative approach to psychotherapy can be documented as far back as 1932 when French delivered an address to the American Psychiatric Association drawing parallels between psychoanalysis and Pavlovian conditioning, citing the similarities between repression and extinction. In 1940, the American Orthopsychiatric Association included therapists who convened to discuss areas of agreement in different theoretical models of psychotherapy. The importance of the therapeutic relationship was one such area of agreement. Dollard and Miller's classic book, *Personality and Psychotherapy* (1950) described the integration of psychoanalytic psychotherapy and learning theory. Alexander (1963) and Marmor (1964) also suggested psychoanalytic theory could be understood within the context of learning theory. Jerome Frank (1960) stressed common factors across psychotherapy models, including expectations for change, self-understanding, and a corrective emotional experience. Other authors began to blend psychoanalytic and behavioural models (London, 1964; Marks & Gelder, 1966; Rogers, 1963; Wolf, 1966). Interest in integrating the different theoretical models of psychotherapy continued, but it is only since the 1980s that psychotherapy integration has been clearly delineated as the *development of a unified paradigm to explain how the affective, behavioural, and cognitive systems interact* (Beck, 1984; Goldfried et al., 2005; Greenberg & Safran, 1984; Safran, 1984). The concept of 'technical eclecticism' was introduced by Arnold Lazarus (1976) in *multimodal therapy*, organised under social learning theory but containing elements from behaviour theory and others.

In 1983, the Society for the Exploration of Psychotherapy Integration (SEPI) was established and began publishing the *Journal of Psychotherapy Integration* in 1991 (Brooks-Harris, 2008). SEPI has an official website at www.cyberpsych.org/sepi. Other publications dedicated to the pursuit of integrative psychotherapy include 'Integrative Psychiatry' and 'In Session', a quarterly publication of the *Journal of Clinical Psychology* summarising different approaches and research findings in treating various clinical issues (Goldfried et al., 2005, p. 39).

Conditions encouraging the pursuit of psychotherapy integration

There are a number of conditions encouraging the field to give increasing attention to integrative psychotherapy in contemporary times. Safran and Messser (1997, cited in Brooks-Harris, 2008) consider 'the shift in the dominant cultural philosophy from modernism to the post modern acceptance of the social construction of reality. When applied to psychotherapy, postmodernism results in pluralism in which no theory is seen as preeminent' (p. 22), offer several other conditions possibly contributing to the renewed interest in integrative psychotherapy. These include: (i) proliferation of therapies; (ii) inadequacy of single theories; (iii) external socioeconomic contingencies; (iv) ascendency of short-term, problem-focused treatment; (v) opportunity to observe various treatments; (vi) recognition that therapeutic commonalities heavily contribute to outcome; (vii) identification of specific therapy effects and evidence-based treatment; and (viii) development of a professional network for integration.

Routes to psychotherapy integration

There are four main routes to integrative psychotherapy: common factors; technical eclecticism or technical integration; theoretical integration; and assimilative integration (Norcross & Goldfried, 2005, pp. 8–9). Brooks-Harris (2008) expanded upon these initial routes to integrative psychotherapy, offering five additional routes: intentional integration; multidimensional integration; multitheoretical integration; strategy-based integration; and relational integration. The first four main paths are described below.

COMMON FACTORS IN PSYCHOTHERAPY

These refer to an aspect of psychotherapy present in most approaches to treatment. This collection of universally applied techniques can be seen regardless of the theoretical approach, because it is common to all of them (Striker, 2010) and the commonalities are more important than the differences. Greencavage and Norcross (1990) suggest a list of common factors would include a therapeutic alliance; exposure of the client to former difficulties followed by a new corrective emotional experience; and expectations by the therapist and client for positive change. Therapeutic qualities such as empathy, attention, and positive regard, giving the client a rationale for problems, and the use of some systematic therapeutic procedure are other conditions. Garfield (1995) strongly agreed the therapist–client relationship was a main common factor. Research on the power of the alliance is reflected in more than 1000 findings (Orlinsky et al., 1994, cited in Miller et al., 2005, p. 94). Other common factors identified in major schools of psychotherapy include: interpretation, insight, and understanding; cognitive modifications; emotional expression and release; reinforcement; desensitisation; relaxation; information; reassurance and support; expectations; exposure and confronting a problem; time; and placebo responses (cited in Brooks-Harris, 2008, p. 24).

FORMS OF PSYCHOTHERAPEUTIC INTEGRATION

Technical eclecticism or technical integration

This is a pragmatic blending of procedures seeking to select the best treatment for the person and the problem based on the client's needs as well as what has worked best for others (Norcross & Goldfried, 2005). Striker (2010) prefers the term 'technical integration' over 'technical eclecticism', stating when there is a systematic basis other than 'idiosyncratic preferences of the therapist' (p. 22) to use these techniques, technical integration is the preferred term.

Technical integration is the least theoretical of the four routes. However, it is neither atheoretical nor antitheoretical. Proponents of technical eclecticism use procedures drawn from different sources without necessarily subscribing to the theories spawning them. Lazarus (1976) is responsible for the term 'technical eclecticism' and made the first major contribution with his systematic, 'multimodal' approach representing a comprehensive view of human functioning. He developed the acronym BASIC-ID, referring to the areas of behaviour, affect, sensation, imagery, cognition, interpersonal function, and drugs (biology) as important areas to consider in psychotherapy integration. Beutler and Clarkin (1990) drew on research as the basis for prescriptive psychotherapy, in which Beutler identified several elements of therapeutic intervention. Prescriptive psychotherapy looks at several dimensions of client 'distinctions, each of which has a corresponding element of therapeutic intervention' (Striker, 2010, p. 23). An example is client behaviour such as resistance.

The therapist finds the approach best suited for the work with this client, choosing a nondirective psychodynamic approach over a more confrontational, cognitive approach. The unifying aspect in prescriptive psychotherapy is the systematic approach by the therapist.

An example of technical integration is Barry Wolfe's (2005) *integrative etiological model of anxiety disorders*, which synthesises elements of psychodynamic, behavioural, cognitive behavioural, and experiential therapies. The goal is the reduction or resolution of the symptoms of an anxiety disorder. Other goals include: (i) enhancing the individual's sense of self-efficacy; (ii) increasing the individual's tolerance for emotional experience; (iii) identifying and modifying the various cognitive and affective defences erected against emotional experience; (iv) restructuring toxic views of the self; and (v) increasing the patient's ability to engage in authentic relationships. The four phases in the treatment process are described below.

Phase one: Establishing the therapeutic alliance

This is a challenging endeavour as the therapist works to desensitise the patient's fear of being known and enhances the patient's ability to trust the relationship and the therapeutic process: 'The provision of a safe relationship that is empathic, genuine, and nonjudgmental serves as a therapeutic bulwark against which the patient leans as he or she negotiates the specific therapy tasks' (Rogers, 1957, cited in Wolfe, 2005, p. 269).

Phase two: Treating the symptoms of an anxiety disorder

The focus of this stage is to help the patient achieve some measure of control over the symptoms of an anxiety disorder. Cognitive behavioural techniques are of most value during this phase of treatment. However, it is important to continue to attend to the therapeutic relationship as the introduction and implementation of these techniques possess meaning for the patient in terms of his or her feelings toward the therapist.

Phase three: Eliciting the tacit self-wounds

The goal of phase three is to determine the tacit self-wounds, and the feared catastrophes and emotions associated with them. The major technique used during this phase is Wolfe's *focusing technique*, a type of imaginal exposure (see Wolfe & Sigel, 1998). Other techniques that may be used during this phase include psychodynamic, interpretive, and insight-oriented interventions.

Phase four: Healing the self-wounds

Attention is now turned to: (i) identifying and modifying the patient's defensive interruption of experiences; (ii) enhancing the patient's self-efficacy; (iii) resolving discrepancies between self-beliefs and immediate self-experiencing; (iv) increasing tolerance for – and ownership of – negative affects; (v) resolution of conflicts preventing the patient from a complete commitment to a particular self-focus; (vi) emotional processing of painful realities; and (vii) increasing the patient's willingness to engage in authentic relationships (Wolfe, 2005, p. 271).

THE CASE OF LYNN: AN EXAMPLE OF THEORETICAL INTEGRATION

Lynn, a woman in her late twenties, suffered from generalised anxiety disorder that had recently evolved into obsessive compulsive disorder (OCD) with compulsive hand washing. This was a first therapy session for Lynn and she clearly was feeling self-conscious and shameful about her feelings and actions with repeated phrases such as, 'I know this is ridiculous but I can't stop it', 'my friends are getting sick of me', and 'you must think I'm crazy'.

Phase one: Establishing the therapeutic relationship

In phase one, the therapist helped to establish the therapeutic relationship by listening to

Lynn's concerns She also assured her she knew these feelings were very real to Lynn and hoped she could help Lynn to find some self-compassion as they worked together to alleviate her anxiety.

Phase two: Treating the symptoms of Lynn's anxiety

In this phase, the therapist introduced the behavioural techniques of exposure and response prevention, evidence-based therapies for the treatment of OCD (Cooper, 1990). Owing to the severity of Lynn's symptoms, the therapist referred her for a psychiatric evaluation and medication was prescribed to enable her to follow the treatment protocol. Lynn needed to be exposed to the feared stimuli (dirt) and told to refrain from hand washing. The therapist also talked with Lynn about her life, and found out a close relative, a young woman about her age, had died a few months prior to the onset of these symptoms, apparently from a rare blood disorder. The patient had never made the connection between both this event in her life and the onset of her OCD. After doing so, and with continued practising of exposure techniques, the hand-washing ritual ceased.

Phase three: Eliciting the tacit self-wounds

Further discussion with Lynn focused on her childhood and family relationships, revealing, as a young child, she witnessed a horrific automobile accident involving her younger sister who was hit by a speeding car. She remembered her 'covered in blood'. She was left in the care of her aunt over the course of the next year as her parents were involved in her brother's recovery. Lynn began to describe other childhood experiences where she felt she lived in the shadow of her sister, denying her own needs and taking on a false independence while feeling frightened and vulnerable. As therapy progressed, it became clear that, following her sister's accident, she had tried not to show negative feelings or displeasure too much for fear of causing her parents even more distress.

Phase four: Healing the self-wounds

Lynn had not thought about her childhood consciously for many years but memories brought obvious feeling of anxiety during the sessions. The therapist addressed these by teaching relaxation and deep-breathing techniques and by tuning in empathically to her affective state. As Lynn gained mastery over anxious feelings, she felt more in control and self-efficacy increased. Continued emotional processing of painful experiences enabled her to realise that her submissive, eager-to-please position in interpersonal relationships was carried over from childhood, and interfered with her ability to be authentic. Continued awareness and psychological work on healing self-wounds helped Lynn take steps to be more honest and less self-deprecating with others, and led to greater satisfaction in interpersonal relationships.

Theoretical integration

Theoretically integrated psychotherapies use a process of synthesising aspects of varied personality theories, combine models of psychology, and integrate various strategies of psychological change from two or more traditional systems. The mutual influence of environment, motivation, cognition, and affective variables may be considered (Striker & Gold, in Gurman & Messer, 2003). The goal of theoretical integration is to create a conceptual framework synthesising the best elements of two or more approaches to therapy. Integration aspires to more than a combination of theories. It seeks an emergent theory comprising more than the sum of its parts and leads to new directions for practice and research (Norcross & Goldfried, 2005).

Cyclical psychodynamic psychotherapy

Also known as cyclical contextual psychotherapy, this is an example of theoretical integration. This model highlights the ways in which individuals persist in thoughts, fantasies, and behaviours that seem out of touch with present reality and are governed by the past rather than the present (Wachtel, 1993, 1997, 2008; Wachtel & Wachtel, 1986). Wachtel (2008), for example, integrated psychoanalysis and behavioural theory, and also included systems theory in cyclical psychodynamics. He described the

> ways that our behavior and experience (including unconscious dimensions) are influenced by the events and emotional nuances of what is transpiring around us as well as our response to that context being determined not by any objective understanding of what was going on by our unique subjective take on those events. It is not a matter of one over the other; it is that each creates and evokes the other. ... consistency is maintained by our perceptual inclination to see the old in the new and by our behavioral inclination to evoke the old in the new (p. 104).

Assimilative integration

This is the most recent of the approaches to psychotherapy integration. It is an approach where solid grounding in one theoretical position is accompanied by a willingness to incorporate techniques from other therapeutic approaches (Striker, 2010). In assimilative integration, a unitary theory is used initially to help understand the client's needs and guide the treatment, but then several different approaches to technique, taken from other theoretical frameworks, help to construct a treatment plan consistent with the theoretical understanding. This treatment plan then undergoes revision as the theoretical understanding of the client is more fully developed over the course of treatment (Striker, 2010).

Several authors addressed the need for the integrative psychotherapy movement to include cultural domains (Brooks-Harris, 2008; Perez, 1999; Rigazio-Digilio et al., 1996). Pederson, 1990, felt multiculturalism was a fourth force in psychotherapy, complementing the traditional forces of psychodynamic, behavioural, and humanistic psychotherapy. An example of an assimilative model of integrative psychotherapy addressing the cultural domain is *multicultural counselling and therapy* (MCT). MCT is described as a meta-theory of counselling and psychotherapy or a 'theory about theories' (Sue et al., 1996, p. 13) with each theory representing a different world view and embedded in a distinct cultural context. Using MCT as a meta-theory helps psychotherapists recognise the cultural values inherent to different theories and to make conscious choices about intervention strategies matching client's cultural values: 'The recognition that culture is relevant to all psychotherapy relationships suggests that MCT may be used as a foundational theory for assimilative integration' (Ivey & Brooks-Harris, 2005, p. 326).

In MCT, there is an assessment of the cultural experiences and contexts shaping clients' identities and an emphasis on the impact of external stressors, such as racism and oppression, on emotional conditions. Cultural variables, such as psychological mindedness and attitudes toward helping, are given diagnostic merit. Group identity variables, cultural orientation or world view, and culture-specific assessment techniques are considered. MCT assessment includes discussion of the impact of psychological dimensions, such as thoughts, actions, and feelings. It also assesses how culture interacts with other contextual dimensions, such as biology, interpersonal patterns, and social systems.

Multicultural counselling and therapy recognises the importance of identity development. The developmental framework for MCT lies within cultural identity theory. This includes attention to models of identity development, such as racial identity development, biracial identity development, ethnic identity development, and white identity development, among others (see Lesser & Pope, 2011 for a more complete description of various identity models). MCT focuses on helping clients appreciate and understand how oppression operates in their lives, and how the dominant culture has shaped their views about themselves and their culture. Recognition of common factors as central change processes is critical. These include consciousness raising, the therapeutic relationship, a shared world view, client expectations, and a ritual of intervention. The universal aspects of healing in most therapeutic models could be integrated with the unique culture of individual clients.

In developing the therapeutic relationship, MCT embraces 'relational adaptation' – adapting the therapeutic relationship to the individual needs and preferences of the client. Attention is given to different clients cultural values about interpersonal communication: 'Relational adaptation allows psychotherapists to create different types of relationships and use different parts of their personality with different clients' (Ivey & Brooks Harris, 2005, p. 328). Additionally, MCT suggests, whenever appropriate, multimodal therapeutic techniques, including family, group, and the involvement of culturally indigenous helpers, such as clergy, peers, or community members, should be considered.

THE CASE OF CAROL: AN EXAMPLE OF ASSIMILATIVE INTEGRATION

The following case illustrates assimilative integration. Multicultural theory is the metatheory guiding the therapeutic process, and interventions from psychodynamic and relational psychodynamic theory are integrated in the treatment of an African-American woman, struggling to accept a bicultural identity.

Carol, an African-American woman age 28, grew up in a small southern town with aspiring parents. She attended predominantly White universities, where, despite her achievement, she felt she was seen as a 'token' by her predominantly White classmates. Living in the East, she felt isolated from her family and, at the prominent law firm where she worked, she experienced instances of racial micro-aggression, as she had in college, and overt racism in her daily life. Plagued with self-doubts, feelings of being alienated from family and friends, and conflicts at work, she entered treatment with a White social worker.

Carol, in the early stage of treatment, talked openly of her experiences with racism. Recently, she had been invited to become a member of the Board of Directors of a major international corporation but her own company refused to support this initiative, stating it was a matter of policy. Carol was not convinced, and viewed this as one more instance of racism. This brought up earlier memories of childhood in her small southern town She mentioned seeing an old movie, *Imitation of Life*, and identifying with the character, a Black girl who tries to pass as White, leaves her family, and fears being found out and rejected. She remembers thinking it would be easier if she were White or not there at all.

> *Carol:* I felt invisible. The school was mainly White. My parents wanted me to have the best education so they sent me to a parochial school. I had a friend named Betsy. She was very pretty and popular and I thought if I were with her, people would like me. My mother chastised me, told me I was acting like I thought I was White. I told her we don't recognize color here, we're all the same. She told me I was kidding myself – color was always there. One day Betsy's cousin from New York came to visit. When she saw me, she refused to play with me because I was Black. Betsy went off with her and left me standing there.
>
> *Social worker:* [Using empathy and interpretation, from psychodynamic theory.] She betrayed you. You must have felt very hurt and alone.
>
> *Carol:* I was so startled I couldn't speak. I wanted to run and hide. But I didn't say anything. And I feel that way now – I lose my voice at work when I feel I'm not being seen for who I am. I'm successful at work but I feel so fake – I don't fit in anywhere - -not in the White world or the Black world either. I feel like I live life on the fence.
>
> *Social worker:* I would like to hear more about your feelings [psychodynamic inquiry[.
>
> *Carol:* Sometimes I feel like I live on the edge of two worlds. It's so hard to pull myself together.
>
> *Social worker:* [Again using psychodynamic inquiry.] Are you wondering whether you'd be happier back home?
>
> *Carol:* At least I'd feel a sense of belonging.

Social worker: [Using intervention from multicultural theory and speaking within a relational theory framework.] It sounds like your present situation at work has brought back feelings you had as a young girl. You were told you didn't fit into one world and then you were having a hard time fitting into another world. Your loyalties are still divided, and you are trying to find an identity that feels right for you. It also has made you feel that, in spite of your success in the White world, racism lurks around every corner.

In this dialogue, Carol struggles with issues of racism, and culture. She is living on the boundaries of two separate cultures. Rather than betray a part of her identity to live in the dominant culture, she isolates herself from both, which leaves her pained and alone. Also evident is how she has not internalised her success, but rather feels fraudulent in her White world of work. This is a common theme among professional women of colour – the more successful they become, the more alienated they may feel from their ethnic and racial communities (Comas-Diaz & Greene, 1994). Bell and Nkomo (2001) write about the success of African-American professional women coming, at least in part, from their resilience in handling the micro-traumas of the everyday racism occurring in routine encounters at work. Having absorbed many of the beliefs of the dominant White culture, Carol appears to be in the early stages of racial identity development.

The social worker tries to talk with Carol within a relational framework, using MCT as a meta-theory. She listens to discussion of cultural experiences and identity development, according to MCT. However, what has been missed in this early stage of counselling is any discussion of the cross-racial helping relationship. The social worker appears colour blind, a stage of White identity development Sue and Sue (2003) describe as not recognising herself as a racial being. This contributes to her inability to see the difference between herself as a White woman and Carol as an African-American woman.

As treatment progressed, Carol spoke more openly about her conflicting loyalties and just how wide the gap between her past and present had become. She described how angry she was at her parents for pushing her to enter the White world, yet denigrating her when she assimilated at the expense of her own racial heritage. The following dialogue from the middle stages of treatment illustrates MCT and her continued struggle with racial identity development, and the challenge both Carol and the worker face in maintaining relational authenticity, a concept from relational theory.

Carol: Recently, I ran into one of the women of color from my previous job. She was angry at me for not staying in touch – she said we had to stick together. I felt uncomfortable. I am very busy, yet I did get in touch with a former White colleague recently. So now I feel torn.
Social worker: Do you feel you have to stick together with other Black women?
Carol: Well, in some ways – the more I continue to advance, the wider the racial gap becomes. I go to this upscale university, and my 16-year-old cousin back home has three kids and is still not married. Yet I don't want to work in the ghetto.
Social worker: [Continuing the multicultural approach.] So, you are talking about racism and where this all leaves you because as an African-American woman you have had some opportunities, but many other African-American women – and men – continue to struggle a lot.
Carol: [Crying.] I feel so guilty. It's awful. My parents didn't achieve as much because they didn't have the opportunities, but I just want to live my life. Sometimes I feel it means forgetting I'm Black. And yet at work, I feel very Black.
Social worker: How do you feel about being Black?
Carol: [Angrily.] How do you feel about being White?
Social worker: [Using relational theory.] I didn't mean to make you angry. To be honest, I'm glad I'm White. I think it's really hard to be Black in this country.
Carol: Right, and so you don't get to ask me how I feel about being Black, okay? I feel proud a lot of the time but right now it's a burden. Sometimes I feel all I've done, I've done for my parents. At other times, however, I feel as though I am leaving them behind. I just want to live my life like a White person gets to do.
Social worker: Carol, sometimes I wonder whether I can understand your feelings enough to help you. [Self-disclosure, a relational theoretical construct.] How do you feel about working with me? Do you wonder whether I can understand or appreciate your feelings? Or do you feel you might

get more understanding from a Black therapist? [Relational theory, using transference and counter-transference.].

Carol: [Crying.] In some ways it is difficult to talk to you but I would like to tell you about my experiences. In all the time I have spent with White people, I feel I have never really been honest about who I am. Sometimes, I don't even know who I am. It's important for me to be honest with you and for you to be able to hear what I have to say. Working with you gives me a chance to practise being a Black woman in a White world – but in a real way. I just want you to be honest with me.

Social worker: [Continuing with relational theory.] Okay, this is hard but I will be honest. Would it surprise you to know sometimes I feel jealous of you even though I said I was glad I was White. [Sharing counter-transference reactions – psychoanalytic theory.] We came from similar backgrounds and I didn't have a lot of the educational opportunities you did because you were African-American. I also feel a sense of shame as a White person for what White people have done to Black people in this country and I get that they deserve more opportunities than White people but it's hard because sometimes I guess I feel like they deserve more opportunities than only some White people. So I get confused also.

Carol: I appreciate your honesty. I never thought about it this way I guess. I always felt White people have all the advantages.

Social worker: I'm not saying they don't, only that sometimes things get complicated. I appreciate your honesty as well.

Carol's case illustrates many components of assimilative integrative psychotherapy. Multicultural theory provides the unitary theoretical understanding framing the therapy, while interventions from *psychodynamic* (including empathy and interpretation, and focusing on feelings and interpersonal relationships), and *relational* (mutual empathy and relationship authenticity, transference and counter-transference, and self-disclosure) theory (or relational psychoanalytic theory). Also noted are the factors referred to by Norcross and Goldfried (2005) as common in most approaches to therapy: the therapeutic alliance, exposure of the client to previous difficulties followed by new, corrective emotional experiences, empathy, positive regard, attention, having a rationale for problems, interpretation, insight, and understanding.

Client-directed psychotherapy

Striker (2010) adds client-directed psychotherapy as an additional route to integrative psychotherapy. This approach gives preference to the client over the preference of the therapist on the dictates of theory. This was driven home to this co-author in the case of a 26-year-old woman, who was handicapped by severe washing, checking, and counting rituals. During the course of a typical day, she performed approximately 54 rituals, which impaired her ability to function vocationally and socially, and caused her great suffering and misery. She awoke at 4.00 am in order to do all her morning rituals and still be at work by 9.00 am. Not surprisingly, she was frequently late for work. Although the client recognised her ritualising was senseless, she felt compelled to continue to do so. This co-author originally treated her with psychodynamic psychotherapy for two years, as was the model being taught in the programme I was attending. Dreams were analysed, as were her fantasies, yet, her depression increased and she did not experience any relief in symptom reduction. Depressed and discouraged, the client happened to see a television programme on OCD that spoke of a successful behavioural treatment. She asked the therapist if she could help her with the approach described on the show. I began to search the literature and discovered some protocols on the treatment of OCD. The result was impressive – the change to a behavioural treatment approach resulted in an elimination of the client's rituals in just eight weeks. Clearly, the client's preference drove the change in the therapeutic work.

PSYCHOTHERAPY INTEGRATION IN THE INTERNATIONAL SPHERE

Wachtel (2008) summarised a symposium addressing the contributions of therapy integration in the international sphere. A special section of the *Journal of Psychotherapy Integration* was published and addressed the state of psychotherapy integration in the USA (Hartston, 2008), Portugal (Vasco, 2008), Switzerland and Germany (Caspar, 2008), Argentina (Fernandez-Alverez, 2008), Chile (Opazo & Bagladi, 2008), and Japan (Iwakabe, 2008). These citations appear in Stiker (2010). Ivey and Brooks-Harris (2005) address issues of race and ethnicity and Franklin et al. (1993) address race specifically in regard to African-American clients (in Striker, 2010).

RESEARCH ON PSYCHOTHERAPY INTEGRATION

Psychotherapy research has begun to emphasise the need for large-scale studies using randomised clinical trials and standardised treatment manuals. This trend presents a new challenge for the integration movement because it is more difficult to manualise and test the efficacy of flexible, integrative forms of psychotherapy. Schottetenbauer et al. (2005) identify the difficulty defining integrative psychotherapy and the variety of ways in which psychotherapists integrate as two major challenges in conducting outcome research studies on integrative psychotherapy. They have identified dialectical behaviour therapy (DBT), mindfulness-based cognitive therapy (MBCT), acceptance and commitment therapy (ACT), and transtheoretical psychotherapy (TP) as four integrative therapies with empirical support with four or more randomised controlled studies. Brief relational therapy (BRT) and multimodal therapy (MT) had some empirical support with one to four randomised control studies. The need to describe integrative psychotherapy in a manner that can be empirically tested and to conduct research is one of the most important challenges to the psychotherapy integration movement in the 21st century (Brooks-Harris, 2008) and the clinical approach to mental health more broadly (see Chapter 33).

CONCLUSION

This chapter has addressed integrative psychotherapy as a framework for clinically based social work practice. Several models were selected to illustrate this approach, although there are additional integrative efforts currently taking place in the world of mental health. Those with empirical evidence are listed in the above research section. Other examples include the integration of meditation and mindfulness and psychotherapy (Kabat-Zinn et al., 1997); spirituality and psychotherapy (Sollod, 2005); pharmacotherapy and psychotherapy (Beitman & Saveanu, 2005); and integrating therapeutic modalities, such as individual, couple, family, and group treatment (Feldman & Feldman, 2005). Integrative models have been used in the treatment of many different clinical syndromes, including anxiety and depression, character disorders, and severe mental disorders, and have been used with specific populations across the life span. Many practitioners select an array of theories and approaches quite intuitively in their clinical work. However, the art and science of integrative psychotherapy is the thoughtful, systematic consideration of theory and intervention matched to client's needs.

REFERENCES

Alexander, F. (1963). The dynamics of psychotherapy in light of learning theory. *American Journal of Psychiatry, 120*, 440–448.

Beck, A.T. (1984). Cognitive therapy, behavior therapy, psychoanalysis, and pharmacotherapy: The cognitive continuum. In J.B.W. Williams & Spitzer, R.I. (eds), *Psychotherapy research: Where are we and where should we go?* New York: Guilford.

Beutler, I.E., & Clarkin, J. (1990). *Selective treatment section: Toward targeted therapeutic interventions.* New York: Brunner/Mazel.

Bell, E.L., & Nkomo, S.M. (2001). *Our separate ways: Black and white women and the struggle for professional identity.* Boston, MA: Harvard Business School Press.

Beutler, L.D., & Clarkin, J. (1990). *Differential treatment selection: Toward targeted therapeutic interventions.* New York: Brunner/Mazel.

Brooks-Harris, J.E. (2008). *Integrative multi-theoretical psychotherapy.* New York: Houghton Mifflin Co.

Comez-Diaz, L., & Green, B. (1994). *Women of color and mental health.* New York: Guilford.

Cooper, M. (1990). Treatment of a client with obsessive-compulsive disorder. *Social Work Research and Abstracts, 26*(2), 26–31.

Dollard, J., & Miller, N.W. (1950). *Personality and psychotherapy.* New York: McGraw-Hill.

Drisko, J.W. (2004). Common factors in psychotherapy outcome: Meta-analytic findings and their implications for practice and research. *Families in Society: The Journal of Contemporary Social Services, 85*(1), 81–90.

Feldman, L.B., & Feldman, S.L. (2005). Integrating therapeutic modalities. In J.C. Norcross & Goldfried, M.R. (eds), *Handbook of psychotherapy integration* (2nd ed.). New York: Oxford University Press, pp. 362–381.

Fernandez-Alverez, H. (2008). Integration in psychotherapy: An approach from Argentina. *Journal of Psychotherapy Integration, 18*, 79–86.

Frank, J.D. (1961). *Persuasion and healing: A comparative study of psychotherapy.* Baltimore, MD: Johns Hopkins University.

Frank, J.D., & Frank, J.B. (1991). *Persuasion and healing: A comparative study of psychotherapy* (3rd ed.). Baltimore, MD: Johns Hopkins University.

Franklin, A.J., Carter, R.T., & Grace, C. (1993). An integrative approach to psychotherapy with Black/African Americans: The relevance of race and culture. In G. Stricker & Gold, J.R. (eds), *Comprehensive handbook of psychotherapy integration.* New York: Plenum, pp. 465–479.

Garfield, S.L. (1995). *Psychotherapy: An eclectic-integrative approach.* New York: John Wiley & Co.

Goldfried, M.R., Pachankis, J.E., & Bell, A.C. (2005). A history of psychotherapy integration. In J.C. Norcross & Goldfried, M.R. (eds), *Handbook of psychotherapy integration* (2nd ed.). New York: Oxford University Press, pp. 24–60.

Goncalves, O., & Ivey, A. (1996). Developmental theory: Clinical implications. In K. Kuehlwein & Rosen, H. (eds), *Cognitive therapy in action.* San Francisco: Josey-Bass.

Greenberg, L.S., & Safran, J.D. (1984). Integrating affect and cognitions: A perspective on the process of therapeutic change. *Cognitive Therapy and Research, 8*, 55–578.

Greencavage, L.M. & Norcross, J.C. (1990). Where are the commonalities among the therapeutic common factor? *Cognitive Therapy and Research, 8*, 559–578.

Gurman, A.S., & Messer, S.B. (eds) (2003). *Essential psychotherapies.* New York: Guilford Press.

Hartston, H. (2008). The state of psychotherapy in the United States. *Journal of Psychotherapy Integration, 18*, 87–102.

Ivey, A.E., & Brooks-Harris, J.E. (2005). Integrative psychotherapy with culturally diverse clients. In J.C. Norcross & Goldfried, M.D. (eds), *Handbook of psychotherapy integration* (2nd ed.). New York: Oxford University Press, pp. 321–342.

Iwakabe, S. (2008). Psychotherapy integration in Japan. *Journal of Psychotherapy Integration, 18*, 103–125.

Kabat-Zinn, J., Chapman, A., & Salmon, P. (1997). The relationship of cognitive and somatic components of anxiety to patient preference for alternative relaxation techniques. *Mind/Body Medicine, 2*, 101–109.

Lazarus, A. (1976). *Multimodal behavior therapy.* New York: Springer.

Lesser, J.G., & Saia, D.P. (2011). *Human behavior and the social environment: Theory and practice* (2nd ed.). Boston, MA: Pearson (Allyn and Bacon).

London, P. (1964). *The modes and morals of psychotherapy.* New York: Holt, Rinehart & Winston.

Marks, I.M., & Gelder, M.G. (1966). Common ground between behavior therapy and psychodynamic methods. *British Journal of Medical Psychology, 39*, 11–23.

Marmor, J. (1969). Neurosis and the psychotherapeutic process: Similarities and differences in the behavioral and psychodynamic conceptions. *International Journal of Psychiatry, 7*, 514–519.

Miller, S.D., Duncan, B.L., & Hubble, M.A. (2005). Outcome-informed clinical work. In J.C. Norcross & Goldfried, M.R. (eds), *Handbook of psychotherapy integration* (2nd ed.). New York: Oxford University Press, pp. 84–102.

National Association of Social Workers (NASW) (2005). *NASW standards for the practice of clinical social work.* Retrieved October 12, 2010 from http://www.naswdc.org/practice/standards/clinical_sw.asp

Norcross, J.C., & Goldfried, M.D. 2005). *Handbook of psychotherapy integration* (2nd ed.). New York: Oxford Press.

O'Neill, J. (1999). Profession dominates in mental health. *NASW News, 44*, 1, 8.

Opazo, R., & Bagladi, V. (2008). Integrative psychotherapy: From Chile with love. *Journal of Psychotherapy Integration, 18*, 126–135.

Orlinsky, D.E., Grawe, K., & Parks, B.K. (1994). Process and outcome in psychotherapy. In A.E. Bergin & Garfield, S.L. (eds), *Handbook of psychotherapy and behavior change* (4th ed.). New York: Wiley, pp. 270–238.

Perez, J.E. (1999). Integration of cognitive-behavioral and interpersonal therapies for Latinos: An argument for technical eclectism. *Journal of Contemporary Psychotherapy, 29*, 169–183.

Rigazio-Digilio, S.A., Goncalves, O.F., & Ivey, A.E. (1996). From cultural to existential diversity: The impossibility of psychotherapy integration within a traditional framework. *Applied and Preventive Psychology, 5*, 235–247.

Rogers, C.R. (1957). The necessary and sufficient conditions of psychotherapeutic personality change. *Journal of Consulting Psychology, 21*, 95–103.

Rogers, C.R. (1963). Psychotherapy today or where do we go from here? *American Journal of Psychotherapy, 17*, 5–15.

Safran, J.D. (1984). Assessing the cognitive-interpersonal style. *Cognitive Therapy and Research, 8*, 333–347.

Safran, J.D., & Messer, S.B. (1997). Psychotherapy integration: A postmodern critique. *Clinical Psychology: Science & Practice, 4*, 140–152.

Schottenbauer, M.A., Glass, C.R., & Arnkoff, D.B. (2005). Outcome research on psychotherapy integration. In J.C. Norcross & Goldfried, M.D. (eds), *Handbook of psychotherapy integration* (2nd ed.). New York: Oxford University Press, pp. 459–493.

Sollod, R.N. (2005) Integrating spirituality and psychotherapy. In J.C. Norcross & Goldfried, M.D. (eds), *Handbook of psychotherapy integration* (2nd ed.). New York: Oxford University Press, pp. 403–416.

Striker, G. (2010). *Psychotherapy integration*. Washington, DC: American Psychological Association.

Striker, G., & Gold, J.G. (2003). Integrative approaches to psychotherapy. In A. Gurman & Messer, S.B. (eds), *Essential psychotherapies*. New York: Guilford Press.

Sue, W.S., & Sue, D. (2003). *Counseling the culturally different: Theory and practice* (4th ed.). New York: John Wiley and Sons.

Sue, D.W., Ivey, A.E., & Pedersen P.B. (1996). *A theory of multicultural counseling and therapy*. Pacific Grove, CA: Brooks-Cole.

Vasco, A.B. (2008) Psychotherapy integration in Portugal. *Journal of Psychotherapy Integration, 18*, 70–73.

Wachtel, P.L. (1993). *Therapeutic communication: Knowing what to say when*. New York: Guilford.

Wachtel, P. L. (1997). *Psychoanalysis, behavioral therapy and the relational world*. New York: Guilford.

Wachtel, P.L. (2000). Reclaiming the disavowed: The evolution of an integrative point of view. In J. Shay & Wheelis, J. (eds), *Odysseys in psychotherapy*. New York: Irvington, pp. 359–392.

Wachtel, P.L. (2001). An (inevitably) self-deceiving reflection on self-deception. In M. Goldfried (ed.), *How therapists change*. Washington, DC: American Psychological Association, pp. 83–101.

Wachtel, P.L., Kruk, J.C., & McKinney, M.K. (2005). Cyclical psychodynamics iand integrative relational psychotherapy. In J.C. Norcross & Goldfried, M.R. (eds), *Handbook of psychotherapy integration* (2nd ed.). New York: Oxford University Press. 172–195.

Wachtel, E.F., & Wachtel, P.L. (1986). *Family dynamics in individual psychotherapy: A guide to clinical strategies*. New York: Guilford.

Wolf, E. (1966). Learning theory and psychoanalysis. *British Journal of Medical Psychology, 39*, 1–10.

Wolfe, B.E. (1992). Self-experiencing and the integrative treatment of the anxiety disorders. *Journal of Psychotherapy Integration, 2*, 29–43.

Wolfe, B.E. (2005). Integrative psychotherapy of the anxiety disorders. In J.C. Norcross & Goldfried, M.R. (eds), *Handbook of psychotherapy integration* (2nd ed.). New York: Oxford University Press, pp. 263–280.

Wolfe, B.E., & Sigel, P. (1998). Experiential psychotherapy of the anxiety disorders. In L.S. Greenberg, Watson, J.C., & Lietaer, C. (eds), *Handbook of experiential psychotherapy*. New York: Guilford Press, pp. 272–294.

16

Crisis Intervention

Barry R. Cournoyer

In the relatively short history of the species, humans individually and collectively have faced thousands of natural and human-caused disasters. How many earthquakes, tsunamis, hurricanes, cyclones, tornadoes, fires, volcanic eruptions, droughts, blizzards, floods, landslides, famines, and disease epidemics have humans experienced [World Health Organisation (WHO), 2009]? How many violent assaults, individual or collective acts of suicide or homicide, and armed conflicts? How many have been enslaved, indentured, kidnapped, trafficked, tortured [European Committee for the Prevention of Torture and Inhuman or Degrading Treatment or Punishment, 2010; United Nations (UN) Global Initiative to Fight Human Trafficking, 2010], and directly or indirectly terrorised by events in the world? How many people have been suddenly displaced from their homes, families, and communities? How many racial, ethnic, and religious communities have been subject to genocidal violence?

How many women and girls have been beaten, abused, raped or sexually assaulted, exploited, or imprisoned in their homes? How many have been publicly stoned, caned, or expelled from their communities (UN Division for the Advancement of Women, 2009)? How many children and elderly or disabled persons have been abused, neglected, or abandoned? How many men and boys have been executed or sentenced to jails and prisons? How many individuals and families have been deported or otherwise forcibly relocated? How many people have been confined to refugee camps?

How many people have died or suffered severe physical injuries and disabilities from work, home, recreational, or transportation-related accidents? How many individuals, families, and communities have been affected by accidents in the nuclear, oil, coal, steel, and manufacturing industries? How many families have been affected by the sudden onset of illnesses, such as strokes, heart attacks, and viral and bacteriological epidemics? How many communities have been affected by sudden and unexpected loss of income, food, or shelter?

Some people assume human life on this world is, or at least should be, relatively safe, predictable, benevolent, and fundamentally fair or just (Janoff-Bulman, 1992). However, the contemporary and historical evidence leads to a different conclusion. Despite the ability to think in complex ways and to create, innovate, and adapt to changing circumstances and opportunities, humans' incredible capacity for adaptation has limitations. Like other species, humans remain relatively fragile creatures whose lives can be threatened and sometimes end suddenly from a variety of events. Planet earth is hospitable in some places at certain times, and inhospitable at others. The environment is sometimes toxic and dangerous. Indeed, humans often engage in neglectful, exploitative, or violent actions toward themselves, other humans, other species, and the earth itself. These are times and circumstances of great uncertainty and considerable injustice due, in large part, to human acts of omission and commission. Many people experience insecurity, uncertainty, and injustice as more the rule than the exception. Indeed, for many human beings, life-threatening crises are ubiquitous.

The police sergeant told me the two children sitting in the back of a patrol car had just witnessed their father kill their mother and then kill himself. The boy was 10 years old and the girl 8. As I walked over to the car, I saw that the boy had his arm around his sister in an effort to provide some comfort. She was shaking or shivering – as if she was very cold. He was motionless. However, their facial expressions were similar. Each was blankly staring off into space. Each was oblivious to the 30 policemen and women, the more than 50 onlookers, the six paramedics, the dozen police cars, the three ambulances, and the fire truck – all with flashing lights and radios loudly blasting voice commands. The children appeared unable to hear the sounds or see the activity all around them. They were in another place, another space, and perhaps another time.

This is not an isolated incident. During their lifetime, as much as 60–90 per cent of some populations experience one or more traumatic events (Breslau et al., 1998; Bruce et al., 2001; Frans et al., 2005). In a Detroit (USA) survey of trauma and post-traumatic stress disorder (PTSD), Breslau et al. (1998) found:

> 37.7% of respondents experienced traumatic assaultive violence (such as rape, torture, or military combat), 59.8% experienced some other traumatic personal injury or shocking experience (such as a life-threatening accident, natural disaster, life-threatening illness, or witnessing a traumatic event), 60.0% experienced the sudden, unexpected death of a loved one, and 62.4% lived through a nonfatal traumatic experience that occurred to a loved one (e.g., daughter raped or spouse seriously injured in an automobile accident) (Kessler, 2000, p. 5).

In areas of the world affected by armed conflict, civil war, or racial, religious, or ethnic violence, the exposure rates are almost certainly higher. Husain et al. (1998) surveyed 791 school-age children in Sarajevo as the long siege of the city ended in 1994. The children completed several measures of stress, PTSD, and depression and responded to survey questions. Their responses indicated, during the previous year, 85% 'had experienced direct or indirect sniper fire', ... 66% 'had lost a member of the immediate or extended family', ... 26% 'had experienced food deprivation, 48% experienced clothing deprivation, 29% reported shortage of water, and 10% reported lack of shelter' (p. 1719).

Despite the ubiquity of life-threatening crises and the extreme nature of some traumatic events, only a proportion of those so exposed subsequently 'develops the problematic cluster of symptoms comprising the syndrome of post-traumatic stress disorder' (Ravindran & Stein, 2009, p. 25). Some studies (Breslau et al., 1991; Kessler et al., 1995) suggest 10–20% of people who experience such severe stressors go on to develop PTSD at some point in their lifetimes. Other studies suggest a lower percentage (Schnyder et al., 2008, as cited by Bryant, 2007), at least in relation to certain severe stressors. However, exposure to military combat (Prigerson et al., 2002) and the experience of sexual assault are associated with higher rates of PTSD (Breslau, 2009).

This chapter addresses the topic of crisis intervention in the context of life-threatening circumstances or traumatic events. Extreme stressors, such as environmental disasters, violence toward individuals and communities, life-threatening accidents, and the onset of a life-threatening illness sometimes trigger active crisis states. Although most people adapt to the stressful circumstances and recover within a few hours or days, some become traumatised so the symptoms of distress continue at severe levels long after the life-threatening events have ended. Although clinical social workers are often involved in services to those affected by post-traumatic distress, in this chapter the focus is on care to individuals, families, and communities during and shortly after the traumatic events. The intervention approaches, principles, and recommendations discussed in this chapter are intended to help social workers provide high-quality, safe, ethical, and effective short-term services in the context of extreme, life-threatening crises.

STRESSFUL LIFE EVENTS AND ACTIVE CRISES

As do members of all living species, humans routinely confront *stressful life events* or *stressors* (Hobson & Delunas, 2001; Holmes & Rahe, 1967; McGrath & Burkhart, 1983; Scully et al., 2000). Many involve loss or uncertainty and most place immediate demands upon those affected. These demands often precipitate a state of active crisis that includes biopsychosocial *distress* – a strong sense of demand, a feeling that something is wrong or missing, and heightened physiological arousal:

> People are in a state of crisis when they face an obstacle to important life goals – an obstacle that is, for a time, insurmountable by the use of customary methods of problem-solving. A period of disorganization ensues, a period of upset, during which many abortive attempts at solution are made (Caplan, 1961, p. 18).

Some stressful life events and conditions constitute an immediate threat to life and well-being. In members of most species, such *life-threatening events* or *life threats* usually trigger extreme reactions in the form of fight, flight, or freeze (Bracha, 2004; Dhabhar, 2009; Turton, 2005). Unlike most other species, however, humans also sometimes misperceive phenomena such that non-life-threatening events are experienced as if they were genuinely dangerous (Raimy, 1975). Nonetheless, whether resulting from an actual or a perceived threat to life or well-being, humans may experience considerable biopsychosocial distress.

In recognition of these factors, Hill (1949, 1958) proposed a model of family crisis where A = the stressful life event or circumstance, B = the resources available to the family and its members, C = the perception of and interpretation of the meaning and significance of the life stressor, and X = a crisis in the form of intense individual and family distress, disequilibrium and sometimes immobilisation. In doing so, he anticipated the importance of perception in contemporary crisis theory:

> Typically, a crisis is described using a trilogy definition; that is, there are three essential elements that must be present for a situation to be considered a crisis: (1) a precipitating event, (2) a perception of the event that leads to subjective distress, and (3) diminished functioning when the distress is not alleviated by customary coping resources (Puleo & McGlothlin, 2010, p. 1).

An *active crisis state* is a condition of biopsychosocial distress resulting from 'a perception or experiencing of an event or situation as an intolerable difficulty that exceeds the person's current resources and coping mechanisms' (James, 2008, p. 3). Although members of various cultures might use different words and images to reference the experience, most people recognise when they are, or recently have been, in a state of active crisis. Following an initial period of shock or daze, humans generally respond to crises with activity, creativity, and adaptability. Most of the time, distress is relatively short-lived as people calm themselves, appraise the situation, develop plans to address the demands and challenges, and take action to avoid, escape, or confront the immediate stressors. In general, humans are remarkably resilient (Bonanno & Mancini, 2008; Coaffee et al., 2009; Delahanty, 2008;

Gillespie et al., 2009; Hobfoll et al., 2009; Hodes et al., 2008; Levine et al., 2009; Mancini & Bonanno, 2006; Williams et al., 2008) (see also Chapter 11). In general, people quickly apply problem-solving and goal-pursuing competencies to address challenges associated with crises (Harvey, 2002; Wainrib & Bloch, 1998). In genuinely life-threatening crisis situations, many people display extraordinary, heroic, and sometimes superhuman capacities (Ripley, 2008).

Obviously, humans do not reflect a uniform capacity to react to and cope with stressful events, lower their levels of extreme distress, recover from loss, or rebound following traumatic events. Owing in part to age, genetic, and biochemical factors, temperament and personality characteristics, and to important social and environmental contexts, people vary in their biopsychosocial responses to crises. Various *risk factors* and *protective* or *resilience factors* operate to exacerbate or mitigate the severity and duration of the signs and symptoms of acute as well as post-traumatic distress. Nonetheless, there are certain common signs and symptoms associated with acute distress.

SIGNS AND SYMPTOMS

The experience of active crisis is sometimes called acute stress or acute stress reaction, or, simply, acute distress. Other terms include acute crisis reaction, combat fatigue, crisis state, or psychic shock. Although the term 'stress' often conveys a negative connotation, some stress is generally a positive human experience. Problems tend to occur when there is too much or too little stress (Selye, 1965). When confronted with a modest demand or challenge that is not life-threatening, urgent, or imminent, a stress response helps to mobilise energy and focus attention on the task at hand. Under such circumstances, humans retain a capacity for rational thought. However, when the demand is urgent, imminent, life-threatening, or apparently insoluble, acute distress may follow. In those circumstances, blood and nutrients shift away from the digestive system and toward the heart, lungs, and the large muscles needed for fight or flight. Simultaneously, the capacity for rational thought decreases (Arnsten, 1998). Diminished rationality under extreme distress may lead to actions or inactions that increase rather than decrease risk of life. For example, after the airliners crashed into the Twin Towers of the New York World Trade Center, many occupants experienced a 'freeze' mode of the 'fight–flight–freeze' response. Less able to think clearly, they remained where they were and died as the buildings collapsed. Others ran down the stairs, exited the buildings, and survived (Ripley, 2008).

If the life-stressor and the associated distress have a negative impact on biopsychosocial functioning, those affected may meet psychiatric diagnostic criteria for *acute stress reaction* (WHO, 1992). If the stressors and the symptoms are more severe, the classifications *acute stress disorder* (American Psychiatric Association, 2000) may be warranted. When the intensity of distress is severe enough and the duration long enough, people may meet the psychiatric diagnostic criteria for an *adjustment disorder* or *post-traumatic stress disorder* (American Psychiatric Association, 2000; WHO, 1992).

In a sense, the International Classification of Diseases (ICD-10) guidelines (WHO, 1992) are more optimistic than the criteria contained in the Diagnostic and Statistical Manual (DSM-IV-TR; American Psychiatric Association, 2000), the system developed in Western countries for the classification and diagnosis of mental disorders. As reflected in the terminology, the ICD-10 anticipates most people recover quickly from the 'reaction' while the DSM-IV-TR seems to anticipate the presence of a 'disorder'. Indeed, the DSM-IV-TR classification seems to suggest, at least implicitly, *acute stress disorder* (ASD) is a precursor to PTSD. Several research studies, however, indicate an ASD diagnosis is not an especially reliable predictor of subsequent PTSD (Creamer et al., 2004; Dalgleish et al., 2008; Kassam-Adams & Winston, 2004; Yasan et al., 2009).

Many social workers are quite familiar with crisis and trauma-relevant psychiatric diagnoses as well as the epidemiological patterns associated with them. Some are also aware of the dangers of excessive or exclusive attention to psychiatric diagnoses, especially if the lived experience, views, and circumstances of those directly affected by crises are neglected.

Inappropriate 'medicalisation' of human problems (Conrad et al., 2010) may interfere with empathic understanding of others and subtly discourage a *person-in-environment* (PIE) perspective (see Chapter 8). A PIE point of view is a hallmark of social work throughout the world and is especially useful within the context of crisis situations and for the purpose of crisis intervention because it consistently considers both people and their social and environmental circumstances. The ever-expanding list of psychiatric diagnoses may tempt social workers to medicalise, psychologise, westernise, or pathologise human reactions to crises. Many social workers recognise these temptations and purposefully attend to social, cultural, and environmental factors as well as individual factors. Attention to both personal and social–environmental aspects of crises increases the chances of: (i) gaining, appreciating, and reflecting genuine understanding of people's felt experience; and (ii) identifying potential pathways and resources that might be used to help.

If social workers expect to find symptoms of severe distress immediately or subsequently following life-threatening events, then they are quite likely to discover them, whether or not clients actually experience them. Similarly, if social workers anticipate all or most people exposed to traumatic events subsequently experience symptoms of PTSD, then they will probably observe them as well. Finding what we expect to find is a central element of the logical fallacy known as *confirmation bias*. Confirmation bias and other forms of fallacious reasoning are obviously not limited to psychiatric diagnoses. If social workers expect to find heroes or heroines, persecutors or perpetrators, bullies or victims, or anticipate miracles will or will not happen, they are likely to discover them as well. The key point here is to recognise and manage the human tendency to notice phenomena that fit one's expectations and fail to notice or ignore those that do not.

Given these precautions, a review of some of the biological, psychological, and social aspects of exposure to life-threatening stressors is warranted. Although they are highly integrated and genuinely inseparable, each area is considered in turn.

BIOPSYCHOSOCIAL *SEQUELAE*

Exposure to life-threatening stressors tends to affect the human biological system in numerous ways. The central nervous system (CNS) contains nerves that carry electrical messages to and from various parts of the body, including the brain. Sensory perceptions, such as sight, sound, smell, taste, and touch, are conveyed through the CNS, which is also used to instruct the body to engage in motor activities, such as running or standing motionless, and screaming or whispering. The autonomic nervous system (ANS) is involved in the regulation of internal organs, such as the heart and circulatory system as well as hormone-producing glands. Through the sympathetic (SNS) and parasympathetic (PNS) nervous systems, the ANS also affects human emotions, including those associated with exposure and reaction to extreme stressors. Indeed, the famous 'fight-or-flight response' is a sympathetic response. In life-threatening circumstances, the SNS engages so the body receives a surge in adrenaline, cortisol, and other hormones. Pupils and bronchioles dilate, and heart rate and blood pressure increase to prepare the body for action needed to survive. Those bodily functions not immediately necessary to fight or flee (e.g., salivation, digestion, and urine and faecal evacuation) are inhibited so the energy may be used by those that are needed. The PNS, on the other hand, restores the body to a state of rest, calm, or 'normalcy' by reducing the secretion of adrenaline, constricting pupils and bronchioles, slowing the heart rate, and reducing blood pressure, and restoring capacities for salivation, urination, and defecation. The SNS and PNS function in a complementary fashion (Gardner, 2008).

During life-threatening events, biological arousal of the SNS in the form of 'fight or flight' has obvious survival value – for individuals and for the human species in general. The evolutionary evidence is incontrovertible. The same can be said for activation of the PNS. Humans must be able to reduce heightened biological arousal to restore their bodies to healthful states and to maximise their abilities to appraise, plan, and act, at least partially, on the basis of rational thought.

Despite the survival value associated with stress reactions, excessively intense or disproportionately lengthy SNS activation can be harmful to the human body. The prefrontal cortex part of the brain is used in thinking rationally, regulating emotions, and making rational decisions while the hippocampus is used for memory storage and retrieval. Chronic distress is associated with diminished capacity in both of these areas. Indeed, people affected by PTSD tend to have smaller hippocampal volume, lower hippocampal function, and more memory impairment than those without PTSD (Bremner et al., 1993, 2003; Chen et al., 2008). Chronic distress is also associated with increased risk of numerous medical conditions, such as impairment of the immune system, obesity, atherosclerosis, cardiovascular diseases, and, of course, depression (Boscarino, 1997; McEwen & Stellar, 1993).

The distress associated with acute crisis reactions sometimes leads people to use natural and synthetic substances to reduce the intensity and duration of symptoms. Alcohol and marijuana, as well as various anti-anxiety medications, have been used to calm agitated bodies and minds. Often comforting in the short run, they typically have little preventive effect *vis-à-vis* subsequent PTSD-related symptoms. However, a few small studies appear to suggest people in acute distress who are administered the β-adrenergic blocker propranolol in the immediate aftermath of the traumatic event experience a lesser degree of subsequent physiological reactivity – one of the symptoms of severe, chronic distress. It is not yet clear however, whether they become less likely subsequently to develop other PTSD-related symptoms (Pitman et al., 2002; Vaiva et al., 2003).

In a study of 696 soldiers who suffered combat-related physical injuries, administration of morphine early in the trauma care process 'was significantly associated with a lower risk of PTSD after injury ... This association remained significant after adjustment for injury severity, age, mechanism of injury, status with respect to amputation, and selected injury-related clinical factors' (Holbrook et al., 2010, p. 110). Similar results were found in a study of physically injured children (Nixon et al., 2010).

Certain psychological phenomena are commonly associated with traumatic events and severe distress. For example, there may be 'an initial state of "daze", with some constriction of the field of consciousness and narrowing of attention, inability to comprehend stimuli, and disorientation' (WHO, 1992, p. 119). Partial or complete amnesia may be evident. In addition, those affected may experience intense anxiety or panic, agitation and hyperactivity, despair, and anger. Emotional withdrawal and psychological dissociation in the form of derealisation, depersonalisation, or personality fragmentation may occur. Psychological defensive operations, such as denial, minimisation, intellectualisation, and avoidance, may be apparent as may some psychotic or psychotic-like phenomena, such as hallucinations or delusional thinking.

Consistent with those in the biological and psychological domains, the social sequelae of extreme distress may be consequential as well. When the physical environment is affected by natural or human-caused disasters, disruption to the social and physical structures may be profound. Families, neighbourhoods, and communities may suddenly lose their homes, streets, schools, hospitals, places of work, and places of worship. They may lose their food, water, energy supply systems. Communication and transportation may be difficult or impossible. The social systems associated with these functions may be disrupted as well. Social, cultural, educational, governmental, communications, religious, and economic organisations can simply cease to exist. Social isolation, fragmentation, neglect, and both violent and nonviolent competition for resources may result. Social sacrifice as well as social opportunism may be apparent.

The sudden loss of a family member alone is sufficient to disrupt biopsychosocial functioning. In an example described earlier in this chapter, the 8- and 10-year-old siblings lost their mother to murder and their father to suicide. In a few minutes' time, the family unit was destroyed. The myriad social-emotional and socialisation functions the parents fulfilled can no longer be addressed through that family structure. How, where, and by whom will those needs be met? What social resources can the community provide? What social capital can be accessed to nurture, protect, and socialise the suddenly orphaned children?

Risk and resilience

Men and women differ in the types of trauma most frequently encountered; molestation and sexual abuse are more frequent in women, while fights, accidents, and threats involving a weapon (and combat) are more frequent in men. Despite this, even when subjected to the same type of trauma as men, women still have approximately twice the risk of developing PTSD symptoms, and their symptoms are more likely to persist than symptoms among men (Nemeroff et al., 2006, p. 2).

Although the picture remains far from clear, it appears studies of military personnel and those of civilians exposed to various traumatic events reflect certain differences. For example, gender (i.e., being female) and race (i.e., being of minority status) emerged as obvious PTSD risk factors in numerous studies of civilians but not as clearly in investigations of military personnel. Even when the severity of trauma is controlled, female soldiers and soldiers of minority racial status are no more at risk than their male or their racial majority counterparts. Interestingly, age also seems to have a differential effect in civilians and soldiers. Although 'there was significant heterogeneity in both military and civilian groups, younger age at trauma was only a risk factor in the military' (Brewin et al., 2000, p. 754).

Despite these differences, many studies suggest certain factors are consistently associated with greater risk of post-traumatic distress. For example, a personal psychiatric history, history of psychiatric problems in one's family, adverse childhood experiences, experience of childhood abuse, previous traumatic exposure, lack of education, low socio-economic status, overall life stress, and low intelligence routinely emerge as risk factors for PTSD. Finally, and certainly not surprisingly, the severity of the trauma and lack of social support reflect increased risk of post-traumatic distress (Brewin et al., 2000).

Shalev (1996) reviewed 38 studies and concluded the intensity and duration of a traumatic experience, such as combat or torture, the dangerousness of an attack, such as rape, and the extent of physical injury resulting from the event were all risk factors for subsequent development of PTSD. In a prospective study, Perkonigg et al. (2000) found assault or sexual trauma were powerful risk factors for PTSD, especially among those who had prior exposure to one or more traumatic events.

Husain et al. (1998) found children who reported sniper fire did not differ significantly in stress, PTSD, or depression scale scores from those who did not report sniper fire. However, when compared to children who did not experience loss of a family member, those children who had lost a family member reflected more PTSD symptoms. Furthermore, 'children who experienced lack of water and shelter were significantly more likely to manifest avoidance and reexperiencing symptoms than those who did not' (Husain et al., 1998, p. 1719).

Although several factors contribute to an increased risk of PTSD, others seem to protect, buffer, or insulate those exposed to traumatic events from subsequent, long-term distress (Cohen & Wills, 1985). In general, being male serves as a protective factor as does majority status, higher education, financial security, and a general sense of self-efficacy, self-esteem, or mastery (Brewin et al., 2000; Coker et al., 2005; Kulka et al., 1990; Norris et al., 2002; Orcutt et al., 2004). A 'hardy' personality that includes a general sense of control or competence, openness to change, and belief life has meaning seems protective as well (King et al., 1998). Training and response preparation seems to help (Basoglu et al., 1997) and people who respond directly to traumatic events with energy and activity seem to do better than those who avoid or respond to them in a passive manner (Benotsch et al., 2000; Norris et al., 2002; North et al., 2001).

Warm and welcoming social support during and following traumatic events is associated with reduced risk of PTSD. Receiving help with basic physical needs and having people provide emotional comfort and sometimes advice seems to mitigate the potentially damaging effects of traumatic exposure (Cohen & Wills, 1985; Flannery, 1990; Fontana et al., 1997; Kaniasty & Norris, 1997; King et al., 1998; Ozer et al., 2003).

The term *resilience* is often used to capture the capacity to 'bounce-back' from adversity. 'A wealth of elements that comprise resilience has been proposed in the literature – including active problem-solving, responsibility, self-esteem, independence, well-being, initiative, humor, insight, creativity, and many others' (Nemeroff et al., 2006, p. 257). Bonanno (2004) observes *resilience:*

> pertains to the ability of adults in otherwise normal circumstances who are exposed to an isolated and potentially highly disruptive event, such as the death of a close relation or a violent or life-threatening situation, to maintain relatively stable, healthy levels of psychological and physical functioning ... resilience is more than the simple absence of psychopathology (p. 20).

It appears some people maintain an adaptive state of biopsychosocial equilibrium during and subsequent to traumatic events, many recover quite quickly, and some actually grow from the experience of responding to and coping with the crisis. Concepts such as 'stress-related growth (Park et al., 1996), adversarial growth (Linley & Joseph, 2004), construed or perceived benefits (McMillen et al., 1995; Tennen et al., 1992), and thriving (O'Leary & Ickovics, 1995)' (Calhoun et al., 2010, p. 1) as well as *post-traumatic growth* (PTG; Calhoun & Tedeschi, 1999, 2006) reflect the notion personal, psychological, social, or spiritual growth may result from the experience of and struggle with traumatic events. In discussing the PTG of some Holocaust survivors, Lev-Wiesel and Amir (2006) observed positive transformations involving 'the reconstruction of meaning, the renewal of faith, trust, hope, and connection, the redefinition of self, self in relation to others, and sense of community' (p. 257). Even coping with the violation of childhood sexual abuse (McMillen et al., 1995) may lead to growth.

When I was 12 years old, my mother had a boyfriend that we both liked a lot. Charles was funny, generous, and kind. My father had abandoned us about three years earlier and Charles helped us out during a time when we had almost nothing to live on. It's also true that he molested me on three occasions. He shouldn't have done that. He violated my human rights and dignity, and he betrayed my mother. He took advantage of my trust and affection, my youth, and my innocence. However, I don't believe that it affected me all that much. He was wrong but it wasn't my fault. I certainly do not feel ashamed or traumatised. In fact, I learned a lot about life from that experience. I became less naïve about men, boys, and people in general. And, I decided that I could choose to believe what I wanted to believe – I didn't have to accept what others said or expected.

CRISIS INTERVENTION

In aiding and comforting others during times of catastrophe, hardship, and loss, humans have always engaged in some form of crisis intervention. As an organised, professional activity, however, crisis intervention is of fairly recent origin. Lindemann (1944, 1956) and Caplan (1961, 1964) are often credited with formulating core concepts of 'crisis theory' and popularising ideas of 'crisis intervention'. Psychiatrist Caplan (1955, 1956) also wrote about social work in the areas of public health and community mental health. Perhaps influenced by social workers, he emphasised the role of social support as a central aspect of crisis intervention and used the term *competence* to reference 'an internal constitutional and acquired quality of individuals that enables them to withstand the harmful effects of hazardous circumstances' (Caplan, 1989, p. 4). In using terms such as mastery, frustration tolerance, self-efficacy, and problem-solving skills, Caplan (1961, 1964) anticipated the current recognition of resilience and biopsychosocial strengths as fundamental to contemporary crisis intervention approaches. Furthermore, he recognised the community and its formal and informal systems of educational, health, legal, and social care as contributing factors that may exacerbate or mitigate adverse effects of traumatic events.

The primary goals of crisis intervention services include: (i) stabilisation; (ii) elimination of or reduction in the intensity, frequency, and duration of symptoms of distress; and (iii) recovery and restoration to, at least, pre-crisis levels of biopsychosocial functioning. Intervention occurs during or immediately following unanticipated traumatic events and, when anticipated, prior to them as well. Services are generally voluntary, short-term, problem and goal focused, and provided within the context of a general view of acute distress as 'normal' in the context of 'abnormal' life-threatening events. Crisis intervention is not viewed as a form of psychological treatment or psychotherapy for ill, troubled, or 'disordered' people reflecting signs and symptoms of one or more psychiatric disorders. Rather, the general expectation is, with some psychosocial support, most people recover from the distress associated with the traumatic events. Indeed, the major intervention tools involve provision of emotional support and empathic understanding within the context of a safe physical environment and a trusting relationship; sharing of information and education about coping strategies; linkage to supportive people and other resources; problem solving and goal-directed action; and sometimes guidance. Some people, however, are especially vulnerable to or seriously affected by the event or its aftermath so referral to health and or mental health care services is warranted.

Services are provided to people in or close to their current location (i.e., their home or current residence, place of work, or at or near the site of the stressful event or situation). Indeed, intervention sometimes occurs close to the place where violence erupted or a disaster happened. However, physical and emotional safety is maximised and, whenever possible, exposure to additional potentially traumatising events and situations is avoided. In adapting to the nature of crisis reactions, information and guidance are communicated in everyday, descriptive language and simple, practical procedures are used (Polk & Mitchell, 2009).

Contemporary models of crisis intervention reflect certain fundamental phases or steps in the provision of services. These resonate with those introduced by Lindemann (1944) and Caplan (1961, 1964). For example,

Gilliland (1982) and James (2008) outline a six-step process:

1. defining the problem;
2. ensuring client safety;
3. providing support;
4. examining alternatives;
5. making plans; and
6. obtaining commitment to positive action.

Hoff et al. (2009) identify the following as basic steps:

1. psychosocial assessment of the individual or family crisis, including evaluation of victimisation trauma and the risk of suicide or assault on others;
2. development of a plan with the person or family in crisis;
3. implementation of the plan, drawing on personal, social, and material resources;
4. follow-up and evaluation of the crisis intervention process and outcomes (Hoff et al., 2009, p. 32).

Polk and Mitchell (2009) use a mnemonic acronym to capture the processes of a 'crisis conversation': SAFER-R refers to *Stabilize*, *Acknowledge*, *Facilitate*, *Encourage*, *Recovery*, and *Referral* (p. 73). The first step is to *stabilize* the situation by, for example, eliminating or minimising noise, unnecessary people, or distracting stimuli. Sometimes a move to a different location is required. Then, *acknowledge* something distressing has occurred by conveying empathic understanding of thoughts and feelings associated with the events and *facilitate* the person's understanding of the situation. Empathic reflections of others' communications often lead them to greater understanding of their own experience and the realities of the situation. As understanding increases, *encourage* the person to develop a rational plan of action. Once formulated, help to implement the plan for crisis resolution. As the person enacts action steps outlined in the crisis plan, progress is apparent and *recovery* is evident. Of course, sometimes, recovery is not evident or despite indications of progress, there may be signs more help is, or soon will be, needed. In both instances, *referral* to additional sources of help may be required. Hospitals, governmental and nongovernmental organisations, religious groups, and occasionally, law enforcement agencies may be asked for further assistance.

In the last few years, controversy has arisen regarding the safety and effectiveness of certain approaches to crisis intervention. In particular, critical incident stress debriefing (CISD) and critical incident stress management (CISM) (Everly & Mitchell, 1999; Mitchell, 1983) have been subject to increased scrutiny. Of particular concern is the practice of *debriefing*. Within the CISM framework, members of a homogenous population exposed to a traumatic event (e.g., fire-fighters who battled a neighbourhood-wide blaze) are organised into small groups within 24-hours of the critical incident. Within the group context, participants *debrief*, that is, they share detailed descriptions of the traumatic events and express associated emotions (Kaplan et al., 2001; Mansdorf, 2008).

Practices similar to debriefing are commonly incorporated within the context of psychotherapy, perhaps especially psychotherapy for people meeting the criteria for PTSD. However, debriefing so soon after a traumatic event with people that may or may not manifest psychiatric symptoms, and may or may not have sought psychotherapeutic treatment, may be questioned on several grounds. Is the practice of debriefing appropriate within the context of crisis intervention – by definition a non-psychotherapeutic service? What are the potential adverse effects of reviewing and perhaps reliving traumatic events during an active crisis state? Can people be traumatised by or their distress exacerbated by the practice of debriefing?

Within the past decade, several reviews of the debriefing, CISD, and CISM research literature have been published (Deahl, 2000; Kaplan et al., 2001). In a Cochrane Collaboration systematic review, Rose et al. (2002) concluded:

> There is no evidence that single session individual psychological debriefing is a useful treatment for

the prevention of post traumatic stress disorder after traumatic incidents. Compulsory debriefing of victims of trauma should cease. A more appropriate response could involve a 'screen and treat' model (para. 7).

According to the CISM model, debriefing occurs within a group rather than an individual context. Therefore, the conclusion of Rose et al. (2002) about 'individual' debriefing may not apply. Nonetheless, caution is warranted when debriefing is considered for use with anyone in the immediate context of traumatic events.

Interest in strengths and resilience combined with concern about pathologising normal processes are contributing to modifications in the provision of crisis intervention services (Mansdorf, 2008). Paton et al. (2000) suggest it:

> is no longer tenable to assume an automatic link between disaster exposure and the experience of pathological reactions or loss. Rather, the possibility of positive reactions and growth outcomes must be accommodated in research and in mitigation and recovery planning (p. 178).

The *integrative model of coping and resiliency* represents one approach to maximise strengths and coping capacities. The model provides a conceptual framework through which to identify, assess, and strengthen coping strategies within each of six domains. The acronym BASIC-Ph refers to the *Beliefs, Affects, Social, Imagination, Cognition,* and *Physical* dimensions of human experience (Lahad et al., 1997).

In the ecosystems approach to crisis intervention, James (2008) seeks to highlight the interactive and interdependent relations among micro-, meso-, macro-, exo-, and chrono-system elements of the environment (see Bronfenbrenner, 1986, 1995) (see Chapter 8). Such an approach:

> reaches far beyond the relational interactions between and among the various members of the crisis client's families and individuals in the client's workplace or immediate surroundings. The approach is continually changing, emerging, evolving, and developing to accommodate the ecological and multicultural contexts within which it exists. It ... encompasses an interdependency among and within people at all different levels of the total environment (James, 2008, p. 569).

The ecosystems approach is consistent with several principles outlined in the Inter-Agency Standing Committee (IASC) *Guidelines on Mental Health and Psychosocial Support in Emergency Situations* (2007). Established by the UN General Assembly, the IASC provides a context in which leaders of relevant UN agencies, nongovernmental organisations (NGOs), and representatives of the Red Cross and Red Crescent societies coordinate activities, make decisions, and develop policies. The IASC Guidelines encourage humanitarian actors to incorporate the following core principles in providing mental health and psychosocial support services in emergency contexts: (i) promote human rights, equity, and nondiscrimination, and maximise fairness in the distribution of services and supports; (ii) maximise participation of people affected by the emergency in humanitarian efforts; (iii) minimise the risk of unintended adverse consequences of mental health and psychosocial support services and *do no harm*; (iv) acknowledge the limitations of externally directed programmes and use available resources and build and strengthen local capacities at the individual, family, community, and societal levels; (v) avoid the dangers associated with stand-alone services and integrate activities and programmes into larger, sustainable care systems; and (vi) recognise people respond differentially to emergency situations and provide psychosocial supports in a multilayered system of care so services match the needs of those affected (IASC, 2007).

CONCLUSION

Crisis intervention services usually involve collaboration and engagement with diverse others, including friends, relatives, neighbours, and both formal and informal groups and organisations throughout a community. Consumers of crisis intervention services include individuals, families, groups, and communities directly or indirectly affected by traumatic events. Services may last a few minutes or a few days. In the context of traumatic events, however, the main foci are on addressing immediate problems and pursuing short-term goals, such as reducing acute distress, mobilising internal resources, linking people with external resources, and establishing or re-establishing connections with supportive people, groups, organisations, and communities. Consistent with a PIE perspective, crisis intervention services are often directed at the immediate problems, needs, and goals of families, natural groups, and communities. The approach is collaborative and, whenever possible, involves joint decision making and planning. Focusing on reducing or mitigating risk factors and promoting resilience or protective factors, crisis intervention may begin in advance of anticipated traumatic events, during, or in the immediate aftermath. Intervention may address the biological, psychological, social, or environmental domains of affected individuals, families, and communities. In most crisis situations, social workers first seek to ensure those in crisis have access to basic needs of safety, food, shelter, medical care, and social support. In so doing, social workers often serve as part of a triage team with other professionals, community leaders, and volunteers.

REFERENCES

American Psychiatric Association (2000). *Diagnostic and statistical manual* (4th ed., text rev.). Washington, DC: American Psychiatric Association.

Arnsten, A.F.T. (1998). Development of the cerebral cortex: XIV. Stress impairs prefrontal cortical function. *Journal of the American Academy of Child and Adolescent Psychiatry, 37*(12), 1337–1339.

Basoglu, M., Mineka, S., Paker, M., Aker, T., Livanou, M., & Gok, S. (1997). Psychological preparedness for trauma as a protective factor in survivors of torture. *Psychological Medicine, 27*(6), 1421–1433.

Benotsch, E.G., Brailey, K., Vasterling, J.J., Uddo, M., Constans, J.I., & Sutker, P.B. (2000). War zone stress, personal and environmental resources, and PTSD symptoms in gulf war veterans: A longitudinal perspective. *Journal of Abnormal Psychology, 109*(2), 205–213.

Bonanno, G.A. (2004). Loss, trauma, and human resilience: Have we underestimated the human capacity to thrive after extremely aversive events? *American Psychologist, 59*, 20–28. doi: 10.1037/0003-066X.59.1.20.

Bonanno, G.A., & Mancini, A.D. (2008). The human capacity to thrive in the face of potential trauma. *Pediatrics, 121*(2), 369–375.

Boscarino, J.A. (1997). Diseases among men 20 years after exposure to severe stress: Implications for clinical research and medical care. *Psychosomatic Medicine, 59*, 605–615.

Bracha, H.S. (2004). Freeze, flight, fight, fright, faint: Adaptationist perspectives on the acute stress response spectrum. *CNS Spectrums, 9*(9), 679–685.

Bremner, J.D., Scott, T.M., Delaney, R.C., Southwick, S.M., Mason, J.W., Johnson, D.R. et al. (1993). Deficits in short-term memory in post-traumatic stress disorder. *American Journal of Psychiatry, 150*, 1015–1019.

Bremner, J.D., Vythilingam, M., Vermetten, E., Southwick, S.M., McGlashan, T., Nazeer, A. et al. (2003). MRI and PET study of deficits in hippocampal structure and function in women with childhood sexual abuse and posttraumatic stress disorder. *American Journal of Psychiatry, 160*(5), 924–932. doi: 10.1176/appi.ajp.160.5.924.

Breslau, N. (2009). The epidemiology of trauma, PTSD, and other posttrauma disorders. *Trauma Violence and Abuse, 10*(3), 198–210. doi: 10.1177/1524838009334448.

Breslau, N., Davis, G.C., Andreski, P., & Peterson, E. (1991). Traumatic events and posttraumatic stress disorder in an urban population of young adults. *Archives of General Psychiatry, 48*(3), 216–222.

Breslau, N., Kessler, R. C., Chilcoat, H.D., Schultz, L.R., Davis, G.C., & Andreski, P. (1998). Trauma and posttraumatic stress disorder in the community: The 1996 detroit area survey of trauma. *Archives of General Psychiatry, 55*, 626–632.

Brewin, C.R., Andrews, B., & Valentine, J.D. (2000). Meta-analysis of risk factors for posttraumatic stress disorder in trauma-exposed adults. *Journal of Consulting & Clinical Psychology, 68*, 748–766.

Bronfenbrenner, U. (1986). Ecology of the family as a context for human development: Research perspectives. *Developmental Psychology, 22*, 723–742.

Bronfenbrenner, U. (1995). Developmental ecology through space and time: A future perspective. In P. Moen, Elder, G.H. Jr, & Luscher, K. (eds), *Examining lives in context: Perspectives on the ecology of human development.* Washington, DC: American Psychological Association, pp. 617–647.

Bruce, S.E., Weisberg, R.B., Dolan, R.T., Machan, J.T., Kessler, R.C., Manchester, G., & Keller, M.B. (2001). Trauma and posttraumatic stress disorder in primary care patients. *Primary Care Companion to the Journal of Clinical Psychiatry, 3,* 211–217.

Bryant, R.A. (2007). Early intervention for post-traumatic stress disorder. *Early Intervention in Psychiatry, 1*(1), 19–26.

Calhoun, L.G., & Tedeschi, R.G. (eds). (1999). *Facilitating posttraumatic growth: A clinician's guide.* Mahwah, NJ: Lawrence Erlbaum.

Calhoun, L.G., & Tedeschi, R.G. (eds). (2006). *Handbook of posttraumatic growth: Research and practice.* Mahwah, NJ: Lawrence Erlbaum Associates.

Calhoun, L.G., Cann, A., & Tedeschi, R.G. (2010). The posttraumatic growth model: Sociocultural considerations, in T. Weiss & Berger, R. (eds), *Posttraumatic growth and culturally competent practice: Lessons learned from around the globe.* Hoboken, NJ: John Wiley & Sons, pp. 1–14.

Caplan, G. (1955). The role of the social worker in preventive psychiatry. *Medical Social Work, 4,* 144–160.

Caplan, G. (1956). *Mental health aspects of social work in public health.* Berkeley, CA: University of California Press.

Caplan, G. (1961). *An approach to community mental health.* New York: Grune and Stratton.

Caplan, G. (1964). *Principles of preventive psychiatry.* New York: Basic Books.

Caplan, G. (1989). Recent developments in crisis intervention and the promotion of support service. *Journal of Primary Prevention, 10*(1), 3–25.

Chen, Y., Dube, C.M., Rice, C.J., & Baram, T.Z. (2008). Rapid loss of dendritic spines after stress involves derangement of spine dynamics by corticotropin-releasing hormone. *Journal of Neuroscience, 28*(11), 2903–2911. doi: 10.1523/jneurosci.0225-08.2008.

Coaffee, J., Wood, D.M., & Rogers, P. (2009). *The everyday resilience of the city: How cities respond to terrorism and disaster.* New York: Palgrave Macmillan.

Cohen, S., & Wills, T.A. (1985). Stress, social support, and the buffering hypothesis. *Psychological Bulletin, 98*(2), 310–357.

Coker, A.L., Weston, R., Creson, D.L., Justice, B., & Blakeney, P. (2005). PTSD symptoms among men and women survivors of intimate partner violence: The role of risk and protective factors. *Violence and Victims, 20*(6), 625–643.

Conrad, P., Mackie, T., & Mehrotra, A. (2010). Estimating the costs of medicalization. *Social Science & Medicine, 70*(12), 1943–1947. doi: DOI: 10.1016/j.socscimed.2010.02.019.

Creamer, M., O'Donnell, M.L., & Pattison, P. (2004). Acute stress disorder is of limited benefit in predicting post-traumatic stress disorder in people surviving traumatic injury. *Behavior Research and Therapy, 42,* 315–328.

Dalgleish, T., Meiser-Stedman, R., Kassam-Adams, N., Ehlers, A., Winston, F., Smith, P. et al. (2008). Predictive validity of acute stress disorder in children and adolescents. *British Journal of Psychiatry, 192,* 392–393. doi: 10.1192/bjp.bp.107.040451

Deahl, M. (2000). Psychological debriefing: Controversy and challenge. *Australian and New Zealand Journal of Psychiatry, 34,* 929–939.

Delahanty, D.L. (2008). *The psychobiology of trauma and resilience across the lifespan.* Lanham: Jason Aronson.

Dhabhar, F.S. (2009). A hassle a day may keep the pathogens away: The fight-or-flight stress response and the augmentation of immune function. *Integrative and Comparative Biology, 49*(3), 215–236.

European Committee for the Prevention of Torture and Inhuman or Degrading Treatment or Punishment (2010). CPT database. Retrieved June 2, 2010, from http://www.cpt.coe.int/en/database.htm

Everly, G.S., Jr, & Mitchell, J.T. (1999). *Critical incident stress management (CISM): A new era and standard of care in crisis intervention* (2nd ed.). Ellicott City; MD: Chevron.

Flannery, R.B. (1990). Social support and psychological trauma: A methodological review. *Journal of Traumatic Stress, 3,* 593–611.

Fontana, A., Rosenheck, R., & Horvath, T. (1997). Social support and psychopathology in the war zone. *Journal of Nervous and Mental Disease, 185,* 675–681.

Frans, O., Rimmo, P.A., Aberg, L., & Fredrikson, M. (2005). Trauma exposure and post-traumatic stress disorder in the general population. *Acta Psychiatrica Scandinavia, 111,* 291–299.

Gardner, D. (2008). *The science of fear.* New York: Dutton.

Gillespie, C.F., Phifer, J., Bradley, B., & Ressler, K.J. (2009). Risk and resilience: Genetic and environmental influences on development of the stress response. *Depression and Anxiety, 26*(11), 984–992.

Gilliland, B.E. (1982). *Steps in crisis intervention.* Memphis, TN: Memphis State University.

Harvey, J.H. (2002). *Perspectives on loss and trauma: Assaults on the self.* Thousand Oaks, CA: Sage Publications.

Hill, R. (1949). *Families under stress.* Westport, CT: Greenwood Press.

Hill, R. (1958). Social stresses on the family: Generic features of families under stress. *Social Casework, 39,* 139–150.

Hobfoll, S.E., Palmieri, P.A., Johnson, R.J., Canetti-Nisim, D., Hall, B.J., & Galea, S. (2009). Trajectories of resilience, resistance, and distress during ongoing terrorism: The case of Jews and Arabs in Israel. *Journal of Consulting and Clinical Psychology, 77*(1), 138–148.

Hobson, C.J., & Delunas, L. (2001). National norms and life-event frequencies for the revised social readjustment rating scale. *International Journal of Stress Management, 8*(4), 299–314.

Hodes, M., Jagdev, D., Chandra, N., & Cunniff, A. (2008). Risk and resilience for psychological distress amongst unaccompanied asylum seeking adolescents. *Journal of Child Psychology and Psychiatry, and Allied Disciplines, 49*(7), 723–732.

Hoff, L.A., Hallisey, B.J., & Hoff, M. (2009). *People in crisis: Clinical and diversity perspectives* (6th ed.). New York: Routledge.

Holbrook, T.L., Galarneau, M.R., Dye, J.L., Quinn, K., & Dougherty, A.L. (2010). Morphine use after combat injury in Iraq and post-traumatic stress disorder. *New England Journal of Medicine, 362*(2), 110–117. doi: 10.1056/NEJMoa0903326.

Holmes, T.H., & Rahe, R.H. (1967). The social readjustment rating scale. *Journal of Psychosomatic Research, 11*(2), 213–218.

Husain, S.A., Nair, J., Holcomb, W., Reid, J.C., Vargas, V., & Nair, S.S. (1998). Stress reactions of children and adolescents in war and siege conditions. *American Journal of Psychiatry, 155,* 1718–1719.

Inter-Agency Standing Committee (IASC) (2007). *IASC guidelines on mental health and psychosocial support in emergency settings.* Geneva: IASW.

James, R.K. (2008). *Crisis intervention strategies* (6th ed.). Belmont, CA: Thomson Brooks/Cole.

Janoff-Bulman, R. (1992). *Shattered assumptions: Towards a new psychology of trauma.* New York: Free Press.

Kaniasty, K., & Norris, F.H. (1997). Social support dynamics in adjustment to disasters. In S. Duck (ed.), *Handbook of personal relationships* (2nd ed.). New York: Wiley. 595–619.

Kaplan, Z., Iancu, I., & Bodner, E. (2001). A review of psychological debriefing after extreme stress. *Psychiatric Services, 52,* 824–827.

Kassam-Adams, N., & Winston, F.K. (2004). Predicting child PTSD: The relationship between acute stress disorder and PTSD in injured children. *Journal of the American Academcy of Child and Adolescent Psychiatry, 43,* 403–411.

Kessler, R.C. (2000). Posttraumatic stress disorder: The burden to the individual and to society. *Journal of Clinical Psychiatry, 61*(suppl 5), 4–12.

Kessler, R.C., Sonnega, A., Bromet, E., Hughes, M., & Nelson, C.B. (1995). Posttraumatic stress disorder in the national comorbidity survey. *Archives of General Psychiatry, 52*(12), 1048–1060.

King, L.A., King, D.W., Fairbank, J.A., Keane, T.M., & Adams, G.A. (1998). Resilience-recovery factors in post-traumatic stress disorder among female and male Vietnam veterans: Hardiness, postwar social support, and additional stressful life events. *Journal of Personality and Social Psychology, 74*(2), 420–434.

Kulka, R.A., Schlenger, W.E., Fairbank, J.A., Hough, R.L., Jordan, B.K., Marmar, C.R., & Weiss, D.S. (1990). *Trauma and the vietnam war generation: Report of findings from the national vietnam veterans readjustment study.* New York: Brunner/Mazel.

Lahad, M., Shacham, Y., & Niv, S. (1997). The community stress prevention center integrative model of coping. In C. Vukadinovic, Trebjesanin, B., & Kranjaic, S. (eds), *Children in times of social crisis.* Belgrade: UNESCO UNDP, pp. 140–164.

Lev-Wiesel, R., & Amir, M. (2006). Growing out of ashes: Posttraumatic growth among holocaust child survivors. In L.G. Calhoun & Tedeschi, R.G. (eds), *Handbook of posttraumatic growth: Research and practice.* Mahwah, NJ: Lawrence Erlbaum Associates. 248–263.

Levine, S.Z., Laufer, A., Stein, E., Hamama-Raz, Y., & Solomon, Z. (2009). Examining the relationship between resilience and posttraumatic growth. *Journal of Traumatic Stress, 22*(4), 282–286.

Lindemann, E. (1944). The symptomatology and management of acute grief. *American Journal of Psychiatry, 101,* 141–148.

Lindemann, E. (1956). The meaning of crisis in individual and family living. *Teachers College Record, 57,* 310–315.

Linley, P. A., & Joseph, S. (2004). Positive change following trauma and adversity: A review. *Journal of Traumatic Stress, 17,* 11–21.

Mancini, A.D., & Bonanno, G.A. (2006). Resilience in the face of potential trauma: Clinical practices and illustrations. *Journal of Clinical Psychology, 62*(8), 971–985.

Mansdorf, I.J. (2008). Psychological interventions following terrorist attacks. *British Medical Bulletin, 88*(1), 7–22. doi: 10.1093/bmb/ldn041.

McEwen, B.S., & Stellar, E. (1993). Stress and the individual: Mechanisms leading to disease. *Archives of Internal Medicine, 153*, 2093–2101.

McGrath, R.E.V., & Burkhart, B.R. (1983). Measuring life stress: A comparison of the predictive validity of different scoring systems for the social readjustment rating scale. *Journal of Clinical Psychology, 39*(4), 573–581.

McMillen, J.C., Zuravin, S., & Rideout, G.B. (1995). Perceptions of benefit from child sexual abuse. *Journal of Consulting and Clinical Psychology, 65*, 733–739.

Mitchell, J.T. (1983). When disaster strikes: The critical incident stress debriefing process. *Journal of Emergency Medical Services, 8*, 36–39.

National Institute of Clinical Excellence (2005). Posttraumatic stress disorder: The management of PTSD in adults and children in primary and secondary care. *National Clinical Practice Guideline*. London: Gaskell and the British Psychological Society.

Nemeroff, C.B., Bremner, J.D., Foa, E.B., Mayberg, H.S., North, C.S., & Stein, M.B. (2006). Posttraumatic stress disorder: A state-of-the-science review. *Journal of Psychiatric Research, 40*(1), 1–21. doi: DOI: 10.1016/j.jpsychires.2005.07.005.

Nixon, R.D.V., Nehmy, T.J., Ellis, A.A., Ball, S.-A., Menne, A., & McKinnon, A.C. (2010). Predictors of posttraumatic stress in children following injury: The influence of appraisals, heart rate, and morphine use. *Behaviour Research and Therapy, 48*(8), 810–815.

Norris, F.H., Friedman, M.J., Watson, P.J., Byrne, C.M., Diaz, E., & Kaniasty, K. (2002). 60,000 disaster victims speak: Part I. An empirical review of the empirical literature, 1981–2001. *Psychiatry, 65*(3), 207–239.

North, C.S., Spitznagel, E.L., & Smith, E.M. (2001). A prospective study of coping after exposure to a mass murder episode. *Annals of Clinical Psychiatry, 13*(2), 81–87.

O'Leary, V. E., & Ickovics, J. R. (1995). Resilience and thriving in response to challenge: An opportunity for a paradigm shift in women's health. *Women's Health: Research on Gender, Behavior, and Policy, 1*, 121–142.

Orcutt, H.K., Erickson, D.J., & Wolfe, J. (2004). The course of PTSD symptoms among gulf war veterans: A growth mixture modeling approach. *Journal of Traumatic Stress, 17*(3), 195–202.

Ozer, E.J., Best, S.R., Lipsey, T.L., & Weiss, D.S. (2003). Predictors of posttraumatic stress disorder and symptoms in adults: A meta-analysis. *Psychological Bulletin, 129*, 52–73.

Park, C. L., Cohen, L. H., & Murch, R. (1996). Assessment and prediction of stress-related growth. *Journal of Personality, 64*, 645–658.

Paton, D., Smith, L., & Violanti, J. (2000). Disaster response: Risk, vulnerability and resilience. *Disaster Prevention and Management, 9*(3), 173–180. doi: 10.1108/09653560010335068.

Perkonigg, A., Kessler, R.C., Storz, S., & Wittchen, H.-U. (2000). Traumatic events and post-traumatic stress disorder in the community: Prevalence, risk factors and comorbidity. *Acta Psychiatrica Scandinavica, 101*, 46–59.

Pitman, R.K., Sanders, K.M., Zusman, R.M., Healy, A.R., Cheema, F., Lasko, N.B. et al. (2002). Pilot study of secondary prevention of posttraumatic stress disorder with propranolol. *Biological Psychiatry, 51*, 189–192.

Polk, D.A., & Mitchell, J.T. (2009). *Prehospital behavioral emergencies and crisis response*. Sudbury, MA: Jones and Bartlett.

Prigerson, H.G., Maciejewski, P.K., & Rosenheck, R.A. (2002). Population attributable fractions of psychiatric disorders and behavioral outcomes associated with combat exposure among us men. *American Journal of Public Health, 92*(1), 59–63.

Puleo, S., & McGlothlin, J. (2010). Overview of crisis intervention. In L.R. Jackson-Cherry & Erford, B.T. (eds). *Crisis intervention and prevention*. Upper Saddle, NJ: Pearson Education, pp. 1–24.

Raimy, V. (1975). *Misunderstandings of the self: Cognitive psychotherapy and the misconception hypothesis*. San Francisco: Jossey-Bass.

Ravindran, L.N., & Stein, M.B. (2009). Pharmacotherapy of PTSD: Premises, principles, and priorities. *Journal of Brain Research, 1293*, 24–39. doi: 10.1016/j.brainres.2009.03.037.

Ripley, A. (2008). *The unthinkable: Who survives when disaster strikes and why*. New York: Crown Publishers.

Rose, S.C., Bisson, J., Churchill, R., & Wessely, S. (2002). Psychological debriefing for preventing post traumatic stress disorder (PTSD). *Cochrane Database of Systematic Reviews, 2*. doi: 10.1002/14651858.CD000560.

Schnyder, U., Wittmann, L., Friedrich-Perez, J., Hepp, U., & Moergeli, H. (2008). Posttraumatic stress disorder following accidental injury: Rule or exception in Switzerland? *Psychotherapy and Psychosomatics, 22*(2), 111–118. doi: 10.1159/000112888.

Scully, J.A., Tosi, H., & Banning, K. (2000). Life event checklists: Revisiting the social readjustment rating scale after 30 years. *Educational and Psychological Measurement, 60*(6), 864–876.

Selye, H. (1965). The stress syndrome. *The American Journal of Nursing, 65*(3), 97–99.

Shalev, A.Y. (1996). Stress versus traumatic stress: From acute homeostatic reactions to chronic psychopathology. In B.A. van der Kolk, McFarlane, A.C., & Weisaeth, L. (eds), *Traumatic stress*. New York: Guilford Press, pp. 77–101.

Tennen, H., Affleck, G., Urrows, S., Higgins, P., & Mendola, R. (1992). Perceiving control, construing benefits, and daily processes in rheumatoid arthritis. *Canadian Journal of Behavioral Science, 24,* 186–203.

Turton, S. (2005). Tend and befriend versus fight or flight: Gender differences in behavioral response to stress among university students. *Journal of Applied Biobehavioral Research, 10*(4), 209–232.

United Nations Division for the Advancement of Women (2009). *The United Nations Secretary-General's database on violence against women.* Retrieved June 2, 2010, from http://webapps01.un.org/vaw-database/advancedSearch.action.

United Nations Global Initiative to Fight Human Trafficking (2010). Publications. Retrieved June 2, 2010, from http://www.ungift.org/ungift/knowledge/publications.html

Vaiva, G., Ducrocq, F., Jezequel, K., Averland, B., Lestavel, P., Brunet, A., & Marmar, C.R. (2003). Immediate treatment with propranolol decreases posttraumatic stress disorder two months after trauma. *Biological Psychiatry, 54*(9), 947–949.

Wainrib, B.R., & Bloch, E. (1998). *Crisis intervention and trauma response: Theory and practice.* New York: Springer Publishing Company.

Williams, R., Alexander, D.A., Bolsover, D., & Bakke, F.K. (2008). Children, resilience and disasters: Recent evidence that should influence a model of psychosocial care. *Current Opinion in Psychiatry, 21*(4), 338–344.

World Health Organisation (1992). *ICD-10 classification of mental and behavioural disorders: Clinical descriptions and diagnostic guidelines.* Geneva: WHO.

World Health Organisation (2009). *EM-DAT: The international disaster database of the Centre for Reseach on the Epidemiology of Disasters.* Retrieved June 2, 2010, from http://www.emdat.be/

Yasan, A., Guzel, A., Tamam, Y., & Ozkan, M. (2009). Predictive factors for acute stress disorder and posttraumatic stress disorder after motor vehicle accidents. *Psychopathology, 42*(4), 236–241. doi: 10.1159/000218521.

17

Empowering and Transformative Practice

Karen S. Haynes

All social work is political. If you are in the USA, all you have to do is click on www.whitehouse.gov and the homepage of the White House is filled with links to advocacy, empowerment, and ways to learn to make a difference: 'The combat mission to Iraq ended: Take a moment to salute the troops'; 'HealthCare.Gov: Take health care into your own hands'; 'Help for Haiti: Learn what you can do'. Although these actions are primarily designed to enlist, empower, and engage individuals, social work not only practises the same on behalf of its clients, but, at the macro-level, empowers and transforms social work itself. This chapter suggests advocacy is at the core of social work practice and is a vital means to empowering clients. Historically, advocacy has been embedded into the values of social work and, while it has fluctuated and waned in practice during periods of prosperity, it is re-emerging as a force in the education of social workers and in their work itself.

In the first few months following the election of the first African-American President of the USA – while not a social worker, he was at least a community organiser with understanding of the core social work principles; those principles of service, social justice, the dignity and worth of persons, the importance of human relationships, integrity, and competence (www.naswdc.org) – the USA as a people had the opportunity to see what public policy might look like as reflected in those values: 'Reeling from the dark ages of social welfare policy of the past 30 years, many who serve, advocate for, or organize with low-income and marginalized populations are understandably hopeful' went one social work commentary (Pyles, 2010). Quickly, actions and plans to begin solving problems in housing, healthcare, and international relations began to take shape, starting with healthcare reform, an issue in which social workers had played a strong advocacy role for decades. In fact, the National Association of Social Workers (NASW) had written a detailed Health Plan and cost analysis for a single-payer system during the national debate on universal health care coverage in 1992 under the Clinton Administration, urging, 'progressive provider and consumer groups must organize and advocate for comprehensive national health care while the climate is right' (Mizrahi, 1992, p. 171).

In fact, the climate was *not* right in 1992. But in 2010, just 15 months after his historic inauguration, President Obama signed into law the Health Care and Education Reconciliation Act of 2010. While it was a 'bittersweet moment' for social workers – the single-payer system they supported having been rejected at the very beginning of the debate – it remained, as NASW suggested, 'a monumental legislative achievement of our time' and 'a significant step toward a comprehensive and universal health care system for our nation' (Gorin, 2010, p. 163). Advocacy as a practice for social workers could breathe a moment and celebrate bittersweet success, but if history has been any reliable indicator, work has only begun with the signatory, not ended with it.

Although *social action* is not synonymous with *political intervention*, social action strategies, when used to intervene in the affairs of government, *are* political strategies. Social workers have been influential in the political arena but politics has not consistently been a central arena for social work practice. Consequently, a historic and ongoing dynamic tension exists between the two institutions.

During the decades of professional development following World War I, the main body of social work may have turned away from reform, but social workers never totally abandoned their transformative agenda. In fact, the intensity of the debate over social reform changes with the general social climate. A lessening of disagreements among social workers on this issue not only will contribute to the unification of the profession but could also produce a multitude of interventions aimed at the formation and renovation of public policy.

No profession is in a better position to judge the impact of social policy than is social work. Although other professions direct their services toward specific problems, social work involves itself with the overall impact on both the individual *and* the community in the social issues of unemployment, inadequate healthcare, lack of education, poor housing, and insufficient income. And social workers themselves have always been uniquely qualified to become advocates. Policy affects social workers, their practice, and their clients. Social workers understand the implementation of policy and know the faces affected by lawmakers' decisions. Social workers are usually characterized as 'do-gooders' who want to help people. The political arena is where a lot of that help can begin.

Nonetheless, the social work profession has not *systematically* and *consistently* sought or been asked to take a significant role in the planning of social programmes or the formulation of social policy. Currently, there is increasing emphasis on professionalism within the field. Social workers should not be criticised for their efforts to attain professional standing because acceptance of social work as a profession is basic to achieving the legitimacy and authority necessary to meet its obligations to those it serves effectively. But the drive toward professionalism may parallel a weakening concern with social reform.

There have been societal and economic moments in recent history when social action has been de-emphasised to the point many questioned whether it really was the business of social work. For example, as early as a 1972 study of 51 US schools of social work, the majority of social work graduate students and educators did not consider social action or the initiation of social change to be a primary function of the profession (Carlton & Jung, 1972). A mid-1980s survey of US undergraduate and graduate bulletins of schools of social work found there were minimal inclusion of course titles reflecting political content or terminology (Haynes & Mickelson, 1985). A review of US Master of Social Work (MSW) programme concentrations indicated five had community organisation concentrations, two had community or social development concentrations, one had social strategies, one had social justice, and one had political social work. Therefore, fewer than 10% of accredited MSW programmes self-described anything resembling a 'politicised' social work concentration. Add to this the data that only approximately 5% of MSW students in these ten programmes were likely enrolled in these political concentrations, and it was clear we were not, in the early 21st century, preparing many political social workers (Haynes, 1996).

Generally, professional schools in the USA do not furnish training in the strategies and techniques fundamental to the effective implementation of social reform. The option of social action is simply not offered to most social work students, and the tools of advocacy are not coupled with study options even when available. In a survey by Wolk et al. (1996) among the reporting programmes, fewer than 20% of BSW and 50% of MSW programmes in the USA offered practice in government relations; fewer than 15% of Bachelor of Social Work (MSW) and 33% of MSW offered practice in policy advocacy and development; and only two BSW and no MSW programmes offered practice in electoral politics. Studies have suggested holders of BSWs and MSWs ranked social policy and social legislation as among the least important areas of knowledge and skill (Biggerstaff & Kolevzon, 1980; Figuera-McDonough, 1993).

This may be changing, however. A study by Verba et al. (1995) on citizen participation models evaluated why some people in the USA become involved in politics whereas others do not, and concluded, among other variables including religious and economic indicators, high levels of political activism were related to higher levels of education. In a study predicting social workers' levels of political participation, building from that study, Ritter (2008) found the two most significant demographic variables for social workers' political engagement were region type (urban) and membership in the NASW. Clearly, as Ritter (2008) suggests, 'this finding should promote efforts to encourage more social workers to join NASW'. This 'change' – if indeed it is a turn toward more advocacy in their practice – could be hailed as a return to the earlier social activism embedded in the founding of the profession.

Domanski (1998) provided an extensive survey of US social work practitioners' political participation conceptualised as a complex process incorporating a range of 44 separate actions that would be considered 'political' actions, classified within ten prototypes (lobbyist, voter, campaigner, collaborator, advocate, individualist, witness, activist, persuader, and communicator; see Domanski, 1998, Table 2, pp. 161–162). The baseline for these respondents' political participation came largely in communications (keeping informed on issues and engaging in discussion with family and friends) and advocacy (providing services to a group involved in social action and advocating to improve services). As survey activities required greater resources and political expertise (persuasion, negotiations, and resolution of policy problems), however, participation decreased.

A comparative study of political practitioners in South Africa, New South Wales, and New Zealand, using Domanski's prototypes and respondents of similar age and gender, showed the most common political participatory actions were in communications and voting:

> Although it is not part of political activity in social work intervention, voting is perhaps the activity most associated with politics. It is the way in which people have their say in a democracy, and it seems social workers want to make their mark (Gray et al., 2002, p. 107).

Historically, the Progressive Era (1895–1915) is often hailed as a proud moment in social work history and advocacy. Early figures in social work have been lauded for their efforts on behalf of social action, and Jane Addams frequently is chosen as a model of the 'involved' social worker. Caseworkers from charity organisations and settlement houses existing in that era have been recognised as having been in the vanguard of social reform of the time. However, even though advocacy once occupied a prominent and visible place in social casework of the time, one must also note many social workers honoured advocacy more with rhetoric or perhaps individual 'citizen participation' models than with practice or macro-level initiatives (Reisch & Andrews, 2002).

Not only was the Progressive Era a prominent time for visible social work advocacy but this was the period when social work became established as an identifiable vocation. This era was probably the liveliest period of social reform and political advocacy in the history of the social work profession, as well as in the history of the USA. Thus, it is not coincidental the social work profession began with a focus on social reform – likely a direct result of the larger societal political climate at the time.

Social work during the Progressive Era reflected two separate, interacting movements. The Charity Organization Society originated in the UK in the late 1860s and, by 1900, was well-established in every major US city and many smaller ones as well (Webb, 2007). The settlement movement, begun in the USA in the 1880s, spread just as quickly during the same time. By 1900 both of these movements were solidly established. Although their overall goals of protecting individual initiative and freedom were essentially the same, their short-range objectives and methods were quite different and frequently conflicted. The Charity Organization Society movement sought to reform on an individual level the character of those who were 'losers' in society, whereas the settlement movement worked to reform the social environment that *made* people 'losers'. The Charity Organization Society movement was not as oblivious to reform as this oversimplification might suggest, but social reform was never its dominant theme, nor was the idea of reforming an individual's character totally absent in the settlement movement (see Webb, 2007, for discussion of UK, Charity Organization Society). Case-level advocacy was prevalent within the settlement movement. Particularly in view of its espoused objective of improving living conditions, the settlement movement epitomised the idea a social agency should serve as an arena for the conversion of private troubles into public issues.

Alongside the New Deal era of the 1930s, there was a fresh wave of political involvement by US social workers. Although social action *strategies* were not necessarily well developed or formalised, the widespread recognition of social *problems* and the simultaneous identification of the public's responsibility for them provided a broad platform for public policy intervention and social work professionals. From the time of the New Deal through the 1950s, social work matured as a profession. During these years, the social casework method was refined, and ego psychology became its dominant approach. United community charities and councils were developed to provide an organised method of meeting community needs. World War II and economic resurgence re-emphasised individual dysfunction and, consequently, micro-level interventions. Social action was not a major emphasis during this period. But it began to return as an emphasis in the 1950s as professional social workers saw many of the issues that concerned them in their individual caseloads could not be dealt with through individual therapeutic methods. US social workers issued calls to undertake social action against the erosion of civil liberties under McCarthyism, against the arms race, and in support of the developing fight for civil rights. Demonstration projects sponsored by the federal government and by foundations in the 1950s and early 1960s, such as the Grey Areas Project and Mobilization for Youth, provided a testing ground for new directions in community programmes and new social work roles.

Attempts to respond to social changes during the 1950s gave rise to three models of social action in social work: (i) citizen social worker, (ii) agent of social change, and (iii) actionist. As delineated by Haynes and

Mickelson (2010), the first model, *citizen social worker*, is the oldest of the three. It called for the professional social worker to use the information and knowledge gained through work with individuals and groups to inform the larger society of needed programmes and policies. The citizen social worker confronted the problems of civil rights, international peace, equality of opportunity, expansion of social programmes, automation and mechanisation, suburbanisation, and the need for preventive services as a concerned citizen rather than as a professional obligation. The second model, *agent of social change*, developed in the late 1950s. Within this model, social action was defined as efforts toward purposeful change. The goal was to achieve desirable social goals using well-developed and well-formulated theoretical systems as guides to action. The third model, *actionist*, shared the traditional social work concern for client groups but rejected detachment, insistence on societal sanction for the profession, and the belief rational planning and cooperation were possible. Actionists believed that social change, particularly for disaffiliated people or groups, could be achieved only by developing and using political, economic, or social pressure.

The 1960s was characterised by reform ideologies and strong political movements run by the 'oppressed' themselves – the Women's Movement, the Black Panther Movement, the Gray Panthers, the Gay Liberation Movement, against a backdrop of protest and anger at the USA's involvement in Vietnam. Some of the reform ideologies and movements of the 1960s continued into the 1970s, but as the decade progressed and the War on Poverty programmes became increasingly bureaucratised, social work practice and social work education began to focus on management and administrative theories, and techniques at the expense of advocacy and reform goals. As federal monies dwindled, competition for funds increased and skills in grant writing, planning, and financial accountability took on more importance than calling on legislators and organising writing campaigns.

This shift of values hardened during the 1980s under 'Reaganomics', which emphasised low taxes, decreased economic regulation, low social service spending, and high military spending. The expansion of public and federal programmes under the 'Great Society' of the 1960s and 1970s was now blamed for increasing the federal deficit and socialist values – and for not 'curing' poverty or other social problems (see Chapter 2).

The decade of the 1990s continued with the erosion of significant human rights. With arguments and appeals to turn back affirmative action legislation, state referenda to deny benefits to illegal aliens, 'new education initiatives' seeking to provide vouchers to parents of schoolchildren, taking public funds away from public schools, and even 'ending welfare as we know it', basic human rights and human dignity became jeopardised. The values social work had always supported, and which social workers embodied even if they were not actively engaged in the political implementation of the Social Security Act, the Medicare, and Medicaid bills, the integration of neighbourhoods and public schools, and expanded opportunities and access for women and persons of colour, became threatened as endangered species.

And in the new millennium, these old policies and politics continued – moving power from the federal government to the states, giving both state and local officials great latitude to shape a full range of federal social, regulatory, and public works programmes. Debates over faith-based programmes, stem cell research, social security, and reform and privatisation prevailed. The ethos of ideologies that government (particularly federal government) is bad, returning decision making to the most local of levels is the 'American way', and reducing taxes will inherently feed the economy and make it stronger led to social fallout and failed communities social workers were expected to repair on an individual client basis. These patterns were also repeated in other parts of the world, such as the UK and Australia.

As it does today, social work historically: (i) depended on heuristic frameworks, including interventions ranging from consciousness raising to the reallocation of resources; (ii) concerned the attainment of basic needs as well as self-actualisation; and (iii) directed strategies toward individual as well as community and societal needs. Given the breadth of these targets of intervention derived from the goals of the profession, the return to a core value of advocacy as empowering and transformative practice continues to legitimise, refresh, and renew social work's role in policy formulation as well as in policy implementation (Haynes, 1996; see Chapter 47).

It seems to be increasingly difficult to retain a professional posture of political neutrality and objectivity when the political agenda is to wage war with the profession of social work and with its clients. The political choices are central to the lives of the clients and, as such, are choices about which the profession of social work ought to have a stake.

It is somewhat heartening that a 2006 US study of MSW students showed more students at graduation held a strong desire to work in core social work areas, and more felt social work should emphasise societal and institutional change over individual change (Limb & Organista, 2006). But there is as yet no professional consensus. However, others must keep the debate alive until political social work, by whatever terminology, is firmly entrenched in social work education and in social work practice.

COMPATIBILITY OF SOCIAL WORK VALUES WITH TRANSFORMATIONAL PRACTICE

As stated in the Preamble to the *NASW Code of Ethics for Social Workers*, 'social workers promote social justice and social change with and on behalf of clients. ... These activities may be in the form of direct practice, community organizing, supervision, consultation administration, advocacy, social and political action, policy development and implementation, education, and research and evaluation' (www.naswdc.org) and the International Federation of Social Workers, in its Code of Ethics, states the social work profession 'promotes social change, problem solving in human relationships and the empowerment and liberation of people to enhance well-being. Utilising theories of human behaviour and social systems, social work intervenes at the points where people interact with their environments. Principles of human rights and social justice are fundamental to social work' (www.isfw.org).

There seems to be little disagreement internationally that the founding principle of social work is related to social justice. To the extent this is and has been true, it represents a posture that redirects and reallocates resources toward a more 'just' distribution. Generally, social work has ascribed to the principle inequities in power, wealth, income, and other essential resources (e.g., healthcare) should not exist unless they work for the benefit of all, including, most importantly, the least well-off members of society. In fact, it is around this basic premise that Specht and Courtney (1994) developed their arguments that North Americans of *all* social classes – the poor and the rich alike – have a trained incapacity to see the community of which they are a part, rather than their individual attitudes, training, and motivation, as either the cause or the solution of many social problems.

Because social justice remains a valued principle within the social work profession, it would appear impossible to argue with a politicised practice, including 'advocacy, social and political action, policy development and implementation ...' and so on, for it is within the realm of budget prioritisation at the federal and, increasingly, at the state level that these decisions, which are clearly value decisions, become focused. Compatible with this social justice principle is an *advocacy-based* social change focus. But many have argued – particularly since the 1970s and into the 1990s – social work has been more concerned with enhancing the profession and less concerned with the issues of racism, sexism, poverty, and access to healthcare (Haynes, 1996, 1998; Mickelson, 1998).

Instead of framing this conflict as conservative and self-serving versus progressive and client-focused, the conflict may more likely be the middle of the two horns of the dilemma: social work practice exists *within* social institutions that, whether public or private, are established and maintained by power groups. However, there is also the view of many practitioners, administrators, policy analysts, and educators, as articulated in a 'Letter to the Editor' column of the NASW News: 'if you accept that social workers have an obligation to advance social justice and that political engagement is a means to accomplish that end, then you have to accept that we will reject conservative thought and conservative politicians' (Newdom, 1993).

A major premise of social work professionalism is objectivity or emotional neutrality. Social workers are strongly encouraged to become aware of and control the degree of their emotional involvement with clients. The development and operationalisation of this value has been said to represent the essence of the 'professional self'. Particularly in a profession such as social work in which the primary tools are the social workers themselves, emotional neutrality is required to differentiate professional exchanges from other kinds of person-to-person encounters. Without neutrality, the expertise of the social worker would not be publicly or legitimately identifiable and sanctioned.

Emotional neutrality may help the worker to continue practising without experiencing despair or 'burnout' in the face of enormous, overwhelming, and depressing social problems. At the macro-level, many decision makers (both administrators and legislators) encourage a posture of neutrality because it supports the objective collection, analysis, and presentation by social workers of 'hard data'. Although the collection and presentation of data are functions the professional must perform, restricting one's efforts to these functions may reduce one's effectiveness in being politically persuasive.

Impartiality is an essential professional value. However, like the values previously mentioned, it has a potential bias, particularly when applied to macro-level interventions. Predicated on a limited definition of injustice, impartiality can lead to unthinking support of the *status quo*, especially if equality and social justice are held to be synonymous with equality of opportunity. Doing 'nothing' – which can frequently be the result of a commitment to impartiality – is, in itself, a political act usually siding with the *status quo* (Haynes & Mickelson, 1985). For example, although social workers supported the civil rights movement and the equal opportunity legislation of the 1960s, many of these measures assumed people started off equally. These laws and the programmes they created attempted to guarantee equality of opportunity or of access without necessarily taking into account that people start life in unequal positions. In fact, measures to guarantee equal opportunity, however laudable, do not automatically guarantee equal outcomes for all.

One potentially negative consequence of emotional neutrality is it may induce social workers to deny or repress emotional experiences or reactions. The isolation and suppression of emotions, however, may only serve to thwart justifiable anger and frustration at the social inequities clearly at the root of many client problems. Thus, it may be possible for social workers to intervene with a low-income, multiproblem client and find short-term, ameliorating solutions, while at the same time ignore the anger they feel toward the societal injustices creating the client's problems. If social workers were to become aware of and to express their feelings of anger at systemic and institutional barriers and inequities, a consensus might emerge that subsequently could lead to cooperative efforts at societal reform.

In every society there is a scarcity of valued resources. As a political concept, impartiality, which has given rise to certain guarantees of equality of opportunity, may influence a more equitable distribution or redistribution of resources by randomising distribution across racial, gender, income, or geographic lines. This may promote equality of opportunity, but it does not alter the total available amount of a given resource.

Despite the importance and indeed, the *nobility* of social values, two important considerations remain: (i) an inability to operationalise these values into programmatic or legislative objectives; and (ii) the leaning of many of these values toward preservation of the status quo rather than social change. It is difficult to imagine these values are inimical to political strategies or ideologies. However, they are commonly misconstrued as being barriers to political intervention by social workers.

MODELS FOR TRANSFORMATIONAL PRACTICE

Knowledge of policy models, assessment techniques, and evaluative tools is essential for *all* social work practitioners, not only for political social work practice. The key is to have sufficient knowledge and skills to generate the self-confidence and a professional mandate to begin the policy analysis to transform practice (Burch, 1999).

Just as the caseworker chooses a model because of its appropriateness to the client's problem while taking into consideration pragmatic constraints of time, money, or situation, so too the political advocate chooses a model focusing on what appears to be the most critical area for intervention, taking into consideration whatever practical realities the environment, budgets, or political climate might dictate.

Policy models should simplify and clarify thinking about social policy and political intervention by identifying the important aspects of a policy and the targets of political intervention and by predicting policy consequences. A useful model should clearly identify the important aspects of a policy using testable concepts with commonly shared meanings. It should be able to explain phenomena, not simply describe them (Stuart, 1999). A few such representations taken from Haynes and Mickelson (2010) and much simplified here would include several models as discussed below.

The institutional model

This model focuses on policy as the *output* of governmental institutions, such as Congress, Parliament, state governments, courts, and political parties. This approach may focus on a structural examination of governmental institutions, but hopefully may go beyond that to include examination of the linkage between structural arrangements and policy content. A typical question of focus might be: How does the division of responsibilities among mental health services affect the content of social welfare policy?

The process model

This model focuses on policy as a political activity, on *how* decisions are made. Of limited use in the analysis of policy, this model is extremely useful to the strategist trying to influence policy. A typical question of focus might be: Does a congressional committee and its members assign greater weight to written testimony and expert opinion or empirical data? Knowledge of the specific types of data considered and the weight given to each might prove to be crucial information to an advocate focused on influencing the outcome of that particular congressional hearing and its legislation.

The group theory model

This model focuses on the interaction between political groups, seen through the struggle among groups to influence policy making. An advocate using this model might build coalitions with the controllers of resources or the formation of political action committees. A typical question of focus might be: If an advocacy group has limited success because of its small numbers, can it form a coalition of agencies representing multiple issues to gain the advantage of collective persuasion?

The elite theory model

This model focuses on public policy as determined by a governing elite, reflecting views belonging to the higher socioeconomic strata. It does not imply elites work against the general public's best interest, but rather it is this group who *defines* the public interest. A typical question of focus might be: How do we convince the elites of the value of the desired policy change and work with them to achieve it, including the option of getting elected to public office and *becoming* one of them?

The rational model

This model focuses on the most efficient ways to achieve the maximum benefits. It assumes costs and benefits of a particular policy can be known, all policy alternatives are available, and social values can be defined and weighed. A typical question of focus might be: How can we compile information and data to use for purposes of persuasion?

The incremental model

This model focuses on current policy as a continuation of past policies, marked only by incremental changes. It is a conservative model, using existing policies as a baseline for determining the range of possible change, but it is also less expensive in terms of time spent reviewing and projecting alternatives and the costs already invested in existing policies. A typical question of focus might be: How can we find new solutions not dramatically different from existing solutions to the same problem?

The problem-solving strategies used in any field are only as good as the theories or models available. Social work does not, however, have one model that is adequate to encompass processes and outcomes as well as the aetiology of the multitude of social problems to be addressed.

Policy evaluation usually requires a review of programmes flowing from the policy being reviewed. Consequently, the practitioner must be cautious about judging the merit of any policy on the basis of an examination of only one programme. Although evaluation has inherent limitations arising from procedures, such as generalising findings, policy evaluation is nonetheless superior to judgements made simply on the basis of political expediency, intuition, or organisational pragmatics. The merit of a particular programme might be measured through examination of that one programme. Still, the success of a particular policy is best determined by multiple programme analyses (see Chapter 28).

To focus on effort as the primary criterion by which to judge the success of a policy means to collect information about what it takes to deliver the policy in terms of staff, equipment, buildings, and so forth. As policies are translated into administrative regulations and procedures, quality control measures often are included. This may be done through separate legislation on accreditation or licensure. In either case, the basic thrust is similar: to evaluate the policy or programme on the basis of the quality of services rendered. Measures of quality focus not on 'how much?' but rather on 'what kind?' To measure a policy's effectiveness, one would ask the central question, 'To what extent are the policy and programme goals being met?' This may be the most useful type of information about a policy's impact, but it also can be the most difficult to gather. Programmes often operationalise shorter-term goals, leaving the achievement of the long-term policy goal to be inferred. For example, although the goal of detoxification might be to reduce alcohol consumption permanently, the measurable indicator might be taken at the point of termination from the programme rather than several years later. When the primary focus of an evaluation is on cost relative to effectiveness, efficiency is the criterion being used.

While in the USA, social work approaches have not taken a radical turn (Reisch & Andrews, 2002), internationally, the profession has continuously attempted to develop transformative models of practice. In particular, critical social work, originating from earlier UK radical perspectives, has gained much currency. According to Gray and Webb (2008), critical social work

> seeks social transformation as forms of justice and emancipation ... [It] seeks to explain and transform various circumstances that social workers and service users find themselves in, while connecting this to a structural analysis of those aspects of society that are oppressive, unjust and exploitive. In this respect, [it] emerged in connection with various intellectual movements, including feminism, race theory, and postcolonial criticism, that identified dimensions of economic and political domination in modern societies (p. 77).

SOCIAL WORKERS AS CHANGE AGENTS AND TRANSFORMERS

As discussed in the beginning of this chapter, social workers are ideally situated to the practice of empowering and transforming social justice. The general social work practitioner is usually equipped with the framework and variety of roles encouraging intervention at the micro- and macro-level, from case (individual) to class (group) advocacy. As also discussed, the general social work practitioner lays claim to a set of values and ethics embedded into the very nature of the work and professionalism of the field of social work. However, not all social work practitioners have the repertoire of knowledge and skills to transform social problems and their solutions from case or micro-level to political interventions. This skill set does not necessarily add additional tasks to the practitioner's role or require the learning of new skills. Activism and class advocacy consists primarily of information dissemination and client empowerment strategies.

Social workers, practising in a variety of settings (hospitals, juvenile homes, the courts, public schools, mental health clinics, and so forth), are in a position to respond quickly and authoritatively when asked about the major difficulties they face in serving clients: lack of time to help people adequately, too large a caseload, and insufficient resources. Each practitioner is an expert on problems, needs, and resources. Clearly, therefore, the practitioner can become an ideal conduit between those who have problems and needs and those who are politically active. Social workers are also good resources for what works. Unfortunately, this invaluable information is not made available at the class advocacy level often enough because the practitioner's knowledge and expertise usually remain at the case level. The missing link to bridge the gap is to aggregate the individual practitioner's diagnoses and data into the meta-information necessary to function in the political sphere (see Chapter 4).

The practitioner can pull together case statistics and scenarios clarifying, expanding, or redefining a problem area in ways an information system cannot. If practitioners become imbued with the idea they have a unique and essential role in the documentation of needs, problems, and resources, they will not only find the usual task of 'paper pushing' less cumbersome, but will also discover this activity becomes essential as part of the political process. Transformative practice may include direct political activism, but the process also includes the foundational task of documentation of the problem and what works.

Because information systems are initiated to serve either agency documentation or clinical diagnostic needs, it is not surprising the use of these for political testimony, legislative support, or administrative rule writing and programme implementation may appear to be an afterthought. However, documentation is a primary step in any problem-solving process in social work, and systems should be designed for multiple purposes, including clinical, administrative, and political activities. Social work staff at all levels should be able not only to input data but also to manipulate it to create categories and groupings answering many questions, problems, and needs in various dimensions.

Presentation at a legislative hearing or testimony using scenarios can have a major impact. Because the practitioner has access to clients who may be affected by a current or future policy, testimony can be enhanced by the inclusion of documented statistics, scenarios, and case illustrations, as well as by the presence of the clients themselves. The practitioner may speak on a client's behalf or have the clients speak for themselves. Either of these tactics can be used in a highly persuasive manner.

Testimony by both the practitioner and the client is an extremely dynamic lobbying tool and is most dramatically done by the practitioners and clients directly affected. It may be more persuasive than the most expensive lobbyist, who, after all, must rely on secondary sources, such as aggregate data or 'second-hand' stories. Thus, the client or social worker who can present facts, personal vignettes, and scenarios, and who also is a constituent, can play a significant role for clients and in major policy settings it is a role no other individual or group can fill.

Expert witnesses are usually called by invitation, and the expert must hold certain credentials – educational or experiential – to be deemed 'expert'. Sometimes legislators will undertake trips to seek information, witness events, or experience a particular social problem so they can themselves provide this first-hand type of information. The role of expert usually excludes clients because the term often implies possession of specific educational credentials and a breadth of professional experience.

Writing letters to legislators is an important professional role practitioners can fill within the construct of their practice. Many practitioners do not realise the potential impact of one letter from a professional, but legislators and their committees understand the value of succinct, knowledgeable education and recommendations from experts working in the field. Many professional organisations, such as the NASW and the Council on Social Work Education in the USA, have staff who review and anticipate important legislation in the field and who provide – via their websites and newsletters – assistance and information on these issues and how to write effective and helpful letters to legislators and legislative hearings and committees.

Inherent in the general social work practitioner's functions is the role of enabler or advocate. Although the advocate role is most commonly used with individual clients to move from case to class, advocacy requires no additional skills other than the ability to aggregate data or mobilise clients. Community organisers build on these basic principles as a practice specialisation, but specialisation is not necessarily required.

Practitioners are also in a central position to identify and evaluate the effects of legislative policies on their organisations and to determine whether the rule-writing and implementation phases have been logically interpreted and consistently followed. This is an important, but rarely used aspect of advocacy – following up on the intent of the law with its effect and implementation – but an important piece that can be an effective part of a practitioner's practice.

It is consistent with social work principles to assist clients in exercising their democratic right to self-determination. Certainly one way to do this is to assist in voter registration. In the USA, voter registration is legal as long as it in nonpartisan. Social workers and human service agencies with a tax-exempt status can participate in nonpartisan voter registration.

It should be evident that the practices and processes advocated throughout this chapter are already in place and part of the intrinsic fabric of social work. They require only the ability – and desire – of the social work professional to translate them from the micro- to the macro-level arena of practice. Furthermore, such intervention in the policy or political arena need not be direct. Repackaging existing information in a slightly different manner and enlisting other individuals in coalition building or problem identification may be all that is necessary. The empowerment of clients may be strategically used or may occur as an outgrowth of other activities. In either case, it is a core social work principle, not an ancillary function.

Advocacy is not a straightforward presentation of all positions on an issue, nor does it have as a goal the enhancement of influence or position. Advocacy is a legitimate, fundamental, and powerful practice in a pluralistic society. There are myths about the political process often discouraging social workers from participating in it as class advocates. One myth is social workers need specialised training in the political process before they can intervene. Specifically, studies have suggested social workers, while more likely to vote, contact legislators by letters or phone, and belonging to organisations taking public stands, are less likely to engage in more direct political behaviours, such as volunteering for a political campaign, contributing financially to a campaign, or testifying before a legislative committee (Andrews, 1998).

Because the US political structure is both representative and pluralistic, it requires, and even demands, some individuals speak on behalf of others and opposing groups resolve conflicts. The very nature of the political process is one of individual interaction, and this clearly implies the importance of social work skills.

Social workers are trained to understand how individuals relate and interact, how groups form and change, how miscommunication can alienate people from each other and from society, and how motivation affects behaviour. These are the resources unique to social work advocacy. Social workers can use this knowledge and their corresponding skills to understand and to intervene in the political process.

There is a great deal one person can do to make programmatic changes and policy changes using the skills of lobbying. With their training and experience in community organising, advocacy, budgeting, planning, and evaluating, social workers already have the basis on which to build the skills necessary to affect change at this larger scale. The old saying 'there is power in numbers' is exactly the message of advocacy. The greater the number and diversity of individuals who are united in support of a policy, the greater the likelihood of making the change.

Organising others is important because social developments are part of a total economic and political system – a political economy in which all strands of life, from the national to local level, intertwine with each other (see Chapter 5). Most problems contemporary communities face manifest themselves at the neighbourhood level but result from city, state, national, and even international factors. Truly one person can start a movement – but a movement embraces many such individuals.

The purpose of monitoring the bureaucracy is to ensure the intent of the legislation is carried out. While specifics will change by country of origin as well as level of bureaucracy, in general the social work lobbyist needs to monitor four areas after a bill has been passed: (i) promulgation of rules; (ii) implementation and adherence to the rules by agencies; (iii) the budget allocation process; and (iv) executive orders and administrative changes. It should not be confused with lobbying per se. Monitoring is the process of keeping a watchful eye on the government to see the legislative intent is carried out, whereas lobbying is the act of influencing legislation. Monitoring and lobbying have some elements in common, yet they are distinctly different activities. It is important for the social worker to understand certain formal and informal steps related to policy adoption and implementation apply to all levels of government: (i) rule-writing and promulgation; (ii) rule implementation; and (iii) budget allocation. In addition, one must be aware of the importance of executive orders and other administrative changes subsequently affecting programme implementation.

Rule-making and rule-implementing processes require consistent monitoring in order to ensure the intent of the law is carried out and the clients targeted by the legislation receive mandated services. Because elected officials, agency staff, public opinion, and society's needs change, social workers must monitor from both outside and inside the bureaucracy. They also need to use social work skills to ensure programme goals and services remain appropriate. Although this type of ongoing monitoring can be difficult and tedious, it is nevertheless essential and is quite compatible with social work skills as well. The same basic problem-solving approach social workers use with clients can be employed in monitoring a programme: Identify the problem, gather information, make an assessment, and develop a plan of action.

Monitoring all of these stages takes time and a great deal of patience and is probably the most detail-oriented of the political interventive techniques, yet it is a necessary step to ensure the original intent of a piece of legislation is indeed implemented. The affect an individual can have on the outcome may be even greater than during the initial legislative process. This is not to say lobbying for the passage of a bill is not necessary, but many mistakenly think once a bill is signed, no further advocacy is necessary.

Innumerable skills carry over easily from social work practice to campaigning, the most obvious being communication skills. Social workers are trained to meet people, listen to their problems, and help them find solutions. Caseloads, lack of time, and lack of familiarity with political campaigns are reasons why social workers do not get involved in campaigns. Ultimately, though, through election of sympathetic officials, the social worker's clientele will benefit.

The most important skills a social worker can contribute to a campaign are in the area of interpersonal relationships and listening skills. These can be used in many facets of a campaign, for example, in canvassing a neighbourhood for support of the candidate or in working with campaign volunteers and with the candidate.

PRESCRIPTIONS FOR ACTION

Empowering and transforming practice is about affecting change, moving from case to class advocacy on behalf of the clients social workers serve. Social work *is* about affecting changes in clients, community, and systems: it is a challenge to think of a social work activity policy does not affect. Policies – federal, state, local, and organisational – affect social work practice in private non-profits as well as in public agencies. Policies in those settings influence the kind of clients who can be served, the amount of fees that can be charged, and the alternative solutions that can be offered.

Consequently, social workers have the choice of either affecting change or allowing policies to affect their ability to help their clients. Social work is not apolitical but inherently part of the political process. And, as the historical overview of the profession may have indicated, the time continues to be ripe for community organisers and social workers to step forward. Times of crisis open the doors for transformation, and that time is now.

Advocacy starts with the education of social workers. In addition to the practice of clinical skills, social work students need to develop advocacy skills through such 'homework assignments' as learning how a bill becomes a law, learning who their elected officials are and the distinction among city, state, and federal issues, finding out how one registers to vote and how they can get others to register, and volunteering to work on political campaigns. Building those skills from the beginning of building a portfolio of practice skills will develop the confidence to use *all* of those skills in the practice of social work.

Educators in social work schools need to 'walk the talk' as well. They must become 'advocates of advocacy' and engage in transforming educational practice with advocacy on behalf of the students they serve and teach as well as, ultimately, the clients they will go on to serve.

Advocacy continues with practitioners. Practitioners must register to vote – and then vote. They must monitor the news on issues governmental bodies are addressing and think about what is *not* being addressed. They can send their letters stating their opinions on how their representatives should vote or how they could better address an issue. They can find fellow social workers to team up with on an issue and share what each other has learnt. All of this creates empowering and transformative practice in social work.

This chapter concludes with several general actions that will begin to affect change in the profession and of the practitioners themselves.

You can make a difference. It is easy to become cynical or helpless in the face of 'unsolvables' – poverty, physical abuse, chemical dependency, and educational achievement gaps. Do not give in. Rather, take your finely tuned skills of diagnosis, assessment and goal setting and begin where the work is doable. Do not be overwhelmed. Remember: you are affecting change for the good.

Just say no. You don't have to take it when changes in policies and regulations mean your practice – in quality, principle, or philosophy – is jeopardised. Whether in privatised models, budget reshaping, or agency downsizing, you can too easily be co-opted to the detriment of quality client services and professionals standards by taking professional roles and converting them to volunteer jobs; by agreeing to higher caseloads; and by cutting technology or professional development from your agency budgets.

Speak out. Advocacy is not just for one day at the legislature, or one letter or telephone call to your local elected officials. You can speak out in elevators, checkout counters, social settings, and social networking. Whenever you hear misinformation and myths, challenge them. If they go unchallenged, stereotyping goes, and only one side is providing the information.

Get angry. There are injustices that hurt humans. There are people who are either ignorant of the issues or inhuman and uncaring – or both. Anger is confrontational, but that is okay. Advocacy is not for wimps. Sometimes it takes courage and confrontation. Sometimes it takes not being 'nice', angering someone. It is justified when the cause is good. Advocacy is not just head work. It is the fire in your gut. It is not just having the facts. It is having the passion to get angry.

Just as important as getting angry is to *keep your sense of humour*. Advocacy can be as erratic, crazy-making, perplexing, and discouraging at the class level of working to affect change as it has always been at the case level. It is all right to take a rest, find new ways of working old systems of change, or even to slip into the background for a while. Over the years, you will deal with many political leaders who are less than supportive to human needs and services, while working in a profession accepting and encouraging political action and affecting change.

There *is* a window of opportunity in these highly political, hyperpartisan, and media-saturated times to both do the work and pass the torch of affecting change to the new generation of social workers. There *is* a window of opportunity to take up the cause, move the profession along, and use your social work skills in the political arena to help others. And that time is *now*.

REFERENCES

Andrews, A.B. (1998). An exploratory study of political attitudes and acts among child and family services workers. *Children and Youth Services Review, 20*(5), 435–461.

Biggerstaff, M.A., & Kolevzon, M.S. (1980). Differential use of social work knowledge, skills, and techniques by MSW, BSW, and BA level practitioners. *Journal of Education for Social Work, 16*(3), 67–74.

Burch, H.A. (1999). *Social welfare policy analysis and choices.* Binghamton, NY: Haworth Press.

Carlton, T.O., & Jung, M. (1972). Adjustment or change: Attitudes among social workers. *Social Work, 17*(6), 64–71.

Domanski, M.D. (1998). Prototypes of social work political participation: An empirical model. *Social Work, 43*(2), 156–167.

Figuera, M.J. (1993). Policy practice: The neglected side of social work interventions. *Social Work, 38*(2), 179–188.

Gorin, S.H. (2010). The patient protection and affordable care act, cost control, and the battle for health care reform. *Health and Social Work, 35*(3), 163–166.

Gray, M., & Webb, S.A. (2008). Critical social work. In Gray, M., & Webb, S.A. (eds), *Social work theories and methods.* London: Sage.

Gray, M., Collett van Rooyen, C.A.J., Rennie, G., & Gaha, J. (2002). The political participation of social workers: A comparative study. *International Journal of Social Welfare,* 11(2), 99–110.

Haynes, K.S. (1996). The future of political social work. In P.R. Raffoul & McNeece, C.A. (eds), *Future issues for social work practice.* Boston: Allyn & Bacon, pp. 266–276.

Haynes, K.S. (1998). The one hundred year debate. *Social Work, 48*(6), 501–509.

Haynes, K.S., & Mickelson, J.S. (1985). Social policy: The hidden power base. Paper presented at the *Council of Social Work Education Annual Program Meeting,* Washington, DC.

Haynes, K.S., & Mickelson, J.S. (2010). *Affecting change: Social workers in the political arena* (7th ed.). Boston: Allyn & Bacon.

Limb, G.E., & Organista, K.C. (2006). Change between entry and graduation in MSW student view of social work's traditional mission, career motivations, and practice preferences: Caucasian, student of color, and American Indian group comparisons. *Journal of Social Work Education, 42*(2), 269–290.

Mickelson, J. (1998). Advocacy. In *Encyclopedia of social work* (19th ed.). Washington, DC: NASW Press.

Mizrahi, T. (1992). Toward a national health care system: Progress and problems. *Health and Social Work, 17*(3), 167–171.

Newdom, F. (2003). On politics and values. National Association of Social Workers News, *48*(4), 3.

Pyles, L. (2010). Global justice in the time of Obama: A call to organize. *Social Work, 55*(1), 90–92.

Reisch, M., & Andrews, J. (2002). *The road not taken: A history of radical social work in the United States.* New York: Brunner-Routledge.

Ritter, J. (2008). A national study predicting licensed social workers' levels of political participation: The role of resources, psychological engagement and recruitment networks. *Social Work, 53*(4), 347–357.

Specht, H., & Courtney, M. (1994). *Unfaithful angels: How social work has abandoned its mission.* New York: Free Press.

Stuart, P.H. (1999). Linking clients and policy: Social work's distinctive contribution. *Social Work, 44*(4), 335–347.

Verba, S., Schlozman, K.L., & Brady, H.E. (1995). *Voice and equality: Civic voluntarism in American politics.* Cambridge, MA: Harvard University Press.

Webb, S.A. (2007). The comfort of strangers: The emergence of social work in Late Victorian England (Part One), *European Journal of Social Work, 10*(1), 39–54.

Wolk, J., Pray, J.E., Weismiller, T., & Dempsey, D. (1996). Political practice: Educating social work students for policymaking. *Journal of Social Work Education, 32*(1), 91–100.

are reshaping the organisational contexts in which social workers practice, which are increasingly characterised by centralised services, managerialism, and auditing and performance monitoring.

In this managerial environment, delivering social work at a community level becomes increasingly challenging. However, this chapter argues that working closer to residents' daily lives in the community would enhance effectiveness, address concerns about declining social capital, and assist the public to understand and appreciate the social worker's role (Stepney & Popple, 2008). Among other advantages, community practice strengthens community norms for engagement; deepens commitment and removes barriers and constraints to change; draws upon local strengths, affiliations, and networks; engages the informal and formal sectors by encouraging community groups to explore possible organisational alliances, liaisons and coalitions, to gather valuable organisational resources and assets for their chosen campaigns (Lee, 1999; Lee & Todd, 2006).

DISCOURSES ON THE MEANING OF 'COMMUNITY'

There is much talk about community in common parlance. Much contemporary thinking about community stems from the Judaeo-Christian theological tradition. In all of the medieval lexicons, the lemma *communitas* is deeply associated with the concept of 'belonging' in its contemporary subjective and objective meaning. However, of all the concepts deployed to characterise, organise, and ground social and political life, the concept of community seems to be one of the most challenging and, until recent times, has been largely neglected by social and political theorists. Raymond Plant (1978) noted that other concepts, such as citizenship, freedom, democracy, rights, and justice, have been subjects of sustained and penetrating analyses.

As Webb (2011) observes the notion of community is central to discussions of public policy and is widely used to legitimate almost any valued social achievement. When the term is used in public discourse, it is used not only to describe or to refer to a range of normative aspects of social life but also to put those aspects into a favourable perspective. Community is presented as a 'social ideal'. It is normatively valued or regarded as a valuable achievement variously through 'community action', 'community development', 'community care', 'community education', 'community planning', 'community empowerment', 'community capacity building', and 'community engagement' (Plant, 1978, p. 79). Raymond Williams (1983) suggests it is a highly 'contestable concept':

> Community can be the warmly persuasive word to describe an existing set of relationships, or ... to describe an alternative set of relationships. What is most important, perhaps, is that unlike all other terms of social organization (state, nation, society, etc.) it seems never to be used unfavourably, and never to be given any positive opposing or distinguishing term (p. 76).

It is for this reason that connotations of the term 'community' can be used to give a positive polish or spin to groups and organisations (Webb, 2009).

In recent times, there has emerged a new wave of radical thought in political philosophy focusing on the nature of community by thinkers such as Jean Luc Nancy, Georgio Agamben, and Roberto Esposito. This thinking challenges the normative concept of community as harmony, solidarity, and a shared sense of place or common bonding experience.

In his influential *The Inoperative Community*, Jean Luc Nancy (1991) lays out a compelling new ontological set of understandings for community which do not rest on unification or harmony and cannot be the fusion of separate subjects into a homogenous whole, nor a movement towards a 'common goal': 'The community that becomes a single thing (body, mind, fatherland, Leader ...)

necessarily ... yields its being-together to a being *of* togetherness' (p. xxxix). A single community, formed of impersonal, homogenised individuals, is untenable within Nancy's thesis. For Nancy, community is instead the existence of a 'Being-in-Common'. The key consideration, which Wittgenstein importantly addressed is, what is 'to be with'. But the 'with' already implies a proximity and distance, a joining but at the same time a removal from the other. For Nancy this is the core of the question of community. Thus community does not have a common being, a common substance, but consists in 'being-in-common'. It is a sharing. So by *common*, Nancy does not denote a uniform substance that binds separate individuals, but rather a 'shared experience'. He characterises community through the sharing of what takes place in the face of the 'terminations and boundaries' of finitude: through 'birth, death, and alterity' (in Prestidge-King, 2005, p. 87). It is in this respect that the 'limit and difference' of social interaction is found.

Esposito (2010) concurs with Nancy, claiming that community is embedded and lived in the communal, by that which is not our own, indeed that which begins where 'my own' subjectivity ends. Hence the idea that communal living is emblematic of a 'shared lack' among members. In developing Nancy's thesis he finds, however, three further meanings of *communitas*, all associated with the term from which it originates: the Latin *munus*. As Campbell (2008) summarises: 'The first two meanings of *munus* – *onus* and *officium* – concern obligation and office, while the third centres paradoxically on the term *donum*, which Esposito glosses as a form of gift that combines features of the previous two' (p. x). Esposito (2008) underscores the specific tonality of this communal *donum* to mark out not simply any gift or donation but a category of gift that necessitates, even demands, an exchange in return: 'Once one has accepted the *munus*', Esposito (2008) writes, then 'one is obliged to return the *onus*, in the form of either goods or services (*officium*)'. *Munus* is, therefore, a much stronger and more intense form of *donum* because it requires a subsequent response from the receiver. Unlike *donum*, *munus* subsequently marks 'the gift that one gives, not the gift that one receives', 'the contractual obligation one has *vis-à-vis* the other' and, finally, 'the gratitude that *demands* new donations' on the part of the recipient. As Campbell (2008) observes: 'Here Esposito's particular declension of community becomes clear: thinking community through *communitas* will name the gift that keeps on giving, a reciprocity in the giving of a gift that doesn't, indeed cannot, belong to oneself' (p. xxi). This debt or obligation of gift operates as a sort of originary defect for all those belonging to a community. In drawing on this perspective to consider its implications for social work, Webb (2011) notes that the nature of social interaction thus rests on a presupposed excess of communal gift giving. This has the net effect of the risk of conflict being inscribed at the very heart of community, consisting as it does in a perpetual form of negotiated interaction. Esposito (2008) summarises this as follows:

> If the members of the communitas are joined together by the same law, by the duties or gift [dono] that they have to give – which is what precisely munus means – immunis is instead he who is exempt or exonerated from them: he who does not have obligations with respect to the other and who can therefore conserve entirely his own proper essence [sostanza] as subject who is owner of himself (p.15).

This new way of conceiving community has far-reaching implications for policy and practice interventions. If the normative conception of community is misleading and the ontological foundation of community rests on a shared sense of lack articulated in a perpetual but tense process of negotiation as gift, donation, and exchange, a radical rethink of community engagement and empowerment is required. It suggests that social work agencies and local government require the undertaking of social impact assessments as a regular and ongoing aspect of policy formation and evaluation (Mowbray, 2004).

At the same time, it begs questions about how social work and local government generate social capital. There are also significant implications for community action and violence. Webb (2011) provocatively argues that the August 'Battle for London' riots in predominantly Black areas of Tottenham and Hackney might be understood through the lens of Esposito's (2008) characterisation of community. Here community is dramatically cast as a field of exhaustive exchange claims set against the State police force, which attempts to immunise itself against excessive community demands through the rule of law. The 'shared lack' in this case is the effect of the killing of a young Black man by the police, which valorises conditions of poverty, inequality, and injustice via the platform of riot as the signifier of community exhortation. Webb (2011) notes 'this new ontological mode of conceiving of community opens up a space of reflection for social work in which political themes and concerns obtain a fresh practical weight and urgency' (p. 8). The important related political themes of neoliberalism and globalisation as outlined in the next section form the political backdrop in which a return to community is invoked via the UK policy of Big Society.

NEOLIBERAL GLOBALISATION AND ITS IMPACT ON LOCAL COMMUNITIES

The impact of neoliberal globalisation is visible in the emergence of global power structures, such as the World Bank, International Monetary Fund, and United Nations, which are instituting structural adjustment programmes that impact negatively on poor countries and marginalised communities. Neoliberal globalisation has produced significant and far-reaching challenges for governments, communities, and individuals, and led to significant changes to relationships at the local and global level. It has reshaped community life. Before examining the changes communities have undergone, these wider economic, political, and social forces reshaping local communities is considered. Neoliberal globalisation, which has refashioned world affairs over the last 30 years, is a combination of two forces, though many argue they are merely different sides of the same coin (O'Hara, 2005).

Globalisation generally refers to the spread of global capitalism through deregulating and opening up markets for competition globally; reducing the role of the nation state in economic affairs; reducing tariffs and subsidies for business; dismantling restrictions to foreign direct investment; and deregulating exchange rates to enable prices to reflect market processes. As a result, regional economies have become increasingly integrated through trade, communication, and transportation, linked through flows of capital, labour, and technology. Large multinational corporations, such as Coca-Cola, Colgate-Palmolive, General Motors, Mitsubishi, Wal-Mart, Volkswagen, and large financial institutions, such as Barclays and HSBC, have played a major part in this regional integration and account for two-thirds of world trade (Held et al., 1999). According to *Fortune* (2006), 500 of these multinational corporations had revenue much larger than most countries. For example, Exxon Mobil collected more revenue in 2005–2006 than individual countries like South Africa, Saudi Arabia, Norway, and Turkey.

Massive media organisations, such as the BBC and CNN, have played a major role in the communication, transmission, and shaping of ideas, cultures, and opinions leading to Canadian philosopher and scholar Marshall McLuhan's idea of the world as a 'Global Village' in which the media facilitates a high degree of integration and sharing of common interests among the world's population (McLuhan & Powers, 1992). He optimistically predicted this sharing of humanity would lead to international cooperation and determination to address problems of mutual concern.

The antiglobalisation movement, however, claims that the concentration of economic power – wealth and influence – in multinational corporations has increased poverty, inequality, and injustice, eroded traditional cultures, and produced a brand-name fetish (Klein, 2000). It has, for example, pointed to the power of the multinational News International Corporation which, until recently, has controlled nearly 40% of British news outlets through its newspaper and broadcast enterprises in the UK.

The antiglobalisation movement is a broad collection of new social movements, pressure groups, social activists, individuals, and organisations, some of which argue for reformist or moderate forms of capitalism, while others advocate a new way of working and living that secures greater equality of life chances for people throughout the world (Cohen & Rai, 2000). Many of these advocators argue that adherence to neoliberal economic policies has damaged the environment and led to the major problems now facing communities everywhere, such as pollution and climate change.

Neoliberalism refers to an economic policy that advocates labour deregulation; deregulation of financial and commodity markets; reduction of budget deficits; privatisation of government services; and cuts in government spending, especially on welfare. Its core premise is 'the market is pre-eminent at producing and distributing goods and services, is best at rewarding managers and workers and is more efficient than the state or bureaucratic planning' (Stepney & Popple, 2008, p. 36). Its advocates argue the economic free market drives the efficient production and distribution of goods and services and, to maintain this approach, government intervention, support, and regulation needs to be kept to a minimum. Calling for a lessening or removal of minimum wage regulations and challenging labour laws, neoliberal economists argue free trade enables countries and their citizens to benefit and prosper:

> [Hence] neoliberal globalisation is attacked for being an extreme philosophy subject to major error and analytical shortcomings. Globalisation is attacked for promoting cultural destruction, financial instability, global inequality, unfair/unhealthy labor conditions, transnational corporate control, and Western (especially US) hegemony in the global economy. Its twin, neoliberalism, is similarly attacked for ignoring public goods and system functions, for reducing the material standard of living of working people, for promoting corporate crises through insufficient governance, and for also leading to inadequate global effective demand (O'Hara, 2005, p. 341).

Detractors of neoliberal globalisation point to rising inequalities at the national and global level (World Bank, 2008). The UN Human Development Report (UN Development Programme; UNDP, 2007) indicated that 40% of the world's population lived on less than US$2 a day, which accounted for 5% of global income. At the other end of the scale, the wealthiest 20% of the world's population enjoyed 75% of global income with the richest 1% receiving as much income as the poorest 57%. Supporters argue the world's population is becoming more affluent and this is leading to improvements in the living standards of the poorest and reductions in illiteracy and infant deaths and malnutrition (UN, 2007). However, many of the improvements are in high and middle-income countries. Despite the economic boom in the world's richest countries in the 1990s, the poorest became poorer due to the impact of famine, political conflict, and the AIDS pandemic, particularly in sub-Saharan Africa (UNDP, 2003). The UN World Food Programme (UNWFP, 2001) estimated that 830 million people went hungry every day and 95% of these were in developing countries.

In the UK, there has been a shift of income from the bottom to the top earners. In 1979, the richest 20% received 35% of income. By 2008–2009, they received 43%. Correspondingly, for the same years, the poorest 20% received 9.6% of income in 1979 and by 2008–2009 this had dropped to 7% (UK Department for Work and Pensions, 2010). At the same time, wealth is increasingly concentrated in fewer hands. According to the 2011 UK Rich List (*Sunday Times*, 2011), the 1000 multimillionaires in the list were

£60.2 billion wealthier than they were in 2010, an 18% rise. Internationally, the pattern is the same. The 50 wealthiest people in the world in 2011 were worth a combined £843.7 billion, up 11.7% on 2010.

THE CHANGING NATURE OF COMMUNITY

So what is the impact of all this on communities? Pertinent to the present discussion, neoliberal globalisation impacts on community through rising individualism and expanding consumerism, and diminishing trust and solidarity and declining social capital.

Rising individualism and declining social capital

Putman (2000) found diminishing sources of social capital among the US population. By social capital he meant the social connections and knowledge that helps people achieve their ambitions and goals, and extends their power and influence collectively. Social capital binds people in their civic and community or neighbourhood life. Putman's (2000) conclusion was based on his finding that, over the previous 25 years, attendance at club meetings had fallen by 58%, family dinners were down by 33%, and having friends visit at home had fallen by 45%. He cited a number of reasons for this diminished social contact, including the fact that women, who have traditionally actively engaged more in neighbourhood and community affairs than men, were more likely to be employed in the labour force than previously. Putman also attributed the decline in community activity to people's disillusionment with politics. However, this latter point is not entirely borne out in the UK where there has been understandable cynicism about parliamentary politics since the British MPs and House of Lords expenses scandals of 2009 and 2010. The right-wing social and economic policies of the present Conservative–Liberal Democratic Coalition Government have met with fierce public opposition through major demonstrations and active campaigns reflecting people's determination to play an active part in influencing policies and bring about change [see, e.g., the work of the organisation '38 degrees', which, through a small team of staff and many volunteers, has successfully organised petitions and engaged in activities that have influenced political decision making in the UK (www.38degrees.org.uk)]. Halpern (2005) observed increasing social capital in Sweden, Japan, and the Netherlands, and decreasing social capital in the UK and Australia, while confirming Putman's (2000) findings in relation to the USA.

Putman (2000) attributed the main decline in community and civic engagement to the impact of television which had led to people spending time alone or with others watching programmes rather than being involved in community and neighbourhood activities. However, Putnam's critics argue that new technologies have increased rather than decreased people's contact with one another. Young people, especially, are relating to each other through social networking sites in the process creating dynamic new communities (Chambers, 2006; Kraut et al., 2006). This development is not restricted to the wealthy or to those living in developed countries as the fastest growing market for mobile phones is in Africa, where sophisticated computer access is available mainly to more affluent urban communities.

As noted above, Western understandings of community are constantly shifting but there remains a tendency to glorify community rather than see the ill that can be done in the name of community or the negative effects of community solidarity. Somerville (2011) epitomises the glorification of community when he says it is about

> connectedness among persons, and the connectedness has to be meaningful to the persons concerned – there has to be a substantive grouping or collectively with which those persons can be identified (by themselves and by others), with the

possibility of recognition of one another as being members of it (Somerville, 2011, p. 7).

Normative sociological perspectives on community focus on either aspects of cultural identity in terms of difference and a sense of belonging, or its relation to social capital as trust and networks of affiliation (Bryson & Mowbray, 2005; Gray, 2010, 2011; Gray & Mubangizi, 2010). Social capital is a vogue concept with a good deal of traction in public policy. In government policy, community refers to a non-institutional context and is identified in terms of geographical location or residence, with the focus being on marginalised or disadvantaged communities requiring targeted intervention. Community in the community work literature is often defined in terms of 'communities of interests' linked – or networked – through religion, ethnicity, class, gender, culture, or occupation. In the UK, two competing discourses are associated with community: Moral communitarianism and community activism.

Moral communitarianism

The growth of communitarianism in Western social policy coincided with the growing disillusionment and concern among the political Left that neoliberal economic policies failed to address the problems created by rampant individualism and neoliberal globalisation (see earlier). The work of Putman (2000), Etzioni (1995), and others pointed to the importance of programmes to maintain and increase social cohesion so as to avoid community breakdown. Communitarianism was epitomised in the UK's New Labour campaign in disadvantaged estates to create a 'new' consensus around 'social inclusion'. Communitarianism was part of New Labour's Third Way programme from 1997 to 2010 wherein poverty was relabelled social exclusion to denote the marginalisation of disadvantaged groups and 'hide' the fact that they were poor. Community interventions – and social services generally – were, in Third Way discourse, about social inclusion – bringing marginalised groups and communities into the mainstream, mainly though making them economically active. Putman's (2000) findings above were used to support New Labour's establishment of the Social Exclusion Unit (SEU), which was in operation from 1997 to 2006 when it merged with the Prime Minister's Strategy Unit. The SEU highlighted the role of community regeneration in addressing poverty. Community regeneration meant bringing people into mainstream society through targeted community-based schemes and welfare-to-work programmes and 'participation in the mainstream' meant being in paid employment (see Chapter 2). The SEU tackled five areas of concern: unemployment, health, crime, education, and housing. A key feature of the government's approach was individual attainment and success in the market economy by building people's capacity through local community involvement (Gray, 2010; Popple, 2007). Responsibility was devolved on to the family and community as public services were streamlined to make way for greater efficiency (Gray, 2010; Harris, 2003).

Thus communitarianism was associated with the neoliberal cuts to welfare, which resulted in an increased discourse about family and community self-reliance; the community – private sector – had to join with or partner government so all citizens – community members – could become active, contributing, participating citizens in a revitalised democracy. This discourse has become further entrenched by the present UK Coalition Government, which was elected in May 2010, and its 'Big Society' programme. The 'Big Society' means more community self-reliance and less government services, more volunteering and local entrepreneurial activity to look after the poor and needy rather than increased government resources. Policy trends – based on communitarianism centred on community ownership, activation, responsibility, empowerment, involvement, and regeneration – reconfigured the way in which services were delivered and social work's role *vis-à-vis* the community.

The UK Coalition Government has entrenched individual and community responsibility by adopting a less interventionist approach to tackling the decline in social capital. Based on the work of political commentator and author of *Red Tory*, Philip Blond (2010), the 'Big Society' replaces the social exclusion model with entrepreneurial community programmes with community groups building affordable houses, tackling youth unemployment, and inviting charities to deliver public services. It is devoid of reference to addressing inequalities or social divisions, views all communities as similar and comparable, and fails to recognise the diversity of communities, and the considerable and growing economic inequalities in the UK noted above. The 'Big Society' approach has much in common with Victorian philanthropy based on mutual aid, charitable giving, and voluntarism (Pearson, 1975). The role of social work under these social policy reforms is unclear as well reflecting its ambivalent relation to working-class forms of organisation. Jordan's (2011) observations are instructive:

> Social work's role in these transformations is far from clear. On the one hand, 'community organizers' might be drawn from the profession, especially if the emphasis of training shifted from the technocratic competences of the New Labour orthodoxy back towards a broader understanding of the social origins of individual problems. The only other clue lies in the proposal, under the heading 'public service reform', to involve social enterprises, charities, and voluntary groups to play a leading role in delivering services and tackling deep-rooted social problems, funding those developments from a Big Society Bank, using unclaimed back assets (p.11).

Any successful engagement with the Big Society programme by social work will necessarily depend on an increase in public spending, rather than the reverse 'austerity measures' that are currently being vigorously pursued. As shown below, social work has long hitched its values to the cause of disadvantaged, marginalised communities through forms of social activism.

Community – transformative – activism

Community activism is a discourse from the margins through which marginalised groups seek collective gains in communities characterised by racial, cultural, ethnic, and religious disadvantage or, put more positively, diversity (Stepney & Popple, 2008). With their anti-oppressive and cross-cultural stance, social workers who are drawn to this discourse see a role for social work in community activism. 'Critical community practice' fits this mould construing the social work role as a radical one cast within the discourse of human rights and social justice (see Chapters 24 and 47). There are those who align the service-user movement with this discourse (see Chapter 43) though it also has links with neoliberal-influenced policy to enhance consumer choice and undermine professional autonomy (Gray, 2010).

The discourse on community activism centres on the community's potential for promoting social solidarity and collective action. It draws from a wide range of sources, including community development theory (Craig et al., 2011; Ledwith, 2011; Mayo, 1977; Popple, 1985; Shaw, 2004), as well as feminist and Black writers who point to communitarianism's failure to address the needs of disadvantaged groups struggling to survive in the most marginalised of communities (Gray & Boddy, 2010). Community activists argue that real advancement for those caught at society's margins requires a radical transformative action (see Chapter 47) and services delivered at a neighbourhood level with local communities and service users having a voice in service delivery.

COMMUNITY SOCIAL WORK

While there is much in common with the discourse of community activism and social work values, not least its anti-oppressive stance, community work is not the main activity of social workers in the UK – and elsewhere – who are employed mainly in highly regulated managerial public service environments, such as child protection services (Jordan, 2011).

Historically, UK community work arose in the 1950s when the Younghusband Report (1959) identified it as a third method of social work alongside casework and groupwork (see Kuenstler, 1961). While by the mid-1960s community development was 'tied intellectually to social work' (Thomas, 1983, p. 21), the deepening economic crisis led the UK government to deploy a range of neighbourhood and community-based interventions aimed particularly at those areas thought to be worse effected by the country's changing fortunes (Popple, 1985). The two most significant of these interventions was the Urban Programme and the National Community Development Project launched in 1968 to work with local residents to improve service delivery and increase community capacity. But community development began to separate from social work since its informal practices did not fit with the professional model pursued by the British Association of Social Workers.

In the 1970s, the Calouste Gulbenkian Foundation (1973) tried to reclaim community work as a method of social work (Jones & Mayo, 1974, 1975; Mayo, 1977). However, the bulk of UK writing on community work that developed in the UK at this time described a Marxist-influenced radical approach to community work (Clark with Asquith, 1985), which did not fit with the government's view of the social work role in local social services.

In the 1980s, community work was further developed in the UK through the Barclay Report (1982), which attempted to re-establish social work's credibility in initiating and sustaining close strengths-based partnerships with communities. The Report was critical of social work's reactive and ameliorative nature and focus on those 'at risk' at a time when policy makers sought holistic planning for families, communities, and community-based agencies. The Report referred to consensus-oriented 'neighbourhood-based approaches', while social workers continued to pursue conflict-oriented Marxist social and community action (Clark with Asquith, 1985). Key texts developed the field of community practice (Francis et al., 1984; Henderson & Thomas, 1981, 1987, 1992; Henderson et al., 1980; Lees & Mayo, 1984; Popple, 1985; Smale et al., 1988; Thomas, 1983).

Subsequently, in the UK in the 1990s onwards, community work developed as a separate discipline from social work trapped in a relentless shift to statutory duties as 'child care tragedies pushed government to more professional standards of practice' (Vincent, 2010, p. 205), following the narrow political and media focus on social work after the Cleveland child abuse inquiry (Holman, 1993; Jack & Stepney, 1995). Nevertheless, a burgeoning literature on community social work continued to develop (Craig & Mayo, 1995; Craig et al., 2011; Ledwith, 2011; Shaw, 2004; Stepney & Popple, 2008; Twelvetrees, 1991).

In the USA, community work was traced to the early Settlement Movement and thus proclaimed as a social work role. Several approaches were developed – community organising, locality development, social action, and urban planning (Alinsky, 1989; Biklen, 1983; Cox et al., 1984, 1987; Dunham, 1970; Kahn, 1982; Kramer & Specht, 1983; Perlman & Gurin, 1972; Ross, 1955; Ross & Lappin, 1967; Rothman, 1979; Rubin & Rubin, 1992; Taylor & Roberts, 1985; Warren, 1983). However, social work became and remains a mainly clinically oriented – mental health – profession in the USA (Gibelman, 1999; Ginsberg, 2005; Specht & Courteney, 1994) and community work is a marginal rather mainstream method of social work practice.

A further body of literature developed in relation to developing countries around community development practice (Batten, 1965). While social workers in some contexts might engage in community development activities, this too is a marginal rather than mainstream method of social work practice (Ife, 1995).

COMMUNITY PRACTICE

Community practice is a generic term describing forms of practice aimed at intervening in individual and community problems at the macro- or community level. It involves:

- establishing priorities 'as locally as possible to fit local circumstances' (Smale et al., 1988, p. 33);
- challenging the way community problems are identified and explained (Stepney & Popple, 2008);
- organising collective action to mount community resistance to initiatives, which it opposes and influence policy making (Homan, 2008);
- developing 'accessible and effective local services in order to meet the needs of individuals more flexibly and appropriately' (Stepney & Popple, 2008, p. 113);
- enabling them to 'generate the cultural resources to act together, to mobilise and organise around their collective interests, and to challenge ... government agencies' agendas' (Jordan, 2007, p. xii);
- reflecting on the connections between the global and local (Ife, 1995, 2000);
- enhancing social capital to counter community breakdown (Stepney & Popple, 2008);
- aligning with local advocacy groups (Ife, 2001); and
- promoting community action (Lee, 1999).

CASE STUDY

Finsbury is an estate of some 7000 people in a large UK city. The estate has a mainly White population, with around 15% people of Afro-Caribbean descent and 10% from Indian ancestry. The estate has suffered from a good deal of economic pressure recently with 20% of the workforce now unemployed while 35% of young people (16–24-year-olds) are out of work. One of the largest employers closed over a year ago as production was switched to a developing country in order to reduce costs and increase the company's competitiveness in an expanding world market. Smaller industrial units have been encouraged to replace the production company but the take up has been marginal and only 25 local people have been able to secure work in the new enterprises. There is an over-representation of children (aged 16 and under) in the local population, which lives alongside people who have lived in the neighbourhood since the estate was built in the 1970s and are now reaching retirement age. Housing is mainly two- and three-bedroomed apartments and houses, the majority of which are social housing. There is a large primary school in Finsbury while older children have to travel to the neighbouring community for their secondary schooling. There are few community facilities on the estate, although there have been efforts recently by residents to petition for the establishment of nursery facilities for babies and pre-school children in the area. There are a number of small local shops, including an Indian cafe and takeaway, hairdressers, betting shop, fish and chip shop, hardware store, and one empty shop building. There is no supermarket at present in Finsbury, although the supermarket chain Tesco has shown interest in placing a new store in the area.

The estate has three pubs, one of which attracts a number of underage young people outside its doors most evenings. Local residents have complained of the noise and disturbance. The city Social Services Department has established a local community social work (CSW) team comprising four social workers and an administrative officer, which is intended to serve the whole community and is based in part of a disused Church Hall. Although there are two doctors surgeries in Finsbury, the nearest health centre is two miles away. There is an open space owned by the local authority which has four football pitches on it together with substandard and outdated changing rooms. The major problems that have been identified by the CSW team are:

- a high level of child protection referrals;
- the local police station is logging a high number of complaints, in particular concerning the young people outside one of the pubs, vandalism to property, and fires started in open spaces;
- publicans at all three pubs are concerned with underage drinking and are enforcing a policy of no drinks to those under 18 years;
- both police and social services are aware of many complaints from neighbours, in particular concerning the relationship problems between children and older people;
- the doctors are concerned about the level of isolation experienced by older people in the neighbourhood; and
- except for the playing fields, there are few public facilities

The problems in Finsbury are not dissimilar to those in neighbourhoods in thousands of communities across the UK. In relation to this case study, it might be asked: What role might the CSW team play in Finsbury? What approach should they take to tackle the problems identified? What could be done to address the needs of the growing older population and the unemployed young people living in Finsbury? What other issues does the team have to deal with?

What role might the CSW team play in Finsbury?

What role could a CSW team of four social workers and an administrative officer undertake in an area of this kind? What would be different about this form of community practice that could potentially deliver better and more effective social work services than conventional methods? The answer has to be that social work practice that is delivered closer to residents requires that the practitioners learn at close hand the issues that are confronting the local community. For example, in this case it is clear that poverty due to high levels of unemployment together with a lack of facilities is creating a situation that has led to problems that are being felt by many residents, both young and older people. Agencies such as the social services cannot, of course, change the course of globalisation and neoliberalism that have created the difficulties that are presented in Finsbury. However, what social workers can do, if appropriately organised and deployed, is to support people in their concerns, campaign with them for change and increased and improved facilities, and provide access to the expertise and contacts that have the potential to bring about greater security for residents.

What is different is the approach the professional workers take to the issues confronting them. While conventional methods of social work might adopt an approach which involves doing to a group or individuals, CSW or community practice is usually focused on the resilience of the community and is engaged in doing with residents. They would develop cooperative strategies and effective interprofessional and interagency relationships, which could tap into formal and informal networks that engage with the concerns of local people. To achieve success in this requires social workers and other practitioners to develop strategies based on joint working and which offer themselves to communities for scrutiny and change. The nearer social workers are to the communities they serve, the greater the opportunities for success, as the residents will also become aware of both the expertise and resources available to social workers as well as their resource limitations.

What approach should they take to tackle the problems identified?

For the most part, community social workers generally take a strengths-based approach focusing on the community's strengths, capacities, and resilience (Gray, 2010). They engaged in doing with – rather than to – residents. Community practice is delivered close to residents so practitioners learn, at close hand, the issues confronting the local community. In this case, the community's problems are largely poverty related, and due to high levels of unemployment and a lack of local facilities. Community social workers can offer social support to help people deal with their daily problems while aligning with their campaigns for increased and improved local facilities.

What could be done to address the needs of the increasing older population and the unemployed young people living in Finsbury?

An ageing population with increasing health and social care needs, and a significantly large number of young people unemployed due to the economic recession is presenting problems in communities in many areas of the developed and developing world. There is greater chance that social work operating with a policy of community practice can begin to address these with local residents of all ages on their side. The mobilisation of resources both external and local to the neighbourhood is more likely to happen when social workers can harness voluntary agencies, and the work of residents in managing their own communities to develop approaches that are creative, sustainable, and inclusive.

What other issues does the team have to deal with?

A reflective community practitioner would realise that the closure of the factory in Finsbury was not due to the action of local residents, but to the nature and power of major corporations to relocate their production to areas where unionisation is weak or non-existent and where wage rates are lower than in developed economies. With this understanding, he or she would join with the residents of Finsbury to help them find proactive solutions to unemployment by exploring opportunities to develop home industries or microenterprises and assisting people enhance their job-seeking skills.

CONCLUSION

Social work services are a small but important element in the delivery of social policy in the UK and elsewhere. In a period of severe public sector financial restraint, the time is right to ask searching questions about the present nature and delivery of social work services. The evidence presented here makes a strong case for reshaping social work so that it better supports people to take action to tackle their problems in a manner that helps them share their difficulties and, where possible, find ways of dealing with these in a manner that combines their collective voices and determination to ask difficult questions and demand responses. Embedding community practice demands a significant and determined commitment from the organisations employing social workers as well as a harmonious policy environment. Community practice means moving social work teams out of centralised offices and locating them in neighbourhood offices based in a range of settings, such as schools, churches, and health centres or co-locating them with other professionals working in these centres.

While community practice has many positives, it needs to be located in a theoretical approach that is mindful of the new European wave of radical ontologies of community as 'shared lack' and remain critical of the notion of neoliberal individualism that has done so much damage to both individuals and communities. In advocating a transformative community practice, social workers would do well to be cognisant of the view by Gray (2011) that there is a need to 'be more guarded about overly optimistic claims about the strength of social capital, community, and community development' (p. 10). What social work needs to consider seriously is an approach to community practice that critiques and addresses structural inequalities, is critically aware of the problems inherent in the present delivery and management of social work, and has at its core a compassion for those who have been damaged by a system that prioritises and sustains the unseemly and greedy pursuit of greater profit and power.

REFERENCES

Alinsky, S. (1989). *Rules for radicals.* New York: Vintage Books.
Barclay Report (1982). *Social workers: Their roles and tasks.* London: National Institute for Social Work/Bedford Square Press.
Batten, T.R. (1957). *Communities and their development: An introductory study with special reference to the tropics.* London: Oxford University Press.
Batten, T.R. (1965). *The human factor in community work.* London: Oxford University Press.

Batten, T.R., & Batten, M. (1967). *The non-directive approach in group and community work*. London: Oxford University Press.

Biddle, W.W., & Biddle, L.J. (1965). *The community development process*. New York: Holt, Rinehart and Winston.

Biklen, D.P. (1983). *Community organising: Theory and practice*. Englewood Cliffs, NJ: Prentice-Hall.

Blond, P. (2010). *Red Tory: How left and right have broken Britain and how we can fix it*. London: Faber.

Bryson, L. & Mowbray, M. (2005). More spray on solution: Community, social capital and evidence-based policy. *Australian Journal of Social Issues, 40*(1), 91–106.

Calouste Gulbenkian Foundation (1973). *Current issues in community work: A study by the Community Work Group*. London: Routledge and Kegan Paul.

Campbell, T. (2008) Translator's introduction: Bios, immunity, life – the thought of Roberto Esposito: *Bios: Biopolitics and philosophy*, Minneapolis: University of Minnesota Press.

Chambers, D. (2006). *New social ties: Contemporary connections in a fragmented society*. Basingstoke: Palgrave.

Clark, C. L. with Asquith, S. (1985). *Social work and social philosophy: A guide to practice*. Routledge and Kegan Paul: London.

Cohen, R., & Rai, S. (2000). *Global social movements*. London: Athlone Press.

Cox, F.M., Erlich, J.L., Rothman, J., & Tropman, J.E. (1984). *Tactics and techniques of community practice*. Itasca, IL: F.E. Peacock Publishers.

Cox, F., Erlich, J.L., Rothman, J., & Tropman, J.E. (eds), (1987). *Strategies of community organization* (4th ed.). Itasca, IL: F.E. Peacock Publishers.

Craig, M., & Mayo, V. (eds) (1995). *Community empowerment: A reader in participation and development*. London: Zed Books.

Craig, G., Mayo, M., Popple, K., Shaw, M., & Taylor, M. (eds). (2011). *The community development reader: History, themes and issues*. Bristol: Policy Press.

Dunham, A. (1970). *The new community organization*. New York: Thomas Crowell and Sons.

Esposito, R. (2008). *Bios: Biopolitics and Philosophy*, Minneapolis: University of Minnesota Press.

Esposito, R. (2010). *Communitas: The origin and destiny of community*. Stanford, CA: Stanford University Press'.

Etzioni, A. (1995). *The spirit of community*. London: Fontana.

Fortune (2006). 'Global 500', 4 July 2006.

Francis, D., Henderson, P., & Thomas, D.N. (1984). *A survey of community workers in the United Kingdom*. Tavistock Place, London: National Institute for Social Work.

Gibelman, M. (1999). The search for identity: Defining social work – past, present, future. *Social Work, 44*(4), 298–310.

Ginsberg, L. (2005). The future of social work as a profession. *Advances in Social Work, 6*(1), 7–17.

Gray, M. (2010). Social development and the status quo: Professionalisation and Third Way cooptation. *International Journal of Social Welfare, 19*(4), 463–470.

Gray, M. (2011). Back to basics: A critique of the strengths perspective in social work. *Families in Society: The Journal of Contemporary Social Services, 92*(1), 5–11.

Gray, M., & Boddy, J. (2010). Making sense of the waves: Wipeout or still riding high? *Affilia*, 25(4), 368–389.

Gray, M., & Mubangizi, B. (2010). Caught in the vortex: Can local government community development workers in South Africa succeed? *Community Development Journal, 45*(2), 186–197.

Halpern, D. (2005). *Social capital*. Cambridge: Polity.

Harris, J. (2003). *The social work business*. London: Sage.

Held, D., McGrew, A., Goldblatt, D., & Perraton, J. (1999). *Global transformations: Politics, economics and culture*. Cambridge: Polity.

Henderson, P., & Thomas, D.N. (eds) (1981). *Readings in community work*. London: George Allen and Unwin.

Henderson, P., & Thomas, D. (1987). *Skills in neighbourhood work*. London: Routledge.

Henderson, P. & Thomas, P. (1992). *Skills in neighbourhood work* (2nd ed.). London: Routledge.

Henderson, P., Jones, D., & Thomas. D.N. (eds), *The boundaries of change in community work*. London: George Allen and Unwin.

Holman, B. (1993). 'Pulling together', *The Guardian*, 20 January.

Homan, M.S. (2008). *Promoting community change: Making it happen in the real world* (4th ed.). Belmont, CA: Thomson Brooks/Cole.

Ife, J. (1995). *Community development: Creating community alternatives: Vision, analysis and practice*. Melbourne: Longman.

Ife, J. (2000). Localized needs and a globalized economy: Bridging the gap with social work practice. Social Work and Globalisation. Special Issue of *Canadian Social Work, 2*(1), 50–64.

Ife, J. (2001). *Human rights and social work: Towards rights-based practice*. Cambridge: Cambridge University Press.

Jack, G., & Stepney, P. (1995). The 1989 Children Act: Protection or persecution? Family and support and child protection in the 1990s. *Critical Social Policy*, *15*(1), 26–39.

Jones, D., & Mayo, M. (eds). (1974). *Community work one*. London: Routledge and Kegan Paul.

Jones, D., & Mayo, M. (eds). (1975). *Community work two*. London: Routledge and Kegan Paul.

Jordan, B. (2007). *Social work and well-being*. Lyme Regis: Russell House.

Jordan, B. (2011) Making sense of the 'Big Society': Social work and the moral order. *Journal of Social Work*, published online 6 May 2011 doi: 10.1177/1468017310394241.

Kahn, S. (1982). *A guide to grassroots leaders organizing*. New York: McGraw Hill.

Klein, N. (2000). *No logo: No space, no choice, no jobs*. London: Flamingo.

Kramer, R.M., & Specht, H. (eds) (1893). *Readings in community organization practice* (3rd ed.). Englewoods Cliffs, NJ: Prentice-Hall, Inc.

Kraut, R., Bryin, M., & Kielser, S. (eds). (2006). *Computers, phones and the internet: Domesticating internet technology*. Buckingham: Open University Press.

Kuenstler, P. (ed.). (1961). *Community organization in Great Britain*. London: Faber and Faber.

Ledwith, M. (2011). *Community development: A critical approach* (2nd ed.). Bristol: Policy Press.

Lee, B. (1999). *Pragmatics of community organization*. Mississauga, ON: CommonAct Press.

Lee, B., & Todd, S. (eds) (2006). *A casebook of community practice: Problems and strategies*. Mississauga, ON: CommonAct Press.

Lees, R., & Mayo, M. (1984). *Community action for change*. London: Routledge and Kegan Paul.

McLuhan, M., & Powers, B.R. (1992). *The global village: Transformations in world life and media in the 21st century*. Oxford: Oxford University Press.

Mayo, M. (ed.) (1977). *Women in the community*. London: Routledge and Kegan Paul.

Mowbray, M. (2004) Beyond community capacity building: the effect of government on social capital. *Observatory PASCAL Place Management, Social Capital and Learning Regions*, retrieved from http://www.obs-pascal.com/

Nancy, J.L. (1991). *The inoperative community*. Minneapolis: University of Minnesota Press.

O'Hara, P.A. (2005). Contradictions of neoliberal globalisation: The role of ideology and values in political economy. *Journal of Interdisciplinary Economics*, *16*(3), 341–365.

Pearson, G. (1975). *The deviant imagination*. Basingstoke: Palgrave Macmillan.

Perlman, R., & Gurin, A. (1972). *Community organization and social planning*. New York: John Wiley and Sons.

Plant, R. (1978). Community: Concept, conception, and ideology, *Politics Society*, 8: 79–107.

Popple, K. (1985). *Analysing community work: Its theory and practice*. Buckingham: Open University Press.

Popple, K. (2007). Community development strategies in the UK. In L. Dominelli (ed.), *Revitalising communities in a globalising world*. Aldershot: Ashgate.

Prestidge-King, C. (2005). A sketch for a new community: The inoperative community and modern politics. *Cross-Sections* (1), 83–93.

Putman, R. (2000). *Bowling alone: The collapse and revival of American community*. New York: Simon and Schuster.

Ross, M.G. (1955). *Community organization*. New York: Harper and Row.

Ross, M., & Lappin, B. (1967). *Community organization theory, principles and practice* (2nd ed.). New York: Harper Ross.

Rothman, J. (1979). Three models of community organization practice, their mixing and phasing. In F.M. Cox, Erlich, J.L., Rothman, J., & Tropman, J.E. (eds), *Strategies of community organization* (3rd ed.). Itasca, IL: F.E. Peacock Publishers.

Rubin, H.J., & Rubin, I.S. (1992). *Community organizing and development*. New York: MacMillan Publishing Company.

Taylor, S.H., & Roberts, R.W. (eds) (1985). *Theory and practice of community social work*. New York: Columbia University Press.

Shaw, M. (2004). *Community work: Policy, politics and practice*. Hull and Edinburgh: Universities of Hull and Edinburgh.

Smale, G., Tuson, G. Cooper, M. Wardle, M., & Crosbie, D. (1988). *Community social work: A paradigm for change*. London: National Institute for Social Work.

Somerville, P. (2011). *Understanding community: Politics, policy and practice*. Bristol: Policy Press.

Specht, H., & Courtney, M. (1994). *Unfaithful angels: How social work has abandoned its mission*. New York: Free Press.

Stepney, P., & Popple, K. (2008). *Social work and the community: A critical context for practice*. Basingstoke: Palgrave.

Sunday Times (2011). 'Rich list 2011', 8 May 2011.

Thomas, D.N. (1983). *The making of community work*. London: George Allen and Unwin.

Twelvetrees, A. (1991). *Community work* (2nd ed.). London: MacMillan Education.

UK Department of Children, Schools and Families (2010). *Building a safe and confident future: One year on: Detailed proposals from the Social Work Reform Board.* London: Department of Children, Schools and Families.

UK Department for Work and Pensions (DfWP) (2010). *Households below average income.* London: DfWP.

UK Department of Education (2011). *The Munro review of child protection: Final report. A child-centred system.* Cm. 8062. London: Department of Education.

United Nations (2007). *Millennium development goals report.* New York: United Nations.

United Nations Development Programme (UNDP) (2003). *Human development report.* New York: UNDP.

United Nations Development Programme (UNDP) (2007). *Human development report.* New York: UNDP.

United Nations World Food Programme (UNWFP) (2001). News Release: *WFP head releases world hunger map and warns of hunger 'hot spots' in 2001*, 8 January. New York: UNWFP.

Vincent, A. (2010). Local area coordination: An exploration of practice developments in Western Australia and Northern Ireland. *Practice: Social Work in Action*, 22(4) 203–216. Retrieved on July 22, 2011 from www.38degrees.org.uk.

Warren, R. (1983). A community model. In R.M. Kramer & Specht, H. (eds), *Readings in community organization practice* (3rd ed.). Englewoods Cliffs, NJ: Prentice-Hall, Inc.

Webb, S.A. (2009). Against difference and diversity in social work: The case of human rights. *International Journal of Social Welfare*, (18)2, 307–316.

Webb, S.A. (2011). *Nothing in common? Guerrilla ontologies in rethinking 'community' and community engagement.* University of Newcastle, unpublished paper.

Williams, R. (1983). Community. *Keywords: A vocabulary of culture and society* (rev ed.). New York: Oxford University Press.

World Bank (2008). *World development indicators.* Washington: World Bank.

Younghusband, E.L. (1959). *Report of the working party on social workers in local authority health and welfare services.* London: HMSO.

SECTION 4
Social Work Values and Ethics

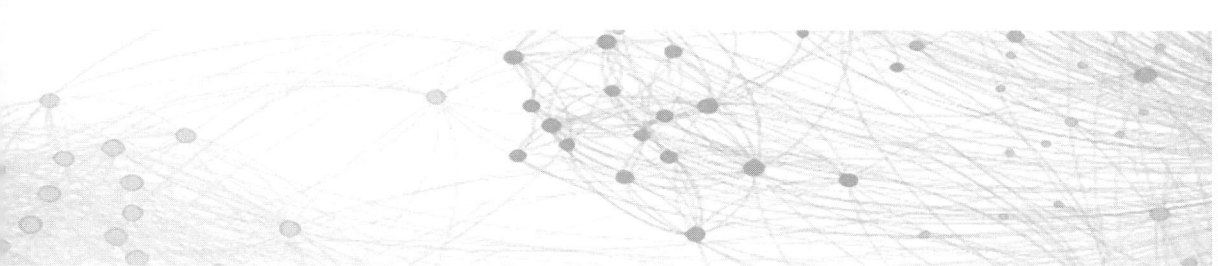

INTRODUCTION

The complex, challenging, and sometimes paradoxical dimensions of social work ethics and values is the subject of Section 4. In observing the long-standing tradition of foregrounding the importance of core values, it identifies and develops themes and issues relating to this area of professional social work. (From the earliest modern construction of social work, the profession has been seen as firmly rooted in values.) Arguably this has been led by significant attention given over to this field in professional training and qualifying courses. In the USA, for example, there have been four books published in the USA that specifically address the teaching of social work values and ethics. Earlier books were Pumphrey's *Teaching Social Work Values and Ethics* in 1959 and then Reamer and Abramson's book *Teaching Social Work Values and Ethics*, as part of the series on Teaching Values and Ethics in 1982. Newer publications include Reamer's *Ethics Education in Social Work* (2001), and Congress, E., Black, P., & Strom-Gottfried, K. (2008) *Teaching Social Work Values and Ethics: A curriculum resource. Alexandria, VA: Council on Social Work Education* (2002). Two of the editors of this *Handbook*, Gray and Webb (2010) recently published *Ethics and Value Perspectives in Social Work* for Palgrave Macmillan.

The section amply demonstrates how an adherence to an ethical stance is one of the defining strengths of social work and makes it most distinctive, perhaps unique. Across the range of chapters, it is shown how social work refuses to drop the notion that society can be a vehicle for the translation of private troubles into public concerns and how the democratically generated search for community, solidarity, and justice is worth pursuing. In a society in which the narrow pursuit of material self-interest is the norm, adherence to an ethical stance is more radical than people realise. In the face of a dominant culture of materialism and obsessive calculative reasoning, social work as a profession is almost unique in remaining committed to values of compassion, justice, and care even in an economic climate of self-interest. A central and unifying theme of this section is that social work is a valuable activity with intrinsic worth, which is confirmed in the fact that the human good consists in certain activities – as opposed to others – with social work being one of these activities. In drawing on some of the leading international authors in the field, this section situates the different ethical standpoints and value perspectives to give the reader a sense of the range and depth of these at work in social work practice. It also gives readers a good feel for the transformative value of social work.

In Chapter 19, Frederic Reamer begins with a brief overview of the nature and purposes of codes of ethics generally, and reviews the literature on the emergence and evolution of codes of ethics in diverse professions, including their various purposes in guiding professional practice. He then examines the emergence and evolution of codes of ethics in social work internationally and provides an overview of prominent codes of ethics before offering a constructive critique of their strengths and limitations, and political and ideological implications. Finally, he anticipates future developments, including the increasingly complex relationship between legal, regulatory, and ethical issues, the impact of limited resources, and ethical questions raised by technological developments in social work practice.

In Chapter 20 on ethical decision making, Donna McAuliffe presents social work as a moral endeavour resting, often tenuously, on a foundation of values intrinsically embedded in frameworks of social justice, human rights, and anti-oppressive practice. Against this backdrop, she examines decision making as part and parcel of a social worker's life, with consequences depending on the nature, impact, and outcome of the decision, and whether there is potential for harm, oppression, or injustice. It is with the latter form of decision that McAuliffe concerns herself: those decisions that have moral consequences – termed 'ethical decisions', which involve questions about rights, duties, responsibilities, and obligations. She asks what makes the decisions social workers are often called on to make sufficiently complex or important to warrant the burgeoning literature on ethical decision-making models. Furthermore, she questions the claims of those writing about ethical decision-making processes as to the potential of their models to improve the effectiveness of ethical options and outcomes.

In Chapter 21, Lena Dominelli discusses anti-oppressive social work practice and the way in which it is adapting to deal with new forms of diversity in social work. Key here is the way in which social work deals with people from nondominant cultures and classes – the poor, discriminated against, marginalised, and oppressed because of race, sex, class, religion, culture, sexual preference, and gender. Dominelli suggests ways in which social workers might work to reduce inequality through transformative anti-oppressive practice.

In Chapter 22, Brid Featherstone and Kate Morris examine the propensity of the ethics of care to meet feminist calls for 'politicising the personal' in relation to issues of diversity and difference in social work. They explore the work of key thinkers within the wide-ranging and influential scholarship on the ethic of care, tracing the journey from its origins within feminist psychology through its contributions to moral theory, political science, and social policy. Writings on the ethic of care focus on concerns of central significance to social work. However, Featherstone and Morris argue that there are compelling reasons for resisting the seductive wiles of an ethic that promises a great deal, delivers quite a lot, but just not some of the key things social work needs.

In Chapter 23, Purnima Sundar, John Sylvestre, and Amandeep Bassi discuss social work's record on dealing with diversity that is frequently described with reference to the philosophy of multiculturalism, noting that, notwithstanding its limitations, in some countries, multiculturalism is celebrated, encouraged, and even accompanied by policies promoting the integration of all members of society, while in others achieving a national identity is paramount, and the adoption of the majority's norms and traditions is promoted. Sundar et al. suggest that the way each society views and responds to differences among its members directly shapes how its social work practitioners work within these contexts to support clients from diverse backgrounds. They show how approaches to social work practice with diverse groups have evolved over time, in a way that mirrors the ideological changes related to diversity that have shaped policies and practices in broader society.

In Chapter 24, Richard Hugman posits that the idea of human rights, although often discussed as if its meaning were self-evident, is a complex and contested field in reality. He examines the complexities of human rights and social justice, the interplay and tensions between them, and some of the challenges in using them to inform good practice. In order to ground the meaning of these ideas, Hugman begins with short outlines of the concepts of human rights and social justice, tracing their important intellectual origins. He also shows that the interplay between these values lies behind continuing debates about the objectives and methods of social work. Having set the scene, he links social work and the Universal Declaration of Human Rights (1948) and examines arguments for social justice as the central concern of social work. He then explores two particular ways in which human rights and social justice create challenges, in so doing considering claims that the idea of human rights, in particular, is a cultural construct. In conclusion, he shows that taking a positive but critical stance towards human rights is vital for social work to be able to think and act more clearly in a diverse and complex world.

19

Codes of Ethics

Frederic G. Reamer

One hallmark of a profession is its promotion of moral conduct among its practitioners and its willingness to establish ethical standards to guide practitioners' behaviour (Callahan & Bok, 1980; Greenwood, 1957; Hall, 1968; Lindeman, 1947). Ideally, professionals exercise morally sound, autonomous judgement when confronted with ethical choices. In principle, ethical standards help professional practitioners identify ethical issues and provide meaningful guidelines to determine ethically acceptable or unacceptable behaviour.

In reality, codes of ethics serve other functions as well. Codes provide measuring rods when licensing or other regulatory bodies assess whether a professional has complied with or departed from standards in the field. Employers may adopt a prominent code of ethics to provide its employees with a moral compass, regulatory bench mark and set of guidelines. Further, codes provide an opportunity for a profession to announce to the public the nature of its mission, moral ideals and principles, and guidelines for proper conduct. Codes of ethics may be ideological or principled language designed primarily to protect the public. Thus, codes serve many purposes and have multiple, sometimes conflicting, aims (Bayles, 1986; Brandl & Maguire, 2002; Freeman et al., 2004; Hugman, 2003; Kultgen, 1982; Lipsky, 1980; Montgomery, 2003).

Codes of ethics are designed to address three major issues (Jamal & Bowie, 1995). First, codes address problems of moral hazard, or instances in which a profession's self-interest may conflict with the public's interest. Such conflicts can occur in a variety of ways. Examples include whether investment company managers should be obligated to disclose conflicts of interest (e.g., when the company makes investments contrary to some clients' financial interests), whether dentists should be permitted to refuse to treat people who have an infectious disease, such as HIV or AIDS, and whether social workers should be expected to disclose to law enforcement officials confidential information about very serious crimes their clients have admitted committing.

Second, codes of ethics address issues of professional courtesy, that is, rules governing how professionals should behave to enhance and maintain a profession's integrity. Examples include whether lawyers should be permitted to advertise and solicit clients, whether psychiatrists should be permitted to criticise unethical or incompetent colleagues, whether psychologists should be prohibited from soliciting colleagues' clients, and whether social workers should be expected to report colleagues who engage in unethical conduct.

Finally, codes of ethics address issues concerning professionals' duty to serve the public interest. For example, to what extent should physicians and nurses be expected to assist vulnerable people when faced with a public emergency? Should dentists donate a portion of their professional time to provide services to low-income people who do not have private dental insurance or a government-sponsored coverage? Should social workers provide *pro bono* services to people in need who have difficulty paying for assistance?

It is important to recognise codes of ethics as political documents as well as guides to professional practice (Lipsky, 1980, Webb & McBeath, 1989). In their purest form, codes of ethics provide professionals with moral inspiration, values, and ethical norms. In reality, codes of ethics also serve political purposes. Many codes are created by voluntary professional associations whose principal purpose is to promote the profession, along with serving the public. These associations may use their codes of ethics to regulate their members' ethical conduct, particularly when members of the public or clients allege ethical misconduct. In addition to using the code of ethics to protect the public, the profession also is using the code to protect itself. In this respect, codes of ethics can be self-serving documents, at least in part. Strict ethics-related prescriptions and proscriptions can serve to limit and constrain practitioners' discretion and autonomous judgement. Further, social work codes of ethics frequently are used even more explicitly for political purposes when they are incorporated formally into legislation and governmental regulations. Many legislative, licensing, and regulatory bodies adopt codes of ethics, not to promote or protect the social work profession but, rather, to protect the public.

THE EVOLUTION OF ETHICAL STANDARDS

Ethical standards in social work have evolved significantly since the profession's formal inception in the late 19th century. Ratified codes of ethics did not exist during the first half century of social work's existence. Although ethical norms emerged during social work's early years, it took decades for them to be codified. The earliest codes of ethics in social work were notoriously simplistic, as were codes in every profession. Early codes of ethics resembled affirmations, oaths, and pledges and, in contrast to contemporary codes, did not seek to provide in-depth, comprehensive coverage of a wide range of complex ethical issues (Banks, 2003).

Ethical standards in social work have developed in stages (Reamer, 2006b). The first stage – the *morality period* – began in the late 19th century, when charity organisation societies were common and social work was inaugurated formally as a profession. During this period, social work was much more concerned about the morality of the client than about the morality or ethics of the profession or its practitioners. Especially in England and the USA, practitioners who were concerned about vulnerable people focused on organising relief and responding to the 'curse of pauperism' (Paine, 1880). This preoccupation often took the form of paternalistic attempts to strengthen the rectitude of the poor whose 'wayward' lives had gotten the best of them.

Several social work organisations formulated draft codes during these early years of the profession's history – for example, the (North) American Association for Organizing Family Social Work and several chapters of the (North) American Association of Social Workers – but not until 1947 did the latter group, the largest organisation of social workers of that era, adopt a formal code (Johnson, 1955). Shortly thereafter, in 1954, the Australian Code of Ethics was first drafted (Congress & McAuliffe, 2006).

After a half century of development, the social work profession was moving into a phase characterised by several attempts to develop consensus about the profession's core values. This was especially prominent between the late 1950s and 1970s (see, e.g., Biestek, 1957; Emmet, 1962; Keith-Lucas, 1963; Levy, 1976; McDermott, 1975; Pumphrey, 1959; Teicher, 1967; Timms, 1983; Younghusband, 1967). Significantly, it was during this *values period*, in 1960, that the National Association of Social Workers (NASW) in the USA ratified the first prominent social work code of ethics. Fifteen years later, in 1975, the British Association of Social Workers (BASW) code was introduced (Banks, 2006; Congress, 2008).

During this period, social work codes of ethics were relatively brief and superficial. Typical was the 1960 NASW Code of Ethics. The code comprised a series of proclamations concerning, for example, every social worker's duty to give precedence to professional responsibility over personal interests; respect the privacy of clients; give appropriate professional service in public emergencies; and contribute knowledge, skills, and support to programmes of human welfare. First-person statements, such as 'I give precedence to my professional responsibility over my personal interests' and 'I respect the privacy of the people I serve', were preceded by a preamble setting forth social workers' responsibility to uphold humanitarian ideals, maintain and improve social work service, and develop professional skills.

Ethical standards in social work matured significantly during a third historical period focusing on *ethical theory and decision making*. Until the late 1970s, social work literature and ethical codes focused primarily on the profession's core values and value base. At this point, the profession underwent another significant transition in its concern about values and ethics. The 1970s saw a dramatic surge of interest in applied and professional ethics. Professions as diverse as medicine, nursing, law, business, journalism, social work, psychology, and criminal justice began to devote sustained attention to the subject. The literature on professional ethics burgeoned, as did academic coursework on the subject and continuing education. As professionals' understanding of ethical issues matured, a number of scholars and practitioners developed, for the first time, conceptually rich ethical decision-making protocols and guidelines (Banks, 2006; Barsky, 2010; Congress, 2000; Dolgoff et al., 2008; Linzer, 1999; Reamer, 2006a, 2006b; Rhodes, 1986). During this period, there was an explicit focus on the application of ethical theories to real-life ethical dilemmas encountered by professionals. Not surprisingly, codes of ethics matured during this period, reflecting this expanded understanding of ethical issues. For example, in the mid-1990s the NASW in the USA embarked on a complete overhaul of its code, first adopted in 1960 and revised in the late 1970s, in an effort to reflect the remarkable growth of new knowledge related to professional ethics. The NASW Code of Ethics ratified in 1996 constituted a sea change in social workers' approach to ethics. Codes in other nations were enhanced as well during this period. For example, the Korean Code of Ethics, first adopted in 1982, was revised in 1992, 1999, and 2001 (Congress & Kim, 2007); the Australian Code of Ethics, first proposed in 1954, was revised in 1999 and 2010; and the BASW Code, first adopted in 1975, was revised in 2002 (Banks, 2006). Significantly, the International Federation of Social Workers (IFSW) Code of Ethics, in conjunction with the International Association of Schools of Social Work (IASSW), was adopted during this period, in 1994, and revised in 2004.

The growth of interest in professional ethics during this period, and professionals' grasp of the need for more sophisticated codes of ethics, was due to a variety of factors (Reamer, 2006b). Complex and controversial technological developments in healthcare and other fields certainly helped to spark ethical debate and analysis involving such issues as termination of life support, organ transplantation, genetic engineering, psychopharmacological intervention, and test-tube babies. What criteria should be used to determine which medically needy patients should receive scarce organs such as hearts and kidneys? When is it acceptable to terminate the life support keeping a family member alive when she is in a persistent vegetative state? Is it ethically justifiable to implant an animal's heart into the body of an infant born with an impaired heart?

Widespread publicity about government scandals also triggered considerable interest in professional ethics and the cultivation of more instructive ethical standards. Beginning especially with Watergate in the USA in the 1970s, the public became painfully aware of various professionals and public officials who abused their authority. The media became saturated with disturbing reports of politicians, physicians, lawyers, clergy, nurses, and social workers who took advantage of clients. One byproduct was professionals' growing awareness of the need for clearer ethical standards.

In addition, the professions' and the public's embrace of the language of rights during this era – women's rights, prisoners' rights, children's rights – helped shape professionals' thinking about the need for more ambitious codification of ethical standards. Contemporary professionals also developed a much better appreciation of the limits of science and its ability to respond to the many complex moral and ethical questions professionals face. Although for some time, particularly since the 1930s, science had been placed on a pedestal, modern-day professionals increasingly began to acknowledge science cannot answer a variety of questions that are, fundamentally, ethical in nature (Sloan, 1980).

Finally, the well-documented increase in litigation and malpractice, along with publicity about unethical professionals, has forced the professions to strengthen ethical standards that distinguish ethical and unethical behaviour. 'Blame culture', especially in the USA, has led to an increase in claims and lawsuits against social workers and a substantial portion of these complaints allege some form of unethical conduct (Houston-Vega, et al., 1997; Reamer, 2001, 2003).

This has led to the development of an emphasis on *ethics risk management*. This stage is characterised mainly by the significant expansion of ethical standards to guide practitioners' conduct and by increased knowledge concerning professional negligence and liability. More specifically, this period includes the development of more detailed, comprehensive codes of ethics. A number of current social work codes of ethics include specific guidelines concerning phenomena such as confidentiality, privacy, privileged communication, and informed consent.

CONTEMPORARY ETHICS CODES IN SOCIAL WORK

Social work codes of ethics exist in three different contexts. First, internationally many professional social work associations have developed codes of ethics. These are voluntary associations of social workers. Thus, these codes typically carry no legal or formal regulatory authority, although the associations may insist on compliance with the code as a condition of membership. Such codes now exist in many nations around the world. The IFSW publicises ethical codes from Australia, Canada, Denmark, Finland, France, Germany, Ireland, Israel, Italy, Japan, Luxembourg, Norway, Portugal, Russia, Singapore, Spain, Sweden, Switzerland, Turkey, the USA, and the UK.

Second, in some nations, social work ethics codes have been developed or adopted by governmental licensing boards or regulatory bodies authorising social work practice. Some governmental licensing boards and regulatory bodies develop their own ethical standards, some formally adopt portions of codes developed by prominent voluntary social work associations, and some formally adopt entire codes developed by prominent voluntary social work associations. These ethical standards become legally enforceable once they are incorporated into licensing statutes or regulations.

Third, many private-sector human and social service agencies have adopted codes of ethics or ethical standards to which employees are bound. Here too, some of these organisations develop their own unique ethical standards and some draw on codes of ethics developed by prominent voluntary professional associations. In some instances, especially when the agency hires employees educated in different professions, agencies will draw on ethical standards from diverse professions, choosing those standards most relevant to their mission, client population, programmes, and services.

Social work codes of ethics are remarkably diverse in their purpose and content. Several prominent examples illustrate this diversity. For example, in the UK, the BASW, a voluntary association, offers a code of relatively modest length defining social work and providing an overview of core values and principles, and guidelines for ethical practice focusing on 'service users', the social work profession, the workplace, and social workers' responsibilities in particular roles (management, education, training, supervision and evaluation, independent practice, and research). Since membership in the BASW is voluntary, this code is not used for regulatory purposes.

In contrast, only recently have social workers in England been held to enforceable ethical standards. In England, a mandatory code of conduct for social workers was first published in September 2002 by the General Social Care Council (GSSCC; the body appointed by the UK Government to regulate professional social work and professional social work education). Registration of social workers commenced in April 2003, and on April 1, 2005, the term 'social worker' became a protected title. From that date, social workers were required to accept a code of conduct and could be disciplined if their actions were deemed to have breached the code. Prior to 2004, any person in the caring professions could use the term social worker irrespective of role or qualification (Reamer & Shardlow, 2009). The English code includes three broad sections: an introduction describing the function of the codes, a code of practice for employers, and a code of practice for social care workers. Significantly, the GSCC document is known as a code of practice, not a code of ethics (see Webster, 2010). The reason England has a code of practice and not a code of ethics is that the GSCC, as charged by Parliament in the Care Standards Act 2000 (Section 62), is required to produce and maintain codes laying down standards of conduct and practice. In fact, the term 'ethics' does not appear in the Care Standards Act. As Shardlow (in Reamer & Shardlow, 2009) suggests, use of the term 'ethics' suggests expected behaviour should be consistent with some *moral* imperatives and the notion of *morality* is the driving force in the determination of acceptable and unacceptable behaviour. A code of ethics expects the individual practitioner is deliberatively *choosing* to exercise moral judgement and make ethical decisions. The term 'code of practice' suggests a more practical, administrative, and managerial tool rather than an inspirational and conceptual guide encouraging and exhorting the individual practitioner.

The GSCC document includes two codes of practice: one is for 'workers' and one for 'employers'. These are 'presented together ... because they are complementary and mirror the joint responsibilities of employers and workers in ensuring high standards' (General Social Care Council (GSCC), 2004). According to Shardlow (in Reamer & Shardlow, 2009), this innovative approach requires a compact between employees and employers to embrace high standards and does not strive primarily to ensure professional practice is ethical practice.

Further, the GSCC does not apply exclusively to social workers. The code of practice is not intended for the exclusive use of professional social workers, as evidenced by its use of the term 'social care workers'. The term 'social care' is not widely used outside the UK, and even within the UK it has diverse meanings. According to Shardlow (in Reamer & Shardlow, 2009), the term 'social care' is sometimes used as a comprehensive term to incorporate all of social services and to provide a mirror to the term healthcare; to differentiate social work from a different category of practice, where 'social care' refers to the provision of interventions such as home care (e.g., provision of meals and domestic tasks, such as cleaning); and increasingly to refer to professional practice with adults, in particular *older adults* whereas the term 'social work' is used to refer to professional practice with children and families. That is, the term 'social care workers' can be taken to refer to a wide range of people employed in social service agencies, many of whom would not usually have a university education.

Similar to the BASW, the Canadian Association of Social Workers (CASW) offers a widely disseminated Code of Ethics to which members are held. In contrast to the English approach, which enforces ethical standards through a national code of practice applying to a diverse group of 'social care workers', the Canadian provinces have the authority to develop and adopt legally enforceable codes of ethics pertaining exclusively to social workers. The CASW Code of Ethics is a relatively short document. It includes a brief preamble, a summary of core social work values and principles related to respect for inherent dignity and worth of persons; pursuit of social justice; service to humanity; professional integrity; confidentiality; and competence. The CASW also publishes a companion document, *Guidelines for Ethical Practice*, which offers detailed guidelines regarding a wide range of ethical issues and challenges. In Canada, enforceable ethical standards exist at the provincial level. Thus, the Alberta College of Social Workers and Association of Social Workers of Northern Canada have the authority to develop their own standards of practice.

In yet another arrangement, the principal set of ethical standards in Australia is promulgated by the Australian Association of Social Workers (AASW), a voluntary professional association. In Australia, the AASW code is the national lodestar, even though the organisation does not have the legal authority to regulate social work. Some social workers choose not to join AASW and, therefore, fall outside the AASW's purview. The AASW (2010) code includes a summary of core values, ethical standards, and a brief guide to ethical decision making. The AASW also publishes extensive practice standards with which members are expected to adhere in conjunction with the Code of Ethics.

In contrast, the Singapore Association of Social Workers Code of Ethics includes a mix of general principles and narrowly focused ethical standards concerning social workers' ethical responsibilities to clients, colleagues, in practice settings, to the social work profession, and to the broader society. This is an example of a code adopted by a voluntary professional association incorporating abstract principles concerning social work's mission and narrowly worded standards concerning such topics as audio recording of clients, sexual misconduct, and informed consent by minors.

In the USA, the NASW Code of Ethics has served as an influential model and resource for many codes of ethics around the world. A number of social work associations, licensing boards, regulatory bodies, and private social and human service agencies have drawn on the NASW code. Within the USA, the NASW Code of Ethics is the best known and most influential set of ethical standards applying to social workers. Ethics codes have also been developed by other social work organisations in the USA, such as the National Association of Black Social Workers, and the Clinical Social Work Association.

In the USA, codes of ethics are used by several bodies governing social workers. The NASW, the largest professional social work association in the USA, uses the NASW Code of Ethics to review and adjudicate ethics complaints filed against NASW members.

Further, many of the individual state licensing boards in the USA have formally adopted the NASW Code of Ethics, or portions of the code, and use it to review and adjudicate ethics complaints filed against licensed social workers. Finally, many public and private social service agencies have adopted the NASW Code of Ethics or portions of the code, as formal agency policy and use the code's standards to guide and assess employees' conduct.

The NASW code includes four major sections. The first section, or 'Preamble', summarises social work's mission and core values. This is the first time in the NASW's history its code of ethics has contained a formally sanctioned mission statement and an explicit summary of the profession's core values. Importantly, the NASW code now includes a specific statement highlighting the profession's mission to 'meet the basic human needs of all people, with particular attention to the needs and empowerment of people who are vulnerable, oppressed, and living in poverty'. Special attention to vulnerable, oppressed, and low-income populations has become a defining feature of social work the code now proclaims.

The section, 'Purpose of the NASW Code of Ethics', provides an overview of the code's main functions and a brief guide for dealing with ethical issues or dilemmas. The code identifies five key purposes: to set forth broad ethical principles reflecting the profession's core values and establish ethical standards to guide social work practice; to help social workers identify relevant considerations when professional obligations conflict or ethical uncertainties arise; to familiarise practitioners new to the field to social work's mission, values, and ethical standards; to provide ethical standards to which the general public can hold the social work profession accountable; and to articulate standards the profession itself (and other bodies choosing to adopt the code, such as licensing and regulatory boards, professional liability insurance providers, and government agencies) can use to assess whether social workers have engaged in unethical conduct.

An important feature of the current NASW code is its overview of resources social workers should consider when faced with difficult ethical decisions. These include ethical theory and conceptually based decision-making frameworks; social work practice theory and research; laws and regulations; agency policies; and other relevant codes of ethics. The code encourages social workers to obtain ethics consultation, when appropriate, from an agency-based ethics committee, regulatory bodies, trained ethicists, knowledgeable colleagues, supervisors, or legal counsel.

Another key feature in this section of the NASW code is explicit acknowledgement that instances sometimes arise in social work in which the code's values, principles, and ethical standards conflict. The code does not provide a resolution for such conflicts and does not specify which values, principles, and standards are most important and ought to outweigh others in instances when they conflict. Further, the code acknowledges reasonable differences of opinion can and do exist among social workers with respect to the ways in which values, ethical principles, and ethical standards should be rank-ordered when they conflict.

The code's third section, 'Ethical Principles', presents six broad ethical principles informing social work practice, one for each of the six core values cited in the preamble: service, social justice, dignity and worth of the person, importance of human relationships, integrity, and competence. Each principle includes a brief annotation.

The code's final and most extensive section, 'Ethical Standards', includes 155 specific ethical standards designed to guide social workers' conduct and provide a basis for adjudication of ethics complaints. The standards are divided into six sections concerning social workers' ethical responsibilities to clients, to colleagues, in practice settings, as professionals, to the profession, and to society at large. The introduction to this section of the code explicitly states some of the standards are enforceable guidelines for professional conduct and some are standards to which social workers should aspire (so-called aspirational, as opposed to enforceable, standards).

In addition to codes of ethics promulgated by voluntary social work associations, licensing and regulatory bodies, and private agencies in many nations, the IFSW provides an overarching, truly international code of ethics. The joint IFSW-IASSW document, *Ethics in Social Work: Statement of Principles*, was first developed in 1994 and revised in 2004 (Congress, 2008). The IFSW represents social work organisations in some 90 nations and places special emphasis on human rights, human dignity, social justice, and professional conduct. It was written deliberately at a fairly high level of abstraction. According to the document, 'by staying at the level of general principles, the joint IASSW and IFSW statement aims to encourage social workers across the world to reflect on the challenges and dilemmas facing them and make ethically informed decisions about how to act in each particular case'. Currently, the IFSW code makes explicit reference to relevant international human rights declarations and conventions: such as the Universal Declaration of Human Rights and the International Covenant on Civil and Political Rights.

THE MULTIPLE USES OF ETHICS CODES IN SOCIAL WORK

Considered as a group, codes of ethics throughout the world serve multiple practical purposes within the social work profession.

Articulate social work's principal mission, values, and ethical principles

Ideally, codes of ethics offer practitioners and the public with a clear, compelling statement of social work's principal aims and moral purposes. In principle, codes of ethics provide a moral touchstone for the profession.

Offer guidance to social workers and employers in addressing ethical issues

Many contemporary social work codes of ethics, unlike earlier codes, include extensive detail regarding a wide range of ethical issues and challenges. In general, code of ethics standards offer guidance concerning three kinds of issues (Reamer, 2003, 2006a). The first includes what can be defined as 'mistakes' social workers might make that have ethical implications. Examples include leaving confidential documents displayed in public areas in such a way they can be read by unauthorised persons or forgetting to include important details in a client's informed consent documents. The second category includes issues associated with difficult ethical decisions, for example, whether to disclose confidential information, without client consent, to protect a third party from harm; barter with low-income clients who want to exchange goods for social work services; or terminate services to a noncompliant, yet vulnerable, client. The final category includes issues relating to social worker misconduct, such as exploitation of clients, boundary violations, or fraudulent billing for services.

Protect consumers from incompetent practice and delineate standards for ethical practice

The expressed purpose of licensing boards and regulatory boards is to protect the public from incompetent or unethical conduct by social workers. Codes of ethics and ethical standards promulgated by these bodies have, as their primary purpose, public protection. Licensing and regulatory bodies use codes of ethics and ethical standards to assess whether social workers have departed from professional standards in the event a citizen files a formal complaint.

Provide a mechanism for the social work profession to govern itself

In some countries, voluntary social work associations use codes of ethics internally to assess whether members have adhered to, or departed from, ethical standards. For example, in the USA, the NASW uses their its Code of Ethics to evaluate and, when necessary, adjudicate ethics complaints filed against NASW members by clients or other parties. NASW may impose sanctions (e.g., suspension, expulsion, notification of a licensing or regulatory body, restitution, and publication of findings) or require various forms of corrective action (e.g., consultation, supervision, and training).

Protect social workers from ethics complaints and litigation

Codes of ethics also serve a preventive function. Presumably, social workers who fully understand prevailing ethical standards are less likely to engage in conduct leading to misconduct, ethics complaints filed with licensing and regulatory bodies, and litigation.

CODES OF ETHICS AS A RISK-MANAGEMENT TOOL

Since the 1990s, social work codes of ethics have been viewed as a risk-management tool used to reduce ethics-related risks in professional practice and minimise the likelihood of harm to clients and other parties (see Webb, 2006). Social workers engage in high-risk behaviour when they practise in a manner inconsistent with prevailing ethical and professional standards (Houston-Vega et al., 1997; Reamer, 2003; Strom-Gottfried, 2000, 2003). Social workers can be held accountable for negligence and ethical violations in several ways. People who believe they have been harmed by social workers can file a negligence claim or lawsuit. Also, disgruntled parties can file formal complaints with social work organisations to which social workers belong and with licensing or regulatory bodies governing social work practice. In exceptional circumstances, criminal charges may be filed (e.g., based on allegations of sexual misconduct or fraudulent billing of a government agency or private insurance company).

Voluntary membership organisations typically process ethics complaints using a peer review model that includes members. The governing body may conduct a hearing during which the complainant (the person filing the complaint), the respondent (the person against whom the complaint is filed), and witnesses have an opportunity to testify. After hearing all parties, discussing the testimony, and consulting relevant codes of ethics, the organisation may impose sanctions or require various forms of corrective action.

Licensing and regulatory bodies also use formal procedures to process and review complaints against licensed social workers. Typically the procedures involve a review of the complaint, investigation, and, when warranted, a hearing conducted by a panel of colleagues offering due process protections (some boards include public members in additional to professional colleagues). In some jurisdictions proceedings are conducted in a court of law. These bodies can impose sanctions and requirements for corrective actions when there is evidence a social worker violated ethical standards set forth in statutes and regulations.

Negligence claims or lawsuits filed against social workers typically allege they engaged in malpractice in failing to adhere to specific standards of care. The standard of care is based on what an ordinary, reasonable, and prudent social worker with the same or similar training would have done under the same or similar circumstances. Departures from the profession's standards of care – as reflected in professional codes of ethics, standards, literature, and expert testimony – may result from a social worker's acts of commission or acts of omission. Acts of commission can occur as a result of misfeasance or malfeasance. *Misfeasance* is the commission of a proper act in a wrongful or injurious manner or the improper performance of an act that might have been performed lawfully. Examples include disclosing clients' confidential information without authorisation, providing substandard services to clients, and terminating services to clients prematurely. *Malfeasance* is the commission of a wrongful or unlawful act. Examples include becoming sexually involved with a client and billing insurance companies for services social workers did not provide. An act of omission, also known as *nonfeasance*, occurs when social workers fail to perform certain duties they ought to have performed. Examples include failing to obtain clients' informed consent before providing services or releasing confidential information and failing to inform clients about exceptions to their confidentiality rights.

Of course, social workers who are accused of malpractice are presumed innocent until proven otherwise. In many jurisdictions, professionals are liable for their actions or inactions (sometimes known as errors or omissions) based on the legal standard of preponderance of the evidence, as opposed to the stricter standard of proof beyond a reasonable doubt used in criminal trials. In general, malpractice occurs when four evidentiary elements are satisfied as follows:

1 *At the time of the alleged malpractice a legal duty existed between the social worker and the client (or whatever party files the complaint):* This element is often the easiest to satisfy. Social workers assume a duty – known technically as a fiduciary duty – to clients once they agree to provide them with professional service. In contrast, a social worker who is asked for advice informally by a casual acquaintance whom the social worker just met at a social gathering, when the social worker was not working, would not have a formal duty of care to this acquaintance.

2 *The social worker was derelict in that duty or breached the duty, either by commission or omission:* Determining whether a social worker was derelict in the performance of a duty typically is more complex. Here questions may arise concerning the nature of the standard of care in social work, that is, what is considered ordinary, reasonable, and prudent practice under the same or similar circumstances. In some instances, the standard of care is clear, for example, with regard to sexual relationships between social workers and clients or fraudulent documentation or billing. However, in many instances social workers may disagree about the nature of the standard of care, and the relevance and application of code of ethics standards. For example, a code of ethics may prohibit inappropriate dual relationships between social workers and former clients. Some social workers might argue this ethical standard prohibits social workers from hiring former clients, for instance, when a former client in a substance abuse treatment programme applies for a job as a case manager. Other social workers, however, might argue in some circumstances hiring a former client would not be unethical and would not constitute an inappropriate dual relationship. Similarly, some social workers might argue code of ethics provisions concerning clients' right to confidentiality prohibit a social worker who counsels a struggling adolescent from sharing confidential information with the client's parents, while others might argue the social worker has a duty to share important information about the client's circumstances with the parents. The fact that code of ethics standards can be interpreted differently by different practitioners is critically important. While some ethical standards are crystal clear (e.g., with regard to a practitioner's sexual involvement with a client), others are inherently vague and open to interpretation. In fact, courts of law recognise that professionals subscribe to various and sometimes conflicting schools of thought, especially with respect to ethical standards. The idea that different professional perspectives are permissible emerged primarily in medicine, when it became clear that physicians subscribe to different philosophies of practice, or schools, each with its own principal

concepts, assumptions, and standards. Rather than try to determine which perspective is 'right', courts of law generally have acknowledged the legitimacy of different perspectives, so long as they are supported by a respectable minority of the profession. When it is difficult to determine whether a respectable minority of a profession endorses a particular school of thought, a judge is likely to explore whether the conduct in dispute falls within a reasonable range of views based on language in a code of ethics and other relevant standards.

3 *The client suffered some harm or injury:* Demonstrating harm or injury can also be difficult in social work. Unlike medicine, for example, where injuries resulting from malpractice are sometimes easy to document with x-rays or lab results, in social work the injuries alleged are often difficult to document empirically. In many instances plaintiffs claim they have experienced some form of emotional harm or injury, as opposed to some form of physical injury. In these cases the plaintiff may have some difficulty substantiating the injury.

4 *The harm or injury was directly and proximately caused by the social worker's dereliction of duty:* Even plaintiffs who can document that they sustained some form of injury – emotional distress or depression, for example – may have difficulty demonstrating that the social worker's alleged dereliction of duty, or departure from ethics-related standards of care, was the direct and proximate cause of the injury.

COMPELLING ETHICAL CHALLENGES

In contrast to earlier codes of ethics, contemporary codes address a wide range of topics regarding social workers' ethical responsibilities to clients, to colleagues, in practice settings, to the social work profession, and to the broader society.

Client rights

Especially since the 1960s, social workers have developed a keen understanding of clients' diverse rights, many of which were established by legislation, regulation, or court ruling and which now are reflected in codes of ethics. These include rights related to confidentiality and privacy, release of information, informed consent, access to services, use of the least restrictive alternative, refusal of treatment, options for alternative services, access to records, termination of services, and grievance procedures.

Cultural and social diversity

One of the most significant developments in social work is the profession's increasingly substantial and nuanced grasp of diversity issues (Anderson & Carter, 2002; Gaine, 2010). Only in recent years have prominent ethics codes incorporated standards related to cultural competence, social diversity, discrimination, and oppression. These standards encourage social workers to recognise that the meaning of key ethical concepts, such as privacy, self-determination, and informed consent varies among different ethnic and cultural groups.

Client self-determination and professional paternalism

The presumption in social work is practitioners should promote and respect clients' right to self-determination (Biestek, 1975; McDermott, 1975). Only recently have prominent social work codes of ethics acknowledged that instances arise when social workers may have a duty to override clients' right to self-determination to protect clients from harming themselves or others. Interference with clients' right to self-determination to protect them from harming themselves raises complex issues of professional paternalism (Reamer, 1983).

Confidentiality, privileged communication, and privacy

One of the most significant developments in the maturation of social work codes of ethics is the proliferation of standards pertaining to confidentiality, privileged communication, and privacy (Dickson, 1998; Polovy & Gorenberg, 1997). Today's codes of ethics pay much more attention to these issues than earlier codes, particularly with respect to issues related to: solicitation of private information from clients; disclosure of confidential information to protect clients from self-harm and protect third parties from harm; release of confidential information; disclosure of information about deceased clients; release of information to parents and guardians of minor clients; sharing of confidential information among participants in family, couples, and group counselling; disclosure of confidential information to media representatives, law enforcement officials, protective service agencies, and other social service organisations protection of confidential written and electronic records, and information transmitted to other parties through the use of computers, email, fax machines, telephones, and other electronic technology; transfer or disposal of clients' records; protection of client confidentiality in the event of a social worker's death, disability, or employment termination; precautions to prevent discussion of confidential information in public or semi-public areas; disclosure of confidential information to third-party payers; disclosure of confidential information to consultants; disclosure of confidential information for teaching or training purposes; and protection of confidential and privileged information during legal proceedings, for example, divorce proceedings, custody disputes, criminal trials, termination-of-parental-rights proceedings, workers' compensation proceedings, and negligence lawsuits. At times, ethical standards relating to confidentiality conflict with one another or with other standards in the code. For example, standards requiring social workers to respect clients' privacy and confidentiality may conflict with social workers' duty to disclose confidential information, without clients' consent, in order to protect a third party from harm.

Informed consent

Current ethical standards focus on informed consent requirements in a variety of circumstances, including release of confidential information, programme admission, service delivery and treatment, videotaping, and audiotaping (Berg et al., 2001; Reamer, 1987; Summers, 1989). Common elements included in ethics standards focus on social workers' duty to give clients specific details about the purpose of the consent, a verbal explanation, information about clients' rights to refuse consent and withdraw consent, information about alternative treatment options, and an opportunity to ask questions about the consent process. The standards in codes of ethics recognise that special challenges arise when clients do not have the cognitive or legal capacity to consent, by virtue of age or impairment, or struggle with literacy.

Service delivery

Ethical standards address social workers' duty to provide service and represent themselves as competent only within the boundaries of their education, training, licence, certification, consultation received, supervised experience, or other relevant experience. They also focus on social workers' obligation to provide services in substantive areas and use practice approaches and techniques that are new to them only after engaging in appropriate study, training, consultation, and supervision from people who are already competent in those practice approaches, interventions, and techniques. Challenging ethical issues arise when social workers consider using nontraditional and unorthodox interventions.

Boundary issues, dual relationships, and conflicts of interest

Literature on boundary issues in professional–client relationships has burgeoned in recent years, and this has influenced expanded content in ethics codes (Herlihy & Corey, 2006;

Reamer, 2001; Syme, 2003). Contemporary ethics codes address issues related to: sexual relationships with current and former clients; counselling former sexual partners; sexual relationships with clients' relatives or acquaintances; sexual relationships with supervisees, trainees, students, and colleagues; physical contact with clients; friendships with current and former clients; encounters with clients in public settings; attending clients' social, religious, or life cycle events; gifts to and from clients; performing favours for clients; the delivery of services in clients' homes; financial conflicts of interest; delivery of services to two or more people who have a relationship with each other (such as couples, family members); bartering with clients for goods and services; managing relationships in small or rural communities; self-disclosure to clients; and becoming colleagues with a former client.

Recording, reporting, and documentation

Ethical and risk-management standards related to documentation have also proliferated in recent years, particularly as they pertain to assessment of clients' circumstances, planning and delivery of services, supervision, and accountability to clients, other service providers, funding agencies, utilisation review staff, and courts of law (Kagle, 1995; Reamer, 2005; Wiger, 2005). Ethics standards focus on the appropriateness of content in clients' records; clients' and other parties' access to records; and storage and retention of records.

Supervision

Ethics standards also focus on supervision issues, especially pertaining to supervisors' competence, documentation of supervision, and dual relationships between supervisors and supervisees (Falvey, 2001). These issues are particularly important when ethics complaints and lawsuits against social workers raise questions about the quality of supervision they received (Reamer, 1989).

Consultation and referral

Occasionally ethical issues arise concerning social workers' consultation with colleagues and referral of clients to other providers. As a result, several ethics codes address social workers' duty to be clear about when consultation with colleagues is appropriate and necessary and the procedures they should use to locate competent colleagues. Codes also address social workers' responsibility to refer clients to colleagues when they do not have the expertise or time to assist clients in need.

Dishonesty, fraud, and misrepresentation

A number of ethical standards in social work focus on social workers' duty to prevent dishonesty and fraud related to, for example, misrepresentation, documentation in case records, billing, and employment applications.

Termination of services

Social workers face ethical risks when they terminate services improperly, for example, when services are terminated prematurely, against a client's wishes, or when a social worker leaves an employment setting. A number of social work ethics codes provide procedural protocols and guidelines to ensure services are terminated ethically.

Practitioner impairment, misconduct, and incompetence

A significant percentage of ethics complaints are filed against social workers who meet the definition of impaired professional, that is, social workers who struggle as a result of substance abuse, mental illness, extraordinary personal stress, or financial or legal difficulties (Reamer, 1992; Strom-Gottfried, 2000, 2003). In addition, social workers sometimes encounter colleagues who are incompetent or engage in misconduct. Consequently, ethics codes include standards pertaining to social workers' duty to address their own and colleagues' impairment, incompetence, and misconduct.

Administration

Only in recent years have social work codes of ethics acknowledged ethical challenges related to administration (Cooper, 2006; Menzel, 2006). Ethical standards focus on resource allocation, management practices, performance evaluation and personnel practices, and social workers' commitment to employers, particularly when social workers believe employer policies, procedures, or administrative orders interfere with their ethical practice of social work (Reamer, 2000).

Evaluation and research

Research and evaluation have become more prominent in social work, particularly with respect to conducting needs assessments, carrying out clinical and programme evaluations, and using research evidence to inform practice (Mertens & Ginsberg, 2008; Sales & Folkman, 2000). Codes of ethics now include extensive guidelines regarding the protection of human participants in research, especially relating to issues of coercion, exploitation, informed consent, conflicts of interest, and confidentiality. These standards are particularly important in light of notorious abuse and exploitation of research and evaluation participants.

Social welfare and social action

One of social work's distinguishing features is its explicit concern about broad social welfare, in addition to social workers' concern about individual well-being. Prominent codes of ethics include standards pertaining to global social welfare, advocacy, social and political action, and preventing discrimination and exploitation.

FUTURE CHALLENGES

The evolution of social work codes of ethics is one of the most remarkable developments in the profession's history. In little more than a century, social work has moved from rather moralistic, sometimes paternalistic, instincts to comprehensive, robust ethical standards designed to guide practice, protect the public, and regulate the profession. Codes of ethics have blossomed as they have expanded from relatively simplistic oaths to sophisticated documents replete with diverse ethical prescriptions, prohibitions, moral ambiguity, and nuance.

The maturation of ethics codes has not occurred in a vacuum. These compelling developments reflect broader societal trends related to ethics and morality, the emergence of a discrete discipline focused on practical and professional ethics, and social workers' deepening grasp of morally complex dimensions of professional practice. Today the net result is a worldwide collection of increasingly comprehensive and influential ethics codes.

That said social workers should not be lulled into a false sense that these mature codes of ethics address all challenging ethical issues in the profession and provide answers to all complex ethical dilemmas. Indeed, no code of ethics is a panacea. Realistically, codes of ethics can identify critically important ethical issues in the profession, set a moral tone, outline broad ethical principles, and provide practical guidance on a wide variety of narrow ethical challenges. Codes of ethics cannot resolve all ethical dilemmas. In fact, it is inevitable that principles and standards contained in codes of ethics will conflict on occasion, requiring social workers to think hard about which ethical duties and obligations take precedence. This is an inherent quality of true ethical dilemmas; by definition, they resist easy solutions. In these instances, codes of ethics provide a valuable inventory of pertinent concepts, principles, and standards. However, in the final analysis, the package comes with this implicit expectation: 'some assembly required'.

As social workers now understand, ethics codes are living documents requiring periodic revision to reflect new knowledge and ethical challenges. During social work's early years the broad discipline of applied, practical, and professional ethics did not exist. Ethical decision-making protocols had not been created and it took decades for the profession to begin to conceptualise about ethical dilemmas, deliberately apply ethics concepts and theories to ethical challenges, and develop rigorous ethical decision-making protocols. Moreover, social work's early pioneers could not have imagined some of the ethical challenges facing today's practitioners. A century ago what social worker could have imagined confidentiality and privacy issues arising when practitioners provide counselling services using the Internet and email, send documents to third parties electronically, store records in computers, and talk with clients on wireless telephones? Further, social work's pioneers could not have anticipated litigation challenging social workers' relationships with former clients or practitioners' decisions to disclose confidential information, without client consent, to a client's sexual partner in order to protect the partner from HIV infection. Social workers of yesteryear had not yet experienced the complicated tension between the use of ethics codes to constrain some forms of practice and the need for social workers to make autonomous moral judgements. These and many other contemporary ethical challenges in social work teach us a compelling lesson: forecasting the ethical challenges the next generation of social workers will encounter is extraordinarily difficult, if not impossible. Technological developments, new social challenges, the emergence of novel social work interventions, and changes in the law are likely to require periodic re-examination and revision of social work codes of ethics. This is as it should be. Ethical standards in the profession should always reflect social workers' perpetual growth of knowledge about the moral purposes of the profession and ways to assist people in need.

REFERENCES

Anderson, J., & Carter, R. (eds) (2002). *Diversity perspectives for social work practice.* Boston: Allyn & Bacon.

Australian Association of Social Workers (2010). *Code of Ethics.* Canberra City, Australia: AASW.

Banks, S. (2003). From oaths to rulebooks: A critical examination of codes of ethics for the social professions. *European Journal of Social Work, 6,* 133–144.

Banks, S. (2006). *Ethics and values in social work* (3rd ed.). Basingstoke: Palgrave Macmillan.

Barsky, A. (2010). *Ethics and values in social work: An integrated approach for a comprehensive curriculum.* New York: Oxford University Press.

Bayles, M. (1986). Professional power and self-regulation. *Business and Professional Ethics Journal, 5,* 26–46.

Berg, J., P. Appelbaum, Lidz, P., & Meisel, A. (2001). *Informed consent: Legal theory and clinical practice.* New York: Oxford University Press.

Biestek, F. (1957). *The casework relationship.* Chicago, IL: Loyola University Press.

Biestek, F. (1975). Client self-determination. In F.E. McDermott (ed.). *Self-determination in social work.* London: Routledge and Kegan Paul, pp. 17–32.

Brandl, P., & Maguire, M. (2002). Codes of ethics: A primer on their purpose, development, and use. *Journal for Quality and Participation, 25,* 8–12.

Callahan, D., & Bok, S. (eds) (1980). *Ethics teaching in higher education.* New York: Plenum Press.

Congress, E. (2000). *Social work values and ethics.* Chicago, IL: Nelson-Hall.

Congress, E. (2008). Codes of ethics. In T. Mizrahi & Davis, L. (Eds.-in-Chief). *Encyclopedia of social work* (20th ed.), vol. 1. Washington, DC: NASW Press and Oxford University Press, pp. 326–331.

Congress, E., & Kim, W. (2007). A comparative study on social work ethical codes in Korea and the United States. *Korean Journal of Clinical Social Work, 4,* 175–192.

Congress, E., & McAuliffe, D. (2006). Social work ethics: Professional codes in Australia and the United States. *International Social Work, 49,* 151–164.

Cooper, T. (2006). *The responsible administrator: An approach to ethics for the administrative role* (5th ed.). San Francisco: Jossey-Bass.

Dickson, (1998). *Confidentiality and privacy in social work.* New York: Free Press.

Dolgoff, R., Loewenberg, F., & Harrington, D. (2008). *Ethical decisions for social work practice* 8th ed.). Belmont, CA: Brooks Cole.

Emmet, D. (1962). Ethics and the social worker. *British Journal of Psychiatric Social Work, 6,* 165–172.

Falvey, J. (2001). *Managing clinical supervision: Ethical practice and legal risk management.* Belmont, CA: Wadsworth.

Freeman, S., Engels, D., & Altekruse, M. (2004). Foundations for ethical standards and codes: The role of moral philosophy and theory in ethics. *Counseling and Values, 48,* 163–173.

Gaine, C. (ed.). (2010). *Equality and diversity in social work practice.* Exeter: Learning Matters.

General Social Care Council (2004). *Code of practice.* London: Author.

Greenwood, E. (1957). Attributes of a profession. *Social Work, 2,* 45–55.

Hall, R. (1968). Professionalization and bureaucratization. *American Sociological Review, 33,* 92–104.

Herlihy, B., & Corey, B. (2006). *Boundary issues in counseling: Multiple roles and responsibilities.* Alexandria, VA: American Counseling Association.

Houston-Vega, M. & Nuehring, E. (with Daguio, E.). (1997. *Prudent practice: A guide for managing malpractice risk.* Washington, DC: NASW Press.

Hugman, R. (2003). Professional values and ethics in social work: Reconsidering Postmodernism? *British Journal of Social Work, 33,* 1025–2041.

Jamal, K., and Bowie, N. (1995). Theoretical considerations for a meaningful code of professional ethics. *Journal of Business Ethics, 1,* 703–714.

Johnson, A. (1955). Educating professional social workers for ethical practice. *Social Service Review, 29,* 125–136.

Kagle, J. (1995) *Social work records* (2nd ed.). Long Grove, IL: Waveland Press.

Keith-Lucas, A. (1963). A critique of the principle of client self-determination. *Social Work, 8,* 66–71.

Kultgen, J. (1982). The ideological use of professional codes. *Business and Professional Ethics Journal, 1,* 53–69.

Levy, C. (1976). *Social work ethics.* New York: Human Sciences Press.

Lindeman, E. (1947). Social work matures in a confused world. *The Compass, 28,* January, 3–9.

Linzer, N. (1999). *Resolving ethical dilemmas in social work practice.* Boston: Allyn & Bacon.

Lipsky, M. (1980). *Street-level bureaucracy: Dilemmas of the individual in public services.* New York: Russell Sage Foundation.

McDermott, F.E. (ed.) (1975). *Self-determination in social work.* London: Routledge and Kegan Paul.

Menzel, D. (2006). *Ethics management for public administrators: Building organizations of integrity.* Armonk, NY: M.E. Sharpe.

Mertens, D., & Ginsberg, P. (2008). *The handbook of social research ethics.* Thousand Oaks, CA: Sage Publications.

Montgomery, V. (2003). Codes of ethics as living documents. *Public Integrity, 5,* 331–346.

Paine, R., Jr. (1880). The work of volunteer visitors of the Associated Charities among the poor. *Journal of Social Science, 12,* 101–114.

Polovy, C. & Gorenberg, C. (1997). Client confidentiality and privileged communications [Law Note]. Washington, DC: National Association of Social Workers.

Pumphrey, M. (1959). *The teaching of values and ethics in social work education.* New York: Council on Social Work Education.

Reamer, F. (1983). The concept of paternalism in social work. *Social Service Review, 57,* 254–271.

Reamer, F. (1987). Informed consent in social work. *Social Work, 32,* 425–429.

Reamer, F. (1989). Liability issues in social work supervision. *Social Work, 34,* 445–448.

Reamer, F. (1992). The impaired social worker. *Social Work, 37,* 165–170.

Reamer, F. (2000). Administrative ethics. In R. Patti (ed.). The handbook of social welfare management. Thousand Oaks, CA: Sage Publications, pp. 69–85.

Reamer, F. (2001). *Tangled relationships: Managing boundary issues in the human services.* New York: Columbia University Press.

Reamer, F. (2003). *Social work malpractice and liability* (2nd ed.). New York: Columbia University Press.

Reamer, F. (2005). Ethical and legal standards in social work: Consistency and conflict. *Families in Society: The Journal of Contemporary Social Services 86,* 163–169.

Reamer, F. (2006a). *Ethical standards in social work: A review of the NASW Code of Ethics* (2nd ed.). Washington, DC: NASW Press.

Reamer, F. (2006b). *Social work values and ethics* (3rd ed.). New York: Columbia University Press.

Reamer, F. & Shardlow, S. (2009). Ethical codes of practice in the US and UK: One profession, two standards. *Journal of Social Work Values and Ethics, 6.* [available at: http://www.socialworker.com/jswve/content/view/120/68/]

Rhodes, M. (1989). *Ethical dilemmas in social work practice.* London: Routledge and Kegan Paul.

Sales, B., & Folkman, S. (2000). *Ethics in research with human participants.* Washington, DC: American Psychological Association.

Sloan, D. (1980). The teaching of ethics in the American undergraduate curriculum: 1876–1976. In D. Callahan and S. Bok (eds). New York: Plenum, pp. 1–57.

Strom-Gottfried, K. (2000). Ensuring ethical practice: An examination of NASW code violations, 1986–97. *Social Work, 45,* 251–261.

Strom-Gottfried, K. (2003). Understanding adjudication: The origins, targets, and outcomes of ethics complaints. *Social Work, 48,* 85–94.

Summers, A. (1989). The meaning of informed consent in social work. *Social Thought, 15,* 128–140.

Syme, G. (2003). *Dual relationships in counseling and psychotherapy.* London: Sage.

Teicher, M. (1967). *Values in social work: A reexamination.* New York: National Association of Social Workers.

Timms, N. (1983). *Social work values: An enquiry.* London: Routledge and Kegan Paul.

Webb, S.A. (2006). *Social work in a risk society.* London: Palgrave.

Webb, S.A., & McBeath, G.B. (1989). A political critique of Kantian ethics in social work. *British Journal of Social Work, 32,* 1015–1036.

Webster, P. (2010). Codes of conduct. In M. Gray & Webb, S.A. (eds), *Ethics and value perspectives in social work.* London: Palgrave. 31–40

Wiger, D. (2005). *The clinical documentation sourcebook: The complete paperwork resource for your mental health practice* (3rd ed.). Hoboken, NJ: John Wiley & Sons.

Younghusband, E. (1967). *Social work and social values.* London: Allen and Unwin.

20

Ethical Decision Making

Donna McAuliffe

Social workers make a range of decisions every day. These decisions, as with all decisions in life generally, will have both intended and unintended consequences. They may be made quickly, or with much deliberation. They may be of little significance, or life-changing. They may involve few or a range of people within a work context, and may be dictated by some or many competing priorities and mandates. Some decisions are made covertly, while others are made under intense scrutiny. Regardless of context, rigorous decision making is a skill that develops with time and practice. In the context of human services and social care, the potential for harm, and requirement to do no harm, needs to be carefully assessed to ensure that all possible implications of decisions that could impact on vulnerable or disadvantaged individuals, families, groups, or communities are taken into account. The understanding that practice, including the making of decisions, relies on a sound ethical foundation first requires a working definition of what ethics is, and why ethics as a definable concept warrants such important consideration.

There are many definitions of ethics, from the position of this being a branch of moral philosophy that incorporates a range of ethical theories developed over time, through to a more applied definition related to the identification of moral norms and standards of behaviour and conduct (Banks, 2006). Essentially, ethics are values in action. They are built on what has been defined as core values of the human and social services, which include valuing difference and diversity, privacy, quality service, humanity, positive change, choice, and the environment (Chenoweth & McAuliffe, 2012). These values have their philosophical roots in extensive bodies of literature dating back to the early writings and works of Confucius, Socrates, Aristotle, and Plato, all of whom deliberated on human nature and virtues, social relationships and moral responsibility, through to philosophers such as Jeremy Bentham and John Stuart Mill who wrote of individual freedom and autonomy, and utilitarian concepts of the greater good. Immanuel Kant's contributions to understanding of duty and obligation through deontological theories, more contemporary works of Martin Buber on reciprocity and John Paul Sartre on individual responsibility; Gramsci, Foucault and Marcuse on power and exploitation; and John Rawls on ideas about distributive justice, all weave a rich tapestry of ideas that influence ethics in the current environment. The very fact that there is such a history of moral philosophy, and that the range of ethical theories are so divergent in many of their foundational premises, challenges any notion that ethics could ever be universal and unchanging. Ethics is, by its very nature, a highly contested terrain, as evidenced by both absolutist and relativist positions on many contemporary issues, which also supports the view that values are culturally derived (Gray et al., 2008). Ethical dilemmas, then, result from situations in which – social, professional, and personal – values collide, and it is not immediately clear which course of action a practitioner should take, or which ethical principle should take precedence. Those decisions which require identification and a systematic working through of competing moral and value dimensions related to any of the previously mentioned core values, and which may have moral consequences are termed 'ethical decisions'. Ethical decision making, then, is defined as:

> the process by which social workers engage in an exploration of values – that may be evident in the personal, professional, social and organisational spheres – in order to establish where an ethical dilemma might lie according to what competing principles, and what factors take priority in the weighing up of alternatives (McAuliffe, 2010, p. 41).

When decision making is placed into the professional space within which social workers carry out their practice, there is an additional layer of responsibility stemming from the relational engagement with others, and the commitment to uphold the core values on which the profession is based. The extensive body of literature laying out the purpose, vision, and ethical foundation of social work has clearly established that the realm of morality (as a broad philosophical concept) is a central point at which knowledge, skills, and values intersect (Bisman, 2004; McBeath & Webb, 1989). While knowledge can be accumulated from many sources, and skills developed with training and professional development, values are much more nebulous and open to personal interpretation (Trevithick, 2008). For decades, social workers have tried to enshrine these values in formalised written documents such as ethical codes, practice standards, and statements of ethical principles. As Congress (2010) points out, 'Many countries continually review their code of ethics in an effort to expand their detail and specificity. However, there is little evidence that codes of ethics reflect cultural differences or keep up to date with societal trends' (p. 29). The International Federation of Social Workers (IFSW, 2004) has led the way in developing statements of general ethical principles that include a commitment to (i) human rights and human dignity, and (ii) social justice. As discussed by Hugman in Chapter 24, many of the debates about human rights and social justice, particularly those taken from a position of political liberalism, highlight the need for these broader perspectives to keep open the question of what is meant by the creation of a just or equitable society. There are many examples worldwide of ways in which social work has moved to claim legitimate moral territory by the development of these templates for ethical practice that then become translated into the 'rules' for the attainment of social justice. Just as it seems undisputed that social work operates in a moral sphere, it is equally undisputed that those coming into social work bring with them their own perspectives and views of the world, ideological positions on matters of right and wrong, and understandings about values and ethical responsibilities. This raises the oft-debated question of whether values can be 'taught', or whether they can be shaped, modelled, or sculptured into what is 'acceptable' in the eyes of the public, or to satisfy those who perform the role of 'gatekeepers' for the profession. While the debate about the malleability of values appears to play out predominantly in educational and academic circles, along with questions about whether values are universal or culturally relevant and locally specific (Healy, 2007), these discussions also take place in the field among social workers who want to reflect critically on these issues. As such, these discussions typically take place in supervision (where this is available), with colleagues and peers, and at times with clients and users of services. Ethical decision making as a process requires social workers to have the ability to hold steady the concept that every situation is uniquely individual, within the understanding that every decision is located within a context, which will inevitably be dominated by societal expectations and moral rules. Bowles et al. (2006) argue that empowered social work practice incorporates an understanding of ethical virtues, knowledge, and skills. They list ethical decision making as one of these skills. It is debatable as to whether or not the educational context, with so much knowledge that needs to be incorporated into often overcrowded curricula, can give students the required space to fully develop these ethical decision-making skills.

This chapter explores ethical decision making not only as it has been constructed as both a process and a defined skill within social work, but also as it relates to a broader interprofessional context. It challenges the premise that models of ethical decision making will in and of themselves lead to appropriate and just decisions. Ethical decision-making processes and models need to be used in conjunction with a range of other skills and processes to achieve an integrated and more holistic approach to resolving difficult moral dilemmas.

HISTORICAL OVERVIEW OF DEVELOPMENTS IN ETHICAL DECISION MAKING: THE INTERPROFESSIONAL CONTEXT

Much has been written about the explosion of literature in the specific field of values and ethics as they relate to social work practice over the past three decades, and this also includes increased attention to the development of models of ethical decision making within the discipline itself (Banks, 2008a). Social work is by no means alone in contributing to this growth in literature, as ethical decision making also has its place in the literature of many other professional disciplines, some (like business, accounting, and environmental practice) seemingly unrelated to social care, yet still with a mandate of social responsibility. There is growing recognition that social work practice rarely operates in disciplinary isolation, and there is a need for more attention to be given to the interprofessional context of the human services environment (Banks & Gallagher, 2009). Pockett (2010) argues social work should be part of the global trend towards interprofessional education and incorporate an understanding of interdisciplinary perspectives in education, specifically curriculum development, and practice. This makes good sense as when social workers make decisions about matters involving ethical dilemmas, it is more often than not the case that they will be actively engaging with others who also have interests in particular outcomes for clients, families, groups, or communities. It is therefore critical for social workers to be aware not only of the ethical decision-making models and processes in the discipline of social work, but also of the frameworks and models used by their professional colleagues. White and Featherstone (2005) document a case in the field of child health to illustrate the unintended outcomes from problematic communication in a multiagency situation, concluding 'the challenge must be to create conditions where every-day practices are open to challenge and scrutiny without trapping people in indecision' (p. 215). To this end, it is necessary to look at an overview of literature across a number of disciplines so a better sense of the interprofessional landscape and how decision making is constructed can be determined.

A scan of the literature over the past decade in the health and allied health professions (the largest employers of social workers in many countries) shows an impressive contribution to ethical decision-making publications. Nursing, as the first example, has contributed a number of models and predominantly uses practical, case-based ethical scenarios to aid in the analysis of clinical and ethical dilemmas (Butts & Rich, 2005; Fry & Johnstone, 2008; Husted & Husted, 2008; Thompson, 2006). Many of these publications set out ethical decision-making processes relating to quite specific nursing fields of practice as diverse as disaster triage (Good, 2008); critical care nursing and oncology (Raines, 2000; Williams, 2002); neurosurgery (Kreuger, 2008); perinatal nursing (Zindler, 2005); and palliative care (Monteverde, 2009). Common themes in the literature on nursing ethics relate to the importance of patient autonomy and informed consent within a context of quality of care and resource allocation (Aitamaa et al., 2010), with comment often made that organisational structures within health systems can impede a focus on these principles. A common question posed in the nursing ethics literature is: what is a good nurse? This question highlights the attention paid to virtue ethics and the ethic of care as foundational theoretical foundations for this discipline.

In the field of psychology and counselling, there are many generalist texts and articles on ethics and ethical decision making (Barnett, 2007; De Cremer, 2009; Morrissey & Reddy, 2006) and then, as with nursing, more specific focus on ethical decision making in areas such as forensic psychology (Bush et al., 2006); clinical neuropsychology (Bush 2007); operational (military) psychology (Stephenson & Staal, 2010); correctional mental health (Bonner & Vandecreeks, 2006); and school mental health (Raines & Dibble, 2010). In this literature, issues of practice competence and reliance on evidence are highlighted, particularly in the dealings with therapeutic interventions in complex cases. Exploration of the use and effectiveness of ethical codes is a constant theme, with conclusions drawn that, while psychology does pay great attention to developing detailed guidelines for practice, it is still difficult to apply generic codes to specific situations. This is a view also seen in the literature of other professions.

In pharmacy, recent studies have found fear of legal implications can result in 'ethical passivity' when it comes to ethical decision making, and also the ethical responsibilities of drug treatment management need to be better understood by pharmacists (Bliss, 2008; Cooper et al., 2008). In the field of medicine, there are many texts and articles relating to bioethics and frameworks for resolving issues around capacity and consent, refusal of treatment, confidentiality, deception, physician-assisted suicide and euthanasia, surrogate decision making, and the rationing of health services (Blakely, 2007; Lo, 2005; Montgomery, 2006). Ethical decision making in the fields of medicine and healthcare tend to favour models such as that developed by Seedhouse and Lovett (1992) where the 'ethical grid' (as an example) leads a health practitioner through four layers to focus on central issues of respecting persons equally, creating autonomy, respecting autonomy, and serving needs first. Models like this are built on what has become a cornerstone of bioethics, known as the four principles approach where autonomy, beneficence, non-maleficence, and justice are the guiding principles (Beauchamp & Childress, 1979). Healthcare ethics is complicated by many contextual factors, including moral uncertainty (is this an ethical dilemma?); moral distress (stress caused by compromising of values); competing interests, conflicts of conscience, and conflicts of interest; dual and divided loyalties; blowing the whistle; and self-interest (Freegard, 2006).

When there are so many ethical decision-making models to examine, it is difficult to resist the temptation to categorise the different constructions of these models, comment on the similarities and differences between them, and analyse the points of philosophical departure making each unique and attractive to those with a particular value position or style of decision making. While a number of authors have done exactly this (Chenoweth & McAuliffe, 2012; Clark, 2011; Cottone & Claus, 2000) and have, in doing so, provided a clear rationale for producing more alternatives, it could be argued such analysis does little more than line the deck chairs up in different configurations. The fundamental question of the value and purpose of ethical decision-making models, and evidence of whether they are indeed of any use for those practitioners who do use them in practice, remains largely undetermined across the professions.

So how then does social work compare in its contributions to the substantive literature on ethical decision making? The simple answer is reasonably well in terms of quantity and quality of analysis and practical applications. Essentially, the literature on this topic dates back over three decades and covers a wide range of depth and scope with a particular emphasis on the following categories:

- texts with a specific focus on ethical decision making in social work as a distinct discipline;
- journal articles or book chapters that outline a specified model of ethical decision making for social work;
- generic social work texts that include analysis of ethical decision-making models and processes within chapters about values and ethics;
- journal articles that report empirical research on ethical decision-making processes in social work, including decision making in specific fields of practice; and
- literature on social work ethics education and teaching, including models of ethical decision making.

First are those full texts devoted entirely to ethical decision making in social work. In his well-researched account of the historical development of values and ethics in social work, Reamer (1998) nominated the period of the 1980s as the beginning of the defined period of ethical theory and decision making where writers such as Levy (1982), Loewenberg and Dolgoff (1982), and Rhodes (1986) set out new methods of resolving ethical dilemmas using systematic ethical problem-solving processes and ranked value hierarchies. The fact that the original Loewenberg and Dolgoff book titled *Ethical Decisions for Social Work Practice* has now moved into its eighth edition bears testimony to the popularity of such texts for students and practitioners (Dolgoff et al., 2009). Following in the tradition of full texts devoted specifically to the topic, Steinman et al. published *The Ethical Decision-making Manual for Helping Professionals* in 1998, followed by Congress (1999) with her *ETHIC* model, Linzer (1999) with *Resolving Ethical Dilemmas in Social Work Practice*, and Robison and Reeser (2000) with *Ethical Decision-making in Social Work* focusing on tracking harms. Rothman (2005) used student decision-making narratives to illustrate the process of justification in *From the Front Lines*, and Miller (2007) contributed *Ethical Decision-making in Social Work and Counselling*. In looking at the history, it could be said these (primarily North American) writers ignited what was to become a chain reaction of model after model of ethical decision making. These texts are popular in ethics education as they generally provide many case scenarios so ethical dilemmas and conflicting ethical principles can be identified, and ethical decision-making models applied. The models set out in these texts are essentially those referred to as 'process models' (McAuliffe, 2010) or 'rational-cognitive models' (Bowles et al., 2006), where students or practitioners are encouraged to work through a linear series of steps to reach an outcome. These texts also provide contextual information about moral philosophy and ethical theory, which is important as a foundation for understanding ethical principles. They also generally try to cover a broad range of fields of practice in the scenarios used, including both statutory and community-based contexts.

The second category of literature includes those journal articles or stand-alone chapters within books setting out a specified ethical decision-making model for social work, or providing an analysis of ethical decision-making tools. Examples of articles or chapters setting out distinct models include Mattison's (2000) *cycle of reflection*; Bowles et al.'s (2006) *360 degree model of ethical decision-making*; and McAuliffe and Chenoweth's (2008) *inclusive model of ethical decision-making*. What is interesting about these models is they have all been developed from a critical analysis of other ethical decision-making models both from within and outside social work, and therefore move away from the more linear models previously mentioned. They have distinct ideological leanings towards virtue ethics and focus largely on critical reflection as a central dimension of sound ethical decision making. These models move much closer to what Gray (2010) describes as relational ethics of care in which the primary conditions include 'attentiveness, receptivity, responsiveness, relatedness, mutuality and reciprocity' (p. 1807). McAuliffe and Chenoweth's (2008) model, for example, has at its core four interlinked central platforms on which all questions need to converge. These principle platforms are accountability, cultural sensitivity, consultation, and critical reflection. A social worker using this model would be expected to keep consideration of these four platforms well in mind so they become integrated into a pattern of decision making congruent with the practitioner's personal framework for practice. The social worker is expected to consult appropriately, keep in mind any issues of cultural discrimination (in the broader sense of that term), be aware of legal or other accountabilities, and engage in active reflective processes designed to expose biases, prejudgements, and any potential for abuse or misuse of power. Bowles et al. (2006) provided an analysis of the inclusive model based on Chenoweth and McAuliffe's (2005) original version and concluded that the circular process had particular merit because:

> lines have ends, circles don't ... ethics and work-life are permanently fused ... ethical challenges should be seen, not as crises to be overcome or averted, but as opportunities to improve the ethical framework within which all social work takes place (Bowles et al., 2006, p. 209).

The third category of literature can be divided into two subsets. The first comprises those generic social work texts (not specifically about values and ethics or ethical decision-making), which includes a chapter on the topic that may cover an analysis of the ethical decision-making models previously mentioned. Examples would include Adams et al. (2002) in which Dominelli's chapter on 'Values in social work: contested entities with enduring qualities' is followed by Sarah Banks' chapter on 'Professional values and accountabilities'. While these generic texts may not go into as much detail about the processes of ethical decision making and the theoretical foundations underlying decision making as texts solely devoted to this topic, they do ensure that a holistic view of social work inclusive of the value dimension is presented.

The second subset comprises those texts that are specifically about social work values and ethics (but not ethical decision making per se), and may include comment on various models. There has been a reasonably even spread of such texts across a number of countries with Reamer (2006) and Guttman (2006) from the USA; Beckett and Maynard (2005), Banks (2006), and Clifford and Burke (2009) from the UK; and Hugman (2005a), Bowles et al. (2006), and Gray and Webb (2010) from Australia, to name some of the more frequently cited examples. These important texts form the backbone of ethics education and ensure students are familiar with the moral philosophy and ethical theories that provide the justification for decisions.

The fourth category of literature includes the reporting of empirical research on the use of ethical decision-making models, effectiveness of ethical decision-making processes, and outcomes in relation to resolution of ethical dilemmas, often within specific fields of practice. There are now two scholarly international journals devoted to publishing research and theoretical commentary on ethics in social work. From the USA comes the *Journal of Social Work Values and Ethics*, published as an e-journal by White Hat Communications and originating in 2004. From the UK comes *Ethics and Social Welfare* (ESW), published by Routledge, with its first edition in 2007. Both of these journals have a focus on the practical application of ethics, and there have certainly been a number of articles exploring various facets of ethical decision making. In her editorial for ESW, Sarah Banks (2008b) acknowledged that 'the development of ethical decision-making models is a theme that we did not identify on our original list of different types of contributions to the journal' (p. 6). She went on to say:

> the development of new critical models is important: models that move beyond simplistic, rational deductive accounts of moral reasoning, that take account of the co-construction of issues and problems; that leave room for emotional and culturally sensitive responses; and encourage reflexivity on the part of professionals to see themselves as engaged participants rather than neutral and impartial decision makers (p. 7).

Banks issues the challenge to authors to consider ways to avoid ethical decision making becoming a skill set to be taken down from the shelf and dusted off for use only at those times of crisis. Rather, it should form an integrated part of practice to ensure that social workers remained connected to those affected by decisions rather than disconnected from them in efforts to remain objective and neutral. The risk for social workers to see themselves as standing outside ethical decisions looking in is high when there is pressure to act with haste, and it is at these times that ethical decision-making models may feel cumbersome and overly rigid. They may be abandoned in the interests of dealing with a situation and moving on to the next case, meeting, or pressing need. It is interesting to note that, despite the number of ethical decision-making models that have been developed, there has not been any research conducted on how social workers actually use ethical decision-making models at their disposal. The empirical research is much more about ethical decision making in a broader sense, with studies exploring, for example, the roles social workers play in interdisciplinary decision-making processes in hospitals (Landau, 2001), the ethical theories on which social workers rely when making ethical decisions (Osmo & Landau, 2006), and the ethical principles taking priority when students from different disciplines (social work and nursing) are given case scenarios to which to respond (Yeung et al., 2010). As expected, these studies found the context of practice was an important determining factor in decision making and critical reflection on the influence of personal values was of paramount importance. One example of a culturally specific case study being run through the 'ethical principle screen' developed by Loewenberg and Dolgoff (2005) quickly showed this model lacked a 'communalist perspective' and was not inclusive of diverse cultural contexts (Healy, 2007).

As social work is a diverse profession, the exploration of the influence of personal and professional values on how decisions are made has been the subject of much interest. Some practice areas seem to have attracted more attention, mainly because of related issues of impaired capacity, competence and informed consent. The negotiation of ethical dilemmas in work with older people, dementia care, mental health, and with children and young people, shows varying degrees of understanding about ethical principles or the moral reasoning driving decision making. A common theme across this body of literature is more needs to be done at the level of professional education to ensure that practitioners are better able to articulate their justifications for actions, and where assessment of risk is a factor (as it is with most of these practice areas), social workers need to be able to balance competing priorities through application of ethical theory and reference to codes of ethics and practice standards (Campbell et al., 2006; Dixon, 2010; Larkin, 2007; Littlechild & Hawley, 2010). There is little difference in the conclusions from those reported in other disciplines. The messages are very similar. Ethics needs to be taken seriously; practitioners regardless of discipline need to engage in ethical dialogue around matters of ethical conduct; the public are to be protected from harm; and rigorous attention to sound and justifiable decision-making processes are expected as a minimum standard. Social work does not, perhaps, engage well in the area of decision-making heuristics (see Chapter 13). This is a growing area of literature in applied psychology and could be of great value in assisting social workers to focus more clearly on the rules underlying decision making. The relevance can be seen if the following use of heuristic cognition is adopted, this being:

> a focus on situations in which people need to act fast, the probabilities or utilities are unknown, and multiple goals and ill-defined problems prevent logic or probability theory from finding the optimal solution. In this view, the mind resembles an adaptive toolbox with various heuristics tailored for specific classes of problems – much like the hammers and screwdrivers in a handyman's toolbox (Gigerenzer, 2008, p. 20).

When related to ethical decision making in social work, it is clear to see how heuristic reasoning might play out. For example, when working in teams, the 'imitate the majority' heuristic (look at the majority of people in the peer group and imitate their behaviour) may win out or the 'take the best' heuristic favouring evidence and validation. The difficulty is the 'rules' (at least in relation to what are perceived to be right or wrong or professional or unprofessional) are often those dictated in written ethical codes, while the relationships and interconnections between people more often dictate final outcomes. In his exploration of ethical decision making as a hermeneutic process Clark (2011) concluded:

> the universal popularity of the algorithms found in textbooks and the plethora of rulebooks favoured by formal organisations suggests they may sometimes be useful. At the very least, any tool, however blunt or clumsy, may sometimes turn out to have some unexpected heuristic value (p. 18).

The warning, however, is quite clear. Rigid adherence to 'technical–rational problem-solving' is not likely to lead to a mutually inclusive outcome for all involved.

The final category of literature is that which covers teaching of ethical decision making in social work. The links between ethical decision making and critical reflective thinking have been evident in the literature for many years. As Gray and Gibbons (2007) point out:

> For students to appreciate the complexity of moral issues, it is necessary for them to be able to accept and deal with uncertainty and ambiguity, and the absence of cookbook solutions, and to learn that when moral conflicts or ethical dilemmas arise, they can only be resolved through dialogue, and a process of moral reasoning, where existing knowledge, theory, skills, values and ethical guidelines are brought together to inform the decision-making process (p. 224).

As well as this focus on dealing with complexity, heuristics and uncertainty, it is also important, as Banks (2005) found in her research with students from Finland, France, and the UK, the development of qualities of moral sensitivity and courage or strength of will were needed from ethics education. It was Reamer (2001) who put forward the necessary goals for ethics education, these being to 'stimulate moral imagination', 'develop analytic skills', 'elicit a sense of moral obligation and personal responsibility', and 'develop ability to respond to ethical controversy and ambiguity' (Reamer, 2001, pp. 20–23). These goals would certainly form the basis of learning objectives for any course in ethics and professional practice, and yet there is a distinct difference of opinion about how this can best be achieved. This brings us back to the earlier question of whether ethics can be 'taught' and, to this end, Hugman (2005b) offers the view 'ethics cannot be *taught*, it must be *learned*' (Reamer, 2001, p. 243). Furthermore, he argues, ethics must be positioned throughout many courses in a programme of study, including field education, so students can learn from a range of experiences both in the classroom and in the field. It is this immersion in ethics as an integrated part of education that will best prepare students for the complexities of practice, and will provide the necessary foundations for critical reflection on practice.

DRAWING TOGETHER THE THREADS: COMMON UNDERSTANDINGS OF CRITICAL ELEMENTS FOR ETHICAL DECISION MAKING

Having presented an overview of the literature on ethical decision making and positioned the discussion within an interprofessional context, it is possible to draw some conclusions about what social workers need to acknowledge and understand about this topic. The intent here is not to put forward yet another ethical decision-making model – there are more than enough of these to keep practice moving for the next few decades – but rather to pull together some threads from what has been a source of rich analysis both theoretical and practical. The key elements of ethical decision making are therefore summarised as follows.

- It is a process with many component parts, constructed differently according to theoretical and ideological perspective, but commanding rigorous attention to identification of competing ethical principles with a view to resolution of an identified dilemma.
- It is a highly reflective and conscious activity drawing on many sources of information and discarding those pieces of information not relevant to the contextual situation at hand, while holding information to inform judgement as of paramount importance.
- It is an individual and collective activity, best undertaken by engaging in dialogue with others and working to understand divergent views while seeking consensus on converging views.
- It involves power and a critical part of an ethical decision-making process is to ensure that power is not misused or abused, and that all those with a vested interest in the decision outcomes are involved in some way in the process of decision making.
- It is not about blindly following a prescribed set of instructions (or ethical code) or steps in a model, but is about personal and professional self-awareness, and intentional development of an integrated and consistent set of principles to guide actions and work in congruence with a framework for practice.
- It takes into account and seeks to challenge those structural factors contributing to oppression and social injustice, and resulting in violations of human rights.
- It must be learned from practice, and the responsibility for this learning lies with the practitioner who remains accountable for his or her conduct, behaviour, and actions connected to rights, responsibilities, duties, and obligations.
- It necessitates both knowledge and skills, drawing on ethical theory and moral philosophy, law and policy, international conventions and cultural world views, ethical codes and standards, research and evidence, to work in ways to maximise human potential and opportunity through collaborative partnerships, open communication, respectful dialogue, and conduct demonstrating competence, caring, and integrity.

CONCLUSION

Ethical decision making has been the subject of significant exploration and it is reasonable to expect more theoretical development and research will follow as professional practice continues to be scrutinised and held under the accountability microscope. This chapter started with the statement that social workers, and those involved in the care professions in a more general sense, have an ethical duty to do good, and not to cause harm. Unfortunately, 'evidence from international and national research studies and other sources has demonstrated that in some cases social work and human services have been provided in a manner which has resulted in harm to clients and those close to clients' (Chenoweth & McAuliffe, 2012, p. 108). To mitigate against the potential for harm, it seems few, if any, professions have not joined the bandwagon of creating ethical codes, checklists, models, and recommendations for the rigorous exploration of best pathways through complex moral dilemmas. As social work continues on its trajectory towards positioning itself as a profession on more equal footing with other disciplines, it is clear, in this particular area, it may well have an edge if the extent and quality of literature on ethical decision making is any benchmark. Social work positions ethics and values at its very core and it is clear the contribution made to the interprofessional practice environment has been sustained and extensive.

The recent literature on cognitive heuristics, decision bias, and ethical context is indicative of a rich terrain and growing body of research that will inevitably impact on our thinking about ethical decision making in social work (Munro, 2010; Webb, 2006). Social work researchers are becoming increasingly aware that professionals and clients are subject to various heuristics and biases that systematically prevent their decision making from being objectively optimal. Not only are social workers choices violating the principle of rational decision making but also violating procedural and formal institutional rules. If there is one overriding lesson from cognitive heuristics research, it is that in decision making, context counts. Clients risk preferences, for instance, will dramatically change depending on whether an option is framed in terms of potential loss or potential gain. Research also shows that the moral intensity of a particular event process can be a major moderator of the ethical decision-making process. Findings show that the availability of consequences associated with an act is likely to be positively related to perceptions of the magnitude of consequences of that act (Hayibor & Wasieleski, 2008).

The commitment social work makes to inclusion of ethical decision making as a defined skill in the education of students requires continued vigilance on the part of those who have responsibility for accrediting university programmes and developing curricula for social work education. Of perhaps greatest importance, however, is for social workers to integrate into their own theoretical and practice frameworks a deep and enduring sense of purpose connected to awareness of their own potential for good and harm, and to ensure the ability to make sound ethical decisions is nurtured and cultivated by ongoing dialogue and connection to others who share a common vision for the future.

REFERENCES

Adams, R., Dominelli, L., & Payne, M. (eds), (2002). *Critical practice in social work*. Basingstoke: Palgrave.

Aitamaa, E., Leino-Kilpo, H., Puukka, P., & Suhonen, R. (2010). Ethical problems in nursing management. *Nursing Ethics, 17*(4), 469–482.

Banks, S. (2005). The ethical practitioner in formation: Issues of courage, competence and commitment. *Social Work Education, 24*(7), 737–753.

Banks, S. (2006). *Ethics and values in social work*. Basingstoke: Palgrave Macmillan.

Banks, S. (2008a). Critical commentary: Social work ethics. *British Journal of Social Work, 38*(6), 1238–1249.

Banks, S. (2008b). Editorial. Ethics and social welfare: The state of play. *Ethics and Social Welfare, 2*(1), 1–9.

Banks, S., & Gallagher, A. (2009). *Ethics in professional life*. Basingstoke: Palgrave Macmillan.

Barnett, J. (ed.). (2007). In case of ethical dilemmas, break glass: Commentary on ethical decision-making in practice. *Professional Psychology: Research and Practice, 38*(1), 7–12.

Beauchamp, T., & Childress, J.F. (1979). *Principles of biomedical ethics*. New York: Oxford University Press.

Beckett, C., & Maynard, A. (2005). *Values and ethics in social work*. London: Sage.

Bisman, C. (2004). Social work values: The moral core of the profession. *British Journal of Social Work, 34*, 109–123.

Blakely, E. (ed.). (2007). *Psychology of decision-making in health care*. New York: Nova Biomedical Books.

Bliss, S.J. (2008). Ethical decision-making in pharmacy. *Drug Topics, 152*(8), 46–56.

Bonner, R., & Vandecreek, L.D. (2006). Ethical decision-making for correctional mental health practitioners. *Criminal Justice and Behaviour, 33*(4), 542–564.

Bowles W., Collingridge M., Curry S., & Valentine B. (2006). *Ethical practice in social work: An applied approach*. Sydney: Allen and Unwin.

Bush, S. (2007). *Ethical decision-making in clinical neuropsychology*. New York: Oxford University Press.

Bush, S.S., Connell, M.A., & Denney, R.L. (2006). *Ethical practice in forensic psychology: A systematic model for decision-making*. Washington, DC: American Psychological Association.

Butts, J.B., & Rich, K.L. (2005). *Nursing ethics: Across the curriculum and into practice*. Sudbury, MA: Jones & Bartlett.

Campbell, J., Brophy, L., Healy, B., & O'Brien, A.M. (2006). International perspectives on the use of Community Treatment Orders: Implications for mental health social work. *British Journal of Social Work, 36*, 1101–1118.

Chenoweth, L. & McAuliffe, D. (2011). *The road to social work and human service practice* (3rd ed.). South Melbourne: Cengage.

Clark, C. (2011). From rules to encounters: Ethical decision-making as a hermeneutic process. *Journal of Social Work*. doi:10.1177/1468017310383003

Clifford, D., & Burke, B. (2009). *Anti-oppressive ethics and values in social work*. Basingstoke: Palgrave.

Congress, E. (1999). *Social work values and ethics: Identifying and resolving professional dilemmas*. Chicago, IL: Nelson Hall.

Congress, E. (2010) Codes of ethics. In M. Gray & Webb, S.A. (eds), *Ethics and value perspectives in social work*. New York: Palgrave, pp. 19–30.

Cooper, R.J., Bissell, P., & Wingfield, J. (2008). Ethical decision-making, passivity and pharmacy. *Journal of Medical Ethics, 34*, 441–445.

Cottone, R.R., & Claus, R.E. (2000). Ethical decision-making models: A review of the literature. *Journal of Counseling and Development, 78*(3), 275–283.

De Cremer, D. (ed.) (2009). *Psychological perspectives on ethical behaviour and decision-making*. Charlotte, NC: Information Age Publications.

Dixon, J. (2010). Social supervision, ethics and risk: An evaluation of how ethical frameworks might be applied within the social supervision process. *British Journal of Social Work, 40*(8), 2398–2413.

Dolgoff, R., Loewenberg, F.M., & Harrington, D. (2009). *Ethical decisions for social work practice* (8th ed.). Belmont, CA: Thomson, Brooks Cole.

Freegard, H. (2006). *Ethical practice for health professionals*. South Melbourne: Thomson.

Fry, S.T. & Johnstone, M.-J. (2008). *Ethics in nursing practice: A guide to ethical decision-making*. Chichester: Wiley-Blackwell.

Gigerenzer, G. (2008). Why heuristics work. *Perspectives on Psychological Science, 3*(1), 20–29.

Good, L. (2008). Ethical decision-making in disaster triage. *Journal of Emergency Nursing*. 34(2), 112–115.

Gray, M. (2010). Moral sources and emergent ethical theories in social work. *British Journal of Social Work, 40*, 1794–1811.

Gray, M., & Gibbons, J. (2007). There are no answers, only choices: Teaching ethical decision making in social work. *Australian Social Work, 60*(7), 222–238.

Gray, M., & Webb, S.A. (2010). *Ethics and value perspectives in social work*. New York: Palgrave Macmillan.

Gray, M., Coates, J., & Yellow-Bird, M. (2008). *Indigenous social work around the world: Towards culturally relevant social work practice*. Aldershot: Ashgate.

Guttman, D. (2006). *Ethics in social work: A context of caring*. New York: Haworth Social Work Practice Press.

Hayibor, S., & Wasieleski, D.M. (2008). Effects of the use of the availability heuristic on ethical decision-making in organization. *Journal of Business Ethics, 80*(1), 151–165.

Healy, L.M. (2007). Universalism and cultural relativism in social work ethics. *International Social Work, 50*(1), 11–26.

Hugman, R. (2005a). *New approaches in ethics for the caring professions*. New York: Palgrave Macmillan.

Hugman, R. (2005b). Exploring the paradox of teaching ethics for social work practice. *Social Work Education, 24*(5), 535–545.

Husted, J.H., & Husted, G.L. (2008). *Ethical decision-making in nursing and health care: A symphonological approach* (8th ed.). New York: Springer Publishing Company.

International Federation of Social Workers (IFSW) (2004). *Ethics in social work: Statement of principles*. Retrieved on December 2, 2010 from http://www.ifsw.org/f38000032.html.

Kreuger, D.L. (2008). Ethical decision-making in neurosurgery: A case study. *Journal of Neuroscience Nursing, 40*(6), 346–349.

Landau, R. (2001). Ethical dilemmas in general hospitals. *Social Work in Health Care. 32*(2), 75–92.

Larkin, H. (2007). The ethics of social work practice in the nursing home setting: A consultant's dilemma. *Journal of Social Work Values and Ethics, 4*(3). Retrieved on March 16, 2011 from http://www.socialworker.com/jswve/content/view/67/54/.

Levy, C. (1982). *Guide to ethical decisions and actions for social service administrators: A handbook for managerial personnel*. New York: Haworth Press.

Littlechild, B., & Hawley, C. (2010). Risk assessments for mental health service users: Ethical, valid and reliable? *Journal of Social Work, 10*(2), 211–229.

Linzer, N. (1999). *Resolving ethical dilemmas in social work practice*. Boston: Allyn & Bacon.

Lo, B. (2005). *Resolving ethical dilemmas: A guide for clinicians*. Philadelphia: Lippincott, Williams & Wilkins.

Loewenberg, F.M., & Dolgoff, R. (1982). *Ethical decisions for social work practice*. Itasca, IL: Peacock Publishers.

Mattison, M. (2000). Ethical decision-making: The person in the process. *Social Work, 45*(3), 201–212.

McAuliffe, D. (2010). Ethical decision-making. In M. Gray & Webb, S.A. (eds), *Ethics and value perspectives in social work*. New York: Palgrave Macmillan, pp. 41–50.

McAuliffe, D., & Chenoweth, L. (2008) Leave no stone unturned: The inclusive model of ethical decision-making. *Ethics and Social Welfare*, *2*(1), 38–49.

McBeath, G.B., & Webb, S.A. (1989). A political critique of Kantian ethics in social work. *British Journal of Social Work*, *20*(1), 491–506.

Miller, P. (2007). *Ethical decision-making in social work and counselling*. Australia: Thomson Nelson.

Monteverde, S. (2009). The importance of time in ethical decision-making. *Nursing Ethics*, *16*(5), 613–624.

Montgomery, K. (2006). *How doctors think: Clinical judgement and the practice of medicine*. New York: Oxford University Press.

Morrissey, S., & Reddy, P. (2006). *Ethics and professional practice for psychologists*. South Melbourne: Thomson Social Science Press.

Munro, E. (2010). Learning to reduce risk in child protection. *British Journal of Social Work*, *40*(4), 1135–1151.

Osmo, R., & Landau, R. (2006). The role of ethical theories in decision making by social workers. *Social Work Education*, *25*(8), 863–876.

Pockett, R. (2010). Interprofessional education for practice: Some implications for Australian social work. *Australian Social Work*, *63*(2), 207–222.

Raines, M. (2000) Ethical decision-making in nurses: Relationships among moral reasoning, coping style, and ethics stress. *JONA's Healthcare Law, Ethics and Regulation*. *2*(1), 29–41.

Raines, J.C., & Dibble, N.C. (2010). *Ethical decision-making in school mental health*. New York: Oxford University Press.

Reamer, F. (1998). The evolution of social work values and ethics. *Social Work*, *43*(6), 488–500.

Reamer, F. (2001). *Ethics education in social work*. Alexandria: Council on Social Work Education.

Reamer, F. (2006). *Social work values and ethics*. New York: Columbia University Press.

Rhodes, M. (1986). *Ethical dilemmas in social work practice*. Boston: Routledge & Kegan Paul.

Robison, W., & Reeser, L.C. (2000). *Ethical decision-making in social work*. Boston: Allyn & Bacon.

Rothman, J.C. (2005). *From the front lines: Student cases in social work ethics*. Boston: Allyn & Bacon.

Seedhouse, D. & Lovett, L. (1992). *Practical medical ethics*. Chichester: John Wiley & Sons.

Steinman, S.O., Richardson, N.F., & McEnroe, T. (1998). *The ethical decision-making manual for helping professionals*. Pacific Grove: Brooks/Cole.

Stephenson, J.A. & Staal, M.A. (2010). An ethical decision-making model for operational psychology. *Ethics and Behaviour*, *17*(1), 61–82.

Thompson, I.E. (2006). *Nursing ethics* (5th ed.). Edinburgh: Churchill, Livingstone, Elsevier.

Trevithick, P. (2008). Revisiting the knowledge base of social work: A framework for practice. *British Journal of Social Work*, *38*(6), 1212–1237.

Webb, S.A. (2006). *Social work in a risk society*. Basingstoke: Palgrave.

Williams, T. (2002). Patient empowerment and ethical decision-making. *Dimensions of Critical Care Nursing*, *21*(3), 100–104.

White, S., & Featherstone, B. (2005). Creating misunderstandings: Multi-agency work as social practice. *Child and Family Social Work*, *10*(3), 207–216.

Yeung, K.S.S., Ho, A.P.Y., Lo, M.C.H., & Chan, E.A. (2010). Social work ethical decision-making in an inter-disciplinary context. *British Journal of Social Work*, *40*, 1573–1590.

Zindler, L. (2005). Ethical decision-making in first trimester pregnancy screening. *Journal of Perinatal Neonatal Nursing*, *19*(2), 122–131.

21

Anti-Oppressive Practice

Lena Dominelli

Social work purports to be a profession with its roots in its activities to enhance people's well-being and uphold the values of human rights and social justice. Yet, it has a legacy of failing to protect children under its care, being involved in imperialist ventures, and not defending the interests of some of the world's most marginalised and excluded peoples. This chapter explores innovations in social work theory and practice that arose largely from grassroots challenges to social work's historical and contemporary oppressive practices. Currently, these are largely encompassed by the umbrella term of anti-oppressive social work, which has recently been enlarged by considerations of an integrated model of social justice drawing on what is referred to as the 'ethical turn' in the social sciences. Inspired by the work of Nancy Fraser and Axel Honneth, it underscores a fresh engagement with the ethics of redistribution and recognition and the way in which social work might make a positive contribution to this agenda. This progressive political agenda paves the way for an integrated model of social justice (Webb, 2010). Theories and practices now widely acknowledged as underpinning what has been termed anti-oppressive practice (AOP) originally grew out of controversies arising in the UK. It has now become a form of social work recognised across the world and is being developed further in other countries. It also has a considerable distance to cover if it is to fulfil its transformational promise of supporting people who access services in receiving the culturally appropriate provisions they both need and want.

SOCIAL WORK'S HISTORY OF OPPRESSION IN PRACTICE

Professional social work was initially developed in Europe (Kendall, 2001) at the end of the 19th century in the interstices of the nation-state (Lorenz, 1994). It became an important tool used by ruling elites to quell rising unrest and counter the popularity of social democratic ideologies as working-class activists sought to address the worst excess of capitalist development in urban cities through organised collective action including political parties, community collaborations and workplace organisations (Dominelli, 1991, 1997, 2010; Ginsburg, 1979). Attempts to contain working class discontent in the slums of London where squalor, poverty, and crime were rife (Stedman Jones, 1971) absorbed a British imperialist ruling class seeking to avoid the popular uprisings that had taken place throughout continental Europe in the 1830s and to control the spread of socialist ideologies at home and abroad. Bismark in Prussia had already demonstrated the value of making available welfare resources to the German working class in undermining the growth of the Social Democratic Party (SDP) in that country (Ginsburg, 1979).

Moreover, imperialist nations like the UK later exported their approaches on social welfare to the colonies where White settlers sought to recreate the institutions and inegalitarian social relations they were familiar with at home, and thereby privilege and enrich themselves. This included social work as an institutional practice. It became part of an empire-building strategy predicated on the destruction of indigenous ways of life, especially in Canada, the USA, New Zealand, and Australia where White settlers demanded private property rights over once communally owned lands, and forced the destruction of local indigenous cultures, languages, and institutions. The infamous residential schools (Haig-Brown, 1988), 'Stolen Generations' of children (Humphreys, 1996), and creation of reserves and legislation privileging White settlers (Grande, 2004; Siggins, 2005), all contributed to the formation of oppressive forms of social work in the colonies (Dominelli, 2004; Gray et al., 2010).

At the inception of the profession in Europe, the existence of private philanthropy to care for 'the sick' and 'the needy' who *deserved* to obtain help from sources external to the family, coincided with the availability of White middle- and upper-class women who could 'do good' by imparting the values of self-sufficiency and thrift to working-class women (Dominelli, 2004; Webb, 2007). The coming together of these three strands – reducing public disorder; limited state interventions in mitigating the harshest elements of an industrial system; and having available a trusted labour force to 'visit deserving families' and show by example how they could pull themselves up by the bootstraps, furthered the development of professional social work (Dominelli, 2010). The need to respond to these crises by offering help while at the same time exerting control over the type of activism the lower-class orders were inclined to engage in gave rise to what Foucault (1980) termed the 'psy' professions or 'social' professions of which social work is one. The emphasis on both care and control also created the contradictions remaining at the heart of the profession today (Corrigan & Leonard, 1978).

Social work has had other earlier origins in the charitable activities undertaken collectively in communities, often under the auspices of religious organisations, by private philanthropists, and nuclear and extended families. Social work, in the sense of spreading resources from those who have to those who have not, can be considered a form of networked social capital that results in a redistribution of social goods, including labour, whether as bonding social capital within small known groups of people like a family; as bridging social capital in small neighbourhood or village communities; or as linking social capital with those further afield. Professional social work transcends the boundaries of bonding and bridging social capital by linking social capital, which covers what has become known as state social work whereby publicly funded welfare resources are exchanged between strangers without the need for personal connections between them, as is typical in private charitable forms of giving. However, a social worker building egalitarian working relations with a person who wishes to access the services they control is drawing on relationships and knowledge acquired mainly at the interpersonal level. In this chapter, social work refers to professional social work regardless of the setting in which it occurs or service user group or individual receiving support.

Social work aimed to solve personal and social problems. From the beginning, there was considerable debate about their causes. How much could be attributed to individual failings and how much to the ways in which society was organised exercised the thinking and practice of the early reformers who established the profession. Eventually, these produced two conflicting approaches to social work: one led by the Charity Organisation Society (COS), which emphasised personal culpability and promoted individual casework or one-to-one work; and the other fostered by the Settlement Movement had a more structural orientation and focused on dealing with poverty, housing, and unemployment through community development (Walton, 1975).

The casework advocated by the COS also sought to raise the professional and scientific status of social work and developed criteria whereby individuals had to behave according to certain accepted principles in order to receive assistance. This has created the 'deserving' and 'undeserving' division among claimants and privileged middle-class attitudes towards life that have been retained in social work. Today, this phenomenon is more likely to be understood as 'looking promising', which is a less stigmatising term for a differentiated approach to claimants (Callahan et al., 2002) that ensures that those who do 'look promising' are considered part of the 'deserving' group of claimants and therefore eligible for social work services and/or social worker support. The Settlement Movement created community centres such as Toynbee Hall in the East End of London encouraging university students to work on social problems with local communities. These ideas were later adopted by Jane Addams in Chicago where she established Hull House for community workers to engage local people in solving their issues. Although community work continues to be part of social work as one of the three basic methods of the profession in many parts of the world (Webb, 2007; Younghusband, 1978), this has ceased to be the case in England and Wales since 1986.

Professional expertise and knowledge also legitimated social workers' right to intervene in the private domain of the family and strengthened top-down views of power relations that have been central to oppressive dynamics reproduced in and through practice. The individualised model promoted by the COS became the hegemonic mode of practice. Although it has since had various transformations ranging from a highly specialised psychodynamic casework to care management, the primary concern with individual shortcomings has remained. This vision of the profession's remit was also incorporated into state social work when it became part of the British welfare state. Despite having ideals premised on the notion people were entitled to services as part of their citizenship status, the state refused to fund the personal social services on a universal basis as recommended in the Beveridge Report, although it did so for health and education (Kincaid, 1973). This reality has not changed since 1945 and is likely to be given new twists favouring market providers by the Coalition Government that assumed power in the UK following the 2010 general elections.

Social work is socially constructed by particular configurations of interest groups and ideologies within specific sociocultural, historical, political, and economic contexts. Understanding these contexts and their impact on practice is integral to anti-oppressive social work. Diverse contexts also make the profession a diverse and heterogeneous one with locality-specific characteristics, even though it may reflect the views of the dominant social group. Meanwhile, similarities in theories and methods enable others outside a specific locality to recognise practitioners' activities as social work. Some authors have argued this gives social work one grand narrative that it seeks to impose all over the world as part of a neo-imperialist mission (e.g., Webb, 2003). Others like Dominelli (2004, 2010) suggest social work has many narratives and assuming one grand narrative writes out the stories of those who have resisted the imposition of a dominant paradigm in the profession, as do indigenous people and those who struggled for anti-oppressive measures to be taken seriously by practitioners and academics. Seeing social work as having a single grand narrative privileges those actively engaged in oppressing people through practice across the world. Thus, it is crucial that the stories of those involved in developing anti-oppressive theories and practice and who provide countervailing narratives should be recognised as significant in developing alternative theories and practices to those endorsed by hegemonic paradigms. The chapter now turns to examining the rise, strengths, and shortcomings of anti-oppressive practice.

ANTI-OPPRESSIVE SOCIAL WORK THEORIES AND PRACTICE

Defining anti-oppressive practice

Defining anti-oppressive practice remains contested because people interpret words and give them different meanings. However, to highlight its specific concerns, Dominelli (1993) defined anti-oppressive practice as:

> a form of social work practice which addresses social divisions and structural inequalities in the work that is done with people whether they be users ('clients') or workers and which aims to provide more appropriate and sensitive services which respond to people's needs regardless of their social status. Anti-oppressive practice embodies a person-centred philosophy, an egalitarian value system concerned with reducing the deleterious effects of structural inequalities upon people's lives; a methodology focusing on both process and outcome; and a way of structuring relationships between individuals that aims to empower users by reducing the negative effects of hierarchy (p. 11).

This definition addresses anti-oppressive practice's contextualised and holistic orientation and its attempt to engage with agency, the complexities of life, and fluid situations people encounter in their lives as they seek to exert control over their social and physical environments while meeting their needs and claiming their entitlements. These considerations provide anti-oppressive practice with an outlook promoting activism and resilience in people and their communities. In addition, anti-oppressive practice:

- is based on human rights and citizenship;
- considers individuals as agents in their own lives and values their uniqueness;
- seeks to address structural inequalities and redistribute resources from those who have to those who do not;
- promotes empowering forms of practice;
- facilitates individual growth alongside community development;
- fosters theoretical and practice innovations;
- centres hegemonic power relations; and
- supports holistic interventions.

The value orientation of anti-oppressive practice

The values of anti-oppressive practice were concerned with the realisation of egalitarian social relations and their reflection in and through professional social work. These were:

- equality;
- agency;
- interdependence;
- solidarity;
- reciprocity;
- empowerment;
- human rights; and
- social justice.

To engage in practice reflecting these values in a critical and sensitive manner, social workers have to understand the dynamics of oppression as they operate at the personal, institutional, and cultural levels. These involve unpacking binaries of superiority and inferiority whereby individuals who are different and or marginalised are 'othered' and working within a holistic contextualised and locality-specific framework. Practising them involves understanding theories about socially constructed realities and empowerment.

The binary classifying people as superior and inferior creates dynamics that divide people into 'them' and 'us' and is integral to identity politics and hegemonic power relations. In oppositional identity politics, this exclusion is used to create protected spaces for reclaiming rights and voices. In hegemonic social relations, those encompassed in the 'us' category are included, those in the 'them' category are excluded. 'Othering' marginalises and disempowers people and is crucial in perpetuating the dynamics of oppression individually, institutionally, and culturally. At the individual level, these are embedded in a person's belief system if they hold themselves and others like them equal, but deny others who are different from them the same treatment. Institutionally, exclusion occurs through policies and practices marginalising, excluding, and limiting others, usually according to bureaucratic means linked to criteria of entitlement that can cause both direct and indirect forms of discrimination to occur. In cultural terms, exclusion fostered through hegemonic values and norms endorses the assumptions behind what is accepted as unquestioned everyday behaviour in a particular society and reproduces it without thought or reflecting critically upon what is taken for granted and affirmed in and through routines in everyday life.

The rise of anti-oppressive practice, the politics of identity, and redistribution

Anti-oppressive social work arose through the endeavours of grassroots activists who participated in the new social movements of the 1960s, 1970s, and 1980s, particularly the feminist movement, the Black activist movement, and the disability movement as they sought to understand why social work, which should have been supporting them and providing them with urgently needed and appropriate services often oppressed them through what was on offer and in how those services were made available to them (Dominelli, 1997, 2004, 2010). These social movements had a trenchant critique of the: inegalitarian capitalist social relations in which services were embedded; society's stigmatising views of people who were outside the dominant White middle-class male norms; and condescension with which services were provided for those who were different.

Marxist theories of political economy, socialist ideologies, particularly those espoused by revolutionaries such as Chairman Mao in China, Che Guevera in Cuba, Regis de Bray in France, Franz Fanon in French-speaking Africa, and Ben Bella in Algeria, became popularised by those in the new social movements and enriched their thinking about different possibilities in the organisation of human relations. In the West, these usually affirmed notions of self-determination through participative democracy and ideas of worker self-management, which also spread into the welfare arena. There, they became translated into claimants determining and controlling the services they utilised. These became significant in the discourses of redistribution permeating discussions about transforming the personal social services and forming alliances to engage working-class activists including those involved in the trade union movement and professionals on the left wing of the political spectrum. Disaffected practitioners, academics, and service users began writing alternative stories for social work, critiquing class-based forms of oppression through easy-to-read magazines, such as *Case Con*, during the 1970s. These critiques brought the politics of redistribution back into social work.

Radical social work, from which anti-oppressive social work developed, had focused on the politics of redistribution and emphasised the class-based nature of the oppression of those who accessed state assistance through the welfare system (Corrigan & Leonard, 1978). They also sought alliances with trade unionists and community activists in arguing for worker-controlled social services. While these received sympathetic support around certain housing and employment issues, such that many gains in workplace relations might be attributed to these forms of resistance (e.g., equal pay for women and an end to discrimination in housing provision for Black people), they failed to galvanise service users, women, and Black activists in the way the new social movements based on a singular identity trait did. Part of this failure was the privileging of White middle-class men and the hierarchy of divisions associated with such social relations. Another was its lack of specific suggestions for alternative services in practice.

The new social movements' concerns about the unequal distribution of power and resources in society were eventually incorporated into identity politics emphasising power relations predicated around identity attributes. Their identity politics concentrated on how power relations were constructed around social divisions based on identity traits like class, race, age, disability, and gender, and used to oppress people or keep them in their place as passive recipients of social goodwill. To create the spaces around which they could analyse and resist oppressive power relations, activists in identity-based groups initiated protected zones from which those different from them were barred (e.g., women-only spaces). While these can be considered exclusionary politics, they were crucial to the formulation of theories about identity and the development of services generated by the group in question without external involvement by those holding hegemonic power. The practices of resistance emanating through these social organisations undermined existing oppressive social relations and became central to the politics of representation aimed at reclaiming marginalised identities.

Questions around identity became concerns that eventually brought people together in groups to understand the answers (e.g., 'Who am I?' 'Why am I being treated in this way?' 'Am I alone in getting such treatment?' 'What can I do about it?'). By working in groups, they were able to explore identity issues in the contexts of the hegemonic social power relations within which they were embedded and expose the commonalities in their oppression alongside the different expressions this took, depending on the social division(s) being considered.

At first, each social division espoused its own social critique, for example, Corrigan and Leonard (1978) on class, Dominelli and McLeod (1989) on gender, Dominelli (1988) and Ahmad (1990) on race, Mama (1989) on gender and race, Oliver (1990) on disability, Morris (1991) on gender and disability, Begum (1992) on race and disability. However, they came to share a focus on unequal power relations and an imperative to change society. Moreover, anti-oppressive practitioners and scholars built on the foundations laid by radical social work (Bailey and Brake, 1975), especially its analyses of privilege and power, for example, Butler (1990) for gender, Spender (1970) for power relations embedded in language, Fryer (1989) for colonising practices linked to race. The politics of redistribution and the politics of recognition were to become integral elements of anti-oppressive practice.

Identity politics underpin the politics of recognition whereby the reclaiming of collective rights affirming social justice have become popularised. They were also significant in shaping the development of anti-oppressive social work. The commitment to eradicating social injustice, however caused, and the labelling of society including social work as oppressive, gave anti-oppressive practice its critical and transformative edge. These concerns also placed anti-oppressive practice on a collision course with the ruling elites, which in the UK, included Members of Parliament responsible for funding social work and legislating upon its activities. In the early 1990s, its detractors, including the then Secretary of State responsible for social services, Virginia Bottomley, rejected the legitimacy of anti-oppressive practice's commitment to social justice and emancipatory social relations and argued for 'business as usual'. Bottomley went so far as to discredit the entire notion of professional social work by declaring 'any street-wise granny can do social work' (in Dominelli, 2009, p. 8).

On the whole, those involved in anti-oppressive practice at the grassroots level were interested in creating services they designed, ran, and controlled. At first, the forays into social work by these new social movements experimented with the creation of services to meet their needs, change the nature of their relationship with professionals in the field, and hold them accountable for the services they provided. Later, they sought to mainstream these practices with varying degrees of success. Contemporary services for women, especially those addressing physical and sexual violence in intimate relationships, were built on early feminist initiatives. Black and ethnic minorities secured employment in the state social work sector and in the social work academy and Black students entered universities in greater numbers. Meanwhile, activist practitioners found employment in the academy. There, they developed theories to explain oppression, conducted research highlighting the hardship endured by those wishing to access the personal social services, and challenged existing hegemonic theories and paradigms for practice.

Those developing anti-oppressive practice also sought to transcend the limitations of radical social work, particularly those linked to: a hierarchy of oppressions privileging class relations and failing to integrate other identity traits into its analysis of political economy; understandings of power relations predicted on zero-sum notions of power based on the thought of Talcott Parsons (1967); the reproduction of traditional views of professional power; and a fragmented approach to service delivery.

In its place, they sought to go beyond the politics of recognition revolving around a single social division to create: holistic practice based on the person in the environment; bottom-up relationships based upon egalitarian relations of power; the validation of local knowledges and wisdom; and an understanding of the links between the location of the person in a social setting and the social relations within which they were embedded (Belenky et al., 1997; Freire, 1970). Rising above the limits of radical social work without losing its incisive critique of society, especially that originating in the politics of redistribution, when combined with the politics of representation, enabled anti-oppressive practice to develop diversity, depth, and richness while remaining rooted in particular localities and contexts. Expanding the theoretical repertoire alongside its practices became important considerations in anti-oppressive practice and is reflected in the writings of various authors (e.g., Braye & Preston-Shoot, 1995; Dalrymple & Burke, 1995; Dominelli, 2002). The theoretical approaches espoused in anti-oppressive practice were and are varied, but they share common features, particularly in their value orientation and goals.

Theoretical considerations about the politics of identity and recognition are situated as part of an 'ethical turn' in the social sciences and have rich implications for social work. If misrecognition stands for the deprecation of an identity as disabled, woman, gay, or Black by the dominant culture and the consequent damage to a group member's sense of self-identity, then poverty and economic exclusion stand at the extreme redistribution end of the recognition–distribution spectrum. Bridget Fowler (2009) suggests the redistribution–recognition debate, originally conducted by Nancy Fraser and Axel Honneth, promises to be as significant 'in the 21st century as the Protestant Ethic debate or the Althusserians/Culturalists debate were in the 20th century' (p. 144). A key issue in the rich exchange between Fraser and Honneth is whether an analytical distinction between different forms of social suffering is needed: on the one hand, the denial of recognition for certain social groups who are subjected to exploitation and prejudice and, on the other, the consequences of vast disparities of stratified wealth and income (Fowler, 2009). Debate about the significance of the politics of recognition and redistribution in producing an integrated model of social justice for social work has recently taken a fresh turn in contributions by Houston (2008), Garrett (2009), and Webb (2010). Together, these critical commentaries, using social work as a concrete case, reveal the explanatory power of the redistribution–recognition interaction by connecting the socioeconomic and sociocultural aspects of injustice. This may have far-reaching implications for anti-oppressive practice in social work. As Webb (2010) notes:

> the defence of social work is often conducted along ethical grounds associated with notions of the 'public good'. However, there are strong economic arguments for suggesting that social work is a vehicle for redistributive justice in practice [and thereby give an innovative thrust to one of its original aims] (p. 10).

As Webb (2010) goes on to note:

> a critical social work oriented towards a social justice framework must have as its object the correspondence of two homologous structures: the ethics of recognition, concerned with cultural injustice and suffering, and an ethics of redistribution, focused on redressing economic injustice (p. 13).

In practising anti-oppressively, social workers can contribute to the transformation of established power relations in the field of economic inequalities and cultural injustice. As shown below, anti-oppressive practice has close affinities with the transformative aspects of redistributive social justice and the affirmative components of the ethics of recognition (see Garrett, 2009; Houston, 2008).

Practising anti-oppressively

For those endorsing the values of and implementing anti-oppressive practice, changing existing social relations is unavoidable. A social-change orientation supporting groups in struggles to end oppression within frameworks aiming to eradicate oppression in all its guises became a key element in anti-oppressive practice. Its holistic and egalitarian approach to the person resulted in practitioners critiquing power relations that depicted those accessing services in narrow, bureaucratic terms. In reifying their personhood, they cast them as dependent on others and denied them agency (e.g., the stigmatisation associated with terms like the handicapped and the elderly). Thus, changing language became another vehicle for destigmatising and changing practice (Spender, 1970). Disabled activists took a key role in struggles associated with these activities by affirming agency through active citizenship and demanding social justice and human rights. The politics of recognition were significant in shaping people's demands for acceptance for whom they were, and not for what they were expected to become under edicts emanating from the dominant social groups. These approaches are particularly evident in indigenous approaches to social work (Gray et al., 2010), especially among the Maori of Aotearoa/New Zealand (Tait Rolleston & Pehi-Barlow, 2001) and the First Nations of Canada (Green & Thomas, 2007) as they reclaim their spirituality, traditional cultures and languages, and ways of helping those in need. A return to indigenous forms of helping is also evident in North America (Grande, 2004), Malaysia (How Kee, 2010), and China (Yip, 2007).

Dominelli (1997) located anti-oppressive practice within emancipatory approaches to social work thereby defining it as an alternative to the therapeutic or maintenance approach espoused by Martin Davies (1983). Anti-oppressive practice's professional commitments to transformative social change, including the redistribution of power and wealth, and the empowerment of service users, were roundly condemned by its opponents who labelled such approaches unprofessional and counter to the history of neutrality and expert knowledge inherent in social work's professionalism (Pinker, 1993). Yet, social change was espoused by anti-oppressive practitioners because the people who accessed services under oppressive conditions demanded such change. Moreover, anti-oppressive practice was consistent with the values of human agency, equality, human rights, active citizenship, and social justice. And, these values were, at least in theory, typical of those espoused by an advanced democratic state. Additionally, anti-oppressive practitioners focused on the entire relationship developed between the person seeking services and their physical and social environments. This meant focusing on inputs – what went into the relationship (resources and people); the processes used in that relationship (how the work was done); and the results of an intervention as evaluated by those receiving services (outcomes) rather than a manager using bureaucratic means to control professional labour and the use of resources (Dominelli, 1996).

For those who practised anti-oppressive practice, the values of equality, human rights, empowerment, active citizenship, and social justice were not simply empty words. They were to pave the way for transformative social action led by people at the grassroots. Action resulting in the formation of alternative services claimants actually wanted was required. The controversies around values and their acceptability for professional practice seem unbelievable today. But it was not until New Labour in the UK mainstreamed at least its rhetoric after its landslide victory in 1997 that these values became acceptable parts of British mainstream practice. This mainstreaming was to become reflected in its modernisation agenda for the public services which later included the personal social services.

As part of this preoccupation, New Labour introduced policies seeking to respond to service-users' agendas. Especially relevant in this respect were the personalisation agenda and individual budgets. These were items the disability movement in particular had been seeking for several decades. Through such demands, they sought to ensure service users' voices were heard and they secured control over service delivery. However, the results have been highly bureaucratised and imposed substantial administrative burdens on service users, for example, turning them into employers responsible for paying the taxes, national insurance, and superannuation contributions of those they chose to employ with money originating from the taxpayer without the support necessary for implementing complicated procedures requiring fairly legalistic knowledge (Dominelli, 2010).

The modernisation approach also individualised service delivery to the extent that getting the specific services a person needed became a matter for individual decision from a range of options available. Raising collective questions about society's responsibilities in facilitating access to services, developing new services, and ensuring accountability for services delivered – whether by the private (market), voluntary, or state sector – fell off the agenda. As part of neoliberalism, affordability and keeping costs down became the key drivers in the state's management of the public sector, firmly embedding business practices in service delivery as the links between the personal and structural became invisible. This outcome also detracted from anti-oppressive practice's potential to secure social change since there was no need to develop an empowering environment when those accessing services and those providing them related to one another. The professional also became redundant though, in theory, this might not be undesirable. Indeed, in the 1970s, radical social workers talked about making this a practice requirement, but when the state simply removes professionals from the scene to save money and does not support service users requiring professional assistance, then conforming to state demands becomes a problem.

Reducing costs resulted in the loss of an original aim of the welfare state – to redistribute social resources from those who have to those who have not. The politics of redistribution no longer featured prominently in the political repertoire of the British nation-state. They were eschewed for 'business as usual', which prioritises economic over social needs and ends with poor people bearing the brunt of diminished funding for welfare services that, in the former welfare state, had been free to all at the point of need.

The radical transformative potential of anti-oppressive practice was undermined by such moves and mainstreaming became a way of sidelining its strengths. Assessing the development of anti-oppressive practice under New Labour thus is not to devalue the significance of the changes it initiated or the contributions its modernisation agenda made to empowering individuals. But progress on these terms needs to be challenged if anti-oppressive practice's mandate for change is to be reactivated and structural inequalities are to be addressed (see Chapter 47). Anti-oppressive practice involves a people-centred approach. It requires concern not only with the personal but also the structural. Anti-oppressive practice avers a focus on the personal at the expense of structural and collective action. It also means reasserting the significance of the politics of redistribution so social resources – whether economic capital or political power – are equitably distributed and social relations changed to accommodate social inclusion and an active citizenry. Reconfiguring professional relationships to make them more egalitarian, empowering service users to place them in positions of power regarding service design and delivery, and validating their knowledge of everyday life practices are important aspects of transformative change. Practitioners working in anti-oppressive ways who understand the use of anti-oppressive values for practice focus upon:

- understanding the dynamics of oppression – their production and reproduction in personal belief systems and forms of behaviour; and their embeddedness in institutional and cultural practices;
- appreciating people as whole human beings living in specific cultural, social, political, economic, and historical contexts;
- working with people to address their problems holistically and involving them in devising solutions;
- understanding the connections between their particular personal beliefs and location in a social structure and how this draws upon institutional policies and cultural practices and impacts on their relationships with service users;
- appreciating the complex links between different forms of oppression and how the dynamics of oppression interact with, feed off each other, and change as people negotiate their interactions with one another;
- creating alliances to change existing oppressive social relations within and outside social work at the personal and structural levels; and
- supporting claims made by those seeking social justice and affirmation of their human rights. Promoting resilience and agency among service users.

Deconstructing socially constructed categories

People accessing and using services are experts in their own culture. The practitioner's task is to engage them in a conversation where both service user and practitioner can develop cultural understanding. Such understanding can only be reached dialogically if presumptions about the culture of others are to be tested and verified. (Dominelli, 2008, pp. 203–204) 'substitution strategy' (p. 8). is helpful here. It is a form of reflective engagement from a critical standpoint to highlight logical absurdities in people's conceptions of one another – especially simplistic binary thinking – which once exposed for their absurdity can then be substituted by cultural facts interactively obtained. In the process, practitioners unravel their confusion when encountering unsettling differences. Sometimes, practitioners can achieve substitution by asking themselves whether they would react to someone from their own culture as they do to someone from a different culture. For example, in 2010, a group of Tamil refugees arrived in Canada in a boat believed to be run by human traffickers. Putting aside the issue of trafficking for a moment, the Canadian public labelled the 490 people on board, which included pregnant women and children, 'terrorists' because the Tamil Tigers were a banned organisation there. So, Tamil refugees were being configured not as individuals in particular circumstances, but as if they were all alike – active members of a militant group of people called 'terrorists'. This 'them–us' binary 'othered' Tamil refugees construing 'them' as a problem warranting exclusion from 'citizenship' in Canada. They had not broken any Canadian laws and were claiming asylum in keeping with Canadian and international law under the 1951 Geneva Convention. A social worker supporting people in this case could use the substitution strategy to expose the oppressive dynamics that the Canadian media used to construct this particular scenario. To stand back from this popular conceptualisation of the asylum seekers, a social worker of European descent using a substitution strategy would ask whether public reaction would be the same if a group of white European origins living in Sri Lanka had entered Canada by similar means, thus substituting 'us' for 'them'. It is unlikely that the public would see such a group as terrorists, even if they accepted that one or two individual terrorists might be amongst them. Moreover, they would be willing to have immigration authorities consider each case on its merits.

Limitations of anti-oppressive practice

Identity issues are crucial to the dynamics of oppression and the struggles to overcome repressive relations. They also account for some of the complexities anti-oppressive practitioners seek to address. Tackling these issues is not easy because identities are created in and through social interactions whereby those interacting are creating both their own identity and that of the other person(s) in the process. For this reason, knowing oneself and understanding the impact of one's own structural positionality and persona on others when interacting with them is an integral part of becoming a practitioner and exuding a sense of confidence about working in accordance with basic anti-oppressive practice principles. However, considerable numbers of social workers feel poorly equipped to deal with these dimensions of anti-oppressive practice. Many practitioners feel thwarted by anti-oppressive practice. They feel personally disempowered because they do not understand: (i) the dynamics of oppression; (ii) the way in which they reproduce these daily in and through their own practice, especially if they declare themselves tolerant, egalitarian, and democratic individuals; (iii) their fears about being labelled oppressive if they make mistakes; (iv) the significance of culture in both same-cultural and cross-cultural relationships; or (v) their feelings of guilt resulting from their privileged or powerful positions in relation to those with and for whom they work.

These fears are normal and can be addressed if practitioners become accountable to those with whom they are working; feel free to ask questions about issues or phenomena they do not know about or understand; and contextualise themselves and service users in locality-specific ways (i.e., by locating themselves in their local cultural, social, political, economic, and physical environments). Anti-oppressive practice's 'substitution strategy' (Dominelli, 2008, pp. 203–204) enables practitioners to deconstruct their taken-for-granted assumptions and stereotypical responses to people by using simple probing questions to understand and value diversity. These would be aimed at unpacking the specifics of a situation and could take the form of: 'Who?' 'When?' 'Where?' 'What?' 'Why?' No one practitioner could know and understand all the cultures that might be present in their practice locality. But if practitioners understood themselves, their own culture, and how it becomes part of the backdrop within which they operate, they could ask these questions. They would not then experience a need to have a toolkit explaining all unfamiliar cultures.

CONCLUSION

Anti-oppressive practice has been criticised for being strong on identifying oppressive social conditions but weaker on practical solutions. Social workers choosing to practise from this perspective would:

- take action to tackle social inequalities in their own organisations or communities and the profession more generally;

- participate in alliances to address structural inequalities on the personal, institutional, and sociocultural levels;
- anticipate risks and controversies associated with anti-oppressive practice wherein their activism might threaten their jobs and jeopardise livelihoods;
- act proactively and form alliances with those aiming to end social inequalities;
- undertake research to acquire evidence for the social construction of inequalities among service users;
- undertake individual and collective actions to eliminate inequalities in and through institutional and cultural practices wherever possible;
- mobilise individuals and communities to challenge perceptions of the inevitability of oppression;
- assist people in understanding the dynamics of oppression by revealing their controlling features visible within increasingly punitive welfare governance systems (see Chapter 4); and
- promote egalitarian social relations and partnerships to facilitate service-user empowerment.

The politics of recognition and redistribution provide anti-oppressive practitioners with powerful tools through which to enact anti-oppressive practice and support service users seeking emancipation from oppressive social structures and practices. The mobilisation of an integrated model of social justice within a social work context offers a critical framework for realising both its political and ethically transformative agenda. Anti-oppressive practice's limited gains to date mean considerable scope remains for further struggles in understanding, realising, and researching emancipatory practice premised on egalitarian principles, human rights, social justice, and the participatory mechanisms of an active and inclusive citizenry.

Anti-oppressive practice is most effectively mobilised as a collective response to injustice and discrimination. The task of developing an integrated strategy for social justice in social work is not a job for individual theorists but rather a collective project for researchers, practitioners, and service users – or what Webb (2010) referred to as 'a (re)assembled Left' – engaged in critical deliberation. Recent literature on the politics of recognition and redistribution in social work highlights the way an integrated model of social justice must inevitably confront existing power relations unavoidably caught in an arena of struggle. Among these, Webb (2010) notes, the aim of these struggles 'is the preservation or transformation of the established power relations in the field of economic inequalities and/or cultural injustice' (p. 16). Anti-oppressive practice can be evaluated on the basis of the degree to which it engages with the politics of recognition and redistribution. When it does so, it attempts to subvert the existing dominant rules within the apparatus of the state and the associated neoliberal economy and provides a way of addressing current injustices.

REFERENCES

Ahmad, B. (1990). *Black perspectives in social work.* Birmingham: Venture Press.

Bailey, R., & Brake, M. (1975). *Radical social work.* London: Edward Arnold.

Begum, N. (1992). Disabled women and the feminist agenda. *Feminist Review, 40,* 71–84.

Belenky, M., Clinchy, B., Goldberger, N., & Tarule, J. (1997). *Women's ways of knowing: The development of self, voice and mind.* New York: Basic Books.

Braye, S., & Preston-Shoot, M. (1995). *Empowering practice in social care.* Buckingham: Open University Press.

Butler, J. (1990). *Gender trouble: Feminism and the subversion of identity.* London: Routledge.

Callahan, M., Dominelli, L., Rutman, D., & Strega, S. (2002). Undeserving mothers? Practitioners' experiences working with young mothers in/from care. *Child and Family Social Work, 7,* 149–159.

Corrigan, P., & Leonard, P. (1978). *Social work under capitalism.* London: Macmillan.

Dalrymple, J., & Burke, B. (1995). *Anti-oppressive practice: Social care and the law.* Buckingham: Open University Press.

Davies, M. (1983). *The essential social worker.* Aldershot: Gower.

Dominelli, L. (1988). *Anti-racist social work.* London: BASW/Macmillan (2nd ed. 1997, 3rd ed. 2008).

Dominelli, L. (1991). *Women across continents: Feminist comparative social policy.* Hemel Hempstead: Harvester/Wheatsheaf.

Dominelli, L. (1993). *Social work: Mirror of society or its conscience?* Inaugural Lecture. Sheffield: Sheffield University, Department of Sociological Studies, 26 May.

Dominelli, L. (1996). Deprofessionalising social work: Equal opportunities, competence and postmodernism. *British Journal of Social Work*, 26, 153–175.

Dominelli, L. (1997). *Sociology for social work*. London: Macmillian.

Dominelli, L. (2002). *Anti-oppressive social work theory and practice*. London: Palgrave Macmillan.

Dominelli, L. (2004). *Social work: Theory and practice for a changing profession*. Cambridge, MA: Polity Press.

Dominelli, L. (2008). *Anti-racist social work*. London: Palgrave Macmillan.

Dominelli, L. (2009). *Introducing social work*. Cambridge, MA: Polity Press.

Dominelli, L. (2010). *Social work in a globalizing world*. Cambridge, MA: Polity Press.

Dominelli, L., & McLeod, E. (1989). *Feminist social work*. London: Macmillan.

Foucault, M. (1980). *Power/Knowledge: Selected interviews and other writings, 1972–77*. New York: Pantheon Books.

Fowler, B. (2009). The recognition/redistribution debate and Bourdieu's theory of practice. *Theory, Culture and Society*, 26(1), 144–156.

Freire, P. (1972). *Pedagogy of the oppressed*. Harmondsworth: Penguin.

Fryer, P. (1989). *Staying power: The history of black people in Britain*. London: Pluto Press.

Garrett, P.M. (2009). Recognizing the limitations of the political theory of recognition: Axel Honneth, Nancy Fraser and social work. *British Journal of Social Work*, 40, 1517–1533.

Ginsburg, N. (1979). *Class, capital and social policy*. London: Macmillan.

Grande, S. (2004). *Red pedagogy: Native American and political thought*. Lanham, MD: Rowman & Littlefield.

Gray, M., Coates, J., & Yellow Bird, M. (2010). *Indigenous social work around the world: Towards culturally relevant education and practice*. Aldershot, Hants: Ashgate.

Green, J., & Thomas, R. (2007). Learning through our children, healing for our children: Best practice in First Nations communities. In L. Dominelli (ed.), *Revitalising communities in a globalising world*. Aldershot, Hants: Ashgate.

Haig-Brown, C. (1988). *Resistance and renewal: Surviving the Indian residential school*. Vancouver: Arsenal Pulp Press.

Houston, S. (2008). Beyond homo economicus: Recognition, self-realization and social work. *British Journal of Social Work*, 40, 841–857.

How Kee, L. (2010). The development of culturally appropriate social work practice in Sarawak, Malaysia. In Gray, M., Coates, J., & Yellow Bird, M. (eds), *Indigenous social work around the world: Towards culturally relevant education and practice*. Aldershot, Hants: Ashgate. 97–106.

Humphreys, M. (1996). *Empty cradles*. London: Corgi.

Kendall, K. (2001). *Social work education: Its origins in Europe*. Alexandria, VA: CSWE.

Kincaid, J. (1973). *Poverty and inequality in Britain*. Harmondsworth: Penguin.

Lorenz, W. (1994). *Social work in a changing Europe*. London: Routledge.

Mama, A. (1989). *The hidden struggle: A study considering statutory and voluntary sector responses to domestic violence against black women in the home*. London: Women's Aid.

Morris, J. (1991). *Pride against prejudice: A personal politics of disability*. London: Women's Press.

Oliver, M. (1990). *The politics of disablement*. London: Macmillan.

Parsons, T. (1967). *Sociological theory and modern society*. New York: Free Press.

Pinker, R. (1993). A lethal kind of looniness, *The Times Higher Educational Supplement*, 10 September.

Siggins, M. (2005). *Bitter embrace: White society's assault of the Woodland Cree*. Toronto, ON: McClleland and Stewart.

Spender, D. (1970) *Man-made language*. London: Pandora and Rivers Oram Press.

Stedman Jones, G. (1971). *Outcast London*. Oxford: Clarendon Press.

Tait-Rolleston, W., & Pehi-Barlow, S. (2001). A Maori social work construct. In L. Dominelli, Lorenz, W., & Soydan, H. (eds), *Beyond racial divides: Ethnicity in social work*. Aldershot, Hants: Ashgate.

Walton, R (1975). *Women in social work*. London: Routledge and Kegan Paul.

Webb, S.A. (2003). Local orders, global chaos. *European Journal of Social Work*, 6(2), 191–204.

Webb, S.A. (2007). The comfort of strangers: The emergence of social work in late Victorian England (Part One). *European Journal of Social Work*, 10(1), 39–54.

Webb, S.A. (2010). (Re)Assembling the Left: The politics of redistribution and recognition in social work. *British Journal of Social Work*, 40(8), 2364–2379.

Yip, K.S. (2007). Tensions and dilemmas of social work education in China. *International Social Work*, 50(1), 93–105.

Younghusband, E. (1978). *Social work in Britain, 1950–1975*. London: Allen and Unwin.

22
Feminist Ethics of Care

Brid Featherstone and Kate Morris

As part of what might be characterised the 'ethical turn' in social work, the feminist ethics of care has achieved a level of influence in the literature (Gray, 2010). This chapter explores the work of key thinkers within the scholarship, tracing the journey from the groundbreaking work of Carol Gilligan in psychology and the first wave of care theorists to a second wave encompassing moral theory, political science, and social policy. It explores how the focus of concern moved from identifying the gendered frameworks underpinning moral decision making to a foregrounding of care practices as part of democratic citizenship. Thus, while the work emerged from an impulse within feminism to value women's lives and practices, contemporary proponents, though clear about the importance of exploring care as gendered, operate from within a commitment to intersectionality and, moreover, do not always use the term feminist, but rather write of the ethic or ethics of care. Indeed, prominent authors, such as Williams (2001), call for a 'political ethics of care' to inform welfare policies. The chapter then explores applications within the social work literature. While recognised as making a contribution to ethics and moral philosophy, and specifically applied to thinking about social workers' practices, the ethics of care has also informed empirical research with service users.

GENDERED MORAL FRAMEWORKS

Carol Gilligan's *In a Different Voice*, published in 1982, revolutionised discussions in moral theory, feminism, and theories of the subject, and was one of the most influential books of the 1980s. It led to an extensive and continuing scholarship (see Hekman, 1995). Gilligan published an empirical and interpretive analysis of the decision-making process of a sample of girls confronted with a range of dilemmas. She challenged the then influential approach of Kohlberg, her teacher, a Harvard psychologist, specialising in moral development, whose studies had concluded women stayed at an inferior stage of moral development with few attaining the highest stages of moral reasoning.

In an analysis developed in the early 1980s, which has since been subject to considerable critique, as explored further below, Gilligan observed gender differences in the moral frameworks within which men and women operated. Men operated within an ethic of justice whereas women operated within an ethic of care. The ethic of care revolved around relationships and responsibilities, whereas an ethic of justice stressed rights and rules. The morality associated with an ethic of care was tied to concrete circumstances rather than philosophical abstractions. Moreover, this morality was best expressed not as a set of principles but as an activity – the activity of care. Different conceptions of selfhood underpinned the differing frameworks. To understand these differing conceptions of selfhood, Gilligan relied on object relations theory and, in particular, the early work of Nancy Chodorow (1978), who, in *The Reproduction of Mothering*, argued the gendered division of caretaking had consequences for boys' and girls' development. In a society where women were devalued, mothers' relations with their sons and daughters developed in contrasting ways. Mothers experienced their daughters as less separate from themselves and girls, in turn, retained their early and intense identification and attachment to their mothers. Moreover, they grew up with a weaker sense of boundaries and with a greater capacity for empathy and sensitivity towards others. Boys, by contrast, were pushed to disrupt their primary identification with their mother. They had to repress and deny the intimacy, tenderness, and dependence of the early bond if they were to assume a masculine identity. Thus they did not define themselves in relational terms, but rather in terms of independence and autonomy. As indicated, Gilligan tied morality to selfhood and Chodorow's analysis was very influential in this. Importantly, Chodorow moved in her subsequent work towards a more plural engagement with masculinities and femininities and, indeed, as explored below, a range of critiques of the notions of selfhood underpinning Gilligan's analysis emerged; see Featherstone (2010) for an overview.

Gilligan was hailed as the harbinger of a new moral theory, who had dealt the final blow to the exhausted masculinist tradition of moral philosophy. However, her work was simultaneously condemned as methodologically unsound, theoretically confused, and even antifeminist (Hekman, 1995). Her findings have been disputed as well as her emphasis on the importance of gender as the basis of the ethic of care. For example, Tronto (1993) noted Patricia Hill Collins' characterisation of the ethic of care as an African-American rather than a gendered phenomenon drawing attention to Carol Stack's research finding there were no gendered differences with African-American men and women.

Overall critics argued Gilligan could be situated within an unhelpful version of 'difference' feminism, which contributed to essentialist thinking about women, problematic assumptions about women's moral superiority to men, and a retreat from earlier emphases on building more socially just settlements between genders and classes (see Segal, 1987). Segal noted also the links between this version of feminism, the defeat of class-based politics in many countries, including the UK, and the dominance of New Right thinking.

However, Hekman (1995) argued Gilligan's work was both an indication of, and a major contributor to, a sea change under way in late 20th century intellectual thought. There was an already-existing move away from the universalism and absolutism of modernist epistemology towards conceptions emphasising particularity and concreteness. The linchpin was the attack on the centrepiece of moral philosophy and modernist Enlightenment epistemology: man as the rational, abstract autonomous constitutor of knowledge. Gilligan identified the ethical code of Western societies as based upon universalisable concepts, such as objectivity and partiality, which reflected a partial and masculine world view. Although not a moral philosopher, Hekman argued that Gilligan had made a major contribution to moral philosophy. This may bear out the truth of Foucault's observation that challenges to established disciplines often come from outside or the margins.

Williams (2001), whose own application of the ethic of care to social policy is explored below, locates Gilligan within a first wave of feminist research on care. She notes Gilligan, among others, signalled a shift away from the emphasis in second-wave feminism on equating care with oppression and exploitation, highlighting its value at a range of levels and its pleasures; see Featherstone (1997) for a discussion of the debates about mothering in the 1990s.

A second development in the scholarship on the ethics of care is represented in the work of the political scientists Joan Tronto (1993) and Selma Sevenhuijsen (2000). Both have tried to resolve a key issue which emerged from Gilligan's work concerning the relationship between an ethic of care and an ethic of justice in wide-ranging attempts to broaden the scope of applicability of a reformulated ethics.

CARE AS A MORAL AND POLITICAL PRACTICE

For Tronto (1993) what distinguished her approach from Gilligan's and others' is her insistence that an ethic of care cannot be understood unless it is placed in its moral and political context. Care should not be reduced to a narrow psychological concern or a kind of practice corruptible by broader social and political concerns. Her definition of care (developed with Berenice Fisher) is as follows:

> On the most general level, we suggest that caring be viewed as a species activity that includes everything we do to maintain, continue and repair our 'world' so that we can live in it as well as possible. That world includes our bodies, our selves and our environment, all of which we seek to interweave in a complex life-sustaining web (Tronto, 1993, p. 103).

She counters Gilligan's emphasis on the mothering relationship as paradigmatic and does not see it either as an individualistic or dyadic activity. Moreover, the activity of caring is largely defined culturally and will vary. It is ongoing and *both* a practice and a disposition.

What is definitive about care seems to be a perspective of taking the other's needs as the starting point for what must be done. In a formulation which continues to be highly influential, Tronto argues, as an ongoing process, care comprises four analytically separate but interconnected phases: caring about, taking care of, caregiving, and care-receiving. From these four elements arise four ethical elements of care: attentiveness, responsibility, competence, and responsiveness.

Thus care as a practice requires more than good intentions. It requires *both* thought and action, which are inter-related and directed towards an end. The emphasis on practice is important – care is neither a principle nor an emotion. This signals her location within a concern to tackle the power inequalities to be found in care. For example, she argues that in the USA caring about and taking care of are often the duties of the powerful and caregiving and care-receiving are left to the most powerless. To operate within an ethic of care would seem to have to involve all of the four elements identified above: caring about, taking care of, caregiving, and care-receiving. Tronto is correct to stress the tendency to sentimentalise and romanticise care when seen solely in dispositional terms, and to seek to link activity and disposition, but it is important to continue to explore the complexities of context in relation to who does what, to whom, why, where, and when; see Williams (2001) and subsequent discussion.

As a political scientist Tronto introduced important concerns in relation to care into the scholarship. What is needed, she argues, is a strong conception of rights. Care and justice must not be separated so care as a practice can inform the practices of democratic citizenship:

> If through the practices of giving and receiving care we were to become adept at caring, I suggest that not only would we have become more caring and moral people, but we would also have become better citizens in a democracy (Tronto, 1993, p. 167).

She argues for the redrawing of three boundaries in order to understand how care might inform political and social practices: the separation between public and private life, morality and politics, and concrete and abstract accounts of morality:

> Care is not a parochial concern of women, a type of secondary moral question, or the work of the least well off in society. Care is a central concern of human life. It is time that we began to change our political and social institutions to reflect this truth (Tronto, 1993, p.180).

In a recent article, Tronto (2010) linked care to public policy debates arguing public policies, as well as less formal care practices, all work through institutions (although she does not define what is meant by institution and this is an important weakness in her analysis). Thus, she suggests, once committed to public policies to improve care, the question 'How can we tell which institutions provide good care?' needs to be answered.

Svenhuijsen (2000) follows Tronto's lead in exploring how care can be placed within the conceptions of democratic citizenship. She argues against some of the feminist tendencies to locate it within a mothering paradigm as care can be seen in all settings. Care should not be counterpoised to justice, but seen as a social process engendering important aspects of citizenship. The process of caring for – or being cared for – makes one aware of diversity, interdependence, and the need to accept difference. This awareness provides an important basis for citizenship and is as likely, or more likely, to be learned through care as through paid work practices.

Gray (2010) has expressed caution about the complex and tension-laden nature of the legacy from the above literature. She notes a lack of clarity about whether it is an ethical theory about the norms relating to the giving and receiving of care or a broader political theory. Hollway (2006), in a critique pertinent to social workers, directly engages with Tronto in particular to express concerns about the notions of selfhood or subjectivity underpinning her analysis. Hollway argues it is too simplistic to think simply in terms of care as a practice as this neglects the 'doer' behind the 'deed'. How do individuals come to care? What sustains them to care well? She argues much of the literature assumes, given the right resources and supports, most people will be able to practice care. However, people are not born with capacities to care and the acquisition of the morality underpinning good caring is a complex process and an integral part of psychological development. The capacity to care cannot be assumed to exist just within individuals. It has to be developed and nurtured. Early caretaking experiences are essential as people are products of their pasts, which cannot be left behind in a voluntaristic project of self-authorship. She argues for a critical realist approach to child development and against a relativist approach to treating theories of child development simply as stories or discourses as social constructionists have done:

> My argument is that certain conditions that start early in life within families (families of all types) are usually *decisive* for later psychological capacities that produce caring (or hostile) relations to difference in others. These capacities may begin in families but they need not end there. Every person's life history is contained in their internal world and this internal world is active in shaping the ways the person encounters current everyday events and relationships, including the challenge of caring for familiars and strangers (Hollway, 2006, p. 3, emphasis added).

The experience of being cared for is essential in developing the capacity to care. Drawing from Kleinian psychoanalytic theory, Hollway (2006) writes of the importance to the baby of being recognised and thus being able to recognise others as similar but different, allowing for the possibility of what she calls 'realistic identification' with the suffering and pain of another. The conditions for realistic identification are established in early childhood and predictive of later capacities. Such identification can avoid the problematic perils of either distancing or over-identification with others in a world where fragility, pain, and suffering abound.

Hollway (2006) takes issue with currents in social theory, within which she locates many ethics of care writers, which reduce subjectivity to an empty category filled by social products. She suggests, for example, Tronto often implies if the political barriers to a care ethic were removed by redrawing existing moral boundaries, then people would naturally care. She suggests Sevenhuijsen takes this a little further when she argues the practice of care can lead to the disposition to care but leaves it unclear if, when, and how such a process takes place.

Despite her emphasis on the importance of early caretaking and the implications for later development, Hollway (2006) does not engage with any literature that might specify what exactly constitutes neglect in any empirically verifiable sense or address what might ameliorate early damage and, if so, how. This is probably related to her indebtedness to Kleinian psychoanalytic thought, which focuses more on unconscious processes and the role of 'phantasy' in mediating behaviours. Although she does emphasise the importance of what 'real' mothers and fathers do and do not do, she does not locate such mothers and fathers concretely, and the focus on unconscious factors seems to preclude any engagement with notions such as resilience which have been used productively by social work writers to explore diverse life pathways. However, her emphasis on the importance to the baby of being 'recognised' is of interest in light of the discussion in a subsequent section of contemporary debates in social work (Houston & Dolan, 2008; Webb, 2010).

A key development within the ethic of care literature was the scholarship which moved it to engage with more applied concerns in social policy and it is here that the work of Williams (2001) is situated. What emerge from her work are important insights about how many contemporary political and economic priorities are based upon a profound misrecognition of what all people, across a range of complex and interlocking differences, need to survive and flourish.

CARE, POWER, AND DIVERSITY

Williams (2001) argues care as a practice involves different experiences, meanings, contexts, and *multiple* relations of power (not just those between the genders). She calls for a 'political ethics' of care in order to engage with the challenges and differences posed by class, gender, disability, 'race', and migration. She locates her analysis within a specific political moment when a New Labour government (1997–2010) was intent on promoting paid work as the pathway to social inclusion, cohesion, and citizenship. She also locates her call within a theoretically sophisticated and substantial feminist social policy scholarship in which care has become a central analytic concept in the comparative study of welfare regimes.

Williams locates herself within the second wave of care scholarship as highlighted above. She suggests while writers such as Gilligan were important, they had limitations. They were almost entirely gender-focused with tendencies towards an undifferentiated category of womanhood, underpinned by essentialism around gender differences. There was also an assumption that the site of care was the heterosexual family and 'the focus on the carer and care as either work or ethic ignored care as a set of relations involving power and featuring both carers and cared-for' (Williams, 2001, p. 476).

The following summarises Williams' (2001) thoughts on the key issues with which a political ethics of care engages. The starting point is recognition of care of the self and others as meaningful activities in their own right, involving everyone – men and women, old and young, able-bodied and disabled. No one is just a giver or receiver of care. Care is an activity binding everyone. In giving and receiving care, everyone can, in the right conditions of mutual respect and material support, learn the civic responsibilities of responsibility, trust, tolerance for human limitation and frailties, and acceptance of diversity. Care is part of citizenship. Interdependence is the basis of human interaction, and autonomy and independence are about the capacity for self-determination rather than self-sufficiency. Vulnerability is a human condition and the experience of vulnerability varies contextually and temporally. Moral worth is attributed to key dimensions of caring relationships, such as dignity and the quality of human interaction, whether based upon blood, kinship, sexual intimacy, friendship, collegiality, contract, or service. Moreover, diversity and plurality in the social process of care is respected and recognised.

Inequalities in caregiving and care-receiving are exposed through questioning who benefits and who loses from existing policies. Inequalities may be constituted through different relations, particularly gender, but also disability, class, occupational status, age, ethnicity, 'race', nationality, religion, sexuality, and marital status. Care requires time, and financial and practical support, while quality, affordability, accessibility, flexibility, choice, and control are key to services based on inclusive citizenship where all involved in the processes of care have a voice. Care is not only personal but also an issue of public and political concern whose social dynamics operate at local, national, and transnational levels:

> The reprivatisation of care services, in conditions of women's increased participation in paid work, has intensified national and international forms of gendered exploitation constituted especially through class, 'race'/ethnicity and migrant status' (Williams, 2001, p. 488).

In Ireland, Lynch, Baker, and Lyons (2009) developed the concept of 'affective equality' to mount a challenge to a dominant neoliberal project founded upon the acceptance and, indeed, intensification of inequalities across a range of domains in Irish society. They draw from the above literature, and in particular Tronto's work, to argue that intellectual thought has shifted from the Weberian and Marxist trilogy of social class, status, and power as the primary categories for investigating the generation of inequalities and exploitation to exploring relations of care, love, and solidarity. The affective domains concerned with relationships of care, love, and solidarity are discrete spheres of social action to be studied in their own right, and are deeply interwoven with the economic, cultural, and political spheres. For example, they offer compelling evidence of how the care worlds of Irish women across a range of social categories are marked by similarities, but are also differentiated in terms of choices and constraints informed by economic resources, social networks, and the priorities of neoliberal welfare systems.

Lynch et al. (2009) situate their work within a very explicit critique of neoliberalism, which is premised *par excellence* on the notion of individual economic actors who seek to maximise their own resources and where care needs are invisible and or assumed to be best met by the market (see Chapter 2). While the ruling economic orthodoxies of the last 30 years (in many countries) have not, as yet, been ejected from their hegemonic position in countries such as the UK or Ireland, they have been subject to serious questioning. Increasing levels of need across diverse constituencies (actively promoted by the austerity policies of specific governments, such as the Irish government and the coalition government in the UK) are opening up some possibilities for articulating alternative understandings of need, dependency, and interdependency, and developing solidarity across differences.

The *feminist* ethics of care literature, as articulated in Lynch et al.'s (2009) work, emphasises any emerging new settlements cannot be based upon the kinds of gendered inequities that underpinned postwar social democracy or New Right thinking. Moreover, taking care seriously does not just oblige reconsideration of caregiving inequities but also highlights the need for a profound rethinking of what is needed by all human beings for their very existence and flourishing.

THE ETHIC OF CARE APPLIED TO SOCIAL WORK

The ethic of care literature has made a contribution to a number of areas in social work explored below: the vibrant debates about the role of codes in guaranteeing ethical practice, the rethinking of ethical traditions, research with service users, and ongoing debates about whether and how social workers can contribute to social justice.

In social work the seven principles of casework, outlined by Biestek in 1961, have been surprisingly influential as ethical codes though, as Banks (1995) highlights, they were not intended as such but rather as pointers towards good practice. A key theme running through these principles – and subsequent additions – was respect for the individual person as a self-determining being. Banks (1995) notes writers such as Plant argue respect for persons underpins not only social work ethics but any system of moral thinking. It is rooted in the categorical imperative formulated by Kant: 'So act as to treat humanity, whether in your own person or that of any other, never solely as a means but always also as an end' (in Banks, 1995, p. 28). The individual is worthy of respect simply because he or she is a person, regardless of what he or she has done, or whether he or she is useful to others.

The focus on the individual was the subject of sustained critique by the radical impulse in social work in the 1970s. For example, Marxists argued the Kantian approach established ethics as impersonal principles and removed them from the world of social relations (Hugman & Smith, 1995). Further allied critiques critical of the focus on the abstract individual emerged from feminist and antiracist writers concerned to stress the importance of social location; see Hugman & Smith (1995) for an overview.

By the 1990s, there appeared to be a clear move towards recognising ethical issues as inevitably specific and contextualised (Hugman & Smith, 1995). While this recognition clearly owed a strong debt to writers within the ethic of care, this debt was not always acknowledged (Orme, 2001, 2002). Orme (2002) developed a wide-ranging analysis drawing from debates within the ethics of care literature in order to develop thinking about community care in particular. Her concerns appeared twofold: to bring the increasingly sophisticated feminist debates about care and justice to the attention of social work in order to contribute to more socially just social work practice but also enrich existing feminist social work theory. Orme argued feminist theories had a limited impact upon social work theory and practice beyond the formula of 'add women and stir' and noted, while this formula had been important in drawing attention to the conditions of women, it was very limited in terms of developing social work practices that were more just and understanding how gender relations operated (see also Fawcett & Featherstone, 2000). She argued contributions within the ethics of care literature and, in particular, debates about the relationship between care and justice opened up important possibilities, outlining the need for a dialogical approach to justice:

> A dialogical approach to justice challenges the binaries not only of care/justice but also those of private/public, carer/cared for … such an interplay allows for perspectives other than gender to inform and complicate ethical choice … traditional ethics heard a single voice of disembodied moral principles, feminist ethics listens to and hears multiple voices because it defines morality and moral knowledge as plural and heterogeneous. This plurality is vital within community care because social work needs to challenge the excessive bureaucratization of confining those who require care, and indeed those who provide it, into constrained homogenized categories of, for example, older people, people with disabilities or those with mental health problems (Orme, 2002, p. 809).

In more recent years, the extensive and vibrant contemporary scholarship on ethics evident, for example, in the contributions to the edited book by Gray and Webb (2010) and the journal *Ethics and Social Welfare* has seen an increasingly influential contribution from those concerned with virtue ethics. Webb (2006) argues, in a neoliberal context, social work ethics needs to recast the moral identity of the social worker in terms of virtue ethics. He argues that virtue ethics is a normative theory emphasising a person's character and the way they reach judgements. It is usually seen as running counter to rule-bound or duty-bound conceptions of moral principles. Derived from the classical writings of Aristotle, virtues are admirable human dispositions that can be learned and distinguish good people from bad (Webb, 2006). Thus the basic question to be asked is not just what constitutes good social work, but rather what is a good social worker?

> Virtue ethics emphasises the priority of the moral agent who has acquired virtues commensurate with the pursuit of a revisable conception of the good life – the *well-fare* of all in a defined community. The virtues are the acquired inner qualities of humans – character – the possession of which, if applied in due measure, will typically contribute to the realisation of the good life ... Virtue ethics is especially distinct from its rivals by pointing the ethical way back to the need for the cultivation of character, and thus to the precedence of the quality of the actor over that of the action (Webb, 2006, p. 219).

Doing the right thing in social work is not a matter of applying moral concepts or rules nor is it an implicit aspect of the work or activity in which the social worker engages. Doing the right thing comes from the social worker as agent practising the virtues. These are generalisable capacities of self, the application of which is acquired through training and experience.

Virtue ethics has been linked to the ethics of care but there are really important differences (Gray, 2010). Above all for care theorists, care is oriented to relationships and practices and is not reducible to dispositions within individuals. Care is an activity *and* an attitude. Moreover, while simplistic assumptions about the differences between men and women are no longer a feature of the literature, a recognition of the continuing power of socially constructed notions of masculinities and femininities in informing who does what kind of caring labour, including in social work, is considered important at an array of levels in the ethics of care literature whereas virtue ethics does not foreground this. Moreover, in the work of Williams (2001) and Lynch et al. (2009), the ethics of care literature brings in important considerations about how gender intersects with a range of inequalities along the lines of class, ethnicity, disability, and sexuality to illuminate the opportunities and constraints available to those seeking to deliver and receive care. They also offer concrete critiques of particular welfare settlements and the politics of neoliberalism, which promotes and intensifies inequalities.

However, there are synergies between ethics of care and virtue ethics. For example, there is an important overlap between Houston's (2010) call for the importance of ethics as communication, Tronto's (2010) appeal for a range of spaces to explore contested needs, and Orme's (2002) call for dialogical justice. Houston (2010) has argued professional virtue is nourished when located in a context of ethics as communication:

> Virtue is linked to the explicit world of interacting subjects. It arises from ethical deliberations on tangible moral dilemmas ... (it) is a product of the social act regulated by conditions, principles and rules. Institutionalizing the latter within our daily decision-making activities over time and in different contexts is... the main way of enhancing moral awareness and virtue in social work (p. 823).

Tronto (2010) argues it is important to focus on institutions as they deliver public policies. Her overriding concern is institutional care, which she sees as best understood in the context of conflict and, therefore, care institutions need explicit institutional arrangements to resolve such conflicts. No caring institution in a democratic society can function well without an explicit locus for the needs-interpretation struggle. She argues for a rhetorical, moral, or political space to ensure the necessary contestation occurs.

Gray (2010) argued the feminist ethics of care is an emergent ethical theory casting ethical dispositions in a different way to the deontological focus on duties and rules, and the consequentialist–utilitarian focus on minimising harm. Thus a social worker influenced by this theory is concerned not with abstract concerns about what is right or wrong or what the rules are, but with engaging with the relationships within which service users are located and their judgements about what the best thing might be for all concerned, taking into account histories of care, attachment, and fairness. She suggests while its contribution to the enriching of contemporary discussions is evident, it is not yet a complete ethical theory. She notes the increasing sophistication of the work and the move away from a concern solely with gender but, alongside Featherstone (2010), she questions whether it has some difficulties when applied to thinking about social work practice. For example, there can still be a tendency to counterpoise the ethic of care and the ethic of justice which can lead to a neglect of the importance of rights for service users and, moreover, there are dangers in the way it is sometimes applied in researching those who care as oppressed thus implying their practices are 'innocent' or uncorrupted by power (see below).

EVERYDAY LIVES, IDENTITIES, AND PRACTICES

While much of the writing above is concerned with social workers themselves, there is a small but growing literature applying insights from the ethics of care in exploring service users' identities and practices; see Orme (2002) for a review. Recent work, focuses on the ordinary, everyday lives of a group of young people facing extraordinary circumstances, such as separation from birth parents. The primary research question was how 'looked after' children and young people understand, negotiate, and wish to express their everyday lives and identities. One consistent finding when exploring their everyday lives was their predominant concerns with their care relationships rather than formal systems. Holland (2010) refers to the former as an ethic of care and the latter as an ethic of justice. She notes the young people's care relationships were broader and more complex than those often captured in assessments and reviews. They were involved in large, complex networks of care and these care relationships, whether positive or negative, were central to their everyday emotional and practical well-being. They were clearly carers as well as cared for, and it was also possible to identify different conceptualisations of care in their narratives. Care was typified by longevity, fairness, reliability, partiality, and everyday acts. Interestingly, in light of the research focus above, social workers were pretty marginal in these young people's lives owing to high staff turnover and, therefore, limited opportunity to build and sustain relationships.

This research highlights the strengths and weaknesses of engaging with the ethic of care literature. On the one hand it signposts the diversity and plurality of relationships and resists one-dimensional, passive objectifying constructions of the young people by noting their caregiving as well as their care-receiving activities. On the other, it can promote an unhelpful binary between the ethic of care and the ethic of justice, and could lead to either/or thinking, which obscures the importance of formal rights under the law.

The following section explores how applying the ethic of care to engaging with family practices can open up really important and often deeply hidden aspects of family practices and oblige the giving of attention to the meanings attached to those practices. Caution is urged against a tendency to use an ethic of care lens to gloss over what might be problematic aspects of family practices.

The ethic of care has had a considerable impact on the family studies literature. Williams (2004) notes the profound shift in this literature from exploring 'the family' as an institution to focusing on families and 'family practices'. Thus the shift to examining what is done – activities and functions – rather than exploring who and what constitutes the family – with close reference to social bonds and relationships – and, at the same time, recognising and respecting diversity. She argues there is considerable value in distinguishing between dominant presentations of the 'normative family' – often promoted by social polices – and lived experiences of family life.

The 'Care, Values and the Future of Welfare' (CAVA) research programme at the University of Leeds explored the extent to which changes in contemporary life have shaped people's commitments to one another and their desire to negotiate the 'proper thing to do'. It suggests people are embedded in the relationships which matter to them, showing little evidence of either moral decline or an individualised drive to self-actualisation. In working through their family life dilemmas, such as divorce, separation, and work, practical ethics emerge for adults and children:

> These are the ethics which enable resilience, facilitate commitment and lie at the heart of people's interdependency. They constitute the compassionate realism of 'good enough' care. They include:
> - fairness
> - attentiveness to the needs of others
> - mutual respect
> - trust
> - reparation
> - being non judgemental
> - adaptability to new identities
> - being prepared to be accommodating and
> - open to communication (Williams, 2004, p. 74).

The adoption of the Family Group Conference (FGC) model by a growing number of UK local authorities has generated a raft of local evaluation studies. One such evaluation of an FGC project (Morris, 2006) suggests the family plans contained an evident articulation of an 'ethic of care' as explored by Williams (2004).

FGC family plans: care examples

Child A had parents whose care was very uneven, at times very poor. The parents were considered not to acknowledge the real extent of their neglect and the social worker noted, prior to the FGC: 'The family finds it very difficult to understand why social services have concerns about their care and this impacts on their ability to engage and their commitment to bring about long term change'. The FGC was attended by the mother, the father, an uncle, an aunt, the grandmother, the key worker, and the health visitor. The family plan involved the extended family in enlisting the support of the paternal grandparents, in monitoring the home environment through extended family arrangements, in parents ensuring they attend appointments, requesting help with housing, and in continuing to use family support services. The family made the following statement: 'A has been our number one priority. He is our only son ... We have all the support from B's family therefore we are in a better position than we were a year ago, we also have close family friends for help and support ...'

Child B and child C were the children of parents with significant drug problems and, as a result, the Local Authority was considering adoption for both children. The grandparents had been given the opportunity to care for the children, but final plans had yet to be agreed. The family plan was to support long-term care by grandparents to facilitate, if possible, a relationship between the children and their parents and to use support from the extended family to support the placement. The family plan says:

> Obviously we would like X and Y to get better and live happily ever after but we live in the real world and *our first priority is the children* [family emphasis] ... B and C have a strong family and are very much loved ...We are fully aware of the commitment needed for ... future and are prepared to raise them into adulthood if necessary .... We do identify future possible difficulties and would deal with these as any family would do ...
> *Just to say which is imperative B and C's needs will always be put first. They are much loved children* [family emphasis].

In the course of the evaluation, it was noted that families were using the FGC as an opportunity to arrive at arrangements to support their capacity to offer some form of nurturing care, or connection to the child, even when direct practical care was not possible. Indeed, it could be suggested the FGC provided an opportunity for a 'safe space' in which to plan and articulate working ethics for the care of children. This has important implications for how practitioners work with families, and how children's needs are met. In particular, further understanding is needed about the professional perspectives in relation to this aspect of family plans. If, for example, professionals do not always anticipate or recognise this capacity within families, valuable opportunities to enhance children's well-being may be being lost or missed (Morris, 2006). Together with this may be a reluctance to use FGCs if professionals are unaware of a family's capacity to use the FGC to 'do right' by its children and to seek to find ways to nurture their children. Professionals may not anticipate this aspect of family life with the families with whom they work and, therefore, may make assumptions about how the family will respond to the opportunities presented by the FGC (Morris & Featherstone, 2010).

However, it is important to hold on to the complexity of practices, desires, and motivations, which can be obscured through using the 'ethics of care' approach, as outlined above, and also to beware of assumptions that people will care adequately if given the appropriate resources and supports, as Hollway (2006) notes. Why might carers be unable to identify with the vulnerability of others and behave oppressively? This is the subject of ongoing work by the authors. The next section offers some thoughts on the contribution the ethics of care literature can make to contemporary debates about social justice in the social work literature.

BEYOND RECOGNITION AND REDISTRIBUTION: THE CONTRIBUTION OF A REFORMULATED ETHICS OF CARE?

Houston and Dolan (2008), in their exploration of a framework for social support for families, make links between a range of literatures, including the ethic of care and virtue ethics. They suggest, following Honneth (1995), human identity is irrefutably intertwined with everyday social recognition and offer a framework for social support based upon this fundamental understanding; see Webb (2010) and discussion later. Such a framework involves the following elements: primary relationships of positive regard, legal rights, and acknowledgement by the community. Where any of these elements are lacking, as they often are in people's lives, social support programmes can play really crucial roles in identification and compensation.

Houston and Dolan's (2008) work highlights the richness brought to the literature on care by writers from applied backgrounds immersed in researching and thinking about what can make a difference to everyday lives, especially of those who are most vulnerable. There is a synergy with virtue ethics evident when they argue: 'Social support is not just an outward but an intentional disposition created around "meaning" and "relationship"' (Houston & Dolan, 2008, p. 467).

Houston and Dolan (2008) employ Honneth's notion of recognition to develop a framework for social support. Notwithstanding its possibilities to enrich debates on a critical social work committed to social justice, Webb (2010) notes this notion has been subject to considerable critique. As McNay (2008) notes, the idea of the struggle for recognition has become one of the most influential ways of depicting social and political movements in the last decade and, in that context, the debate between Honneth and the feminist writer Nancy Fraser (see Fraser & Honneth, 2003) has been of seminal importance. While both thinkers aim to ground the normative political implications of their work in a critical analysis of contemporary power relations, there is a basic disagreement between them about how to characterise the dynamics of contemporary social and political conflict:

> For Honneth, all such conflicts, including those over economic distribution, are variants of a fundamental struggle for recognition that itself is the key to understanding the long-term development of social interaction in capitalist societies. Against this, Fraser argues that struggles for recognition, such as identity politics, are analytically distinct from conflicts over redistribution. Both are fundamental to social justice but are irreducible to each other (McNay, 2008, p. 271).

Honneth argues material inequality is a facet of a more profound disrespect, indeed a lack of recognition which has its origins in early infant–mother dynamics, whereas Fraser argues for the need to distinguish analytically between different forms of suffering (Fowler, 2009). Moreover, for Fraser, lack of recognition springs from damaging cultural representation of particular groups, such as women, whereas a lack of material resources springs from power inequalities in relation to the distribution of resources.

Important critiques have been made of the grounds mobilised by *both* Honneth and Fraser to locate their analyses (see McNay, 2008). But Fraser's arguments about the need for a politics incorporating both redistribution and recognition are persuasive in a contemporary context of obscene concentrations of wealth and intensifying inequalities. Drawing from Lister (2001), it might be argued, however, that while socially just welfare policies and practices need to be informed by discourses of recognition *and* redistribution, recognition needs to be understood along three dimensions. One concerns 'the politics of voice' and here Lister (2001) notes the demands from poverty activists to be involved in debates about poverty and not just treated as its objects. This is not about the assertion of group difference but concerned with respect and understanding citizenship as a practice as well as a status since the exclusion of those in poverty from debates can be seen to reinforce their exclusion from full citizenship. Another dimension of recognition concerns the recognition given by welfare systems to different kinds of activities. Insights from the ethic of care are of key importance here. Recognition and redistribution issues are intertwined in how care work is dealt with in most welfare settlements where wage-earning is privileged in terms of status and money over childrearing. Moreover, waged care work is low status and poorly paid (Lynch et al., 2009). Finally, recognition needs to be considered in relation to group difference and the demands which may need to be made in relation to *particular* needs. Such demands *can* provide a bridge to recognition of the common humanity of different groups and the equal worth of all citizens. Lister's (2001) optimism here is in contrast with the concerns raised, for example, by Webb (2010) about how preoccupations with difference can rest upon and reinforce a perverse, divisive, and ghettoising identity politics. While many feminists, such as Lister (2001), would share Webb's (2010) concerns, for feminists there can be no escape from trying to grapple with difference, particularly in terms of relations between men and women and between women themselves. For example, liberal feminist notions of equality were often premised on the assimilation of women into existing male-stream norms paraded as universal. In effect, women had to change to be like men in order to be treated equally, for example, in relation to their work patterns (Lister, 2003). Variants of feminism emerged in reaction focused variously on challenging men to change to become more like women and valorising women, asserting a defiant 'difference', even if such defiance trapped them in tired old binaries. Over the decades, political struggles and rigorous scholarship has ensured notions of equality and difference have been shaken up, radically rethought and, moreover, linked to concrete strategies in particular contexts; see, for example, William's (1996) thoughtful discussion about the differences 'that make a difference'.

The ethic of care literature illustrates the enormous conceptual and political leaps made by feminists on what has often been a painful journey from naming difference, understanding the need to map its different dimensions but not to reify it and, ultimately, to reformulate it within a rethinking of the universal. To return to Orme (2001, 2002), the writer who has most consistently mapped this journey in relation to thinking about a socially just social work problematic, she notes the journey from a focus on a narrow and problematic notion of difference – the ethics of care versus justice – towards a generous and 'solidaristic' concern with mapping the contours of dialogical justice. She argues this involves engaging with a very diverse range of voices, including, for example, men who are violent to women.

CONCLUSION

A number of authors have called for social workers to have some grounding in moral philosophy (Gray, 2010; Houston, 2003).

The ethic of care, with or without the prefix of feminist, is considered by some authors, alongside other approaches, to have an important contribution to make in harsh political and practice environments. The literature has often been located within specific contexts where neoliberalism has been the dominant economic and political project, but also where social work has become defined more and more narrowly and heavily circumscribed in remit.

As outlined in this chapter, there is evidence that the ethics of care offers an explicit critique of neoliberalism and associated policies. Such an ethics starts from the recognition of human interdependence and highlights the problematic assumptions pervading the notion of independence often promoted. It renders visible the care practices fundamental to human survival and flourishing, practices often obscured or left to the harsh disciplines of the market, and it is part of a scholarship continuing to work through really important questions around difference and solidarity. It counters assumptions that particular family practices are characterised by selfishness, moral carelessness, and deficit, and has provided important methodologies and analytic frameworks for those working with families who are subject to considerable concern and state intervention. But it is also important to note the ethic of care can be used in an unhelpful way to pit care against justice and to reinforce rather than interrogate difference, thus institutionalising essentialist and fixed identities.

REFERENCES

Banks, S. (1995). *Ethics and values in social work.* London: BASW.

Biestek, F.P. (1961). *The casework relationship.* London: Allen and Unwin.

Chodorow, N. (1978). *The reproduction of mothering.* California: University of Yale Press.

Fawcett, B., & Featherstone, B. (2000). Introduction. In B. Fawcett, Featherstone, B., Fook, J., & Rossiter, A. (eds). *Practice and research in social work: Postmodern feminist perspectives.* London: Routledge.

Featherstone, B. (1997). Introduction. In W. Hollway & Featherstone, B. (eds), *Mothering and ambivalence.* London: Routledge.

Featherstone, B. (2010). Ethic of care. In M. Gray & Webb, S.A. (eds), *Ethics and value perspectives in social work.* Basingstoke: Palgrave, pp. 73–84.

Fowler, B. (2009). The recognition/redistribution debate and Bourdieu's theory of practice. *Theory, Culture and Society, 26*(1), 144–156.

Fraser, N., & Honneth, A. (2003). *Redistribution of recognition: A politico-philosophical exchange.* London: Verso.

Gilligan, C. (1982). *In a different voice: Psychological theory and women's development.* Harvard, MA, Harvard University Press.

Gray, M., (2010). Moral sources and emergent ethical theories in social work. *British Journal of Social Work, 40*, 1794–1811.

Gray, M. & Webb, S.A. (eds), (2010). *Ethics and value perspectives in social work.* Basingstoke: Palgrave.

Hekman, S. (1995). *Moral voices, moral selves.* Cambridge, MA: Polity Press.

Holland, S. (2010). Looked after children and the ethic of care. *British Journal of Social Work, 40*(6), 1664–1680.

Hollway, W. (2006). *The capacity to care.* London: Routledge.

Honneth, A. (1995). *The struggle for recognition: The moral grammar of social conflicts.* Cambridge, MA: Polity Press.

Houston, S. (2003). Establishing virtue in social work: A response to McBeath and Webb. *British Journal of Social Work, 33*, 819–824.

Houston, S. (2010). Discourse ethics. In M. Gray & Webb, S.A, (eds), *Ethics and value perspectives in social work.* Basingstoke: Palgrave, pp. 95–107.

Houston, S., & Dolan, P. (2008). Conceptualising child and family support: The contribution of Honneth's critical theory of recognition. *Children and Society, 22*, 458–469.

Hugman, R., & Smith, D. (1995). Ethical issues in social work: An overview. In R. Hugman & Smith, D. (eds), *Ethical issues in social work.* London: Routledge.

Lister, R. (2001). Towards a citizens' welfare state: The 3 + 2 'R's' of welfare reform. *Theory, Culture and Society, 18*(2–3), 91–111.

Lister, R. (2003). *Citizenship: Feminist perspectives* (2nd ed.). Basingstoke: Palgrave.

Lynch, K., Baker, J., & Lyons, M. (2009). Introduction. In K. Lynch, Baker, J., & Lyons, M. (eds), *Affective equality: Love, care and injustice.* Basingstoke: Palgrave.

McNay, L (2008). The trouble with recognition: Subjectivity, suffering and agency. *Sociological Theory, 26*(3), 271–296.

Morris, K. (2006). *Camden FGC service: An evaluation of outcomes.* London: Borough of Camden.

Morris, K., & Featherstone, B. (2010). Investing in children, regulating parents and supporting whole families. *Social Policy and Society, 9*(4), 557–586.

Orme, J. (2001). *Gender and community care: Social work and social care perspectives.* Basingstoke: Palgrave.

Orme, J. (2002). Social work: Gender, care and justice. *British Journal of Social Work, 32,* 799–814.

Segal, L. (1987). *Is the future female?* London: Virago.

Sevenhuijsen, S. (1998). *Citizenship and the ethics of care.* London: Routledge.

Tronto, J. (1993). *Moral boundaries: A political argument for an ethic of care.* New York: Routledge.

Tronto, J. (2010). Creating caring institutions: Politics, plurality and purpose. *Ethics and Social Welfare, 4*(2), 158–171.

Webb, S.A. (2006). *Social work in a risk society.* Basingstoke: Palgrave.

Webb, S.A. (2010). (Re)Assembling the left: The politics of redistribution and recognition in social work. *British Journal of Social Work, 40*(8), 2364–2379.

Williams, F. (1996). Postmodernism, feminism and the question of difference. In N. Parton (ed.), *Social theory, social change and social work.* London: Routledge.

Williams, F. (2001). In and beyond New Labour: Towards a new political ethics of care. *Critical Social Policy, 21*(4), 467–493.

Williams, F. (2004). *Rethinking families.* London: Calouste Gulbenkian Foundation.

23

Diversity and Social Work Practice

Purnima Sundar, John Sylvestre, and Amandeep Bassi

Attention to cultural, religious, and ethnoracial diversity and the philosophy of multiculturalism is most common to the Western world as it fits with the democratic ethos of human and citizenship rights. Multiculturalism is an approach:

> that acknowledges and values diversity in society and describes the various tangible (that is, economic) and intangible (for example, social) benefits that result from different ethnic, cultural, racial and religious groups living together. Its goal is to support the full political, social and economic integration of all members of society (Sundar, 2008, p. 98).

Multiculturalism arose as a response to the increasing diversity among people in Western societies, and individual and collective efforts to work effectively with and through cultural, religious, and ethnoracial differences. The essential debate in the discourse of multiculturalism is the extent to which nations tolerate immigrants' retention of their culture of origin or require assimilation into the dominant or national culture, which, for most Western nations, is tied to Christian values.

Generally, the social work profession supports the philosophy of multiculturalism despite the challenges that might arise for practitioners personally, professionally, organisationally, or socially. Most professionals are challenged to understand the roles ethnicity, race, culture, religion, and language play in the lives of the people they serve and social work is no exception. Many mainstream social service agencies, where social workers are employed, continue to experience pressure to provide culturally sensitive and appropriate services to meet the needs of newcomers, as well as those of more established ethnoracial, religious, and cultural diasporas (Bernard & Moriah, 2007; Herberg, 1993; Sue, 2001).

Different countries approach immigration and the management of diversity in different ways. This chapter examines how these diverse approaches to multiculturalism are linked to social work practice. It begins by providing an introduction to two broad approaches to multiculturalism, followed by a description of how different nations view ethnoracial, religious, and cultural diversity broadly in terms of their orientations to multiculturalism, and examples of some corresponding approaches to policy development for responding to this diversity. The chapter then reviews the more common historical and contemporary ways the field of social work has attempted to manage ethnoracial, religious, and cultural diversity within helping relationships. It is then argued that, despite their theoretical soundness and laudable goals, both multiculturalism and 'cultural competence' are ways of managing diversity that are limited in their execution. The chapter concludes by suggesting some future directions towards which the field may move in order to work not simply *across* but *through* differences to ensure appropriate social work practice and positive outcomes for clients of all backgrounds.

DIVERSITY ACROSS THE GLOBE

Ethnoracial, religious, and cultural diversity are often linked to the philosophy of multiculturalism, which emphasises the tangible (e.g., economic) and intangible (e.g., social and political) benefits emerging when diverse ethnoracial, religious, and cultural groups live and work together (James, 2003; Sundar, 2008). In some places, multiculturalism is encouraged and supported by policies aiming to promote the social, economic, and civic integration of all members of society while also encouraging people to retain traditions and customs unique to their own group. Other countries view respecting a national identity as paramount and promote assimilation to or the adoption of majority norms and cultural traditions (Soroka et al., 2006). This section begins by distinguishing between two general ways of understanding multiculturalism before discussing these differences by describing how immigration and diversity are understood and managed in four places across the Western world: in several different European countries, the USA, Australia, and Canada. These broad characterisations are offered with full recognition, within various places, approaches and policies are not monolithically implemented and, frequently, prevailing approaches are hotly contested. Also they must be seen in light of the events following the 9/11 attack on the Twin Towers in New York City and the fear of terrorism linked to Islamic fundamentalism that has gripped, and also been promoted within, the Western world in its aftermath.

APPROACHES TO MULTICULTURALISM: FROM BELOW AND ABOVE

Although the term *multiculturalism* is often equated with cultural pluralism, it can also be defined as an ideology shaping a country's identity and influencing how people understand and interact with one another (Sundar, 2008). Bannerji (2000) distinguishes between multiculturalism from above (where state-sponsored structures and policies promote diversity and inclusion) and multiculturalism from below (where activities designed to support intercultural relations are initiated by individuals, groups, and communities in the absence of system-level support). These broad approaches are expressed in particular societies in a variety of different ways, reflecting their unique histories, political and economic structures, and social systems. Thus, in practice, multiculturalism is a complex, protean terrain in which policy priorities vary in different places, and can shift from one elected national government to the next. Though certain to be flawed at the level of a detailed fine-grained analysis, a broad characterisation based on historical trends and overarching policy directions can be instructive for understanding the context of social work practice. Table 23.1 provides an overview of these approaches and how they are expressed in policy and linked to social work practice.

Multiculturalism from below

Multiculturalism from below is most often found where *difference blindness* is practised. In these societies, individual rights and

Table 23.1 Approaches to diversity and social work practice

Approach to diversity	Country or region	Social, historical, and political context	Multicultural policy orientation	Approaches to social work practice
Multiculturalism from below or weak multiculturalism	Europe (esp. France, Britain, and Germany)	Strong national identities (both within and across countries) Entrenched cultural norms and values	Assimilationist Tendency toward absence of official multicultural policies; emphasis on immigration and antidiscrimination policies	Range from cultural sensitivity to antiracism
	USA	Strong national identity Tension between established and evolving cultural norms and values	Assimilationist Absence of official multicultural; emphasis on immigration and antidiscrimination policies	Range of practitioners using antiracism or anti-oppression Predominant focus on cultural competence
	Australia	Emergent national identity Multiple cultural norms and values	Increasingly assimilationist Presence of some official multicultural policies	Range of practitioners using antiracism or anti-oppression Predominant focus on cultural competence
Multiculturalism from above or strong multiculturalism	Canada	Complex and multiple national identities Evolving multiple cultural norms and values	Management and promotion of difference Presence of official multicultural policies	Range of practitioners using antiracism or anti-oppression Predominant focus on cultural competence

privileges are expected to be applied to everyone in the same way, without consideration of ethnoracial, cultural, or religious differences (Bissoondath, 2002). The emphasis is on individual opportunity, civic integration, and the assimilation of newcomers who are encouraged to adopt the norms and traditions of the host society (Soroka et al., 2006). Referred to as 'weak' multiculturalism (Grillo, 2007), ethnoracial, religious, and cultural diversity is tolerated within the private sphere – family and community, while system-level policies remain geared towards assimilation in the public domain – education and law enforcement, for example. Countries practising multiculturalism from below tend to focus on establishing antidiscrimination policies to facilitate assimilation.

Western Europe

Multiculturalism from below is exemplified in European countries with strong national and ethnic identities, such as Britain, Germany, and France. In these countries, historically, there has been an expectation newcomers will adopt the norms and traditions of the host culture, at least publicly, and customs from 'back home' be relegated to the private sphere. Whereas Europeans have a long history of migrating to other places (like the USA, Canada, Africa, and Australia, Latin America, and parts of Asia), in recent years a number of nations within Europe (e.g., Norway, Germany, and Britain) have come to play host to newcomers themselves (Kivisto, 2002). For example, in Britain, immigration after World War II began when newcomers from their current and former colonies started to enter the country from places like the Caribbean, India, and Africa. At the risk of over-generalising, some European countries (e.g., Germany) have historically viewed immigration as time-limited with guest workers invited to fill temporary labour shortages and so, because their contribution has been viewed primarily in terms of short-term economic needs, immigrants are typically not expected to form permanent attachments to the host society (Bauböck et al., 2007). Hence, several laws within the European Union have historically prevented immigrants and their children from becoming citizens or attaining legal residency (Rodriguez-Garcia, 2010). Often these are people of colour, who, in spite of their diverse origins, have been referred to collectively as 'Black' (Kivisto, 2002). Yet there are 'model minorities'. For example, in Britain, those who are 'English' and reflect the 'Englishness' of the empire are favoured over those who are different (Bannerji, 2000). Strong opposition to immigration in Germany and France – and discrimination and racism – have resulted in violence and social segregation (Kivisto, 2002). There have been policies to manage these challenges, such as Britain's Race Relations Act of 1976 (Kivisto, 2002) but overall, multiculturalism is seen as a threat to national unity by those with expectations for assimilation and civic integration through a common language and culture now the norm (Bissoondath, 2002; Rattansi, 2004; Soroka et al., 2006).

The USA

Unlike European countries, which have long-established and entrenched traditions, the USA is a land of immigrants with a shorter history and early migration enforced by the slave trade. The first wave of voluntary immigration is considered to have taken place from 1820 to the Civil War, mostly drawing newcomers from Western Europe (Kivisto, 2002). The second wave of immigrants from eastern and southern parts of Europe between 1880 and 1924 was the largest and, since 1965, the third wave has comprised people of colour arriving from South – Latin – America and various parts of Asia. North Americans have forged a national identity 'as a settler nation with an ever-changing ethnic composition [and], an overarching *American* [US] identity had to be … reconciled with a multitude of particular ethnic identities' (Kivisto, 2002, p. 44, emphasis added). Consequently, newcomers were encouraged to identify first as Americans and 'other' only secondarily. The term 'melting pot' came to characterise US multiculturalism, though, rather than a 'mix of cultures', being 'American' was reinforced as the newcomer's new and distinctive identity (Bannerji, 2000; Kivisto, 2002). More recently, the term *transnational America* (first coined by writer and intellectual Randolph Bourne) has emerged to suggest newcomers do not simply shed their ethnic and cultural roots in the melting pot. Rather, the 'pot' transforms and changes due to the newcomer's contact with American society. Instead of becoming '100% American', newcomers are increasingly embracing a transnational identity as 'ampersand Americans'. For example, American *and* Mexican, and, in this way, identify with both ethnic and cultural traditions (Kivisto, 2002).

Against this backdrop of almost continuous immigration, there are some groups with a more tenuous connection to this 'American' identity, such as Native Americans, African-Americans, and non-Christian people of colour (Kivisto, 2002). Discrimination and racism persist in the USA, and people from particular ethnoracial groups are often not viewed as 'true Americans'. While multiculturalism is not accompanied by any official policies at the federal level, the US government has attempted to mediate some of this system-level prejudice by supporting a number of antidiscriminatory, affirmative-action policies.

Australia

Although recognised as a society characterised by wide ethnoracial, religious, and cultural diversity, Australia has not consistently favoured multiculturalism. Up until the 1950s, Australia was committed to its assimilationist 'White Australia' policy (Gray & Agllias, 2010; Kivisto, 2002) but, in the late 1950s, economic need led to an influx of Asian immigrants. In addition to managing this demographic shift, the adoption of multiculturalism as a national identity was key in supporting the psychological separation of the Australian colony from 'mother England' (Tilbury, 2007). In 1996, this progressed under the leadership of soon-to-become Prime Minister John Howard (1997–2006), to Australia's vision for multi*racialism* in the new century through a Statement on Racial Tolerance. This document provided a foundation for inclusion-based policy recommendations focused on four core principles: civic duty, cultural respect, social equity, and productive diversity (Australian Multiculturalism for a New Century: Towards Inclusiveness, 1999).

Despite acknowledging ethnoracial, religious, and cultural differences, multicultural policies have always encouraged all members of society to embrace the 'Australian way of life and values'. In recent years, there has been an even more deliberate 'retreat from multiculturalism' (see, e.g., Tilbury, 2007), characterised by heated debates on immigration in Australia and a vigorous promotion of Australian values tied to the country's Judeo-Christian identity, even though Australia has been seen largely as a secular nation. Whereas Australia had for a time been compared with Canada in terms of its recognition of differences and corresponding multicultural policies (see later), most recently there has been a shift to 'breaking down cultural distinctiveness' (Galligan & Roberts, 2003, p. 4) and moving towards a more 'American' way of doing things (e.g., see Lopez, 2005). For example, neoliberal welfare policy in Australia has followed the USA in giving faith-based organisations a pivotal place in social provision owing to their promotion of Judeo-Christian values and a collective commitment to addressing ethnic conflict (more specifically, the 'war on terror'). There are thus parallels between Australia, the USA, and Britain, all of whom increasingly emphasise the need for difference blindness and national allegiance as tools to fight against world terrorism (Lopez, 2005).

Multiculturalism from above

Multiculturalism from above is found where there is *recognition* and *valuing of differences* among people (Kymlicka, 1995; Taylor, 1994). Referred to as 'strong' multiculturalism (Grillo, 2007), it is characteristic of democracies promoting equality of treatment and recognition of ethnoracial, religious, and cultural diversity in the public sphere, supported by official antidiscriminatory policies relating *inter alia* to religious freedom. Multiculturalism from above is most apparent in Canada.

Canada

Like the USA, Canada was settled by European immigrants who took ownership of land previously inhabited by native peoples. Canada is unusual since it was founded by two main charter groups: the English and the French. In this sense, then, Canadians have always understood themselves in plural terms (Kivisto, 2002). Unlike the US 'melting pot', Canada is a 'mosaic' of people who share a national identity, but also maintain their original ethnic traditions and customs (Clarke, 1997). While Canadians see themselves as celebrating diversity, decisions concerning 'who gets in' have always and continue to be informed by political and economic concerns, specifically labour needs (Kelley & Trebilcock, 1998). Historically, Canada has used explicitly racist policies, such as the Chinese Head Tax, to limit the number of people from certain ethnoracial and cultural groups from entering the country. In 1967, a new regulation called the 'points system' was introduced to ensure fairness in immigration decisions. Within this framework, a number of personal attributes along with education, skill level, and knowledge of the two official languages – English or French – are assessed and assigned 'merit points' with the likelihood of entry determined by the number of points earned. As a result, there has been an increase in the number of non-White immigrants to Canada in the past 40 years. Thus in Canada, 'multiculturalism is a state initiated enterprise'

(Bannerji, 2000, p. 16) with policies, such as the Canadian Multicultural Policy (1971) and the subsequent Multiculturalism Act (1988), part of the national strategy to promote diversity (Calliste & Dei, 2000; Kobayashi, 2005; Wood & James, 2005). Although some question the extent to which multiculturalism is fully realised, and indeed multiculturalism has persisted as a source of strong debate within the country, Canada is unique in its commitment to a shared national identity side by side with minority ethnic and cultural traditions (Bannerji, 2000; McLaren, 1994). This 'unity within diversity' forms the institutional basis of Canadian society.

While the recognition-of-differences perspective represents an alternative to assimilationism, it has been criticised for its superficial treatment of people's identities and unwillingness to grapple with structural barriers to social integration (e.g., Abu-Laban, 2002; Bannerji, 2000). All nations struggle with tensions surrounding immigration and how to balance economic benefits with perceived threats to the national identity. The relative merits of multiculturalism – or diversity of any sort – are all too easily trumped by perceived threats to national security. In Europe, the USA, and increasingly Australia, the priority is retention of a strong national identity accompanied by clearly entrenched cultural values and social norms. Most countries have multicultural and antidiscriminatory policies, yet racism, discrimination, and religious intolerance continue (Abu-Laban, 2002; Bauböck et al., 2007; Patni, 2006). Clearly, a 'new worldview' on immigration and diversity is needed (Rodriguez-Garcia, 2010).

DIVERSITY AND SOCIAL WORK PRACTICE

A pivotal requirement of social work ethics is tolerance or acceptance of difference, but it was not until the 1960s that the professional literature began to highlight the importance of recognising race and ethnicity in service provision (Proctor & Davis, 1994). Prior to then, social workers adopted a 'civilising role' (Christensen, 2003), with the goal of early social work in certain contexts being focused on problematising differences and then working to bring the values, norms, and behaviours of 'others' in line with White, Eurocentric, mainstream norms. As the field evolved, however, a recognition of the reality of race and racism in people's lives and the role of multiple identities in the experience of marginalisation grew with a number of prominent approaches emerging, including the cultural inferiority, colour blind, cultural sensitivity, antiracist, anti-oppressive, and cultural competence approaches discussed below (see Table 23.2).

The cultural inferiority approach

In the 1960s, a deficits-based *cultural inferiority approach* emerged and continued to dominate the field until the early 1980s (Casas, 1985). Specific models of practice included the pathological model (Padilla, 1981), the deviant model (Rubington & Weinberg, 1971), the disorganisational model (Moynihan, 1965), the culturally deficient model (Padilla, 1981), and the genetically deficient model (Hernstein, 1971). Despite slight variations, all shared the view members of ethnoracial and cultural groups were genetically inferior on the evolutionary scale and pathological when compared to the White dominant group. In the cultural inferiority approach, assimilation was thought to be the best way to integrate members of diverse ethnic groups into the dominant population (Maiter, 2009). The role of social workers was to help newcomers integrate into mainstream society. With a growing awareness of the racism inherent in these practices, the colour blindness approach began to emerge.

The colour blind approach

Through the 1970s, a growing awareness of the racial discrimination inherent in practices

Table 23.2 Summary of approaches to working across difference

Model or framework	Main ideas	Goal(s) of intervention	Strengths	Limitations
Cultural inferiority approach	Pathology among members of ethnoracial and cultural groups is due to their genetic inferiority relative to people who are White	Control the behaviours of 'others' and teach them the ways of the Eurocentric majority in order to ensure their assimilation into mainstream society		Supports a pseudoscientific theory of racial classification with White people ranked above people of colour. Social work is viewed as an arm of social control to bring 'others' in line with mainstream norms
Colour blind approach	Differences based on race are ignored and all members of society are seen as equal	Promote equal opportunity and support people from diverse ethnoracial and cultural groups in achieving economic and social success	Acknowledges racism inherent in past social work practices	Denies the existence of racism and racial inequality in society. Compromises effective service by erasing race (a critical component of one's identity) the clinical relationship
Cultural sensitivity approach	Practitioners should strive to acquire, develop and use an 'accurate cultural perceptual schema' when working across difference	Provide service that is informed by both surface and deep structures	Highlights the importance and relevance of culture in social work practice	Disregards the effects of oppression and racism in the lives of people of colour. Views people who are white as cultureless while 'others' have culture – as a result, the latter is in a subordinate position to the former
Antiracist social work	Race, power and economics are linked inextricably. Racism as a social attitude introduced by people with power to justify and sustain their exploitation of people without power. Individual problems are due to an unjust society	Work at individual, community, organisational and structural levels to dismantle systems that depend on racial divisions to function, and to reconstruct them in more egalitarian ways	Highlights issues related to race in service provision. Provides an understanding of the impact of racism on individuals' lives and the broader system in which these relationships exist	Antiracist social work practice can be slow to produce change, particularly at organisational and system levels. Although race is critical to an understanding of oppression, there are other salient aspects of a person's identity that can place her or him at risk for marginalisation

(*continued*)

Table 23.2 Summary of approaches to working across difference (*Continued*)

Model or framework	Main ideas	Goal(s) of intervention	Strengths	Limitations
Anti-oppressive practice	Identity is multiple and complex Oppression results when those in positions of privilege establish and sustain systems in which some have access to power and resources and others are marginalised	Recognise the existence of oppression in its varied forms Work at individual and system levels to overcome oppressive relationships and ensure a just society	Attends to a number of identifications that are possible sites of oppression, which provides a rich understanding of marginalisation Acknowledges the role of system-level inequities that contribute to problems at the individual level	There is little research evidence linking anti-oppressive practice to positive outcomes for clients
Cultural competence	Practitioners require self-awareness, knowledge and particular skills to work effectively across difference	Deliver services at individual and organisational levels that are appropriate and responsive to the cultural concerns of diverse groups	Works to respond to needs of diverse populations Involves service users in planning and delivery of services	Ethnicity and culture are presented as static and fixed Views culture as something only people of colour or 'others' have Despite strengths of individual social workers, institutional barriers may prevent real change Lack of evidence linking cultural competence and positive health and mental health outcomes

derived from cultural inferiority models prompted a shift in the field toward colour blindness. The *colour blind approach* ignored race (Cooper, 1973; Davis & Proctor, 1989; Thomas & Sillen, 1976) and promoted equal opportunity (Frankenberg, 1993). This denial of race failed to take into account the reality of structural inequality and barriers to resources and opportunities in daily life (Yee & Dumbrill, 2003). Furthermore, because race was a critical aspect of identity and social experience, erasing it from the clinical relationship would obscure important issues confronting clients (see Chapter 15, case study of Carol).

The cultural sensitivity approach

The recognition that race – and other differences – played a significant role in the lives of people of colour led to culturally sensitive services and a more inclusive approach to working with minority groups (Dhooper & Moore, 2001; Dyche & Zayas, 1995; Gushue & Constantine, 2007; Proctor & Davis, 1994; Tsang & George, 1998). Cultural sensitivity was seen as the ability of practitioners to 'acquire, develop, and actively use an accurate cultural perceptual schema in the course of multicultural counselling' (Ridley et al., 1994, p. 130). It emphasised two main dimensions of culture: surface and deep structures. Surface structures comprised 'superficial' characteristics, like music and food, while deep structures comprised traditions, social customs, history, and environmental aspects of culture that were strong determinants of culturally sensitive interventions (Resnicow et al., 2000). However, the cultural sensitivity approach disregarded the effects of oppression and issues of race and class for people of colour (Maiter, 2009). Compared to the backdrop of a 'culture-free' mainstream, 'cultured' individuals were different from the norm and culture as a deficit placed people in a subordinate position to the mainstream, becoming too a euphemism for race (Park, 2005). Over time, several more approaches evolved to deal with difference, including antiracist social work, anti-oppressive practice, and cultural competence.

Antiracist social work

Antiracist social work was rooted in an economic understanding of the relationship between race and power, where race was defined as the observable, physical features shared by members of a particular group and distinguished them from members of other groups (Henry et al., 2000). Although biological in origin (skin colour and hair texture), classifications based on race came to be seen as socially constructed meaning a person's identity was both formed and sustained through social interaction. In and of themselves, racial differences were meaningless. Racism resulted from the way people understood such differences and individuals or groups interacted with one another (Berger & Luckmann, 1967; Burr, 1995; Pincus, 2006). Originating in Britain through the late 1980s and 1990s, antiracist social work was a political and academic movement that viewed the problems of the individual as largely rooted in a socially disruptive and unjust society (Bonnett, 2000). Hence, antiracist social work practice worked to 'transform the unequal social relations shaping social interaction between black and white people into egalitarian ones' (Dominelli, 1994, pp. 33–34). The goal was to deconstruct social systems relying on racial divisions to function, and reconstruct them in more egalitarian ways. Social workers practising from this perspective sought to understand the experience and impact of racism in the lives of people of colour, and the role this played in the problems they experienced. The antiracist approach highlighted issues related specifically to race in service provision, and offered an understanding of the impact of racism on the individual and the broader system in which these relationships exist. However, it was slow to produce results, particularly at the structural level where entrenched powers resisted change. This was discouraging for individual practitioners and others taking up this approach. As well, critics of this approach suggested, whereas race was an important entry point to understand oppression, there were other salient aspects of an individual's identity placing her or him at risk for marginalisation, such as class, gender, sexual orientation, and religion.

In recent years, a number of authors have noted a growing European backlash against multiculturalism within both policy and public discourse, with words such as 'cultural' or 'ethnic' generating negative responses (Favell, 1998; Grillo, 2007; Joppke, 2004; Modood, 2005). Over the last 30 years, however, social workers across Europe have developed and become increasingly committed to antiracist social work (Husband, 2007). Although a popular political and academic movement, at times antiracist practice has been criticised on the basis it contributes to racial polarisation and essentialises people's ethnic identities (Rattansi, 2005). Furthermore, particular ethnic communities have felt antiracist practice has made them feel *more* marginalised and neglected given the focus on and language of race (Modood, 2005). A shift to anti-oppressive practice and its focus on a number of identities in addition to race has perhaps helped to mediate some of these concerns (see Chapter 21).

Anti-oppressive practice

Similar to antiracist social work, *anti-oppressive practice* has its roots in social constructionism (see earlier). It views people's identities as shaped, negotiated, and sustained through complex, continuously evolving social processes and focuses on power and oppression, rather than solely on race. Those with power and privilege have material (e.g., money and property) and symbolic advantages (e.g., facility with the dominant language) over those without (Dei, 1996; Perry, 2001). These advantages are used to establish and sustain systems of oppression where people are categorised as dominant or superior, or subordinate or inferior based on various social distinctions (e.g., class, caste, race, and gender; Calliste & Dei, 2000). Oppression occurs when 'these relations of domination consist of the systematic devaluing of the attributes and contributions of those deemed inferior, and their exclusion from the social resources available to those in the dominant groups' (Dominelli, 2002, p. 8; see also Chapter 21). The goal of anti-oppressive social work practice is to identify oppression and how people, groups, and institutions either contribute to or resist power in different situations and thus work to overcome oppressive relationships at the individual and structural levels. This approach expands the focus of antiracism by attending to a number of identifications (in addition to race) as possible sites of oppression and, therefore, can provide a richer understanding of an individual's experience of marginalisation. As well, this approach acknowledges the role of structural inequities contributing to problems for individuals and groups. A considerable limitation, however, is evident here. While there exist useful discussions of how practitioners incorporate anti-oppression in their practice (e.g., see Baines, 2007), there is little research or evidence of its long-term effectiveness and impact on client outcomes.

Cultural competence

Through the 1990s to the present, *cultural competence* has emerged influenced by three main factors: (i) the lack of fit between traditional, Eurocentric models of service provision and the needs of diverse clients; (ii) an increased demand on the part of diverse communities to be involved in their own service delivery and planning; and (iii) the growing visibility of ethnoracial, religious, and cultural groups broadly, as well as within schools of social work (Chau, 1990; Este & Bernard, 2003). Social work practice is deemed culturally competent when practitioners demonstrate a particular level of self-awareness, knowledge, and skill related to the client's ethnicity, race, religion, and cultural background (Lum, 1999; McPhatter, 1997; Williams, 2006; Yan & Wong, 2005). According to Whaley and Longoria (2008), cultural competence is the 'delivery of services ... responsive to the cultural concerns of racial and ethnic minority groups, including their language, histories, traditions, beliefs and values' (p. 169).

At the present time, cultural competence is considered to be critical for service providers working with diverse clients in multicultural environments. According to the National Association of Social Workers' (the US body of professional social workers, the largest in the world) Code of Ethics (2008) (item 1.05) *not* becoming culturally competent is a violation of the ethical responsibilities of social workers. Practitioners not only need to learn about a culture but also develop skills in engaging deeply in cross-cultural encounters (Berlin & Johansson, 2006). Rather than simply viewing cultural competence as the process of learning specific skills, however, many view cultural competence as a continuous learning process involving confronting bias, dealing with resistance, and growing through mistakes (Bussema & Nemec, 2006; Ecklund & Johnson, 2007; Heppner, 2006; Tang, 2007). A common thread is the importance of self-examination, in-depth exploration, and ongoing reflexive practice (Chipps & Simpson, 2008; Mahoney & Carlson, 2006).

Despite its popularity, there are a number of critiques of this approach. First, current conceptualisations of cultural competence tend to present ethnicity and culture as static and fixed (Dean, 2001). Given culture shifts and changes with time and across individuals, particularly those who are biracial or bicultural (Keddel, 2009), working to truly 'know' a person's culture is impossible. As well, believing members of particular cultural groups are homogeneous can contribute to a practitioner's belief clients and their problems can be placed into neat categories (Bussema & Nemec, 2006), and understanding difference is as simple as memorising a list of 'facts' about any given group.

Second, the cultural competence approach tacitly assumes social workers are White, middle-class and, culturally neutral and without their own 'cultural baggage' (Jeffery, 2005). Indeed 'culture' is not simply something people of colour possess (Park, 2005). Add to this the growing number of racialised practitioners, and the rationale for positioning cultural competence as something mainstream, cultureless social workers gain in order to facilitate their work with 'others' becomes increasingly problematic.

Third, most models of cultural competence ignore organisational and system-level factors contributing to the marginalisation of diverse groups. Oftentimes it becomes the responsibility of social workers who themselves belong to such groups to insist on cultural competence in their organisations (Este, 2007). Even where such initiatives are supported, their implementation can be uneven and superficial because of a lack of attention to issues related to racism, discrimination, and White privilege (Pease, 2010; Pon, 2009; Sue, 2001) as well as a dearth of resources for such changes (Bankhead & Erlich, 1996).

Finally, there is a remarkable lack of strong evidence relating cultural competence to positive outcomes for clients (Vega & Lopez, 2001). In fact, none of these approaches has produced much in the way of significant social change. Despite the history of structural analyses within social work, along with these new approaches, effective practice at broad systemic levels has always lagged behind and has never been as developed and effective as community, group, and individual level changes.

FROM WORKING *ACROSS* TO WORKING *THROUGH* DIFFERENCE

While antiracist and anti-oppressive approaches work to challenge the notion of a neutral, apolitical professional, most curricula in social work education are predicated on the idea of a culturally neutral social worker and a culturally different 'other' (Jeffrey, 2005). Indeed anti-oppressive and antiracist practice can only work if there is always an oppressed or victimised or racially different 'other'. While acknowledging differences are inevitable, below a less divisive approach is advanced to work *through* – rather than across – difference.

Working 'across' difference in social work

While multiculturalism aims to manage cultural diversity at a *systemic* level, cultural competence does so at the *interpersonal* and *organisational* levels. Though sound in theory, neither of these approaches has solved the problem of diversity in practice, and to date have not appeared to produce the positive outcomes promised (e.g., see Jansen, 2005). Despite decades of discussion around multiculturalism and related attempts to establish policies to support it, racism, social exclusion, and oppression persist throughout society. Further, notwithstanding the theories, rhetoric and practice of antiracism, anti-oppression, and cultural competence, dealing with diversity remains a thorny and obstinate challenge for social work.

A possible reason for this lack of success may centre upon the strong emphasis both multiculturalism and cultural competence place on *difference*. When difference is the explicit reason for exclusion, it cannot also be its solution. The obdurate reality of difference, whether socially constructed or not, means it is not easily reconciled, and so long as it is the focus, so long will the gulf of difference remain. The discourses of difference creating a juxtaposition between 'us' and 'them' is reproduced at all levels, not least in the training of 'culturally competent' social workers where the goal is for 'us' to know 'them' in order to provide appropriate support.

At the same time, this emphasis on difference tends to homogenise and essentialise individuals *within* groups since the goal is to understand their unique attributes and then use this knowledge to respond to their needs in a standard set of ways. This *cultural essentialism* sees each culture as having 'a unique, fixed essence that can be understood independently of context or intercultural relations, and which makes a ... group act the way it does' (Modood, 1997, p. 10). Judgements are then made on the basis of common stereotypes all members are meant to share (Abu-Laban, 2002) while 'containing' or controlling the impact of diversity on society (Bedard, 2000; Hage, 2000).

By centring both this difference and sameness, multiculturalism and cultural competence continue to position those from diverse ethnoracial and cultural groups on the fringes of our communities. In the case of multiculturalism, 'while "tolerating", "accommodating", "appreciating" and "celebrating" differences, it allows for the preservation of the cultural hegemony of the dominant cultural group' (Henry & Tator, 2006, p. 49). Further, it deals with 'surface structures' unsupported by public legislation, thereby ensuring a lack of accountability (Jansen, 2005). Thus, for example, despite policies to encourage employment equity, people of colour continue to be underemployed and underpaid relative to their mainstream counterparts (Kobayashi, 2005). Cultural competence deals with difference and sameness in the same superficial way – practised in some organisations but not in others, and resting solely on individual practitioners' knowledge of and skills in dealing with others' culture in the absence of any research on effectiveness (Koehn & Swick, 2006). The result is often a neutral, watered down introduction to 'multicultural social work' in which practitioners develop only a superficial understanding of racism and marginalisation experienced by members of diverse groups (Pon, 2009; Williams, 2006). This approach not only requires a continued focus on difference, but is also self-congratulatory about responding in appropriate or relevant ways to the needs of 'others' in clinical practice. Failed attempts are considered exceptions to the rule, or the fault of the 'other' who is, for some reason, not amenable to support (Dei et al., 2004).

Social work needs, then, to find ways to ensure that, although difference may be the starting point of a conversation, it is not the endpoint. In the field of social work, it is clear, while not without strengths, a cultural competence approach (as it is most commonly formulated) is routinely practised as 'otherising', given its emphasis on differences between groups and its tendency to homogenise people within each of these groups without identifying processes for achieving alignment and understanding between cultures. In an assimilationist context, being competent *about* other cultures is at odds with a promotion of the common ground and adherence to a national identity sought by the broader culture. Within a multicultural context, difference is privileged without a means of constructing a sense of social inclusion within a broader unity. In essence, in both circumstances, the emphasis is on the difference between 'me' and 'you', or 'us' and 'you', without a means of creating a 'we'. Indeed, according to Webb (2009):

> This tendency towards different differences being affirmed leads to the point of divisiveness. The predilection towards highlighting difference can lead to a latent form of xenophobia in peoples, a partitioning rather than an understanding ... precisely the thing that social workers imagine they are not going to do (p. 310).

Cultural competence, then, is an extension of prior approaches working *across* differences in superficial ways, rather than moving *through* these differences to achieve common service goals within a rich therapeutic relationship.

Learning to work 'through' differences in social work

Given the problematic nature of this focus on difference, it may be tempting, as some have suggested, to abandon the notion of difference altogether and become 'indifferent to difference' (e.g., Webb, 2009). This view runs the risk of ignoring the very real implications of being constructed as a diverse 'other' in the lives of people of colour. Instead, then, a possible alternative can be found by returning to an understanding of race, ethnicity, and culture as social constructions. Though influenced by broad sociohistorical events and narratives (e.g., see Dei, 1996), they are, more importantly, played out through interactions between social workers and their clients. During these interactions, both client and social worker are actively involved in the co-construction of identities, and potentially the co-construction of the 'other'. Crucially, there are times when differences in race and culture will be critically important to the issue being worked through by the client and the social worker, but there will be other times when these differences are of little importance. Even when these differences are relevant, *how* they are relevant can shift from client to client, and from encounter to encounter. In these interactions it is perhaps less important for a social worker to be competent *about* someone's culture, and more important for him or her to be competent in working with clients to understand how they wish to be understood and supported in the social work encounter. Thus, a social worker's main challenge is not to work *across* differences but to learn to work *through* differences as they arise and are relevant within particular helping situations. In this way, differences are acknowledged and attended to, and then depending on the situation, either addressed further or put aside thereby creating space to address *other* relevant presenting issues as they arise. Sundar, Todd, Danseco, Searson, and Cunning (under review) have proposed a *relational* approach seeing competence not as a possession – a bank of skills or knowledge one possesses to work with others – but as what is displayed in therapeutic encounters when social workers demonstrate their ability to align their understanding according to how clients present themselves in particular interactions. From this relational perspective, cultural competence is not a characteristic of the social worker, but is demonstrated in and is an outgrowth of the worker–client relationship. Also critical, however, is the nature of the relationship and the extent to which the social worker is skilful in eliciting talk to establish whether diversity issues are relevant or not, and, if so, how. In this relationship, the goal is not to achieve mastery over a situation through definitive knowledge, but to achieve mutual understanding so client and social worker might work *through* their differences together, with an honest and realistic appreciation for the implications of these differences in the life of the client. The social worker is not simply a blank canvas upon which the client acts but is an active actor with a culture needing to be named and understood. The focus is on how cultural difference is understood and expressed in the helping *relationship* through the co-construction of identities. By engaging in a commitment to work through rather than across differences, there is space to explore and address cultural differences, power dynamics, and oppressive relationships so as to move to a common space where new understanding makes positive outcomes possible.

CONCLUSION

People in Western society increasingly live in heterogeneous environments where multiculturalism has arisen as an approach to diversity at various levels. This chapter has examined the resultant tensions. It has argued, for the most part, multiculturalism has produced superficial responses, despite antidiscriminatory, equal-opportunity legislation, and is tolerated so long as it does not conflict with a country's national identity or way of life. Likewise, it has critiqued successive attempts to deal with diversity in social work and suggests an approach that involves working through rather than across difference in the helping relationship. Favouring a social constructionist perspective, it challenges social workers to take a more nuanced, complex, and riskier approach and not shy away from difference – as in previous approaches like colour blindness or even cultural sensitivity, but rather advocates for a careful and respectful *engagement* of difference in order to move towards a rich social worker–client relationship, positive client outcomes, and a more just society.

REFERENCES

Abu-Laban, Y. (2002). Liberalism, multiculturalism, and the problem of essentialism. *Citizenship Studies, 6*(4), 459–482.

[Australian] National Multicultural Advisory Council (NMAC) (1999). *Australian multiculturalism for a new century: Toward inclusiveness.* Canberra: Australian Government Publishing Service.

Baines, D. (2007). *Doing anti-oppressive practice: Building transformative politicized social work.* (ed.), Halifax, Nova Scotia: Fernwood Publishing.

Bannerji, H. (2000). *The dark side of the nation: Essays on multiculturalism, nationalism and gender.* Toronto, ON: Canadian Scholars' Press Inc.

Bankhead, T., & Erlich, J. (2005). Diverse populations and community practice. In M.Weil (ed.), *The handbook of community practice.* Thousand Oaks, California: Sage Publications, pp. 59–83.

Bauböck, R., Kraler, A., Martiniello, M., & Perchining, B. (2007). 'Migrants' citizenship: Legal status, rights and political participation. In R. Pennix, Gerger, M., & Kraal, K. (eds). *The dynamics of international migration and settlement in Europe: A state of the art.* Amsterdam: Amsterdam University Press, pp. 65–98.

Bedard, G. (2000). Deconstructing whiteness: Pedagogical implications for anti-racism education. In A.M. Calliste & Dei, G.J. (eds), *Power, knowledge, and anti-racism education: A critical reader.* Halifax, Nova Scotia: Fernwood Publishing, pp. 41–56.

Berger, P., & Luckmann, T. (1967). *The social construction of reality: A treatise in the sociology of knowledge.* New York: Anchor Press/Doubleday.

Berlin, E., & Johansson, S. (2006). Working conditions and cultural competence when interacting with children and parents of foreign origin: Primary Child Health Nurses' opinions. *Scandinavian Journal of Caring Sciences, 20,* 160–168.

Bernard, W.T., & Moriah, J. (2007). Cultural competency: An individual or institutional responsibility. *Canadian Social Work Review/Revue Canadienne de Service Social, 24*(1), 81–92.

Bissoondath, N. (2002). *Selling illusions: The cult of multiculturalism in Canada* (2nd ed.). Toronto, ON:: Penguin Books.

Bonnett, A. (2000). *White identities: Historical and international perspectives.* Harlow: Prentice-Hall.

Burr, V. (1995). *An introduction to social constructionism.* New York: Routledge.

Bussema, E., & Nemec, P. (2006). Training to increase cultural competence. *Psychiatric Rehabilitation Journal, 30*(1), 71–73.

Calliste, A. & Dei, G. (2000). *Power, knowledge, and anti-racism education: A critical reader.* Halifax, Nova Scotia: Fernwood Publishing.

Casas, J.M. (1985). A reflection on the status of racial/ethnic minority research. *The Counseling Psychologist, 13,* 581–598.

Chau, K. (1990). A model for teaching cross-cultural practice in social work. *Journal of Social Work Education, 26*(1), 124–133.

Chipps, J., & Simpson, B. (2008). The effectiveness of cultural-competence training for health professionals in community-based rehabilitation: A systematic review of literature. *Worldviews on Evidence-Based Nursing, 5*(2), 85–94.

Christensen, C.P. (2003). Canadian society: Social policy and ethno-racial diversity. In A. Al-Krenawi & Graham, J.R. (eds), *Multicultural social work in Canada.* Don Mills, ON: Oxford University Press. 70–94.

Clarke, G.E. (1997). White like Canada. *Transition, 73,* 98–109.

Cooper, S. (1973). A look at the effect of racism on clinical work. *Social Casework, 54,* 76–84.

Davis, L.E., & Proctor, E. (1989). *Race, gender, and class: Guidelines for practice with individuals, families, and groups.* Englewood Cliffs, NJ: Prentice Hall.

Dean, R. (2001). The myth of cross-cultural competence. *Families in Society: The Journal of Contemporary Social Services 82*(6), 623–630.

Dei, G. (1996). *Theory and practice: Anti-racism education*. Halifax, Nova Scotia: Fernwood Publishing.

Dei, G., Karumanchery, L., & Karumanchery-Luik, N. (2004). *Playing the race card: Exposing white power and privilege*. New York: Peter Lang.

Dhooper, S.S., & Moore, S.E. (2001). *Social work practice with culturally diverse people*. Thousand Oaks, California: Sage Publications.

Dominelli, L. (1994). Anti-racist perspectives in the social work curriculum. In L. Dominelli, Patel, N., & Bernard, W.T. (eds), *Anti-racist social work education: Models of practice*. UK: SSSU, pp. 22–35.

Dominelli, L. (2002). *Anti-oppressive social work theory and practice*. Basingstoke: Palgrave Macmillan.

Dyche, L., & Zayas, L.H. (1995). The value of curiosity and naiveté for cross cultural psychotherapists. *Family Process, 34*, 389–399.

Ecklund, K., & Johnson, W. (2007). The impact of a culture-sensitive intake assessment on the treatment of a depressed biracial child. *Clinical Case Studies, 6*(6), 468–482.

Essed, P. (1990). *Everyday racism: Reports from women of two cultures*. Trans. C Jaffeac. Claremont, CA: Hunter House.

Este, D. (2007). Cultural competency and social work practice in Canada: A retrospective examination. *Canadian Social Work Review, 24*(1), 93–104.

Este, D., & Bernard, W.T. (2003). Social work practice with African Canadians: An examination of the African Nova Scotian community. In A. Al-Krenawi & Graham, J. (eds), *Multicultural social work in Canada: Working with diverse ethno-racial communities*. Don Mills, Ontario: Oxford University Press, pp. 306–337.

Favell, A. (1998). *Philosophies of integration: Immigration and the idea of citizenship in France and Britain*. London: Macmillan.

Frankenberg, R. (1993). *White women, race matters: The social construction of whiteness*. Minneapolis: University of Minnesota Press.

Galligan, G., & Roberts, W. (2003). *Australian multiculturalism: Its rise and demise*. Paper presented to the Australasian Political Studies Association Conference. University of Tasmania, Hobart.

Gray, M., & Agllias, K. (2010). Australia: The world in one place. In U.A. Segal, Mayadas, N.S., & Elliott, D. (eds), *Immigration worldwide: Policies, practices, and trends*. New York, NY: Oxford University Press, pp. 153–170.

Gray, M., & Webb, S.A. (eds), (2010). *Ethics and value perspectives in social work*. Basingstoke: Palgrave.

Gushue, G.V., & Constantine, M.G. (2007). Color-blind racial attitudes and white racial identity attitudes in psychology trainees. *Professional Psychology: Research and Practice, 38*, 321–328.

Hage, G. (1998). *White nation: Fantasies of white supremacy in a multicultural society*. London: Routledge.

Henry, F., & Tator, C. (2006). *The colour of democracy: Racism in Canadian society* (3rd ed.). Toronto, ON: Thomson Nelson.

Henry, F., Tator, C., Mattis, W., & Rees, T. (2000). *The colour of democracy: Racism in Canadian society* (2nd ed.). Toronto, ON: Harcourt Canada.

Heppner, P. (2006). The benefits and challenges of becoming cross-culturally competent counseling psychologists: Presidential address. *The Counseling Psychologist, 34*(1), 147–172.

Herberg, D. (1993). *Frameworks for cultural and racial diversity: Teaching and learning from practitioners*. Toronto, ON: Canadian Scholars Press.

Hero, R., & Tolbert, C. (1996), A racial/ethnic diversity interpretation of politics and policy in the states of the US. *American Journal of Political Science, 40*, 851–871.

Hiebert, D. (2003). Are immigrants welcome? Introducing the Vancouver Community Studies Survey. *Research on Immigration and Integration in the Metropolis, Working Paper Series, 03-06*, 1–69.

Hernstein, R. (1971). I.Q. *Atlantic Monthly, 228*, 43–64.

Husband, C. (2007). Social work in an ethnically diverse Europe: The shifting challenges of difference. *Social Work and Society, 6*(1), 1–13.

James, C. (2003). *Seeing ourselves: Exploring race, ethnicity, and culture* (3rd ed.). Toronto, ON: Thompson Educational Publishing, Inc.

Jansen, C. (2005). Canadian multiculturalism. In C. James (ed.), *Possibilities and limitations: Multicultural policies and programs in Canada*. Halifax, Nova Scotia: Fernwood Publishing, pp. 21–33.

Jeffery, D. (2005). What good is antiracist social work if you can't master it? Exploring a paradox in anti-racist social work education. *Race Ethnicity and Education, 8*(4), 409–425.

Joppke, C. (2004). The retreat of multiculturalism in the liberal state: Theory and policy. *British Journal of Sociology, 55*(2), 237–257.

Keddell, E. (2009). Narrative as identity: Postmodernism, multiple ethnicities and narrative practice approaches in social work. *Journal of Ethnic and Cultural Diversity in Social Work, 18*, 221–241.

Kelley, N. & Trebilcock, M. (1998). *The making of the mosaic: A history of Canadian immigration policy*. Toronto, ON: University of Toronto Press, Inc.

Kivisto, P. (2002). *Multiculturalism in a global society*. Oxford: Blackwell Publishing.

Kobayashi, A. (2005). Employment equity in Canada: The paradox of tolerance and denial. In C. James (ed.), *Possibilities and limitations: Multicultural policies and programs in Canada*. Halifax, Nova Scotia: Fernwood Publishing, pp. 154–162.

Koehn, P., & Swick, H. (2006). Medical education for a changing world: Moving beyond cultural competence into transnational competence. *Academic Medicine, 81*(6), 548–556.

Kymlicka, W. (1995). *Multicultural citizenship*. New York: Oxford University Press.

Lopez, M. (2005). Reflections on the state of Australian multiculturalism and the emerging multicultural debate in Australia 2005. *People and Place, 13*(3), 33–41.

Lum, D. (1999). *Culturally competent practice: A framework for growth and action*. Pacific Grove, CA: Brooks/Cole.

Mahoney, J., & Carlson, E. (2006). A framework for cultural competence in advanced practice psychiatric and mental health education. *Perspectives in Psychiatric Care, 42*(4), 227–237.

Maiter, S. (2009). Using an anti-racist framework for assessment and intervention in clinical practice with families from diverse ethno-racial backgrounds. *Journal of Clinical Social Work, 37*, 267–276.

McLaren, P. (1994). White terror and oppositional agency: Towards a critical multiculturalism. In D.T. Goldberg (ed.), *Multiculturalism: A critical reader*. Cambridge: Blackwell, pp. 45–74.

McPhatter, A.R. (1997). Cultural competence in child welfare: What is it? How do we achieve it? What happens without it? *Child Welfare, 76*(1), 255–278.

Modood, T. (1997). Introduction. In T. Modood & Werbner, P. (eds), *The politics of multiculturalism in the New Europe*. London: Zed Press, pp. 1–25.

Modood, T. (2005). Establishment, multiculturalism and British citizenship. *The Political Quarterly, 65*(1), 53–73.

Moynihan, D.P. (1965). *The Negro family: The case for national action*. Washington, DC: US Department of Labor, Office of Policy, Planning and Research.

Padilla, A.M. (1981). Competent communities: A critical analysis of theories and public policy. In O.A. Barbarin, Good, P.R., Pharr, O.M., & Siskind, J.A. (eds), *Institutional racism and community competence*. Rockville, MA: US Department of Health and Human Services, pp. 20–29.

Park, Y. (2005). Culture as deficit: A critical discourse analysis of the concept of culture in contemporary social work discourse. *Journal of Sociology and Social Welfare, 32*(3), 11–33.

Patni, R. (2006). Race-specific vs. culturally competent social workers: The debates and dilemmas around pursuing essentialist or multicultural social work practice. *Journal of Social Work Practice, 20*(2), 163–174.

Pease, B. (2010). *Undoing privilege: Unearned advantage in a divided world*. London: Zed Books.

Perry, P. (2001). White means never having to say you're ethnic: White youth and the construction of 'cultureless' identity. *Journal of Contemporary Ethnography, 30*(1), 56–91.

Pincus, F. (2006). *Understanding diversity: An introduction to race, class, gender, and sexual orientation*. Boulder, CO: Lynne Rienner Publishers.

Pon, G. (2009). Cultural competence as new racism: An ontology of forgetting. *Journal of Progressive Human Services, 20*, 59–71.

Ponterotto, J.G., & Cassas, M. (1991). *Handbook of racial/ethnic minority counseling research*. Springfield, IL: Charles C. Thomas.

Proctor, E.K., & Davis, E.L. (1994). The challenge of racial difference: Skills for clinical practice. *Social Work, 39*, 314–323.

Qureshi, A., & Collazos, F. (2008). Cultural competency training in psychiatry. *European Psychiatry, 23*, S49–S58.

Rattansi, A. (2004). Dialogues on difference: Cosmopolitans, locals, and 'others' in a post-national age. *Sociology, 38*(3), 613–621.

Resnicow, K., Soler, R., Braithwaite, R.L., Ahluwalia, J.S., & Butler, J. (2000). Cultural sensitivity in substance use prevention. *Journal of Community Psychology, 28*, 271–290.

Ridley, C.R., Medoza, D.W., Kanitz, B.E., Angermeier, L., & Zenk, R. (1994). Cultural sensitivity in multicultural counselling: A perceptual schema model. *Journal of Counseling Psychology, 41*, 125–136.

Rodriguez-Garcia, D. (2010). Beyond assimilation and multiculturalism: A critical review of the debate on managing diversity. *Journal of International Migration and Integration, 11*, 251–271.

Rubington, E., & Weinberg, M.S. (1971). *The study of social problems*. New York: Oxford University Press.

Soroka, S., Johnston, R., & Banting, K. (2006). Ties that bind? Social cohesion and diversity in Canada. In *Belonging? Diversity, recognition and shared citizenship in Canada*. The Institute for Research on Public Policy (IRPP) is a nonpartisan Canadian public policy institute located in Montreal, Quebec, Canada, pp. 1–40.

Sue, D. (2001). Multidimensional facets of cultural competence. *The Counseling Psychologist, 29*(6), 790–821.

Sundar, P. (2008). Multiculturalism. In M. Gray & Webb, S.A. (eds), *Social work theories and methods*. London: Sage. 98–108.

Sundar, P., Todd, S., Danseco, E., Searson, L., & Cunning, S. (forthcoming). Toward a culturally-responsive approach to child and youth mental health practice: integrating the perspectives of service users and practitioners. *Canadian Journal of Community Mental Health.*

Tang, G. (2007). Commentary on 'Extending cultural competence through systems change: Academic, hospital, and community partnerships'. *Journal of Transcultural Nursing, 18*(1), 79S–83S.

Taylor, C. (1994). The politics of recognition. In C. Taylor & Gutmann, A. (eds), *Multiculturalism.* Princeton, NJ: Princeton University Press. 25–74.

Thomas, A., & Sillen, S. (1976). *Racism and psychiatry.* Secaucus, NJ: Citadel Press.

Tilbury, F. (2007). The retreat from multiculturalism: The Australian experience. *Pluralism, Inclusion and Citizenship,* 3rd Global Conference, Interdisciplinary. net, Salzburg. Retrieved November 16, 2010 from http://www.inter-disciplinary.net/ati/diversity/pluralism/pl3/Tilbury%20paper.pdf

Tsang, A.K., & George, U. (1998). Towards an integrated framework for cross-cultural social work practice. *Canadian Social Work Review, 15,* 73–93.

Vega, W., & Lopez, S. (2001). Priority issues in Latino mental health services research. *Mental Health Services Research, 3*(4), 189–200.

Webb, S.A. (2009). Against difference and diversity in social work: The case of human rights. *International Journal of Social Welfare, 18,* 307–316.

Whaley, A., & Longoria, R. (2008). Assessing cultural competence readiness in community mental health centers: A multidimensional scaling analysis. *Psychological Services, 5*(2), 169–183.

Williams, C. (2006). The epistemology of cultural competence. *Families in Society: The Journal of Contemporary Social Services 87*(2), 209–220.

Wood, M., & James, C. (2005). Multicultural education in Canada: Opportunities, limitations, and contradictions. In C. James (ed.), *Possibilities and limitations: Multicultural policies and programs in Canada.* Halifax, Nova Scotia: Fernwood Publishing, 93–107.

Yan, M., & Wong, Y. (2005). Rethinking self-awareness in cultural competence: Toward a dialogic self in cross-cultural social work. *Families in Society: The Journal of Contemporary Social Services 86*(2), 181–188.

Yee, J., & Dumbrill, G. (2003). Whiteout: Looking for race in Canadian social work practice. In A. Al-Krenawi & Graham, J. (eds), *Multicultural social work in Canada: Working with diverse ethno-racial communities.* Don Mills, Ontario: Oxford University Press. 98–121.

Human Rights and Social Justice

Richard Hugman

In 2000 the International Federation of Social Workers (IFSW) and the International Association of Schools of Social Work (IASSW) put forward the following definition of social work:

> The social work profession promotes social change, problem solving in human relationships and the empowerment and liberation of people to enhance well-being. Utilising theories of human behaviour and social systems, social work intervenes at the points where people interact with their environments. Principles of human rights and social justice are fundamental to social work (IFSW/IASSW, 2000/2001).

This statement replaces an earlier definition, formulated in 1982. Attention to this current definition is focused especially on the final sentence, which makes a very bold claim. The principles of human rights and social justice were not previously emphasised in this way, but within this definition are made central to the purposes of social work around the world. Therefore, the first decade of the 21st century CE (all dates throughout this chapter are in the 'Common Era') can be seen as the time in which international social work embraced these ideas and placed them at centre stage in understanding the nature of the profession. Four questions immediately arise. First, what is the origin of these principles and what values do they embody? Second, how were these principles addressed prior to the international definition (if indeed they were)? Third, what aspects of social work internationally call for such a strong declaration of these particular principles and, by implication, the values lying within them? Fourth, what are the implications of claiming these principles as foundational for social work? For the purposes of this discussion, a principle should be seen as a basic set of standards or norms, which underpins and structures more detailed argument about thoughts and beliefs, while a value is a statement of what is regarded as good, something to be pursued because of its inherent qualities (see, e.g., Banks, 2006, pp. 6, 27). The ideas and practices of human rights and social justice perform both these functions, and these two facets are used interchangeably not only in social work but also in wider ethical and political debates. An underlying challenge in thinking about ethics is that principles and values are often highly contested between different perspectives.

In seeking to answer these questions, this chapter does several things. It takes an historical perspective on the development of the profession's claim to human rights and social justice as its core principles. In doing so, it also considers the background of these principles in social philosophy (i.e., both in ethics and in politics and the relationship between the two). In order to accomplish this, each of these principles is examined separately in some detail before then going on to look critically at some of the issues for practice and policy that arise from integrating them into a single moral foundation for social work. In particular, the focus here is on the way in which social work has tended to assume the connection between the two, as 'human-rights-and-social-justice' (see, e.g., Lundy, 2006). However, although this usage has gained currency in recent discussions of social work values, often it can beg many questions (see, e.g., Bowles et al., 2006). For example, are these ideas actually compatible and, if so, in what ways? What has to be done to achieve such integration? What happens when this integration is challenged?

Underlying this approach to the topic is a commitment to the idea that, if we were going to make the claim to these foundations, it must be something in which we would engage consciously so the challenges and contradictions emerging from the process could be used creatively to form a distinctive social work approach (see Hugman, 2005). A principle, as a 'set of basic norms or standards', is a position from which choices are made for more specific thought and action. Yet all principles are inherently contestable and agreement cannot be assumed. In other words, although in everyday practice social workers must use principles without constantly rethinking and reworking them, if social work does not continually consider and debate these ideas in appropriate ways, it will fail to recognise that they are tools to be used to achieve the goals set out in the international definition. This is the task to which this chapter is directed.

THE ORIGINS OF SOCIAL WORK'S CORE VALUES

Thinking about human rights and social justice has a very long history. Philosophers trace such ideas back to classical Greece, in particular to Socrates, Plato, and Aristotle, and, although this is more contentious, also in some respects to Confucius in ancient China (Hansen, 2004; Hinman, 2008). The common concern of these philosophers was in finding the way to achieve a society in which people were able to live a fully human life. Thus they were concerned with questions about what a person needed in order to be able to achieve or have in order to live such a life (the basis, as we see below, of human rights) and how a society should best be organised to achieve this (the basis of social justice). However, although the Greek thinkers, in particular, are often regarded as the originators of the ideals of democracy, both the Greek and Chinese traditions can be seen as shot through with contradictions. For example, they largely accepted the social subordination of women, social class divisions, and also slavery (often based on racial or cultural differences). Nonetheless, they set out many of the values that later provided the building blocks for modern thought.

Contemporary understanding of human rights and social justice have emerged during the modern period in Europe. These ideas were developed over several hundred years, but two particular bodies of work have been most influential in modern values and ethics, which come from the 18th and 19th centuries. These are the deontology of Kant in Germany (1724–1804), and the utilitarianism of Bentham (1748–1832) and Mill (1806–1873) in the UK (Hinman, 2008). Indeed, these ideas can be seen as the origins of contemporary understanding of human rights and social justice, respectively. So these philosophical approaches are examined briefly before looking in more detail at their impact on the origins and development of modern social work.

At the heart of Kant's approach is the value of human agency and autonomy. For Kant, all human beings are of equal moral worth, with all being entitled *on these grounds alone* to moral dignity. From this Kant argued all people have an ethical duty to each other, to act in ways that respect and uphold our humanity (Banks, 2006, pp. 29–30). ('Deontology' means the science or systematic theory of duty.) So the responsibility to tell the truth, for example, is grounded in the fact of the moral status of both the other person and ourselves. If we were to lie, we would fail in our duty to the humanity of the other and of our own self. The implication is that the idea of human rights, although not formally part of Kant's thinking, is the logical conclusion of his ideas of moral worth and dignity. From this, because a core aspect of achieving humanity is through the maximum possible liberty for individuals to develop and exercise agency, in an increasingly complex and contractual society, expectations that each person might have of others need to be set out clearly in law, in political and institutional structures, and so on. In this way, the foundations for the modern claim to *human rights* were laid. We return to this point below in a closer look at human rights in social work.

The Utilitarians must also be seen as liberals, since they shared with Kant the value of the liberty of each person based on an understanding of moral worth. However, their approach differed markedly from deontology since they recognised that each person has their own view of what is good. In a finite world, it may not be possible for each person always to achieve all that they wish to and so some basis has to be found for finding a balance between competing objectives. Bentham saw this in terms of the maximisation of pleasure and the minimisation of pain (MacIntyre, 1998, p. 226). Mill refined this idea, with an emphasis on the balance between human flourishing and misery. This approach is 'consequential', since it determines what is good through a consideration of outcomes. Such an approach underpins the idea of social justice through the notion of a balance to be found between competing claims about which things in life enable people to flourish as much as possible. As shown below in a more detailed consideration of social justice in social work, other values necessarily must be introduced into any utilitarian consideration, which makes it highly contested.

As an historical project, social work emerged within societies where these two ethical frameworks reflected the dominant moral and political world view. The processes of industrialisation and urbanisation were accompanied by increasing formal political democracy and the development of the rule of law. But, at the same time, there was also the rapid growth of large-scale poverty, among both the new city-dwellers and those in rural communities. Two responses to these growing aspects of human need can be considered as the antecedents of modern social work: the Charity Organization Society (COS) and Settlement House movements (Payne, 2005). Examples of these two approaches can be found across Northern Europe, North America, and Australasia.

The COS approach aimed to provide aid and assistance to those who were in poverty using the logic of 'science' to define need and to identify who should receive assistance and how it should be given. This involved the provision of relief and assistance to individuals and families through the practice of 'casework' (indeed, this is the origin of the concept). Trained and supervised fieldworkers visited families to give advice and social education to those who received material and financial help from these organisations, with the intention that this help would be more effective.

In contrast, the Settlement House movement involved people from more advantaged social backgrounds living and working in poorer areas. Their goal was to contribute experience and knowledge, through forms of community work and community education – in terms current one century later they could even be described as promoting 'social capital' and 'empowerment' (compare Addams, 2002 [1907], with Adams, 2008). While the language may have changed, the underlying emphasis of the early Settlement Movement on the humanitarian and democratic basis of social work is extremely clear.

It would not be correct to identify either deontology or utilitarianism specifically with one or other of these major early forms of social work. While early casework and the COS focused on promoting individual agency in dealing with poverty and need, there are also aspects of utilitarianism in their selection of those who were deemed appropriate to receive such help and those who were not. In contrast, because the Settlement Movement worked with groups and communities, it necessarily emphasised more aggregate responses to needs, which carries a utilitarian logic of finding a balance between views and interests, but, at the same time, it sought to enhance human agency and dignity, especially within liberal democracy. In this sense, early social work was already bringing together the beginnings of its twin focus on human rights and social justice.

The next historical turning point for these principles in social work is in the aftermath of the world war of 1939 to 1945. Again, this is especially pronounced in social work ideas in the global North. For example, to consider social justice, there was a 'rediscovery of poverty' in the major cities of Northern Europe and North America, revealed through the social changes arising from the conflict (Fox Piven & Cloward, 1971; Jones, 1983). Social workers were involved both in the identification of these needs and in the formation of policies and practices to respond to them. In many countries of Northern Europe, it could be said that social work's growth as a profession at this time came often through its increasing role in the provision of social services to those who were in need. The welfare states of Scandinavia and the UK, for example, both benefited from and provided the institutional basis for the development of social work.

On the international stage, social workers were also very involved in the postwar responses to global issues at structural and political levels. Although social work has been 'international' since the 1920s (Healy, 2008), it had largely concentrated on its own development and in the provision of responses to specific issues (such as the foundation of Save the Children Fund by a social worker, Jebb, in 1919; see Healy, 2008, pp. 166, 169). However, in the postwar 'reconstruction', social workers were involved in various ways not only in establishing programmes for people who were then called 'displaced persons' but also in the formation of the United Nations (UN) and some of its agencies, such as the World Health Organization (WHO) and the United Nations Children's Fund (UNICEF) (Eilers, 2008; Kendall, 2008). A central part of the thinking within these activities was the emergence of the understanding of human rights now commonly accepted in social work discussions, as set out in *The Universal Declaration of Human Rights* (UN, 1948). Moreover, social work established a set of close relationships with the UN, as since 1947 the IASSW and from 1959 the IFSW have had special reporting status at the Economic and Social Council (ECOSOC), which is one of the major decision-making bodies of the UN.

Over the succeeding 50 years, the two principles of human rights and social justice have become much more consciously part of debates about the purposes of social work. For example, between the ethical document of the IFSW 1994 and the joint IFSW/IASSW statement in 2004, increasingly explicit statements about these principles as part of social work ethics and values can be seen. By 2004, they had become the main framework for the document (especially in section 4) with the *Universal Declaration of Human Rights* identified (section 2) as a major point of reference for thinking about the basis of social work ethics internationally. This emphasis then affects the way in which national codes of ethics are formulated, so that many now incorporate these aspects of the IFSW/IASSW documents (Banks, 2006, pp. 81–86). By 2004, this approach in the profession in various countries fed back into the revision of the ethical documents produced by IFSW and IASSW working jointly. Having established the background of thinking about human rights and social justice, and their incorporation into social work ethics, each principle – and its application – is now examined in more detail, before considering the ways in which these principles might be brought together.

HUMAN RIGHTS

Wronka (1992) defines three 'generations' of human rights (called thus because, he argues, they have developed sequentially over time) as follows.

1 *First-generation rights* – civil and political rights, such as the right to vote, or meet with whom one chooses, to practise a religion or not, to freedom of speech, to equality before the law, to be free from fear of arbitrary arrest or torture, and so on. Some of these rights are 'positive' (i.e., they are the right to do something) and some are 'negative' (the right not to have something happen).
2 *Second-generation rights* – social, cultural, and economic rights, such as the right to food, clothing, housing, employment, health, or education. These rights are not as individualistic as the first generation and they are more widely contested.
3 *Third-generation rights* – community and collective rights, such as the right to social and economic development, to be able to express one's own culture, to enjoy the natural world free from pollution – perhaps even to leave it in a liveable state for future generations. These rights are the most highly contested.

Ife (2008) argues that the first-generation understanding of rights dominates everyday ways of thinking. It is, he says, widely used in politics and in the media because it has a long record and also because it is most widely supported. The international 'human rights agenda' is usually defined in these terms (Ife, 2008, p. 31). For O'Neill (2005), this stems largely from the way in which rights require the identification of a corresponding bearer of obligations. First-generation rights are more easily agreed, because they require everyone as a bearer of obligations not to impede the liberty of others. Second- and third-generation rights require the designation of specific individuals or institutions as obligation bearers, hence there is a lack consensus on such matters.

However, for Ife (2008), the second- and third-generations of rights have as much importance for social work, because these can be seen to be direct expressions of many of the issues with which social work is usually concerned. Yet, it is only relatively recently that social work has addressed them as such, although issues such as food and water, clothing, shelter, health and so on, have been recognised as core human *needs* since the early days of the profession. For Ife (2008, Chapter 5), human needs provide a strong basis for identifying and responding to human rights claims because these are the things that are necessary in order to live a fully human life. However, at the same time, his discussion points to the importance of identifying what is a right and what is a particular expression of meeting a need. This can be seen in the difference between asserting the right to food, clothing, or shelter and whether that constitutes a right to this particular dish, garment, or house. There are strong parallels here with the arguments of development theorists such as George (1988) and Nussbaum (2000) about whether these things should be seen as rights – the discussion returns to this point below.

It is precisely this ambiguity and struggle in gaining widespread support for so much of the rights claims with which social workers are involved that prompts Lundy (2006) to assert that seeing these necessities for a fully human life only as 'needs' is inadequate (p. 123). It is vital, she argues, that such things are addressed as rights because attention is then focused on the structural reasons why people might lack access to them. While some might disagree with Lundy (2006) regarding the ascription of the notion of need to those things humans require *necessarily* implying they are the personal and private responsibility of each individual person, it can be agreed that in the great majority of historical circumstances this has actually been the case. So the idea of rights strengthens the claims of those who are impeded by life circumstances from meeting their needs unaided to receiving some assistance from those around them. The rights emphasised by Lundy (2006) as the focus of social work, in this sense, are clearly the second generation in Wronka's (1992) framework. Considered further below are the implications this understanding of rights in social work has for the connection of human rights and social justice.

For Reichert (2003), the pursuit of rights similarly finds its realisation in practice through challenging discrimination and the unequal distribution of resources. Her discussion identifies particular aspects of social structures as the source of challenge to rights, in disparities arising from issues of gender, race, and culture, and other sites of inequality. While some of her argument is based in second-generation rights, in the way in which these inequalities relate to access to resources to meet human needs, some are also grounded in the third generation in so far as this is concerned with collective identity and other communal aspects of life (an indication that the 'generations' model has some limitations). So, although issues, such as interpersonal and family violence against women, concern the rights of women not to be assaulted and to live free from fear in their own home, both the causes of the issue and the rights they can claim are also matters of community and collective problems, such as the social status of women. Issues particularly affecting Indigenous communities or ethnic minority groups should be seen in the same way.

Ife (2008) argues that there is a pattern to the way in which different forms of social work practice are related to the different generations of rights. He links the first generation, civil and political rights, particularly to advocacy. An example of how this might appear in practice can be seen in the work of Australian social workers, who, together with psychiatrists, nurses, and other health professions, challenged the lengthy periods of detention for asylum seekers common in Australia between 2001 and 2007 (Briskman et al., 2009). Welfare rights work, support for women who have experienced domestic violence and support for ex-prisoners are examples of advocacy work based on this understanding of human rights.

The practices Ife (2008) links to second-generation rights are those of social services provision, including direct work with service users, organisational work, and policy development. This is crucial, because this encompasses a great deal of social work practice, such as family casework, especially in the global North, and for some colleagues who are involved in this type of social services delivery 'human rights' may not be recognised as a core concern (personal communication). However, as Staub-Bernasconi (2007) argues, in most countries such services may exist as programmes but are not fully recognised as rights, so they can be limited or even withdrawn as matters of 'policy' – thus the claim to rights is important for ensuring that services are maintained and developed (see also Midgley, 2007).

Third-generation rights, although perhaps on the face of it apparently less concrete, nevertheless are also addressed by social work. Ife (2008) identifies community development as the central practice here – and he subsumes other practice approaches within this, including social development, economic development, environmental action, community organising, and so on. These are all collective practices and so appropriately related to collective rights. It may be that, as with the assertion of a rights approach in other areas, such as work with refugees (see earlier) or environmental programmes, these forms of social work have been weakened or even delegitimised in the global North as 'politics' as opposed to 'professionalism' (Hugman, 1998).

Nonetheless, they still have relevance for social work everywhere in so far as needs arise from the failure for people to enjoy community rights.

The centrality of human rights to practice and policy in social work is recognised by international social work organisations, such as the IFSW and the IASSW, both of which have 'human rights committees'. In addition to advocacy on the civil and political rights of individual social workers and others, at times these organisations have played active roles within the UN system, using the status of representation (see earlier), for example, contributing to the debates leading to the international covenants on civil and political rights, and on social and economic rights, as well as UN instruments such as the *Convention on the Rights of the Child* (CRC), the *Convention for the Elimination of Discrimination Against Women* (CEDAW), the *Declaration on the Rights of Disabled People,* and the *Declaration of the Rights of Indigenous People* (Healy, 2008; Ife, 2008).

SOCIAL JUSTICE

It should be noted clearly that the idea of *social* justice is a relatively recent one. Indeed, not only throughout history have scholars, politicians, and others simply debated the notion of *justice*, but this is also still the case in modern philosophy, law, political science and so on (compare with Hinman, 2008; MacIntyre, 1998). In this wider intellectual sphere, justice is widely seen as having two aspects. The first is the restitution of harm done to social relationships. This can take the form of retributive action, such as exacting a punishment for wrong or harmful actions, or it might be focused more on restoring the social relationships that have been harmed or it may comprise both. The second aspect of justice concerns distribution, which may be of material resources or of access to social resources. Thus, the principle of justice affects many areas of life.

In his succinct history of the idea of justice, Reisch (2002) notes that, to a large extent, the meaning of the principle depends on how the relationship between society and individual people is viewed. While social workers might agree that the values of justice are fairness, balance, and so on, what this actually means in practice will be based on whether they wish to give primacy to other ideas, such as needs, merit, opportunity, responsibility, and other questions with both moral and nonmoral aspects.

Reisch (2002) identifies an important difference between the political ethics of classical philosophers and much religious thought. The former, he notes, accepted inequality as just, based on understandings of social roles and status. In this view, the good society is one in which people fulfil their proper social role and this can be seen in the ideas of both Plato and Confucius. In contrast, religious teachings (e.g., Buddhism, Christianity, Hinduism, Judaism, and Islam) have tended to emphasise the moral equality of all people (even though historically the practices of religious institutions have not always conformed to this principle). An example of this is the teaching of Aquinas (1225–1274), who argued that a society in which those who have more than they need are expected to give to others who are in serious need is, in these terms, a just society and those individuals who make such a response are just. Secular thought began to identify equality as a core feature of a just society in the modern period (Reisch, 2002). So, it can be agreed, what lies at the heart of the concept of justice is the goal of 'balance' between the needs and interests that each of us has in achieving a fully human life. What remains contested is how this can be achieved, how (as in the Platonic notion) people can seek both to be just individuals and live in a just society and whether this demands equality.

Embedded in Reisch's (2002) analysis is a broad understanding in social work of the way in which the opportunity to exercise choices and take responsibility is socially structured and, therefore, not fully within the control of any individual person. Indeed, one of the arguments for a concept of *social* justice is the unequal distribution of resources giving some people considerable control and denying any such power to others. But this understanding is countered by those who deny that there are social goods to be redistributed (Grace, 1994). From this latter perspective, matters such as health, education, and well-being are regarded as personal rather than social responsibilities. Within that view, which can be understood as radical liberalism, in so far as justice concerns the distribution of material goods, it can only be seen in terms of a responsibility not to stand in the way of others who are seeking to achieve whatever goals they have set for themselves. Beyond that, such a position asserts that to require some people to provide for the needs of others (such as through taxation-based services) is to rob them through the coercive use of power, however much this might be sanctioned by a parliamentary democracy, and hence should be seen as unjust. From this perspective, claims to social justice may deny some people their human rights. [It is this point that O'Neill (2005) addresses in relation to the lack of consensus in designating obligation bearers for second- and third-generation rights; see earlier.]

Against this radical form of liberalism, the arguments of Rawls (1972) have had a profound impact on social work ideas (as much as they have on philosophy, political science, economics, and so on; Hugman, 1998). While seeking to maintain a liberal notion of individual liberty, Rawls (1972) also argued that a just society was one in which there were limitations to the ways in which inequalities might prevent people from achieving a good human life. He proposed two connected principles, which support each other:

1. each person has a right to the maximum amount of personal liberty consistent with the liberties of others;
2. inequalities (social and or economic) must benefit the least advantaged and be open to everyone fairly under conditions of equal opportunity.

Without the second principle to moderate the first, Rawls (1972) was concerned that life chances simply become a matter of luck, which is entirely contrary to any definition of justice (Hinman, 2008, pp. 236–237). So to achieve this it is necessary to create social structures and relationships favouring those who are disadvantaged either by nature or by existing social arrangements. The limit Rawls (1972) sets on the redistribution required by such an approach, therefore, is when it begins to harm the widely agreed notion of personal liberty. An example of unjust redistribution would be where a person was forced to give up goods necessary for him or her to meet his or her own needs.

Some writers within social work seek to go even further than this, stating that a society that is based on any acceptance of inequality must be regarded as inherently unjust (Jordan, 1991; Solas, 2008). For both Jordan (1991) and Solas (2008), nothing short of radical equality can achieve social justice. Thus they are both critical of Rawls (1972) as not going far enough. This argument is grounded in an analysis of social structures and social relationships as the cause of human need and suffering, whether such need is experienced at the level of the individual or is collective. For example, people might be in poverty because of specific circumstances affecting their own lives, or their poverty may be highly affected by the fact they are members of a recognisable social grouping, such as being a disabled person, being a woman, or being a member of an ethnic, racial, or cultural minority. Of course, for some people these collective identities can coalesce to compound disadvantage.

Various writers on social justice identify this principle as a core dimension to the nature of social work, referring to the Settlement House Movement and the association of social work in the early 20th century with humanitarian and democratic work both in the global Northern countries and in international work (e.g., in the League of Nations, the precursor to the UN; Jordan, 1991; Reisch, 2002; Solas, 2008; also see Healy, 2008 and

Payne, 2005). If, as seems to be reasonable, England's (1986, p. 13) statement is accepted that social work does not exist for people with problems but for people who cannot cope unaided with their problems, then this should not be too contentious. While some of the individual and collective problems with which social work is appropriately concerned will be the outcome of poverty or other lack of material resources, those not usually related to the lack of access to other sorts of goods, such as education, health, and so on. For most service users, the things in life leading them to seek assistance from social work almost always are not simply a matter of personal responsibility, but are also seriously affected by social structures and relationships. It is for this reason social work around the world tends to have an overwhelming concern with those who experience material and structural disadvantage.

From this understanding, it may be possible to begin to see a parallel between the three generations of human rights and justice. The first of these is the clearest. Civil and political rights have a close relationship with justice in the formal operation of institutions, such as the law and government. The person who does not receive a fair trial, for example, has both been treated unjustly *and* has had his or her human rights denied. Claiming the failure to achieve social, cultural, and economic rights, or community and collective rights as injustice, however, is considerably more contentious. The idea of *social* justice emerges in these areas but debate can be found in the very nature of the goods in question as social because, even within the same society or culture, it is reasonable for people to hold different views about what constitutes the right and the good. So the next section examines the relationship of human rights and social justice in more depth.

PROBLEMS OF INTEGRATION

Earlier in this chapter it was noted there was a tendency in social work to regard human rights and social justice either as interwoven or even as if they were two aspects of one overall concept, without much debate about the problems of reconciling core elements of each idea. However, because of the questions raised by critiques of the concept of social justice, it is necessary to show how such links can be sustained if social work is going to continue to build on such a connection.

To recap, the principle of human rights is grounded in the claim that what it is to be human is shared by all people equally and absolutely. Anything that people can agree is a right must be available to everyone, while allowing everyone to enjoy the maximum possible personal liberty to pursue their own life goals. In contrast, social justice necessitates structures setting limits on the capacity of some people to pursue certain life goals because, it may be argued, the conditions under which they can do so unfairly exclude others from achieving their life goals. This, as has been noted from Reisch (2002), is a particular conception of justice. It is the one tending to inform modern social work theory and practice. In this understanding, the responsible agents must be the democratic institutions of a society, whether these are government or nongovernment organisations (although the latter will almost inevitably be dependent in some way on government, for freedom to operate if not for direct funding). The underlying reality is that resources are finite, so any redistribution must demand a change from the *status quo* leading to some people being required to give up something they currently have (Jordan, 1991; Solas, 2008). Although even most radical liberals accept that there are limits to ownership (Hinman, 2008), in a world in which more than one billion people live on less than US$1.25 per day, and wealth is increasingly unequally distributed, this cannot happen unless those who currently have most come to have less in the future (George, 1988; Singer, 2002).

A further issue crucial to how social workers think about the connections between human rights and social justice is culture.

Different cultures emphasise different values, leading to disparate ideas about the goods to be pursued in life, and within cultures people may reasonably disagree with each other about how a particular value is understood. For example, arguments about the role of adult men in relation to other members of families are as relevant in the global North as in the South (Hugman, 2008).

Moreover, statements about human rights are inevitably couched in terms of individual people. Where a culture emphasises collectivities as the basic moral unit, from outside the idea that the life choices of individuals should be subordinated to those of the group can be seen as a denial of rights. Indeed, given that the determination of what is in the group's interests may be made by those with particular identities (by sex, by age, by sexuality, and so on), claims to culture and tradition can be critiqued as supporting sectional power and even oppression. In turn, arguments for cultural difference and the importance of collectivities can reject the idea of human rights as neocolonialism, seeing the concept as a 'western imposition' (Healy, 2008). Thus, it can be seen, it is difficult to draw comparisons between the second- and third-generation human rights and equivalent aspects of social justice.

One important attempt to find a way through this potential impasse is the 'capability' approach, as argued by Nussbaum (2000, 2006). Nussbaum's argument contains certain assumptions:

1   what it is to be human is common across cultures because it is based on a set of basic human needs;
2   denial of opportunity to meet these needs prevents people from achieving a truly human life;
3   the role of culture is to give concrete expression to how needs should appropriately be met in different social circumstances;
4   cultures change over time; and
5   rights and justice must be enjoyed by individuals as well as by collectivities.

From this base, Nussbaum defines 'capabilities' as those things which people must be capable of achieving in order to be said to be living a truly human life. These are: life of normal length; bodily health; bodily integrity (which includes being free from assault); senses, imagination and thought; emotions; practical reasoning; affiliation; living well with other species; play; and control over ones environment (Nussbaum, 2000, pp. 78–80; see also Chapter 41). For Nussbaum, whether or not the language of rights is used, everyone has a claim to these capabilities. So any social arrangements preventing people from achieving them are to be challenged. Indeed, one of the contributions claimed by Nussbaum (2000) for the capabilities approach is that it bypasses debates about whether human rights are a neocolonial global Northern imposition.

A further contribution to this way of thinking about the link between rights and needs is made by Asad (2000), who cautions that human rights can be a rather thin and sometimes brittle concept to use in the promotion of human well-being, because the claims of human rights rest on the logic of law and contract. Yet even in global Northern countries, access to law may be distributed unevenly, on the basis of gender, ethnicity, age, and so on. The interdependence of human relationships means values of 'compassion, patience, commitment, selflessness, and so on' are also necessary in everyday social practices if we are to overcome oppression (Asad, 2000, section 51).

When social work defences of culture and tradition are examined from the global South (e.g., see Mafile'o, 2006), these are often arguments against the inappropriate use of particular expressions of rights amounting to the imposition of global Northern culture. The important point is that the general idea of rights has to be separated from the specific forms they take within particular cultural contexts. It is significant, for example, that Nussbaum (2000), herself from the north-eastern USA, based some of her concrete examples on work undertaken with women's groups in India, where women sought to use culturally appropriate means to challenge ideas about disparities in gender relationships within families.

When approaches in social work combining or reconciling human rights and social justice are encountered, similar attention is found to the way in which people live their lives in context. For example, Lundy (2006), who, as noted above, writes of human rights and social justice as a single approach, wants social workers to consider that they must think in terms of rights when looking at how people will meet their basic human needs. A claim to needs, Lundy (2006) argues, can too easily be reduced to a matter of preference or can imply that these are questions for each person or family in isolation, which do not have implications for the wider society. Against this, Lundy (2006) reasserts a view that has been central to much social work theory, that social structures and social relationships are the primary cause of people not being able to meet their needs. Thus only the idea of rights can make this clear and give social work moral force. As noted above, the predominant focus in social work is on those people (individually or in groups) who suffer material or social disadvantage and, although social workers respond primarily to those who require assistance to deal with these circumstances (as compared to others who may face the same life challenges but can cope in responding to them), the basis of doing so is that all people are *entitled* by virtue of being human to having these basic needs met.

This view of basic needs (i.e., those common for all people to be able to live a decent human life) and their relationship to rights is extremely close to Nussbaum's (2000) notion of capabilities. This suggests that her approach could possibly open up a range of possibilities for thinking more deeply about the basis for integrating the principles of human rights and social justice in social work. But, given that her intention is to go round the idea of human rights as being too enculturated, it is still necessary to ask if a more robust reconciliation of the two principles might be possible.

In attempting to deal with this challenging question, Baldry (2010) has proposed that social workers should see human rights and social justice not as separate and absolute values, but as moderating each other in a more dynamic relationship. While she does not actually use the term, this is a more pluralist concept (compare with Hinman, 2008), since, where there are tensions between values, these can be employed creatively: it is not necessary, in fact it could be counterproductive, for one to 'trump' the other. The basis of Baldry's (2010) argument is:

1 human rights are concerned with access to those things necessary for a truly human life;
2 social justice is concerned with the way society distributes social and material resources to meet human needs in a finite world.

Seen in this way, human rights are effectively 'what' social justice seeks to have distributed fairly and equitably. That is, the basic question of social justice is why some people are denied human rights, which may take the form of access to material resources, and what can be done to redress this. In turn, social justice grounds human rights in the realities of a finite world. As has been emphasised throughout this chapter, finding the right balance between the liberties of some individuals and the needs of others for that which they cannot obtain unaided is what makes this a highly contested set of principles. It can, and often must, lead to giving primacy to the interests of those who are not as able to achieve what is necessary to live a truly human life (whether seen as human rights or capabilities) even if this were to run directly counter to the interests of those who do have sufficient access to these things. Of course, having this sort of emphasis as a defining characteristic of social work can lead to the profession being questioned from certain political perspectives (Hugman, 1998). Yet, this is a value position social workers should and often do share with colleagues in other professions, such as law, medicine, nursing, allied health, and education.

QUESTIONS FOR THEORY AND PRACTICE

The international definition of social work with which this discussion began (IFSW/IASSW, 2000/2001) was made broad deliberately as the profession is a (sometimes messy) combination of ideas and practices combining macro- and micro-perspectives. It involves analysis and intervention at both the structural and interpersonal levels of social life. That is, both human rights and social justice are central to thinking about micro- and macro-practices, about the structural *and* the interpersonal. An example can be seen in the ways in which social workers can respond to family and domestic violence. A solely interpersonal understanding leads to practice remaining confined in a focus on individual behaviours and ignores the importance of context, while concentrating exclusively on structural issues such as poverty misses the unique factors of a particular relationship (that such situations concern people). Effective intervention therefore needs to take all aspects into account, with appropriate and relevant attention to helping people to change behaviours in the context of also challenging poverty, poor housing, the tangible expression of patriarchy and racism, and so on. So social work must contribute to programmes assisting women and children in dealing with domestic violence, working with men to challenge and change oppressive behaviours, seeking changes in material circumstances (housing, employment, access to healthcare), and supporting communities to gain strength in dealing with all these issues. Even though not every individual social worker will be involved in all these forms of practice, this view points to a claim that all these practices are part of social work. So a concern with human rights and social justice is as much a part of counselling as it is of community development.

If Baldry (2010) is taken seriously, social workers must think about social work practice as multidimensional. Old debates between macro- and micro-perspectives can tend to suggest claims to the primacy of particular ways of seeing social work, as dealing with individual or collective needs, or as incorporating skills related to one or the other level. On the one side is the argument that working with individuals and families inherently locates the responsibility for need with those of people as individuals. On the opposite side collective approaches can be seen as failing to recognise and respond to the unique moral value of each person. Both these extreme positions fail to grasp the complexities of the needs with which social workers are concerned. Integration of human rights and social justice is a necessary goal, because social work must be concerned with actual human lives while at the same time recognising the structural roots of human need.

Social workers must also resist the temptation to try to make one or other of these principles paramount, over and above the other. Both Jordan (1991) and Solas (2008) have argued that social justice ought to be the defining value of social work. It is possible to understand their case as a challenge to social work not to lose sight of social justice, as in some respects this could be said to be a risk, particularly in global Northern countries: it is impossible to have human rights without social justice. But this cannot be at the expense of subordinating or ignoring human rights (with its underlying ethics of the equal moral worth and dignity of all people) in order to achieve a just society. What is needed is for social work theory and practice to engage with a more conscious consideration of both principles and the difficult task of holding them together in a creative tension.

CONCLUSION

Principles of human rights and social justice are claimed by the international professional organisations as foundational to social work. This chapter has identified the central arguments and examined the implications of the different bases for them. This has shown social work to be faced with the difficult task of making the two principles work together. However, it has also been shown this can be done, although it requires careful and explicit recognition that such a task has to be undertaken. What comes out of this inquiry is a strong sense that both principles are necessary for a conception of good social work. But social work cannot rest on them. Together these principles set up a dynamic tension it must address explicitly if social workers are to realise them in practice. Human rights and social justice do not connect automatically and unproblematically. From the nature of the profession, it is correct to identify these as foundational principles. Social work cannot give up on either. But nor can it avoid the responsibility to engage actively with them, to understand them in order that the profession can ensure they do indeed inform good practice.

ACKNOWLEDGEMENT

I am very grateful to Eileen Baldry for her inspiration in developing a core idea to make these principles work together.

REFERENCES

Adams, R. (2008) *Empowerment, participation and social work* (4th ed.). Basingstoke: Palgrave-Macmillan.

Addams, J. (2002 [1907]). *Democracy and social ethics*, edited by C.H. Siegfried. Chicago, IL: University of Illinois Press.

Asad, T. (2000). What do human rights do? An anthropological enquiry. *Theory and Event*, 4(4), electronic journal. Retrieved May 25, 2007 from http://muse.jhu.edu/journals/theory_and_event/v.0004/4.4asad.html

Baldry, E. (2010). Mental health disorders and cognitive disability in the criminal justice system. Keynote address to the *Community Legal Centres NSW Conference*, Sydney, 6 May.

Banks, S. (2006). *Ethics and values in social work* (3rd ed.), Basingstoke: Palgrave-Macmillan.

Bowles, W., Collingridge, M., Curry, S., & Valentine, B. (2006). *Ethical practice in social work: An applied approach*. St Leonards, New South Wales: Allen & Unwin.

Briskman, L., Latham, S., & Goddard, C. (2009). *Human rights overboard: Seeking asylum in Australia*. Melbourne: Scribe Publications.

Eilers, K. (2008). René Sand (Belgium) President 1946–1953. In F.W. Seibel (ed.), *Global leaders for social work education: The IASSW Presidents 1928–2008*. Ostrava: Verlag Albert, pp. 57–70.

England, H. (1986). *Social work as art: Making sense for good practice*. London: Allen & Unwin.

Fox Piven, F. & Cloward, R.A. (1971). *Regulating the poor: The functions of public welfare*. New York: Pantheon Books.

George, S. (1988) *A fate worse than debt: A radical analysis of the third world debt crisis*. Harmondsworth: Penguin Books.

Grace, D. (1994). Social justice: New route to Utopia? In M. Wearing & Berreen, R. (eds), *Welfare and social policy in Australia*. Sydney: Harcourt-Brace, pp. 81–95.

Hansen, C. (2004). The normative impact of comparative ethics: Human rights. In K.-L. Shun & Wong, D.B. (eds), *Confucian ethics*. Cambridge: Cambridge University Press, pp. 72–99.

Healy, L. (2008). *International social work: Professional action in an interdependent world* (2nd ed.). New York: Oxford University Press.

Hinman, L.M. (2008). *Ethics: A pluralistic approach* (3rd ed.). Belmont, CA: Thompson-Wadsworth.

Hugman, R. (1998). *Social welfare and social value*. Basingstoke: Macmillan.

Hugman, R. (2005). *New approaches in ethics for the caring professions*. Basingstoke: Palgrave-Macmillan.

Hugman, R. (2008). Ethics in a world of difference. *Ethics and Social Welfare*, 2(2), 118–132.

Ife, J. (2008). *Human rights and social work: Towards rights-based practice* (2nd ed.). Melbourne: Cambridge University Press.

International Federation of Social Workers (1994). *The ethics of social work: Principles and standards*. Electronic document. Retrieved August 3, 2010 from http://www.ifsw.org/f3000020.html

International Federation of Social Workers/International Association of Schools of Social Work (2000/2001). *The definition of social work*. Electronic document. Retrieved August 3, 2010 from: http://www.ifsw.org/f38000138.html

International Federation of Social Workers/International Association of Schools of Social Work (2004). *Ethics in social work: Statement of principles.* Electronic document. Retrieved August 3, 2010 from http://www.ifsw.org/f38000324.html

Jordan, B. (1991). *Social work in an unjust society.* Brighton: Harvester-Wheatsheaf.

Jones, C. (1983). *State social work and the working class.* London: Macmillan.

Kendall, K. (2008). Herbert D. Stein (Belgium) President 1968–1976. In F.W. Seibel (ed.), *Global leaders for social work education: The IASSW Presidents 1928–2008.* Ostrava: Verlag Albert, pp. 105–121.

Lundy, C. (2006). Social work's commitment to social and economic justice: A challenge to the profession. In N. Hall (ed.), *Social work: Making a difference. social work around the world IV.* Berne/Oslo: IFSW/FAFO, pp. 115–128.

MacIntyre, A. (1998). *A short history of ethics* (2nd ed.), London: Routledge.

Mafile'o, T. (2006). Matakainga (behaving like family): The social worker–client relationship in Pacifika social work. *Social Work Review/Tu Mau, 18*(1), 31–36.

Midgley, J. (2007). Development, social development, and human rights. In E. Reichert (ed.), *Challenges in human rights: A social work perspective.* New York: Columbia University Press, pp. 97–121.

Nussbaum, M. (2000). *Women and human development.* New York: Cambridge University Press.

Nussbaum, M. (2006). In defence of global political liberalism. *Development and Change, 37*(6), 1313–1328.

O'Neill, O. (2005). The dark side of human rights. *International Affairs, 81*(2), 427–439.

Payne, M. (2005). *The origins of social work.* Basingstoke: Palgrave-Macmillan.

Rawls, J. (1972). *A theory of justice.* Oxford: Clarendon Press.

Reichert, E. (2003). *Social work and human rights.* New York: Columbia University Press.

Reisch, M. (2002). Defining social justice in a socially unjust world. *Families in Society: The Journal of Contemporary Social Services, 83*(4), 343–354.

Singer, P. (2002). *One world: The ethics of globalisation.* Melbourne: Text Publishing.

Solas, J. (2008). Social work and social justice: What are we fighting for? *Australian Social Work, 61*(2), 124–136.

Staub-Bernasconi, S. (2007). Economic and social rights: The neglected human rights. In E. Reichert (ed.), *Challenges in human rights: a social work perspective.* New York: Columbia University Press, pp. 138–161.

United Nations (1948). *The universal declaration of human rights.* New York: UN.

Wronka, J. (1992) *Human rights and social policy in the twenty-first century.* Lanham, MA: University Press of America.

SECTION 5

Social Work Research

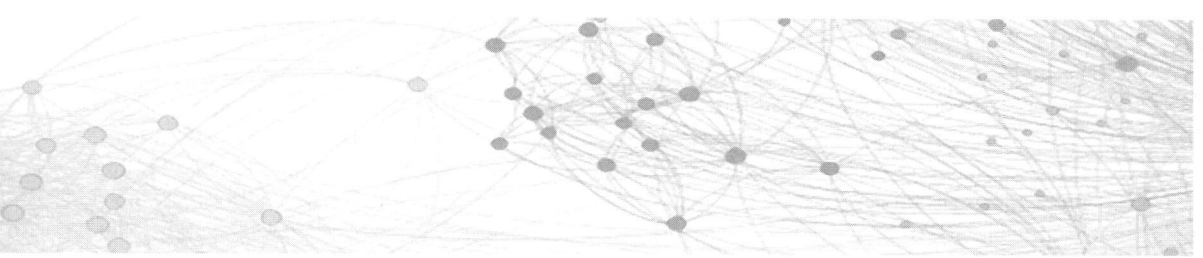

INTRODUCTION

Section 5 provides an extensive and contemporary coverage of social work research. It draws attention to innovative and cutting-edge material focusing on some of the most pressing issues in this rapidly expanding area. It is constantly claimed that insufficient effort is given to research in building the knowledge base for professional practice, particularly in the social work training curriculum. Indeed, the movement towards developing a profession more confidently grounded in research has been one of the most significant international trends in social work during the past decade. As Beddoe (2011) notes, social workers identify research-based activities as part of the professionalisation project of social work. Research activity is perceived as significant to the legitimacy of the profession in contestable spaces, evidence of the contribution of social work, and vital to the maintenance and development of excellent practice. 'Research mindedness' has long been an important concept in social work. This section demonstrates how, in an increasingly complex policy and practice world, social workers are required not only to provide high-quality services, but also to base them on prior evidence of effectiveness and value for money. This means that social workers must possess the ability and knowledge to appraise critically and make sound judgements about the relevance of research for practice. This requires that social workers should be able to view policy and practice issues in a particular way – they need to be 'research minded'. The section presents a range of research-for-practice approaches, from quantitative to qualitative research, and assesses their relevance and effectiveness in informing social work interventions. In bringing together contemporary material from key writers in the field, it examines some of the controversies, debates, and dilemmas surrounding social work research. It asks what is distinctive about social work research and what contribution does it make to both practice interventions with service users and society at large? It picks up the questions of what is knowledge, and how we know. It considers how the social work community has responded to questions of how we can know what we know and, in particular, asks if it makes helpful sense to think of social work knowledge and research as socially constructed. It also offers a reader-friendly overview of different perspectives in social work research.

In 'mapping the social work research agenda', Daniel Gredig, Ian Shaw, and Peter Sommerfeld, identify several 'cutting-edge issues' relating to social work research, including social work's relationship to science, the relationship of research to practice, the social work practitioner's underuse of research, methodological debates between qualitative and quantitative research approaches, research governance and research ethics, and building research capacity to establish research quality in social work. The authors address the thorny questions around whether tacitness is inherent in research for practice or whether it can be formalised into systematic frameworks. From here the question arises as to whether tacit, implicit understanding is in tension with more explicit, planned research-based practice.

In Chapter 26, Bruce Thyer examines the origins of evidence-based practice in medicine and its spread to social work, highlighting the philosophical assumptions and theory of evidence-based social work, and the processes it involves. He draws attention to approaches that do not constitute evidence-based practice, such as lists of empirically supported treatments, practice guidelines prepared by professional associations, best practices, and the empirical clinical practice model. He considers applications of evidence-based practice to social work practice, education, and research, and the role of the Cochrane and Campbell Collaborations in evidence-based practice, including how systematic reviews are undertaken through searching databases, appraising quality using the hierarchy of evidence, synthesising experimental studies through meta-analysis, and disseminating research to the appropriate practitioners through vehicles such as the Cochrane and Campbell Collaborations and their libraries of systematic reviews of effectiveness. Thyer provides current examples of systematic reviews relevant to social work and considers how social workers can get involved in the Campbell and Cochrane Collaborations. Finally, he outlines common myths and misconceptions, and several controversies about evidence-based practice.

In Chapter 27, Brian Taylor outlines and discusses the purpose, place, and challenges of research into the effectiveness of social work interventions. He discusses the hierarchy of evidence and the central place of randomised controlled intervention studies in determining the internal validity of intervention effectiveness and also considers other experimental and quasi-experimental research designs and their application in social work, such as longitudinal cohort studies where experiments with controls are not possible. Challenges in intervention research are debated, including the ethical, legal, and procedural issues in experimental designs, defining interventions, issues in masking (blinding) participants to interventions, the importance of external as well as internal validity, and measures of outcome or functioning by which to measure change. Examples are included of social work intervention studies to illustrate points made.

In Chapter 28, Donald Forrester examines evaluation research. In contemporary debates on evidence-based practice, it has been claimed that programme evaluation or evaluative research does not constitute research proper nor does it produce gold-standard evidence. The practice evaluation movement predates evidence-based practice and has concerned itself with effectiveness research. Forrester examines the enduring importance of practice evaluation in social work and proposes measures for sound, rigorous, and generalisable evaluative research. He also highlights the relationship between practice evaluation and service audits. In the UK, for example, the multiprofessional audit is distinguished from other forms of practice evaluation by an 'audit' having a standard against which a service is being measured, whereas in 'evaluation' a service is evaluated without clear measurement standards or criteria and generally involves the use of more diverse evaluation methods.

In Chapter 29, Deborah Padgett examines qualitative research methods in and outside of social work grounded in the epistemic self-consciousness of the late 20th century. She traces their US origins to Jane Addams and the Chicago pragmatists, and the influence of philosophy, linguistics, and the social sciences, such as anthropology and sociology. She considers various qualitative approaches, such as narrative, discourse, and conversation analyses; grounded theory (post-positivism and constructivism); ethnography (critical clinical and auto-ethnography); Heideggerian phenomenology; case study analysis; and evidence-based practice and meta-analytic reviews, including the Campbell Collaboration and the challenges of qualitative meta-syntheses. Padgett highlights several concerns for a practice-based 'qualitative' profession, including social work exceptionalism, community-based advocacy research, and the dangers of conflating social justice values (which can be associated with any methods but is foregrounded in qualitative research) with rejection of 'rigour' (i.e., favouring 'relevance'). She shows that, despite – or perhaps due to – the vast proliferation of epistemic stances and methodological approaches, there remain a number of commonalities in the practice of qualitative research. These include: a thorough review of the literature to establish the 'problem', the use of research questions rather than hypotheses, some type of purposive sampling, in-depth interviewing (often supplemented with observation and or the use of documents), coding and thematic development, and use of direct quotes to illustrate and ground the findings. Although not always evident in the report or described as such, most qualitative researchers attend to strategies for rigour or attempts to ensure trustworthiness. Padgett reviews the rise of mixed methods and their epistemological implications and examines social work research as a mixed-method approach. She concludes with envisioning the future of cross-national, cross-language, cross-disciplinary, and multimethod research, outlining the tensions between social work's predilections towards bridging divides while maintaining professional boundaries.

In Chapter 30, Mark Baldwin clearly articulates the purpose and underpinning values of participatory action research (PAR) as one of the few research methods embracing the principles of participation and reflection, and empowerment and emancipation of groups seeking to improve their social situation. He discusses the epistemological underpinnings of PAR as a collaborative approach between researchers and stakeholders and presents case examples demonstrating its purposes and similarities with social work helping processes, posing the question of whether social work practice is itself a form of PAR. The chapter offers guidelines for the assessment of the readiness of the service-user group and practice-based researcher to engage in participatory research, and for monitoring ongoing process.

In Chapter 31, Elaine Sharland discusses systematic reviews that bring with them the promise of connectedness between diverse and multidisciplinary elements of the research base, and between research and evidence-based policy and practice. Drawn originally from health, then education, and championed by the Cochrane and Campbell Collaborations, systematic reviews are now increasingly advocated in social work. They stand for rigour and transparency in identification, quality appraisal, and synthesis of research. Arguably they can render existing research more accessible, its findings collectively more robust and so, more useful. It is claimed that these approaches can tell us *what works* for social work. Enthusiasm for systematic review in social work, however, has been tempered with criticism. Its tenets are too positivist and its criteria for inclusion more often than not too restrictive to embrace social work research at all. Its capacity to capture social work complexity is too flimsy and its potential to diminish methodological diversity and strangle professional reflexivity too dangerous. This excellent chapter draws on her experience of conducting and directing systematic reviews in social work; Sharland's chapter explores not *'what can systematic review do with social work?'* but *'what does social work need from systematic review?'*. In light of recent developments in the field of meta-analysis, she examines how systematic review can best fit the characteristics and serves the purposes of social work research, policy, and practice.

REFERENCE

Beddoe, L. (2011). Investing in the future: Social workers talk about research. *British Journal of Social Work, 41*(3), 557–575.

25

Mapping the Social Work Research Agenda

Daniel Gredig, Ian Shaw, and Peter Sommerfeld

To this day, different understandings of the nature and purpose of social work research have evolved, reflecting diverse conceptions of the nature and purposes of social work itself (Parton & Kirk, 2010; Powell & Ramos, 2010). Given this situation of diverse understandings and the presence of divergent positions in the literature on social work reseach, this chapter attempts to offer readers an entry point into the discussion on social work research by providing a possible understanding of the nature and subject matter of social work research, the specificities of research on social work, the evolution of research in this field, and the purpose and utilisation of reseach findings, and to speculate on future prospects. The aim of mapping social work research and outlining its agenda is to set the ground for the discussion of the more specific issues, enlarged on in the following chapters in this section. Without being comprehensive, the chapter endeavours to be inclusive and approaches the subject from different perspectives, deliberately referring to discourses held in various parts of the world. In so doing, it does not zoom quickly into the centre of contemporary debates about research on and in social work, but rather steps back and turns first to some more general philosophical anthropological grounds underlying the understanding of science and research and then specifically research on social work.

APPROACHING SOCIAL WORK RESEARCH

Knowledge and science

The first question to examine is, what is knowledge, and how is it created? Philosophical anthropology (Plessner, 1975) describes the condition of human existence as a special class of living organisms, because human beings – owing to the special cognitive faculty of the human brain – are not simply in the world but rather must establish mediated relations with their environment via knowledge. The concept of *establishing* a relationship to the world through which knowledge about that world is created already lays bare the whole problematic nature of the human cognitive faculty. Knowledge is not simply there but is *created* through interaction with an already existing world, (see, for example, Piaget's 'genetic epistemology', Piaget, 1974). This interaction and experiencing is fundamentally shaped and moulded socially and culturally. The social process of establishing a relation with the world makes possible and channels individuals' cognitive development and knowledge horizons. Accordingly, Petzold (2008) describes the evolution of human cultures as driven by an interplay of curiosity and *poiesis* (from the ancient Greek verb for 'to make'), shaping, producing, creating, and forming life conduct and the world. Human knowing is therefore created via related observation and shaping of life conduct in circular processes of cognition and (social) action – social and individual processes described by Weizsäcker (1992) as a circular movement (*Kreisgang*).

Science is an attempt to extend the systematically constrained possibilities of human knowing. In awareness of the given constraints of the human faculty for understanding, science introduces rules, which seek to take these limitations into account and, at the same time, extend the possibilities of human understanding. These rules require:

- explication of position and perspective, and thus explicit reference to other perspectives;
- explication of the knowledge path and the results thereby gained; and
- logical consistency of argument and theory development.

These rules serve a central structural principle of the practices of 'science', namely, the introduction of the discourse as an arena where the claim of an assertion to be accurate is recognised or rejected by intersubjective exchange. The mode of this discourse is criticism, that is, close examination and, by consequence, confirmation or refutation of the assertions made. Over time, this leads to systematisation of the findings with reference to a certain part of reality. In the discursive *Kreisgänge,* there arises a body of solid knowledge or, at least, knowledge held to be solid, stored mainly in the theories of a field structuring new discovery processes inasmuch as questions and criticisms will be formulated with reference to it.

Scientific research

Among the different routes to knowledge open to human beings, scientific research is a mode of systematic inquiry aiming at overcoming the constraints inherent in (individual) human everyday ways of knowing. Hence, basically, scientific research can be understood as a process of knowledge production aiming at robust, sound, and trustworthy knowledge (Creswell, 1994; Richards, 2005) while meeting the above-mentioned criteria or rules of science.

The relationship between research and theory is neither simple nor uniform. A widely (albeit not universally) held position is taken in this chapter that accepts a revaluing of the role of observation as the final arbiter. This includes a rejection of the largely discredited assumption that observation can be theoretically neutral and an acceptance of all observation as 'theory-laden'. However, arguing for theory-laden observation does not necessarily entail relativism and the authors hold a cautious version of a correspondence view of truth, which holds research can represent – albeit imperfectly – social phenomena as an independent reality (Chapter 4 in Hammersley, 1995; Phillips, 1990b).

The relationship between theory and observation has been shown to be more complex than earlier thought. Theories are 'underdetermined' by nature, such that it is impossible to claim a particular theory is 'the *best* theory'. A variety of equally compatible theories can be constructed with given available evidence. This has led to the almost unanimous rejection of 'foundationalism' – the view that research findings of indisputable validity can be a foundation for policy. But this includes discarding any notion that theories are always fallible, whereas the empirical base for them is not. Lakatos

(1970) labelled this position 'dogmatic falsificationism'. He rightly rejected the caricature he expressed as 'science grows by repeated overthrow of theories with the help of hard facts' (Lakatos, 1970, p. 97). Observations are so in the light of a given theory and 'there are and can be no sensations unimpregnated by expectations' (Lakatos, 1970, p. 99). While one may be warranted in holding a particular view, one cannot assert that something is true, that their warrant is unchallengeable, or that it will for ever be warranted: '*nothing* can guarantee that we have reached the truth' (Phillips, 1990a, p. 43). But, although there are no *absolute* justifications, this does not mean there are *no* justifications. In light of the foregoing, the view there is a steady accumulation of findings and theories, and science grows thus, has been effectively challenged by Kuhn, Popper, Lakatos, and others.

Research processes and results are always significantly jeopardised by interests, the social location of the inquirer, powerful stakeholders, and, in Guba's (1990) surprisingly realist phrase, 'nature's propensity to confound' (p. 19). Yet some version of objectivity remains as a 'regulatory ideal' (Phillips, 1990a, p. 43) and research should be subject to methodological control, that is, applying accepted procedures of data generation, analyses, and interpretation. Which methods are accepted as sufficient is subject to ongoing critical discussion in the scientific community and thus also a matter of ongoing change and development (e.g., Diekmann, 1995; Friedrichs, 1990; Lüders & Rauschenbach, 2001). Researchers should proceed on a normative, 'as if' basis, seeking to justify through explicit and plausible rationales all the decisions taken and procedures applied in the process of knowledge production and, in so doing, aim to avoid internal inconsistencies and contradictions.

Theory development and scientific research (in the following simply referred to as 'research') are two sides of the same coin. Theory development, in brief, is descriptive or explanatory modelling of the world or, at least, small parts of the world, from a position of observation that is distant in the sense it is not immediately involved in 'quotidian life'. Stepping out offers another observation perspective (observation of second or third order), which is privileged in some respects, but limited in others. This stepping out of the 'natural' flow of the processes in the world, including human behaviour, offers not only another perspective but also time allowing more intensive and extensive study, stimulating the search for appropriate observation instruments and methodologies. Research is the *observational part of science* for establishing a sufficient basis of evidence through an instrumental methodology.

Research has two widely accepted functions, which represent two different modes of knowledge creation: to *discover* and to *test* or *examine* in the sense of finding out if our assumptions are correct. If it is possible for human beings to know the world only in mediated form, and in the form of a channelled perspective (Plessner), the classical question for the discoverer remains always potent: 'What lies beyond the horizon?' The *discovery* mode gives priority to curiosity. But discoveries are also the most effective critique of previous theories and give rise to a need for new models. The other mode is *examination*. In this form of knowledge creation, the emphasis is on testing and confirming (using research, or systematic and controlled observation) whether the statements, pictures, models, and theories that have been formed of the world are plausible or not. In philosophy of science, these modes of knowledge generation are associated with different positions (e.g., hermeneutics on the one hand and critical rationalism on the other).

Besides this, there are authors postulating a third modus, referring to the possibility of acquiring knowledge also and perhaps predominantly directly in action (in practice). The structure of the question: 'What should be done in order to solve practical problem X?' is a route to knowledge with its own special quality. For example, following Lewin and Dewey in a continuation of North

American pragmatism, Argyris et al. (1990) proposed that the knowledge mode *poiesis* produces different questions, methods, and findings if it is pursued in science, that is, pursued nevertheless 'freed from action', methodologically controlled, and systematically.

Research in and on social work

First, a very broad approach to research on social work might include all research activities relating to this domain and delivering insight into this vast, diverse, and confusing field. But more systematic and specific approaches to the structure of this field can be derived from different perspectives. One approach is to derive the object of social work research from the understanding of social work as discipline. Scholars who argue social work is a scientific discipline delineate the formal object of social work in different ways. Introduced here are different ways to create an inclusive description of the object of social work research, each of them being rather wide but still systematising, overlapping, and not mutually contradictory.

A first understanding states that the formal object of social work intertwines two dimensions: *social problems* to be treated, as much as *interventions and services* offered by social workers to users in order to prevent, relieve, or solve their problems and facilitate a self-determined life-conduct (Hornstein, 1998). While in such an understanding the investigation of social problems is an interdisciplinary endeavour, the investigation of services, service delivery, use of services, and outcomes of services delivered are specific for social work as a discipline. From this, categories can be drawn allowing for gathering the subject matters of social work research in a small number of categories. One suggestion is to offer four categories, each of them covering a quite large field of research investigating:

1. social problems – a societal or macro perspective;
2. the life-world and living conditions of (potential) service users – a more user-centred perspective;
3. professional action and social work professionals; and
4. social work organisations within social policies.

Some authors confound the investigation of social problems and living conditions of target persons and users to one category (e.g., Gredig & Marsh, 2010). Others add the investigation and reflection on the science of social work as a fifth category (e.g., Thiersch & Rauschenbach, 1984).

An alternative approach derives wide categories from a perspective putting theory of profession and professional action centre stage. This approach assumes professional social work action can be roughly summarised as:

1. assessment or co-construction of the problem to be treated in a cooperation of service user and professional;
2. building a working agreement or commitment;
3. defining goals;
4. decision on and implementation of courses of action; and
5. evaluation of the ongoing process.

Knowledge professionals rely on has to enable them to co-construct the problem in cooperation with the users (Schnurr, 2005) or, in other words, to interpret (Oevermann, 1996) and 'understand' the case, and lead through this process and perform courses of action in order to support problem solving and foster a self-determined life-conduct. So professionals need and use knowledge-for-understanding and knowledge-for-action (Gredig & Marsh, 2010). These bodies of knowledge are multifaceted and include knowledge stemming from different sources, one of them being scientific research. Scientific knowledge contributing to knowledge-for-understanding can be named 'explanatory knowledge', including findings on the nature, prevalence, and causes of social problems, as well as on the life-worlds of (potential) service users. Scientific knowledge contributing to knowledge-for-action can be named 'interventionist knowledge', including findings generated in research bearing on professional action. In this view, social work research contributes with:

- explanatory knowledge on social problems;
- interventionist knowledge regarding social work action (including outcomes).

Aspects of this kind of approach have been elaborated in one of the very few empirically developed classifications of kinds of social work research, distinguishing two defining dimensions (Shaw & Norton, 2007):

- Dimension 1: On whom is the primary substantive focus of the research?
- Dimension 2: What is the primary problem focus of the research?

Examples of substantive fields include adult offenders and victims (within the larger grouping of service users and carers); people as members of communities or as citizens; and social work practitioners and managers, in their capacity as members of professional or policy communities. Examples of problem *foci* include:

- understand and explain issues related to equality, diversity, poverty, and social exclusion;
- understand, develop, assess, and evaluate social work practices, methods, or interventions;
- understand and promote learning and teaching about social work, or related professions.

A fourth approach can depart from a systematic view on the contexts of social work, visualised in a triangle. The first angle of the triangle is professional action and the professional knowledge bearing on action. This includes the professional procedures (methods and theories on the way things work, i.e., ends–means knowledge) and knowledge concerning the results achievable using those procedures (effectiveness). The conditions under which this action is realised represent the second angle of the triangle, and this is at the level of society (policy, legislation, and the public) and the organisation (workplace). The third angle is the co-producers, which means not only (although prominently) the users and their social problems but also other people involved in the problem-solving process, especially other professionals and voluntary workers (Sommerfeld, 1998). The research area defined in this way comprises the professional problem-solving process as found as an ideal type in Abbott (1988) but also as found in Sidler's (2004) systematic view. This process comprises *problem constitution*, or understanding the genesis of the problem (Hornstein, 1998), including the procedures of social work as they code and construct the problem, that is, *problem assessment* or diagnosis or understanding of the case, *problem treatment*, including the knowledge and procedures or methods actually applied, and *evaluation of the results* (with regard to their effectiveness and suitability). Sidler (2004) proposed a further important element, also highlighted by Maier (2009), as meriting special attention: the values and goals with which the professional problem-solving process is connected and which are negotiated between the society and the profession. These cannot be established scientifically, but science can participate in the necessary teleological (ultimately normative) discourses by describing, discussing, and possibly critiquing the objectives and reference values of practice in their societal contexualisation.

Distinctive features of social work research?

Placing social work research within wider notions of research and still wider understandings of human knowledge emphasises ways in which social work research is part of, and shares important characteristics with, a larger picture. Social work research does not differ in the least when it comes to these general epistemologies. Research on social work does not produce knowledge directly but rather empirical information on the state and composition of the world, using various methods of observation and analysis. Scientifically solid knowledge arises only in connection with: (i) theories – in diverse forms ranging on a continuum from a declared prior understanding to hypotheses – to which the research already refers in developing the research questions and design, and (ii) the scientific discourse. Social work research operates in the discovery and examination modes and – although further debate is probably needed – possibly also in the *poiesis* mode, that is, when the knowledge sought pertains to, for example, 'What is to be done in order to help a person released from prison to master the tasks for a successful conduct of life?' 'What type of probation service is needed, in relation to what legal and societal conditions, in order to achieve optimum results?' Seeking to answer questions deriving from these different modes of knowledge creation, social work research utilises available scientific research methods and may contribute towards further development of those methods. Suitable methods for particular research questions have to be selected, which means the methods have to produce knowledge relevant to the question. In this particular sense, the differences between quantitative and qualitative methodologies do not drive social work research, but reflect different modes of knowledge creation and thus serve different purposes (Shaw, 2010).

So is social work research much the same as other forms of social research? Are there specific research designs and methods for social work? Are debates about qualitative or quantitative research designs and methods of primary or secondary significance? These questions anticipate issues discussed in the chapters that follow.

Social work research is identifiable through a set of features, none of which exclusively or exhaustively defines it, but which typify its scope and character. These general features include a broad range of research methods, and recurring but diverse linkages between research methods and research questions. Social work research is underpinned by a quest for usefulness and theoretical contributions. Hence research should not be categorised as only 'pure' or 'applied'. It is also marked by a pervasive, if variously understood, concern with social inclusion, justice, and change.

Yet there are temptations and risks associated with strong claims to social work research's distinctive character – in much the same way as there are risks with corresponding claims for social work in general. Historically, the social work community has deliberated with some care as to whether and in what sense it is a profession. This has frequently included defences against critical accounts of how social work is seen or thought to be seen by others. For an incisive account of the historical context of such concerns, especially in the USA, Lubove (1965) remains unsurpassed, and Kirk and Reid (2002) helpfully revisit the debates of the early 20th century. Nokes' (1967) deliberation on the nature of the professional task in British welfare professions is also a much better starting point than some later analyses, as is Noel Timms' (1968) early tract on *The Language of Social Casework*. Paul Wilding (1982) provided a consummate, if uncomfortable, assessment of how social welfare professionals exercise power.

There has, until recently at least, been less interest in the academic analogue of whether social work is a *discipline*. But there is probably an unresolved question of whether social work is or wishes to be seen as a social science discipline in quite the same way as, for example, geography or sociology. (There is also a question whether social work is a discipline in a similar sense to other disciplines associated with a profession, such as medicine or clinical psychology.) There is no controversy – at least in countries where social work education and training programmes exist – as to whether social work is a discipline in the sense of 'a branch of instruction'. But in the sense of a 'department of knowledge' social work's disciplinary identity raises numerous awkward questions. Even those unequivocally committed to the scientific character of social work have sometimes regarded the social work research community as 'scattered across many academic hamlets' (Kirk & Reid, 2002, p. 218).

Furthermore, social science disciplines are not fixed and abiding realities. Whether social work becomes recognised as a distinct field in a given country is the result of dynamic, socially negotiated processes, shaped by the construction and ordering of knowledge claims within social work and social science communities, and reflecting power differentials mediated through structural mechanisms tending to exclude 'new kids on the block', such as social work (Shaw et al., 2006).

Yet the bottom line for such discussions is not so much what makes social work research distinctive but what makes social work research distinctively *good*. Social work research will be distinctively good when it:

- aims for methodological excellence in whatever it does;
- promotes social work inquiry marked by rigour, range, variety, depth, and progression;
- sustains an active conversation with the social science community;
- achieves a thoroughgoing consistency with broader social work purposes;
- gives serious attention to aspects of the research enterprise close to social work; and
- aims to unsettle its preconceptions by taking seriously aspects of the research enterprise seemingly far from social work (Shaw, 2007).

The account of the field of social work research outlined above poses several substantial and recurrent questions for debate. These are reviewed below and elaborated in subsequent chapters in this section of the Handbook.

SOCIAL WORK RESEARCH AS ADVOCACY

In the last twenty to thirty years, claims to interest and participation in the core acts of research and evaluation have extended to a wider constituency than academic and professional evaluators. The most potent challenge in this regard has come from the user-researcher movement. 'User' in this context refers not so much to the research user (a wider category including policy communities, practitioners, and elected members), but to service users. While there is much talk of empowerment evaluation in the USA – associated most noticeably with the work of David Fetterman – more radical forms of this development have been prevalent in the UK, Canada, and Australia and, to some degree, in networks such as the International Association of Schools of Social Work and the International Federation of Social Workers. In the UK, at least, there has been a gradual incorporation of user–researcher interests within mainstream organisations and networks. There is also a gradual recognition within the UK's Economic and Social Research Council that these issues cannot be ignored (e.g., Frankham, 2009).

Most user research is part of a wider family of critical research involving systematic inquiry into 'the contradictions ... of practice' (Popkewitz, 1990, p. 46). The critical researcher reconstructs the rules of inquiry to reflect understanding of language categories as historically related to larger social and moral issues of production and reproduction: 'Methodology is concerned with the moral order ... presupposed in the practice of science. It is the study of what is defined as legitimate knowledge' (Popkewitz, 1990, p. 51).

Within social work research there is a distinction – sometimes insufficiently emphasised – between participatory and advocacy forms of user research. Examples of the former are well captured in Reason and Bradbury's (2002) *Handbook of Action Research* and Reason's (1994) earlier strong collection. Perhaps the most sustained and powerful voice for advocacy forms of user research is the UK academic and user activist, Peter Beresford (e.g., Beresford, 2007, see Chapter 44). The field continues to develop, with recent work spreading in various directions. The terminology has diversified and includes 'user-led', 'user-controlled', 'survivor', and 'emancipatory' research, in addition to terms referring more generally to participatory or action research (see Chapter 30). Health, learning disability, older people, and young people are all areas where important work has been done, though mental health has been one of the more prolific fields for such research (e.g., Arthur, 2008; Mayes, 2010; Palmer, 2009). There is also a more recent tendency towards formalising user research, through textbooks (e.g., McLaughlin, 2006, 2009) and articles attempting to set out the research skills needed for user research. Parallel discussions aim to relate user research to mainstream research (e.g., Glasby & Beresford, 2007; McLaughlin, 2010; Miller, 2006). A continuing strand focuses on the general stance of user research (e.g., Beresford, 2007).

What conclusions can be drawn? First, empirical evidence available suggests there is a deeply held diversity among academic researchers regarding user involvement in research. Take the following quotations from academics speaking about users and research in a study of social work research in UK universities (Shaw & Norton, 2007).

> It was the methodology, because it wasn't just about writing, it was about actually involving people in what the writing was going to say.
>
> You want to involve service users but the way that you have set it up and the methodology you intend to use and the design isn't going to work so you have to be pragmatic.
>
> I think we're beginning to make user involvement a kind of, a test for quality and I think that is extremely poor methodology. I think what you have to do, just as with anything else, is justify user involvement as part of the methodology.

Here there are three quite different positions in relation to user involvement in research – the *sine qua non* position, in which good research must always involve service users in some substantial form; the pragmatic position; and the inner science criteria always come first position. There is no apparent way these can be collapsed into a unified position.

The authors retain a degree of caution about each of these positions as stand-alone benchmarks of good social work research. Systems researcher, Norma Romm (1995) holds a basic premise that 'the process of attempting to "know" about the social world already is an intervention in that world which may come to shape its constitution' (p. 137). She says 'The view that theory is applied in practice and may be tested in that practice, can amount to an unreflected/unreflexive endorsement of a theoretical position' (Romm, 1996, p. 25). 'One is not just applying "findings", but intervening in the social discussion in a specific way, that is, in a way which authorises particular conceptions' (Romm, 1995, p. 145). She is not only doubtful on these grounds about the wisdom of traditional research application perspectives, but also raises questions about positions taken on participatory and advocacy research. For example, most but not all participatory approaches advocate reflective deliberation as a means of reaching agreement. Romm (1995) chides by saying such approaches 'fail to consider that their "understanding" already gears practical activity in a certain direction, and excludes other options for action' (pp. 151–152). What she means is participatory models direct research processes towards dialogue, debate, and accommodation of interests and do not press researchers to consider the fairness of the accommodation reached, and whether contention or confrontation are ever appropriate. Approaches that fall within advocacy research positions recognise this problem, and are cautious about pseudo-compromises. Yet even here there is a risk that 'knowing' predisposes certain action: 'By "knowing" that there "is" an inevitable and unnegotiable conflict of interests, one may contribute to rendering this so – through the political action that one adopts' (Romm, 1995, p. 163).

SOCIAL WORK RESEARCH OVER TIME

How should the relationship between the historical development of social work research and its relation to social work be understood? Social work research adjoins – and is challenged by – other contemporary fields and disciplines. It also has a history – indeed, histories – suggesting the nature of social work research is not always similar from time to time or from place to place. Feminist histories of social work research go to figures such as Jane Addams, when the politics of gender were brought to the fore especially through 'settlement sociology' (Lengermann & Niebrugge, 2007). Mainstream academic histories may cite Charles Loch in the UK or Edith Abbott in the USA. Histories of social work research also vary by country. Nordic histories trace the origins of later distinctions in earlier moments and people. The recent development of social work in countries of the Asia Pacific Rim will produce its own research narratives. One stream within the UK has been the policy research tradition going back to the Fabian impact on policy from the late years of the 19th century, with Beatrice and Sydney Webb, and the relationship of social work to the emerging discipline of social policy. Other histories set social work in a related or more widely encompassing social category – human services in the USA, social care in the UK, and social pedagogy in Germany, the Baltic States, and elsewhere in Europe.

But despite this multiplicity of histories, it is possible to argue for a common approach to 'doing history' in social work research. To insist on the importance of history is not simply a point about methodology, but has regard to a way of thinking – of 'focusing "upstream" on the historical roots of contemporary relationships' (Mallinson et al., 2003, p. 773). Walter Lorenz (2007) and, to some extent, Abbott (1995) have pressed this point effectively. Lorenz (2007) complains it is as if social workers were too embarrassed to examine their history seriously, afraid of the disorder they might find, too eager to distance themselves from their pre-professional beginnings and, as a consequence, they remain homeless and 'disembedded' (p. 598). He concludes, 'All social work practices are deeply embedded in historical and cultural habits from which ... [social workers] cannot detach ... [them]selves at will' (Lorenz, 2007, p. 601). He aptly infers social workers should be practising history 'in the dual sense of positioning ... [them]selves in a historical context and of giving [their] ... interventions a historical dimension' (Lorenz, 2007, p. 601).

Standard accounts of the history of social work research lack depth. Some of the central questions are scarcely asked: 'What role does research play in the collective memories of social work?' 'How does social work research relate historically to the emergence of research in other social science disciplines?' 'What are the main themes in a critical narrative of social work research's past and its relation to other disciplines?' 'Were certain knowledge conditions necessary for the emergence and development of social work research?' 'What roles have university departments played in this narrative?' (see Chapters 6 and 7 in Platt, 1996).

RESEARCH UTILISATION

However, scarce as history on social work research may be, an identifiable claim has accompanied research in the field of social work since its origins. From well over one hundred years ago, researchers on social problems, living conditions of service users, social reform, and interventions of social workers were challenged to support social workers' action and make a difference to the lives and welfare of service users. From the outset, social work research has deliberately chosen to sit 'uncomfortably between the social sciences and the world of practice and policy' (Shaw et al., 2010, p. 7) and committed itself to be 'useful' for social work. In fact, conceptualisations of the inter-relation between scientific knowledge and professional action, especially how research findings 'translate into day-to-day practice' (Boaz & Blewett, 2010, p. 39), are still evolving. Pursuing a thought expressed by Bill Reid, a broad distinction can be made between concepts viewing research as a 'model' for practice' and concepts viewing 'research as a knowledge base' for practice (Parton &

Kirk, 2010, p. 28). Most approaches to using research as a *model for practice* basically involve transferring scientific methods and techniques to social work practice. This view can be traced back to the first attempts to rationalise charity and to Mary Richmond's (1917) suggestion to make each case an object of systematic social investigation. Good direct practice, so the argument goes, integrates various procedures from scientific inquiry, including careful observation, gathering data about the case from different sources, forming hypotheses on the causes of the client's problems based on these data, deriving interventions from the interpretation of the case, undertaking systematic intervention, and evaluating outcomes (Parton & Kirk, 2010).

Similarly, from the late 20th century in the German-speaking context, *Rekonstruktive Sozialpädagogik* (reconstructive social pedagogy; Jakob & Von Wensierski, 1997) gathered concepts focusing on the use of qualitative research methods in direct practice. This approach emphasises that adopting methods from qualitative social research facilitates processes of understanding and reflection in direct practice (e.g., Schweppe & Graßhoff, 2006), since both qualitative research methods and social work direct practice methods are geared toward understanding (e.g., Miethe, 2007; similarly for the Anglo-Saxon context, e.g., Reissman & Quinney, 2005). Shaw (2011) criticises this unmediated 'transfer' approach and attempts an extensive 'translation', 'interruption', and 're-inhabiting' of qualitative methods for social work practice. Some features of utilising scientific techniques as a 'model of practice' were also part of the assumptions of the empirical practice movement originating in the USA in the 1960s, which foregrounded the use of research methods in order to enhance assessment, guide intervention planning, and evaluate progress (Reid, 1994; Reid & Zettergren, 1999).

Within the strand of 'utilisation of research findings', a range of concepts has been formulated to conceptualise how the outcomes of scientific research can be integrated into the knowledge base of professional social workers and thus guide professional practice. These approaches differ regarding the sequence of research and utilisation and task sharing between researcher and practitioner. Also, they highlight different kinds of knowledge. Relating to the latter, and for the purposes of this contribution, one can distinguish between concepts concentrating on the utilisation of explanatory knowledge and those focusing on the use of interventionist knowledge. One example of conceptualisations starting from a consecutive process and strict task sharing between researcher and practitioner is the model of Knowledge-Transfer. This model centres on explanatory knowledge and assumes scientific knowledge, once produced, is simply to be applied by practitioners. This conceptualisation posits a linear, unidirectional relationship between research and practice, wherein researchers are senders and practitioners receivers of knowledge (Dewe et al., 1993; Otto, 1971). However, developments in the analogous field of 'policy transfer' push the model towards a more nuanced argument. So also do arguments for methods of generalisation appropriate to qualitative methods. Eisner (1991), for example, concludes: 'Since no generalization can fit an individual context perfectly, modification is always necessary. This modification requires judgement on the part of intelligent practitioners' (p. 212). The expression 'transfer of learning' captures exactly this implicit distinction.

An example of a similar conceptualisation, also starting from a consecutive process and (more or less) strict task sharing between researcher and practitioner, while concentrating on interventionist knowledge, is the model of evidence-based practice (see Chapter 26). Although exhibiting varying forms, evidence-based practice foregrounds the utilisation of the best available evidence on the efficacy of interventions. It rests on the core assumption that professional decision making takes into account expectations and values of service users, draws on practitioner knowledge, judgement, and expertise, and also relies on interventionist knowledge (e.g., Gambrill, 1999; Mullen et al., 2007). Some advocates of evidence-based practice claim explicitly this mode of practice will fulfil social work's 'long-professed but too-little-acted-upon mandate to be a science-based discipline' (Thyer, 2008, p. 342).

Other conceptualisations distance themselves from a consecutive arrangement of research and utilisation, and instead plead for a research process blending research procedures with change processes in practice. The best-known example is action research. While covering far-reaching ground (Palshaugen, 2007), the varying notions of action research hold a shared position that research should not only investigate social realities and practices but should also change these directly, that is, by means of the same process (Dick, 2007) blending research and change in practice.

Various concepts attempt to reconcile research and practice and provide a smooth transition for scientific knowledge into practice while assuring the participation of practitioners (and service users) in the research process (see Chapter 30). One example is the rich but diversely employed concept of practice research (Pain, 2012; Saurama & Tukiala, 2009; The Salisbury Statement, 2009; Thyer, 1989). Some concepts of practice research aspire to a seamless combination of research activities, counselling of practitioners, and change management in practice in one single, comprehensive process.

Finally, there are conceptualisations highlighting the importance of development as the core element in the process leading from research to practice. In these, intervention design or intervention development is the element bridging scientific knowledge production and professional practice (Rothman & Thomas, 1994). This is implicit in the concept of intervention research seen as closely aligned to evidence-based practice (e.g., Fraser et al., 2009) and explicit in research-based intervention development (Gredig, 2011; Gredig & Sommerfeld, 2008; Hüttemann & Sommerfeld, 2007) (see Chapters 26–31, all of which bear on the issue of utilising research findings in some of its current manifestations).

SOCIAL WORK RESEARCH FUTURES

Drawing these reflections together, the key trends in the issues reviewed in this chapter are captured so as to say something about the value, limits, and limitations of social work research. 'Limits' and 'limitations' are, of course, two very different questions – the first has regard to the implications of the nature of social work research, while the latter is more a matter of empirical judgement. The chapter ends with some (risky) attempts to anticipate future movements and trends. Identifying these is not easy, because there are few cross-national trends and considerable diversity between, for example, Nordic countries, southern Europe, the Asia Pacific region, the USA, the Francophone world, the UK, and so on. The present authors have also tried to stay clear of aspirational statements or normative wish-lists but venture four possible trends within recent social work research and evaluation:

1. the purpose of research and especially evaluative research has come to be seen as encompassing wider purposes than accountability models;
2. research is increasingly viewed as entailing more than the core act of inquiry, and including more diverse stakeholders and a life history extending beyond the core research act;
3. in some but by no means all parts of international social work, community research has also come to be regarded as entailing theoretical reflection;
4. claims to interest and participation in the core act of evaluation have come to be seen as extending to a wider constituency than academic researchers.

Looking forward is much more hazardous. Danish physicist Niels Bohr remarked 'Prediction is very difficult, especially about the future'. Bearing in mind his caution, the relative emphases placed on different issues in this chapter are the best indicators of the questions likely to remain in the foreground for the foreseeable future.

First, a differentiation and expansion of existing strands and issues in social work research is anticipated. There will continue to be more detailed and hopefully solid research on social problems and the living conditions of (potential) service users. It would be a success story if findings were to provide more in-depth insights into professional action, outcomes of courses of action, and the efficacy and effectiveness of interventions. Social work research will continue to investigate the changes and impacts of social policies on social work organisations, professional practice, and service users. It does not need special vision to realise that research on the role of technology, the social media, and the Internet will continue to grow, with the focus extending to the impact of virtual communities on everyday life – not least for practitioners and service users – and their potential for service delivery (Hill & Shaw, 2011). These trends will, in turn, have growing influence on how research is published. Furthermore, the discussion doubtless will continue on the issues sketched above – quality standards for social work research, the participation of diverse stakeholders in research, and the utilisation of findings. Further, more comparative and cross-border research activities – conducted partly as a consequence of globalising trends and partly in the hope they will offer mutual lessons and learning between countries and even continents – are expected. However, a range of new challenges are anticipated. These newer issues can be provisionally identified as follows.

Research on large-scale social problems

For the short- and medium-term future, social work research will be called to focus on social problems deriving from larger global developments already in evolution and finding expression in new or additional forms and patterns of inequality and social strain. For example, on the global–local dynamic, shifts of economic power and political influence and leadership on a global scale; new forms of power relations and conflicts arising in the context of global warming, water shortages, and the quest for (alternative) sources of energy; demographic changes in high-income countries; changing patterns of migration; local responses to social change relating to xenophobia or racism; and faith issues – all resulting in new social questions and challenges.

Research on changes in the life-world and the conditions of life of citizens and service users

Major social trends will impact on the conditions of life for today's disadvantaged groups but, in addition, the effects of newly arising or accentuated social problems will need to be understood if they are to be targeted by social work. In the near future, for example, researchers will have to observe the social consequences of the global financial and economic crisis from 2007 onwards, governments' crisis management and state indebtedness, substantial changes to the funding of higher education in the West, as well as ensuing discrepancies between rich and (newly) poor or working poor. Highly likely is research on changes in the everyday life of large sectors of national populations creating new challenges for the self-determined conduct of individual lives. Perhaps social work research will need to draw attention to and find evidence of new life struggles, forms of solidarity, and battlefronts.

Research on professional action and social work professionals

The profession will not only be faced with new problems but also pressure from national governments to develop innovative interventions with demonstrable effectiveness.

In some national contexts, social work researchers will have to foster knowledge on and effective courses of action in social service delivery despite scarce resources. Several chapters reflect on the possible directions research may take for advocacy (see Chapter 17) and rights-based approaches (see Chapter 24), and whether social work researcher will and should adopt clear political positions (see Chapter 47). Social work researchers may be urged to investigate new configurations where professionals work with volunteer and user movements, to respond to new challenges. Further, the present predominance of social work research and evaluation as a Western phenomenon may alter following the economic recession of the early years of the century and its worldwide repercussions. This may well see countries such as China, India, Brazil, and Russia emerging as leading economic powers with significance for how the state–citizen relationship plays out in social work research.

Research on social work organisations within social policy

Also envisaged is the unfolding of broad-ranging research on impacts of current developments in welfare regimes on frontline social workers involved in welfare provision (see Chapters 2, 3, and 4), changes in organisational culture, and the role of service users (see Chapter 44). As the full force of these impacts becomes evident, social work will need to consider where it is likely to find its 'best' – and 'worst' – allies. While this chapter – and the *Handbook* as a whole – have been written largely in the familiar scientific voice, this may not be true of future professional discourse following the emergent interest in issues of 'voice' in professional writing. Some claim social work can lead the way in writing in a more accessible linguistic style (e.g., Witkin, 2000, 2001; and *Qualitative Social Work* – special issue, December, 2007). Whether social work research will stand the test of scientific respectability in the face of these postmodern developments concerns the wider question of the future identity of social work as an occupation and profession. It will also be difficult to weigh the balance of consequences arising from changes within social work, such as evidence-based practice, or more generally, such as globalisation, climate change, the 'technological revolution', and the rise of militant Islam, against national trends resulting from changes of governments, political conflict, and unforeseen crises.

In closing, four cautions are offered to the social work research community: First, *be mindful of diverse perspectives*. Pursued within this chapter is a perspective on social work research informed by thinking in the UK, Germany and Switzerland. How will perspectives owing an intellectual, political, and social debt to Eastern Europe or southern Europe, or Spanish-speaking communities in the USA differ from present – Western, mainly US and UK – ways of thinking dominant in social work?

Second, *resist pressures towards homogeneity*, for example, in the development of international quality frameworks for social work research. An unintentional outcome of yielding to such pressures might be limiting rather than strengthening nationally and regionally diverse modes of social work research (Stern, 2006), notwithstanding the worthwhile cultivation of international networks, doctoral research, and academic mentoring programmes.

Third, *maintain a healthy mistrust of government*. In offering her 'final thought' on the political climate in western democracies, Chelimsky (2006) noted:

> Evaluation is a fragile reed to send up against all those giant oaks … and evaluators need to be ingenious, lucky and much better protected than they currently are if they are to survive in any government. Alas, we make a lot of enemies, although we try hard not to … (p. 53).

Public mistrust of government is not new. It precipitated the Magna Carta and Bills of Rights in England, France, and the USA. 'Public distrust is … a positive not a negative element in a democratic society. In that larger sense, the search for political balance and open government makes evaluators of us all' (Chelimsky, 2006, p. 4).

Finally, as hinted earlier in relation to the problematic nature of the human cognitive faculty and the understanding of science as an attempt to extend the systematically limited possibilities of human knowing, any research has limits. There are other grounds for bearing the limits of science in mind. There will always be an element of uncertainty in scientific knowledge. *Understanding uncertainty* is, needless to say, a major achievement of science, but *living with* uncertainty (e.g., from probabilistic or contextually contingent explanations) will always call for negotiation, judgement, and deliberation. The limits of research also stem from its time-consuming nature in comparison with the speed of shifting political priorities. Even in times of political stability, recognition of the value of research derives as much from extrinsic as intrinsic criteria (Shaw & Norton, 2007).

In conclusion, in the words of novelist Hilary Mantel, from a lecture given at the University of York on November 19, 2008, who described herself as 'a long thinker and a quick writer', social workers would do well to see themselves as 'long thinkers' and players in a long-term game. To conclude on a cautiously upbeat note:

> Science can be socially framed, possess political meaning, and also occasionally be sufficiently true or less false, in such a way that we cherish its findings. The challenge comes in trying to understand how knowledge worth preserving occurs in time, possesses deep social relations, and can also be progressive ... and seen to be worthy of preservation (Jacob, 1992, p. 501).

REFERENCES

Abbott, A. (1988). *The system of professions: An essay on the division of expert labor*. Chicago, IL: The University of Chicago Press.

Abbott, A. (1995). Boundaries of social work, or social work of boundaries? *Social Service Review, 69*(4), 545–562.

Argyris, C., Putnam, R., & McLain Smith, D. (1990). *Action science*. San Francisco: Jossey-Bass.

Arthur, B. (2008). Cutting the dash: Experiences of mental health and employment. *Journal of Public Mental Health, 7*(4), 51–59.

Beresford, P. (2007). The role of service user research in generating knowledge-based health and social care: From conflict to contribution. *Evidence and Policy, 3*(3), 329–341.

Boaz, A., & Blewett, J. (2010). Providing objective, impartial evidence for decision making and public accountability. In I. Shaw, Briar-Lawson, K., Orme, J., & Ruckdeschel, R. (eds), *Sage Handbook of Social Work Research*. London: Sage, pp. 37–48.

Chelimsky, E. (2006). The purposes of evaluation in a democratic society. In I. Shaw, Greene, J.C., & Mark, M.M. (eds), *Sage Handbook of Evaluation*. London: Sage, pp. 33–55.

Creswell, J.W. (1994). *Reseach design: Qualitative and quantitative approaches*. London: Sage.

Dewe, B., Ferchhoff, W., Scherr, A., & Stüwe, G. (1993). *Professionelles soziales Handeln: Soziale Arbeit im Spannungsfeld zwischen Theorie und Praxis*. Weinheim, München: Juventa.

Dick, B. (2007). Action research as an enhancement of natural problem solving. *International Journal of Action Research, 3*(1&2), 149–167.

Diekmann, A. (1995). *Empirische Sozialforschung: Grundlagen, Methoden, Anwendungen*. Reinbek b. Hamburg: Rowohlt.

Eisner, E. (1991). *The enlightened eye: Qualitative inquiry and the enhancement of educational practice*. New York: Macmillan.

Frankham, J. (2009). Partnership research: A review of approaches and challenges in conducting research in partnership with service users. In N.C.F.R. *Methods* (eds), Retrieved January 10, 2010 from http://eprints.ncrm.ac.uk/778/1/Frankham_May_09.pdf

Fraser, M.W., Richman, J.M., Galinski, M.J., & Day, S.H. (2009). *Intervention research: Developing social programs*. New York: Oxford University Press.

Friedrichs, J. (1990). *Methoden empirischer Sozialforschung*. Opladen: Westdeutscher Verlag.

Gambrill, E. (1999). Evidence-based practice: An alternative to authority-based practice. *Families in Society: The Journal of Contemporary Social Services, 80*(4), 341–350.

Glasby, J., & Beresford, P. (2007). In whose interests? Local research ethics committees and service user research. *Ethics and Social Welfare, 2*(3), 282–292.

Gredig, D. (2011). From research to practice: Research-based intervention development in social work. Developing practice through cooperative knowledge production. *European Journal of Social Work, 14*(1), 53–70.

Gredig, D., & Marsh, J.C. (2010). Improving intervention and practice. In I. Shaw, Briar-Lawson, K., Orme, J., & Ruckdeschel, R. (eds), *Sage handbook of social work research*. London: Sage, pp. 64–82.

Gredig, D., & Sommerfeld, P. (2008). New proposals for generating and exploiting solution-oriented knowledge. *Journal Research on Social Work Practice, 18*(4), 292–300.

Guba, E.G. (1990). The alternative paradigm dialog. In E.G. Guba (ed.), *The paradigm dialog*. Newbury Park: Sage, pp. 17–30.

Hammersley, M. (1995). *The politics of social research*. London: Sage.

Hill, A., & Shaw, I. (2011). *Social work and ICT*. London: Sage.

Hornstein, W. (1998). Erziehungswissenschaftliche Forschung und Sozialpädagogik. In T. Rauschenbach & Thole, W. (eds), *Sozialpädagogische Forschung: Gegenstand und Funktionen, Bereiche und Methoden*. Weinheim, München: Juventa, pp. 47–80.

Hüttemann, M., & Sommerfeld, P. (2007). Forschungsbasierte Praxis: Professionalisierung durch kooperative Wissensbildung. In P. Sommerfeld & Hüttemann, M. (eds), *Evidenzbasierte Soziale Arbeit. Nutzung von Forschung in der Praxis*. Baltmannsweiler: Schneider Verlag Hohengehren, pp. 40–57.

Jacob, M.C. (1992). Science and politics in the late twentieth century. *Social Research, 59*(3), 487–503.

Jakob, G., & Von Wensierski, H.-J. (eds), (1997). *Rekonstruktive Sozialpädagogik*. Weinheim, München: Juventa.

Kirk, S., & Reid, W. (2002). *Science and social work*. New York: Columbia University Press.

Lakatos, I. (1970). Falsification and the methodology of scientific research programmes. In I. Lakatos & Musgrave, A. (eds), *Criticism and the growth of knowledge*. Cambridge: Cambridge University Press.

Lengermann, P., & Niebrugge, G. (2007). Thrice told: Narratives of sociology's relation to social work. In C. Calhoun (ed.), *Sociology in America: A history*. Chicago, IL: University of Chicago Press, pp. 63–114.

Lorenz, W. (2007). Practising history: Memory and contemporary professional practice. *International Social Work, 50*(5), 597–612.

Lubove, R. (1965). *The professional altruist*. Cambridge: Harvard University Press.

Lüders, C., & Rauschenbach, T. (2001). Sozialpädagogische Forschung. In H.-U. Otto & Thiersch, H. (eds), *Handbuch der Sozialarbeit/Sozialpädagogik* (2nd ed.). Neuwied, Kriftel: Luchterhand, pp. 562–575.

Maier, K. (2009). Für eine integrative praktische Wissenschaft Soziale Arbeit. In E. Mührel & Birgmeier, B. (eds), *Die Sozialarbeitswissenschaft und ihre Theorie(n)*, Wiesbaden: VS Verlag für Sozialwissenschaften, pp. 41–52.

Mallinson, S., Popay, J., Elliott, E., Bennett, S., Bostock, L., Gatrell, A., et al. (2003). Historical data for health inequalities research. *Sociology 37*(4), 771–780.

Mayes, D. (2010). When it pays to be bi-polar. *Mental Health and Social Inclusion, 14*(1), 20–23.

McLaughlin, H. (2006). *Understanding social work research*. London: Sage.

McLaughlin, H. (2009). *Service user research in health and social care*. London: Sage.

McLaughlin, H. (2010). Keeping service user involvement in research honest. *British Journal of Social Work, 40*(5), 1591–1608.

Miethe, I. (2007). Rekonstruktion und Intervention: Zur Geschichte und Funktion eines schwierigen und innovativen Verhältnisses. In I. Miehte, Fischer, W., Giebeler, C., Goblirsch, M., & Riemann, G. (eds), *Rekonstruktion und Intervention. Interdisziplinäre Beiträge zur rekonstruktiven Sozialarbeitsforschung*. Opladen: Barbara Budrich, pp. 9–33.

Miller, E. (2006). Challenges and strategies in collaborative working with service user researchers: reflections from the academic researcher. *Research Policy and Planning, 24*(3), 197–208.

Mullen, E.J., Bellamy, J.L., & Bledsoe, S.E. (2007). Evidenzbasierte Praxis in der Sozialen Arbeit. In P. Sommerfeld & Hüttemann, M. (eds), *Evidenzbasierte Soziale Arbeit. Nutzung von Forschung in der Praxis*. Baltmannsweiler: Schneider Verlag Hohengehren, pp. 10–25.

Nokes, P. (1967). *The professional task in welfare practice*. London: Routledge and Kegan Paul.

Oevermann, U. (1996). Theoretische Skizze einer revidierten Theorie professionalisierten Handelns. In A. Combe & Helsper, W. (eds), *Pädagogische Professionalität*. Frankfurt a.M.: Suhrkamp, pp. 70–182.

Otto, H.-U. (1971). Zum Verhältnis von systematisiertem Wissen und praktischem Handeln in der Sozialarbeit. In H.-U. Otto & Utermann, K. (eds), *Sozialarbeit als Beruf: Auf dem Weg zur Professionalisierung?* München: Juventa.

Pain, H. (2011). Practice research: what it is and its place in the social work profession. *European Journal of Social Work*, 14(4), 545–562.

Palmer, D. (2009). 'No one knows like we do': The narratives of mental health service users trained as researchers. *Journal of Public Mental Health, 8*(4), 18–28.

Palshaugen, O. (2007). On the diversity of action research. *International Journal of Action Research, 3*(1&2), 9–14.

Parton, N., & Kirk, S. (2010). The nature and purposes of social work. In I. Shaw, Briar-Lawson, K., Orme, J., & Ruckdeschel, R. (eds), *Sage handbook of social work research*. London: Sage, pp. 23–36.

Petzold, H.G. (2008). Evolutionäres Denken und Entwicklungsdynamiken im Feld der Psychotherapie. *Integrative Therapie, 4*, 353–396.

Phillips, D.C. (1990a). Postpositivistic science: myths and realities. In E.G. Guba (ed.), *The paradigm dialog*. Newbury Park: Sage, pp. 31–45.

Phillips, D.C. (1990b). Subjectivity and objectivity: An objective inquiry. In E. Eisner & Peshkin, A. (eds), *Qualitative inquiry in education*. New York: Teachers College, Columbia University, pp. 19–37.

Piaget, J. (1974). *Abriss der genetischen Epistemologie* (Org.: 1970, Paris ed.). Olten: Walter Verlag.

Platt, J. (1996). *A history of sociological research methods in America, 1920–1960*. Cambridge: Cambridge University Press.

Plessner, H. (1975). *Die Stufen des Organischen und der Mensch: Einleitung in die philosophische Anthropologie*. Berlin: W. De Gruyter.

Popkewitz, T.S. (1990). Whose future? Whose past? In E.G. Guba (ed.), *The paradigm dialog*. Newbury Park: Sage, pp. 46–66.

Powell, J., & Ramos, B. (2010). The practice of social work research. In I. Shaw, Briar-Lawson, K., Orme, J. & Ruckdeschel, R. (eds), *Sage handbook of social work research*. London: Sage. 231–245.

Reason, P. (1994). (ed.), *Participation in human inquiry*. London: Sage.

Reason, P., & Bradbury, H. (2002). *Sage handbook of action research*. London: Sage.

Reid, W., & Zettergren, P. (1999). A perspective on empirical practice. In I. Shaw & Lishman, J. (eds), *Evaluation and social work practice*. London: Sage, pp. 41–62.

Reid, W.J. (1994). The empirical practice movement. *Social Service Review, 68*(2), 165–184.

Reissman, C., & Quinney, L. (2005). Narrative in social work: A critical review. *Qualitative Social Work, 4*(3), 391–412.

Richards, L. (2005). *Handling qualitative data: A practical guide*. London: Sage.

Richmond, M. (1917). *Social diagnosis*. New York: Russell Sage Foundation.

Romm, N. (1995). Knowing as an intervention. *Systems Practice, 8*(2), 137–167.

Romm, N. (1996). Inquiry-and-Intervention in systems planning: Probing methodological rationalities. *World Futures, 47*, 25–36.

Rothman, J., & Thomas, E. (1994). *Intervention research*. New York: The Haworth Press.

Saurama, E., & Tukiala, A.-K. (2009). The alternative story: The quest for practice research. Paper presented at the conference *Research and Social Work in Urban Areas* held at Antwerp, Belgium, September 24–26.

Schnurr, S. (2005). Evidenz ohne Reflexivität? Zur Debatte um Evidenzbasierte Praxis in der Sozialen Arbeit. *Zeitschrift Forschung und Wissenschaft Soziale Arbeit, 5*(2), 19–31.

Schweppe, C., & Graßhoff, G. (2006). Rekonstruktive Sozialpädagogik und sozialpädagogisches Handeln. In T. Badawia, Luckas, H., & Müller, H. (eds), *Das Soziale gestalten. Über Mögliches und Unmögliches der Sozialpädagogik*. Wiesbaden: VS Verlag, pp. 185–198.

Shaw, I. (2007). Is social work research distinctive? *Social Work Education, 26*(7), 659–669.

Shaw, I. (2010). Logics, qualities and quality of social work research. In I. Shaw, Briar-Lawson, K., Orme, J., & Ruckdschel, R. (eds), *Sage handbook of social work research*. London: Sage, pp. 246–263.

Shaw, I. (2011). *Evaluating in practice* (2nd ed.). Aldershot, Hants: Ashgate Publishing.

Shaw, I., & Norton, M. (2007). *Kinds and quality of social work research in higher education*. London: Social Care Institute for Excellence.

Shaw, I., Arksey, H., & Mullender, A. (2006). Recognizing social work. *British Journal of Social Work, 36*(2), 227–246.

Shaw, I., Briar-Lawson, K., Orme, J., & Ruckdeschel, R. (2010). Mapping social work research: Pasts, presents and futures. In I. Shaw, Briar-Lawson, K., Orme, J., & Ruckdeschel, R. (eds), *Sage handbook of social work research*. London: Sage, pp. 1–20.

Sidler, N. (2004). *Sinn und Nutzen einer Sozialarbeitswissenschaft: Eine Streitschrift*. Freiburg i. Br.: Lambertus.

Sommerfeld, P. (1998). Spezifische Sozialarbeitsforschung: Ein Resümee zu den dargestellten Forschungsprojekten. In E. Steinert, Sticher-Gil, B., Sommerfeld P., & Maier, K. (eds), *Sozialarbeitsforschung: was sie ist und leistet*. Freiburg i.Br.: Lambertus, pp. 182–192.

Stern, E. (2006). Contextual challenges for evaluation practice. In I. Shaw, Greene, J.C., & Mark, M.M. (eds), *Sage handbook of evaluation*. London: Sage, pp. 292–314.

The Salisbury Statement (2009). Retrieved January 10, 2010 from http://www.socsci.soton.ac.uk/spring/salisbury/The_Salisbury_Statement_on_practice_research_May_2009.pdf.

Thiersch, H., & Rauschenbach, T. (1984). Sozialpädagogik/Sozialarbeit: Theorie und Entwicklung.

In H. Eyferth, Otto H.-U., & Thiersch, H. (eds), *Handbuch zur Sozialarbeit/Sozialpädagogik.* Neuwied: Luchterhand, pp. 984–1016.

Thyer, B. (1989). First principles of practice research. *British Journal of Social Work, 19*(4), 309–323.

Thyer, B.A. (2008). The quest for evidence-based practice? We are all positivists! *Journal Research on Social Work Practice, 18*(4), 339–345.

Timms, N. (1968). *The language of social casework.* London: Routledge and Kegan Paul.

Weizsäcker, C.F. v. (1992). *Zeit und Wissen.* München: Hanser Verlag.

Wilding, P. (1982). *Professional power and social welfare.* London: Routledge and Kegan Paul.

Witkin, S.L. (2000). Writing social work. *Social Work Education, 45*(5), 389–394.

Witkin, S.L. (2001). Reading social work. *Social Work Education, 46*(1), 5–8.

26

Evidence-Based Practice and Social Work

Bruce A. Thyer

In the late 1980s, a group of physicians concerned with enhancing the scientific foundations of clinical medicine formed a loose-knit organisation called the *Evidence-based Medicine Working Group* (EBMWG). They proposed a systematic process by which individual clinicians could help make more research-informed decisions about the care of individual clients, a process that de-emphasised unsystematic clinical experience, intuition, and theory as sufficient sources of information, by themselves, for making decisions (e.g., about what assessments to conduct, or interventions to offer), in favour of an approach more informed by published and high-quality clinical research, in situations where such evidence was available. Other sources of information are not repudiated by this approach. For example, it was noted 'Clinical experience and the development of clinical instincts are a crucial part of becoming a competent (clinician)' and 'many aspects of clinical practice cannot or will not, ever be tested' (EBMWG, 1992, p. 2421). The essence of evidence-based practice (EBP) is:

> that clinicians should regularly consult the original literature (and be able to critically appraise the methodological and results sections in solving clinical problems and in providing optimum ... care. It also follows that clinicians must be ready to accept and live with uncertainty and acknowledge that management decisions are often made in the face of relative ignorance of their true impact ... The new paradigm puts a much lower value on authority. The underlying belief is that (clinicians) can gain the skills to make independent assessments of evidence and thus evaluate the credibility of opinions offered by experts. The decreased emphasis on authority does not imply a rejection of what one can learn from colleagues and teachers ... A final assumption of the new paradigm is that physicians whose practice is based on an understanding of the underlying evidence will provide superior (client) care (EBMWG, 1992, p. 2421).

The Evidence-based Medicine Working Group went on to publish a series of papers refining and further describing their model of EBP, which culminated in a small book by Sackett et al. (1997), followed by a second edition (Sackett et al., 2000), which defined evidence-based practice as 'the integration of best research evidence with clinical expertise and patient values' (Sackett et al., 2000, p. 1). Best research evidence is described as clinically relevant research, especially from clinical research on the validity of assessment measures and on the safety and efficacy of interventions. Clinical expertise refers to one's ability to use clinical skills and past experience to assess clients, the 'benefits of potential interventions, and their personal values and expectations' (Sackett et al., 2000, p. 1). Patient values were defined as 'the unique preferences, concerns and expectations each patient brings to a clinical encounter and which must be integrated into clinical decisions is they are to serve the patient' (Sackett et al., 2000, p. 1). It was further claimed 'When these three elements are integrated, clinicians and patients form a diagnostic and therapeutic alliance which optimizes clinical outcomes and quality of life' (Sackett et al., 2000, p. 1).

It is worth emphasising early on in this chapter that EBP reflects the *integration* of the best available research evidence into clinical decision making, decisions made *jointly* with clients. Research evidence is one of several components of EBP, with clinical expertise, past experiences, and the client's values, expectations, preferences, and concerns also playing large roles in the process. EBP requires consideration of the best research evidence when making decisions, but does not dictate that research considerations should trump these other equally important factors.

The EBP model involves five steps, as described in Sackett et al. (2000, pp. 3–4) and listed below.

1 Convert our need for information (about evaluating the client, or selecting an intervention) into an answerable question.
2 Track down the best available evidence to answer that question.
3 Critically evaluate this evidence for its credibility and applicability to our client's situation. In general, more reliable or credible forms of evidence are accorded greater (but not exclusive) weight than less credible evidence. For example, the findings of a well-designed randomised controlled trial (RCT) would be considered more informative than those from a quasi-experimental study, or the results of a well-designed meta-analysis would be seen as more credible than those from a single RCT.
4 Integrate our critical appraisal of this evidence with the other equally important factors comprising EBP – one's clinical skills, client's preferences, values, and circumstances, professional ethics, available resources, feasibility, and so on, to jointly arrive at a course of action on behalf of the client.
5 Review the outcomes of our efforts, in terms of client outcomes, and our effectiveness in carrying out the overall EBP process.

Note the wording in step 2 'Track down the *best* available evidence to answer that question'. Emphasising the word 'best' implies only evidence of the methodologically highest quality can be used to inform practice. This is an incorrect understanding. Instead, also emphasise the word 'available' and put them together to read 'best available'. What constitutes 'best' evidence will vary according to the practice question being asked. If the question pertains to assessing the past effects of a social work intervention, then certainly some forms of evidence are seen in mainstream science as yielding potentially more valid findings than others. Some writers in the EBP field have proffered up hierarchies of so-called 'best' evidence, with many prescribing something like the following rough order.

Generally more valid (less potential for bias) evidence

Systematic reviews and meta-analyses
Independent multisite randomised controlled experiments
Individual randomised controlled experiment
Quasi-experimental outcome studies
Case-control and cohort outcome studies
Pre-experimental outcome studies
Single-subject studies
Descriptive studies
Epidemiological studies
Qualitative inquiry
Credible theories
Credible clinical opinions

Generally less valid (e.g., more potential for bias) evidence

Now, any such proposed hierarchy is not intended to make a rigid proclamation of merit. A given study might possess the desirable design features of a randomised controlled experiment (listed high on the above hierarchy), but if the outcome measures are of poor validity, the assessments are not blinded, or the statistical power may be too low, then a better designed quasi-experimental outcome study will possibly yield more useful information to guide practice. Indeed, it is not necessary that true experiments (those involving random assignment of participants to the various treatment and control groups) be conducted in any field in order to arrive at legitimate causal inferences. One need be concerned with developing *plausible* causal inferences, not irrefutable ones, from a compilation of the available evidence. For example, through a combination of clinical observations, theory, epidemiological work, descriptive studies, case control, cohort studies, and quasi-experiments, it is now quite clear smoking increases one's chances of developing lung cancer. This conclusion is most certainly valid even though no experiment has ever been conducted that randomly assigned young persons to be smokers or abstainers, and later determined that those assigned to smoke had an elevated likelihood of contracting lung cancer.

Evidence-based practice urges the practitioner to locate and critically evaluate the best available evidence. If you only look for the 'best', thinking that this means you must locate good experiments or meta-analyses, in many areas of social work practice you will fail to find such studies. This has led some critics of EBP to conclude the model is impractical, for example, Plath (2006) states 'The first barrier is the limited amount of high quality social work research that can be drawn upon as evidence for practice' (p. 65). This is a misreading of the process of EBP on two levels. A practitioner is asked to locate available evidence bearing on one's answerable question (e.g., what psychosocial intervention works best with depressed clients?). Much will be revealed. Then the practitioner is differentially directed to evaluate the most credible of this available evidence. If no systematic reviews or meta-analyses can be located, look for multisite experiments. If none of these can be located, evaluate any existing RCTs, then quasi-experimental studies. And so on. In EBP there is *always* evidence available, even if it consists of theory or informed clinical opinions. Social workers are urged to give differential weight to the stronger studies, as they are usually better able to reduce bias, control for threats to external validity, and yield replicable conclusions. Another mistake made by Plath (2006) is to suggest practitioners must rely on 'social work research'. Fundamental to EBP is to locate *all* relevant evidence, regardless of the disciplinary origins of the authors of pertinent studies. It would be absurd to imply that child protection social workers need not review important research conducted by psychologists, nurses, medical doctors, and others contributing to the child abuse literature. Scientific findings do not have rigid disciplinary barriers. Just because social work as a discipline has contributed little to a given area of practice research does not mean social workers cannot draw upon the substantial research literature published by members of other disciplines. Indeed, the very notion of a coherent and identifiable corpus of social work research is a dubious one (see Thyer, 2002, for a review of this complex issue).

With all forms of evidence, any independently replicated finding is usually seen as a more credible result than one which has been reported only once. The above hierarchy is suggested when one's question deals with learning about the potential effects of a given treatment, or in trying to locate potentially useful interventions. If one is asking different questions, this hierarchy is of little use. For example, if one's question deals with say 'how valid is the Beck Depression Inventory when assessing levels of depression among Hispanic clients', the above ranking is meaningless, and a different one is needed that deals with the reliability and validity of assessment measures. If the question involves assessing clients' experiences of a given treatment (e.g., 'how do persons with chronic mental illness experience participating in a programme of Assertive Community Treatment'), randomised experiments might be of little utility in answering such a question, and qualitative studies may be a preferred methodology, of potentially much greater value (see Chapter 29).

Evidence-based practice was quickly taken up by significant elements in the medical education and practice communities, and rapidly spread through the healthcare professions in the USA, Canada, UK, and indeed around the world. This process model of EBP made its initial appearance in the social work literature in articles by Macdonald (1998) and Gambrill (1999), in parallel with its incorporation into clinical and nonclinical fields such as nursing, dentistry, social policy, supervision, public health, criminal justice, political science, and public administration. In social work, a large literature has appeared addressing the topic of EBP. A search of the PsycINFO database conducted in October of 2010, using 'social work', or 'social welfare', and 'evidence-based practice' or 'evidence based practice' as terms contained in an abstract, found over 200 articles, books, chapters, and editorials, reflecting a fairly substantial body of scholarship. Many international social work journal articles address the topic, with contributions from Holland (e.g., Garretsen et al., 2005), Germany (Otto et al., 2009), China (Yunong & Fengzhi, 2009), Sweden (e.g., Blom, 2009) and Australia (Gray et al., 2009; Plath, 2006). Thyer and Kazi's (2004) edited book titled *International Perspectives on Evidence-based Practice in Social Work* contains chapters describing the state of evidence-based social work practice in the USA, England, Scotland, Northern Ireland, South Africa, Israel, Hong Kong, Canada, and Australia. A small industry has arisen, discussing and implementing EBP across the spectrum of social work, including its applications within scholarship, teaching, internships, supervision, administration, community practice, and policy.

Some of this discussion has been critical in nature (e.g., Webb, 2001, 2002) but the overall impression is one of positive growth of this perspective, albeit with some critics of EBP taking a distinctly alarmist perspective at the success of this model. For example, Gray et al. (2009) argue it is too soon to call this a movement and evidence-based social work is emergent, with an increasing number of social workers attempting to grapple with EBP. They see in the growing literature on evidence-based *social work* a great deal of debate about the merits or otherwise of evidence-based *practice*, much on education as the place where the change begins, little on its actual practice in social work, and even less on its implementation.

When locating evidence, a social worker can take a bottom-up or a top-down approach. The bottom-up approach involves locating, reading, and critically evaluating individual studies. This brings one closest to the 'facts' but can be very time consuming, if not impractical for the average practitioner, in areas enjoying a rich foundation of contemporary research. Articles appearing in recent issues of high-quality, peer-reviewed journals are typically considered more credible sources of contemporary evidence than chapters, books, unpublished reports, or conference papers. There are a variety of legitimate reasons for this preferential valuing, but as with the evidentiary hierarchy in general, it is not an absolute or rigid rule. Most professional social workers receive training in locating and critically appraising research literature, so this is not an unreasonable task. Finding articles depends on having access to high-quality, web-based search engines, such as PsycINFO or Web-of-Science, usually available through public libraries, universities and colleges, and via some agencies. Simply reviewing recent issues of available journals is not a systematic or recommended approach to searching the literature, for the purposes of following the EBP process model.

The top-down approach to searching the literature approach involves trying to locate a recently published systematic review (SR) relevant to your answerable question. A SR

> aims to comprehensively locate and synthesize research that bears on a particular question, using organized, transparent, and replicable procedures at each step in the process. Good systematic reviews take ample precautions to minimize error and bias ... a systematic review follows a protocol (a detailed plan) that specifies its central objectives, concepts, and methods in advance. Steps and decisions are carefully documented so that readers can follow and evaluate reviewers' methods (Littell et al. 2008, p. 1).

Two highly credible organisations involved in preparing and disseminating SRs are the Cochrane (www.cochrane.org) and Campbell Collaborations (www.campbellcollaboration.org). Cochrane prepares SRs in the general area of healthcare, and Campbell in the fields of social welfare, education, and criminal justice. Each maintains a library of SRs available via its website, along with protocols of SRs in development, and the titles of future SR topics. Below are listed the titles of some representative completed reviews in the Campbell library:

- advocacy interventions to reduce or eliminate violence, and promote the physical and psychosocial well-being of women who experience intimate partner abuse;
- behavioural and cognitive behavioural training interventions for assisting fostercarers in the management of difficult behaviour;
- cognitive behavioural therapy for men who physically abuse their female partner;
- cognitive behavioural treatment for antisocial behavior in youth in residential treatment;
- cognitive behavioural interventions for children who have been sexually abused;
- court-mandated interventions for individuals convicted of domestic violence;
- effects of second responder programmes on repeat incidents of family abuse;
- financial benefits for child health and well-being in low-income or socially disadvantaged families in developed world countries;
- independent living programmes for improving outcomes for young people leaving the care system;
- interventions intended to reduce pregnancy-related outcomes among adolescents;
- work programmes for welfare recipients;
- school-based education programmes for the prevention of child sexual abuse.

Each of these SRs provides a comprehensive critical appraisal of high-quality studies addressing the past effectiveness of the intervention mentioned, with respect to the specified problem. You can see how access to such a summary would be of immense value as a shortcut to undertaking a bottom-up search yourself. Each SR is completed by a team of three or more experts, and is comprehensively edited and peer reviewed before being posted on the Campbell Library website. To the extent there is a gold standard of evidence, these reviews approximate such an ideal.

Although the Cochrane Library of SRs has a focus on healthcare, it too contains a very large number of completed reviews relevant to social work practice, and may be consulted by social workers seeking a top-down appraisal of the evidence evaluating the effectiveness of selected interventions used with clients experiencing particular difficulties or issues. Here are a few representative Cochrane Systematic Review Titles currently available:

- individual and group-based parenting programmes for improving psychosocial outcomes for teenage parents and their children;
- individual and group-based parenting programmes for the treatment of physical child abuse and neglect;
- kinship care for the safety, permanency, and well-being of children removed from the home for maltreatment;
- treatment fostercare for improving outcomes in children and young people;
- family therapy for depression;
- marital therapy for depression;
- psychosocial and psychological interventions for treating postpartum depression.

These Campbell and Cochrane-sponsored systematic reviews provide a summary of the evidence and generally indicate whether the intervention is useful, not useful, harmful, or if the evidence is unavailable or inconclusive, with respect to a given condition (see Chapter 31). That is *all* they do. In particular it is worth emphasising the systematic reviews which EBP so heavily relies upon *do not tell practitioners what to do!* Such a decision cannot be made, according to the EBP model, by consulting the research evidence alone. The client plays a crucial role, as do the other components of EBP, such as one's practice skills, professional ethics, and resources (see Chapter 31 for further discussion of systematic reviews).

Evidence-based practice is the latest model of efforts to better integrate research findings into social work practice. Indeed, from the very beginnings of professional social work, a reliance on social and behavioural science research findings were what was said to distinguish professional practice from the less systematic efforts of volunteers, religiously motivated individuals, and the philanthropically inclined. Arnold Toynbee (1912) proclaimed, 'To make benevolence scientific is the great problem of the present age' (p. 74). At the (North American) National Conference on Social Work in 1918, Ellwood (cited in Karpf, 1931) outlined the development of social work. According to him, 'it began with a theological stage, passed through a metaphysical stage, and is entering upon its scientific stage' (Karpf, 1931 p. 71). He held

> the scientific stage will be reached when social work passes fully under the domination of science; when it becomes transfused with the spirit and transformed by the method of modern science ... The social worker must learn to become a scientific social worker also. Simple good will and human sympathy are no sufficient guide for the social worker. They may furnish warmth but not light (Karpf, 1931 pp. 71–72).

And, perhaps alarmingly to the postmodernists, Warner et al. (1930) boldly asserted 'Social work interprets human troubles in terms of natural processes, that is "laws" of cause and effect' (pp. 560–561). Distinguished North American social worker Frank Bruno (1936) carried this positivist view even further:

> Social work holds as its primary axiom that knowledge of human behavior can be acquired and interpreted by means of the senses and that inferences drawn from such knowledge can be tested by the principles of logic. The difference between the social work of the present and of all preceding ages is the assumption that human behavior can be understood and is determined by causes which can be explained. We may not have at present a mastery of the methods of understanding behavior, but any scientific approach to behavior presupposes that it is not in its nature incomprehensible to sensory perception and inference therefrom (pp. 192–193).

There is much in the above quote worth noting. The reliance upon the findings of science, and of the value of the scientific method as a useful means of discovery, are two major points emphasised by these early social workers. The assertion the data of social work research comes from the senses indicates the empiricist philosophical foundations of the emerging field. The gaps and preliminary nature of much of our knowledge is evident, and the influence of Comte's positivism is also clear (see Thyer, 2008). From Todd's (1920) *The Scientific Spirit and Social Work* to Kirk and Reid's (2002) *Science and Social Work*, our profession has seen a consistent valuing of scientific findings and of the scientific method over the past century. Indeed, the contemporary Codes of Ethics of both the major British and North American social work associations indicate social workers both rely upon and engage in research.

Prior to the establishment of the EBP model, there were two separate and distinct precursor movements that deserve attention, given their historical importance and overlap with some of the tenets of EBP. These are reviewed below.

PRECURSORS TO EVIDENCE-BASED PRACTICE

Empirical clinical practice

There are at least two clear precursors to the adoption of EBP within the field of social work. The first of these was called *empirical clinical practice* (ECP), which was the title of a book authored by social workers Siri Jayaratne and Rona Levy in 1979. ECP contained several seemingly sensible contentions.

The first was social workers should consult the empirical research literature, most notably empirical outcome studies, for guidance in selecting interventions for clients. Here is what these authors said in this regard:

> The clinician would first be interested in using an intervention strategy that has been successful in the past. As all research builds on previous findings, so too should all clinical practice. When established techniques are available, they should be used, but they should be based on objective evaluation rather than subjective feeling (Jayaratne & Levy, 1979, p. 7).

> The clinician-researcher must have an ability to evaluate, incorporate, and use the research of others .... Here the clinician-researcher asked the questions: Am I familiar with the literature in this area? What are the reported positive and negative effects of this approach? How does the literature say I can best implement these strategies? How much confidence do I have in the reported results? A professional should not have to keep inventing the wheel ... the clinician researcher must be well acquainted with the literature and research procedures that may not be personally used in his or her own practice (Jayaratne & Levy, 1979, p. 13).

The second principle of ECP was that social workers should empirically evaluate the results of their own intervention efforts on behalf of clients, primarily using the approach called single-system research designs described as follows (Jayaratne & Levy, 1979, p. 3):

1. formulating the problem;
2. designing the study;
3. putting the plan into operation;
4. collecting the data;
5. analysing the data;
6. drawing conclusions; and
7. presenting the results.

In many ways the parallels between EBP and ECP are striking. However, keep in mind these were independently derived initiatives, with the former arising in medicine in the early 1990s and the later from social work in the late 1970s and early 1980s. ECP had a good run. In 1982 the Council on Social Work Education, the social work accreditation body in the USA, mandated Bachelor of Social Work (BSW) and Master of Social Work (MSW) students be taught research designs suitable for evaluating their own practice. Many social work educational programmes adopted the principles of ECP and a vigorous social work literature on ECP flourished for a decade or so (Faul et al., 2001; Ivanoff et al., 1987; Reid, 1994; Thyer, 1996), including critical commentaries (e.g., Witkin, 1991). During the past decade, however, discourse on ECP has largely been superseded by both EBP and another related initiative known as empirically supported treatments.

Empirically supported treatments

The American Psychological Association is organised into special interest groups called Divisions. One of these is Division 12, devoted to clinical psychology, also known as the Society of Clinical Psychology. In the early 1990s, the then-President of Division 12 constituted a *Presidential Task Force on the Promotion and Dissemination of Psychological Procedures* (Task Force), which was charged with two challenges. The first was to devise a defensible set of evidentiary standards by which various treatments could be measured, in terms of their effectiveness. Those which met this standard would be designated by this group as an *empirically validated treatment* (a term later revised to empirically supported treatment, or EST). After much wrangling by the Task Force, a rather low bar was set. Put simply, a given intervention had to meet the following standard in order to be called an EST:

- the intervention was supported by at least two well-designed RCTs of adequate sample size, conducted using some form of treatment manual or protocol (to enhance replicability), with positive effects obtained by at least two independent researchers or teams;
- the treatment had to be superior to pill or psychological placebo, or to an established treatment; or
- the treatment had to be equivalent to an established treatment; and
- the client samples had to be well-described.

Armed with these standards, the Task Force then began to see which psychosocial interventions met this level of evidence. In due course, journal publications and a website appeared which contained lists of these putative ESTs, as did a large compendium immodestly called *A Guide to Treatments that Work* (Nathan & Gorman, 2007). The EST initiative of Division 12 remains alive, but not quite thriving, and its latest materials may be viewed on its designated website (www.div12.org/PsychologicalTreatments/index.html). Almost all the conditions found on this website are so-called mental disorders, not other types of psychosocial problems, but the information found herein is reasonably up to date and does make a good resource for tracking down treatments modestly well supported by research evidence. The EST approach has been criticised, of course, with both legitimate and strawman arguments, and like ECP, EST seems to have been overtaken by, and to some extent, transmogrified into EBP (see McHugh & Barlow, 2010). As two eminent psychologists have put it,

> In a short span of time, psychology has seen the term *empirically-validated treatment* evolve into *empirically-supported treatment*, and further into *evidence-based treatment* (EBT) … and further consideration has led to the rise of the umbrella term *evidence-based practice*' (Goodheart & Kazdin, 2006, p. 3).

Please note the purported equivalence of ESTs and EBP in the above quote. Yet the discerning reader will have picked up, based on the prior material presented in this chapter, these two initiatives are quite conceptually distinct approaches. Evidence-based practice is the *process* that helps individual clinicians and their clients arrive at important decisions about what assessment methods and interventions may be useful in a particular case. Empirically-supported treatments was an effort to designate selected interventions as having reached some evidentiary bar, and are, therefore, to be preferentially used. EST's 'product' is a list of treatments. EBP's 'product' is a process to guide practice decision making. In fact, *nowhere in the primary literature on EBP will one find lists of approved or endorsed therapies or interventions*. Indeed, the creation of such a list would be completely antithetical to the EBP approach, because such lists of ESTs fail to take into account other very important factors used in the decision-making process, factors such as client preferences and values, one's clinical expertise, and professional ethical standards. EBP decisions reflect the *integration of these factors*, and go far beyond the simple appraisal of the amount of support a given treatment may enjoy. In a very real sense, there are no such things as 'evidence-based practices'. EBP does not produce such lists and does not support them, inasmuch as these lists ignore all the crucial factors going into the decision-making process. There are lists of empirically supported treatments, but these are not a part of EBP. Below are some additional common misconceptions of EBP that deserve attention and correction.

WHAT EVIDENCE-BASED PRACTICE IS NOT

Practice guidelines or treatment manuals

It should be clear EBP does not involve formal lists of supposedly approved or organisationally endorsed treatments. It also does not involve practice guidelines or treatment manuals. Practice guidelines (PGs) are 'systematically developed statements to assist practitioner and patient decisions about appropriate care for specific clinical circumstances' (Institute of Medicine, 1990, p. 27). Synonymous terms include practice protocols, practice standards, and practice algorithms. PGs pre-dated the emergence of EBP by several decades. A special issue (May, 1999) of the journal *Research on Social Work Practice* was devoted to the topic of social work and practice guidelines, with a seminal article by Howard and Jenson (1999) leading the subsequent articles discussing the pros and cons of the topic. Rosen and Proctor (2003) edited a later volume entitled *Developing Practice Guidelines for Social Work Intervention: Issues, Methods, and Research Agenda*. However, I am aware of no sustained efforts by any professional social work organisations or prominent individuals to create PGs for social workers. In some ways, this is a good thing, as PGs should be problem oriented and interdisciplinary in focus. It is foolish to have separate PGs for the disciplines of social work, psychology, psychiatry, nursing, and marital therapy, all focused on the effective assessment and treatment of, say, depression. Rather, it would be more scientifically tenable for the members of all these relevant disciplines to work collaboratively and come up with a PG to help depressed clients to provide guidance to members of all these professions (see Thyer, 2003). Furthermore, the construction of PGs is very uneven in a scientific sense and they are often laden with turf-protective features. Some PGs are based on the consensus of so-called experts, not necessarily on a careful appraisal of the research evidence. Such PGs are practically useless, reflective of theory, ideology, and egos, rather than solid research findings. For example, PGs developed by psychiatric organisations over-emphasise drug treatment and tend to ignore effective psychosocial interventions. Should organised psychology develop PGs, it is possible the converse will prove true. To be clear, nowhere in the primary source literature on EBP will you find PGs recommended or incorporated into this model.

Lists of empirically supported treatments

Similarly, readers will search the primary EBP literature in vain for lists of approved therapies, interventions, or assessment methods. Such lists are the hallmark of the EST movement originating in psychology, but that was a separate development, both historically and conceptually, from EBP. In fact, it would be completely antithetical to the EBP process model for anyone to come up with a list of endorsed treatments, suggesting in any way these be the first-choice treatments for clients with a given condition. Why? Because such a list would ignore the other important considerations affecting the decision-making characteristic of EBP. For example, on the EST website one can read 'cognitive therapy' is said to be empirically supported for the treatment of depression. Well, it is, according to the evidentiary standards of the EST initiative, but, by itself, this does not indicate what the practitioner should do when faced with a client who is seriously depressed. For example, if the client also experienced a significant developmental disability, he or she might lack the requisite intellectual skills to fully engage in cognitive therapy. Thus for *this* depressed client, cognitive therapy, for all its research support, would not be a treatment of choice. Similarly, suppose it has been shown that legally mandated chemical castration dramatically reduces the risk of recidivism among sex offenders (see Harrison, 2007). Would a social worker wish to participate in a treatment team providing such therapy? It may well be that some would decline on ethical grounds relating to the coercive and invasive nature of the treatment. Again, research evidence alone is an insufficient guide to conduct EBP. In his widely cited, incisive commentary and critique of EBP, Webb (2001) claimed, 'According to this view, social work decisions should rest *solely* on evidence leading to effective outcomes' (p. 62, emphasis added). This is simply incorrect. No citation was provided to support this criticism, and I would be very surprised to find one given the untenability of that position, scientifically, ethically, and professionally.

Best practices

'Best practices' is an even more elusive term than practice guidelines. At its best, it is synonymous with empirically supported treatments. At its worst, it is a self-proclaimed assertion, widely promoted, which may have little basis in scientific evidence. Again, nowhere in the primary EBP literature will you find recommendations for so-called 'best practices' for the same reasons EBP eschews lists of ESTs.

Behaviourism

Also in his critique, Webb (2001) included as a negative feature of the EBP model its supposedly close association with the philosophy and practice of behaviourism. For example:

- 'the inference being, of course, that only behaviourist approaches which are objective will suffice' (p. 59).
- 'an evidence-based infrastructure derived solely from a behaviorist worldview and an empirically generated methodology' (p. 60).
- 'five distinctive background sources can be identified which feed directly into the diverse appeals of the value of evidence-based practice ... These are ... 1 behavioural social work ...' (p. 60).
- 'By rooting decision making within a behavioural mind-set ...' (p. 63).
- 'evidence is not simply punched into a black box, with a decision as an output as the more behaviorally-minded would have it' (p. 68).

Behaviourism pre-dated EBP by close to a century, and the latter was developed by physicians with no evident associations with a behaviourist orientation (see Chapter 9). Any similarities between behaviourism and EBP arise from the grounding of each distinct approach on a reliance on the scientific method of inquiry, empirical research, and a generally positivistic philosophy of science. Some behaviourists (the author among them) appreciate this congruence between the two approaches, and support both orientations to practice. But EBP (which is largely theory-neutral) is not behaviourism (grounded in social learning theory), and reflects a scientific world view, not a strictly behavioural one.

Managerialism

Grave concerns have been expressed by some critics of EBP that this approach reflects the implementation of a managerialist perspective on the provision of social care. Administrators (or worse yet, bureaucrats and politicians) will decide what interventions are to be delivered by the practitioners in a given agency, and this will reduce professional autonomy, and the opportunity for effective, responsive, services. Webb (2001) describes some of these concerns:

- 'evidence-based practice reduces professional judgment to decisionism' (p. 72).
- 'attempting to root out value laden, professional judgment or 'opinion-based ideas ...' (p. 72).
- 'replaces traditional criteria of professional judgment, as well as rules of experience developed unsystematically in everyday working contexts' (p. 73).
- 'Evidence-based practice links directly into what Harris (1998) calls 'new managerialism' in British social work' (p. 73).
- 'a double discursive alliance of *scientism* and *managerialism* in social work' (p. 74).
- 'We thus have the assimilation of a form of 'scientific management' in social work' (p. 74).
- 'neutralizing social work's role in moral and political discourse and undermining its professional autonomy' (p. 76).

These are indeed serious concerns, and seemingly reflect more how the British government has imposed new practices on its systems of social welfare and care. It is not clear how they are derived from the process model of EBP. EBP actually enhances professional autonomy, judgement, and decision making, since it is a model to be used by individual practitioners. Any unilateral imposition by administrators of what treatments must be offered would, again, fly in the face of the EBP model, since this would seemingly ignore all but research-based considerations in dictating interventions. And that is not what EBP is all about.

Based on a medical model

Evidence-based practice is a theoretically neutral practice model. It contains no assumptions regarding the causes of psychosocial problems, and is instead more focused on evaluating the effects of interventions, and on the validity of methods of assessment. To the extent these methods are clearly theoretically derived, then the results of systematic reviews commissioned in support of EBP may have some indirect bearing on corroborating or refuting those theories. In particular, it is worth emphasising EBP is not based on a medical model. Nowhere in EBP does it assert the conditions it focuses upon have a biological etiology or interventions need to be biologically based, or physicians are the most authoritative providers of services. Lacking these crucial features of a medical model, it is clearly incorrect to allude to EBP as somehow being tainted with this characterisation. Gray et al., (2009, p. 26) concur that EBP is not based on a medical model.

CONTROVERSIES

Evidence-based practice has met with fierce resistance from some social work circles, most notably from advocates of postmodernist philosophies of science or those contending qualitative research methods are a preferred methodological orientation for social work research. For example, Witkin (1991) contends, 'Virtually any intervention can be justified on the grounds that it has as much support as alternative methods' (p. 158). This is a version of the Dodo-bird verdict, which similarly asserts the essential equivalence of almost all forms of psychotherapy. If this were one's position, then following the EBP process model to help in selecting interventions, or relying on systematic reviews to help ascertain the evidence relating to the comparative effectiveness of one form of intervention over another, would indeed be useless undertakings. Perhaps similarly useless would be the existence of professional training programmes in the human services which provide social workers with the skills and techniques used to help clients and effect system-wide change? Such is the logical conclusion if one were to accept the Dodo-bird hypothesis. Fortunately, common sense supported by sound research convincingly refutes this nihilistic contention (e.g., Reid et al., 2004; Siev et al., 2009; Tolin, 2010). This chapter is not the venue to engage in a thorough discussion of the contention all treatments yield equal effects, but it is important to know this perspective is one important source of resistance to the idea of EBP.

Another major source of contention is the accusation EBP is grounded in 'positivism', as if this were somehow akin to being a convicted child abuser. What does this supposedly controversial philosophical position labelled contend? It is actually quite a simple notion:

> A paradigm introduced by Auguste Comte that held that social behavior could be studied and understood in a rational, scientific manner – in contrast to explanations based in religion or superstition (Rubin & Babbie, 2008, p. 642)

Positivism is of course the dominant philosophy of science upheld by mainstream social and behavioural science, thus those who hold differing views (e.g., postmodernism, social constructivism, critical reflection, phenomenology, reflexivity, critical realism, and so forth) take issue with the fundamental assumptions and derivative conclusions upon which EBP is predicated. This source of resistance is being played out by all the major disciplines in which EBP is making inroads, even medicine. Within education, for example, Hammersley (2001) has published a widely cited critique of the possible role of systematic reviews in determining governmental policy. He expressed concerns over the notion some forms of inquiry in EBP are more privileged than others (e.g., randomised controlled trials over qualitative inquiry), which will lead to lessened governmental funding for the latter. He also described many of positivism's purported shortcomings, expressed general scepticism that empirical research could fruitfully inform educational practices, and later expanded these views in a social work journal (Hammersley, 2003). A spirited exchange between the views of Ian Chalmers (2003, 2005), who conceived of the Campbell Collaboration, and Martyn Hammersley (2001, 2005), a critic of EBP, have enriched the dialogue on these contrasting perspectives, and has been picked up and echoed in much of the analogous social work literature (Gray et al., 2009). Space does not permit a discussion of the pros and cons of positivism as a philosophy of science for social work, but I will venture my own view. Positivism and its derivative applications, such as traditional empirical research and EBP, have much to offer our discipline. My asserting this says nothing about the merits of alternative approaches, and most certainly does not condemn them. I am content to let others pursue other ways of knowing in peace, and I eagerly await the constructive contributions they provide the social work discipline in terms of improving the effectiveness of social care. If these are forthcoming I will be delighted, inasmuch as my primary concern is in the improvement of the social condition of clients and society as a whole. The source of these improvements (e.g., quantitative inquiry versus qualitative research) or the nature of the philosophical positions undergirding them (e.g., positivism versus constructivism) is, frankly, not too important. I personally advocate for the positions I do because I judge them to offer the best route to advance the profession and society. Not for any other reason.

CONCLUSION: CURRENT STATUS OF EVIDENCE-BASED PRACTICE IN SOCIAL WORK

In less than 15 years, EBP has made considerable inroads into social work practice. Practitioners are becoming more familiar with the EBP process model and terminology, and a number of social work academic programmes have adopted EBP as their curriculum's organising structure, while others place it in a less central role but still have it prominently featured. The highly regarded social policy and social work programme at the University of Oxford is one of the foremost institutions to integrate EBP, and now offers the M.Sc., M.Phil., and D.Phil. in Evidence-based Interventions. Similarly, in the USA, the respected MSW programme at Washington University in Saint Louis is focused on training in EBP (Howard et al., 2003).

Continuing education and in-service training programmes are being provided to practising social workers (Parrish & Rubin, 2011) on how to conduct EBP, and a formal Institute for Evidence-based Social Work has been established at the University of Toronto (Regehr et al., 2007). A nationally conducted survey of MSW faculty in the USA found a large majority (73%) to have favourable views on the approach. However, there was much confusion in distinguishing among EBP and ESTs, with over 65% indicating they believed EBP included designating certain interventions as empirically supported, and only 22.5% defining EBP (correctly) as '... a process that includes locating and appraising evidence as a part of practice decisions' (Rubin & Parrish, 2007, p. 116). *The Society for Social Work and Research* includes the promotion of EBT as among its organisational goals, and its annual convention programme contains considerable content on EBP. The US *National Association of Social Workers* is paying some positive, albeit limited, attention to the emergence of EBP, noting 'EBP plays a key role in social work mental health care education, training and treatment' (Pace, 2008, p. 1).

Special issues of *Research on Social Work Practice* (September 2007) and of the *Journal on Social Work Education* (Fall 2007) were devoted to the teaching of EBP in social work, and another special issue, to be published by the *Clinical Social Work Journal*, is well under way. The *Journal of Evidence-based Social Work*, published by Taylor and Francis, began publishing in 2004 and appears quarterly.

It is becoming increasingly evident EBP has implications and applications far beyond clinical social work and mental disorders. This process model is not linked in any way to using formal diagnoses. For example, EBP-style answerable questions may be developed concerning the validity of social work assessment methods, to the aetiology of non-mental health psychosocial problems (e.g., domestic violence, child abuse, and homelessness due to poverty) and to the effectiveness of large-scale social policies. The website for *Social Programs that Work* (noted at the end of this chapter) provides links to a wide array of social policy-related issues, and the new journal *Evidence and Policy* (http://www.policypress.co.uk/journals_eap.asp) provides another useful platform for extending EBP to more macro-level applications.

In these fiscally conservative times, there is ever-increasing pressure for social work programmes to be able to demonstrate they are capable of improving the lives and well-being of the clients they are asked to serve. During President Obama's (2009) inauguration speech, he made the following statement:

> What the cynics fail to understand is that the ground has shifted beneath them – that the stale political arguments that have consumed us for so long no longer apply. The question we ask today is not whether our government is too big or too small, *but whether it works – whether it helps families find jobs at a decent wage, care they can afford, a retirement that is dignified. Where the answer is yes, we intend to move forward. Where the answer is no, programs will end. And those of us who manage the public's dollars will be held to account – to spend wisely,* reform bad habits, and do our business in the light of day – because only then can we restore the vital trust between a people and their government (President Barack Hussein Obama, Inauguration Address, 20 January 2009, emphasis added).

Similar sentiments have been widely expressed within the UK. For example, almost a decade ago, the UK Secretary of State for Education and Employment issued a press release which contained the following view:

> Social science should be at the heart of policy-making. We need a revolution in relations between the government and the social research community – we need social scientists to help determine what works, and why, and what types of policy initiatives are likely to be most effective (Department for Education and Employment, 2000, p. 1).

Helping to determine what works in social work and social welfare, and what does not, and to improve services, is the goal of EBP. This is a maturation of a perspective present during the origins of professional social work over a century ago. It is unclear if EBP can strengthen our profession's ability to provide more effective services. History tells us professions rise and fall, and elements within disciplines can even disappear entirely. Several decades ago a major component of UK social work was called psychiatric social work (analogous to the thriving field of clinical social work in the USA today). Psychiatric social work in the UK has virtually disappeared (Brewer & Lait, 1980), and other important fields of traditional social work practice, such as probation, are being supplanted by individuals without social work degrees. Proactive steps on the part of social work are needed to enhance the credibility of what social workers do. EBP may provide some guidance towards that goal.

REFERENCES

Blom, B. (2009). Knowling or un-knowing? That is the question in the era of evidence-based social work practice. *Journal of Social Work, 9*, 158–177.

Brewer, C., & Lait, J. (1980). *Can social work survive?* London: Temple Smith.

Bruno, F. (1936). *The theory of social work.* New York: Heath.

Chalmers, I. (2003). Trying to do more good than harm in policy and practice: The role of rigorous, transparent, up-to-date evaluations. *Annals of the American Academy of Political and Social Science, 589,* 22–40.

Chalmers, I. (2005). If evidence-informed policy works in practice, does it matter if it does not work in theory? *Evidence and Policy, 1,* 227–242.

Department for Education and Employment (DfEE) (2000). Blunkett rejects anti-intellectualism and welcomes sound ideas. *DfEE News, 43/00.* London: Author.

Evidence-based Medicine Working Group (1992). Evidence-based medicine: A new approach to teaching the practice of medicine. *Journal of the American Medical Association, 268,* 2420–2425.

Faul, A.C., McMurtry, S.L., & Hudson, W.W. (2001). Can empirical clinical practice techniques improve social work outcomes? *Research on Social Work Practice, 11,* 277–299.

Gambrill, E. (1999). Evidence-based practice: An alternative to authority-based practice. *Families in Society: The Journal of Contemporary Social Services, 80,* 341–350.

Garretsen, H., Bongers, I., & Rodenburg, G. (2005). Evidence-based social work in the Dutch welfare sector. *British Journal of Social Work, 35,* 655–665.

Goodheart, C.D., & Kazdin, A.E. (2006). Introduction. In C.D. Goodheart, Kazdin, A.E. & Sternberg, R.J. (eds). *Evidence-based psychotherapy: Where practice and research meet.* Washington, DC: American Psychological Association, pp. 3–10.

Gray, M., Plath, D., & Webb, S.A. (2009). *Evidence-based social work: A critical stance.* New York: Routledge.

Hammersley, M. (2001). On 'systematic' reviews of research literatures: A 'narrative, response to Evans and Benefield. *British Educational Research Journal, 27,* 543–554.

Hammersley, M. (2003). Social research today: Some dilemmas and distinctions. *Qualitative Social Work, 2*(1), 25–44.

Hammersley, M. (2005). Is the evidence-based practice movement doing more good than harm? *Evidence and Policy, 1,* 1–16.

Harris, J. (1998). Scientific management, bureau-professionalism, new managerialism: The labour process of state social work. *British Journal of Social Work, 28*(6), 839–862.

Harrison, K. (2007). The high-risk sex offender strategy in England and Wales: Is chemical castration an option? *Howard Journal of Criminal Justice, 46,* 16–31.

Howard, M.O., & Jenson, J. (1999). Clinical practice guidelines: Should social work develop them? *Research on Social Work Practice, 9,* 283–301.

Howard, M.O., McMillen, C.J., & Pollio, D.E. (2003). Teaching evidence-based practice: Toward a new paradigm for social work education. *Journal of Social Work Education, 13,* 234–259.

Institute of Medicine (1990). *Clinical practice guidelines: Directions for a new program.* Washington, DC: National Academy Press.

Ivanoff, A., Blythe, B.J., & Briar, S. (1987). The empirical clinical practice debate. *Social Casework, 68,* 290–298.

Jayaratne, S., & Levy, R.L. (1979). *Empirical clinical practice.* New York: Columbia University Press.

Karpf, M.J. (1931). *The scientific basis of social work.* New York: Columbia University Press.

Kirk, S.A., & Reid, W.J. (2002). *Science and social work: A critical appraisal.* New York: Columbia University Press.

Littell, J.H., Corcoran, J., & Pillai, V. (2008). *Systematic reviews and meta-analysis.* New York: Oxford University Press.

Macdonald, G. (1998). Promoting evidence-based practice in child protection. *Clinical Child Psychology and Psychiatry, 31,* 71–85.

McHugh, R.K., & Barlow, D.H. (2010). The dissemination and implementation of evidence-based psychological treatments. A review of current efforts. *American Psychologist, 65,* 73–84.

Nathan, P.E., & Gorman, J.M. (eds) (2007). *A guide to treatments that work* (3rd ed.). New York: Oxford University Press.

Obama, B.H. (2009). *Inauguration Address, 20 January 2009.* Retrieved October 20, 2010 from http://www.npr.org/templates/story/story.php?storyId=99590481

Otto, H-U., Polutta, A., & Ziegler, H. (2009). Reflexive professionalism as a second general of evidence-based practice: Some considerations on the special issue 'What Works? Modernizing the knowledge base of social work'. *Research on Social Work Practice, 19,* 472–478.

Pace, P.R. (2008). Evidence-based practice moves ahead: EBP plays a key role in social work mental health care education. *NASW News, 53*(1), January, 1.

Parrish, D.E., & Rubin, A. (2011). An effective model for continuing education training in evidence-based practice. *Research on Social Work Practice, 21*(1), 77–87.

Plath, D. (2006). Evidence-based practice: Current issues and future directions. *Australian Social Work, 59,* 56–72.

Regehr, C., Stern, S., & Shlonsky, A. (2007). Operationalizing evidence-based practice: The development of an Institute for Evidence-based Social Work. *Research on Social Work Practice, 17,* 408–416.

Reid, W.J. (1994). The empirical practice movement. *Social Service Review, 68,* 165–184.

Reid, W.J., Kenaley, B.D., & Colvin, J. (2004). Do some interventions work better than others? A review of comparative social work experiments. *Social Work Research, 28,* 71–81.

Rosen, A., & Proctor, E.K. (eds) (2003). *Developing practice guidelines for social work intervention: Issues, methods, and a research agenda.* Columbia: Columbia University Press.

Rubin, A., & Babbie, E.R. (2008). *Research methods for social work* (6th ed.). New York: Thomson.

Rubin, A., & Parrish, D. (2007). Views of evidence-based practice among faculty in Master of Social Work programs: A national survey. *Research on Social Work Practice, 17,* 110–122.

Sackett, D.L., Straus, S.E., Richardson, W.S., Rosenberg, W., & Haynes, R.B. (1997). *Evidence-based medicine: How to practice and teach EBM.* New York: Churchill-Livingstone.

Sackett, D.L., Straus, S.E., Richardson, W.S., Rosenberg, W., & Haynes, R.B. (2000). *Evidence-based medicine: How to practice and teach EBM* (2nd ed.). New York: Churchill-Livingstone.

Siev, J., Hubbert, J., & Chambless, D.L. (2009). The Dodo bird, treatment technique, and disseminating empirically supported treatments. *The Behavior Therapy, 32*(4), 69–75.

Thyer, B.A. (1996). Guidelines for applying the empirical clinical practice model to social work. *Journal of Applied Social Sciences, 20,* 121–127.

Thyer, B.A. (2002). Developing discipline-specific knowledge for social work: Is it possible? *Journal of Social Work Education, 38,* 101–113.

Thyer, B.A. (2003). Social work should help develop interdisciplinary evidence-based practice guidelines, not discipline specific ones. In A. Rosen & Proctor, E.K. (eds). *Developing practice guidelines for social work intervention.* New York: Columbia University Press, pp. 128–139.

Thyer, B.A. (2008). The quest for evidence-based practice: We are all positivists! *Research on Social Work Practice, 18,* 339–345.

Thyer, B.A., & Kazi, M.A.F. (eds) (2004). *International perspectives on evidence-based practice in social work.* Birmingham: Venture Press.

Todd, A.J. (1920). *The scientific spirit and social work.* New York: Macmillan.

Tolin, D. (2010). Is cognitive-behavioral therapy more effective than other therapies: A meta-analytic review. *Clinical Psychology Review, 30,* 710–720.

Toynbee, A. (1912). *Lectures on the industrial revolution of the eighteenth century in England.* London: Longmans, Green.

Warner, A.G., Queen, S.A., & Harper, E.B. (1930). *American charities and social work* (4th ed.). New York: Thomas Y. Crowell.

Webb, S.A. (2001). Some considerations on the validity of evidence-based practice in social work. *British Journal of Social Work, 31,* 57–79.

Webb, S.A. (2002). Evidence-based practice and decision analysis in social work: An implementation model. *Journal of Social Work, 2*(1), 45–63.

Witkin, S.L. (1991). Empirical clinical practice: A critical analysis. *Social Work, 36,* 158–163.

Yunong, H., & Fengzhi, M. (2009). A reflection on reasons, preconditions, and effects of implementing evidence-based practice in social work. *Social Work, 54,* 177–181.

WEBSITES

www.campbellcollaboration.org

The international Campbell Collaboration (C2) is a non-profit organisation that aims to help people make well-informed decisions about the effects of interventions in the social, behavioural and educational arenas. C2's objectives are to prepare, maintain, and disseminate systematic reviews of studies of interventions. It acquires and promotes access to information about trials of interventions. C2 builds summaries and electronic brochures of reviews and reports of trials for policy makers, practitioners, researchers and the public.

www.cochrane.org

An international not-for-profit organisation, providing up-to-date information about the effects of health care. It produces the Cochrane Database of Systematic Reviews, part of The Cochrane Library, the definitive resource for evidence-based health care.

www.scie.org.uk/

The Social Care Institute for Excellence (SCIE) aims are to improve the experience of people who use social care by developing and promoting knowledge about good practice in the sector. Using knowledge gathered from diverse sources and a broad range of people and organisations, it develops resources which it shares freely, supporting those working in social care and empowering service users.

ebbp.org
The website for Evidence-based Behavioral Practice, sources of training materials to help bridge the gap between behavioral health research and practice.

www.sswr.org
The website for the Society for Social Work and Research.

www.evidencebasedprograms.org/
Social programs that work: what works and what doesn't work in social policy: findings from well-designed randomized controlled trials.

www.cebc4cw.org/
California Clearinghouse for Evidence-based Child Welfare

www.rip.org.uk/
Research in Practice website, supporting research-informed practice with children and families. A UK site.

www.equator-network.org
Website devoted to reporting various rating scales used to evaluate the quality of individual research studies.

Intervention Research

Brian J. Taylor

'The origins of social work in Western democracies might be viewed as rooted in efforts to apply the question "what works?" to the endeavours of Christian and socialist charitable activities in the 19th century' (Taylor, 2010, p. 66). This statement raises interesting historical and philosophical debates but what is clear is that the development of effective interventions to help other human beings in need lies at the heart of social work practice. Social work is not only an academic discipline studying people, their needs, or the impact of government policies but is also a professional discipline committed to using the most effective psychosocial interventions to help individuals, families, groups, and communities to better their lives, safeguard those who are vulnerable to abuse or serious harm, and contribute to protecting citizens from the harmful effects of crime. Social work intervenes to reduce the likelihood of harm, stimulate self-help, provide therapeutic interventions, enhance and maintain - or at least reduce deterioration of - functional abilities, and safeguard those at greatest risk. In short, the professional focus of social work is on intentional, planned intervention to help people achieve beneficial change. It is important, therefore, for the profession to use interventions with proven effectiveness to achieve beneficial change for clients, families, and communities. This means professional decisions need to be justified and based on sound evidence (Taylor, 2006). Ethically it might be regarded as inappropriate to waste the time and energies of clients, families, and professionals engaging in interventions with limited or no effect, let alone positively unhelpful. Politically, the profession needs to be able to demonstrate the effectiveness of its psychosocial interventions if it is to receive funding support through governments and charitable bodies and, once it does, social workers are ethically obliged to be accountable for what they do (Bloom et al., 2003; Fisher, 1973). As the International Federation of Social Workers (IFSW) (2000) notes, 'Social work bases its methodology on a systematic body of evidence-based knowledge derived from research and practice evaluation …' (p. 1). But deciding on appropriate research methods to determine what works in practice has been the subject of much debate since varying approaches to the theory of knowledge – epistemology - influence the choice of research design and method. For example, viewing research as essentially about creating generalisable knowledge means notions of *truth*, *belief*, and *justifiable argument* will influence the approach to how such knowledge is created (Darragh & Taylor, 2008). Developments in intervention research have gone some way to assisting social workers in basing their work on interventions developed through sound research. This chapter addresses the challenges and opportunities facing social work in demonstrating its effectiveness through intervention research. To highlight these challenges, the fundamentals of intervention research are discussed first.

DEVELOPMENTS IN INTERVENTION RESEARCH

Intervention Research (IR) or *Social Intervention Research* (SIR) involves a clustering of research designs and approaches brought together in the design and development of new interventions, as well as in the evaluation and improvement of existing interventions (Fraser et al., 2009). Rothman and Thomas (1994) described intervention research as embodying: (i) empirical research on service intervention, (ii) knowledge utilisation, and (iii) research directed towards intervention development. Schilling (1997) took a broader view, seeing intervention research as encompassing: (i) studies attempting to understand social phenomena; (ii) studies of helping processes; (iii) longitudinal studies of clients before and after social work intervention; (iv) studies to systematically design and develop interventions; and (v) full-scale experiments. Fraser (2004) outlined the six-phase engineering perspective of Rothman and Thomas (1994) as encompassing the key elements of intervention research: (i) problem analysis and project planning; (ii) information gathering and synthesis; (iii) intervention design; (iv) early development and pilot testing; (v) evaluation and advanced development; and (vi) dissemination.

Social work interventions may be complex, and take place in complex environments. Factors such as multiple stressors, co-morbidities, poverty, and strained relationships with family and neighbours create a complexity presenting challenges to the design, development, and evaluation of effective interventions. Such complexity might be described in terms of the multidimensional, interacting components, the difficulty of the behaviours required of providers and recipients, the levels – individual, group, and organisational – targeted, the variability and unpredictability of outcomes, and the flexibility often demanded in tailoring interventions to fit practice (Craig et al., 2008). In addressing the limitations of intervention research Craig et al. (2008) noted evaluation in complex environments required:

> early phase piloting and development work, a less linear model of evaluation process, integration of process and outcome evaluation, recognition that complex interventions may work best if they are tailored to local contexts rather than completely standardised and greater use of the insights provided by the theory of complex adaptive systems (p. 694).

A key issue in conceptualising what constitutes intervention research is whether research comes *before* the development of an intervention or whether a model of research running *in parallel with* its development is used. For the researcher wanting to report robust results in an academic journal, and for those commissioning and funding research, the former approach is often preferred. For managers wanting to see change for clients within their organisations achieved quickly and efficiently, the latter approach has attractions. Models of integrating intervention development activity in parallel with research activity in the USA tend to be called *intervention research* while in Europe they are often referred to in terms of *quality improvement* or *service development* (Davidoff et al., 2008). The term *action research* is also commonly used to describe an iterative process of gathering data about a generalisable intervention of interest to a wider audience while, at the same time, feeding an ongoing intervention development process (see Chapter 30). Recent developments using these various names – and drawing on their different research approaches – constitute the basic *building blocks* of intervention research and program or service development activity with varying emphases and terminology, within and across cultures and countries. In order to provide a useful and clear international perspective of enduring value on research in social work, this *Handbook* provides separate chapters on the main elements of these building blocks, many of which have been incorporated into the more recent broad conceptualisations of *intervention research*. Evidence-based social work, in particular, is concerned with knowledge utilisation (see Chapter 26) where knowledge means research-based knowledge. Evidence-based practice – or EBP as it is commonly known – is the accepted terminology within the health and social and behavioural sciences. It is taken as given that any substantive research, audit, or service-development activity will commence with an appropriately thorough review of the literature or state-of-the-art review as Rothman and Thomas (1994) refer to it. The state of the art in this regard is the *systematic review* and the emerging technologies of *meta-analysis* of quantitative data and *meta-synthesis* of qualitative data (see Chapters 29 and 31 respectively).

There is a plethora of research to inform social work practice. For example, longitudinal studies of social problems and human well-being are plentiful in democratic countries, although there are challenges in countries where governments are less open to publication of evidence showing their society is less than perfect. Key dimensions of iterative intervention research and development processes – such as problem analysis and project planning, piloting of interventions, and ongoing evaluation – may be highly political (see Chapter 30). Studies of helping processes often usefully and appropriately use qualitative methods (see Chapter 29) while experimental studies – as discussed in this chapter – form the meat of the most robust studies of interventions and their effectiveness (see also Chapter 26). However, they must be viewed in light of recent developments in designing, developing, and evaluating complex social care interventions, the types of designs available (discussed below), and the potential benefits of mixed methods studies in this endeavour.

TYPES OF RESEARCH DESIGN

Intervention research integrates a range of research designs in the design, development, and evaluation of social interventions. Among these are observational designs and quasi-experimental designs.

Observational designs

Observational designs do not have a control group of any kind against which to measure the change in the group of participants who are receiving the intervention. In a *before-and-after* – or pre- and post-test – design, the outcome measure(s) is used with the clients or families both before and after the intervention in order to measure change. However, a study using this design cannot conclude with certainty any change observed is attributable to the intervention. There may be other changes occurring to these families (for example, social changes in the neighbourhood, general economic change, or changes in government policy) causing the observed change or, indeed, negating the effectiveness of the intervention.

A BEFORE-AND-AFTER DESIGN

Khoury-Kassabri et al. (2010) assessed the outcomes of a group intervention program with violent juveniles. Forty-eight juveniles referred to the juvenile probation service because of violent crime completed the 16 sessions of the intervention which lasted 1.5 hours each. Participants completed questionnaires addressing their attitudes toward violence, perpetration of violent behavior toward others, and sociodemographic factors, before and after the group intervention.

One design is to follow a group of people over time comparing those who received an intervention with those who did not. This is known as a *cohort* or *longitudinal study*. Such studies require a large number of participants and a long time period to produce useful results.

A LONGITUDINAL DESIGN

Substance use behaviours of young people attending a special school are reported over a four-year period from the age of 12–16 years. The researchers investigated these behaviours by surveying a cohort of young people with a statement for moderate learning disabilities annually during the last four years of compulsory schooling. The findings showed these young people consistently reported lower levels of tobacco, alcohol, and cannabis use compared with those attending mainstream school. No other illicit drug use was reported. These findings had implications for the context and timing of targeted substance education and prevention initiatives for young people with moderate learning disability attending a special school (McCrystal et al., 2007).

Quasi-experimental designs

Quasi-experimental studies are where the researcher has some control over which people receive the intervention or else over how a control group is created, but where participants are not allocated randomly. In general, quasi-experimental studies would be regarded as stronger in terms of design than the observational studies described above.

Non-randomised controlled intervention design

A *non-randomised controlled intervention design* may be appropriate where it is possible to measure the participants both before and after the intervention, but not influence which received the intervention. For example, a control group might be formed from individuals (or families) corresponding to each individual or family in the intervention group. The matched pairs would be created in relation to relevant factors. This provides some additional rigour by comparison with the observational studies above. However, a weakness is that the factors on which the pairs are created may not represent all of the relevant factors. Also, inevitably, there will be limitations of what can reasonably be achieved in terms of degree of matching in relation to the number of clients or families available from which to select.

A QUASI-EXPERIMENTAL DESIGN

Solution-focused brief therapy [to improve academic underachievement and school nonattendance for at-risk school pupils] was evaluated through a quasi-experimental pretest-posttest comparison group design in which 26 students receiving the intervention were compared to 26 students who did not. Compared to students who did not receive the intervention, students in the treatment group increased their grade point average from pretreatment to posttreatment. No differences were found between the two groups on attendance (Newsome, 2004).

Interrupted time series design

An *interrupted time series design* is where multiple observations are made over a period of time, where there are periods with and without intervention. The design focuses on the likelihood the response to an intervention will probably be stronger while the intervention is being carried out (or increase during the intervention) and is likely then to reduce when the intervention stops. Measurements at appropriate points could identify these changing levels of response, and thus give a measure of the effectiveness of the intervention. It is traditional to describe the measures before the intervention as time A and the measures during the intervention as time B. As an example, one might measure the level of a family problem before the parenting program (time A), then measure it again during the intervention (time B). After the program finishes (time A again), the level of the problem could be measured again. A gradual reduction in the effect of the program over time would be expected. The intervention could be repeated (time B again) at a later date, giving an A-B-A-B design which, as a design, would be more convincing than the simpler AB or ABA design where the effect observed was due to the intervention rather than other factors. The *interrupted time series design* (ITS) is particularly suited to identifying the aspects of interventions influencing outcomes. The ITS is a design suited to identifying variables and developing understanding of principles of effective practice, whereas the experimental designs below are better suited to testing the overall effectiveness of interventions. ITS designs are also suited to community interventions (Fawcett et al., 1995).

Experimental designs

It will be apparent the above designs suffer from weaknesses in not fully addressing the need to ensure all factors are taken into account in order to ensure the outcomes being measured are caused by the intervention. Hence experimental designs tend to be more suited to the study of social work interventions since people are allocated randomly between whether they receive the intervention or not, which might be called a *randomised controlled intervention study*. If people are allocated randomly, then they each have an equal chance of being allocated to the group receiving the intervention or to the control group. Hence in the long run (with enough participants) the group receiving the intervention and the control group will, on average, be similar in every respect so any effect can be confidently attributed to the intervention and not to any other factor.

Randomised controlled intervention studies

The simplest form of a *randomised controlled intervention study* is to have two parallel groups one of which receives the intervention and one of which does not. A slightly more complex design is to have two groups each receiving a different intervention. Sometimes a design might have three groups, two receiving different interventions and one receiving no intervention.

A RANDOMISED CONTROLLED INTERVENTION DESIGN

Objective: To evaluate the effectiveness of cognitive therapy for post-traumatic stress disorder related to terrorism and other civil conflict in Northern Ireland.

Design: Randomised controlled trial.

Setting: Community treatment centre, Northern Ireland.

Participants: 58 consecutive clients with chronic post-traumatic stress disorder (median 5.2 years, range 3 months to 32 years) mostly resulting from multiple traumas linked to terrorism and other civil conflict.

Interventions: Immediate cognitive therapy compared with a waiting list control condition for 12 weeks followed by treatment. Treatment comprised a mean of 5.9 sessions during 12 weeks and 2.0 sessions thereafter.

Main Outcome Measures: Primary outcome measures were clients' scores for post-traumatic stress disorder (post-traumatic stress diagnostic scale) and depression (Beck Depression Inventory). The secondary outcome measure was scores for occupational and social functioning (work related disability, social disability, and family related disability) on the Sheehan Disability Scale.

Results: At 12 weeks after randomisation, immediate cognitive therapy was associated with significantly greater improvement than the waiting list control group in the symptoms of post-traumatic stress disorder (mean difference 9.6, 95% confidence interval 3.6 to 15.6), depression (mean difference 10.1, 4.8 to 15.3), and self reported occupational and social functioning (mean difference 1.3, 0.3 to 2.5). Effect sizes from before to after treatment were large: post-traumatic stress disorder 1.25, depression 1.05, and occupational and social functioning 1.17. No change was observed in the control group.

Conclusion: Cognitive therapy is an effective treatment for post-traumatic stress disorder related to terrorism and other civil conflict (Duffy et al., 2007, p. 1147).

Cluster randomised controlled intervention design

There are variants on this randomised controlled intervention design. A *cluster randomised controlled design* is where clusters rather than individuals are randomised. Thus, for example, a list of social work offices might be compiled and the offices randomly allocated as to whether they are experimental or control. The social workers in the experimental offices are then trained in the intervention while those in the control offices are not. The results are measured in terms of individual clients or families, although the randomisation was not at the level of individuals or families.

A CLUSTER RANDOMISED CONTROLLED INTERVENTION DESIGN

Background: Falls and resulting injuries are particularly common in older people living in residential care facilities, but knowledge about the prevention of falls is limited.

Objective: To investigate whether a multidimensional intervention program would reduce falls and fall-related injuries.

Design: A cluster randomised, controlled, non-blinded trial.

Setting: 9 residential care facilities located in a northern Swedish city

Clients: 439 residents 65 years of age or older.

Intervention: An 11-week multi-professional program included general and resident-specific, tailored strategies. The strategies comprised educating staff, modifying the environment, implementing exercise programs, supplying and repairing aids, reviewing drug regimes, providing free hip protectors, having post-fall problem-solving conferences and guiding staff.

Measurements: The primary outcomes were the number of residents sustaining a fall, the number of falls and the time to occurrence of the first fall. A secondary outcome was the number of injuries resulting from falls.

Results: During the 34-week follow-up period, 82 residents (44%) in the intervention program sustained a fall compared with 109 residents (56%) in the control group (risk ratio, 0.78 [95% CI, 0.64 to 0.96]). The adjusted odds ratio was 0.49 (CI, 0.37 to 0.65), and the adjusted incidence rate ratio of falls was 0.60 (CI, 0.50 to 0.73). Each of three residents in the intervention group and 12 in the control group had a femoral fracture (adjusted odds ratio, 0.23 [CI, 0.06 to 0.94]). Clustering was considered in all regression models.

Conclusion: A multi-professional and multi-dimensional prevention program targeting residents, staff, and the environment may reduce falls and femoral fractures (Jensen et al., 2002, p. 733).

The *cluster randomised controlled design* can be useful to avoid the possibility of 'contamination' between those providing the intervention and may be the only feasible experimental approach for this reason. For example, if the intervention were randomised on an individual level, those social workers being trained to deliver the new intervention might talk informally with those providing a service to those individuals in the control group. Thus those providing a service to the control group might unwittingly adopt some of the ideas or practices of the planned new intervention the researchers are trying to measure as being the essential difference between the two groups. Clarity about the essential difference in the intervention between the groups makes it possible to understand how effective the intervention is for future practice. A *cluster randomised controlled design* requires a larger sample than the standard randomised trial design because there are factors between clusters to be balanced as well as those at participant level (Everitt et al., 2001).

USING A WAITING LIST CONTROL GROUP

For the randomised controlled intervention study of the effectiveness of cognitive therapy for post-traumatic stress disorder related to terrorism and other civil conflict illustrated in a prior example (see above), a waiting list control rather than a comparison with another psychological or pharmacological treatment was chosen. To determine whether Cognitive Therapy was more effective than no treatment, at 12 weeks clients allocated to immediate Cognitive Therapy were compared with clients initially allocated to the waiting list condition. This was done because the researchers anticipated many of the clients referred to the centre would be those who had failed more commonly available psychological treatments, such as counselling or debriefing, or pharmacotherapy. A design comparing cognitive therapy with alternative treatments would have excluded such people. Also, cognitive behaviour therapy has already been shown to be superior to supportive counselling in non-terrorism related post-traumatic stress disorder. Potential clients would have been on a waiting list to receive Cognitive Therapy for longer than 12 weeks at this time, due to demand on this publicly-funded service (adapted from Duffy et al., 2007, pp. 1147–1150).

CHALLENGES FOR SOCIAL WORK

Social workers raise many challenges to designing, developing, and measuring the effectiveness of social work interventions. Some of these challenges are discussed below as follows:

1. Defining the intervention (intervention fidelity)
2. Defining outcome measures
3. Principles of internal and external validity
4. Eliminating confounding factors
5. Ethical issues
6. Refinements to intervention research in light of risk, protective, and mediating factors.
7. Reconciling 'contradictory' evidence: the hierarchy of evidence

Defining the intervention (intervention fidelity)

There is an immediate challenge to intervention research in social work where practice is eclectic, that is, diverse models – and forms of knowledge – are used to inform practice in particular situations as seems most helpful at the time. The needs and context of the individual may require a range of interventions, for example, compulsory child protection activity on behalf of society combined with family support as the social worker attempts to help a family function more effectively (see Chapters 32 and 39). Often little value is placed on using a pure or proven form of intervention. Several systematic reviews (see www.cochrane.org) attest many of the interventions used in social work practice. Included among those used by social workers are family therapy models (e.g., Bjornstad & Montgomery, 2005); counselling models, including cognitive behavioural therapy (e.g. Macdonald et al., 2006); marital therapy for depression (Barbato & D'Avanzo, 2006); psychosocial treatments for deliberate self-harm (Hawton et al., 1999); parenting-training programs (Coren & Barlow, 2001); supported housing (e.g., Chilvers et al., 2006); kinship care (Winokur et al., 2009); supporting foster parents in managing difficult behaviour (Turner et al., 2007); cognitive stimulation, validation therapy (reality orientation) and narrative review methods (reminiscence) for people with dementia (Martin et al., 2011; Neal et al., 2003; Woods et al., 2005), and smart home technology for health and social care support (Martin et al., 2008).

PARENTING PROGRAMS

Barlow et al. (2006) synthesised the effectiveness of brief – between 6 and 30 weeks – individual or group-based parenting programs for parents with a history of abuse or at high risk of abuse with a view to preventing the (re)occurence of child maltreatment. Parenting programs were defined as standardised interventions delivered to parents with the aim of changing parenting attitudes and practices, improving parenting skills, reducing parenting stress, improving maternal psychosocial functioning, improving family dynamics, or reducing child behavioural problems. The review included parenting programs that had been modified to meet the specific needs of high-risk parents by, for example, adding components focused on anger and stress management, or that involved structured interaction with children. The findings showed insufficient evidence to support the use of parenting programs to reduce physical abuse or neglect (i.e., using objective assessments of abuse such as reports of child abuse and children on the children protection register. There is, however, limited evidence showing some parenting programs may be effective in improving some outcomes *associated* with physically abusive parenting (Barlow et al., 2006, abstract).

In order to evaluate the effectiveness of an intervention, the starting point is to specify and define the intervention under consideration. The lack of sound research on and, therefore, evidence of the effectiveness of social work interventions is due, in part, to the limited attention given to specifying and defining the model of intervention used. The challenge of defining clear treatment protocols is an aspect of social work research receiving increased attention within the realms of social intervention research (Fraser, 2004) and in service developments such as *care pathways*. This is important for intervention fidelity so realistic comparisons are possible across contexts.

Defining outcome measures

Once the intervention of interest has been clearly specified and defined, the next challenge is to decide on ways to measure the outcomes of the intervention so as to demonstrate to managers and those funding social work services – usually the general public through government taxation, or charities and their donors – its activities are worthwhile and effective. Social work goals, such as *better family functioning* where there has been abuse or discord, or *a more independent, satisfying life* for a person with disability or in older age, are not as readily measured as, for example, recovery from medical conditions or educational achievements. One approach is to use more easily measurable aspects of the life of the individual or family. An example would be school attendance in a situation where an effect of family problems has been poor attendance. Another example might be reduction in stays in a psychiatric hospital where there are mental health problems amenable to a psychosocial intervention, such as individual counselling.

OUTCOME MEASURES

Diggle *and* McConachie (2002) reviewed studies of parent-mediated early intervention for young children with autism spectrum disorder. The outcomes they measured included: child's progress with language; child's positive behavioural change; parents' interaction style; parental confidence; and reduction in levels of parental stress.

One approach to outcome measurement in intervention research is to use standardised psychometric scales measuring a particular attribute or behaviour, such as knowledge, ability, personality, motivation, attitudes, and social functioning. Examples of well-known standardised scales widely used in social work research and practice include the Beck Depression Inventory (BDI), the General Health Questionnaire (GHQ), and the Mini-Mental State Examination (MMSE).

There has been steady development of *quality of life measures* to evaluate the general social well-being of individuals and communities. Quality of life measures include objective dimensions, such as physical and mental health, symptoms of the 'problem' or 'issue' bringing the person to the attention of a social worker, ability to function in terms of daily living, including employment, education, and housing. Quality of life measures may include more subjective dimensions focusing on the individual's sense of well-being or life satisfaction. This may include their sense of satisfaction with the domains of work and social engagement as well as overall measures of social well-being. Quality of life tools increasingly embody clients' subjective perceptions of their well-being. Generally, however, subjective perceptions of success – the perception of clients or helpers – might not necessarily mean specified outcomes have, indeed, been achieved. Emotional factors and relationships can skew perceptions, particularly at vulnerable moments of crisis, being helped and helping. Hence objective measures, such as standardised psychometric scales, are also needed in intervention research.

USING A PSYCHOMETRIC OUTCOME MEASURE

Lee et al. (2010) developed the Satisfaction With Life (SWL) scale – a brief, easily completed, freestanding scale – addressing important domains related to subjective quality of life of people with severe and persistent mental illness. This 18-item self-report scale asks questions regarding current perception of satisfaction on four domains: living situation; work; social relationships; and self and present life. Each item has a Likert 5-point scale from 0 = not at all to 4 = a great deal. The SWL scale takes 5–10 minutes to administer.

In intervention research, outcome measures define the threshold at which *success* will be deemed to have occurred. The development and testing of psychometric scales is a key contributory element to intervention research and is underdeveloped in social work (see Miller et al., 2010). Nevertheless, research has been undertaken relating specifically to social care outcomes in relation to child care (Knapp, 2006; Sleed et al., 2006), mental health (Chambers et al., 2009; Chisholm & Knapp, 2006), disability (Felce et al., 2008; Mansell et al., 2007), and older adults (Comas-Herrera et al., 2007; Knapp, 2007; Smith et al., 2007). There are useful studies of health and social care benefits and costs (Beecham et al., 2010) and cost-benefit analyses of psychosocial interventions generally (Layard et al., 2007).

Because of the challenges in defining meaningful and useful outcome measures, sometimes proxy measures are used instead. These are common, where more readily measurable outcomes of interventions are used instead of the eventual outcome desired, as in evaluative research (see Chapter 28). It is tempting for governments, funders, and organisations to use service outputs as a measure instead of harder-to-measure outcomes. For example, organisations have been known to set the number of children on the child protection register as a target. But does a reduction in the number of children on the child protection register represent less rigorous activity in registering abuse, more effective social work in helping dysfunctional families, or more efficient (or premature) de-registration? Such service output measures have inherent weaknesses and care needs to be exercised to differentiate between outcome measures for clients, proxy outcomes achieved by a service, the outputs (or productivity) of the service, and the effectiveness of interventions.

PROXY OUTCOME MEASURES

In a community-based scheme to help young adults with disabilities to gain employment, the measures used to evaluate effectiveness included:

- Number gaining paid employment – both full-time and part-time (true outcome measure)
- Number gaining voluntary employment *or* entering an education or training scheme
- Number of qualifications gained (proxy outcome measures).
- Number of work experience placements undertaken in relation to the number of participants on the scheme (scheme output measures).

The number gaining paid employment was low, and it gave a more useful profile of the effectiveness of community-based interventions (such as personal assistants for young adults with physical disability, coaching for young adults with mental health problems, relevant short courses, and supervised work placements) to use a range of proxy outcome measures in addition (Taylor et al., 2004).

Internal and external validity

Validity has no single agreed definition but generally refers to the extent to which a study corresponds to the truth or actual situation. *Internal validity* and *external validity* are important in intervention research. *Internal validity* is the extent to which the research is really measuring what the researcher claims it is measuring. In other words, it is concerned with the extent to which the design is a good test of the hypothesis under consideration, and alternative causal explanations are excluded. In terms of intervention research, this means a study with good internal validity evokes confidence in that the outcomes being measured are attributable to the intervention of interest. *External validity* refers to the extent to which the findings of a study can be generalised to other settings or from a laboratory to natural settings. In terms of intervention research, a key challenge for external validity lies in the number of *realistic* factors when viewed from the perspective of other settings in which the intervention might be carried out. Limited or controlled factors, perhaps to improve *internal validity,* might simultaneously reduce *external validity*. In trials to test the effectiveness of pharmaceutical interventions it is common to reduce confounding factors, for example by having participants resident in a controlled environment, so as to improve *internal validity* and thereby have good evidence as to the effectiveness of the intervention. The inherent weakness of this design is *external validity* is likely to be reduced because, for example, the treatment might be less effective in the *real world* of poverty, multiple pressures, or a challenging treatment regime, for example. Conversely, intervention studies deeply rooted in the *real world* may gain credibility in terms of *external validity* but be weak in the *internal validity* required to demonstrate the outcomes were caused by the intervention being studied (see Chapter 28).

In terms of rigour, one source of possible error is if participants drop out of receiving the intervention. Some might begin in one group and end up in the other, particularly if they drop out of the intervention group, and the control group is defined as those receiving no service. In analysing data, the most rigorous studies handle this in terms of *intention to treat* where data on participants is included in the group to which they were originally allocated. This provides a more rigorous test of the effectiveness of the intervention.

Eliminating confounding factors

Having defined the intervention, the outcomes to be measured, and the outcome measures to be used, the next major challenge is how to eliminate confounding factors. How does one know the effect being measured is attributable to the planned intervention and not to unrelated lifestyle choices or other events in the life of the individual, family, group, or local community? The quality of a research design is often determined by the way in which it eliminates confounding factors so as to be sure improvements result from the intervention rather than other surrounding factors.

Masking of participants to avoid bias

What has not been addressed thus far is the possibility of the participants, or the social workers providing the intervention, skewing the results through their actions either unwittingly or through bias. The researcher must be confident clients receiving help and those providing help have not confounded the results of the study through attempts to make the intervention being studied appear more or less successful than it really was. In principle this could be addressed by *blinding* or *masking* the participants to which intervention they were receiving. In medicinal trials this might be done by giving both the intervention and control groups identical-looking tablets, although only those tablets given to the intervention group would contain the active ingredient under study.

For social work interventions, the *masking* of participants is a particularly problematic aspect of achieving robust evidence of the effectiveness of interventions. If families have any experience of services they will know the difference between a novel family group conferencing approach and the way the social worker has previously handled this type of situation. Therapeutic psychosocial interventions, such as varieties of counselling and group work, are influenced by client motivation and, as an ethical principle, social workers normally explain the proposed intervention to prospective clients.

Ethical challenges in using randomised controlled intervention designs

To know about the effectiveness of social work interventions, the rationale for using some type of *randomised controlled intervention design*, as outlined above, is overwhelming, other aspects of quality being equal. With rigorous intervention research, it is possible to gain sound evidence of the effectiveness of interventions so social workers are not wasting time and resources of clients, organisations, the profession, and society with activities unlikely to be productive. There are a number of ethical issues to be addressed in relation to using experimental studies in social work. Research ethics committees now consider poor science to be poor ethics. In other words, a design inefficient for its purposes is unethical since it would impose an inappropriate burden on participants in relation to the expected value to be derived from it, in addition to the ethical issues in the proper use of resources by the funding body.

One ethical issue is respecting the choices of participants. Generally speaking, clients allocated to the intervention group can, of course, refuse to participate, and would revert to receiving either no service or the normal service. Where there are safeguarding concerns there may be legal or procedural issues in setting up such a study if the new intervention were an alternative to some statutory system, such as holding a case conference.

There are ethical issues to consider in deliberately depriving the control group of an intervention in order to carry out a study. This might be addressed by the profession deciding whether or not sufficient is known about an intervention to regard is as being effective. If the proposed intervention were regarded as not known to be effective, then social workers would not be deliberately depriving the control group as they would not yet know whether or not it was effective. There is also an argument that the study could be justified in terms of the welfare of future clients, who would thereby be offered a more knowledgeable and effective service.

Another common approach to this ethical issue of depriving people of an intervention is to use *waiting list controls* (see example above). If people were on a waiting list for a service then they might be picked at random to receive the service more quickly, while those not picked would be regarded as the control group who would receive the same service in due time. In this case none would be disadvantaged by the study taking place by comparison with the service that they would have received, although some might be advantaged. Another approach to this ethical issue is that the control group receives the normal intervention, as opposed to the traditional *no intervention*. This standard is now being introduced in medical trials, and is viewed generally as more acceptable in terms of social work ethics. It should be noted, however, with this approach the new intervention needs to be sufficiently more effective than normal practice to demonstrate a significant effect. This presents even more challenge to social work in terms of outcome measures fine enough to differentiate between the levels of outcome.

Studying mediating factors in interventions

As mentioned at the outset, social work is replete with studies attempting to understand or explain social problems. Many of these studies are cross-sectional surveys which can provide correlations between social problems and socio-demographic factors. Thus we know parental self-esteem and locus of control, the child having a disability, poverty, and housing are *risk factors* for child abuse (Taylor, 2010). Some risk factors are described as *static*, that is, they are regarded as not amenable to intervention, such as the child having a disability in relation to child abuse. Other risk factors are described as *dynamic*, meaning they might be amenable to intervention, such as parental self-esteem. Such *dynamic risk factors* are the focus for social work interventions, and thus for experimental studies of effectiveness as described above. Longitudinal studies, as mentioned in some of the visionary complex models for intervention research, are well suited to identifying such causal factors of social problems.

There is increasing interest in *protective factors*, which might be viewed as a complement to risk factors. For example, having one caring, trusted adult has been found to be a major factor in the resilience of children with disrupted lives in a recent guide for professional practice based on a systematic review (Bostock, 2004). This could be described as a *protective factor*. This developing aspect of social work research might be viewed as within the general interest in a *strengths approach* to practice which seeks to reduce the pathologising of need by giving attention also to client and family strengths as a key aspect of surviving the present crisis and then thriving in future life challenges.

Risk and protective factors can be considered within experimental studies of the effectiveness of interventions. If the sample size were large enough, then a *sub-set analysis* could be conducted so as to differentiate between the effectiveness of the intervention on one sub-group as opposed to another. For example, an experimental study of the effectiveness of a mental health intervention might have a large-enough sample to be able to draw different conclusions depending on the age or gender of participants.

A SUB-GROUP ANALYSIS

Hunot et al. (2007) undertook a systematic review of psychosocial interventions for generalised anxiety disorder, including a meta-analysis of 22 studies. From the data, it was possible to examine the effects on adults in general compared with those over 65 years, whether clients received less or more than eight sessions, and whether it was a group or individual form of the intervention.

A particular aspect of individual risk and protective factors of interest to experimental studies of effectiveness is to consider what factors mediate (or influence) the effectiveness of the intervention. Sometimes such *mediating factors* are psychological constructs derived from particular practice theories supporting interventions, such as *the therapeutic alliance* in some counselling models, *attachment theory* in interventions with families, or *group cohesion* in relation to a group work intervention. Such mediating factors are of particular interest to intervention research and the profession because understanding them can help to develop practice theory underpinning interventions, and hence improve teaching of practice. Knowledge of which factors enhance or mitigate the intervention can usefully inform the way in which the intervention is carried out.

MEDIATING FACTORS

Acceptance and commitment therapy (ACT) has a small but growing database of support. One hundred and one heterogeneous outpatients reporting moderate to severe levels of anxiety or depression were randomly assigned to traditional cognitive therapy (CT) or to ACT. To maximise external validity, the authors used very minimal exclusion criteria. Participants receiving CT and ACT showed large, equivalent improvements in depression, anxiety, functioning difficulties, quality of life, life satisfaction, and clinician-rated functioning. Whereas improvements were equivalent across the two groups, the mechanisms of action appeared to differ. Changes in 'observing' and 'describing' one's experiences appeared to mediate outcomes for the CT group relative to the ACT group, whereas 'experiential avoidance,' 'acting with awareness,' and 'acceptance' mediated outcomes for the ACT group. Overall, the results suggest ACT is a viable and disseminable treatment, the effectiveness of which appears equivalent to that of CT, even as its mechanisms appear to be distinct (Forman et al., 2007, abstract).

The hierarchy of evidence for design of studies of effectiveness

There is increasingly widespread recognition of a *hierarchy of evidence* (Centre for Reviews and Dissemination, 2009) which rank orders the quality of research design of studies to measure the effectiveness of interventions. However, this widely-known and accepted hierarchy does not address the quality of data collection tools or similar factors that may undermine the rigour of a robust study in design terms. The *hierarchy of evidence* does not purport to address quality issues in relation to other research questions for which other research designs may be more appropriate. This hierarchy is the subject of debate within the profession although it is widely accepted among researchers as a scheme to rank order the robustness of the design of studies of effectiveness of planned interventions (Guyatt et al., 2008; Petticrew & Roberts, 2006) (see Chapter 26). It might be helpful to debate whether a new name could be found to more accurately reflect its purpose. This might more readily allow for wider recognition of possible other hierarchies, such as clarifying the strengths and weaknesses in particular contexts of data collection tools and qualitative studies (Taylor et al., 2007) (see Chapters 29 and 31).

HIERARCHY OF STUDY DESIGNS TO ASSESS THE EFFECTS OF INTERVENTIONS

Randomised controlled trials: The simplest form of RCT is known as the parallel group trial which randomises eligible participants to two or more groups, treats according to assignment, and compares the groups with respect to outcomes of interest. Participants are allocated to groups using both randomisation (allocation involves the play of chance) and concealment (ensures that the intervention to be allocated cannot be known in advance). There are different types of randomised study designs, such as:

Randomised cross-over trials: Where all participants receive all the interventions, for example, in a two-arm, cross-over trial one group receives intervention A before intervention B, and the other group receives intervention B before intervention A, i.e., the sequence of interventions is randomised.

Cluster randomised trials: A cluster randomised trial is a trial where clusters of people rather than single individuals are randomised to different interventions. For example, whole clinics or geographical locations may be randomised to receive particular interventions, rather than individuals.

Quasi-experimental studies: The main distinction between randomised and quasi-experimental studies is the way in which participants are allocated to the intervention and control groups. Quasi-experimental studies do not use random assignment to create the comparison groups.

Non-randomised controlled studies: Individuals are allocated to a concurrent comparison group, using methods other than randomisation. The lack of concealed randomised allocation increases the risk of selection bias.

Before-and-after study: Comparison of outcomes in study participants before and after the introduction of an intervention. The before-and-after comparisons may be in the same sample of participants or in different samples.

Interrupted time series: Interrupted time series designs are multiple 'interrupted' – usually by an intervention or treatment – observations over time.

Observational studies: A study in which natural variation in interventions or exposure among participants (i.e., not allocated by an investigator) is investigated to explore the effect of the interventions or exposure on health outcomes.

Cohort study: A defined group of participants is followed over time and comparison is made between those who did and did not receive an intervention.

Case-control study: Groups from the same population with (cases) and without (controls) a specific outcome of interest, are compared to evaluate the association between exposure to an intervention and the outcome.

Case series: Description of a number of cases of an intervention and the outcome (without comparison with a control group). These are not comparative studies (Centre for Reviews and Dissemination, 2009, p. 11, Box 1.3, edited).

CONCLUSION

Social care interventions are complex, as are the environments in which they are implemented. Social intervention research is centrally concerned with the design and development of interventions that work. Hence evaluating the effectiveness of the intervention under development is a pivotal stage in the social intervention research process leading to changes and improvements in interventions for practice. Equally important is the ability to specify the intervention and to design intervention protocols to ensure the same procedures are followed to make for cross-study comparisons. Hence intervention fidelity is an important aspect of social intervention research. As outlined in this chapter, social workers have raised many challenges for social intervention research and may confuse it with evaluation research (see Chapter 28). These challenges include defining the intervention and intervention protocols, specifying meaningful outcome measures, implementing robust research designs with internal and external validity to eliminate confounding factors, and maintaining intervention fidelity since social workers tend to tailor interventions to fit the context.

Progress in intervention research has produced a growing number of randomised controlled intervention studies on which social workers draw, as well as systematic reviews of interventions with proven effectiveness. Morally and legally, social workers are required to use the best-available evidence to inform their decision making regarding which interventions best fit client values, preferences, and needs (see Chapter 26). The lack of rigorous randomised experimental studies in social work might be due, in part, to their costs but also they require advanced research expertise and large research teams, and the use of control groups might not be possible for legal or ethical reasons. Hence the challenge for social work researchers to create robust research designs is likely to persist given the realities of practice, resource constraints, professional ethics, legal regulations, and research scepticism among practitioners. Nevertheless, intervention research has provided a new perspective on the integration of a range of research designs and knowledge transfer approaches. Intervention research in related health and behavioural science disciplines is generating a wealth of data on effective interventions for social work to draw upon. Perhaps the main challenge facing the profession is to achieve more widespread involvement in these research initiatives as one dimension of developing higher level skills through post-qualifying studies (Taylor et al., 2010). It is only by basing their practice on robust evidence social workers can be confident they are being as effective as possible in the ways they decide to offer help to people and in how they put forward their argument to governments, charities, and other funders as to the value of their service to individuals, families, groups, and communities in every country and culture.

REFERENCES

Barbato, A., & D'Avanzo, B.B.D. (2006). Marital therapy for depression. Cochrane Database of Systematic Reviews 2006, Issue 2. Art. No.: CD004188. DOI: 10.1002/14651858.CD004188.pub2

Barlow, J., Johnston, I., Kendrick, D., Polnay, L., & Stewart-Brown, S. (2006). Individual and group-based parenting programmes for the treatment of physical child abuse and neglect. Cochrane Database of Systematic Reviews 2006, Issue 3. Art. No.: CD005463.

Beecham, J., Perkins, M., Snell, T., & Knapp, M. (2010). Health and social care costs for young adults with epilepsy. *Health and Social Care in the Community*, *18*(5), 465–473.

Bjornstad, G.J., & Montgomery, P. (2005). Family therapy for attention-deficit disorder or attention-deficit/hyperactivity disorder in children and adolescents. Cochrane Database of Systematic Reviews 2005, Issue 2. Art. No.: CD005042. DOI: 10.1002/14651858.CD005042.pub2

Bloom, M., Fischer, J., & Orme, J. (2003). *Evaluating practice: Guidelines for the accountable professional*. Boston: Allyn and Bacon.

Bostock, L. (2004). *SCIE Guide 6: Promoting resilience in fostered children and young people*. London: Social Care Institute for Excellence.

Centre for Reviews and Dissemination (2009). *Systematic Reviews: CRD's Guidance for Undertaking Reviews in Health Care*. York: University of York. Retrieved September 26, 2010 from http://www.york.ac.uk/inst/crd/systematic_reviews_book.htm

Chambers, J., Yiend, J., Barrett, B., Burns, T., Doll, H., Fazel, S., Jenkinson, C., Kaur, A., Knapp, M., Plugge, E., Sutton, L., & Fitzpatrick, R. (2009). Outcome measures used in forensic mental health research: A structured review. *Criminal Behaviour and Mental Health*, *19*, 9–27.

Chilvers, R., Macdonald, G., & Hayes, A. (2006). Supported housing for people with severe mental disorders. Cochrane Database of Systematic Reviews 2006, Issue 4. Art. No.: CD000453. DOI: 10.1002/14651858.CD000453.pub2

Chisholm, D., & Knapp, M. (2006). Client Sociodemographic and Service Receipt Inventory: European version. In G. Thornicroft, Becker, T., Knapp, M., Knudsen, H.C., Schene, A., Tansella, M., & Vasquez-Barquero, J.L. (eds), *International outcome measures in mental health: Quality of life, needs, service satisfaction, costs and impact on carers*. London: Gaskell, pp. 85–91.

Comas-Herrera, A., Wittenberg, R., Pickard, L., & Knapp, M. (2007). Cognitive impairment in older people: Future demand for long-term care services and the associated costs. *International Journal of Geriatric Psychiatry*, *22*, 1037–1045.

Coren, E., & Barlow, J. (2001). Individual and group-based parenting programmes for improving psychosocial outcomes for teenage parents and their children. Cochrane Database of Systematic Reviews 2001, Issue 3. Art. No.: CD002964. DOI: 10.1002/14651858.CD002964

Craig, P., Dieppe, P., Macintyre, S., Michie, S. Nazareth, I., & Petticrew, M. (2008). Developing and evaluating complex interventions: the new Medical Research Council guidance. *British Medical Journal*, *337*, 694–696. a1655. Retrieved December 10, 2010 from http://www.bmj.com/content/337/bmj.a1655.full

Darragh, E., & Taylor, B.J. (2008). Research and reflective practice. In P. Higham (ed.), *Post qualifying social work practice*. London: Sage.

Davidoff, F., Batalden, P., Stevens, D., OGrinc, G., & Mooney, S. (2008). Publication guidelines for quality improvement in health care. *Quality & Safety in Health Care*, *17*(Supplement 1), i3–i9.

Diggle, T.T.J., & McConachie, H.H.R. (2002). Parent-mediated early intervention for young children with autism spectrum disorder. Cochrane Database of Systematic Reviews 2002, Issue 2. Art. No.: CD003496.

Duffy, M., Gillespie, K., & Clark, D.M. (2007). Post-traumatic stress disorder in the context of terrorism and other civil conflict in Northern Ireland: randomised controlled trial. *British Medical Journal*, *334*(7604), 1147–1150.

Everitt, B.S., Landau, S., & Morven, L. (2001). *Cluster analysis* (4th ed.). New York: Oxford University Press.

Fawcett, S.B., Paine, A.L., Francisco, V.T., & Vliet, M. (1995). Promoting Health through Community Development. In D. Glenwick & Jason, L.A. (eds), *Promoting health and mental health: Behavioural approaches to prevention*. New York: Haworth Press.

Felce, D., Perry, J., Romeo, R., Robertson, J., Meek, A., Emerson, E., & Knapp, M. (2008). Outcomes and costs of community living: Semi-independent living and fully staffed group homes. *American Journal of Mental Retardation*, *113*, 87–101.

Fischer, J. (1973). Is social work effective? A review. *Social Work*, *18*, 5–20.

Forman, E.M., Herbert, J.D., Moitra, E., Yeomans, P.D., & Geller, P.A. (2007). A randomized controlled effectiveness trial of acceptance and commitment therapy and cognitive therapy for anxiety and depression. *Behavior Modification*, *31*(6), 772–790.

Fraser, M.W. (2004). Intervention research in social work: Recent advances and continuing challenges. *Research on Social Work Practice*, *14*, 210–222.

Fraser, M.W., Richman, J.M., Galinsky, M.J., & Day, S.H. (2009). *Intervention research: Developing social programs*. New York: Oxford University Press.

Hawton, K.K.E., Townsend, E., Arensman, E., Gunnell, D., Hazell, P., House, A., & van Heeringen, K. (1999). Psychosocial and pharmacological treatments for deliberate self harm. Cochrane Database of Systematic Reviews 1999, Issue 3. Art. No.: CD001764. DOI: 10.1002/14651858.CD001764.

Hunot, V., Churchill, R., Teixeira, V. & Silva de Lima, M. (2007). Psychological therapies for generalised anxiety disorder. Cochrane Database of Systematic Reviews 2007, Issue 1. Art. No.: CD001848. DOI: 10.1002/14651858.CD001848.pub4

International Federation of Social Workers (2000). *Definitions of Social Work*. Adopted by the IFSW General Meeting in Montréal, Canada. Retrieved September 26, 2010 from www.ifsw.org/en/p38000208.html

Jensen, J., Lundin-Olsson, L., Nyberg, L., & Gustafson, Y. (2002). Fall and injury prevention in older people living in residential care facilities: A cluster randomized trial. *Annals of Internal Medicine*, *136*(10), 733–741.

Khoury-Kassabri, M., Sharvet, R., Baver, E., & Livneh, C. (2010). An evaluation of a group treatment program with youth referred to the juvenile probation service because of violent crime. *Research on Social Work Practice*, *20*(4), 403–409.

Knapp, M. (2006). The economics of group care practice: a reappraisal. *Child and Youth Services*, *28*, 259–284.

Knapp, M. (2007). Why do we spend so much on health care when social care is the real challenge of an ageing population? *Journal of Health Services Research and Policy*, *12*(3), 192.

Layard, R., Clark, D., Knapp, M., & Mayraz, G. (2007). Cost-benefit analysis of psychological therapy. *National Institute Economic Review, 202*, 90–98.

Lee, K.K., Brekke, J.S., Yamada, A.M., & Chou, C.P. (2010). Longitudinal invariance of the satisfaction with life scale for individuals with schizophrenia. *Research on Social Work Practice, 20*(2), 234–241.

Macdonald, G., Higgins, J.P.T., & Ramchandani, P. (2006). Cognitive-behavioural interventions for children who have been sexually abused. Cochrane Database of Systematic Reviews 2006, Issue 4. Art. No.: CD001930. DOI: 10.1002/14651858.CD001930.pub2

McCrystal, P., Percy, A., & Higgins, K. (2007). Substance use behaviors of young people with a moderate learning disability: A longitudinal analysis. *The American Journal of Drug and Alcohol Abuse, 33*(1), 155–161.

Mansell, J., Knapp, M., Beadle-Brown, J., & Beecham, J. (2007). *Deinstitutionalisation and community living: Outcomes and costs*. Report of a European Study (volume 1). Executive Summary. University of Kent, Canterbury: Tizard Centre.

Martin, M., Clare, L., Altgassen, A.M., Cameron, M.H., & Zehnder, F. (2011). Cognition-based interventions for healthy older people and people with mild cognitive impairment. Cochrane Database of Systematic Reviews 2011, Issue 1. Art. No.: CD006220. DOI: 10.1002/14651858.CD006220.pub2

Martin, S., Kelly, G., Kernohan, W.G., McCreight, B. & Nugent, C. (2008). Smart home technologies for health and social care support. Cochrane Database of Systematic Reviews 2008, Issue 4. Art. No.: CD006412. DOI: 10.1002/14651858.CD006412.pub2

Miller, L.A., McIntire, S.A., & Lovler, R.L. (2010). *Foundations of psychological testing: A practical approach* (3rd ed.). London: Sage.

Neal, M., & Barton Wright, P. (2003). Validation therapy for dementia. Cochrane Database of Systematic Reviews 2003, Issue 3. Art. No.: CD001394. DOI: 10.1002/14651858.CD001394

Newsome, W.S. (2010). Solution-focused brief therapy groupwork with at-risk junior high school students: Enhancing the bottom line. *Research on Social Work Practice, 14*(5), 336–343.

Petticrew, M., & Roberts, H. (2006). *Systematic reviews in the social sciences: A practical guide*. Oxford: Blackwell.

Rothman, J., & Thomas, E.J. (1994). *Intervention research: Design and development for human science*. New York: Haworth Press.

Schilling, R.F. (1997). Developing intervention research programs in social work. *Social Work Research, 21*(3), 173–180.

Sleed, M., Beecham, J., Knapp, M., McCauley, C., & McCurry, N. (2006). Assessing services, supports and costs for young families under stress. *Child: Care, Health and Development, 32*, 101–110.

Smith, S., Lamping, D., Banerjee, S., Harwood, R., Foley, B., Smith, P., Cook, J., Murray, J., Prince, M., Levin, E., Mann, A., & Knapp, M. (2007). Development of a new measure of health-related quality of life for people with dementia: DEMQOL. *Psychological Medicine, 37*, 737–746.

Taylor, B.J. (2006). Factorial surveys: Using vignettes to study professional judgement. *British Journal of Social Work, 36*(7), 1187–1207.

Taylor, B.J. (2010). *Professional decision making in social work*. Exeter: Learning Matters Post Qualifying Social Work Series.

Taylor, B.J., McGilloway, S., & Donnelly, M. (2004). Preparing young adults with disability for employment. *Health & Social Care in the Community, 12*(2), 93–101.

Taylor, B.J., Dempster, M., & Donnelly, M. (2007). Grading gems: Appraising the quality of research for social work and social care. *British Journal of Social Work, 37*(2), 335–354.

Taylor, B.J., Mullineux, J.C., & Fleming, G. (2010). Partnership, service needs and assessing competence in post qualifying education and training. *Social Work Education: The International Journal*, 29(5), 475–489.

Turner, W., Macdonald, G., & Dennis, J.A. (2007). Behavioural and cognitive behavioural training interventions for assisting foster carers in the management of difficult behaviour. Cochrane Database of Systematic Reviews 2007, Issue 1. Art. No.: CD003760. DOI: 10.1002/14651858.CD003760.pub3

Winokur, M., Holtan, A., & Valentine, D. (2009). Kinship care for the safety, permanency, and well-being of children removed from the home for maltreatment. Cochrane Database of Systematic Reviews 2009, Issue 1. Art. No.: CD006546. DOI: 10.1002/14651858.CD006546.pub2

Woods, B., Spector, A.E., Jones, C.A., Orrell, M. & Davies, S.P. (2005). Reminiscence therapy for dementia. Cochrane Database of Systematic Reviews 2005, Issue 2. Art. No.: CD001120. DOI: 10.1002/14651858.CD001120.pub2

28

Evaluation Research

Donald Forrester

Evaluation research is distinctively concerned with 'what works' in policy and practice intervention. Evaluation is literally the process of discovering the value of something. For social work, it is the attempt to use research to discover whether the activities of social workers achieve their intended goals. This purposeful endeavour can be aimed at anything from large-scale evaluation of services or programmes to an individual worker using research methods to try to find out whether a piece of work they have done has made a difference for a specific client. Given this range of uses, evaluation research is defined, not by any specific methodology, but by a focus on understanding what difference social work makes. Rather than attempting to describe evaluation methods or techniques covered excellently in a number of other places (see, for instance, Robson, 2002; Seale, 1999), this chapter focuses on key issues within evaluation as a social work research activity. In particular, it attempts to outline a characteristically and distinctively social work approach to evaluation. It does this by considering two particular dilemmas within evaluative research. The first can be framed in a number of ways, but is characterised in this chapter as the tension between the advantages of closeness to practice – and a consequent understanding of the context of that which is evaluated – on the one hand, and the need to avoid bias and strive for more objective measures of 'outcome' on the other. On its own, either focus has limitations as a form of evaluative research and, it is argued, research on what works in social work needs to embrace both approaches. This is characteristic of good evaluative research in social work. The second dilemma is the complexity of deciding what a valid outcome is and the ramifications of this for social work research. Some believe that social work evaluation typically is more complex than most types of research on what works, particularly because social work involves multiple interests with different views on the purposes of the service and, therefore, the standards it should be measured against (Butler & Pugh, 2004; Humphries, 2003). Hence, excellent evaluative research in social work embraces this complexity. The chapter concludes with some examples of evaluative social work research involving these distinctive and characteristic approaches from social work's past and proposes directions to develop evaluative research building on a lost tradition by combining attempts to reduce bias, consider context, and address the multiple interests and viewpoints characterising social work research.

EVALUATION RESEARCH: ISSUES OF CONTEXT AND SCIENCE

For ease of discussion, this section considers a rather simplistic antithesis between context-specific research and scientific approaches aimed at creating generalisable knowledge. This is not intended to be an accurate depiction of the field of evaluation research as there are, of course, myriad approaches, with many subtle variations and fine distinctions between them. Rather, it is hoped that exploring elements of approaches at opposing ends of the spectrum of evaluation research will allow an argument for a combination of the best elements of objective and context-specific approaches.

Evaluation has often been argued to be a distinct approach to researching what works. For instance, in the USA, the American Evaluation Society is a professional membership organisation for 'evaluators', and similar organisations can be found in Canada, the UK, Africa, and other locations (see links at the end of the chapter). These societies characterise evaluation as a professional discipline and seek to support those carrying out evaluations to use the most rigorous methods but, in contrast to 'pure' research, understanding fully the context for the intervention being researched is considered crucial. Thus, one of the key principles of evaluative practice is that 'evaluators should seek a comprehensive understanding of the important contextual elements of the evaluation' (American Evaluation Association, 2010). This focus on context has been clearly articulated by Pawson and Tilley (1997) in the development of 'realist evaluation'. They argue that outcomes are a product of an interaction between the specific mechanism of an intervention (what it is and how it may work) and the context in which it is delivered (which can be understood broadly as all aspects of the context for a service, including location, timing, client group, and other relevant factors). As the interaction between these will always be dependent on the specifics of a situation, they are deeply sceptical about attempts to develop generalisable knowledge about interventions. Evaluations identify what works in a specific situation, rather than general rules about what 'works'.

An illuminating example provided by Pawson and Tilley (1997) relates to the use of closed-circuit television (CCTV) in car parks to deter car crime and the many mechanisms by which one might believe CCTV would reduce car crime. These include, for instance, deterring crime, catching and imprisoning key offenders, reminding those who park cars of the risks by their presence, and so on. There are also a variety of contexts in which car parks may be situated, including shopping centres, leisure centres, times or areas of relative prosperity or poverty, societies where cars are widespread or rare, and so on. Given this complexity, Pawson and Tilley (1997) argue it is not possible to draw general conclusions about whether CCTV 'works' in reducing crime. Rather it is possible to understand different types of situations, identify patterns of impact, and begin to relate elements of context and mechanism influencing outcomes. Or, to put it another way, they are arguing for a move away from looking at 'what works' to a focus on 'what works for whom, in what circumstances, in what respects and how' (Pawson et al., 2005, p. 22).

At this broad level, there is little that is contentious about the realist approach of Pawson et al. (2005). However, one of the conclusions arising from their argument is that they consider some of the methods valued by the more scientific tradition within the social sciences to be of limited validity. In particular, they are highly critical of the usefulness of randomised controlled trials (RCTs) and other attempts to develop generalisable knowledge related to RCTs, such as conventional systematic review methodologies (see Pawson et al., 2005; see Chapter 31).

An RCT is a methodology familiar to most readers, but one should not assume such knowledge. The author debated the pros and cons of RCTs for three years with a leading academic of a qualitative inclination before discovering she did not actually know what an RCT was. The methodology for RCTs is one of the greatest intellectual achievements of the 20th century. It has allowed the development of much of modern medicine and it is likely to remain a key way of finding out what works indefinitely. This is, in part, because RCTs are characterised by an elegant simplicity. They aim to answer one question – whether the thing being studied makes a difference – by excluding all other potential explanations. The simplest example of an RCT would be a pill, let us say aimed at reducing headaches. An RCT takes a group of people and randomly chooses half to receive the pill and half to receive an identical pill with no medicinal value (a placebo). As the membership of each group is entirely random and the members do not know what they are being given, the only difference between the groups should be related to whether they received the pill. As a result, provided the sample is large enough to avoid chance differences, any difference between the groups in the number of headaches (or potential side effects) can be attributed to the pill. (It is also usually desirable to check there are no chance differences between the groups.) If there is no difference, then it suggests the pill does not work or, conversely, a reduction in headaches can be attributed to the pill.

The importance of randomisation lies in the range of explanations for results. Most headaches just disappear or people may take action to reduce the headache – like going to bed, having a shoulder rub, or some other potentially headache-reducing activity – and there is powerful evidence showing merely believing a pill will reduce a headache will work even when it contains no active medicinal ingredient (the placebo effect). In the world of social work, there are even more powerful conflating variables. People often come into contact with social workers at times of crisis – and following a crisis things tend to get better. Crucially, clients are not passively waiting for social work 'help'. Rather, they are, in general, actively trying to resolve the problems they have. As a result, with or without a social worker, things might get better. Conversely, social workers often work with people whose chronic difficulties, such as long-term mental illness, learning difficulties, or alcohol problems, may not change much following a social work intervention. Yet it is possible that, without the intervention, situations might have worsened. Social workers are often successfully maintaining people in the community – rather than making them 'better' (Davies, 1994) – and this would be identified by an RCT but not by simple measures of their welfare before and after social work input.

Furthermore, there are myriad forms of bias – defined as potential other explanations for an outcome – associated with evaluative research. These include the fact that those delivering a service will tend to consider that it works and report positively about it and that service users tend to report positively about services they receive (at least for services they have a choice about receiving) but this does not help differentiate the relative impact of the service. In short, there is no well-established link between the views of those who use a service and its impact. In addition, being employed to evaluate a service and working closely with those who deliver a service produces formal and informal pressures to identify the positives about a service. This can lead data collection and analysis to be biased toward a particular set of findings, such as those the funder or workers might wish to hear (see Torgerson & Torgerson, 2008). Indeed, unless evaluations are independently funded, it is relatively rare for them to conclude a service is *not* worthwhile, appreciated, and effective. One is often left wondering whether such evaluations constitute genuine research or a more complicated element of the policy-making process designed to justify funding decisions (see Butler & Pugh, 2004; Taylor & Balloch, 2005).

The major advantage of RCTs is, therefore, that they are the best method for eliminating bias: most other explanations for findings are excluded. Thus, for instance, an evaluation of a family centre which found that parents and children liked it, staff thought it was a high-quality service, referring professionals believed it worked effectively with families, and, after working with the centre, the parents tended to be less stressed and the children did better at school would create a positive picture of a family centre. However, there are myriad other potential explanations for the findings (for instance, families using the centre might be those ready to make a positive change whether they worked with the family centre or not, and their positive views of the centre might have been expressed for any service offered at that point). Randomly allocating families to the centre and to a 'normal service' and then following-up their welfare would provide a much stronger measure of the centre's impact because other explanations would be excluded. Conversely, if there were positive changes compared to a control group in an RCT, it would be possible to conclude they were a result of the centre's work.

This is not a theoretical issue. The first RCT of social work examined intensive long-term social work for teenage boys 'at risk' of delinquency and followed them up for some years. The boys and the workers talked very positively about the service, but on the key measures relating to crime, employment, and other outcomes, there was either no difference or the children receiving the intervention had done worse (see Oakley, 2000). This study was, in fact, riven with methodological limitations, but it illustrates the potential power of RCTs for correcting misperceptions about interventions and their effectiveness. More recently, in the USA, Intensive Family Preservation Services (IFPS) aimed at preventing the need for children to enter care were claimed to be highly effective because studies consistently found low proportions of children referred to the service subsequently entered care. A large RCT found not only was this true for children who had not received the intervention, but also no measurable impact of the IFPS could be identified (see Forrester et al., 2008). Task-centred approaches grew out of William Reid's research, including RCTs reporting shorter more focused work produced better outcomes than the open-ended approaches that were popular in social work (discussed further later; Reid & Shyne, 1969). The list could go on, but a key point here is that RCTs' resistance to bias means they seem far more likely to produce unexpected findings and, in particular, to challenge beliefs about what works and thus lead to the development of new and more effective approaches.

Indeed, the RCT's ability to identify evidence that a service does *not* work marks it out as a particularly important evaluative methodology. It sometimes seems the difficulty of obtaining positive results in RCTs has contributed to social work's reluctance to use the approach. Yet, social work is most likely to progress as a discipline by discarding ineffective approaches. Indeed, this is precisely the approach taken by medicine, which has become far more effective for testing and discarding approaches – from using leeches to remove blood through to recommending babies be put to sleep on their chests. One of the dispiriting aspects of modern social work is how rare it is for an approach actually to become discredited and stop being used.

At this point it may be helpful to differentiate between three different issues, namely, bias, context, and generalisability. Thus far it has been argued RCTs are an unusually robust way of excluding bias in research. However, it is now worth considering the degree to which research needs to understand context in order to be meaningful. Finally, issues around the generalisability of knowledge are reviewed. Following these discussions, the chapter moves to a broader look at a particular dilemma within social work evaluation, namely, who defines what success is.

Arguing that RCTs are an extremely good way of reducing potential bias in evaluative research does not address the central critique inherent in the evaluative tradition – and particularly in approaches such as realist evaluation – namely, whatever the findings of an RCT, the social world does not allow for generalisable knowledge. Even if an intervention works in one RCT, it may or may not work in another carried out in different circumstances (see Cartwright & Munro, 2010). This is certainly true. However, this is not a consideration confined to – or even particularly acute for – RCTs. All research tends to make generalisable claims for its truth. For instance, Goffman's (1986) study of stigma in certain groups led him to explore more general truths about the ways in which people manage their 'spoilt' identities. Even poststructuralists, such as Foucault, were trying to make more general points about the relationships between power and knowledge in exploring the construction of madness or sex (Foucault, 1978, 2001). Indeed, at the extreme level, why would anyone bother to read or write an article without some inherent or explicit claim to generalisability? If a piece of research were of no interest for any context beyond that being studied then why would anyone else be interested in it? On the other hand, much of the evidence of the most rigorous science is in fact open to questions about variability. For instance, there is increasing interest in physics in the possibility the basic laws of science may vary over time or space. Furthermore, even within the medical tradition, the impact of medicines may vary depending on context and a particular patient's conditions or behaviour. Even a medicine found to be very effective in many RCTs might not work for particular individuals or in certain contexts. The generalisable rules about effectiveness of medicines created by RCTs are, therefore, best conceived as detailed indications of general trends in relation to a medicine, rather than absolute rules. In fact, while issues of context are explored in detail later, and they are enormously important, all research – whether evaluative or not – makes claims to wider import. The complexities of these claims are well captured by Simon Singh (1997) in *Fermat's Last Theorem*:

> An astronomer, a physicist, and a mathematician were holidaying in Scotland. Looking out from a train window, they saw a black sheep in the middle of a field. 'How interesting', said the astronomer, Scottish sheep are black'. 'No, no', said the physicist, '*Some* Scottish sheep are black'. The mathematician looked at them, looked out of the window and said, 'As a mathematician, I say that in Scotland there is at least one field, containing at least one sheep, *at least one side of which is black*' (p. 134 original emphasis).

The key point is, once one strays beyond the certainties of maths and logic, then one is dependent on empirical observations and the degree to which one can make generalisable assertions based on empirical evidence is a matter of degree and judgement rather than scientific rules. In the quotation above, one might suggest the mathematician is taking a position akin to the evaluator with a focus on context. He is emphasising the potential uniqueness of each sheep (or indeed, each side of a sheep) and the need to understand it in depth. The astronomer is rather cavalierly attempting to draw a general conclusion based on a very limited sample. The physicist takes a position with which most in social work would be most comfortable: in policy and practice terms, it is akin to reviewing the research and drawing a conclusion based on the balance of the evidence. Thus, if one were establishing a service to help people with alcohol problems, one would find a lot of support for the motivational interviewing approach. This would, therefore, seem a sensible way of working on which to base the service. At the extreme, programme evaluators might suggest an evaluation produced specifically for a service and not published or used in any other way makes no claims to generalisability. However, even here there is, in general, some claim to temporal generalisability. The evaluation may attempt to identify whether a service works or what people think about it at one point, and this may be used to make decisions about management structure or funding based on the – quite reasonable – idea findings at one point in time are likely to be generalisable to the (near) future. In practice, many evaluations provide information likely to be of more general significance.

One of the important contributions of the evaluative tradition is to problematise the process of generalisability. Having considered their critique, it seems sensible to have a healthy scepticism about simplistic attempts at creating generalisable knowledge. For instance, meta-analyses of multiple RCTs are likely to conflate similar interventions in very different contexts and, unless this is taken into account within the analysis, they may not be appropriate for psychosocial interventions. The same may be true of simplistic approaches to systematic reviews. However, this should not lead to throwing the baby of generalisable knowledge out with the bathwater of a failure to consider context. Rather, it suggests a critical and rounded approach should be taken to understanding the evidence in general and, in particular, the full context of research studies.

The importance of context

The concept of context is a key theme of this chapter. Up to this point, the argument has, in broad terms, defended the potential contribution of rigorous research methods, such as RCTs and systematic reviews (SRs), by suggesting they are uniquely strong ways of reducing error and bias or eliminating other false explanations for empirical findings. It has been argued that, while there are limitations and caveats in all attempts to create generalisable knowledge, these are not specific issues for RCTs or SRs, but issues for all knowledge. These issues are best addressed through informed and thoughtful application of research evidence rather than blanket rules either for or against the generalisability of knowledge from particular sources. Hence, the chapter now turns to consider some potential limitations in RCTs as an approach and the ways in which these limitations are shaping new understandings of the experimental method. It does this by a detailed consideration of the use of RCTs to explore what works, and for whom, in relation to people with alcohol problems. In doing so, it considers a critique of RCTs from within the experimental tradition. There is an active tradition of critiques of RCTs from within social work (and related disciplines); however, in large part, these considerations are irrelevant to this discussion. For instance, RCTs have been argued to take an insufficiently critical view of the nature of the issues with which social workers deal (for instance, what is 'child abuse' or 'schizophrenia'; Humphreys, 2003; Taylor & Balloch, 2005), since they tend to involve rather individualistic interventions (for instance, at the level of the individual or the family; Butler & Pugh, 2004; Pitts, 2011) and ignore broader social causes of problems. In a nutshell, they individualise highly complex social issues and work within a broadly 'medical model' (Betts et al., 2009; Webb, 2001).

On one level, all of these criticisms are true. However, on a more profound level, they are irrelevant. This is because all of these criticisms are of the *questions* RCTs attempt to answer rather than the appropriateness of the RCT as *a method to answer them*. Thus, for instance, a long tradition of research indicates the nature of depression varies across cultures (and probably time) and depression is influenced by myriad complex social factors, including levels of poverty, gender, social isolation, and caring responsibilities. All of these are important points, and they might suggest we should not be focusing on whether cognitive behavioural therapy works for people who are depressed. On the other hand, if one wants to know how practitioners can help people referred to them who are depressed, then it is perfectly reasonable to ask what works best, and RCTs have a key part to play in answering this question. Thus, most of the criticisms of RCTs from within social work have, in fact, been criticisms of the appropriateness of the questions posed and answered by RCTs rather than the appropriateness of RCTs as a way of answering such questions. It is absolutely right for social workers to take a critical view of unhelpfully individualised questions and methodologies. Elsewhere, the author has argued that the evaluative tradition could be enriched by taking such criticisms seriously and developing more rounded, social, and critical versions of RCTs and other 'medical' methodologies (Forrester, 2010). However, this is not to say it is never appropriate to find out what helps individuals and, if one were interested in this question, RCTs have – as outlined above – an important contribution to make in providing answers.

In terms of developing a more nuanced and constructive engagement with RCTs, it is more useful to look in detail at developing criticisms of RCTs from within the experimental tradition than those posed by individuals who do not have experience of RCTs. There is currently something of a crisis of confidence within the experimental tradition generally and, in particular, a rethinking of the nature and place of experimental methods. This is particularly pronounced in the field of substance misuse intervention. A key reason for the current re-examination of the RCT approach within the substance misuse field is related to what is termed the 'Dodo Bird' effect.

The Dodo Bird effect is the finding that, often when credible therapies are compared, they have the same impact: they *all* seem to work. It is named after the Dodo in *Alice in Wonderland* who stated, 'everyone has won, so all shall have prizes'. The key issue here is that there does not seem to be much difference between therapies. Thus, in the alcohol misuse field, large-scale RCTs compared theoretically different interventions to identify not just whether a specific way of intervening worked, but what worked for whom. For instance, in the largest ever trial of psychotherapies carried out in the USA, 'Project MATCH' compared a brief four-session version of motivational interviewing, with a longer cognitive behavioural therapy intervention with a still more intensive counselling approach aimed at facilitating involvement in 12-step treatment (such as Alcoholics Anonymous; Project MATCH Research Group, 1997a, 1997b, 1998a, 1998b). The United Kingdom Alcohol Treatment Trial (UKATT) compared brief motivational interviewing for individuals with a longer intervention aimed at individuals plus their family and friend support systems [Social Behaviour Network Therapy (SBNT); Russell et al., 2005]. For both trials, all the interventions worked – but there was almost no difference in how well they worked, with whom they worked best, or other significant differences.

Why does this matter – and why has it led to a fundamental reconsideration of the place of RCTs in the substance misuse field? The Dodo Bird effect is difficult to explain within the underlying rationale for RCTs. If everything has been kept similar and there are variations in the intervention being provided, then it is hard to understand why not only were very different interventions equally effective, but beyond that, why there did not seem to be any matching between key issues (such as the seriousness of the alcohol problem) and very different interventions. Given the different theoretical frameworks, levels of intensity, and methods of working, one would have expected some important differences. The failure to find either significant differences or matching effects has led influential researchers, such as Orford (2008), to call for a fundamental re-examination of research in relation to substance use and misuse. It is worth considering these issues in greater depth before attempting to reformulate a place for RCTs within the field of evaluative research.

There can only be one explanation for the Dodo Bird effect. For some reason, there were far more similarities across conditions than differences. This may be true for a number of reasons. First, participants may have been similar. Having chosen to participate, their agreement to take part in an RCT might indicate high levels of motivation and readiness to change in any case. (It is particularly important to note most of the reduction in alcohol use occurred prior to the first therapeutic session.) Secondly, the research itself might have been a powerful intervention. In the UKATT, participants received eight hours of research interviews – compared to four hours of motivational enhancement therapy (the briefest intervention). Research interviews – with an empathic non-judgemental listener talking to participants about their drinking and the difficulties it may be causing them, and then agreeing to come back and talk about their drinking again in the future – might, in fact, be a powerful intervention in its own right. Thirdly, despite their apparent similarities, the different interventions might have had more in common than it might seem. For instance, all of them involved an empathic listener having a structured conversation focused on helping someone who had identified his or her drinking as a problem. Perhaps these similarities were more important than the apparent differences between approaches. Finally, maybe the interventions under study missed the crucial elements of the helping relationship. Perhaps the theoretical approach was less important than the human qualities of the therapist. Considerations such as these have led Orford (2008) and others to suggest a new broader approach needs to be taken to understanding alcohol problems and how to help people, where the problem of alcohol use and professional help is viewed in the contexts within which they happen. It requires a better understanding of processes of change beyond the context of treatment and encourages a focus on more qualitative or mixed method research approaches.

At this point, it is worth returning to the evaluative tradition: for these are precisely the types of consideration at the heart of 'evaluative' methods. A focus on understanding of context (including for the client, the project, and the research) addresses precisely these issues. At the heart of the arguments in this chapter is, therefore, a conviction that evaluation research in social work should combine the best of both traditions. It should strive to reduce bias and exclude other explanations, but should simultaneously attempt to understand the specific contexts within which clients, services, and research operate. There is a rich – though largely lost – tradition of such research within social work, and some examples are discussed below. However, before considering these examples, it is worth focusing on a second reason why a complex, multifaceted, and multimethod approach is particularly appropriate for social work evaluation research. This is the question of who defines what is meant by a service or intervention 'working' and 'working for whom'.

Who decides what 'works'?

One of the first questions for any evaluation is what constitutes a good outcome – how is 'works' being defined and by whom. In much traditional research, this is taken as unproblematic. For instance, if one were evaluating an intervention for drug problems, reduced drug use – however it was measured – would be assumed to be the goal. In social work, there is often less clarity about who defines the goals of an intervention and, therefore, what outcomes should be measured (Humphreys, 2003). This complexity arises from the ambivalent nature of social work itself, which is typically characterised by a need to incorporate the views of three different parties: clients or service users, society or the state, and the professional judgements of the worker. In some instances, all three of these may be in accord and in such circumstances there may be an easy agreement about what a service aims to achieve. A social worker in a substance misuse service might well be in such a situation. However, social work is more typically characterised by actual or, at least, potential disagreement about both means and ends. Indeed, to some degree, social work's role can be seen as mediating between these different views. For example, a social worker is working with a seven-year-old child who experienced serious neglect while living with her mother who misused drugs. The child may have a very strong bond and wish to return to his mother's care, and the mother may share this feeling. The social worker may believe – on the basis of her professional knowledge and experience – that a return home would not be in the best interests of the child. However, the social worker may believe the child requires intensive therapeutic work in order to help him come to terms with the neglect he has suffered, but the state (in the form of the social worker's manager) may say funding for this is not available. The manager may also argue that a serious attempt to return the child home should be made – in part to save the cost of public care and in part because society, through its laws, suggests this is necessary.

This example illustrates a fundamental aspect of social work, namely, social workers' limited discretion or decision-making authority (see Chapters 4, 13, and 14), while social work itself is a contested arena where the social work role involves – as an essential element of the work – an ability to wrestle with and, if possible, reconcile differing legitimate viewpoints. Put another way, social work is an irreducibly political activity: it can never simply be the delivery of technically proficient 'interventions', but involves negotiation and decision making within restrictive and contested environments (Taylor & Balloch, 2005; Webb, 2001). Importantly, neither of these voices is the correct one and the social worker's professional judgement is hugely important, as is her ability to resist potentially abusive or oppressive policies and practices based, in large part, on the degree of professional independence or autonomy she has within the particular practice context or organisational environment. Furthermore, the legitimacy of an independent professional point of view does not mean professional judgement should always have precedence. In a classic text, Ignatieff (1990) outlines how the maxim of 'the professional knows best' can lead to dehumanising and disrespectful care services. This point is also powerfully made by those from the service-user movement, who have emphasised the position of service users as members of an oppressed group and championed their right to control or have a voice in the services provided for them (see Chapter 44). Hence professional viewpoints should not take precedence over the views of service users and other key stakeholders, such as agency managers. At the same time, however, it is not generally appropriate for the voice of the service user to take unqualified precedence. Sometimes the service user's ability to make rational decisions may be compromised, for instance, because of their age, ability, or emotional distress or mental illness. Often the social worker has to make difficult judgements about the degree to which the age or mental illness or learning difficulties of clients may limit their ability to make informed decisions (see Chapter 20), but usually agencies provide guidelines for such decisions in contemporary new public management environments. In addition, society more generally has a legitimate say in such debates. This is most obviously true in the way society decides to resource social services. Ultimately, needs significantly exceed resources (at least in contemporary neoliberal economies) and societies – through the state and those employed to run services on behalf of society – make decisions about the limits of provision (both in theory and in practice). Thus, social workers may assess need but government ultimately has a major say in which needs are met. However, government – on behalf of society – has a more profound role than this. It also creates the laws that define the parameters of social work relationships and the powers and duties of the social worker.

What is the relevance of these arguments to evaluative research? In a nutshell, when deciding to evaluate whether a service 'works', the first issue is to explore what is understood by the term 'works'. In particular, who is defining what works and is there consensus or conflict around defining the nature of the outcomes to be evaluated? There are many examples of good social work research focusing on only one of the three 'voices' within social work. Research stretching back to the 1960s has emphasised the importance of the voice of the service user. In more recent years, this has, in large part, been superseded by research with or by service users as part of a broader political movement identifying those using services as an oppressed group and viewing research as an opportunity to challenge this oppression by giving voice and power to service users. Equally, there has been research focusing solely on the views or experiences of social workers, for instance, by interviewing them or gathering information from their files. There is also research seeking to evaluate whether services work according to the outcomes defined by those funding the service, such as the government or local authority. Often this research will take into account the views of those using services, but it is not uncommon for the research to focus primarily or entirely on the achievement of specific outcomes.

Social work research can be good – or even excellent – in relation to any of these types of research. However, in general terms, the best social work research tends to embrace some of the complexity in defining whose outcomes are being evaluated by trying to give voice to or explore different perceptions in relation to 'outcomes'. This is a challenging task. For instance, Sheppard (2001) interviewed depressed mothers allocated a family social worker and their social workers, and the accounts were so different it was not possible to triangulate the data and draw conclusions. Instead, the researchers had to describe the views of workers and mothers quite separately. In other research, the differing views of workers and clients, or clients and funders, have been incorporated into multiviewpoint and often multimethod research to produce interesting and insightful comments.

Highlighting the influence of different interest groups on the definition of what works in social work research does not lead to a simplistic resolution of the issue of 'what works'. There is no one right way to do research, and research focusing on a particular viewpoint can still be excellent. However, for evaluative research – or research interested in exploring what works in social work settings – some attempt to wrestle with these complexities seems a minimal requirement. This may take the form of including multiple perspectives within the study, or involving different voices in defining the measures used. If only one perspective is being considered, this needs to be acknowledged because it might influence the findings and limit their ability to evaluate other legitimate views on whether a service 'works'. As it stands, this seems to be an important consideration in outlining a vision for social work evaluation. When these considerations are combined with the importance of understanding context and reducing bias in research, they lead to a characteristic and perhaps distinctively social work approach to evaluation.

EVALUATION RESEARCH AND SOCIAL WORK

In summary, good evaluative research attempts to minimise other potential explanations for findings, including those produced by bias within the researchers, those delivering the service, or the research design. RCTs and related methodologies are particularly robust ways of doing this, though they are not the only useful methods for excluding other potential explanations. Hence, there are two challenges in using them that have been insufficiently recognised within the scientific tradition. The first is the challenge associated with generalising knowledge. It has been argued that this is a more general problem for human knowledge and there is no simple answer to the difficulty. Rather, the most appropriate response is a critical and thoughtful approach to weigh up the extent and nature of the evidence. Formulations of what the evidence reveals for practice or policy purposes should, therefore, be characterised by being thorough, transparent, accountable, and balanced. This is a somewhat different approach to the scientific tradition, which relies on the procedures of systematic review to address thoroughness and transparency but has little to say about the judgements required to consider the applicability of findings from one setting for another (see Chapter 31). This complexity is required because of the importance of context for understanding the nature of an intervention and, therefore, the significance (in the broadest sense, rather than mere statistical significance) of the findings. Hence research should combine an attempt at rigour in avoiding bias with detailed attention to the context of the intervention. Finally, it relates this to an important element of the context of the intervention and the research, namely, the fact that social work is characterised by multiple perspectives and interests, and that, as a result, the outcomes to be achieved – and therefore the focus of evaluative research – may be contested. Indeed, it may not be possible to resolve this, as different parties may have radically different views in relation to what services should be aiming to achieve, for instance, where social workers are working in interprofessional teams (see Chapter 42). Social work research cannot aim to resolve these challenges, any more than social work practice can always do so. However, it can engage in a respectful and dialogical process of giving voice to multiple perspectives and evaluating differing outcomes. Good evaluative research should, therefore, be characterised by:

1. an attempt to reduce potential sources of bias, particularly in relation to measuring outcomes of interventions;
2. paying significant attention to the context of the service and the research itself; and
3. considering differing perspectives on outcomes.

This is a challenging formulation of evaluative research within social work. However, such an approach is likely to lead to better evaluative research and a more distinctively social work approach to such evaluation, which, if pursued, would place social work in a position to make an important contribution to the wider traditions of evaluation and research. To provide some flesh to these theoretical bones, it is worth considering a couple of examples of work characterised by these factors. In doing so, it is suggested developing such an approach will require rediscovering a lost tradition rather than inventing something wholly new.

Reid and Shyne: brief and extended casework

Reid and Shyne's (1969) classic study is one of the foundational pieces of research for the creation of task-centred social work. However, it is much more than this. It is a case study in excellent research using innovative and interesting approaches with lasting applicability. Reid and Shyne's study compared brief casework (a maximum of eight sessions) with the more common (at the time) open-ended casework. One hundred and twenty families were randomly assigned to receive one or the other type of input. The study is most famous for finding that families receiving brief casework had better outcomes. Yet, this is only one of a number of fascinating aspects of the study. A second area worth highlighting is the considerable attention spent exploring the nature of the interventions themselves. Thus, interviews were taped and analysed in a manner that would seem revolutionary if published today (Forrester et al., 2008). This analysis provides a detailed and rigorous account of what the social workers were doing, variations between conditions and between workers, and an exploration of the relationship between patterns of social worker communication and outcomes. Furthermore, outcomes were explored quantitatively and qualitatively, and included service-user evaluations of outcome, the views and ratings of workers, and independent researcher judgements. Finally, the study provides a detailed account of the context within which services were provided. It is little wonder this study had such a profound impact on social work but what is surprising is that this tradition of research was not continued and developed. Reid and Shyne's focus on understanding the detail of social work practice, its complex relationship with client outcomes, and their exploration of a variety of views on such outcomes provides an excellent starting point for evaluative social work research. It was not the only example of such an approach. The next example, carried out in the UK, has similar qualities.

Tilda Goldberg: helping the aged

As noted elsewhere, social work pays scant attention to its own history, and nowhere is this more apparent than in the history of social work research. In part, to address this gap, this chapter considers an outstanding early contribution to the social work evaluative tradition: *Helping the Aged* by Tilda Goldberg (1970). *Helping the Aged* was the first attempt to carry out an RCT on social work in the UK – and one of the first internationally. The study focused on whether qualified social workers produced better outcomes for older people than unqualified workers. Older people were randomised to qualified project social workers or normal service (from nonqualified workers). As an RCT, *Helping the Aged* was flawed. The 'intervention' (social work training) was poorly specified. Furthermore, it was confounded with a variety of other factors (for instance, the qualified workers chose to apply for jobs within the study and they had a protected caseload). These failings meant it was difficult to interpret the main finding that there were relatively few significant differences between the groups in relation to the welfare of the older people. Yet while *Helping the Aged* was, in some respects, a flawed research study, it had considerable strengths. The failure of the RCT design was related to the fact that the use of RCTs in psychosocial interventions was in its infancy. Today, research would focus far more on specifying the nature and quality of the intervention (see Chapter 27). However, *Helping the Aged* remains an important study because, in addition to the outcome data, the study looked in detail at the context within which services were delivered and the views of different participants, including older people themselves and the workers. As a result, what emerged was a richly textured and detailed account of the very real difficulties of the older people. This was combined with a successful attempt to consider 'outcomes' on a variety of different levels and from different perspectives to provide an RCT combining multiple perspectives, different methods of data collection, and detailed attention to the context for clients, service, and research. As a result, not only did the research remain full of important insights, but it was also possible to understand how and why the comparison at the heart of the RCT failed to produce results. For instance, there was ample evidence documented that the service received in the two conditions varied in important ways beyond the qualification of the worker. This thorough and comprehensive approach to the research meant *Helping the Aged* was not only inherently an excellent piece of research, but also contributed to it being influential in developing a whole research tradition in the UK ultimately contributing to the development of community care and, more recently, 'personalisation' (i.e., giving those in need control over the budgets for their needs).

On one level this was a triumph. However, the tragedy was that social work ignored this rich and rigorous approach to evaluative research. These studies were undertaken increasingly within the field of social policy or economics. In the UK, there have been no further attempts to carry out RCTs on social work within local authority fieldwork settings (where the bulk of social workers practice) and a scant few examining specialist services with particular groups (see McCambridge et al., 2007). The situation is only marginally better in the USA, where a recent review of social work articles in key journals found a large proportion of theoretical pieces and only 2.3% reporting on RCTs (Holosko, 2010). Overall, the turn away from rigorous evaluation and the tendency to bifurcate between the quantitative RCT and qualitative traditions has been little short of a tragedy. It means there is surprisingly little rigorous research indicating what works – and even less identifying what does not work – in social work practice. This leaves social work weakened in public debates about the profession's contribution and results in the colonisation of areas that should be key foci for social work by psychological approaches with rigorous evidence of effectiveness and lists of evidence-based interventions (see Chapter 26). This is not a tragedy because it leaves social work marginalised and weakened. It is a tragedy because it leads to a simplistic, uncritical, and often highly individualised set of responses to issues that would benefit from the more holistic approach characterising social work. Ultimately, it is the people who use social work services – often without any choice in the matter – who are harmed by the profession's failure to create a body of work exploring rigorously and holistically social work's contribution to helping them.

CONCLUSION: BACK TO THE FUTURE?

The work of Reid and Shyne and Goldberg provide examples of the type of evaluative research required in social work. Tilda's legacy – financial and intellectual – is being developed through the work of the Tilda Goldberg Centre, which aims to develop an evaluative research tradition based on the precepts set out in this chapter. However, it is no means alone in developing this approach. There has been an increasing awareness that the arid and unhelpful 'method wars' across the social sciences ultimately created little progress (see Little, 1998). Within social work internationally, there seems to be far more interest in exploring myriad methods, in finding the most appropriate method for the question under study, and in using an eclectic approach to ensure the needs of those using and funding services are best met. Looking once again at the profession's history of research produced two examples of the benefits of pragmatic and eclectic social work approaches from key studies within the social work tradition. Learning from such studies might help the future development of new and innovative ways of taking forward evaluation in social work. This more pragmatic approach, combining the best of different approaches to evaluation, offers the best path toward a more characteristic, distinctive, and constructive vision of evaluative social work research.

REFERENCES

Adams, K.B., Matto, H.C., & LeCroy, C.W. (2009). Limitations of evidence-based practice for social work education: Unpacking the complexity. *Journal of Social Work Education*, 45(2), 165–186.

American Evaluation Association (2010). *Guiding principles for evaluators.* Retrieved December 1, 2010 from http://www.eval.org/Publications/GuidingPrinciples.asp

Butler, I., & Pugh, R. (2004). The politics of social work research. In R. Lovelock, Lyons, K., & Powell, J. (eds). *Reflecting on social work: Discipline and profession.* Aldershot, Hants: Ashgate.

Cartwright, N., & Munro, E. (2010). The limitations of randomized controlled trials in predicting effectiveness. *Journal of Evaluation in Clinical Practice*, 16(2), 260–266.

Davies, M. (1994). *The essential social worker* (3rd ed.). Aldershot, Hants: Ashgate.

Forrester, D. (2010). Playing with fire or rediscovering fire? The perils and potential for evidence based practice in child and family social work. In P. Ayre & Preston-Shoot, M. (eds). *Children's services at the crossroads: A critical evaluation of contemporary policy for practice.* Lyme Regis, Dorset: Russell House Publishing.

Forrester, D., Kershaw, S., Moss, H., & Hughes, L. (2008). Communication skills in child protection: how do social workers talk to parents? *Child and Family Social Work, 13*(1), 41–51.

Foucault, M. (1978). *The history of sexuality: An introduction*. New York: Pantheon Books.

Foucault, M. (2001). *Madness and civilization: A history of insanity in the age of reason* (2nd rev. ed.). London: Routledge.

Goffman, E. (1986). *Stigma: Notes on the management of spoiled identity*. Place: Touchstone.

Goldberg, E.M., Mortimer, A., & Williams, B.T. (1970). *Helping the aged: A field experiment in social work*. National Institute for Social Work Training, No. 19. London: George Allen & Unwin.

Holosko, M.J. (2010). What types of designs are we using in social work research and evaluation? *Research on Social Work Practice, 20*(6), 665–673.

Humphreys, B. (2003). What *else* counts as evidence in evidence-based social work? *Social Work Education, 22*(1), 81–91.

Ignatieff, M. (1990). *The needs of strangers*. London: The Hogarth Press.

Little, M. (1998). Whispers in the library: A response to Liz Trinder's article on the state of social work research. *Child and Family Social Work, 3*, 49–56.

McCambridge, J., Forrester, D., Waissbein, C., & Strang, J. (2007). What is the extent and nature of quantitative research in British social work?: A brief survey of one journal's publications 2000–2004. *International Social Work, 50*, 265–271.

Oakley, A. (2000). *Experiments in knowing: Gender and method in the social sciences*. Oxford: Polity Press.

Orford, J. (2008). Asking the right questions in the right way: The need for a shift in research on psychological treatments for addiction. *Addiction, 103*(6), 875–885.

Pawson, R., Greenhalgh, T., Harvey, G., & Walshe, K. (2005). Realist review: A new method of systematic review designed for complex policy interventions. *Journal of Health Services Research and Policy, 10*(Suppl 1), 21–34.

Pawson, R., & Tilley, N. (1997). *Realistic evaluation*. London: Sage.

Pitts, J. (2011). Evidence based practice: What worked for whom in youth justice? Presentation at *Conference on Experimental and Quasi-Experimental Methods in Social Work*, Tilda Goldberg Centre, Economic and Social Research Council, University of Bedfordshire, 24 February.

Project MATCH Research Group (1997a). Matching alcoholism treatments to client heterogeneity: Project MATCH posttreatment drinking outcomes. *Journal of Studies on Alcohol, 58*, 7–29.

Project MATCH Research Group (1997b). Project MATCH secondary a priori hypotheses. *Addiction, 92*, 1671–1698.

Project MATCH Research Group (1998a). Matching alcoholism treatments to client heterogeneity: Treatment main effects and matching effects on drinking during treatment. *Journal of Studies on Alcohol, 59*, 631–639.

Project MATCH Research Group (1998b). Matching alcoholism treatments to client heterogeneity: Project MATCH three-year drinking outcomes. *Alcoholism: Clinical and Experimental Research, 22*, 1300–1311.

Reid, W.J., & Shyne, A.W. (1969). *Brief and extended casework*. New York: Columbia University Press.

Robson, C. (2002). Real *world research* (2nd ed.). London: Blackwell Publishing.

Russell, I., Orford, J., Alwyn, T., Black, R., et al. (2005). Effectiveness of treatment for alcohol problems: Findings of the randomised United Kingdom Alcohol Treatment Trial (UKATT). *British Medical Journal, 331*(7516), 541–544.

Seale, C. (ed.). (1999). *Researching society and culture*. London: Sage.

Sheppard, M. (2001). *Social work practice with depressed mothers in child and family care*. Norwich: The Stationery Office.

Singh, S. (1997). *Fermat's last theorem*. London: Fourth Estate.

Taylor, D., & Balloch, S. (2005). The politics of evaluation: An overview. In D. Taylor, & Balloch, S. (eds). *The politics of evaluation: Participation and policy implementation*. Bristol: The Policy Press.

Torgerson, D.J., & Torgerson, C.J. (2008). *Designing randomised trials in health, education and the social sciences: An introduction*. Basingstoke: Palgrave.

Webb, S.A. (2001). Some considerations on the validity of evidence-based practice in social work. *British Journal of Social Work, 31*(1), 57–79.

EVALUATION ASSOCIATIONS AND ORGANISATIONS

African Evaluation Association: http://www.afrea.org/home/index.cfm

The American Evaluation Association: http://www.eval.org/

The Canadian Evaluation Society: http://www.evaluationcanada.ca/site.cgi?s=1

United Kingdom Evaluation Society: http://www.evaluation.org.uk/

29

Qualitative Social Work Research

Deborah K. Padgett

For some time now, qualitative methods have crossed the threshold from the margins to the mainstream in social work research. Between 1990 and 2002, the proportion of qualitative studies in *Social Work Abstracts* increased almost 20 times over from 0.21 to 4.0% (Shlonsky & Gibbs, 2004). This proportion, while still small, has undoubtedly increased in the intervening years. With popularity have come debates about the epistemological bases of knowing through qualitative means and the role of such methods in practice-based professions such as social work. Notwithstanding such differences, there are few if any individuals who question the importance of qualitative methods as a key contributor to knowledge development for improving practices and policies (Padgett, 2009). In social work research, these methods have been used in virtually all arenas of practice, from child welfare to elder care, from individual psychotherapy to community-based change projects, and from intervention studies to naturalistic field observation. Whether used in conjunction with quantitative methods (a 'mixed methods' design) or as stand-alone, these approaches offer unique and complementary perspectives on the complex and dynamic aspects of human lives.

The considerable benefits qualitative methods bring to social work research include an emphasis on: (i) treating *study participants as the experts*; (ii) capturing their experiences and beliefs *in their own words*; (iii) using *flexible designs and inductive thinking* allowing for creativity and insight; and (iv) employing perspectives on *how* and *why* social care services do or do not work to complement quantitative studies designed to test *whether* these services work and their degrees of effectiveness. As social and healthcare programmes face greater scrutiny than ever before, it can be argued successful implementation depends upon designing programmes to meet the needs of clients as they experience and give voice to them.

In this chapter, various perspectives on qualitative social work research are described. A few caveats are necessary at the outset, especially in this era of global perspectives and epistemic self-consciousness. First, most of what is reported on herein originated in the English-language literature. This is an admitted limitation.

Second, it is difficult to speak of qualitative methods without engaging with the central issue of epistemology and the postmodern critiques of post-positivism (the latter constituting the foundation of Western science).

The debates surrounding such differences continue to form the backdrop to many discussions *about* qualitative methods in social work yet are far less evident in reports of empirical studies *using* these methods. With respect to the latter, the sheer enormity of the literature makes any summarisation futile (and probably outdated before it is published). Thus, much of this chapter reviews issues of methodological diversity and what they imply for the growth of knowledge development in social work. The chapter begins with a self-reflexive acknowledgement at the outset that the author subscribes to a pragmatic point of view rather than a specific paradigmatic allegiance.

Third, and related to the above, discussions about qualitative methods in social work raise questions about what is meant by 'research' and, consequently, the boundaries between research and practice. Such concerns rarely attend parallel discussions of the relationship between quantitative methods and practice (where presumably the boundaries are clearer). Finally, qualitative methods, like social work itself, are transdisciplinary, both in origin and in their ongoing use and evolution. This eclecticism enlivens but also complicates discussions of epistemology and methodology.

HISTORIC EVOLUTION: GROWING DIVERSIFICATION AND EPISTEMOLOGICAL COMPLEXITY

The term 'qualitative methods', as well as the ways in which these methods are known and practised, are of relatively recent origin. In prior years, these methods were more likely to be known by their disciplinary origins (e.g., *ethnography* in anthropology, *grounded theory* in sociology). Qualitative methods as such began to be elucidated and codified in the 1970s, influenced by Glaser and Strauss's (1967) grounded theory yet also undergoing evolution and change reflecting the intellectual currents of the ensuing decades. Subsequently, much of what is known about qualitative methodology today was developed by researchers from diverse professional fields, especially education and nursing. The provenance of these methods in social work is relatively recent, with edited readers by Riessman (1993), Sherman and Reid (1994), Shaw and Gould (2002), and Padgett (2004), and a textbook by Padgett (1998a, 2008). The journal *Qualitative Social Work* began publishing in 2002.

The epistemic self-awareness of the late 20th century owes much to the postmodern intellectual revolution and the rise of constructivism and critical theories (class, race, gender, and queer; Denzin & Lincoln, 2005). Seeding doubt about the hegemony of Western science, these movements lent qualitative methods heightened legitimacy as less controlling and distancing, and more attuned to the messy and subjectively negotiated realities of human lives. The invocation of Schön's (1983) vivid metaphor contrasting scientists working on 'high hard ground' with researchers who slog through the muck of the 'real world' is used to illustrate this attraction to qualitative methods (Ely, 1991). Schön's (1983) groundbreaking writing on the 'reflective practitioner' has resonated deeply with social work professionals who resist the dominance of the scientific method and standards of evidence holding the randomised clinical trial as the single and ultimate gold standard (Floersch, 2004; Fook, 1996; Scott, 2002; Shaw & Gould, 2001; van Heugten, 2004).

The epistemological debates among qualitative researchers came to the fore with the first edition of the *Handbook of Qualitative Methods* (Denzin & Lincoln, 1994). In this and more so in later editions (Denzin & Lincoln, 2000, 2005), the *Handbook's* editors heralded a new era of rejecting positivism in favour of emancipatory and interpretivist approaches. Despite or because of this call for paradigm purity, some qualitative researchers have sought a middle ground by tapping into pragmatic philosophy promulgated by

John Dewey, Charles Peirce, and Richard Rorty. Centred in Chicago in the early 20th century, the pragmatists eschewed the grand theories and ideologies of the day (Marx, Freud, and Skinner) and aligned themselves with a more utilitarian view of knowledge production. Social work researchers in the USA take pride in the contributions of Jane Addams as a key member of the Chicago pragmatist movement (Menand, 2001).

As the 21st century began, the landscape of qualitative methods was vibrant and inclusive of a variety of epistemological and philosophical stances fostered by postmodern critiques. For example, the venerable tradition of ethnography gave rise to critical ethnography (Madison, 2005) and autoethnography (Ellis, 2004). Grounded theory expanded to include constructivist (Charmaz, 2006) and postmodern (Clarke, 2005) versions. An interweaving of philosophy, psychology, and linguistics spawned phenomenological, narrative, discourse, and conversation analysis (Giorgi, 1985; Riessman, 1993). And case study analyses endured as having a unique role in the methodological toolkit (Stake, 1995; Yin, 2009). Qualitative studies in social work represent all of these diverse approaches (see, e.g., the edited volumes mentioned above as well as the journal *Qualitative Social Work* for numerous exemplars).

Quickly gaining ground have been participatory action research (PAR) and community-based participatory research (CBPR). A hybrid of advocacy and research dedicated to community empowerment and betterment, PAR and CBPR are not inherently qualitative but often use these methods as consonant with their values (Israel et al., 2005). CBPR is best seen as a meta-method able to incorporate several qualitative approaches as well as mixed (qualitative–quantitative) methods under the rubric of one study. Perhaps not surprisingly, social work researchers have embraced PAR and CBPR as a natural extension of their interests in empowerment and community development (Pinto et al., 2007; Stahl & Shdaimah, 2008).

QUALITATIVE METHODS IN SOCIAL WORK RESEARCH

The compatibility argument and the embrace of qualitative methods

The importance of qualitative methods came to the fore in the social work literature by the mid-1990s with a number of experienced researchers (e.g., contributors to volumes mentioned earlier) arguing qualitative methods were more conducive to the goals of a practice-based profession. Drawing upon an oft-made distinction from anthropology, Gilgun (1994) referred to 'idiographic' vs. 'nomothetic' goals of inquiry, the former less focused on broad generalisability and thus consonant with qualitative methods. As evidenced in a special issue of *Social Work Research* devoted to qualitative methods (1995, vol. 19, issue 1), the welcome mat was laid down for qualitative methods with optimism they would prove to be 'rich, relevant, and rigorous' (Fraser, 1995, p. 25). In the same year, Sheppard (1995) published an influential article in the *British Journal of Social Work* asserting qualitative methods (and analytic induction in particular) had the best fit with social work practice assessment.

The increase in popularity of qualitative methods in social work provided an opportunity (or an obligation) to revisit the traditional divide between research and practice previously attributed to the dominance of quantification and measurement (Padgett, 2004; Sherman & Reid, 1994). Many advocates of these methods point to their natural affinity with the fundamental tenets of social work practice: empathic, nonjudgmental, intuitive, individualising, and holistic (Riessman, 1993; Rodwell, 1998). That these methods are low-threshold (in comparison to a household survey or experiment) and low-tech (compared to statistical analyses) makes them even more attractive. The recent emphasis in the UK and elsewhere on paying attention to the needs and wishes of service users (Hardwick & Hardwick, 2007) has given impetus to the community-based action approaches favouring qualitative methods (Gray & Schubert, 2010). This affinity was, in turn, framed as presenting an unparalleled opportunity to conduct research *in* practice using the familiarity of qualitative techniques as an entrée and a reflection-in-action technique as the particular method (Fook, 1996; Gould, 1999).

Exhortations to view qualitative methods as more compatible with social work values are compelling – the openness to advocacy embraced by many qualitative researchers (deemed unwelcome bias in quantitative research) is one obvious commonality. Considering the nature of most practice settings – crowded waiting rooms, harried staff, shortages of resources, frustrated community representatives – it is no surprise any type of research is a challenge. The less intrusive, low-tech approaches of qualitative methods can clearly make such an effort go more smoothly.

Special ethical concerns for a practice-based profession

How do qualitative social work researchers who are also trained practitioners behave in an ethical manner? Qualitative methods are not inherently more ethical than quantitative methods, but their approach to 'subjects' (better known as 'study participants') implies greater sensitivity to the issues. Clearly, practice ethics and research ethics have overlapping domains of interest but they also have differences. In one noteworthy distinction, social work practitioners who are acting as researchers must notify study participants of their legal duty to report child abuse (a responsibility trumping any promise of confidentiality).

Defining what is (and is not) research can be difficult in the practising professions since many practice-related activities also resemble research (observing and listening, collecting and recording information, aggregating and analysing data). And, for some in social work, worrying about where to draw the line (or why a line is needed at all) is problematic (Crawford et al., 2002; Fook, 2002; Shaw, 2008). Shaw and Gould (2001), for example, argue in favour of a reflective approach to social work research promoting practice itself as a form of research.

Determining what 'research' is can be crucial since, when formally recognised, it is subject to oversight and ethical expectations differing from those of practice. Influenced by the 1964 Declaration of Helsinki (which called for protection of human subjects), the boundaries have become defined by ethics committees having purview over research involving human subjects. Although originally meant to address potentially harmful medical experiments, jurisdiction of these committees has spread to include virtually all research dealing with human subjects (at least in the USA). Qualitative social work researchers, like their counterparts in anthropology, sociology, and oral history, have pointed out the lack of fit emanating from governmental regulations originally intended for medical experiments, but to no avail (Padgett, 2008). Their counterparts in other countries have not been held to such strict biomedical standards. In the UK, for example, social work research is governed by the National Health Service ethics committees only if it is health-related (Hardwick & Hardwick, 2007). As the NHS model expands in influence, some social work researchers in the UK have argued for adopting independent criteria distinct from the biomedical model (Dominelli & Holloway, 2008).

From an ethical standpoint, community-based action research tests the boundaries of research and practice in new ways, of which only a few can be anticipated in advance. The most obvious revolve around confusion over the roles of community partners (who shift between being 'subjects' and 'investigators'), the fluidity of what is 'practice' and 'research' when engaged in community advocacy, and concomitant difficulties for providers shifting between their 'research' and 'practice' roles.

In the USA, the threshold definition of 'research' revolves around intent (Padgett, 2008). That is, 'research' involves activities undertaken to develop and build knowledge through wider dissemination. These same activities are not considered research if they are carried out solely to improve practices and programmes. An individual practitioner or an entire programme may self-evaluate using the latest research methods but if what is learned is intended only for internal use, the evaluation is not considered 'research'. Once intent is established, the researcher is obliged to seek voluntary informed consent and adhere to all necessary protections of the human 'subjects' in the study. This applies to all types of research, whether micro-level studies of practice or community-based participatory research.

Conducting qualitative research for, in, and about practice: distinguishing micro-, meso-, and macro-levels

Expressing concern that the boundaries between research and practice were becoming blurred in potentially detrimental ways, Padgett (1998a) objected to the idea such a trend could lead to ethically challenged and diluted (or distorted) practice and research. If all social work qualitative research is presumed to be *for* practice, it is also true not all such research is directly *about* or *in* practice (e.g., an ethnographic study of homeless youths' survival strategies). Differences in opinion arise when the research is being conducted *in* practice by the practitioner while simultaneously delivering the service (Bein & Allen, 1999; Padgett, 1998b). Consider a hypothetical example of a social worker employed by a programme serving new mothers suffering from post-partum depression. If the social worker opts for qualitative methods to study her one-on-one counselling, the dilemmas are both methodological and ethical. Will she observe her client as she is counselling her? Conduct an in-depth interview after each session? Ixer (1999) refers to this temporal problem of studying practice while being engaged in it, arguing one must at some point remove oneself long enough to reflect on it.

Ethics committees frown on practitioners directly evaluating their work with clients when done for research and dissemination purposes in the belief the client cannot truly give informed consent and could reasonably feel coerced under the circumstances (fearing loss of services if she were to refuse). Self-evaluation for 'internal purposes' (i.e., to improve one's practice) is not at issue here. Some of the same issues could come up in a qualitative programme evaluation, but it is less likely programme-level outcomes would require the practitioner-researcher to be in direct contact with the clients while she is working with them. Indeed, the degree of fit between qualitative methods and evaluation at the programme (meso-) level has achieved wide recognition, both in examining process as well as outcome (Padgett, 2008b; Patton, 2002). And, as mentioned earlier, these methods are well suited for use outside of the usual settings where practice takes place (e.g., in communities where service users live and work). To sum up, social work qualitative research can be usefully conducted for and in practice at multiple levels from micro to macro, but a single cautionary note comes from micro-level applications conducted by the researcher-practitioner *in situ*.

Qualitative methods in value-based professional advocacy work

One of social work's distinguishing features is its embrace of social justice values (Bisman, 2004; Reisch, 2007). This hallmark of the profession is likely to give traditional quantitative researchers pause since it points to a conflict with the bias-free ideal of empirical research. Qualitative researchers do not make such claims, preferring to start from the premise values and biases are inherent to the process (how and whether they address this is open to many options). A demonstration of how social justice values, such as empowerment, can be incorporated into qualitative study of homelessness in the USA (Padgett & Henwood, 2009) is one such illustration. Participatory and action research approaches go a step further and embrace the values of empowerment and social betterment as central tenets extending to every aspect of the study (Freire, 1970; Israel et al., 2005).

There is little question qualitative methods present fewer obstacles to pursuing advocacy and qualitative researchers tend to be far more comfortable with social justice as part of their agenda. At the same time, they are not the only means to such an end (e.g., statistics documenting health disparities can be used in a call for increased access to care). And, from a methodological standpoint, the balance of 'rigorous versus relevant' can tilt too far in either direction and undermine both aims.

CURRENT PRACTICES IN QUALITATIVE METHODS: COMMONALITIES AND DIVERSITIES

Overview of the most common approaches in qualitative inquiry

Despite – or perhaps due to – the proliferation of epistemic stances and methodological approaches, there remain a number of commonalities in the practice of qualitative research. These include: a thorough review of the literature to establish the 'problem', the use of research questions rather than hypotheses, purposeful sampling, in-depth interviewing (supplemented with observation and or use of documents), coding and thematic development, and use of direct quotes to illustrate and ground the findings.

Within these broad rubrics are many variations and choices. With respect to an orienting framework, for example, a qualitative study may be truly inductive with few if any theoretical or conceptual frameworks or it may entail a set of pre-defined concepts or a template around which the research questions, data collection, and analyses revolve. In between these extremes, most qualitative studies use *sensitising concepts* and ideas from the literature but these must subsequently earn their way into the findings (Charmaz, 2006).

Purposeful sampling at the outset of a study may entail *extreme or deviant case, intensity, maximum variation, homogeneous, typical case, critical case, criterion,* and *snowball* variants – the choice depending upon the study's goals and the nature of the population being studied (Patton, 2002). Analysis-driven sampling techniques occurring later in a study may include any of these initial sampling techniques with the additional possibilities of *theoretical sampling* (used in grounded theory when inductively derived analytic concepts are used to guide the choice of additional participants) and *confirming or disconfirming sampling,* which takes the logic of theoretical sampling a step further to seek out specific examples to test the validity of the grounded theory.

Modes of data collection include in-depth interviews (individual and focus group), observation with varying degrees of participation, and use of documents, such as records, minutes, diaries, and web pages. Observation and field note-taking may include photography and video recording as well as site-specific observation and 'shadowing' individuals to learn about their daily lives (Kusenbach, 2003). Individual interviews may be in-person, on the telephone, or via the internet (videoconferencing, email, blogs, and chat rooms). Documents may be in hard copy or scanned and digitised.

Coding and thematic development may follow an *a priori* template with limited inductive thinking, resembling content analysis in the straightforward examination of manifest meanings (key words, phrases, and so on; Boyatzis, 1998). At the opposite end of the continuum of interpretive latitude, the researcher may explore latent meanings and narrative structures to produce themes arcing across the data. Such is the case with phenomenological approaches that do not fracture texts into codes but instead capture the 'lived experience' of study participants (Giorgi, 1985).

In the vast middle ground of data analytic options is some version of grounded theory (Charmaz, 2006; Glaser & Strauss, 1967). Relatively few researchers strictly follow the protocols of grounded theory to completion, i.e., the production of a grounded theory or explanatory model of the phenomenon under study, but most engage in some version of *constant comparative analysis*, an inductive–deductive iterative process of closely examining data and, through use of memos, searching for contrasts and commonalities.

More common is the open coding of texts with gradual filtering and refining producing a set of codes which are then analysed further to yield themes. Central to this process is *memoing*, or recording one's interactions with the data and thoughts directed to thematic development (Charmaz, 2006). In case study analyses (whether single- or multi-case), the focus is different insofar as the integrity of the case is maintained (Yin, 2009). For example, an intensive case study of exemplary after-school programmes would analyse all available data on each programme before looking for cross-case patterns.

The use of qualitative data analysis (QDA) computer software has become common, with options including NVIVO, ATLAS.ti, HyperRESEARCH, and The Ethnograph (Lewins & Silver, 2007). QDA software offers invaluable assistance in managing and retrieving raw data of diverse forms (interview transcripts, photographs, video, and audio). Because of the cost, regularity of upgrades, and learning curve required, an investment in this software is clearly justified when the researcher is committed to more than one qualitative study and or has large quantities of data to manage and analyse.

While lending technological cachet to what has traditionally been a low-tech enterprise, this software has one fundamental difference from its statistical counterparts: it does not analyse the data. As with all other aspects of qualitative inquiry, the researcher-as-instrument must assume responsibility. What QDA software does offer is a highly efficient means of coding, organising, and retrieving coded text, and searching for patterns. For researchers who prefer not to use the software, most data-processing programmes permit copying and pasting text (albeit in a less systematic and more labour-intensive way).

Secondary analysis of qualitative data is an option garnering attention (Thorne, 1998). It is sensible to assert the vast and growing archives of qualitative data should be mined for new and different purposes and give researchers (either the originating team or new ones) a chance to benefit from earlier efforts. Of course, the immersion and interconnectedness of researcher and participant, one of the most rewarding and informing aspects of qualitative research, are missing from secondary analyses.

In pursuit of rigour

Though not always evident in the report or described as such, most qualitative researchers attend to *strategies for rigour* to enhance their studies' trustworthiness. Such strategies lend credence by minimising the biases accompanying the researcher-as-instrument as well as the closeness of the researcher–researched relationship. The interpretive latitude afforded a qualitative researcher varies with the type of approach (e.g., ethnography differs from grounded theory) but none encourages undisciplined and ungrounded findings.

Six strategies for rigour proposed by Padgett (1998) were drawn from the literature on qualitative methods: *prolonged engagement, triangulation of data* (use of multiple sources), *peer debriefing and support, negative case analysis, member checking* (referring back to study participants to verify one's findings), and *keeping an audit trail*. Few studies use all six (and some strategies will not fit a particular approach), but their appropriate application inspires greater confidence in concerted efforts being made.

Other criteria of quality social work researchers find useful include 'pragmatic validity' or utility for service users and 'ecological validity' (Shadish et al., 2002).

Standards for assessing quality

Pursuing strategies for rigour is necessary but not sufficient for ensuring a qualitative study is of high quality. Not surprisingly, evaluative standards tend to differ according to the epistemological and methodological approaches adopted by the qualitative researcher. Overall, a study should be *trustworthy* (i.e., devoid as much as possible of unfounded interpretations and misrepresentations of what study participants are saying and doing). The conundrum arises when trying to identify what the criteria for quality are and should be. In quantitative studies, the standard invocations of reliability, internal validity, and external validity set forth expectations the study's methods were rigorously controlled and its findings generalisable – all of which are ill-suited to the flexibility and locality which are the strengths of qualitative research. Leading qualitative methodologists have offered alternative criteria, such as credibility, transferability, and auditability (Lincoln & Guba, 1985).

Over the years, a number of checklists for quality have emerged to guide evaluations of qualitative studies (Barbour & Barbour, 2003; Inui & Frankel, 1991; Patton, 2002; Sandelowski & Barroso, 2003). Cutting across these guidelines are a few central concerns: are the findings grounded in the data? How were the inevitable intrusions of bias addressed? Were decisions about sampling and analysis reasonable and logical? How systematic and auditable were the study's procedures? Are the interpretations strong and insightful?

Erickson (1986) sums it up as *adequacy* of data richness, data variety, disconfirming evidence, and interpretations. Existing as a kind of transcendent criterion, adequacy is not about quantity but, rather, sufficiency.

Attending to cultural and other forms of diversity in a global context

It is somewhat ironic qualitative methods originated in cross-cultural venues – anthropologists staked their reputations on intensive immersion among 'foreign' peoples in exotic places (the latter most often colonial possessions of Western nations). Required to learn the native language or hire a translator, they were assumed to overcome the barriers of language as part of fieldwork designed to describe and interpret a culture.

The explosion of popularity of qualitative methods after the 1970s owes much to their embrace by applied professions, such as nursing, education, and social work. As qualitative methods 'came home' to focus on local issues and populations, they became more diverse in method and epistemology, yet they also became interview-intensive to the exclusion of the participant observation – previously their singular hallmark. An unintended consequence was the shrinking importance of addressing language and cultural barriers amid the marked increase in monolingual studies (most conducted in English).

This trend also made it easier to overlook the importance of ethnic and racial differences as methodological and ethical issues. Recent attempts to remedy this include a volume where indigenous voices are showcased as part of qualitative methods pursued in a postcolonial context (Denzin et al., 2008). Meanwhile, the interests of social work researchers have always included the cross-cultural realm: native peoples, immigrants, and refugees for whom language and culture differences (not to mention poverty and discrimination) presented significant barriers to adapting to the dominant society.

The methodological dilemmas of cross-cultural qualitative research centre on ensuring the linguistic accuracy of translation as well as the cultural validity of interpretations. They also include ongoing debates about whether the interviewer and interviewee should be matched by ethnicity (or gender or age, and so forth). A skilled interviewer regardless of demographic characteristics can often overcome a 'mismatch' and obtain rich and meaningful data. At the same time, there are invariably occasions when matching makes sense (e.g., having African-American interviewers in a study of racism and identity). Ethical issues of cross-ethnic, cross-cultural research include stoking fears needlessly when requiring signed informed consent (if the participant is not a legal resident) and the need to have all consent and other forms in the participants' native language.

The rise of globalisation has had a notable impact on enlarging the scope of research to include issues transcending national boundaries, e.g., infectious diseases such as HIV and AIDS, drug and sex trafficking, refugees fleeing disasters and wars, and so on. The advantages of qualitative methods – sensitivity to cultural differences, accessibility through listening, and empathy – make entrée in such circumstances far easier than a randomised clinical trial. By and large, social work qualitative researchers have focused on 'local' diverse populations (e.g., First Nations in Canada, the Maori people in New Zealand, Cambodian refugees in the Western USA, Palestinian Arabs in Israel, and lower castes in India).

Reflecting the diversity in qualitative methods, as well as their geographic applications, social work researchers have employed ethnography in Jordan (e.g., Al-Makhamreh & Lewando-Hundt, 2008), grounded theory in New Zealand and Korea (e.g., Yang, 2008), case studies in the UK (Holland, 2000), hermeneutic phenomenology in the USA (e.g., Armour et al., 2009), analysis of documents in Hong Kong (Lam et al., 2007), narrative analysis in India, action-oriented evaluation in Canada (Whitmore, 2001), and mixed methods in Australia (O'Leary & Gould, 2008). These examples give a small glimpse into the globally expanding compendium of qualitative social work research.

Systematic reviews and qualitative methods

Systematic reviews have become commonplace with the rise of evidence-based policies and practice (see Chapter 31). The well-known Cochrane reviews in healthcare and Campbell Collaboration reviews in social welfare provide methodologically rigorous standards for establishing effectiveness. A number of centres have emerged including the Centre for Reviews and Dissemination at the University of York (Great Britain), the Evidence for Policy and Practice Information and Coordinating Centre at the University of London, and the Joanna Briggs Institute at the University of Adelaide in Australia.

Specific to social work are the Social Care Institute for Excellence (SCIE) in London and the Institute for Evidence-Based Social Work at the University of Toronto in Canada. As faculty involved in the latter, Saini and Shlonsky (2012) have produced a textbook on conducting systematic syntheses of qualitative research in social work. Gould (2010) also offers examples of how qualitative studies can be incorporated into these syntheses.

Systematic reviews have been open to qualitative methods as providing valuable information on how and why interventions work, not just whether they work according to standards of statistical significance (Noyes et al., 1993). Dixon-Woods and colleagues propose qualitative studies contribute different kinds of evidence for practice and policy, answering not 'what works' but 'what is at work' with clients and patients (Dixon-Woods et al., 2006, p. 32).

Given the nature of qualitative research, such syntheses present special challenges.

First, the feasibility of qualitative syntheses has been challenged by some who object on epistemological grounds that consensual definitions of 'quality' or 'rigour' are elusive at best (McDermott et al., 2004). Second, the absence of standard conventions for reporting qualitative methods and evaluating the quality of studies makes meaningful aggregation and synthesising difficult (Saini & Schlonsky, 2012; Taylor et al., 2007). As noted by Taylor et al. (2007), central to the question of synthesis is the existence of consensual standards for rigour and quality and, as yet, there are no quality checklists comparable to the hierarchy of evidence used in quantitative research.

To the extent evidence-based practice guidelines become incorporated into practice decision making, the absence of qualitative studies from meta-syntheses renders their contributions invisible and the views of service users (voiced in their own words) absent (Saini & Shlonsky, 2012). Forging ahead, published syntheses of qualitative studies have begun to appear in a number of areas, including falls prevention among elders (McInnes & Wimpenny, 2008), the experience of having hepatitis C (Treloar & Rhodes, 2009), and parenting programmes (Kane et al., 2007).

Mixed methods: bringing qualitative and quantitative methods together

The rise in popularity of mixed methods has followed closely on the heels of the boom in qualitative inquiry. The development of mixed methods designs has largely originated in qualitative research (Creswell, 2007) but their adoption by quantitative researchers has been remarkable. They have become *de rigueur* among researchers seeking to take advantage of what both approaches have to offer (Padgett, 2008).

Space precludes a detailed exposition of the many options in mixing methods (most revolving around whether the mixing is done sequentially or concurrently and whether one 'side' is dominant over the other 'side' or both given equal due). There are a number of textbooks (Creswell, 2007; Tashakkori & Teddlie, 2003) as well as a dedicated journal (*Journal of Mixed Methods Research*) available for guidance in this area.

Compared to nursing and education, this topic has received less attention in the social work literature on methods. It is unclear why this is the case, but it may be due to reticence on the part of postmodern-oriented methodologists in social work who view mixing methods as epistemologically incorrect. Meanwhile, it appears social work researchers are *de facto* pragmatists since there are growing numbers of mixed methods designs among the empirical studies published in the social work literature (Gioia, 2004; Padgett, 2009; Yoon, 2009).

THE FUTURE OF QUALITATIVE SOCIAL WORK RESEARCH: REFLECTIONS ON TRENDS

The abundance of qualitative studies found in social work journals and conference proceedings attests to the explosive popularity of the methods. Equally impressive have been the social work researchers who have advanced thinking about and doing qualitative methods (featured in *Qualitative Social Work* but also found in a variety of social work journals). At some risk of overstatement, a few trends are offered below. First, as noted throughout this chapter, the growth, diversification, and sophistication of approaches used by qualitative social work researchers continues unabated. Second, disagreements about quality and rigour will not likely produce consensus in the near term. This is not bad news *per se*, but it does represent a challenge to qualitative researchers seeking legitimacy in a quantitative world (Padgett, 2004). Third, the timely co-occurrence of social policy changes favouring the views of service users, and the methodological wherewithal to capture these opinions in their own words and contexts, presents unprecedented opportunities for qualitative social work research. As such, this trend directly challenges both the hegemony of quantitative methods, and the traditions of expertise and authority accorded practitioners. Last but not least, as global issues become front and centre – interdependent economies, climate change, small- and large-scale wars, and public health crises – cross-national, cross-language, cross-disciplinary, and multimethod research is urgently needed. The examples cited earlier in this section point to promising moves in this direction – the place of social work research *vis-à-vis* other professions depends on rising to meet these challenges. Qualitative methods offer one means of producing relevant and rigorous research conducted *by* social workers, *in* and *for* the profession and, most importantly, *to the benefit of* disadvantaged individuals and communities. The rewards – knowledge development and a positive influence on socially just policies and practices – are many.

REFERENCES

Al-Makhamreh, S.S., & Lewando-Hundt, G. (2008). Researching 'at home' as an insider-outsider: Gender and culture in an ethnographic study of social work practice in an Arab society. *Qualitative Social Work*, *7*, 9–23.

Armour, M., Rivaux, S.L., & Bell, H. (2009). Using context to build rigor: Application to two hermeneutic phenomenological studies. *Qualitative Social Work*, *8*, 101–122.

Barbour, R.S., & Barbour, M. (2003). Evaluating and synthesizing qualitative research: The need to develop a distinctive approach. *Journal of Evaluation in Clinical Practice*, *9*, 179–186.

Bein, A., & Allen, K. (1999). Hand in glove: It fits better than you think. *Social Work*, *44*, 273–277.

Bisman, C. (2004). Social work values: The moral code of the profession. *British Journal of Social Work*, *34*, 109–123.

Boyatzis, R.E. (1998). *Transforming qualitative information: Thematic analysis and code development*. Thousand Oaks, CA: Sage.

Charmaz, K. (2006). *Constructing grounded theory*. Thousand Oaks, CA: Sage.

Clarke, A. (2005). *Situational analysis: Grounded theory after the postmodern turn*. Thousand Oaks, CA: Sage.

Crawford, F., Dickinson, J., & Leitman, S. (2002). Mirroring meaning making: Narrative ways of reflecting on practice for action. *Qualitative Social Work*, *1*, 170–190.

Creswell, J.W. (2007). *Qualitative inquiry and research design* (2nd ed.). Thousand Oaks, CA: Sage.

Denzin, N.K., & Lincoln, Y.S. (eds) (1994). *Handbook of qualitative research*. Thousand Oaks, CA: Sage.

Denzin, N.K., & Lincoln, Y.S. (eds) (2000). *Handbook of qualitative research* (2nd ed.). Thousand Oaks, CA: Sage.

Denzin, N.K., & Lincoln, Y.S. (eds) (2005). *Handbook of qualitative research* (3rd ed.). Thousand Oaks, CA: Sage.

Denzin, N.K., Lincoln, Y.S., & Tuhiwai Smith, L. (eds) (2008). *Handbook of critical and indigenous methodologies*. Thousand Oaks, CA: Sage.

Dixon-Woods, M., Bonas, S., Jones, D.R., Miller, T., Sutton, A.J., Shaw, R.L., Smith, J.A., & Young, B. (2006). How can systematic reviews incorporate qualitative research? A critical perspective. *Qualitative Research*, *6*, 27–44.

Dominelli, L., & Holloway, M. (2008). Ethics and governance in social work research in the UK. *British Journal of Social Work*, *38*, 109–124.

Ellis, C. (2004). *The ethnographic I: A methodological novel about auto-ethnography*. Walnut Creek, CA: Altamira Press.

Erickson, F. (1986). Qualitative methods in research on teaching. In M.C. Wittrock (ed.), *Handbook of research on teaching* (3rd ed.). New York: Palgrave, pp. 119–161.

Floersch, J. (2004). A method for investigating practitioner use of theory in practice. *Qualitative Social Work*, *3*, 161–177.

Fook, J. (ed.). (1996). *The reflective researcher: Social workers' theories of practice research*. Sydney: Allen & Unwin.

Fook, J. (2002). Theorizing from practice: Towards an inclusive approach for social work research. *Qualitative Social Work*, *1*, 79–95.

Fraser, M. (1995). Rich, relevant and rigorous: Do qualitative methods measure up? *Social Work Research*, *19*, 25–27.

Freire, P. (1970). *The pedagogy of the oppressed*. New York: Continuum.

Gilgun, J. (1994). 'Hand in glove': The grounded theory approach and social work practice research. In E. Sherman & Reid, W.J. (eds), *Qualitative research*

in social work. New York: Columbia University Press, pp. 115–125.
Gioia, D. (2004). Mixed methods in a dissertation study. In D.K. Padgett (ed.), *The qualitative research experience*. Belmont, CA: Thomson, pp. 119–146.
Giorgi, A. (ed.). (1985). *Phenomenology and psychological research*. Pittsburgh, PA: Duquėsne University Press.
Glaser, B.G., & Strauss, A.L. (1967). *The discovery of grounded theory: Strategies for qualitative research*. Chicago, IL: Aldine.
Gould, N. (1999). Qualitative practice evaluation. In I. Shaw & Lishman, J. (eds), *Evaluation and social work practice*. London: Sage, pp. 63–80.
Gould, N. (2010). Integrating qualitative research in practice guideline development. *Qualitative Social Work, 9*, 93–109.
Gray, M., & Schubert, L. (2010). Turning base metal into gold: Transmuting art, practice, research and experience into knowledge. *British Journal of Social Work, 40*, 2308–2325.
Hardwick, L., & Hardwick, C. (2007). Social work research: 'Every moment is a new and shocking valuation of all we have been'. *Qualitative Social Work, 6*, 301–314.
Holland, S. (2000). The assessment relationship: Interactions between social workers and parents in child protection assessments. *British Journal of Social Work, 30*, 149–163.
Inui, T.S., & Frankel, R.M. (1991). Evaluating the quality of qualitative research. *Journal of General Internal Medicine, 6*, 485–487.
Israel, B.A., Eng, E., Schulz, A.J., & Parker, E.A. (eds) (2005). *Methods in community-based participatory research for health*. San Francisco, CA: Jossey-Bass.
Ixer, G. (1999). There's no such thing as reflection. *British Journal of Social Work, 29*(4), 513–527.
Kane, G.A., Wood, V.A., & Barlow, J. (2007). Parenting programmes: A systematic review and synthesis of qualitative research. *Child care, health and development, 33*, 784–793.
Kusenbach, M. (2003). Street phenomenology: The go-along as ethnographic research tool. *Ethnography, 4*, 455,485.
Lam, C.M., Wong, H., & Leung, T.F. (2007). An unfinished reflexive journey: Social work students' reflection on their placement experiences. *British Journal of Social Work, 37*, 91–105.
Lewins, A. & Silver, C. (2007). *Using software in qualitative research: A step-by-step guide*. London: Sage.
Lincoln, Y.S., & Guba, E.G. (1985). *Naturalistic inquiry*. Beverly Hills, CA: Sage.

Madison, S. (2005). *Critical ethnography: Method ethics and performance*. Thousand Oaks, CA: Sage.
McDermott, E., Graham, H., & Hamilton, V. (2004). *Experience of being a teenage mother in the UK: A report of a systematic review of qualitative studies*. Centre for Evidence-Based Public Health Policy, Glasgow: University of Glasgow.
McInnes, E., & Wimpenny, P. (2008). Using qualitative assessment and review instrument software to synthesize studies on older peoples' views and experiences of falls prevention. *International Journal of Evidence-Based Health Care, 6*, 337–344.
Menand, L. (2001). *The metaphysical club: A story of ideas in America*. New York: Farrar, Straus, & Giroux.
Noyes, J., Popay, J., Pearson, A., Hannes, K., & Booth, A. (1993). *Qualitative research and Cochrane reviews*. The Cochrane Collaboration.
O'Leary, P., & Gould, N. (2008). Men who were sexually abused in childhood and subsequent suicidal ideation: Community comparison, explanations, and practice implications. *British Journal of Social Work, 39*, 950–968.
Padgett, D.K. (1998a). *Qualitative methods in social work research* (1st ed.). Thousand Oaks, CA: Sage.
Padgett, D.K. (1998b). Does the glove really fit? Qualitative research and clinical social work practice. *Social Work, 43*, 373–382.
Padgett, D.K. (ed.). (2004). *The qualitative research experience*. Belmont, CA: Thomson.
Padgett, D.K. (2008). *Qualitative methods in social work research* (2nd ed.). Thousand Oaks, CA: Sage.
Padgett, D.K. (2009). Qualitative and mixed methods in social work knowledge development. *Social Work, 54*, 101–105.
Padgett, D.K., & Henwood, B.F. (2009). Obtaining large-scale funding for empowerment-oriented qualitative research: A report from personal experience. *Qualitative Health Research, 19*, 868–874.
Patton, M.Q. (2002). *Qualitative research and evaluation methods* (3rd ed.). Thousand Oaks, CA: Sage.
Pinto, R., Schmidt, C., Rodriguez, P., & Solano, R. (2007). Using principles of participatory research: Groundwork for a collaboration in Brazil. *International Social Work, 50*, 53–65.
Reisch, M. (2007). Social justice and multi-culturalism: Persistent tensions in the history of U.S. social welfare and social work. *Studies in Social Justice, 1*, 67–92.
Riessman, C.K. (1993). *Narrative analysis*. Newbury Park, CA: Sage.
Riessman, C. K. (2005). Exporting ethics: A narrative about narrative research in South India. *Health: An Interdisciplinary Journal for the Social Study of Health, Illness and Medicine, 9*, 473–490.

Rodwell, M.K. (1998). *Social work constructivist research*. New York: Garland Publishing.

Saini, M., & Shlonsky, A. (2012). *Systematic synthesis of qualitative research*. New York: Oxford University Press.

Sandelowski, M., & Barroso, J. (2003). Classifying the findings in qualitative studies. *Qualitative Health Research, 13*(7), 905–923.

Schön, D.A. (1983). *The reflective practitioner: How professionals think in action*. New York: Basic Books.

Scott, D. (2002). Adding meaning to measurement: The value of qualitative methods in practice research. *British Journal of Social Work, 32*, 923–930.

Shadish, W., Cook, T., & Campbell, D. (2002). *Experimental and quasi-experimental designs for generalized causal inference*. Boston: Houghton Mifflin.

Shaw, I. (2008). Ethics and the practice of qualitative research. *Qualitative Social Work, 7*, 400–414.

Shaw, I., & Gould, N. (eds) (2001). *Qualitative research in social work*. London: Sage.

Shaw, I.F., & Gould, N.G. (eds) (2002). *Qualitative research in social work*. Thousand Oaks, CA: Sage.

Sheppard, M. (1995). Social work, social science and practice wisdom. *British Journal of Social Work, 25*, 265–293.

Sherman, E., & Reid, W. (eds) (1994). *Qualitative research in social work*. New York: Columbia University Press.

Shlonsky, A., & Gibbs, L. (2004). Will the real evidence-based practice please step forward? Teaching evidence-based practice in the helping professions. *Journal of Brief Therapy and Crisis Intervention, 4*, 137–153.

Stahl, R., & Shdaimah, C. (2008). Collaborations between community advocates and academic researchers: Scientific advocacy or political research? *British Journal of Social Work, 38*, 1610–1639.

Stake, R. (1995). *The art of case study research*. Thousand Oaks, CA: Sage.

Tashakkori, A., & Teddlie, C. (eds) (2003). *Handbook of mixed methods in social and behavioral research*. Thousand Oaks, CA: Sage.

Taylor, B.J., Dempster, M., & Donnelly, M. (2007). Grading gems: Appraising the quality of research for social work and social care. *British Journal of Social Work, 37*, 335–354.

Thorne, S. (1998). Ethical and representational issues in qualitative secondary analysis. *Qualitative Health Research, 8*(4), 547–555.

Treloar, C., & Rhodes, T. (2009). The lived experience of hepatitis C and its treatment among injecting drug users: Qualitative synthesis. *Qualitative Health Research, 19*, 1321–1334.

van Heugten, K. (2004). Managing insider research: learning from experience. *Qualitative Social Work, 3*, 203–219.

Whitmore, E. (2002). 'People listened to what we had to say': Reflections on emancipatory qualitative evaluation. In I.F. Shaw & N.G. Gould (eds), *Qualitative research in social work*. Thousand Oaks, CA: Sage, pp. 104–118.

Yang, S. (2008). Cane of love: Parental attitudes toward corporal punishment in Korea. *British Journal of Social Work, 39*, 1540–1555.

Yin, R. (2009). *Case study research* (4th ed.). Thousand Oaks, CA: Sage.

Yoon, I. (2009). A mixed method study of Princeville's re-building from the flood of 1999: Lessons on the importance of invisible community assets. *Social Work, 54*, 19–28.

30

Participatory Action Research

Mark Baldwin

This chapter shows that, rather than the generation of new knowledge – the purpose of conventional research – participatory action research (PAR) is driven predominantly by a desire for positive social change. Growing out of social and educational research, it is one of the few research approaches embracing the principles of participation and critical reflection. Its aim is to empower and emancipate groups of people seeking to improve their situation and, to this end, involves collaboration between researchers and stakeholders as co-researchers. It closely parallels the purpose of social work as conceptualised in the International Federation of Social Workers (IFSW)/International Association of Schools of Social Work (IASSW) definition (see Chapter 24).

The chapter begins with a review of the conceptual foundations of PAR, highlighting its benefits and shortcomings. It then examines PAR's compatibility with the values and methods of social work providing illustrative examples of its appropriateness for investigating many of the questions social work practitioners, academics, students, and service users ask. Notwithstanding critiques of PAR, the chapter asks whether social work is a form of participatory research in its own right and, if so, what kinds of social work practice it suggests.

WHAT PARTICIPATORY ACTION RESEARCH CLAIMS TO BE

The *Handbook of action research* defines PAR as:

> a participatory process concerned with developing practical knowing in the pursuit of worthwhile human purposes. It seeks to bring together action and reflection, theory and practice, in participation with others, in the pursuit of practical solutions to issues of pressing concern to people, and more generally the flourishing of individual persons and their communities (Reason & Bradbury, 2008, p. 4).

There are several important aspects to this definition of PAR as a form of cooperative or collaborative enquiry. First, PAR conducts research *with* people not *on* them (Heron & Reason, 2001). Those involved in the problem under study are part of the research process. Second, co-researchers join together to develop knowledge to inform practice and solve concrete problems. As such, PAR aims to ensure the actions of those involved are better informed, if not changed through the research process. Third, PAR is a process of knowledge development involving action and reflection. It is a creative process of testing knowledge in action and through critical reflection on action. Lastly, PAR aims to solve concrete problems and, in so doing, make a positive difference in the lives of those involved in the research process and those who benefit from it (Wadsworth, 1998). Hence PAR is transformative rather than merely informative. As Gergen and Gergen (2008) argue, PAR is about 'world making' not 'world mapping' (p. 159). Research should, in their view, show people how the world could be and not just how it is. In wanting to make a difference, participatory action researchers often make claims to the emancipatory nature of the PAR process. There are examples, in the world of social work, of PAR changing practice through critical reflection (Baldwin, 2001; Bryan, 2002; Jones, 2004; Kreitzer et al., 2009) and transforming the lives of marginalised groups through challenging rather than perpetuating oppression (Baldwin, 1997; Bryan, 2002; Chowns, 2008; Cassano & Dunlop, 2005; Fenge, 2010).

van Rooyen and Gray (1995) provide a useful critique of participatory research and its compatibility with social work foreshadowing Reason and Bradbury's (2008) definition cited above. They defined PAR as an 'experiential research process where people are collectively involved on an equal basis in collective action aimed at knowledge development, education, social change and empowerment' (van Rooyen & Gray 1995, p. 89). Their review of the literature describes three aspects of participatory approaches which are the source of their strength as a research methodology. These are:

> the collective investigation of problems involving the active participation of those affected by them; the collective analysis of data so that participants gain an enhanced understanding of both the problems identified and their underlying structural causes; the collective action of participants to yield both short and long term solutions to their identified problems (van Rooyen & Gray, 1995, p. 3).

Three inter-related aspects of PAR are now examined before going on to describe how it works in practice:

1 *its participatory world view* fitting the social constructionist argument that people construct reality in relationship with one another;
2 *the focus on action* and making a difference to how people behave; and
3 *the nature of knowledge created through participatory action processes* not just valuing formal theory, but also other ways of knowing and making sense of the world.

Participatory world view

Participatory action research takes a social constructionist perspective holding to the belief all knowledge is socially created. There is no reality independent of human beings and, therefore, it suggests all knowledge is relative since it is co-constructed by human beings in relationships with others and, furthermore, humans in interaction with one another co-create their reality from their particular worldview (Reason, 1994). Hence human relationships are fundamental to the co-construction of reality, and research methodology should reflect this inextricable relationship. For researchers to see themselves as separate from the researched is to deny this relationship. Researcher-led methodologies, where objective measures are used (see Chapter 27) wherein the researcher's interpretation of the data is paramount are examples of the separation of researcher and research subjects. They imply research subjects' knowledge has lesser importance. From a PAR perspective, knowledge thus gained is less likely to have *meaning* for the subjects of the research because it has not been constructed from *within their experience*. They are, therefore, less likely to find use for research findings or to see them as relevant to their particular situation. In PAR ownership of research data and the knowledge generated is crucial, based on the belief people are also less likely to change their behaviour in directions suggested by research if they have not been part of the research experience. Hence they are more likely to reject the findings of research if they have not participated in the production of knowledge directly relevant to their concerns (Baldwin, 2000). Subject participation, on the other hand, is more likely to generate a sense of ownership and ensure the outcomes of the research are 'empowering and sustaining' (van Rooyen & Gray, 1995, p. 97). For this reason, PAR claims to generate locally relevant, useful knowledge capable of solving real-world problems.

In this sense, the influence on the development of participatory research from 'in-depth, community level anthropological research' (van Rooyen & Gray, 1995, p. 88) is discernible. This tradition is apparent through much of the ethnographic research used within a participatory framework. For example, Carol Stack, the white US researcher, is described as using a participatory ethnography in her work with Black Americans (Edmonson Bell, 2001). The participative nature of her research, built on a value base which esteemed hearing the voice of the poorest and most marginalised in the community, rather than the usual community leaders, is a powerful example of the way in which PAR can use anthropological and ethnographic traditions, within a participatory world view, to hear the voice of marginalised people.

Focus on participatory action

An action focus is pivotal to PAR built on the idea people's involvement in research directly concerning them is likely to generate useable knowledge and enhance the possibility of problem-solving action based on the research findings. People's participation has the added impact of removing power differentials between researchers and research subjects – seen as participants in the PAR process (Healy, 2001; Reason & Heron, 1995). Whereas the aim of conventional research is the generation of objective knowledge, in PAR the subjective perceptions, interests, and experiences of participants or co-researchers are paramount and the driving force is the search for practical solutions likely to make a difference in the lives of participants, who are, more often than not, oppressed or marginalised social groups. For this reason, Reason and Bradbury (2008) argued PAR is: (i) *political* in 'asserting people's right and ability to have a say in decisions which affect them and which claim to generate knowledge about them' (p. 9); and (ii) *empowering* in enabling marginalised people to 'see that they are capable of constructing and using their own knowledge' (p. 9).

THE NATURE OF KNOWLEDGE CREATED THROUGH PARTICIPATORY ACTION RESEARCH

Rather than privileging objective or propositional knowledge, as in orthodox research, Heron and Reason (2008) suggested an extended epistemology for PAR including: (i) *experiential knowledge* gained through direct encounters with people, places, and objects; (ii) *practical knowledge* related to competence or skill – knowing 'how to' do something; (iii) *propositional or explanatory knowledge* comprising theories 'about' something; and (iv) *presentational knowledge* expressed through speech, writing, and art to symbolise and convey meaning (Reason, 1994; see also Heron, 1996). Propositional knowledge – or formal theory – has dominated Western epistemology with its positivist scientific rationality. Being gleaned by expert researchers from individual subjects alienated as objects of research, it is not grounded in subjective, experiential, and practical knowledge. In recognising the dangers of this separation, PAR provides a participatory model to ensure propositional knowledge is grounded in the experience of service users as co-researchers and co-constructed by them through democratic decision-making processes. It also requires reflection upon and validation of other forms of knowledge within the extended epistemology outlined above and emphasises the part feelings play in generating or blocking knowledge development in the reflective inquiry-action learning cycle (Boud & Knights, 1996). Honing the critical faculties of participants is, therefore, an important outcome of PAR (Baldwin, 2000, 2004; Bryan, 2002; Chowns, 2008; Glennie & Cosier, 1994; Jones, 2004).

THE PURPOSE OF PARTICIPATORY ACTION RESEARCH AND ITS USE IN PRACTICE

Reason and Bradbury (2008) refer to three purposes for PAR. First, it brings an 'action dimension' back to research generating useful knowledge in practice. As a collaborative research process, it uses cycles of reflection and action to create new forms of knowledge and understanding where the aim is to link rather than separate knowing and doing. This is why participatory action researchers claim the potential to produce useful, practical, locally relevant, emancipatory knowledge freeing research participants to transform their lives through the actions they take in and as a result of the research process. Second, it challenges the status quo by giving voice to local people's perspectives and shifting views on what constitutes 'useful' knowledge (Swantz, 2008). It promotes 'inclusive participation … to address embedded social and economic inequalities' (Gaventa & Cornwall, 2008, p. 173) giving it the appearance of political action or community development rather than research or knowledge development. Third, it moves away from the modernist, positivist mindset many PAR protagonists argue is dominated by 'crude notions of economic progress' (Reason & Bradbury, 2008, p. 7). Most influential in this regard was the work of psychologist Schön (1984) who believed reflection in action was a better way of making sense of the 'swampy lowlands' of professional practice than the scientific method with its pursuit of certainty (Harre, 1981). From his study of diverse professions, Schön found multiple realities and myriad ways of knowing constituting the everyday lives of professionals. PAR is equipped uniquely for this uncertain world: Its collaborative processes of knowledge creation validate multiple voices and constructions of reality, where participants *own* the knowledge created. More important in professional practice is making sense of participants' subjective experience and behaviour in particular situations rather than the generation of 'new' knowledge or solution of broader social problems.

Illustrative examples of participatory action research in practice

In the context of professional social work practice, PAR can provide support for social workers working in threatening organisational contexts (Baldwin, 2000, 2001; Heron, 1996), such as Black practitioners working in predominantly White organisations, given its commitment 'to improving practice in organisations and bringing about political change to improve the lives of black people in a racist society' (Bryan, 2002, p. 1). It enhances multidisciplinary practice in contexts, such as child protection, where engaging groups of practitioners in collaborative inquiry is essential to interprofessional teamwork (Glennie & Cosier, 1994). Jones (2004) demonstrated its usefulness in improving assessment practices with prospective foster parents. Baldwin (2001) used cooperative inquiry to explore social workers' use of professional knowledge, skills, and values within a challenging new policy framework perceived to be undermining their autonomy. They experimented with new forms of practice, collected data on their effectiveness, over a six-month period, developed understanding of the nature of the problems with which they were dealing, and gained confidence in the process, in particular, valuing the opportunities to reflect critically on their practice. Three further examples are discussed below to illustrate PAR's use in social work. Each depicts PAR as a strongly collaborative and empowering approach, congruent with the ethos, values, aims, and practice of social work.

Daycare on the move (Baldwin, 1997)

Baldwin (1997) describes his research with colleagues involved in a daycare centre for people with learning difficulties, where a person-centred model of service provision was used (Williams, 2006). Senior staff members were concerned service users were being stigmatised and labelled in the local community. Consequently, they had bought into a consultancy package, which was based on a participatory, action-oriented approach to change, and had engaged the researcher as an external participant tasked with providing an evaluation of the change process. Drawing on O'Brien and Lyle's (1987) framework, Baldwin (1997) endeavoured to assess the extent to which service users had been able to:

1. exercise their right to share the centre with everyone else;
2. make real choices affecting their lives;
3. develop their skills and abilities;
4. be treated with respect and play a valued role in society; and
5. grow in relationships.

The collaborative PAR process involved staff-facilitated groups of service users, staff, and other stakeholders. It was overseen by a core group comprising representatives of all constituencies. Centre users were placed in changeover groups taking the process through the early stages of action and reflection when options for change were explored and debated. Each changeover group provided the core group with ideas for change, whereupon they were collated, critically reflected upon, checked with each group for accuracy and, after some cycling, presented to all involved as an action plan. This initial process was far from easy. There was a commitment from most staff but this was complicated as many centre users did not initially have the capacity to make choices or offer opinions. The depth of marginalisation of these centre users was remarkable, although, through the use of a participatory research approach, this marginalisation was largely overcome. With sensitive and empowering facilitation, the groups moved from being unable to understand the concept of choice to being assertive about what they wanted individually and collectively for the centre.

The next phase involved networking groups based on areas for future activity identified as appropriate and desirable by the changeover groups. They then took the activity (or occupation) as a research focus. The degree of sophistication of this cooperative inquiry was remarkable. It followed the principles of PAR in being participatory (all members of the group were involved as equal partners), involving action and reflection (going out and finding information, followed by an opportunity to share and make sense of what had been learnt), and creating useable knowledge.

An example was the catering group, who decided to research the viability of a business providing light lunches, with a view to marketing their enterprise to the local authority for staff on training days. They explored menus, ingredients, purchasing, preparation, cooking, equipment, health and safety, and potential markets. Each person's interests and capabilities – in what became known as the Catering Crew – contributed the motivation to start a successful business providing delicious lunches (tried and tested by the author!).

This was a PAR project because: (i) it was inclusive, democratic, and participatory; and (ii) rather than merely map the existing world of service users, it created a new world for them (Gergen & Gergen, 2008). Some centre users had very poor communication skills and dedicated efforts were made by staff and user colleagues to ensure their involvement. One service user, who was believed to be mute, began to speak when being filmed and literally found his voice through the PAR process.

Cycles of action and reflection meant the process of cooperative inquiry resulted in effective learning about the practicalities of running a small enterprise. The author observed and highlighted the different forms of knowledge found most helpful. Presentational knowledge was used in imaginative ways by staff and centre users alike. The view of the 'mute' man, presented on video, was one such example. The validation of different forms of knowledge in the extended epistemology of PAR was vital in ensuring everyone's voice was heard (Heron & Reason, 2008).

Developing culturally appropriate social work in Ghana (Kreitzer et al., 2009)

Baldwin (1997) showed PAR can be developmental or emancipatory in process and intent. Another study, facilitated by Canadian academic Kreitzer as the subject of her Ph.D. research, was primarily developmental but had emancipatory potential. She involved a group of nine Ghanaian social workers – one academic, five Bachelor of Social Work (BSW) and Diploma graduates, two BSW students, and a local community leader in a PAR project aimed at developing culturally appropriate social work education in Ghana (Kreitzer et al., 2009). The initial stages of the research involved developing understanding of social work in Ghana so as to explore ways to make it more consistent with African culture and values. Kreitzer's research involved developing an understanding of the tension between Western and African perspectives by collecting African social work literature for the group and, based on group discussions, developing her critique of Western, hegemonic social work ideas *vis à vis* Ghanaian social work. Thus the extent to which a democratic, collaborative process was followed and knowledge and learning was co-constructed could be subject to some critique. Nevertheless, the justification for using PAR was located within its transformational potential. The group endeavoured to construct methods to ensure democratic communication, worked hard to reach consensus on important matters, such as information gathering and critical analysis, and generated research themes geared towards constructing action plans. These then determined the focus of the work.

One theme was the exploration of 'past influences that have affected education in Ghana' (Kreitzer et al., 2009, p. 152). Exploration through cycles of study and reflection challenged the group to 'critically examine underlying [Western] assumptions' (Kreitzer et al., 2009, p. 153) affecting their personal and professional development. This action-and-reflection phase enabled the group to explore traditional Ghanaian beliefs and cultural practices so collectively they could decide which were appropriate to local social work education and practice. In so doing, they also studied the effects of globalisation and the way in which neoliberal International Monetary Fund policies had led to cuts in government spending on education and welfare services thus marginalising social work in Ghana.

The group's inquiry focused on: (i) foreign and local influences on social work education in Ghana and social work's position on the 'periphery' (Kreitzer et al., 2009, p. 156); (ii) restructuring the Ghanaian Association of Social Workers (GASOW), which had become weak and disorganised; (iii) researching African social work literature and getting these texts into university libraries; (iv) evaluating the effectiveness of social welfare institutions and social work practice in Ghana, noting the undue British influences and the implications of changes for social work education; and (v) developing a new culturally appropriate postcolonial social work curriculum, which balanced the traditional and colonial systems. After a ten-month period, the following outcomes were achieved.

1. The 'core themes of the research were incorporated into the existing courses'; new ones reflecting 'the social needs of Ghanaian society' (Kreitzer et al., 2009, p. 159) were added; reading lists were revised to include the new-found African texts; and new teaching methods, such as the use of video, were developed.
2. To raise the profile of social work, the research group made a public education video with assistance from Ghana TV.
3. The GASOW was revivified with a new, more active executive.

While there are some concerns about the written evaluation of this project, such as questions regarding participants' insider–outsider status, power, and control of the PAR process, and the possibility some were marginalised as a consequence, Kreitzer et al. (2009) concluded the 'PAR process, as experienced by this group of people, generated a wealth of knowledge and experience' (p. 161). The process was described as *inter alia* chaotic, confusing, serious, and conflictual, but the outcome of a clear process to disseminate learning and conscientise participants so changes to the curriculum could be made to the benefit of Ghanaian society made it worthwhile. This is a substantial claim for a research project and it perhaps overplays the importance of the research process in particular and social work in general as a force for the benefit of society as a whole.

Collaborative inquiry with children (Chowns, 2008)

In engaging in a process of research with children facing the life-threatening illness of a parent, Chowns (2008), a palliative care social worker-researcher, pushes the boundaries of what she identifies as an acceptable subject group because the voices of these particular children were rarely heard. Hence she thought it necessary to employ an approach to research respecting the marginalised nature of the group and the need to engage in a process in which their voices could be heard and make a difference, at the very least, in their own lives. Chowns (2008) described the research as 'a collaborative inquiry that sought to enable children to be listened to, and respected for their expertise and experience' (p. 562). She focused on two particular aspects, namely, power and competence. She covered the ethical issues involved, namely, informed consent, confidentiality, and the ownership of knowledge generated, noting her value position as well as a number of different methods for ensuring ethical issues were addressed. These included acknowledging the children's rights and abilities and seeking their consent before talking to parents. In addition, she engaged in a number of trust exercises enabling the young people to address their hopes and fears, starting from an 'assumption of ability rather than vulnerability' (Chowns, 2008, p. 566). She conveyed the message their voice was important thus addressing the power differentials in research involving young people. At all stages, children were given permission to veto the content of discussions and the recording of them. As in Baldwin (1997), a great deal of emphasis was placed on group processes and facilitation, and on building trust and modelling good practice, which Chowns (2008) saw as fundamental to the success of the project. The vehicle for demonstrating the knowledge, as in the example above, was video.

The children generated ideas for discussion, although the process was facilitated by adults. In light of the possibility of distressing feelings being generated by the process, opportunities for feedback, reflection, and offloading were introduced. These included trust exercises, games, discussions, and opportunities for feedback at the beginning and end of each session when participants were given the chance to examine positive and negative aspects of the process. Other than the skill of reflection, the children learnt to express themselves in coherent and sophisticated ways over the course of the project. They also showed the video at conferences and learnt skills of presentation. Hence 'the project ... enabled a marginalised group of service users – children – to communicate their research directly to the wider public' (Chowns, 2008, p. 565). While ongoing critique is necessary (see later) about the degree to which this process constituted 'research', there is a strongly made argument the process enabled these young people to create new knowledge for and about themselves and this made a difference in their lives. For instance, the effect on the young people's self-esteem was considerable, enabling them 'to properly value themselves as worthwhile contributors to society, rather than as passive victims needing help' (Chowns, 2008, p. 565). Chowns (2008) also noted their critical faculties were honed, particularly through practising 'other-centred behaviour' (p. 566). Another fundamental aspect of PAR was the collaborative ethos, which was significant, not just in building critical capability, but also for mutual capacity building. There were some profoundly moving examples of the ability to empathise and draw out deep feeling between the children in the account. The learning from this research process concluded young children were able to use the participatory aspect of the research process to express personal feelings, such as fear or grief, they found difficult to articulate. Again, some observers may wish to define this more as group work than research. What makes this research from the PAR perspective is the engagement of the researcher in helping young people understand the research process, that is, how to collect information so as to find new and effective ways of solving the problems more traditional helping approaches had left them struggling with, such as grief management. The key outcome of the research is the new knowledge generated through the process making a difference in these young people's lives.

Chowns (2008) encountered views from parents, schools, and the wider community regarding young people's capacity or competence to express their feelings and beliefs, thus questioning their reliability as co-researchers. However, she believed the children would be no more reliable or unreliable than any other group of participants. Hence, she started with the 'assumption of ability' favouring 'capacity and competence' (Chowns, 2008, p. 566). The process of the research, the video produced, and the opportunities for the children to present their work to adults at professional practitioner conferences, changed those involved despite the project's 'limited power to change the broader *context* in which it took place' (Chowns, 2008, p. 568). Since competence was not acknowledged, generally, by other key adults in the children's lives – parents, school teachers, and the wider community, Chowns (2008) concluded 'knowledge may be power, but if that knowledge is not respected or sanctioned as knowledge by those currently in power (adults), then it may yet not bring power to the knowers (children)' (p. 568). She noted, in constructing children 'as knowers, actors and equals ... the espoused values of social work and collaborative inquiry [we]re the same' (Chowns, 2008, p. 568). Collaborative inquiry tried to shift the power dynamic not through research as method but through modelling collaboration. This made it akin to empowering social work practice (e.g. Dalrymple & Burke, 2006; Dominelli, 2002; Guttierez et al., 1998). The discussion now turns to the overlapping nature of social work practice and participatory action research.

PARTICIPATORY ACTION RESEARCH: AN APPROACH SUITABLE FOR SOCIAL WORK?

Participatory action research and social work are linked in three ways: (i) there are similarities between the aims, values, and skills of PAR and social work (Barbera, 2008; Healy, 2001); (ii) social work favours collaborative, cooperative research approaches involving service-user participation (see Chapter 44); (iii) the social work process could be seen as a form of PAR and vice versa; (iv) both are political in representing the interests of oppressed and marginalised groups; (v) both capitalise on strengths; (vi) both focus on process and outcomes; and (vii) both recognise the importance of critical reflection.

Definitional similarities

The two principal international social work organisations, the IASSW and the IFSW, agreed on the following definition of social work:

> The social work profession promotes social change, problem solving in human relationships and the empowerment and liberation of people to enhance well-being. Utilising theories of human behaviour and social systems, social work intervenes at the points where people interact with their environments. Principles of human rights and social justice are fundamental to social work (IFSW/IASSW, 2000/2001).

And on the following statement on *values*:

> Since its beginnings over a century ago, social work practice has focused on meeting human needs and developing human potential. Human rights and social justice serve as the motivation and justification for social work action. In solidarity with those who are disadvantaged, the profession strives to alleviate poverty and to liberate vulnerable and oppressed people in order to promote social inclusion (IFSW/IASSW, 2000/2001).

The statement on *theories* states: 'The social work profession draws on theories of human development and behaviour and social systems to analyse complex situations and to facilitate individual, organisational, social and cultural changes' (IFSW/IASSW, 2000/2001). Finally, the statement on *practice* includes: 'Social work addresses the barriers, inequities and injustices that exist in society' (IFSW/IASSW, 2000/2001).

Returning to the definition of PAR provided in the *Handbook of Action Research* (Reason & Bradbury, 2008) and other commentaries on its purpose and aims, several connections emerge: (i) Reason and Bradbury (2008) emphasise the participatory nature of PAR in much the same way that social work emphasises working in solidarity with those who are disadvantaged; (ii) PAR emphasises the importance of practical change as does the definition of social work; (iii) the IFSW/IASSW (2000/2001) definition refers to enhancing well-being, while Reason and Bradbury (2008) refer to 'human flourishing' (p. 1) and the contribution of PAR to 'increased well-being' (p. 4); and (iv) Reason and Bradbury (2008) talk about creating 'theories which contribute to human emancipation' (p. 4) while the definition of social work refers to the values of alleviating poverty and liberating 'vulnerable and oppressed people in order to promote social inclusion' (IFSW/IASSW, 2000/2001). These correspondences between the two activities at the level of definition are profound, but the similarities do not stop there.

Service-user involvement

Much of the rhetoric from social care policy, practice guidelines, and academic writing about social work emphasises the importance of working in participation with service users. Indeed, in the UK, for instance, this was written into law (e.g., in the Children's Act, 1989 and National Health Service and Community Care Act, 1990) and governs how social workers should work with children, their families, and with adults. This directly reflects the centrality of participation as a value and process not only for effective social work but also for successful PAR, as discussed earlier.

Shared political objectives

Proponents of social work and PAR see both as areas of political activity, with an eye to the ways in which unequal power relationships create and maintain poverty and oppression. In the radical tradition, social work is viewed as a political activity seeking to: (i) liberate some sections of the community the welfare state machinery maintained in poverty (Bailey & Brake, 1975); (ii) involve them in decision making about the distribution of scarce resources (Baldwin, 2011); (iii) work with marginalised people constructed as quasi-consumers in a market of care (Ferguson & Woodward, 2009); and (iv) question the supremacy of global capitalism and the way in which it marginalises and oppresses people (Ferguson & Woodward, 2009; Ferguson et al., 2005).

Capitalising on strengths

Another aspect of commonality is a focus on strengths (see Chapter 11), with its emphasis on the expertise and autonomy of service users in assessing and meeting their own needs (Baldwin & Teater, 2012; Teater, 2010). Social workers do, however, need to be wary of trumpeting the strengths perspective in isolation from other considerations, such as structural inequalities, as it could, in isolation from a broader political analysis, be seen to be congruent with 'contemporary neoliberal notions of self-help and self-responsibility' (Gray, 2011, p. 10). The UK's ruling Conservative Party policy on 'The Big Society' would be a good example of this. The more empowering version of the strengths perspective is reflected in the writing of a number of action researchers, such as Brydon-Miller (2008), who acknowledges the importance of participant autonomy and voice in the construction of knowledge and research practice. However, this is difficult to sustain in neoliberal environments seeking to curtail autonomy (see Chapter 4).

Focus on process and outcomes

Some forms of participatory research are more concerned with processes leading to direct outcomes for oppressed and marginalised people than with knowledge development and this brings the approach close to the values of contemporary social work where service-user participation is seen as empowering and transformative. One important outcome is giving marginalised groups a 'voice', as in the example above of children living with a parent who has a life-threatening condition (Chowns, 2008), where those involved also gained confidence in the value of the knowledge they had generated, not just for them, but also for others, such as fellow practitioners, or where children are concerned, their parents. PAR encourages 'people from minority groups to have a "voice" in defining knowledge, theory and practice in their lives' (Fenge, 2010, p. 878) and might also provide social workers working in hostile environments with a powerful means of understanding and addressing their feelings of powerlessness. By aligning themselves with service users, clients and social workers alike can gain a voice.

Focus on critical reflection

Writers such as Schön (1984) and Boud and Knights (1996) have been highly influential in the development of critical reflection in social work (Fook, 2002; Gould & Baldwin, 2004; Gould & Taylor, 1996) and Heron's (1996) cooperative inquiry, later expanded with Peter Reason into the approach now known as action research, further popularised critical reflection (Heron & Reason, 2001). Hence Gaventa and Cornwall (2008) and Brydon-Miller (2008) refer to PAR as a process of reflection emphasising its importance in developing critical consciousness and dealing with power relationships within the research process. However, neither PAR nor radical social work is mainstream. PAR has struggled to maintain a place in the research hierarchy, although there is some evidence of its success in the market for books and journals, such as Reason and Bradbury (2008) and the *Journal of Action*

Research (now into its eighth volume), both of which have elicited contributions from many disciplines across the globe. Radical social work perspectives retain their appeal due to their critique of mainstream social work practice and the global managerialist agenda (Ferguson & Lavalette, 2008; Ferguson & Woodward, 2009; Ferguson et al., 2005). They are rediscovering their voice in some parts of the world, such as the UK, where the radical Social Work Action Network (SWAN) has proved successful in attracting social workers' interest in its publications (e.g., Ferguson & Lavalette, 2008) and conferences (see Chapter 47). Likewise, PAR is marginal in social research, partly because of wariness as to its efficacy. For example, Frideres (1992) offers a strident attack on the nonscientific basis of participatory research claiming it is 'moral and ideological' (p. 4) in its search for a 'legitimizing strategy' (p. 5). He sees knowledge gleaned from PAR as 'idiosyncratic' (Frideres, 1992, p. 8) reflecting 'the opinion or conviction of a specific individual' (p. 7). He goes on to claim PAR undermines the privileging of scientific knowledge which is 'an ethical consideration ... [rather than] a research issue' (p. 8) and rebrands PAR as an education or community development medium claiming it transcends 'the bounds of research ... [in] mixing ideology and politics with scientific research' (p. 9). Whether or not PAR constitutes research is clearly debatable and, as in the examples above, it is not always clear what new *knowledge* has been produced. Rather it is clearer how existing knowledge has been used for the betterment of participants, either to enhance their understanding or improve their skills. For academics who accept PAR as a legitimate form of research, there are still problems requiring resolution. For example, Healy (2001) questions whether PAR reduces power differentials in research relationships. While PAR claims researchers should eliminate power differences, activities, such as initiating activism, promoting involvement, and facilitating meetings all involve the exercise of power. Failure to acknowledge this means power becomes invisible or is driven underground. She laments the lack of reflection on the overt forms of power recreated by PAR, such as consciousness-raising, which presupposes research participants are uneducated or ignorant and need the researcher to make sense of their oppression. She asks how overarching claims of PAR's potential to change the world might be measured, noting examples of projects contributing to local change but a lack of evidence of PAR initiatives changing the social order. Further, Healy (2001) suggests PAR is too conflictual and oppositional in its approach to dealing with the results of structural oppression, since social workers have to make pragmatic decisions about which battles to fight, partly because they risk losing their jobs if they take on the wrong power brokers. There are limited opportunities for social workers to act as co-researchers in contemporary Western environments where market forces, managerialism, and privatisation threaten professional autonomy, ascribe highly prescriptive roles, and leave little time for the reflective approach of PAR. PAR is time and resource intensive making it unattractive to research funders. Finally, it does not transfer easily across cultures built as it is on a Western ethos of 'conflict, protest and dissent as features of social progress' (Healy, 2001, p. 102), which is not necessarily applicable, for example, in some Asian contexts.

While noting the consistency between the core values of social work and PAR, Barbera (2008) warns there is an ethical issue in the risks participants take in speaking up, whether they are practitioners or members of the community. Social workers could lose their jobs and members of the community could fall foul of the authorities as shown in her case example from Chile, post-Pinochet. The need for participants to make informed decisions about the consequences of participation is clear. PAR exponents Rennie and Singh (1995) warn, at its worst, PAR could result in co-option of key members of communities to more powerful agendas, thus undermining community cohesion. Participation holds the danger of being exploitative and tokenistic. It can provide an impression of involvement but actually have the effect of legitimising powerful political and business agendas rather than those of marginalised communities. Another powerful proponent of PAR, McTaggart (1999) notes the problems of publication and dissemination as having potential to alter or at least diffuse the voice of participants because of the problem of collective recording. Ultimately, whose voice is heard?

Another interesting critical consideration for participatory action researchers is the notion of insiders and outsiders (Cassano & Dunlop, 2005). In describing PAR with South Asian immigrant women, Cassano and Dunlop (2005) note how an external researcher, acting as facilitator for a PAR group, had her position undermined by the director of a voluntary organisation. There is also an issue, not discussed in any detail, of the problems associated with outsider status, where the facilitator can skew the cooperative inquiry process by their presence – as in the Kreitzer et al. (2009) example earlier. In other contexts, where researchers are insiders, there might be questions about the degree to which they can be neutral in the research process (van Rooyen & Gray, 1995). The problem for PAR is it purports to be democratic and collaborative, and this aspect is crucial to the validity and meaning of knowledge generated by the participatory research process. If there are unacknowledged power relationships from outsiders towards insiders, then the danger is this validity and meaning is undermined. Vigorously identifying the potential for such occurrences and building checks and balances at every stage of a PAR project is then essential to avoid this. In light of such critique, van Rooyen and Gray (1995) argue researchers committed to PAR have a duty to ensure consistency and clarity through use of 'systematic methodologies' (p. 93), especially if they want to avoid perceptions PAR is merely a 'problem-solving process' (p. 93) like community work rather than a mainstream research methodology. Likewise, Healy (2001) believes participatory action researchers must be transparent given the considerable opportunities for social workers to engage in collaborative research (Baldwin, 2000, 2004; Jones, 2004); positive feedback from service users engaged as co-researchers in cooperative or collaborative inquiry (Baldwin, 1997; Chowns, 2008); and encouraging outcomes in multidisciplinary environments (Glennie & Cosier, 1994; Jones, 2004). Indeed, wherever human beings experience the blunt end of discrimination, due to racism, gender inequalities, homophobia, disabling environments, ageism, classism, Indigeneity, or any of the other ways in which people's lives are devalued as a result of unequal power relationships, social workers and participatory action researchers will be found. However, they will be people who recognise the negative impacts of global capitalism and want to make a difference by changing the world. There are others, for example from some of the new social movements, with whom participatory action researchers and social workers will also collaborate, but, in the fields of social work and research practice, such a political perspective is still comparatively unusual.

CONCLUSION: SOCIAL WORK AS A FORM OF PARTICIPATORY ACTION RESEARCH

This chapter described and defined PAR illustrating its compatibility with social work's aims, values, processes, and, to a lesser degree, its practice. While academic freedom gives some leeway to researchers committed to social justice, social work practitioners might not have the same leeway within neoliberal welfare regimes (Ferguson et al., 2005). Those in nongovernment organisations engaged in community action and social development might enjoy more freedom than those working in public social services where most social workers are employed. There are signs of resistance in some quarters which are encouraging for social workers who treasure the profession's radical roots, but there is little to suggest organisations employing social workers are likely to provide opportunities for them to engage in radical practice let alone participatory research despite the profession's avowed commitment to work 'in solidarity with those who are disadvantaged' to address the 'barriers, inequities and injustices that exist in society' (IASSW, 2001).

This barrier to realising the values of the profession in the current climate is unfortunate. There are distinct signs around the globe that people are unhappy with the authoritarian imposition of ways of living upon then. This is evident in the renewal in democratic fervour in some South Mediterranean and Middle East countries where long-standing authoritarian leaders are being threatened or pushed aside by popular revolt. Also evident is a growing realisation among public sector workers, service users, and the general public in countries such as the UK of the effect of the authoritarian imposition of welfare retrenchment and ideologically driven policy carving huge chunks out of the welfare state. In this context, social work as a profession could be working in alliance with the losers in such authoritarian regimes whether driven by autocracy or global capitalism. In the UK, the spectre of privatisation of potentially all services delivered by local government for the last 100 years looms. The UK coalition government has opened up all services for marketisation: 'We will create a new presumption – backed up by new rights for public service users and a new system of independent adjudication – that public services should be open to a range of providers competing to offer a better service' (David Cameron, in the *Daily Telegraph*, 21 February 2011). A profession driven by the values of social justice and human rights is completely at odds with an ideology which favours markets and the pursuit of financial gain for the few. Social workers habitually work with people who are marginalised, oppressed, and poor. PAR is illustrative in its intentions and in its practice of a different way of understanding and instigating social change. Although it may be difficult in such organisations to offer resistance, PAR does provide a positive and pragmatic call to action.

REFERENCES

Bailey, R., & Brake, M. (eds), (1975). *Radical social work*. London: Edward Arnold.

Baldwin, M. (1997). Day care on the move. *British Journal of Social Work, 27*, 951–958.

Baldwin, M. (2000). *Care management and community care: Social work discretion and the construction of policy*. Aldershot, Hants: Ashgate.

Baldwin, M. (2001). Working together, learning together: The role of co-operative inquiry in the development of complex practice by teams of social workers. In P. Reason & Bradbury, H. (eds), *Handbook of action research*. London: Sage, pp. 287–293.

Baldwin, M. (2004). Critical reflection: Opportunities and threats to professional learning and service development in social work organizations. In N. Gould & Baldwin, M. (eds), *Social work, critical reflection and the learning organisation*. Aldershot, Hants: Ashgate.

Baldwin, M.J. (2008). Promoting and managing Innovation; Critical reflection, organizational learning and the development of innovative practice in a national children's voluntary organization. *Qualitative Social Work, 7*(3), 330–348.

Baldwin, M. (2011). Resisting the EasyCare model: Building a more radical, community-based, anti-authoritarian social work for the future. In M. Lavalette (ed.), *Radical social work today: Legacy, relevance and prospects*. Bristol: Policy Press.

Baldwin, M., & Teater, B. (2012). *Social work in the community: Making a difference*. Bristol: Policy Press.

Barbera, R. (2008). Relationships and the research process: Participatory action research and social work. *Journal of Progressive Human Services, 19*(2), 140–159.

Boud, D., & Knights, S. (1996). Course design for reflective practice. In N. Gould & Taylor, I. (eds), *Reflective learning for social work*. Aldershot, Hants: Arena, pp. 23–34.

Bryan, A. (2002). *Exploring the experiences of black professionals in welfare agencies and black students*

in social work education. Ph.D. thesis, University of Bath.
Brydon-Miller, M. (2008). Ethics and action research: Deepening our commitment to principles of social justice and redefining systems of democratic practice. In P. Reason & Bradbury, H. (eds), *The Sage handbook of action research: Participative inquiry and practice* (2nd ed.). London: Sage, pp. 199–210.
Cassano, R., & Dunlop, J. (2005). Participatory action research with South Asian immigrant women: A Canadian example. *Critical Social Work*, 6(1). Retrieved October 28, 2010 from http://www.uwindsor.ca/criticalsocialwork/participatory-action-research-with-south-asian-immigrant-women-a-canadian-example
Chowns, G. (2008). No – you don't know how we feel: Collaborative inquiry using video with children facing the life-threatening illness of a parent. In P. Reason & Bradbury, H. (eds), *The Sage handbook of action research: Participative inquiry and practice* (2nd ed.). London: Sage, pp. 562–572.
Dalrymple, J., & Burke, B. (2006). *Anti-oppressive practice: Social care and the law* (2nd ed.). Maidenhead: Open University Press.
Dominelli, L. (2002). *Anti-oppressive social work: Theory and practice*. Basingstoke: Palgrave.
Edmonson Bell, E. (2001). Infusing race into the US discourse on action research. In P. Reason & Bradbury, P. (eds), *Handbook of action research: Participative inquiry and practice*. London: Sage, pp. 48–58.
Fenge, L. (2010). Striving towards inclusive research: An example of participatory action research with older lesbians and gay men. *British Journal of Social Work*, 40, 878–894.
Ferguson, I., & Lavalette, M. (2008). *Social work after Baby 'P': Issues, debates and alternative perspectives*. Liverpool: Hope University.
Ferguson, I., Lavalette, M., & Whitmore, E. (eds), (2005). *Globalisation, global justice and social work*. Abingdon: Routledge.
Ferguson, I., & Woodward, R. (2009). *Radical social work in practice: Making a difference*. Bristol: Policy Press.
Fook, J. (2002). *Social work: Critical theory and practice*. London: Sage.
Frideres, J.S. (1992). Participatory research: An illusionary perspective. In J.S. Frideres (ed), *A world of communities: Participatory research perspectives*. North York: Captus University Publications, pp. 1–13.
Gaventa, J., & Cornwall, A. (2008). Power and knowledge. In P. Reason & Bradbury, H. (eds), *The Sage handbook of action research: Participative inquiry and practice* (2nd ed.). London: Sage, pp. 172–189.
Gergen, K., & Gergen, M. (2008). Social construction and research as action. In P. Reason & Bradbury, H. (eds), *The Sage handbook of action research: Participative inquiry and practice* (2nd ed.). London: Sage, pp. 159–171.
Glennie, S., & Cosier, J. (1994). Collaborative inquiry: Developing multi-disciplinary learning and action. *Journal of Inter Professional Care*, 8(3), 255–263.
Gould, N., & Baldwin, M. (2004). *Social work, critical reflection and the learning organisation*. Aldershot, Hants: Ashgate.
Gould, N., & Taylor, I. (1996). *Reflective learning for social work*. Aldershot, Hants: Arena.
Gray, M. (2011). Back to basics: A critique of the strengths perspective in social work. *Families in Society: The Journal of Contemporary Social Services*, 92(1), 5–11.
Guttierez, L., Parsons, R., & Cox, E. (eds) (1998). *Empowerment in social work practice: A sourcebook*. Pacific Grove, CA: Brooks/Cole.
Harre, R. (1981). The positivist–empiricist approach and its alternatives. In P. Reason & Rowan, J. (eds), *Human inquiry: A sourcebook of new paradigm research*. Chichester: John Wiley.
Healy, K. (2001). Participatory action research and social work: A critical appraisal. *International Social Work*, 44, 93–105.
Heron, J. (1996). *Co-operative inquiry: Research into the human condition*. London: Sage.
Heron, J., & Reason, P. (2001). The practice of co-operative inquiry: Research 'with' rather than 'on' people. In P. Reason & Bradbury, P. (eds), *Handbook of action research: Participative inquiry and practice*. London: Sage.
Heron, J., & Reason, P. (2008). Extending epistemology within a co-operative inquiry. In P. Reason & Bradbury, H. (eds), *The Sage handbook of action research: Participative inquiry and practice* (2nd ed.). London: Sage.
International Federation of Social Workers [IFSW]/International Association of Schools of Social Work [IASSW] (2000/2001). *The definition social work*. Electronic document. Retrieved August 3, 2010 from: http://www.ifsw.org/f38000138.html
International Association of Schools in Social Work (IASSW) (2001). Historic agreement on international definition of social work, *IASSW Newsletter*, 1.
Jones, J. (2004). *Report of an action research project to improve the quality of family placement assessments*. Mindful Practice Ltd. Retrieved August 13, 2010 from www.mindfulpractice.co.uk

Kreitzer, L., Abukari, Z., Antonio, P., Mensah, J., & Kwaku, A. (2009). Social work in Ghana: A participatory action research project looking at culturally appropriate training and practice. *Social Work Education*, *28*(2), 145–164.

McTaggart, R. (1999). Reflection on the purposes of research, action, and scholarship: A case of cross-cultural participatory action research. *Systemic Practice and Action Research*, *12*(5), 493–511.

O'Brien, J., & Lyle, C. (1987). *A framework for accomplishment*. Decatur, GA: Responsive Systems Associates.

Reason, P. (ed.) (1994). *Participation in human inquiry*. London: Sage.

Reason, P., & Bradbury, P. (eds) (2001). *Handbook of action research: Participative inquiry and practice*. London: Sage.

Reason, P., & Bradbury, H. (eds) (2008). *The Sage handbook of action research: Participative inquiry and practice* (2nd ed.). London: Sage.

Reason, P., & Heron, J. (1995). Co-operative inquiry. In J. Smith, Harre, R., & Langenhove, L. (eds), *Rethinking methods in psychology*. London: Sage.

Schön, D. (1984). *The reflective practitioner: How professionals think in action*. New York: Basic Books.

Social Work Action Network (2010). Home page. Retrieved August 13, 2010 from http://www.socialworkfuture.org

Swantz, M. (2008). Participative action research as practice. In Reason, P., & Bradbury, H. (eds), *The Sage handbook of action research: Participative inquiry and practice* (2nd ed.). London: Sage.

Teater, B. (2010). *Applying social work theories and methods*. Maidenhead: Open University Press, McGraw Hill.

van Rooyen, C., & Gray, M. (1995). Participatory research and its compatibility to social work. *Social Work Practitioner-Researcher*, *8*(3), 87–93.

Wadsworth, Y. (1998). What is participatory action research? Action Research International, Paper 2. Retrieved September 29, 2010 from http://www.scu.edu.au/schools/gcm/ar/ari/p-ywadsworth98.html

Williams, P. (2006). *Social work with people with learning difficulties* (2nd ed.). Exeter: Learning Matters.

31

Systematic Review

Elaine Sharland

Echoing a wider tide of criticism, the UK Economic and Social Research Council (ESRC) complained in 2008:

> Despite some notable exceptions, social work and social care policy and practice have developed largely without an adequate, closely connected research evidence base. It is essential that a stronger connection is made [to] deliver high quality evidence to the policy and practitioner communities (ESRC, 2008, p. 1).

Described as 'the cornerstone of evidence based policy and practice in modern welfare democracies' (Social Care Institute for Excellence Fisher et al., 2006, p. vi), systematic reviews bring with them the promise of such connectedness – between diverse and multidisciplinary elements of the research base – and between research, policy, and practice. They are, nonetheless, relatively recent arrivals in social work, though more established in allied disciplines of health and education. Their pledge is to identify, appraise rigorously, synthesise, and communicate to those who need to know the findings and implications of robust research. Like evidence-based practice (see Chapter 26), in which they are embedded, systematic reviews have their passionate advocates and their detractors, on epistemological, methodological, political, and professional grounds.

This chapter offers a critical reflection on systematic reviews, from the perspective of social work. It is written with the benefit of experience, the author having co-conducted several systematic reviews in this field, but also with the luxury of independence from any single orthodoxy (Sharland & Taylor, 2006, 2007; Taylor et al., 2006). At the heart of discussion lies the nature and needs of social work as a research discipline and a professional field. Hence the central question is not 'How can systematic review cope with social work research?' but 'How can systematic review work for social work?'

The discussion begins with an outline of the key characteristics of systematic review, setting them in wider contexts, and giving a profile of the surrounding debates. Potentially the most helpful for scrutinising systematic review from the particular perspective of social work is the TAPUPAS framework, developed by Pawson et al. (2003). It was designed to capture generically the qualities of all forms of social care knowledge, not just research. It is still exploratory, with some further work done and more needed to explore how it may be operationalised in detail (Long et al., 2006). For now, TAPUPAS appears to offer an overarching quality framework with the potential capture many of the characteristics of social work research described above, along with its intrinsic and extrinsic qualities. The name of the framework amalgamates the seven quality dimensions it comprises:

- *Transparency* (openness to scrutiny)
- *Accuracy* (grounding in events, sources, and experiences)
- *Purposivity* (fitness of method to purpose)

These are broadly familiar intrinsic quality criteria deployed in social sciences:

- *Utility* (fitness for use)
- *Propriety* (ethics and legality) may capture intrinsic qualities of research conduct and also the extrinsic ethical purposes of social work research
- *Accessibility* (intelligible presentation) (accessibility and utility are extrinsic dimensions of quality, focused on the relevance and timeliness of the knowledge presented, and their value to the knowledge user)
- *Specificity* recognises all social care knowledges should meet source-specific (in this case research) standards, however defined.

The remainder of the chapter uses the lens of TAPUPAS to look critically at how systematic review might work for social work.

SYSTEMATIC REVIEWS: CHARACTERISTICS, CONTEXT, AND CONTEST

The nature and context of systematic reviews

Important at the outset is to clarify what is meant by 'systematic review', and how these are distinguished from 'traditional' reviews of research literature. Put simply:

> A systematic review is a summary of research that uses explicit methods to perform a thorough literature search and critical appraisal of individual studies to identify the valid and applicable evidence. It ... can be applied to any field of research (Thyer, 2010, slide 11).

As a whole, the systematic review process aims, and claims, to be as transparent, consistent, and bias-free as possible (Boaz et al., 2002; Gough & Elbourne, 2002; Oakely, 2006; Petticrew & Roberts, 2006). Reviews are carried out to explicit and agreed standards, and to principles of accountability and transparency, replicability, and potential for update. They are led by tightly defined, specific research questions, and protocols are developed from the beginning to guide each stage of the process. They involve exhaustive searches of all relevant literature – usually including 'grey' literature – apposite to the review question, and deploy explicit criteria to include and exclude research and appraise its quality. The methods used for synthesis vary, ranging from narrative approaches to statistical meta-analysis of data from comparable studies aggregated to measure the size of effect of interventions. However, meta-analysis of this sort is rarely achievable in social work, where study populations, contexts, interventions, and outcomes, even if calculable, are almost invariably too diverse to allow statistical comparison to this level. The exceptions are in the USA, where some social work interventions have the advantage of discrete programme funding and evaluation according to experimental designs (Littell et al., 2008), but the corresponding disadvantage that their findings have limited transferable value elsewhere. For these reasons, meta-analysis is a minority focus of the present discussion.

Systematic reviews originated in the fields of health and education, part and parcel of the push towards evidence-based practice, grounded on scientifically demonstrated efficacy (Petticrew & Roberts, 2006; Sheldon, 1997). During the last 20 years, systematic reviews of healthcare interventions have been strongly promoted by the international Cochrane Collaboration and reviews of psychology and criminal justice interventions by its sister organisation, the Campbell

Collaboration. Both restrict their remit to examining the efficacy of interventions, relying on studies using experimental methods, mainly randomised controlled trials. Since the mid-1990s, however, there has been diversification. In particular, the UK Centre for Evidence for Policy and Practice Information (EPPI) in the Institute of Education at the University of London has been responsible for extending the fields of social intervention reviewed, to include education, as well as the types of review question asked and the range of studies included. Their review methodologies embrace qualitative as well as quantitative research, in response to questions both wider and deeper than 'what works?' More recently, and drawing closely on the EPPI model, SCIE – whose purpose is to collect, synthesise, and communicate up-to-date knowledge about what works in social care – has developed dedicated guidelines for systematic review in social care (Coren & Fisher, 2006; Rutter et al., 2010).

Like evidence-based practice more broadly, systematic reviews have been increasingly popular with governments and funders commissioning research for use in professional fields. In UK social work, for example, SCIE has commissioned in excess of 20 systematic reviews of professional practice, services, and education, many of them leading directly to practice guides for dissemination. In other cases, government departments responsible for children, families, adult social care, and international development have commissioned systematic reviews directly.

The appeal of systematic reviews in these quarters can be explained on several related counts (Solesbury, 2001). Since they aggregate and synthesise findings across many studies, they have the potential to make existing research both more generalisable and more accessible to policy and practice users (Dixon-Woods et al., 2004; Thomas & Harden, 2003). Moreover, they speak to contemporary preoccupations with public service accountability through demonstrable evidence-based practice (Braye & Preston-Shoot, 2005b; Nutley et al., 2002). For those responsible for spending public monies on policies and services that are both effective and cost effective, systematic reviews promise to yield the best substantiated and most trustworthy evidence on which to base decisions. There are only two blots on the horizon. First, systematic reviews are costly, time consuming and require capacity development in information management and technical skills for searching, mapping, quality appraising and synthesising research. In resource-starved public spending environments, there may well be resort to lighter touch 'rapid evidence reviews' instead. Second, even where skills and funding allow, identifying and retrieving relevant research in social sciences remains challenging. Increasing online availability of journals is helpful, as is access to electronic bibliographic databases. But the sensitivity and specificity of the latter are variable and often compromised by poor-quality abstracts. In social work the challenges are accentuated by lack of a dedicated international bibliographic database with the capability and facilities of others in, for example, medicine, nursing and psychology (Taylor, 2009; Taylor et al., 2007).

Contested territories

Notwithstanding their favoured status with policy makers, systematic reviews have their detractors, many of them passionate. The vehemence of debate, as with evidence-based practice, at times seems underscored by misunderstanding, at times by parody, and is accentuated through the force of rhetoric. As Hammersley (2001) observed, both evidence-based practice and systematic review have become 'slogan(s) whose rhetorical effect is to discredit opposition' (p. 1). Against such disavowal, MacLure (2005) has railed at the 'clarity bordering on stupidity' (p. 393) of systematic reviews. Oakley's (2006) rejoinder dismisses critics of systematic review and randomised control trials as 'resisters', simply confused or defensive, while Thyer (2010) explains away criticism as 'myths and misconceptions'. The arguments are heightened in the fields of education and social welfare, where problems and interventions are complex and situated, and where the nature and status of knowledge and evidence themselves are contested, as is their relationship to practice. Key axes of contention are epistemological and methodological, and political and related to professional practice.

Epistemology and methodology
The introduction of systematic reviews into fields such as education and social work has exposed a trail of epistemological and methodological fault lines within the research community and beyond. At one end of the terrain, the Cochrane (2008) and Campbell (2010) models – with Macdonald (2003), Littell et al. (2008), and Thyer (2009, 2010) strong advocates in social work – are largely positivist in their approach to review and primary research. 'Positivist' here denotes the belief knowledge accumulation is aggregative, generalisable factual evidence of the causes and effects of interventions may be discovered, and predictive theories generated. Cochrane and Campbell adhere strongly to their hierarchy of evidence which places randomised controlled trials highest among sources of primary research evidence, and until now have included only these in their systematic reviews. According to the Cochrane and Campbell hierarchy, qualitative research generates a much lower form of evidence, expert opinion lower still, and theory lowest of all. From the perspective of social work, adherence to the Cochrane and Campbell criteria would mean the vast majority of social work research conducted outside the USA would simply be excluded from review. It is noteworthy both the Cochrane and Campbell Collaborations are now considering the development of methodologies to synthesise qualitative research, so though the hierarchy of evidence remains intact, practices for inclusion in systematic review may change (The Cochrane Collaboration, 2010).

However, to date, and despite Thyer and Myers' (2011) observation there are many Cochrane and Campbell systematic reviews relevant for social work, unsurprisingly there have been none of core social work research, as characterised in discussion later.

At the opposite pole stand postmodernist critics of 'methodology's [failed] hope for certainty' (Stronach & MacLure, 2007, p. 4; see also MacLure, 2005). They reject the notion of an objectively knowable external world and, along with rule-bound enslavement to measuring it, predicting it, and generalising from its diversity. Meanwhile, Hammersley (2001), though not encamped with postmodernists and not averse to synthesis of diversity, has also been an animated critic of systematic review. He rejects its claims to objectivity, the apparent eradication of researcher judgement, and argues it fails to deliver on transparency. Instead, he favours a fully interpretative approach to knowledge generation, typified by narrative reviews that describe what there is without imposing hierarchical judgements about evidential status.

On the middle ground, EPPI (Gough & Elbourne, 2002; Thomas & Harden, 2003) and others, such as Nutley et al. (2002), Petticrew and Roberts (2006), and Popay et al. (2006), have all turned their minds to developing review methodologies intended for application across various policy sectors, such as education, health, and criminal justice, and including social care. All are committed to core principles of systematic review, in particular to rigorous appraisal of the quality of research evidence but they reject the Cochrane hierarchy of evidence, favouring instead a 'horses-for-courses' approach, with the inclusion of qualitative as well as quantitative research in systematic reviews, as best befits the review question. Systematic review questions, in turn, need not be restricted to 'what works'. They might equally explore social problems, processes, and experiences of intervention (Fisher et al., 2006; Harden & Thomas, 2005). These approaches explicitly retain some positivistic principles, aiming towards knowledge accumulation and generalisability, and working through a set of preset, formalised – some would say formulaic – procedures but they recognise 'there are considerable interpretative steps along the way' (Gough & Elbourne, 2002, p. 234) and, in the case of Popay et al. (2006), explicitly foreground the use of theory to guide interpretation.

Finally, Pawson (2002c), from the position of critical realism, rejects both what he regards as the straitjacket of positivism and the analytical flaccidity of narrative review, proposing in their place a framework for 'realist synthesis'. Here, the transmission of lessons from one study to another occurs through a process of constant comparison and theory building, rather than appraisal of each study in its own right and assembling empirical generalisations. By contrast with mainstream systematic review, which for the most part sidelines theory, Pawson's (2002c) model is theory led, on the conviction 'theory and evidence work best when they meet in the middle' (p. 356). These formulations and their significance for systematic review in social work in particular, are discussed further below.

Politics and professional practice

Epistemological and methodological contests, especially when they take place in research disciplines close to policy and practice, are rarely free from politics and, by definition, have wider implications for the professional fields of and to which they speak. Chief among the political criticisms levelled at systematic review has been it is an instrument of governmentality and managerialism. For Solesbury (2001), systematic reviews can be seen as specific expressions of neoliberal utilitarian pragmatism and fixation on 'what works'. For Hammersley (2001), the systematic review movement extends the myth of the audit society to research, threatening to monopolise research funding and distort the research enterprise. In the main, however, political critique has subsumed systematic review under the broader umbrella of evidence-based practice, which 'may merely serve to provide a source of legitimacy that contributes to the authority of social work managers' (Yunong & Fengzhi, 2009, p. 179). Here the political and the professional begin to merge, with the complaint practice wisdom, professional judgement, discretion, and reflexivity are undermined by the imposition of 'expert' and decontextualised knowledges from outside, that is, the appliance of science (Webb, 2001).

These wider political and professional criticisms, along with corresponding vigorous defence (Oakley, 2006; Thyer, 2010; Thyer & Myers, 2011) are beyond the scope of this chapter. So too are broader considerations of knowledge management, which challenge mechanistic or simplistic assumptions of a direct path between research production, dissemination, and utilisation (Gray & Schubert, 2011; Gray et al., 2009; Nutley et al., 2003). However, what is core to present discussion is the extent which systematic reviews are capable of contributing to practice-oriented disciplines and to practice itself, in policy and political contexts. Here a primary criticism, albeit levelled mainly at the Cochrane and Campbell Collaborations, has been systematic reviews lack the capacity to capture the complexity characterising real social problems and interventions (Boaz et al., 2002). Added to this, the findings of systematic reviews, grounded as they may be in robust research from some contexts, may make little sense for others. Whatever the structural facilitators or barriers to research utilisation, if systematic reviews do not speak, and speak accessibly, to policy and practice realities recognisable in context, their findings have little hope of uptake among policy makers or practitioners.

KINDS AND QUALITY OF SOCIAL WORK RESEARCH

Social work practice typically deals with 'wicked problems' (Webb, 2006), so-called because they are complex and multilayered, located at the interface between the individual and the social, situated within complex organisational and structural contexts – often under conditions of uncertainty, concerned with process and experience as well as outcomes, and framed through competing value systems. This too is the stuff of social work research. If systematic review is to engage productively with social work, it must find appropriate ways of embracing the nature and quality of social work research.

Characterising social work research and determining how its quality can be judged have been the subjects of lively debate in recent years. Differences centre around whether or not social work should be considered a distinctive discipline, whether pure or applied, and how its intrinsic epistemic quality, as well as its extrinsic value, might be appraised. The detail and nuance of much of that debate is beyond the scope of this chapter. For present purposes, discussion draws specifically on the work of Shaw and Norton (2007) and Shaw et al. (2010) to outline the key characteristics of social work research, and additionally on Pawson et al. (2003) to examine the quality of social work research, and the qualities required of systematic reviews in particular.

Characterising the research field

Shaw and Norton (2007) and Shaw et al. (2010) argue social work research may be both 'pure' and 'applied', that is, driven by considerations of contributing to fundamental knowledge and use, respectively. This is a pluralistic research field, drawing on many allied disciplines for its hybrid epistemological, methodological, theoretical, and empirical palette. What characterises social work research and brings to it coherence is its distinctive configuration around four key, inter-related dimensions: its purpose, contexts, practice or methods, and domains.

Starting with *purpose*, the aim of social work research may well be (as exponents of evidence-based practice would have it) to provide impartial evidence to inform decision making and improve practice and organisational learning. Beyond this, however, Shaw et al. (2010) point out the purpose of social work research may be also to generate or enhance theory about social work and social care, or to fulfil a critical, moral purpose reflecting its practice values. The latter may include highlighting lived experience, advancing practice wisdom, foregrounding service users, and promoting empowerment, social justice, and social change.

Moving to the *contexts* characterising social work research, here Shaw et al. (2010) refer to the working environments shaping both social work practice and knowledge development. These may be specific institutional and policy environments, as well as wider structural, cultural, political, and ethical contexts. In particular, there are the dual contexts of government and governmentality, whereby social work research might not only evaluate government-led strategies, but itself become the means of governance (Shaw & Zlotnick, 2010).

As for the *practice* or *methods* of social work research, Shaw et al. (2010) observe these tend not to be original to social work, but are adapted to serve the characteristic purposes of this field, hence their heterogeneity. They can include, for example, either quantitative or qualitative evaluation of the effectiveness of interventions, methods for highlighting the experience of social work problems, practices, and processes, and for promoting service-user and carer participation.

Lastly, there are the *domains* characteristic of social work research. The term 'domain' is intended to be more context-free than 'services' or 'agencies', to capture the problems social work confronts at multiple levels and the means of addressing them. Hence the domains of social work research may include, for example, children and adults, ageing and disability, health and well-being, and family, community, and nation. Characterised in this way, it is abundantly clear how diverse and complex a research field this is. The challenges for systematic review to embrace it are significant, all the more so when the question of research quality is brought into play.

The quality of social work research

As noted in the preceding discussion, the strongest claims made for evidence-based practice in general, and systematic review in particular, rest on their capacity to deliver to those who need it not just evidence but the best evidence to inform their decision making and practice. These claims have generated animated debate, much of it paradigmatic, about how quality may be judged. From the characterisation of social work research presented above, stems the obvious conclusion its quality should be judged according to its purposes, contexts, practices, and domains.

Here Shaw and Norton (2007) make the useful distinction between inner and outer science (also expressed as intrinsic and extrinsic research quality). The former refers to the inherent qualities of research in itself, that is, the extent to which it adheres to accepted epistemic norms. These norms or criteria may be methodological, concerned with the choice of methods fit for purpose to the research question, and the rigour with which they are deployed. But they are not restricted to methodology alone. They also refer to the quality of conceptualisation and theorisation, the extent to which research is informed by an existing knowledge base, and to which conclusions drawn are justified by the evidence discovered. Distinct from these inherent qualities, the outer science or extrinsic quality of research concerns its value – either value for use – or value determined according to some other purpose. Thus the value of social work research may rest directly in its relevance and utility for those who need to use it in context. Equally, however, its value may rest in the contribution of the research process or product to service-user involvement, social justice, or social change.

So systematic review in social work must not only cater to the diversity and complexity of the research field, it must also address the quality of research in a nuanced and inclusive way appropriate to the field. A plethora of detailed schema for appraising research quality in the social sciences has been developed, as further discussion will elaborate. Potentially the most helpful for scrutinising systematic review from the particular perspective of social work is the TAPUPAS framework, developed by Pawson et al. (2003). It was designed to capture generically the qualities of all forms of social care knowledge, not just research. It is still exploratory, with some further work done and more needed to explore how it may be operationalised in detail (Long et al., 2006). For now, TAPUPAS appears to offer an overarching quality framework with the potential capture many of the characteristics of social work research described above, along with its intrinsic and extrinsic qualities. The name of the framework amalgamates the seven quality dimensions comprising it: 'Transparency' (openness to scrutiny), 'Accuracy' (grounding in events, sources, and experiences) and 'Purposivity' (fitness of method to purpose) are broadly familiar intrinsic quality criteria deployed in social sciences. 'Propriety' (ethics and legality) may capture intrinsic qualities of research conduct and also the extrinsic ethical purposes of social work research. Both 'Utility' (fitness for use) and 'Accessibility' (intelligible presentation) are extrinsic dimensions of quality, focused on the relevance and timeliness of the knowledge presented, and their value to the knowledge user. Finally the dimension of 'Specificity' recognises all social care knowledges should meet source-specific (in this case research) standards, however defined.

SYSTEMATIC REVIEW: WORKING FOR SOCIAL WORK

An inclusive approach to inclusion

Defining and setting clear boundaries around the review question is a *sine qua non* for systematic reviews. But it is rarely straightforward in social work, where the problems and interventions under review are themselves rarely bounded. A brief look at the catalogue of systematic reviews commissioned and published by SCIE, for example, confirms their topic areas, including 'partnership', 'human growth and development', and 'complex healthcare needs', are not always readily definable, let alone their boundaries agreed. Moreover, the review questions themselves call into the field of vision wider research not directly addressed to the questions, but usefully shedding light on them. Tight focus on the nature and effectiveness of interprofessional education, for example, excluded the much more developed body of empirical and conceptual work on interprofessional practice, the possibilities for and challenges of which education is intended to prepare students (Sharland & Taylor, 2007). Against inclusivity, however, come the priorities of manageability, achieving the review task within resources, and generating a digestible and informative report.

The pragmatic response to these tensions is simply to give explicit justification for review boundaries, wherever drawn, to acknowledge their strengths and limitations and proceed. However, a more radical solution also suggests itself. Central to the claims to systematicity of positivist – including EPPI – approaches to systematic reviews is tightly defined criteria for inclusion or exclusion of research studies are determined at the outset by the review question and remain intact throughout. More akin to interpretative research paradigms would be to adopt a more fluid rather than linear review process, with boundaries, and inclusion and exclusion criteria redefined as the review progresses and findings or concepts emerge (Dixon-Woods et al., 2004). The fluidity of this process presents huge challenges for reviewing within limited resources. It may also compromise transparency and some notions of rigour but the gains in utility, accessibility, and fitness for purpose, that is, making the findings meaningful in context, may be worth it.

Tackling the problem of inclusivity versus exclusivity also shines the spotlight on 'hierarchies of evidence', held dear by Cochrane and Campbell, and the butt of ridicule from systematic review's most vehement critics. The work of EPPI and others to promote inclusion of qualitative empirical research has already been discussed. It sits alongside arguments in the wider methodological literature qualitative research is of equal, not secondary status to quantitative, and systematic reviews excluding it are much the lesser for doing so (Popay & Roen, 2003). In the particular case of social work, there are no remaining advocates for what Pawson (2006) calls the 'RCT or bust' approach to systematic reviews. While there are few who dispute the contribution randomised controlled trials (RCTs) can make to answering 'what works' review questions, even Macdonald (2003), one of the strongest advocates for randomised controlled trials in social work, concedes inclusion of other experimental designs may have to suffice. Beyond this, the case for inclusion of qualitative research in social work systematic reviews – in addition to, rather than instead of quantitative research – is compelling. Pragmatically, as discussed, since by far the majority of empirical research in the discipline, especially outside the USA, is qualitative, to exclude this would be to exclude from (re)view most of what is there to be seen. More fundamentally, if the characterisation of social work research drawn above holds, the field calls out for robust qualitative as well as quantitative research and review.

More challenging is the question of whether conceptual or theoretical work should be included in systematic reviews, and if so how. Much of the social care literature includes 'think pieces', reflecting, conceptualising and, in some cases, theorising on the basis of practice experience or accumulated knowledge of the field, but not directly from primary empirical research. The question of the relationship between evidence and theory is, of course, familiar from much wider methodological debates. Cochrane and Campbell approaches exclude non-empirical work, on the grounds it does not constitute 'evidence'. By contrast, EPPI (Gough & Elbourne, 2002) and Popay et al. (2006) recognise theory – for example about how, why, and for whom interventions work – informs review questions, decisions about which empirical studies to include, and about how to interpret and synthesise their findings. Nonetheless, reflecting from the inside as well as out, theory feels very much the silent guest in systematic review. Non-empirical work is not included for appraisal or synthesis in its own right. There is little guidance nor yet debate about how to judge its quality, nor how to use it to appraise and synthesise empirical evidence. On grounds of utility alone, inclusion and more prominent engagement with theory in systematic reviews of social work research would add value. It would help research users to make sense of empirical findings, and to reflect critically on whether and how messages from review can be transferred from wider contexts to their own.

The qualities of research quality

Since the key purpose of systematic review is to identify not simply any research evidence but specifically 'the most valid and applicable evidence' (Thyer, 2010) in answer to a review question, appraising the quality of included research is core to their business and fitness for purpose. Necessarily, this involves using what TAPUPAS calls 'source specific' – in this case research – quality criteria. For social work reviews, assuming the arguments developed above hold, these criteria must embrace both quantitative and qualitative research, and must address the intrinsic and extrinsic qualities of research. Achieving this in a fashion that is not mechanistic or formulaic but is fit for purpose (Shaw & Norton, 2007) is a further challenge for systematic review in social work.

Quality criteria

Quality standards for quantitative research, as deployed by the Cochrane (2008) and Campbell (2010) Collaborations, are well established and broadly agreed, with research rigour and the robustness of evidence associated primarily with inner science qualities, such as reliability, validity, and capacity for statistical generalisation. The heterogeneity of qualitative methodologies has been less easy to capture through common quality standards, though there has been a range of attempts to do so (Boaz & Ashby, 2003; Daly et al., 2007; Harden et al., 1999; Popay & Roen, 2003; Solesbury, 2001; Spencer et al., 2003). Indeed, Harden (2007) found no fewer than 31 different tools diversely designed for this purpose, some even intended to combine quality standards for qualitative with quantitative research (Mays & Pope, 2000; Wallace et al., 2004). Whether consensus on generic standards across diverse qualitative methodologies, let alone qualitative and quantitative, is ultimately achievable may be in doubt (Dixon-Woods et al., 2004; Pawson, 2006; Sutton et al., 1999). Nonetheless, it is sufficiently possible to look across their commonalities to see how well collectively they may serve systematic review in social work.

Looked at through the lens of TAPUPAS, transparency, first, is a quality criterion highlighted by most, with the emphasis on the quality of reporting and clarity of research questions, aims, objectives, and methods. Next, accurate presentation of findings and conclusions is also strongly called for, with 'internal validity' or 'credibility' denoting faithful representation of what is found, be it the effect size of interventions or the lived experiences of research subjects. As for purposivity, the fitness of research methods used for exploring the questions being asked is held by all to be central to research quality – recognising, of course, the specific criteria used to judge purposivity will vary according to the research question and context in each case. The quality standard of *propriety* is most commonly articulated in the broader methodological literature in terms of informed consent, confidentiality, and researcher 'sensitivity' to participants (Mauthner & Birch, 2002; Wallace et al., 2004). Given, however, social work research may also aspire to moral purposes, the quality standard of propriety might well be extended to give distinctive credit, for example, to participative or service-user led research promoting social inclusion and empowerment (Braye & Preston-Shoot, 2005a; Long et al., 2006).

By contrast with the above quality criteria, the broader methodological literature pays rather scant attention to appraisal either of the accessibility or the utility of research evidence. Seen through the TAPUPAS lens, both of these qualities are essential if social work research and review are to be capable of communicating complexity without compromising it, and of conveying what it is useful to know in decision-making settings. Of course, research accessibility does not guarantee utilisation (Boaz & Ashby, 2003; Nutley et al., 2003; Ruckdeschel & Chambon, 2010) but, as Shaw and Norton (2007) proposed, social work research should be judged not on whether it achieves desired impact, but on whether and how it aims to be useful. As yet, although there are some examples to which social work might usefully look (Furlong & Oancea, 2005), the criteria for doing so are less well developed than they might be.

At least as important as the question of which quality criteria should be applied to social work research in systematic review is the question of how and in what combination. Before embarking on this discussion, there are notes of caution to be sounded. Stake and Schwandt (2006) wisely warn against the pitfalls of 'criteriology', whereby 'quality as experienced' becomes submerged beneath 'quality as measured'. For social work, Shaw and Norton (2007) and Shaw et al. (2010) counsel quality criteria should not be applied mechanistically, weighted one against the other, but rather at a level of generality doing justice to the integrity of the whole.

Quality in the balance

At present, guidance for those conducting systematic reviews pays much more attention to 'what counts' in research quality than to 'how much it counts'. Whatever the formulae in use, these judgements are inevitably interpretative and contestable. Cochrane and Campbell regard intrinsic qualities of rigour in experimental design and method as paramount. EPPI (2006) review guidelines for research quality appraisal, adapted for social care by SCIE (Coren & Fisher, 2006), also require much more detailed scrutiny of intrinsic than extrinsic quality, making judgements of the latter less painstaking and, arguably, privileging them less. Returning, for example, to the SCIE review of interprofessional education (Sharland & Taylor, 2007), faithful adherence to EPPI rules meant the reviewers paid detailed attention to methodologically rigorous North American evaluations whose transferability to other contexts may well be limited, while consigning potentially relevant and useful evidence from other less robust studies to the quality shadows.

A more radical approach is suggested by Boaz and Ashby (2003), drawing on the work of Edwards et al. (1998). They propose methodological rigour, so highly valued by positivist systematic review, constitutes the 'noise' of empirical research and it should not be allowed to drown out the research 'signal', which is where its true value lies. Sandelowski et al. (1997) and Pawson (2006) similarly warn 'nuggets' of evidence are all too easily discarded on grounds of methodological rather than substantive flaw. Seen through the lens of TAPUPAS, these arguments favour the qualities of purposivity and utility, but, at the same time, they may compromise accuracy, transparency, and other 'source-specific', technical quality standards. The point here is to identify rather than to resolve the conundrum of which aspects of research quality should be privileged in systematic reviews, and to highlight this as an interpretative not an algorithmic or self-evident process. Given the diversity and complexity of social work research, no one-size-fits-all formula will be fit for purpose and judgements may well be best made on a review-by-review basis. That said, if systematic reviews are to be fit for social work purpose, these judgements should themselves be made as transparent and appropriate as possible to the review question at hand.

Yet more provocative a challenge for research quality appraisal, however, arises from the arguments of Pawson (2002b, 2002c, 2006) and, to some extent, Hammersley (2001). The thrust of these is that systematic reviews in fields such as education and social work should not merely include qualitative and theoretical content, but should follow qualitative and theorised research processes too. This calls into question not just the appraisal of research quality but also the nature of research synthesis.

Research synthesis

To say systematic reviews, if they are to summarise research evidence, require research synthesis, is a statement of the obvious verging on tautology. This makes it all the more surprising, until recently, research synthesis has received relatively little attention in systematic review guidance or literature. If it is to be done in a way both useful and fit for purpose for social work, it requires significant time, and not a little critical thought about both content and process.

The content of synthesis

In the case of Cochrane and Campbell reviews, where included evidence comes from randomised controlled trials, with interventions and their effects, in theory at least, comparable across samples, meta-analysis is the synthetic tool of choice and demands sophisticated statistical skills. Synthesis of social work research, some of which is quantitative and experimental, but much of it qualitative, presents some quite other challenges.

As Dixon-Woods et al. (2004) point out, in the past the development of reviews bringing together evidence from both qualitative and quantitative research has been inhibited by the apparent schism between positivism and constructivism. Against this, they argue there is a strong rationale for 'cross-fertilisation to develop more encompassing methods incorporating the most useful element of each and allow for greater transparency' (Dixon-Woods et al., 2004, p. 31). This shift from the paradigmatic to the technical challenges of integrating qualitative and quantitative research dovetails with longer standing developments in the wider methodological field (Brannen, 1992; Popay & Williams, 1997). EPPI (Gough & Elbourne, 2002; Harden & Thomas, 2005) and Popay et al. (2006) have developed models for systematic review synthesis to incorporate and combine qualitative and quantitative research. Given the characteristics of social work research, the case for doing this in systematic review for social work seems incontestable.

More interesting a question, when holding up the critical lens of TAPUPAS, is where theory should sit within the content of the material synthesised. This discussion has highlighted the 'wicked problems' lying at the heart of social work research, along with the need for research users to understand not just 'what works' but also how, for whom, and where. So if systematic reviews are to be fit for purpose and useful, it seems likely research synthesis requires something more than the aggregation of evidence characteristic of Cochrane and Campbell (Hammersley,

2001). To use the distinction drawn by meta-ethnographers Noblitt and Hare (1988), this needs to be a theorised and 'interpretative' rather than simply an 'aggregative' or 'integrative' process of knowledge production. Far from marginalising theory – as has been the wont of systematic review and evidence-based practice – review synthesis needs fully to include and engage with theoretical as well as empirical work. Configured this way, theory-led research synthesis can guide the interrogation of empirical evidence from each study in the light of others. As a result, systematic reviews can provide the opportunity for testing existing theory and for generating new theory to advance understanding of research evidence in the most useful and productive way (Campbell et al., 2003; Pawson, 2002a, 2002b, 2002c; Popay et al., 2006).

Following these principles, one approach to which systematic review in social work might turn is Pawson's (2003c) model of 'realist synthesis'. Theory led, this scrutinises empirical research evidence to uncover the mechanisms of change explaining how interventions work, for whom, and in what contexts. Pawson's model seeks to avoid both the pitfalls of decontextualisation (characteristic of meta-analysis) and overcontextualisation (typical of narrative review). For social work, it may allow practitioners and policy makers to distinguish between research evidence generated in contexts quite different from their own, and the transferable messages genuinely to inform their situated practice and decision making. Though Pawson's model is designed for review of evaluation research, the same theory-led and iterative principles might well be applied to other systematic review questions in social work. Making this happen, however, involves rethinking not just the content of systematic review but the process too.

The process of synthesis

Some systematic reviewers of social work research have recognised already a process of 'analytic induction', or some combination of inductive and deductive reasoning and reflection, may best fit the purpose of social work research synthesis (Braye & Preston-Shoot, 2005b; Wallace et al., 2004). In essence, this would be an iterative process in terms of which understandings emergent from research findings are drawn together, scrutinised in the light of further findings, revised and retested, perhaps through a process of 'constant comparison'. Not least this mirrors the processes of reflective practice desirable in social work. It allows reviewers to challenge a priori definitions of 'the problem', to open their minds to alternative understandings, and to hear otherwise unheard voices.

It is in support of this kind of argument, however, Pawson (2006) delivers the biggest challenge to systematic review conventions, throwing down the gauntlet: 'research quality can only be determined within the act of synthesis' (p. 135). His strong claim is research quality cannot be judged piecemeal, according to predefined standards of intrinsic worth. Instead 'standards are forged in the cumulation of enquiry' (Pawson, 2002a, p. 7), the quality of each study rests in the explanatory contribution it makes to the composite picture. This stands in stark contrast to the deductive processes of positivist systematic review, typical not only of Cochrane and Campbell but also of EPPI, where the quality of each study is judged individually, whether on intrinsic or extrinsic criteria, prior to and distinct from the process of synthesis.

For social work, seen through the lens of TAPUPAS, the dynamic, iterative approach of realist synthesis has a distinct appeal but it also presents very considerable challenges. Primary among these are the practicalities: visiting and revisiting judgements of individual research quality or value would be labour intensive and time consuming beyond the point likely to be achievable within realistic resources. Standards of transparency, accuracy, and accessibility may also be very difficult to uphold through such an iterative process. Moreover, as layers of interpretation and iteration become thicker, reviews may risk becoming truer to their own logic than to the research they seek to represent.

CONCLUSION: WAYS FORWARD?

This chapter has not been intended either as an apology or a manifesto for systematic review in social work. Rather, it has tried to extract systematic review from the depths of orthodoxy at one end and scorn at the other, on the principle it may help to forge the connections between research, policy, and practice that have yet to serve social work well. Systematic review is one tool in the kit of knowledge management. Like primary research, systematic reviews should always complement, never replace, practice and policy knowledges, and organisational, service-user, and carer knowledges (Pawson et al., 2003). Nor will their findings ever obviate the need for professional judgement but, arguably, they can provide a crucial link in the chain of knowledge production, transfer, exchange, and utilisation.

In this spirit, this chapter has taken a close look at systematic review from the perspective of social work, with a mind to the kinds and quality of social work research, the problems it grapples with, and the purposes it most needs to fulfil. Unsurprisingly, there turns out to be no one-size-fits-all formula guaranteeing systematic reviews will 'work for social work' but it is possible to identify some of the key qualities required if they are to be useful and fit for purpose for social work.

First and foremost, systematic review needs transparently to recognise itself, and to be recognised, as an interpretative not a calculative activity, and one in which theory should lie not at the margins but at the heart. Reviews need to ask questions that include and extend beyond 'what works', and in answering them to draw on empirical research across all paradigms. When judging the quality of research evidence, whichever specific criteria are used, these need to capture both intrinsic and extrinsic research qualities. Taken together, they need to avoid drowning out the 'signal', that is, what might be most relevant and useful to know, with the 'noise' of methodological scrupulousness. Nonetheless, as a matter of propriety as well as transparency and accuracy, reviews must be rigorous in their own terms, and faithful in representing their sources, particularly perhaps those sources giving voice to service users and carers (Braye & Preston-Shoot, 2005a).

Characterised like this, the project of systematic review in social work is, to some extent, well catered for already by wider developments in the field. The efforts of EPPI, for example, have gone a long way towards opening up the range of review questions asked and research admissible for evidence. But some challenges have yet to be met, including the foregrounding of theory. Most obviously, there is the conundrum of the review process, which is not just a procedural matter but reflects and shapes the essence of the review. There seems a strong argument for resisting the boundedness and linearity of more positivistic systematic review processes in favour of more iterative approaches. The latter could include revising review boundaries and inclusion and exclusion criteria, and even revising the review question in the light of evidence emerging. More profoundly, an iterative approach could include reconsidering the quality or value of each study, even each piece of evidence, in the light of theorised synthesis of all.

While the potential for iterativity in systematic reviews of social work research is appealing, it is equally daunting. The complexity of the enterprise could be huge, as would be the time and cost entailed. In a research field not known for its abundance of investment (Marsh & Fisher, 2005), this is likely to be unrealistic at best, self-defeating at worst. In this sense, social work will be best served by an approach that avoids orthodoxy of any sort. Systematic reviews will be best fit for purpose for social work if they respond with integrity and flexibility to the kinds and quality of research and review questions, and to the needs and resources of research users.

REFERENCES

Boaz, A., & Ashby, D. (2003). *Fit for purpose? Assessing research quality for evidence based policy and practice.* Working Paper 11. London: ESRC UK Centre for Evidence Based Policy and Practice.

Boaz, A., Ashby, D., & Young, K. (2002). *Systematic reviews: What have they got to offer evidence based policy and practice?* Working Paper 2. London: ESRC UK Centre for Evidence Based Policy and Practice.

Brannen, J. (ed.) (1992). *Mixing methods: Qualitative and quantitative research.* Aldershot: Avebury.

Braye, S., & Preston-Shoot, M. (2005a). Emerging from out of the shadows? Service user and carer involvement in systematic reviews. *Evidence and Policy*, 1(2), 173–194.

Braye, S., & Preston-Shoot, M. (2005b). On systematic reviews in social work: observations from teaching, learning and assessment of law in social work education. *British Journal of Social Work*, 37(2), 312–332.

Campbell, R., Pound, P., Pope, C., Britten, N., Pill, R., Morgan, M., & Donovan, J. (2003). Evaluating meta-ethnography: A synthesis of qualitative research on lay experiences of diabetes and diabetes care. *Social Sciences and Medicine*, 56, 671–684.

Campbell Collaboration (2010). *Resource Centre.* Retrieved August 12, 2010 from http://www.campbellcollaboration.org/resources/research.php

Cochrane Collaboration (2008). *Cochrane Collaboration Handbook.* Retrieved August 12, 2010 from http://www.igh.org/Cochrane/tools

Cochrane Collaboration (2010). *Joint Colloquium of the Campbell and Cochrane Collaborations,* Keystone, CO, USA, 18–22 October 2010. Retrieved 7 October 2010 from http://www.cochrane.org/events/cochrane-collaboration-calendar/joint-colloquium-campbell-and-cochrane-collaborations-keyston

Coren, E., & Fisher, M. (2006). *The conduct of systematic research reviews for SCIE knowledge reviews.* SCIE Research Resource 1. London: SCIE.

Daly, J., Willis, K., Small, R., Greene, J., Welch, N., Kealy, M., & Hughes, E. (2007). A hierarchy of evidence for assessing qualitative health research. *Journal of Clinical Epidemiology*, 60, 43–49.

Davies, P. (2003). Systematic reviews: how are they different from what we already do? In L. Anderson & Bennet, N. (eds), *Evidence-informed policy and practice in educational leadership and management: Applications and controversies.* London: Paul Chapman Publishing, pp. 25–38.

Dixon-Woods, M., Agarwal, S., Young, B., Jones, D., & Sutton, A. (2004). *Integrative approaches to qualitative and quantitative evidence.* London: Health Development Agency.

Economic and Social Research Council (ESRC) (2008). *Commissioning brief for the strategic adviser for social work and social care research.* Swindon: ESRC.

Edwards, A.G.K., Russell, I.T., & Stott, N.C.H. (1998). Signal versus noise in the evidence base for medicine: an alternative to hierarchies of evidence. *Family Practice*, 15(4), 319–322.

Evidence for Policy and Practice Information and Co-ordinating Centre (EPPI-Centre) (2006). *Methods and databases.* Retrieved August 15, 2010 from http://eppi.ioe.ac.uk/cms/Default.aspx?tabid=177

Furlong, J., & Oancea, A. (2005). *Assessing quality in applied and educational research.* Swindon: ESRC. Retrieved August 24, 2010 from http://www.esrcsocietytoday.ac.uk/ESRCInfoCentre

Fisher, M., Qureshi, H., Hardyman, W., & Homewood, J. (2006). *Using qualitative research in systematic reviews: Older people's views of hospital discharge.* How Knowledge Works in Social Care. Report 9, London: SCIE.

Gough, D., & Elbourne, D. (2002). Systematic research synthesis to inform policy, practice and democratic debate. *Social Policy and Society*, 1(3), 225–236.

Gray, M., & Schubert, L. (2011). Sustainable social work: Modelling knowledge production, transfer and evidence-based practice. *International Journal of Social Welfare.* doi: 10.1111/j.1468-2397.2011.00802.x

Gray, M., Plath, D., & Webb, S.A. (2009). *Evidence-based social work: A critical stance.* London: Routledge.

Hammersley, M. (2001). On 'systematic' reviews of research literatures: A narrative response to Evans and Benefield. *British Educational Research Journal*, 27(5), 543–553.

Harden, A. (2007). The quality of qualitative evidence: A review of assessment tools. Paper presented at *The Seventh International Campbell Collaboration Colloquium,* May 14–15, London, England.

Harden, A., & Thomas, J. (2005). Methodological issues in combining diverse study types in systematic reviews. *International Journal of Social Research Methodology*, 8(3), 257–271.

Harden, A., Weston, R., & Oakley, A. (1999). *A review of the effectiveness and appropriateness of peer delivered health promotion interventions for young people.* London: EPPI-Centre.

Littell, J., Corcoran, J., & Pillai, V. (2008). *Systematic reviews and meta-analysis.* New York: Oxford University Press.

Long, A., Grayson, L., & Boaz, A. (2006). Assessing the quality of knowledge in social care: Exploring the potential of a set of generic standards. *British Journal of Social Work, 36*(2), 207–226.

Macdonald, G. (2003). *Using systematic reviews to improve social care.* London: SCIE.

MacLure, M. (2005). Clarity bordering on stupidity: Where's the quality in systematic review? *Journal of Education Policy, 20*(4), 393–416.

Mauthner, M., & Birch, M. (2002). *Ethics in qualitative research.* London: Sage.

Marsh, P., & Fisher, M., with Mathers, N., & Fish, S. (2005). Using knowledge in social care. *Report 10: Developing the evidence base for social work and social care practice.* London: SCIE.

Mays, N., & Pope, C. (2000). Assessing quality in qualitative research. *British Medical Journal, 320,* 50–52.

Noblitt, G., & Hare, R. (1988) *Meta-ethnography.* Thousand Oaks, CA: Sage.

Nutley, S., Davies, H., & Walter, I. (2002). *Evidence based policy and practice: Cross sector lessons from the UK.* Working Paper 9. London: ESRC UK Centre for Evidence Based Policy and Practice.

Nutley, S., Walter, I., & Davies, H. (2003). From knowing to doing: A framework for understanding the evidence-into-practice agenda. *Evaluation, 9*(2), 125–148.

Oakley, A. (2006). 'Resistances to 'new' technologies of evaluation: education research in the UK as a case study. *Evidence and Policy, 2*(1), 63–87.

Pawson, R., Boaz, A. Grayson, L., Long, A., & Barnes, C. (2003). *Types and quality of knowledge in social care.* Knowledge Review 3. London: SCIE.

Pawson, R. (2002a). *Assessing the quality of evidence in evidence-based policy: Why, how and when?* Working Paper 1, London, ESRC UK Centre for Evidence Based Policy and Practice.

Pawson, R. (2002b). Evidence-based policy: in search of a method. *Evaluation, 8*(2), 157–181.

Pawson, R. (2002c). Evidence-based policy: the promise of realist synthesis. *Evaluation, 8*(3), 340–358.

Pawson, R. (2003c). *Does Megan's law work? A theory-driven systematic review.* Working Paper 8. London: ESRC UK Centre for Evidence Based Policy and Practice.

Pawson, R. (2006). Digging for nuggets: How 'bad' research can yield 'good' evidence. *International Journal of Social Research Methodology, 9*(2), 127–142.

Pawson, R., Boaz, A. Grayson, L., Long, A., & Barnes, C. (2003). *Types and quality of knowledge in social care.* Knowledge Review 3. London: SCIE.

Petticrew, M., & Roberts, H. (2006). *Systematic reviews in the social sciences: A practical guide.* Oxford, Blackwell.

Popay, J., & Roen, K. (2003). *Using evidence from diverse research designs.* SCIE Report 3. London: The Policy Press.

Popay, J., & Williams, G. (1997). Qualitative research and evidence-based healthcare. *Journal of the Royal Society of Medicine, 91*(Suppl 35), 32–37.

Popay, J., Baldwin, S., Arai, L., Britten, N., Petticrew, M., Rodgers, M., & Sowden, A. (2006). *Narrative synthesis in systematic reviews: Methods Briefing 22,* ESRC Methods Programme. Retrieved August 15, 2010 from http://www.ccsr.ac.uk/methods/projects/documents/Popay.pdf

Ruckdeschel, R., & Chambon, A. (2010). *The uses of social work research.* In I. Shaw, Briar-Lawson, K., Orme, J., & Ruckdeschel, R. (eds), *The Sage handbook of social work research.* London: Sage, pp. 195–209.

Rutter, D., Francis, J., Coren, E., & Fisher, M. (2010). *SCIE Research Resource 1: SCIE.*

Systematic Research Reviews: Guidelines (2nd ed.). Retrieved July 15, 2011 from http://www.scie.org.uk/publications/researchresources/rr01.asp

Sandelowski, M., Docherty, S., & Emden, C. (1997). Focus qualitative methods: Qualitative meta-synthesis: issues and techniques. *Research in Nursing and Health, 20,* 365–371.

Sharland, E., & Taylor, I. (2006). Social care research: A suitable case for systematic review?. *Evidence and Policy, 2*(4), 503–523.

Sharland, E., & Taylor, I. (2007). *Interprofessional education for qualifying social work.* Knowledge Review 10. London: SCIE.

Shaw, I., & Norton, M. (2007). *The kinds and quality of social work research in UK universities.* Using Knowledge in Social Care Report. London: SCIE.

Shaw, I., & Zlotnick, J. (2010). Research and government. In I. Shaw, Briar-Lawson, K., Orme, J., & Ruckdeschel, R. (eds), *The Sage handbook of social work research.* London: Sage, pp. 115–130.

Shaw, I., Briar-Lawson, K., Orme, J., & Ruckdeschel, R. (eds) (2010). *The Sage handbook of social work research.* London: Sage.

Sheldon, B. (1997). Introduction. In L. Grayson (ed.) *Evidence-based medicine: An overview and guide to the literature.* London: The British Library.

Solesbury, W. (2001). *Evidence based policy: Whence it came and where's it going.* Working Paper 1. London: ESRC UK Centre for Evidence Based Policy and Practice.

Spencer, L., Ritchie, J., & Dillon, L. (2003). *Quality in qualitative evaluation: A framework for assessing research evidence.* Occasional Paper 2, London: Government Chief Social Researcher's Office. Retrieved August 5, 2010 from www.policyhub.gov.uk/docs/a_quality_framework.pdf

Stake, R., & Schwandt, T. (2006). On discerning quality in evaluation. In I. Shaw, Greene, J., & Mark, M. (eds), *Sage handbook of evaluation.* London: Sage, pp. 404–418.

Stronach, I., & MacLure, M. (1997). *Educational research undone: The postmodern embrace.* Buckingham: Open University Press.

Sutton, A., Jones, D., Abrams, K., Sheldon, T., & Song, F. (1999). Systematic reviews and meta-analysis: A structured review of the methodological literature. *Journal of Health Services Research and Policy, 4*(1), 49–55.

Taylor, B. (2009). Invited commentary on papers by Holden et al. and Shek on the quality of social work abstracts. *Research on Social Work Practice, 19*(3), 366–369.

Taylor, B., Wylie, E., Dempster, M, & Donnelly, M. (2007). Systematically retrieving research: A case study evaluating seven databases. *Research on Social Work Practice, 17*(6), 697–706.

Taylor, I., Sharland, E., Sebba, J., & LeRiche, P. (2006). *Learning, teaching and assessment of partnership work in social work education.* Knowledge Review 10. London: SCIE.

Thomas, J., & Harden, A. (2003). Practical systems for systematic reviews of research to inform policy and practice in education. In L. Anderson & Bennet, N. (eds), *Evidence-informed policy and practice in educational leadership and management: Applications and controversies.* London: Paul Chapman Publishing, pp. 39–54.

Thyer, B. (2009). Introductory principles of social work research. In B. Thyer (ed.), *The handbook of social work research methods.* London: Sage.

Thyer, B. (2010). Evidence-based practice, social development, and social work: Myths and misconceptions. Paper presented at the *Joint World Congress on Social Work and Social Development,* June 10-14, Hong Kong.

Thyer, B., & Myers, L. (2011). The quest for evidence based practice: A view from the United States. *Journal of Social Work, 11*(1), 8–25.

Wallace, A., Croucher, K, Quilgars, D., & Baldwin, S. (2004). Meeting the challenge: developing systematic reviewing in social policy. *Policy and Politics, 32*(4), 455–470.

Webb, S.A. (2001). Some considerations on the validity of evidence based social work. *British Journal of Social Work, 31*(1), 59–79.

Webb, S.A. (2006). *Social work in a risk society: Social and political perspectives.* London: Palgrave.

Yunong, H., & Fengzhi, M. (2009). A reflection on reasons, preconditions, and effects of implementing evidence-based practice in social work. *Social Work, 54*(2), 177–181.

SECTION 6

Social Work in Context

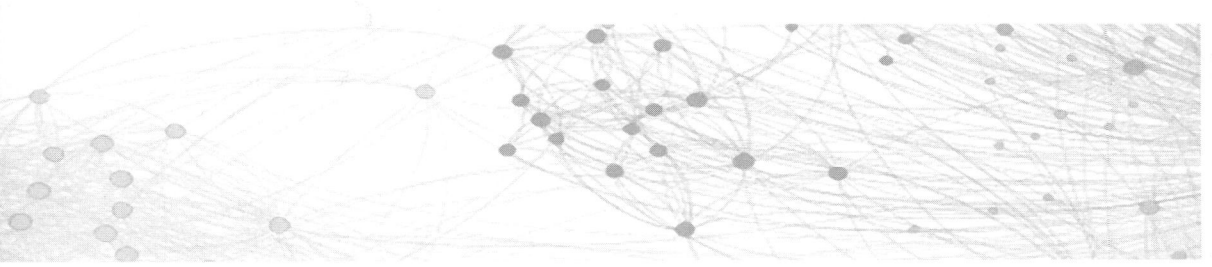

INTRODUCTION

Social work is inevitably encumbered by its public, legal, and social role, that is, it is situated within rich and complex set of structures, institutions, and processes that sustain social, cultural, and economic life-worlds. The term 'social context' refers to the social relationships that exist in a given social space or time, reflecting the environment in which something is produced, thereby indicating its purpose or agenda. The 'contexts' of social work are wide ranging and dynamic, including the variety settings or institutions in which practitioners work or the types of service they implement and the sorts of service users with whom they engage. Social work occurs in a range of organisational contexts and it is shaped by public policies, service resources, legal requirements, and service-user expectations. The way social work in context is deployed here is framed by specifying work with different sorts of client or service-user group. It is recognised that this is only a partial coverage of all client groups and that any comprehensive coverage would require a volume dedicated solely to this material. The range of contexts covered captures the main populations and categories of service-user interventions. They include several important areas of social work practice – child and family, mental health, and work with older and disabled people, immigrants and refugees, the alcohol and drug dependent, and those passing through the juvenile and criminal justice systems. The section ends with a discussion of family support services that traverse these diverse contexts.

In Chapter 32, Stan Houston provides an overview of social work with children and families. He examines the challenges of contemporary social work practice with children and families, which focuses primarily on improving protection, and balancing the need for protection with prevention, in order to enhance the quality of care and improve the life chances of children and young people. Considerable resources have been allocated to the prevention of problems within the family with initiatives, such as Sure Start in the UK, which emphasise the role of the community in reducing disadvantage in the poorest areas. For the most part, however, social workers have been involved in risk assessment and resource management at the local level rather than in community-based practice. Houston shows how social work increasingly operates within the government's agenda of containment and management of the poor and socially excluded.

In Chapter 33, Barbara Fawcett examines the challenges of contemporary social work practice in mental health where service priorities relate to the promotion of independence, improvement in the consistency of care, and provision of user-centred services. She argues that the distinction between medical and social models as they impact on social work has deleterious effects, often causing boundary tensions between different service providers. Fawcett offers a new framework to help overcome some of these intrinsic tensions and maps out a conceptual model for service provision and resourcing in a multiprofessional team context.

In Chapter 34, Nancy Hooyman examines social work with older people. The rapidly growing older population is more heterogeneous by health and economic status, gender, race, sexual orientation, and family and living arrangements than any other age group. Although many adults face vulnerabilities and inequities as they age, most elders are resilient, even in the face of chronic illness. Hooyman reviews this diversity, discusses concepts of productive, active ageing and elder-friendly communities for 'ageing in place', and suggests new leadership roles for social workers in enhancing the well-being of elders and their families within the context of chronic care and healthcare reform. She brings a critical and creative lens to promote optimal ageing and emphasises strategies to address inequities across the life course through cultural competence and anti-oppressive practice throughout.

In Chapter 35, Romel Mackelprang examines the challenges of contemporary social work practice in the field of disability. He notes the tremendous strides made as a result of disability activism and wider acceptance of social models of disability, and outlines the place of professional social work within the wider consumer-oriented, service-user movement. He draws attention to research that highlights the need for social integration and community access and addresses social workers' roles as key agents in providing services, promoting human rights, and advocating for adequate societal resources for people with disabilities and for families with disabled children.

In Chapter 36, Doreen Elliott and Uma Segal examine the challenges of contemporary social work practice with immigrants and refugees. They point to the intersection between civil society and the social policy agenda as a focus for tension between the mandate from refugees and immigrants to address their needs appropriately as service users, and legitimately enter into their life-world. They develop a mandate for the state to secure social citizenship in practice, while simultaneously reflecting the political values and priorities of government. Social work's problematic engagement in meeting the needs of refugees and asylum seekers is critically exposed as a fraught intersection between the core values of social work and the political priorities of the state. The ratcheting up of the 'politics of dissuasion' by receiving states over the last decade has been a pragmatic and calculated political response to popular xenophobia and racism. It has been a concrete expression and reproduction of the social marginalisation of refugees and asylum seekers. This has, for example, included the calculated pauperising of refugees and refused asylum seekers. This is only one very recent instance of the state involving social work organisationally, and social workers personally, in distinguishing between the deserving and undeserving recipients of social welfare. Elliott and Segal conclude with some constructive suggestions for how social work can effectively work with immigrants and refugees from an ethical and practical perspective.

In Chapter 37, Holly Matto presents a critical, cross-disciplinary review of the major treatment approaches currently in use across the USA and abroad. She presents the most up-to-date empirical literature undergirding current treatment approaches, along with discussion on the gaps in the evidence base and how these issues affect social workers' clinical decision-making abilities and treatment application. Matto identifies factors that may influence macro-level adoption and implementation of each intervention (e.g., staff training and supervision, organisational management practices, and capacity to adopt treatment fidelity tools across institutional settings). She highlights programmatic and policy implications along with multiple diverse case applications to illustrate application of content.

In Chapter 38, Nicola Carr reviews changes in the approaches to juvenile and criminal justice in the past decade across a number of countries and case contexts. She shows that there is clear empirical evidence that the mere establishment of criminal laws and their enforcement only partly explains the extent of offending by an individual – or in a community – and argues that, from a social work perspective, prevention should be the prime focus, while policy and practice trends need to be examined to identify how they might ameliorate or exacerbate factors that give rise to offending. Carr identifies the distinctive role that social work can play in this.

In Chapter 39, Steven Walker examines the importance of family support services in an age when there is increasing deprofessionalisation of the human services or social care context with a higher priority allocated to the assessment of risk than social intervention. He maps out the challenges faced by social workers in their fundamental role of family support in the economic context of shrinking public sector resources combined with heightened expectations of child protection services. He critically examines the anticipated expanded role and function of voluntary, charitable, and faith groups in the provision of family support in terms of the limits to their knowledge and skills, and in the recasting of their relationship with statutory services. Equally, he illustrates the strengths and resourcefulness of the nonstatutory sector to provide a rich and complex analysis of the range of provision, service-user experiences, effectiveness, and future prospects for collaborative, multidisciplinary family support. Walker's chapter is underpinned by a rich exploration of reference to non-orthodox, multicultural methods and models of family support celebrated by indigenous groups, anti-racist concepts, and non-Western forms of community organisation.

Child and Family Social Work

Stan Houston

In Anglophone countries, such as the UK, the USA, Australia, New Zealand, and Canada, children and families experience a number of common needs. At the outset, these needs must be seen in the context of developments in neoliberalism, where childhood is becoming increasingly commodified (Dominelli, 2004), that is, despite the notable advances towards the social investment state and early prevention, childhood is seen as a pivotal institution in maintaining optimal economic outcomes within the global market. Hence disrupted childhoods can result in psychological and social problems in adulthood requiring expensive public welfare investments. By way of contrast, children who mature into 'model' adult-workers are more likely to be seen as profitable, cost-effective commodities. The neoliberal world continues to be defined by consumption, competition, and profit, and the early part of the life cycle is not exempt from its effects. This notion of childhood as a depersonalised and objectivised commodity with economic significance is also witnessed in the clothing industry, the purchase of children in international adoption, commercial surrogacy, and in the sex trade. It is also formative to the social policy aims of countries such as Australia, the USA, and the UK where, through the lens of the social investment state, governments shift investment from 'the demand side of the economy (the production of things) to the supply side (preparing (child) citizens to participate in economic production)' (Spratt, 2008, p. 415).

If this is the dominant economic context within which children mature, there are also cultural discourses impacting on their developmental trajectories. One such discourse is the social construction of deviant identities. It is particularly connected with young people's so called anti-social behaviours. The 'devil wears a hoodie' (Robinson, 2010) is one way of concretising this construction in a manner demonising a small group of young people in Britain. Ironically, the populist attempt by the former member of the opposition, now the current prime minister, David Cameron, to show a caring side of conservative politics was revealed in his clarion call to 'hug a hoodie'. What is more, despite his predecessor's, that is, Tony Blair's sound bite to be 'tough on crime but also tough on the causes of crime', the reality is, in the UK, there has been an increasing raft of punitive measures put in place to curb 'hoodie'-like behaviour (Hendrick, 2003).

Children's needs are also being approached through moral panics about risk even in Nordic countries, such as Finland, where a wide-ranging welfare paradigm has been historically evident (Harrikari & Satka, 2006). The pattern of the untimely and tragic death of a child, in circumstances of caregiver abuse, followed by a frenzied media response and public castigation of the professionals involved with the family, is most visible across Western states. This pattern reflects the ascendancy of child protection concerns over promotional forms of intervention within communities. The risks of child abduction, the focus on paedophiles in the community, and an overarching 'precautionary stance' has meant risk has been conflated with danger rather than keeping alive its opportunistic dimensions. In this connection, discernibly centralised, policy initiatives have been promulgated across states to protect children. It seems the rationale for these responses lies in the need to preserve the public's confidence in state welfare provision but possibly at the cost of infantilising children and their carers.

Despite these moral panics, many risks to children and young people are real and substantive. Significant populations exhibit signs of broken attachment, trauma, and the effects of domestic violence. What is more, many children and families experience poverty as the inequalities between the social classes in Western states increase, affecting mortality rates, life expectancy, and outcomes related to health and social well-being. For example, 'families growing up in Australia's poorest postcodes are up to seven times more at risk of child abuse and neglect, and likely to suffer from low incomes, long-term unemployment, early school leaving, physical and mental disabilities and prison admission' (Costello, 2009, p. 119). Similarly, in the USA, there is a growing concern about the impact of reduced welfare entitlements on the poorest families: 'Being in poverty (there) continues to be a central defining characteristic of those children and families referred to child protection services' (Spratt, 2008, p. 415).

The association between multiple deprivations, early on in life, and later outcomes in terms of mental health careers, criminality, and engagement with state welfare services is notable as the aforementioned quotation suggests, although factors such as resilience, temperament, and 'windows of opportunity' can subvert predicted pathways.

It is axiomatic these questions of health and social well-being must also be seen in the context of changing family structures. There are more people living alone, experiencing divorce, cohabiting, and facing single parenthood. The traditional nuclear family can no longer be taken for granted as people now choose to construct familial relationships in mixed and varied ways. Complex, intermeshed family structures are becoming more prevalent, reflecting the attainment of greater personal freedoms and choices. However, for some, the dissolution of these older structures has not led necessarily to greater stability. In some cases, there has been a lack of role models, insufficient preparation for childrearing, and a diminution in skills of intrafamilial conflict resolution.

In this chapter, the author critically appraises how social work has typically responded to the needs of children and young people, including those mentioned above. It is argued child and family social work is haemorrhaging (Lonne et al., 2009), in a situation of professional and institutional crisis, despite its best efforts and committed staff. This argument is substantiated by taking account of the work of a number of critical commentators on the child welfare system. Later on, this crisis is explained by drawing on critical social theory – a source much needed by social work as it attempts to navigate its way through the miasma of neoliberalism. With this critical understanding in place, the focus turns to some 'green shoots of encouragement' or examples of 'best practice'. Representing signposts for future developments in child and family social work, they mirror alternative conceptions of social work practice as found in many European and Nordic countries, where neoliberalism has been softened by social democracy, and where constructions of childhood emphasise the ideal of personhood and citizenship.

ORGANISATIONAL RESPONSES TO NEED: A PROFESSION IN CRISIS?

Although the organisational responses to need (listed below) are centrally placed within the Anglophone countries, they are also being emulated, to some degree, in other parts of the world. Critically, they are emblematic of wider social changes taking root in many societies. In this section, these responses are considered through the work of a range of critical commentators and an attempt is made to capture their essence under the following headings: (i) risk fixation; (ii) 'panoptical' modernisation; (iii) information categorisation; (iv) procedural managerialism; and (v) preventive regulation. This typology of responses is not meant to present an exhaustive depiction of child and family social work in all its guises and settings. Rather, it shows some of the mainstream attempts to respond to the complex, demanding, and ethically fraught situations social workers encounter daily, particularly when they operate from a statutory context. While the tone of this description is critical and suggestive of a crisis, a later section offers a counterbalance by focusing on some positive developments within the field.

Risk fixation

The preoccupation with risk in social work is reflected in the prevalence of risk assessment, intervention, management, and governance processes, as referrals of a child protection nature show a massive increase in many Anglophone countries (Parton & Mathews, 2001). These processes, particularly in the USA, are often directed towards a calculative form of reasoning lying in tension with the use of a more time-honoured commitment to professional judgement and intuition. Calculative reasoning aims to predict and quantify risk. It finds a home in actuarialism, where mathematical and statistical methods are used to arrive at supposedly reliable and valid predictions of danger. However, it is a form of numeration that may not fit neatly with the vagaries, vicissitudes, and inflections of meaning comprising the social world. Child and family social work attempts to grapple with the often indeterminate, messy nature of this world, where ethical dilemmas abound. Children and parents' rights often clash. Safeguarding and promotional perspectives vie for attention when it comes to planning decisions and funding allocations. Social workers feel the strain created by the discordant and ubiquitous care and control themes in their daily practice. In the USA, as elsewhere, these tensions have been rooted historically and pervasively felt. Given this context, we might query the attempt to apply calculative processes in social work. The existential issues with which social work grapples are 'meaning saturated' and need to be examined through an interpretive lens comfortable with artistic judgement.

Stephen Webb (2006) provides an erudite, sociological analysis of this fixation with risk in social work. For him, we are living in a 'risk society' permeating every aspect of social life. Moreover, it is a society driven by neoliberalism. In the neoliberal, risk society, risk has become privatised and, in the private domain of life, there is a need for 'security against risk and uncertainty' (Webb, 2006, p. 47) for the subject's ontological well-being is at stake. Security, here, is assuaged through expert systems, regulatory practices, social care governance, and technologies of care, including various types of risk assessment schedule. Yet, despite efforts on these fronts, 'the entrenchment of child protection work as the forensic core of child and family social work, together with continued agency preoccupation with the management of risk, result in an antipathy evident amongst those receiving the systems' ministrations' (Spratt, 2008, p. 420).

Panoptical modernisation

Paul Michael Garrett (2003) adeptly launches a polemical review of the impact of modernisation on children's services in the UK. His analysis is relevant to other nation-states equally caught up in this process to varying degrees. Garrett's analysis centres on the neoliberal trends remaking child and family social work in a manner fitting children into preformed, conceptual categories. Thus, 'micro engagements with users of the services are increasingly being plotted by centrally devised assessment schedules and measured by quantitative performance indicators' (Garrett, 2003, p. 4). Compartmentalisation and categorisation, he argues, are the twin engines driving a raft of assessment schedules and rating scales more about authoritarian, class-based control than the acquisition of objective knowledge about children's needs.

Protocols inherent within the 'Looked After Child' system, and in the 'Framework for the Assessment of Need', for example, have been designed to make certain children and young people are prepared adequately for the world of work, ensuring they become compliant employees and, therefore, able to function as flexible agents in changing markets. These protocols can also be used, argues Garrett, to detect propensities within young people towards antisocial and criminal behaviour and, therefore, can be seen as part of an increasing panoply of surveillance measures within society. Following Foucault (1975), these trends might be recast as 'panopticism in the service of modernisation', panopticism referring to a centralised form of surveillance (see later).

In a later work, Garrett (2009) builds on his critique to argue children's services are being transformed according to an ASBO (antisocial behaviour order) infused politics. In this neoliberal dispensation, this discourse is both authoritarian and populist. It denotes the regulation of 'problem' populations seen as products of a failed socialisation process. For Garrett (2009), 'any trace of progressive elements detectable in the endeavour to transform children's services has been located within a neoliberal framework which is likely to constrain, nullify, or at best render ephemeral the more potentially positive components' (p. 1).

Information categorisation

There is strong evidence to suggest social work assessment is being driven increasingly by information technology and performance management. These impetuses ostensibly occlude the imperative to be centred on the needs of service users. In this regard, Nigel Parton (2008) examines the changing use of knowledge in social work, concluding a 'data base' way of thinking is overtaking traditional qualitative narratives in social work. Hence, social work's mission to focus on the subject, her (sic) meanings, and the social environment in which she operates has been somewhat eclipsed by an informational discourse. The pervasive impact of information technologies is witnessed in the 'gathering, sharing and monitoring of information' (Parton, 2008, p. 254) about individual service users. Meaning has become subjugated by 'operationality', threatening the very essence of relational social work. Yet, for Parton (2008), this is not a deterministic, dystopian surge by any means. Because of the socially constructed nature of technology, reflective spaces are always being manifest allowing for humanistic discourses to interface with technological imperatives.

The electronic 'Common Assessment Framework' in England and Wales is a primary example of a technology of classification and categorisation in child and family social work. However, far from imposing uniformity and standardisation, and echoing Parton's (2008) thesis, it is at the mercy of the professional operative's predilections, interpretations, and variegated responses (Pithouse et al., 2009; White et al., 2009).

In many jurisdictions the electronic turn has not taken place with the same vigour. Yet, the daily practice of social workers reveals the gathering and processing of information, manually, forms the hub of their role. Report writing, record keeping, and disseminating information at meetings, have become central to child welfare practice. Notably, the amount of time available for face-to-face contact with service users has waned in the face of this imperative.

Procedural managerialism

The proceduralisation and bureaucratisation of child welfare services in the state sector has had insuperable effects, including the rise of 'audit and blame cultures'. It is also witnessed in the attempt by administrations to measure social workers' actions and to set targets to achieve specified goals. Curtailing professional discretion, and attempting to ameliorate indeterminacy, these processes replace trust in the professionals with trust in systems. They show an over-reliance on a particular form of rationality: one exhibiting a means–end relationship. This is where a designed goal is identified purposively and a strategy developed to meet it but, crucially, no attempt is made to appraise the propriety of the goal itself. Expedience, efficiency, effectiveness, and overall gain are the central preoccupations.

The net effect is other forms of rationality, encapsulated in critical thinking (Munro, 2007), communicative reason (Houston, 2002), and emotional and relational intelligence (Howe, 2008), have withered by comparison. The dominance of a means–end rationality has meant, when a problem arises, procedural, managerial solutions are applied automatically, almost as a knee-jerk reaction. It is similar to a carpenter who only has a hammer and, therefore, responds to every problem as if it were a nail. In doing so, bureaucratic defensiveness arises, and the quest for organisational efficiency subjugates ethical deliberation, reflective thinking, and practice wisdom. Management systems, meeting structures, and planning fora, while all playing a vital role in decision-making, have perhaps occluded the 'relational', subjective domain within which social work establishes its *raison d'etre*.

Preventive regulation

Attempting to strike the right balance between child protection and preventive family support has been a formative consideration in many countries throughout the world (Parton & Mathews, 2001). Reforms within the USA, Australia, and the UK have struggled to achieve this balance to appease the public outrage about horrendous child deaths, on the one hand, and concern about an overly intrusive state welfare system, on the other. Underpinning child welfare ideologies, within nation-states, have shaped debates on the issue. Thus, Khoo (2002) discovered child welfare services in Sweden, with its universalist orientation, tended to focus more on family preservation compared to a narrow focus on protection and permanency-planning in Canada, where a liberal welfare regime operated.

In England and Wales, the debate has been shaped in a particular direction. Parton (2006) takes up the theme observing the state has changed by adopting a preventive–surveillance focus. By this he means the notion of 'prevention' has been reformulated radically in the wake of a renewed focus on the *regulation* of children and their agency. So-called 'at risk' populations of children are to be identified and targeted for early intervention in order to avert problems occurring in later life. This development brings about a sense preventive services are now being mandated rather than offered voluntarily. The intention, here, is to maintain the social fabric of society and lessen the economic drain on its welfare resources. Such trends have also been apparent in the USA, where there have been large-scale initiatives to target populations deemed to be at risk. Community-based programmes, such as 'Head Start' play a central role in this context.

Critically, the identification of at-risk groups of children and adults involves measures of surveillance leading to the storage of sensitive information about children and families. However, 'in the process, the child as victim and the child as villain are both seen as in need because, for both, it is their health and development which should be the focus' (Parton, 2006, p. 169). The danger in all of this, for Parton (2006), is this form of prevention ensnares and imprisons children as problem populations, who are required to be fixed. His concerns are echoed more widely (Baldwin et al., 2006) in the social work profession, which sees the move as contributing to the stigma children and families experience.

TOWARDS A SOCIOLOGICAL UNDERSTANDING OF CHILD WELFARE

The trends outlined above reflect societal changes in late modernity where, as has been argued, neoliberalism is to the fore in shaping social policy and social work. It is contended child and family social workers must make sense of these changes before they can begin to engage with their inherent contradictions. They can approach this challenge through the lens of critical social theory, a key source of knowledge for understanding the prevailing currents in social life. The five trends mentioned earlier are now considered briefly through this lens. The word restriction in this chapter means this is a signposting exercise to guide the reader rather than presenting a comprehensive exegesis.

The fixation with risk in society, the first of the trends identified, can be understood more fully through the work of Anthony Giddens (1991) and Ulrich Beck (1992). Both of these thinkers view current social formations in the Western world as typifying a 'risk society'. Giddens (1991) says:

> Modernity is a risk culture. I do not mean by this that social life is inherently more risky than it used to be; for most people that is not the case. Rather, the concept of risk becomes fundamental to the way both lay actors and technical specialists organise the social world. Modernity reduces the overall riskiness of certain areas and modes of life, yet at the same time introduces new risk parameters largely or completely unknown to previous eras (pp. 3–4).

Like Giddens (1991), Beck (1992) opines we continue to live in the modern world, albeit a late form of reflexive modernity. Through the process of individualisation, social agents have been freed increasingly from a range of social constraints. As a consequence, they have become more reflexively aware, more able to shape their lives and their social environments. However, these agents are confronted by risks of differing hues and dimensions. The reflexive challenge becomes one of having to prevent, minimise, and channel risk. In reflexive modernity, the central preoccupation is with safety and averting danger. A crisis in confidence in the capacity of experts to predict future hazards emerges devolving risk back to the lay person. That said, 'for those who struggle or are unable to find ... certainties or take responsibility, expert interventions, such as social work, are justified through categories of risk' (Webb, 2006, p. 47).

Panoptical regulation, by way of contrast, can be explored through Michel Foucault's (1975) ideas on surveillance in the contemporary world. For Foucault, modern society presents new instruments of disciplinary power. An example of such is hierarchical observation. This is the capacity of professionals and officials to oversee populations through a controlling gaze. Foucault expresses this idea by exploring the function of the 'panopticon': a physical structure enabling officials to observe completely inmates in an institution. Much like a central tower, the panopticon stands erect in the centre of the institution with an observation point at its pinnacle. Never knowing for sure whether they are being observed or not, the inmates start to control themselves. Its mere presence constrains. Discipline becomes internalised. Beyond its physical location within the institution, though, the panopticon rises as a representative symbol of modern society, or, to put this another way, the carceral, disciplinary society, in which professionals, such as social workers, carry out pervasive monitoring activities in respect of designated populations.

The third noted trend, informational categorisation, might be approached in the broader context of the rise of the information society. In this regard, Jean-Francois Lyotard (1984) suggested knowledge has become the prime mover in production of goods and services. It has assumed the role of a commodity in the postindustrial society. In a different vein, Peter Otto and Philipp Sonntag (1985) commented on the proliferation of occupations centred round information and how it was processed. A connection can be made here with Paul Michael Garrett's (2005) thesis the electronic turn in England and Wales is becoming central to the remaking of child and family social work. A concomitant perspective has been taken by Nico Stehr (2002). He argued knowledge had penetrated all of the domains of social life and had become a central, productive force. Moreover, for Manuel Castells (2000), key advances in information technology were having a radical effect on the make-up of the networks processing information anywhere in the world through multifaceted flows or conduits of communication.

Procedural managerialism, the fourth trend referred to, reflects a strategic form of action instrumental by its very nature. Jürgen Habermas (1987) has noted the pervasive, colonising effects of this type of action in modern society. According to Habermas (1987), it has displaced (to a large degree) a more accustomed, everyday form of action between subjects relying on open, reciprocal communication where the aim is to reach consensus between the parties. Such action is located in the 'life-world', which is 'the transcendental site where speaker and hearer meet, where they reciprocally raise claims their utterances fit the world ... and where they can criticise and confirm those validity claims, settle their disagreements, and arrive at agreements' (Habermas, 1987, p. 126). Elsewhere, Houston (2002) has argued child and family social work must retain a strong foothold in the 'life-world' of service users to fulfil its ethical responsibility to them.

Lastly, the trend of preventive regulation might be interpreted in terms of a new form of government of aberrant selves. Nikolas Rose (1999), a card-carrying Foucauldian, posits modern liberal society exercises governmentality over its subjects. Governmentality is the way society uses power to shape language, ways of doing things, approves modes of conduct, and, in doing so, shapes the self and the person's inner subjectivity. The 'psy' professionals, which include psychologists, counsellors, and psychotherapists, along with education and welfare institutions, are active arms in directing subjects towards an examination of their self-conduct. As a result, the self becomes implicated in the power inherent within oppressive structures and subjected to a top-down form of regulation.

This systematised use of governmentality in targeting social populations aims to bring about normality and prudentialism, *prevent* the rise of aberrant selves and social ills, and promote the 'good' society. It directs social work to adopt practices based on moralisation and normalisation (Donzelot, 1980). The former refers to the use of preventive social work interventions, including the distribution of material assistance, to rectify moral failings in children and families. The latter alludes to the inculcation of normative standards through educative programmes.

Further sociological insights into the child welfare system have been articulated by Paul Michael Garrett (2009) when he draws on the theories of Pierre Bourdieu and Antonio Gramsci. Bourdieu (1977) presents a sophisticated battery of concepts, which are appropriated to explain how social workers are influenced by their 'habitus' (their internalised dispositions), their 'fields' (the structured sites and positions in which they are located), and their allocation of 'capital' (or the assets and resources available to them). Gramsci's idea of hegemony is employed to show how neoliberalism gives rise to ideologies shaping, constraining, and imbuing social workers' consciousness. Practices taken-for-granted, conversations held, procedures invoked, and progressive innovations are all part of an *engineered* consensus. Garrett's (2003) elucidation of these ideas is helpful because it debunks conventional practice wisdom, unchallenged shibboleths, and social work's received ideas.

At this point, the reader might be forgiven for thinking critical social theory is a dismal branch of knowledge, one embroiled in pessimistic analyses and forecasts. While there may be some truth in this observation, this avenue of scholarship is also concerned primarily with the agency of individuals, that is, their creative capacity, virtuosity, and intentionality. Individuals can go against the tide of structural constraint, albeit to some degree. Their actions over time can lead to novel social habits. Choices, decisions, motives, and reasons are all powerful undercurrents driving the dynamics of social relations, even in highly prescribed and proscribed sites, such as the child protection system. With this in mind, let us now examine what I have termed the 'green shoots of encouragement': contemporary practices opening up alternative visions of child welfare and mollifying some of the constraining elements of children's services examined above. To keep alive an awareness of prospects and possibilities is vital for a profession criticised to a tiresomely excessive degree, with diminished confidence in its skills base, and forced into defensive posturing. 'Without a vision the people die', said the prophet Jeremiah.

SOME GREEN SHOOTS OF ENCOURAGEMENT

Four so-called 'green shoots of encouragement' are delineated in this section: (i) embracing the notion of children's spaces; (ii) adopting reflective family support; (iii) engaging in relationship-based practice; and (iv) using devolved problem-solving. Each of these conceptualisations offers an alternative vision of children's services to the prevailing reality set out in the foregoing sections. Moreover, they can be propitiously aligned with the critical social theory adopted above to analyse these described trends.

Children's spaces

One of the most engaging, groundbreaking perspectives on child welfare is contained in Peter Moss and Pat Petrie's (2002) book entitled *From children's services to children's spaces*. Here, the authors set out an alternative construction of childhood leading, in turn, to a different form of public provision and set of practices. The book's thesis is grounded in an eclectic array of ideas, including social constructionism, a social theory influenced greatly by Michel Foucault referred to earlier. It posits actors construct their social world rather than having it imposed upon them. Applied to the notion of childhood, it means, while this stage of the life cycle may be a biological reality, the way it is approached and lived is socially and culturally shaped. According to constructionist perspectives, there is no essential, unitary childhood, no fixed age and stage, and developmental trajectory. The authors also draw on Nikolas Rose's governmentality thesis (see earlier) to suggest 'the power that results from a combination of government and experts, knowledges and procedures is considerable, making childhood the most intensively governed sector of human existence' (Moss & Petrie, 2002, p. 34).

Moss and Petrie (2002) relativise childhood through social constructionism so as to make grand narratives stutter, the familiar strange, and the taken-for-granted uncomfortable. This, they contend, is to challenge the existing technical, commodifying, disciplinary, regulatory, normalising, and surveillance-led system prevailing in children's services (described earlier), particularly in relation to the construction of deviant identities. Based on this theoretical rationale, Moss and Petrie (2002) argue for a shift from the traditional mode of children's services to a new radicalised vision of children's spaces. Spaces refer to enabling physical locations but also social, discursive, and cultural positions. They constitute domains of social practice and relationship based on human rights allowing for critical dialogue about the needs of children but involve children as co-constructors of these needs. This idea of children's spaces views children as rich, competent, and powerful. It is in direct opposition to the dominant, discursive regime seeing them as weak, enfeebled, and needy, or mad, bad, and sad commodities. Furthermore, it promotes an enlarged vision of helping comprising pedagogical, aesthetic, environmental, and cultural activities. Moss and Petrie (2002) cite developments in child care policy in Sweden, and the use of social pedagogy in some European countries, as exemplifying many of these trends.

Reflective family support

A second promising possibility comes from the work of Pat Dolan, John Canavan, and John Pinkerton (2006). These authors take up the theme of family support arguing it has become 'a major strategic orientation in services for children and families', now having a 'global currency' (Dolan et al., 2006, p. 11). However, they argue it has been under-theorised. Moving into a *reflective* mode, and advocating it be adopted by other aficionados, they begin to conceptualise family support through the lens of social support theory (Cutrona, 2000). From here, various types of support are enumerated, namely, concrete, emotional, advice, and esteem support. The closeness, reciprocity, and durability aspects of these different forms are then identified and considered. Finally, Dolan et al. (2006) undertake a stratified perspective, showing how family support has relevance within micro-, meso-, and macro-contexts, addressing practice, policy, and legislative change. Such an enlarged definition of family support helps the social work practitioner to conceptualise alternatives to the risk-fixated discourse outlined earlier. It also assists in making sense of the needs of families where changing relationships and structures (see earlier) are to the fore. This direction of inquiry is led by continuous *reflection,* which Dolan et al. (2006) see as a constant attempt to make sense of family support interventions. They note reflective practice, drawing on adult learning theory, is hampered by the bureaucratic, procedural context described earlier. It is also stymied by the tendency to typify relationships, that is, to set out routine, expected responses for both practitioners and users of the service. For Dolan et al. (2006), family support presents an alternative paradigm to this formulaic, bureaucratic model. It alternatively constructs family support as a negotiated consensus between the professional and family members, where reflection 'in' and 'on' action is germane: 'The purpose is to get practitioners to describe and analyse a critical incident, evaluate the outcome, identify learning points and then act on them' (Dolan et al., 2006, p. 18). This should be a cyclical activity as reflection and practice are inter-related dimensions. What is being described here is very different from the model of preventive regulation (previously described) almost imposing intervention on families in a top-down, centralised, authoritarian manner. This model shows very little understanding of family support as a reflective, negotiated, fluid process, one that is part of a socially constructed subsidiarity. Taking up this latter theme, a central authority should perform only those tasks that cannot be performed at a more local level (see also Walker, Chapter 39 in this volume).

Relationship-based practice

Gillian Ruch (2005) has made a convincing case for relationship-based practice in child and family social work. Her thesis counters the contemporary tendency to make information management and proceduralism (see earlier) the twin pillars of social work practice. Put in a different way, her timely work challenges the 'prevailing trends which emphasise reductionist understandings of human behaviour and narrowly conceived bureaucratic responses to complex problems' (Ruch, 2005, p. 111). Ruch proceeds to delineate the distinctive elements of relational social work practice: first of all, it is an interpretive activity consonant with the essence of social work. What is important here is the attempt to achieve a holistic understanding of both the rational and irrational aspects of the service user's behaviour. Secondly, it draws from traditional psychosocial and psychodynamic theories. The indivisibility of the internal and external worlds (which is a primary tenet of these theories), and the interplay between the psychological and the social, frames analysis in a holistic manner, and makes a linkage with empowerment-led and anti-oppressive practice possible. On top of that, the psychosocial model sees 'relationship' as the pivotal axle around which helping responses revolve. In a third way, relational approaches acknowledge the pervasive feelings of anxiety, uncertainty, and ambivalence percolating 'face-to-face' activity in social work and offer strategies for dealing with them. One such strategy, according to Ruch (2005), is the use of reflection, mirroring the theme of the previous section. Reflection, with its social constructivist roots, synergises with a relational stance in a manner generating a renewed understanding of the service user, the professional self, the organisational context, and the epistemologies underpinning practice.

Devolved problem solving

Devolving problem solving to families, and what Habermas has referred to as the 'life-world' (see earlier), finds an important expression in the Family Group Case Conference. Much has been written about it since its inception in New Zealand. Within this forum, the welfare of the child, who may have experienced some level of trauma as a result of child abuse or neglect, is considered both by the family network and the professionals.

The aim is to reach agreement and consensus between all the parties by affording the family protected time to come up with a workable plan the state professionals can then consider. In this regard, it is emblematic of Habermas' plea for structures mediating between the 'life-world' and the state or the 'system' as he terms it. Such structures as these restrain the operation of a crude form of procedural–managerialism in child and family social work (see earlier) by actively involving the 'life-world'. A different form of action takes place within the latter domain compared to the instrumental nature of some current, procedural modes of practice. It reflects processes of inter-subjectivity, meaning, understanding and, crucially, the give and take of equalling communication. Such processes cement bonds of relationship and are much needed in child and family social work, where the potential for relationship breakdown is high. Better outcomes for the child are likely to accrue when consensus, between parents and social workers in child protection, over the interpretation of concerns, is achieved. The format of the conference also provides an empirically validated model for empowering service users that can be extrapolated beyond child protection to other parts of the child and family care continuum of service provision including: (i) restorative practices for young people caught up and potentially labelled by the criminal justice system; (ii) school-based meetings involving young people who face exclusion; and (iii) planning meeting for children and young people with special physical, health or learning needs.

CONCLUSION

This chapter set out some of the needs of children and young people within Anglophone countries. State-organised attempts to meet them were then described and critically analysed through the lens of critical social theory. As a follow on, some 'green shoots of encouragement' were highlighted. These descriptions of different approaches to practice reflect the empowering tenets within critical social theory emphasising a democratisation of relationships, both within the private and public sphere, and the need to preserve citizenship in the face of neoliberalism, and its assault on childhood. The chapter has, therefore, attempted to provide a sociological view of child and family social work. So much of the negative focus on social work in the child abuse inquiry reports and case management reviews has looked for individual culpability. It has created a forensic psychologism of deficit, scapegoating, and blame. Set against these trends, the power of critical social theory and sociology to look for deeper, institutional, and structural reasons for the current malaise in the profession needs to be harnessed. Sociology debunks and promulgates a healthy sense of disenchantment. It poses difficult questions and subjects prevailing discourses to deconstruction. It sets individual problems within a corporate context and thus challenges the 'fundamental attribution of blame' (where causality centres on internal personality traits as opposed to environmental factors). It shows meanings are situated, social constructions and language is unstable. In addition, it portrays the contradictory nature of modern society: its capacity to bring about good, but also its disciplinary gaze, its drive for homogeneity in human populations, and its inculcation of individuals within configurations of knowledge and power. But more than all of this, this invitation to sociology has attempted to argue the person lies in society but society also lies in the person. Because of this indelible imbrication, child and family social workers must embrace sociology as a form of consciousness, or a type of imagination, to assist in the navigation of neoliberalism's acquisitive waters.

REFERENCES

Baldwin, N. (plus signatories) (2006). Social exclusion plan: Response. *The Guardian*, 25 September, p. 33.

Beck, U. (1992). *Risk society: Towards a new modernity*. London: Sage.

Bourdieu, P. (1977). *Outline of a theory of action*. Cambridge: Cambridge University Press.

Castells, M. (2000). *The rise of the network society: The information age – Economy, society and culture*. Cambridge, MA: Blackwell.

Costello, S. (2009). Reconstructing social work practices with families. In J. Allan, Briskman, L., & Pease, B. (eds), *Critical social work: Theories and practices for a just world*. Sydney, NSW: Allen and Unwin, pp. 117–131.

Cutrona, C. (2000). Social support principles for strengthening families: Messages from America. In Canavan, J. Dolan, P., & Pinkerton, J. (eds), *Family support: Direction from diversity*. London: Jessica Kingsley.

Dolan, P., Canavan, J., & Pinkerton, J. (eds) (2006). *Family support as reflective practice*. London: Jessica Kingsley.

Dominelli, L. (2004). *Social work: Theory and practice for a changing profession*. Cambridge: Polity Press.

Donzelot, J. (1980). *The policing of families: Welfare versus the state*. London: Hutchinson.

Foucault, M. (1975). *Discipline and punish: The birth of the prison*. London: Tavistock.

Garrett, P.M. (2005). Social work's 'electronic turn': Notes on the deployment of information and communication technologies in social work with children and families. *Critical Social Policy*, 25, 529–553.

Garrett, P.M. (2003). *Remaking social work with children and families: A critical discussion on the modernisation of social care*. London: Routledge.

Garrett, P.M. (2009a). Transforming children's services: Questioning Habermasian social work: A note on some alternative sources. *British Journal of Social Work*, 39, 867–883.

Garrett, P.M. (2009b). *Transforming children's services: Social work, neoliberalism and the 'modern' world*. Berkshire: Open University Press.

Giddens. A. (1991). *Modernity and self identity: Self and society in the late modern age*. Stanford: Stanford University Press.

Habermas, J. (1987). *The theory of communicative action* (vol. 2) – *Lifeworld and system: A critique of functionalist reason*. Boston: Beacon, Press.

Harrikari, T., & Satka, M. (2006). A new regime of governing childhood? Finland as an example. *Social Work and Society*, 4, 209–216.

Hendrick, H. (2003). *Child welfare: Historical dimensions, contemporary debate*. Bristol: The Policy Press.

Houston, S. (2002). Beyond the iron cage of bureaucracy: Hyperrationality and social work. *Social Work and Social Sciences Review*, 9, 5–22.

Howe, D. (2008). *The emotionally intelligent social worker.* London: Palgrave.

Khoo, E. (2002). Child welfare of child protection: Uncovering Swedish and Canadian orientations to social intervention in child maltreatment. *Qualitative Social Work, 4,* 451–471.

Lonne, B., Parton, N., Thomson, J., & Harries, M. (2009). *Reforming child protection.* London: Routledge.

Lyotard, J.F. (1984). *The postmodern condition.* Manchester: Manchester University Press.

Moss, P., & Petrie, P. (2002). *From children's services to children's spaces: Public policy, children and childhood.* London: RoutledgeFalmer.

Munro, E. (2007). *Child protection.* London: Sage.

Otto, P., & Sonntag, P. (1985). *Wege in die informationsgesellschaft.* Munich: dtv.

Parton, N. (2006). *Safeguarding childhood: Early intervention and surveillance in a late modern society.* Basingstoke: Palgrave.

Parton, N. (2008). Changes in the form of knowledge in social work: From the 'social' to the 'informational'. *British Journal of Social Work, 38,* 253–269.

Parton, N., & Mathews, R. (2001). New directions in child protection and family support in Western Australia; A policy initiative to re-focus child welfare practice. *Child and Family Social Work, 6,* 97–113.

Pithouse, A., Hall, C., Peckover, S., & White, S. (2009). A tale of two CAFs: The impact of the electronic common assessment framework. *British Journal of Social Work, 39,* 599–612.

Robinson, J. (2010). The *political perspectives social construction of deviant identities: The devil wears a hoodie.* In D. Kassem, Murphy, L., & Taylor, E. (eds), *Key issues in childhood and youth studies.* London: Routledge.

Rose, N. (1999). *Governing the soul: The shaping of the private self.* London: Free Association Books.

Ruch, G. (2005). Relationship-based practice and reflective practice: Holistic approaches to contemporary child care social work. *Child and Family Social Work, 10,* 111–123.

Spratt, T. (2008). Possible futures for social work with children and families in Australia, the United Kingdom and the United States. *Child Care in Practice, 14,* 413–427.

Stehr, N. (2002). *Knowledge and economic conduct.* Toronto, ON: University of Toronto Press.

Webb, S.A. (2006). *Social work in a risk society: Social and political perspectives.* Basingstoke: Palgrave.

White, S., Hall, C., & Peckover, S. (2009). The descriptive tyranny of the common assessment framework: Technologies of categorization and professional practice in child welfare. *British Journal of Social Work, 39,* 1197–1217.

33

Mental Health

Barbara Fawcett

Social workers operating in the arena of mental health are continually required to face new challenges and to manage conflicting responsibilities. These responsibilities include protecting the public, upholding human rights, working with families, addressing severe mental distress, incorporating the views of service users, operating within an evidence base, and making underfunded systems work. Social workers also have to contend with a tendency for complexity and uncertainty to be subsumed into forms of procedural guidance which simplify and reduce the knowledge, skills, and values of social work. In this chapter, conceptualisations and responses to mental distress – variously termed mental ill-health, madness, mental illness, and mental disorder – are appraised. The aim is to enable social workers to reflect on, explore the wider canvass of, pose critical questions about, and identify creative opportunities for responsive mental health practice. There is also an accompanying emphasis on analysis and action, with the latter not being prescriptive, but instead highlighting the importance of flexibility and context.

TERMINOLOGY AND MEDICALISATION: AN HISTORICAL OVERVIEW

As a starting point, it is useful to look at what constitutes good mental health. Notably, the framing of emotions and behaviours within the language of health is taken for granted, at least in Western nations. This was not always the case. In Western culture, from the Middle Ages to the 16th century, hearing voices or 'strange' behaviour tended to be linked to religion and associated either with divine inspiration or with the machinations of the Devil.

During the 18th century, the onset of the period commonly referred to as the Enlightenment brought about a seismic change in how many of those in the West viewed the world and what they regarded as acceptable knowledge. This movement, over time, privileged rational scientific thought and positivist objective thinking over religion, emotion, and subjective knowledge and paved the way for science to present its own understandings of 'madness'. However, despite the emphasis on objectivity and reason, then as now, prevailing social values and beliefs influenced the scientific enterprise. The work of Henry Maudsley in England serves as a good example. Maudsley was strongly influenced by the eugenics movement and social Darwinism. By citing the legitimising backing of science, he influentially and 'scientifically' linked mental disorder with moral impropriety, crime, and hereditary defects (Skultans, 1979). Unregulated experimentation was also undertaken and Ugo Cerletti, one of the founders of electroconvulsive therapy (ECT), has famously been described as administering a 110-volt discharge for 0.2 seconds to an unwilling patient (Fawcett et al., 2011).

Although, initially, asylums were not initially created as hospitals in the modern sense, science and medicine increasingly started to play an influential role. This was based on the 'scientific' belief, promulgated by Maudsley and others, that mental disturbance was due to a biologically disordered brain, which, for many, was associated with poor heredity and a tainted gene pool. This biodeterministic model of medical psychiatry, as Pilgrim and Rogers (1999) point out, was not questioned until the trauma of the First World War brought its legitimacy into question. As they wryly state, the 'shell shock' (later called battle neurosis, then post-traumatic stress disorder) experienced by officers and gentlemen could not be explained by reference to the tainted gene pool model of psychiatry. This paved the way for talking therapies, initially based on psychoanalytic frames of reference, although early on a distinction was drawn between neurosis, regarded as amenable to these forms of therapy, and psychosis, still seen to require physical forms of treatment. During the 20th century, the significance ascribed to talking therapies waxed and waned, with the introduction of the major tranquillisers in the 1950s serving to boost an already buoyant resurgence of biodeterminism (Pilgrim & Rogers, 1999). During the 20th and 21st centuries, medicalised understandings of mental distress have been challenged and these are reviewed later in this chapter. However, the dominant orientation clearly remains predicated on clinical frames of reference and medicalised practices. It is this dominant understanding that locates the discussion within the health arena and it is predominantly within these parameters that social workers operate.

What constitutes mental health?

To return to the question posed at the outset, good mental health has been regarded as relating to a number of inter-related aspects. These include the possession of a sense of self-worth, having self-confidence and self-esteem, being self-aware, having maturity of judgement, being able to form affectionate relationships, possessing the ability to generate and sustain supportive networks, being able to tackle life's tasks and deal with complex demands and, most important of all, having the capacity to grow as a person. Clearly, these aspects of self are mediated by socioeconomic factors, as well as by the interaction of aspects related to gender, 'race', ethnicity, sexuality, and disability. They are also influenced by context and by what is regarded as appropriate or inappropriate, as acceptable or as a problem, at any given moment. In *The Unbearable Lightness of Scones,* Alexander McCall Smith wittily paints the verbal picture of one of the characters, Mathew, on holiday in Australia being caught by a rip tide and taken out to sea. A dolphin saves him, but running down the sand dunes towards the road, dripping wet and ecstatic after his miraculous rescue, he is picked up by a local police patrol car and rapidly assessed by the occupants as a homeless lunatic and responded to accordingly. His attempts to explain are rewarded by 'sit back and keep calm, we don't have to use handcuffs do we, you keep calm, everything's going to be alright, they'll fix you up nicely at the hospital' (McCall Smith, 2009, audio CD).

It is notable, despite the rise in literature relating to 'well-being' and the importance of attaining a work–life balance, that greater emphasis is placed on deciding what constitutes mental ill-health rather than mental health and on concentrating on problems rather than building on what is working well (see Chapter 11). Concern tends to be generated if individuals threaten their own safety or that of others, if they appear to have lost self-control, and if their behaviour is unpredictable and difficult to understand. However, as highlighted, prevailing values, traditions, cultural practices, and political or religious orthodoxies also play a part, as do socially generated tolerations of difference.

PERSPECTIVES ON MENTAL HEALTH AND MENTAL DISTRESS

Clinical perspectives

Medical orientations

As discussed above, those understandings which dominate thinking in relation to mental distress, mental ill-health, or mental illness have developed primarily within a Western frame of reference that prioritise medical understandings. Medical approaches can be seen to form a continuum from organic brain disease models, which focus specifically on brain architecture and chemical imbalances, at one end of the spectrum, to biopsychosocial models at the other, which, in addition to physiological and biological factors, take psychological, social, and environmental aspects into account. Within the parameters of the health spectrum, all models view mental distress as an illness or disorder and a psychiatric diagnosis is given on the basis of prevailing symptoms. These are categorised and indexed in relation to established criteria, such as the Diagnostic and Statistical Manual, with the fifth version (DSM-5) due for publication in 2013 (American Psychiatric Association, 2013 forthcoming). Each version reviews and, where relevant, adds to, amends, or deletes the disorders specified. Although work is continuing on DSM-5V, revision of the current definition of mental disorder is being considered with the proposed definition taking cultural factors more fully into account as well as emphasising the importance of underlying psychobiological dysfunction (http://www.dsm5.0rg).

The Diagnostic and Statistical Manuals link specified disorders with established criteria to enable informed professional judgements to determine diagnoses. Clinical depression, for example, is diagnosed on the basis of the appearance of patients; their speech and motor activities, energy levels, and prevailing mood; and the duration and severity of the symptoms. The condition of schizophrenia is diagnosed on the basis of the presence of an impairment in reality testing. The corresponding evidence relates to the observed presence of delusions, hallucinations, incoherence, disorganised behaviour, catatonic stupor, and/or disorganised associations. Again the severity and duration of the symptoms and the absence of initiating organic factors are taken into account. Treatment, following diagnosis, can involve a combination of prescribed medication as well as a range of therapies. Medications range from psychotropic products, such as Modecate, Stelazine, chlorpromazine, and risperidone, used to treat diagnoses of schizophrenia, to preparations such as Prozac for diagnoses of depression or anxiety. Many commentators have drawn attention to the side effects of the major tranquillisers and it is notable that these can include stiffening, weakening, and contracting of the muscles, restlessness, involuntary movements or shaking, often referred to as tardive dyskeniesia, drowsiness, skin rashes, considerable weight gain, jaundice, as well as low resistance to sunlight and infections generally. Associated forms of therapy can include talking therapies, such as counselling, psychoanalysis, psychotherapy, and forms of cognitive behaviour therapy. However, there is still a tendency for these responses to be directed towards those regarded as being at the nonpsychotic end of the clinical spectrum.

There are clearly many advantages associated with a medicalised approach. Depression, for example, is presented as an illness like any other and emphasis is placed on its amenability to standardised forms of treatment where, as with physical illnesses, pharmacology plays a major role. Communities and families are not regarded as being at fault in any way and individuals are not viewed as being responsible for their behaviour while they are ill. There are also resources to be accessed and, although stretched, particularly in remote and rural areas, all use a shared understanding of what mental illness is about, how it is categorised, and associated treatment responses. Private insurance claims are also based on medical diagnosis and the resultant prognosis. Problems are seen to relate predominantly to there not being enough resources, facilities, in-patient beds, or assertive outreach teams to provide services or to facilitate early intervention to ameliorate the longer term effects of the illness.

However, there are some disadvantages and these include individuals losing autonomy and emphasis being placed on control and regulation, particularly in terms of taking medication. Individuals can also lose personhood and be referred to generically as 'the' mentally ill or individually as 'a schizophrenic', losing their personal identity. The current emphasis placed on early intervention has also been critiqued by a number of researchers. Bentall and Morrison (2002), Warner (2008), and Spandler and Carlton (2009), for example, question the almost automatic association between early intervention and positive outcomes, and draw attention to the tensions between early intervention policies and practices and the very different strategies employed by those engaged in mental health promotion and prevention. These researchers draw from their research findings to maintain that evidence on the effectiveness of early intervention is at best weak and at worst non-existent. Spandler and Carlton (2009), in particular, comment on the human rights issues inherent in exposing people to a psychiatric career and the administration of drugs with potentially harmful side effects to people who may not go on to develop psychosis.

Factors influencing clinical practice: 'evidence', 'risk', and 'vulnerability'

Within clinical assessment parameters, areas such as 'evidence', 'risk', and 'vulnerability' have been ascribed a particular significance and judgements relating to these aspects have assumed a major role in decision-making processes. Social workers will be familiar with policy and practice guidance documentation emphasising how 'evidence' is to be used and 'risk' and 'vulnerability' assessed. It is, therefore, pertinent to unpack these terms and to look at the implications of particular definitions at this point.

Evidence and 'evidenced-based practice'

Evidence – and more particularly evidence-based practice – has gained considerable ground in the clinical arena of mental health over the past two decades. Simply put, the argument is that practice should be based on research findings demonstrating positive outcomes. On one level, this appears to promote good practice but on another it provokes a number of further questions. These range from the fairly obvious 'who determines what constitutes evidence or positive outcomes' to whether a direct relationship between research evidence and practice can ever be assumed (see Chapter 26). When looking at the former question, the argument presented is that, provided the research is carried out within prescribed methodological parameters, then authoritative knowledge can be seen to have been produced. However, it is notable that a hierarchy has been applied to different forms of evidence with quantitatively orientated randomised controlled trials being regarded as the 'gold standard'. Qualitative research emphasising meaning making and experiential knowledge is relegated to the lower ranges (see Chapter 31). Critics, such as

Webb (2001), maintain that evidence-based practice linked to a scientific rationale fails to take account of the contexts in which practitioners operate. Despite emphasis being placed on making connections between information, research findings, and evidence-based practice, he maintains that practitioners do not work in rationally, logically orientated working environments. Instead, they are beset by differential interests, complexities, and the demands of particular situations.

There have been attempts to create environments amenable to particular research-based approaches and these have tended to focus on practitioners applying fairly rigid clinical techniques, including prescribed versions of cognitive behaviour therapy, with accompanying goal-attainment scales to users of a particular service (Fawcett et al., 2010). However, one-size-fits-all approaches have tended to downgrade professional knowledge and skills, and to disregard experience. Most importantly, they have failed to take the particular situation and views of those using the service into account. This reductionist application of evidence-based practice (EBP) has been strongly critiqued by others. Gray et al. (2009), for example, argue that EBP should be applied flexibly to take full account of contingencies. In terms of the original definition by Sackett et al. (2000), rather than EBP prescribing a form of intervention, it can be used to ensure the best available evidence is taken into account and tailored to fit clients' needs, values, interests, situations, and preferences by a professional with expertise in the area of the client's problems (see Chapter 26).

Overall, although there are provisos, as well as examples of empirically based practice being rolled out in an organisationally well-intentioned but ultimately counterproductive manner, it is important not to dismiss EBP. As Fawcett et al. (2010) argue, although the goal of practice being based solely on rational, scientific underpinnings is elusive and the idea of evidence is far more complex than often portrayed, research findings can and should play an important role in informing practice. However, attention has to be paid to moving away from a hierarchical approach and, although continuing to emphasise the importance of ongoing critical scrutiny, to embrace methodological rigour and a range of orientations, approaches, and methods, including participatory action research approaches (see Chapter 30).

'Risk' 'Risk' is also a concept that within clinical frames of reference assumes a mantle of scientific credibility. Risk assessments are used to identify, measure, and prioritise risk and to identify strategies for its effective management. Although risk can be viewed positively as something challenging and enhancing personal development, within mental health the emphasis is predominantly negative and risk assessments and risk-management plans have the function of risk-managing individuals towards normalising social trajectories. Webb (2006) questions the objective authority ascribed to risk assessments and argues that these are influenced by unacknowledged value-laden assumptions. He also points to their use as rationing devices, including some and excluding others. Clearly, the view that 'risk' can be subject to a form of cost–benefit analysis has its adherents as well as its critics. However, the point to be made is that the prevailing interpretation constitutes one among many others.

'Vulnerability' 'Vulnerability', like 'risk', is a term frequently used in clinical practice. It is usually employed to position certain individuals in such a way that they are seen to require intervention. It is a word which is interrogated infrequently and, as such, often carries with it the overtones of deficit. Warner (2008) interestingly inverts its usual application and uses it to refer to the community rather than to an individual. She argues the stigmatising view, that mental health service users pose a high risk to the public, carries with it a view of the public as vulnerable, as collectively exhibiting deficits, and as requiring intervention. Beckett (2006)

also regards the public as vulnerable, but relates this to the fragile and contingent nature of personhood. She rejects the clinical view of vulnerability and maintains all are 'vulnerable', in some respects, and most people are potentially or actually 'vulnerable' in relation to a very wide range of 'risks' and new forms of social exclusion. She makes links between vulnerability and citizenship, defining citizenship as a process of proactive engagement, where the aim is to achieve human rights for all citizens with these rights being determined on the basis of a universal acceptance of the vulnerability of all (see Chapter 24).

Skolbekken (2008) also challenges commonly held views of vulnerability. As Fawcett (2009) highlights, he examines the links between risk calculation and medicalisation, and maintains that not only is the increasing medicalisation of problems that were previously regarded as social being witnessed, but that this process also identifies which newly discovered vulnerabilities will be addressed and which will be ignored. Accordingly, as everyone increasingly develops a variety of 'conditions', constant medical surveillance or prevention is required to address increasing vulnerabilities. However, Skolbekken (2008) argues this attention is both directed and partial, and a consequence of increasing medicalisation leads to resources being directed towards the lifestyles of the affluent rather than on lifesaving medicines for those living in poverty.

Psychological perspectives

Psychological perspectives broadly but not definitively range from behavioural to cognitive behavioural, from psychodynamic to psychoanalytical, and from humanistic to discourse analysis. While the former have links to medicalised frames of reference, the latter have clear points of overlap with forms of sociological analysis. These ranges are outlined below.

The behavioural–cognitive behavioural range

Behavioural understandings tend to view the symptoms together with the behaviour which follows from them as constituting the problem or disorder. Symptoms are generally regarded as resulting from maladaptive learned responses or unhelpful learning or conditioning processes. Emphasis is placed on changing both the learning and the accompanying responses. Approaches have included forms of behaviour modification based on principles of classical conditioning (where a particular behaviour is associated with a specific stimulus) and operant conditioning (where desired behaviours are positively reinforced). Specific associated techniques include systematic desensitisation, where an individual is gradually induced to overcome a fear or problematic response and 'flooding', where an individual is fully exposed to what they fear most (see Chapter 9).

Over recent years, cognitive behavioural approaches have largely replaced forms of behavioural therapy in the arena of mental health. These vary considerably, but are based mainly on work undertaken by pioneers such as Beck (1967, 1976). He highlighted the effects of negative thought processes and, in relation to depression, identified three major components. These relate to the presence of negative automatic thoughts, which reinforce unhelpful perceptions emphasising failure or the inability to perform a task, systematic logical errors or overgeneralisations about events. Accordingly, this can result in the magnification and globalisation of a throwaway comment or nonverbal gesture and entrenchment of depressogenic schemata, where past and present experiences are organised in a negative manner and re-emphasised. This exacerbates low self-esteem and a lack of confidence. To remedy debilitating or inappropriate thought processes, cognitive therapies generally focus on enabling an individual to become aware of and to question unhelpful ways of operating, and to plan and practise different strategies. Sutton (2000) outlines a range of techniques used by cognitive behaviour therapists to enable an individual to change entrenching thinking patterns. These include countering irrational beliefs about individual capabilities by a process of supportive rational questioning; monitoring and addressing negative 'self-talk' by learning positive 'self-talk'; and testing the evidence for negative self-perceptions by means of a 'reality check'.

The psychoanalytic–psychodynamic range

Psychoanalysis has seen many different interpretations since the work of Freud who produced his groundbreaking works in the latter part of the 19th and early part of the 20th centuries (see Freud, 1949 edition). Basic concepts include the placing of emphasis on an individual's personal history, on the dynamic relationship between the conscious and the unconscious parts of the mind, and on the importance of maintaining a balance between the id, ego, and superego. Where a balance is not maintained, the ego can resort to defence mechanisms, which include projection, splitting, sublimation, and rationalisation. Unlike clinical understandings, psychoanalytic frameworks regard abnormality and normality as being connected. As a result, rather than emphasis being placed on distinguishing between those who are ill and those who are well, everybody is regarded as requiring psychoanalytical interpretation and guidance to some degree.

Psychoanalysis assumes our behaviour is predominantly determined by unconscious thoughts, drives, and desires. The unconscious can become accessible to the conscious mind by means of specific techniques, which include transference, dream interpretation, and free association. Repression is a means by which difficult experiences are relegated to the unconscious and this is regarded as a means of ego defence. Sexual energy plays an important role in determining future intrapersonal and interpersonal conduct. Accordingly, the way in which the infant passes through the five psychosexual stages (the oral, anal, phallic, Oedipal, and latency) in the first six years of life is seen to influence later personality significantly. Regression, where individuals who have progressed to subsequent stages fall back on behaviour associated with earlier stages, and fixation, where individuals remain locked into a particular stage, are associated with particularly problematic progression. Psychoanalysts, such as Jung (1964), Adler (1927), and Klein (1932), have all famously hallmarked their own interpretations of psychoanalysis. Jung, for example, moved away from an emphasis on childhood experiences and the personal unconscious, and instead focused on interpretations of the collective unconscious; Adler largely replaced the focus on sexuality with the 'will to power'; and Melanie Klein developed the child- and parent-orientated 'object relations' school of psychoanalysis (Gross, 2007; Payne, 2005; Sutton, 2000).

Psychodynamic approaches generally, in contrast to psychoanalysis, pay less attention to the inter-relationship between the id, ego, and superego, and concentrate instead on self-realisation by means of ongoing processes of therapeutic intervention. This often focuses on active listening and the promotion of self-reflection and personal insight. Attachment theory is linked to psychodynamic approaches and associates emotional well-being, emotional maturity, and social competence with the early formation of secure and emotionally responsive attachments between children and significant adults. As a result, many mental health difficulties experienced by children, young people, and adults are seen as having their roots in various forms of insecure or nonexistent attachments experienced in childhood (Payne, 2005).

The humanistic to discourse analysis range

The humanistic approach was developed initially by Carl Rogers (1951) as a holistic way of viewing mental health. He argued individuals face key 'would/should' dilemmas and the tensions between what they should do and what they feel is best for them can result in anxiety and depression. According to Rogers, dilemmas such as these must be addressed if individuals are to be able to control their life and achieve self-actualisation. Incongruence, which is the taking on board of values which do not suit to obtain positive regard from important figures, is regarded as a negative strategy, while congruence, which concerns a person's attempts to achieve harmony in their way of being, enables individuals to work towards the goal of self-actualisation.

Maslow (1968) is concerned more with the motives driving people than with the effect of the opinion of others upon self-concepts. He focused on establishing key patterns and famously produced what is now termed Maslow's Hierarchy of Needs. He saw different needs as comprising a pyramidical structure, with fundamental physiological needs at the base, followed by safety, belonging, love, esteem, and self-actualisation needs at the pinnacle. He regarded problems in relation to the last three needs as being possible triggers for the experiences of depression and anxiety.

Discourse analysis is associated with social constructionism (discussed below). As with the other approaches outlined, there are many variations, but common threads include an emphasis on anti-essentialist and nonpositivist forms of thinking, historical and cultural relativity, and the overriding importance of context in the analysis of social interaction. Edley and Wetherell (1997), both significant pioneers in this area, have pointed to a distinction between 'top-down' and 'bottom-up' forms of analysis. Top-down orientations are seen to be concerned with interpretative repertoires and with the positioning of the subject within discursive regimes in order to highlight the interplay of the various discourses. Bottom-up perspectives are regarded as drawing from ethnomethodology and conversation analysis where emphasis is placed on the accomplishments of conversation and 'talk' generally. Edley and Wetherell (1997) maintain that the paying of eclectic attention to both aspects facilitates detailed study of the ways in which people are simultaneously the master and slave of discourse. In relation to mental health, as with social perspectives generally, this form of analysis focuses on how an individual acquires a diagnosis of mental illness and critically interrogates the part played by prevailing values, cultural influences, power–knowledge frames, historical precedent, and context.

Social perspectives

It is very easy, when looking at social perspectives, to set these up in opposition to medical or clinical understandings of mental health. Although there are differences in relation to analysis and emphasis, there is a great deal of overlap. This is particularly the case as Western medicalised conceptualisations of mental distress formulated as mental ill-health and mental illness, have dominated thinking in this arena for so long. Nevertheless, an exploration of social perspectives does facilitate critical reflection and analysis, and draws attention to health inequities and power imbalances operating within mental health systems.

It also needs to be acknowledged that social perspectives do not include the biopsychosocial approach, as the latter can be seen to be firmly located within a clinical frame of reference (Fawcett & Karban, 2005). Social perspectives, in contrast, draw from discourse analysis, from critical sociological and postmodern deconstructive critiques and also, importantly, from the lived experiences and experiential knowledge of those who refer to themselves as mental health consumers or service users and mental health system survivors. When looking at the key points emerging from social perspectives, one which comes to the fore is that of problem identification not being straightforward. Here sociological analyses focusing on social causational, social constructionist and also ecological systems orientations make a major contribution.

Social causationalism
This is a form of enquiry which looks at what might have preceded, influenced, or caused mental distress, mental ill-health, or mental illness. Aspects can include sexual abuse, child abuse, trauma, bereavement, poor

educational experiences, family conflict, and marital disharmony, and this list is far from exhaustive. These stressors are also influenced by social position, cultural and religious beliefs, gender, sexuality, race, disability, and age, with many of these areas intersecting and converging. It needs to be noted that biopsychosocial approaches often do explore possible social causative factors, but the difference in relation to social perspectives is that, within the latter, predominant emphasis is placed on social determinants and on ways of addressing these within a social framework. However, social causationalist perspectives often also subscribe to medicalised understandings, using this analysis to add a distinctive social dimension. To give an example, Indigenous people in Australia have markedly higher rates of hospital admission for psychosis than non-Indigenous people and Indigenous people are also ascribed a higher rate of psychiatric morbidity, that is, they are more likely to be diagnosed with a psychiatric condition than non-Indigenous people (Meadows et al., 2007). A social causational perspective would relate this to inequalities associated with multiple losses, the trauma of the Stolen Generations, racism, and dislocation from traditional forms of community support. A socially orientated response would be to work with community groups to develop and implement sustainable, inclusive, and multilevel strategies to address pervasive inequalities.

Increasingly the World Health Organisation (WHO) is acknowledging the effects of global inequality and is emphasising the role social determinants play in the arena of mental ill-health. The 2009 WHO Report entitled *Mental Health, Resilience and Inequalities* states:

> levels of mental distress among communities need to be understood less in terms of individual pathology and more as a response to relative deprivation and social injustice, which erode the emotional, spiritual and intellectual resources essential to psychological wellbeing (Freidli, 2009, p. iii).

In the WHO Report (Freidli, 2009), the major challenge is seen to be addressing inequalities across WHO member states by intervening in the social, cultural, and economic conditions that support family and community life. Accordingly, educational and employment opportunities, and work conditions need to be significantly improved and partnerships between health and other sectors enhanced, with particular attention being paid to aspects that affect mental health and well-being. The Report emphasises 'mental health is produced socially' and 'the presence or absence of mental health is above all a social indicator and therefore requires, social as well as individual solutions' (Freidli, 2009, p. 38). The challenges posed for social work, particularly in terms of ensuring a social focus, are evident.

Social constructionism

There are many versions of social constructionism with some being influenced by critical theory and others by discourse analysis. However, a commonality relates to applying a deconstructive analysis or unpacking 'taken-for-granted' views. Burr (1995) states:

> Defining illness and disease is not simply a matter of identifying the presence of pathology. It is a deeply social matter involving the interpretation of our experience within our particular cultural context of assumptions, norms and values as well as the economic structure of our society. It is also a matter of power relations. The body's 'deficiencies' only show up as such when persons are constrained to live in environments designed to suit the needs and activities of others (p. 40).

Accordingly, emphasis is placed on how medicalised orientations came to be seen as 'the' way to frame and respond to mental distress. In line with discourse analysis, social constructionist perspectives concentrate on how individuals can be positioned in relation to prevailing values, ideologies, and cultural and social attitudes. To continue with the example given above, not including Indigenous people in the formulation of mental health strategies infers a lack of respect and can assume homogeneity, constructing a group in a negative manner. Social constructionist perspectives pay attention to power imbalances, to who is being positioned or constructed, how this is taking place, and who is doing the constructing. Commentators such as Joan Busfield (1996) maintain that there is a direct relationship between power imbalances, devaluation, and an individual, group, or community not being heard. For example, if individuals have been given a diagnosis of psychosis, their concerns about treatment and associated side effects and the overall effect on their lives, are more likely to be disregarded and dismissed.

Social constructionist perspectives also subject those precepts drawn from transcultural psychiatry to critical appraisal. Accordingly, the argument that if different cultures were more fully understood, then the possibility of misdiagnosis would be reduced and more culturally sensitive services developed, is critiqued. The criticism is made that it fails to take account of power imbalances, unacknowledged racist and colonising practices, and the views and experiences of those receiving the services. Returning to Indigenous perspectives, Meadows et al. (2007) state in relation to Australia:

> many Aboriginal people find the language of psychiatry alien and stigmatizing. Classification can lead to invisibility and allow the real health needs of Aboriginal people to be ignored. Similarly conventional psychiatric care is not sufficient for, and on its own may be damaging to Aboriginal people, who rarely utilize mainstream services (p. 98).

Those who can be seen to have adopted a social constructionist perspective range from psychotherapist Thomas Szasz (1973) to sociologist Allan Horwitz (2002). Szasz (1973), at his most controversial, declared mental illness to be a myth, used to justify persecution in the name of mental health. He argued that those called mentally ill should only be compulsorily detained if they commit imprisonable offences and then the place of detention should be prison. Otherwise, he maintained individuals should be able to express themselves however they wish, with those feeling they require support negotiating this on an individual contractual basis. Instead of the term 'mental illness', Szasz (1973) suggested the phrase 'problems with living' offered a less constraining and more productive way forward. Horwitz (2002), in a very different way, regards mental illnesses as social constructions, but argues *something* is being constructed. He advocates subjecting mental health labels to deconstructive appraisal, to continually scrutinising what is regarded as dysfunctional by taking full account of social contexts to ensure individuals are not making understandable responses to aberrant social situations, and to check continually whether it is the individual or the social-systemic conditions that requires change. However, as already highlighted, although social constructionism applied to mental distress can take many forms, it is the deconstructive element that has the greatest potential to bring about challenge and change.

Ecological systems perspectives

Ecological systems perspectives originally emanated from the biological sciences where they directed attention towards the organism in its environment. Applications to the social field have significantly widened the range and there are now many versions of ecological systems orientations. Brofenbrenner (1988), a pioneer in this arena, concentrates on the inter-relationship between four ecological systems. These are the micro-system, which relates to the immediate setting, the meso-system, which is associated with the linkage between two or more micro-systems, the exo-system, which refers to those aspects which influence the micro-system, and the macro-system, which encompasses those wider social and cultural aspects that influence other systems. Gilgun (1996a, 1996b) makes links between human ecology, human processes, and developmental psychopathology. She notes the limitations of approaches that concentrate on internally orientated, non-ecological, disease-orientated perspectives and directs attention towards strengths-based, ecological systems. She argues a combination of developmental psychopathology viewed from within an ecological social work framework, informed by a combination of ecological systems, strengths-based approaches, and phenomenological orientations, can inform programme development and significantly influence policy and practice. Accordingly, she suggests it is not risk factors per se that determine outcomes and no single adversity or combination of adversities guarantees poor developmental outcomes. She argues that poor outcomes appear to occur as a result of the presence of a host of risk factors, and the relative absence or ineffectiveness of protective factors. She sees protective factors as often being embedded in subtle processes within families, neighbourhoods, and schools, and maintains that the determination of whether assets are protective or not depends on the interpretations of the individuals concerned rather than on the assessments of outsiders. Drawing from her research findings, she focuses on the long-term importance of increasing protective factors and of decreasing risk processes at individual and social levels.

The type of ecological systems theory adopted clearly influences both process and outcome. However, Houston's (2002) interpretation, which draws from Jack (2000), links ecological theory with the refocusing of services towards prevention, client-determined support, the development of capacity, social capital, and the tackling of oppressive social barriers. In Chapter 8, Jack examines how an ecological perspective, in association with a systems-orientated approach, provides the basis for the development of holistic, anti-oppressive practice. This orientation clearly has considerable relevance for the promotion of positive mental health and for the provision of a constructive framework for practice. Within medical contexts it is referred to as the biopsychosocial perspective (see comment earlier).

Service-user, consumer, and survivor perspectives

Those who use mental health services have largely lacked a collective voice. However, in most Western nations, consumer, user, and survivor movements gained momentum in the early 1980s. Although not all would claim an allegiance with Disability Rights Movements, aspects such as the need for service users to play an integral part in the design and operation of services, the attention drawn to oppressive and disabling social barriers, and the importance of citizenship, have featured significantly (see Chapter 44). Sayce (2002), in particular, develops what she calls a 'Disability Inclusion' model where she focuses on the importance of rights and citizenship and the tackling of discriminatory social barriers. Within this model, the right to self-determination features strongly – as it does in most social work interventions. It suggests those with a mental health diagnosis should issue advance directives to ensure that they retain control over what happens to them should they become subject to compulsory detention and treatment.

Service-user, consumer, and survivor perspectives also focus on a service-user definition of recovery. Unlike clinical definitions of recovery, emphasise those aspects of particular significance to the individual and prioritise meaning making, identity, and self-esteem. As a result, recovery is not about becoming symptom free, but about reclaiming an individually determined and socially valued lifestyle, retaining control over decision-making processes, and using advance directives if necessary (Double, 2002; see Chapter 11).

Service-user, consumer, and survivor perspectives are also influencing research. They have directed attention towards users or survivors negatively located as passive 'subjects' of research, rather than as active participants. As a result, there have been calls for inclusive participatory approaches, which focus not only on the purpose of a research project but also on how it is to be carried out and the use to be made of the findings (see Chapter 30). It is also notable that research into funded consumer-run programmes carried out in the USA in particular, have shown that benefits include peer support, encouragement, the power to persevere, a sense of belonging, the sharing of coping strategies, a renewed sense of hope and energy, affordability, educative sharing, and a heightened sense of self-worth. These benefits are associated with a reduction in the use of mental health services and with increased consumer confidence and self-determination (Meadows et al., 2007; Van Tosh & Del Vecchio, 2000).

As Fawcett and Karban (2005) note, user and survivor movements range from those who want to effect change within existing clinical services to those who are more interested in developing different forms of user-driven and managed support. The 'Hearing Voices' networks provide an example of different forms of support where those who hear voices come together to overcome isolation and to share strategies for managing their voices (Romme & Esher, 1993). Having begun in the Netherlands, they are now spreading globally as an adjunct or alternative to clinical services.

Different ways of conceptualising mental health are also emerging from within psychiatry. The development of 'postpsychiatry' by psychiatrists Pat Bracken and Phil Thomas (2005) can be seen to be particularly significant. They state:

> As doctors, we are taught to encounter phenomena such as voices, self-harm, madness, suicidal feelings and paranoia as psychopathology – symptoms of disease processes. Our 'diagnosis and treat' medical model is an easy fix. Our diagnoses explain quickly; our drugs deaden immediately. But increasingly, service users tell us that this approach robs their experiences of meaning and strips them from the lived contexts (social, cultural, personal) in which they have arisen ... our argument is that our models (especially the medical model) are part of the problem when it comes to users overcoming the idea that they have a 'life less worthy' (p. 7).

Bracken and Thomas (2004) prefer to talk about states of madness, distress, or alienation rather than mental illness. Their perspective does not herald a return to the anti-psychiatry movement of the 1970s (Fawcett, 2007). They insist they do not aim to replace the medical techniques of psychiatry with new therapies. Rather than positing a set of fixed ideas or beliefs, they want to provide a set of signposts enabling all engaged in the field of mental health to look constructively and critically at contemporary mental health systems and to move on. As part of this process, they draw attention to faith in the ability of science and technology to resolve human and social problems. They argue attention has to be paid to social and cultural contexts, to placing ethics before technology, and to working to minimise medical control of coercive interventions. They see poverty, racism, unemployment, loneliness, relationship difficulties, spiritual conflicts, sexual abuse, and domestic violence as being at the heart of mental health crises. These, they maintain, are social not individual problems and require social responses. Accordingly, they place emphasis on community involvement and on prioritising a form of active citizenship which foregrounds hope, trust, dignity, and meaningful engagement (Fawcett, 2007).

THE CONTEXT OF MENTAL HEALTH SOCIAL WORK

Across the globe, improving mental well-being, preventing mental ill-health, and responding to mental distress in all its manifestations are key concerns. As highlighted in this chapter, there are a number of prevailing perspectives that variously challenge, promote consistency, and foster mutual viability. The WHO, as highlighted earlier, is promoting measures which focus on mental health promotion and mental ill-health prevention and on reducing inequalities within and between nations. Their emphasis on the social determinants of mental health supports a whole-population approach that views beneficial outcomes, not in relation to the absence of mental illness, but rather in terms of the active encouragement of individual and social resilience, well-being, and positive mental health.

Clearly contexts of practice are far from static. Nevertheless, there remain differences in terms of how nations are responding to the challenges presented. In the USA, for example, there is a predominant emphasis on clinical practice and on consumer choice supported by private health insurance. However, systemic challenges are presented by those who lack insurance and who, for a variety of reasons, are excluded from the mainstream.

In the UK, the prevailing tensions between clinical forms of practice, 'postpsychiatry', and service-user perspectives, paint a vibrant, sometimes turbulent, but overall dynamic canvass. The research of Huxley et al. (2005) into the stress and pressures experienced by mental health social workers notably highlights their commitment to service users. The importance they attach to face-to-face contact is also seen to be a major factor in staff retention. Beinecke and Huxley (2010) have also pointed to the differences in the composition of the mental health workforce in the UK and the USA. They note in this field in the USA, social workers are the largest professional group, while in the UK, this position is held by community nurses. They view this situation as having been influenced by mental health being a promoted specialist social work area in the USA and highlight the influence of private, as opposed to public, mental health practice. They maintain that in the future, social workers are well placed to address emerging demands for coordination, case management, advocacy, negotiation, and networking, as well as placing the client at the centre of service planning. Within the context of workforce considerations, they argue that greater attention needs to be paid to areas where skills and values both converge and diverge, and that supply issues (i.e., the availability of particular professionals) should not determine workforce outcomes.

In Australia, despite the presence of a series of National Mental Health Plans, the picture differs from state to state. Emphasis is placed on both public and private provision, but services generally have been described as fragmented and consumer and carer involvement as underdeveloped (Mental Health Council of Australia, 2005). Similarly, there are far fewer social workers operating in the mental health arena than in the USA. Across the board, however, although not as highly developed as in the UK, consumer perspectives are gaining ground and many public services are now employing consumer advocates. Roper (2003) points to how the role of consumer advocates within public mental health services can be compromised by factors such as negative attitudes towards consumer providers held by nonconsumer staff and by tensions resulting from operating as an employee of a service as well as an advocate. However, he emphasises that staff training, a good use of resources, and effective communication and support systems can re-orientate priorities and enable agencies and organisations to foster important links with consumer movements. Research on peer support and user-run services has also highlighted significant development and good outcomes, with these including positive changes in community attitudes (Campbell, 2005; Salzer et al., 2002; Solomon, 2004).

WAYS FORWARD FOR SERVICE PROVISION AND RESOURCING: ROLES FOR PROFESSIONALS

Given the discussion thus far, there are a number of distinct but overlapping trends that can be applied to policy and social work practice in the mental health field. Some of these place continued emphasis on clinical practice. Some serve to broaden the contemporary picture and incorporate various aspects drawn from social orientations. Some challenge and others, by means of constructive critique, focus on reconfiguring the mental health landscape.

It is also possible to frame these trends within modern and postmodern terms of reference. Clinically oriented approaches, where emphasis is placed on rationality, on the production of universally applicable diagnostic frames and categorisation processes, and on the privileging of 'expert' knowledge over experiential knowledge are all predicated on a world view based on modernist elements of certainty and foundational thinking. Deconstructive appraisals tend to draw from postmodern forms of analyses and to take apart to reconstruct. As highlighted earlier, although there are tensions, an understanding of all these orientations, together with an appreciation that the spectrum encapsulating clinical frames is broadening, can re-energize and reinvigorate practice, and open up policy and practice spaces for strategic development.

One example of how this might be taken forward is suggested by Fawcett et al. (2011) and Fawcett and Hanlon (2009). What is proposed is a form of analysis and action to enable social workers to develop and support inclusive processes that have the capacity to reconfigure entrenched ways of operating or to develop new initiatives. The aspects highlighted are not meant to be prescriptive and draw from what social workers already know as being embedded in anti-oppressive and antidiscriminatory practice and critical reflection (see Chapter 21).

Clearly, any action requires prior analysis of what is going on and an appraisal of who benefits and why. This draws attention to power relations and to entrenched or situationally specific power imbalances. It also foregrounds the effects of these on all those involved and promotes the identification of areas of strength, as well as areas for development or change. It is about clarifying what is going on and the range of expectations and understandings operating as well as the commonalities and differences between all of those involved. There might, for example, be differences of opinion about ensuring effective service-user representation on service development and planning committees. As a result, the analysis might focus on examining the different rationales and finding common ground. The 'action' element then explores how to facilitate participation and how to ensure all players are involved in decision-making processes. Throughout, it is about: (i) identifying areas for negotiation; (ii) looking at how flexible, negotiatory processes can be developed to operate at a range of levels, where tradeoffs can take place, and where, perhaps, there have been small successes; and (iii) exploring how these can be built upon, sustained, and further developed. It is about being innovative and pragmatic and either creating situations or using situations which present themselves to take forward what has been learned and to transform analysis into action. So another example would be to forge a consensus around a single issue, which could be a festival about mental health and well-being that could then, at different points, be linked to other initiatives, such as a community mental health forum, an inclusive 'fun run', and consumer, social worker, and mental health practitioner lunches, and so on. These activities would also incorporate the establishment of representative opportunities across different groups at various levels, always making sure agreed action has a clear focus and achievable goals can be built on. As highlighted earlier, an ongoing priority is to ensure the spaces identified by the analysis are used strategically and these can also include those found in local councils, service provider agencies more generally, local media outlets, educational establishments, and central government schemes. Throughout, emphasis is placed on foregrounding involvement in decision-making processes at all levels, making sure decisions made are clearly followed through and supported, and that regular feedback and evaluatory processes are available (Fawcett et al., 2011).

Social work in mental health takes place in diverse forums. Many have a clinical emphasis. Sometimes social workers feel their role is limited and prescribed and at other times that there is room for interpretation and reinvention. However, it can be maintained a focus on analysis and action, whatever the scale and whatever the perceived room for manoeuvre, always opens up further possibilities for practice development.

CONCLUSION

This chapter has drawn attention to different conceptual movements in the mental health arena as a means of promoting and supporting social work practices that prioritise inclusivity, fluidity, and flexibility. Attention has also been paid to the importance of: (i) analysis; (ii) the taking of strategic decisions; (iii) consumer participation; and (iv) taking action in ways that use situationally specific aspects. Social workers are often in the firing line and can feel overwhelmed by competing pressures. Nevertheless, the importance of, to use a cliché, continually looking outside the box, of taking account of a range of perspectives, and continually involving consumers and service users in processes that affect them, cannot be underestimated.

REFERENCES

Adler, A. (1927). *The practice and theory of individual psychology*. New York: Harcourt Brace Jovanovich.

American Psychiatric Association (APA) (2013 forthcoming). *DSM-5: The future of psychiatric diagnosis*. Retrieved October 8, 2010 from http://www.dsm5.org/Pages/Default.aspx

Beck, A. (1967). *Depression: Clinical, experimental and theoretical aspects*. New York: Harper and Row.

Beck, A. (1976). *Cognitive therapy and emotional disorders*. New York: International Universities Press.

Beckett, A.E. (2006). *Citizenship and vulnerability*. Basingstoke: Palgrave.

Beinecke, R.H., & Huxley, P.J. (2010). Mental health social work and nursing in the USA and the UK: Divergent paths coming together. *International Journal of Social Psychiatry, 55*(3), 214–225.

Bentall, R.P., & Morrison, A.P. (2002). More harm than good: The case against using anti-psychotic drugs to prevent severe mental illness. *Journal of Mental Health, 11*(4), 351–356.

Bracken, P., & Thomas, P. (2004). Out of the clinic and into the community. *OpenMind, 126,* 13.

Bracken, P., & Thomas, P. (2005). *Postpsychiatry: Mental health in a postmodern world*. Oxford: Oxford University Press.

Brofenbrenner, U. (1988). Interacting systems in human development. Research paradigms: Present and future. In N. Bolger, Caspi, A., Downey, G., & Moorehouse, M. (eds), *Persons in context: Developmental processes*. Cambridge: Cambridge University Press, pp. 25–49.

Burr, V. (1995). *An introduction to social constructionism*. London: Routledge.

Busfield, J. (1996). *Men, women and madness: Understanding gender and mental disorder*. Basingstoke: Palgrave.

Campbell, J. (2005). *Emerging research base of peer run support programmes*. St Louis: Missouri Institute of Mental Health.

Double, D. (2002). The limits of psychiatry. *British Medical Journal, 324,* 900–904.

Edley, N., & Wetherell, M. (1997). Jockeying for position: On the construction of masculine identities. *Discourse and Society, 8*(2), 203–215.

Fawcett, B. (2007). Consistencies and inconsistencies: Mental health, compulsory treatment and community capacity building in England, Wales and Australia. *British Journal of Social Work, 37*(6), 1027–1042.

Fawcett, B. (2009). Vulnerability: Questioning the certainties in social work and health. *International Social Work, 52*(4), 473–485.

Fawcett, B., & Hanlon, B. (2009). The 'return to community': Challenges for human service professionals. *Journal of Sociology, 45*(4), 433–444.

Fawcett, B., & Karban, K. (2005). *Contemporary mental health: Theory, policy and practice*. London: Routledge.

Fawcett, B., Goodwin, S., Meagher, G., & Phillips, R. (2010). *Social policy for social change*. South Yarra: Palgrave.

Fawcett, B., Weber, Z., & Wilson, S. (2011). *Mental health, landscapes and vistas across the lifespan: A critical appraisal*. Basingstoke: Palgrave.

Freidli, L. (2009). *Mental health, resilience and inequalities*. Copenhagen: WHO.

Freud, S. (1949). *An outline of psychoanalysis*. London: Hogarth Press.

Gilgun, J.F. (1996a). Human development and adversity in ecological perspective, part 1: A conceptual framework. *Families in Society: The Journal of Contemporary Social Services, 77*(7), 395–402.

Gilgun, J.F. (1996b). Human development and adversity in ecological perspective, part 2: Three patterns. *Families in Society: The Journal of Contemporary Social Services*, 77(8), 459–476.

Gray, M., Plath, D., & Webb, S.A. (2009). *Evidence-based social work: A critical stance*. London: Routledge.

Gross, R. (2007). *Themes, issues and debates in psychology* (2nd ed.). London: Hodder and Stoughton.

Horwitz, A. (2002). *Creating mental illness*. Chicago, IL: The University of Chicago Press.

Houston, S. (2002). Re-thinking a systemic approach to child welfare: A critical response to the framework for the assessment of children in need and their families. *European Journal of Social Work*, 5(3), 301–312.

Huxley, P., Evans, S., Gately, C., Webber, M., Mears, A. Pajak, S., Kendall, T., Medina, J., & Katona, C. (2005). Stress and pressures in mental health social work: The worker speaks. *British Journal of Social Work*, 35, 1063–1079.

Jack, G. (2000). Ecological Influences on parenting and child development. *British Journal of Social Work*, 30, 703–720.

Jung, C.G. (1964). *Man and his symbols*. London: Aldus-Jupiter Books.

Klein, M. (1932). *The psycho-analysis of children*. London: Hogarth.

Maslow, A.H. (1968). *Towards a psychology of being* (2nd ed.). New York: Van Nostrand Reinhold.

Meadows, G., Singh, B., & Grigg, M. (2007). *Mental health in Australia* (2nd ed.). Melbourne: Oxford University Press.

McCall Smith, A. (2009). *The unbearable lightness of scones*. Disk 2, Hachette Digital.

Mental Health Council of Australia (MHCA) in Association with the Brain and Mind Research Institute and the Human Rights and Equal Opportunities Commission (2005). *Not for service report*. Canberra: MHCA.

Payne, M. (2005). *Modern social work theory* (3rd ed.). Basingstoke: Palgrave.

Pilgrim, D., & Rogers, A. (1999). *A sociology of mental health and illness* (2nd ed.). Buckingham: Open University Press.

Rogers, C.R. (1951). *Client-centred therapy: Its current practice, implications and theory*. Boston: Houghton-Mifflin.

Romme, M., & Escher, S. (1993). *Accepting voices*. London: MIND Publications.

Roper, C. (2003). Consumer perspective employment in the psychiatric service system: A Victorian view on safety issues. *Australian Journal for the Advancement of Mental Health*, 2(1), 1–6.

Sackett, D.L., Straus, S.E., Richardson, W.S., Rosenberg, W., & Haynes, R.B. (2000). *Evidence-based medicine: How to practice and teach EBM* (2nd ed.). New York: Churchill-Livingstone.

Salzer, M.S., & Mental Health Association of Southeastern Pennsylvania Best Practices Team (2002). *Best practice guidelines for consumer delivered services*. Philadelphia: Mental Health Association of South Eastern Pennsylvania.

Sayce, L. (2000). *From psychiatric patient to citizen (overcoming discrimination and social exclusion)*. Basingstoke: Palgrave.

Skolbekken, J-A. (2008). Unlimited medicalization? Risk and pathologization of normality. In A. Petersen & I. Wilkinson (eds), *Health, risk and vulnerability*. London: Routledge, pp. 16–29.

Skultans, V. (1979). *English madness, ideas on insanity, 1850–1890*. London: Routledge and Kegan Paul, pp.16–29.

Solomon, P. (2004). Peer support-peer provided services underlying processes, benefits, and critical ingredients. *Psychiatric Rehabilitation Journal*, 27, 392–401.

Spandler, H., & Carlton, T. (2009). Psychosis and human rights: Conflicts in mental health policy and practice. *Social Policy and Society*, 8(2), 245–257.

Sutton, C. (2000). *Child and adolescent behaviour problems: A multidisciplinary approach to assessment and intervention*. Guilford: BPS Books.

Szasz, T. (1973). *Ideology and insanity*. Harmondsworth: Penguin.

Van Tosh, L., & Del Vecchio, P. (2000). *Consumer operated self-help programmes: A technical report*, Rockville, MD: US Centre for Mental Health Services.

Warner, J. (2008). Community care, risk and the shifting locus of danger and vulnerability in mental health. In A. Petersen & Wilkinson, I. (eds), *Health, risk and vulnerability*. London: Routledge, pp. 30–47.

Webb, S.A. (2001). Some considerations on the validity of evidence-based practice in social work. *British Journal of Social Work*, 31(1), 57–79.

Webb, S.A. (2006). *Social work in a risk society*. Basingstoke: Palgrave.

34

Older People

Nancy R. Hooyman

The dramatic growth of the population age 65 and older worldwide is often referred to as a demographic imperative because it affects all social institutions: families, the workplace, educational settings, housing, and health and mental healthcare systems. Addressing older adults' needs is challenging, since they are more heterogeneous by gender, race, ethnicity, sexual orientation, and functional ability than any other age group. Although many adults face vulnerabilities and inequities as they age, most elders are resilient, even in the face of chronic illness. This chapter describes demographic changes in developed and developing countries, highlights the increasing diversity of older adults in Western societies, and reviews trends in physical, mental, and social well-being and emerging concepts of active ageing (i.e., ageing in a healthy manner across the life course), and elder-friendly communities for 'ageing in place occurring in the USA and Western European countries. It concludes with a discussion of emergent leadership roles for social workers to enhance the well-being of elders and their families within the context of chronic care and healthcare reform. Such leadership is critical, since social workers in developed countries in all practice arenas increasingly interact with older adults and their families in child welfare, family services, schools, community centres, mental health facilities, and among the homeless.

Social workers, key members of interdisciplinary healthcare teams, are not prepared to meet the growing demand for geriatric care. The US National Institute on Aging has projected a need for 60,000 to 70,000 geriatric social workers by 2020. In 2001, only 3% of the 150,000 members of the National Association of Social Workers (NASW) in the USA identified their primary area of practice as geriatric. By 2005, 9% of a sample of licenced NASW members identified ageing as their field of practice. Among these, fewer than 5% had received gerontological social work training (US Bureau of Labor Statistics, 2004; Whitaker et al., 2006). Unless social work education programmes become more effective in engaging faculty to teach gerontological competencies and in recruiting students to specialise in gerontology, the current situation will grow into an elder care workforce crisis (ElderCare Workforce Alliance, 2009).

DEFINITIONS

Defining old age is a challenge, given the increasing heterogeneity of the older population (now encompassing two to three generations) and the greatest growth of the oldest-old segment, particularly centenarians. Significant differences are found among the 'young-old' (ages 65–74), the 'old old' (ages 75–84), and the 'oldest old' (age 85 and over). However, ageing cannot be defined merely chronologically, which only partially reflects the biological, psychological, and social–cultural processes as people age. A more relevant distinction is functional age or the ability to perform activities of daily living (ADLs), such as eating, bathing, walking, and dressing, that require cognitive and physical well-being [World Health Organization (WHO), 2002].

AGEING AS A GLOBAL PHENOMENON

> Global aging is among the most pivotal changes of our time. Stark demographic differences among nations will significantly shape almost every aspect of national and international life. Demographics affect growth rates, intergenerational distribution of income, the structure of markets, the balance of savings and consumption, and many other economic variables. Socially, the world will change as well, as families come to have three, four, sometimes even five generations alive at one time. International relations, too, will change as some countries grow and others shrink. The stakes are high (George P. Schultz, Stanford University, March 2007).

All world regions are experiencing an increase in the absolute and relative size of their older populations, but the current numbers and expected growth of this group differ substantially between industrialised and developing countries. The most extreme societal ageing will occur in Europe and developed Asian countries, such as Japan. In contrast, the developing world will remain comparatively young, creating a more pronounced demographic divide between developed and developing countries. This gap will diminish by 2050, when developing countries will be as old as today's developed countries (Hayutin, 2007).

The number of persons aged 65 and older worldwide is projected to increase from 495 million or 7% of the world population currently to 974 million or 12% in 2030 (United Nations, 2009 a,b). This growth is due primarily to a reduction in fertility rates worldwide, even in developing countries of Africa and South America. It is estimated 120 countries will reach total fertility rates below replacement levels (i.e., 2.1 children per woman) by 2025, compared to 22 countries in 1975 and 70 in 2000 (WHO, 2002). Additionally, the global mortality rate for adults has fallen by about 1% a year for the past 40 years, with women making greater gains than men (Brown, 2010).

Ageing in developing countries

The projected increase of the older population is even higher for developing nations than developed ones, 475 million in 2009 to 1.6 billion in 2050, when about 80% of the world's older adults will live in developing countries (United Nations, 2009b). This parallels the trend that the most rapid world population growth across all ages is occurring in developing countries (Bloom & Canning, 2007). Even though fertility rates are declining worldwide, huge differences occur between countries and regions. Children under 15 represent 37% of the population in less developed regions, 22% in more developed areas (United Nations, 2009a). Nevertheless, the most dramatic future change in developing countries will be a successively larger percentage of older people than younger people. Adults aged 65 and older will increase from 3.8% of the population of less developed countries in 2005 to 14.6% in 2050, and 17% in 2075, nearly a fivefold increase. The growth rate for those aged 80 and older is even higher than for the young-old: 3.9% per year worldwide, 3.8% in the least developed countries, and 3.3% in the most developed. In fact, the less developed regions of the world will show a nearly fivefold increase in their oldest population, from 3.8% in 1975 to 17% in 2075 (Kinsella & Velkoff, 2001; United Nations, 2009b).

Because of its huge population, China currently has the largest number of people 65 and older (102 million) and of 80 and older in the world (13 million vs. 9.2 million in the USA). By 2050, the oldest-old in China will comprise 100 million. These dramatic increases are attributable mostly to China's continued low birthrate, 12 births per 1000 population compared with 21 worldwide. As a result, the median age of China is projected to rise from 33 in 2005 to 42 by 2030 (Kaneda, 2006; Population Reference Bureau, 2008).

Ageing in developed countries

Currently, 60% of older adults live in developed countries, which is projected to increase to 75% by 2020. Japan has the highest proportion of elders in the world (22%), followed by Italy (20%), Germany and Greece (19%), and Sweden (18%); Population Reference Bureau, 2008a). Older adults will comprise 30% of Japan's population by 2050, with one million of these elders age 100 and older. The median age in Italy will be 52.5 followed closely by Japan at 52.3 by 2050. The USA will show a much smaller increase from a median age of 36.5 to 41.5 in 2050.

The increasing size of the older population is a primary factor affecting current interest in the field of gerontological social work in developed countries. For example, in 1900, people aged 65 and older formed approximately 4% of the US population, less than 1 in 25. Today, slightly more than 100 years later, this segment has grown to almost 39 million, or 12.8%. During this period, the number of older adults grew thirteenfold, compared with a threefold increase in those under age 65. The growth of the older population slowed slightly in the 1990s owing to the relatively small number of children born during the Great Depression. But with the first baby boomers (those born between 1946 and 1964) turning 60 in 2006 and 65 in 2011, the population over the age of 65 is again growing significantly to comprise 19.3% of the total population by 2030. This represents a 100% increase over 30 years, compared with a 30% growth in the total population (Administration on Aging (AOA), 2011; US Census Bureau, 2009b).

As is the case to other developed countries, a major reason for such growth in the USA is increased life expectancy beyond age 65 combined with reduced fertility, with most gains in life expectancy occurring in the younger ages. In 1900, the average life expectancy at birth (i.e., the average length of time one could expect to live if one were born that year) was 47 years compared to 78.1 years currently. About four out of five individuals can now expect to reach age 65, at which point there is a better than 50% chance of living past age 80. Additionally, life expectancy at birth is projected to increase to 82.6 in 2050 (AOA, 2011; US Census Bureau, 2009a). Gains in the early years of life are largely attributable to advances in medicine and eradication of many acute diseases, particularly influenza and pneumonia, which caused high infant and childhood mortality in the past.

Although less dramatic than increases earlier in the life course, gains in life expectancy after age 65 also occurred from about 12.3 to 18.7 years between 1900 and 2008 (Those who make it to age 65 have gained an additional 18.6 years). Survival beyond age 65 may grow dramatically in future cohorts, when heart disease and cancer become more often chronic or long-term diseases rather than fatal. 65 were gained, (AOA, 2011). The outcome is an increase number of people who survive to advanced old age, typically with multiple chronic illnesses. Nevertheless, life expectancy at age 65 is lower in the U.SA. than in Japan, Switzerland, and Canada, for both men and women. In particular, Japanese men can expect to live 1.2 years longer than American men, and Japanese women 3.2 years longer than American women at age 65 (Federal Interagency Forum, 2010).

As is the case in other developed countries, the 'oldest-old' population age 85 and older in the USA has grown most rapidly. In 2008, of the 38.9 million persons age 65 and older, 36% were age 75–84 and 14.3% 85 and older. The oldest-old are projected to increase to 24% of the older population by 2050, largely due to baby boomers' turning 85 after 2030. Baby boomers are also expected to survive to age 100 at rates never before achieved; one in 26 North Americans can anticipate living to age100 by 2025, compared with 1 in 500 in 2000 (AOA, 2011; Federal Interagency Forum, 2010). These increases in life expectancy are reflected in the growth of multigenerational (three or four generations) families both in the USA and globally. Since 1990, the number of multigenerational households in the USA has grown by 60% and since 2000, by 30%. Nearly 6.6 million US households comprise three or more generations living together, with about 78,000 four-generation households nationwide (Generations United, 2009). Latino and Asian elders are more likely to live with extended family than other groups in the USA, reflecting in part cultural values. Although multigenerational households have always been common in developing countries, what has shifted is the current rise in multigenerational households in the USA and Western Europe. This is partially influenced by economics, with many young adults known as 'boomerang kids' moving back home with their parents, because of limited job prospects and a housing crunch. Alternatively, a greater number of older people are living with adult children because of declines in their income resulting from the worldwide recession (Yen, 2010).

PHYSICAL WELL-BEING: DIVERSITY BY AGE, FUNCTIONAL ABILITY, GENDER, RACE, SEXUAL ORIENTATION, AND SOCIAL CLASS

By age and functional ability

In planning and implementing health care and social services for older adults, it is essential to take account of the widely differing needs and characteristics between the current cohort of oldest-old (e.g., those age 85 and older) and the baby boomers (AOA, 2011; US Census Bureau, 2009b). In comparison with previous cohorts, the first wave of baby boomers is generally rejecting the concept of 'seniors', dependence, disability, and frailty, placing more emphasis on being productive, engaged, and powerful, and redefining the chronological definition of old. In a 2009 survey of young baby boomers (turning 50) and older baby boomers (turning 64), for example, both groups agreed old age starts around age 80 (Del Webb, 2010).

Baby boomers will have higher expectations of what society will offer them as they age. They are often informed, health-conscious consumers who are more committed to fitness than their predecessors. Accordingly, they are likely to make more demands on the health care system, not just for themselves but for those for whom they are caring. Their family structures are more diverse because of the effects of divorce, remarriage, blended families, and more single parents, unmarried heterosexual couples, and lesbian/gay/bisexual/transgender (LGBT) couples. They value 'staying connected' to their family, locale, and community and increasingly seek ways to 'age in place' (Gurwitt, 2010).

As has been the case for boomers earlier in life, they often seek to redefine lifestyles, and are more familiar with service-driven models of business or care compared to past generations. They want more choices of living environments and responsive, flexible, readily accessible, and culturally appropriate services. They tend to be technologically savvy, although socioeconomic status often determines access to technology and the extent to which they are technology-driven.

More diverse in terms of race, ethnicity, sexual orientation, social class, and functional ability, baby boomers experienced more disparities in access to healthy ageing than have prior cohorts of elders. Contrary to popular images of baby boomers as wealthy consumers, many have experienced losses of home value and retirement income as a result of the recession and are working longer than anticipated out of economic necessity, which may affect their assets available for service and living options. They are also likely to be providing informal care for a relative who is over the age of 80 and is at high risk of physical disability and dementia.

Although baby boomers are projected to have lower rates of disability, a minority of them, particularly smokers, those who are obese, and those experiencing a lifetime in poverty with little access to preventive services, will cope with multiple chronic illness. From 2011 to 2030, baby boomers will be healthier than prior cohorts, but in 2031, when they begin to turn 85, their health care needs will increase and the impact of escalating health expenditures will be felt. As baby boomers age, healthcare spending could reach $4.4 trillion by 2018, or 20.3% of the US gross domestic product, compared with 17.6% in 2009 (Centers for Medicaid and Medicare Services, 2009). Such increasing expenditures will take place in the context of healthcare reform and growing demands for a competent eldercare workforce; these trends are primary concerns for providers and policymakers (Institute of Medicine, 2008).

The concept of functional ability is central to understanding the oldest-old's health and long-term care needs. Within respondents aged 70 and older in a large study of community-dwelling elders aged 60–99, the prevalence of chronic diseases did not differ significantly, but those aged 80 and older reported greater functional limitations than did the younger respondents (Lee et al., 2008). Health status not only encompasses the presence or absence of disease, but also the degree of disability in an individual's level of functioning. Functional ability is measured by ADLs (or eating, dressing, bathing, or toiletry) and Instrumental Activities of Daily Living (IADLs; or preparing meals, shopping, managing money, and taking medication). Thus, activities older people can do, or think they can do, are useful indicators of the services and environmental changes needed to function as autonomously as possible. About 20% of older people are estimated to have a mild degree of disability in their ADLs, 14% with IADLs, with 2.5% (typically among the oldest-old) so disabled they need help with five or more ADLs (AOA, 2009; Federal Interagency Forum on Aging-Related Statistics, 2010). Generally, an older person's functional limitations depend on their gender, age, and lifestyle, such as whether they exercise, smoke, and maintain average weight [Centers for Disease Control (CDC) & Merck Foundation, 2008; Christ & Diwan, 2009]. Since 43% of Medicare beneficiaries have three or more conditions and 23% have five or more, their ability to function in the least-costly living environment is of concern to policy makers (Reuben, 2009). Not surprisingly, the oldest-old predominate among residents of long-term care facilities, such as skilled nursing homes, assisted living and adult family homes, because of their higher incidence of physical frailty, cognitive impairment, and living alone. Among the 1.6 million elders in skilled nursing facilities, about 50% are aged 85 and older (AOA, 2011).

Although rates of disability have diminished over the past 25 years, the sheer number of frail elders with multiple physical and mental illness is straining health care systems as well as families' caregiving capacities. This trend of declining disability may be slowed or even reversed, however, due to older adults' relatively low exercise rates, growing rates of obesity and its accompanying chronic diseases, and increasing levels of functional impairment (Alley and Chang, 2007; Reuben, 2009; Schoeni et al., 2008). The root cause of almost 35% of US deaths in 2000 was attributed to three behaviours: smoking, poor diet, and physical inactivity. These behaviours are risk factors for the nation's leading chronic disease killers: heart disease, cancer, stroke, and diabetes. Despite the known benefits of exercise, however, only about 22% of older North Americans participate in regular physical activity (30 minutes or more at least five times per week; Chipperfield, 2008; Federal Interagency Forum, 2010). Of additional concern, high blood pressure, elevated cholesterol, diabetes, smoking, and physical inactivity are conditions and behaviours related to cognitive decline. These patterns are of concern to policy makers and providers since medical care for chronic diseases is costly, with almost 95% of healthcare expenditures for older adults spent on managing long-term illnesses (CDC & the Merck Foundation, 2008).

By gender

Women predominate among older adults globally and in the USA, where they represent 58% of the population aged 65 and older and 68% of those over age 85. Women age 65 and older outnumber men in that age group by a ratio of three to two, at age 85 and over by five to two, and among centenarians by three to one. At age 65, women can expect to live an additional 19.9 years compared to 17.2 more years for their male counterparts. Even at age 85, female life expectancy is 1.2 years longer than that for males. However, men who survive beyond age 85 tend to have fewer chronic illnesses, disabilities and functional limitations, and enjoy a life expectancy similar to that of women (Federal Interagency Forum, 2010).

Sex differences in life expectancy have declined since 1980, when females born that year could expect to live 7.4 years more than men; in 2008 the difference narrowed to about 5 years. Females born in 2005 are expected to reach age 80.7, whereas males in that birth cohort will reach age 75.4 (US Census Bureau, 2009a). Differences continue to be greater between African-American females and males, with their current life expectancies at birth of 76.9 and 70, respectively. Even in the year 2050, however, male life expectancy will be less than 80 years, whereas women will achieve 84.3 years (AOA, 2011).

By race

Today, over 19% of the US population over the age of 65 are persons of colour (8.3% African-American, 7% Latino, 3.4% Asian or Pacific Islander, and less than 1% American Indian or Native Alaskan) and this is projected to increase to nearly 24% by 2020; populations of colour include a smaller proportion of older people and a larger percentage of younger adults than the White population. This difference results primarily from the higher fertility and mortality rates among the non-White population under age 65 than among their White age peers. However, the proportion of non-White older persons is predicted to increase at a higher rate than the Caucasian population. This is partly because of the large percentage of children in these groups, who, unlike their parents and especially their grandparents, are expected to reach old age (AOA, 2011). Not surprisingly, rates of disability and chronic illness vary across populations of colour and by social class, with highest rates among low-income and less educated African-Americans and Latino elders (Federal Interagency Forum, 2010; Ferraro & Kelley-Moore, 2005; National Center for Health Statistics, 2007).

By sexual orientation

Estimates of the number of older lesbian, gay, bisexual, and transgender adults range from as low as 3% to as high as 18–20%. This translates into at least 2 million older lesbians and gay men, which will likely increase to over 6 million by the year 2030 (Butler, 2006). The general invisibility of being old is heightened for those who are old and LGBT – the most 'invisible of an already invisible minority' (Blando, 2001). Because of this double stigma of being 'twice hidden,' some studies suggest the ageing experience is more difficult for LGBT adults; others indicate lifelong marginalisation and skills in managing a stigmatised status may stimulate adaptive strategies to the challenges of ageing (Gabbay & Wahler, 2002; McFarland & Sanders, 2003; Thompson, 2006). What is clear is LGBT elders still encounter legal and attitudinal obstacles in receiving and giving care, largely because of lacking the legal protection of marriage, although some barriers have been removed by President Obama's Executive Order to eliminate discrimination in hospital visitations (Services and Advocacy for Gay, Lesbian, Bisexual, and Transgender Elders, 2010; Zodikoff, 2006).

By social class

The poverty rate among adults age 65 and older decreased from 9.7% to 8.9% from 2008 to 2009, while increasing for those younger than age 64 (US Census Bureau, 2010). This largely reflects the success of Social Security and Medicare in reducing poverty, but also growing unemployment and underemployment among younger populations. Older adults' improved economic status, however, masks the 6% of elders classified as near-poor as well as growing poverty among women, elders of colour, the oldest-old, and those living alone. Older women are almost twice as likely to be poor than are men. Older African-Americans (20%) and Latinos (19%) are far more likely to be poor than are Whites (7.6%). Among elders living alone, 17% are poor compared to 3% living with familes (AOA, 2009). Given the number of older adults who lost jobs and investments in the Great Recession, poverty among older adults grew slightly in 2010–11.

MENTAL WELL-BEING

Given the growth of the oldest-old, an expanded number of older adults will experience cognitive decline and dementia within the next 40 years, making their care a significant health care imperative and expenditure.

However, irreversible and universal cognitive decline with ageing is a myth (Alzheimer's Association, 2010) and recent research and care have shifted the focus toward improving cognitive health through physical activity and "brain exercises" (CDC & the Merck Foundation, 2008).

Paradoxically, older adults have lower rates of mental disorders than younger individuals and generally report higher emotional well-being and positive affect. Normal psychological development with ageing includes some changes in cognitive processes as well as maturation of coping responses and stability in personality traits. The majority of elders experience such changes without major disruptions in their behaviour or mental health. Most mental health disorders in old age are chronic and recurring conditions across the life course, not due to ageing (Ryff & Singer, 2009; Zarit, 2009). However, some older people experience more severe problems in cognitive function, coping ability, and emotional stability as they age.

The prevalence of mental disorders among older persons living in the community ranges from 15 to 25%, with depression and anxiety as the primary mood disorders. Rates of depression are highest for older persons with serious chronic disease, and those in hospitals and skilled nursing facilities, in part due to social isolation and co-occurring medical conditions and disability. However, most older persons with chronic psychiatric conditions live in the community. Overall, less than 25% of older adults who need mental health services receive treatment. Barriers to treatment include a shortage of geriatric mental health professionals and inadequate reimbursement for mental health services (Gellis, 2006; Gellis & McCracken, 2008; Rosen et al., 2008; Zarit, 2009).

Although not part of normal ageing, the likelihood of experiencing Alzheimer's disease and other dementias increases with advancing age. As many as 2 million Americans over age 85 have severe dementia, and up to 5 million are mildly to moderately impaired. Rates of dementia are even higher in nursing home populations: almost 30% of those age 65–74 and 45% of those age 85 and older. Because of problems in differentially diagnosing dementia and variations in the testing criteria, prevalence rates are only estimates. Nevertheless, epidemiological studies document the increasing incidence of dementias with age, especially between ages 75 and 90 (Kukull et al., 2002).

Alzheimer's disease (AD) accounts for 60–80% of all irreversible dementias. About 14% of all persons age 65 and over, and 29% of those age 85 and older have clinical symptoms of AD (Alzheimer's Association, 2009). With the increased survival of older adults beyond age 85, it is estimated as many as 11–16 million Americans will be diagnosed with AD by 2050. The sheer growth in the size of the older population accounts for this dramatic increase in both the USA and most regions of the world. For example, in China and India, the number of elders with dementia is expected to double between 2005 and 2025, and to triple by 2050 (Alzheimer's Disease International, 2006). In the USA, the incidence of AD is higher among Latinos and African-Americans, which does not appear to be due to genetic factors. Moderate (30%) to high (96%) rates of depressive symptoms are found among persons with dementia, which is associated with increased severity of cognitive deficits and risk of death (Armore et al., 2007). Since symptoms of depression may overlap with those of dementia, detection and assessment can be challenging and point to the need for geriatric training for health and mental healthcare providers (Unutzer et al., 2003).

One of the most important considerations with dementia is to give social and emotional support to the family as well as the patient, since approximately 70% of all people with AD are cared for by family (Alzheimer's Association, 2009). Across all types of chronic illness, families are the primary providers of long-term care. Yet their needs for support have only been recognised within the past two decades.

SOCIAL WELL-BEING

The central role of family caregivers is not surprising, since the family is the primary source of support for older adults; nearly 94% have living family members. These include partners, adult children, grandchildren or great-grandchildren, and siblings. Approximately 80% of adults over the age of 65 have children, but this percentage is declining because of reduced fertility rates (Cruikshank, 2009; Uhlenberg & Jong Giervelt, 2004). However, the majority has at least one child living close by and sees them regularly. About 66% of older adults live in a family setting – with a partner, child, or sibling – although not necessarily in a multigenerational household (Davidson, 2006).

In the USA nearly 55% of the population age 65 and older is married and lives with a spouse in an independent household. Marriage rates are highest among Asian and Pacific Islanders, then Whites, followed by Latinos and African-Americans (American Community Survey, 2007; Calasanti & Kiecolt, 2007). Less is known about the proportion living with a gay or lesbian partner. Significant differences exist, however, in living arrangements by gender and age. Given the higher rates of widowhood among women than men, older men (81%) are more likely to live in a family setting, typically with a spouse or partner than are women (61%). Because of women's longer life expectancy, higher rates of widowhood, and fewer options for remarriage, only 42% of women age 65 and older are married and living with a spouse, compared to 73% of men. These percentages decline dramatically with age for women, with only 15% of women age 85 and older married compared to 60% of men. Accordingly, women are twice as likely as their male counterparts to live alone, and represent 80% of the 30% of community-dwelling elders who live alone (AOA, 2011; Connidis, 2006; Federal Interagency Forum, 2010).

Grandparents and other extended family members have traditionally provided care for grandchildren across families of colour and in many other countries and cultures. Such care generally supplemented parental care or supported the parents while they worked outside the home or faced short-term disruptions. What has changed relatively recently is the rapid growth of grandparents (or great-grandparents) who are the primary caregivers for grandchildren because their adult children are unable or unwilling to provide care, often because of substance abuse, HIV and AIDS or incarceration. With over 2.5 million grandparents providing such primary care, skipped-generation households (the absence of the parental generation) are currently the fastest growing type in the USA (Generations United, 2007; Simmons & Dye, 2003). These shifts represent an increase of over 30% in custodial grandparenting (i.e., those who have legal custody) since 1990 (US Bureau of the Census, 2006). Grandparents also increasingly perform a primary caregiver role in developing countries with a high incidence of HIV and AIDS, such as South Africa and Cambodia. Financial and other supports for grandparent caregivers are a growing and critical need.

AGEING IN A HEALTHY MANNER

Although many adults face vulnerabilities as they age, most elders are resilient (e.g., able to thrive despite adversity in their lives). A shift is occurring from the past widely held perspective that ageing represents inevitable decline, dependency and illness to a more optimistic view that people can, to some extent, influence their own ageing through lifestyle choices in across the life course (Butler, 2010). Although genetic and societal factors, such as educational and employment opportunities, affect how we age, even the oldest-old and others with dementia, chronic illnesses, disabilities or living in poverty can experience active ageing in ways rarely imagined in the past. For the majority of older adults, including those with chronic diseases, maintaining autonomy and choices about being able to do the things they want at home and the community is a primary component of ageing in a healthy manner, regardless of their physical and mental health status (Phelan et al., 2004).

Active ageing is influenced by individual behaviours, the physical and social environment, including informal and formal support networks, economic security, and access to and use of health and social services across the life course. Most older adults, even those with chronic illness, experience health benefits from exercise. There is considerable evidence of the relationship between regular, vigorous exercise and the reduction in a person's chances of dying from heart disease and cancer, as well as lower hospital admissions for serious illness (Butler, 2010; Manini et al., 2006). However, structural variables of race, class, gender, and sexual orientation influence opportunities for active ageing, such as access to education, employment, and healthcare beginning from childhood. Health disparities earlier in the life course are generally exacerbated in old age, pointing to the need for social workers to bring their advocacy skills to bear in reducing inequities across the life course.

The concepts of resilience and active ageing are congruent with social work's strengths-based approach to build on elders' internal, family, social, community, and cultural capacities (WHO, 2002). There is also increasing recognition of the health benefits from older adults' contributing to society and remaining integrated in their communities (Butler, 2010). Elders are our society's most underutilised asset, with wisdom, skills, and life experience to contribute. This has translated into growing numbers of civic engagement initiatives, such as voluntarism, intergenerational programmes, and cross-generational political advocacy – all of which have implications for social work roles to promote inclusion of older adults (Hendricks & Hatch, 2006; Martinson & Minkler, 2006).

FUTURE DIRECTIONS AND SOCIAL WORK'S LEADERSHIP ROLE

Community-based initiatives

Looking toward the future, it is vital to differentiate social work's leadership role in addressing the oldest-old's immediate health and long-term care needs from baby boomers' needs and preferences. Social workers, along with other healthcare professions, require competencies to work effectively with the oldest-old, with chronic illness, disability cognitive deterioration – and often in hospitals and skilled nursing facilities – but also with the young-old who have different expectations about the quality of their ageing experience and prefer to 'age in place'. Gerontological social work knowledge, values and skills are essential to enhance physical, social and psychological well-being within the contexts of active ageing, chronic care and healthcare reform.

Because of the centrality of the social and physical environment to elder's well-being, a wide range of living options address differences in preferences and needs for the young-old and oldest-old. Elder's decisions about where they live are influenced by their health status, extent of functional ability, geographic location, finances, and families. The majority of older adults, particularly the young-old, prefer to remain in their own homes and communities as they age. Some social and health services assist many of them to do so, particularly those who have the financial resources to purchase such supports. Substantial work is being conducted nationally to promote 'ageing in place' housing models for 'active elders' and diverse models of long-term living approaches for those who need care. As one example, 'virtual' villages are 'built' environments designed to facilitate supportive community networks and sharing of services that support elders living in their own homes. In over 50 village organisations nationally, individuals join together and pay a fee to support staff and/or volunteers to meet members' needs for transportation, home maintenance, and basic services (Accius, 2010; Anderson, 2009; Krishnan, 2010; Wick & Zanni, 2009). Design features, even computerised smart homes or medical cottages with security monitors, make homes accessible and safe both for elders and younger individuals with disabilities. These universal design considerations promote the building of housing friendly to all ages of all abilities. Elder-friendly environments are increasingly conceptualised as communities for all, cultivating interdependence, fostering asset exchanges among all members, and promoting a sense of meaning (Gurwick, 2010; Kirk, 2009; Wick & Zanni, 2009).

Social workers are well positioned to build intersections of both formal and informal sources of support since an elder-friendly community is more than its physical aspects. They can bring their community development and outreach skills to mobilise older adults and their informal networks to develop local resources, including cross-generational alliances, to remain in their own homes and neighbourhoods. For example, *Aging your Way*, an asset-building approach in which social workers play central community organising roles, is occurring in 12 diverse Seattle neighbourhoods. Social workers have the competencies to promote the concept of living interdependently, and strategies to ensure social support and interpersonal connections are a core value of any living situation. With their person–environment perspective, social workers can also facilitate home modifications and the use of assistive technology, including computer-based options.

In-home services are central to most elders' preferences to 'age in place'. Some of these services, such as meals on wheels, home repairs, and friendly visitors, are provided through the federally funded Aging Network, particularly senior centres. A growing number of communities are redefining senior centres to be community hubs for networks of social relationships and supports. The Medicaid Waiver programme has funded in-home services to keep adults who meet the criteria for skilled nursing care in their own homes.

Social workers, for example, have provided leadership in designing and implementing consumer-directed care, which ensures decision-making autonomy to elders and younger adults with disabilities. This model posits frail adults and their families have the right and ability to assess their own needs and determine how to meet them. Most importantly, social workers, by building on the strengths of all elders, even those with limited functional ability, can reaffirm older adults' dignity and worth (Doty et al., 2010).

Long-term care living environments

Not all older adults, especially those with functional limitations, are able to – or even prefer – to remain in their own homes (Lee et al., 2008). For older adults with chronic illness and disabilities, or who simply prefer a more structured safe environment, the number and variety of living options promoting health and preventing, or managing, disabilities and long-term disease are growing dramatically. Retirement communities and homes traditionally have provided only limited healthcare. Some retirement homes, however, are delivering skilled nursing services, when needed, in residents' apartments to allow 'ageing-in-place.'

Other living environments providing help with activities of daily living and health care are assisted-living facilities (ALFs) and adult family homes (ADFs). Skilled nursing facilities (SNFs) offer skilled care, rehabilitation, subacute care and long-term care. Since 1985, the percentage of the oldest-old who live in SNFs is decreasing substantially. This change is attributed to declines in both disability and poverty rates, which has reduced the numbers of elders relying on Medicaid for long-term care and to the growth of more community-based options (Alecxih, 2006). Continuing care retirement communities (CCRCs) offer a continuum of services, from dining and apartment maintenance for relatively independent elders to comprehensive ALF and SNF services, if needed, thus affording care for a full spectrum of 'ageing in place'. These options are generally beyond the reach of low-income older adults, which points to the need for social workers to work to ensure the growing number of living options is available to all elders, including those who have been historically disadvantaged.

Along with these evolving community-living environments, new models for SNFs are also being implemented. The traditional institutional model for SNF buildings, staffing, and culture is patterned after nursing units in hospitals. Decision making is generally 'top-down' and daily routines are determined by and for staff with limited resident input. Starting in the 1990s, a 'culture change' movement is occurring to give residents and direct care staff more autonomy. One model for decentralisation is to organise the physical environment into smaller functional units called neighbourhoods, with a cluster of residents' rooms and a large kitchen, dining, and activities area. Staff are permanently assigned to a neighbourhood and are cross-trained, resulting in more integrated and less hierarchical roles than the traditional medical model (Boyd, 2003). Other types of culture change, as promoted by the national Pioneer Network, occur without extensive physical restructuring by promoting greater resident decision-making autonomy and improved supervision, training, and work conditions for direct care staff (Angelelli & Higbie, 2005; Grant, 2006). Similarly, social workers can play pivotal roles in changing the organisational culture of care of long-term care facilities to be resident-centred and to empower and partner with the direct care staff.

Models of care coordination

To meet the complexity and heterogeneity of older adults' needs, it is imperative to design, sustain, and disseminate evidence-based models of collaborative care. Collaborative care models are essential to take account of the wide diversity of care needs of older adults – those who are healthy, 'pre-frail' or who have chronic illness and disabilities, including dementia. Models of care attending to existing conditions as well as addressing modifiable factors for disability for older adults 'at-risk' of the development or exacerbation of chronic, potentially debilitating conditions are critical. Effective collaborations provide care that considers the psychosocial context, draw upon the full range of medical and social support services within and outside of health care systems, and promote coordination across different organisations and providers. Barriers to designing such models are numerous, with the current fee-for-service Medicare reimbursement policy as a primary obstacle.

As more adults live longer with disability, social workers are central to community-based models for chronic disease management, rather than acute care or cure, and to fostering social supports essential to health-promoting behaviours. New models of coordinated care less bound to health care systems and more accessible to local communities are needed. As an exemplar, *Improving Mood – Promoting Access to Collaborative Treatment for Late-Life Depression* (IMPACT), is a care coordination model for hospital patients with concurrent depression and mental illness. A depression care manager, who may be a social worker, provides patient education in the hospital with follow-up, treatment support, and brief psychotherapy after discharge. Older adults in the IMPACT intervention showed a greater reduction in depression than those receiving usual care (Capers, 2004).

As another example of the importance of care coordination, social workers' psychosocial skills are critical when older people must be moved between the acute care of hospital settings to long-term care settings – and perhaps back again. They often experience discontinuities of care and a lack of coordination, adding to their vulnerability. As an exemplar, the *Care Transitions Intervention* gives patients specific skills and tools reinforced by a 'transition coach', often a social worker, who follows them across settings for the first 30 days after leaving the hospital. Such a psychosocial approach has reduced re-hospitalisation, significantly cutting healthcare costs and enhancing quality of life (Coleman & Berenson, 2004). Strategies are needed to increase older adults' self-care capabilities and self-efficacy. To illustrate, an evidence-based community-based innovative treatment programme for depression where social workers play a primary role fostering elder's efficacy and problem-solving skills during in-home visits is the *Program to Encourage Active, Rewarding Lives for Seniors* (PEARLS). Not only has it reduced depressive symptoms but also cut hospitalisation rates (Ciechanowski et al., 2004).

Another exemplary integrated care model based in the community is *PACE (Program of All-Inclusive Care of the Elderly)*, which coordinates primary and long-term care within an adult day health model for frail adults who are eligible for nursing home placement. PACE focuses on preventing such placement, offering specific health and social services as needed, and maintaining frail elders in the community. Interdisciplinary teams that include social workers are central to coordinating care through adult day health centres and case management. PACE not only saves costs, but older participants also demonstrate enhanced quality of life, satisfaction with care, improved functional status, and ability to live longer in the community (Dobell & Bloom, 2009; Grobowski, 2006; Hansen, 2008; Kane et al., 2006; Naylor, 2006). A culturally competent integrated community-based care model is the El Porto Latino Alzheimer's Project which offers a single-entry point for comprehensive services for Latino elders with dementia and their family caregivers, and is coordinated by a social work care advocate (Aranda, 2006).

Whether based in health care systems or the community, social workers are often the lead professionals supporting multigenerational families, particularly related to psychosocial interventions to reduce the stress of cross-generational caregiving across the life course. Social work strength-based assessments increasingly take account of the needs of the total caregiving system as client, not just the elder. Psychoeducational programmes, support groups, and respite care are relatively effective interventions in reducing caregiver stress, all of which have implications for social work roles (Gonyea et al., 2006; Kuhn & Fulton, 2004; Mittelman et al., 2004). Increasingly, social workers recognise the vital role played by direct care staff as caregivers, and seek ways to improve their work conditions and include them in care teams (Dawson, 2010; Eldercare Workforce Alliance, 2009; Wilson & Bavineau, 2010).

Health promotion and disease prevention programmes offer emerging roles for social workers to apply their skills in motivating behavioural changes. One such exemplary programme nationally, Enhance Wellness, has effectively addressed the challenge of motivating healthy behaviour changes. A team of two professionals, typically a social worker and a nurse, assess an elder's strengths and risks, then develop a care plan in which the older adult, not the professional, chooses the health behaviours they want to work on. Allowing elders to set their own goals and providing support have resulted in reduced length of hospital stays, lower medication use, fewer mood disorders, and enhanced self-efficacy. Social workers can also help to evaluate fitness programmes, building the evidence base about prevention in old age (Enhance Fitness, 2011).

In sum, social workers are well positioned to promote active ageing and well-being for all older adults – both baby boomers and the oldest-old. As a first step, social workers must be prepared to meet the geriatric workforce challenge, since the need for gerontologically competent social workers far exceeds the supply. The John A. Hartford Foundation Geriatric Social Work Initiative is working to ensure all social workers have foundation gerontological competencies, as well as to prepare specialists with advanced geriatric practice behaviours. Another opportunity for social work is to address not only increased longevity but also life course inequities for women, persons of colour, and LGBT individuals. With its person-in-environment perspective and strengths-based values, social work is pivotally placed to advocate for structural and policy changes to reduce lifetime inequities that preclude optimal ageing in the setting of one's choice.

REFERENCES

Accius, J.C. (2010). The village: a growing option for aging in place. *AARP Fact Sheet 177*. Washington, DC: AARP Public Policy Institute.

Administration on Aging (AOA) (2011). *Profile of older Americans*. Washington, DC: US Government Printing Office.

Alecxih, L. (2006). *Nursing home use by 'oldest old' sharply declines*. Presentation to National Press Club by the Lewin Group. Retrieved August 9, 2010 from http://www.lewin.com/content/publications/NursingHomeUseTrendsPaperRev.pdf

Alley, D.E., & Chang, V.W. (2007). The changing relationship of obesity and disability. *Journal of the American Medical Association, 17*, 2020–2027.

Alzheimer's Association (2009). *Alzheimer's disease facts and figures*. Retrieved April 15, 2009 from http://www.alz.org

Alzheimer's Association (2010). Alzheimer's disease facts and figures. *Alzheimer's and Dementia: The Journal of the Alzheimer's Association, 6*(2), 158–194.

Alzheimer's Disease International (2006). *Dementia in the Asia Pacific region: The epidemic is here*. Report submitted September 21, 2006. Retrieved December 15, 2006 from http://www.alz.co.uk/research/files/areport

Amore, M., Tagariello, P. Laterza, C. Savola, E.M. (2002). Beyond nosography of depression in elderly. *Archives of Gerontology and Geriatrics*, supplement Suppl 1, 13–22.

Aranda, M., (2006). Older Latinos: A mental health perspective. In B. Berkman (ed.), *Handbook of aging in health and social work*. New York: Oxford University Press, pp. 283–292.

Anderson, D. (2009). The village movement comes home to Seattle. *Seniors Digest, Seattle-King County Division*. Retrieved May 23, 2010 from http://www.poststat.net/pwp008/pub.49/issue.1044/article.4309

Angelelli, J., & Higbie, I. (2005). Unfolding the culture change map and locating ourselves together. *Journal of Social Work in Long-term Care*, 3, 121–135.

American Community Survey (2007). *The marriage measures guide of state-level statistics*. Retrieved November 2009, from http://aspa.hhs.gov/hsp/07/marriagemeasurse.html

Amore, M., Tagariello, P., Laterza C., & Savoia, E.M. (2007). Subtypes of depression in dementia. *Archives of Gerontology and Geriatrics*, 44 (Suppl.), 23–33.

Basia, B., Snyder, S., Thompson, M., & LoGerfo, J. (2010). From research to practice: EnhanceFitness, an innovative community-based senior exercise program. *Topics in Geriatric Rehabilitation*, 26(4), 299–309.

Boyd, C. (2003). The Providence Mt. St. Vincent experience. *Journal of Social Work in Long-term Care*, 2, 245–268.

Blando, J.A. (2001). Twice hidden: Older gay and lesbian couples, friends and intimacy. *Generations*, 25, 87–89.

Bloom, D., & Canning, D. (2007). Demographic change, fiscal sustainability and macroeconomic performance. *Public Policy and Ageing Report*, 17, 18–23.

Brown, D. (2010, April 30). Global mortality rate down dramatically, study of past 40 years shows. *Washington Post*. Retrieved May 18, 2010 from http://washingtonpost.com/wp/dyn/

Bureau of Labor Statistics (2004). *Social workers*. Retrieved September 15, 2008 from http://stats.bls.gov/oco/ocos060.htm

Butler, R. (2010). *The longevity prescription: Eight proven keys for a long and healthy life*. New York: Avery.

Butler, S. (2006). Older gays, lesbians, bisexuals and transgender persons. In B. Berkman (ed.), *Handbook of social work in health and aging*. New York: Oxford, pp. 273–282.

Calasanti, T., & Kiecolt, K.J. (2007). Diversity among late-life couples. *Generations*, 31, 10–17.

Capers, M. (2004). Conference Panel: Depression and illness: Coordinating care, *SMHSA News*. Retrieved February 28, 2007 from http://www.SAMHSA_News/index.html

Centers for Disease Control and Prevention and the Merck Foundation (2008). *The state of aging and health in America 2008*. Whitehouse Station, NJ: The Merck Company Foundation.

Centers for Medicaid and Medicare Services (CMS) (2009). *Medicare Program Stats, 2009*. Retrieved July 10, 2010 from http://www.cms.hhs.gov/MedicareProgramRatesStast/downloads/MedicareMedicaidSummaries2009

Chipperfield, J.G. (2008). Everyday physical activity as a predictor of late-life mortality. *The Gerontologist*, 56A (Special Issue II), 47–53.

Christ, G., & Diwan, S. (2008). *Chronic illness and aging: The demographics of aging and chronic diseases*. Council on Social Work Education, Section 1.

Ciechanowski, P., Wagner, E., Schmaling, K., Schwartz, S., Williams, B., Diehr, P., Kulzer, J., Gray, S., Collier, C., & LoGerfo, J. (2004). Community-integrated home-based depression treatment in older adults. *Journal of the American Medical Association*, 291, 1569–1577.

Coleman, E.A., & Berenson, R.A. (2004). Lost in transition: Challenges and opportunities for improving the quality of transitional care. *Annals of Internal Medicine*, 14, 533–536.

Connidis, I.A. (2006). Intimate relationships: Learning from later life experience. In T. Calasanti & Slevin, K. (eds), *Age matters*. New York: Routledge, pp. 123–153.

Cruikshank, M. (2009). *Learning to be old: Gender, culture and aging*. New York: Rowman & Littlefield.

Davidson, K. (2006). Flying solo in old age: Widowed and divorced men and women in later life. In J. Vincent, Phillipson, C., & Downs, M. (eds), *The futures of old age*. London: Sage, pp. 172–179.

Dawson, S. (2010). Are we prepared to care? *CSWE Gero-Ed Center Aging Times*, 6(1), 1.

Del Webb Baby Boomer Survey (2010). Retrieved August 10, 2010 from http://www.deboomersurvey.com/

Dobell, D., & Bloom, S. (2009). *Integrated care for frail elders: The PACE example*. Institute for Research Public Policy. Retrieved August 10, 2010 from http://www.irpp.org/events/archive/20090403/dobell.pdf

Doty, P., Mahoney, K.J., & Sciegaj, M. (2010). New state strategies to meet long-term care needs. *Health Affairs*, 29(1), 49–56.

Eldercare Workforce Alliance (2009). *A strong eldercare workforce for America's seniors is essential to real health care reform*. Retrieved August 28, 2010 from http://www.eldercareworkforce.org/

Enhance Fitness (2011). *What is Enhance Fitness?* Retrieved September 2011, from www.projectenhance.org/enhance fitness_aspx

Federal Interagency Forum on Aging-Related Statistics (2010). *Older Americans 2010: Key indicators of well-being*. Retrieved September 9, 2010 from http://www.agingstats.gov/agingstatsdotnet/Main_Site/Data/2010_Documents/Docs/OA_2010.pdf

Gabbay, S., & Wahler, J. (2002). Lesbian aging: Review of a growing literature. *Journal of Gay and Lesbian Social Services*, 14, 1–21.

Gellis, Z.D. (2006). Older adults with mental and emotional problems. In B. Berkman & D'Ambruoso, S. (eds),

Handbook of social work in health and aging. New York: Oxford University Press, pp. 129–140.

Gellis, Z.D., & McCracken, S.G. (2008). Depressive disorders in older adults. In S. Diwan (ed.), *Mental health*. Washington, DC: CSWE Gero-Ed Center. Master's Advanced Curriculum Project. Retrieved August 11, 2009 from http://depts.washington.edu/geroctr/mac/14substance.html

Generations United (2007). *Definitions of grand families*. Washington, DC. Retrieved May 10, 2009 from http://ipath/gu.org/Grand8101303.asp

Generations United (2009). *Numbers of multigenerational families on the rise*. Retrieved May 10, 2009 from http://www.pbs.org/americanfamily/gap/multi.html

Gonyea, J., O'Connor, M., & Boyle, P. (2006). Project care: A randomized controlled trial of a behavioral intervention group for Alzheimer's disease caregivers. *The Gerontologist, 46*(6), 827–832.

Grant, L.A. (2006). *Culture change in for-profit nursing homes*. The Commonwealth Fund. Retrieved November 11, 2006 from http://www.cmwf.org/spotlights/spotlights_show.htm?doc

Grabowski, D.C. (2006). The cost-effectiveness of noninstitutional long-term care services: Review and synthesis of the most recent evidence. *Medical Care Research and Review, 63*(1), 3–28.

Gurwick, R. (2010). Staying connected. *AARP Bulletin, 51*(2), 24, 26–29.

Hansen, J.C. (2008). Community and in-home models. *Journal of Social Work Education*, 44, 83–88.

Hayutin, A.M. (2007). Graying of the global population. *Public Policy and Aging Report*, 17, 12–17.

Hendricks, J., & Hatch, L.R. (2006). Lifestyle and aging. In R. Binstock & George, L. (eds), *Handbook of aging and the social sciences*. New York: Academic Press, pp. 301–319.

Institute of Medicine (2008). *Retooling for an Aging America: Building the health care workforce committee on the future health care workforce for older americans*. Washington, DC: The National Academies Press.

Kane, R.L., Homyak, P., Bershadsky, B., & Flood, S. (2006). Variations on a theme called PACE. *Journals of Gerontology: Biological Sciences, 61B*, 689–693.

Kaneda, T. (2006). *China's concern over population aging and health*. Retrieved October 15, 2006 from http://www.prb.org

Kelley-Moore, J., & Ferraro, K.F. (2005). A 3-D model of health decline: Disease, disability and depression among black and white older adults. *Journal of Health and Social Behavior, 46*(4), 376–391.

Kinsella, K., & Velkoff, V.A. (2001). *An aging world: 2001: U.S. Census Bureau Series*. Washington, DC: US Government Printing Office, 95/01–1.

Kirk, P.A. (2009). Naturally occurring retirement communities, thriving through creative retrofitting. In P.S. Abbott, Carman, N., Carman, J., & Scarfo, B. (eds), *Re-creating neighborhoods for successful aging*. Baltimore, MD: Health Professions Press. 115–143.

Krishnan, S. (2010). Grass-roots NEST to help elderly stay in home. *The Seattle Times*, Retrieved November 20, 2011 from http://seattletimes.nwsource.com/html/localnews/2012168526_nest21m.html

Kuhn, D., & Fulton, B. (2004). Efficacy of an educational program for relatives of persons in the early stages of Alzheimer's disease. *Journal of Gerontological Social Work, 42,* 109–130.

Kukull, W.A., Higdon, R., Bowen, J.D., McCormick, W.C., Teri, L., Schellenberg, G., van Belle, G., et al. (2002). Dementia and Alzheimer disease incidence: A prospective cohort study. *Archives of Neurology, 59,* 1737–1746.

Langa, K.M., Larson, E.B., Karlawish, J.H., Cutler, D.M., Kabeto, M.U., Kim, S.Y., et al. (2008). Trends in the prevalence and mortality of cognitive impairment in the United States. *Alzheimer's and Dementia, 4,* 134–144.

Lee, S.J., Go, A.S., Lindquist, K., Bertenthal, D., & Covinsky, K.E. (2008). Chronic conditions and mortality among the oldest-old. *American Journal of Public Health, 98,* 1209–1214.

Manini, T.M., Everhart, J.E., Patel, K.V., Schoeller, D.A., Colbert, L.H., Viser, M., et al. (2006). Daily activity energy expenditure and mortality among older adults. *Journal of the American Medical Association, 296,* 171–179.

Martinson, M., & Minkler, M. (2006). Civic engagement and older adults: A critical perspective. *The Gerontologist, 46*(3), 318–324.

McFarland, P.L., & Sanders, S.A. (2003). A pilot study about the needs of older gays and lesbians: What social workers need to know. *Journal of Gerontological Social Work, 40,* 67–80.

Mittelman, M.S., Roth, D.L., Coon, D.W., & Haley, W.E. (2004). Sustained benefit of supportive intervention for depressive symptoms in caregivers of patients with Alzheimer's disease. *American Journal of Psychiatry, 161*(5), 850–856.

National Center for Health Statistics (NCHS) (2007). *The United States*. Hyattsville, MD: NCHS.

Naylor, M.D. (2006). Transitional care: A critical dimension of home health care quality agenda. *Journal for Healthcare Quality, 28,* 48–54.

Phelan, E., Anderson, L., LaCroix, A., & Larson, A. (2004). Older adults' views of 'successful aging': How do they compare with researchers' definitions? *Journal of the American Geriatrics Society, 53,* 211–216.

Population Reference Bureau (2008). *2008 World population data sheet.* Washington, DC: USAID.

Reuben, D.B. (2009). Medical care for the final years of life: 'When you're 83, it's not going to be 20 years'. *Journal of the American Medical Association, 302*(24), 2686–2694.

Rosen, D., Smith, M., & Reynolds, C. (2008). The prevalence of mental and physical health disorders among older methadone patients. *The American Journal of Geriatric Psychiatry, 16,* 488–497.

Ryff, C.D., & Singer, B. (2009). Understanding health aging: Key components and their integration. In V.L. Bengtson, Silverstein, M., Putney, N.M., & Gans, D. (eds), *Handbook of theories of aging.* New York: Springer, pp. 117–144.

Schoeni, R.V., Freedman, V.A., & Martin, L.G. (2008). Why is late-life disability declining? *The Milbank Quarterly, 86,* 47–69.

Schulz, G.B. (2007). *Stanford Center on Longevity.* From the preface of a report by the Stanford Center on Longevity, 7, p. 6.

Services and Advocacy for Gay, Lesbian, Bisexual, and Transgender Elders (SAGE) (2010). *Improving the lives of LGBT older adults: Executive summary, introduction, and overview of key challenges.* Retrieved August 12, 2010 from www.sageusa.com

Simmons, T., & Dye, J. (2003). *Grandparents living with grandchildren: 2000.* Washington, DC: US Census Bureau.

Thompson, E.H. (2006). Being women, then lesbian, then old: Femininities, sexualities, and aging. Review essay. *The Gerontologist, 46,* 300–305.

Uhlenberg, P., & de Jong Gierveld, J.J. (2004). Age-segregation in later life: An examination of personal networks. *Ageing and Society, 24*(1), 5–28.

Uhlenberg, P. (2009). Children in an aging society. *Journal of Gerontology, 64B*(4), 489–496.

United Nations (2009a). *Opportunities and challenges for an aging world.* AARP United Nations Briefing Series. Retrieved April 15, 2009 from www.aarpinternational.org/2008UNBriefingSeries

United Nations (2009b). *World population to exceed 9 billion by 2050.* Retrieved April 15, 2009 from http://www.un.org/esa/population/publications/wpp2008/pressrelease.pdf

Unutzer, J., Katon, W., Callahan, C.M., Williams, J.W., Hunkeler, E., Harpole, L., et al. (2003). Depression treatment in a sample of 1801 depressed older adults in primary care. *Journal of the American Geriatrics Society, 51,* 505–514.

US Census Bureau (2009a). *Population division, interim statistics: Population projections by age, sex and race for 2008.* Retrieved March 11, 2009 from http://factfinder.census.gov/servlet/ DatasetMainPageServlet?program=PEP&Submenuid=&lang=en&ts

US Census Bureau (2009b). *Statistical abstract of the United States: 2009.* Retrieved March 11, 2009 from http://www.census.gov/compendia/statab/2009edition.html

US Census Bureau (2010). *Facts for Features: Grandparents Day 2010,* July 12, 2010. Retrieved November 20, 2011 http://www.census.gov/newsroom/releases/archives/facts_for_features_special_editions/cb10-ff16.html

Voisine, J.M., Walker, L.M., & Jeffrey, S.M. (2009). Home is where the heart is: Living arrangements for older adults. *The Consultant Pharmacist, 24,* 134–145.

Whitaker, T., Weismiller, T., & Clark, E. (2006). *Assuring the sufficiency of a frontline workforce: A national study of licensed social workers. Special report: Social work services for older adults.* Washington, DC: National Association of Social Workers. Retrieved January 25, 2008 from http://workforce.socialworkers.org/studies/aging/aging.pdf

Wick, J.Y., & Zanni, G.R. (2009). Aging in place: multiple options, multiple choices. *The Consultant Pharmacist, 24,* 804–806, 808–809, 811–812.

Wilson, N., & Bavineau, J. (2010). Vital yet undervalued: Recruiting and retaining qualified direct care workers. *CSWE Gero-Ed Center Aging Times, 6*(1), 1.

World Health Organization (WHO) (2002). *Active ageing: A policy framework.* Geneva: WHO.

Yen, H. (2010). 'Boomerang kids' flocking back home number of multigenerational families living together rises during economic downturn. Deseret News. Retrieved September 15, 2010 from http://www.deseretnews.com/article/700017476/Boomerang-kids-flocking-back-home.html

Zarit, S.H. (2009). A good old age: Theories of mental health and aging. In V.L. Bengtson, Silverstein, M., Putney N.M., & Gans, D. (eds), *Handbook of theories of aging.* New York: Springer, pp. 675–692.

Zodikoff, B.D. (2006). Services for lesbian, gay, bisexual and transgender older adults. In B. Berkman (ed.), *Handbook of social work in health and aging.* New York: Oxford Press, pp. 569–576.

35

Disability

Romel W. Mackelprang

People with atypical conditions and attributes labelled as disabilities have been present from humanity's beginnings. For millennia, people and communities defined the meaning and subsequent treatment of people with atypical physical and behavioural attributes according to local beliefs and customs. With the development of organised societies, beliefs about people who were 'different' from the mainstream evolved and generalised to larger communities, usually with negative implications. However, in the 19th century, the foundation was laid that led to a collective identity for people with physical, behavioural, mental, and sensory atypicalities (Mackelprang, 2010a). This chapter introduces readers to historical and contemporary perspectives on disabilities. It addresses the place of disability in the world and the responsibilities, opportunities, and challenges faced by the social work profession in working with disability and disabled persons.

DEFINING DISABILITY

Definitions of disability diverge widely and the incidence and prevalence are difficult to estimate. For example, learning disabilities may qualify individuals for extended test-taking time, but not be considered disabilities in qualifying one for government supports. In a society in which eyeglasses are readily available, a visual impairment may not be considered a disability, whereas it may be a severe disability when corrective lenses are not available for people to engage in everyday life tasks. Of course, definition difficulties are common when attempting to define other diversities as well. For example, Barak Obama is widely considered to be African-American, yet he was raised by his Caucasian mother's family. Definitions relative to gender identity, sexual orientation, as well as disability are far from universal.

In a report for the World Bank, Mont (2007) states prevalence estimates range from 1% in Kenya to 20% in New Zealand. He contends how one measures disability is dependent on the purposes for measuring. Nagi (1969) provided a framework for defining disability containing four elements: (i) *pathology* interrupting physical or mental processes; (ii) *impairment* limiting a person's ability to function possibly resulting in; (iii) *functional limitation* relative to the ability to perform or engage in life tasks; and (iv) *disability* or the inability to perform socially expected activities. In 1980, the World Health Organization's *International Classification of Impairments, Disabilities, and Handicaps* (ICIDH), provided a framework joining disease and disability, defining them as internal conditions. However, the latter part of the 20th century saw challenges to these deeply seated beliefs defining disability as internal pathology. For example, the policy of the New Zealand Ministry of Health, Office of Disability Issues (2001) seeking to create an inclusive society states:

> Disability is not something individuals have. What individuals have are impairments. They may be physical, sensory, neurological, psychiatric, intellectual or other impairments. Disability is the process which happens when one group of people create barriers by designing a world only for their way of living, taking no account of the impairments other people have (p. 7).

The first major United Nations human rights initiative of the 21st century, the 2007 UN Convention on the Rights of Persons with Disabilities, represents a marked a paradigm shift to a civil rights approach to disability (United Nations, 2007a). The UN explains:

> The drafters of this Convention were clear that disability should be seen as the result of the interaction between a person and his or her environment. Disability is not something that resides in the individual as the result of some impairment. This convention recognizes that disability is an evolving concept and that legislation may adapt to reflect positive changes within society. Disability resides in the *Society* not in the *Person* (United Nations, 2007b).

A final way of defining disability as an element of diversity has arisen from the disability rights movement. As Johnson (2006) states:

> Disability and nondisability are also constructed through the language used to describe people ... There is a world of difference between using a wheelchair and being treated as a normal human being (who happens to use a wheelchair to get around) and using a wheelchair and being treated as invisible, unintelligent, frightening, passive, dependent, and nothing more than your disability ... We think the way our culture defines something like race or gender (or disability) is simply the way things are in some objective sense (pp. 19–20).

This approach avers that people with disabilities deserve the same treatment as non-disabled people.

HISTORICAL PERSPECTIVES ON DISABILITY

Though disability characteristics vary widely, people with disabilities share commonalities, including societal treatment and life experiences. From the beginning of recorded human history, disability has been defined negatively. Cave wall carvings suggest Neolithic tribes performed skull surgeries to release evil spirits from people who displayed atypical behaviours. Ancient Zoroastrians envisioned a more perfect world without disabilities. The Greeks and Romans believed disabled people were not human and advocated for putting them away or leaving them to die. However, this perception was not universal. For example, Julius Caesar, who had epilepsy, claimed to have visions during his seizures and was a fully accepted member of Roman society. Muslim and Judeo-Christian scripture portrayed disability as arising from sin, spiritual deficiency, or God's displeasure. During the Middle Ages in Europe, people with disabilities were often ostracised and isolated, while concomitantly some believed people's infirmities gave them trials to overcome helping them achieve salvation. These perspectives have common threads, collectively, reflecting a 'moral model' in which disability is explained as a result of sin or evil, or is out of harmony with nature (Albrecht, 1992; Miles, 2002; Morris, 1986; Plato, 1991).

As Western cultures progressed from the Middle Ages through the Reformation and Enlightenment eras, competing perspectives on disability were introduced. Rational, scientific thought competed with spiritual and religious explanations of the world, including disability. Christian thought contended human reasoning was madness, while secularists considered divine reasoning madness (Foucault, 2006; Khalfa, 2006). These eras produced an alternate view wherein disability was considered a physical, mental, or other health problem. This view is commonly referred to as the 'medical model' (see Chapter 33). As early as 1600, Francis Bacon refuted the idea 'madness' was a form of moral punishment. Philosophers of this era, such as John Locke, believed human nature was basically good and, with continued improvements, societal ills, such as disease, disability, and war, could be eliminated. For people with disabilities, the medical model focuses on the internal impairments limiting them and interventions are directed at curing, fixing, or repairing individuals, thus eliminating their abnormalities. Institutions and treatments – ostensibly devoted to treating and curing 'defective' people – became a means to isolate and objectify them (DePoy & Gilson, 2004; Foucault; 2006; Snyder & Mitchell, 2006).

> The story of Jennie Marsh (pseudonym) illustrates the medical model approach. Born with cerebral palsy, Jennie recalls her relationships with health care professionals as an adolescent: 'I was barely human. One time, as a fourteen-year-old, I was paraded in front of a whole class of doctors so they could see my "abnormal gait." I was wearing only my panties. They would never have done that to a nondisabled girl, but it was OK to parade me almost naked. And the crazy thing is, it wasn't until years later that I realized they had dehumanized me' (Mackelprang & Salsgiver, 2009, pp. 84–85).

Industrialisation and urbanisation contributed to acceptance of the medical model. As people's worth became increasingly connected to their economic productivity, those with atypicalities limiting their productivity became increasingly burdensome. Institutions replaced family care and often became warehouses with inadequate funding and subhuman living conditions. Others were forcibly removed from their communities (Foucault, 2006).

The Belgian social statistician Adolphe Quetelet (1796–1874) was influential in framing a new comprehensive view of disability. He applied the mathematical concepts of the bell curve and normal distribution to human beings, presenting the average man (sic) as society's ideal. The typical man (sic) became defined as desirable and deviations from the norm were considered abnormal, thus providing the rationale for systematic efforts to fix those with physical and mental differences (DePoy & Gilson, 2004; Longmore, 1987; Snyder & Mitchell, 2006).

By the late 1800s, social Darwinism gained prominence with proponents arguing, just as physical environments promote biological evolution, social policies and practices should be used to promote desired attributes in society (Mackelprang & Salsgiver, 2009). These philosophies gave rise to eugenics, whose adherents argued for eliminating the poor, nonproductive, and undesirable while advocating the procreation of those with desirable traits (Wiggam, 1924). Eugenicists were instrumental in laws and policies forbidding interracial marriage, mandating the sterilisation of disabled people, and leading to the proliferation of large institutions with degrading living conditions (Longmore, 1987).

During this period, disability was perceived negatively, even among those who fought for the rights of other devalued groups. Early feminists, such as Charlotte Perkins Gilman and Margaret Sanger, equated disability with corruption and scourge, and taught a lack of opportunities for women who produced disabled offspring (Snyder & Mitchell, 2006). The 1924 *Buck v. Bell* decision of the Supreme Court of the United States legitimised the forced sterilisation of disabled persons (Mackelprang & Salsgiver, 2009). An early 20th century Chicago ordinance stated:

> No person who is diseased, maimed, mutilated, or in any way deformed so as to be an unsightly or disgusting object or improper person to be allowed in or on the public ways or other public places in this city, shall therein or thereon expose himself to public view' (cited in Longmore, 2003, p. 36).

People born with disabilities were especially susceptible to being ostracised from society. In 1935, the small grassroots organisation, the League of the Physically Handicapped, staged protests against disability discrimination. Jane Addams, the first US Nobel prize winner and a founder of social work in the USA, was ashamed of her disability, describing herself in childhood as 'a delicate little girl of six with the further disability of a curved spine' (Addams, 1910, p. 6), and as an 'ugly duckling' (p. 7). Her poor self-image was manifest in the her own words:

> My great veneration and pride in my father manifested itself in curious ways. On several Sundays ... the Union Sunday School of the village was visited by strangers. My father taught the large Bible class ... and to my eyes at least, was the most imposing figure in his Sunday frock coat, his fine head rising high above all the others. I imagined that the strangers were filled with admiration for this dignified person, and I prayed with all my heart that the ugly, pigeon-toed little girl, whose crooked back obliged her to walk with her head held very much to one side would never be pointed out to these visitors as the daughter of this fine man. In order to lessen the possibility of a connection being made, on these particular Sundays I did not walk beside my father (Addams, 1910, p. 7).

Had Jane Addams lived in Nazi Germany in the 1930s–1940s, she may have been murdered by the government before reaching adulthood. The ultimate implementation of negative disability attitudes in Western cultures occurred in the Nazi T4 programme wherein between 75,000 and 200,000 people with disabilities were systematically murdered. In fact, Franz Stangl, commandant of the infamous extermination camps at Sobibor and Treblinka, gained his expertise using gas to exterminate people while serving as an administrator at Hartheim, a hospital converted into an extermination centre for disabled people (Garscha & Kuretsidis-Haider, 1997; Levy, 1993). However, few medical personnel in the disability killing centres were prosecuted and this element of the Holocaust has been largely ignored, arguably because the lives of disabled people are less valued than nondisabled people (disability now, n.d.).

Negative attitudes towards disability based on the moral and medical models continue today. Consider end-of-life laws and policies. In the Netherlands, euthanasia is extended to people with disabilities as well as those who are terminally ill. In the USA, courts have consistently sanctioned people with physical disabilities, such as quadriplegia, to terminate their lives upon request (Mackelprang & Mackelprang, 2005). In some areas of Ghana, blind people are not allowed in the community without assistance. In Tanzania, albinos live in fear of being murdered because of spiritual beliefs. In a nine-month period in 2008, 47 Tanzanians were arrested for alleged murders of albinos prompting the president to call the treatment of albinos and the president called the treatment of albinos a stain on the country (Canada.com, 2008).

Against a backdrop of pervasive devaluation for millennia, there have been incremental changes in disability policies dating back more than a century. As early as the late 1800s, Germany and France implemented social security policies for elderly and disabled persons. Ironically, conflicts and wars have been a primary motivator. Soldiers injured in war have been the initial recipients of disability benefits with the eventual extension to others. For example, the 1916 US Defense Act providing rehabilitation services to veterans was expanded by the 1920 National Rehabilitation Act to include non-veterans (Mackelprang & Salsgiver, 2009).

In areas of the world, such as North America and Europe, the 1960s and 1970s ushered in a new civil rights movement, and the disability rights movement in which people rejected traditional disability notions. A basic premise of the disability rights movement was that the primary problems disabled people faced were rooted in society and *not* in individuals. Only human rights, not handouts or charity, would meet the needs for people with disabilities. Disability rights proponents rejected the moral and medical models' societal explanations of disability which kept them subjugated. An alternate model, the 'social model' was proposed with the foundational premise the primary problems facing disabled persons arose from external social factors, such as discrimination and devaluation rather than internal personal deficiencies. The social model continues to employ this civil rights approach to disability argues, as with other oppressed groups like First Nations Peoples, ethnic minorities, women, and GLTBs, disabled persons need access to human rights and dignity, not separation or special treatment (see Chapter 21). Consider the following questions as illustrative comparisons.

1. Have Australian Aborigines been denied rights because they need to be taken care of – or because of pervasive devaluation?
2. Was much of the world colonised by European and North American countries because Indigenous Peoples were deemed to need the guidance of colonisers – or for other reasons?
3. Have people with mental health and intellectual disabilities been warehoused because society needs protection – or because of prejudices?
4. Were the millions of Africans forced into slavery really less than human – or were they defined as such to justify exploitation and for economic gain?
5. Have women been denied basic rights, such as the right to vote and to own property, because men are more capable – or for other reasons?
6. Are high suicide rates among lesbian and gay youth a result of their inherent mental inadequacies – or of societal attitudes and social policies?
7. Is unemployment and poverty endemic among disabled persons because of their lack of ability to work – or due to social and economic policies deterring them from working?
8. Have people like Steven Hawking become successful 'in spite' of their disabilities – or have the life experiences associated with their disabilities contributed to their greatness?

Questions like some of those posed above do not always have simple answers. However, they challenge the simple and inaccurate assumptions that have led to imperialist, racist, sexist, heterosexist, and ableist policies and practices.

The late 20th and early 21st centuries have signalled change in social perceptions of disability. In 1980, the United Nations adopted a model of disability based on functional limitations and individual impairment. However, in 1981, the United Nations General Assembly Resolution 31/123 declaring The International Year of Disabled Persons acknowledged the 'the right of persons with disabilities to take part fully in the life and development of their societies, enjoy living conditions equal to those of other citizens, and have an equal share in improved conditions resulting from socio-economic development' (United Nations Enable, 2004). This was followed by the International Decade of Disabled Persons (1983–1992), global regions, including the Asian and Pacific Decade of Disabled Persons (1993–2002), the African Decade of Disabled Persons (2000–2009), and the Arab Decade of Disabled Persons of (2003–2112). Similarly, individual countries implemented disability rights laws, including the Canada Act and the Canadian Charter of Rights and Freedoms (1982), the Americans with Disabilities Act (1990), the Australian Disability Discrimination Act (1992), Bolivia Law No. 1678 (1995), United Kingdom Disability Discrimination Act (1995), Japan's Disabled Persons' Fundamental Law (1993), the India Persons with Disabilities Act (1995), the Jordan Law for the Welfare of Disabled Persons (1993), the Israel Equal Rights for People with Disabilities Law (1998), and the Constitution of the Republic of Ghana (1992). The 2001 United Nations General Resolution 56/108 instituted the convention on disability rights. In March 2007, the Convention on the Rights of Persons with Disabilities was adopted with 82 countries as signatories. The United Nations (2007b) calls the protocol 'the first comprehensive human rights treaty of the 21st century' (p. 1), that signals a 'paradigm shift' in attitudes and approaches to persons with disabilities in which people are viewed as subjects with rights rather than objects to be acted upon. The UN Convention is a legally binding human rights instrument with explicit, social development goals (United Nations, 2007a, 2007b). Increasingly, disability is being seen as a human rights issue in the international community. The laws and policies cited above all acknowledge the discrimination and marginalisation of disabled persons. Unfortunately, as acknowledged in the United Nations Convention, poverty, exclusion, and violations of basic human dignity remain widespread. While the international community has acknowledged the problems and challenges, implementing laws and eliminating barriers are taking decades. People with disabilities continue to face socially imposed obstacles. All too often, newly physically disabled people in developing countries lay in bed for months or years without access to wheelchairs. People with mental health disabilities live on the streets throughout the world. In the USA, people with disabilities, such as quadriplegia, are incarcerated in nursing facilities with no access to community living. In the 1980s and 1990s, dramatic decreases in life expectancy in Africa as a result of HIV and AIDS occurred in a context in which life-prolonging medications widely distributed in the USA and Europe were denied to Africans (United Nations Development Programme, 2004). Only in the last decade have some of those life-prolonging medications been made available to Africans.

DISABILITY GROUPINGS

An important tenet of the social model is people with disabilities share similar life experiences. While the medical and social models categorise people to study and treat them, those who employ the social model can use disability groupings to understand commonalities consistent with an ethnographic perspective of self-identification and cultural classification. Thus, like other diverse groups, identifying diverse disability groups helps one understand group experiences and culture without stereotyping. Further, it helps people with disabilities, social workers, and others to find a framework for understanding the specific ableist attitudes and discrimination disabled folks in these groups may experience. There is no universally accepted disability categorisation system and this chapter uses a system used by Mackelprang and Salsgiver (2009) identifying seven groups: mobility disabilities, deafness and hearing impairments, visual disabilities, developmental disabilities, mental health disabilities, cognitive disabilities, and health-related disabilities.

Mobility disabilities

Mobility disabilities include those present from birth, such as spina bifida and cerebral palsy, as well as others that can be acquired at any time of life, such as amputation, spinal cord injury, and stroke. In some areas of the developing world, polio remains a common source of mobility disabilities. One of the fastest growing contributors to the prevalence of mobility disabilities is the ageing of populations worldwide, especially in developed countries. Common issues faced by people with mobility disabilities include physical access, housing, and transportation. For people in developing countries, where mobility aids, such as wheelchairs, are scarce, some people may be confined to their homes because of the lack of resources. Mobility disabled people are often discriminated against in employment because of negative social attitudes and lack of physical access (Russell, 2001). For example, teacher Judy Heumann, a leader in the US disability rights movement, relates how she was unable to find a teaching job. The common explanation was her mobility disability from polio made it so she could not teach when, in reality, it was lack of physically accessible buildings and employer attitudes keeping her from working (Mackelprang & Salsgiver, 2009).

Deafness and hearing impairments

An estimated 70 million people are deaf, 80% of whom live in developing countries (World Federation of the Deaf, 2005). For every deaf person, there are scores of hard-of-hearing people, many of whom acquire their impairments later in life. Most children born deaf are born to hearing parents and a major challenge for these children is identifying them promptly, providing access to visually based communication, such as sign language, ensuring adequate education, and providing examples and role models. For people who develop hearing impairments later in life, adequate technologies can help them stay connected with the hearing world. Deaf culture can be a significant resource for people who are deaf from birth or early in life. People with postlingual hearing loss may experience grief and loss and be slow to acknowledge they have hearing impairments.

Visual disabilities

Though some people are born with visual disabilities, the majority acquire them later as a result of conditions such as glaucoma, cataracts, and diabetic retinopathy. Stroman (1982) and tenBrock (1993) discuss prejudicial and stereotypical attitudes about people who are blind and visually impaired reinforcing the notion blindness is a terrible fate and blind people 'live in the dark' literally and metaphorically. People with visual impairments are perceived as helpless and pitiable, providing justification for keeping them dependent. Large (1993) cites how internalised ableism can lead some blind and visually impaired persons to adopt stereotypes similar to the way some ethnic minorities, women, and gays and lesbians respond to stereotyping (Pharr, 1988; Solomon, 1976).

Developmental disabilities

An estimated 5–10% of children have developmental disabilities (DDs; Moeschler & Shevell, 2006). The common characteristic of DDs is they occur in childhood. However, DDs have most commonly been associated with intellectual disabilities, traditionally referred to as mental retardation, as well as autism-spectrum conditions. Dudley (1987) identifies three misconceptions professionals and others have about people with DDs. First, they have little or no awareness of their disability. Second, they are passive or indifferent to pejorative language used against them. Third, they are unaware of demeaning treatment and pervasive discrimination to which they are subjected. In the USA and other developed countries, people with intellectual disabilities have been institutionalised and separated from society. As a rejoinder to these stereotypes, people such as Wolfensberger (1972) and Simpson (1996, 2007) have offered the alternate approach of 'normalisation' to working with people with DDs. Originally, normalisation was applied primarily to people with DD, but its concepts have universal appeal. In essence, normalisation involves providing the same opportunities for disabled persons as for nondisabled people. It has been instrumental in closing large institutions traditionally incarcerating large numbers of people with DD and integrating them into communities. Given opportunities for self-expression, DD people have built a strong self-advocacy movement. For example, *People First* is an organisation in the USA run by people with DD to promote their rights and fight discrimination. Given adequate opportunities, people with DDs, who would have been institutionalised for life a generation ago, are living active, productive lives.

Mental health disabilities

People living with mental health disabilities are among the most stigmatised in society. In Judeo-Christian history, they were considered possessed by demons. Contemporarily, terms such as mental *illness* and *psychiatric* illness or disability connote medically associated pathology. A relatively new professional 'recovery' movement has taken a step forward, contending people can recover from the 'catastrophic' effects of mental illness to lead productive lives (Anthony, 1993). Mental health disabilities, including thought (e.g., schizophrenia), mood (e.g., depression), and anxiety disorders have a significant impact on the lives of millions worldwide. However, these classifications are *not* objective or scientific realities, but instead reflect contemporary perceptions. Consider the Native American with whom the author worked. When hospitalised after an automobile accident, he was labelled schizophrenic by a psychiatrist when he reported his visions and spiritual experiences following his accident. In his local community, he had long been considered a spiritual leader because of similar experiences. Mental health disabilities can have serious impacts on people's lives and they often benefit from professional services to manage the problems associated with their impairments. However, they are not defined by their disabilities, nor do they necessarily need to 'overcome' their conditions to be productive. Many famous and accomplished people, including Winston Churchill (depression), Michelangelo (obsessive compulsive disorder), Edgar Allen Poe (bipolar), and Vincent Van Gogh (anxiety) have lived with mental health disabilities. Psychologist Kay Jamison (1995), actress Patty Duke (Duke & Hochman, 1997), and others (Mackelprang & Salsgiver, 2009) with mental health disabilities have documented how their disabilities have led to life experiences contributing to their accomplishments. Rather than exclusively focusing on ameliorating or overcoming symptoms, people with mental health disabilities benefit from supportive communities and from environments maximising their capabilities and self-determination, and minimising discrimination.

Cognitive disabilities

Cognitive disabilities, such as attention deficit disorder, learning disabilities, and traumatic brain injury affect people's ability to process or comprehend what they see, hear, or sense (Bruyere et al., 2000). Cognitive disabilities are usually 'invisible', and often unrecognised by individuals, families, and the educational system (Dunham et al., 1996; Kronick, 1981). Lack of recognition results in the inability to use alternate strategies to compensate for differences, and can precipitate a cascading effect of low self-esteem, avoidance, and underachievement (Naylor et al., 1994). Roland's experiences provide an example. As a high school student, he was told by a math teacher he was not 'smart enough' to be successful in college. During his first year at university, he struggled mightily. However, his tenacity prompted him to seek the testing that revealed he had 'attention deficit disorder'. With this knowledge, professional assistance, and accommodation, he developed compensatory learning strategies. In his last two years of college, he earned a 3.9 GPA (on a 4.0 scale), was accepted into every top public health graduate programme to which he applied, and subsequently earned his Ph.D. He relates the primary obstacles he faced include lack of insight and the attitudes of others.

HEALTH-RELATED DISABILITIES

The incidence and prevalence of chronic health conditions leading to health-related disabilities will continue to increase dramatically during the 21st century. Among these are infectious conditions, such as AIDS and HIV, congenital conditions, such as spina bifida, cancers, and autoimmune conditions, such as rheumatoid arthritis and multiple sclerosis. Advancements in healthcare are prolonging lives and improving quality of life. However, traditional medical approaches keep people subservient and dependent on healthcare providers. The social model approach places treatment and life decisions with individuals and uses professionals as expert consultants and educators. Interventions consider individuals holistically, functionally, and socially rather than focusing on disease. The social model also accounts for societal factors. For example, in the USA, HIV and AIDS was largely ignored by the federal government for years because it primarily affected gay men and ethnic minorities. Life expectancy is much shorter in developing countries than in the USA and Europe, and in many cultures HIV is still considered shameful. Social policies and societal reactions have tremendous impact on the lives, including life expectancy, of people living with HIV.

SOCIAL WORK AND DISABILITY: HISTORICAL AND CONTEMPORARY PERSPECTIVES

Social work's commitment to the dignity and worth of individuals and groups, as well as its dedication to human rights and social justice, position the profession to partner with disabled individuals and groups to bring to fruition the promise of recently enacted disability rights laws and policies. At its core, the international social work community is committed to promoting individual rights and social justice (see Chapter 24). To obtain these objectives, the profession has (i) embraced people with diverse characteristics and from diverse backgrounds, and (ii) advocated for people and groups who are devalued, discriminated against, or deemed to be at risk. Historically, social work has defined disabled people as a devalued and at-risk population along with other marginalised groups, such as people in poverty, racial and ethnic minorities within societies and cultures, women, and lesbian, gay, bisexual and transgender (LGBT) populations (Gilson et al., 2002). Social workers have worked in settings such as social services, child welfare, mental health, residential institutions, hospitals, and criminal justice where vulnerable populations, including those with disabilities, are over-represented. However, in contrast to women, people from diverse ethnic backgrounds, and lesbians and gays, people with disabilities have not been embraced as colleagues and members of the profession. For example, a nationwide study of accredited programmes of the US Council on Social Work Education (CSWE) revealed 4% of baccalaureate social work students, 2% of Masters students, and 0.4% of doctoral students had disabilities (Mackelprang et al., 1996). The author's experience is illustrative of the profession's ambivalence:

> In the late 1980s, the author, as a young educator attempting to develop a scholarly agenda and achieve tenure, submitted an article to an NASW journal on including disabled persons in the social work profession. The article was rejected with one reviewer's comments, stating, 'Reject, reject, reject, do you really think we want those people in our profession?' The lesson learned from this experience for disabled social work academics with invisible disabilities was to remain securely in the closet. For social work educators with visible disabilities, the message was to minimize the impact of the disability to the extent possible.

In recent decades, disability has increasingly been accepted as an element of diversity in the profession, albeit with some ambivalence. As recently as the mid-1990s, the CSWE placed groups such as women and racial groups as diverse 'population groups', while placing disability in the same category as racism and poverty, that is, as problems to be eliminated (CSWE, 1992). Furthermore, the US National Association of Social Workers (NASW) includes disability in its definitions of populations-at-risk. However, its diversity and equity website (NASW, 2009) embraces sex, race, and ethnicity, and sexual orientation but not disability in its diversity definitions. Contemporarily, CSWE has made significant strides in adopting a social model of disability and accepting disabled social workers in its ranks, including a disability council within its formal structures (Mackelprang, 2010a). The International Federation of Social Workers has, at its 2010 general meeting, introduced a policy paper on the rights of disabled people acknowledging the treatment of more than 600 million people with disabilities worldwide 'is marked by marginalisation, discrimination, profound exclusion, and ultimately extermination' (Chenoweth et al., 2010). This draft policy statement embraces the United Nations Convention on the Rights of People with Disabilities in calling for social workers worldwide to work on behalf of disability rights. A next step would be to include a statement embracing disabled people in the profession as partners and equals.

SOCIAL WORK AND DISABILITY: ENVISIONING A FUTURE

As we move through the 21st century, the social work profession can be a major player in improving the lives of disabled persons individually and collectively. Below are principles to guide the profession in meeting its obligations in coming decades.

Disability as diversity

The profession has long acknowledged disability as a population at risk and social workers have long advocated on behalf of disabled persons. The next step is to embrace disabled people as equals and to accept disability and disability culture repudiating nondisabled values of overcoming diversity. In chronicling the development of disability culture, Longmore (2003) states:

> disabled people began to celebrate themselves. Coining self-affirming slogans such as 'Disabled and Proud,' 'Deaf Pride,' and 'Disability Cool,' they seized control of the definition of their identities. This has been not so much as a series of personal choices as a collective process of reinterpreting themselves and their issues. It is a political and cultural task ... For example, some people with physical disabilities have been affirming the validity of their own experience. Those values are markedly different from, and even opposed to nondisabled majority values. They declare they prize not self-sufficiency but self-determination, not independence but interdependence, not functional separateness but personal connection, not physical autonomy but human community (p. 222).

Disabled persons working in the social work profession

Embracing disability includes welcoming disabled persons into the social work profession. Colonialists believed Gandhi achieved greatness in spite of his Indian ethnicity while contemporarily it is accepted his ethnicity contributed to his political impact. Is it possible Franklin Roosevelt's polio contributed to his effectiveness as a politician and as President of the USA? Just as the profession has been enriched through the inclusion of majority and minority groups in multiple countries and cultures, the profession will benefit from including people with disabilities who bring their unique life experiences and perspectives to the profession. Rather than exclusively 'overcoming' disabilities, disabilities can contribute to people's lives. Stephen Hawking did not demonstrate his brilliance until after the onset of his disability. Arguably, his disability has contributed to his scientific greatness.

Assume competence

Colonialist European practices were based on a racist foundation considering colonised people and cultures inferior to White attributes and values as evidenced by Rudyard Kipling's (1899) 'White Man's Burden'. Concomitantly, until a century ago, women in the USA and Europe were marginalised and denied the right to vote or hold political office. Contemporarily, disabled persons must still fight for self-determination. People with mental health and intellectual disabilities are especially at risk of others' taking control of their lives (see Chapter 33). The profession's responsibility to advocate for the civil rights and self-determination of disabled individuals and groups is as great as it is for other devalued groups. To maximise self-determination, two elements are critical. First, social workers must start from the assumption that disabled people are competent and have the right to control decision making over their life. The burden of proof rests with those who want to wrest control when people become incapacitated or unable to make decisions. Second, it is critical social workers facilitate access to adequate resources, including assistive technology, treatments, and non-institutional living options. It is ironic and unjustifiable, in spite of a US Supreme Court decision (*Olmstead v. L.C.*, 1999) acknowledging the right of disabled people to live outside of institutions, thousands of disabled Americans remain in nursing facilities because resources to support them in the community continue to be diverted to the medical institutions incarcerating them at far greater expense.

Assume equal worth and value

This principle may seem self-evident in a profession valuing the dignity and worth of each individual. However, there are underlying disability assumptions in society placing disabled lives as less valued than nondisabled lives. Johnson's (2005) autobiographical musings in *Too Late to Die Young* recounts reactions people had to her. Because of the effects of muscular dystrophy on her body, common reactions include 'most people would give up', and 'if I had to live like you I think I'd kill myself' (Johnson, 2005, p. 3). Yet McBride, like others with disabilities, has no desire to end her life. In research with disabled youth, Altshuler et al., (2008) and Mackelprang and Altshuler (2004) found youth report levels of self-esteem, life satisfaction, and health on par with nondisabled youth. Their primary problems were associated with societal related factors, such as extreme difficulty in finding employment. Yet, as these researchers presented their findings, professionals and loved ones asked questions like 'what is the *real* story behind the results' and made comments such as 'I don't believe these children are *really* that happy'. The oft-implied assumption of nondisabled people is these youths' lives are less than satisfying. Nowhere are these assumptions more apparent than in end-of-life decisions in which disabled persons have sought help with assisted suicide. In case after case of disabled young people, who have been awarded the 'right' to end their lives, courts have granted permission for them to kill themselves while ignoring the fact these people have been incarcerated in nursing facilities with little ability to control their lives (Mackelprang & Mackelprang, 2005). The courts have also failed to see the irony in the fact they would never permit the same choice from nondisabled persons and, if nondisabled young people were subjected to similar living conditions, they might also choose to end their lives. The disability rights organisation, *Not Dead Yet* (http://notdeadyetnewscommentary.blogspot.com/) describes practices such as these as 'a deadly double standard for people with severe disabilities'. Thus, it is incumbent on the profession to purge remnants of ableist attitudes and partner with disabled allies to promote equal opportunity, human rights, and the social inclusion of people with disabilities.

Developing disability competence within the profession

Diverse cultures are based on multiple personal and social identities extending beyond race and ethnicity (Ridley et al., 2001). Disability culture has its roots in shared experiences and is influenced largely by disability communities' intersections with dominant societies and cultures. Disability culture is relatively new and evolving as disabled people repudiate traditional pathology-based explanations of disability. Disability culture promotes interdependence and self-identity, and rejects the notion people must 'overcome' their disabilities. The common experiences of devaluation, oppression, and marginalisation are providing a common bond and resilience within disability communities (Fine & Asch, 1993; Longmore, 2003; Mackelprang & Salsgiver, 2009; Snyder & Mitchell, 2006).

Language is an important cultural component and the language of Disability culture and Disability pride challenges traditional disability views. Euphemisms such as differently-abled, handicap-able, and physically challenged are rejected in disability culture. Descriptors such as wheelchair-*bound*, *afflicted* with spina bifida, polio *victim*, and *tragically* deaf are similarly rejected. By contrast, Deaf cultures throughout the world are characterised by their languages that are sometimes unique and independent from the predominant oral languages in their respective countries. Being culturally Deaf is a source of identity and pride. In the USA, Deaf culture has long been signified by 'big D' deaf as opposed to a 'little d' to signify deafness as a hearing impairment. Members of Deaf culture also reject terms such as 'person with deafness' in favour of 'd/Deaf person'. In the non-Deaf disability community, some use spelling such as disAbility to connote disAbility pride and to emphasise dis*Ability* as diversity over *dis*ability as problematic. Some argue person-first disability language implies pathology analogous to calling a Black person a 'person with blackness', or man 'a person with maleness', or a lesbian a 'person with gayness'. Disability language might be best approached by using context-specific terminology. The use of terms such as *disAbility* and *Disabled person* can be used when referring to Disability culture and pride. In contrast, *disability* and person-first language can be used in other contexts, such as when a person with multiple sclerosis seeks healthcare or when advocating for adequate services for people with mental health disabilities (Mackelprang, 2010a, 2010b).

By embracing Disabled people as members of the profession, partnering with disability rights organisations, such as independent living centres, and advocating for the rights of disabled persons and groups, the profession can develop and maintain the knowledge and values for culturally competent practice. These associations are mutually beneficial in the same manner social work partnerships with other diverse organisations have enhanced the profession. Disability competence within the social work community will require organisations at international, national, regional, and local levels to embrace these partnerships and the social model of disability as diversity.

Disability-competent social work practice

An essential element of competent social work practice is practitioner self-awareness and understanding. Awareness of one's beliefs and attitudes are especially important when working with people and groups different from oneself. This self-reflection can prevent or alter ethnic, sexist, heterosexist, and other stereotypes. In working with individuals, families, and groups with disabilities, as well as within Disability culture, answering four questions can help social workers recognise and mitigate their ableist beliefs, some of which they may not even realise they have.

1   *What are the prevalent attitudes I carry about disability as a group and people with disabilities?* These attitudes are often reflected in the language one uses to describe disability. For example, many people think of someone who uses a wheelchair for mobility as confined or wheelchair bound. Put downs and pejorative language, such as 'That's so retarded' and 'She was crippled by fear', often have negative disability connotations.
2   *To what degree are my beliefs stereotypical and or ableist?* Ableist beliefs are often based on attitudes such as pity rather than dislike or hatred. For example, most societies and cultures have a strong commitment to *investing* in their children through education. In contrast, disabled children are routinely excluded or segregated.

When education is provided, it is often perceived as a service or charity rather than an investment that will 'pay off' in productive citizens.

3 *When necessary, what can I do to educate myself, challenge ableist attitudes, and work effectively with people with disabilities?* This involves learning about and acknowledging people's potentials and strengths (see Chapter 11). Working with people with disabilities includes multiple roles beyond clients or patients, and includes disabled colleagues and peers, as well as mentors and supervisors.

4 *What is my responsibility to affirm the rights of disabled persons to fully participate in society?* Social workers' responsibility to advocate for social justice extends beyond individuals with disabilities to disabled people as a group. Disability rights are human rights and social workers' responsibility involves all levels from individuals to the disability population as a group (see Chapter 8).

Culturally competent practice with disabled persons and communities can be complex. Some elements of disabled people's lives mirror the lives of other diverse groups. However, disability also has unique implications. Below are a few tools social workers might consider. Important elements of positive identity development are families and communities conveying positive identity and self-worth. This can be especially important for 'minorities' and those who are subjected to discrimination from larger society. For example, ethnic minority children who experience racism in larger societal contexts, such as Aboriginal children in Australia, or Black children in the US Jim Crow south, have usually had the safety of family and community to buffer the exigencies of racism and devaluation. However, children who are born with disabilities or who acquire them early in life are typically raised in nondisabled families and communities, who may not convey disability-positive messages and identities associated with Disability culture. Social workers can be resources to individuals and families, exposing them to disability-positive messages and helping them redefine ableist attitudes and beliefs. In some instances, social workers may be called upon to prevent harm.

For example, in one West African country in which the author has worked, a young child Joa with significant orthopaedic impairments was referred shortly after birth to a religiously based orthopaedic centre. The child ended up staying at the orthopaedic centre for several years because, had Joa returned home to his rural village, the likelihood he would have been allowed to die was very high. Institutionalisation is a last resort, but in this instance, a life-saving one.

A second tool for effective practice is exposure to Disability-positive role models who can teach disability-positive attitudes and challenges ableist beliefs and disability stereotypes. In Joa's case, he was exposed to several older children as well as staff and other adults with disabilities. These same people were also role models for other disabled youth and parents who used the Centre. The perpetuation in role modelling was evidenced in the fact some of the disabled staff members were previously clients of the Centre when they were children. Unlike other minority groups, one can join the disability minority group, thus benefit from mentors, at any time in one's live. On a larger level, disabled people are joining collective voices to provide role models and convey the message disability can be a source of pride. For example, the *Its Our Story* project (http://www.youtube.com/user/itsourstoryproject) provides videos and examples of the struggle for disability rights from those who have been in the forefront. The Disability Social History Project (http://www.disabilityhistory.org/) provides disability-positive view of disability in contrast to prevailing approaches to disability.

A third tool for effective practice within disability contexts involves taking a civil rights approach to convey disability-positive messages and promote social justice and integrity rather than charity and pity. Laura Hershey, a former 'poster child' for the annual US Muscular Dystrophy Association telethon articulates this approach:

The MDA (Muscular Dystrophy Association) justifies the telethons as a very effective fundraising tool and they argue that the money does a lot of good. And I have a totally different analysis of it which is that it helps to perpetuate negative stereotypes about people with disabilities and that we don't need pity. We don't need people that give to charity in order to feel like they've done something to "help the disabled." What we need is equality, justice, and civil rights (http://www.youtube.com/watch?v=PpBcUAlbR8U).

The human rights approach to disability eschews language conveying pity and stereotypes, such as *wheelchair bound* and *tragically mentally ill*, for language conveying respect (e.g., wheelchair user and mental health disability). They would much rather people invest in their successes than provide them with handouts and charity.

There is no absolute disability uniform language and it is incumbent on social workers to learn about and use language conveying respect for those with whom they work. Sometimes colloquialisms provide insight into culture. For example, for decades disabled people in the USA have used the term TAB (temporarily able bodied) to signify nondisabled people can join their world at any time. In work with Deaf people, bilingual social workers can facilitate communication *and* provide insights into deaf communities, and Deaf culture to hearing colleagues.

A fourth element of culturally competent practice involves learning about and respecting the perspectives and identities of people with disabilities. There is great diversity within disability and it has dramatically different meanings for different people. Some people with disabilities do not identify as such. This is especially true for people who acquire disabilities when they are older. At the other end of the spectrum, others fully embrace their disabilities, Disability identity, and Disability culture. For example, individuals who are born deaf may become immersed in Deaf culture while those who become deaf in later life do not consider themselves part of the deaf community or Deaf culture. People born with disabilities, such as cerebral palsy or visual impairments, grow up without knowing anything different while those who acquire similar disabilities will often experience grief and adjustment.

It is critical for social workers to learn about people's perceptions rather than make assumptions. This includes a commonly held assumption all disabled people would give up their disability if given the opportunity. Consider the sentiments of the late Justin Dart, who is widely considered the father of the Americans with Disabilities Act who stated, 'I count the good days in my life from the time I got polio' (in Fay & Pelka, 2002). Below is a short excerpt that Dart wrote to be read at his funeral and intended to be used to challenge to disability activists to carry on his legacy after his death.

> Dearly Beloved:
> Listen to the heart of this old soldier ... I do not go quietly into the night ... Let my final actions thunder of love, solidarity, protest–of empowerment ... I adamantly protest the richest culture in the history of the world which still incarcerates millions of humans with and without disabilities in barbaric institutions, backrooms and worse, windowless cells of oppressive perceptions ... I call for solidarity among all who love justice, all who love life, to create a revolution that will empower every single human being to govern his or her life, to govern the society and to be fully productive of life quality for self and for all ... I do so love you, my beautiful colleagues in the disability and civil rights movement ...Thanks to you, I die in the joy of struggle. Thanks to you, I die in the beautiful belief that the revolution of empowerment will go on ... Justin Dart (cited in Fay & Pelka, 2002).

Dart's sentiments are representative of a fifth tool – using *universal access* in the struggle for disability rights and human rights in general. Rather than focusing on specific vulnerable or disadvantaged groups, universal access promotes a just society built for all. Civil rights laws have been necessary to redress wrongs and promote the rights minority ethnic groups, women, disabled people, gays and lesbians, and others. However, laws singling out specific groups can silo those groups and make them vulnerable to retaliation. Societies beginning to embrace universal access for all people will need to rely less and less on laws and policies, such as affirmative action, and provide reasonable accommodation for people and groups who do not fit societies' norms by embracing people with diverse characteristics – typical and atypical, majority and minority. When social workers advocate for disability rights, they are concomitantly advocating for women's rights, racial equality, and gay rights.

CONCLUSION

Disability laws and social policies, advances in technology, and slowly changing societal attitudes are providing disabled persons new opportunities to participate fully in society. Though they continue to face significant social and economic problems, there is hope. The role of disability and disabled persons in social work is continually evolving. Along with racially and ethnically diverse groups, women, and LGBTs, the profession recognises disabled persons and populations have been subjected to discrimination and devaluation. Increasingly, the voices of disabled social workers and allies, who advocate for the social model of disability, are being heard. Social model adherents look forward to the day disabled social workers are fully embraced in the profession and in society. As societies embrace the diverse tapestries of their members, including ethnically diverse groups, males and females, gays and straights, disabled and nondisabled, young and old, *all* people will benefit.

REFERENCES

Addams, J. (1910). *Twenty years at Hull-House: with autobiographical notes.* New York: The MacMillan Co.

Albrecht, G. (1992). *The disability business: rehabilitation in America.* Newbury Park, London: Sage.

Altshuler, S.A., Mackelprang, R.W., & Baker, R.L. (2008). Youth with disabilities: A standardized portrait of how they are they faring. *Journal of Social Work in Disability and Rehabilitation, 7*(1), 20–42.

Anthony, W.A. (1993). Recovery from mental illness: The guiding vision of the mental health service system in the 1990's. *Psychosocial Rehabilitation Journal, 16*(4), 11–23.

Bruyere, S., Davis, S., & Golden, T.P. (2000). *Working effectively with persons who have cognitive disabilities.* Ithaca, NY: ILR Program on Employment and Disability, Cornell University.

Canada.com (2008). *Crackdown vowed after Tanzanian albino girl killed, mutilated.* Retrieved October 21, 2008 from http://www.canada.com/topics/news/world/story.html?id=d9487de6-5eeb-4b6e-b21f-4863db51113c

Chenowith, L., Molderings, B. & Gutman, C. (2010). Draft policy statement on disability: IFSW policy statement on people with disabilities. *General Meeting of the International Federation of Social Workers.* Hong Kong, China. June 14–16, 2010.

Council on Social Work Education (CSWE) (1992). *Curriculum policy statement for baccalaureate and master's degree programs in social work education.* Alexandria. VA: CSWE.

DePoy, E. & Gilson, S. (2004). *Rethinking disability: Principles for professional and social change.* Belmont, CA. Brooks Cole.

disability now (n.d.) *T4: Hitler's holocaust rehearsal.* Retrieved November 12, 2010 from http://www.disabilitynow.org.uk/living/features/t4-hitlers-holocaust-rehearsal

Dudley, J.R. (1987). Speaking for themselves: People who are labeled as mentally retarded. *Social Work, 32*(l), 80–82.

Duke, P., & Hochman, G. (1992). *A brilliant madness: Living with manic-depressive illness.* New York: Bantam Books.

Dunham, M.D., Roller, J.R., & McIntosh, D.E. (1996). A preliminary comparison of successful and nonsuccessful closure types among adults with specific learning disabilities in the vocational rehabilitation system. *Journal of Rehabilitation, 26*(1), 42–48.

Fay, F., & Pelka, F. (2002). Justin Dart's obituary. *Ability Magazine.* Retrieved September 24, 2007 from http://www.abilitymagazine.com/JustinDart_remembered.html

Fine, M., & Asch, A. (1993). Disability beyond stigma: Social interaction, discrimination, and activism. In M. Nagler (ed.), *Perspectives on disability: Text and readings on disability* (2nd ed). Palo Alto, CA: Health Markets Research, pp. 61–74.

Foucault, M. (2006). *History of madness* (J. Murphy & J. Khalfa, trans.). London: Routledge.

Garscha, W., & Kuretsidis-Haider, C. (1997). War crimes trials in Austria. Presented at the *21st Annual Conference of the German Studies Association*, Washington, DC.

Gilson, S., DePoy, E., MacDuffie, H., & Meyershon, K. (eds) (2002). *Integrating disability content in social work education: A curriculum resource.* Alexandria, VA: Council on Social Work Education.

Jamison, K.R. (1995). *An unquiet mind: A memoir of moods and madness.* New York: Alfred A. Knopf.

Johnson, A.G. (2006). *Privilege, power, and difference* (2nd ed.). New York: McGraw-Hill.

Johnson, H.M. (2005). *Too late to die young.* New York: Henry Holt.

Khalfa, J. (2006). Introduction. In M. Foucault. *History of madness.* London: Routledge, pp. xiii–xx.

Kipling. R. (1899). *White Man's Burden.* Retrieved from http://www.online-literature.com/kipling/922/

Kronick, D. (1981). *Social development of learning disabled persons.* San Francisco: Jossey-Bass.

Large, T. (1993). The effects of attitudes upon the blind: A reexamination. In M. Nagler (ed.), *Perspectives on disability.* Palo Alto, CA: Health Markets Research, pp. 165–168.

Levy, A. (1993). *The Wiesenthal file.* Grand Rapids Michigan: William B. Eerdmans Publishing Co.

Longmore, P. (1987). Elizabeth Bouvia, assisted suicide and social prejudice. *Issues in Law and Medicine, 3*(2), 141–168.

Longmore, P.K. (2003). *Why I burned my book and other essays on disability.* Philadelphia. Temple University.

Mackelprang, R.W. (2010a). Disability controversies: Past, present and future. *Journal of Social Work in Disability and Rehabilitation, 9*(2–3), 87–98.

Mackelprang, R.W. (2010b). Cultural competence with persons with disabilities. In D. Lum (ed.), *Culturally competent practice: A framework for understanding diverse groups and justice issues* (4th ed.). Pacific Grove, CA: Brooks/Cole, pp. 437–465.

Mackelprang, R.W., & Altshuler, S. (2004). A youth perspective on life with a disability. *Journal of Social Work in Disability and Rehabilitation, 3*(3), 39–52.

Mackelprang, R.W., & Mackelprang, R.D. (2005). Historical and contemporary issues in end of life decisions: Implications for social work. *Social Work: Journal of the National Association of Social Workers, 50*(4), 315–324.

Mackelprang, R.W., & Salsgiver, R. (2009). *Disability: A diversity model approach in human service practice.* Chicago, IL: Lyceum.

Mackelprang, R.W., Ray, J., & Hernandez-Peck, M. (1996). Social work education and sexual orientation: Faculty, student and curriculum issues. *Journal of Gay and Lesbian Social Services, 5*(4), 17–31.

Miles, M. (2002). *Community and individual responses to disablement in south Asian histories: Old traditions, new myths?* Stockholm-Johanneshov, Sweden: Independent Living Institute.

Moeschler, J.B., & Shevell, M. (2006). Clinical genetic evaluation of the child with mental retardation or developmental delays. *Pediatrics, 117*(6), 2304–2316.

Mont, D. (2007). *Measuring disability prevalence.* SP Discussion Paper #0706. Washington, DC. The World Bank.

Morris, R. (1986). *Rethinking social welfare: why care for the stranger?* New York: Longman.

Nagi, S.Z. (1969). *Disability and rehabilitation.* Columbus, OH: Ohio State University Press.

National Association of Social Workers (2009a). Diversity and equity. Retrieved February 10, 2010 from http://www.socialworkers.org/diversity/default.asp

Olmstead v. L.C. (1999). 527 U.S. 581

Naylor, M.W., Staskowski, M., Kenney, M.C., & King, C.A. (1994). Language disorders and learning disabilities in school-refusing adolescents. *Journal of the American Academy of Child and Adolescent Psychiatry, 33*(9), 1331–1338.

New Zealand Ministry of Health, Office of Disability Issues (2001). *The New Zealand disability strategy.* Wellington: New Zealand Ministry of Health

Pharr, S. (1988). *Homophobia: A weapon of sexism.* Inverness, CA: Chardon Press.

Plato (1991). *The Republic: The complete and unabridged Jowett translation.* New York: Vintage Books.

Ridley, C.R., Baker, D.M., & Hill, C.L. (2001). Critical issues concerning cultural competence. *The Counseling Psychologist, 29*(6), 822–832.

Russell, M. (2001). Disablement, oppression, and the political economy. *Journal of Disability Policy Studies, 12*(2), 87–116.

Simpson, M. (1996). Normalisation and the psychology of mental retardation. *The Sociological Review, 44*(1), 99–118.

Simpson, M. (2007). The developmental concept of idiocy. *Intellectual and Developmental Disabilities, 45*(1) 23–32.

Snyder, S., & Mitchell, D. (2006). *Cultural locations of disability.* Chicago, IL: University of Chicago.

Solomon, B. (1976). *Black empowerment: Social work in oppressed communities.* New York: Columbia University Press.

Stroman, D.E. (1982). *The awakening minorities: The physically handicapped.* Lanham, MD: University Press of America.

TenBroek, J. (1993). Pros and cons of preferential treatment of blind persons. *Future Reflections, 12*(1). Retrieved September 12, 2006 from http://www.nfb.org/Images/nfb/Publications/fr/fr1/93win.htm

United Nations (2007a). *Convention on the rights of persons with disabilities and optional protocol.* Retrieved May 19, 2007 from http://www.un.org/esa/socdev/enable/conventioninfo.htm

United Nations (2007b). *Enable: Frequently asked questions.* Retrieved December, 7, 2010 from http://www.un.org/esa/socdev/enable/faqs.htm

United Nations Enable (2004). *The international year of disabled persons 1981.* Geneva: United Nations. Retrieved June 26, 2007 from http://www.un.org/esa/socdev/enable/disiydp.htm

United Nations Development Programme (2004). *Human development report 2004: Cultural liberty in today's diverse world.* Retrieved September 25, 2007 from http://hdr.undp.org/reports/global/2004/?CFID=8711891&CFTOKEN=5d8aabb2a38bd631-3EE282C8-1321-0B50-35921A0EDEC5CB17&jsessionid=e630b49c209120534d47

Wiggam, A.E. (1924). *The fruit of the family tree.* Indianapolis. In Bobbs-Merrill Company Publishing.

Wolfensberger, W. (1972). *The principle of normalization in human services.* Toronto, ON: National Institute on Mental Retardation.

World Federation of the Deaf (2005). *Home.* Retrieved August 29, 2007, from http://www.wfdeaf.org/

World Health Organization (WHO) (1980). *International classification of impairments, disabilities, and handicaps.* Geneva: WHO.

Immigrants and Refugees

Doreen Elliott and Uma A. Segal

Social work operates at the intersection of society and the individual, and in dealing with migrant populations of all kinds, refugees, asylum seekers, and undocumented labour migrants, the conflict between the core values of social work and the political priorities of nation-states are all too evident, making this a challenging task. This chapter critically reviews issues relating to the roles of social workers working with migrant populations, arguing that in order to provide effective services, social workers need to understand the context of their client's experience, as well as the complexity of world politics and economics that influence the way governments of nation-states formulate immigration policies. It begins by outlining several major issues affecting global migration in the world today before discussing their implications for the role of social workers.

IMMIGRATION'S HIGH PROFILE IN POLICY MAKING AND PUBLIC OPINION

Everyone has an opinion it seems, about international migration. It causes much media attention and emotions run high in the rich industrialised nations which increasingly exhibit a 'fortress mentality' with strict immigration policies, many using detention of immigrants while their status is verified, and almost all having some varying degrees of exclusion mechanisms to limit immigration. This attitude is fuelled by fear of job loss and competition, cultural differences, loss of security, especially after the 9/11 attacks on the World Trade Center in New York, and the 'outsider' and the unknown. It may be said that xenophobia and racism only too often drive negative responses to immigrants. The expression 'fortress Europe' has been used to describe European Economic Community (EEC) policies about immigration (Lorenz, 1998). The Global Commission on International Migration (GCIM), a collaboration between the United Nations and a number of countries, recognised this increasingly problematic response in its final report in 2005. In regard to the process of collecting data, the commission noted that, in every country it visited, immigration was high on the political agenda and an issue of explosive public debate, in several countries having determined the course of elections (GCIM, 2005). However, a review of the data raises the question of whether this is much ado about nothing.

International migrants as a percentage of the world population increased over the last decade of the 20th century and the first decade of the 21st century, from 2.9% of the total world population to 3.1%. With a world population having reached seven billion in 2011, international migrants of all categories numbered approximately 214 million people or one in 35 people globally (GCIM, 2005). The annual rate of change of international migration did increase somewhat over the two decades from 1990 to 2010 from 1.3% to 1.8% [United Nations Department of Economic and Social Affairs (UNDESA), 2009]. These data indicate a very small percentage of migrants compared to the total world population, although it should be taken into consideration that this percentage is unequally distributed across the globe. In fact, in the developed regions of the world, the migrant population is 10.3% of the total population (UNDESA, 2009). This operates in reverse for forced migrants (refugees, asylees, and internally displaced persons; IDPs), most of whom stay in their own region of the world. The developing world hosts 80% of forced migrants and 75% of refugees live in countries neighbouring their country of origin [United Nations High Commissioner for Refugees (UNHCR), 2011]. The data certainly paint a different picture than the world's media.

People migrate for many reasons. Some people migrate for financial reasons, to better their lives economically for themselves and their children, and achieve a higher standard of living. Some migrate for survival, to flee poverty and civil war. Natural and human-made disasters and the changing environment giving rise to shortages of food and water also play a big role in population movements. Others migrate to join family members who have emigrated beforehand. Finally, since the beginning of humankind, the urge to discover and experience adventure has continuously been a motivation for migration. The fact remains that the reason for migration largely determines the legal classification that the international community places on individuals, and the label given greatly affects their reception, prospects, and subsequent status in a host country. Segal et al., (2010) offer an explanatory model that addresses the factors involved in global immigration movements.

WHO ARE THE GLOBAL MIGRANTS?

It is important to get a picture of who the global migrants are and also of the politicisation of their status. By legal and common definitions they fall into various categories. An *immigrant* is defined as an individual who has lived outside her or his country of birth for more than one year with a view to permanent settlement in the country of residence (GCIM, 2005). Within this category of immigrant there are many subpopulations. For example, they may be the following.

- Temporary labour migrants or guest workers, who migrate for short periods to different parts of the world and send remittances back home, for example, immigrants in United Arab Emirates who are migrants from countries such as the Philippines, or India; female migrants are often domestic workers, while males work as building labourers.
- Agricultural workers from Mexico working in the USA picking fruit in California or working in landscape maintenance, mowing lawns in Texas.
- Migrants in Europe from North Africa or Asia.
- Skilled professionals, such as nurses, doctors, and IT workers migrating from less-developed countries, such as India, to the rich countries where such skills are in short supply because of demographic changes resulting in a lower birth rate and an ageing labour force.
- Corporate global executives, academics, or those with other high-level occupations from developed nations who have chosen, for various reasons, to work in a country other than their country of origin. Global corporations by their very nature operate across the globe. Their employees may spend a great deal of time working in countries other than their country of origin, and they become transnationals in that often they are

short-term migrants operating simultaneously in more than one country.
- Family migrants who migrate to rejoin family members.
- One of a small group of international adoptees.
- Unaccompanied children who may either be voluntary or forced migrants. While children without caregivers have always been part of refugee flows, their parents perhaps dying on the way, or having been killed in civil strife, the number of children travelling alone has increased in recent years. Some of these children are forced migrants and victims of human trafficking. Others may be fleeing civil strife where they may be kidnapped to serve as soldiers. Whatever their motivation, they join large refugee flows and hope to cross nation-state boundary lines with the large group (Levinson, 2011).

Table 36.1 shows global migration data for different regions of the world. Europe hosts the largest number of refugees, but North America, including the USA and Canada, has a higher percentage compared with the population. Australia, with immigrants being 18.7% of the population, hosts the highest percentage of immigrants in the population (Gray & Agllias, 2010).

While the term *immigrant* is generally used to indicate a voluntary migrant and the term *refugee* is used to indicate forced migration, both immigrants and refugees are immigrants, and clearly the category of 'immigrant' covers a wide range of human experience. As shown below, the term *refugee* covers just one category of forced migration.

Table 36.1 Global Migration Data

Region	No. of immigrants in millions	% of region's population
Europe	56.1	7.7
Asia	49.9	1.4
North America	40.8	12.9
Africa	16.3	2.0
Latin America	5.9	1.1
Australia	5.8	18.7

Source: Adapted from GCIM, 2005, p. 84.

Refugees are a category of migrants defined by two major international legal instruments, the 1951 Convention and the 1967 Protocol, each having 144 countries as signatories who have promised to uphold these international laws (UNDESA, 2009). Article 1A(2) of the 1951 Convention defines a refugee as any person who:

> As a result of events occurring before 1 January 1951, and owing to a well-founded fear of being persecuted for reasons of race, religion, nationality, membership of a particular social group or political opinion, is outside the country of his [or her] nationality and is unable, or owing to such fear, is unwilling avail him [or her]self of the protection of that country; or who, not having a nationality and being outside the country of his [or her] former habitual residence as a result of such events, is unable or, owing to such fear, is unwilling to return to it (UNHCR, 2005, p. 5).

The definition was originally intended to provide for the one million European displaced people following World War II. The major powers, including Britain, France, and the USA, were keen to limit the definition, and hence their responsibility for refugees in other parts of the world. However, subsequent events led to a continuing stream and large population of refugees remaining in camps or cities long after the war had ended, and this needed to be addressed. In 2011, war and political conflict is still a significant factor producing refugee flows. Refugees from Afghanistan and Iraq produce almost 50% of those identified as refugees today (UNHCR, 2011).

The 1967 Protocol officially extended the definition of refugee beyond the 1951 convention date, although in practice, of necessity, the date had long been ignored. The 1969 Organization of African Unity (OAU) Convention Governing the Specific Aspects of Refugee Problems in Africa extended the definition of refugee beyond Europe to Africa and was significant in that it also extended the definition of refugee from a person who is persecuted to one who experiences generalised conflict:

> the term 'refugee' shall also apply to every person who, owing to external aggression, occupation,

foreign domination or events seriously disturbing public order in either part or the whole of his [or her] country of origin or nationality, is compelled to leave his [or her] place of habitual residence in order to seek refuge in another place outside his [or her] country of origin or nationality (UNHCR, 2005, p. 6).

The 1984 Cartagena Declaration similarly extended the definition of refugee to Central and South America and introduced the concept of human rights' violations:

the refugee definition or concept of a refugee to be recommended for use in the region is one which, in addition to containing the elements of the 1951 Convention and the 1967 Protocol, includes among refugees persons who have fled their country because their lives, safety or freedom have been threatened by generalized violence, foreign aggression, internal conflicts, massive violation of human rights or other circumstances which have seriously disturbed public order (UNHCR, 2005, p. 6).

In the two decades from 1990 to 2010, the percentage of refugees among international migrants declined from 11.9% of the migrant population to 7.6% (UNDESA, 2009). In 2011, there are 10.5 million refugees, with an additional 4.8 million under the care of UNRWA, the United Nations Relief and Works Agency for Palestinian Refugees in the Near East (UNHCR, 2011).

Asylum-seekers are individuals who have requested international protection for fear of persecution and loss of life, but whose claim for refugee status remains undecided. They may be in a country of asylum by having fled their country of origin, by having overstayed their visa or other entry papers, or by having gained illegal entry into a country (UNHCR, 2008). There are currently 850,000 asylum seekers waiting a decision on their future, including 150,000 unaccompanied children (UNHCR, 2011).

Internally displaced persons are migrants who have been forced to leave their homes and who have not crossed an international border. This forced migration may occur as a result of natural disasters, human-made disasters, war, violations of human rights, and generalised violence. In 2011 there were 15.4 million IDPs needing protection as a result of armed conflict (UNHCR, 2011).

Victims of human trafficking are 'trafficked' for a variety of reasons, including sexual exploitation, forced labour, and forced domestic service, which is largely hidden from public view. However, there have been a number of high-profile media reports where victims have escaped brutal circumstances, forced marriage, organ removal where organs are sold for high prices, child soldiers, sexual exploitation of children, and child begging. Human trafficking reaps profits of an estimated at US$65 billion worldwide. It is estimated that 2.5 million people are victims of human trafficking at any one time and, of those, 1.2 million are children. Human trafficking victims of all ages come from 127 countries and are dispersed across national borders and often continents to another 137 recipient countries [United Nations Office on Drugs and Crime (UNODC) & United Nations Global Initiative to Fight Human Trafficking (UNGIFT), 2008]. Women are disproportionately involved since sexual exploitation involves approximately 79% of all human trafficking followed by approximately 18% forced labour. It has also become evident from recent studies that some women transition from being victims to become perpetrators (UNODC, 2009).

Another category of global migrants is people who do not have the correct documents to be able to legally stay in the country where they are currently living. They are known by various labels, such as *irregular*, *undocumented*, *unauthorised*, or *illegal immigrants*. Many undocumented immigrants have been smuggled across an international border. Migrant smuggling is different from human trafficking in various ways. Migrant smuggling always involves crossing international borders for the purposes of illegal immigration on the part of the individual being smuggled and financial gain for the smuggler. Human trafficking may be carried out through normal migration routes, following which the passport is usually confiscated by the person or group providing transportation upon arrival in the destination country. A victim of human trafficking is always exploited; an individual who is smuggled across borders is not necessarily exploited, and the relationship with the smuggler may end before the border is crossed or soon after. That is not to say that crimes may not be committed against the smuggled individual, in terms of method of transportation, or being left in the desert once the exchange of money has taken place (UNODC, 2009).

Smuggling is not the only way in which an individual may become an undocumented immigrant. Individuals may have entered the country legally as tourists, students, seasonal workers, or asylum seekers but outstay their visas. Also an individual may have crossed borders with false documents to seek employment, for family reunion purposes where lines for legal immigration take years, or to avoid criminal prosecution in another country (McCreight, 2006). Individuals may have entered the country legally as tourists, students, seasonal workers, or asylum seekers but outstay their visas.

Stateless persons are individuals not considered nationals by any State under relevant national laws. UNHCR has extended its role of protection and assistance for refugees to include prevention of statelessness and to find solutions for those who are stateless. An example of stateless people is the approximately 300,000 Urdu-speaking Bihari people living in Bangladesh since it was given independence from Pakistan in 1971. Owing to reasons of culture and language, they never assimilated with the local community and lived for almost 40 years in squalid, unhygienic, poverty-stricken conditions in camp-like ghettos, but were not recognised as refugees. Bangladesh finally gave about 50% of the population citizenship in 2008 (Farzana, 2008). It is estimated by the UNHCR that there are approximately 12 million people worldwide living in a stateless condition. However, at the end of 2010, documentation was so poor that only 3.5 million living in 65 countries could be documented (UNHCR, 2011).

Table 36.2 summarises the main categories of forced migration. Not all categories are represented because of space limitations, but the main categories are shown with the numbers of people affected globally to highlight the extent of forced migration from a global perspective.

WHO BEARS THE GLOBAL BURDEN? UNEQUAL BURDEN ON THE GLOBAL SOUTH

What we're seeing is worrying unfairness in the international protection paradigm. Fears about supposed floods of refugees in industrialized countries are being vastly overblown or mistakenly conflated with issues of migration. Meanwhile it's poorer countries that are left having to pick up the burden (António Guterres, UN High Commissioner for Refugees, in UNHCR, 2011, p. 6).

The world's poorest countries host the largest number of refugees: Pakistan hosted almost two million refugees (1,900,600) at the end of 2010; the Islamic Republic of Iran hosted just over one million (1,073,400); and the Syrian Arab Republic hosted over half a million (594,000). The 49 least-developed countries gave asylum to two million refugees

Table 36.2 Numbers of people forcibly displaced globally at end of 2010

Category of forced migrant defined by UNHCR	Estimated No.
Refugees under UNHCR	10.5m
Refugees under UNRWA*	4.8m
Asylum-seekers	845,000
Internally displaced persons (IDPs) Conflict generated	14.7m
Stateless people	12m
Natural disaster and human made disaster-related IDP's	25.0m
Victims of Human Trafficking	2.5m
Number of forced migrants worldwide	*43.7m

Source: UNHCR (2011), UNODC & UNGIFT (2008).
*This number is a UN estimate and not a total of the column due to overlapping categories and some additional categories not included in this estimate.

(UNHCR, 2011). Popular myth has it that all the world's refugees and migrants are knocking at the doors of the Western industrialised nations but this is not so. In fact, at the end of 2010, 75% of the world's refugees were living in a country neighbouring the country from which they had fled and 80% (approx. 8.3. million) of the global refugee population was hosted by developing countries in 2009 (UNHCR, 2011). Only 17% lived outside their region of origin (UNHCR, 2011). Thus the countries who can least afford it bear the greatest burden of settlement. This disparity between the global North and the global South in this era of neoliberal globalisation is well known in terms of distribution and use of resources, but the question is constantly posed in the global North, why should the developed world share the burden of responsibility for forced migrants caused by wars or environmental changes far from their national borders? The same question is extended to voluntary migrants, particularly in their use of social welfare programmes. Responses include an ethical and historical imperative: for many years since the age of Elizabeth I of England and Phillip II of Spain, who were competitive in plundering the resources of the New World, the global North has exploited the resources and labour of the global South. Second, another argument, less altruistic, but nevertheless important, is self-interest. Creating the conditions that enhance world peace and global prosperity is in everyone's interest. Third, members of the United Nations subscribe to the Universal Declaration of Human Rights and other human rights conventions and, therefore, have an humanitarian obligation to assist the global community in the implementation of those rights. Fourth, globalisation has brought nations of the world closer together in terms of interdependence of economies; a problem in one economy reverberates throughout the global trade communication lines and every country suffers. Globalisation has brought better understanding and sharing of popular and other culture through modern communications. Hence it is less easy to exclude and objectify suffering in a distant land. Fifth, global sustainable development requires collaboration in new areas: as the demographics of the global North change with falling birthrates, immigrant labour becomes a necessity for sustainable development, and new approaches to link immigration and labour market policies are needed. Migration becomes a mutually beneficial arrangement for the distribution of labour in the global economy.

A report issued by the British Broadcasting Corporation (BBC) in the spring of 2011 illustrates the meeting of two very different worlds of global North and global South through the eyes of immigrants. It shows the geographical proximity of the North to the South in certain areas of the globe, and the continuing attitude of a major power in avoiding responsibility for a group of immigrants who speak the same language. Lampedusa Island is located in the Mediterranean Sea at the southernmost latitude of Europe, between Sicily and Tunisia, although closer to Tunisia than Sicily with the nearest landmass being Malta. Now known as the 'Arab Spring', the uprising started in Egypt and spread to other Arab countries, such as Tunisia, Libya, and Syria, with the goal of bringing down the repressive regimes ruling those countries. Lampedusa has a long history of being a playground for rich vacationers from Europe. After the uprising, vacationers and citizens of Lampedusa were faced with the prospect of an 'invasion' of more than 5000 migrants seeking asylum arriving on small boats from Tunisia. Conditions in Tunisia were violent. Many of the asylees were foreign workers in Tunisia, trying to exit from the country or be faced with possible threats to their lives. They were escaping on humanitarian grounds and were also overwhelming the small island that had previously dealt with only small numbers of asylees entering Europe in this way. Hygiene arrangements were insufficient, food was scarce, and the island population was split between those, such as the Mayor, who tried to prevent the boats from landing sending them off to sea again with little food or water, and those islanders who provided food and shelter for the migrants. There was concern for their major industry, the tourist trade. A visit by the Italian Prime Minister resulted in a large vessel waiting offshore to take the asylees to the mainland of Italy to be processed. Many spoke French, since French is spoken in Tunisia, so the logical next step was to try to enter France. French President Sarkozy challenged international law and foreign relations with Italy by closing his country's borders to this immigrant group. Signatories to the 1951 Convention agree to the principle of *non-refoulement* in terms of which migrants fleeing for their lives would not be turned away and sent back to the conditions that prompted their need to flee in the first instance. Thus a major power avoided its responsibility to forced migrants once again and the island of Lampedusa is faced with continuing problems, loss of tourism and income, and community conflict over how to treat this population that will likely last for many generations (BBC, 2011).

THE POLITICISATION OF HUMAN TRAGEDY: DEFINING WHO BECOMES A REFUGEE OR IMMIGRANT

Intense politicisation has surrounded both the role of the international voluntary migrant and the forced migrant. It is important for social workers to understand some of the reasons for this politicisation, since it has important effects on the acceptance and integration of immigrants and refugees in host communities and affects immigration policies in host countries. With regard to refugees, international protection has always been a reluctant function of the developed industrialised economies. Under the auspices of the United Nations Relief and Rehabilitation Agency (UNRAA), which operated from 1943 to 1947, refugees were repatriated without any consideration of their reintegration into their country of origin or of the political situation there and most of those returned to Russia were imprisoned in Stalin's gulags in Siberia (Loescher, 2001; UNHCR, 2000). UNRAA's successor agency, the United Nations International Refugee Organization (IRO) operated from 1946 to 1952 and was successful in replacing the policy of repatriation to an uncertain future with the durable solution of resettlement to a third country. However, even this humanitarian triumph was a function of cold war politics since the change in policy then suited the Western powers to take the high road in contrast to the forced placement and containment of peoples within the Soviet Union. The Office of the UNHCR took over in 1952 and was envisaged as a temporary agency to deal with the remaining displaced people in Europe following World War II. However, numerous political crises occurred in a changing political landscape both in Europe and beyond, and the definition of refugee had to be extended by the 1967 Protocol, the 1969 Organization of African Unity Convention, and the Cartagena declaration as late as 1984. The United Nations, of course, remains in business today, since numerous political crises continue to occur with consequent migration flows and its task has grown from protecting about one million people when it was first formed to more than 40 million globally today (UNHCR, 2010). Another example of the reluctance of the major powers to take responsibility for forced migrants beyond their borders is illustrated by the Palestinian refugee situation. The establishment of IRO and UNHCR ignored the existence of Palestinian refugees displaced through the partitioning of Palestine in 1947 and the founding of the State of Israel in 1948. Established in 1949, the United Nations Relief and Works Agency (UNRWA) was limited to assistance, while the UNHCR founded three years later was mandated to protect and assist and also to find lasting – durable – solutions. Largely ignored by the international community, Palestinian refugees today have increased from the 750,000 in 1948 to 4.8 million in 2010 (UNRWA, 2010).

Today, mixed migration flows have complicated the definitions and blurred the boundaries between forced and voluntary migrants. Refugees as defined by the Convention; 'environmental' migrants fleeing from extreme poverty, lack of food and water, caused by natural or human made disasters and global environmental changes; victims of human trafficking; and unaccompanied separated children may all be moving in the same migration flows. They may be displaced by similar events, but not all qualify for international protection under the convention. Civil disturbances and violence sometimes follow the environmental changes and some migrants may be displaced for these reasons. Increased suspicions of migrants as terrorists has led to tightening of nation-state borders and has created more restrictive immigration policies in the global North. Governments have been guilty of alarmist positions, fearful of environmental migrants as creating global conflict. Examples of this position are The Stern Report (UK Department of the Treasury, 2006) published by the British government and the US Department of Defense (2011) Quadrennial Defense Review. The latter identifies five major national security risks, one of which is climate change and the economic and political changes it may bring. The Stern Report also identifies migration as a security risk. Yet in the midst of this politicisation are the unmet needs of forced and voluntary migrants worldwide, as well as the long waiting times, often amounting to many years, for family reunions, and the hardening of media and popular attitudes to immigrants. The issue of immigration as a global security risk is not evidence based and more data are needed. History would suggest that the very presence of mineral resources, rather than the lack of these, creates conflict. Furthermore, argues Martin (2010), most environmental migrants are rural and apolitical peoples and they generally move peacefully. Nevertheless, when powerful government positions are taken, policies are changed and so are people's lives.

INTEGRATION OF IMMIGRANTS IN HOST COUNTRIES

Social workers and other human service workers need to be aware of the numerous barriers to integration for immigrants and some of these are reviewed here. While a number of countries have well-developed immigration policies, few countries or regions have sufficiently developed immigration integration policies, and this is especially true of labour market integration for immigrants [Organisation for Economic Co-operation and Development (OECD), 2006]. Recent studies have shown that integration can be a significant challenge. One of the factors that contribute to this challenge is the gap between public perceptions and the reality of the data with reference to immigrants. Negative public attitudes and media attention are often focused on certain groups, such as those immigrants who look or dress differently, have a different religion, and speak a different language. An example of the challenge to integration for immigrants is a European study that demonstrated that citizens of Denmark, Norway, Germany, and Sweden thought that the immigration population was 60–70% more than it actually was and, in France and the UK, citizens assumed the immigration population to be one and a half to two times more than the actual figure [European Economic Commission (EEC), 2009]. Another study in Britain showed that people believed there were four times more than the actual number of immigrants in the country and that immigrants were 50% of the population (EEC, 2009). In fact, UK statistics for 2011 show the foreign-born population as 11.5% of the population (UK Office of National Statistics, 2011).

Research studies in the European Economic Community (EEC) have demonstrated that certain factors are linked with more positive views on immigrants and less ethnic exclusionism. These are: younger age, higher socioeconomic status, higher education, and salaried employees as opposed to manual workers. Rural dwellers were more likely than urban dwellers to support social exclusionism, and those who have more personal contact with immigrants were more likely to be positive in their view of immigrants. In contrast to Mediterranean, Eastern European, and Baltic countries, those from Nordic countries were less in favour of ethnic exclusionism. Those who attended church regularly and those who are on the right of the political spectrum also tended to favour ethnic exclusionism. From an economic perspective, low gross domestic product per capita in a nation-state was positively related to ethnic exclusionism (Coenders et al., 2004).

Negative media influence also contributes to a hostile environment and includes using incorrect and inflammatory terminology, such as 'illegal asylum seekers'. This is, of course, a contradiction in terms and confuses asylum seekers with illegal immigrants. Often immigrants are over-represented in reports about crime and positive stories, such as immigrants' economic contribution to society, are rarely published (EEC, 2009).

Integration into the labour market is also a challenge. Recent evidence has emerged that even second- and third-generation immigrants still experience barriers in the labour market. For instance, they have no local references, no social capital in the form of contacts, friends, families, and social networks to enable their locating job opportunities. Often local job-finding agencies do not have the expertise to evaluate foreign equivalencies for qualifications, and with pressure to get a job, the immigrant often accepts a job at less than their skill level (OECD, 2006). Poverty forces them into urban ghettos and alienation from the host society may follow.

Different global regions have had various responses to integration. The EEC has responded to these challenges at the policy level in various ways, including the publication of a *Handbook on Migration Integration* covering policies and practices relating to 'mass media and integration; awareness-raising and migrant empowerment; dialogue platforms; acquisition of nationality and the practice of active citizenship; immigrant youth, education and the labour market' (EEC, 2009, p. 22). This integration initiative covers common principles for which member states have agreed best and innovative practices. The initiative also makes funding available and promotes the goals of establishing baselines and outcome measures of the effectiveness of integration policies and practices. An example of a measurement tool is the Migration Integration Policy Index (MIPEX) produced by the British Council and the Migration Policy Group with additional funding from the European Fund for the Integration of Third-Country Nationals. It is an instrument with seven factors formed from 148 policy indicators as a measure of a country's integration policies. The factors measuring integration in this instrument are: labour market mobility; family reunion; education; political participation; long-term residence, including, for example, security of status and associated rights; access to nationality; and anti-discrimination policies. The 2010 study gives a rank order of effectiveness for integration policies in all EEC countries with the addition of Norway, Switzerland, Canada, and the USA as of 2010. The research design included national experts in the immigration policy field in each country who completed a questionnaire evaluating their country's policies (MIPEX, 2010). According to this index, where 100 is the highest score, the rank of order of countries is as follows: Sweden was the top of the list with a score of 83, followed by Portugal (79), Canada ranked third (72), USA ranked ninth with a score of 62, Italy ranked tenth (60), and Germany and the UK both with a score of 57, ranked equally at 12th (MIPEX, 2010). Of course, the methodology of the study can be critiqued in that scholars from the country may be inclined to rank their own country higher or that their responses may very well be dependent on their political positions. Other scholars evaluate US outcomes relating to the country's effectiveness on integrating migrants much more favourably than the MIPEX Index. In a comparative study of European and US integration policy, also funded by the European Community, Jiménez (2011) found that, despite there being no cohesive federal integration policy (he argues it is *laissez-faire* with the exception of policy towards refugees who receive some initial assistance), immigrants fared well on several counts over two or three generations in that housing segregation was decreased, the socioeconomic status of the second and third generations was better than that of their parents, and language acquisition was not a problem by the third generation.

Another example of an integration policy is that of the Australian government that has a programme called *Settlement Grants Programme* (SGP) supporting integration for certain categories of immigrant, for instance, humanitarian immigrants who are not refugees but are victims of similar circumstances to refugees, and dependents of skilled immigrants in rural areas who do not speak English. Eligible individuals, communities receiving immigrants, and nongovernmental organisations working with immigrant groups may apply for these funds. For the financial year 2011–2012, the programme is significantly funded with AUD38 million (Commonwealth of Australia, 2007).

These examples of global integration policies for immigrants demonstrate the attempts being made to ensure that immigrants are integrated but not required to assimilate. Issues such as the wearing of headscarves by women, the requirement to speak the host country language implemented through admission or citizenship tests, and the challenge of integrating Islam in mainly Christian countries, as well as negative media communications and xenophobic reactions of host country citizens, all present an enormous social and economic challenge. The European Community makes it clear in its integration policy statements that integration is a function of a mutual adjustment on the one side on the part of the host country and its communities, and on the other of individual immigrants and immigrant families.

BENEFIT OR COST? THE FISCAL IMPACT OF MIGRATION ON HOST COUNTRIES

Immigration has a clear benefit for the countries of the global North where the birthrate is declining and people are living longer. The ratio of workers to retirees is becoming less sustainable, and immigrants serve to alter the balance, providing much-needed labour and population growth. The immigration policies of several counties, such as Canada and Australia, have recognised this fact and have become more focused on the admission of highly skilled migrants. While tabloid headlines refer to immigrants as a burden on a host country's economy, data from research studies prove the opposite. Immigrants pay unemployment and social security taxes, and unauthorised immigrants will not be able to receive the benefits of their payments. Immigrants spend the money they earn and generate stimulus for local economies.

The Immigration Policy Center of the American Immigration Council (AIC) has reviewed studies of legal and unauthorised immigrants across many states in the USA. Numerous studies have shown that the net cost–benefit is positive both for legal and unauthorised immigrants. A 2008 Arizona study showed that there was a net gain of US$940 billion for the state economy and, in Arkansas in 2007, the net gain was US$2.96 billion. Immigrant households in California in 2008 contributed US$589 per capita per annum more than the US-born household. In a 2007 study in Florida, immigrants contributed $1500 more per capita than they received in benefits totalling US$10.49 billion in federal taxes and US$4.5 billion in state and local taxes. Other studies from New Jersey, New York, Utah, Washington DC, Washington state, and Wisconsin are also reported along similar lines with a net gain for the state in every case (AIC, 2010). The AIC (2010) also reports studies for unauthorised immigrants. In Colorado 2006, unauthorised immigrants contributed US$30 million in state income tax, US$13 million in property tax, and US$151 million in sales taxes. In Illinois a 2002 study of unauthorised immigrants showed that they spent US$2.89 billion in the local economy. It is argued that this stimulated a further US$2.89 billion and sustained 31,908 local jobs. In Texas in 2006, unauthorised immigrants contributed US$17.7 billion to the state economy. Just as for legal immigrants, other studies for Oregon, New Mexico, Missouri, Iowa, and others are reported with the same net benefit for the local economies (AIC, 2010). It should be noted that each of these studies is independent and uses differing methodologies. Gray and Agllias (2010) report similar results for Australia.

The *New York Times* reported in 2008, how immigrants were saving social security in the USA. The report suggests that the contribution of undocumented immigrants is even better than for legal immigrants, since they enter the country at a younger age, produce more children resulting in an increase in the working-age group paying payroll taxes, but unfortunately for them they do not collect retirement benefits later. Their collective contributions will close 15% of the social security deficit (*New York Times*, 2008).

IMMIGRANTS AND WELFARE

A statement by Milton Friedman that free immigration is incompatible with a welfare state has been often quoted. In this section, welfare benefits are examined in relation to immigrant populations in the USA. The question may very well be asked: 'is Friedman's quip not a complete overstatement when the data are examined', apart from the fact that free immigration does not exist anywhere at present.

Using data drawn from the 2010 American Community Survey, Table 36.3 indicates consumption of welfare benefits in the USA comparing the native-born with the foreign-born population. The foreign-born population is divided into three columns, all foreign-born immigrants (FB), foreign-born naturalised citizens (FBN), and foreign-born non-naturalised citizens (FBNN) as there are some important differences to be noted in these latter two groups. The poverty rate for native citizens at that time was 13.5%. The FB rate was much higher at 16.4% compared with the FBN rate which was 9.8%; this figure, however, was affected by the much higher rate of the FBNN group. This disadvantage of the FBNN group is reflected throughout most of the rows in Table 36.3. Rows two to four relate to income levels and again the same pattern is noted that immigrants (FB) as a whole fall below the native-born population, and the FBNN group is at a significant financial disadvantage. However, the established immigrant group (FBN) in fact earns more than the native group where there is household income. This is contrary to popular myth about immigrants. It is also correlated with row nine relating to higher education. Row five shows the percentage of the populations receiving public assistance in cash benefits. Here the results are mixed. The percentage of the foreign-born population as a whole who receive public assistance is greater than the native-born population as a whole. Then, however, the FBN percentage is less than native born, which seems to indicate that, once established, the foreign-born population is less of a burden than popular myth would have it believed. Row six suggests that the FBN group, while fewer of them receive assistance, when they do receive it the mean annual amount received is more than the native-born population and the FBNN group is much more than all the other categories. It is possible that one factor influencing these data is that the FB take time to get on their feet and may use public assistance to do so (this population of FB includes both forced and voluntary migrants). As would be expected, a consistency is observed in row seven relating to receipt of food stamps. Row eight shows the mean annual social security dollars received and these are less for the FB populations. This possibly relates to the fact that immigrants start paying in to the system later in life, plus with fewer earnings as observed in rows two through four, they qualify for lower payments of social security in retirement. The pattern deviates in row nine concerned with education. The FB group as a whole and the established FBN group have higher education than native-born citizens. Finally, related to employment, the FBN group has more in employment and less unemployed than the native group, and the FBNN group has more in employment than the native group, but as an earlier row tells us, they earn less so we can conclude that the FBNN group earns less than the other groups. Differences between the FBN and the FBNN groups may be accounted for by the fact that the FBN will have had longer to be in the country and build social and economic capital, while the FBNN group may still be in the early stages of immigration. Also the FBN group is likely to be more highly skilled considering the fact that they are more highly educated, but also that their skill level would influence their receiving citizenship. Another possibility is refugees who may be included in the FBNN group, often have to accept jobs below their experience and educational level because their qualifications do not transfer or their language skills are insufficient for high-earning positions.

What do we conclude simply from Table 36.3 in relation to immigrants and welfare? First, established immigrants are more educated, paid better, and less likely to receive welfare than native-born citizens. Secondly, this advantage does not follow them through into retirement since retirement funds are dependent on time to grow as people who move jobs frequently experience a disadvantage too. Thirdly, there is a group of immigrants, the FBNN group, who does not fare as well as the established citizen group. Fourthly, the data for the USA do not support popular myth about immigrants being a burden on the welfare system.

Table 36.3 Comparison of Native and Foreign Born (FB) Populations (2009)

Row #		All	Native	FB	FBN Naturalised citizen	FBN Not a citizen
1	Below 100% of poverty level	13.5	13.0	16.4	9.8	21.3
2	Mean household income of households with income in US$	71,159	71,560	68,769	80,737	57,384
3	Mean household income of all US households	51,425	51,998	47,633	56,431	40,201
4	Mean retirement income	20,838	21,000	18,100	18,683	15,689
5	Percent of population receiving cash public assistance	2.4	2.4	2.6	2.2	3.0
6	Mean annual public assistance received in US dollars	3,363	3,245	4,062	3,920	4,175
7	Percent of population receiving food stamps/SNAP	8.5	8.4	9.3	7.7	11.0
8	Mean Social security US dollars received	14,966	15,122	13,307	13,870	11.112
9	Percentage holding graduate or professional degree	10.1	10.0	11.0	12.9	9.4
10	Percent employed	59.9	59.4	62.8	61.6	63.8
11	Percent unemployed	4.7	4.7	4.5	3.5	5.2

Source: United States Census Bureau (2010)

Nannestad (2007) reviewed 15 years of research into immigration and welfare in the global North, excluding Canada, Australia, and New Zealand. While acknowledging that the data were mixed, the studies show immigration is not advantageous to citizens of welfare states, but is advantageous to immigrants. This gives a different picture from the data presented above. Clearly, much more research is needed, as Nannestead (2007) points out, particularly from social scientists, in a field presently dominated by economists.

ROLE OF SOCIAL WORK

With the growing numbers of migrants globally, it is increasingly likely that social workers will meet immigrants or refugee families and individuals on their caseloads. This is especially so for social workers based in large cities of developed economies. Social workers, therefore, need to be well prepared to practise effectively with migrants. A global awareness and culturally competent understanding needs to be taught in professional social work education and is vital for the delivery of effective services. Understanding the context of practice is essential for effective work with migrants as are the ability to see the local in the global and the global in the local, and a human rights education and awareness.

New ways of viewing social work intervention with migrants is needed. The old dichotomy of micro- and macro-practice is no longer relevant, where services are predominantly delivered on the lines of individual and family intervention focusing mostly on case management, language, and housing acquisition, and where necessary for treatment of post-traumatic stress disorder. For example, the ability to work with home-town associations that are formed by migrants in diaspora communities to assist development projects in their home communities. The skill to work at the level of policy making is essential for social workers. Too few social workers are engaged in policy advocacy and are under-represented in think tanks, immigration research, and policy making. The field of immigration scholarship and research is dominated by social geographers, lawyers, and political scientists. Social work needs to focus on research in the field if the profession is to participate in policy making and ensure improvement of services to clients who are migrants. Social workers also have an important public education and advocacy role to help the public understand the value of immigrants for the receiving economies. Because most refugees stay in the region of origin, there needs to be an increasing role for international aid agencies. This offers an employment market for social workers interested and able to do this work

New progressive ideologies, models, and paradigms are needed to meet the need for more effective social service delivery. A social development approach is one model that offers considerable potential for new intervention levels and for taking the role of social work to a new level of policy influence. It has the potential both for transforming social work at global and local levels, and for more global reciprocal change and collaboration. This is especially important in social work with migrants whose life experience goes far beyond local boundaries. As applied to social work, the social development approach offers an empowerment, strengths-based, asset-building perspective consistent with micro- and macro-practice approaches (Elliott, 2010; Elliott & Mayadas, 1996; Mayadas & Elliott, 2000, 2001, see Chapter 6). Other approaches are needed if social work is to remain relevant in assisting and advocating for immigrants and refugees.

CONCLUSION

This chapter has reviewed some current issues in global migration and the role of social work. It is premised on the view that social workers need to understand the context of their clients' backgrounds and to expand the area of practice to include more research and policy advocacy in international migration. Topics reviewed include: the politicisation of migrant status and the consequences for individuals and families; the unequal global burden of international migration flows are considered to put the debate in context regarding fear in the rich countries of being overwhelmed by migrants; the integration of migrants in host societies, the costs and benefits of international migration for a host country, and the impact on welfare are also considered. Much has of necessity been omitted given lack of space. However, it is hoped that the reader will be motivated to explore this issue further and play whatever part they can in developing the role of social work still further.

REFERENCES

American Immigration Council (AIC) (2010). *Assessing the economic impact of immigration at the federal and state level.* Immigration Policy Center: AIC. Retrieved July 17, 2011 from http://www.immigrationpolicy.org/just-facts/assessing-economic-impact-immigration-state-and-local-level

British Broadcasting Corporation (BBC) (2011). BBC News Europe 22 March 2011, *Italy's Lampedusa island hit by migrant crisis.* Retrieved July 24, 2011 from http://www.bbc.co.uk/news/world-europe-12816340 downloaded 7/24/2011

Coenders, M., Lubbers, M., & Scheepers, P. (2004). *Report 1 for the European Monitoring Centre on Racism and Xenophobia* Ref. no. 2003/04/01. University of Nijmegen, Nijmegen Institute for Social and Cultural Research, Department of Social Science Research Methodology, Department of Sociology. Retrieved June 15, 2011 from http://fra.europa.eu/fraWebsite/attachments/Report-1.pdf

Elliott, D. (2010). A social development model for incorporating disaster planning, management and relief in the social work curriculum. In D. Gillespie & Danso, K. (eds), *Disaster planning, management and relief: New responsibilities for social work education.* Alexandria, VA: Council on Social Work Education.

Elliott, D., & Mayadas, N.S. (1996). Social development and clinical practice in social work. *Journal of Applied Social Sciences, 21*(1), 61–68.

European Economic Commission (EEC) (2009). *Handbook on integration for policy makers and practitioners.* J. Niessen & Huddleston, T. of MPG (authors), on behalf of the European Commission (Directorate General for Justice, Freedom and Security). Retrieved June 28, 2011 from http://www.migpolgroup.com/public/docs/173%20Integration_Handbook_III_15%2004%2010_EN.pdf

Farzana, K.F. (2008). Neglected stateless Bihari community in Bangladesh: Victims of political and diplomatic onslaught. *Journal of Humanities and Social Sciences, 2*(1), 1–19.

Commonwealth of Australia (2007, revised 2011). *Australian Immigration Fact Sheet 92 Settlement Grants Programme.* Retrieved July 2, 2011 from http://www.immi.gov.au/media/fact-sheets/92funding.htm

Global Commission on International Migration (GCIM) (2005). *Migration in an interconnected world: New directions for action.* Report of the Global Commission on International Migration. Retrieved June 28, from http://www.gcim.org/en/finalreport.html

Gray, M., & Agllias, K. (2010). Australia: The world in one place. In U.A. Segal, Elliott, D., & Mayadas, N.S. (eds), *Immigration worldwide.* New York: Oxford University Press, pp. 153–170.

Jiménez, T.R. (2011). *Immigrants in the United States: How well are they integrating into society?* Washington, DC: Migration Policy Institute. Retrieved February 7, 2011 from http://www.migrationpolicy.org/pubs/integration-Jimenez.pdf

Levinson, A. (2011). *Unaccompanied immigrant children: A growing phenomenon with few easy solutions.* Washington, DC: Migration Policy Institute. Retrieved November 7, 2011 from http://www.migrationinformation.org/Feature/display.cfm?ID=823

Loescher, G. (2001). *The UNHCR and world politics: A perilous path.* New York: Oxford University Press.

Lorenz, W. (1998). Social work, social policies and minorities in Europe. In C. Williams, Soydan, H., & Johnson M.R.D. (eds), *Social work and minorities: European perspectives.* London: Routledge, pp. 247–264.

Martin, S. (2010). Climate change, migration and governance. *Global Governance 16,* 397–414.

Mayadas, N.S., & Elliott, D. (2000). International perspectives on social work practice. In P. Allen-Meares & Garvin, C. (eds), *The handbook of direct practice.* Thousand Oaks, CA: Sage, pp. 633–650.

Mayadas, N.S., & Elliott, D. (2001). Psychosocial approaches, social work and social development. *Social Development Issues, 23*(1), 5–13.

McCreight, M.V. (2006). Smuggling of migrants, trafficking in human beings and irregular migration in comparative perspective. *European Law Journal, 12*(1), 106–129.

Migration Integration Policy Index (MIPEX) (2010). *Migration integration policy index.* British Council and the Migration Policy Group. Retrieved July 7, 2011 from http://www.mipex.eu/

Nannestad, P. (2007). Immigration and welfare states: A survey of 15 years research. *European Journal of Political Economy, 23*(2), 512–532.

New York Times (2008). Editorial. How immigrants saved social security. Retrieved October 7, 2011 from http://www.nytimes.com/2008/04/02/opinion/02wed3.html

Organisation for Economic Co-operation and Development (OECD) (2006). Policy brief. *From immigration to integration: Local approaches.* Retrieved June 28, 2011 from http://www.oecd.org/dataoecd/5/55/37726512.pdf

Segal, U.A., Mayadas, N.S., & Elliott, D. (2010). *Immigration worldwide: Policies, practices and trends.* New York: Oxford University Press.

UK Department of the Treasury (2006). *The Stern review.* Retrieved June 16, 2011 from http://webarchive.nationalarchives.gov.uk/+/http://www.hm-treasury.gov.uk/d/Executive_Summary.pdf

UK Office for National Statistics (2011). *Migration statistics quarterly report No 9: May 26th 2011. Coverage UK: Theme: Migration.* Retrieved February 7, 2011 from http://www.statistics.gov.uk/pdfdir/mig0511.pdf

United Nations Department of Economic and Social Affairs (UNDESA) (2009). *Trends in International Migrant Stock: The 2008 Revision (United Nations* database, POP/DB/MIG/Stock/Rev.2008). Population Division: UNDESA. Retrieved June 28, 2011 from http://www.un.org/esa/population/publications/2009Migration_Chart/ittmig_wallchart09_table.xls

United Nations High Commissioner for Refugees (UNHCR) (2000). *The State of the world's refugees 2000: Fifty years of humanitarian action.* Retrieved June 6, 2011 from http://www.unhcr.org/3ebf9ba80.html

United Nations High Commissioner for Refugees (UNHCR) (2005). *Refugee status determination: Who is a refugee?* Retrieved May 19, 2011 from http://www.unhcr.org/publ/PUBL/43144dc52.pdf

United Nations High Commissioner for Refugees (UNHCR) (2008). *Global trends: Refugees, asylum-seekers, returnees, internally displaced and stateless persons.* Retrieved June 28, 2011 from http://www.unhcr.org/statistics/STATISTICS/4852366f2.pdf

United Nations High Commissioner for Refugees (UNHCR) (2011). *Sixty years and still counting: Global trends 2010.* Retrieved June 11, 2011 from http://www.unhcr.org/4dfa11499.html

United Nations Office on Drugs and Crime (UNODC) (2009). *Global report on trafficking in persons.* Retrieved June 11, 2011 from http://www.unodc.org/documents/human-trafficking/Global_Report_on_TIP.pdf

United Nations Office on Drugs and Crime (UNODC) & United Nations Global Initiative to Fight Human Trafficking (UNGIFT) (2008). *Human trafficking: An overview.* New York: United Nations. Retrieved June 11, 2011 from http://www.ungift.org/docs/ungift/pdf/knowledge/ebook.pdf

United Nations Relief and Works Agency (UNRWA) (2010). *UNRWA in Figures 2010.* Retrieved June 11, 2011 from http://www.unrwa.org/userfiles/file/statistics/UNRWA_in_figuresJune_2010_English.pdf

US Census Bureau (2010). S0501. *Selected characteristics of the native and foreign-born populations data set: 2005–2009.* American Community Survey 5-Year Estimates Survey: American Community Survey. Retrieved July 16, from http://factfinder.census.gov/servlet/STTable?_bm=y&-geo_id=01000US&-qr_name=ACS_2009_5YR_G00_S0501&-ds_name=ACS_2009_5YR_G00_&-_lang=en&-_caller=geoselect&-state=st&-format

US Department of Defense (2011). *Quadrennial defense review.* Retrieved June 16, 2011 from http://www.defense.gov/qdr/transcripts_flourncy_20090429.html

37

Drug and Alcohol Interventions

Holly Matto

This chapter presents a critical, cross-disciplinary analysis of the major drug and alcohol treatment interventions currently in use across the USA and other countries. It examines the most up-to-date empirical literature and highlights programmatic and policy implications relating to drug and alcohol interventions. Most dominant in this literature is the medical model of addiction that conceptualises substance abuse as a disease characterised by intense emotional distress, lack of impulse control, and disruption in the reward centres of the brain. In terms of the medical model, it is believed brain changes caused by drug use render the individual unable to control drug-using behaviour, leading to significant impairment in occupational, interpersonal, medical, and psychological functioning (Goodman, 2008). As the disease progresses from use, to abuse, to dependency, drug-using behaviour moves from impulsive actions to compulsive drives (Koob, 2006). Other models of addiction see the condition as a sociocultural phenomenon, emphasising the importance of the environment on the development and maintenance of drug-using behaviour. For example, community engagement models suggests addiction is facilitated by cognitive, emotional, and interpersonal attachments to an *addiction community*, with the level of attachment mediated by substance users' cognitive and affective orientation to context referents (network members) within that community. This approach suggests assessing the relevant social processes and leveraging (intervention) within the social network is necessary to facilitate pro-recovery identity change and subsequent behavioural commitments to a recovery-oriented community (Matto & Spera, 2009; Matto et al., 2006, 2007). Increasingly recognised is the importance of *integrating* models to address the biopsychosocial phenomenon of addiction more effectively and competently. Indeed, consistent across perspectives, drug and alcohol use is recognised as a serious public health problem with significant medical, psychological, social, and economic consequences. This section presents recent empirical data to document the scope of the problem.

PREVALENCE OF DRUG AND ALCOHOL ABUSE

According to the US Preventive Services Task Force, young adults aged 18–20 years have the highest rate of illicit drug use, with marijuana as the most frequently used drug of choice in the US (6% of the 12+ population). Cocaine is the next most frequently used drug with 1% of the US population reporting use in the past month. Other drugs, such as hallucinogens, inhalants, heroin, other stimulants, are used less frequently. Rates are significant for special populations, like pregnant women, 5% of whom report illicit drug use in the past one month (Polen et al., 2008). Substance use prevalence estimates vary by country. Table 37.1 shows additional cross-country substance use prevalence estimates.

The US Centers for Disease Control and Prevention's (CDC) Task Force on Community ranks *heavy drinking* (consuming more than two drinks per day for men or more than one drink per day for women) and or *binge drinking* (consuming five or more drinks at one time for men, or four or more drinks at one time for women) as the *third* leading cause of preventable death in the USA. Rates of heavy drinking are estimated at 5% of the total US population and 15% of the population binge drink. The majority (90%) of the alcohol consumed by young people aged 12–20 involved binge drinking. Young adults, aged 18–24, are a high-risk group for developing alcohol dependence.

The global medical, psychological, social, and economic consequences of substance use are significant. Alcohol use has a significant impact on health worldwide and accounts for 2.3 million early deaths across the globe per annum. It is the third leading cause of preventable death, with the majority of alcohol-related

Table 37.1 Annual prevalence of use as a percentage of the population aged 15–64 (unless otherwise indicated)

Drug	USA	England and Wales*	Spain*	Italy	Australia	Ireland	Germany†
Alcohol[b]	8.80 (2008)	10.20 (2009)	10.00 (2006)	8.00 (2006)	10.10 (2009)	11.30 (2009)	9.70 (2009)
Marijuana[a]	12.50	7.90	10.10	14.60	10.60	6.30	4.70
Cocaine[a]	2.60	3.00	3.00	2.20	1.90	1.70	0.70
Opiates[a]	0.58	0.81	0.13	0.72	0.40	0.50	0.21
Ecstasy[a]	1.00	1.80	1.10	0.70	4.20	1.20	0.40
Amphetamines[a]	1.30	1.10	0.90	0.60	2.70	0.40	0.50

Drug	Switzerland	France	Netherlands	Canada	Belize‡	Bahamas
Alcohol[b]	10.20 (2008)	12.60 (2007)	9.60 (2007)	8.20 (2009)	§	§
Marijuana[a]	9.70	8.60	5.40	13.60	8.50	5.50
Cocaine[a]	0.80	0.60	0.60	1.90	0.90	0.20
Opiates[a]	0.61	0.47	0.31	0.50	§	0.22
Ecstasy[a]	0.30	0.50	1.20	1.70	0.30	0.10
Amphetamines[a]	0.60	0.20	0.30	1.50	1.40	0.40

* Ages 16–59.
† Ages 18–64.
‡ Ages 12–65.
§ No report.
[a] UNODC, World Drug Report 2010 (United Nations Publication, Sales No. E.10.XI.13).
[b] OECD Health Data (Liters Per Capita Age 15 and Older).

deaths caused by (i) auto accidents; (ii) homicide; and (iii) suicide [World Health Organisation (WHO), 2009a,b]. Injuries account for one-third of the burden of disease risk associated with alcohol use. Higher levels of drinking are associated with higher rates of emergency department visits for violence-related injuries across countries. Injuries are the main cause of death up to age 45 and alcohol use is the main cause of injuries among 15–44-year-olds (WHO, 2009a). Some estimates show Europe has the highest per capita alcohol consumption and has highest percentage of death attributable to alcohol worldwide. Past year prevalence rates of alcohol dependence was 5.5% for Western Europe and 10.9% for Eastern Europe compared to 3.6% worldwide (Rehm et al., 2009). Globally, tobacco use is the second biggest health risk for mortality (9%), after high blood pressure (13%). Tobacco is related to 18% of all deaths in high-income countries and alcohol use is implicated in 5% of all disease worldwide, right after childhood underweight (6%) and unsafe sex (5%; WHO, 2009b).

PREVENTION PROGRAMMING: A MULTILEVEL APPROACH

Individuals who abuse substances are likely to engage in other high-risk behaviours and are less likely than those who do not abuse substances to engage in positive, health-promoting behaviours. Ettner et al. (2010) found a negative relationship between alcohol consumption and health-promotion behaviours, such as wearing a seat belt and keeping preventative physical examinations. Others have found substance users are at high risk for injuries and accidents, exposure to violence (Rolfe et al., 2006), and engaging in risky sexual behaviours (Cooper, 2002). Consistently, neuroscience findings suggest drug use may lead to heightened reactivity in the limbic system (emotional centres of the brain) with a concomitant disconnect from the regulatory prefrontal structures that would allow for behavioural control, rendering the drug-using individual at higher risk for making poor behavioural health decisions.

Harm reduction

Substance abuse harm reduction approaches recognise this constellation of risk factors and work to mitigate the deleterious consequences (e.g., involvement with criminal justice system, medical illness, and homelessness) associated with substance use (Mancini et al., 2008). In contrast to abstinence-only models, there is an understanding that addiction recovery is a process, with relapse part of the process, and engagement and relationship-building central to managing behavioural risks. Strategies include employing outreach and engagement activities to mobilise community resources and to build capacity to reduce harm. The focus is on safe practices and use reduction and not total substance abstinence as a primary outcome.

'Harm reduction' began in the Netherlands to reduce disease among HIV drug users, and spread in acceptance to other Western countries (Inciardi & Harrison, 2000). However, the approach meets challenges as an acceptable practice to some health and human service providers, most 12-Step facilitation programmes, and other care providers who fundamentally believe the substance behaviour must be the primary focus of targeted intervention (i.e., abstinence as outcome), and without a primary focus on stopping use, individuals may be supported to continue in their using behaviours.

School-based psycho-educational prevention programmes

There is a growing body of evidence-based substance abuse prevention programmes. The literature, to date, suggests school-based programmes with a focus on the consequences of use are not effective. Rather, the most effective programmes include resistance skill training, community and family interventions, use peer leadership modules, and include teacher training protocols (Spoth et al., 2008). Specifically, family and school interventions combined are more effective than school interventions alone (Spoth et al., 2005). Life skills training in school settings and community-based programmes focusing on multiple domains, such as family interventions and youth mentoring, are effective prevention programmes for high-risk youth (Roe & Becker, 2005). The Iowa Strengthening Families Programme (Spoth et al., 2001, 2004) is one example of an integrated prevention programme, where seven sessions are conducted in the school setting, and others are conducted with the family.

Along these lines, National Institute on Drug Abuse's *Preventing Drug Use among Children and Adolescents* suggests the following areas to be included in comprehensive assessment and prevention programming: (i) exploring drug abuse problem severity; (ii) reasons for use and biopsychosocial consequences of use, and risk and protective factors to include personal adjustment; (iii) peer environment; (iv) home environment; and (v) community and neighbourhood characteristics. In addition, engaging in a neighbourhood assessment examining perception of neighbourhood norms related to drug use and recovery behaviours, employment opportunities, and nondrug-related activities should be included in prevention programming.

Communities that Care is a manualised evidence-based community-engaged drug abuse prevention model based on a risk-protection framework, targeted for children and adolescents. The approach makes use of a community prevention coalition, made up of community leaders, to identify community-level risk and protective factors to be targeted for prevention programming to reduce youth behaviour problems and promote positive youth development in the community. Evidence from research studies has shown the model to be effective in reducing substance abuse and delinquent behaviour by age 14 and to improve community behavioural health statistics overall (Hawkins et al., 2008). Community-level prevention plans focus on youth aged 10–14 and their families. Communities are trained to use tools to identify risk and protective factors, and to match evidence-based prevention and intervention programmes and policies to the identified needs, to implement the strategies, and to evaluate the outcomes. Programmes focus on school, youth, and community, and examples include: life skills training, school-based bullying programmes, strengthening families, and academic tutoring (Hawkins et al., 2008, 2009).

Ager et al. (2008) describe a successful prevention programme for African-American youth living in an urban housing project, designed to develop pro-social behaviour from community-influenced antidrug social norms shaped by the youth's creation of an antidrug video in their neighbourhood. The programme involves inspirational speakers from the community, role playing, and youth-initiated videotaping of drug-related themes in their neighbourhood. Ager et al. (2008) cite the following factors as significant to the programme's success: 'family involvement, community engagement, adapting drug education content to fit community characteristics, using the camcorder as a central vehicle for learning, community field assignments, and evaluation-based learning' (p. 313). Similarly, in the young adult student population, antismoking videos on college campuses have shown to be effective in changing attitudes and social norms about smoking behaviour (Simmons et al., 2004).

In England, the National Healthy School Program includes similar evidence-based, holistic components, adopting a 'whole school approach' to drug-use prevention. Normative education is the cornerstone of the approach, with interventions aimed at changing drug-use norms of peers. In Turkey's Action Plan (2007–2009) for drug-use reduction, several priorities shape national policy and programming including supply and demand reduction; changing community attitudes; drug-related crime reduction; strengthening treatment capacity; and improving coordination of agencies relevant to drug addiction. The 2008 UK Drug Strategy, *Drugs: Protecting families and communities*, emphasises strong community enforcement that includes helping community residents take charge in safely and anonymously reporting drug dealers in their communities by increasing neighbourhood policing efforts. There is also significant attention to improving the drug treatment opportunities in the correctional system and to enhance social reintegration of drug-using offenders. Germany's Drug Action Plan (2003) emphasises priority goals in areas of prevention, treatment, harm reduction, and supply reduction, with a focus on strengthening international cooperation to reduce supply, limit drug access to youth, and improve treatment access for all who need services.

Changing social norms across institutional settings and neighbourhoods

Expectancies related to alcohol use have been found to develop as early as eight years old (Kraus et al., 1994). Drug-free social norms within the school, peer groups, and larger community, as well as emotional and instrumental social support from non-abusers, are significant protective factors in decreasing drug-use initiation. Changing these perceived norms can be more influential than behavioural programmes teaching only drug-refusal skills to youth.

Akerloff and Kranton (2010) in their recent book, *Identity Economics*, suggest norms or social rules directing behaviour in a social context acquired through community socialisation, lead to behavioural enactment. It is identity that is constructed through social relationships and interactive processes leading to the adoption of a particular prescribed set of behaviours. Identity utility, the gains achieved when actions conform to the norms and ideals of that constructed identity or, alternatively, the losses when they do not, reinforces and maintains a set of behaviours. This behavioural economics approach applied to substance use prevention programming implies it is essential to examine the larger societal value of a social category or identity (i.e., 'addict'), rather than focus solely on behavioural modification. Studies have found recovery-related social identity has a significant effect on a treatment-seeker's intention to change substance using behaviour (Matto et al., 2007). Thus social context is implicated at multiple levels of identity construction and, therefore, needs to be understood and leveraged in identity deconstruction and reconstruction phases. This approach suggests prevention interventions should focus on other social categories – other than 'addict' – that can be developed ultimately to change behavioural decision making, so the distribution of gains or losses associated with an addict identity changes in favour of abstinence, and construction of a recovery-related identity.

Environmental prevention strategies

Environmental and macro-focused perspectives on drug abuse are contributing new ways of thinking about use, abuse, and dependency, its effects on individuals, families, and communities, and methods for intervening at macro-levels. Environmental approaches for drug-use prevention typically include targeted media initiatives, community collaborations, and coalition building (Collins et al., 2007), and policy enactment focused on regulating supply and access to alcohol (Gruenwald et al., 2003). One example of an evidence-based multisite environmental drug-abuse prevention approach is the development of a community coalition among the US Air Force and civilian communities. Sponsored by the Office of Juvenile Justice and Delinquency Prevention, the Enforcing Underage Drinking Laws (EUDL) initiative, is a community-based environmental approach to decrease military service members' alcohol use (Spera et al., 2010). EUDL strategically engages elected officials, police, human service agencies, alcohol and beverage control departments, and other organisation representatives. Interventions include: (i) a community-based awareness and media campaigns to reduce drinking; (ii) increasing driving under the influence (DUI) checks in the community; (iii) monitoring local liquor establishments to ensure they are not selling to underage airmen; (iv) using covert underage buying operations to; and (v) enhancing participating in nondrinking activities.

INDIVIDUAL, GROUP, AND FAMILY TREATMENT: BIOMEDICAL, COGNITIVE, AND RELATIONAL APPROACHES

There will always be individuals in our communities whose substance use has progressed to levels requiring formal treatment services. These individuals may seek out formal treatment themselves or make the decision at the encouragement of family, they may be court-mandated to seek out such services, or they may receive treatment as part of another institution's service-delivery plan (e.g., drug users in the correctional system, child welfare system, or mental health system).

In the USA, depending on the medical presentation of the addiction, as determined by the American Society of Addiction Medicine (ASAM) patient placement criteria, clients are likely first to enter detoxification, with primary focus on medical stabilisation, and then may transition to rehabilitation, which may be short-term residential (30–90 days) or a therapeutic community (three months to one year). After inpatient stay, clients may further transition to intensive outpatient or traditional outpatient counselling, which typically meets several days a week for a few hours each day. After formal treatment services, clients will typically transition to continuing care services, which may include community-based supports, continued monitoring, and recovery maintenance. Research increasingly shows peer support during aftercare is one of the most important factors in maintaining sobriety, after release from formal care (White, 2009).

A variety of evidence-based biomedical, cognitive, and relational (family and significant other) treatment approaches are available in these treatment settings. At treatment entry, clients should be assessed routinely for motivation or readiness for change. Prochaska and DiClemente's (1983) transtheoretical model of change offers a well-used and long-studied framework for understanding clients' readiness for change, suggesting six stages to include: pre-contemplation; contemplation; preparation; action; maintenance; and relapse. Regardless of treatment type, a client's readiness to engage in, and commit to change, will significantly influence recovery outcomes. The next section discusses a range of evidence-based formal treatment approaches to drug addiction.

Biomedical and psychosocial integrated treatment

Drug abuse changes the neurochemistry and hormonal balance in the brain. For example, dysregulation occurs in the brain's reward system, with D1, D2, and D3 dopamine receptors disrupted in cocaine addiction (Koob, 2006). The cycle of drug use and subsequent withdrawal activates the hypothalamic-pituitary-thalamus (HPA) axis, the body's stress response system. Gamma-aminobutyric acid (GABA), an inhibitory neurotransmitter to diminish anxiety and distress, is reduced during withdrawal, while at the same time, an excitatory hormone and neurotransmitter, corticotrophin-releasing factor (CRF) is increased during withdrawal, leaving the body in a hyperaroused, particularly agitated state (Koob, 2006). Neurobiological processes that constitute vulnerability include dysregulated dopamine (reduced D2 receptors specifically) and abnormalities in the orbitofrontal and ventromedial prefrontal cortex (Wiers & Stacy, 2006). These neurobiological changes associated with the addictive process impair the motivation–reward system and the ability to regulate affect, and lead to behavioural impulse control problems (Goodman, 2008). Therefore, pharmacotherapy and behavioural treatments aim to restore and enhance self-regulation capacity by operating on the implicated brain structures via direct structural or neurotransmitter modification (pharmacotherapy) and via indirect functional changes using behavioural interventions seeking to modify cognitive processing and teach new behavioural skills to 'retrain' the brain. For example, there is the potential to use real-time functional magnetic resonance imaging technology (fMRI) to help clients via immediate in-scanner feedback to strengthen targeted brain structures and train parts of their brain to achieve identified goals.

Innovations and clinical applications of pharmacotherapy interventions for drugs of abuse work at a neurochemical level to diminish the effect of the drug or to directly or indirectly stimulate the receptors and neurotransmitters implicated in the neurobiology of addiction. While clinical evidence for the use of such biological interventions holds much promise for managing the ill-effects of dependency, it should be seen as one component of a comprehensive treatment plan. Pharmacotherapy should be implemented with behavioural interventions to target medication adherence and compliance strategies as well as to increase treatment retention. For example, in the large COMBINE (Combining Medication and Behavioural Interventions for alcoholism) multisite controlled trial, support was found for naltrexone and naltrexone + behavioural interventions on abstinence outcomes (Galanter & Kleber, 2008).

Pharmacotherapy typically uses *agonist* compounds, a direct drug substitute (e.g., methadone for heroin, and nicotine replacement gum, patch, inhaler, and nasal spray for smoking) and *antagonists* that block the reinforcing effects of the drug by blocking agonist access to the receptors (e.g., disulfiram for alcohol, and naltrexone for opioids), or a combination of both (O'Malley & Kosten, 2006), to change the drug-dependent person's neurochemistry. Suboxone (combination of buprenorphine and naloxone) is used to treat opioid dependency and operates as a partial agonist at the mu-opioid receptors, and an antagonist at the kappa-opioid receptors and an antagonist, through naloxone, at the mu-opioid receptors. Another pharmacoptherapy option for opioid dependency is methadone maintenance, shown to be effective in stabilising neurochemistry and hormonal composition by decreasing the intensity of peaks and dips in brain changes (O'Malley & Kosten, 2006). Data from the North American Opioid Maintenance Initiative study show promising new opioid agonist opportunities. Specifically in a double-blind study of injectable hydromorphone and diacetylmorphine, mu-opioid receptor agonists, both were found to be more effective than methadone for hard-to-treat patients (Oviedo-Joekes et al., 2010).

Motivational interviewing

Motivational interviewing (MI) is relational, and cooperative in style, and focuses on clinician-driven qualities of empathy and collaboration, with attention to client autonomy in treatment decision making. A core MI intervention, the decisional balance, involves asking clients to explore perceived discrepancies between their own values, goals, and problem behaviours. Specifically, clients are asked how behaviours uphold or undermine their values and goals via careful examination of the pros and cons of continuing to drink or use drugs versus maintaining a commitment to recovery (Apodaca & Longabaugh, 2009; Miller & Rollnick, 2002). Brief motivational interventions can be used in diverse settings (Anstiss, 2009). For example, Bernstein et al. (2005) found cocaine and heroin users benefited from a single contact by a peer educator who was seeking services in a medical setting. The study brief intervention was effective at reducing drug use at six-month follow-up, suggesting brief MI can be employed in service settings other than primary substance abuse treatment agencies.

Motivational enhancement therapy (MET) is similar in focus to MI, and focuses on mobilising client internal opportunities for change. In the FRAMES model, clinicians provide direct *Feedback* to the client; recognise the *Responsibility* for change is at the client level; offer *Advice* and encouragement; help the client generate a *Menu* of options for change; employ *Empathic* counselling; and work to *Support* client self-efficacy (Miller, 2006). Specifically, counsellors using an MET approach help clients identify discrepancies between values and behaviours, clarify choice, and review consequences of behaviour (Carroll et al., 2009). Project MATCH (Matching Alcoholism Treatments to Client Heterogeneity), an important randomised controlled trial, examined differential effects of 12-step Alcoholics Anonymous participation, cognitive behavioural therapy, and MET on abstinence. The study found few differences between the three treatment conditions except outpatients who received 12-step facilitation during after care had highest abstinence rates at one-year follow up (Project MATCH Research Group, 1998).

Cognitive behavioural therapy

Based on social learning theory and operant and respondent conditioning principles, cognitive behavioural therapy (CBT) helps clients examine thoughts, emotions, and behaviours and the sequencing of these capacities as related to continued drinking or drugging patterns. Clients are encouraged to recognise and cope with high-risk situations and to identify triggers that lead to relapse. Techniques include functional analysis of the consequences of drug use, modifying interpretations about drug use, skills training in intrapersonal and interpersonal domains, changing reinforcement schedules of rewards, enhancing emotional self-regulation, enhancing the integrity and use of a social support network, coping skills training for cravings, planning for crises, development of safety plans, and strengthening refusal skills. In doing so, clients are asked to examine specific thoughts, feelings, and behaviours associated with the problem and to identify the 'before', 'during', and 'after' experiences associated with drug episodes (Carroll, 1998; Carroll et al., 2008). Often, elements of MET and CBT have been combined. For example, MET/CBT-5 (SAMHSA Treatment Improvement Protocol Series) is an evidence-based treatment that includes two individual sessions of MET and three group sessions of CBT to treat adolescent substance abuse (Sampl & Kadden, 2001). MET sessions helped adolescents identify desired changes; CBT sessions taught coping skills.

Another evidence-based approach using CBT principles is relapse prevention (RP; Larimer et al., 1999; Marlatt & Gordon, 1985). RP emphasises client empowerment and efficacy in managing precipitants to relapse in effort to mitigate the risk of future drug use. Specific interventions include identifying high-risk situations and skills training to cope with those situations; and increasing client self-efficacy and refusal skills (Larimer et al., 1999). Marlatt and colleagues have recently expanded their original RP model to include mindfulness components (Mindfulness-Relapse Prevention), and empirical results have been promising. Bowen et al. (2006) examined mindfulness training in a sample of incarcerated substance abusers and found recidivism reduction and decreased substance use after treatment participation. Other studies have shown mindfulness works to reduce negative affect, stress system reactivity, and actual substance use (Zgierska et al., 2008). Specifically, Garland et al. (2010) recently found mindfulness training decreased distress during the period from alcohol-related cue exposure to recovery from craving experience, and mindfulness training in alcohol-dependent patients was most effective for those patients with higher baseline stress levels. In efficacy trials of mindfulness-based relapse prevention for adults with alcohol and other drug disorders, components such as mindfulness language have been associated with drug abstinence (Collins et al., 2009).

For clients with substance abuse diagnoses and a co-occurring mental illness, research suggests integrated mental health and substance abuse treatment is more effective than parallel or sequential treatments (Mueser et al., 2006). One example of an integrated treatment for post-traumatic stress disorder and substance abuse is Seeking Safety (Najavits, 2007, 2009; Najavits et al., 2009). Seeking Safety is a manual-guided CBT administered in group or individual format. There is a growing body of research documenting its effectiveness with a variety of subpopulations, such as incarcerated women, homeless female veterans, male veterans, and a population of African-American men, and adolescent girls (Najavits et al., 2007; Weaver et al., 2007).

Dual-processing approach

The substance abuse literature consistently shows negative emotional states and subjective stress are highly predictive of relapse and significantly influence behavioural motivation (Goldin et al., 2008; Tanabe et al., 2009). Further, cognitive control resources (i.e., cognitive coping skills or relapse prevention training) have been shown to exert minimal impact on behavioural decision-making in the presence of intense affective material (Bolla et al., 2003). Thus, implicit cognitive processes play a significant role in drug-use behaviour, decreasing self-regulation capacities, and increasing risk of relapse (Wiers & Stacy, 2006; Uhl et al., 2008). Specifically, high levels of stress associated with drug use and relapse can compromise prefrontal cortex functioning (Fein et al., 2002).

A dual-processing treatment approach is based on dual representation theory (Brewin, 2001; Brewin et al., 1996), and is a 12-session psychosocial intervention combining a visual processing (structured drawing activities to engage in sensory-based cue exposure) and a verbal processing component (structured CBT) (Matto, 2005). The visual experience allows an individual to be actively engaged in a physical process that stimulates sensory circuitry in the brain. The verbal processing component facilitates cognitive control over these varied internal, sensory-based reactions. Clinical goals are evidence-based, and include: strengthening self-regulation capacity; decreasing cue reactivity through in-session sensory-based cue exposure experiences; increasing cognitive control and affective–cognitive integration through application of cognitive behavioural techniques; and understanding and managing environmental sensory-based triggers that may be operating out of conscious awareness (at an implicit level). Empirical evaluation has found reductions in cravings and increases in self-efficacy for those participating in the treatment (Matto et al., 2010; Strolin-Goltzman et al., 2007).

Multidimensional family therapy

The US Center for Substance Abuse Treatment's Treatment Improvement Protocol (TIP) Series recommendations (SAMHSA) includes a family treatment approach, multidimensional family therapy (MDFT), that combines individual and family counselling sessions with telephone and case management services. Treatment aims to enhance conflict resolution skills in the substance abusing youth, while simultaneously helping the parents to enhance their parenting efficacy and to help the family develop their support network and community linkages (Rowe et al., 2002). A similar approach, the family support network (FSN) treatment, uses a combined MET and CBT protocol, and adds case management and family support groups to the model, designed to address the individual as embedded within a family network and a community of services.

Empirical support shows efficacy for a variety of approaches, and depending on the outcome of interest by study design, equal effects across approaches have been found. For example, Rowe et al. (2004) found family treatment and CBT are both effective treatments for adolescent substance abusers with externalizing disorders. A third approach to treating substance abuse from a relational model is network therapy (NT; Galanter, 1993a, 1993b; Galanter et al., 2002). NT recruits nonsubstance-abusing significant others to co-facilitate change with the therapist around a client's treatment plan, and is implemented in addition to individual counselling.

Intervening in families to strengthen behavioural control and parenting discipline in families where there is at least one parent with a substance use disorder can significantly reduce the odds of the child developing a substance use disorder later in the life course. However, there are very few evidence-based treatment interventions for children of substance-abusing parents. Alateen, is a 12-step based self-help group for children who have an alcoholic parent(s), the Strengthening Families Programme, provides education for parents, and support and skills training for the family as a whole, and SAMHSA's Children's Programme Kit (SAMHSA, 2007), is a coping skills training support programme. Betty Ford's children's programme is a four-day programme also aimed at children, aged 7–13 years, who have a substance-abusing parent(s). Empirical evaluation of the programme showed a significant increase in social skills, and a decrease in loneliness (Moe et al., 2008).

COMMUNITY-BASED INTERVENTIONS

Community reinforcement approaches

A family-inclusive and behavioural-based treatment model that has shown promising empirical support is the Community Reinforcement and Family Training (CRAFT) approach (Meyers et al., 2002). CRAFT is used by family members who desire to engage a loved one in treatment and help facilitate commitment to recovery, typically when the loved one is resistant to treatment. The approach uses a nonconfrontational, motivational style to teach the loved one some strategies to engage the substance using family members in treatment. Overall, a community reinforcement approach is behavioural and employs environmental contingencies as reinforcers for sobriety. Emphasis is on problem-solving, communication, and drug or drinking resistance skills training (Miller et al., 2001; Smith & Meyers, 2009). A variation on traditional Community Reinforcement Approach is CRA + contingency management (Carroll & Rounsaville, 2006). Vouchers are awarded on a point system, for drug-free test results, and can be redeemed for items purchased in the community. Typically treatment duration is 24 weeks. Contingency management models have been effective in achieving abstinence goals, and increasing treatment retention and medication compliance (Carroll & Rounsaville, 2006).

A community reinforcement approach for adolescents, the Adolescent Community Reinforcement Approach (A-CRA) intervention, combines individual adolescent counselling sessions (ten sessions) with individual parent or caregiver counselling sessions (two sessions), and combined sessions with the adolescent and parent or caregiver (two sessions). The primary focus of the approach is to manipulate environmental reinforcers in favour of drug abstinence, and to use other community resources that promote a drug-free lifestyle and foster pro-social supports around the adolescent (Godley et al., 2007). In a randomised controlled trial of the A-CRA intervention, treatment participation was significant in mediating the relationship between retention and abstinence outcomes (Gossop et al., 2003).

Drug courts and community-based treatments for offenders

Current data estimate up to 80% of youth with juvenile justice system involvement have a relationship with drugs and/or alcohol according to Columbia University's National Center on Addiction and Substance Abuse (CASA; 2010). CASA's 'criminal neglect' data suggest there are significant drug use rates in the incarcerated youth population. For example, the study found more than three-quarters of youth in the juvenile justice system were using drugs or alcohol when the crime for which they were incarcerated was committed and substance-related problems at the time they entered the juvenile justice system According to CASA (2010), 65% of prisoners, overall, meet the Diagnostic and Statistical Manual of Mental Disorders (DSM-IV) diagnostic criteria for alcohol or drug disorder; and an additional one-fifth had some reportable level of drug and/or alcohol involvement related to their incarceration. However, only 11% of these prisoners received substance abuse treatment for their drug/alcohol problems. Other estimates suggest less than half of drug-using individuals in the correctional system participate in drug treatment while in prison (Mumola & Karberg, 2006).

Studies show, however, community-based substance abuse treatment for individuals in the criminal justice system is effective in increasing drug abstinence rates and reducing prison re-entry (Taxman et al., 2007), with significant cost savings to society. In fact, National Institute on Drug Abuse (NIDA) estimates for every $1 spent on treatment for drug-addicted individuals in the correctional system, there is a $12 savings in crime and health costs (CASA, 2010). VanderWaal et al. (2008) assert effective service delivery to the incarcerated substance-abusing population must be comprehensive, strengths-focused, and community-based

Policy changes to promote a more comprehensive, community-based treatment plan for incarcerated youth have been proposed. For example, CASA's *Model Bill of Rights for Children in the Juvenile Justice System* proposes states adopt legislation to promote comprehensive, targeted, and evidence-based treatment and resource opportunities for incarcerated youth with substance abuse problems. Specific priorities of the model bill include:

> Right to rehabilitation, treatment, education, family and social services, least restrictive alternative, reintegration (support services in aftercare); also, right to non-discrimination, safety and security, counsel, protection from self-incrimination, evidence-based practice (scientifically supported treatments that are tracked), speedy review' (CASA, Model Bill of Children's Rights).

The US states of California, Connecticut, Massachusetts, and New York have all introduced legislation in this proposed direction.

Therapeutic communities

According to Farbing and Johnson's (2008) review of substance abuse treatment interventions in the correctional system, Scared Straight programmes and Boot Camps are not effective in reducing substance use or reducing recidivism. Developing non-incarcerated lifestyle community supports is most effective. One of the most successful interventions in showing long-term abstinence rates is the Swedish Prison Study's 2–5-year follow-up of prisoner participation in a therapeutic community (TC). This was consistent with other studies finding TCs were effective in increasing abstinence and reducing recidivism rates. TCs are structured, residential programmes and include 12-Step participation, professional counselling incorporating cognitive behavioural and skill-training techniques, and group counselling. The most frequently used technique in the Swedish substance-abusing population who received treatment for their drug problem is MI, implemented from a stages of change model (Farbing & Johnson, 2008).

12-Step programmes and other community-based continuity of care practices

The mounting empirical literature consistently reinforces the importance of comprehensive community-based care for individuals and families with substance-abuse problems. In facilitating the transition from formal services provision to community care, the literature suggests client attachment to and engagement with a recovery community is critical for recovery success. Even continuing care services using telephone communication as a means of contact have been shown to be beneficial in decreasing abstinence rates at three months follow-up (Godley et al., 2010).

Social influence theory suggests social network drug use will influence other network members' drug-use patterns, and the quality (closeness) of network relationships and frequency of time spent with network drug users is associated with individual member use (Reifman et al., 2006). Behavioural choice theory (Moos, 2006) suggests substance use persists in the absence of alternative, viable community interests such as attachments to religious, occupational, and educational opportunities. Therefore, effective community-based programmes, such as sober-living homes and 12-Step self-help programmes are a significant component in any comprehensive treatment plan (Moos, 2006).

Recovery coaches and comprehensive community-based intensive service models are increasingly recognised as best practice for those in the child welfare system. It is estimated up to three-quarters of families in the child welfare system experience some type of alcohol or other drug-related problems (Brook & McDonald, 2007). Recovery coaches have been shown to increase reunification rates and treatment access for this population (Ryan et al., 2006). Brook and McDonald (2007) propose a practice model for working with substance-involved families in the child welfare system, which includes direct services to the families, assistance to agencies involved in the family's service plan through monthly court hearings, and monthly family conferences. For example, the Illinois Demonstration Project showed that the majority of families with substance abuse issues in the child welfare system have several serious co-occurring problems, such as domestic violence, mental health challenges, and housing instability. Family reunification is less likely to occur in the child welfare system if, in such families, these problems are not sufficiently addressed. When recovery coaches helped families obtain needed case management services, transported families to their appointments, frequently contacted their families, and met with their families' treatment providers, reunification rates increased. Findings suggest that integrated service programmes that ameliorate problems in target areas may enhance abstinence and family reunification outcomes (Marsh et al., 2006).

For all clients, attention should be paid to the influence of larger community macro-factors on clients' capabilities to stay clean and on their perceived employment prospects and recovery routine upon discharge. The Betty Ford Institute Consensus Research Conference on Extending the Continuum of Care recent position statement includes a section on 'utilization of community support' (McKay et al., 2009), stating: 'collectively, there is growing focus on the ecology of addiction recovery – how the relationships between individuals and their physical, social, and cultural environments promote or inhibit the long-term resolution of severe AOD problems' (White, 2009, p. 147).

As already outlined, it is important to integrate biological *and* environmental perspectives in treatment design to fit with the biopsychosocial realities of substance abuse. Social workers should acknowledge and work to mitigate the day-to-day logistical barriers that may impede treatment-seekers' opportunities to be involved in treatment. Social workers should help individuals with addiction fit into a productive societal niche upon re-entry into the community after participating in a treatment programme. Advocacy for such re-entry programmes should be central to social work in this field (e.g., summer youth employment programmes and youth offender community re-entry programmes with sufficient length for follow-up and support). It is necessary not only to assess how an individual treatment-seeker 'engages' in treatment and transitions back into the community, but also how the treatment provider, as an agency embedded within the community, engages with the larger community-wide recovery network. The extent to which the individual will have access to services and supports when discharged from any given programme may depend, for example, on how the agency and its programme is regarded by other agencies and community-based social institutions, and the extent to which there is community-wide reciprocal exchange in services and support. In the absence of these efforts, there is considerable risk of blaming families for lack of treatment involvement or relapse, when environmental barriers may prohibit opportunities for individuals and families to be continuously involved and committed to recovery.

Understanding how agencies adopt, implement, and evaluate the success of evidence-based programming in their agency context is a growing area of research focus. Proctor et al. (2009) outline a conceptual model to examine how agencies adopt and implement evidence-based practices. Their conceptualization includes the following domains: intervention and implementation strategies (systems environment, organisational, group learning, supervision, and individual client or consumer); implementation outcomes (feasibility, fidelity, penetration, acceptability, sustainability, uptake, and costs); service outcomes (efficiency, safety, effectiveness, equity, patient-centredness, and timeliness); and client outcomes (satisfaction, function, and symptomatology) (p. 29). Glasgow (2006) presents a RE-AIM framework for understanding and evaluating the use of evidence-based practices in community settings. RE-AIM is: *Reach* (of the programme to the appropriate target population); *Effectiveness* (of the programme on target outcomes); *Adoption* (of the programme by agencies and by staff within agencies); *Implementation* (how the programme is delivered); and *Maintenance* (sustainability of the programme). Adoption, implementation, and evaluation of evidence-based practice is likely to continue to be a significant focus in substance abuse research though the translational opportunities for these interventions will certainly vary by organisational context.

Finally, there is a tendency in the literature to bifurcate thinking into substance abuse *prevention* and *intervention* efforts when, in fact, there is in reality a crucial interdependency and progression in and out of these larger categories. It would, perhaps, be more consistent with the human presentation of addiction if formal prevention and intervention programme philosophies and assumptions more closely mirrored the transtheoretical stages of change, where prevention is considered pre- and post-formal intervention. In doing so, greater emphasis on service coordination, follow-up, extended support, and continuing care would naturally be a part of service transactions.

CONCLUSION

Drug and alcohol use disorders pose significant biopsychosocial consequences to individuals, families, and communities. Without primary, secondary, and tertiary intervention efforts, public health risks will remain high. However, empirical work in the substance abuse field offers optimism. There are effective, evidence-based approaches to reduce drug-use initiation, to intervene with targeted groups who have been identified as having a drug or alcohol problem, and to promote healthy individuals, families, and communities. Treatment has been shown to be cost-effective. Specifically, the literature offers several important recommendations for social work: (i) prevention and intervention efforts should be comprehensive and target multiple systems (family, peers, school, community); (ii) prevention efforts should focus on strategically changing drug-related social norms within these systems; (iii) pharmacotherapy, when used, should usually be implemented along with behavioural or psychosocial interventions; (iv) motivational interviewing and other brief interventions can be used effectively in diverse health and human service and institutional settings (e.g., correctional system; physician's offices); and (v) continuing care, social support, and positive recovery–community engagement is critical for maintaining sobriety upon discharge from formal treatment services.

REFERENCES

Ager, R.D., Parquet, R., & Kreutzinger, S. (2008). The Youth Video Project: An innovative programme for substance abuse prevention. *Journal of Social Work Practice in the Addictions*, 8(3), 303–321.

Akerloff, G.A., & Kranton, R.E. (2010). *Identity economics*. Princeton, NJ: Princeton University Press.

Anstiss, T. (2009). Motivational Interviewing in primary care. *Journal of Clinical Psychology in Medical Settings*, 16(1), 87–93.

Apodaca, T.R., & Longabaugh, R. (2009). Mechanisms of change in motivational interviewing: A review and preliminary evaluation of the evidence. *Addiction*, 104(5), 705–715.

Bernstein, J., Bernstein, E., Tassiopoulos, K., Heeran, T., Levenson, S., & Hingson, R. (2005). Brief motivational intervention at a clinic visit reduces cocaine and heroin use. *Drug and Alcohol Dependence*, 77, 49–59.

Bolla, K.I., Eldreth, D.A., London, E.D., Kiel, K.A., Mouratidis, M., Contoreggi, C. Matochik, J.A., Kurian, V., Cadet, J.L., Kimes, A.S., Funderburk, F.R., & Ernst, M. (2003). Orbitofrontal cortex dysfunction in abstinent cocaine abusers performing a decision-making task. *NeuroImage*, 19(3), 1085–1094.

Bowen, S., Witkiewitz, K, Dillworth T.M, Chawla, N., Simpson, T.L, Ostafin, B.D., et al. (2006). Mindfulness meditation and substance use in an incarcerated population. *Psychology of Addictive Behaviors*, 20, 343–347.

Brewin, C.R. (2001). A cognitive neuroscience account of posttraumatic stress disorder and its treatment. *Behaviour Research and Therapy*, 39, 373–393.

Brewin, C.R., Dagleish, T., & Joseph, S. (1996). A dual representation theory of posttraumatic stress disorder. *Psychological Review*, 103(4), 670–686.

Brook, J., & McDonald, T.P. (2007). Evaluating the effects of comprehensive substance abuse intervention on successful reunification. *Research on Social Work Practice*, 17(6), 664–673.

Carroll, K.M. (1998). A cognitive-behavioral approach: Treating cocaine addiction. Rockville, MD: National Institute on Drug Abuse.

Carroll, K.M., Ball, S.A., Martino, S., Nich, C., Babuscio, T.A., Nuro, K. Gordon, M.A., Portnoy, G.A., & Rounsaville, B.J. (2008). Computer-assisted delivery of cognitive-behavioral therapy for addiction: A randomized trial of CBT4CBT. *American Journal of Psychiatry* 165, 881–888.

Carroll, K.M., Martino, S., Ball, S.A., Nich, C., Frankforter, T., Anez, L.M., Paris, M., Suarez-Morales, L., Szapocznik, J., Miller, W.R., Rosa, C., Matthews, J., & Farentinos, C. (2009). A multisite randomized effectiveness trial of motivational enhancement therapy for Spanish-speaking substance users. *Journal of Consulting and Clinical Psychology*, 77(5), 993–999.

Carroll, K.M., & Rounsaville, B.J. (2006). Behavioral therapies. In W.R. Miller & Carroll, K.M. (eds), *Rethinking substance abuse: What the science shows, and what we should do about it*. New York: Guilford Press, pp. 223–319.

Center on Addiction and Substance Abuse (2010). *Behind bars II: Substance abuse and America's prison population*. New York: Columbia University Press.

Collins, S.E., Chawla, N., Hsu, S.H., Grow, J., Otto, J.M., & Marlatt, G.A. (2009). Language-based measures of mindfulness: Initial validity and clinical utility. *Psychology of Addictive Behaviors*, 23(4), 743–749.

Collins, D., Johnson, K., & Becker, B. (2007). A meta-analysis of direct and mediating effects of community coalitions that implemented science based substance abuse prevention interventions. *Substance Use and Misuse*, 42, 985–1007.

Cooper, M. (2002). Alcohol use and risky sexual behavior among college students and youth: Evaluating the evidence. *Journal of Studies on Alcohol*, 14, 101–117.

Ettner, S.L., French, M.T., & Popovici, I. (2010). Heavy drinking and health promotion activities. *Social Science and Medicine*, 71, 134–142.

Farbing, C.A., & Johnson, W.R. (2008). Motivational interviewing in the correctional system. In H. Arkowitz, Westra, H.A., Miller, W.R., & Rollnick, S. (eds), *Motivational interviewing in the treatment of psychological problems.* New York: The Guilford Press, pp. 304–323.

Fein, G., Di Sclafani, V., & Meyerhoff, D.J. (2002). Prefrontal cortical volume reduction associated with frontal cortex function deficit in 6-week abstinent crack-cocaine dependent men. *Drug and Alcohol Dependence, 68,* 87–93.

Galanter, M. (1993a). Network therapy for addiction: A model for office practice. *American Journal of Psychiatry, 150,* 28–36.

Galanter, M. (1993b). *Network therapy for alcohol and drug abuse.* New York: Basic Books.

Galanter, M., Dermatis, H., Keller, D.S., & Trujillo, M. (2002). Network therapy for cocaine abuse: Use of family and peer supports. *American Journal on Addictions, 11,* 161–166.

Galanter, M., & Kleber, H.D. (2008). *Textbook of substance abuse treatment* (4th ed.). Arlington, VA: American Psychiatric Publishing, Inc.

Garland, E., Gaylord, S.A., Boettiger, C.A., & Howard, M.O. (2010). Mindfulness training modifies cognitive, affective, and physiological mechanisms implicated in alcohol dependence: Results of a randomized controlled pilot trial. *Journal of Psychoactive Drugs, 42*(2), 177–192.

Glasgow, R.E. (2006). RE-AIMing research for application: ways to improve evidence for family medicine. *Journal of the American Board of Family Medicine, 19,* 11–19.

Godley, M.D., Coleman-Cowger, V.H., Titus, J.C., Funk, R.R., & Orndorff, M.G. (2010). A randomized controlled trial of telephone continuing care. *Journal of Substance Abuse Treatment, 38*(1), 74–82.

Godley, S.H., Meyers, R.J., Smith, J.E., Karvinen, T., Titus, J.C., Godley, M.D., Dent, G., Passetti, L., & Kelberg, P. (2001, reprinted 2002, 2003, and 2007). *The adolescent community reinforcement approach for adolescent cannabis users, Cannabis Youth Treatment (CYT) Series, Volume 4.* DHHS Pub. No. (SMA) 07-3864. Rockville, MD: Center for Substance Abuse Treatment, Substance Abuse and Mental Health Services Administration.

Goldin, P.R., McRae, K, Ramel, W., & Gross, J.J. (2008). The neural bases of emotional regulation: Reappraisal and suppression of negative emotion. *Biological Psychiatry, 63,* 577–586.

Goodman, A. (2008). Neurobiology of addiction: An integrative review. *Biochemical Pharmacology, 75,* 266–322.

Gossop, M., Marsden, J., Stewart, D., & Kidd, T. (2003). Reduction or cessation of injecting risk behaviours? Treatment outcomes at 1-year follow-up. *Addictive Behaviors, 28*(4), 785–793.

Gruenwald, P.J., Holder, H.D., & Treno, A.J. (2003). Environmental approaches to prevention. In A.W. Graham,. Schultz, T.K., Mayo-Smith, M.F., Ries, R.K., & Wilford B.B. (eds), *Principles of addiction medicine* (3rd ed.). Chevy Chase, MD: American Society of Addiction Medicine, pp. 838–394.

Hawkins, J.D., Brown, E.C., Oesterle, S., Arthur, M.W., Abbott, R.D., & Catalano, R.F. (2008). Early effects of Communities That Care on targeted risks and initiation of delinquent behavior and substance use. *Journal of Adolescent Health, 43,* 15–22.

Hawkins, J.D., Oesterle, S., Brown, E.C., Arthur, M.W., Abbot, R.D., Fagan, A.A., & Catalano, R.F. (2009). Results of a type 2 translational research trial to prevent adolescent drug use and delinquency: A test of Communities That Care. *Archives of Pediatric and Adolescent Medicine, 163*(9), 789–798.

Inciardi, J.A., & Harrison, L.D. (2000). *Harm reduction: National and international perspective.* Thousand Oaks, CA: Sage.

Koob, G.F. (2006). The neurobiology of drug addiction. In W.R. Miller & Carroll, K.M. (eds), *Rethinking substance abuse: What the science shows, and what we should do about it.* New York: Guilford Press, pp. 25–45.

Kraus, D., Smith, G.T., & Ratner, H.H. (1994). Modifying alcohol-related expectancies in grade-school children. *Journal of Studies on Alcohol, 55,* 535–542.

Larimer, M.E., Palmer, R.S., & Marlatt, G.A. (1999). An overview of Marlatt's Cognitive-Behavioral Model. *Alcohol Research and Health, 23*(2), 151–160.

Mancini, M.A., Linhorst, D.M., Broderick, F., & Bayliff, S. (2008). Challenges to implementing the harm reduction approach. *Journal of Social Work Practice in the Addictions, 8*(3), 380–408.

Marlatt, G.A., & Gordon, J.R. (1985). *Relapse prevention: Maintenance strategies in the treatment of addictive behaviors.* New York: Guilford Press.

Marsh, J.C., Ryan, J.P., & Choi, S. (2006). Integrated services for families with multiple problems: Obstacles to family reunification. *Children and Youth Services Review, 28*(9), 1074–1087.

Matto, H.C. (2005). A bio-behavioral model of addiction treatment: Applying dual representation theory to craving management and relapse prevention. *Substance Use and Misuse, 40*(4), 529–541.

Matto, H.C. (2007). An innovative treatment: Stage I Evaluation of a dual processing treatment protocol on self-regulation capacities of chronic substance dependent adults. *Best Practices in Mental Health, 3,* 41–51.

Matto, H.C., Miller, K.A., & Spera, C. (2006). Measuring the influence of social context referents in substance abuse treatment: An instrument validation study. *Journal of Social Work Practice in the Addictions, 6*(3), 13–23.

Matto, H.C., Miller, K.A., & Spera, C. (2007). Examining the relative importance of social context referents in predicting intention to change substance abuse behavior using the EASE. *Addictive Behaviors, 32*(9), 1826–1834.

Matto, H.C. & Spera, C. (2009). Estimating person–environment transactions on intention to change drug using behaviors. *Journal of the American Psychiatric Nurses Association, 15*(3), 182–190.

Matto, H.C., Strolin-Goltzman, J., & Mogro-Wilson, C. (2010). Dual Processing Treatment Modality: An innovative treatment to decrease physiological craving in substance abusers. *Journal of Groups in Addiction and Recovery, 5*(2), 113–123.

McKay, J.R., Carise, D., Dennis, M. L., Dupont, R., Humphreys, K., Kemp, J., Reynolds, D., White, W., Armstrong, R., Chalk, M., Haberle, B., McLellan, T., O'Connor, G., Pakull, B., & Schwarzlose, J. (2009). Extending the benefits of addiction treatment: Practical strategies for continuing care and recovery. *Journal of Substance Abuse Treatment, 36,* 127–130.

Meyers, R.J., Miller, W.R., Smith, J.E., & Tonigan, J.S. (2002). A randomized trial of two methods for engaging treatment-refusing drug users through concerned significant others. *Journal of Consulting and Clinical Psychology, 70*(5), 1182–1185.

Miller, W.R. (2006). Motivational factors in addictive behaviors. In W.R. Miller & Carroll, K.M. (eds), *Rethinking substance abuse: What the science shows, and what we should do about it.* New York: Guilford Press, pp. 134–150.

Miller, W.R., Meyers, R.J., Tonigan, J.S., & Grant, K.A. (2001). Community reinforcement and traditional approaches: Findings of a controlled trial. In R.J. Meyers & Miller, W.R. (eds), *A community reinforcement approach to addiction treatment.* Cambridge: Cambridge University Press. 79–103.

Miller, W.R., & Rollnick, S. (2002). *Motivational interviewing: Preparing people for change.* New York: Guilford Press.

Moe, J., Johnson, J.L., & Wade, W. (2008). Evaluation of the Betty Ford Children's programme. *Journal of Social Work Practice in the Addictions, 8*(4), 464–489.

Moos, R.H. (2006). Social contexts and substance use. In W.R. Miller & Carroll, K.M. (eds), *Rethinking substance abuse: What the science shows, and what we should do about it.* New York: Guilford Press, pp. 182–200.

Mueser, K.T., Drake, R.E., Turner, W., & McGovern, M. (2006). Comborbid substance use disorders and psychiatric disorders. In W.R. Miller & Carroll, K.M. (eds), *Rethinking substance abuse: What the science shows, and what we should do about it.* New York: Guilford Press, pp. 115–133.

Mumola, C.J., & Karberg, J.C. (2006). *Substance abuse and treatment, state and federal prisoners, 2004* (NCJ 213530). Washington, DC: US Department of Justice, Office of Justice Programs.

Najavits, L.M. (2007). Seeking safety: An evidence-based model for substance abuse and trauma/PTSD. In K.A. Witkiewitz & Marlatt, G.A. (eds), *Therapists' guide to evidence-based relapse prevention: Practical resources for the mental health professional.* San Diego: Elsevier Press, pp. 141–167.

Najavits, L.M. (2009). Seeking Safety: An implementation guide. In A. Rubin & Springer, D.W. (eds), *The clinician's guide to evidence-based practice.* Hoboken, NJ: John Wiley.

Najavits, L.M., Rosier, M., Nolan, A.L., & Freeman, M.C. (2007). A new gender-based model for women's recovery from substance abuse: Results of a pilot outcome study. *American Journal of Drug and Alcohol Abuse, 33,* 5–11.

Najavits, L.M., Schmitz, M., Johnson, K.M., Smith, C., North, T., Hamilton, N., Walser, R., Reeder, K., Norman, S., & Wilkins, K. (2009). Seeking Safety therapy for men: Clinical and research experiences. In Katlin, L.J. (ed.), *Men and Addictions.* Hauppauge, NY: Nova Science Publishers.

OECD (2011). *Health at a Glance 2011: OECD Indicators, OECD Publishing.* doi:10.1787/health_glance-2011-en

O'Malley, S.S., & Kosten, T.R. (2006). Pharmacotherapy of addictive disorders. In W.R. Miller & Carroll, K.M. (eds), *Rethinking substance abuse: What the science shows, and what we should do about it.* New York: Guilford Press.

Oviedo-Joekes, E., Guh, D., Brissette, S., Marsh, D.C., Nosyk, B., Krausz, M., Anis, A., & Schechter, M.T. (2010). Double-blind injectable hydromorphine versus diacetylmorphine for the treatment of opioid dependence: A pilot study. *Journal of Substance Abuse Treatment, 38*(4), 408–411.

Polen, M.R., Whitlock, E.P., Wisdom, J.P., Nygren, P., & Bougatsos, C. (2008). *Screening in primary care settings for illicit drug use: Staged systematic review for the U.S. Preventive Services Task Force.* Evidence Synthesis No. 58, Part 1. (Prepared by the Oregon Evidence-based

Practice Center under Contract No. 290-02-0024.) AHRQ Publication No. 08-05108-EF-s. Rockville, MD, Agency for Healthcare Research and Quality, January.

Prochaska, J.O., & DiClemente, C.C. (1983). Stages and processes of self-change in smoking: Toward a more integrative model of change. *Psychotherapy: Theory, Research and Practice, 20*, 161–173.

Proctor, E.K., Landsverk, J., Aarons, G., Chambers, D., Glisson, C., & Mittman, B. (2009). Implementation research in mental health services: An emerging science with conceptual, methodological, and training challenges. *Administration Policy Mental Health, 36*, 24–34.

Project MATCH Research Group (1998). Matching alcoholism treatments to client heterogeneity: Project MATCH three-year drinking outcomes. *Alcoholism: Clinical and Experimental Research, 22*(6), 1300–1311.

Rehm, J., Mathers, C., Popova, S., Thavorncharoensap, M., Teerawattananon, Y., & Patra, J. (2009). Alcohol and global health 1. *Lancet, 373*(9682), 2223–2233.

Roe, S., & Becker, J. (2005). Drug prevention with vulnerable young people: A review. *Drugs: Education, Prevention and Policy, 12*(2), 85–99.

Reifman, A., Watson, W.K., & McCourt, A. (2006). Social networks and college drinking: Probing processes of social influence and selection. *Personality and Social Psychology Bulletin, 32*, 820–832.

Rolfe, A.J., Dalton, S.I., Krishnan, M.A., Orford, J.F., Mehdikhani, M., Cawley, J.V., & Ferrins-Brown, M. (2006). Alcohol, gender, aggression and violence: findings from the Birmingham untreated heavy drinkers project. *Journal of Substance Use, 11*, 343–358.

Rowe, C.L., Liddle, H.A., Greenbaum, P.E., & Henderson, C.E. (2004). Impact of psychiatric comorbidity on treatment of adolescent drug abusers. *Journal of Substance Abuse Treatment, 26*, 129–140.

Rowe, C., Liddle, H.A., McClintic, K., & Quille, T.J. (2002). Integrative treatment development: Multidimensional family therapy for adolescent substance abuse. In F.W. Kaslow & Lebow, J. (eds), *Comprehensive handbook of psychotherapy*. New York: John Wiley & Sons, pp. 133–161.

Ryan, J., Marsh, J. Testa, M., & Louderman, R. (2006). Integrating substance abuse treatment and child welfare services: Findings from the Illinois alcohol and other drug abuse waiver demonstration. *Social Work Research, 30*, 95–107.

Sampl, S., & Kadden, R. (2001). *Motivational enhancement therapy and cognitive behavioral therapy for adolescent cannabis users: 5 sessions, cannabis youth treatment (CYT) series, Volume 1*. Rockville, MD: Center for Substance Abuse Treatment, Substance Abuse and Mental Health Services Administration. BKD384.

Simmons, V.N., Webb, M.S., & Brandon, T.H. (2004). College student smoking: An initial test of an experiential dissonance-enhancing intervention. *Addictive Behaviors, 29*(6), 1129–1136.

Smith, J.E., & Meyers, R.J., (2009). Community reinforcement and family training. In G.L. Fisher & Roget, N.A. (eds), *Encyclopedia of substance abuse prevention, treatment, and recovery*. Thousand Oaks, CA: Sage Publications.

Spera, C., Franklin, K., Uekawa, K., Kunz, J., Szoc, R., Thomas, R., & Cambridge, M. (2010). Reducing drinking among junior enlisted Air Force members in five communities: Early findings of the EUDL Programme's influence on self-reported drinking behaviors. *Journal of Studies on Alcohol and Drugs, 71*(3), 373–383.

Spoth, R., Greenberg, M., & Turrisi, R. (2008). Preventive interventions addressing underage drinking: State of the evidence and steps toward public health impact. *Pediatrics, 121*, Supplement 4, S311–S336.

Spoth, R., Redmond, C., & Shin, C. (2001). Randomized trial of brief family interventions for general populations: adolescent substance use outcomes four years following baseline. *Journal of Consulting and Clinical Psychology, 69*(4), 627–642.

Spoth, R., Randall, G.K., Shin, C., & Redmond, C. (2005). Randomized study of combined universal family and school preventive interventions: patterns of long-term effects on initiation, regular use, and weekly drunkenness. *Psychology of Addictive Behaviors, 19*(4), 372–381.

Spoth, R., Redmond, C., Shin, C., & Azevedo, K. (2004). Brief family intervention effects on adolescent substance initiation: school level curvilinear growth curve analyses six years following baseline. *Journal of Consulting and Clinical Psychology, 72*(3), 535–542.

Strolin-Goltzman, J., Matto, H., & Mogro-Wilson, C. (2007). A comparative analysis of a dual processing substance abuse treatment intervention: Implications for the development of Latino-specific interventions. *Hispanic Health Care International, 5*(4), 162–168.

Tanabe, J., Tregellas, J.R., Dalwani, M., Thompson, L., Owens, E., Crowley, T., & Banich, M. (2009). Medial orbitofrontal cortex gray matter is reduced in abstinent substance-dependent individuals. *Biological Psychiatry, 65*, 160–164.

Taxman, F.S., Perdoni, M., & Harrison, L. (2007). Treatment for adult offenders: A review of the state of the state. *Journal of Substance Abuse Treatment, 32*(3), 239–254.

Uhl, G.R., Drgon, T., Johnson, C., Fatusin, O.O., Liu, Q-R., Contoreggi, C., Li, C-Y., Buck, K., & Crabbe, J. (2008). 'Higher order' addiction molecular genetics: Convergent data from genome-wide associations in humans and mice. *Biochemical Pharmacology, 75,* 98–111.

VanderWaal, C.J., Taxman, F.S., & Gurka-Ndanyi, M.A. (2008). Reforming drug treatment services to offenders: Cross-system collaboration, integrated policies, and a seamless continuum of care model. *Journal of Social Work Practice in the Addictions, 8*(1), 127–153.

Weaver, C.M., Trafton, J.A., Walser, R.D., & Kimerling, R.E. (2007). Pilot test of seeking safety with male veterans. *Psychiatric Services, 58,* 1012–1013.

White, W.L. (2009). The mobilization of community resources to support long-term addiction recovery. *Journal of Substance Abuse Treatment, 36,* 146–158.

Wiers, R.W., & Stacy, A.W. (2006). *Handbook of implicit cognition and addition.* Thousand Oaks, CA: Sage.

World Health Organization (WHO) (2009a). *Alcohol and injuries: Emergency department studies in an international perspective.* Geneva: WHO.

World Health Organization (WHO) (2009b). *Global health risks: Mortality and burden of disease attributable to selected major risks.* Geneva: WHO.

Zgierska, A., Rabago, D., Zuelsdorff, M., Coe, C., Miller, M., & Fleming, M. (2008). Mindfulness meditation for alcohol relapse prevention: A feasibility pilot study. *Journal of Addiction Medicine, 2*(3), 165–173.

38

Criminal and Juvenile Justice

Nicola Carr

Social work in the criminal justice system with adults and young people is distinct from other forms of social work for a number of significant reasons. With this type of frontline practice, social work is mandated by courts of law. In other words, people are made subject to court orders requiring them to work with a social worker or probation officer for a set period. While consent is typically sought by the court before making an order, for the most part, clients of social workers in the criminal justice system have an involuntary status (Trotter, 1999).

Social work within the criminal justice system usually takes place under the auspices of justice rather than welfare or health agencies. For example, in England and Wales social workers in the criminal justice system are employed by *Probation Trusts*. This is reflected similarly in the job titles and, increasingly, the qualifications of social workers in the criminal justice system. In the Anglo-American and Australian spheres, the term 'Probation Officer' is used to denote the separate and distinct role of social workers within these systems.

The origins of social work in the criminal justice system are usually traced back to the late Victorian period and what were termed 'court work missionaries' (Nellis, 2004; Vanstone, 2004) or volunteers with a religious mission to 'save the souls' of those before the courts. Typically, the work of the early court work missionaries involved an undertaking to a member of the judiciary to work with a person who appeared frequently before the courts to help them to desist from crime and thereby avoid further court appearances. Various historical accounts note such work focused on temperance and welfare assistance (Fulton & Parkhill, 2009; Smith & Vanstone, 2002). In the context of the UK, this work was eventually formalised through the introduction of the *Probation of Offender's Act* (1907), which set out the role of the 'Probation Officer' to 'advise, assist and befriend' those placed under his or her supervision by the Courts.

JUSTICE BASED AND WELFARE ORIENTED?

This early model of probation practice was replicated a range of jurisdictions. Vanstone (2008) notes probation was introduced into countries in North and South America,

Europe, Africa, and Asia between 1878 and 1920. The 'welfarist' orientation of such work remains a key but contested tenet of practice. Generally, however, social work in the criminal justice system takes place at the juncture between the 'welfare' and 'justice' systems, and the practice of probation, at least in the Anglo-American sphere, has been influenced by the shifting sands of these paradigms. This is illustrated by changes in probation practice in a number of contexts. In England and Wales, for example, since the 1990s, there has been an evident shift in the discourse surrounding probation practice with a repositioning of probation as a form of 'community punishment' as opposed to its previous construction as an 'alternative to punishment' (Brownlee, 1998).

Attendant on these changes has been a shift in probation's focus from 'advising, assisting and befriending' individuals towards an emphasis on 'protecting the public'. *Public protection* is variously conceived as the panoply of strategies employed to assess, manage, and intervene to manage risk posed by individual *offenders*. Across numerous contexts, 'public protection' is situated as the top priority of probation practice, emphasising a shift in orientation away from probationers as clients towards the 'public' as the ultimate clients or consumers of the service (Smith & Vanstone, 2002).

Such changes, many commentators have argued, are reflected in the increased punitiveness of criminal justice rhetoric and policies. Specifically, in the Anglo-American sphere (Garland, 1985, 2001), this shift is visible in terminology within probation practice towards the routine use of the term 'offender' to describe clients of probation. Another has been the change in the requirements, in some countries, for probation officers to be qualified social workers. For example, England and Wales introduced a separate training route for probation officers in the 1990s to reflect the shift in policy from a welfarist to a justice-oriented service (Burke, 2010; Knight & Ward, 2001). A similar requirement does not exist in Australia, however, where criminal justice work is not a core component of mainstream social work practice.

While punitive trends are by no means uniform, one of the most tangible effects has been the exponential rise in prison populations in the Anglo-American sphere (Garland, 2001; Simon, 2007; Wacquant, 2001). One of the notable aspects of increased levels of incarceration has been the disproportionate levels of imprisonment among minority populations. For instance, in the USA, Simon (2007) reported, based on the current prison population figures, one in three Black men and one in seven Hispanic men would go to prison in their lifetime. Similarly, 'disproportionate minority contact' has been observed and gained critical attention in other countries, including the UK (Bhui, 2009; Feilzer & Hood, 2004) and countries with Indigenous minorities, such as Canada (La Prairie, 1996) and Australia (Cuneen, 2008). Wacquant (2001) pillories the US 'justice by race' policy, which criminologists tactfully refer to as 'racial disproportionality'. He shows in no uncertain terms how, in the USA, crime and poverty are intimately linked in a sustained strategy of 'imprisoning the poor', with young Black people prime targets of this criminalisation strategy. The rise in imprisonment often goes hand in hand with a deterioration in the labour market:

> More than a third of Blacks aged between 20 and 29 years are either in prison, under the authority of a judge responsible for the execution of sentences, or awaiting trial. In the big cities, the figure is substantially higher than 50%, and in some places, in the heart of the ghetto, in excess of 80% (Wacquant, 2001, p. 120).

As part of this 'prison industrial complex', Wacquant (2001) shows the rate of incarceration for African-Americans has reached levels unknown in any other society and remarkably is higher now than the 'total incarceration rate in the Soviet Union at the zenith of the Gulag and in South Africa at the height of the anti-apartheid struggle' (p. 97). For Wacquant (2001), the prison is a surrogate ghetto with

African-Americans now living 'in the first prison society of history' (p. 121).

The inter-relationships between racism and other structural inequalities has been long observed and further critical analyses note those who come into contact with and are processed through the criminal justice system tend overwhelmingly to be from disadvantaged socioeconomic backgrounds (Scraton & McCullogh, 2008; Simon, 2007). All these factors have implications for the role of social work within the criminal justice system, with both adult and juvenile populations. This is particularly pertinent to strategies advocating an 'antiracist practice' perspective. However, as will be shown, these issues are drawn increasingly into focus in the context of an individualised, colour-blind, risk-focussed orthodoxy which has gained dominance in practice over a number of years (Hong Chui & Nellis, 2003; Mair, 2004).

The shift from welfarism to a more justice-oriented approach within probation practice is linked with broader social, political, and cultural trends. Obviously this varies according to context, but in the Anglo-American sphere this has been linked to an increased politicisation of *crime* and *justice* with a focus on punitive sanctions rather than on rehabilitation or welfare provision (Bottoms, 1995; Garland, 2001). More broadly, the efficacy of rehabilitative interventions in reducing recidivism has faced a number of sustained critiques leading to a broad pessimism about *rehabilitation* (Miller, 1989).

Sentencing options and anti-oppressive practice

The Courts have a range of sentencing options with clients on probation representing only a proportion of all those sentenced before the courts. The largest numbers of those under probation supervision are people sentenced to community orders, such as a Probation or Community Service Order involving unpaid work in the community. The second largest population of probation clients usually comprises people leaving prison, who are required to adhere to licence conditions following release. In England and Wales, for example, of the total number of people under probation supervision in 2009, approximately two-thirds were being supervised following a court sentence; the remaining third were subject to post-custodial supervision on licence (Ministry of Justice, 2010).

Licence conditions typically include a stipulation on where the ex-prisoner can live and the requirement they attend regular meetings with a probation officer. As community sentences are legal sanctions and release from prison on parole is conditional, the failure of a client to attend appointments or comply with the instructions of the probation officer can lead to the person being returned to court through breach proceedings or a recall to prison in the case of prisoners released on licence. This aspect of probation practice illustrates most vividly the nonvoluntary element of the intervention and more so than ever within probation there has been an increased emphasis on compliance and enforcement in an attempt to persuade sentencers and the public that probation is a 'tough' sentencing option and constitutes 'punishment' in the community. Such changes in emphasis are arguably further illustrative of the changing nature of probation practice (Nicholls, 2007).

Reflecting the constituency of people who are processed through the criminal justice system, the majority of those placed under the supervision of the Probation Service are male and aged between 18 and 40. This is borne out by data from the National Offender Management Service (NOMS) in London which records that approximately 74% of those under the supervision of the probation service are in this age group (NOMS, 2010). In some contexts, the probation service works with young people under the age of 18. For example, a range of community sentences can be applied to those aged 16 and over. However, increasingly there has been a division between probation practice with adults (over 18) and young people under the age of 18, evident in the development of separate justice administrative systems for this population. In England and Wales, for example, a separate agency, the *Youth Justice Board* (YJB), is responsible for policy and funding of this area. The YJB was responsible for overseeing the youth justice system in England and Wales. It aimed to prevent offending and re-offending by children and young people under the age of 18, and to ensure custody for them was safe, secure, and addressed the causes of their offending behaviour. In 2000, the commissioning of custodial provision for children and young people was transferred to the Board from the Home Office with two-thirds of the YJB's budget going into the cost of custody. In late 2010, the UK government announced that the YJB was to be scrapped as part of the 'quango cuts' policy with the influential Howard League describing 'the Board's track record as having been " pretty poor", and accusing it of failing to protect children in custody and failing to match its stated aim of reducing the unnecessary use of imprisonment' (http://www.guardian.co.uk/society/2010/oct/14/quango-youth-justice-board-scrapped). The separate and distinct sphere of youth justice is discussed later in this chapter.

Social work practice within the criminal justice system is, therefore, distinct from other areas of social work, given its particular focus and the predominance of male, and in the USA, often Black clients. This leads to specific challenges in terms of ensuring practice is tailored towards individual need, in particular when clients do not fit this profile. For example, the distinct needs of women in the criminal justice system have been highlighted in a range of work and the responsiveness of probation practice to diverse needs has been challenged (Agllias, 2004; Shaw & Hannah-Moffatt, 2004).

Within the wider context of anti-oppressive practice, specific challenges arise for social work practitioners within the criminal justice system, namely, how to consider the individual in an holistic manner that gives due recognition to context and need while recognising that offending occurs within a wider inequitable sociostructural context (Hannah-Moffat, 2008) (see Chapter 21). Such contextualisation becomes more difficult in increasingly individualised, risk-aversive practice environments with a focus on individual responsibility and emphases on the cognition of the 'offender' rather than on wider structural factors (Carlen, 2008). The following section deals with some of the core components of social work practice within the criminal justice system, including the centrality of risk assessment as the means through which interventions are targeted. The evidence base for interventions with 'risk' as an overarching framework is critically analysed, and examples of innovative practice and a move beyond the risk paradigm are explored.

RISK-BASED APPROACHES

Pre-sentence reports and risk assessment

In common with other areas of social work practice, assessment is one of the core tasks of social work practitioners within the criminal justice system. The most common forms of assessment are initiated following a request from the court for an assessment of the defendant following conviction and prior to sentencing. Such reports are referred to as *pre-sentence reports* (PSRs) and their purpose is to provide a background context in relation to the defendant and the nature of their offending in order to assist the court in arriving at a sentencing decision. Another important area of assessment is for sentenced prisoners for whom release on parole (i.e., conditional release prior to the end of their prison sentence) is being considered. Such reports are normally referred to as *parole reports*.

Usually the format of a PSR is determined by regulations and service standards. Most reports contain an analysis of the offence or offences for which the defendant has been convicted. An offence analysis will contain information *inter alia* on the individual's account of the offence and its circumstances resulting from an exploration of precipitating factors and any particular characteristics of an offence, for example, whether a specific victim was targeted or not. The report will also include an analysis of patterns of offending, where appropriate. So, for example, such an assessment would note whether alcohol or drug misuse was a factor in offending or, in the case of violent offences, whether there had been an increase in severity of offending over time. It provides background information not only on the crime but also on the defendant. Such information should include the person's living circumstances, employment, level of education and training, and network of social supports. Reflecting a wider trend within social work and in the criminal justice system in particular, the assessment of risk is a critical component of the overall assessment (Bullock, 2011; Kemshall, 2010; Robinson, 2003; Webb, 2006). Within social work in the criminal justice system, there are two main domains in which risk is assessed: risk of re-offending and risk of harm. These components relate to the gravity or seriousness of any future offending behaviour and the likelihood of such behaviour occurring.

The PSR concludes with a recommendation to the court as to the most appropriate sentence, having taken into consideration the defendant's offending history, the circumstances of the presenting offence, and the assessment of risk of re-offending and harm. The sentence and programme of work proposed in any report should be consistent with the assessment of the level of risk posed. Increasingly, specific risk assessment tools and frameworks are used to structure and guide assessment.

A range of risk assessment frameworks combining elements of actuarial and clinical risk assessment have been developed and are used in probation practice. An actuarial assessment of risk is a statistically derived measure based on a range of factors, such as age at first conviction. A clinical assessment of risk is based on the practitioner's assessment typically derived from interviewing, observation, professional judgement, and knowledge (Beech et al., 2003; Kemshall, 2003; Robinson, 2003). Such assessment tools are used by measuring a range of *risk factors* at the assessment stage to assist in preparing a PSR. Dependent on the sentence received, these tools are also intended to guide the areas of intervention and, through re-measurement, to collect data on change over time.

Analysis of what constitutes a *risk factor* in relation to further offending is based on a body of work exploring the relationships between a range of variables and involvement in offending (e.g., Andrews et al., 2006; Farrington, 1994, 2007). A range of risk factors associated with offending have been identified in a wide body of literature (e.g., Farrington, 2007; Kemshall, 2003; McGuire & Priestly, 1985). Typical examples of predictive risk factors for re-offending include individual characteristics, such as low intelligence, hyperactivity, impulsivity, negative attitudes, and antisocial peer friendships. Further risk factors have been located in family characteristics, such as a history of family involvement in criminal behaviour, and educational experiences, such as low achievement, beginning in primary school. Furthermore, a prior history of offending indicates a high risk of possible re-offending (Andrews et al., 2006; Farrington, 1994, 2007).

Risk assessments involve an analysis of *static* and *dynamic* risk factors. A static risk factor cannot be changed, such as age at first conviction. A dynamic risk factor is amenable to change, for example, substance misuse. Dynamic risk factors are further classified as *stable* or *acute*, with the latter being more subject to fluctuation. Heightened emotional distress is an example of an acute dynamic risk factor (Beech et al., 2003).

Examples of risk assessment tools in probation practice include: the Level of Service

Inventory-Revised (L-SIR; Andrews & Bonta, 1995) used by criminal justice social workers in Scotland and by practitioners in parts of Australia, New Zealand, and the USA; the Assessment, Case Management, and Evaluation (ACE) tool used by the Probation Board for Northern Ireland; and the Offender Assessment System (OASys) used by the Probation Service in England and Wales.

As risk assessments are predicitions of future behaviour, they may be incorrect. A *false positive* (i.e., predicting a person poses a risk of re-offending and/or harm when they do not) or a *false negative* (predicting a person does not pose a risk when they do) are possible incorrect outcomes and raise ethical issues regarding the use of actuarial measures (Kemshall, 2003). The use of assessment tools in probation practice has been considered from a range of perspectives. In research with practitioners, some point to the benefits of using a standardised tool that provides a common assessment framework (Fitzgibbon, 2008; Mair et al., 2006). The use of structured tools also enables practitioners to make defensible, evidence-based assessments (Gottfredson & Tonry, 1987; Kemshall, 2003). However, such tools have also been critiqued for their overly prescriptive nature, their 'tick-box' approach, and the amount of time required to complete them (Mair et al., 2006).

EFFECTIVE PRACTICE APPROACHES

Evidence-based practice

The use of such assessment tools in probation practice is consistent with the emphasis placed on *evidence-based practice*, which has gained increasing currency from the 1990s onwards and is usually taken to refer to a body of research demonstrating effectiveness in reducing offending, also referred to in the literature as 'what works?' (Ward & Maruna, 2007; see Chapter 26). There has been much debate within the probation services and further afield about exactly 'what does work' to reduce or stop people from offending, and there have been wide-scale policy and practice developments across several countries, including the UK, Canada, and Australia, to demonstrate effectiveness in reducing offending (Mair, 2004).

One of the key drivers for *effective, evidence-based practice* has been the increased emphasis placed on 'public protection' as a key function of probation work from the 1990s onwards. Along with greater expectations regarding the role of the probation service, there has been a shift from the original ethos of 'advising, assisting, and befriending' towards a *risk management* approach. Individuals subject to probation are assessed as to whether they are likely to re-offend and whether their offending is likely to cause harm (assessed as its seriousness). This then determines the manner in which individual offenders are 'managed' and the type of interventions they receive.

One of the key tenets of *effective practice* elucidated in a range of literature is that interventions should be targeted at the level of risk posed to the public. In the simplest terms, the higher the assessed risk of re-offending and harm, the greater the level of intervention required or the more severe the sentencing option. This overarching orthodoxy is referred to as the *Risk–Need–Responsivity* (RNR) model of offender rehabilitation (Ward & Maruna, 2007).

Risk–need–responsivity

The RNR model is predicated on the understanding that interventions should be based on the assessed level of risk and targeted at *criminogenic needs*, or the factors related to offending. For example, if alcohol misuse was a factor in someone's offending, then it would be considered a *criminogenic need*. Interventions are deemed to be most effective (with effectiveness demonstrated in a reduction in recidivism) when targeted at level of risk and criminogenic needs.

The *responsivity* component of this model refers to the interaction of the individual with the environment in which rehabilitation occurs. This principle means interventions to address offending behaviour should be targeted to the individual's learning style, level of motivation, and personal and social circumstances. In an overview of the RNR model, Ward and Maruna (2007) helpfully distinguished between *specific responsivity* and *general responsivity*. Specific responsivity refers to the individual characteristics of the offender, such as those already outlined, and general responsivity refers to the *mode* of treatment, for example, the particular form in which a programme is delivered and the underlying evidence base for this. The components of this model are shown in Figure 38.1.

Cognitive behavioural programmes

From the 1990s onwards, an emergent body of research indicated cognitive behavioural approaches had demonstrated effectiveness in reducing offending. The 'what works' findings gained increasing currency following a series of conferences promoting their results and, what has been characterised as, the 'persuasive advocacy of experts' (Ward & Maruna, 2007). In the UK, the Home Office published a review of *What Works* in 1997 (Vennard et al., 1997) and produced a practice guide entitled *Evidence Based Practice: A Guide to Effective Practice* in the following year (Chapman & Hough, 1998). This was followed by wide-scale investment in these methodologies and approaches, including investment in the training of staff in groupwork delivery and the development of 'accredited programmes'.

In addition to the principles outlined in the RNR model, the 'what works' literature also explores the types of interventions deemed to be effective in reducing offending, such as cognitive behavioural approaches (McGuire, 2005), which integrate aspects of behavioural and cognitive psychology, including learning theory (see Chapter 9). These approaches explore the way in which thoughts (cognition) and feelings (emotion) interact with behaviour. The basic premise of cognitive behavioural interventions is that aspects of cognition – negative thought patterns or maladaptive problem-solving skills – influence affect (feelings) and, therefore, behaviour

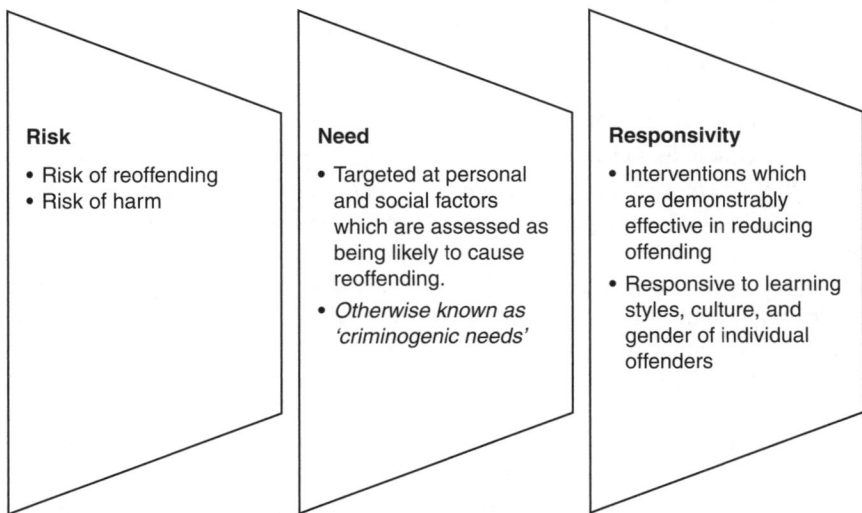

Figure 38.1 Risk-Need-Responsivity Model

(McGuire, 2005). Some of the literature on effective practice found delivering programmes in group settings produced positive results, that is, a reduction in offending behaviour. One example of an offending behaviour modification programme based on these principles is *Think First*, which targets 'general offending' – involving offences such as theft, burglary, and damage to property. *Think First* focuses on the development of behaviour management skills, such as problem-solving, raising victim awareness, and resisting pressures to offend, as the key to behaviour change. These skills are learnt, practised, and reinforced throughout the programme, which is delivered over four pre-group sessions, followed by 22 groupwork sessions (each lasting for approximately two hours). This is then followed by seven individual post-group sessions (McGuire, 2005). A person with an offending history who is considered to have a medium to high risk of re-offending is eligible for referral to this programme and a requirement to attend a programme can be specified by a Court and included as a condition of a community order.

While the early evidence base of the *What Works?* initiative has been the subject of some critique (Farrant, 2006; Israel & Hong Chui, 2006; Mair, 2004), one of the more recent systematic reviews conducted under the auspices of the Campbell Collaboration has demonstrated the effectiveness of *some* cognitive behavioural interventions targeted at offending (Lipsey et al., 2007). Lipsey et al.'s review, which included 58 eligible studies (evaluating 'generalized offending programmes'), identified a number of factors which influenced the level of *effect* of treatment including: (i) the prior risk categorisation of the participant; (ii) how well the treatment was implemented; and (iii) the presence or absence of certain treatment elements (e.g., the presence of an anger management component to the programme was associated with larger treatment effects). Perhaps counter-intuitively, programmes that included a 'victim-impact' component had lower treatment effects (Lipsey et al., 2007). However, this review also highlights the highly specific conditions in which some programmes can demonstrate effectiveness. For example, the study sample included programmes which were implemented as part of a research process in the first instance. In other words the transferability of programmes from the research environment to practice remains unknown (Lipsey et al., 2007).

Increasingly, there has been a great deal of attention paid to specific aspects of probation practice, such as risk and effectiveness and, in many areas, this has led to practice becoming much more prescribed. Risk- and effectiveness-based approaches have led to highly regulated practices, such as the use of pre-scribed cognitive behavioural groupwork programmes. The influences of these changes have been experienced widely in practice, but they have not been universally accepted. In fact, a range of literature points to critiques of these orthodoxies (see later).

QUESTIONING ORTHODOXY?

Problems with the evidence base

Despite appearances, *risk assessment* in the field of criminal justice is by no means an exact science. Predicting the future is an uncertain activity. The assessment of risk is based on a range of factors derived from research evidence on the relationship between offending behaviour and the sociodemographic profiling of offenders. On the basis of this evidence, high-risk factors for offending are low intelligence, poor educational attainment, lack of empathy, impulsiveness, poor social and cognitive skills, and family disruption (Farrington, 2007). However, while these factors may be present in a population of people who have become involved in offending, it is difficult to predict prospectively which people with these characteristics or experiences will engage in offending behaviour. In other words, risk assessment tends to work through retrospective rather than prospective analysis. This suggests using 'epidemiological risk factors' to predict future offending is necessarily fraught as some people with a range of risk factors *may* commit offences while others may not.

Importantly for anti-oppressive social work practice, it risks targeting and stigmatising specific populations deemed to be at greater risk of offending. As a result, some argue that risk assessment tools used within the criminal justice system are inherently biased against minorities (Lewis, 2009; Hannah-Moffat, 1999). At the same time, there is a lack of research on *resilience* and *protective* factors mitigating risk (Farrington, 2007). Finally, the ethical dimension of conceiving of people as 'risk' subjects raises questions regarding the purposiveness of interventions (Ward & Maruna, 2007).

Criminogenic need

The RNR model employs a narrow concept of 'need', specifically, *criminogenic need* or factors associated with the risk of re-offending. Thus, the distinction between 'risk' and 'need' within this model is hard to discern and *criminogenic needs* and *dynamic risk factors* are often conflated (Ward & Maruna, 2007). The RNR rehabilitation model ties intervention effectiveness inextricably to *criminogenic need* rather than a holistic assessment of individual, family, group, or community needs as related not only to personal but also environmental and structural factors. These wider *non-criminogenic* needs are deemed to be unrelated to individual offending behaviour.

Ward and Maruna (2007) observe a number of difficulties with this approach. First, the failure to meet wider needs will influence a person's motivation to engage in change to address the reasons or factors that brought them into contact with the probation service in the first place and may adversely affect a person's ability to engage effectively. Second, the location of the problem within the *individual* ignores the wider structural context and the social embeddedness of offending behaviour. Thirdly, the 'what works' agenda has led to an over-reliance on cognitive behavioural methods (Bhui & Buchanan, 2004; Kendall, 2004) and an overly prescribed approach to practice with a lack of attention paid to the importance of the practitioner–client relationship in affecting change (Bhui, 2001; Burnett & McNeill, 2005).

IMPLICATIONS FOR SOCIAL WORK PRACTICE

Relationship-based practice

For many years, the relationship between the person on probation and their probation officer, formed through individual casework, has been the cornerstone of practice. As discussed above, over the last decades there has been a move towards 'evidence-based practice' and a more managerial approach to working with offenders. This has led some commentators to argue the client–worker 'relationship' has become lost or marginalised in probation work (Burnett & McNeill, 2005). However, research on desistance from crime – or the *processes by which people come to stop or refrain from further offending* – point to the continued importance of the relationship between the probation officer and probationer in supporting and motivating desistance from offending (Burnett & McNeill, 2005; Rex, 1999):

> Because desistance is about the subjective meaning of age, maturation, social bonds, life events and identities for individuals, a desistance-focussed perspective in practice fundamentally requires recognition of diversity and heterogeneity in people's pathways to desistance (Weaver & McNeill, 2007, p. 91).

Maruna et al. (2004) distinguish between *primary* and *secondary* desistance: *primary desistance* refers to a desistance from offending and *secondary desistance* refers to a change in self-identity. The distinction recognises the importance of changes in self-identity in the move towards a cessation of offending. This suggests desistance is an ongoing process rather than a stable state or single event. Research shows a range of factors are important in promoting desistance, including maturation, life transitions, the development of positive social bonds, and changes in subjective narratives and personal attitudes (McNeill, 2003).

Ways to support desistance in probation practice have gained increasing attention in recent years highlighting some key components (McNeill, 2006; Rex, 1999), such as the significance of the relationship between the probation officer and probationer in promoting change (Rex, 1999) and the importance of strengths- and assets-based approaches (Farrall, 2002; McNeill, 2006; see Chapter 11). One example of the latter is the *Good Lives (Rehabilitation) Model* (Ward & Maruna, 2007), which sees offending as an illegitimate means to obtain specific goals or goods. The focus of the rehabilitative approach, therefore, should be to assist individuals to achieve these goals or goods through legitimate means. Addressing and leveraging motivation to change is central to this approach. Focusing on access to the means for achieving desired goals, rather than risk alone, is seen as a prime motivator that also enhances likelihood of engagement. The development of the evidence base to support the *Goods Lives Model* remains a work-in-progress (Ward & Maruna, 2007). However, the resurgence of strengths-based approaches to practice points to some cause for optimism, not least because of its resonance with social work practice more broadly.

Social work in juvenile justice

The range and type of social work practice with young people in the juvenile justice system is clearly determined by the nature, structure, and intersection of the criminal justice and welfare systems. Traditionally, approaches towards young offenders have been characterised as 'welfare' or 'justice' oriented, or more commonly a mix of both. Indeed, in a comparative analysis of the youth justice system, Muncie (2006) argues the rationale for youth justice often oscillates between or is an amalgamation of sometimes contradictory principles. This is particularly evident when young people become involved in offending also present with a range of welfare and child protection concerns, specifically child protection, or justice, are sometimes by no means straightforward. Furthermore, sometimes a decision must be made whether a young offender is to be treated within the juvenile or criminal justice system and this usually depends on the severity of the crime. A key determining factor as to whether a young offender is treated within the justice system is the age at which the young person is deemed to assume *criminal responsibility*.

The age of criminal responsibility is reflective of the historical origins of the legal system and the manner in which 'children' and 'childhood' are viewed by societies (Muncie & Goldson, 2006). Therefore, it varies widely from country to country. For example, in Belgium the age of criminal responsibility is 18 years (Put & Walgrave, 2006), while in England it is 10 years (Muncie & Goldson, 2006).

Besides the age of criminal responsibility, the type of justice system is also relevant. In many countries, separate 'youth justice systems' aim to recognise that, while children and young people may be legally responsible for a crime as reflected in the age of criminal responsibility, the type of intervention required differs from that for adults who have transgressed the law. Therefore, youth justice systems tend to combine aspects of a welfare-oriented approach with a justice or court-mandated response (Whyte, 2009).

Part of the rationale for a different approach is the recognition that children and young people who become involved in crime, also have welfare needs and may also be the subject of child protection concerns. Secondly, longitudinal data from a range of sources on patterns of offending suggest most people 'grow out' of petty crime and one of the most effective means of preventing further offending is to divert young people from formal processing in the criminal justice system in the first instance (McAra & McVie, 2007; Muncie, 2009). Therefore, many systems place an emphasis on strategies of prevention, diversion, and early intervention (Whyte, 2009).

Critically, however, the manner in which such diversionary or preventative strategies are implemented is crucial. Drawing on findings from a prospective longitudinal study on youth offending (the *Edinburgh Study of Youth Transitions and Crime*), McAra and McVie (2007) concluded reductions in offending are linked to 'minimal intervention and maximum diversion' (p. 315). These authors found *diversion* from involvement in, rather than *processing through*, the criminal justice system was more closely associated with desistance from future offending.

Increasingly, however, some commentators argue social work practice in juvenile justice, as discussed in the earlier section on the adult system, has become premised on the notion of 'risk' rather than 'need' (Goldson, 2000b). Critiques of the *risk factor prevention paradigm* point to a number of difficulties with the associated evidence base used to underpin prevention and early intervention programmes (Case, 2006; Haines & Case, 2008; Webster et al., 2006). One of the key areas of criticism relates to the imputation of causality – while a range of *factors* may associated with offending, these are often correlates of offending rather than causal factors. (Haines & Case, 2008). Available evidence also suggests that clusters of risk factors and their inter-relationships are likely to be more important than individual factors, and that several factors are likely to overlap, for example, poor school attendance may be linked to poor parental supervision, which may in turn be associated with low educational attainment (O'Mahony, 2009).

Several authors have also argued that the construction of *risk factors* in respect of offending, such as poor school attendance, limited parental supervision, and low educational attainment, should instead be interpreted as indicators of need (Scraton & Haydon, 2002). The cumulative effects of viewing children through the lens of 'risk' and 'youth justice' have a number of consequences. One is of net widening, whereby young people deemed to be 'at risk' of future offending are channelled into a justice system, which, paradoxically, seeks to divert young people from this system in the first instance. Over time, a number of studies have highlighted the negative effects for young people of involvement with the criminal justice system, including a range of poor outcomes.

Yet, in many countries the range of interventions directed towards young people in a criminal justice context is relatively far-reaching and progresses along a continuum. This continuum comprises early intervention programmes, ostensibly targeted towards young people at risk of offending or, in some cases, below the age of criminal responsibility, through to direct interventions sanctioned through the criminal justice system, including court-directed supervision. It is also notable, in some contexts the numbers of young people in custody has increased in line with the broader trends evident within the adult criminal justice system. The youth custody population in England and Wales is one prominent example; here, the number of children and young people in custody rose markedly in the 1990s and 2000s (Morgan, 2010). In 2002 United Nations data recorded that England and Wales had a rate of custodial detention for under 18s of 18.26 for every 100,000 of its population. The USA detained almost double this figure (38.40 per 100,000). This contrasted with European countries such as Denmark with a rate of 0.11 per 100,000 (Muncie, 2005).

As in the adult criminal justice system, the direction of intervention in the youth justice system is governed by risk. Some authors have characterised the merging of approaches as one of the 'adulteration' of juvenile justice (Muncie, 2005). Indeed, this is evidenced also in similarities of approaches in practice, including the application of risk assessment frameworks, such as ONSET (used by the Youth Justice Board in England and Wales to assess risk factors for early intervention) and ASSET (used for young people who come into contact with the criminal justice system) (Baker, 2008). In many cases also, the range of interventions applicable to young people, in terms of court-ordered supervision, while bearing different names, demonstrate a striking similarity to adult orders. In fact, some community-based sanctions available for young people are more intensive than anything similar for adults. Examples of this are the *intensive supervision and surveillance programmes*, which, in some contexts, require a young person to engage in supervised activities, observe curfews, and comply with the directions of the youth justice worker. Part of the stated rationale for such intensive and intrusive programmes is they should be directed towards young people involved in frequent offending (Gray et al., 2005). However, evidence also suggests the imposition of certain sentences on young people is used as a means to address welfare needs that could or should have been met within the welfare system (Goldson, 2000; Muncie, 2009).

In some jurisdictions, (e.g., New Zealand and Northern Ireland) restorative justice approaches are used for young people within the criminal justice system. Such approaches are premised on the understanding that crime causes harm and restoration should focus on repairing it (Zehr, 1990). A range of literature on restorative justice situates such approaches as the corollary to the more commonplace retributive model of justice. Where restorative justice operates, its incorporation within formal criminal justice systems differs from country to country (Doherty, 2010). However, the basic principles involve a facilitated meeting between the perpetrator of a crime and the victim – or a representative of the victim, where the emphasis is on 'making good' the harm caused. The manner in which this restoration occurs is dependent on the process. In some instances, for example, it may involve an apology or a commitment to undertake unpaid community work.

The use of restorative approaches within the criminal justice system broadly, and within youth justice systems in particular, has been the subject of positive endorsement, particularly when juxtaposed against the retributive justice model (Daly, 2002; Morris, 2002). However, a note of caution is voiced by some observers who argue the question of restoration does not adequately address some of the underlying structural issues causing young people to engage in offending behaviour.

Rights-based approaches

While there is undoubtedly evidence of *adulteration* of aspects of youth justice systems and practice, one of the key principles underpinning the rationale for separate justice systems for young people in various forms is recognition of the United Convention of the Rights of the Child (UNCRC), wherein a young person under 18 should be considered a child. The UNCRC is a universally ratified document and, in addition to the main convention, there are a number of nonbinding treaties pertaining specifically to juvenile justice. These include standards on the 'Minimum Rules for the Administration of Juvenile Justice' (1985), guidelines on the prevention of delinquency, and a set of rules relating to children who are deprived of their liberty. The utility of rights-based approaches to young people involved in youth justice systems has been recognised (e.g., Scraton & Haydon, 2002). This is underlined particularly under Article 3 of the UNCRC, which states: 'in all actions concerning children, the best interest of the child shall be a primary consideration'. A range of commentary suggests that this approach would be in keeping with the value base of social work practice in respect of young people, in general, and for those who come into difficulties, in particular (Haydon & Scraton, 2000; Goldson & Muncie, 2006; Kilkelly, 2008).

CONCLUSION

In a study on the history of rehabilitation, Garland (2001) documented a number of trends in attitudes in the UK and USA towards crime, criminal justice, and criminal justice policy in the past 40 years. The main trends are the collapse of the rehabilitative ideal; the return of the victim; the (re)emergence of more punitive criminal justice policies (particularly in relation to imprisonment); and the commercialisation of crime control. In short, welfare and criminal justice systems have become more punitive because of broader social trends, such as the rise of neoliberal regimes (see Chapters 2). As a result, the State has attempted to exercise more control not only in the criminal justice sphere but also in the welfare sector more broadly to demonstrate its authority (Garland, 2001; Simon, 2007; Wacquant, 1999, 2007, 2009). These trends are visible within social work in the juvenile and criminal justice systems in the increased emphasis on public protection (which the offender has foregone) and risk aversion (Webb, 2006). Challenges to the orthodoxy of the RNR model are evident in a range of literature seeking to promote a more holistic social work approach but this is difficult to achieve in a hostile neoliberal practice environment. It is clear more nuanced studies exploring professional practice in real-life situations are needed to determine whether professional discretion softens more punitive rhetoric (Cheliotis, 2006; Kemshall, 2002, 2010; see Chapter 4). Kemshall (2002) refers to the distinction between a normative policy-making rationality and the situated rationality of service users and frontline workers. The question remains whether probation practice in different jurisdictions, at the micro-level, is more nuanced than these generalised approaches suggest.

REFERENCES

Agllias, K. (2004). Women in corrections: A call to social work. *Australian Social Work, 57*, 331–342.

Andrews, D.A., & Bonta, J. (1995). *The level of service inventory – revised*. Toronto, ON: Multi-Health Systems.

Andrews, D.A., Bonta, J., & Wormith, J.S. (2006). The recent past and near futures of risk and/or need assessment. *Crime and Delinquency, 52*(1), 7–27.

Baker, K. (2008). Risk, uncertainty and public protection: Assessment of young people who offend. *British Journal of Social Work, 38*(8), 1463–1480.

Beech, A.R., Fisher, D.D., & Thornton, D. (2003). Risk assessment of sex offenders. *Professional Psychology: Research and Practice,* 34(4), 339–352.

Bhui, H.S. (2001). New probation: Closer to the end of social work? *British Journal of Social Work, 31*(4), 637–639.

Bhui, H.S., & Buchanan, J. (2004). 'What works?' and complex individuality. *Probation Journal,* 51(3), 195–196.

Bhui, H.S. (ed.) (2009). *Race and criminal justice.* London: Sage.

Bottoms, A. (1995). The philosophy and politics of punishment and sentencing. In C. Clarkson & Morgan, R. (eds), *The politics of sentencing reform.* Oxford: Clarendon Press, pp. 17–49.

Brownlee, I. (1998). *Community punishment: A critical introduction.* London: Longman.

Bullock, K. (2011). The construction and interpretation of risk management technologies in contemporary probation practice. *British Journal of Criminology, 51*(1), 120–135.

Burke, L. (2010). Probation qualifications framework: Getting the right balance. *Probation Journal, 57*(1), 3–8.

Burnett, R., & McNeill, F. (2005). The place of the officer-offender relationship in assisting offenders to desist from crime. *Probation Journal,* 52(3), 247–268.

Carlen, P. (ed.) (2008). *Imaginary penalities.* Cullompton: Willan.

Case, S. (2006). Young people 'at risk' of what? Challenging risk-focused early intervention as crime prevention. *Youth Justice,* 6(3), 171–179.

Chapman, T., & Hough, M. (1998). *Evidence based practice: A guide to effective practice.* London: Her Majesty's Inspectorate of Probation.

Cheliotis, L. (2006). How iron is the cage of new penology?: The role of human agency in the implementation of criminal justice policy. *Punishment and Society, 8*(3), 313–340.

Cunneen, C. (2008). Indigenous incarceration: The violence of colonial law and justice. In P. Scraton &

McCulloch, J. (eds), *The violence of incarceration*. London: Routledge, pp. 209–224.

Daly, K. (2002). Restorative justice: The real story. *Punishment and Society, 4*(1), 55–79.

Doherty, K. (2010). The development of restorative justice in Northern Ireland. In W. Taylor, Earle, R., & Hester, R. (eds), *Youth justice handbook: Theory, policy and practice*. Cullompton: Willan, pp. 243–252.

Farrall, S. (2002). *Rethinking what works with offenders*. Cullompton: Willan Publishing.

Farrant, F. (2006). Knowledge production and the punishment ethic: The demise of the probation service. *Probation Journal, 53*(4), 317–333.

Farrington, D. (1994). Human development and criminal careers. In M. Maguire, Morgan, R., & Reiner, R. (eds), *The Oxford handbook of criminology*. Oxford: Clarendon, pp. 511–584.

Farrington, D. (2007). Childhood risk factors and risk-focussed prevention. In M. Maguire; Morgan, R., & Reiner, R. (eds), *The Oxford Handbook of Criminology* (4th ed). Oxford: Clarendon, pp. 602–640.

Feilzer, M., & Hood, R. (2004). *Differences or discrimination?* London: Youth Justice Board.

Fitzgibbon, D.W. (2008). Fit for purpose? OASys assessments and parole decisions. *Probation Journal, 55*(1), 55–69.

France, A., & Crow, I. (2005). Using the 'risk factor paradigm' in prevention: Lessons from the evaluation of communities that care. *Children and Society, 19*, 172–184.

Fulton, B., & Parkhill, T. (2009). *Making the difference: An oral history of probation in Northern Ireland at its centenary and in the 25th year of the Probation Board for Northern Ireland*. Belfast: Probation Board for Northern Ireland.

Garland, D. (1985). *Punishment and welfare: A history of penal strategies*. Aldershot: Gower.

Garland, D. (2001). *The culture of control*. Oxford: Oxford University Press.

Goldson, B. (2000). 'Children in need' or 'young offenders': Hardening ideology, organizational change and new challenges for social work with children in trouble. *Child and Family Social Work, 5*(3), 255–265.

Goldson, B., & Muncie, J. (2006). Rethinking youth justice: comparative analysis, international human rights and research evidence. *Youth Justice, 6*(2), 91–106.

Gottfredson, D.M., & Tonry, M. (eds) (1987). *Prediction and classification: Criminal justice decision making*. Chicago, IL: University of Chicago Press.

Gray, E., Taylor, E., Roberts. C., Merrington, S., Fernandez, R., & Moore, R. (2005). *Intensive supervision and surveillance programme final report*. London: Youth Justice Board.

Haines, K., & Case, S. (2008). The rhetoric and reality of the 'risk factor prevention paradigm' approach to preventing and reducing offending. *Youth Justice, 8*(1), 5–20.

Hannah-Moffat, K. (1999). Moral agent or actuarial subject. *Theoretical Criminology, 3*(1), 71–94.

Hannah-Moffat, K. (2008). Re-imagining gendered penalities: The myth of gendered responsivity. In P. Carlen (ed.), *Imaginary penalities*. Cullompton: Willan, pp. 193–218.

Haydon, D., & Scraton, P. (2000). 'Condemn a little more, understand a little less': The political context and rights implications of the domestic and European rulings in the Venables–Thompson case. *Journal of Law and Society, 27*(3), 416–448.

Hong Chui, W., & Nellis, M. (2003). *Moving probation forward: Evidence, arguments and practice*. Harlow: Pearson Longman.

Israel, M., & Hong Chui, W. (2006). If 'Something Works' is the answer, what is the question?: Supporting pluralist evaluation in community corrections in the United Kingdom. *European Journal of Criminology, 3*(2), 181–200.

Kemshall, H. (2002). *Risk, social policy and welfare*. Buckingham: McGraw Hill/Open University Press.

Kemshall, H. (2003). *Understanding risk in criminal justice*. Maidenhead Berkshire: Open University Press.

Kemshall, H. (2010). Risk rationalities in contemporary social work policy and practice. *British Journal of Social Work, 40*(4), 1247–1262.

Kendall, K. (2004). Dangerous thinking: A critical history of correctional cognitive behaviouralism. In G. Mair (ed.), *What matters in probation*. Cullompton: Willan, pp. 53–89.

Kilkelly, U. (2008). Youth courts and children's rights: The Irish experience. *Youth Justice, 8*(1), 39–56.

Knight, C., & Ward, D. (2001). Qualifying probation training: Implications for social work education. *Social Work Education, 20*(2), 176–186.

La Prairie, C. (1996). Reconstructing theory: Explaining Aboriginal over-representation in the criminal justice system in Canada. *Australian and New Zealand Journal of Criminology, 30*(1), 39–54.

Lewis, S. (2009). The probation service and race equality. In H. Bhui (ed.), *Race and criminal justice*. London: Sage, pp. 102–121.

Lipsey, M.W., Landenberger, N.A., & Wilson, S.J. (2007). Effects of cognitive behavioural programmes for criminal offenders. *Campbell Systematic Reviews*, 2007:6.

Mair, G. (2004). *What matters in probation.* Cullompton: Willan.

Mair, G., Burke, L., & Taylor, S. (2006). 'The worst tax form you've ever seen'? Probation officers' views about OASys. *Probation Journal, 53*(1), 7–23.

Maruna, S., Immarigeon, R., & LeBel, T. (2004). *After crime and punishment: Pathways to ex-offender reintegration.* Cullompton: Willan.

McAra, L., & McVie, S. (2007). Youth justice?: The impact of system contact on patterns of desistance from offending. *European Journal of Criminology, 4*(3), 315–345.

McGuire, J. (2005). The Think First programme. In M. McMurran & McGuire, J. (eds), *Social problem solving and offending.* Chichester: Wiley, pp. 183–206.

McGuire, J., & Priestly, P. (1985). *Offending behaviour: Skills and stratagems for going straight.* London: Batsford.

McNeill, F. (2003). Desistance-focused probation practice. In W. Hong Chui & Nellis, M. (eds), *Moving probation forward.* Harlow: Pearson Longman, pp. 146–161.

McNeill, F. (2006). A desistance paradigm for offender management. *Criminology and Criminal Justice, 6*(1), 39–62.

Miller, J. (1989). Does nothing work? In P. Priestly & Vanstone, M. (eds), *Offenders or citizens? Readings in rehabilitation.* Cullompton: Willan, pp. 185–191.

Ministry of Justice. (2010). *Offender management caseload statistics 2009.* London: Ministry of Justice.

Morgan, R. (2010). Children and young people in custody. In W. Taylor, Earle, R., & Hester, R. (eds), *Youth justice handbook: Theory, policy and practice.* Cullompton: Willan, pp. 132–142.

Morris, A. (2002). Critiquing the critics: A brief response to restorative justice. *British Journal of Criminology, 42*(3), 596–615.

Muncie, J. (2005). The globalization of crime control – the case of youth justice: Neo-liberalism, policy convergence and international conventions. *Theoretical Criminology, 9*(1), 35–64.

Muncie, J. (2006). Governing young people: Coherence and contradiction in contemporary youth justice. *Critical Social Policy, 26*(4), 770–793.

Muncie, J. (2009). *Youth and crime* (3rd ed.). London: Sage.

Muncie, J., & Goldson, B. (2006). *Comparative youth justice.* London: Sage.

National Offender Management Service (2005). *A Guide to Interventions in the National Probation Service.* London: NOMS.

National Offender Management Service (2010). *London borough offender profile report 2009.* London: Ministry of Justice.

Nellis, M. (2004). 'Into the field of corrections': The end of English probation in the early 21st century? *Cambrian Law Review, 35,* 115–133.

Nicholls, G. (2007). Enforcement. In Canton, R., & Hancock, D. (eds), *Dictionary of probation and offender management.* Cullompton: Willan Publishing, pp. 120–121.

O'Mahony, P. (2009). The risk factors prevention paradigm and the causes of youth crime: A deceptively useful analysis? *Youth Justice, 9*(2), 99–114.

Put, J., & Walgrave, L. (2006). Belgium: From protection towards accountability. In J. Muncie & Goldson, B. (eds), *Comparative youth justice.* London: Sage, pp. 111–127.

Rex, S. (1999). Desistance from offending: experiences of probation. *Howard Journal of Criminal Justice, 38*(4), 366–383.

Robinson, G. (2003). Risk and risk assessment. In W.H. Chui & Nellis, M. (eds), *Moving probation forward: Evidence, arguments and practice.* Harlow: Pearson Longman, pp. 108–125.

Scraton, P., & Haydon, D. (2002). Challenging the criminalisation of children and young people: Securing a rights based agenda. In J. Muncie, Hughes, G., & McLaughlin, E. (eds), *Youth justice: Critical readings.* London: Sage, pp. 311–328.

Scraton, P., & McCulloch, J. (eds) (2008). *The violence of incarceration.* London: Routledge.

Shaw, M., & Hannah-Moffatt, K. (2004). How cognitive skills forgot about gender and diversity. In G. Mair (ed.), *What matters in probation.* Cullompton: Willan Publishing, pp. 90–122.

Simon, J. (2007). *Governing through crime.* Oxford: Oxford University Press.

Smith, D., & Vanstone, M. (2002). Probation and social justice. *British Journal of Social Work, 32*(6), 815–830.

Trotter, C. (1999). *Working with involuntary clients.* London: Sage.

Vanstone, M. (2004). *Supervising offenders in the community: A history of probation theory and practice.* Aldershot, Hants: Ashgate.

Vanstone, M. (2008). The international origins and initial development of probation. An early example of policy transfer. *British Journal of Criminology, 48*(6), 735–755.

Vennard, J., Hedderman, C., & Sugg, D. (1997). *Changing offenders' attitudes and behaviour: What works?* London: Home Office Research Findings No. 61, Research and Statistics Directorate.

Wacquant, L. (1999). *Prisons of poverty (contradictions).* Minnesota: University of Minnesota Press.

Wacquant, L. (2001). Deadly symbiosis: When ghetto and prison meet and mesh. *Punishment and Society, 3*(1), 95–133.

Wacquant, L. (2007). *Urban outcasts: A comparative sociology of advanced marginality.* Cambridge: Polity Press.

Wacquant, L. (2009). *Punishing the poor: The neoliberal government of social insecurity.* Durham: Duke University Press.

Ward, T., & Maruna, S. (2007). *Rehabilitation.* London: Routledge.

Weaver, N., & McNeill, F. (2007). Desistance. In R. Canton & Hancock, D. (eds), *Dictionary of probation and offender management.* Cullompton: Willan Publishing, pp. 90–92.

Webb, S.A. (2006). *Social work in a risk society.* London: Palgrave.

Webster, C., MacDonald, R., & Simpson, M. (2006). Predicting criminality? Risk factors, neighbourhood influence and desistance. *Youth Justice,* 6(1), 7–22.

Whyte, B. (2009). *Youth justice in practice: Making a difference.* Bristol: Policy Press.

Zehr, H. (1990). *Changing lenses: A new focus for restorative justice.* Scottdale, PA: Herald Press.

Family Support Services

Steven Walker

As a mainstay of social work, family support has a long history. As a response to rapidly changing contexts, prompted by European enlargement, globalisation, and political attempts to converge diverse social work practices, it requires some fresh consideration. As the global social work context enlarges and embarks on the development of neoliberal policy in an environment of financial austerity, the opportunity arises to engage with critically and share knowledge of diverse geopolitical experiences. The family is always inevitably caught up in these complex policies and politics. While this chapter uses the British experience to evaluate how social work practice has fluctuated between a reactionary child protection stance and a more preventive and supportive mode of family support, the lessons have international application.

Social work is intimately linked to diverse national policies, legislation, and sociocultural traditions that try to support families in some way or another. Nevertheless, the political perception that globalisation could undermine national sovereignty leads to suspicion that closer socioeconomic integration could threaten social work's professional autonomy. This makes the task of identifying best social work practice and designing appropriate family support policies a challenging one. Many continental European models of social welfare imply a residual role for the state and have a history of faith, charitable, and nongovernmental provision. Almost the reverse was evident in the development of the modern British welfare state.

Following the Children Act 2004 and the launch of the 'Every Child Matters: Change for Children' programme, England has embarked on the most ambitious changes in children's services for over a generation. While the government presented the changes as a response to the Laming Report into the death of Victoria Climbié, they are much more than this. They build on a number of ideas and policies that had been developed over a number of years, which emphasise the importance of intervening in children's lives at an early stage in order to prevent problems in later life. In the USA, this has been mirrored by the aggressive 'No Child Left Behind' policy initiative (Lagana-Riordan & Aguilar, 2009).

Parton (2008) provides a critical analysis of the assumptions underpinning the changes in England and argues that the relationships between, and respective responsibilities of, parents, children, professionals, and the state are being reconfigured as a result of the priority given to the accumulation, monitoring, and exchange of electronic information. What we are witnessing, Parton argues, is the emergence of the 'preventive–surveillance' state, where the role of the state is becoming broader, more interventive, and regulatory at the same time.

Evidence provides a compelling picture of changing family characteristics, which have accelerated over the past 30 years across developed countries (Home Office, 2009; National Children's Home, 2009). Rising trends in divorce, single-parent households, and cohabitation signal significant structural change in the pattern of contemporary family relationships. The increased volume, complexity, and severity of child and adolescent mental health problems as symptoms of family discord has also attracted much more recent concern (Carr, 2000; Gordon & Grant, 1997; Walker, 2005; Webster-Stratton, 1997).

The widening gap between rich and poor highlight the needs of those families socially excluded, marginalised, and disempowered. Growing numbers of mothers in work, an ageing population, rising youth homelessness, and increasing reports of domestic violence, child abuse, and the prevalence of substance misuse are cited as evidence of the pressures and strains put on modern, consumerist, Western family life (Walker 2007).

Racism and xenophobia have increased as European Union enlargement has accelerated migration, armed conflict has precipitated increased numbers of asylum seekers, and worldwide economic and social dislocation has prompted more refugee applications to wealthier countries. These changes in the world geopolitical texture have produced moral panics and hasty policy changes to tackle the phenomena or, at least, the symptoms. There has always been an interest among social work professionals in providing earlier and more appropriate support to families where help with children is needed in order to prevent the development of more serious problems, or to deflect the need for statutory intervention (Baradon et al., 1999; Gardner, 1998; Gibbons & Wilding, 1995; Iwaniec, 1995). As societies become more developed, diverse, and culturally enriched, the need for a culturally appropriate response from social workers is evident.

COMPARATIVE CONTEXTS

Family support in Britain has tended to attract much less attention in terms of government policy emphasis or research and development than the more clearly defined systems for children in need of statutory protection and or those looked after by local authorities. Over the past 20 years, a series of legislative and policy initiatives have shaped contemporary social work provision for children and families UK Department of Health (DOH), 1995, 1999, 2000; Quinton, 2004] underpinned by the 1989 UN Convention on the Rights of the Child. The DOH's (1995) refocused children's services initiative together with the Quality Protects Programme (1999), New Assessment Guidance (2000), and Sure Start (1998) family support service were all evidence of a policy shift designed to influence social work practice, prompted by research into family support services and the limitations of the child protection system (DOH, 1995; Thoburn et al., 1998). Initiatives such as these are not unique to Britain. In a critique of these policy shifts Katz and Pinkerton (2005) argue for the importance of locating family support within an understanding of the changing nature of the state and welfare provision driven by economic and market forces and political expediency in the context of changes in family life.

Within these broad findings, detailed studies have detected intrafamilial changes in traditional patterns of kinship relationships and contact and support, where significant numbers of families have lost touch or were unable to rely on help when it was needed

(Coleman et al., 1997; McGlone et al., 1998; Quinton, 2004). Further complexity is revealed by research into subgroups of the population which, although sparse, offers evidence of the nature and variety of contemporary family life. Modood and Berthoud (1997) found, while all ethnic groups had high levels of contact with nonresident parents, Asian and African-Caribbean people had higher levels of contact with aunts and uncles. The potential of other family members and grandparents to serve as helpful resources is indicative of a need for the widening of the focus for social workers who are now expected to assess strengths within the wider family constellation and work preventively (Statham et al., 2006).

The Western model of mental illness tends to ignore the religious or spiritual aspects of the culture in which it is based. However, Eastern, African, and Native American cultures tend to integrate them (Fernando, 2002). Spirituality and religion have only recently featured in the mainstream social work literature, yet they can be critical components of a family's well-being, offering a source of strength and hope in trying circumstances (Furness & Gilligan, 2010). Social workers need to address this dimension as part of the constellation of factors affecting children and adolescents, avoiding stereotyping, and bearing in mind the positive and sometimes negative impact spiritual or religious beliefs might have on their well-being (Gray & Webb, 2010; Wong & Vinsky, 2009).

The diverse nature of family life in contemporary Britain and in other societies, therefore, requires sophisticated analysis of the broad trends reported in social surveys, otherwise abrupt policy changes can fail to address fully the needs of every family requiring support. Racist and cultural stereotypes of the role played by extended families distort the picture of unique family situations, which are complex and fluid and inhibit proper assessment of the needs of Black and other ethnic minority families, travellers, and refugee families, all of whom face additional problems in the context of prejudice, institutional racism, and discrimination (Dominelli, 1999; Kiddle, 1999; Vostanis & Cumella, 1999).

Renewed interest in early intervention and prevention in the context of authoritative evidence (Thoburn et al., 2000; Tunstill et al., 2004; Walker, 2001a), together with rapid sociological change affecting the ability of parents to cope, has managed to keep the issue of family support highlighted but, at the same time, surrounded by different definitions and strategies. An examination of the characteristics of models of assessment, analysis of methods of support, and evaluation of measures of effectiveness, permits some conclusions to be drawn on where family support as a feature of professional social work practice is heading.

MODELS OF ASSESSMENT

Family support can be defined as self-help or volunteer help with little statutory involvement, or it can mean a continuum of advice, support, and specialist help geared to provide early preventive intervention, parenting support, education, and marital therapy (Houston & Dolan, 2008). The intervention can be directed at individual parents, couples, the child, the whole family, or groups. Invariably, given the prevailing patriarchal social structures, parent support is still largely *mother* support. The place of preventive family support work can usefully be conceptualised using a three-stage model identifying different levels of intervention (Crisp, 1994; Hardiker, 1995). The *primary* level offers universally available services to strengthen family functioning provided by a mix of state welfare providers and parent education services often organised by voluntary organisations. The *secondary* level provides services targeted to families in early difficulties, such as relationship counselling for couples, informal family centres, and home visiting schemes by voluntary agencies to help families with young children. At the *tertiary* level, intensive work – either by the statutory or voluntary sector to prevent family breakdown – can include those who are experiencing severe difficulties and who are on the threshold of care proceedings.

Services geared towards the needs of specific age groups of children, young people, or adults can determine the type of help offered and whether it is perceived as family or individual support. This becomes particularly important in the area of child and adolescent mental health, where the initial assessment of the presenting problem could be formulated on an individual or family basis. Social workers trained in family therapy are particularly alert to the potential for scapegoating individual children within family systems functioning in negative and punitive ways (Dallos & Draper, 2000; Walker, 2001a; Walker & Akister, 2004).

While it has been established a confluence of several risk factors in childhood can create the conditions for later psychosocial difficulty, including socioeconomic disadvantage, child abuse, and parental mental illness, there are also protective mechanisms to mitigate the chance of some children going on to develop antisocial behaviour or serious mental health problems. These can be obscured by the imperative for medical diagnosis or the over-reactions of untrained volunteer helpers. This highlights the importance of assessment methods taking account not just of individual characteristics within the child but equally within the family, community, and broader environment. It is unlikely this holistic level of assessment is available to unqualified volunteers.

A social model of Europe, incorporating the continental European heritage of social pedagogy and social action in social work practice, could enlarge the panorama of assessment activity (Walker, 2002). In combination, a sophisticated assessment identifying strengths and protective factors, together with a more explicit social mandate, could create a chain of indirect links to foster resistance to adversity. Organising services across the spectrum of multi-agency provision in partnership between social work professionals and parents offers the opportunity to bring out dormant protective factors to interrupt the causal chain of events so often set in train under entrenched child protection work (Little & Mount, 1999). A positive environment, which promotes children's emotional well-being, is preferable to reacting to the consequences of neglect or abuse. Service-driven models of social work assessment for children and families are the product of a reactive system geared to responding to concerns relating to child protection, developmental harm, or disturbed symptoms within a deficit framework. This leads to a focus on risk assessment, which can be experienced by parents as undermining, or psychiatric treatment, which constructs the child as suffering an individual mental illness requiring individual treatment. The literature on assessment and UK Department of Health (DOH, 1999) guidance are, nevertheless, improving to emphasise multifaceted assessment (Baradon et al., 1999; Statham & Kearney, 2007; UK Department for Education and Skills, 2003), but they are still influenced by psychiatric classifications located in a medico-biological model and psychotherapeutic concepts linked with attachment theory. There is less emphasis on psychosocial factors, including the effects of poverty, racism, unemployment, social exclusion, and poor housing. However, there is evidence of some fresh thinking in this area (Walker, 2010; Walker & Beckett, 2011), where attempts to offer a more sophisticated model of assessment are being made, stressing the interactive quality of assessment variables and the need for enhanced interpretive and planning skills. The emphasis is on the need for analysing and weighing the information generated during the assessment process and ensuring this is underpinned by partnership practice and service-user involvement (Thompson, 2002).

A number of themes have emerged from the research literature relating to the context of family and children's difficulties. These include the importance of multifactorial causal explanations and the contribution of structural variables to childhood problems (Donnellan & Jack, 2010; Okitikpi & Aymer, 2008; Sutton, 1999). The importance of variation in the perception of children's behaviour depends on the theoretical model used and the evidence on assessment methodology is crucial in determining the course and type of family support offered.

METHODS OF SUPPORT

Social workers have the opportunity to employ communication and relationship skills in direct family support work, which they traditionally find rewarding and which service users find more acceptable than intrusive, investigative risk assessment (Crisp et al., 2003). The social work role in multi-agency assessment and planning becomes significant in this context, where several perceptions can be expressed, based on diverse evidence and different levels of professional anxiety. Social workers managing and supporting these processes with individuals or groups in planning meetings, case conferences, or case reviews require advanced negotiation and decision-making skills, which are the hallmarks of professional training and supervision. As the volume and complexity of family problems increases, there is concern the voluntary and nongovernmental sectors will be unable to match the level of skills to the level of need expressed and, therefore, creative ways of thinking are generating effective resources, such as the Family Group Conference approach to child welfare. Developed in New Zealand, it is based on a cultural–religious Indigenous concept among Maori people emphasising the relationship between celestial and terrestrial knowledge. According to Maori belief, the origin of the Family Group Conference was a rebellious initiative by the children of *Ranginui*, the great Sky Father, and *Papatuanuku*, the matriarch Earth Mother. Protected in a darkened cocoon by their parents, the children desired freedom to explore the outer limits of the universe. The family conference included close and distant relatives and grandparents, all of whom were regarded as part of a single spiritual and economic unity (Fulcher, 1999). Thus each Maori child's cultural identity is explicitly connected to their genealogy or *whakapapa*. The Family Group Conference has been incorporated into mainstream child protection and adult mental health services in the UK and elsewhere, where extended family members are invited to participate in care planning and become part of the family support system rather than excluded from it (Brown, 2003; Featherstone, 2004).

Various initiatives aimed at children and their families living in disadvantaged areas are evidence of the practical implementation of the implicit preventive aspects of this policy, which was based on evidence of success from the US Head Start scheme (Gross et al., 1995). Gross et al.'s (1995) study demonstrated long-term reductions in antisocial activity, marital problems, child abuse, adult mental health difficulties, and unemployment in later life in a group of children who received the intervention, with a comparison group of children who did not receive the intervention. The Sure Start initiative was the British equivalent and the signature family support policy of the early 21st century. Recent research to evaluate its impact has produced positive findings (Hutchings et al., 2007). However, a systematic review of Family Group Conferences shows, to succeed as a family support intervention, they need to be part of a range of helping services and the start of a continuum of support (Shlonsky, 2010).

Measuring or quantifying the impact of preventive family support work is complex and achieving systematic results is expensive. Therefore, there is little in the way of evidence of long-term effectiveness in Britain or the rest of Europe. However, while outcome measures from various government projects are intangible (Robbins, 1998), there are signs small-scale social action projects could show changes in relationships between parents and professionals, as well as demonstrate how to work in partnership and engage positively with parents, all of which contribute to better family support and user-focused approaches.

The expansion of parent education or training programmes in the face of exponential demand for help from parents to deal with a range of child and adolescent difficulties from toddler tantrums to self-harm, suicide, and drug and alcohol addiction has meant this form of intervention is popular and expected to be offered as part of a repertoire of contemporary family support measures. Studies of parent education programmes, while limited in number, show they can be an effective way of supporting families by improving behaviour in pre-adolescent children (Lloyd, 1999; Miller & Prinz, 1990). They highlight the impact of group-based behaviourally oriented programmes in producing the biggest subsequent changes in children's behaviour and are perceived by parents as non-stigmatising. Programmes where both parents are involved and which include individual work with children are more likely to result in long-term changes. However, while enjoying a growth in popularity in Britain and other European countries, parent education programmes are generally not subject to rigorous evaluation (Donnellan, 2003, Nybell et al., 2009). In a number of studies, 50% of parents continue to experience difficulties. Further, it is not clear to what extent changes are due to the format or method of intervention, group support or practitioner skill. High attrition rates from some programmes are attributed to practitioner variables, such as their level of qualification and experience, and qualities such as warmth, enthusiasm, or flexibility (Barlow, 1998). It may also be that some programmes are inappropriate for parents lacking motivation, especially when they are compelled to attend under the pressure of child protection concerns.

Few British studies have used randomised controlled trials. This inhibits identification of the most beneficial elements of a programme and, because most provision is geared to rectifying problems in disadvantaged groups, available research evidence reflects this bias. While over ten years old, those that have been conducted, nevertheless, have yielded important qualitative data from stakeholders' perspectives (Ghate & Daniels, 1997; Morrow, 1998). It has been argued managerialist preference for evaluating work on the basis of the three Es (efficiency, effectiveness, and economy), which reflects service managers' agenda for quantitative outcome measures, fails to reflect the whole picture (Leonard, 1997; Walker, 2001b). Others argue these data need to be supplemented with the three Ps (partnership, pluralism, and process), which better reflect professional social work principles seeking to incorporate service-users' perspectives (Beresford, 2001; Dominelli, 2004; Powell & Lovelock, 1992). Further studies paying attention to normative models of parenting in the community would counter this bias by identifying skills leading to successful parenting and focus on what went right rather than what went wrong.

CULTURE AND ETHNICITY

Antiracist practice focuses attention on the family life cycle of Black and other ethnic minority families, especially transitional points, strengths, and acceptable support (Bhui & Olajide, 1999; Thoburn et al., 2005, Walker, 2005). The views of parents and children are largely absent from the research, particularly in families with lone parents, gay and lesbian parents, and step parents. There is also very little systematic incorporation of culture and ethnicity as factors influencing parenting styles. Also overlooked are the particular issues faced by parents of disabled children with emotional and behavioural problems or gender influences within families and within professional groups. Families for whom parent education is unlikely to be a sufficient response to child-management difficulties are those which feature maternal depression, socioeconomic disadvantage, and the social isolation of the mother. Extrafamilial conflict, combined with relationship problems, contribute to problem severity and chronicity, and, therefore, influence the ability to introduce change. While parental misperception of the deviance of their children's behaviour is a significant impediment to engaging in constructive family support (Rubin & Chung, 2006; Walker, 2001c), the prospects for unqualified staff attempting to help without professional supervision are further diminished.

Parenting education or training programmes seem to be a response to a demand for a variety of support, including information, child development knowledge, and skills development in managing children of all ages with diverse physical and psychological abilities. It is a role undertaken in social work practice in the context of other work, most likely general family assessments or specific risk assessments, where concerns have reached the threshold of statutory intervention. The gap between demand and provision is increasingly being met in the voluntary and private sector, which is absorbing more and more complex work with fewer qualified staff. This is likely to increase in the UK as more work is devolved to private, faith, and charitable providers where social work staff are rarely employed and less skilled people who are cheaper to employ face challenging work. Yet social work skills deployed early enough are ideally suited to provide appropriate family support based on best practice evidence (Walker, 2003).

The value of Western individualistic concepts in alleviating suffering and alienation is questioned by collectivist and land-based cultural groups. In their work with Aboriginal communities in the Canadian Arctic, Beatch and Stewart (2002) show how significant problems related to depression, addiction, and family violence are linked with cultural loss through colonisation, environmental destruction, and assimilation by Western influences. Aboriginal healing includes strengthening cultural belonging, identity, and community-based self-determination. Indigenous outlooks indicate a preference for ecological systems approaches, holistic processes, belonging at the community level, and reliance on traditional beliefs and values. A culturally appropriate approach requires social workers to adapt and synthesise their work with prevailing Indigenous ideas in order to maximise effectiveness, although some argue psychosocial ideas do not fit many of these contexts (Gray et al., 2010).

Multiple caregiving of young children in Australian Aboriginal cultures has attracted concerns based on Western notions of attachment theory, especially the need for secure attachment relationships with primary carers. However, this concept is inappropriate since research has demonstrated Aboriginal children can sustain and thrive with multiple attachment figures and this is wholly consistent with Aboriginal social norms (Yeo, 2003). Indeed, there are sometimes lengthy absences from parents related to important sacred initiations or religious ceremonies necessary for the child or young person's spiritual development. These findings resonate with research in the UK and elsewhere studying the developmental progress of Black children raised in single-parent households with multiple attachment figures (Daycare Trust, 2000).

EFFECTIVENESS OF FAMILY SUPPORT

The literature on the effectiveness in family support tends to focus on the evaluation of specific service interventions, but it should be acknowledged broader fiscal and social policies impact on children and their families and, therefore, contribute for good or bad to the context of children's welfare in general, and family well-being in particular (Shaw et al., 2004). Recent research on child poverty ranked Britain bottom in a comparison of the current 15 European Union countries with 32% of children living in poor households (Gilbert, 2003; Micklewright & Stewart,

2001). This is an important part of the equation of demand, needs, and resources when evaluating provision.

It has long been argued early intervention is the key to effectiveness because it stops problems getting worse when they become harder to tackle, and more costly in terms of damage to children's development, family relationships, use of scarce resources, and prevention of antisocial consequences in the long term (Bayley, 1999). However, Eayrs and Jones (1992) pointed out the accumulated evidence for the effectiveness of early intervention programmes is not as optimistic as was once hoped. On occasion there is the possibility such programmes can be damaging, deskilling parents and undermining their confidence. On the other hand, 16 years ago a meta-analysis of early education interventions demonstrated children from disadvantaged backgrounds were less at risk from developing maladjustment, school failure, and delinquency after participating in these programmes delivered in an educational context (Sylva, 1994). More recent research supports this conclusion (Dolan, 2006). The location of family support is critical in engaging parents and children. Schools are emerging as an acceptable and accessible nonstigmatising venue for individual or group-based activity where attached social workers can engage in interprofessional work (Quinney, 2006).

A major review of consumer studies of family therapy and marital counselling analysed a variety of large- and small-scale studies, individual case studies, and ethnographic studies of specific therapeutic methods (Carr, 2000; Treacher, 1995). It concluded workers who neglected the service-user perspective and undervalued the personal relationship aspects of their family support work in favour of concentrating on inducing change ran the risk of creating considerable dissatisfaction among service users. This reinforced findings from an earlier study into the effectiveness of family therapy, which found advice and directive work needed to be balanced with reflective and general supportive elements typical of a professional social work approach (Howe, 1989). A subsequent meta-analysis of family therapy demonstrated effectiveness with specific problems, such as adolescent substance abuse and anorexia nervosa (Stanton & Shadish, 1997; Vostanis, 2007).

Systems theory can be useful in understanding the interactive nature of some family problems. It is also important in helping to take account of the natural history, social system, and environmental context of children's problems in relation to their developmental stage. What becomes clear is there are no standardised ways of measuring childhood functioning or isolating all the family variables that can influence change. What is consistent is the general absence and rarity of service-user evaluation of, and involvement in, the design of family support (Statham, 2000). This further reinforces the need to establish professional social work methodologies, which incorporate shared social work values and preserve the cultural autonomy of groups in different societies. Taking the service-user perspective into account in determining effectiveness has become a feature of contemporary policy in social and health care contexts, but practice evidence does not support this policy aspiration (Barnes & Warren, 1999; Crawford & Kessel, 1999; Everitt & Hardiker, 1996; Kelson, 1995). In seeking to evaluate family support, it is problematic to define who the service user is. One of the challenges in defining effectiveness in family support interventions is clarifying for whom it is effective.

Family support usually means 'mother support' as fathers' absence is a feature of the helping context, despite efforts to engage men in programmes to effect change. There is evidence of activity to engage men in work but what little has been undertaken has rarely been subject to rigorous evaluation (Holt, 1998). Mothers' evaluation of family support might differ in more or less ways than the evaluation of the children and/or father irrespective of whether the focus of intervention was on an individual child, adult couple, or the whole family (Walker, 2001d). A school-based behavioural problem might be resolved but at the expense of a deterioration in the parent–child relationship. Robust methods of differential evaluation by all participants, referrers, users, and providers would enhance the sophistication of up-to-date data on effectiveness.

FAMILY SUPPORT AND SOCIAL WORK

There is evidence of a shift in the locus of family support largely outside statutory social work services where most professional social workers are located due to the neoliberal retrenchment of local government social service provision and expanding reliance on faith-based, voluntary, charitable, private, and community-based organisations and activities. In its widest definition, family support is being transformed by the government-backed expansion of the voluntary sector to more integrated community-based services while professional social work is being more narrowly defined at the child protection end of the spectrum. At the same time, professional social work, under the influence of evidence-based practice, is under pressure to prove its practice effectiveness in a broadened context of family support which does not easily yield short-term effectiveness measures (see later). Further, these local, organic, often self-help activities are decentring orthodox, professionally centred, Western models in favour of locally relevant, culturally sensitive – Indigenous, community, and African and Eastern 'traditional' – methods in non-Western contexts or when working with non-Western cultures in Western contexts (Gray et al., 2010). One of the significant conclusions to be drawn from considering this broadening of family support in relation to contemporary social work practice is the impressive amount of community-based activity and diverse range of interventions alongside a worrying lack of reliable evidence on social work's effectiveness (Gray et al., 2009; Walker & Akister, 2004). The drive to create a research-minded profession so as to improve professional practice standards and protect professional autonomy is producing a confusion of research studies varying in empirical quality and methodological rigour, yet producing potentially useful data hidden within the quantity being produced. Practitioner research in social work is being encouraged as a means of influencing social policy, management, and practice, using evaluative concepts moulded by service-user expectations (Adams et al., 2002; Tovey, 2007). Service-user expectations call for empowering strategies, creative solutions beyond narrow service-led resources, and refined relationship-building and networking skills. They are challenging the service-management orthodoxy for short-term, focused assessments aimed at identifying risk and need according to a limited range of skills and resources provided by nonstatutory agencies. They offer opportunities for more satisfying work over longer time periods where service users are respected, valued, and supported in a consistent and reliable way (Walker & Beckett, 2003).

Research into children's perceptions of family support services shows a focus on strengths, competencies, and resources – rather than problems – and provides a fuller picture of their circumstances. It also highlights the importance of the personal relationship children establish with their social worker or counsellor (Sandbaek, 1999; Walker, 2001d). It is also consistent with the child's right in terms of the United Nations Charter to be consulted and to express their views about services provided for them (United Nations, 1989). The implications seem to be, by enlarging the focus of assessment (and effectiveness measures), it is possible to see children not just as problems but also as positive and constructive contributors to family life. Strengths-based interventions build on and amplify strengths wherever possible (see Chapter 11). Research into interventions targeting the child, teacher, and parent demonstrates that interactional approaches produce the most sustained reduction in conflict at home, at school, and in peer relationships (Webster-Stratton, 1997). Working from the child's perspective and recognising and building on the child's strengths provides new opportunities for social work with children and families, and bring to the fore issues adults might not be fully aware of or to which they do not pay enough attention.

However, for the most part, research suggests family support programmes tend to focus on single outcome measures, such as changes in the child's behaviour, rather than take interactional dimensions into account, such as improved parent–child interactions or use of community resources (Gardner, 1998). This reflects a problem orientation rather than the strengths or solution focus outlined earlier.

Family support is a multidisciplinary enterprise. Its focus is short-term, nonstigmatising intensive services, including advice, information, parental guidance, and direct work with children in their own homes or in locations of their choosing. Parents voluntarily seek help and support, and listen to, and act upon, advice. This contrasts with the often negative and antagonistic relationship in statutory child protection services. In family support services, it is easier to take a strengths focus when asking what works for families – *what went right* and how might success be replicated, rather than a risk-focused assessment. Clifford et al. (2002) are highly critical of contemporary risk-based assessment protocols on the grounds they:

- rely heavily on psychological models and overlook social and structural factors impacting upon personal and group problems;
- do not offer a coherent framework of theoretical principles, which include antidiscriminatory values, especially relating to social divisions;
- do not emphasise 'reflexivity' since workers and agencies are not highlighted as key agents, focusing instead on the interaction between child, parent, and 'environment' as a 'catch-all', with insufficient attention to the complex interaction of specific social systems over time;
- overemphasise the new needs assessment frameworks without acknowledging workers' initial – and ongoing – assessments of risk;
- overlook the politics of assessment, especially the power dynamics between individual workers, the managerial requirements of organisations in local contexts, and formally recognised child-and-family-focused needs assessment frameworks.

Given that a large focus of family support services involves work with racially and ethnically diverse communities with low socioeconomic status, further research is needed in this area (Trevino, 1999). The needs of gay and lesbian families are virtually absent in the literature on family support reflecting homophobic and discriminatory practices in health and social care generally and social work in particular. This gap needs to be filled on the grounds of equity and equality to ensure appropriate support can be offered to every family, however defined, and to value and learn from different parenting styles and practices (Salmon & Hall, 1999).

CONCLUSION

Family support in usually seen as distinct from child protection rather than as part of a connected architecture of resources activated as different family needs emerge. Therefore, contemporary policies to develop community-based voluntary family support services where multiproblem families are dealt with by largely untrained family support workers run the risk of precipitating child protection failures which in light of existing problems in the child protection system might lead inadvertently to further retrenchment of professional social work and a reactionary framework of welfare policy. The future direction of family support services appears to be heading in the direction of a minimalist, crisis, reactive system of disparate providers as further welfare state retrenchment takes place in the forthcoming decade of austerity, public sector cuts, and increased voluntary activity. The move to a local, community-based focus is positive in light of the old African proverb 'it takes a whole village to raise a child' but pigeonholing social workers into narrowly prescribed risk-based child protection underutilises their expertise and skills in fostering harmonious, mutually enriching relationships between and within families and communities.

REFERENCES

Adams, R., Dominelli, L., & Payne, M. (2002) *Critical practice in social work.* Basingstoke: Palgrave.

Baradon, T., Sinason, V., & Yabsley, S. (1999). Assessment of parents and young children – a child psychotherapy point of view. *Child Care Health and Development, 25*(1), 37–53.

Barlow, J. (1998). Parent training programmes and behaviour problems: Findings from a systematic review. In A Buchanan & Hudson, B. (eds), *Parenting, schooling, and children's behaviour: Interdisciplinary approaches.* Aldershot, Hants: Ashgate, pp. 221–236.

Barnes, M., & Warren, L. (1999). *Paths to empowerment.* Bristol: The Policy Press.

Bayley, R. (1999). *Transforming children's lives: The importance of early intervention.* London: Family Policy Studies Centre.

Beresford, P. (2001) Service users, social policy and the future of welfare. *Critical Social Policy, 21*(4), 494–512.

Bhui, K., & Olajide, D. (eds) (1999). *Mental health service provision for a multi-cultural society.* London: Saunders.

Brown, L. (2003). Mainstream or margin? The current use of Family Group Conferences in Child Welfare Practice in the UK. *Child and Family Social Work, 8*(4), 331–340.

Carr, A. (2000). *What works with children and adolescents?* London: Routledge.

Clifford, D., Burke, B., Feery, D., & Knox, C. (2002): Combining key elements in training and research: Developing social work assessment theory and practice in partnership. *Social Work Education, 21*(1), 105–116.

Coleman, M., Ganong, L., & Cable, S. (1997). Beliefs about women's intergenerational family obligations to provide support before and after divorce and remarriage. *Journal of Marriage and the Family, 59*(1), 165–176.

Craford, K. (2006). *Social work and human development.* Exeter: Learning Matters.

Crawford, M., & Kessel, A. (1999). Not listening to patients: The use and misuse of patient satisfaction studies. *International Journal of Social Psychiatry, 45*(1), 1–6.

Crisp, S. (1994). *Counting on families: Social audit report on the provision of family support services.* London: Exploring Parenthood.

Crisp, R., Anderson, R., Orme, J., & Lister, P.G. (2003). *Knowledge review: Learning and teaching in social work assessment.* Bristol: Policy Press/Social Care Institute for Excellence.

Dallos, R., & Draper, R. (2000). *An introduction to family therapy.* Buckingham: Open University Press.

Dolan, P. (2006). Assessment, intervention and self appraisal tools for family support. In P. Dolan, P., Pinkerton, J., & Canavan, J. (eds), *Family support as reflective practice.* London: Jessica Kingsley, pp. 196–213.

Dominelli, L. (ed.) (1999). *Community approaches to child welfare.* Aldershot, Hants: Ashgate.

Dominelli, L. (2004). *Social work: Theory and practice for a changing profession.* Cambridge: Policy Press.

Donnellan, C. (2003). *Parenting issues.* Cambridge: Independence Publishers.

Donnellan, H., & Jack, G. (2010). *The survival guide for newly qualified child and family social workers.* London: Jessica Kingsley.

Eayrs, C., & Jones, R. (1992). Methodological issues and future directions in the evaluation of early intervention programmes. *Child Care, Health and Development, 18*, 15–28.

Everitt, A., & Hardiker, P. (1996). *Evaluating good practice.* Basingstoke: Palgrave.

Featherstone, B. (2004). *Family life and family support.* Basingstoke: Palgrave.

Fernando, S. (2002). *Mental Health, Race and Culture* (2nd ed.). Basingstoke: Palgrave.

Fulcher, L.C. (1999). Cultural origins of the contemporary group conference. *Child Care in Practice, 6*, 328–339.

Furness, S., & Gilligan P. (2010). *Religion, belief and social work: Making a difference.* Bristol: Policy Press.

Gardner, R. (1998). *Family support: Practitioner's guide.* BASW, Birmingham: Venture Press.

Ghate, D., & Daniels, A. (1997). *Talking about my generation.* London: NSPCC.

Gibbons, J., & Wilding, J. (1995). *Needs, risks and family support plans: Social services departments responses to neglected children.* Norwich: University of East Anglia.

Gilbert, P. (2003). *The value of everything.* Lyme Regis: Russell House Publishing

Gordon, G., & Grant, R. (1997). *How we feel: An insight into the emotional world of teenagers.* London: Jessica Kingsley.

Gray, M., Coates, J., & Yellow Bird, M. (eds) (2010). *Indigenous social work around the world: Towards culturally relevant education and practice.* Aldershot, Hants: Ashgate.

Gray, M., Plath, D., & Webb, S.A. (2009). *Evidence-based social work: A critical stance.* London: Routledge.

Gray, M., & Webb, S.A. (2010) *Ethics and value perspectives in social work.* London, Palgrave.

Gross, D., Fogg, L., & Tucker, S. (1995). The efficacy of parent training for promoting positive parent–toddler relationships. *Research in Nursing and Health, 18,* 489–499.

Hardiker, P. (1995). *The social policy contexts of services to prevent unstable family life.* York: Joseph Rowntree Foundation.

Holt, C. (1998). Working with fathers of children in need. In R. Bayley (ed.), *Transforming children's lives: The importance of early intervention.* London: Family Policy Studies Centre, pp. 64–69.

Home Office (2009). *Social trends.* London: HMSO.

Houston, S., & Dolan, P. (2008). Conceptualising child and family support: The contribution of Honneth's critical theory of recognition. *Children and Society, 22,* 458–459.

Howe, D. (1989). *The consumer's view of family therapy.* London: Gower.

Hutchings, J., Gardner, F., Bywater, T., Daley, D., Whitaker, C., Jones, K., Eames, C., & Edwards, R.T. (2007). Parenting intervention in Sure Start services for children at risk of developing conduct disorder: pragmatic randomised controlled trial. *British Medical Journal, 334,* 678–682.

Iwaniec, D. (1995). *The emotionally abused and neglected child: Identification, assessment and intervention.* Chichester: Wiley.

Katz, I., & Pinkerton, J. (2005). Perspective through international comparison in the evaluation of family support. In Katz, I & Pinkerton, J. (eds), *Evaluating family support: thinking internationally, thinking critically.* Chichester: NSPCC/Wiley.

Kelson, M. (1995). *Consumer involvement initiatives in clinical audit and outcomes.* London: College of Health.

Kiddle, C. (1999). *Traveller children: A voice for themselves.* London: Jessica Kingsley.

Kurtz, Z. (1996). *Treating children well: A guide to using the evidence base in commissioning and managing services for the mental health of children and young people.* London: Mental Health Foundation.

Lagana-Riordan, C., & Aguilar, J.P. (2009). What's missing from No Child Left Behind? A policy analysis from a social work perspective. *Children and Schools, 31*(3), 135–144.

Leonard, P. (1997). *Postmodern welfare: Reconstructing an emancipatory project.* London: Sage.

Little, M., & Mount, K. (1999). *Prevention and early intervention with children in need.* Aldershot, Hants: Ashgate.

Lloyd, E. (ed.). (1999). *Parenting matters: What works in parenting education?* London: Barnardos.

McGlone, F., Park, A., & Smith, K. (1998). *Families and kinship.* London: Family Policy Studies Centre.

Micklewright, J., & Stewart, K. (2001). Poverty and social exclusion in Europe. *New Economy, 8*(2), 104–109.

Miller, G., & Prinz, R. (1990). Enhancement of social learning family interventions for childhood conduct disorders. *Psychological Bulletin, 108,* 291–307.

Modood, T., & Berthoud, R. (1997). *Ethnic minorities in Britain.* London: Policy Studies Institute.

Morrow, V. (1998). *Understanding families: Children's perspectives.* London: National Children's Bureau.

Nybell, L.M., Shook, J.J., & Finn, J.L. (eds) (2009). *Childhood, youth, and social work in transformation: Implications for policy and practice.* New York: Columbia University Press.

Okitikpi, T., & Aymer, C. (2008). *The art of social work practice.* Lyme Regis: Russell House Publishers.

Parton, N. (2008). The 'Change for Children' programme in England: Towards the 'preventive-surveillance state'. *Journal of Law and Society, 35*(1), 166–187.

Powell, J., & Lovelock, R. (1992). *Changing patterns of mental health care.* London: Avebury.

Quinney, A. (2006). *Collaborative social work practice.* Exeter: Learning Matters.

Quinton, D. (2004). *Supporting parents: Messages from research.* London: Department of Health/DFES.

Robbins, D. (1998). The refocusing children's initiative: an overview of practice. In R. Bayley (ed.), *Transforming children's lives: The importance of early intervention.* London: Family Policy Studies Centre, pp. 86–90.

Roth, A., & Fonagy, P. (1996). *What works for whom? A critical review of psychotherapy research.* London: Guilford Press.

Rubin, K.H., & Chung, O.B. (2006). *Parenting beliefs, behaviours, and parent–child relations: A cross cultural perspective.* Hove: Taylor & Francis.

Salmon, D., & Hall, C. (1999). Working with lesbian mothers: Their healthcare experiences. *Community Practitioner, 72*(12), 396–397.

Sandbaek, M. (1999). Children with problems: Focusing on everyday life. *Children and Society, 13,* 106–118.

Shlonsky, A. (2010). A fine balancing act: Kinship care, subsidized guardianship, and outcomes. In B. Kerman, Maluccio, A.N., & Freundlich, M. (eds), *Achieving permanence for older children and youth in foster care.* New York: Columbia University Press.

Shardlow, S., & Payne, M. (1998). *Contemporary issues in social work: Western Europe.* Aldershot, Hants: Arena.

Shaw, I., Arksey, H., & Mullender, A. (2004). *ESRC research, social work, and social care.* London: SCIE.

Stanton, M., & Shadish, W. (1997). Outcome, attrition and family-couples treatment for drug abuse: A meta-analysis and review of the controlled comparative studies. *Psychological Bulletin, 122,* 170–191.

Statham, J. (2000). *Outcomes and effectiveness of family support services: A research review.* London: Institute for Education, University of London.

Statham, J., Cameron, C., & Mooney, A. (2006). *The tasks and roles of social workers: A focused overview of research evidence.* London: Thomas Coram Research Institute.

Statham, D., & Kearney, P. (2007) Models of assessment. In J. Lishman (ed.), *Handbook for practice learning in social work and social care: Knowledge and theory* (2nd ed.). London: Jessica Kingsley, pp. 101–114.

Sutton, C. (1999). *Helping families with troubled children.* Chichester: Wiley.

Sylva, K. (1994). School influences on children's development. *Journal of Child Psychology and Psychiatry and Allied Professions, 35*(1), 135–170.

Thoburn, J., Ashok, C., & Procter, J. (2005). *Child welfare services for minority ethnic families: The research reviewed.* London: Jessica Kingsley.

Thoburn, J., Wilding, J., & Watson, J. (2000). *Family support in cases of emotional maltreatment and neglect.* London: HMSO

Thompson, N. (2002) *Building the future: Social work with children, young people and their families.* Lyme Regis: Russell House Publishers.

Tovey, W. (ed.) (2007). *The post qualifying handbook for social workers.* London: Jessica Kingsley.

Treacher, A. (1995). Reviewing consumer studies of therapy. In A. Treacher & Reimers, S. (eds), *Introducing user-friendly family therapy.* London: Routledge, pp. 128–149.

Trevino, F. (1999). Quality of health care for ethnic/racial minority populations. *Ethnicity and Health, 4*(3), 153–164.

Tunstill, J., & Aldgate, J., with Hughes, M., & Peel, M. (2004). *Family support at the centre: The role of family centres in the local service network.* London: Royal Holloway College, University of London.

UK Department for Education and Skills (2003). *Every child matters.* London: HMSO.

UK Department of Health (1995). *Child protection: Messages from research.* London: HMSO.

UK Department of Health (1999). *Quality protects programme: Transforming children's services 2000–01.* LAC Circular (99)33. London: HMSO.

UK Department of Health (2000). *Framework for the assessment of children in need.* London: HMSO.

Vostanis, P. (ed.). (2007). *Mental health: Interventions and services for vulnerable children and young people.* London: Jessica Kingsley.

Vostanis P., & Cumella, S. (1999). *Homeless children: Problems and needs.* London: Jessica Kingsley.

Walker, S., (2001a). Consulting with Children and Young People. *International Journal of Children's Rights.* 9, 45–56.

Walker, S. (2001b). Tracing the contours of postmodern social work. *British Journal of Social Work, 31,* 29–39.

Walker, S. (2001c). Domestic violence: Analysis of a community safety alarm system. *Child Abuse Review, 10,* 170–182.

Walker, S. (2001d). Family support and social work practice: Opportunities for child mental health work. *Social Work and Social Sciences Review, 9*(2), 25–40.

Walker, S. (2002). Family support and social work practice: Renaissance or retrenchment? *European Journal of Social Work, 5*(1), 43–54.

Walker, S. (2003). *Social work and child and adolescent mental health.* Lyme Regis: Russell House.

Walker, S. (2005). *Culturally competent therapy: Working with children and young people.* Basingstoke: Palgrave.

Walker, S. (2007). Family therapy and systemic practice. In J. Lishman (ed.), *Handbook for practice learning in social work and social care: Knowledge* and theory (2nd ed.). London: Jessica Kingsley, pp. 216–234.

Walker, S., & Akister, J. (2004) *Applying family therapy: A guide for caring professionals in the community.* Lyme Regis: Russell House.

Walker, S., & Beckett, C. (2003). *Social work assessment and intervention.* Lyme Regis: Russell House.

Walker S., (2010). *The social workers guide to Child and Adolescent Mental Health.* London: Jessica Kingsley.

Walker, S., & Beckett, C. (2011). *Social work assessment and intervention* (2nd ed.). Lyme Regis: Russell House.

Webster-Stratton, C. (1997). Treating children with early-onset conduct problems: A comparison of child and parent training interventions. *Journal of Consulting and Clinical Psychology, 65*(1), 93–109.

Wong, Y., & Vinsky, J. (2009). Speaking from the margins: A critical reflection on the 'spiritual-but-not-religious' discourse in social work. *British Journal of Social Work, 39* (7), 1343–1359.

SECTION 7

Future Challenges for Social Work

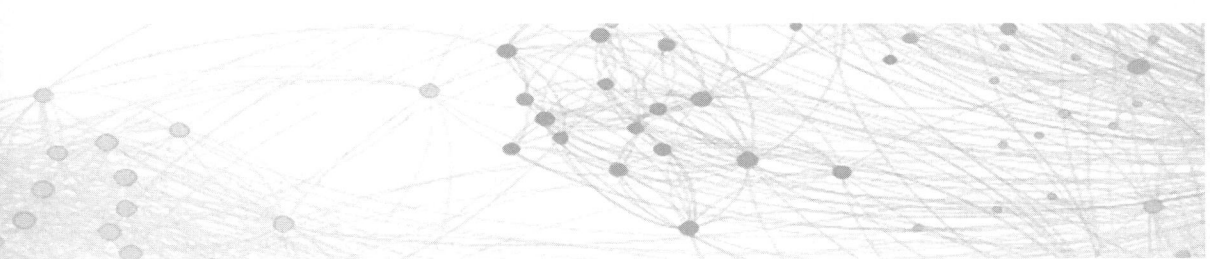

INTRODUCTION

The final section on future challenges for social work is probably one of the most exciting and innovative parts of the *Handbook*. The section is ambitious in its remit and concentrates on various possibilities, new directions, and futures advances that are likely to occur in social work. It argues that the changing roles and tasks of social work over the next decades are likely to be determined by economic and political drivers that will have significant long-term effects. Just to give a feel for this, it is likely that issues around sustainability and environment will increasingly shape service delivery and policy changes in social work. Mary (Mary, N. (2008). *Social work in a sustainable world*. Chicago, IL: Lyceum Books) addresses exactly this context of social work and the responsibility of the social worker within the larger global community. Though not covered in this *Handbook*, one role of the social worker is to advocate for these 'greener' mandates. Gray et al. (Gray, M., Coates, J., & Hetherington, T. (eds). (2012 forthcoming). *Environmental Social Work*. London: Routledge) make a compelling case for the way in which environmental concerns and issues are beginning to influence theory, practice, and education in social work. It is likely that the inter-relatedness of social work both in relation to other professions and wider social issues will become ever more pressing. Thinking about interdependence is smart thinking. People have all become interdependent in various important ways. Societies are creating global problems, like climate change and the financial crisis, which no country can address on its own. So these problems are orphan problems that remain unaddressed by many world institutions and professional organisations. 'We don't care' is possibly the major future challenge societies are facing. Inertia, hopelessness, and inaction as symptoms of late-modern times will inevitably impact on social work. The 'thick stuff' of social worker–client interaction may change as a result of these broader future-oriented societal problems. The power to define the client's problems may shift to 'we don't care what happened, we only care what is going to happen'.

We need high-quality analysis and research to respond to these new challenges. There is general agreement that the recent trend toward theory-driven research that is contextual and process oriented is encouraging for social work. There is also a shared concern that the pressures on social work to achieve improvements based on a narrow, performance culture rationality will inevitably suppress innovation and weaken the quality of direct work. This section deals with challenging questions regarding the short- and medium-term prospects for social work in an increasingly consumer-driven culture: Will it result in an increased professionalisation of a 'clinical' and evidence-based approach to social work based on ability to pay? Has the service-user movement made a significant and lasting contribution to how services are resourced and delivered? As part of this shift, has the role of expert changed in social work? Given the increased emphasis on integrated services, what are the prospects for interprofessional approaches to social work and how will they impact upon professional boundary making and turf wars? These are questions about the sustainability of social work itself, if defined as an ability or capacity of the profession to be maintained or to sustain itself. Crucial in considerations about the future of social work is how the profession's changing role and tasks will be affected by the increased deployment of new communication technologies: Is a virtual client service provision a real possibility? What are the prospects for a transnational social work that addresses global agendas relating to human rights and social justice? Is this a vanity or a significant move forward in developing new overarching policy agendas? These are the sort of vexed issues and questions that are addressed in this final section.

Chapter 40 examines the future(s) of social work. Few readers are likely to disagree with Paul Michael Garrett that social work practitioners' working practices and ways of viewing their role are shifting and transforming. In this sense, therefore, social workers are confronted with an uncertain future. More fundamentally, the professional 'habitus' of individual social workers is being remade. Globally also, the profession is now situated within an economic and social context determined by the recession and attempts to ensure that economic 'meltdown' does not occur. Against this backdrop, Garrett examines the changing nature and role of social work. He maps the significant challenges facing social workers and dwells on a range of key themes and preoccupations. These include: changing work and organisational structures; the increasing use of e-templates and various ways of deploying e-technologies within social work; the prevalence of surveillance practices; and moves to commodify social work services by increasingly shifting these services into the private sector. In response to global instabilities and transformations, Garrett – mainly referring to developments in England and the Republic of Ireland – suggests that social work might seek to recreate itself as a more political activity committed to defending (and enhancing) public sector provision. This would entail social workers and social work educators trying to align themselves with other groups that are seeking to construct a counter-hegemonic bloc which may have the capability of resisting discredited neoliberal solutions. Moreover, such a strategy would involve the fostering of critical engagement across a number of diverse fields.

In Chapter 41, David Stoesz and Howard Karger discuss various trends, changes, and developments in the area of professional education in social work. Drawing on their own research, they develop a controversial thesis on the nature of professional education and show how a 'critical approach' to professional education is best achieved via 'scientific scholarship' and rigour. In laying out the foundations for this approach, Stoesz and Karger show how, from initial conceptualisation to the consideration of outcomes, social work professional education is often more doctrinaire and mechanical than thoughtful, balanced, questioning, informed, and incisive. They argue that students are socialised into practice without a critical understanding of direct social work interventions and treatment. Rather, they are trained through derivative, frequently inadequate, and always 'reductionist textbooks'. Drawing on empirical research, they show that it is the rarest student who reads therapeutic theory in the words of the original theorists, or confronts the problems of effectiveness, or understands the ambiguities of research, or considers the social and political imperatives that are realised in mental health treatment, the dominant form of social work practice in the USA. Indeed, it is the rarest social work instructor who contributes to this discussion in a forum beyond the sheltered workshops of academic social work. In the concluding section, Stoesz and Karger give examples of new directions for professional social work education within an international context.

Imogen Taylor addresses the emerging area of interprofessional practice in Chapter 42. Collaboration with other professions has always been important in social work, but over the past ten years the interprofessional agenda has been brought to the forefront of policy and practice agendas. The response to the growth in the complexity of health and social care practice has increasingly identified the potential for comprehensive integrated services. Taylor examines interprofessionality from the perspective of health and social care brought about by Third Way policy on partnership development and the need to overcome 'silo effects'. Given enduring professional concern with identity, status, and discretion and accountability, in competitive managerial environments, interprofessionalism might constitute the Achilles' heel of social service partnerships. Despite differing professional perspectives, there is some normative agreement that interprofessionalism is a 'good thing' though a great deal of work is required to ensure that a coordinated approach is used. Interprofessionalism is used not only to benefit service users but also to influence policy issues. Taylor develops a framework for integrated services in health, education, and social work that has the potential to overcome many of the barriers and resistance to change.

In Chapter 43, Thomas Ley's very contemporary analysis concentrates on new technologies for practice, particularly ways in which the 'electronic turn' brought on by developments in information and communication technology (ICT) are reconfiguring work practices relating to communicating with and profiling clients; collating, storing, and sharing information; streamlining data collection; controlling and Taylorising work practices; targeting client, customer, consumer, or service-user need to enhance efficiency; engaging in advocacy; enhancing accountability; and so on. Most important is the marketisation of the public sector – and the role of the corporate sector in this – and ICT as an essential tool to promote restructuring with public sector welfare bureaucracies with access to new customers via smart cards, for example. Of concern are threats to civil liberties and human rights, the engagement of consenting families, electronic assessments, and over-simplification of complex problems with the aid of preconfigured categories in drop-down menus.

Chapter 44 addresses service-user participation. Long-time advocate for service-user participation, Peter Beresford examines the changed view of service users in social policy as unreliable, untruthful, and suspect and the new emphasis on 'conditionality' and responsibility before rights. The focus has shifted to changing the behaviour of people (i.e., welfare service users) through more stringent controls, such as welfare-to-work programmes. Despite the rhetoric of participation and empowerment, thus far, welfare users have had minimal involvement in welfare reform. Thus Beresford questions the populist intent of the UK's New Labour's approach to social policy, noting the role played by the media in shaping reactionary populist attacks that play on individual fears and anxieties, which do not reflect a full or accurate picture. He argues that political notions of participation do not match social work's normative framework of involving people in the process, giving them a voice, taking their wishes into account, and so on. The extent to which the New Labour-Democratic Coalition government was interested in real participation by service-user groups remains open to question. For New

Labour, participation effectively meant 'choice' and 'take up' of services. If people choose to participate in this way, then services can be said to be responsive to consumer wants and needs. But service users and their organisations can and want to offer their own analyses, interpretations, and plans for action. They want to develop their own practices, services, and organisations instead of just being subject to those of others.

In Chapter 45, Narda Razack turns her attention to the changing contours of international social work. She examines the definition and nature of international social work and contemporary developments in this area, demonstrating the changing nature of social work at the beginning of the 21st century. Having entered its second century, she claims that contemporary social work is a global profession, increasingly shaped by global phenomena. International social work is thus increasingly shaped by the interaction between the local and the global, by the inequalities between the North and South, and by calls to see international exchanges as mutual learning processes to counter the perpetuation of colonising practices and Western dominance.

From their considerable experience in the development of social work education in Africa, Osei-Hwedie and Morena Rankopo examine social work in developing countries in Chapter 46, including its successes, problems, and pitfalls. They employ an example of the development of social work in Botswana. Taking an international perspective on social work in developing countries, they examine what makes Africa different and unique, and the struggles with developing social work there mainly brought about by its colonialist past and the struggle for relevance that goes on even today. They highlight the issues in making an international professional entity like social work with its Western ways relevant to local cultures with diversely different – African or non-European – world views and the influence of people from the USA and elsewhere that have moulded and shaped social work in Africa as well as the diversity between north and south Africa and the reasons why people write mainly about sub-Saharan Africa.

The final chapter (Chapter 47) by Iain Ferguson examines the challenging but compelling nature of the politics of social work. Deemed a past project of social work in these neoliberal times, Ferguson examines why social work is inherently political and proposes ways in which its political agenda is being rekindled and revivified by contemporary developments in dehumanising practice contexts. If there is one single conclusion to be drawn from this chapter, it is the need for social workers to acknowledge openly the political nature of their profession and to grapple with its consequences. Ferguson claims this does not mean social work is reducible to politics but that its failure consciously to address the political roots and role of social work makes it more likely that, by default, social workers will succumb to political ideologies and agendas inimical to the ethical core of the profession. For that reason, Ferguson believes, whatever their specific limitations might be, over the past decade, emergent approaches seeking to challenge a dominant ideology of 'non-political' professionalism are a welcome part of social work's political coming of age.

40

The Future(s) of Social Work

Paul Michael Garrett

At the time of writing, autumn 2010, it remains difficult to imagine the future(s) of social work. It remains clear however, the forms which the profession assumes in the years to come, across a range of jurisdictions and institutions, cannot be detached from the global economic crisis which erupted in 2007. This 'big picture' dimension cannot be elided, in this final section of the *Handbook*, when one begins to ponder social work in the future. That is to say, there is no partition around the sector which safeguards it – and those working in it – from other more pervasive and dominant economic and social tendencies and trajectories.

The global economic crisis represented what historian Eric Hobsbawm (2008) termed the 'most serious crisis of the capitalist system since 1929–33' (p. 28). In September 2008, when the financial crisis seemed to deepen – as stock markets around the world began to falter and plummet and a number of banking, mortgage, and insurance companies failed – even the US administration was prompted to intervene decisively and to pass the Emergency Economic Stabilisation Act 2008, a measure which provided for greater government intervention and seemed to run entirely counter to the rhetoric of neoliberalism.

Indeed, these emergency measures introduced in North America, Europe, and elsewhere, appeared to indicate something of a Keynesian resurgence.

What remains apparent, however, is the economic crisis is *not* over. Indeed, there are some indications the US economy is 'on the brink of a double-dip recession' (Elliott, 2010, p. 30). According to the US Census Bureau, one in seven Americans now live on or below the poverty line: 43.6 million people or 14.3% of the population were in poverty in 2009, up from 39.8 million the previous year ('Four million Americans fall into poverty in one year', *The Guardian*, 17 September, 2010, p. 6; see Chapter 2). More than a quarter of African-Americans and Latinos live in poverty, and the statistics on children are equally stark in terms of what is revealed about the intersecting of class and 'race': nearly 36% of all Black children and 33% of Latino children were poor in 2009 ('Lean times for the poor', *The Irish Times*, 23 September, 2010, p. 15).

Despite these extraordinary figures, the sense of inchoate international panic, so detectable in 2007–2008, has abated. However, it remains sensible to try to perceive the crisis which erupted a few years ago as a *long* crisis, the outcome of which is still to be determined. Importantly also, the most severe social costs (public spending cuts) of the bank bailouts are still to impact, particularly in Britain, which is about to experience the deepest cuts in public spending since the 1920s. In this economic and global context, social work services in Britain, Ireland, and further afield, will come under additional pressures because more children and their families are likely to need assistance (see also 'Councils expect social problems from recession', *The Guardian*, 19 December, 2008, p. 13; 'Slump will bring home violence', *The Guardian*, 20 December, 2008, p. 8).

Expressed somewhat more theoretically, and perhaps aiding attempts to understand the trajectory – or 'future(s) – of social work in *particular* societies, the present time may be conceived as a series of interlinked 'conjunctures'. This idea, located within the matrix of ideas associated with Antonio Gramsci, refers to a period during which various 'social, political and economic and ideological contradictions at work in society come together to give it a specific and distinctive shape' (Hall, in Hall & Massey, 2010, p. 57), when different 'levels of society, the economy, politics, ideology, common sense, etc, come together or "fuse"' (Hall, in Hall & Massey, 2010, p. 59). A conjuncture is also a 'critical turning point or rupture in a political structure, primarily signifying a crisis in class relations' (Rustin, 2009, p. 18; see also Garrett, 2008a, 2009a). John Clarke et al. (2007) helpfully elaborate:

> [conjunctures are] particular formations of time and space in which multiple forces, pressures, tendencies and possibilities are condensed ... Taking conjunctures as containing multiple forces and multiple possibilities enables us to see how political projects attempt to construct coherence out of this multiplicity and create the apparent necessity of a particular future (Clarke et al., 2007, p. 36).

That is to say, a conjuncture represents a moment which provides an opportunity to construct a new hegemonic settlement.

In both the countries forming the focus of this chapter, it could be argued conjunctural analysis might help understanding and enable speculation on the nature of the crises and tentative analysis of the situation of social work within these two different but closely associated jurisdictions. Clearly, Britain and the Republic of Ireland are two entirely different social formations which are, because of contrasting histories and economic positioning, experiencing the current crisis in dissimilar ways. Thus, the patterning of the conjunctures are, therefore, immensely different and this will also impact on how social work is shaped in the future. Unlike Britain, in Republic of Ireland, the Roman Catholic Church – itself now experiencing a crisis – has historically fulfilled a key role within the hegemonic bloc governing Irish society. However, in both Britain and Ireland, as elsewhere, the global economic crisis is manifestly having an impact on social work. More broadly, connected to how the crisis is unfolding, in both countries, have been new attempts to defining the meaning and aim of 'welfare'. This entails, as Clarke (2004) maintained, even prior to the present crisis, 'attempts to create new settlements – to fix meanings, to institutionalize them in new political–cultural formations and to naturalize them as necessary, inevitable and the best way of "doing welfare"' (pp. 25–26). This also relates to questions pivoting on more encompassing discourses concerning how to be 'modern' both within and beyond social work (Garrett, 2008b, 2009b).

BRITAIN

One of the key contextual developments for the evolution of the future of social work in Britain is, of course, the election of a new government. In the general election, held in May 2010, there was a much smaller swing to the Conservative Party than had been expected: a mere 4%. The party took 10.7 million votes, a 36% share of the ballot and

306 seats – 20 short of the number required to form an overall majority. The Labour Party plummeted to 8.6 million votes, down by six points at 29% of the vote: the former governing party was left with 258 parliamentary seats in the House of Commons. The Liberal Democrats saw a swing of only 1%, despite the party's expectation and that of sections of the media, and a popular vote of 6.8 million: it increased its share of the vote to 23% and this gave the party 57 seats (see also Watkins, 2010). Following a short period of negotiations, a Conservative/Liberal Democrat coalition government, headed by David Cameron, was formed.

Surveying the defeat of the Labour Party, Susan Watkins (2010) asserted it took place 'within the wider story of the disintegration of European social democracy, from above – leaders enlisted in the neo-liberal project – from below: deindustrialization, privatization, and downward pressure on wages from immigrant workers' (p. 90). Certainly, in terms of the Labour leadership's adherence to neoliberal measures, there was a good deal of evidence available. For example, under 'Blair and Brown, the City of London was pumped up into the most deregulated trading centre in the world' (Watkins, 2010, p. 13). Furthermore, as illuminated in a number of key articles within the academic literature, the neoliberal agenda has heavily impinged on social work and associated areas of social care (Carey, 2007; Ferguson & Lavallette, 2004; Harlow, 2004; Harris, 2003; Jones, 2001).

Attention has been drawn, therefore, to how neoliberal policies – reflected in unfilled vacancies and a high turnover of and dependence on agency staff – are having a deleterious impact on the ability of practitioners to deliver effective services. For example, the Joint Area Review (JAR), published after the death of Peter Connolly in the London Borough of Haringey, concluded this 'high turnover of qualified social workers in some social care teams has resulted in heavy reliance on agency staff ... results in lack of continuity for children and their families and of care planning' (Ofsted, Healthcare Commission, Her Majesty's Inspectorate of Constabulary, 2008, p. 13; see also Garrett, 2009c). Peter Connolly – initially referred to in media reports simply as 'Baby P' – was a 17-month-old boy who died on 3 August 2007 from severe injuries which were inflicted while he was in the care of his mother, her partner, and a lodger in the household, Jason Owen. On 11 November 2008, two men were found guilty of causing or allowing the death of a child or vulnerable person. The mother had already pleaded guilty to the same charge. Peter had been subject to a child protection plan from 22 December 2006, following concerns he had been abused and neglected. He was still subject to this plan when he died. Related to this incident, the British Association of Social Workers revealed 'nationally about 11% of posts were vacant, rising to 30% in some of the most stressful urban communities' ('Social worker chiefs call for end to demonization of their colleagues', *The Guardian*, 13 November 2008, p. 15).

The private sector has become increasingly important with regard to the 'delivery' of care for older people following the NHS and Community Care Act 1990 (Harris, 2003). This has, of course, been particularly the case in the residential and nursing sector where large corporate providers increased their share of the market. In this context, Scourfield (2007) argued residential care was now 'a commodity ... there to be traded and exploited for its surplus value like any other commodity' (p. 162) and, as a consequence, 'the quest for profitability means business values, reductions in costs and income generation have been prioritised over above the quality of care' (p. 170). The private sector role has also begun to colonise children's homes and related services and it has been maintained there has been something of a 'stampede of private equity firms into the foster-care sector' (Mathiason, 2007, n.p.). The *Care Matters* agenda, which mapped the future direction of services for children and young people in public care for the former

Labour administration, also emphasised the role of the private sector, not only in terms of the promotion of 'social work practices', but also in a more pervasive sense (Secretary of State for Education and Skills, 2006; see also Garrett, 2008a, 2010a).

More generally within the sphere of social work and social care, as McLaughlin's (2007, 2010) work has highlighted, the habitus of practitioners was subjected to drastic changes during the period of Labour governments (Bourdieu, 2002; see also Garrett, 2007a, 2007b). Following the establishment of the Social Care Register in April 2003 it became:

> clear from the Codes of Practice that being a social care worker is not seen as a nine-to-five job, in which there is left a clear separation of work/home/private life. Indeed, the criteria gives both employers and the General Social Care Council (GSCC), via the registration process, unprecedented regulation over the workforce, whether in office, pub or at home (McLaughlin, 2007, p. 1274).

Developments such as this can, perhaps, be interpreted as reflecting, in complex and complicated ways, some of the thinking of Henry Ford, the US car manufacturer, who was keen – during the period of rapid mass industrialisation around the time of the First World War – to intervene in the private lives of his employees and to exert some degree of control over how they spent their lives when not at work. Indeed, as Gramsci observed, these tendencies were then only 'latent' yet they could become 'at a certain point, state ideology' (in Forgacs, 1988, p. 191). Moreover, given the neoliberal aspiration to erode the boundary between home and work, mostly prompted by the need to create new temporal spaces for capital accumulation, social work practitioners may, over time, find their workplace 'abolished altogether, or rather dissolved into life' (Bauman, 2002, p. 149). The trend is likely to continue given the coalition government's discontinuation of the GSCC, following an announcement in July 2010 soon after taking office, with its powers to be transferred to the Health Professions Council.

The JAR, referred to earlier, also brought into a wider public domain a theme which had, perhaps, previously largely been confined to academic journals, that is what has been referred to as social work's 'electronic' or 'e-Turn' (see, e.g., Garrett, 2004a; see also Chapter 43). For example, the JAR reported, in Haringey, some 'allocations of cases within social care services' were even 'made electronically and without discussion with social workers' (p. 7). Moreover, the 'existing social care electronic recording system operated by the council lacked sufficient flexibility and, although this impedes effective practice by social workers, there has been insufficient priority given to resolving this issue by managers' (Ofsted, Healthcare Commission, HM Inspectorate of Constabulary, 2008, p. 14). In *The Guardian*, for example, Simon Jenkins maintained the 'belief has long been bred in the bone of the children's minister, Ed Balls, that any computer can solve the world's ills at the click of a mouse. It is a dangerous lie' (Jenkins, 2008, p. 37). Importantly, following research conducted by Sue White et al. (White et al., 2008), there has been wider coverage of the amount of time social workers are compelled to spend in front of computer screens (see also Munro, 2008). Related to the deployment of ICTs, there has also been a related concern about the State's new 'watchfulness' and how technologies are increasingly being deployed to conduct surveillance of the 'risky' and the *potentially* risky (Pollack, 2010; see Chapter 4). Within children's services this was reflected in the deployment of new systems of dataveillance, such as the much criticised ContactPoint (Garrett, 2004b, 2004c). Ministers spent tens of thousands of pounds – including £15,700 on mugs and £45,000 on pens – to promote the controversial scheme, according to a freedom of information request ('Ministers spend £61,000 on mugs and pens to promote database', *The Guardian*, 30 April, 2010). The new government is committed to 'scrapping' Contactpoint 'as soon as possible and it is also 'considering its replacement with an alternative approach to support vulnerable children' (Department of Education, 10 June, 2010; see also Garboden, 2010).

The former Labour administration was, of course, keen to emphasise its expenditure on social work, social care, and associated services. Nevertheless, it appeared to fail to reach its own 'targets' to reduce the numbers of children who were poor. Furthermore, in October 2008, the Audit Commission reported the Children's Trusts, created by the government, had been 'confused and confusing'. Five years after the publication of the declarative *Every Child Matters* (Chief Secretary to the Treasury, 2003) programme there was 'little evidence of better outcomes for children and young people' (p. 1). Professionals, it seemed, were 'working together' but this was 'often through informal arrangements outside the trust framework. Trusts get in the way: a third of directors of children's services say the purpose of the trusts is "unclear", and the uncertainty is hampering their efforts to deliver better services' (Audit Commission, 2008, p. 1). Indeed, these findings illustrate the fact spending patterns – and the lauding of 'new' initiatives and programmes – often fail to reveal (and may even conceal) some of the more significant aspects of 'reforms'.

For the Labour Party, an embedded neoliberal rationality characterised its vision of the future. This is not, of course, to argue the former government's *entire* project of organisational, thematic, and professional 'reform' – focused on social work – was unambiguously rooted in neoliberalism. Nonetheless, neoliberalism served – often implicitly – to provide the dominant, or hegemonic, core for the 'transformation' of children's services and associated sectors and spheres, for example (see Garrett, 2009d). Some academics and political commentators maintained New Labour's neoliberalism was 'an uncomfortable and strained construction rather than an essential political character' (Clarke et al., 2007, p. 146). However, following Blair's ascendancy to the leadership of the party, it was to become increasingly comfortable with the neoliberal agenda. What Stuart Hall (2003) referred to as the 'subaltern programme, of a more social-democratic kind, running alongside' (p. 19) became much more subdued and increasingly marginal and marginalised.

Social work in an age of eternal austerity within a 'permanently shrunken state'

None of this is, of course, to suggest the arrival of a new ConDem administration, with its 'cocktail of born-again monetarism and regressive social policies' (Elliott, 2010, p. 26), is likely to be preferable for social workers in Britain. Indeed, the emphasis which David Cameron has placed on the role of philanthropy and charity in providing what are now public services, has made it plain his party's vision of the 'future' is likely to be even more damaging than that imagined by the defeated Labour administration (see also Finlayson, 2007; Toynbee, 2010a). Indeed, a review, set up by the new coalition government is presently considering what 'role might ... *volunteer* social workers play?' (Department of Education, 2010, p. 2, emphasis added), and is due to deliver its final recommendations in April 2011 (Department of Education, June, 2010). Nonetheless, even prior to the general election, the Conservative Party was intent on trying to win the support of social workers (see Conservative Party Commission on Social Workers, 2007). Since coming to power, the government has also stated it will support the 15 recommendations of the Social Work Task Force (2009), which was appointed by the Labour government and reported in 2009. It has also instigated a review of child protection, headed by Eileen Munro – Professor of Social Work at the London School of Economics – which also involves exploring issues related to, for example, early intervention, reducing bureaucracy, and providing more professional freedom in order to 'liberate' their skills and talents. Indeed, this idea that, for social work practitioners, 'liberation' and 'creative' work now lies beyond what is presented as a discredited and moribund public sector was frequently a key component of the Labour Party's approach to 'transforming' social work within children's services (see Garrett, 2009d).

However, when seeking to gain some insights into how social work future(s) might evolve in Britain, it is vital to understand the political discourse which the Conservatives, aided by their coalition partners, are seeking to deploy to explain the social problems often prompting the involvement of social workers. Following the death of Peter Connolly, a number of ideas were discussed which drew attention to how the tragedy – seemingly a reflection of a wider societal crisis – could be explained. For the former Conservative Party leader, Iain Duncan Smith (2008), the child's death was a symbol of a 'broken society' which he, and David Cameron, was seeking to fix. He – along with a number of other signatories – had a letter published in *The Guardian*, in December 2008, imploring then prime minister Gordon Brown to seize 'the opportunity of initiating a long-term inquiry to examine how we can stop some of today's children becoming the abusing parents of tomorrow' (n.p.). This aspiration for earlier and more substantial interventions into the lives of children and their families was also supported by then Shadow Secretary for Work and Pensions, Chris Grayling, who called for out-of-work parents to have their home lives and prospects investigated in the context of Conservative Party plans to 'tackle underclass Britain' ('Never-worked' families face Tory scrutiny, *The Observer*, 7 December, 2008, p. 5).

Ideas rooted in the notion of Britain being a 'broken society' are central to the hegemonic endeavours of the new ConDem administration. However, in terms of how the politics of the 'broken society' is being assembled and orchestrated, other themes and keywords are also important. For example, it could be argued discourses revolving around 'underclass' stereotypes are significant. Indeed the linkage was made explicit in political and media responses to the death of Peter Connolly (see Garrett, 2009c). *The Observer*, for example, argued the 'fate' of the child had 'focused the spotlight once again on child protection services and loopholes in the net designed to protect the most vulnerable children, *as well as broader questions of how to reach an underclass of inadequate parents* raising children in volatile circumstances' ('Put more children at risk into care', *The Observer*, 16 November 2008, p. 2, emphasis added). These were, it was asserted, 'families that were straight out of *nightmares* ... an *underclass* ... untouched by the affluence of modern Britain' ('Why children are left to die beyond help's reach', *The Observer*, 16 November, 2008, p. 18). Moreover, a number of newspaper articles attempted to forge a connection between Peter Connolly and his family, and Shannon Matthews and her mother, Karen. Shannon, her mother had alleged, had been kidnapped. Later it was revealed Karen had hidden the child along with an accomplice, Michael Donovan. She was charged with child neglect and, in December 2008, with Donovan was found guilty on charges of kidnapping, false imprisonment, and perverting the course of justice. In *The Observer*, it was maintained the case of Peter Connolly 'ran in parallel to that of Shannon, a more horrific shadow'. She 'loved Shannon to bits' but had her kidnapped ('Inside the dark, dangerous world of Karen Matthews', *The Observer*, 7 December, 2008, pp. 29–32). The same piece then went on to argue it 'was easy to present her as a representative of a feckless *underclass, a broken society*, a generation of parents only concerned for their own childish emotions' (p. 31, emphasis added). The newspaper presentation of Karen Matthews, frequently fused to that of Peter Connolly, was characterised by, what can be termed, a certain class loathing and contempt. This was, perhaps, most apparent in an article by columnist, Sophie Heawood, published in

The Independent on Sunday in mid-November, where she argued:

> It's what seems to be an *underclass*, a level of British society that is not just struggling with poverty – this is way beyond being poor – but often getting by with *subnormal intelligence* levels, living in a world *with no professional aspirations* whatsoever, for generations, where criminality is normality, with people who seem to have not just fallen through the net of literacy or personal improvement, but missed out on education or social development altogether (Heawood, 2008, p. 42, emphases added).

Her solution to these problems was that her readers should:

> join a mentoring scheme to befriend a struggling child ... And how about mentoring adults? Could we create more real-life schemes, and not just TV shows, where people like Karen Matthews can get to know people from less troubled backgrounds? It's the entrenchment of the *underclass* that keeps people there (Heawood, 2008, p. 43, emphasis added).

Perhaps related to this cultural and political ambiance on parenting, there have also been calls for more children to be placed in care (see 'More children need to be placed in care, says Barnardo's boss', *The Guardian*, 28 June, 2010, p. 7). More provocatively, there has also been a call to sterilise parents who abuse children (Perberton, 2010).

It could be argued New Labour's 'ASBO – Anti-Social Behaviour Orders – politics', with its so-called 'neighbours from hell' (Home Office, 2007), also provided the discursive foundation for much of this and the 'broader questions' the new ConDem government is now seeking to define and address (Garrett, 2007c). For the Conservatives especially, the 'broken society' is 'the baleful outcome of social-democratic politics' and the 'source of the corrosion of social life can be found in the excesses of government' (Finlayson, 2010, pp. 25–26). Unsurprisingly, perhaps, given this political orientation, the 'effects of neoliberal competitiveness and inequality are ... ignored' (Finlayson, 2010, p. 26). Nevertheless, and in contrast to the theorists of the 'broken society', it is analytically preferable to conceptualise the current crisis as part of 'social recession' – in both Britain and Ireland. That is to say, the cause of the current problems 'is not the 'intrusive state but the intrusive economy' (Finlayson, 2010, p. 27).

For the ConDem administration, however, the chief way to respond to the 'broken society' is to construct a 'big society'. According to Cameron, this 'is about a real cultural shift – we know that the era of big government ... didn't work. We want to build a Big Society where local people feel empowered' (Cabinet Office, 2010a, p. 1). The Deputy Prime Minister has also placed an emphasis on 'social mobility' (Cabinet Office, 2010b). However, it remains clear the government is intent on cutting jobs and services within the public sector and the political aspiration is to usher in 'eternal austerity' and a 'permanently shrunken state' (Toynbee, 2010b, p. 27; see also Samuel, 2010). In this context, it will be the very poorest – many of whom are, of course, in contact with social workers – who are likely to suffer the most ('Poor families bear brunt of austerity drive', *The Guardian*, 25 August 2010; 'Cuts will hit poor 10 times harder than rich – report', *The Guardian*, 11 September 2010, p. 1).

THE REPUBLIC OF IRELAND

It is undeniable, for a few years, the Irish economy expanded enormously and some Irish citizens *have* experienced the 'best of times', even if the benefits of economic growth have never been shared equitably (Fahey et al., 2007; see also Allen, 2009). Nevertheless, despite the clear transformations taking place in Irish life, there was always a palpable fragility associated with the economic boom. More fundamentally, capitalism is, of course, inherently unstable and, as early as 2003, it was suggested the country had entered a 'post-Celtic phase as each day brings fresh news of an increase in inflation or unemployment' (Mayer, 2003, p. 27). In the latter quarter of 2008, the economy entered a recession. This was largely related to global economic events, but the Republic inhabited a position of specific vulnerability because of how the 'boom' of the 'Celtic Tiger' phrase had been fuelled by an 'overheated' property market and a reliance of inward investment, particularly from US-based multinational corporations (Allen, 2009). Indeed, as historian Roy Foster (2007) maintained, the US microelectronics industry has, effectively, 'colonized Ireland' (p. 424).

Despite neoliberalism's rhetorical tendency to inflate the scale of its success, it has also been apparent many – often the users of social services – continued to experience considerable hardship and poverty *even* throughout the years of economic growth (Conference of Religious of Ireland, 2006). Furthermore, it is widely acknowledged the public welfare sphere – and especially the hospital and educational domains – are underfunded and, as a consequence, many staff have poor morale (Allen, 2007). The health sector, particularly, has been subjected to processes of privatisation with, in March 2003, tax relief on the building of private hospitals being introduced. Since then three different groups have come together to create such hospitals: builders (or property developers), hospital consultants, and financiers. Moreover, this has served to create a form of 'medical apartheid' with the poor being left to 'queue and pray', while those able to afford private medical care could be fast tracked (Allen, 2007, p. 175; see also Tussing & Wren, 2006). Related to these developments, concerns are being frequently expressed about the often poor quality of care afforded to older people in a poorly regulated nursing home sector.

Public anxiety is now also apparent over how the years of unplanned growth – in terms of housing and the transport infrastructure – has taken its toll on the nation's ecology (see also Leonard, 2009). Moreover, Irish society has yet adequately to address a plethora of social ills which continue to provide part of the day-to-day context for the work of social workers and those situated in associated areas of work: racism, for example, is encountered in embedded and socially pervasive ways by Irish Travellers (Fanning, 2002; Helleiner, 1997, 1998; Mac Laughlin, 1996; see also 'Traveller men's lives shorter by 15 years', *The Irish Times*, 3 September 2010, p. 3). In recent years some newer migrants have, in some instances, also encountered racism and xenophobia (Christie, 2006; Crowley & Mac Laughlin, 1997; Lentin, 2007; Lentin & McVeigh, 2006; White, 2009). Prior to the recent downturn, this may have been somewhat muted because of the buoyant economy, but workers from outside the jurisdiction have still been discriminated against – structurally and legally – and rendered subordinate within the Irish labour market (Dundon et al., 2007).

Women in the Republic continued to be denied the right to choose whether or not to have an abortion (both within the northern and southern jurisdictions; Fletcher, 1995; Kelly & Nic Giolla Choille, 1997; Mahon et al., 1998; Oaks, 2002; Smyth, 1992). Furthermore, the issue of clerical sexual abuse has commanded much attention in recent years (Commission to Inquire into Child Abuse, 2009; Commission of Investigation, 2009; Garrett, 2010b; Murphy et al., 2005). More broadly, the ruling political bloc has come under scrutiny due to public concerns about corruption and the 'brown envelope', or bribery culture. This culture, a product as much of privatisation as of the specific character of elite – and largely male – business–political–cultural networks, has led to the establishment of numerous expensive tribunals which have meandered in their enquiries for a number of years. Strikingly, though, these investigations led to the resignation of the previous *Taoiseach* and head of government, Bertie Ahern, in 2008.

Again seeking to perceive the present situation as a complex conjuncture, it can be argued the Republic, an unstable social and economic formation, is now entering a period of destabilised – but still combative and socially toxic – neoliberal hegemony (Forgacs, 1988; see also Foster, 2009). As Sean Phelan (2007a, 2007b) has persuasively argued, this hegemony – although sharing some of the characteristics of more internationally dominant features of neoliberalism – can be interpreted as having possessed a distinct *national* character (Harvey, 2005; Saad-Filho & Johnston, 2005). Thus, for him, to grasp the operation of neoliberalism, within the Republic, it is important to identify 'five key rhetorical strategies structuring the articulation of elite neoliberal discourses' (Phelan, 2007a, p. 36). These have centred on corporate 'social partnership' arrangements and mechanisms which 'bring together' business, compliant trade unions, and other 'stakeholders' with a view to promoting consensus and harmonious economic and social arrangements (Allen, 1999, p. 2000); the spectre of the 'bad old days', which risk being conjured up once again if neoliberal 'truths' are questioned; the pre-emption of critique by the skilful appropriation of 'fragments of critical discourses' (Phelan, 2007a, p. 39; see also Phelan, 2007b); a feigned non-ideological posture; and the bogus notion neoliberalism is a 'threatened' or minority discourse which is embattled and constantly needing to 'fight its corner'.

In December 2009, a budget was introduced which was widely perceived as the 'toughest in the history of the state' (Foster, 2009, p. 26). Welfare benefits were reduced, but the main targets were public sector workers whose salaries were cut by up to 15%. Moreover, these salary reductions followed levies introduced earlier in the year which cut into the salaries of workers such as nurses, civil servants, teachers, lecturers, and social workers. Nonetheless, such drastic austerity measures, unsurprisingly, are impairing the economy's ability to grow and failing to address the economic crisis. In September 2010, it was announced the national output had fallen again in the second quarter of the year. Moreover, unemployment stands at 13% percent and the 'emigrant boat and plane have re-emerged' as social safety valves, with the number of people leaving the state rising by a quarter between 2006 and 2008 ('Emigration must be confronted', *The Irish Times*, 23 September, 2010, p. 15). However, a budget – scheduled for December 2010 – is expected to cut even deeper into public spending. How, therefore, can social work's situation be perceived at this particular conjuncture? To even begin to consider this issue, it is important – albeit if only briefly – to locate social work historically in the Republic of Ireland.

A crisis for the state, a crisis for social work services?

From the advent of the partially independent state in 1922, elite groups were hesitant to embrace the new profession because it was viewed, especially by primary definers within the Roman Catholic Church, as a harbinger of modernity. Perhaps, more specifically, they were fearful of what they saw as its potential ability to intervene in the 'private' sphere of family life (Kearney & Skehill, 2005; Skehill, 2004). As the remarkably influential John Charles McQuaid (1895–1973), Catholic Archbishop of Dublin and Primate of Ireland (1940–1973) stated in the early 1950s: 'Our people do not want lady analysts of their lives and motives. Trouble is certain to develop if almoners undertake psychological investigation in our homes and hospitals' (in Skehill, 2004, p. 163). Perhaps, also, the idea persisted social work was a peculiarly 'protestant' endeavour and, as such, it was – as McQuaid's remark suggests – contrary to the 'Catholic' ethos of the inchoate state. In time, however, such concerns diminished. However, the specific role accorded to the family, recognised in the Irish Constitution, *Bunreacht Eireann* in 1937, has continued to place some limitations on how social workers and the courts can intervene in this 'private sphere' to safeguard the rights of children. Indeed, despite the aspirations for children encompassed within the project for national freedom, the new state, which defeated more potentially progressive social forces during the civil war, was rooted in a corrosively conservative form of hegemony (Lloyd, 1999). Furthermore, the harsh treatment afforded to children – more specifically, the children of the urban and rural poor – illuminates the failures of the partially post-colonial state. Indeed, by 1924, there were more children in the quasi-penal industrial schools in the Free State than there were in all of the industrial schools in England, Scotland, Wales, and Northern Ireland put together (Raftery & O'Sullivan, 1999).

Social work in the Republic is now broadly similar to social work activity in Britain and this is reflected in social workers sharing many of the same professional concerns (see, e.g., Burns & Lynch, 2008; Lynch & Burns, 2008). For example, many are critical that the nature of the 'work' in social work has, in recent times, been altered by managerialism and a 'quality agenda' seemingly intent on eroding professional autonomy and judgement (Kemp, 2008). Similar to Britain, recent research has also revealed social workers' concern about the lack of opportunity to form relationships with service users (Burns, 2008).

Significantly, social work is still mostly work undertaken by women: 83.2% of posts are filled by women ($n = 1928$) and 18.8% by men ($n = 338$). Moreover, student entrants to accredited programmes, in 2004, revealed a further tilt in the direction of females [87% women as against 13% men; National Social Work Qualification Board (NSWQB), 2006]. Nevertheless, there are, not surprisingly, certain national defining characteristics. Social work, within the state sector, is administratively situated within the Health Service Executive (HSE), an executive agency responsible for providing public hospital care. Perhaps contentiously, it might be maintained social work is somewhat more functional and less associated with ideas connected to emancipatory practice than, for example, social work in Britain. Indeed, it has been noted 'little evidence exists of practices or policies in social work to accommodate increased diversity' (Walsh et al., 2010, p. 1984). However, this is a complex issue, because there are significant local differences in terms of how social work is shaped and practised within and across the state (Kemp, 2008), for example, in terms of the divergences between urban and rural locations.

Social work education within the state is regulated by the NSWQB, which is scheduled to be subsumed within a new and more substantial regulatory Health and Social Care Professionals Council in 2010. The NSWQB has been responsible for producing surveys of the workforce and these provide a useful snapshot of some of the key issues impacting on social workers. The third of these surveys was issued in 2006 and revealed, in 2005 when the survey was conducted, there were 2237.4 whole time equivalent (WTE) posts in the Republic (2316 people). What was apparent, however, even during this period *prior* to the current recession, was the number of temporary posts: 426 (17.4%) up from 326 (16.4%) when the previous survey was undertaken in 2001. Indeed, this prompted the NSWQB to ponder why the profession was beginning to be characterised by a 'syndrome of permanent temporary posts'? It concluded this development might have been a consequence of 'employment ceilings' introduced by the government (see also Burns, 2008). More recently, the government – although maintaining it will increase the number of practitioners in the aftermath of the publication of the Ryan Report (Commission to Inquire into Child Abuse, 2009) – has remained intent on drastically reducing the number of public sector workers, including social workers ('Public service has 10,000 fewer staff, figures show', *The Irish Times*, 11 September, 2010, p. 6).

Clearly connected to social worker shortages within the Republic, there have been concerns about gaps and shortfalls in specific services. For example, a topical and contentious issue in terms of the provision of child and family services in the HSE is 'the absence of a nationwide out-of-hours crisis intervention service' (Office of the Minister for Children and Youth Affairs, 2008, p. 13; see also Lunny et al., 2008). More generally, a number of defects have been identified across services for children and families. At present, for example, one in five children in care do not have an allocated social worker and approximately a third of those in care also lack a care plan (HSE, 2009). In addition, 'awareness' and 'consistent implementation' of *Children First* (Department of Health and Children, 1999) – the protocol guiding arrangements for interprofessional working and the protection and welfare of children – remains 'a continuing challenge' (Office of the Minister for Children and Youth Affairs, 2008, p. v). Indeed, in this context two key issues are significant:

> the absence of consistency in the delivery of child welfare and protection services across the country and, more importantly, the absence of any standards against which delivery of services can be benchmarked and monitored ... [It is] incontrovertible that there are major inconsistencies in the implementation of the *Children First* guidelines throughout the country (Office of the Minister for Children and Youth Affairs, 2008, pp. 14–15).

Over recent months, concerns have been expressed about the deaths of children in public care, the inability of the HSE to produce reliable data on these deaths, and the failure to monitor children located in foster-care placements.

CONCLUSION

Templates for the future – be they encompassing visions of how society should operate or simply particular discrete fields such as social work which evolve at particular conjunctures – must engage with and incorporate ingrained expectations and ways of understanding and acting. In terms of social work, these embedded ways of comprehending practice need not be unambiguously progressive and may be rooted in a defence of professional privilege. However, these ingrained expectations may also be grounded in a set of values and code of ethics which are potentially oppositional to neoliberalism. Perhaps the key point is the new political or policy imperatives being devised by, for example, the new ConDem administration in the UK will 'not arrive in empty spaces – they arrive in the middle of already crowded and contested spaces where other discourses jostle for dominance' (Clarke et al., 2007, p. 50). In this context, therefore, it remains important to understand those seeking to promote neoliberal approaches are intent on a 'long war' and on ensuring change takes place and becomes embedded over many years, even decades. That is to say, the aspiration is to try and create, within each individual worker and new entrant to the field, a new sense of professional milieu or habitus conducive to neoliberalism (see also Bourdieu & Wacquant, 2004). Nonetheless, social workers in Britain, Ireland, and beyond cannot be relied upon merely to 'translate' plans and blueprints for change – unambiguously – into practice. The ability of practitioners to resist neoliberal inflected future(s) is, however, likely to depend on their ability to make linkages with other workers in other sectors and with the users of services.

REFERENCES

Allen, K. (1999). The Celtic Tiger, inequality and social partnership. *Administration, 47*(2), 31–55.

Allen, K. (2007). *Corporate takeover of Ireland*. Dublin: Irish Academic Press.

Allen, K. (2009). *Ireland's economic crash: A radical agenda for change*. Dublin: Liffey Press.

Audit Commission (2008). *Every Child Matters – are we there yet?* Press Notice, 29 October. Retrieved September 11, 2010 from http://www.audit-commission.gov.uk/pressoffice/pressreleases/Pages/20081029everychildmatters.aspx

Bauman, Z. (2002). *Society under siege*. Cambridge: Polity Press.

Bourdieu, P. (2002). Habitus. In J. Hillier & Rooksby, E. (eds). *Habitus: A sense of place*. Aldershot: Ashgate, pp. 27–34.

Bourdieu, P., & Wacquant, L.J.D. (2004). *An invitation to reflexive sociology* (2nd reprint, 1st English translation 1992). Cambridge: Polity.

Burns, K. (2008). Making a difference: Exploring job retention issues in child protection and welfare social work. In K. Burns & Lynch, D. (eds), *Child protection and welfare social workers: Contemporary themes and practice perspectives*. Dublin: Farmar, pp. 60–75.

Burns, K., & Lynch, D. (eds) (2008). *Child protection and welfare social work*. Dublin: Farmar.

Cabinet Office (2010a). *Prime Minister launches the Big Society Bank and announces the first four big society communities*. Press Notice, 19 July. Retrieved July 20, 2010 from http://www.cabinetoffice.gov.uk/newsroom/news_releases/2010/100719-bigsociety.aspx

Cabinet Office (2010b). *Deputy Prime Minister to champion social mobility*. Press Notice, 18 August. Retrieved August 19, 2010 from http://www.cabinetoffice.gov.uk/newsroom/news_releases/2010/100818-socialmobility.aspx

Carey, M. (2007). White-collar proletariat? Braverman, the deskilling/upskilling of social work and the paradoxical life of the agency care manager. *Journal of Social Work*, 7(1), 93–114.

Chief Secretary to the Treasury (2003). *Every Child Matters*. London: Stationery Office, Cm 5860.

Christie, A. (2006). Whiteness and the politics of 'race' in child protection guidelines in Ireland. *European Journal of Social Work*, 13(2), 199–217.

Clarke, J. (2004). *Changing welfare, changing states: New directions in social policy*. London: Sage.

Clarke, J., Newman, J., Smith, N., Vidler, E., & Westmarland, L. (2007). *Creating citizen-consumers: Changing publics and changing public services*. London: Sage.

Commission of Investigation (2009). *Report into the Catholic Archdiocese of Dublin*. Dublin: Department of Justice, Equality and Law Reform.

Commission to Inquire into Child Abuse (2009). *Commission to inquire into child abuse report*. Dublin: Stationery Office.

Conference of Religious of Ireland (CORI) (2006). *Developing a fairer Ireland: Policies to ensure economic development, social equity and sustainability*. Dublin: CORI.

Conservative Party Commission on Social Workers (2007). *No more blame game: The future for children's social workers*. Retrieved December 23, 2007 from http://www.fassit.co.uk/leaflets/No%20More%20Blame%20Game%20-%20The%20Future%20for%20Children's%20Social%20Workers.pdf

Crowley, E., & Mac Laughlin, J. (eds) (1997). *Under the belly of the tiger: Class, race, identity and culture in a global Ireland*. Dublin: Irish Reporter Publications.

Department of Education (2010). *Review of child protection: Better frontline services to protect children*. Press Notice, 10 June. Retrieved June 11, 2010 from http://www.education.gov.uk/inthenews/inthenews/a0061426/review-of-child-protection-better-frontline-services-to-protect-children

Department of Health and Children (1999). *Children First: National guidelines for the protection and welfare of children*. Dublin: Stationery Office.

Duncan Smith, I. (2008). The legacy of broken lives. *The Guardian*, 13 November, p. 32.

Dundon, T., Gonzalez-Perez, M.A., & McDonough, T. (2007). Bitten by the Celtic tiger: Immigrant workers and industrial relations in the new 'globalized' Ireland. *Economic and Industrial Democracy*, 28(4), 501–522.

Elliott, L. (2010). A brand of austerity about as progressive as Thatcher's. *The Guardian*, 26 August, p. 30.

Fahey, T., Russell, H., Whelan, C.T. (eds) (2007). *Best of times: The social impact of the Celtic tiger*. Dublin: Institute of Public Administration.

Fanning, B. (2002). *Racism and social change in the Republic of Ireland*. Manchester: Manchester University.

Ferguson, I., & Lavallette, M. (2004). Beyond power discourse: Alienation and social work. *British Journal of Social Work*, 34(3), 297–312.

Fletcher, R. (1995). Silences: Irish women and abortion. *Feminist Review*, 50, 44–66.

Finlayson, A. (2007). Making sense of David Cameron. *Public Policy Research*, March–May, 3–11.

Finlayson, A. (2010). The broken society versus the social recession. *Soundings*, 44, 22–35.

Forgacs, D. (ed.) (1988). *A Gramsci reader*. London: Lawrence and Wishart.

Foster, R.F. (2007). Changed utterly? Transformation and continuity in late twentieth-century Ireland. *Historical Research*, 80(209), 419–442.

Foster, R.F. (2009). A hungover Celtic tiger. *The Guardian*, 14 December, p. 26.

Garboden, M. (2010). Facebook-style site in bid to replace ContactPoint. *Community Care*, 19 August. Retrieved August 19, 2010 from http://www.communitycare.co.uk/Articles/2010/08/19/115106/facebook-style-site-in-bid-to-replace-contactpoint.htm

Garrett, P.M. (2004a). Social work's 'electronic turn': Notes on the deployment of information and communication technologies in social work with children and families. *Critical Social Policy*, 25(4), 529–554.

Garrett, P.M. (2004b). The electronic eye: Emerging surveillant practices in social work with children and families. *European Journal of Social Work*, 7(1), 57–71.

Garrett, P.M. (2004c). New Labour's new electronic 'telephone directory': The Children Act 2004 and plans for databases on all children in England and Wales. *Social Work and Social Sciences Review*, 12(1), 5–22.

Garrett, P.M. (2007a). Making social work more Bourdieusian: Why the social professions should critically engage with the work of Pierre Bourdieu. *European Journal of Social Work*, 10(2), 225–243.

Garrett, P.M. (2007b). The relevance of Bourdieu for social work: A reflection on obstacles and omissions. *Journal of Social Work*, 7(3), 357–381.

Garrett, P.M. (2007c). Making 'anti-social behaviour': A fragment on the evolution of 'ASBO Politics' in Britain. *British Journal of Social Work*, 37(5), 839–856.

Garrett, P.M. (2008a). Thinking with the Sardinian: Antonio Gramsci and social work. *European Journal of Social Work*, 11(3), 237–250.

Garrett, P.M. (2008b). How to be modern: New Labour's neoliberal modernity and the *Change for Children* programme. *British Journal of Social Work*, 38(2), 270–289.

Garrett, P.M. (2009a). The 'whalebone' in the (social work) 'corset'? Notes on Antonio Gramsci and social work educators. *Social Work Education*, 28(5), 461–475.

Garrett, P.M. (2009b). Marginalized youth, the 'modern' professional and the 'modern' workplace: A note on the need for a critical approach to 'modernizing' strategies. *Social Work and Society*, 6(2). Retrieved January 10, 2010 from http://www.socwork.net/2008/2/special_issue/garrett

Garrett, P.M. (2009c). The case of 'Baby P': Opening up spaces for debate on the 'transformation' of children's services. *Critical Social Policy*, 29(3), 533–547.

Garrett, P.M. (2009d). *'Transforming' children's services? Social work, neoliberalism and the 'modern' world*. Maidenhead: McGraw Hill/Open University.

Garrett, P.M. (2010a). Creating happier children and more fulfilled social workers: Neoliberalism, privatization and the reframing of leftist critiques in Britain. *Journal of Progressive Human Services*, 21, 83–101.

Garrett, P.M. (2010b). 'It is with deep regret that I find it necessary to tell my story': Child abuse in industrial schools in Ireland. *Critical Social Policy*, 30(2), 292–306.

Hall, S. (2003). New Labour's double-shuffle. *Soundings*, 24, 10–25.

Hall, S., & Massey, D. (2010). Interpreting the crisis. *Soundings*, 44, 57–72.

Harlow, E. (2004). Why don't women want to be social workers anymore? New managerialism, postfeminism and the shortage of social workers in Social Services Departments in England and Wales. *European Journal of Social Work*, 7(2), 167–179.

Harris, J. (2003). *The social work business*. London: Routledge.

Harvey, D. (2005). *A brief history of neoliberalism*. Oxford: Oxford University.

Heawood, S. (2008). The world around Baby P is wrong, why are we afraid to say so. *The Independent on Sunday*, 16 November, pp. 42–43.

Health Service Executive (2009). *Review of adequacy of services for children and families*. Retrieved January 10, 1010 from http://www.lenus.ie/hse/bitstream/10147/85813/1/ReviewofAdequacy2008.pdf

Helleiner, J. (1997). Women of the itinerant class: Gender and anti-traveller racism in Ireland. *Women's Studies International Forum*, 20(2), 275–287.

Helleiner, J. (1998). Contested childhood: The discourse and politics of traveller childhood in Ireland. *Childhood*, 5(3), 303–325.

Hobsbawm, E. (2008). The £500bn question. *The Guardian*, 9 October, p. 28.

Home Office (2007). *Innovative new help to tackle 'neighbours from hell'*. Press Notice, 11 April. Retrieved January 11, 2010 from http://www.respect.gov.uk/article.aspx?id=9072

Jenkins, S. (2008). Officialdom cannot hammer straight the crooked timber of mankind. *The Guardian*, 14 November, p. 37.

Jones, C. (2001). Voices from the front line: State social workers and New Labour. *British Journal of Social Work*, 31(4), 547–562.

Kearney, N., & Skehill, C. (eds) (2005). *Social work in Ireland: Historical perspectives*. Dublin: Institute of Public Administration.

Kelly, K., & Nic Giolla Choille, T. (1997). Listening and learning: Experiences in an emigrant advice agency. In P. O'Sullivan (ed.), *Irish women and Irish migration*. London: Leicester University. 168–192.

Kemp, T. (2008). Questioning quality: a critical analysis of the development and implementation of the 'quality agenda' and its impact on child protection social work practice in Ireland. In K. Burns & Lynch, D. (eds), *Child protection and welfare social workers: Contemporary themes and practice perspectives*. Dublin: A & A Farmar, pp. 97–110.

Lentin, R. (2007). Illegal in Ireland, Irish illegals: Diaspora nation and racial state. *Irish Political Studies*, 22(4), 433–453.

Lentin, R., & McVeigh, R. (2006). Irishness and racism: Towards an e-reader. *Translocations: The Irish Migration, Race and Social Transformation Review*, *1*(1), 22–40.

Leonard, L. (2009). Social partnership's boiling point: Environmental issues and social responses to neoliberal policy in Ireland. *Critical Social Policy*, *29*(2), 279–293.

Lloyd, D. (1999). *Ireland after history*. Cork: Cork University.

Lunny, L., McHugh, J., & Brosnan, K. (2008). *Monageer Inquiry*. Retrieved January 3, 2009 from http://www.omc.gov.ie/documents/child_welfare_protection/MonageerReport.pdf

Lynch, D., & Burns, K. (2008). Contexts, themes and future directions in Irish child protection and welfare work. In K. Burns & Lynch, D. (eds), *Child protection and welfare social workers: Contemporary themes and practice perspectives*. Dublin: A & A Farmar, pp. 1–9.

Mac Laughlin, J. (1996). The evolution of anti-traveller racism in Ireland. *Race and Class*, *37*(3), 47–64.

Mahon, E., Conlon, C., & Dillon, L. (1998). *Women and crisis pregnancy*. Dublin: Government Publications Office.

Mathiason, N. (2007). Children's homes hit by buyout fears. *The Observer*, 14 October. Retrieved October 15, 2007 from http://society.guardian.co.uk/children/story/0,,2191473,00.html.

Mayer, E. (2003). An outsider's view of modern Ireland: Michel Houllebecq's atomised. *Studies*, *92*(365), 27–34.

McLaughlin, K. (2007). Regulation and risk in social work: The General Social Care Council and the Social Care Register in context. *British Journal of Social Work*, *37*(7), 1263–1277.

McLaughlin, K. (2010). The social worker versus the General Social Care Council: An analysis of care standards tribunal hearings and decisions. *British Journal of Social Work*, *40*(1), 311–327.

Munro, E. (2008). Lessons learnt, boxes ticked, families ignored. *The Independent on Sunday*, 16 November, p. 45.

Murphy, F.D., Buckley, H., & Joyce, L. (2005). *The Ferns report*. Dublin: Stationery Office.

National Social Work Qualification Board (NSWQB) (2006). *Social work posts in Ireland*. Dublin: NSWQB.

Oaks, L. (2002). Abortion is part of the Irish experience, it is part of what we are: The transformation of the public discourses on Irish abortion policy. *Women's Studies International Forum*, *25*(3), 315–333.

Office of the Minister for Children and Youth Affairs (2008). *National review of compliance with Children First: National guidelines for the protection and welfare of children*. Dublin: Stationery Office.

Ofsted, Healthcare Commission, Her Majesty's Inspectorate of Constabulary (2008). *Joint area review: Haringey Children's Services Authority Area*. Retrieved January 3, 2009 from http://www.ofsted.gov.uk/oxcare_providers/la_download/(id)/4657/(as)/JAR/jar_2008_309_fr.pdf

Perberton, C. (2010). Sterilise parents who abuse children. *Community Care*, 24 August. Retrieved August 26, 2010 from http://www.communitycare.co.uk/Articles/2010/08/24/115157/sterilise-parents-who-abuse-children-top-professor-says.htm

Phelan, S. (2007a). The discourses of neoliberal hegemony: The case of the Irish Republic. *Critical Discourse Studies*, *4*(1), 29–48.

Phelan, S. (2007b). The discursive dynamics of neoliberal consensus: Irish broadsheet editorials and the privatization of Eircom. *Journal of Language and Politics*, *6*(1), 7–28.

Pollack, S. (2010). Labelling clients 'risky': Social work and the neoliberal welfare state. *British Journal of Social Work*, *40*(4), 1263–1278.

Raftery, M., & O'Sullivan, E. (1999). *Suffer the little children: The inside story of Ireland's industrial schools*. Dublin: New Island Books.

Rustin, M. (2009). Reflections on the present. *Soundings*, *43*, 18–35.

Saad-Filho, A., & Johnston, D. (eds) (2005). *Neoliberalism: A critical reader*. London: Pluto.

Samuel, M. (2010). TUC: 100 cuts in coalition's first 100 days. *Community Care*, 18 August. Retrived August 19, 2010 from http://www.communitycare.co.uk/Articles/2010/08/18/115099/TUC-100-unfair-cuts-in-coalition39s-first-100-days.htm

Scourfield, P. (2007). Are there reasons to be worried about the 'caretelisation' of residential care. *Critical Social Policy*, *27*(2), 155–181.

Secretary of State for Education and Skills (2006). *Care matters: Transforming the lives of children and young people in care*. London: HMSO.

Skehill, C. (2004). *History of the present of child protection and welfare social work in Ireland*. Lewiston: Edwin Mellon.

Smyth, A. (1992). *The abortion papers*. Dublin: Attic Press.

Social Work Task Force (2009). *Building a safe, confident future: The final report of the Social Work Task Force*. Retrieved December 23, 2010 from http://publications.dcsf.gov.uk/eOrderingDownload/01114-2009DOM-EN.pdf.

Toynbee, P. (2010a). The 'big society' is a big fat lie – just follow the money. *The Guardian*, 7 August, p. 27.

Toynbee, P. (2010b). Loyal, public service merits more than this cold trashing. *The Guardian*, 24 August, p. 27.

Tussing, A.D., & Wren, M.A. (2006). *How Ireland cares: The case for health care*. Dublin: New Island.

Walsh, T., Wilson, G., & O'Connor (2010). Local, European and global: An exploration of migration patterns of social workers into Ireland. *British Journal of Social Work, 40*(6), 1978–1995.

Watkins, S. (2010). Blue Labour. *New Left Review, 63*, 5–17.

White, E.J. (2009). Paradoxes of diaspora, global identity and human rights: The deportation of Nigerians in Ireland. *African and Black Diaspora: An International Journal, 2*(1), 67–83.

White, S., Hall, C., & Peckover, S. (2008). The descriptive tyranny of the common assessment framework: Technologies of categorization and professional practice in child welfare. *British Journal of Social Work, 39*(7), 1197–1217.

# Social Work Education

David Stoesz and Howard Karger

Social work and social work education are facing profound challenges due to significant economic, social, and technological change experienced over the past 50 years. The overexpansion of social work programmes has created an 'educational bubble' not unlike the housing bubble preceding the recession of 2008. This bubble is evident in the inability of the profession to generate sufficient faculty – academics – to teach in accredited programmes. It is also visible in acute problems confronted by many social work graduates who face high loan debt while struggling with deteriorating job prospects and low salaries.

Primary among the problems facing social work is the globalised economy and protracted economic recession, which has caused many, if not most, Western welfare states to reduce provision to citizens (Beland, 2010). Various strategies have been employed to cut costs, including market-based approaches to the delivery of social programmes and services, the proliferation of 'case management' (casework) as the intervention of choice, and the use of information and communications technologies that are changing how practitioners and service users interact and provide services (Lonne et al., 2009; McDonald, 2006; Oorschot et al., 2008). The same factors that have redefined social welfare have also been evident in professional education, including attempts to make qualifications and standards in higher education more consistent within the European Union through the Bologna Process that is somewhat similar to the US system (Bologna Process, 2010).

Introduced in 1999 and signed by almost 50 countries, the Bologna Process (or Accords) was designed to standardise European educational standards to increase their portability (i.e., to promote workforce migration across Europe), to increase the appeal of non-Europeans to study at European universities, and to bring about a convergence between US and European tertiary education systems. Bologna adopted a framework whereby bachelor-level professional qualifications would be replaced by a three-tiered system based on Bachelor's, Master's, and Doctoral degrees. In effect, this meant replacing the bachelor-level professional qualification with masters-level qualifications. The role of undergraduate education would be to prepare students for a postgraduate professional qualification. It would also provide students with a useful liberal arts background in literature, history, philosophy, social science, mathematics, and humanities (Bologna Process, 2010; Dominelli, 2007). The Bologna Process has had a profound effect on shaping social work education throughout Europe and in other parts of the world. Moving the bar upward in terms of professional qualifications has had a particularly profound effect on countries, such as Australia, where the four-year BSW has been the accepted practice degree.

International standardisation of higher education notwithstanding, reductions in funding due to the global recession threaten the prospect of a unified higher education system replicating the US experience. All of these factors converge in social work education, a training system that has been hierarchical, bureaucratic, professional, and primarily public. While this model may have been congruent with the industrial era, substantial questions arise as to its suitability with respect to the 'information age', to say nothing of the developing world (Stoesz, 2005).

THE WELFARE STATE LEGACY

Fundamentally, social work is a product of industrialisation in democratic–capitalist nations and the welfare state infrastructure that developed within them. To be sure, not only did welfare states evolve variable structures (Chatterjee, 1996), but they changed over time as well (Gilbert, 2002). Regardless, a broad outline is discernible: (i) markets were the primary vehicles for distributing goods and services; (ii) democratic government provided a mechanism for correcting the skewed distribution of resources and opportunities; (iii) public social programmes protected citizens against insecurities related to illness, age, poverty, disability, unemployment, and discrimination; and (iv) professional expertise evolved to advocate for greater protection against insecurity, manage social programmes, and assist needy citizens. Emerging early in the 20th century, social work consolidated its professional status during the mid to latter part of that century (Lubove, 1965), only to encounter considerable doubt about its viability in the 21st century (if not before as reflected in Britain's Colwell Inquiry in the 1970s).

Social work's paradox – a continual struggle for stature despite expansion of the welfare state – can be traced to an iconic address by Abraham Flexner in 1915. At the National Conference of Charity and Corrections, Flexner, an acknowledged expert on North American medical education, spoke on the professional status of social work. His synopsis of what constitutes a profession remains relevant today:

> professions involve essentially intellectual operations with large individual responsibility; they derive their raw material from science and learning; this material they work up to a practical and definite end; they possess an educationally communicable technique; they tend to self-organization; they are becoming increasingly altruistic in motivation (Flexner, 1915, p. 22).

Flexner observed social work involved routine activity, much of which did not originate in social work but with other disciplines: Social work 'appears not so much a definite field as an aspect of work in many fields. ... Would it not be at least suggestive therefore to view social work as in touch with many professions rather than a profession in and by itself?' (Flexner, 1915, pp. 585–586). He further observed 'the education [of social workers] is not technically professional so much as broadly cultural in a variety of realms of civic and social interest' (p. 587). He concluded with a sage bit of advice: 'To some extent the evolution of social work towards the professional status can be measured by the quality of publications put forth in its name' (p. 590). Those who hoped Flexner would anoint social work a bona fide profession clearly left the conference disappointed.

In the decades following World War II, welfare states expanded at unprecedented rates, consuming ever larger portions of nations' gross domestic product. Although the US welfare state lagged behind its European counterparts, advocates of social and economic justice believed it would eventually assure basic protections as a right of citizenship. Indeed, inexorable expansion of social programmes was codified in social philosophy on both sides of the Atlantic. In broad strokes, the British philosopher T.H. Marshall (1964) had reflected, while the 18th century assured *civil* rights to citizens and the 19th guaranteed *political* rights, the 20th would deliver *economic* rights. In the USA, Harold Wilensky and Charles Lebeaux (1965) thought 'under continuing industrialization all institutions will be oriented toward and evaluated in terms of social welfare aims. The "welfare state" will become the "welfare society", and both will be more reality than epithet' (p. 127). Social worker Leon Ginsberg (1998) echoed a similar refrain:

> the development of the welfare state is a natural and parallel outgrowth of the industrialization of the world. Just as physical things became more complicated following the Industrial Revolution, so did social relations. The rise of metropolitan areas, the decline of the extended family, the recurring incidence of economic crises, and the increasing need for objective help from strangers in the form of government aid, all made the welfare state and its current patterns inevitable (p. 70).

With various social programmes growing annually at double digit rates, the crying demand for a professional workforce virtually guaranteed the expansion of social work education.

SOCIAL WORK EDUCATION

Social work education's response to the growing welfare state was to adopt a public utility model of higher education whereby a single national accrediting organisation validates professional programmes based on a more-or-less standardised curriculum. The result was an array of cookie-cutter programmes with little consideration of their actual need, let alone the quality of the education (Karger & Stoesz, 2003). In the USA, the Council on Social Work Education (CSWE) orchestrates a system of professional social work education accrediting close to 500 undergraduate and 225 graduate programmes with little regard for their impact on the social work labour force, the special skills needed in certain regions, or the aptitude of academic faculty. (A cynical interpretation would conclude the driving force in this growth is CSWE's dependence on accreditation fees.) In any case, rapid programme growth outstripped manpower requirements and, in 2009, only 56% of full-time social work faculty in the USA had a Ph.D. or DSW in social work (CSWE, 2011).

Social work educators bet that an infinite supply of prospective students could be lured with the promise of employment and future salaries justifying tuition-induced debt. The CSWE leadership gambled that additional educational programmes were justified by an inexhaustible supply of prospective students (Taylor, 2010). As a result, hundreds of North American social work programmes have been accredited irrespective of the labour market demand for the 14,000 BSW and 19,000 MSW students who graduated in 2008. They were also accredited irrespective of market saturation (Stoesz et al., 2010). For example, North Carolina has a population of less than 10 million people yet has 22 BSW and 11 MSW programmes. By comparison, Texas has a population of 25 million with 30 BSW and 13 MSW programmes (CSWE, 2011). Moreover, it is unlikely that North Carolina social work graduates will find a robust job market given that the state ranked 30th among all US states in per capita welfare spending in 2006 (Public Policy Institute of New York State, 2007).

The same unrestrained growth is also evident in Southeast Queensland (Australia), where a population of less than three million people is expected to provide sufficient jobs and student numbers to support seven social work programmes. Accrediting bodies in both Australia [the Australian Association of Social Workers (AASW)] and the USA

(CSWE) have clearly failed to consider labour market demand and market saturation in their decision to accredit social work programmes. Ironically, CSWE requires prospective programmes to provide comprehensive needs assessment as part of the accreditation process. Fearful of being labelled 'anticompetitive', AASW does not require a needs assessment as a prerequisite for accreditation.

The over-supply of social work graduates in many areas of the USA has predictable results. Nationally, the median pay for social workers with less than five years of experience was US$43,700 in 2009. The pay band was also relatively narrow since highly experienced (30–39 years) social workers earned US$63,000, or only US$20,000 more than new graduates. BSW graduates earned US$30,000 or less (National Association of Social Workers, 2010). Although the same low salary base for social workers is not yet evident in South East Queensland, the increasing number of graduates points to an employer's job market.

More than 100 years after its creation, social work continues to struggle for credibility and legitimacy in tertiary education. While a number of smaller US colleges and universities have begun social work programmes within the last 15 years – or more typically have augmented their bachelors of social work degree with a Masters of Social Work – none has started an independent school of social work with a dean. In fact, the long-term trend has been to demote schools of social work into departments or to merge them into existing academic units. Consequently, the number of social work deans in the USA is roughly half of what it was 20 years ago. Moreover, not a single prestigious US university has started a social work programme in more than 50 years. In fact, some of the most highly ranked US universities, such as Harvard, Yale, Princeton, Massachusetts Institute of Technology (MIT), and Stanford do not have a social work programme. Nor are any of these institutions rumoured to be starting one. In 2003, the University of Oxford closed down its programme for the professional training of social workers at Barnett House after running for ninety years. Founded in 1913, this was one of the UK's premier centres of excellence for social work training. Social work's tenuous status in the academy is ironic in light of the enormous expansion of social programmes occurring in the 20th century.

The consequences of adopting this system of social work education are global insofar as the North American model has been widely adopted by many countries worldwide. A discernible pattern emerges sustaining a superficial status quo and, at worst, inviting a vertiginous descent toward vocational training. All too often social work education attracts the weakest students. According to the Educational Testing Service which administers the Graduate Record Examination (GRE), US applicants to graduate social work programmes have the second lowest score of any discipline, and the mathematical score is the worst among all disciplines (Stoesz et al., 2010).

A similar trend has occurred in parts of Australia. All graduating high school students in Queensland leave with a ranking called an OP score (the lower the number the better the score). In 2004 the OP score required for admission into social work at the University of Queensland was four. By 2011 the range of admissible OP scores in South East Queensland social work programmes ranged from 12 to 17 (Chenoweth et al., 2010).

The theoretical underpinnings of social work education are a hodgepodge of theories derived from other disciplines, such as psychology, sociology, medicine, and the hard sciences. Internships reify the status quo by insisting that only MSWs can supervise students. The expectation that faculty hold MSWs has come to symbolise a preference for practice over research and scholarship, the cardinal distinction between professional education and vocational training. The failure to require a research thesis in most US social work programmes means entire generations of students are denied the opportunity to engage in academically supervised research in their field of practice.

The problems in social work education are endemic. For instance, Eileen Gambrill (2010) has noted that the dearth of field experiments has meant most of social work's knowledge base is derived from less than optimal investigative methods. Assigning referees and editors of little accomplishment to vet the professional literature leaves better scholars shaking their heads in frustration when they encounter reviews of their manuscripts that are superficial, inept, and contradictory, encouraging more adept scholars to publish outside of social work journals (Pardeck & Meinert, 1999). Stoesz et al. (2010) examined publication rates of deans and directors in US schools of social work (the vast majority of whom are full professors) and found that most have curriculum vitae that would not warrant promotion and tenure at most mid-range US universities. Hence, many US social work programmes are burdened with leaders whose academic stature is below those from higher status disciplines (Stoesz et al., 2010). Hence, less accomplished administrators and weak journal editors gravitate into leadership positions within CSWE where they promulgate standards and oversee accreditation procedures. With a monopoly on accreditation, CSWE has no competition from a potentially more innovative and rigorous accrediting authority and is able to operate with impunity, castigating those who question its supremacy, and vilifying those who dare to challenge its hegemony (Stoesz et al., 2010).

The Australian context is different since the professional body – the AASW – accredits social work programmes. This scheme is replete with its own set of problems as social work practitioners often fail to understand the constraints of a university context. The AASW accreditation process is also more concerned with practice issues in the curriculum than with research productivity and knowledge building.

THE CHALLENGES FACING SOCIAL WORK

Given the state of US social work education, it is not surprising it has drifted away from addressing compelling public interest issues. Having failed to develop its own theory base and cultivate its research capacity (as well as demonstrate the efficacy of its own methods), social work is frustrated by its lack of influence in public policy decisions relating to welfare (Karger & Hernandez, 2004). Despite token opposition, social work has adjusted to the transformation of the welfare state occurring on a worldwide basis since the 1980s, including the shift from welfare to workfare marking US and Australian social policy. At the policy level, social programmes are assessed largely in relation to their symbolic value. Bill Epstein (2010), an acerbic observer of social welfare, refers to this as *social efficiency*:

> the demand that social welfare be minimal and conform to popular tastes. The controlling influence of social efficiency explains the persistence of inadequate and ineffective programs. ... The promise of big payoffs in good citizenship for small investments of actual resources has inspired the enormous range of personal social services, community organization, and community development that have been dedicated to reducing American poverty and inequality. Yet, these programs have routinely failed to ameliorate social problems, even while they have persisted as morality plays, rites, rituals, totems and ceremonies they endorse the society's values (p. 3).

The hostile policy environment where social workers practice is replicated on the agency level. Earlier models of social service delivery relying on the wisdom, practice experience, and professionalism of social workers has been replaced by a highly interventionist, bureaucratic model of micromanagement known as New Public Management (NPM), which has 'profoundly transformed the inner world of service delivery' (Yeatman, 2009, p. 20). Subservient to a regime based on performance management, limiting liability, and the ongoing search for efficiency, NPM diminishes the self-determination that is supposedly part of professional social work. It also limits the capacity of organisations and workers to define quality practice, thereby forcing a model of welfare delivery potentially removed from core social work values. Cooper and Lousada (2005) note 'the welfare system creates a "structure of illusion" which serves to both obscure and render "accountable" the increasingly impoverished business of doing welfare' (p. 16). In professional education, NPM translates into administrative regimes where schools of social work are managed as social agencies as opposed to academic units in a university. Effectively, the dean becomes the executive director, the faculty is reduced to staff, and the students become clients (Stoesz et al., 2010).

The role of government in the affairs of disadvantaged citizens is becoming more residual. In effect, the state is 'governing at a distance', having substantially shifted its political alliances away from citizens and towards capital interests (Rose, 1999). Consequently, in many countries the state has little interest in the social work profession, which has been reduced to a vestigial role in a failing and expensive welfare state. (One can catch glimpses of this in Australia where the state refuses to register social work as a profession.) Internationally, social work does not play a pivotal role in defining welfare policy in the same way that lawyers play a role in law reform or doctors in healthcare policy. Social workers are therefore forced to practise in an increasingly hostile policy and organisational environment devaluing their work. It is little wonder many social work education programmes are finding it increasingly difficult to convince academically high-performing students to choose a social work career (Stoesz et al., 2010).

The social work profession is rooted in an almost obsolete industrial-era welfare state. Its agency structure is hierarchal and it typically delivers services in a bricks-and-mortar framework rather than by a variety of means, such as online services, or through innovative arrangements, such as employee-owned companies. Moreover, in an age of accountability, public sector fiscal austerity, and specialisation, after more than 100 years social work remains unable to exactly define its mission and goals to the public at large, or even to its own members. Even 100 years after its birth, the International Federation of Social Workers (2000) felt compelled to define or redefine social work yet again. Hence, the profession is finding it difficult to defend itself against territorial incursions made by psychologists, community sociologists, occupational therapists, nurses, human service graduates, counsellors, and other disciplines making inroads in traditional social work venues, such as hospitals, family service agencies, child welfare services, community centres, and counselling agencies (Karger & Stoesz, 2003).

Despite the almost 100 years since Flexner's speech, social work continues to synthesise (some might argue lift) content from medicine, psychology, and other disciplines rather than lay claim to its own unique theory or knowledge base. Theories dance across the social work stage like acts in a Vaudeville show: psychoanalysis, ego psychology, Rankian, systems theory, problem-solving, ecological theory, role theory, the unitary approach, empowerment theory, feminist social work, strengths perspective, cognitive behavioural approaches, and the latest enthusiasm, evidence-based practice. Each quickly captures the profession's imagination and just as quickly vanishes from sight after a few short years. More durable than ephemeral theories are the core values of the profession.

The implications of this are enormous: social work has frittered away the institutional legacy of the welfare state by a strategy of indiscriminate expansion of educational programmes. Since 1985 the rapid growth of US social work programmes on all three levels – baccalaureate, masters, and doctoral – is unsurpassed in the history of social work education. In 1985 there were 89 CSWE-accredited MSW programmes, 351 BSW programmes, and 19 programmes in candidacy. By 2009 that number had exploded to 195 MSW and 470 BSW programmes plus another 33 in various stages of candidacy. This represented a 52% growth rate. Similarly, the number of US doctoral programmes grew from 47 in 1985 to 69 in 2009, a 47% increase (CSWE, 2007, 2009; Rubin, 1986). A similar growth pattern is evident in Australia which has 25 social work programmes in a nation of 21.5 million people.

As noted earlier, the overexpansion of social work programmes is especially evident in Brisbane and South East Queensland, where in 2003 Brisbane (population of two million) had only one social work programme. By 2008 there were three social work programmes within the city and another four within a 30-mile radius.

While this rapid growth may be viable in the short run, it is unsustainable in the longer term. Attracting and graduating ever larger numbers of students creates an oversupply of social workers, some undoubtedly with less than competent skills. In other cases, the rush to start or grow social work programmes has led to understaffed and under-resourced enterprises. Graduating students with little regard for employability effectively subverts wage and salary scales, thus making it more burdensome for new graduates to meet their student loan obligations. Since most social work programmes are funded on a capitation or per student basis, the reflexive response to increased competition is to lower admission standards and retain marginal students already admitted. The pressure to lower admission standards is exacerbated in regions where several schools of social work compete for a static applicant pool. Job prospects for social work graduates are further diminished when corollary social service type disciplines (e.g., family studies, child development, human services, counselling, and marriage and family studies) are added into the mix. The possibility of recapturing lost occupational territory is diminished as corollary disciplines acquire larger and larger shares of traditional social work territory.

A similar set of problems is found in Australian social work education. According to Chenoweth et al. (2010), enrolment in social work degree programmes across Australia has grown only modestly over the last five years. At the same time, 'academic entry standards in social work have dropped substantially during the past five years, with social work now averaging near the lowest of the helping professions' (Chenoweth et al., 2010, p. 5). Alice Lieberman and Margaret Severson (1998) sum up the overall dilemma: 'Are our clients suffering, and will they continue to do so, because of the need of graduate programs to fill student slots by dipping even lower into their applicant pools?' (p. 6).

CAPABILITY

Social work in the USA is in the midst of a colossal contradiction: While its mission involves the primacy of self-determination, much of social work practice segregates clients from the mainstream by viewing their behaviour through the lens of 'dependence' and 'dysfunction' (Saleebey, 2006). Accordingly, the future of social work is contingent upon adopting alternative views of function and independence in the context of intervention and service delivery. One promising point of departure can be found in the concept of 'capability' articulated in the philosophy of Amartya Sen and Martha Nussbaum. Capability means more than subsistence, as Nussbaum (2000) writes:

> a life has been so impoverished that it is not worthy of the dignity of the human being, that it is a life in which one goes on living, but more or less like an animal, unable to develop and exercise one's human powers (Nussbaum, 2000, p. 72).

Realising opportunity in modern, democratic–capitalist nations must be reconciled with pluralism, Sen (2009) observes 'the capability perspective is inescapably concerned with a plurality of different features of our lives and concerns' (p. 233). He goes on to acknowledge it 'does point to the central relevance of the inequality of capabilities in the assessment of social disparities, but it does not, on its own, propose any specific formula for policy decisions' (Sen, 2009, p. 234). A capability approach in social welfare thus requires multiple options from which people can choose to fulfil their aspirations, and the menu from which people select should include those options essential for prosperity. The capability approach is multidimensional, capturing most of what it means to be human.

1 *Life*: Being able to live to the end of a normal human life.
2 *Bodily health*: Being able to have good health, including reproductive health.
3 *Bodily integrity*: Being able to move about and be secure in one's safety.
4 *Senses, imagination and thought*: Being able to use the senses to imagine, think, and reason, and to nurture these through education.
5 *Emotions*: Being able to have attachments to those we love and care about.
6 *Practical reason*: Being able to form a conception of what is good and incorporate it in one's life.
7 *Affiliation*: Being able to live freely among others.
8 *Other species*: Being able to live among animals, plants, and the world of nature.
9 *Play*: Being able to laugh, play, and engage in recreational activities.
10 *Control over one's environment*: Being able to engage politically and acquire property in order to govern one's life (Nussbaum, 2000, pp. 78–80).

Sen's (2009) recognition of pluralism makes these benchmarks dynamic, infusing them with all the contradictions and complexities which make human life so rich and paradoxical.

The application of the capability approach to social work is relatively new, but its implications can be radical. Margaret Sherraden (2010) has adapted capability to poverty analysis, observing, with respect to economic justice, 'financial capability requires both the *ability to act* (knowledge, skills, confidence, and motivation) and the *opportunity to act* (through access to beneficial financial products and institutions)' (p. 2). Thus, capability involves two reciprocal elements: ability and opportunity. Ignorance precludes optimal choice just as the absence of achieving objectives yields futility. At the same time, people enjoy the latitude of making bad choices from which they can learn to make more prudent decisions. Significantly, choice is essential for accountability. Markets in products or services do not exist if consumers do not enjoy the option of selecting a provider they prefer. Thus, pluralism requires multiple sources from which consumers can select, whether it is the family's transportation, the school the children attend, or social services sought for family members. As Sen's research on human development demonstrates, indicators of prosperity are many, including longevity, education, and income. Several well-being indices have demonstrated how multiple indicators can be employed, such as KidsCount, the Child Well-Being Index, and the Index of Social Health.

INNOVATION

It is an indictment of modern social work that so many of the opportunities it might exploit are now charted by advocates outside the profession. For example, Stephen Goldsmith (2010), former mayor of Indianapolis, Harvard professor, and once advisor to New York City Mayor Michael Bloomburg, has proposed *civic entrepreneurship* as a method to jumpstart innovation in troubled communities, a notion not unlike community organising. As a mayor, Goldsmith came to appreciate the inertia symptomatic of an institutionalised status quo maintained by an archaic infrastructure. Key to breaking up the social service monopoly was the identification of 'positive disruptors', or provocateurs 'who leapfrog over well-intentioned tinkering at the margins in order to propel daring yet measurable progress' (Goldsmith, 2010, p. 29). As the Director of

Innovations in American Government Program at Harvard's Kennedy School of Government, Goldsmith's staff inventoried dozens of instances where imaginative citizens mobilised resources to address local social problems, the template of which is explicated in *The Power of Social Innovation*. Among the innovations cited are KickStart, which provides inexpensive foot-pumps to drought-stricken farmers in Kenya; the partnership between New Profit, a social venture fund, and the Monitor Group, which consults with community-based organisations; City Year, which provides volunteers to urban service organisations; and two icons of the entrepreneurship movement: Teach For America, begun by Wendy Kopp, and the Harlem Children's Zone, organised by Geoffrey Canada.

Goldsmith recognises extant social services often impede progress, not only because of their advocates' wrong intentions, but also because they succumb to the status quo. The failure to provide consumer choice, the absence of competitive funding, and the neglect of accountability are all evidence of an institutionalised complacency sustaining the status quo rather than optimising innovation. On the other hand, the commodification or privatisation of services is often a less dependable funding source than governmental social services. It also ultimately allows government to abdicate its responsibility to populations in need. Nevertheless, 'transforming a social service delivery system' requires 'positive disruptors' who advocate for 'enhancing the human resource pipeline, improving management, inducing a technical innovation, or providing realignment' (Goldsmith, 2010, p. 220).

David Bornstein, author of *How to Change the World* (2004), and Susan Davis (2010), an advocate for the Grameen Bank, argue *social entrepreneurship* represents a new generation of organisational activity, the use of collective agency to address pressing social problems:

> Social entrepreneurship represents a fundamental reorganization of the problem-solving work of society: a shift from control-oriented, top-down policy implementation to responsive, decentralized institution building. It draws on a core insight of the twentieth century: namely, that a dynamic marketplace of ideas and initiative is the basis of a thriving economy (Bornstein & Davis, 2010, p. 94).

A critique of government lurks within the social entrepreneurship model. Public social programmes may anchor the welfare state, but they are hardly champions of innovation. Legislated by a majority of elected representatives, government social programmes are by necessity the product of an attempt at a cultural consensus. Invariably, public policies may take decades to be enacted, and many suffer from inadequate resources upon implementation. Finally, public programmes involve stakeholders who become dependent upon them: 'Once a program is rolled out, with a budget and a constituency to defend it, it will remain there almost regardless of its effectiveness' (Bornstein & Davis, 2010, p. 36). By contrast, social entrepreneurial models are opportunistic, flexible, innovative, and accountable.

In addition to charting the topography of social entrepreneurship, Bornstein and Davis (2010) cite examples of nongovernmental ventures: Ashoka has provided fellowships to an entire cadre of international development innovators; Geoffrey Canada organised the Harlem Children's Zone to provide an organisational conveyor belt for low-income, minority children; Wendy Kopp founded Teach For America, which has not only encouraged thousands of college graduates to work in troubled public schools, but also incubated a new cohort of educational leaders, such as the founders of the KIPP (Knowledge is Power Program) Schools. As these innovations have become institutionalised they have become incorporated within business schools, such as the Center for the Advancement of Social Entrepreneurship at the Fuqua School of Business at Duke University, and in public policy through initiatives such as Promise Neighborhoods promoted by the Obama Administration.

Comparable innovations in schools of social work are a rarity if they exist at all.

It is remarkable social work rarely features in *any* of these developments, the exception being Michael Sherraden's promotion of asset strategies to abate poverty. His concept of Individual Development Accounts has been implemented through federal policy in the USA as well as internationally by nongovernmental organisations (NGOs). Arguably, the profession is more intent on serving staff, maintaining programming, and sustaining administrators than deploying the latest innovations to optimise services to needy citizens (Stoesz, 2005). Social administration, as evident in the social work curriculum, consists largely of traditional methods for operating government programmes, managing non-profit organisations, writing grants for external support, and supervising existing staff. In sum, these discourage thinking outside the parameters of traditional organisational frameworks. According to Goldsmith (2010), a new professional culture poses a fundamental problem precisely because such innovation presumes features – choice, competition, and accountability – subverting the status quo. He asserts:

> Many existing social service providers find themselves frozen in the status quo by their own frames of reference – they assume that their clients cannot live without them. This view becomes a self-fulfilling prophesy as those who need help look increasingly like problems to be managed rather than people with unrealized potential (Goldsmith, 2010, p. 165).

A corrective for this exists in the empowerment perspective gaining credence in professional education. That concept, however, rings hollow for the simple reason that empowering individuals, families, and communities presumes consumer choice and citizen accountability. Insofar as social work remains embedded in a public utility model of service provision, it will not only continue to be associated with a suboptimal status quo, but will likely also impede innovations emanating from other disciplines.

A FUTURE FOR SOCIAL WORK EDUCATION

In its current iteration, social work education in the USA has reached a dead end. Standardised practices in public bureaucracies judged to be effective solely by the authority of professional experts, and which fail to consult consumers about the services they desire, to say nothing of their experiences after receiving them, summarises the paradigm of professional social work education. In the developing world, the USA – and arguably Western – model of social work education is an irrelevant, if not damaging, artefact of imperialism (Midgley, 1981).

Social work education should be the source of professional renewal, yet its adoption of the industrial-era paradigm of professionalism necessitates a radical departure as it currently exists. While vaulting social work into the 21st century will be resisted by those invested in the status quo, the upgrade in professional education is well within possibility since its components have been exploited by other professions, such as medicine, public health, and engineering. The guideposts for professional prosperity have been widely known since they are part of the public domain.

To turn things around, social work must better *articulate its philosophies*. As Flexner observed, professions derive their own understandings of the world that they endeavour to change. Sometimes social work mistakenly interprets normative approaches, such as the empowerment or ecological approach, as equivalent to philosophies. However, such 'approaches' are generalised intentions, lacking the subject, values, and assumptions of a formal philosophy. Until now much of social work philosophy qualifies as moral metaphysics, good intentions without the necessary philosophical components. In addition to ambiguity, it is also possible for philosophy to impede the professional project, as in the case of postmodernism. Eschewing formal categories and investigative methods, postmodernism establishes its credibility on the narratives of free individuals engaged in authentic discourse. While such dialogue is implicit in all social phenomena, it is not perforce 'professional' since it lacks identifiable categories, rejects standardised methods, and cannot replicate results. While there is nothing wrong with conversation, narrative alone does not qualify the activity of a group of practitioners as professional. Adopting philosophy from other disciplines might serve in the short run, but the result is always derivative and never has quite the fidelity to social work a home-grown philosophy would have.

Just as any pluralistic society has differing ideas for the good life, so social work would be expected to generate different, even competing, philosophies. Glimmers of this are evident in the USA when, during the 20th century, social work scholars argued about social work's objectives being 'cause' or 'function' yet this debate did not generate formal philosophies (Lee, 1937). Mature disciplines expect different schools of thought to evolve, and these are a source of intellectual renewal. Social work's failure to construct philosophies and debate them is evidence of its intellectual failing. An accreditation monopoly insisting that all schools of social work are the same actually impedes the evolution of various schools of thought so essential for a vibrant professional community.

Second, *social work must develop its own theories*. A theory is a logically deduced system of abstracted propositions. As such, it specifies variables and their hypothesised relationships. Compounding its philosophical netherworld, many of social work's theories fail to qualify as such. Systems and ecological theory, for example, do not specify variables and their relationships cannot be formally assessed. Other theories defy empirical substantiation. Psychoanalytic theory proposes concepts, such as the unconscious, that cannot be independently validated. Related to its infatuation with postmodernism (Meinert, 1998), social work has subscribed to oppression as a way to understand the marginalisation of specific groups. Here the problem of classification looms large. Moreover, context alters the circumstances of populations: Gays living on Fire Island are likely to be less oppressed than those living in the rural West; Native American communities with tribe-owned gambling casinos on their reservations might fare somewhat better than those without them. What can we make of the superior income and educational outcomes of Asian-Americans compared to other groups, including Whites? (Mishel et al., 2007). Under such circumstances, theories should provide the opportunity for adjudicating divergent intellectual claims, but this rarely occurs in social work (Stoesz, 1989).

A mature profession employs research as the arbiter of divergent claims. An immature discipline refuses to consider divergent views may emerge, or in the extreme, eliminates the possibility of debate altogether. Optimally, theories provide the intellectual infrastructure for a 'school of thought', which provides the signature to a given professional school, attracting students and faculty who wish to further examine a given problem. It is not surprising such schools have failed to emerge in social work. Ambiguous philosophy and inadequate theory impede their emergence. Moreover, standardised accreditation requirements create cookie-cutter programmes and work against faculty and students aggregating at a given school to construct a distinct school of thought.

Third, *cultivate the research capacity of social work*. A data-driven society requires any professional group dependent on public funds to employ state-of-the-art methods to advance the public good. In developed nations an epistemic convention has evolved establishing a hierarchy of research generating the highest quality information. Social work in developed nations has been able to exploit governmental data sets, such as national departments of welfare and labour, as well as those by NGOs, such as the Organization for Economic Cooperation and Development. While these are important for establishing a discipline's legitimacy, field experiments are essential for determining optimal intervention methods, a recognition that led to the establishment of the Campbell Collaboration in 1999 where representatives from several nations (including several social welfare professions) met. A decade later the collaboration had systematically reviewed extant research, but few of the studies were truly experimental in the classical scientific sense. Thus, while experimental studies had become the gold standard in biomedical research, such research was seldom conducted in social work. Instead of developing research capacity, social work promoted methods of limited value, such as single-subject design. Given the expansion of social work programmes in the developed nations, the failure to develop comparable research capacity *vis-à-vis* field experiments and large-scale surveys is striking. Although other ways of knowing, such as qualitative or naturalistic inquiry are important forms of research, when decision makers evaluate social programmes and public policy, they often want hard quantitative data, and hence they must rely on the research of analysts who are non-social workers.

In developing nations, some social workers contend quantitative methods are inappropriate or harmful to Indigenous ways of knowing (Gray et al., 2008). This antagonism has enjoyed widespread popularity in social work. To the contrary, development economist Esther Duflo of MIT's Jameel Poverty Action Lab has conducted field experiments in developing nations around compelling issues, such as education, leadership by women, and micro-finance, the results of which have convinced national aid agencies as well as the World Bank to employ randomised controlled trials as a way to evaluate the effectiveness of foreign assistance (Parker, 2010). This is not to suggest all research needs be experimental. While there is value in conducting surveys and engaging in social action research, they cannot be replicated, which is the *sine qua non* of professionalisation.

Fourthly, *demonstrate the effectiveness of social work methods.* Any profession that insists its methods are effective simply by virtue of its authority substitutes propaganda for sound knowledge. When combined with professional values, the result can be a professional ideology not only divorced from the reality experienced by consumers of services, but practitioners as well. Professional ideology creates the possibility the received wisdom of leaders is peddled as professional knowledge. Because a profession is self-governing, the result can be an echo chamber of professional pronouncements. Since the 1990s, this problem has prompted the emergence of evidence-based practice (EBP) in social work education. EBP presents a poignant problem for social work educators because three outcomes are possible for research on interventions: (i) the intervention has the desired, salubrious effect; (ii) the intervention has no effect; and (iii) the intervention damages study participants. If there were a good chance resources might be inconsequential or harmful to consumers of social services, programme administrators would be understandably sceptical about EBP, and likely to question the propriety of the concept (Gray et al., 2009).

Efficacy of professional activity is not limited to programme intervention. Any profession working in the public realm should be concerned about the perceptions of other stakeholders. Chief among these are consumers of social services. However, social work systematically avoids sampling clients to determine their satisfaction with the services provided. When this evaluation is executed, it is often under the auspices of staff not connected with social work services. Nor do social workers survey other important groups, including taxpayers who foot the bill for public services. A third stakeholder consists of department heads depending on management information systems to monitor programme activity, but social workers are rarely at the forefront in developing such systems. Regrettably, social service information systems tend to compare poorly with those in other fields, such as health, prison services, and education.

CONCLUSION

Social work emerged as the professional complement to the industrial-era welfare state and managed itself through bureaucratic, hierarchical structures mandating standardised practices irrespective of the input of important stakeholders, such as consumers, taxpayers, and department heads. Social work education replicated the industrial model of professional preparation by establishing national accreditation organisations, which, through a monopoly on accrediting schools of social work, assured a standardised product. This North American model has been replicated in many places around the globe. Because it presumes the vast resources of the welfare state, this model is of questionable value to developing nations, although it may have more value in terms of personalised services.

A social work practice base replacing a focus on dysfunction and dependence with capability and innovation is more apropos of the 21st century. However, reforming social work education requires reinventing the basic components of the profession with respect to essential elements of professional education: philosophy, theory, research, and practice efficacy. Failing to renew itself, social work will struggle to compete with other disciplines and may well fade away as a profession, a casualty of a postindustrial state in which other disciplines demonstrate their willingness to consider consumer preference, the persistence to craft effective interventions, and the ability to compete for public resources.

REFERENCES

Beland, D. (2010). *What is social policy?* Malden, MA: Polity Press.

Bologna Process (2010). Retrieved August 11, 2010 from http://www.ond.vlaanderen.be/hogeronderwijs/bologna/

Bornstein, D. (2004). *How to change the world.* New York: Oxford University Press.

Bornstein, D., & Davis, S. (2010). *Social entrepreneurship: What everyone needs to know.* New York: Oxford University Press.

Chaterjee, P. (1996). *Approaches to the welfare state.* Washington, DC: National Association of Social Workers.

Chenoweth, L., Karger, H., Lonne, B., & McDonald, C. (2010). *Educational options for professional social work: An Australian case study.* Unpublished manuscript. Griffith University, Brisbane, Australia.

Council on Social Work Education (2007). *Statistics on social work education.* Alexandria, VA: Council on Social Work Education.

Council on Social Work Education (2009). *Accreditation news, reports and archives.* Retrieved February 28, 2009, from http://www.cswe.org/CSWE/accreditation/Accreditation+News+Reports+And+Archives

Council on Social Work Education (2011). *Statistics on social work education: 2009.* Alexandria, VA: Council on Social Work Education.

Cooper, A., & Lousada, J. (2005). *Borderline Welfare: Feeling and Fear of Feeling in Modern Welfare.* London: Karnac.

Dominelli, L. (2007). Contemporary challenges in social work education in the United Kingdom, *Australian Social Work, 60*(1), 29–45.

Epstein, W. (2010). *Democracy without decency.* University Park, PA: Penn State Press.

Flexner, A. (1915). *Is social work a profession?* New York: Proceedings, National Conference of Charities and Corrections.

Gambrill, E. (2010). Evidence-informed practice: Antidote to propaganda in the helping professions? *Research on Social Work Practice, 20*(3), 302–320.

Gilbert, N. (2002). *Transformation of the welfare state.* New York: Oxford University Press.

Ginsberg, L. (1998). *Conservative social welfare.* Chicago: Nelson Hall.

Goldsmith, S. (2010). *The power of social innovation: How civic entrepreneurs ignite community networks for good.* New York: Jossey Bass.

Gray, M., Coates, J., & Yellow Bird, M. (eds) (2008). *Indigenous social work around the world: Towards culturally relevant education and practice.* Aldershot, Hants: Ashgate.

Gray, M., Plath, D., & Webb, S.A. (2009). *Evidenced-based social work: A critical stance.* London: Routledge.

International Federation of Social Workers (IFSW) (2000). *Definition of social work: Review of the international definition of social work.* Retrieved June 20, 2011 from http://www.ifsw.org/f38000138.html

Karger, H., & Hernandez, M. (2004). The decline of the public intellectual in social work. *Journal of Sociology and Social Welfare, 31*(3), 51–68.

Karger, H., & Stoesz, D. (2003). The growth of social work education programs, 1985–1999: Its impact on economic and educational factors related to the profession of social work. *Journal of Social Work Education, 39*(2), 279–295.

Lee, P. (1937). *Social work as cause and function*. New York School of Social Work, Columbia University.

Lennon, T. (1991). *Statistics on social work education: 1990*. Alexandria, VA: Council on Social Work Education.

Lennon, T. (2004). *Statistics on social work education: 2003*. Alexandria, VA: Council on Social Work Education.

Lieberman, A., & Severson, M. (1998). Should there be a moratorium on the development of social work education programs? Yes! *Journal of Social Work Education, 34*, 167.

Lonne, B., Parton, N., Thomson, J., & Harries, M. (2008). *Reforming child protection*. London: Routledge.

Lubove, R. (1965). *The professional altruist*. Boston: Harvard University Press.

Marshall, T.H. (1964). *Class, citizenship and social development*. Chicago: University of Chicago Press.

McDonald, C. (2006). *Challenging social work: The context of practice*. Basingstoke, Hampshire: Palgrave Macmillan.

Meinert, R. (1998). *Postmodernism, religion and the future of social work*. New York: Routledge.

Midgley, J. (1981). *Professional imperialism: Social work in the Third World*. London: Heinemann.

Mishel, L, Bernstein, J., & Allegretto, S. (2007). *The state of working America*. Washington, DC: Economic Policy Institute, 163.

National Association of Social Workers (NASW) (2010). *Report on 2009 compensation and benefits study: Summary of key compensation findings*. Silver Springs, MD: NASW.

Nussbaum, M. (2000). *Women and human development*. New York: Cambridge University Press.

Oorschot, W., Opielka, M., & Pfau-Effinger, B. (2008). *Culture and the welfare state*. Cheltenham: Edward Elgar.

Pardeck, J., & Meinert, R. (1999). Scholarly achievements of the social work editorial board and consulting editors: A commentary. *Research on Social Work Practice, 9*(1), 86–91.

Parker, I. (2010). The poverty lab. *New Yorker*, May 17.

Public Policy Institute of New York State (2007). State and local per-capita welfare spending, FY2005-2006. Retrieved June 20, 2011 from http://www.ppinys.org/reports/jtf/welfarespending.htm

Rose, N. (1999). *Powers of freedom: Reframing political thought*. Cambridge: Cambridge University Press.

Rubin, A. (1986). *Statistics on social work education in the United States: 1985*. Alexandria, VA: Council on Social Work Education.

Saleebey, D. (2006). *The strengths perspective in social work practice*. Boston, MA: Allyn & Bacon.

Sen, A. (2009). *The idea of justice*. New York: Cambridge University Press.

Sherraden, M. (2010). *Financial capability*. St Louis: Center for Social Development.

Stoesz, D. (1989). A theory of social welfare, *Social Work, 34*(2), 22–29.

Stoesz, D. (2005). *Quixote's ghost: The right, the liberati, and the future of social policy*. Oxford: Oxford University Press.

Stoesz, D., Karger, H., & Carillo, T. (2010). *A dream deferred: How social work education lost its way and what can be done about it*. New York: Transaction Books/Aldine.

Taylor, M. (2010). Academic bankruptcy. *New York Times*, August 15.

Wilensky, H., & Lebeaux, C. (1965). *Industrial society and social welfare*. New York: Free Press.

Yeatman, A., with Dowsett, G.W., Fine, M., & Gursansky, D. (2009). *Individualisation and the delivery of welfare services: Contestation and complexity*. Basingstoke: Palgrave Macmillan.

42

Interprofessional Practice

Imogen Taylor

> Many have chronicled how organisation destroyed skilled craft labor; a machine based division of labor allows the unskilled to accomplish highly skilled tasks. The same process, many feel, now applies to the professions ... organisations clearly seek to maximise both the quantity of expertise institutionalised in these arrangements and the economic returns to that quantity (Abbott, 1988, p. 325).

Over 20 years ago, US sociologist Abbott, in his seminal text *The System of Professions*, was prescient in suggesting organisations compete with the professions for control of work. He traced the cultural and social forces bearing on the professions and argued, since one profession can pre-empt another's work, the histories of the professions are inevitably interdependent. Taking a systems perspective and analysing three detailed case histories: information, law, and psychotherapy, Abbott (1988) examined how a chain of effects might begin in external events or within the professions themselves, and how new groups could emerge. This chapter presents a case study of interprofessional education in the UK, the forces at work in its emergence and their implications for the social work profession as it grapples with interprofessional learning and practice.

Interprofessional practice and collaboration with other professions has always been important in social work but, over the past two decades, this agenda has come to the forefront of policy and practice. This has resulted from the catastrophic failures by different professionals to work together, with tragic and high-profile consequences for children and vulnerable adults, and with serious consequences for the professions themselves. In the UK, these have provided the opportunity for influences from the Left and Right to come together, including, for example, neoliberalism and new public management and their concerns with economy, effectiveness, and efficiency, and the resultant backlash against professionals. In the USA, Brandon and Knapp (1999) described the redesigning of professional norms and expectations in realignment with changing demands for interprofessional practice and went so far as to suggest 'the sum total of this multidimensional realignment activity constitutes a loose but definable social movement' (p. 877). They proposed the movement towards interprofessional education followed one step behind organisational change and universities risked becoming irrelevant if they failed to allow other training institutions to enter the field of interprofessional training.

In the UK, an indication of the profile of interdisciplinarity was the commissioning of a study in 2008 of interdisciplinary approaches to strengthening the research base in social work and social care. The study was led by the prestigious and influential UK Economic and Social Research Council (ESRC), in collaboration with the Social Care Institute for Excellence and the Scottish Institute for Research and Innovation in the Social Services (Sharland, 2011). It resulted in a series of proposals to promote both disciplinarity and interdisciplinarity in social care and social work research. Few professions have escaped this changing agenda, but social work appears to have been a target for a particularly potent combination of government, employers, and the media calling for social work to reshape professional education. Portentously, Abbot (1988) had issued warnings about the media's role in 'creating a substantial public discourse about professions, while the state itself plays an ever-increasing role as audience' (p. 143), an increasingly familiar phenomenon in the global North.

Internationally, there is a burgeoning literature on interprofessional practice and its preparation. Indeed, Bronstein et al.'s (2010) study of interdisciplinary collaboration in social work education in the USA, Israel, and Canada revealed 'the call for interdisciplinary collaboration has become commonplace among health, education and human service professionals around the world' (p. 458). In discussing interprofessional education in Australia, Pockett (2010) suggested it was comparatively well developed in the UK, Sweden, and Canada, and fast developing elsewhere. Lorenz (2009) urged social workers to think globally about interprofessional education using multinational Europe as a metaphor for interprofessional collaboration. He drew parallels between European intercultural relativity and interprofessional education:

> Interprofessional education has to accompany all professional exchanges across borders as a critical, constructive process that focuses on differences in theory and practice within the different professional fields to overcome their problems of adjustment to changing user needs and cultural requirements (Lorenz, 2009, p. 432).

International changes can be seen in several developments beyond social work. As far back as 1988, the World Health Organisation (WHO) published *Learning Together to Work Together for Health* and, in 2010, this was followed by *Frameworks for Action on Interprofessional Education and Collaborative Practice* claiming interprofessional education was a prerequisite for improved healthcare outcomes across the globe. Well-established and newly developing international networks followed, including the Centre for Advancement of Interprofessional Education (CAIPE), the European Interprofessional Education Network in Health and Social Care (EIPEN), the Canadian Interprofessional Health Collaborative (CIHC), the Japanese Association for Interprofessional Education (JAIE), and the Australian Interprofessional Practice and Education Network (AIPPEN). Some countries have institutionalised interprofessional requirements in accreditation arrangements and competence frameworks. For example, UK social work degree programmes have been required to teach 'partnership working' since 2002. Interprofessional collaboration is built into the National Occupational Standards for Social Work (UK Department of Health, 2002) in the UK and in the USA into the Educational Policy and Accreditation Standards of the Council on Social Work Education (CSWE, 2008).

This chapter aims to contribute to knowledge for social work education by suggesting it is centrally important internationally for educators engaged in responding to the interprofessional agenda to be alert to the forces for change and their implications for the profession. It begins with a brief discussion of definitional issues as fuzzy discourse can itself mask significant concerns. The pedagogic research base upon which the evidence for this chapter draws is then presented, citing in particular two research studies on interprofessional education (Taylor et al., 2008a) Sharland and Taylor, 2007. The chapter then moves to a discussion of theory, heeding

Eraut's (2003) warning: 'Theory for theory sake is futile but practice that is not underpinned by a sound theoretical underpinning is tantamount to incompetence' (in Hean et al., 2009, p. 260). Activity theory, drawing particularly on the work of Finnish educational theorist and researcher Yrjo Engeström, is used to illuminate the case study of a systemic exploration of interprofessional education as it relates to social work. In light of the lack of attention to power differentials in activity theory, these are addressed separately, since power differences are a crucial factor in interprofessional education and practice. Abbott (1988) warned that, as organisations and government seek to maximise economic returns for professional expertise, less powerful and organised professions were more vulnerable than long-standing professions. Hence social work is at risk given the far-reaching and erosive changes afoot. Finally, the chapter concludes by pointing towards key areas for further research and development.

DEFINITIONS AND DISCOURSE

A multiplicity of terms is used to discuss interprofessional practice and learning leading to conceptual confusion. In this way, important conceptual differences, and their implications, are masked so that changes are made without the consequences being fully understood. (Sharland & Taylor, 2007). Thus an insidious erosion of the profession might happen without the profession being fully aware of it. Significantly, Barr and Sharland's (2011) close examination of definitions of interprofessional education found two different approaches in need of reconciliation. On the one hand, there was 'interprofessional education' (IPE) defined as: 'Occasions when two or more professions learn with, from and about each other to improve collaboration and the quality of care' (Freeth et al., 2005, p. 11) while on the other, there was 'common learning' (CL). Despite these different approaches, a common language – denoting shared concepts and practice competencies – was used across professional boundaries to generate a more flexible and mobile workforce responsive to service-delivery needs. Both approaches required professional educators to re-conceptualise and restructure curricula and make the necessary cultural shifts in higher education and professional practice. However, each approach followed a quite different and possibly irreconcilable trajectory, creating tensions around professional identity.

'Interprofessional education' generally emphasises the distinctiveness of the professions while extolling the advantages of complementary practice as the basis for interprofessional collaboration. Hence existing professional identities and differences essentially remain intact and the focus of IPE is on learning about both commonalities and differences at the micro practitioner and macro organisational levels, and how to bridge them to work together. In contrast, 'common learning' emphasises commonalities and transfer across professional boundaries, with practice shaped by the needs of the end user and the agency rather than the concerns of the professional. In this approach, there is a blurring of professional boundaries and the development of new kinds of professional and paraprofessional worker.

In the UK, the differences between IPE and CL are accentuated by the different fields of practice in which they are most likely to occur with IPE more germane to learning for practice with adults in health and social care (Sharland & Taylor, 2007) supported by the historical dominance of the health professions and, in particular, medicine. In this arena, the health and social care interface is a site for professional conflict (Hall, 2005; Hudson, 2002). In contrast, and particularly following new children's legislation in 2005 (UK Department for Education and Skills, 2005), CL has become associated with services for children and families and New Labour's promotion of the 'integrated' children's services agenda with the introduction of practice tools such as the Common

Assessment Framework and the Common Core of Skills and Knowledge for the Children's Workforce. Integration was defined by government as:

[a] set of processes and actions by which partners ensure outcome-focused front-line delivery. It means a holistic approach within which needs can be identified and priorities – national and local – can be addressed (UK Department for Education and Skills, 2005, p. 11).

The discourse of 'outcomes' paved the way for new kinds of 'holistic' paraprofessional or professional children's workers focusing on service-user needs making it difficult to tell one from another, in effect challenging traditional professional identities (Taylor et al., 2008a, 2008b).

PEDAGOGIC RESEARCH BASE

Within the fast-changing UK policy context under the then New Labour government (1997–2010), two pedagogic studies, which included a literature review of in total 56 studies (Taylor et al., 2008a, 2008b) pointed to irreconcilable differences between IPE and CL. While comparisons between IPE and CL were not part of the studies' original aims, once the irreconcilability hypothesis began to emerge from the findings of these two separate studies undertaken within two years of each other, the data were subjected to further comparative analysis to explore compatibilities and differences between IPE and CL.

The first study was a systematic review of international research into IPE for qualifying social work commissioned in 2006 by the Social Care Institute for Excellence (Sharland & Taylor, 2007). It examined current knowledge of and participation in IPE in qualifying social work and the effectiveness of IPE in qualifying social work education, that is, barriers and facilitators to successful outcomes. The studies included in the review met the definition of IPE; addressed qualifying level social work education; were published after 1995; and included empirical research. The review focused on particular IPE programmes as well as surveys of IPE provision and practitioner attitudes. In all, 42 relevant studies were examined, 24 of which were from the UK with the remainder from the USA or Canada. They were biased towards health services for adults, including mental health, HIV and AIDS, and palliative care. Under-represented practice areas included work with older people, domestic violence, and learning difficulties. None involved preparation for collaborative work in child protection. Among these, a subset of 13 merited in-depth quality appraisal.

The second study comprised a knowledge review and survey of higher education preparation for 'integrated services'. Called the 'Integrated Children's Services (ICS) in Higher Education' project, the study was commissioned in 2007 by the Higher Education Academy (Taylor et al., 2008b) to support the development of practice for ICS in university-level education in a range of professional fields associated with children. These included teaching, early years development, careers, nursing, midwifery (and a range of allied health professions), medicine, psychology, youth and community work, and social work. Given the diversity of these fields, a wide-ranging project Stakeholder Reference Group was established with 29 members from sector skills councils, regulatory bodies, and academic and professional bodies. An online and telephone practice survey was initially undertaken with an opportunistic sample of 36 higher education institutions (HEIs) from England, Wales, and Northern Ireland, of which ten were pre-1992 research-intensive HEIs; 26 had developed since 1992 and included ten newly created (since 1993) further education colleges and teacher-training institutions accredited by universities to run social work programmes. In-depth interviews were held with 47 staff drawn from the 36 HEIs leading relevant initiatives (i.e., 'whole system' initiatives reflecting a significant commitment from the HEI); whole programmes, for example, new degrees; and single modules or parts of a module. These were offered at foundation, undergraduate, postgraduate, or continuing professional development (CPD) levels or, indeed, addressed a range of levels simultaneously. The knowledge review also included relevant UK research studies going back to 1989 (the date of the Children Act) and, of the 51 studies screened on the basis of the title and abstract, 12 met the criterion of addressing ICS in university-accredited programmes and included empirical and conceptual pieces. Having introduced the research underpinning this chapter, the next section outlines the theory base.

ACTIVITY THEORY

The field of interprofessional learning has been consistently criticised for being theory-less (e.g., Barr et al., 2005; Sharland & Taylor, 2007). Several researchers and theorists have responded to this challenge (Hean et al., 2009, Payler et al., 2007, 2008). Hean et al. (2009) found an increasing number of publications after 2005 on the theoretical underpinnings of interprofessional learning to the extent 'the plethora of theories has become a confusing and un-navigable quagmire' (p. 251). They also presented a helpful framework integrating key micro-level learning theories from the wider field of education. However, they did not address sociological or psychological theories dealing with issues of professionalism, socialisation, and group identity. A seminar funded by the ESRC (2009) was devoted to validating their framework though theories relating to the social context of learning were not considered. Subsequently, Hean et al. (2009) suggested a move beyond micro-level analysis to macro-level understanding, where learning was viewed as a collective exercise within a practice organisation. Most apposite were 'situated learning' theories which addressed learning impacts within specific 'learning organisations' (Lave & Wenger, 1991). However, drawing on practice in a children's hospital in Helsinki and Latour's actor network theory, Engeström (2001) suggested it was difficult to find such well-bounded learning communities. Where the aim was to change practice, to be fully adequate in a particular situation, learning had to be located within a heterogeneous network of non-human and human actors which it turned into:

> black boxes without identifiable internal systemic properties and contradictions. If we want to successfully confront the various actors involved in the care, we must be able to touch and trigger some internal tensions and dynamics in their respective institutional contexts, dynamics that can energise a serious learning effort on their part (Engeström, 2001, p. 140).

For Engeström (2001) learning needed to occur in a changing mosaic of interconnected activity systems where the challenge was to acquire a new way of working:

> activity theory has evolved through three generations of research. The emerging third generation of activity theory takes two interacting activity systems as its minimal unit of analysis, inviting us to focus research efforts on the challenges and possibilities of inter-organizational learning (p. 133).

Engeström (2001) started from the premise that any theory of learning must answer at least four central questions: (i) who are the subjects of learning, and how are they defined and located; (ii) why do they learn and what makes them make the effort; (iii) what do they learn and what are the contents and outcomes of learning; and (iv) how do they learn and what are the key actions or processes of learning? He combined these four central questions with five 'principles of activity theory'. In considering his approach, it is important to note that, while situated interprofessional learning also occurs in 'learning organisations', for student social workers at all levels, the main educational source is the HEI located within a broader – local and national – social work practice environment and – global or international – professional community.

For Engeström (2001), the prime unit of analysis and first principle is a 'collective, artefact-mediated and object-oriented activity system seen in its relation to other network systems' (p. 136). In the case of social work, this system comprised the HEI-based actor stakeholders (subjects) who led the planning and development of interprofessional learning (the 'object') understood by subjects as either IPE or CL. These actor stakeholders operated within the rules and cultural norms of the external communities shaping their interactions and, in so doing, deployed 'artefacts', such as internally mandated curriculum design interacting with externally driven accreditation processes, to mediate their actions.

The second principle is the activity system is 'multi-voiced', representing multiple points of view and interests as the division of labour creates different positions and subjects bring different cultures and traditions. For Engeström (2001), 'multi-voicedness is a source of trouble and a source of innovation, demanding actions of translation and negotiation' (p. 136). In the case of social work, the unusually large number of members of the stakeholder reference group established in the Integrated Children's Services in Higher Education project described earlier exemplified this.

The third principle is an activity system with a cultural history that has been shaped and transformed over quite lengthy periods of time. In this study, the relatively long history of IPE beginning in the 1990s contrasted with the more recent rapid policy change, aptly described by UK social policy researcher John Clarke (2004) as 'policy churn' (p. 145).

The fourth principle is 'historically accumulating structural tensions within and between activity systems' (Engeström, 2001, p. 137) generate disturbance and conflict, particularly when the activity system adopts a new element from outside and this collides with the old system. An example of this is where the relative newcomer of CL collides with the more established IPE.

Finally, the fifth principle is, as an activity system is transformed, it generates expansive learning, a rethinking of goals, activities, and relationships, and begins to respond in new and enriched ways, producing new patterns of activity to expand understanding and change practice. Given the solidified boundaries between professions, this presents the greatest challenge for interprofessional education.

Engeström's (2001) analytical matrix and activity theory generally would seem to resonate particularly well with social work and its long-standing and distinctive focus on the person-in-environment. There are clear parallels between activity theory and systems theory in social work. Activity theory has been criticised for being more suited for evaluation purposes rather than as a guide to action (Jarvis et al., 2003) and, similarly, systems theory in social work has been criticised for being more useful for assessment purposes than as a guide for intervention.

The two interacting activity systems in interprofessional education were the non-HEI key actor stakeholders promoting IPE and CL, and their relationships, positions, and perspectives. This system, in turn, impacted on the HEI actors, particularly the curriculum planners who, in their respective activity systems within HEIs, were involved in the design, development, and implementation of IPE, CL, or both. While each is addressed separately, it is important to see them as interactive rather than unidirectional, despite the power imbalances between the two activity systems.

NON-HIGHER EDUCATION INSTITUTION STAKEHOLDERS

The non-HEI actor stakeholders included policy makers, regulators, employers, and service users and carers who formed a multi-voiced activity system exerting pressure on one another to bring their interests into alignment to gain access to tools to mediate their objectives to shape IPE and CL.

The policy makers

Since the 1990s, the key policy makers with an investment in IPE focused on health and social care. Of the 42 relevant studies in Sharland and Taylor's (2007) research, 32 were health related while only five (not drawn from the UK) focused on children and families and, of these, none involved preparing practitioners to work collaboratively in child protection, a predominant social work practice area. Of these, only evaluations of the Department of Health pilots in health and social care (Miller et al., 2006) paid any significant attention to external stakeholder participation. Since the introduction of *Every Child Matters* (UK Department for Education and Skills, 2003), which heralded an unprecedented series of new policies calling for urgent and comprehensive change to improve outcomes for children in England, a new focus on CL as an approach to learning for practice with children and families took hold. Parallel developments in IPE and CL, albeit with IPE off the starting blocks first, led by different government departments, had quite different implications for the subjects of learning and why, what, and how they learned (Engeström, 2001).

Government in the UK has been a key actor in both approaches but each has been led by different government departments with differing trajectories, impacts, and implications. First, and with a considerably longer history, the emphasis on IPE for health and social care professions emerged in 1990 under the then Conservative government, with groundbreaking legislation to support the new activity of care management and community care led by the Department of Health. Importantly, care management was an occupation which, in different areas of the country, could be undertaken by people from different professions (e.g., social work, nursing, and occupational therapy) or, indeed, by people without professional qualifications. Care management, although a new and hybrid role in the 1990s, did not result in a plethora of specific educational programmes; instead IPE was promoted.

The IPE approach continued under New Labour (1997–2010) with legislation reinforcing the importance of collaboration. Notably the National Health Service Plan (UK Department of Health, 2000) emphasised the importance of collaboration between the National Health Service (NHS), higher education providers, and regulatory bodies to promote partnership at all levels to ensure a seamless service of patient-centred care. Following the NHS Plan, and with significant levels of government funding, 13 pilot sites were established to develop and implement IPE, representing partnerships between NHS Trusts, Workforce Development Consortia (some linked to Strategic Health Authorities), and HEIs. The message was clear: health and social care professions should expect IPE at every stage of workforce development (UK Department of Health, 2001a, 2001b, 2004). In general, the focus remained on curriculum development, supporting organisational structures, and student outcomes with little explicit attention to the improved quality of practice or better outcomes for users and carers (Sharland & Taylor, 2007).

In contrast, the field of practice with children and families focused on the development of a range of practice tools designed to shape integrated working. The genesis of these developments was the Laming Inquiry (2003) into the tragic child abuse death of 'Victoria Climbié' in England, which, in itself, generated a huge amount of media attention and public discourse about the professions, particularly social work. This led to *Every Child Matters* (UK Department for Education and Skills, 2003) and subsequently *The Children's Plan* (UK Department for Children, Schools and Families, 2007), which underlined the need for professionals to be trained in a common core of knowledge and skills to work collaboratively in multidisciplinary teams (Edwards, 2005). Developments were led by the newly created Department for Children, Schools and Families, with its somewhat counter-intuitive title reflecting an attempt to reinforce the message about the importance of collaboration. A second major child abuse scandal in London, the case of 'Baby Peter', served to reinforce the media position on professional failings, and social work was once again on the firing line (Garrett, 2009a). The state, operating from an increasingly interventionist position, not only brought back Lord Laming to lead a review of child protection, but also enforced the questionable, illegal public sacking of the then Director of Children's Services for the London borough where Baby Peter had died. This review set a number of actions in train, including the Social Work Taskforce (2009) which led to the Social Work Reform Board and its far-reaching review of social work education and practice where the final outcomes have yet to be determined.

Key new practice tools were designed to respond to the *Every Child Matters* agenda and reinforced capacity to deliver enhanced services (Garrett, 2009b). Among them was the *Lead Professional*, a single contact point for children, coordinating the delivery of agreed actions. Significantly, this role could be taken by many different types of practitioners, including social workers, healthcare professionals, or teachers, and was defined by function and skill, rather than by profession or practitioner grouping. The *Common Assessment Framework* aimed to identify, at the earliest opportunity, children's needs not covered by universal services to provide timely and coordinated support to meet those needs. The *Common Core of Skills and Knowledge for the Children's Workforce* identified six areas of knowledge and skill required to practise at a basic level of expertise and aimed to 'help establish a greater shared language and understanding across different parts of the workforce' (UK Department for Education and Skills, 2005, p. 3). Finally, the *Integrated Qualifications Framework* aimed to establish comparative qualifications to enable practitioners to move freely between roles within the sector.

This plethora of tools was designed to underpin practice outcomes and, by implication, to shape learning for practice.

The regulators

The second group of external stakeholders were the well-established accrediting bodies, including powerful health players like the General Medical Council, the Nursing and Midwifery Council, and the Health Professions Council, who also played an important role in the development of IPE, together with the General Social Care Council, a relative newcomer in 2003. The professions worked through their respective Councils, in consultation with the powerful higher education Quality Assurance Authority, to establish HEI curricular expectations regarding IPE. In contrast though, and several years later, when developing CL to respond to the integrated children's services agenda, accrediting bodies by then tended to be seen as part of the problem rather than the solution. For example, frustration was expressed by employers with accrediting bodies, such as the General Teaching Council and the General Social Care Council, being too inflexible to allow for a range of routes into professional programmes. As a result, new regulatory stakeholders were introduced, including the Sector Skills Councils and other emerging quangos, such as the Children's Workforce Development Council, who represented new fields of practice in relation to the children's workforce. They were seen as garnering new levels of funds and power, at the expense of the traditional accrediting bodies and roles and responsibilities were blurred. 'Multi-voicedness' was indeed both a source of trouble and of innovation (Engeström, 2001) and this continued in 2010 when, although it was after the study on which this chapter was based took place, very soon after its election, the Coalition Government acted swiftly to absorb the Children's Workforce Development Council into the 'new'

Department of Education and to set in train the transfer in 2012 of the regulatory functions of the General Social Care Council to the Health Professions Council. The Health Professions Council is an 'independent' UK regulator, which regulates 15 health professions. Social work will be by far the largest member group, constituting 40% of the membership of what will likely become the Health and Care Professions Council. Social work has viewed with concern the move from a unitary to a multiprofessional regulator. However, the aim of the parallel development in England of the College of Social Work (2011) is to establish an independent and strong organisation to represent and support the profession. These changes in regulatory body may have an impact on IPE but collaboration at the level of the regulator would appear to be difficult to enact. For the first time, in 2004, the established accrediting bodies at the time had explicitly acknowledged the importance of their own collaboration in relation to IPE. The General Social Care Council, the General Teaching Council for England, and the Nursing and Midwifery Council began to meet with practitioners to develop a shared values statement. However, it took four years to produce a draft statement, *Working Together in Children's Services: A Statement of Shared Values for Interprofessional Working* (General Social Care Council, General Teaching Council, & Nursing and Midwifery Council, 2008), and this remained a draft for use as guidance. This development was also significant since it engaged the General Teaching Council, although teachers came relatively late to the interprofessional table. In 2006, the Universities Council for the Education of Teachers had commissioned a position paper on the implications of *Every Child Matters* for university-based teacher education, warning it presaged a 'transformation of educational provision at all levels' (Kirk & Broadhead, 2007). However, the Coalition Government took over before the intended transformation had been accomplished.

The employers

Moving now to the increasingly significant employer stakeholders, IPE employers were predominantly represented by health, in the form of NHS Trusts with a strong emphasis on partnerships with HEIs. Research into IPE showed no evidence of significant direct employer influence but rather of employers being ready to leave IPE development to the professional and accrediting bodies working with the HEIs, and primarily to the large Schools of Medicine, Nursing, and other allied professions which included many senior practising health clinicians. In contrast, the children's services employers were vocal about the need for CL, particularly those from Local Authorities wanting HEIs to 'qualify the unqualified' estimated to be as much as 80% of the workforce. The employers' concern was fuelled by media attention to the quality of direct practice with children and families following the child abuse deaths of Victoria Climbié and 'Baby Peter'. This media-driven frenzy created a demand for instant and far-reaching responses compared to the slow burn of IPE in health and social care over more than a decade. The employers were particularly concerned to develop work-based learning, a field in which the 'new' (post-1992) HEIs had more experience, particularly in tertiary education. There were examples of co-configuration of new kinds of relationships and associated innovative structures. For example, six Local Authorities formed a partnership to commission (through open tender) an HEI to design and accredit work-based learning for children's services employees within the Local Authority, provided by Local Authority trainers. This transfer of power from the HEI to the employers was very unusual and potentially highly significant in diluting the power of the HEIs.

Service users and carers

The final group of stakeholders with a voice in IPE or CL were service users and carers, but they were largely missing in both arenas. In 2003, the Department of Health formalised its requirement for users and carers to be involved in the design, delivery, monitoring, and review of the new social work qualifying programmes (UK Department of Health, 2002). However, minimum evidence of user and carer involvement in IPE or CL was found (Taylor et al., 2008a, 2008b).

HIGHER EDUCATION INSTITUTION STAKEHOLDERS

The second activity system comprised the university-based educators, a relatively more homogeneous group than the external stakeholders. It is the similarities and differences in the characteristics of the HEIs who responded to IPE and CL, the nature of the educators involved, and the ways they responded to external pressures in terms of what they delivered and how they did it, which is largely of interest here, always keeping in mind the earlier point about the interactive relationships between activity systems.

First, there was a difference between the characteristics of the HEIs who responded to IPE and CL. In the 1990s, IPE engaged the interest of some leading and long-established research intensive HEIs, as well as some established post-1992 'new' HEIs (although not the newest post-1993 HEIs associated with tertiary education). There were unusually large amounts of money, initially from the Department of Health, to support the development of IPE initiatives and their evaluation. There was also generous funding through the introduction of the Higher Education Funding Council Centres for Excellence in Teaching and Learning where several focused on further developing IPE. The high-status profession of medicine was involved in some, though not all, health and social care IPE programmes. Other health disciplines involved included nursing, occupational therapy, and physiotherapy, all of which represented large numbers of students, as well as much smaller numbers of social work students. IPE was predominantly at undergraduate or postgraduate level (rather than continuing professional development) and was classroom based.

However, in CL in the field of children's services, the picture was quite different. Funding was available to employers to upgrade the children's workforce but, in general, it was not available directly to the HEIs to support CL programme development, or to fund evaluations of new developments. The 'new' HEIs were particularly active in this arena by a ratio of 3:1 compared to the 'old' research-intensive universities. Of note, the newest HEIs, including the tertiary further education providers and some HEIs that had previously been teacher-training colleges, in collaboration with employers, were forming new kinds of partnerships to develop CL. The main 'disciplines' involved included the longer-established fields of social work and children's nursing as well as newly emerging areas, including, for example, early years and youth work, where education programmes had been available for some time but were given a new lease of life by these developments. Teacher education was minimally involved and medicine was not involved at all. Developments were predominantly at pre-professional, undergraduate, or foundation (tertiary) level, with a particular emphasis on flexible, modular, work-based structures. There was relatively little development at the more prestigious and lucrative postgraduate levels.

Actor leaders were identified as important in both IPE and CL change agendas. The Best Evidence Medical Education Review of IPE in health and social care (Hammick et al., 2007) discussed the value of 'transition drivers' to act on a top-down call to initiate, develop, and deliver IPE. These might be senior figures, such as Pro-Vice Chancellors or Deans, with the power and influence to bring together interested groups from across the HEI and key external stakeholders operating at comparable senior levels, who, crucially, could commit resources.

Knotworking (Engeström, 2001) was particularly evident among CL educators where, possibly due to more comfort and familiarity in the new HEIs with enterprise and innovation, actors collaborated across loosely connected systems and CL programmes rapidly evolved with resulting inevitable improvisation, particularly with reference to 'placements'. The 'knotworkers', crossing disciplinary and organisational boundaries, were keen in research interviews to talk about seemingly quite isolated and, at times, risky practice. Some had formal roles created to support the development of the CL agenda across parts of the HEI, such as 'Head of Interprofessional Learning' or 'Head of Enterprise and Partnership'. These appointments circumvented the problem of one faculty or department being seen to take a lead over others and provided a mandate for a lead person to work across HEI internal structures, co-configuring and knotworking to resolve internal disturbances created by the rapid development of new structures. The disciplinary background of the knotworkers was largely invisible and appeared irrelevant.

Then there were differences in curriculum content and processes put in place by the actor leaders in the HEIs to respond to the interprofessional agenda. The substantive content of teaching in IPE and CL was of a different order. In IPE the focus was on learning first and foremost to be a professional and, secondly, to work interprofessionally. In CL the drive to 'qualify the unqualified' resulted in the development of a new brand of multiskilled children's or family worker. IPE curricula tended to address professional roles and responsibilities, attitudes to other professions, team roles, leadership, and conflict management. CL curricula, in addition to attention to working collaboratively with others within organisations, included a focus on the whole child, child development, and children's trajectories, seen by curriculum planners as a unifying or common focus for different kinds of learners.

In relation to curricular processes, both IPE and CL were characterised by an impressive range and variety (Barr & Sharland, 2011) of qualifying programmes to integrate interprofessional learning throughout – 'horizontally' across classroom and practice curricula or, more commonly, limiting it to discrete modules or projects of which:

> [s]ome are classroom based, some practice based, some span the two; some are compulsory, some optional, some assessed, some not; some focus on attitudes, some on skills, some on professional roles, values, identities – and combinations of any or all … the practical, resource and cultural challenges are significant. Negotiations between social work and other parties can be protracted (Barr & Sharland, 2011, p. 206).

Common learning programmes, in particular, implemented some significant changes, which brought them closer to employers in order to compete in the HEI marketplace. The 'how' of learning was particularly important to employer stakeholders. For example, in relation to timetabling, there were examples of weekend teaching, or teaching throughout the calendar year rather than in traditional semesters or terms. In relation to place of learning, the emphasis was on learning in the workplace with minimal need for attendance at the HEI. In relation to level of learning, work-based initiatives tended to combine learning for the same group of student employees across a range of levels (e.g., foundation, undergraduate, and even postgraduate levels). These developments challenged higher education culture, norms, and practices, and some disturbance was reported by academics (Taylor et al., 2008b). They also challenged HEI planning practices as new programmes were heavily dependent on employers purchasing student places and, in times of budget cuts, planning more than one year ahead was difficult for employers. This emphasis on short-term goals challenged Engeström's (2001) principle of historicity whereby activity systems were transformed over time. Policy churn (Clarke, 2004) was inevitably developing into practice churn.

So far, using activity theory, the two activity systems and aspects of the results of their interactions have been explored but, as mentioned earlier, the two systems were not equally weighted and within the systems, the different stakeholders had variable power and influence. However, activity theory does not adequately address issues of power relations and responses to power differentials. Returning again to a systems analysis, Abbott (1988) noted no one familiar with the history of the professions could ignore the importance of power in jurisdictional competitions.

POWER IN INTERPROFESSIONAL PRACTICE

In their discussion of activity theory and adult learning, Jarvis et al. (2003) suggested that activity theory paid insufficient attention to psychological processes. In relation to power relations in IPE and CL, researchers, such as Dickinson and Carpenter (2005) and Colyer (2008), have discussed the value of social identity theory in understanding the barriers to interprofessional learning and education, drawing on theorists, such as Tajfel (1981), who proposed that members of one group compared themselves with other groups to establish positive distinctiveness. A UK-based researcher with a long track record of examining partnership working in health and social care, Hudson (2002), suggested that a weak professional identity might result in increased vulnerability to powerful actor stakeholders: 'Where professional identity is weak or ill-defined, there may be little scope for resisting bureaucratic requirements, whereas a distinctive and well-organised profession may be more able to retain an independent approach' (p. 11). Lorenz (2009) further suggested that identity is important to crossing boundaries and to what he termed 'interculturalism', which also implied an encounter with 'the other':

> The encounter with other cultures can only be productive on the basis of a secure, differentiated and effective sense of identity in individuals and societal groups ... but this security does not develop in isolation. It develops from border crossings, from seeing one's identity in context and from developing methods of negotiating differences that respect the dignity and the rights of 'the other' (p. 438).

A weak professional identity has been associated with role blurring and, in her research in healthcare in Canada, Hall (2005) found role blurring led to confusion which could cause practitioners to feel underutilised (their roles usurped), or overutilised (they were doing everything and had usurped others). This focus on professional identity would indicate the importance of timing in introducing learning to work interprofessionally in relation to the formation of a professional identity, a matter which has been picked up in evaluations of IPE in the UK at pre-qualifying social work level (see, e.g., Miers et al., 2005).

British social work psychotherapist and academic Cooper (2009) adopted a psychodynamic perspective on interprofessional working and eloquently suggested the obstacles to working together interprofessionally might be profoundly rooted in our love of ourselves and our professions, and our dislike of those 'not like us', dynamics which are also central to the production of professional identities:

> 'Ethical engagement in pursuit of better interprofessional functioning is about the willingness to continually re-enter this arena of emotional difficulty even if progress is slow, or we continue to fail in familiar ways' (p. 536).

Warmington et al.'s (2004) literature review for the ESRC learning in and for interagency Project identified an avoidance of areas of emotional difficulty in interagency and interprofessional practice suggesting both IPE and CL should pay attention to managing conflict and difference, topics which may not be given enough attention in social work education programmes.

Abbott (1988) argued interprofessional power was unsuccessful due to the presence of dominant actors, including dominant professions and the state as serious competitors to professions, restricting the power of individual professions. He also suggested 'the clients or payers' (p. 140) restricted interprofessional power. However, as previously noted, Taylor et al. (2008a, 2008b) found service user and carer clients were largely invisible in IPE and CL. The fact that these clients were not 'payers' or consumers who could purchase services elsewhere, was of likely significance here. IPE continues, in part, due to the ongoing support of the powerful health professions and, indeed, the endorsement of a regulator, such as the General Medical Council. However, Abbott (1988) warned of health's diminishing dominance in the USA: '[US] medicine which looked so successful for so long, is now crumbling before a combination of invaders and external forces – business administrators, the various medical professions, the insurance companies, large corporations and the government' (p. 141). The same could equally be said of the UK Coalition Government and its onslaught on the NHS.

HEIs are themselves sites of power, which have helped to develop and sustain the professions (Taylor, 1997), as well as serve as arenas for interprofessional competition and conflict (Abbott, 1988). Analysis in this chapter has shown, in the UK at least, IPE has most often been associated with the higher status research universities, in part, due to their focus on the health agenda, whereas CL and the children's agenda has been more closely associated with the 'new' universities and tertiary education providers. On one level, this kind of division of labour may be functional and such complementarity may help avoid competition. On the other, it splits the field of social work and potentially reinforces the risk of hybrid practitioners being developed with the more powerful part of the higher education sector in effect excluded from such developments.

CONCLUSION

Engeström (1999) emphasised the importance of culture in changing practice: 'People face not only the challenge of acquiring established culture; they also face situations in which they must formulate desirable culture' (p. 35). This implies notions of a culture where there is choice and control, where increased understanding and ownership of the different cultures perpetuated by IPE and CL may support the overall project for expansive learning to produce new patterns of activity to enhance partnership and interprofessional collaboration to improve practice for the end user. However, application of activity theory to the pedagogic studies undergirding this chapter (Taylor et al., 2008a, 2008b) has illuminated key differences in the development of interprofessionalism between IPE and CL. On the one hand, in IPE, the culture is one of discrete, collaborative professionals who maintain strong and separate identities, and although as discussed, these are difficult to sustain in interprofessional learning and practice, and may well be a site of tension and conflict, at best 'multi-voicedness' may be a source of innovation, assuming there are processes for translation and negotiation (Engeström, 2001, p. 136). On the other hand, in CL, the culture is one where hybrid practitioners will not be negotiating professional identity and conflict, and will be more likely to respond to the fast pace of change in policy and practice because they are operating under the direction of the employer and the state, without the mediating influence of a profession. Furthermore, crucially in today's context, the employer, the state, and the HEIs are vulnerable to economic factors, and the hybrid practitioner is likely to be less costly to employ than the professional practitioner, and less costly to teach by those engaged in higher education.

Activity theory analysis would suggest the two kinds of activity system of IPE and CL were essentially operating in parallel, and the 'who, what, and how of learning' were different (Engeström, 2001). These differences would not so clearly have emerged if the micro-level learning theories identified by Hean et al. (2009) had been used as these focus on interpersonal dynamics, important as these are. At best, the differences revealed in the activity theory analysis would have presented only as contextual information the very influential macro-interactions between HEIs and the external systems, and the resulting outcomes for IPE and CL. This chapter has shown there clearly are different agendas at work in IPE and CL with different outcomes for interprofessional learning and practice.

In the UK, the hybrid practitioner engaged in CL has been more common in children and family services, although health and social care is not immune from attack. For example, Lewy (2010), in her discussion of interprofessional working in health in the UK, drew attention to the development of the generic healthcare practitioner and the risk of this being a: 'political move to erode professional status and therefore provide a substandard health care workforce' (p. 8). She gave the example of responses to cutbacks in government healthcare in 2007 and the resultant increase in generic foundation degrees (tertiary level) to deliver a mass workforce with no professional status, known as 'the Christmas Tree effect' (p. 8). Lewy (2010) warned about the effect of the tendency to just produce more workers rather than evaluate the workforce organisation and plan strategically how to use workers differently:

> The development of a cheaper, broader multi-skilled workforce may result in less flexibility with the outcomes of horizontal enlargement of generic skills. Thus rather than having a large, flexible multi-skilled workforce they have a large general knowledge based inflexible workforce (p. 8).

This warning about the effects of hybridity on organisations would be an important one to carefully evaluate in practice.

Hudson (2002) would likely attribute the above scenario to what he denotes as the 'pessimistic tradition', which is concerned particularly with role blurring and is largely sceptical of the feasibility of effective joint working between professionals. The pessimistic hypothesis presented herein holds CL will come to predominate in this era of economic restraint and short-termism, largely due to the power and influence of the state: 'Perhaps most surprising, the state itself is a serious competitor to dominant professions, providing various of the services they sell, usually through untrained officials at fractions of the prices professions charge' (Abbott, 1988, p. 141). In the UK, the state is buttressed by the media while employers, particularly in child welfare, are increasingly becoming extensions of the state apparatus. The failure of social workers to perform interprofessional practice in high-profile child abuse cases reinforces their usurpation by lesser-trained functionaries willing to use the plethora of practice tools available, and work flexibly across boundaries (see Chapter 14). The risk, of course, in this scenario is of oversimplifying and reducing highly complex matters, such as child abuse, where the application of professional judgement by experienced practitioners is essential to practice, which could, indeed, be dangerous for children.

Lorenz (2009), in his discussion of intercultural relativity and interprofessional education from a European perspective, further illuminated the pessimistic scenario. On the one hand, one might be sceptical of the risk of professions being immutable and self-contained entities with fixed areas of responsibility and hierarchies, which might discriminate and exclude. On the other, one might be wary of the quest for quick fixes and highly technical solutions, where professionals are interchangeable, equally able to complete the same tasks, competent regardless of training, and easily replaceable.

Hudson (2002) also argued for an 'optimistic hypothesis' and proposed three main reasons for this. First, for *normative* reasons, interprofessionality is a good thing and fragmentation can lead to harmful consequences for service users. Secondly, for *policy* reasons, governments have supported engaging with interprofessionality. Thirdly, for *academic* reasons, professional disciplines must make a more constructive contribution to debates about interprofessionality. However, there is a clear problem with this 'optimistic' hypothesis since, although interprofessionality may be viewed as a good thing, academics and researchers have yet to produce clear evidence of the costs and benefits of its outcomes. Over ten years ago, Brandon and Knapp (1999) suggested it was essential to have clear evidence of the relative benefits and costs of different ways to implement learning for interprofessional practice, and this remains true today (Sharland & Taylor, 2007).

Hudson (2002) suggested it is the role of the academics to test optimistic hypotheses and build the evidence base against which to test the hypotheses. The optimistic hypothesis in relation to IPE and CL is they could co-exist at different levels and across divergent fields of practice if the respective roles and responsibilities of hybrid practitioners were clearly defined in relation to each other and to professionals, and where the skill mix was fit for purpose. Confusion and lack of clarity in roles and responsibility, and in lines of accountability, have been shown to be significant in inquiries into failures in interprofessional practice (see, e.g., Laming, 2003). Pursuing this agenda in interprofessional learning must involve attention to issues of power and conflict, as discussed earlier.

Lorenz (2009) shifted the focus from outcomes for professionals to outcomes for the end user believing professionals were being swept away for economic reasons and, to survive and grow in a context of intense competition for resources, IPE must embrace possibilities for expansive learning, and this must include attention to outcomes for the end user. Lewy (2010) also drew attention to the end user, suggesting that, although as a vision interprofessional learning is ideal, it:

> [n]eeds to be supported for its value in moving health care forward and supporting staff and patients. It should not be misinterpreted and used as a management tool undermining professions because this effectively destroys the essence of what the agenda was developed to achieve (p. 8).

The outcomes of IPE or CL for the end user remain largely untested. Furthermore, as shown in the themed edition of *Social Work Education* (2011, 30/2) focusing on evaluations of the outcomes of social work education, social work educators are only just beginning to address these. Greater certainty regarding the outcomes of IPE and CL is needed if social workers are to be confident and competent promoters of interprofessional education and practice.

REFERENCES

Abbott, A. (1988). *The system of professions*. London: University of Chicago Press.

Barr, H., Koppel, I., Reeves, S., Hammick, M. & Freeth, D. (2005). *Effective Interprofessional Education: Argument, Assumption & Evidence*. London: Blackwell with CAIPE.

Barr, H., & Sharland, E. (2011). Implementing interprofessional education in qualifying social work. In J. Lishman (ed.), *Social work education and training*. London: Jessica Kingsley, pp. 199–210.

Brandon, R.N., & Knapp, M.S. (1999). Interprofessional education and training: Transforming professional preparation to transform human services. *American Behavioural Scientist, 42*(5), 876–891.

Bronstein, L., Mizrahi, T., Korazim-Korosy, Y., & McPhee, D. (2010). *International Social Work, 53*(4), 457–473.

Clarke, J. (2004). *Changing welfare, changing states*. London: Sage.

College of Social Work (2011) Home page. Retrieved July 24, 2011 from http://www.collegeofsocialwork.org/

Colyer, H. (2008). Embedding interprofessional learning in pre-registration education in health and social care: evidence of a cultural lag. *Learning in Health and Social Care, 7*(3), 126–133.

Cooper, A. (2009). Soapbox: Interprofessional working: Choice or destiny? *Clinical Child Psychology and Psychiatry, 14*(4), 531–536.

Council on Social Work Education (CSWE) (2008). Educational policy and accreditation standards. Retrieved April 16, 2011 from http://www.cswe.org

Dickinson, C., & Carpenter, J. (2005) 'Contact is not enough': An inter-group perspective on stereotypes and stereotype change in interprofessional education. In *The theory–practice relationship in interprofessional education*. Occasional Paper 7, 23–30. London: The Higher Education Academy Centre for Health Sciences and Practice.

Edwards, A. (2005). Relational agency: learning to be a resourceful practitioner. *International Journal of Educational Research, 43*(3), 168–182.

Engeström, Y. (1999). Innovative learning in work teams: Analysing cycles of knowledge creation in practice. In. Y. Engeström, Miettinen, R., & Punamaki, R.L. (eds), *Perspectives on activity theory.* Cambridge: Cambridge University Press.

Engeström, Y. (2001). Expansive learning at work: Towards an activity theoretical reconceptualisation. *Journal of Education and Work, 14*(1), 133–156.

Eraut, M. (2003). The many meanings of theory and practice. *Learning in Health and Social Care, 2,* 61–65.

Freeth, D., Hammick, M., Reeves, S., Koppel, I., & Barr, H. (2005). *Effective interprofessional education: Development, delivery and evaluation.* Oxford: Blackwell.

Garrett, P.M. (2009a). The case of 'Baby P': Opening up spaces for debate on the 'transformation' of children's services. *Critical Social Policy, 29*(3), 533–547.

Garrett, P.M. (2009b). *'Transforming' children's services? Social work, neoliberalism and the 'modern' world.* Maidenhead: McGraw Hill/Open University.

General Social Care Council, General Teaching Council & Nursing and Midwifery Council (2008). *Working together in children's services: A statement of shared values for interprofessional working.* Retrieved July 23, 2011 from http://www.derbyshirescb.org.uk/

Hall, P. (2005). Interprofessional teamwork: Professional cultures as barriers. *Journal of Interprofessional Care, 19*(1), 188–196.

Hammick, M., Freeth, D., Koppel, I., Reeves, S., & Barr, H. (2007). *A best evidence systematic review of interprofessional education.* BEME Guide 9. Dundee: BEME & AMEE.

Hean, S., Craddock, D., & O'Halloran, C. (2009). Learning theories and interprofessional education: A user's guide. *Learning in Health and Social Care, 8*(4), 250–262.

Hudson, B. (2002). Interprofessionality in health and social care: The Achilles heel of partnership. *Journal of Interprofessional Care, 16*(1), 7–17.

Jarvis, P., Holford, J., & Griffin, C. (2003). *The theory and practice of learning.* London: Kogan Page.

Kirk, G., & Broadhead, P. (2007). *Every child matters and teacher education: Towards a UCET Position Paper.* London: Universities Council for the Education of Teachers.

Laming, L. (2003). *Inquiry into the death of Victoria Climbié,* London: HMSO.

Lave, J., & Wenger, E. (1991). *Situated learning: Legitimate peripheral participation.* Cambridge: Cambridge University Press.

Lewy, L. (2010). The complexities of interprofessional learning/working: Has the agenda lost its way? *Health Education Journal, 69*(1), 4–12.

Lorenz, W. (2009). Europe, the professions and interprofessional education: An exploration of interculture relativity. *Journal of Interprofessional Care, 23*(3), 432–441.

Miers, M., Clarke, B., Pollard, K., & Thomas, J. (2005). Learning together: Student and staff experience of interprofessional groups. *Interprofessional Learning Research Programme: Pre-qualifying Curriculum Evaluation, Study 2.* Bristol: Centre for Learning and Workforce Research in Health and Social Care, University of the West of England.

Miller, C., Woolf, C., & Mackintosh, N. (2006). *Evaluation of common learning pilots and allied health professions first wave sites: Final report.* London: Department of Health.

Payler, J., Meyer, E., & Humphris, D. (2007). Theorising interprofessional pedagogic evaluation: Framework for evaluating the impact of interprofessional continuing professional learning in professional education development on practice change, *Learning in Health and Social Care, 6*(3), 156–169.

Payler, J., Meyer, E., & Humphris, D. (2008). Pedagogy for interprofessional education: What do we know and how can we evaluate it? *Learning in Health and Social Care, 7*(2), 64–78.

Pockett, R. (2010). Interprofessional education for practice: Some implications for Australian social work. *Australian Social Work, 63*(2), 207–222.

Sharland, E. (2011). All together now? Building disciplinary and interdisciplinary research capacity in social work and social care. *British Journal of Social Work,* published May 19, advance access.

Sharland, E., & Taylor, I. (2007). *Interprofessional education for qualifying social work.* London: Social Care Institute for Excellence.

Social Work Taskforce (2009). *Building a safer, confident future: The final report of the social work taskforce.* London: Department for Children, Schools and Families. Retrieved April 16, 2011 from http://publications.dcsf.gov.uk/eOrderingDownload/01114-2009DOM-EN.pdf

Tajfel, H. (1981). *Human groups and social categories.* Cambridge: Cambridge University Press.

Taylor, I. (1997). *Developing: Partnerships for practice,* Buckingham: Open University Press and Society for Research into Higher Education.

Taylor, I., Sharland, E., & Whiting, R. (2008a). Building capacity for the children's workforce: Findings from the knowledge review of the higher education response. *Learning in Health and Social Care Special Issue: Learning for Integrated Services, 7*(4), 184–197.

Taylor, I., Whiting, R., & Sharland, E. (2008b). *Integrated children's services in higher education project: Knowledge review*. Retrieved April 16, 2011 from http://icshe.escalate.ac.uk

UK Department for Children, Schools and Families (2007). *Building brighter futures: The Children's Plan*. London: HMSO.

UK Department for Education and Skills (DfES) (2003). *Every child matters: Change for children*. Nottingham: DfES.

UK Department for Education and Skills (2005). *Statutory guidance on inter-agency collaboration to improve the well-being of children*. London: HMSO.

UK Department of Health (2000). *The NHS Plan: a plan for investment, a plan for reform*. London: Department of Health.

UK Department of Health (2001a). *A health service for all the talents*. London: Department of Health.

UK Department of Health (2001b). *Working together, learning together*. London: Department of Health.

UK Department of Health (2002). *Requirements for social work training*. London: Department of Health.

UK Department of Health (2004). *The NHS improvement plan: Putting people at the heart of public service*. London: HMSO, Cm 6268.

Warmington, P., Daniels, H., Edwards, A., Brown, S., Leadbetter, J., Martin, D. & Middleton, D. (2004). *Interagency collaboration: a review of the literature*. Retrieved on April 26, 2012 from www.bath.ac.uk/research/liw/resources/interagency_collaboration_a_review_of_the_literature_initial.pdf

World Health Organization (WHO) (1988). *Learning together to work together for health*. Geneva: WHO.

World Health Organization (WHO) (2010). *Frameworks for action on interprofessional education and collaborative practice*. Geneva: WHO.

New Technologies for Practice

Thomas Ley

Information technology (IT) is increasingly shaping relationships between human service managers, frontline practitioners, and service users within a networked social service environment. This chapter addresses the unavoidable impact of complex technological advances and draws on contemporary research literature from the UK, USA, Australia, Germany, and other European countries. Informed by a Science and Technology Studies (STS) paradigm, it examines how social, political, and cultural values affect scientific research and technological innovation, and how these, in turn, affect organisational culture and professional social work practice. STS researchers are interested in a variety of problems, including the relationship between scientific and technological innovations and society, and the emerging risks of technology. They often point to the way new innovations are 'technologically rich, but socially poor'. It is shown how the institutionalisation of narrow technological framings of risk and uncertainty presents ethical dilemmas for social workers. The resort to technology attempts to normalise uncertainty, legitimate standardised practices, and create stability. This is described as a formalisation process. It concludes with a critical analysis of the marketisation and re-bureaucratisation of the public sector, and consequent threats to civil liberties, workplace skills, and professional autonomy.

SOCIAL WORK IN THE DIGITAL AGE: 'ELECTRONIC TURN' IN THE PROFESSION?

In the last few decades, no other innovation has had such a big impact on working and living environments than information and communication technologies (Rosenberg, 2004). These are restructuring economies and their forms and modes of production (Castells, 1996). The World Wide Web (www) or internet as a key element of the digital age is also reshaping organisational systems and processes. It has created new e-commerce business models and social networking sites. The impact of new communication technology, such as the internet, is often ambivalent. On the one hand, a regulatory and surveillance culture supported by new technology has emerged in which networked information systems are capable of bringing organisations and professionals very quickly to account. On the other hand, a new form of activism has emerged whereby social movements and direct action are speedily transmitted and mobilised through new social media, such as Facebook and Twitter.

The daily use of digital media and consumption of digitally delivered information has significantly reshaped the way in which social workers communicate with one another, access information, process knowledge, and intervene in the daily lives of clients. Service-users' lives are similarly reshaped, though with the digital divide many do not have access to or the computer skills needed for the internet (Iske et al., 2005). Those who do have access can be both confounded or empowered, by either an overload or richness of information, which shapes their perceptions and interactions with professionals. However, professional social work remains constrained and highly regulated, and IT has enabled new 'systems of governance' to monitor, regulate, and survey service-user behaviour, professional performance, and organisational effectiveness. The net effect may well be a chicken-and-egg scenario. Since the 1970s, organisational and technological change has developed in an intricately connected way to the point where it is inconceivable to operate without computers and IT. This is loosely referred to as the 'electronic turn' in social work and social care (Garrett, 2005, p. 531).

Scientific reflection on the informatisation – the process of increasing dependence on information in post-industrial societies – has produced a range of discourses on information, knowledge, or network society mainly resulting from analyses of digital capitalism. Despite the inescapable force of informatisation – through computerisation – on social workers' daily lives, in-depth analyses of the complexity of factors shaping organisational processes, practice interventions, and service-user behaviour are rare in mainstream social work.

Much of the literature on the role of technology in social work was written in the 1980s and early 1990s and focused on client information systems, decision-support systems, and the computer's role in social work education (Colombi et al., 1993; Glastonbury, 1985; Rafferty et al., 1996; Schoech, 1999; Steyaert et al., 1996). Furthermore, two journals focus on this specialised issue – *New Technology in the Human Services* (from 1984 to 2003), and *Technology in Human Services* (from 1985 to the present). Human Services Information Technology Applications (HUSITA) was formed as an international virtual hub dedicated to promoting the ethical and effective use of IT in social work (see links to these websites at the end of the chapter). However, until very recently, there has been relatively little research on the impact of IT on social work (see more recent literature later in text).

Rather than seeing information technologies as merely educational or pedagogical functional devices, this chapter aims to enhance understanding of IT by conceptualising it first as a *'thing-in-itself' for work or a tool for work*, and secondly as an *organisational technology*. While IT is increasingly shaping professional knowledge and the relationship between organisations, professionals, and service users, it is also changing the role, responsibility, and function of social work (Burton & van den Broek, 2008; Garrett, 2009; Harlow & Webb, 2003). Within the research findings there is no clear position on whether IT in general and case management systems in particular are advantageous either to the profession or to the organisation. Moreover, the contemporary discourse on IT and social work is often accompanied by the discourse of management and business. In this respect, the concepts of efficiency and effectiveness on the one hand and IT on the other are intertwined and discernible. This is described below as an emergent process of formalisation in the field of professional social work.

DOES *IT* REALLY MATTER? AN EXTENDED DEFINITION OF TECHNOLOGY

The methodological significance and practical value of IT in social work is a long-standing issue and a matter of intense debate. At one extreme, technology is seen as an objective, external force with deterministic impacts on organisational culture and professional practice. The contrary position focuses on the social embeddedness of technology, seeing it only as the outcome of strategic choice and social action (Peckover et al., 2008). In this respect science and technology are conceived as cultural practices with an emphasis on scientific culture. According to STS, these perspectives are respectively described as technical and social determinisms. From the perspective of technical determinism, social work is considered to be more affected by IT than professional methods and habitus. Thus social work is overdetermined by technology. The social determinism viewpoint argues that IT cannot deal adequately with the complexity of social work practice. Thus social work is underdetermined by technology due to its complexity and it does not significantly affect frontline work. In this respect it is little more than symbolic innovation. Those who highlight the overbearing influence of technologies have to cope with problems of ambivalent technological inscriptions and their 'interpretative flexibility' (Pinch & Bijker, 1987). Those who focus on the social actors underestimate the role of material agency or 'non-human actors' (computers, mobile phones, computer registered work cards, and speed cameras) in the subject–object relation (Latour, 1994). These two positions can be found in frontline practice as well as in social work research. Both views are incomplete. Therefore, a re-conceptualisation of technology and its mediation by the social is needed to take both perspectives into account. Technology in its broadest sense can be:

> defined as tools made by humans, as efficient means to an end, or as an ensemble of material artifacts. But technology also encompasses instrumental practices, like the creation, fabrication and the use of means and machines; it includes the whole ensemble of material and non-material techno-facts; it is closely connected with institutionalized needs and ends-in-view that technologies serve (Rammert, 1999, p. 23).

In summary, technological innovation 'in the making' reveals a multiplicity of heterogeneous decisions made by a large number of different and often conflicting groups, within social work and the information management systems.

Since the classic writings of Aristotle, four constituting elements of technology have been distinguished:

> the first element is the stuff or material, out of which a techno-fact is made; the second element is the form or shape, that is given to it; the third element is the end or use, for which it is determined; the fourth element is the efficient action, done by the tool-using human (Rammert, 1999, p. 23, see also Heidegger, 1962).

Evidence-based protocols, formalised quality management systems (Beckmann et al., 2007) as well as diagnostic assessment instruments (Timmermann & Berg, 1997) in social work are best subsumed under this broad concept of technology. *Information technology* in particular can be defined as digital information and networked data processing, including the technical base of hardware and software. Digitalisation is not merely the technical means to pre-structure work-based operational procedures, but also involves the medial form of intra- and inter-organisational communication. In terms of a social pragmatic approach, it is about the rich relations constituting technology and media that make the difference. Technology encompasses instrumental practices, like the creation, fabrication, and use of means and machines, but also includes the whole ensemble of material and non-material techno-facts. Rammert (1999) regards the shifting relation between the social and the technical to be gradual rather than a substantial difference. In setting out definitions for his analysis of 'technologically mediated experiences', he suggests:

> Technicization means more reliability, tighter coupling of elements, less dependency on contexts, and more efficiency of control. Techniques to attain technicized relations are the simplification and specification of complex causal relationships by separating, purifying, and schematizing the

elements, the fixing of the relations by repetition in time or incorporation in matter, and the closure of a system by encapsulation and 'black boxing' (p. 29).

'The stuff that technology is made of' as a mediating phenomenon for the social, according to Rammert (1999), has to meet three conditions:

> A *use relation* has to be found or created between a bodily experience and an outer environment that is mediated by something. A *relation of inter-objectivity* has to be established between two elements that assures an expectable and tightly-coupled output from an input. There must be *a memory or an archive* that marks and fixes the evaluated relations in a way that can be repeated often and reproduced in any context (p. 37).

ACTORS, FUNCTIONS, AND ATTRIBUTIONS OF IT IN SOCIAL WORK

Social workers and their clients have to deal with IT in numerous contexts. For example, e-government, online counselling or (self-help) online forums have become part of the digital initiation and delivery of social services to clients. In addition, social workers (have to) use various forms of software and web applications for the purpose of documenting, planning, evaluating, and accounting for their work. Information and communication technologies (ICT) are reconfiguring work practices through the following.

New requirements for the individual staff member

- Communicating with and profiling of clients.
- Collating, storing, and sharing information.
- Streamlining data collection.
- Enhancing accountability.

New public management processes

- Controlling and monitoring work practices.
- Enhancing efficiency.
- Targeting clients, customers, consumers, or service user needs (through use of statistical data).

New politics

- Engaging in (cyber) advocacy and activism as a chosen political strategy (McNutt, 2000, Hick & McNutt, 2002).
- Enhancing client autonomy through IT, for example, through Computer-Assisted-Self-Interviewing (Morgan & Fraser, 2010).

At a network level, IT in social work takes various forms and rites of passage at different levels of the actor–organisation dynamic. As shown in Figure 43.1, these can be depicted as a triangular relationship between clients, organisations, and professionals (Ley & Seelmeyer, 2008, p. 340).

From the *client*'s perspective, the focus is on them as capable 'active citizens' using various IT media to enhance their autonomy and participation in civil society or as 'dependent' with psychosocial needs. The latter shifts the focus to the therapeutic relationship between clients and professionals, for example, in online counselling (Murphy et al., 2009). From an *organisational* perspective, IT has enabled service users to access services in novel ways, such as national call centres like Findhelp Information Services 211 in Canada or local call centres in England (Coleman & Harris, 2008, p. 581). Coleman and Harris (2008) have been highly critical of these developments because of the interconnection between consumerism, technology, and business models. From a *professional* perspective, IT has enabled tightly prescriptive case management systems, which have altered professional relationships.

Rafferty and Steyaert (2009) distinguished four key themes in this context, as follows:

1 *Information systems supporting practice* (as outlined above).
2 *The learning professional and learning organisation* associated not only with case management systems (see later), but also with discourses of knowledge management or evidence-based practice where IT plays a crucial role (Dunlop & Holosko, 2006).

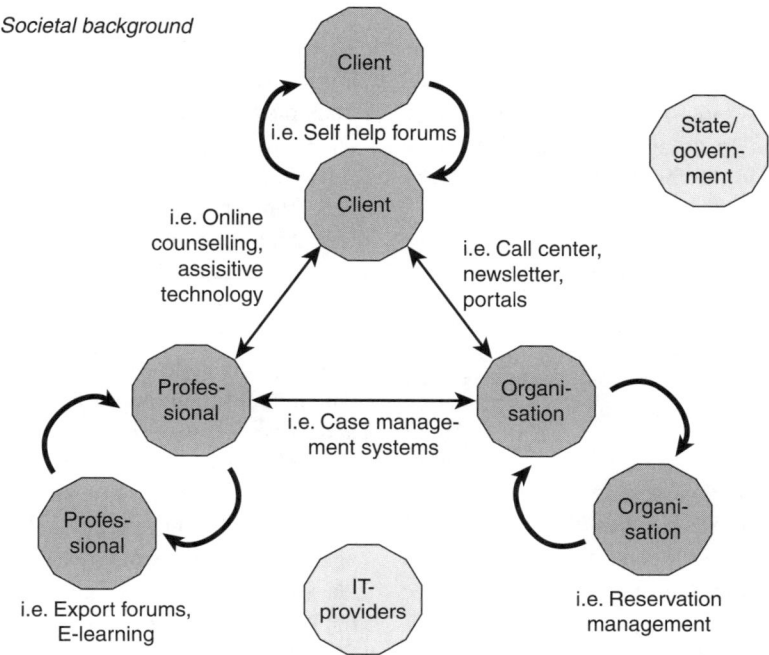

Figure 43.1   Analytic matrix of information technology (IT) applications in social work

3   *Independent living*, for example, the use of assistive technologies for disabled or elder persons to increase their mobility and provide alternative communication channels – even though many technologies are predominantly designed to exclude (Blaschke et al., 2009; Rafferty & Steyaert, 2009).
4   *the information society*, where issues of 'social inclusion', 'social exclusion', regulation and surveillance, and the 'digital divide' must be taken into account.

EXPERT SYSTEMS FOR EXPERTS? CASE MANAGEMENT SYSTEMS AS SUBJECT MATTER

Information systems began to appear in social work organisations in the 1980s, initially in organisational administration and financial accounting. Browsing the literature, one finds numerous terms for this object, including case management systems (CMS), management information systems (MIS), integrated information systems (IIS), decision support systems (DSS), and expert systems (ES). In the core all of these systems are database-driven file- and information-systems, but the naming prioritises different purposes and ends-in-view. In the 1990s, the use of IT in social work practice accompanied shifts in social policy, moving public services into a new era of accountability and monitoring. This new public managerialism eclipsed technological innovations and professional agendas supportive of professional practice. Technology was tied to prescriptive welfare programmes with 'inscripted' aims or ends-in-view (Akrich, 1992; Akrich & Latour, 1992). Case management systems led to a proliferation of manuals, forms, and assessments. They can be understood as 'techno-scientific scripts', which are neither exclusively technical nor scientific (Akrich, 1992; Akrich & Latour, 1992; Timmermans & Berg, 1997). In effect, these integrated information systems reify the possibility of a concrete end-user, since they are formal networked abstract data sets that anticipate any number of endless clients or 'customers'.

However, in concrete terms, different user role concepts and observer positions are inscripted and, as a result, divergent user requirements, motivations (to fill in data) and expectations on the usage and usefulness of IT emerge. In the discussion on these 'technologies of care', Webb (2006) argues:

> As new technologies of care converge the causal power of the networked information becomes more important than the specific interests it represents, the flows of power. It becomes vital to be present in the network and not be excluded from it (p. 165).

Until recently, most of the information systems in social work have had a 'documentary character', that is, they have been aids to recordkeeping. As Webb (2006) notes, 'Hard copy is replaced by electronic data flows ... The rhetoric of time is important – planning making lists, scheduling and reporting, all figure significantly. Working life becomes a networked enterprise' (p. 167). Information systems have led to extended classification systems, detailed care planning, cost–performance analysis, as well as case- and organisation-oriented evaluation and monitoring. Case management systems direct the 'workflow of social services'. The prevailing software has, in fact, a more descriptive than a prescriptive character. In short, 'it generally looks back rather than forward'. However, this is changing with the current discourses about risk assessment – especially in the context of child protection – and evidence-based practice. These specialised tools are meant to aid professional decision making (Dunlop & Holosko, 2006).

In several countries, a software market has been established for social services. In Germany, for example, there are over 300 software products (Halfar & Kreidenweis, 2008; http://www.social-software.de). Nonetheless there are significant differences in the national welfare systems as well as in the various fields of intervention. This suggests the differences are dependent on the mode of implementation, for example, whether it is policy driven, like the national social work practice agenda in the UK (White et al., 2010), or part of system-wide institutional innovations. Despite this, social work institutions become market participants depending on engineering companies and the process of software design. Open source activities are very rare in the field of social work. In Germany, for example, two out of 300 products can be classified in this way. The concept open source describes practices in production and development promoting access to the end product's source materials, which could be trend setting for social work and more adequate for communities of practice. Moreover, only a few academics are involved in processes of software development, or to be more precise it is not on the agenda of social work research to develop classification systems and taxonomies for the practical fields (e.g., Fitch, 2007; Fitch & Shaffer, 2007). Webb (2006) contends, 'the information architectures and classification tools that underlie many of the new technologies impacting on frontline practice are designed by a small elite, with decisions on what is represented and what is not' (p. 165). It is the power of naming and defining which is inherent to the exclusive access to constructing and designing the software. In order to fully understand how IT applications exert a decisive influence on social work, it is necessary to examine the systems themselves and their formal structure. From this vantage point, it is possible to grasp how the processes of embedding (or non-embedding) in organisational (and societal) contexts might be best analysed. The whole process of informatisation can be broadly conceptualised through the 'double character' of software. That is, first the dimension of the formal prescriptive structure and, secondly, the dimension of practical signification. In this context of practical embedding, software assigns the user responsibility to arrange, organise, and classify on the one hand while offering scope for autonomous acquisition on the other. The term 'software' itself is a good metaphor for this, because there are two connected concepts involved: the mouldable, enabling media (soft) and the structuring, restrictive machine (ware). To arrive at a good impression of computer-assisted practice, the following heuristic comparison to traditional practice might be helpful to the reader (see Kreuger et al., 2006). Table 43.1 shows that traditional practice and computer-assisted practice implicate different modes of action, which require different competences and capabilities, and lead to different results and consequences for social workers and their clients.

and thus tackling the question of how technologies are embedded in professional action. However, in recent years, discussion on social work theory and research has increased (Broadhurst et al., 2010a; Kutscher et al., 2011; Ley & Seelmeyer, 2011; Shaw & Clayden, 2009). The following analysis of formalisation, discretion, and documentation will take an approach that draws on science and technology studies, and organisational and professional theories.

PROCESSES OF FORMALISATION, DISCRETION, AND DOCUMENTATION

In analysing the ambivalent relation between IT and social work, it is possible to adopt very different fields of research, for instance, philosophy of technology (Heidegger, 1962); media theories or science and technology studies (Bowker & Star, 2000; Latour 1994, 1996; Rammert, 1999); computer science (usability engineering and artificial intelligence) or social informatics (Kling, 2007); organisational theories, especially neoinstitutionalism (Benders et al., 2005); micropolitics or structuration theory (Orlikowsky, 1992); social policy (Garrett, 2004; Webb, 2006); or more application-oriented social work informatics (Parker-Oliver & Demiris, 2006). As yet, there is no unique study systematically relating technology studies and the professional perspective of social work

THE BASIC PROCESS OF FORMALISATION

A strong claim made in this chapter is that technological advancement in social work fundamentally rests on a process of formalisation, which objectifies the professional task. The professional task is reduced to means, rather than ends, and to raw materials or 'things that are ready to hand'. Thus end values are increasingly shorn from contexts of meaning. To re-present 'reality' in software, information about clients and interactions (i.e., between client and social worker as well as between client 'systems of support') has to be transformed into a new *formalised order*. The transformation of social work actions into technical artefacts requires the reduction of complex realities to abstract categories. This process is characterised – as the computer scientist Arno Rolf notes – by

Table 43.1 Comparison of traditional and computer-assisted practice

Traditional practice	Computer-assisted practice
Person-in-environment situates knowledge	Avoids situated, indexical expressions
Centres on physically embodied client	Avoids embodiment
Open to multiple orientations	Open primarily to code-only orientations
Focuses on process	Focuses on product
Involves caring	Involves monitoring
Orients to total person	Orients to person as text

Source: adapted from Kreuger et al. (2006, p. 30).

the steps of 'semiotisation', 'formalisation', and 'algorithmisation' (Ley & Seelmeyer, 2008, pp. 344–346; Rolf, 2003) as follows:

- *Semiotisation* means the *attribution of signs,* such as language, *to things or actions.* It is the prerequisite for understanding contexts and communicating and acting in social environments.
- *Formalisation* means the transformation of *action into operation.* Actions are characterised by uniqueness and dependent on context and situation. Operations describe routine actions which have been repeated many times. Transformation of action into operation has to be described and defined by an observer whose perspective and aims inevitably influence the description. Sesink (2003) describes the basic process of formalisation as follows:

  > Through formalised abstraction, a part of reality is reduced to its essential structures. From the outset, only causal (formal) references may appear as being essential. ... Aspects of the reality to be modelled, which defy this kind of formalisation – that is all material, individual, singular and exclusive aspects – appear to be inessential/insignificant. ... Formal models are free of meaning and have not a soul in sight (computer scientists would probably say 'devoid of context'); respectively meaning is replaced by function (p. 59, analogously translated by the author).

- *Algorithmisation* or *the transformation from operation to algorithm* implements these formalised models into software providing a precise, final description of a step-by-step solution to determine certain factors. Algorithmisation is the last step in the process of reduction and the final level of abstraction from reality. Owing to the implementation of case management systems, the observer fixes the described operations in computer systems in advance of any material contact with people.

These steps of transformation can be described as a process that moves from *narrative to code* (Parton, 2006; Regan, 2003; Peckover, White et al., 2008). This transformation has important consequences: the process of mapping actions into software regimes leads to the splitting, fragmentation, and depersonalisation of the rich stuff of lived experience. Again, in the words of Latour (1994), social actions are inscribed into technical artefacts. The act of formalisation is a process of objectivation and subsumption, which ignores the contingency of social life. In Habermasian terms, these systemic and functional imperatives advanced via technology threaten the integrity of the 'life-world'. They hollow out the richness of the life-world. The knock-on effects of this leads to problems of negative 'labelling'. As Bowker and Star (2000) observe:

> We have a moral and ethical agenda in our querying of these [classification] systems. Each standard and each category valorises some point of view and silences another. This is not inherently a bad thing – indeed it is inescapable. But it is an ethical choice, and as such it is dangerous, not bad, but dangerous (pp. 5–6).

In summary, the process of formalisation (see Figure 43.2) leads to consequences at different levels: working in computerised work sites (and with techno-scientific scripts in general) enforces processes of *classification*. At an organisational level, these processes then become countable and accountable (Burton & van den Broek, 2008; Carrilio, 2008) and a basis of monitoring and, therefore, *standardising* (work) procedures. From the client's perspective, this involves *processes of labelling* with a shift from a preoccupation with needs to a preoccupation with risks. This leads to a form of actuarial practice whereby the client is reduced to the calculation of standardised risk factors, which, in turn, enforce strategies of profiling that conflict with a more holistic view of professional assessments (Webb, 2006). These basic actions of categorisation as increasingly inevitable and ubiquitous in social work practice are best described as *processes of routinisation*.

Modes of knowledge, discretion, and decision making

With regard to the question of how professional social work generates its knowledge about the case, one can distinguish between two constitutive logics: the logic of subsumption and the logic of reconstruction (see also the epistemological differentiation of deduction and

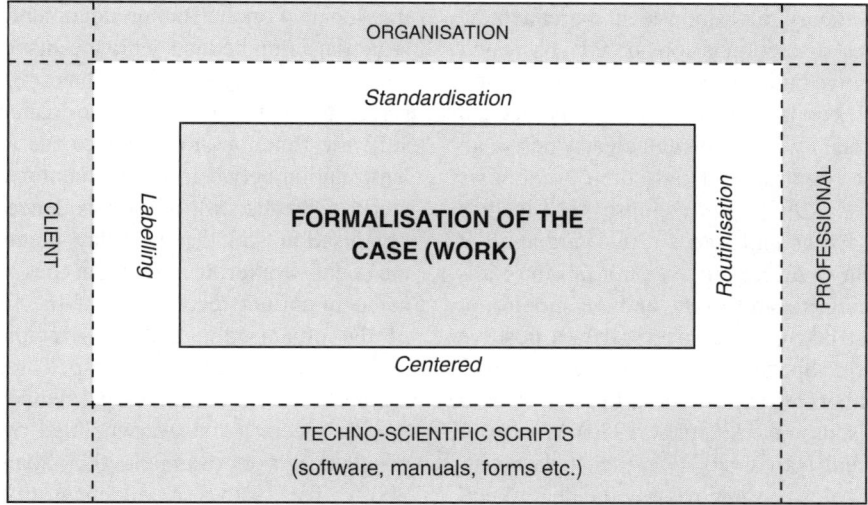

Figure 43.2 The process of formalisation and its consequences.

induction or the methodological debate of statistical and clinical prediction) (Schrödter, 2005). The logic of subsumption (deduction) refers to the mode of knowledge typically found in classification systems. Classification systems comprehend established terms which can be operationalised (such as the 'ICD 10' in medical science and the 'child behaviour check list' frequently used in youth welfare services in Germany). In their studies on the effectiveness of actuarial risk assessment models, Baumann et al. (2005) refer to this as part of a methodological debate between clinical versus statistical prediction. Their findings suggest the effect on everyday practice and case-related behaviour of social workers by actuarial feedback was minimal. This criticism of actuarial knowledge ended up in what was called the 'risk assessment wars' (Johnson, 2006) and we can anticipate debates about the significance of actuarialism as an ongoing issue in social work (Gray et al., 2010). However, throughout this chapter, it has been suggested professional social work cannot be reduced to diagnostic classification. It always includes rich and complex components which cannot be standardised, such as hermeneutical and interpretative understanding of cases. These are, in fact, two contradictory requirements and diverging modes of practice knowledge for professional actions, which simultaneously exclude but depend on each other (Schrödter, 2005).

A focus on decision making helps clarify this interdependency. The relationship between social work practice and its different forms of knowledge is often discussed in terms of the problems of *decision making*. This especially applies if a professional task is constructed along the following lines (Otto & Schnurr, 1999).

- *Contingent* meaning diffuse, 'badly structured', complex, and hard to comprehend as a whole.
- *Related to values*, such as integrity, autonomy, and justice. Furthermore, there is a drift to situations where different values and maxims, which are often conflicting and antagonistic, have to be given equal attention and balanced against each other. Taking the example of child welfare, the child's right to education versus the protection of familial privacy or the child protection vs. the family support model (Hall et al., 2010; Parton, 2009).
- *Fraught with risk* reflected in the paradox of professional action 'patiently waiting vs. intervening'.

Because of these dimensions, the professional task cannot be clearly defined through prescriptive routines, performance rules, or codes of practice. Thus, as Michael Lipsky's

(1980) theory of 'street-level bureaucracy' indicates, discretion is considered a basic and constitutive precondition for decision making in professional social work. It is needed when social workers cannot clearly derive an explicit treatment from their diagnosis (Handler, 1992). In response to Lipsky's theory, Evans and Harris (2004) argued that the myth of discretion does not fall into 'all-or-nothing' formulations, and we should not consider discretion as necessarily a positive condition. Space for discretion can be created either reflexively or arbitrarily (for a basic discussion, see Lipsky, 1980). Moreover, Evans and Harris (2004) argue, '(t)he existence of rules is not inevitably the death-knell of discretion. Rather, by creating rules organisations create discretion' (p. 883).

Hence it might be helpful to take a closer look at organisational rules and the way they are formalised. According to contemporary research findings from organisational studies, there are at least two types of formalisation: enabling and coercive formalisation (Adler & Borys, 1996; for a discussion on of quality management in social services, see Beckmann et al., 2007). The coherence of discretion and formalisation can therefore be located in the contrarinesses of enabling and coercion on the one hand, and reflexivity and arbitrariness on the other. In this context, a basic research question for social work might be: 'How is professional discretion – as a link between organisational governance and face-to-face professional work – shaped by case management systems? In short, is there a changing environment of case intervention strategies in computerised work sites within social work?'

THE DOCUMENTAL CHARACTER OF SOCIAL WORK

According to the above-mentioned dimensions, documentation in social work cannot be understood as a simple individual task for the social worker. Rather documental construction is embedded with the institutional network of an organisation. Thus it is appropriate to focus on how case-management software functions to influence the ambivalent relation between management and casework, or better still, the ambivalence of the organisation and the everyday practices of the social worker. It is apparent that, without some important recognition of the function of the organisation and its principles, the entire situation cannot be grasped (see, e.g., Schoech et al., 2006). At first glance, social workers seem to be overwhelmed by routinised paper work (Samuel, 2005; Shaw et al., 2009). This shows a tendency to the re-bureaucratisation of social work (Burton & van der Broek, 2008) and, therefore, to the managerial and technocratic aspiration to monitoring the whole working processes of social work. On the other hand, when looking to the oft-noted, insufficient quality of data (Shaw et al., 2009), this points to two revealing research findings: (i) 'bad' organisational reasons for 'good' clinical records (Heath & Luff, 1996, pp. 354–363) or, conversely, (ii) 'good' organisational reasons for 'bad' clinical records (Garfinkel, 1967, pp. 186–207). As Garfinkel (1967) suggests, the contents of clinical folders are often collected with a view to the future possibility that the clinician–patient relationship might have to be reconstructed in accordance with expectations of sanctionable performances. These contingencies provide a good example of the 'bad clinical records' for 'good reasons' case scenario. Heath and Luff (1996) reformulate this paradox:

> Despite the widespread introduction of information technology into primary health care within the United Kingdom, medical practitioners continue to use the more traditional paper medical record often alongside the computerised system. The resilience of the paper document is not simply a consequence of an impoverished design, but rather a product of the socially organised practices and reasoning which surround the use of the record within day to day consultative work. The practices that underpin the use of the medical records may have a range of important implications, not only

for the general design of systems to support collaborative work, but also for our conceptions of 'writers', 'readers', 'objects' and 'records' utilised in those designs (p. 354).

While Garfinkel traces the insufficient quality of data back to the respect for the client and the integrity of their working alliance, Heath and Luff (1996) ascribe this lack of perfect recording to respect for the daily and socially embedded routines of professionals. For Heath and Luff (1996), the organisational legitimacy of professional practice is at stake.

Keeping in mind the above-mentioned managerial and technocratic fictions on the one hand and the daily, bulky frontline practices on the other, it seems appropriate to characterise case management systems in particular and any care technologies in general as 'boundary objects' (Star & Griesemer, 1989):

> Boundary objects are objects which are plastic enough to adapt to local needs and constraints of the several parties employing them, yet robust enough to maintain a common identity across sites. They are weakly structured in common use, and become strongly structured in individual-site use. They may be abstract or concrete. They have different meanings in different social worlds but their structure is common enough to more than one world to make them recognizable means of translation. The creation and management of boundary objects is a key process in developing and maintaining coherence across intersecting social worlds (p. 393).

Boundary objects are embodied in a specific artefact (physical or conceptual) which is recognisable as such to members of more than one community. According to this approach, the relationships between different stakeholders, such as manager, frontline social worker, software developer, and politician, in their social worlds become apparent. Furthermore, the structuration via artefacts (and their interpretative flexibility) becomes transparent through common and individual use. Lastly, the maintenance of and collaboration between joint working trajectories are brought into sharp relief. Thus, documentation is not only transforming the organisational aims, but also ways of professional acting in computer-supported cooperative work. Indeed, seeing documentation as a 'rationale' for a shared point of access to facilitate intra- and inter-agency collaboration (Fitch, 2009) becomes fragile under the perspective of boundary objects, since even though the technology is a shared entity, it is used or viewed differently by each of the stakeholders. Perhaps it is for this very reason that information technology becomes such a contestable issue in social work.

EMPIRICAL STUDIES OF THE IMPACT OF IT ON SOCIAL WORK

As mentioned above, there is little robust research on the transformation of social work via IT. The existing research literature comprises mainly qualitative case studies on the implementation and usage of IT – not reviewing the whole (descriptive) literature, but, for example, Bolay and Kuhn, 1993 (Germany); Gillingham, 2009 (Australia), and for the UK see later). Quantitative research, and in particular research on the efficacy and effectiveness of IT in social work, based on current knowledge, is largely missing. The Integrated Children's System in the UK provides a good example on which to concentrate for the following reasons:

1 It is part of the UK's e-Government strategy and a central element of the nationwide, political *Every Child Matters* reform agenda, including measures which aim to improve information gathering, sharing, and multi-agency working. Among these are the children's database (nowadays the Integrated Children's System; ICS), the Common Assessment Framework (CAF), and the now defunct ContactPoint (CP).
2 An ethnographic approach seems to be best suited to capture this complex phenomena. Ethnographically oriented workplace studies (Luff et al., 2000) are, at least in science and technology studies, approaches to standardisation in action that can be used for user-orientated software design as well as for basic research that can unpick the paradoxes and ambivalences of social work practice.

Three aspects of this research potential are highlighted below (Broadhurst et al., 2010a, 2010b, Peckover et al., 2008, 2009; Pithouse et al., 2009; Shaw et al., 2009; Wastell et al., 2010; White et al., 2010).

From policy to practice: adapting to local universalities

The basic idea of the ICS, CAF, and CP was to establish a 'common language' for all social institutions in the UK which are related to child welfare (see Garrett, 2009). But as Peckover et al. (2008) illustrate:

> these initiatives are shaped by existing organisational cultures and practices, and the local contexts in which these take place. The different interpretations ... are themselves constructed by the local and situated cultures, services, histories and practices into which these policy initiatives are being introduced (p. 145).

As a consequence of the untidy implementation process, the diffusion of software and its usage is highly differential. Furthermore, the research findings suggest 'despite its nomenclature there is nothing "common" about the CAF. It is a strategic document which child welfare practitioners used in different ways and for different purposes' (Peckover et al., 2008, p. 143). After all, some of the differences arise because the CAF was designed and used as a tool for 'assessment' and 'referral'. This ambiguous inscription into the technology has then to be made explicit by the practitioner and encloses the social practice. Oddly enough, there are still two tales reported: the 'CAF of policy' and the 'CAF of practice': 'the formal construct of policy and the applied CAF as constructed by multiple organizations ... wherein there is no singular model' (Pithouse et al., 2009, p. 600).

Sharpening professional and moral dilemmas

Technological innovation and implementation have the effect of increasing the working requirements for social workers. Thus it is commonly observed using these systems is 'taking them away from the day job' (Peckover et al., 2008, p. 142). This is characterised as:

> quite simply, a tension between 'putting (data) in' and 'going out' to see families. Often this is resolved in favour of 'going out', which may leave practitioners at risk of being blamed for failing properly to record their involvement. Sometimes, however, when there is clear, non-negotiable instruction from managers about using the Index, it is resolved in favour of 'putting in' (Peckover et al., 2008, p. 379).

This shows the contradictory demands of practice intervention from the organisational perspective. At a professional level, there is a shift to fragmentation of working procedures (Hall et al., 2010) and an enforcement of an informal logic (and an unequal balance between narrative and code: White et al., 2008) which implies a shift from early needs to risk factors in the labelling of clients situations (Broadhurst et al., 2010a; Webb, 2006). According to this assumption:

> [...] risk management is an inherently complex, contingent and negotiated activity. Social work practitioners are obliged to comply with risk reduction technologies, but informal processes continue to play a critical role in shaping decisions and actions in this relationship-based profession (Broadhurst et al., 2010a, p. 1046).

Thus, in a contradictory fashion, the tendencies towards double-binds and errors inherent in professional decision making appear to be intensified through IT (Broadhurst et al., 2010b).

Performing the performance

After an awkward and slow beginning, the implementation process of the virtual organisation seems to be under way and is steadily building up its own reality *sui generis*. A rigid performance management regime increasingly ignores the rich nature of professional tasks and discretion prescribing as it does its own narrow aims and purposes (White et al., 2010). Practitioners can only equip themselves strategically under the preconditions of the 'iron cage' of performance management

(Wastell et al., 2010), by either adapting to or undermining the new requirements through tactics of resistance.

To end metaphorically, in terms of the ICS case example discussed above: IT has different 'faces' or frames. First, technology can be seen as a *projection screen* for desires, fictions, frustrations, and dependencies. Second, IT can be seen as a *quick fix*, sharpening the short-termist professional culture through new IT-generated demands, but sharpening, too, professional and moral dilemmas. Third, IT can be seen as an *iron cage*, constructing a small world with its own rules of calculating reason and internal procedures while neglecting the complexity and richness of the social world around it.

CONCLUSION

As is often the case, the research findings described above reveal more questions than answers. But it is reasonable to project the ongoing informatisation of social work as part of a deepening technological culture which has both an impact on social work at the level of everyday practice, and is also a part of a transformation of social service organisations. It has been shown how the impact is felt continuously on professional forms of knowledge, perception, and patterns of interpretation. This chapter has outlined the divergent functions, attributions, and constellations of IT and social work from which basic processes of formalisation, professional discretion, and the documental character of social work institutions are radically redrawn. For social work research there remain a number of challenging questions.

- How does IT affect the quality of social service delivery? What impacts does it have on relations of trust and working alliances between professionals and their clients?
- How and under what circumstances does professional social work become formalised? Which modes of formalisation tend to deprofessionalise social work? Which modes of formalisation enhance spaces of professional discretion, flexibility, and autonomy in casework?
- How are modes of professional and instrumental reasoning interwoven, especially under the emergence of evidence-based practice and risk assessment regimes (Broadhurst et al., 2010a)?
- How can ethical threats to data privacy, civil liberties, and human rights be handled without falling into a panoptical and risk-averse vision of social work?
- Which ethical standards can be provided by professional institutions and trade unions for a publicly acceptable usage of IT in value-driven social work (National Association of Social Workers, 2005)?
- How can social work theory, research, and practice develop a position whereby it can contribute to software design for developing information systems and enhancing the knowledge base of social work?
- What are the consequences of this complex research agenda for social work education and professional training (Hill & Shaw, 2011)?

Without reverting to vulgar social or technical determinism, the issues in this chapter have raised some long-standing concerns that relate to controversial debates in social work; to summarise briefly: are we seeing a new kind of IT-enabled, 'reflexive practitioner' in social work, or are we stuck with the reductionist effects of technology, in which the oversimplification of complex social problems occurs via preconfigured categories and framings? This last scenario has the social worker in a functional engineering role as an executing technocrat of human services. Perhaps the answer rests in a wider set of sociopolitical considerations outlined by Simpson (1995):

> The new role of technology would then ideally be the outcome of something like a consensus arising from a discursive will formation, ever vigilant to uncover and criticize sources of domination and distortion, and, also committed to discuss what should *count* as domination and distortion, given communitarian insights (p. 175).

REFERENCES

Adler, P.S., & Borys, B. (1996). Two types of bureaucracy: Enabling and coercive. *Administrative Science Quarterly, 41*(1), 61–89.

Akrich, M. (1992). The de-scription of technical objects. In W.E. Bijker & Law, J. (ed.), *Shaping technology – building society – Studies in sociotechnical change*. Cambridge, MA: MIT Press, pp. 205–224.

Akrich, M., & Latour, B. (1992). A summary of a convenient vocabulary for the semiotics of human and nonhuman assemblies. In W.E. Bijker & Law, J. (ed.), *Shaping technology – building society – Studies in sociotechnical change*. Cambridge, MA: MIT Press, pp. 259–264.

Baumann, D.J., Law, J.R., Sheets, J., Reid, G., & Graham, J.C. (2005). Evaluating the effectiveness of actuarial risk assessment models. *Children and Youth Services Review, 27*, 465–490.

Beckmann, C., Otto, H-U., Schaarschuch, A., & Schrödter, M. (2007). Quality management and formalization in social service organizations: A survey on home-based family intervention services. *Social Work and Society, 5*(1), 78–92.

Benders, J., Batenburg, R., & van der Blonk, H. (2006). Sticking to standards: Technical and other isomorphic pressures in deploying ERP-systems. *Information und Management, 43*(2), 194–203.

Blaschke, C.M., Freddolino, P.P., & Mullen, E.E. (2009). Ageing and technology: A review of the research literature. *British Journal of Social Work, 39*(4), 641–656.

Bolay, E., & Kuhn, A. (1993). *'Wilde PC' am Arbeitsplatz. Implementation von EDV in Institutionen sozialer Arbeit durch Mitarbeiter. Eine arbeits- und kultursoziologische Untersuchung*. Opladen: Westdt. Verlag.

Bowker, G.C., & Star, S.L. (2000). *Sorting things out: Classification and its consequences*. Cambridge, MA: MIT Press.

Broadhurst, K., Hall, C., Wastell, D., White, S., & Pithouse, A. (2010a). Risk, instrumentalism and the humane project in social work: Identifying the informal logics of risk management in children's statutory services. *British Journal of Social Work, 40*(4), 1046–1064.

Broadhurst, K., Wastell, D., White, S., Hall, C., Peckover, S., Thompson, K., Pithouse, A., & Davey, D. (2010b). Performing 'initial assessment': Identifying the latent conditions for error at the front-door of local authority children's services. *British Journal of Social Work, 40*(2), 352–370.

Burton, J., & van der Broek, D. (2008). Accountable and courtable: Information management systems and the bureaucratization of social work. *British Journal of Social Work, 38*(1), 1–17.

Carrilio, T.E (2008). Accountability, evidence, and the use of information systems in social service programs. *Journal of Social Work, 8*(2), 135–148.

Castells, M. (1996). *The information age: Economy, society and culture, Part 1: The rise of the network society*. Oxford: Blackwell.

Coleman, N., & Harris, J. (2008). Calling social work. *British Journal of Social Work, 38*(3), 580–599.

Colombi, D., Rafferty, J., & Steyaert, J. (eds) (1993). *Human services and information technology: A European perspective*. Antwerp: European Network for Information Technology.

Dunlop, J.M., & Holosko, M.J. (2006). *Information technology and evidence-based social work practice*. New York: Haworth Press.

Evans, T., & Harris, J. (2004). Street-level bureaucracy, social work and the (exaggerated) death of discretion. *British Journal of Social Work, 34*(6), 871–895.

Fitch, D., & Shaffer, J. (2007). An alternative database table design. *Journal of Technology in Human Services, 25*(3), 57–79.

Fitch, D. (2007). Structural equation modeling the use of a risk assessment instrument in child protective services. *Decision Support Systems, 42*(4), 2137–2152.

Fitch, D. (2009). A shared point of access to facilitate interagency collaboration. *Administration in Social Work, 33*(2), 186–201.

Garfinkel, H. (1967). 'Good' organizational reasons for 'bad' clinic records. In H. Garfinkel (ed.), *Studies in ethnomethodology*. Englewood Cliffs, NJ: Prentice-Hall, pp. 186–207.

Garrett, P.M. (2004). The electronic eye: Emerging surveillance practices in social work with children and families. *European Journal of Social Work, 7*(1), 57–71.

Garrett, P.M. (2005). Social work's 'electronic turn': Notes on the deployment of information and communication technologies in social work with children and families. *Critical Social Policy, 25*(4), 529–553.

Garrett, P.M. (2009). *'Transforming' children's services? Social work, neoliberalism and the 'modern' world*. Maidenhead: McGraw Hill/Open University.

Gillingham, P. (2009). The use of assessment tools in child protection: An ethnomethodological study. Unpublished Ph.D. thesis, School of Nursing and Social Work, The University of Melbourne.

Glastonbury, B. (1985). *Computers in social work*. Basingstoke: Macmillan.

Gray, M., Plath, D., & Webb, S. A. (2010). *Evidence-based social work*. London: Routledge.

Halfar, B., & Kreidenweis, H. (2008). *IT-Report für die Sozialwirtschaft 2008/2009*. Eichstätt: Katholische Universität, Arbeitsstelle für Sozialinformatik.

Hall, C., Parton, N., Peckover, S., & White, S. (2010). Child-centric Information and Communication Technology (ICT) and the fragmentation of child welfare practice in England. *Journal of Social Policy, 39*(33), 393–413.

Handler, J.F. (1992). Discretion: Power, quiescence, and trust. In K. Hawkins (ed.), *The uses of discretion*. Oxford: Clarendon Press, pp. 331–360.

Harlow, E., & Webb, S.A. (2003). *Information and communication technologies in welfare services.* London: Jessica Kingsley Publishers.

Heath, C., & Luff, P. (1996). Documents and professional practice: 'Bad' organisational reasons for 'good' clinical records. In *Cooperating Communities: Proceedings of the ACM 1996 Conference on Computer Supported Cooperative Work.* New York: ACM, pp. 354–363.

Heidegger, M. (1962). *Die Technik und die Kehre. Pfullingen: Neske* [The question concerning technology and other essays]. San Francisco: Harper and Row.

Hick, S., & McNutt, J. (2002). *Advocacy, activism, and the internet – community organization and social policy.* Chicago, IL: Lyceum Books.

Hill, A. & Shaw, I. (2011) *Social work and ICT.* London: Sage.

Iske, S., Kutscher, N., & Klein, A. (2005). Differences in internet usage: Social inequality and informal education. *Social Work and Society, 3*(2), 215–223.

Johnson, W. (2006). The risk assessment wars: A commentary. *Children and Youth Services Review, 28*(6), S704–714.

Kling, R. (2007). What is social informatics and why does it matter? *The Information Society: An International Journal, 23*(4), 205–220.

Kreuger, L.W., Stretch, J.J., & Kelly, M.J. (2006). Is computer-assisted EBP generating 'fast' practice? *Journal of Evidence-Based Social Work, 3*(2), 27–38.

Kutscher, N., Ley, T., & Seelmeyer, U. (2011). Subjekt – Technik – Kontext. In Arbeitskreis 'Jugendhilfe im Wandel' (ed.), *Jugendhilfeforschung. Kontroversen – Transformationen – Adressierungen.* Wiesbaden: VS-Verlag, pp. 187–214.

Latour, B. (1994). On technical mediation: Philosophy, sociology, genealogy. *Common Knowledge, 3*(2), 29–64.

Latour, B. (1996). Social theory and the study of computerized work sites. In W. Orlikowski, Walsham, G., Jones, M., & Degross, J. (eds) *Information technology and changes in organizational work.* London: Chapman and Hall, pp. 295–307.

Ley, T., & Seelmeyer, U. (2008). Professionalism and information technology. *Social Work and Society, 6*(2), 1–14.

Ley, T., & Seelmeyer, U. (2011). Informationstechnologien in der Sozialen Arbeit. In H-U. Otto & Thiersch, H. (ed.), *Handbuch Soziale Arbeit: Grundlagen der Sozialarbeit und Sozialpädagogik.* München: Reinhardt, pp. 652–659.

Lipsky, M. (1980). *Street-level bureaucracy: Dilemmas of the individual in public services.* New York: Russell Sage Foundation.

Luff, P., Hindmarsh, J., & Heath, C. (2000). *Workplace studies.* Cambridge: Cambridge University Press.

McNutt, J.G. (2000). Coming perspectives in the development of electronic advocacy for social policy practice. *Critical Social Work, 1*(1). Retrieved January 31, 2011 from http://www.uwindsor.ca/criticalsocialwork/coming-perspectives-in-the-development-of-electronic-advocacy-for-social-policy-practice-0

Morgan, A., & Fraser, S. (2010). Looked after young people and their social work managers: A study of contrasting experiences of using Computer-Assisted-Self-Interviewing (A-CASI). *British Journal of Social Work, 40*(2), 445–461.

Murphy, L., Parnass, P., Mitchell, D.L., Hallett, R., Cayley, P., & Seagram, S. (2009). Client satisfaction and outcome comparisons of online and face-to-face counselling methods. *British Journal of Social Work, 39*(4), 627–640.

National Association of Social Workers (NASW) (2005). *NASW and ASWB standards for technology and social work practice.* Retrieved January 31, 2011 from http://www.socialworkers.org/practice/standards/NASWTechnologyStandards.pdf

Orlikowski, W.J. (1992). The duality of technology: Rethinking the concept of technology in organizations. *Organization Science, 3*(3), 398–427.

Otto, H.-U., & Schnurr, S. (1999). *Sozialpädagogische Professionalität in marktförmig gesteuerten Organisationskontexten: Formen der Aneignung managerialistischer Rationalitätsmuster in der öffentlichen Jugendhilfe.* DFG-Antrag. Unpublished manuscript, Bielefeld.

Parker-Oliver, D., & Demiris, G. (2006). Social work informatics. *Social Work, 51*(2), 127–134.

Parton, N. (2006). Changes in the form of knowledge in social work: From the 'social' to the 'informational'? *British Journal of Social Work, 38*(2), 253–269.

Parton, N. (2009). How to explore and develop child welfare systems: The English experience. Retrieved January 31, 2011 from http://www.fruehehilfen.de/fileadmin/user_upload/fruehehilfen.de/pdf/Prof._Nigel_Parton_English.pdf

Peckover, S., White, S., & Hall, C. (2008). Making and managing electronic children: E-assessment in child welfare. *Information, Communication and Society, 11*(3), 375–394.

Peckover, S., Hall, C., & White, S. (2009). From policy to practice: The implementation and negotiation of technologies in everyday child welfare. *Children and Society, 23*(2), 136–148.

Pinch, T., & Bijker, W. (1987). The social construction of facts and artefacts. In W.E. Bijker, Hughes, T.P., & Pinch, T. (ed.), *The social construction of technological systems: New directions in the sociology and history of technology.* Cambridge, MA: MIT Press, pp. 17–50.

Pithouse, A., Hall, C., Peckover, S., & White, S. (2009). A tale of two CAFs: The impact of the electronic Common Assessment Framework. *British Journal of Social Work*, 39(4), 599–612.

Rafferty, J., & Steyaert, J. (2009). Editorial. *British Journal of Social Work*, 39(4), 589–598.

Rafferty, J., Steyaert, J., & Colombi, D. (eds) (1996). *Human services in the information age*. New York: The Haworth Press.

Rammert, W. (1999). Relations that constitute technology and media that make a difference: Toward a social pragmatic theory of technicization. in: Techné: Research in Philosophy and Technology, 3(4), 23–44. Retrieved January 31, 2011 from http://scholar.lib.vt.edu/ejournals/SPT/v4_n3pdf/RAMMERT.PDF

Regan, S. (2003). Technology and systems of referral taking in social services. In E. Harlow & Webb, S.A. (ed.), *Information and communication technologies in welfare services*. London: Jessica Kingsley Publishers, pp. 83–111.

Rolf, A. (2003). Interdisziplinäre Technikforschung und Informatik. *Technikfolgenabschätzung Theorie und Praxis*, 12(3/4), 59–67.

Rosenberg, R.S. (2004). *The social impact of computers*. Amsterdam: Elsevier Academic Press.

Samuel, M. (2005). *Social care professionals overwhelmed by paper work*. Retrieved January 31, 2011 from http://www.communitycare.co.uk/Articles/2005/12/14/52187/Social-care-professionals-overwhelmed-by-paper-work.htm

Schoech, D. (1999). *Human services technology*. New York: Haworth Press.

Schoech, D., Basham, R., & Fluke, J. (2006). A technology enhanced EBP model. *Journal of Evidence-Based Social Work*, 3, 55–72.

Schrödter, M. (2005). Wer macht bessere Diagnosen: Der Mensch oder die Maschine? Zu den interventionspraktischen Möglichkeiten und Gefahren diagnostischer Klassifikationssysteme. 1–18 Retrieved January 31, 2011 from http://www.uni-bielefeld.de/paedagogik/agn/ag8/Schr%F6dter,%20Mark%202005%20-%20mechanische%20und%20klinische%20Prognose.pdf

Sesink, W. (2003). Wozu Informatik? Ein Antwortversuch aus pädagogischer Sicht. In F. Nake, Rolf, A., & Siefkes, D. (ed.), *Informatik zwischen Konstruktion und Verwertung*, pp. 59–62. Retrieved January 31, 2011 from http://mtv.cs.tu-berlin.de/siefkes/Hersfeld/Hersfeldheft.pdf

Shaw, I., & Clayden, J. (2009). Technology, evidence and professional practice: Reflections on the Integrated Children's System. *Journal of Children's Services*, 4(4), 15–27.

Shaw, I., Bell, M., Sinclair, I., Sloper, P., Mitchell, W., Dyson, P., Clayden, J., & Rafferty, J. (2009). An exemplary scheme? An evaluation of the Integrated Children's System. *British Journal of Social Work*, 39(4), 613–626.

Simpson, L.C. (1995) *Technology, time and the conversations of modernity:* London, Routledge.

Star, S.L., & Griesemer, J.R. (1989). Institutional ecology, 'translations' and boundary objects: Amateurs and professionals in Berkeley's Museum of Vertebrate Zoology, 1907–39. *Social Studies of Science*, 19(3), 387–420.

Steyaert, J., Colombi, D., & Rafferty, J. (eds) (1996). *Human services and information technology: An international perspective*. Aldershot: Arena.

Timmermans, S., & Berg, M. (1997). Standardization in action: Achieving local universality through medical protocols. *Social Studies of Science*, 27(2), 273–305.

Wastell, D., White, S., Broadhurst, K., Peckover, S., & Pithouse, A. (2010). Children's services in the iron cage of performance management: Street-level bureaucracy and the spectre of Švejkism. *International Journal of Social Welfare*, 19(3), 310–320.

Webb, S.A. (2006). *Social work in a risk society*. Basingstoke: Palgrave Macmillan.

White, S., Hall, C., & Peckover, S. (2009). The descriptive tyranny of the common assessment framework: Technologies of categorization and professional practice in child welfare. *British Journal of Social Work*, 39, 1197–1217.

White, S., Wastell, D., Broadhurst, K., & Hall, C. (2010). When policy o'erleaps itself: The 'tragic tale' of the Integrated Children's System. *Critical Social Policy*, 30(3), 405–429.

WEBSITES

All websites were retrieved on January 31, 2011.

Findhelp Information Services 211 in Canada: http://www.211canada.ca

German portal for software in social work: http://www.social-software.de

Archive of the *Journal of New Technology in the Human Services*: http://www.southampton.ac.uk/chst/projects/nths_archive/abstract.htm

Archive of the *Journal of Technology in Human Services*: http://wweb.uta.edu/faculty/schoech/cussn/jths/

HUSITA (HUman Services Information Technology Applications): www.husita.org

Overview for ICS, CAF, and CP: http://www.warwickshirechildren.com/CYPP/ICS%20CAF%20and%20ContactPoint.pdf

Service-User Involvement

Peter Beresford

This chapter is concerned with social work and user involvement. Both are complex, contradictory, and ambiguous activities and domains. Social work traditionally lies at the intersections between state, society, family, community, government policies, and individual citizen and noncitizen. Historically, it has had support and control roles, and been identified as both liberatory and regulatory in process, nature, and purpose. It has been both bureaucratised and subjected to managerialist restructuring by state and service system, and reconceived as a radical force by proponents of social justice, equity, and equality.

While these contradictory pressures and ambitions continue to operate, social work has also been overlaid internationally by new ideas and practices presented in terms of 'user involvement'. These have similarly had a range of ideological origins. The aim of this chapter is to explore the origins and nature of this development, the theory and practice associated with it, and to consider its relations with various ideological approaches to social work. A central aim of the chapter is to try to untangle potentially progressive and regressive aspects of social work and user involvement. Each also tends to be affected by its interaction with the other. The chapter seeks to make sense of the inter-relations of the two and the impacts they may have on each other as a starting point for exploring what may be the most helpful ways of taking forward social work and user involvement internationally.

THE EMERGENCE OF SERVICE-USER INVOLVEMENT

Service-user involvement has become part of the lexicon of social work. However, there is no consensus about its meaning, purpose, or nature. In some countries, it is a requirement for learning and practice, is frequently cited, and has gained high visibility. At the same time, it is also important to clarify from the start that, in some countries, user involvement is barely understood, underdeveloped, and many service users perceive, and are critical of, the discourse of 'service-user involvement', seeing it as tokenistic and manipulative. Sometimes both these statements are true of the same country. Equally, there are major differences between countries, with some – like the UK and Nordic countries – having a reputation for well-developed user involvement, while others are less familiar with the idea and practice. There is no agreed language or conceptualisation for user involvement. This was signalled in 2010 when the International Federation of Social Workers (IFSW, 2010) took the initiative of developing a paper on 'Service User/Consumer Involvement and Social Work' and put it on its website as part of a consultation linked to its worldwide conference in Hong Kong. Not only did the paper get little response, but as can be seen in the title, it was difficult even to find a common language to which social workers in different countries would be able to relate. As it says, other terms are also used for user or consumer involvement, like partnership, engagement, and participation. In some countries, rather than service user, there is talk of self-help, advocacy, and mutual aid activities and groups, which have a far longer history. This issue was further highlighted in a straw poll carried out through an international social work discussion list when writing this chapter. Different terms for 'service user' emerged as having a different significance at different times, in different countries, and for different stakeholders. 'Client', 'service consumer', and in some settings, 'patient' were all mentioned. In the USA, for example, advocacy groups tended to favour the term 'consumer', while social workers used the word 'client'.

A key part of the IFSW (2010) paper was explaining different meanings attached to user and consumer involvement. As it said, this could include:

1. consulting with and listening to what service users, clients or consumers have to say;
2. developing links with service-user or consumer groups and organisations;
3. involving service users or consumers in social work and other social policy organisations so these are better informed by them; and
4. service users or consumers individually and collectively having more say over their lives and in services they use;
5. involving service users or consumers in 'co-producing' social work as a joint activity (IFSW, 2010, n.p.).

International social work organisations, like the IFSW, set out lofty goals and principles for social work including claims that it:

1. promotes social change and the empowerment and liberation of people to enhance well-being and promote social inclusion;
2. sees the principles of human rights and social justice as fundamental;
3. enables all people to develop their full potential, enrich their lives, and prevent dysfunction, through focusing on problem solving and change; and
4. bases its activities on humanitarian and democratic ideals, with values prioritising respect for the equality, worth, and dignity of all people (IFSW, 2010, n.p.).

User involvement is still not a core theme of social work and its organisations internationally, although it is reflected in such liberatory principles and values. While these may not refer explicitly to user involvement, they are clearly compatible with it and are likely to be advanced by it. What they are not always so clearly connected with are the day-to-day realities of modern state social work.

SOCIAL WORK REFORM

The London School of Economics (LSE), established in 1895, can be seen as the founding home of global social work, having influenced social work internationally ever since (Titmuss, 1968). It was here that the first school of social work was established. This tradition ended with the passing of the 20th century when professional social work education was abandoned by the LSE. Nonetheless, in 2010, in the UK, the Coalition Conservative/Liberal government commissioned Professor of Social Policy at the London School of Economics, Eileen Munro (see Chapter 14), to undertake a major review of child protection, the most contentious area of social work. The UK Department for Education (2010), in reporting on her initial findings, stated:

> professionals have told the review that more focus [in child protection social work] is being given to complying with process and regulations than to providing a service that meets the needs of children and young people ... an over-bureaucratised system, focused on meeting targets, has reduced the capacity to spend time with children and young people. Children and young people themselves have told us that they still regularly have to manage frequent changes of social worker, that help is often not quickly available and that their wishes and feelings can go unheard (http://www.education.gov.uk/munroreview/ retrieved October 1, 2010).

In her first report, Professor Munro (2010) highlighted the failure of modern reforms in social work:

> At the front line, where all these changes come together, the effect has been to produce the current unbalanced state of affairs. Social workers and other professionals have told the review that more managerial focus is being given to complying with top-down regulation, and often further locally designed procedures, than to providing a personalised service that matches the variety of needs of children and young people. The review will learn from innovations where local leaders and managers have supported social workers and other professionals to create less prescriptive working environments with more room for professional judgment (p. 12).

> The role of social workers has been insidiously eroded so that the concept of 'case management' whereby social workers assess and refer on rather than doing work themselves is creeping into child and family work (UK Department for Education, 2010, p. 31).

> There is frustration that an imbalance has developed between the demands of the management and inspection process and professionals' ability to exercise judgment, arising from efforts to deal with uncertainty and often shaping practice in adverse ways. Furthermore, previous reforms have tended to address single aspects of the child protection system without anticipating the effect that these will have on other parts of the system, unintentionally reinforcing some aspects of practice, while downplaying others (UK Department for Education, 2010, p. 41).

While offered as findings, Munro's observations merely restate serious concerns about the 'direction of travel' of state social work which have long been highlighted by both social work practitioners and commentators (e.g., Ferguson & Lavalette, 2009). They were also signalled in the final report of the Social Work Task Force set up following the inquiry into the high-profile Baby Peter tragedy (UK Department for Children, Schools and Families/Department of Health, 2009).

Both in the UK and internationally, welfare reform has been part of broader ideological developments associated with 'new public management' and managerialism, originating with New Right politics, which continues to be embodied in the thinking of neoliberal governments – like the UK Coalition – and they have taken place despite long-standing criticism and determined opposition from social workers and service users alike (Beresford & Croft, 2004). While the Munro report suggests social work's failings were unintended consequences of the managerialist approach to service provision, critics – of welfare reform – have argued that they were a direct consequence of the reforms themselves, which aimed to reduce professional autonomy and increase control of social workers through information technology systems and the social care bureaucracy (Dustin, 2007; Ferguson & Woodward, 2009). Ambiguities about the nature and purpose of social work, present from the profession's earliest beginnings, have not helped matters. It always seems to have had both regressive and progressive aspects to it, being concerned both with support and liberation and control and regulation.

SOCIAL WORK'S HISTORICAL AMBIGUITY

Historically, social work has been ambiguous in its inspiration, nature, and purpose. Nineteenth-century organisations and pioneers associated with the origins of social work were as much concerned with trying to regulate poor people as with challenging their disadvantage. They often reflected utilitarian philosophy and middle-class fears about the improvidence and thriftlessness of 'the poor'. 'Able-bodied paupers', 'clever beggars', and 'the residuum' were seen as a degraded force whose 'demoralisation' posed a threat to civilisation, social order, and even the gene pool (Stedman Jones, 1971). Canon Barnett, social reformer and first warden of Toynbee Hall (after whom Oxford University named the site of its social work department), said 'the principle of our work is that we aim at decreasing, not suffering but sin' (Stedman Jones, 1971, p. 270). The Charity Organisation Society, frequently identified as a key pioneer of social work, attacked the London School Board for providing shoes for barefoot children to attend school for encouraging parental neglect. Charitably supported free dispensaries and outpatient treatment by London hospitals were condemned for holding up the development of 'provident' habits (Stedman Jones, 1971, pp. 270–271). But social work also owed its origins to friendly societies, mutual aid and self-help schemes, and trade unions, as well as philanthropists and traditional social reformers (Rogowski, 2010).

In the past, social work has been identified by some Marxists as the 'soft cop' of state control. Marxists, however, have also played a key role in the development of the idea and practice of radical social work (Bailey & Brake, 1975; Langan & Lee, 1989). More recently, in countries such as the UK, social work was reviled by governments of the political New Right, like Mrs Thatcher's, which sought to reconstruct it as an expression of managerialist consumerism. However, over the same period, service-user movements, like the disabled people's and psychiatric system survivor movements, have emerged and these have become involved actively in the development of social work, contributing to and influencing its practice, education, planning, research, and evaluation (Beresford, 1999; Braye & Preston-Shoot, 2003; Denvall et al., 2010; Warren, 2007). Social work has always had the potential both to control and to liberate, and the role of social workers still often embraces both activities. So long as social work continues to have powers to restrict people's rights, for example, as parents and mental health service users, this ambiguity is likely to remain central. Demanding greater discussion than it tends to be given is the question of whether social work should still have such powers of control. But, even beyond this, its ambiguity is always likely to be a feature, since its role and ramifications often can be read in two ways. For example, is supporting disabled people to re-enter the labour market, an expression of social workers' ability to enhance their self-determination and right to the same opportunities, rights, and responsibilities as nondisabled people? Or is it simply a means of maintaining the status quo through their enforced integration into a harsh and discriminatory labour market? Does social work's advocacy role play a positive part in improving access to services and income for individual service users or simply reinforce existing inequalities and inequities of access to the system?

COMPETING STRANDS OF SOCIAL WORK

Its contending liberatory and regulatory roles are reflected also in the competing strands of or approaches to social work. This can be seen in the UK and elsewhere in the parallel development of state-reformed care management and radical social work. The important role of management and managerialist ideas in shaping social services and social work was already beginning to be recognised in the UK by 1989. The establishment of social services departments in England in 1971 constituted an early expression and reinforcement of this. Managerialism needs to be acknowledged as a key force in shaping modern social work and social services. It is one frequently seen by its critics as undermining the progressive and liberatory values, potential, and aspirations of social work and social policy more generally (Clarke et al., 1994; Gibbs, 2000; Jordan, 1990; Lowndes, 1997). Such (new) managerialism has been strongly associated with the political New Right values of economy, effectiveness, and efficiency, emphasising the benefits of the private market and the failings of public provision and state intervention.

Care management

This has been associated with the recasting of professional social work in managerialist terms of 'care management' (Gorman & Postle, 2003; Postle, 2002). Care management became the new form of social work in the early 1990s under Thatcher-inspired social care reforms. This resulted in 'changes to the values, regimes and objectives of social work' (Gibbs, 2000, p. 231). It reinforced the gendered nature of social work and social services, confirming traditional male dominance in its hierarchy and ideology. It saw a shift in power from professionals to managers and has been linked with constant organisational restructuring and the strengthening of central government control over the aims, activities, and finances of social work agencies. This has taken place in the statutory and independent sectors, generally through direct control in the first case and funding policy in the second.

Donna Dustin (2007) has described the shift in social work to care management as the 'McDonaldization of social work'. She concludes that the influence of McDonaldization has permeated social work with adults and children since it has resulted in changes to the role of social workers in local authority social services and the entire service-delivery system. She explores care management through the four key principles associated with McDonaldization (Ritzer, 2000): (i) *efficiency*, based on narrow economic and bureaucratic judgements; (ii) *predictability*, through reliance on standardisation and a procedural approach; (iii) *calculability*, reducing everything to numbers; and (iv) *surveillance*, closely controlling and monitoring social workers. Her book recounts social workers' stories about the fundamental change in social work practice heralded by care management, which deskilled practitioners, restricted professional discretion, limited their relationship with service users and focus on the individual, and undermined a preventative approach. Social workers described a system based on highly prescriptive procedures, checklist approaches, dependence on technology and computerised systems, and cost containment. Instead of being providers of support, social workers became purchasers of services. Instead of being distributors of resources, they were now meant to be guardians of funds for their organisations. The rhetoric was of 'needs-led' provision, but the reality was the dominance of budgetary considerations over service-users' expressed need and professionals' informed judgements (Dustin, 2007).

Radical social work

In 2010, radical social workers celebrated the 35th anniversary of Bailey and Brake (1975), the book which led to the emergence of the radical social work movement and went on to be published internationally, generating a movement with local, national, and international groupings, campaigns, and literature, including its own journal and magazines, such as *Case Con*. A book was then produced marking this anniversary (Lavalette, 2010).

Radical social work has taken different expressions in different contexts. In Canada for example, it developed as 'structural social work' and in Australia as 'critical social work'. The founders of radical social work drew a distinction between the new movement and what they described as 'traditional social work', which they criticised for its overemphasis on an individualistic, psychological orientation and its preoccupation with pathology and casework. (Significantly although such social work focused on the individual, there was little or no involvement of either the individual service user or service users collectively.) They called for a more self-critical form of social work, one critically exploring relations with the state and service users and prepared to be radical, rather than merely reformist. They challenged social work's origins and assumptions, for example, calling on social workers to 'challenge the relevance and long-term effectiveness of received ideas in social-work and social-work education – many of which remain rooted in the rapacious benevolences of Victorian philanthropy' (Bailey & Brake, 1975, back cover).

Radical social work can be seen as a development that was increasingly influenced by women's, Black people's, civil rights, and lesbian, gay, bisexual, and transgender (LGBT) movements, as well as growing out of more traditional leftist and trade union campaigning and organising (Langan & Lee, 1989; Williams, 1989). It was a development committed to social justice and equality. It was also linked with and drew on feminist and Black critiques of social work (Dominelli, 2002; White, 2006). It was concerned with individual and collective rights, and individual and collective struggles, including industrial action, leading it to ask difficult and now unfashionable questions, such as 'How far can the needs of the single member be subsumed in the interests of the community? How far can the requirements of political organization and conscientization of the oppressed override the immediate need to salve the distress of one family or individual?' (Bailey & Brake, 1975, back cover).

Proponents of radical social work saw it as having a real role to play in 'empowering' service users (Langan & Lee, 1989, p. 9) and bringing about social change. Yet the movement struggled to gain large-scale support from social work practitioners, to influence the state social work agenda significantly, or to bring about progressive change in the workplace. Its most effective and enduring impact was probably in social work education and academic social work discussion (Croft & Beresford, 1989). However, this changed with the rebirth of radical social work early in the 21st century. This was heralded by the publication in the UK of a Social Work Manifesto in 2004 (Jones et al., 2004). It made clear that the impetus for radical social work's revival was the determined shift to the market and new managerialism in modern state social work and a desire instead to pursue an egalitarian and social justice based approach to social work (Jones et al., 2004). This provided the basis for the establishment of the Social Work Action Network (SWAN), which described itself as:

> a loose network of social work practitioners, academics, students and social welfare service users united in their concern that social work activity is being undermined by managerialism and marketisation, by the stigmatisation of service users and by welfare cuts and restrictions (SWAN, 2010).

Radical social work has again sought to establish itself as an international movement, with groups developing in different parts of the world and SWAN gaining a presence at global social work events. It is explicitly framed as an alternative to the prevailing trends in state social work as a new radical social work book sets out:

> At the start of the twenty-first century social work finds itself at a crossroads. In Britain social work is shaped by managerialism and marketisation and social welfare services face retrenchment and substantial cuts. In this current climate the book examines the radical tradition to assert that 'another social work is possible' and assess its relevance for the movement today (Lavalette, 2010, back cover).

USER INVOLVEMENT

While the early exponents of radical social work in the 1970s expressed a strong commitment to service users, there was little user involvement, as it might now be understood, in this early movement. Mary Langan's and Phil Lee's *Radical Social Work Today* published in 1989 charted progress on this issue in one of its chapters (Croft & Beresford, in Langan & Lee, 1989), highlighting how much work still needed to be done. This was despite the fact that the issue of user involvement had been raised from service-users' perspectives for some time (Beresford & Croft, 1980; Oliver, 1983).

The emergence of service-user movements

While there seemed to be little crossover between radical social work and service users, a key founding document of the UK disabled people's movement was published only a year after radical social work's first major text (Union of the Physically Impaired Against Segregation/Disability Alliance, 1976). This lack of overlap or linkage between the emerging service-user movement and moves to radicalise social work is interesting. Even though radical social workers have always concerned themselves with changed relationships between practitioners and service users or 'clients', in some countries and in the view of some commentators, it was under the banner of self-help that some service-user groups first mobilised as a result of the failures of professional and state intervention (Borman, 1975; Katz & Bender, 1976). Others, particularly people from the service-user movements themselves internationally, drew much more direct links between their movements and the women's, Black, civil rights, and development movements (Campbell, 1996; Campbell & Oliver, 1996; Charlton, 1998; Coleridge, 1993).

While service-user movements tend to be seen as coming to prominence in the 1980s, most had earlier origins (Campbell, 2009; Wallcraft et al., 2003). For example, the UK disabled people's movement's beginnings can be traced to the 1960s coinciding with efforts to escape from institutions and live more equal lives in mainstream society (Campbell & Oliver, 1996; Oliver, 1990, 1996). Disabled people pioneered self-help and developed new organisations, which were subject to the control of disabled people themselves, rather than led by nondisabled people or professionals, and these formed the basis of the disabled people's movement. Movements developed of looked-after young people in state care, older people, people with learning difficulties, people living with HIV and AIDS, mental health service users, and of people who had had drug and alcohol problems.

There are now local, regional, national, and international service-user organisations (Beresford, 1999). While service-user movements vary in nature and purpose, they tend to be based on formal, democratically constituted organisations. Such movements have developed worldwide (Charlton, 1998; Stone, 1999). While, for example, the disabled people's and mental health service user and survivor movements can be seen to have a number of significant differences, all service-user movements seem to have important values and goals in common. They all highlight the importance they attach to:

1 service users speaking and acting for themselves;
2 working and organising cooperatively to achieve change;
3 having more say over their lives and the support they received;
4 challenging stigma and discrimination;
5 having access to alternatives to prevailing medicalised interventions and understandings;
6 valuing user-controlled organisations, support, and services; and
7 focusing on people's human and civil rights and their citizenship – this has emerged later, but is increasingly evident of the survivors' movement; and

8   being part of mainstream life and communities, and able to take on responsibilities as well as securing entitlements (Beresford & Harding, 1993; Campbell, 1996).

Service-user movements have been described as liberatory, 'new social', and 'post-materialist' (Oliver, 1996; Oliver & Zarb, 1989). Tom Shakespeare has said: 'Most of the [liberation] struggles mentioned ... are about resource allocation; women, black people and disabled people are crucially concerned with their economic exploitation and poverty' (Shakespeare, 1993, p. 258). Certainly consistent themes among all service-user movements have been 'self-organising' to secure the rights and interests of people as service users and to increase the say and control they have over their lives, and services and agencies intervening in them. Notably, they have been concerned with democratisation and inclusion. The disabled people's movement has also been conspicuous in developing new theory in relation to disability and challenging the exclusion and discrimination disabled people face, through the 'social model of disability' and the philosophy of 'independent living' (Oliver, 1996).

The emergence of service-user movements has significantly changed how service users have been understood by social work, including radical social work. As mentioned, the supporters of radical social work have always placed an emphasis on service users or clients and the need to align with them. Langan and Lee (1989), for example, argued that one of the major achievements of the original radical social work movement was that it 'pushed the interests of the client to the fore' (p. 7). There was talk of 'clients' as 'political allies' (Taylor, 1972, p. 5). Roy Bailey, one of the founding parents of radical social work, emphasised its role in supporting 'those who seek to oppose the stigma and stereotyping of the recipients of social work, and who resist authoritarian attempts by the state to undermine their dignity' (in Langan & Lee, 1989, p. xviii). However, the role of service users in the early days of radical social work seems to have been more symbolic than as active partners in its construction.

Service-user influence in social work

More recently, however, service users have become much more actively involved in social work generally, although the patchiness of this development needs to be recognised. User involvement has developed in social work policy, planning, practice, education, and research. In some countries, like the UK, there are state requirements for such involvement. Service-user organisations over the years have gained in numbers, scale, diversity, and inclusivity. They have learned to organise in new, accessible, and creative ways, gaining collective skills, confidence, and knowledge, as well as supporting the empowerment of individual service users. These movements have developed their own arts and cultures, as well as their own collective history, user-controlled services, and research. They have pioneered new kinds of services, as well as new kinds of roles, from personal assistant to user researcher. They have begun to make an impact on social work policy and provision and brought about changes in legislation and public and professional attitudes, for example, through the philosophy of independent living, the social model of disability, and innovations like self-advocacy and direct payments. Social work literature and theory has begun to be affected by them, and social work discussions more routinely to include them, although major variations still operate internationally. While their influence and impact should not be overstated, it equally can no longer be ignored (Beresford & Campbell, 2004; Campbell & Oliver, 1996; Charlton, 1998; Denvall et al., 2010; O'Hagan, 1994; Oliver, 2009). The famous US disability rights leader Ed Roberts, for example, began as a Black civil rights leader, and then made the decision to transfer his organising and mobilising skills to the disabled people's movement (Campbell & Oliver, 1996; Charlton, 1998). There are comparable examples of people active in service-user movements who have also been active in the women's, LGBT, and environmental movements.

STATE-LED INVOLVEMENT

Just as two strands have been highlighted in modern social work, the move to marketised managerialism in state social work and the recrudescence of radical social work, so similarly the emergence of service-user movements has not been the only development in the field of user involvement. A parallel development, emerging somewhat later, but frequently framed in the same terminology of participation and involvement can also be identified, this time fostered by the state. This approach to involvement, emanating from the state and service system, has frequently and probably most accurately been seen to be based on a managerialist–consumerist model. It begins with the market ideology of the new political right combined with the 'new public management' ideas from the 1980s (Simmons, et al., 2009). It is concerned with gaining public, patient, and service-user information, and experience to inform services and provision. It has predominated in both state and (nongovernment) service system discussions and developments in user involvement. It is concerned primarily with individual and individualising involvement, and follows from ideological commitments to the market, purchase of service, and the marketisation of welfare, emphasising *consumer choice*. This contrasts with the democratic or empowerment approach developed by service users and their movements, which is concerned with increasing the say and control that people have over their lives and the policies and services intervening in them. This approach to user involvement, described above, has been based particularly on collective action, originates with service users and their organisations, and highlights power and the redistribution of power in society and services, emphasising democratisation and *citizen control* (Beresford, 2001; Kemshall & Littlechild, 2000).

There can be little doubt that increasing state interest in user involvement has gained some measure of public support. In the UK, it has been officially associated with a rhetoric of devolution, decentralisation, 'shifting control from Whitehall', activating citizens, and challenging paternalism. In the fields of health and social care, where user involvement has been particularly developed, it has gained a significant response from service users over the years, both individually and collectively, with relatively large-scale participation in high-profile consultations, people joining participatory structures like LINKS (now replaced by 'Health Watch'), the successor to PALS (Patient Advice and Liaison Services), and responding to invitations to 'get involved'. It has acted as an opportunity, an impetus, and sometimes a funding source for service users seeking to feed in their views and experience, and for these to influence and improve policy and provision.

Increasing offers of involvement from the state have provided windows of opportunity for service-user organisations and movements. They have also raised awareness and interest in getting involved. However, service users have been expressing growing concerns about what is actually achieved by the latter. This is often compounded by a lack of feedback and a sense that decisions were already made before their views were sought. Increasingly, there is talk among service users of being 'over-consulted' and 'all-consulted-out'. Service users frequently interpret their experience of formal user involvement as 'tokenistic' and a 'tick-box exercise' (Campbell, 1996, 2009). Such views are regularly encountered among members of service-user organisations which are under constant pressure to respond to an ever-growing range of consultative and participatory initiatives. Some explanation of this is likely to be found in the often conflicting reasons why people get involved and the rationale of most involvement exercises. When asked why they get involved, service users are most likely to say it is to achieve change in line with securing their rights and needs (Branfield et al., 2006). Such change is often neither feasible with, nor on the agenda of, managerialist–consumerist initiatives for involvement. Thus, while there have long been many provisions for user involvement in UK social work, Mike Oliver, the disability activist, writing in 2009, said the aim of his book written nearly 30 years ago, *Social Work With Disabled People* (Oliver, 1983) to 'switch social work intervention away from impaired individuals and target the disabling society had not been achieved in social work' (Oliver, 2009, p. 51). In 1986, the British Association of Social Workers adopted this social model, but Oliver concluded that the individual model still dominated social work, as it did other professions, and that disability issues were still inadequately dealt with in social work education (Oliver & Sapey, 2006):

> Social work has failed to meet disabled people's self-articulated needs. Twenty years ago, I predicted that if social work was not prepared to change in terms of its practice relating to disabled people it would eventually disappear altogether (Oliver, 1983) ... It seems likely that the forecast is about to come true. We can probably now announce the death of social work at least in relation to its involvement in the lives of disabled people (Oliver, 2009, p. 51).

There is still strong support for social work among many service users in the UK because they value the social approach which they associate with good practitioners who work with them (Beresford et al., 2005; Branfield et al., 2005). However, at the same time, adult service users now have much less contact with social workers: the 'approved' social worker role, for example, has been replaced by the 'approved mental health professional' who may come from other disciplines. The move to care management has meant much social work with adults is concerned with rationing and restricting, rather than providing support and, more recently, there has been a loss of professional social work jobs and their replacement with unqualified staff to make assessments and provide 'care packages'.

CONCLUSION: CONNECTING SOCIAL WORK AND SERVICE-USER INVOLVEMENT

Four inter-related but distinct domains and developments have so far been delineated in this chapter. These are:

1. state social work;
2. radical social work;
3. service-user movements; and
4. state-user involvement.

It has been shown that social work has continued to be a contested area with competing pressures from marketised managerialism and social work's long-standing commitment to social justice and social change. Similarly, it becomes clear that increasing interest in public, patient, and user involvement in public policy does not mean that issues are uncontested there either. Instead, what emerges within the frameworks and terminology of user involvement are complex, fierce, but also often unacknowledged, tensions and conflicts. Underpinning these are the competing value systems of the two major sources of interest in such involvement. These are:

1. state managerialist–consumerist involvement;
2. service-user or citizen interest in democratisation and empowerment.

While there may be some overlaps and blurring, at heart the methods and purposes of these two ideologies tend to be different. What also becomes apparent is that these two ideologies are at work in both social work and user involvement. Thus, as has been seen, the marketised managerialism of state social work is reflected in the form of its care management practice (with all its limitations) and the managerialist–consumerist nature of the user involvement that has come to be associated with it. There is an irony in the fact that pressure to marketisation in both cases is state-led.

That leads to a final key issue, that is, the state and nature of user involvement in radical social work. As noted, in radical social work's original expression, this was limited, but more recent developments in the UK (such as the Social Work Action Network and major national events held in Nottingham in 2006 and 2008 to explore social work's and social care's value base) have given priority to user involvement and the equal involvement of service users in an effective and meaningful way (Barnard, et al., 2008; Beresford, 2006a, 2006b; Ferguson & Woodward, 2009). There seems to have been a genuine commitment to such involvement in both their process and purpose. This reflects a 'step change' in radical social work's relation with service users from its earlier manifestations. Service users have been involved across activities and at all levels in these initiatives. They have included service users actively involved in service-user organisations and movements, as well as others without particular affiliation or involvement. There has been recognition of the importance of enabling diverse involvement and addressing issues of equality and difference. Partnerships have begun to develop, and service users and their organisations have been involved as part of the overall liberatory and democratising project of this renewed radical social work. As with radical social work, Marxist analysis and leftist critiques played a significant part in the development of the thinking of the disabled people's and service-users' movements (see, e.g., Oliver, 1990; Shakespeare, 1998). Service users' democratising approach to user involvement is the natural ally of radical social work. To this end, it is important for radical social work to maintain its link with service-user movements and their underpinning ideologies and philosophies as opposed to becoming restricted to state-led approaches to involvement, whose essentially consumerist nature appears to be fundamentally opposed to the principles and spirit of radical social work. Together they offer the opportunity to advance some of the key goals of participatory radical social work. To:

1 take account of the essentially political nature of social work;
2 recognise the micro-politics of social work;
3 start with the primacy of the relationship and human qualities in social work;
4 draw on a social model;
5 prioritise supportive not controlling social work;
6 start with participatory social work education;
7 advance participatory social work practice;
8 be practice-led;
9 see social work as co-production between workers and service users;
10 recognise the universal value of social work for all, rather than a narrow disadvantaged group;
11 address diversity and equality; and
12 work towards diverse involvement (Beresford, 2011; Ferguson & Lavalette, 2009; Ferguson & Woodward, 2009; Lavalette, 2010).

The ideologies currently at work in social work and user involvement are those of the supermarket and the liberation movement. The two do not sit very comfortably together. Yet, often they are misunderstood and confused with one another. A worrying example which has developed in the UK is that of 'personalisation' in social work and social care. This is meant to mean ensuring service users have 'more choice and control' over their lives and support. What has actually happened is that the liberatory ideology underpinning the direct payments originally developed by disabled people (with state money allocated to service users to select their own support to help them live independently, with an infrastructure of advocacy and advice and help to do so) has been converted into a consumerist cash voucher system rebranded as a 'personal budget'. What it tends to mean in practice is cuts in collective services, reductions in support received, and job losses for qualified social work staff (Beresford, 2009). That is why there is a need for greater clarity about these issues internationally so people can make rational judgements, as both service users and practitioners, about what kind of social work they want and how to be involved most effectively to secure and sustain it. Hence we can expect that the future of (radical) social work is intimately tied to the success of the service-user movement. While there tends to be an overemphasis on the control role of social work in state settings – of which service users may be unwilling recipients – the evidence suggests that service users greatly value good social work practice (Branfield et al., 2005). This raises the question of whether service users see social workers as having a role to play in their success. So far at least the evidence seems encouraging for social work.

REFERENCES

Bailey, R., & Brake, M. (eds) (1975). *Radical social work*. London: Edward Arnold.

Barnard, A. Horner, N., & Wild, J. (eds) (2008). *The value base of social work and social care*. Maidenhead: Open University Press.

Beresford, P. (1999). Making participation possible: Movements of disabled people and psychiatric system survivors. In T. Jordan & Lent, A. (eds), *Storming the millennium: The new politics of change*. London: Lawrence and Wishart, pp. 34–50.

Beresford, P. (2001). Service users, social policy and the future of welfare. *Critical Social Policy*, 21(4), 494–512.

Beresford, P. (2006a). Service user values, in community care. Nottingham Trent University, Confirming our value base in social work and social care, Sutton, *Community Care*, 16–22 March, p. 6.

Beresford, P. (2006b). Nottingham meeting gladdens: The heart, Opinion, Stand Up For Social Care Campaign. *Community Care*, 16–22 March, p. 20.

Beresford, P. (2009). Social care, personalisation and service users: Addressing the ambiguities. *Research, Policy and Planning*, 27(2), 73–84.

Beresford, P. (2011). Radical social work and service users: A crucial connection. In M. Lavalette (ed.), *Radical social work today: Social work at the crossroads*. Bristol: Policy Press, pp. 95–114.

Beresford, P., & Campbell, P, (2004). Participation and protest: Mental health service users/survivors. In M.J. Todd & Taylor, G. (eds), *Democracy and participation: Popular protest and new social movements*. London: Merlin Press, pp. 326–342.

Beresford, P., & Croft, S. (1980). *Community control of social services departments*. London: Battersea Community Action.

Beresford, P., & Croft, S. (2004). Service users and practitioners reunited: The key component for social work reform. *British Journal of Social Work*, 34, 53–68.

Beresford, P., & Harding, T. (eds) (1993). *A challenge to change: Practical experiences of building user led services*. London: National Institute for Social Work.

Beresford, P., Shamash, O., Forrest, V., Turner, M., & Branfield, F. (2005). Developing social care: Service users' vision for adult support. Report of a consultation on the future of adult social care. *Adult Services Report 07*. London: Social Care Institute for Excellence in association with Shaping Our Lives.

Borman, L.D. (ed.) (1975). *Explorations in self-help and mutual aid*. Illinois: Centre for Urban Affairs, Northwestern University.

Branfield, F., Beresford, P., with Andrews, E.J., Chambers, P., Staddon, P., Wise, G., & Williams-Findlay, B. (2006). *Making user involvement work: Supporting service user networking and knowledge*. York: Joseph Rowntree Foundation, York Publishing Services.

Branfield, F., Beresford, P., Danagher, N., & Webb, R. (2005). *Independence, wellbeing and choice: A response to the Green Paper on adult social care*. Report of a consultation with service users. London: National Centre for Independent Living and Shaping Our Lives.

Braye, S., & Preston-Shoot, M. (2003). *Empowering practice in social care*. Buckingham, Open University Press.

Campbell, J., & Oliver, M. (1996). *Disability politics: Understanding our past, changing our future*. London: Routledge.

Campbell, P. (1996). The history of the user movement in the United Kingdom. In T. Heller, Reynolds, J., Gomm, R., Muston, R., & Pattison, S. (eds), *Mental health matters*. Basingstoke: Macmillan.

Campbell, P. (2009). The service user/survivor movement. In J. Reynolds, Muston, R., Heller, T., Leach, J., McCormick, M., Wallcraft, J., & Walsh, M. (eds), *Mental health still matters*. Basingstoke, Palgrave/Macmillan, pp. 46–52.

Charlton, J.I. (1998). *Nothing about us without us: Disability, oppression and empowerment*. California: University of California Press.

Clarke, J., Cochrane, A., & McLaughlin, E. (1994). *Managing social policy*. London: Sage.

Coleridge, P. (1993). *Disability, liberation, and development*. UK and Ireland: Oxford.

Croft, S., & Beresford, P. (1989). Decentralization and the personal social services. In M. Langan & Lee, P. (eds), *Radical social work today*. London: Unwin Hyman, pp. 97–119.

Denvall, V., Heule, C., & Kristiansen, A. (eds) (2010). *Mobiliserande socialt arbete (Mobilising social work)*, Malmö: Gleerups.

Dominelli, L. (2002). *Feminist social work theory and practice*. Basingstoke: Palgrave Macmillan.

Dustin, D. (2007). *The McDonaldization of social work*. Aldershot: Ashgate.

Ferguson, I., & Lavalette, M. (eds) (2009). *Social work after baby P: Issues, debates and alternative perspectives*. Hope for Social Work Series. Liverpool: Liverpool Hope University.

Ferguson, I., & Woodward, R. (2009). *Radical social work in practice: Making a difference*. Bristol: Policy Press.

Gibbs, A. (2000). New managerialism, In M. Davies (ed.), *The Blackwell encyclopaedia of social work*. Oxford: Blackwell, pp. 229–231.

Gorman, H., & Postle, K. (2003). *Transforming community care: A distorted vision?* Birmingham: Venture Press.

International Federation of Social Workers (IFSW) (2010). *Service user/consumer involvement and social work*. Consultation Paper (Prepared by Peter Beresford). Berne: IFSW. Retrieved September 30, 2010 from http://www.ifsw.org/p38001933.html

Jones, C., Ferguson, I., Lavalette, M., & Penketh, L. (2004). *The social work manifesto*. Retrieved September 2, 2010 from http://www.socialworkfuture.org/index.php/swan-organisation/manifesto

Jordan, B. (1990). *Social work in an unjust society*. London: Harvester Wheatsheaf.

Katz, A.H., & Bender, E.I. (eds) (1976). *The strength in us: Self-help groups in the modern world*. New York: New Viewpoints.

Kemshall, H., & Littlechild, B. (2000). *User involvement and participation in social care*. London: Jessica Kingsley.

Langan, M., & Lee, P. (eds) (1989). *Radical social work today*. London: Unwin Hyman.

Lavalette, M. (2010). *Radical social work today: Social work at the crossroads*. Bristol: Policy Press.

Lowndes, V. (1997). Changes in public service management: New institutions and new managerial regimes. *Local Government Studies*, *23*(2), 42–46.

Munro, E. (2010). *The Munro review of child protection, part one: A systems analysis*. London: Department for Education.

O'Hagan, M. (1994). *Stopovers: On my way home from mars*. London: Survivors Speak Out.

Oliver, M. (1983). *Social work with disabled people*. Basingstoke: Macmillan.

Oliver, M. (1990). *The politics of disablement*. Basingstoke: Macmillan.

Oliver, M. (1996). *Understanding disability: From theory to practice*. Basingstoke: Macmillan.

Oliver, M. (2009). *Understanding disability: From theory to practice* (2nd ed.). Basingstoke: Palgrave Macmillan.

Oliver, M., & Sapey, B. (2006). *Social work with disabled people* (3rd ed.). Basingstoke: Palgrave.

Oliver, M., & Zarb, G. (1989). The politics of disability: A new approach. *Disability, Handicap and Society*, *4*(3), 221–241.

Postle, K. (2002). Working 'between the idea and the reality': Ambiguities and tensions in care managers' work. *British Journal of Social Work*, *32*(3), 335–351.

Ritzer, G. (2000). *The McDonaldization of society: An investigation into the changing character of contemporary social life* (rev. ed.). London: Sage.

Rogowski, S. (2010). *Social work: The rise and fall of a profession*. Bristol: Policy Press.

Shakespeare, T. (1993). Disabled people's self-organisation: A new social movement? *Disability and Society*, *8*(3), 249–264.

Shakespeare, T. (ed.) (1998). *The disability reader: Social science perspectives*. London: Cassell.

Simmons, R., Powell, M., & Greener, I. (eds) (2009). *The consumer in public services: Choice, values and difference*. Bristol: Policy Press.

Social Work Action Network (SWAN) (2010). Home Page. Retrieved September 2, 2010 from http://www.socialworkfuture.org/

Stedman Jones, G. (1971). *Outcast London: A study in the relationship between classes in Victorian society*. Oxford: Clarendon Press.

Stone, E. (ed.) (1999). *Disability and development: Learning from action and research in the majority world*. Leeds: The Disability Press.

Taylor, I. (1972). Client refusal: A political strategy for radical social work. *Case Con*, *2*, 59–68.

Titmuss, R.M. (1968). *Commitment to welfare*. London: George Allen and Unwin.

UK Department for Education (2010). *Munro review of child protection*. Retrieved October 1, 2010 from http://www.education.gov.uk/munroreview/

UK Department of Children, Families and Schools and Department of Health (DCSF/DH) (2009). *Building a safe confident future: The final report of the Social Work Task Force*. London: DCSF/DH.

Union of the Physically Impaired Against Segregation (UPIAS)/Disability Alliance (1976). *Fundamental principles of disability: Being a summary of the discussion held on 22nd November, 1975 and containing commentaries from each organization.* London: UPIAS and the Disability Alliance.

Wallcraft, J., Read, J., & Sweeney, A. (2003). *On our own terms: Users and survivors of mental health services working together for support and change.* London: Sainsbury Centre for Mental Health.

Warren, J. (2007). *Service user and carer participation in social work.* Exeter: Learning Matters.

White, V. (2006). *The state of feminist social work.* London: Routledge.

Williams, F. (1989). *Social policy: A critical introduction – Issues of race, gender and class.* Cambridge: Polity Press.

International Social Work

Narda Razack

International social work is challenging to describe and defies systematic inquiry, yet it serves as a point of departure for those who wish to maintain that the professionalisation of the field is more than academic. 'Internationalisation' has become an effective legitimation device for networks of professional practitioners and academics around the world. Yet international social work continues to be an enigma to many in the profession, since it has not been embraced as a rigorous academic component across a range of research and practice learning dimensions, including the social work curriculum. Rather it has become a terrain for spirited debate as some suggest it signifies a misguided 'quest' for universality (Gray & Fook, 2004), while others focus on comparative social development (Hokenstad et al., 1992), and, more recently, international exchanges and collaboration (Lager et al., 2010).

Webb (2003) sums up the push towards a global social work in the following:

> There is now talk of a global social work; an international social work; a transnational social work; globalized welfare and cross national activities in social work. The 2009 IASSW conference in Adelaide, Australia, for example, further proselytized this trend with its title of 'Global Social Work' (p. 192)

Nevertheless, international social work is firmly on the agenda in contemporary neoliberal environments, where there is a renewed fervour to internationalise universities and globalise the curriculum. A major priority of universities around the world faced with massive funding cuts is international student recruitment, where students have to pay exorbitant tuition fees to ensure that university programmes remain financially viable (Paton, 2010). Globalising the curriculum, however, is not a primary focus and, as will be seen, racism and other structural problems have emerged (Ziguras, 2009).

This chapter argues that international social work is a contested terrain, which is fluid, dynamic, and shifting, as its focus is a global analysis of ever-changing sociocultural issues. Hence it contends that international social work urgently requires a theoretical framework from which to critically analyse global social issues, the heightened dynamic of institutional internationalisation, ongoing fervour for international placements and collaborations, and increasing attention to globalising the curriculum. An understanding of the variations in social work in diverse contexts is critical for social work teaching, research, scholarship, practice, and professional development.

To connect the threads of the varied readings of international social work, this chapter begins with a focus on its historical significance, including the relevance of contemporary analyses of globalisation and international development. In taking account of this complexity, the chapter explores international exchange and research collaborations from a critical standpoint to highlight the risks of perpetuating racist, imperialistic, and re-colonising practices. The conclusion reached is that international social work constitutes a growing body of work relating to the social work profession's internationalising agenda in a rapidly changing global context.

HISTORICISING INTERNATIONAL SOCIAL WORK: THE PROFESSION'S INTERNATIONALISING AGENDA

To arrive at common understandings of international social work, it is necessary to recognise how it was conceived and applied originally and historically. According to Kendall (2000), social work is an international enterprise since from its inception it was an international venture which included different countries, notably in Great Britain, Europe, and North America. It also mirrored the United Nation's organisational structure and its division of the globe into five major regions (Gray & Rennie, 2007). From the outset, the profession set its sights on world coverage and had a presence in many non-Western colonised contexts through the imperial powers' civilising mission.

Since its inception, social work was founded by white Northerners invested in philanthropy, benevolence, and missionary work for those deemed 'the wretched of the earth' (Fanon, 1963). Social work struggled to maintain its status within the academy from its early beginnings and borrowed from other disciplines to formulate its theory and knowledge base. The profession was initially premised upon modernist assumptions about ontology and epistemology. Although positivism was a dominant force, social work was still marginalised as a discipline and viewed as unscientific because of its primary focus on qualitative research and community development. Social work's embeddedness in modernism is still reflected in some of its approaches (Gray et al., 2008; Haug, 2005) and professional competencies and standardised practices (Gray & Webb, 2008). This history is important and a discursive and dialogical framework is needed to grapple with the implications of social work's historical beginnings in benevolent charity and missionary work.

Social work began simultaneously in Europe and the USA (Rogers, 2004). The first school of social work was established in Amsterdam in 1899 and offered a two-year programme (Kendall, 1998). Further schools in New York, London, and Berlin soon followed (Healy, 2001; Webb, 2007). Each country developed a special emphasis to reflect its sociocultural context. For example, in Sweden the focus was on public administration, in Germany on social pedagogy, and in France on public health. The US approach was more individual and therapeutically focused, while the Europeans focused on environmental issues (Midgley, 1981), and Canada tended to followed US approaches.

Social work began to spread to other countries with the international transfer of its values and ideologies, which were steeped in colonialism and tended to overlook the violence and genocide inflicted on colonised populations by imperial powers. In its origins, international social work grew out of the imperial West's conception of its civilising mission as intellectual forms of dominance by the North on the South (Said, 1978). As an institutional welfare response, the development of social work was guided by liberal political theory (Wilensky &

Lebeaux, 1958; see Chapter 2). For example, the British welfare state after World War II was the culmination of social and industrialising processes which had catapulted large portions of the metropolitan population into poverty and unemployment. Social work became embedded in this Western industrial model of welfare provision though diverse models of welfare statism were adopted in developed Western countries (Esping-Andersen, 1990).

Healy (2001) traced the first major shift in international social work to the period between the world wars. Arising from the profession's close links with the United Nations (UN), the beginnings of the profession's formal expansion began with the institution of professional conferences, the first of which was held in Paris in 1928 and led to the establishment of the first International Committee comprising 51 mainly European schools of social work in Berlin in 1929 (Gray & Rennie, 2007). Further international meetings followed and international professional associations were formed: The International Committee became the International Association of Schools of Social Work (IASSW) in 1954 and the International Federation of Social Workers (IFSW) was founded in 1956. A related body, the International Council on Social Welfare (ICSW), was established in Paris in 1928.

These events constitute critical landmarks of international activity in social work, documented in rich detail by Healy (2001) along with profiles of pioneers and founders of various international organisations (see also, http://www.ifsw.org/p38001894.html). As Healy (2001) notes:

> The profession of social work has had a long history of international action, beginning almost at the inception of the profession. There have been impressive accomplishments, both by organizations and by individuals. If there is a negative side, it is that it is a history of ups and downs, not a seamless story of progress (p. 75).

Stoesz et al., (1999) also documented the international social development focus emerging after World War II when the afore-mentioned international committees were formed to foster professional collaboration, consultation, and exchange. But progress was eroded with the rise of nationalism, the conflicts of World War II, and the 'economic devastation of the worldwide depression' (Lager et al., 2010, p. 16), which led to the closure of many schools of social work in Europe. Prior to entry into World War II, the US congress passed a law which helped to facilitate international collaboration in a bilateral exchange with South America for training in social welfare (Kendall, 1995).

The second major shift for international social work involved the creation of the UN Relief and Rehabilitation Administration (UNRRA) in 1943 (Lager et al., 2010) and, by the end of the war, there were rich opportunities for global social work with its structures modelled on the UN's regional structure (Kendall, 1978). Its dominant Western ideals were exported to more non-Western countries like Jordan and the Sudan following World War II, as the UN and UNICEF assisted in social work's international development. The West dominated the field through exportation, management, and control over theoretical and practice approaches. Northern countries were heavily implicated in relations of power with their Southern counterparts, and these processes of dominance continue to influence modern-day education and practice. Thus the postwar spread of international social work is directly attributable to the profession's strong links with the UN (Healy, 2008). UN agencies have assisted in sending teams of advisers to establish social work programmes in formerly colonised countries (see later) and, for some, the intellectual domination of the West, specifically the USA, over the rest constitutes a new pattern of colonisation:

> Motivated by the demands of modernization, they [US social workers] designed curricula which replicated the content of western social work training, urged that social work courses be established in universities and recommended the adoption of western professional standards. In spite of economic, social and cultural differences between the

industrial and developing countries, few questioned the relevance of these approaches to the Third World or attempted to provide courses which were suited to local needs or conditions (Midgley, 1981, p. 60).

Social workers continue to involve themselves in international service organisations and social welfare activities with several journals, such as *International Social Work* and the *International Journal of Social Welfare*, attesting the profession's international commitment, and the various associations maintaining the international perspective. These two international journals endeavour to publish international articles but are published in the West and in English, thereby limiting access for the majority of the world.

Social work's professional international bodies – the IFSW and IASSW – work closely with organisations like the UN and the UN Educational, Scientific, and Cultural Organization (UNESCO), which, as already noted, share their interests in responding to global issues. These organisations, however, were conceptualised in the West and continue to reflect Western hegemonic values through their operational procedures and practices, as the language used at meetings and conferences is largely English and because the cost of travel representation, although subsidised, continues to be problematic for those in less economically secure countries. According to Mohan (2005), international social work entails exclusionary practices that debase its foundations and are 'confined to exchanges of mutual interests, annual and biannual conferences and related rituals of self promotion' (p. 246). He rightly insists that social work ought to rethink whether its normative rights-based approaches are applicable to the complexities inherent in a diverse and divisive world. The exportation of Western knowledge, values, and ideology has helped to sustain hegemony and control, constructing social work on universal ideals of human rights, social justice, and advocacy but, as discussed below, how these ideals get translated to fit local realities remains an important issue for international social work.

THE DEVELOPMENT OF SOCIAL WORK IN CANADA: A CASE EXAMPLE

By the early 1920s, Canadian social work followed Western cultural influences in 'sporting a new sense of nationalism' (Jeffery, 2002, p. 58) as social reform was being shaped by White elite bourgeois Canadians bent on changing immigrants and lower-class people to conform to their own national image. Jeffery (2002) focused her analytical description of the history and origins of social work on the performers who carried out the work. She critiqued the early beginnings of the making of White bourgeois subjects working on charity and settlement work as a 'process of moral and social reform', where the aim was to reshape the 'ethical subjectivities of both immigrant and native-born Canadians' (Jeffery, 2002, p. 58). She also provided footnoted accounts of the few radical social workers who were aware of injustices and inequalities, and advised practitioners to engage in critical discussions on how the White subject is produced to avoid racial stereotypes when working with others. She concluded the making of the bourgeois White subject was still being produced within social work.

The shift from performing charity work to being a university discipline occurred as the first Canadian social work education programme was established at the University of Toronto in 1914 (see Jeffery, 2002). Significantly, although social work was managed by mainly White women, in the university department the staff included male and female faculty. The school relied heavily on US and British practice models and texts, a situation which has changed slowly with recent publications promoting policy and practice perspectives within the political context of Canadian social work (Graham et al., 2000; Hicks, 2002). Signs exist therefore that the hegemony imposed through the adoption and reliance on US and British writings are being challenged.

As in many Western countries, earlier settlement work dominated the profession in Canada, with Christian family life being nurtured (Jeffery, 2002). White middle-class respectability and a paternalistic approach to working with immigrants were pronounced. The most virulent forms of racism were practised on Aboriginal people. The children were forcibly taken away from their parents and homes to residential schools where they were forced to renounce their native culture and language and assimilate to 'Christian' values within a context of nation building involving brutally harsh policies of land confiscation and denial of basic rights including genocide. Aboriginal communities have continued to resist such imperialism. It is quite apparent that Indigenous communities continue to feel the plague of Western dominance on a global scale (Gray et al., 2008). However, modern-day racism and imperialism have become entrenched within the profession because the values and ideology, in part, originate from this destructive history.

The overall lack of reflection on this violent history in the mandates and mission statements of international social work is striking. There is a basic recognition that continued references to the world being a 'global village' (Mishra, 1999; Thompson, 1999) means engagement in global responses to social issues must be sought. Despite the emphasis on globalisation and internationalisation in the Canadian terrain, for example, social work responses have, so far, been very limited as policies remain nationally driven. For example, the US Council on Social Work Education (CSWE) has explicit guidelines for schools to include international content in the curriculum (CSWE, 1992). CSWE is committed to an integral approach to international social work and there are mandates to ensure this directive is implemented (CSWE, 1992). In the UK, Khan and Dominelli (2000) document two significant areas in which changes in social work have occurred. The first is the 'application of market principles to the public sector' (Khan & Dominelli, 2000, p. 95), which includes privatisation, retrenchment, competencies relating to performance, and especially linking organisational goals to competition for financial resources. The second relates to the changing context for social work because of the international growth in social inequalities and an 'intensification of disadvantage' (Khan & Dominelli, 2000, p. 95). These are mirrored across the globe and, as societies become more culturally and ethnically diverse, it is critical to explore how educators might incorporate these realities in educational programmes. US academics continue to play a major role in shaping the international social work discourse because of the prevalence of their texts and articles. This production of knowledge continues to be largely devoid of analyses of racism and imperialism.

WHAT THEREFORE REALLY *IS* INTERNATIONAL SOCIAL WORK?

Beginning with definitions from scholars who have studied and written about international social work, Healy (2001) states:

> International social work is defined as international professional action and the capacity for international action by the social work profession and its members. International action has four dimensions: internationally related domestic practice and advocacy, professional exchange, international practice, and international policy development and advocacy (p. 7).

For Healy (2001), these four categories signify how international social work *should* unfold and why these areas are critical. Interestingly, international exchange involving the formulation of theoretical ideas is missing from the list. While international social work remains a complex concept, the meanings are historically related to areas like comparative social welfare, international practice, cross-cultural understanding, professional exchange activities, and human rights and advocacy. Healy's (2001) simplifies a very complex phenomenon as international social work is a complex entity which defies rigid constructs. At the very least, social work might be viewed as an international profession simply because it is taught and practised in most developing and developed countries. From a postcolonial perspective, however, a major antecedent of social work, especially international social work, is the history of missionary activity carried out by Christian churches in conjunction with the spread of European imperialism and colonisation. It emerged 'out of philanthropic activities directed at poor people living in the slums of the rapidly industrializing cities of North America and Europe' (Midgley, 1997, p. 162).

Defining international social work has been a subject for much debate (Gray, 2005; Gray & Webb, 2008; Healy, 2001; Hokenstad et al., 1992). At the time of going to press, the belated IFSW/IASSW project to review the 2000 definition of social work is still underway. Haug (2001) struggled to understand this question while enrolled in a Canadian social work graduate programme with a concentration on international social work. She and a number of her professors began to query the meaning of international social work, and through her readings, she came to realise that international social work was seldom defined. However, definitions limit the context of ongoing critiques and ability to indigenise perspectives according to territory. Haug (2001) realised there was a lack of critical analyses of power and privilege, which signified a huge gap in the international social work discourse (see also Razack, 2002). The literature in fact speaks to the 'doing', or 'international action' as Healy (2001) calls it, in normative and prescriptive ways rather than addressing the critical nature of international social work and how it ought to be defined, not only in the context of the profession but also in national and local cultural contexts. Gray et al. (2008) critique the approach to 'indigenizing' social work as it can be appropriated from Indigenous people and cautioned that social work ought to refer instead to localising knowledge to fit particular contexts. A place to begin this analysis of the international social work discourse is, therefore, with an exploration of its concepts and foundational ideals.

Hokestad et al. (1992) proposed a variety of meanings for international social work. They noted the interchangeable use of the term with international social welfare, sometimes also referred to as comparative social welfare or comparative social policy. For them, it comprised a focus on the profession and its practice in different parts of the world, including the various roles social workers assumed; practice methods used; problems confronted; and challenges encountered. Clearly emphasising a benevolent imperial form of helping, they focused on a distinctive area of practice where social workers could apply skills and knowledge to assist people in 'the developing nations, or Third World' (Hokestad et al., 1992, p. 4).

Although social work is a recognised international profession, practised in unique ways all over the world, the theoretical foundations of international approaches have not been seriously integrated into the social work curriculum. Some schools have added electives on international social work (Healy, 2008) and many schools in the global South are determined to indigenise their curricula (Gray et al., 2008; Mwansa, 2011; see Chapter 46). Consequently, social work has not adopted or implemented an international perspective.

More recent research indicates some attention to internationalism but only in additive frames (Healy, 1995; Midgley, 1997), such as special courses and some content in other courses, but this results in a lack of integration or consideration of international social issues as a major feature of the social work curriculum. Thus, despite exhortatory statements as to its importance, there is no solid conceptual framework for incorporating awareness of a global reality for understanding social issues into the social work curriculum (Asamoah et al., 1997).

As borders become more permeable through technology development, the global market economy, and the constant movement of peoples across the globe, anti-imperialist understandings from international perspectives are crucial in social work. Social issues know no boundaries and global interdependence is relevant to social problem analysis. These definitions and explanations of international social work need constant critical analysis. Yet, with their roots in charity work and settlement housing as the profession became secured during the era of the industrial revolution (Midgley, 1990), social work in Europe and North America remains associated with the dominant ideology and economic realities of these eras, clearly driven by powerful Western countries.

Social work in developing countries is left with the vestiges and psychological legacy of imperialism and colonisation, where indigenous inhabitants were taught to measure themselves by the 'White man's' definitions. It was, therefore, conceptualised under and within these colonial conditions and incorporated the regime of benevolence and kindliness to 'make it better' for the 'other'. This does not mean social work was a disingenuous profession but, despite the good intentions and benevolence of White women and men who administered to the deserving poor, they did so based on their own positions of power. Hence, social work is not innocent of historical abuses associated with colonial practices, especially and foremost among Aboriginal peoples, and these historical truths need to be included in any analysis of international social work which will, otherwise, be seen as a further attempt at masking colonisation.

Mwansa (2011) describes the colonial history of social work education in Africa as dictated by foreigners from Western society rather than indigenous knowledge (see Chapter 46). Social work education was exported to many countries and the West continues to be the prime – though not the only – exporter of social work. Though not itself a unitary body of knowledge, Western theories, concepts, and practices seep through borders and enter countries in far and distant places. Critics argue this desire for Western knowledge is so fierce and has been so cunningly enforced by the West that those in the South seek to emulate the North despite their gains through independence from colonising nations. Entrenched notions of the infinite superiority of Western ideology and practices continue to reign long after the – formal – ending of colonisation (Midgley, 1981).

Midgley (2008) revisited his earlier work on *Professional Imperialism* written 25 years previously, re-igniting debates about the motivation of professionals sincere in their intentions to develop professional social work education in new contexts. He questioned whether professional imperialism had been adequately addressed and described the meagre efforts at reciprocity, limited curriculum transformation, and the insidiousness of not being open to learning from colleagues in 'underdeveloped' countries. New technologies, ease of travel, and the continuous prestige of schools in the North has enabled the exportation of Western knowledge on an even larger scale.

Nevertheless, developing countries do not unthinkingly adopt Western theories and concepts of social work and have resisted through efforts to indigenise the profession in many countries. Tsang et al., (2000) attempted to recognise reciprocity and mutuality in their project introducing social work in China. Likewise in many South American countries foreign concepts and practices are being reconciled with local values, needs, and problems (Resnick, 1995). However, these attempts have to grapple with the indomitable forces of internationalisation and globalisation. Lorenz (2005) aptly noted the international perspective was not an alternative to the local perspective, but 'on the contrary, it is the necessary reference point for understanding local developments in their fuller significance' (p. 100). Internationalisation and globalisation are features of international social development which have become an important component of international social work. The next section explains how this came about.

GLOBALISATION AND INTERNATIONAL DEVELOPMENT

Midgley (1999) noted 'social work and social development are not synonymous but interlinked' (p. 201). Consequently, they have become ever more closely aligned for several reasons. Firstly, and primarily, social workers and faculty who go abroad often conduct their work through international humanitarian organisations and agencies as project consultants, teachers, and community development and international aid workers. Vast amounts of money are channelled through well-established organisations like World Vision, Oxfam, CARE, and the International Red Cross to fund local development aid programmes (Haug, 2001). These international nongovernmental organisations work closely with multilateral bodies like the UN. Secondly, and inevitably, international social workers collaborate with development and aid workers, UN personnel, and refugee counsellors who work in a variety of settings abroad. Thirdly, these various contexts need to be examined because they are not adequately included in the social work curriculum. Added to this imperative is the increasing impact of information technology, transnational corporations, world travel, and migrant flows bringing social workers increasingly closer on a global scale. Hence the history of international development work and globalisation forms an important part of the international social work discourse.

Nawal El Saadawi (1997) noted the 'globe is shrinking ... But the concept of universality should be redefined. It should not mean central control, monopoly, and domination of one country over another. Real human universality and unity should be democratic, and respect differences, interests and multiple systems' (p. 31). Herein lie the dangers of globalisation and its counterpart westernisation (see earlier), which all too frequently colour the landscape of international development amounting to little more than the inculcation of neoliberalism through, for example, structural adjustment programmes. Hence 'development' is a highly contentious ideological construct steeped in Western values and directed at specific social and economic change in the Third World (Grillo & Stirrat, 1997). Midgley (2000), however, uncritically located development in the context of social work:

> Social development first emerged as a coherent approach to social welfare in the 1950s when it was adopted by several developing countries supported by the United Nations. This approach seeks to link economic and social policies and to promote social welfare (or social development as it was known) within the framework of a planned economic development (p. 23).

Such social development perspectives insist on the integration of economic and social policy but distortions in development continue. Clearly, there are differences as to how development has been perceived and implemented, especially within the profession of social work. Despite the significant improvement in the conditions of the world's poor through international development, in some regions of the world the 'deprivation actually deepened' (Heron, 1999, p. 242). The situation appears to have worsened for many people in the world, especially through structural adjustment polices introduced in 'developing' countries as a way to repay large debts incurred through borrowing from the International Monetary Fund and the World Bank (Lyons, 1999). The economies of many countries (e.g., Greece and Portugal) continue to face significant upheavals while other countries like China and, to a lesser extent, India are now being heralded as the new and emerging superpowers despite their own struggles with poverty and other socioeconomic problems,

The profession of social work expanded and infiltrated most parts of the 'underdeveloped' world after industrialisation in an effort to educate and assist those in poor and destitute conditions mainly through its close links with the development of social welfare rather than social development. However, there is a strong push to integrate social work and social development (Asamoah et al., 1997; Cox, 1995). This is driven by increasing requests from students in developed countries, mainly in the North, to do field placements in humanitarian organisations working in less developed countries in the South. Thus, increasingly, social workers have to face issues which transcend local and national boundaries, and academic programmes need to reflect these changing realities.

INTERNATIONAL EXCHANGES AND COLLABORATIONS FROM A CRITICAL STANDPOINT

International exchanges and research collaborations constitute the main means for cross-cultural and comparative research and practice. One of the primary goals of international social work is the development of cross-cultural understanding, language skills, and awareness of the plight of the most marginalised in the world. There is recognition of the need for interdependence (Hokenstad et al., 1992), strong linkages and partnerships (Campfens, 1996; Midgley, 1992), internationalising programmes (Estes, 1992), and knowledge about cross-cultural differences and intercultural sensitivity (Altbach, 2007; Holmes & Mathews, 1993; Krajewski-Jaime et al., 1996). More cynically, however, these programmes constitute a form of education or development tourism for students and academics in 'pursuit of the exotic' (Woolf, 2007, p. 504).

Despite noble goals, the main discussion tends to revolve around the mechanics of international exchanges and collaborations rather than critical attention being paid to who benefits most (see Razack, 2002, 2005, 2009, 2012). Thus guidelines for international student exchanges continue to comprise the body of this literature (Lager et al., 2010). In a recent analysis of an exchange programme, Singh (2011) found a proliferation of glossy advertisements for study abroad programmes (together with intensive international student recruitment) providing grist for the mill to boost the economy of universities.

Healy (1988), however, saw some international goodwill at the heart of attempts to internationalise the curriculum in the profession's profound commitment to global justice. There is any number of issues to satisfy the profession's concerns in this era of globalisation: The much debated 'war on terror', neoliberal threats to welfare, unrest in the Middle East, dislocated populations worldwide, family disruption, poverty, homelessness, environmental pollution, HIV and AIDS, social inequalities, violence, and other global political and socioeconomic challenges. These problems transcend local and national boundaries, and social workers ought to be aware of and responsive to these realities (Estes, 1992). They are the proper terrain of international social work, rather than the limited focus on one-dimensional international student exchanges and research collaborations from the North to the South or from the West to the rest. Moreover, the racial overtones of international research and exchanges are not fully realised.

Theoretical and historical discourses on 'race' have enormous implications for international social work. Canadian society tends to react to overt and virulent expressions of racism rather than respond to its systemic, institutional manifestations. The global profiling of Arabs, Arab-looking individuals and Muslims permeate the current climate and promote racism and intolerance. Noting the importance of cross-cultural learning (see earlier) requires an understanding of how culture has become in official discourses a euphemism for race (Lentin, 2000; Park, 2005 see Chapter 23). New and disguised forms of racism accompany the multiculturalism of societies, where immigration has significantly altered 'race' relations (see Chapter 36):

> The increasing 'multiculturality' of Western societies is accompanied by a parallel inability to effectively deal with its inevitable consequences – the racist discrimination of ethnically or 'racially' different minorities, who highlight the alterity between the dominant and subordinate groups inherent in today's nation state (Lentin, 2000, p. 92).

Population mobility has intensified the need to study globalised 'race' relations (Bonilla-Silva, 2000). Furthermore, Western nations maintain superiority over peripheral nations and this form of hegemony constitutes an 'informal imperialism' or 'dominance without empire' (Bonilla-Silva, 2000, p. 194). Hence a focus on culture can act as a new form of racism where normative standards are applied to groups of people, marginalising some and exalting others. Whites are constantly positioned at the top of the hierarchy of 'race' relations because they construct ideological categories of racial superiority and inferiority. The White majority media frequently portrays Blacks as criminals or deviants (Benjamin, 2003). Aboriginal people are depicted as perpetual drunks and other groups who tend not to fit the model of the White majority are similarly stereotyped (e.g., Arabs and Arab-looking people, and Roma Jews in Europe). hooks (1995) describes the killing rage she and many African-Americans feel when subjected to racism, and adds that addictions, and more dangerously, apathy and 'hard-heartedness' are ways to cope with this rage. Many White people are not attuned to these everyday realities of racism because they believe overt racist acts are uncommon. They also tend to be unaware of their complicity within institutional and structural forms of racism.

In international social work, there is an underlying belief that those who go abroad will acquire increased understandings for how to work with people from different cultures. In many cosmopolitan cities, the dominant group, recognising an increasingly diverse population, adopts a 'management of diversity approach' devoid of analyses of power and paying lip service to the entrenched racism people of colour and other oppressed groups experience. Workshops and sensitivity training sessions are common responses to gain the necessary skills and understandings to work with those who are deemed 'inferior' in society (Bloommaert & Verschueren, 1998). It is tempting for those from the North to want to leave this multicultural context, rife though it is with opportunities to work through oppression, and instead head South to seek to sharpen their skills in foreign countries steeped in colonial legacies and oftentimes political disarray. Going abroad to work with the 'other' is sometimes considered a more authentic learning experience producing more sophisticated cross-cultural skills and understandings perceived to be of benefit to work with the native other at home (Razack, 2004). These geopolitical divisions between North and South have long featured in the social sciences and led Raewyn Connell in *Southern Theory* (2007) to posit the cardinal points of cartography to capture inequalities between ethnicities, peoples, and nation-states. This 'world picture' perspective reveals sharp divides in stressing the relationality of the changing context in terms of power and knowledge across time and place. Margaret Jolly's reviews capture this divisive North-South relation as follows:

> The South appears in such global theories primarily as a source of data for Northern theorists rather than as sites of knowing and self-conscious social reflection, places where important social theories are also developed. Through a survey of nineteenth and twentieth-century 'Southern theory' from Latin America, Iran, Africa, India and Indigenous Australia, Connell aspires to restore the fullness of the world to social science, to include its many voices in a more democratic global conversation (Jolly, 2008).

This trend is likely to intensify in this era of globalisation and transnationalism, where funding grants and invitations to work in postcolonial sites are increasing for Northern academics giving them the opportunity to act as 'experts', and export their expertise wholesale to another country. 'Race' and racism may not be primary considerations for the academics in international social work, as they focus more on project development and programme construction. However, some researchers have shared their experiences of trying to work in collaboration with their partners in the South and describe the difficulty in trying to build an equitable North–South partnership (Altbach, 2004; Canto et al., 2001). Whitmore and Wilson (1997) discussed how their Northern superiority inevitably crept into the process of collaboration, despite their good intentions. Generally, however, international collaborative processes tend not to be analysed from 'race'-critical standpoints. This is a major oversight since racism and colonialism are intertwined in a shared discourse on ideas of the 'other', constituting a combination of older prejudices and legacies of power, borne out of colonial relations, and mixed in with contemporary sociocultural and economic conditions (Williams & Chrisman, 1994). Subtle forms of hegemony are apparent in contemporary practice abroad through the adoption of Northern practices in the South, and, 'subjectivity and ideology [which] are absolutely central to [this] process of domination' (Loomba, 1998, p. 31). Racism continues to be prevalent in many countries, and settler societies like Canada and Australia, being dominated by a White majority, have not shifted significantly (Hage, 2000; Lawrence, 2002; Paisley, 2002). The ideology of those who have political and economic power infiltrates policy, practice, theory, laws, and regulatory standards and, as in the colonial era and in contemporary society, the ruling ideology continues to be adopted by the colonised. In Canada, Aboriginal voices are ignored, non-White bodies are racialised, and these peoples are viewed as substandard, 'not as good as' the White ruling class (Bonilla-Silva, 2000). The minority population has to learn the norms and standards of the dominant group. In going South, many believe their theories and practices are a 'cut above' those from the developing world (Razack, 2004). One needs, therefore, to ask whether Western social work students or academics can escape this racism and hegemony in going abroad to learn and teach. Such questions force the profession to pay close attention to Shohat's (1992) question: 'where is the "post" in postcolonial?', since a refashioning of colonisation can occur in these North–South encounters.

In international exchanges and collaborations, Western social workers are caught in the web of 'race' relations because of their unearned privilege, and their innate tendency to be either ignorant or adequately informed of the fact of 'race', or of their complicity within repressive societal structures (Razack, 2004). Those who are deemed to be marginal in society are also capable of being oppressive and need to be acutely aware of how they contribute to imperialism. Kaplan (1997) aptly states that it is inevitable that Western tools will be taken up by colonised peoples because they are present in the North and in the South. As Frankenberg (1993) states, Whites are taught not to see 'race' and, therefore, view themselves as colourless. Other (non-White) people are thus 'raced'. Concepts of whiteness and privilege are pivotal to international social work but they are largely invisible in the international social work literature. It is common for social workers to adopt a liberal view to refute and deny racialised differences showing a tendency to resort to feeling White liberal guilt when discussing 'race', and this impedes conversation and action (Dominelli, 1998; Razack & Jeffery, 2003; Williams, 1999). White people share a fundamental belief that 'white raciality is cultureless' (Perry, 2001, p. 58) and, therefore, taken for granted. Perry (2001) argues there is power in adopting a position that there is no culture, for in doing so, racial superiority is inscribed. Weedon (1999) similarly contends whiteness allows the problem of racism to be the problem of Black people and not fundamentally a part of the problem of White people. Racism has structural as well as individual advantages for White people who tend to be invisible to the privileged position of whiteness. Racism therefore needs to be problematised: theorising whiteness allows for critical analysis of how it operates on the international social work terrain.

Frankenberg (1993) views the social construction of whiteness as being similar to the social construction of racism asserting whiteness 'refers to a set of locations that are historically, socially, politically, and culturally produced and, moreover, are intrinsically linked to unfolding relations of domination' (p. 6). Harding (1991) indicates that those White people who have an increased knowledge and awareness about the world of the oppressed can 'become marginal' to their own group, or viewed as having 'traitorous identities' by the oppressors. Frankenberg (1993) refers to this position as 'privilege cognizant' (p. 123), meaning viewing difference only at an intellectual level from their privileged locations, rather than getting politically involved. Misrecognition of privilege leads to the constant 'reinscription of whitely scripts' through the firm belief in their authority and ways of being in the world (Bailey, 1998).

Razack (2004) found many of the White participants in her study spoke of their discomfort while abroad. Yet, ironically, many reinscribed 'whitely scripts' in their travels abroad. Hence knowledge of the social construction of whiteness and its role within Third World politics is needed in international social work discourse. Analysing North–South encounters abroad demands knowledge of the history of colonisation and postcolonial theory even to begin to try and understand how 'race', whiteness, and hegemonic power unfold in international social work. Critical 'race' theory, which includes analyses of whiteness, shifts the discourse of 'race' and racism from the Black–White dynamic to one that includes multiple voices and experiences (Solorzano & Yosso, 2002). It also gives voice to those who are on the margins of society and recognises their knowledge, histories, and experiences (Delgado Bernal, 2002). It is, therefore, critical to understand how privilege is enacted abroad, how 'identities that move' from North to South become unsettled in the process, and how postcolonial realities operate in international work sites. How do Northern social workers position themselves in Southern spaces? When they decide to go to these 'developing' countries for work, do they realise these are postcolonial spaces in which the White body is implicated historically within these structures?

CONCLUSION

This chapter examined international social work from a critical standpoint. It began with an observation about the tendency to compartmentalise international social work into limited descriptive elements thereby eluding the fluidity and dynamism inherent in this body of work. If there were one critique worth highlighting it would be the lack of a definitive corpus of theory informing this critical area of social work. To redress this oversight, theories of 'race' and racism, colonisation, postcolonialism, and White privilege and their critical insights were offered as essential knowledge sources for international social work, especially in nonhegemonic and anti-imperialistic work with professional partners abroad. A focus on countering hegemonic structures and alliances between and among nations resulting from the negative effects of neoliberal globalisation is needed given this toxic influence is still very pervasive to social work in developing countries and where indigenous or local practices and theories are not given sufficient attention. Martinez-Brawley (1999) highlight the dangers of imperialism in the benevolent caring role of social workers as they travel and consult with partners abroad on programmes and curricula. Engaging in continuous critical reflection and research on different world views is essential given social work's role in perpetuating 'dominant, often Eurocentric, theoretical assumptions and methods' (Martinez-Brawley, 1999, p. 334). International social work, and international exchanges and collaborations, especially from North to South, may be seen as engaging in colonising activity in its efforts to learn and glean from the 'other'. According to Spivak (1999), a form of 'pretentious internationalism' is pervasive in the way the West attempts to respond to world realities.

Racism in internationalisation has not been under scrutiny in the international social work literature. Rather the language remains couched in the rhetoric of differences, attending to cross-cultural sensitivities, and 'managing diversity'. The production of the racialised subject in these exchanges and linkages as a result of these international endeavours is not a central concern for the profession premised on recognising the needs of the 'client' by allowing for individual self-determination, and advocacy for social justice and respect for human rights. In international social work, many students and academics are located in work sites which promote these values, but how can such values be critically analysed with a view to exposing the workings of power and dominance when there is no space to discuss and engage in how the history of imperialism, colonisation, and racism continues to impact on contemporary social work?

During the last few decades, 'subjugated' voices have become more centralised in intellectual and theoretical debates, which may enhance international social work. Developing countries are struggling to reclaim indigenous or local practices after being fed an exclusive diet of Western colonial knowledge (Gray et al., 2008; Webb, 2003). Traces of colonialism and imperialism linger, however, as there continues to be a flow of information about pedagogy and practice from industrial to developing nations. The dilemmas created by Western hegemony are not unique to developing countries for, even in large metropolitan cities where there is diversity, social work teachings and practices are largely devoid of analysis and awareness of global realities (Healy, 2000). The profession needs to facilitate critical thinking and awareness of how dominance is produced, organised, and sustained.

REFERENCES

Altbach, P. (2004). Globalization and the University: Myths and realities in an unequal world. *Tertiary Education and Management, 10*, 3–25.

Altbach, P. (2007). The imperial tongue: English as the dominating academic language. *International Higher Education, 49*(2), 2–4.

Asamoah, Y., Healy, L., & Mayadas, N. (1997). Ending the international–domestic dichotomy: New approaches of a global curriculum for the millennium. *Journal of Social Work Education, 33*, 389–401.

Bailey, A. (1998). Locating traitorous identities: Toward a view of privilege-cognizant white character. *Hypatia, 13*(3), 26–37.

Benjamin, A. (2003). *The Black/Jamaican criminal: The making of ideology.* Unpublished Ph.D., Ontario Institute for Studies in Education, University of Toronto, Canada.

Bloommaert, J., & Verschueren, J. (1998). *Debating diversity: Analysing the discourse of tolerance.* New York: Routledge.

Bonilla-Silva, E. (2000). 'This is a white country': The racial ideology of the Western nations of the world-system. *Sociological Inquiry, 70*(2), 188–214.

Canto, I., & Hannah, J. (2001). A partnership of equals? Academic collaboration between the United Kingdom and Brazil. *Journal of Studies in International Education, 5*(1), 26–41.

Campfens, H. (1996). Partnerships in international social development: Evolution in practice and concept. *International Social Work, 39*, 201–223.

Council of Social Work Education (1992). *Handbook of Accreditation Standards and Procedures.* (4th ed.). Alexandria, VA: CSWE.

Connell, R. (2007). *Southern Theory: The global dynamics of knowledge in social science.* Australia: Allen & Unwin.

Cox, D.R. (1995). Social development and social work education: The U.S.A.'s, continuing leadership in a changing world. *Social Development Issues, 17*(2/3), 1–18.

Delgado Bernal, D. (2002) Critical race theory, Latino critical theory, and critical raced-gendered epistemologies: Recognizing students of color as holders and creators of knowledge. *Qualitative Inquiry, 8*(1), 105–126.

Dominelli, L. (1998). *Anti racist social work: A challenge for white practitioners and educators.* Philadelphia: Temple University Press.

Esping-Andersen, G. (1990). *The three worlds of welfare capitalism.* Princeton, NJ: Princeton University Press.

Estes, R.J. (1992). *Internationalizing social work education: A guide for resources for a new century.* Philadelphia: University of Pennsylvania.

Fanon, F. (1963). *The wretched of the earth.* Harmondsworth: Penguin.

Frankenberg, R. (1993). *White women, race matters: The social construction of whiteness.* Minneapolis, MN: University of Minnesota Press.

Graham, J., Swift, K., & Delaney, R. (2000). *Canadian social policy: An Introduction.* Scarborough, Ontario: Prentice Hall.

Gray, M. (2005). Dilemmas of international social work: Paradoxical processes in indigenisation, imperialism and universalism. *International Journal of Social Welfare, 14*(2), 230–237.

Gray, M., Coates, J., & Yellow Bird, M. (2008). *Indigenous social work around the world: Towards culturally relevant education and practice.* Burlington, VT: Ashgate.

Gray, M., & Fook, J. (2004). The quest for a universal social work: Some issues and implications. *Social Work Education, 23*(5), 625–644.

Gray, M. & Rennie, G. (2007). International social work: Bodies with organs. *Aotearoa New Zealand Social Work Review, 19*(2), 42–58.

Gray, M., & Webb, S.A. (2008). The myth of global social work: Double standards and the local-global Divide. *Journal of Progressive Human Services, 19*(1), 61–66.

Grillo, R.D., & Stirrat, R.L. (eds), (1997). *Discourses on development: Anthropological perspectives.* New York: Oxford.

Hage, G. (2000). *White nation: Fantasies of white supremacy in a multicultural society.* New York: Routledge in association with Pluto Press.

Harding, S. (1991). *Whose science? Whose knowledge? Thinking from women's lives.* Ithaca, NY: Cornell University Press.

Haug, E. (2001). *Writing in the margins: Critical reflections on the emerging discourse of international social work.* Masters of Social Work thesis, Department of Social Work, Calgary, Alberta.

Haug, E. (2005). Critical reflections on the emerging discourse of international social work, *International Social Work, 48*(2), 126–135.

Healy, K. (2000). *Social work practices: Contemporary perspectives on change.* London: Sage.

Healy, L. (1988). Curriculum building in international social work: Toward preparing professionals for the global age. *Journal of Social Work Education, 24*(3), 221–228.

Healy, L. (1995). Comparative and international overview. In T. Watts, Elliott, D., & Mayadas, N. (eds), *International Handbook on Social Work Education.* Westport, CT: Greenwood Press.

Healy, L. (2001). *International social work: Professional action in an interdependent world.* New York: Oxford.

Healy, L. (2008). *International social work.* New York: Oxford University Press.

Heron, B. (1999). *Desire for development: The education of white women as development workers.* Unpublished Ph.D. thesis, Ontario Institute for Studies in Education, University of Toronto, Canada.

Heron, B. (2007). *Desire for development: Whiteness, gender and the helping imperative.* Waterloo, Ontario: Wilfrid Laurier Press.

Hick, S. (2002). *Social Work in Canada: An Introduction.* Toronto, ON: Thompson Educational Publishers.

Hokenstad, M.G., Khinduka, S.K., & J. Midgley (eds) (1992). *Profiles in international social work.* Washington, DC: NASW Press.

Holmes, T.R., & Matthews, G. (1993). Innovations in international cross-cultural social work education. *Arete, 18*(1) 43–47.

Hooks, B. (1995). *Killing rage: Ending racism.* New York: H. Holt and Company.

Jeffery, D.I. (2002). *A terrain of struggle: Reading race in social work education.* Unpublished doctoral dissertation, Department of Sociology and Equity Studies, OISE/University of Toronto.

Jolly, M. (2008). The South in *Southern Theory:* Antipodean Reflections on the Pacific. *Australian Humanities Review,* 44, March. Retrieved from http://www.australianhumanitiesreview.org/archive/Issue-March-2008/jolly.html?pagewanted-all

Kaplan, E.A. (1997). *Looking for the other: Feminism, film, and the imperial gaze.* New York: Routledge.

Kendall, K. (1978). *Reflections on social work education 1950–1978.* New York: International Association of Schools of Social Work.

Kendall, K. (1995). Foreword. In T. Watts, Elliott, D., & Mayadas, N. (eds), *International handbook on social work education.* Westport, CT: Greenwood Press, pp. xiii–xvii.

Kendall, K. (1998). *IASSW: The first fifty years 1928–1978 and a tribute to the founders.* Alexandra, VA: International Association of Schools of Social Work.

Kendall, K. (2000). *Social work education: Its origins in Europe.* Alexandria, VA: Council on Social Work Education.

Khan, P., & Dominelli, L. (2000). The impact of globalization on social work in the UK. *European Journal of Social Work, 3*(2), 95–108.

Krajewski-Jaime, E.R., Brown, K.S., Ziefert, M., & Kaufman, E. (1996). Utilizing international clinical practice to build inter-cultural sensitivity in social work students. *Journal of Multicultural Social Work, 4*(2), 15–30.

Lager, P., Mathiesen, A.G. Rodgers, M.E., & Cox, S.E. (2010). *Guidebook for international field placements and student exchange: Planning, implementation, and sustainability.* Alexandria, VA: Council on Social Work Education.

Lawrence, B. (2002). Rewriting histories of the land: Colonization and indigenous resistance in eastern Canada. In S. Razack (ed.), *Race, space and the law: Unmapping a white settler society.* Toronto, ON: Between the Lines, pp. 21–46.

Lentin, A. (2000). Race, racism and anti-racism: Challenging contemporary classifications. *Social Identities, 6*(1), 91–106.

Loomba, A. (1998) *Colonialism/postcolonialism: The new critical idiom.* New York: Routledge.

Lorenz, W. (2005). Social work and a new social order: Challenging neo-liberalism's erosion of solidarity. *Social Work and Society, 3*(1), 93–101.

Lyons, K. (1999). *International social work: Themes and perspectives.* Brookfield, VT: Ashgate.

Martinez-Brawley, E. (1999). Social work, postmodernism and higher education. *International Social Work, 4*(3), 333–346.

Midgley, J. (1981). *Professional imperialism: Social work in the third world.* London: Heineman.

Midgley, J. (1990). International social work: Learning about the Third World. *Social Work, 35*(4), 295–301.

Midgley, J. (1992). The challenge of international social work, In M.C. Hokenstad, Khinduka, S.K., & Midgley, J. (eds), *Profiles of international social work.* Washington, DC: NASW Press, pp. 13–27.

Midgley, J. (1997). *Social welfare in a global context.* California: Sage.

Midgley, J. (1999). Social development in social work: Learning from global dialogue. In C.S. Ramanathan & Link, R. (eds), *All our Futures: Principles and resources for social work practice in a global era.* Toronto, ON: ITP, pp. 193–205.

Midgley, J. (2000). Globalization, capitalism and social welfare: A social development perspective. *Canadian Social Work Review, 2*(1), 13–28.

Midgley, J. (2008). Promoting reciprocal international social work exchanges: Professional imperialism revisited. In Gray, M., Coates, J., & Yellow Bird, M. (2008). *Indigenous social work around the world: Towards culturally relevant education and practice.* Aldershot, Hants: Ashgate, pp. 31–48.

Mishra, R. (1999). *Globalization and the welfare state.* Cheltenham: Edward Elgar.

Mohan, B. (2005). New internationalism: Social work's dilemmas, dreams, and delusion. *International Social Work, 48*(3), 241–250.

Mwansa, L.K. (2011). Social work education in Africa: Whence and whiter? *Social Work Education, 30*(1), 4–16.

Paisley, F. (2002). Cultivating modernity: Culture and internationalism in Australian feminism's Pacific age. *Journal of Women's History, 14*(3), 105–132.

Park, H. (2005). Culture as deficit: A critical discourse analysis of the concept of culture in contemporary social work discourse. *Journal of Sociology and Social Welfare, 32*(3), 11–33.

Paton, G. (2010). Cash-strapped universities 'turning to foreign students'. *The Telegraph,* 27 July 2011. Retrieved July 28, 2011 from http://www.telegraph.co.uk/education/educationnews/7989155/Cash-strapped-universities-turning-to-foreign-students.html

Perry, P. (2001). White means never having to say you are ethnic: White youth and the construction of 'cultureless' other. *Journal of Contemporary Ethnography, 30*(1), 56–91.

Razack, N. (2002). Critical race discourse and tenets for social work. *Canadian Social Work Review, 19*(2), 257–271.

Razack, N. (2004). *Perils and possibilities: Racism, imperialism and nationalism in international social work.* Unpublished Ph.D. dissertation, School of Administration and Social Work, Flinders University, Adelaide, Australia.

Razack, N. (2005). Spatialized locations, identities and nationality in international work. *Social Justice: A Journal of Crime, Conflict and World Order, 32*(4), 87–104.

Razack, N. (2009). Decolonizing the pedagogy and practice of international work. *International Social Work, 52*(1), 7–19.

Razack, N., & Badwall, H. (2012). Professional Approaches: social work theories, methods and practices. In K. Lyons, Hokenstad, M.C. Huegler, N., & Pawar, M. (eds), *Handbook of International Social Work.* London: Sage.

Razack, N., & Jeffery, D. (2003). Critical race discourse and tenets for social work. *Canadian Social Work Review, 19*(2), 257–272.

Resnick, R. (1995). South America. In N. Mayadas, Watts, T., & Elliott, D. (eds), *International handbook of social work education.* Westport, CT: Greenwood Press.

Rodgers, M. (2004). The Christian context of international social work practice. *Social Work and Christianity*, *31*(2), 209–231.

Saadawi, N. El. (1997). *The Nawal El Saadawi reader*. New York: Zed.

Said, E.W. (1978). *Orientalism*. New York: Routledge.

Shohat, E. (1992). Notes on the post-colonial. *Social Texts*, *31/32*, 99–113.

Singh, P. (2011). *Destination unknown: A case study of the Ontario-Maharashtra-Goa Exchange (OMG) Program*. Master's thesis, Faculty of Education, York University.

Solorzano, D.G., & Yosso, T.J. (2002). Critical race methodology: Counter-storytelling an analytical framework for education research. *Qualitative Inquiry*, *8*(1), 23–44.

Spivak, G.C. (1999). *A critique of postcolonial reason: Toward a history of the vanishing present*. Cambridge, MA: Harvard University Press.

Stoesz, D., Guzzetta, C., & Lusk, M. (1999). *International development*. Toronto, ON: Allyn and Bacon.

Thompson, G. (1999). Situating globalization. *International Social Sciences Journal*, *160*, 139–152.

Tsang, K.T., Yan, M.C., & Shera, W. (2000). Negotiating multiple agendas in international social work: The case of the China–Canada collaborative project. Social Work and Globalization. *Canadian Social Work Review*, *17*, 147–161.

Webb, S.A. (2003). Local Orders and Global Chaos in Social Work. *European Journal of Social Work*, *6*(2), 191–204.

Webb, S.A. (2007). The comfort of strangers: The emergence of social work in late Victorian England (Part One). *European Journal of Social Work*, *10*(1), 39–54.

Weedon, C. (1999). *Feminism, theory and the politics of difference*. Oxford: Blackwell Publishers Ltd. 152–177.

Whitmore, E., & Wilson, M. (1997). Accompanying the process: Social work and international development practice. *International Social Work*, *40*(1), 57–74.

Wilensky, H.L., & Lebeaux, C.N. (1958). *Industrial society and social welfare: The impact of industrialization on the supply and organization of social welfare services in the United States*. New York: Russell Sage Foundation.

Williams, C. (1999). Connecting anti-racist and anti-oppressive theory and practice: Retrenchment or appraisal? *British Journal of Social Work*, *29*, 211–230.

Williams, P., & Chrisman, L. (eds) (1994). *Colonial discourse and post-colonial theory: A reader*. New York: Columbia University Press.

Woolf, M. (2007). Impossible thinkings before breakfast: Myths in education abroad. *Journal of Studies in International Education*, *11*(3/4), 496–509.

Ziguras, C. (2009). Indian students in Australia: How did it come to this? *Global Higher Education blog*. http://globalhighered.wordpress.com/2009/08/11/indian-students-in-australia-how-did-it-come-to-this/

Social Work in 'Developing' Countries

Kwaku Osei-Hwedie and Morena J. Rankopo

The idea of social work as a formal helping system to improve the well-being of individuals, families, groups, communities, and societies is now widely accepted across the globe. Social work, however defined, is recognised as a formal approach to address the personal and social problems of individuals, families, groups, and communities. Social work practice and education was generally exported from Western contexts, mainly from the UK and USA, to other parts of the world (Askeland & Payne, 2006; Hokenstad & Midgley, 1997; Kendall, 1995, 2000; Midgley, 2001; Mwansa, 2011; Yuen-Tsang & Ho, 2007). Social work education across the world has been, and continues to be, dominated by modern Western knowledge, which has, to a large extent, ignored and displaced developing nations' indigenous knowledge systems (Gray & Coates, 2008; Gray et al., 2008). However, debates over an appropriate social work knowledge and skill base compatible with culturally relevant educational curricula and practice models have intensified over the past two decades (Gray et al., 2008; Nimmagadda & Balgopal, 2000; Osei-Hwedie & Rankopo, 2011; Yan & Cheung, 2006). The search for culturally appropriate, indigenous social work practice and education is a complex undertaking given the lack of resources in developing countries, which makes it difficult to evolve innovative curricula departing from dominant modernist Western models. This is further complicated by the dynamics of neoliberal globalisation and its associated pressures for the universalisation and internationalisation of social work education and practice (Gray & Webb, 2008; Gray et al., 2008; Midgley, 2001). Whereas the immediate task has been to make social work meaningful to practitioners and clients, cognisance must be taken of transitions in the international arena with respect to knowledge, skills, theories, and practice models, since social work in developing contexts generally is, albeit sometimes reluctantly, part of the global social work family.

Social work expanded to the developing countries, now often referred to in the international social work discourse as the South, mainly through the technical assistance provided by developed countries, now commonly known as the North (Kendall, 1995, 2000).

It is interesting to note Raewyn Connell's *Southern Theory* (2007) which maps the geopolitical divisions between North and South in terms of knowledge production and transfer. She constructs a 'world picture' to identify cardinal points of cartography as illustrative of inequalities between people, states, and ethnicities within the North-South divide. This reveals a sharp divide which stresses the relationality of changing contexts in terms of power and knowledge across time and space, with the South often featuring as little more than a source of data collection for Northern researchers, rather than a site for meaningful, self-conscious reflection in its own right. The expansion of social work was made possible because educators in the developed countries of the North, particularly the USA and UK, had access to resources necessary to provide technical assistance to the developing countries of the South (Gray et al., 2008). Consequently, the English language became the dominant language used in global social work education. Thus, the term 'social work' is commonly defined in English and translated into other languages across the world. According to Kendall (1995), the first technical assistance project of the US government was in social work education when 15 directors of schools of social work from South America were brought to the USA for a training tour of social work educational institutions. This project was led by the Department of State, the Children's Bureau, and the (North) American Association of Schools of Social Work and its success led to similar initiatives in Africa and Asia. Moreover, the United Nations is recognised for spreading social work through awarding international scholarships to students from the developing countries and engaging US academicians to assist in the establishment of schools of social work in the South. The United Nations supported the Association of Schools of Social Work Education in Africa which led to debates on the indigenisation of social work education on the continent (United Nations, 1969, 1971).

Social work expanded rapidly over the 20th century due to improved international relations across the globe. Governments of many developing countries rapidly put in place formal social welfare systems in their effort to address social and economic debt. New technologies and global institutions facilitated the growth of social work in developing countries (Kendall, 1995; Lin & Wang, 2010; Midgley, 2000, 2008; Mwansa, 2011; Yuen & Ho, 2007). Although the exact number of qualified social workers may not be known, Midgley estimated there were 1700 professional schools of social work in over 100 countries across the world in the mid-1990s. This was a huge leap from 46 schools in ten countries in 1929; 373 schools in 46 countries in 1950; and 459 schools in 66 countries in 1975 (Midgley, 2001, p. 23). Writing before the South African International Association of Schools of Social Work (IASSW) and International Federation of Social Workers (IFSW) Conference of 2008, Healy (not dated) stated that there were 'members in more than 70 countries spread across all the inhabited continents' (p.11). In 2010, Japan (82) and South Africa (19) had the most registered members in Asia and Africa, respectively (IASSW 2010).

The chapter begins with a discussion of the history of social work education and practice in Asia and Africa generally, and the specific evolution of social work education and practice in Botswana. Whereas the Botswana case study may not sufficiently represent the development of social work in Asia and Africa, it outlines adequately the prospects and problems in ongoing efforts to localise social work practice and education in a globalising environment. That is what Webb (2003) referred to as the need to maintain the emphasis on local orders of encumbered practice in social work given the ensuing push to meet global agendas and fashions. The chapter further highlights theoretical and conceptual issues relevant to debates on the cultural relevance of social work education and practice in Africa and Asia.

THE HISTORY OF SOCIAL WORK IN AFRICA AND ASIA

Social work as a formal discipline started in Europe and North America over a century ago. Its roots have been traced to the activities of philanthropists, missionaries, and volunteers for charity organisation societies, state boards of charity, and settlement houses (Brieland et al., 1985; Kendall, 2000). Early social work interventions viewed social problems from a Judeo-Christian and bourgeois value perspective, which emphasised limitations or deficiencies within the individuals or communities in which they lived as the root cause of social problems with personal problems resulting from individuals' failure to take advantage of opportunities in their social environment (Ambrosino et al., 2005; Bloom, 1990). Social work in the developing countries of Africa and Asia was generally imported from their colonial masters in the first quarter of the 20th century and, as such, did not emerge from existing – local or national – socioeconomic and political conditions of the times (Gray et al., 2008; Kendall, 1995, 2000; Midgley, 2000; Yuen-Tsang & Ho, 2007). Social work education was adopted to facilitate the civilisation and improvement of the living conditions of the natives (Lin & Wang, 2010; Mwansa, 2011) and to take control of as many territories as possible for the economic advancement of the colonial powers (Sachs, 2005). As part of the colonising process, missionaries played a critical role in spreading social work to the developing countries. In addition to preaching and converting the 'heathens', they were involved in exploration of minerals and sent information to the colonial powers. Further, they were instrumental in developing rudimentary formal basic social services, such as primary schools, health clinics, hospitals, and social welfare institutions (Kendall, 2000; Midgley, 1981; Mwansa, 2011; Rea Zambesia, 1970).

In Asia, social work education was founded first in China in 1922 followed by India in 1925 (Kendall, 2000). According to Kendall (2000), while China was the pioneer of social work in Asia, the discipline which had been launched at the Yenching University (formerly located in Peiping) was short lived as it was wiped out by the communist regime. Thus, social work in China, unlike in India, did not have any lasting value and, as such, India is widely recognised as the founder of social work education in Asia. The Bachelor of Arts in social work at Yenching was founded by a North American social worker, Ida Pruitt, and focused on training hospital workers. The curriculum contained a mix of sociology and social work courses with a dominant North American influence. The combination of sociology and social work became the dominant model in most other Asian countries.

In the case of India, the roots of social work are traced to a North American missionary, Clifford Manshardt, the founder of the Tata Institute. Guided by his Christian values, he established the Nagpada Neighbourhood House, which brought together diverse races in a low-income settlement to promote a spirit of brotherhood, and breakdown racial and social class barriers, and was later transformed into the Tata Institute of Social Sciences where a graduate social work programme was launched in 1936. Manshardt became the founding director of the institute assisted by Dr J.M. Kamurappa, an Indian educated at Columbia University in New York. The curriculum drew on a strong British model of social sciences, India being a British colony, with a strong North American influence in social work. However, the curriculum varied from the British and North American models in the sense that it introduced labour welfare workers based on the unique experiences of rapid industrialisation in India.

In Taiwan, the first social work programme was launched in 1954 as a two-year course known as the 'social administrative programme' in the Department of Sociology (Lin & Wang, 2010, p. 870). Throughout the 1950s and 1960s, there was an inadequate supply of qualified social work educators, resulting in little professional social work content in existing social work programmes. Most courses were taught by sociology faculty. As the country transformed from an agricultural to industrialising economy, poverty became a major social issue to the government resulting in the launch of community development. The pioneer of community development in Taiwan in the 1960s, Mr Chang Hon-Chiung, was educated in the USA. The first 15 graduates of the Research and Training Centre of Community Development were sent to the USA, the Netherlands, and the UK for further advanced training in social work. This marked the beginning of professional social work education. The 1970s witnessed the transformation of social work education as more social work content was added to existing programmes and eventually a fully fledged social work degree programme was launched in 1979 at Tunghai University. Many universities followed suit with the introduction of departments of social work with separate curricula and enrolments from sociology. This was a milestone in the professionalisation of social work in Taiwan (Lin & Wang, 2010).

According to Kendall (2000), the first social work education programme in Africa was launched in South Africa in 1924 at the University of Cape Town and Transvaal University College followed by the University of Pretoria in 1929. This was a three-year diploma course modelled after the British social studies programme with more social science content, particularly sociology, than social work. It was followed by a degree programme at the University of Stellenbosch in 1939. Initially, some universities encouraged the admission of all races but this later changed as the White minority government legalised racial discrimination. The Jan van Hofmeyer School of Social Work established in Johannesburg in 1941 is recognised as the first school to promote the training of non-White South Africans (Gray, 2000). A North American missionary, Dr Ray Phillips, who held a Ph.D. from Yale University, was the founder of the school. During the apartheid era, there were separate social work educational institutions for Black and White South Africans.

According to Mwansa (2011), Egypt was the second country to adopt social work education in 1936 followed by Algeria in 1942, Ghana in 1945, Zambia in 1950, Uganda in 1954, Tanzania in 1958, Ethiopia in 1959, Upper Volta (now Burkina Faso) in 1960, and Tunisia and Zimbabwe in 1964. Other countries followed in the 1960s and early 1970s. In Botswana, social work education started as a two-year certificate in social welfare and community development at the Botswana Agricultural College through the influence of the United Nations. The programme was transferred to the University of Botswana in the 1985–1986 academic year with the introduction of the one-year certificate, two-year diploma, and four-year Bachelor of Social Work, respectively (Department of Social Work, 1985).

THE EVOLUTION OF SOCIAL WORK IN BOTSWANA

Country profile

Formerly Bechuanaland Protectorate (1885–1965), Botswana is a landlocked country covering 581,730 square kilometres in the Southern African subcontinent. Its neighbours are South Africa to the south, Namibia to the west, Angola to the north-west, Zambia to the north, and Zimbabwe to the east. Almost two-thirds of the land is occupied by the Kalahari Desert. The current population is estimated to be about 2 million people with 61% residing in urban areas (CIA World Factbook, 2011). Botswana gained independence on the 30 September 1966 following democratic elections. The last general elections were held in 2009 at which the ruling Botswana Democratic Party maintained the uninterrupted rule it has enjoyed since independence. There are currently four opposing political parties with a splinter faction of the ruling party, the

Botswana Movement for Democracy, being the current Leader of the Opposition (CIA World Factbook, 2011). Botswana has sustained rapid economic growth over the past three decades.

At independence, the country was among the 25 poorest countries in the world but the situation changed drastically following the discovery of minerals, especially diamonds (Edge, 1998). By 2001, about 54% of the population lived in the urban areas, mainly due to employment opportunities, given recurrent droughts in the rural areas. Botswana is currently a middle-income country, according to the United Nations classification (Rankopo et al., 2007). The greatest challenge is the high HIV and AIDS prevalence with an adult prevalence rate of 23%. Women are twice as vulnerable to HIV infection as men. However, due to effective national HIV and AIDS interventions, annual surveillance reports indicate that HIV prevalence among pregnant women aged 15–49 years dropped from 38.2% in 2001 to 32.4% in 2006. In 2009, the national HIV prevalence stood at 17.3% (National AIDS Coordinating Agency (NACA), 2009). Poverty is another issue for social work in Botswana, and social workers are associated with the registration of destitute persons and the distribution of food rations and clothes to the needy (Hedenquist, 1992).

Prior to contact with colonialists, traditional welfare services were provided within a communitarian context with households supporting each other in times of need. Poor members of the community were assisted by affluent members through institutionalised systems, such as the *mafisa*, through which, for example, those rich in cattle loaned livestock to those who had none. The chief, the highest political authority, occasionally collected levies from his subjects to be used for public undertakings and sustenance of communities in times of famine and drought (Mwansa et al., 1998; Osei-Hwedie, 1994a). Thus, until the 1800s, the economy of Tswana societies was based on extensive cattle and food crop production supplemented by hunting (Parsons, 1984). This agrarian and close-knit community lifestyle was destined to change when the British arrived in 1885 and the British Protectorate of Bechuanaland was formed under the leadership of three *dikgosi* (kings/chiefs) Bathoen I, Sechele II, and Khama III. This era also marked the beginning of contact between the Batswana and missionaries. Notable among them was David Livingstone who started primary schools and health services in the Kweneng region. In the Bangwato region, King Khama III, for example:

> was steadfast in imposing his Christianized will on the tribe. He banned alcohol from tribal lands (with varying success), put moratoriums on the sale of cattle outside the Bamangwato territory and tribal land as concessions to foreign mining and cattle interests, and abolished polygamy. The abolition of polygamy was perhaps his most controversial move. Some argue that as Christianity later spread among the other tribes of the protectorate and polygamy was universally abolished, the societal 'glue' that kept families together (extended as they were through polygamy) dried up (http://en.wikipedia.org/wiki/Khama_III).

British colonisation, with the complicity of Khama III (circa 1837–1923 whose grandson – Sir Seretse Khama – became the first president of the Republic of Botswana at the end of the colonial period in 1966), marked the beginning of a process of rapid sociocultural, political, and economic change in Tswana society (Mwansa et al., 1998). Despite Bechuanaland's strategic importance for British expansion from South Africa to the north, the country did not offer any significant economic opportunities. British interests focused mainly on South Africa and territories to the north, including Southern and Northern Rhodesia.

Social services, such as education and health, were basic and rudimentary, and mainly provided by tribal organisations through local initiatives – *mephato* (different age regiments) and *dikgosi* (chiefs). According to Osei-Hwedie (1997), during this period, indigenous volunteerism and mutual aid were the key avenues to service provision and whatever services were provided did not develop into a coherent system of social provision countrywide. According to Wass (1969), the first welfare officer, Jack Leech, was appointed in 1946 to administer welfare services for war veterans, the destitute, juveniles, and to form youth clubs. The Welfare Unit was located in the Department of Education. In the 1960s, welfare officers were appointed to work in the slums of Lobatse and Francistown, focusing on their unsanitary conditions. In the early 1960s, the colonial government gradually recognised the importance of community development in rural areas. Thus, in 1963, the government piloted community development and, in 1964, sent six locals for training in Tanzania with the support of the United Nations (Wass, 1969).

From community development to social work education

Initial training of social workers was in community development offered at the Botswana Agricultural College from 1972 to 1984. In 1974, a few social work courses were offered in the community development curriculum, and the programme was renamed a certificate in social welfare and community development (Hedenquist, 1992). Ngwenya (1992) called this a marriage of convenience, leading to social work being subsumed under community development and losing its critical identity until 1985, when training in social work began at the University of Botswana with three programmes: a two-year certificate, a two-year diploma, and a four-year degree in social work. The certificate programme, until its termination in 2001–2002, was a paraprofessional training programme for assistant social workers. Initially, it was a two-year programme between 1985 and 1994 and targeted junior secondary school leavers. It was later revised to a one-year programme in the 1994–1995 academic year and enrolled senior secondary school leavers but was discontinued in 2002 when the university resolved to terminate all certificate programmes. The Diploma in Social Work is a two-year programme targeting senior secondary school graduates with a pass in English and mathematics. Both of these were stand-alone programmes. The Bachelor of Social Work is a four-year programme targeting senior secondary school graduates with a credit in English and mathematics. A two-year master's degree in social work (MSW) was introduced in 1999 and has produced 50 graduates since 2001 (University of Botswana, 1985, 2010).

All of these programmes offer content on social work methods, a small fraction of social science courses, block fieldwork placements, and general elective courses or electives (as required by university rules). For a time, the certificate and diploma programmes offered home economics as a core course, since social workers were required to work with women's groups to promote small enterprises, but there were subsequently dropped when the Diploma in Home Economics and B.Ed. (Home Economics) programmes were introduced' (Tummala, 1995). In addition, the BSW programme has annual seminars on diverse topics such as globalisation and social work, diversity, disaster management, adoption and fostercare, and human rights (University of Botswana, 2009).

The process of transforming social work training and education was long and sometimes rapid. One of the authors of this chapter, Morena Rankopo, was a pioneer of the BSW programme in 1985–1986. At the time, it was more of a Bachelor of Arts in Social Work with social work content accounting for about 50%, while sociology accounted for most of the remainder. A British Professor, Malcolm J. Brown, a clinical social work educator, was recruited as founding head of department from Queens University (Belfast, Ireland) in 1986. He immediately reviewed the curriculum and, by the following year, a completely new programme was launched and subsequently renamed the Bachelor of Social Work degree. This curriculum review was participatory as students and other stakeholders were involved in the process.

Africanisation of social work

A major curriculum review was undertaken under the leadership of Dolly Ntseane between 1989 and 1991 following the recruitment of more African faculty. Notable among these was one of the authors of this chapter, Professor Kwaku Osei-Hwedie. A Ghanaian, educated in the USA, he later became a leading writer on the indigenisation of social work in Africa. His passion to Africanise the social work curriculum was a product of his personal and professional reflection on the appropriateness of universal social work education and the tensions between Western social work knowledge as espoused in mainly North American and British textbooks in use at the time and the realities of social development in Africa (Osei-Hwedie, 1990). Second, the curriculum review make further critical exploration possible enhanced by his work with the Institute of Indigenous Theory and Practice in Cape Town in the mid-1990s (Osei-Hwedie, 1994b), and later the Joint Universities Committee of social work educators in South Africa (Osei-Hwedie, 1995) and the Association of South African Social Work Education Institutions (ASASWEI) until his retirement in 2010. At the same time, the University of Botswana benefited from a staff exchange programme through a Canadian International Development partnership that saw the recruitment of Canadian Professor Miriam Hutton, an expert on curriculum design and accreditation processes in North America. Hutton was very receptive to developing an African social work curriculum and provided leadership to develop developmental social work programmes at the University of Botswana (see Hutton, 1992; Hutton & Mwansa, 1996).

Dilemmas in seeking acceptance, recognition, and cultural relevance

The curriculum review in 1999–2000, when the University of Botswana semesterised its academic programmes, saw culturally relevant social work education entrenched, despite the difficult journey arising from the tensions within the university to develop internationally recognised yet locally relevant education programmes (University of Botswana, 1999). Social work education in Botswana, as part of community development or a fully fledged professional programme, had struggled for acceptance and recognition by the government, practitioners, and academics alike. The graduates of the social and community development programme were seen as not having the necessary skills for practice, unsure of their duties and procedures, with their skills being vague and unfocused (Republic of Botswana, 1978). The post-1984 social work curriculum was deemed irrelevant by practitioners and some local academicians, who preferred a stronger community development focus and more African content. Ngwenya (1992) referred to 'the agony of irrelevance' and lamented the lack of strategic curriculum development associated with social work's role and identity crisis. Fellow academics agreed (Hutton, 1994; Lucas, 1993; Raditlhokwa, 1993). Lucas (1993), educated at the University of Regina in Canada, believed social work did not challenge the State about the problems created by societal structures and environmental conditions. Raditlhokwa (1993), educated at Carlton University in Canada, accused social work of 'professional elitism', seeing it as a politically conservative, state-dominated and controlled activity perpetuating oppressive policies and programmes and structural inequalities while serving the interests of the elite. Hutton (1994) saw social work in Botswana as out of step with local needs, inflexible, and not easily adaptable to change. It focused exclusively on meeting individual needs in an environment where community was the basis of social living.

Against the backdrop of these severe critiques of social work in Botswana, academics at the University of Botswana endeavoured to reshape social work education and practice. From the criticisms levelled at social work education, it became abundantly clear there was a need for a culturally relevant curriculum developed out of, and in harmony with, local needs. However, the problem was how to design and implement such a programme and make society, in general, and academics and students, in particular, understand the necessity to change the nature of social work as a profession: What should social work be responding to on the ground and what teaching materials would be suitable given the criticisms of the foreign sources in use? Hence curriculum change flowed from the assumption that foreign knowledge and theory was not appropriate and, in the absence of local materials, teaching was to be guided by the experiences of academics, students, and practitioners. Further, community was to be the basis for curriculum organisation along with the inclusion and integration of cultural issues in social work courses (Hutton, 1994; Osei-Hwedie, 1997). Thus efforts toward cultural relevance began in Batswana social work in the early 1990s. At this time, the connection with South African universities became highly strategic and fruitful.

South Africa was going through transformation to a new sociopolitical dispensation and, globally, the theory of social development was growing, spurred on in social work by the work of James Midgley (see Gray, 2006; Gray & Lombard, 2008). The new dispensation in South Africa in the post-apartheid era gave academics in Botswana a 'reference point and a support base for a new social development orientation' (Osei-Hwedie & Rankopo, 2008, p. 211). The shift in emphasis from the individual to the community – based on the idea that social and physical environments, and related conditions and structures must be the basis of any meaningful social work education and practice – spurred on the quest for cultural relevance in social work. This was connected to social conditions exacerbated by HIV and AIDS, abject poverty, disease, illiteracy and ignorance, inequality and lack of economic opportunity, rapid social change, especially rapid urbanisation and changing family systems, and recurrent drought (Osei-Hwedie & Rankopo, 2008). However, the process of making social work culturally relevant was not easy for several reasons.

First, there were pressures from university management, academics, and students who wanted their programmes and qualifications to be externally accredited and internationally recognised (Osei-Hwedie et al., 2006). The university authorities wanted the programmes to be internationally competitive, while academics wanted international recognition and students wanted internationally marketable knowledge and skills (Osei-Hwedie & Rankopo, 2008). If this were to happen, social work education would have to conform to European and North American standards. Second, apart from South Africa and Zimbabwe, there were no efforts in other African countries to change social work education radically. Whereas there was sympathy for changes in post-apartheid South Africa, many people did not see the need for 'radical change' in politically stable Botswana. Third, the approved curriculum was a compromise. In most instances, course titles, outlines, and content also had to satisfy regional and international requirements, and reflect wider knowledge and needs. Fourth, there was also serious debate among social work academics on the overall importance of cultural relevance and the necessity for comprehensive local content. Some contended that courses should be taught from standard Western textbooks with reference to African or Batswana cultures whenever necessary. This was contrary to the initial position taken to emphasise the local. In the long run, courses on helping and problem solving were not based on local knowledge, values, skills, and experiences but assumed social work methods were universal. Thus, the local focus became secondary. Lastly, the development of culturally relevant social work was a dynamic, politically charged process. As members of the social work board, we were alive to these undercurrents. Vested interests and power plays had to be reckoned with. From its inception, there were fierce battles due to the cultural diversity of the social work academic team representing two major influences, North American and British social work education. The goal of the university to win international recognition pushed the social work programme to resemble, as closely as possible, social work programmes in North America and Europe. This view was also supported by students who believed that they could use for employment or further study overseas. Thus, the university management looked to North America to provide leadership on the reformulation of the curriculum. Professor Miriam Hutton, from the University of Manitoba in Canada, was recruited through the University of Manitoba–University of Botswana exchange programme to lead the exercise from 1991 to 1995. Politics emerged in the quest to reformulate the certificate, diploma, and BSW programmes and make them more relevant to the African context. Some African staff members teamed up against the Canadian professor, whom they feared would further Americanise the programmes. However, other colleagues were quite comfortable with her as they believed her vast experience from Canada would enhance international recognition of the programme. At that time, there were also Fulbright scholars from the USA who influenced junior staff to look to the USA as a model of social work. After all, most of the textbooks used at the time were from the USA. There was preference for Professor Osei-Hwedie to lead the department, as it was believed that he would be better placed to reshape the curriculum as he had shown interest in the indigenisation debate. But he had just been recruited and was reluctant to enter the political fray despite the strong push toward localisation within the University. The experience showed that the development of culturally relevant social work education and practice requires flexibility, politicking, patience, and the willingness to compromise. In the case of Botswana, the final outcome fulfils the university's strategic interests aimed at international recognition.

One of the issues in international recognition is accreditation. Since Botswana has no social work council or board, there is no formal national authority accrediting social work educational programmes. There is only one university offering social work, which makes it impossible to have inter-university discussions on national social work education. This has also made it necessary to look to South Africa, with its highly developed social work sector in the region, for cooperation, direction, and guidance. Botswana has been admitted as a full member of the Association of South African Social Work Education Institutions (ASASWEI), and through this body, a member of the International Association of Schools of Social Work (IASSW). There are continuing formal discussions as to how the University of Botswana's social work programmes might be accredited by the South African Council of Social Service Professions regulating social work or another internationally recognised body.

While graduates from the University of Botswana BSW and MSW continue to gain entry to universities across the world for postgraduate study, problems arise when graduates seek jobs in those countries due to the non-accreditation of these programmes. Even though few graduates seek jobs in North America and Europe, employers want the programmes to conform to the standards set by international regulating bodies. Culturally relevant social work assumes local programmes must satisfy local needs first. The problem, though, is that satisfying local needs de-emphasises the international dimension, thereby creating problems for international recognition and accreditation. A case in point is a European country that does not recognise the University of Botswana's social work degrees, since they do not conform to that country's social work education model. In an attempt to rectify this, guidance was sought on how Botswana's programmes might gain recognition in that country in particular, and Europe in general. The response was an agency familiar with accreditation standards would undertake a consultancy, at a handsome fee in local terms, to study Botswana's programmes and advise on what was needed to meet the accreditation standards of that country. At the time of writing, no final decision had been taken owing to financial constraints, even though the university encourages such accreditation. The implication is, for such an accreditation to be formally granted, the programme must have the course content required and dictated by the external body, a representative of Western imperialism.

THEORETICAL DEFINITIONS AND CONCEPTS OF CULTURAL APPROPRIATENESS

Cultural relevance and indigenisation in social work

Developing nations in Africa and Asia continue to seek solutions to poverty, chronic disease, urbanisation, unemployment, inequality, and a lack of economic opportunities. However, despite massive socioeconomic investments and political development aimed at modernisation, about half of the population are poor and remain economically deprived, politically marginalised, and generally ill-fed, ill-housed, undereducated, and extremely vulnerable to preventable diseases, such as HIV and AIDS, and malaria. Against that backdrop, scholars are searching for culturally relevant ways to tackle these problems to improve the welfare of people (see Gray et al., 2008).

For a long time, Western values and ideas have dominated the development discourse irrespective of culturally embedded African and Asian values and ideas. Scholars in developing countries maintain that, in a globalising world, societies need to develop and sustain their local knowledge, values, and resources as the basis for maintaining their comparative advantage in competing with others, and for their own development (Mangaliso, 2005; Osei-Hwedie, 2005; Osei-Hwedie & Rankopo, 2008). Hence, as Osei-Hwedie and Rankopo (2008) note, in relation to Botswana, culturally embedded qualities, values, and forms of social provision, are a critical resource for social development.

Midgley (1983) is widely recognised as one of the pioneers of indigenisation as a way of countering professional imperialism in developing nations. He defined indigenisation as 'appropriateness' arguing 'professional social work roles must be *appropriate* to the needs of different countries and social work practice' (p. 170 emphasis added). Osei-Hwedie (1996a, 1997) extended this notion beyond the idea of development addressing local needs Osei-Hwedie (1996a, 1997) extended this notion beyond the idea of development addressing local needs and extended it to the creation of culturally appropriate social work education and practice. Hence social work knowledge, values, norms, philosophies, and procedures should arise within local contexts rather than be applied from outside – as had been the case for much of social work's development in Africa and Asia. More recently, the language has changed from indigenisation to *cultural relevance* in social work education and practice across the world (Gray et al., 2008, emphasis added). Hence the IFSW included the notion of cultural relevance in its revised definition of social work noting 'Indigenous knowledge' refers to 'the critical importance of shaping social work to suit economic and *cultural realities*, particularly in developing countries' (Hare, 2004, p. 416, emphasis added). Essentially, indigenisation means locally determined and culturally relevant social work practice rather than homogenised 'one-size-fits-all' models, which may not satisfy all cultural contexts and solve unique socioeconomic problems (Osei-Hwedie & Rankopo, 2008).

It must be noted, however, while the notion of 'culturally relevant social work practice and education' is most widely preferred (see Gray et al., 2008; Hart, 2009; Rankopo & Osei-Hwedie, 2011; Rehklau & Lutz, 2007), over the years, others have used related terms, such as localisation, authentisation, radicalisation, re-conceptualisation, normalisation, and conscientisation to clarify the meaning of indigenisation (Alfero, 1973; Costa, 1987; Gray et al., 2008; Kendall, 1973; Osei-Hwedie, 1996b; Resnic, 1976; Walton & Abo El Nasr, 1988; Webb, 2003). Basically, in this discourse, indigenisation is seen as a process of *localisation*, which is thought to be achieved more easily from the ground up through grassroots participation rather than from the top down through the imposition of Western theories and models totally foreign to local cultural contexts. *Authentisation*, on the other hand, sees indigenisation as focusing on local knowledges and resources, and processes rooted solely in local systems, with the implication authentic approaches are consequently original and culturally relevant and vice versa (Osei-Hwedie, 1996).

Radicalisation is associated with social work shedding its liberal character of promoting piecemeal reforms and adopting an approach allowing for the comprehensive transformation of oppressive and socially exclusive practices (Mupedziswa, 1992; Mwansa, 1992). It frequently embodies techniques of re-conceptualisation, normalisation, and conscientisation befitting the radical review and reframing of Western social work theories, concepts, models, and processes based on Paulo Freire's (1970) adult education model. The reformulation of Western knowledge, concepts, values, and philosophies to bring them into alignment with the developmental and empowerment efforts of poor and marginalised peoples is the focus of *re-conceptualisation*. Mupedziswa (1992) contends it focuses on rethinking, restructuring, and strengthening social work practice by adapting and merging local and foreign ideas.

These concepts are not mutually exclusive and interweave to describe various attempts to support the development of culturally relevant social work practice and education, as well as research and knowledge development. Despite diverse attempts at indigenisation, however, it has proved difficult for scholars to agree on what, exactly, constitutes culturally relevant African social work, or what indigenised social work in developing countries in general might look like. Nevertheless, the wholesale importation of social work from the North to the South has brought about the need for 'restructuring' and 'repositioning' in relation to local needs and, in the process, 'relevance' has become a battleground for academics. One dissenter observes local social workers' discomfort with terms like 'appropriateness' and 'relevance', since attempts at 'localisation' are seen as contrary to individuals' and society's wish to modernise, industrialise, and compete in an economically globalised world (Bar-On, 2003). Without its connection to the 'local' (Gray & Allegritti, 2002, 2003), the notion of 'cultural relevance' might be seen as stemming from social work's humanistic, homogenising tendencies and its assumption that, as a science of professional practice based on human rights, the profession can be globalised (Osei-Hwedie & Rankopo, 2008). Despite the acceptance of indigenisation or cultural relevance in social work, some authors are either uncomfortable with it or reject the notion that indigenous people prefer locally relevant to Western forms of social work education and practice (for further discussion of the debate on indigenisation, see Bar-On, 2003; Gray, 2010; Gray & Coates, 2010; Yunong & Xiong, 2008). This ambivalence runs throughout the social work literature. However, despite dissenting views, the notion of 'cultural appropriateness' is helpful in developing social work as a problem-solving framework in developing countries with their unique cultures, needs, institutional structures, and patterns of social relationships. For example, many cultures in developing countries, Botswana included, are communalistic and find fulfilment in the broader community context. Thus, social work in developing countries should focus on community development approaches, since communities carry a great deal of importance, rather than on the individualistic casework method. Thus the domain of social work must be the values, norms, social processes, and relationships of diverse local communities and cultures in which local culturally relevant social work approaches must be grounded (Gray et al., 2008; Nagpaul, 1993; Nimmagadda & Balgopal, 2000; Osei-Hwedie, 1996b; Sin, 2008; Tsang & Yan, 2001).

INTERNATIONALISATION, GLOBALISATION, AND UNIVERSALISATION

Despite all these positive developments in the evolution of the social work profession in the developing countries of Africa and Asia, the global development of social work is facing many challenges, namely, internationalisation, globalisation, and universalisation (Gray, 2005; Midgley, 2001). The primary goal of international social work is to transfer social work methods or knowledge between countries (Barker, 2003); spread the idea of social work as a profession; and promote the exchange of staff to practice social work in different parts of the world (Hokenstad, 1992; Midgley, 1992). Proponents of international social work contend, since social work involves scientific inquiry, it has common elements that should be identified and maintained across the world. Humanitarian agencies that provide emergency relief services also help promote the idea of helping people across diverse cultures and geographical locations. However, international social work is not a neutral process but has serious imperialistic tendencies (Gray, 2005; Nagpaul, 1993; Healy, 2001). The indigenisation literature has demonstrated that the transfer of social work knowledge between countries is heavily dominated by the Western academics of mainly the UK and USA. Proponents of internationalism have 'the implicit assumption that developing countries were incapable of finding their own models, resulting in indigenous forms of social care being 'silenced, devalued, displaced, ignored, made invisible, and disqualified' (Gray, 2005, p. 235). As Midgley (1992) correctly argues, 'it is time to challenge the one-way international flow of ideas and practices and to learn from the Third World' (p. 300). This can be achieved when social work educators and practitioners from the developed and developing countries enter into reciprocal staff exchange programmes where genuine learning can take place between social workers in the two global regions (Midgley, 2008). He cautions that there would still be barriers as 'some social workers with considerable expertise and experience in international social work find it difficult to accept that they can learn from colleagues in what are sometimes describes as "underdeveloped" countries' (Midgley, 2008, p. 43). Related to internationalisation, are debates on how social work should respond to the consequences of globalisation which have altered the contexts within which social work operates as well as its values and roles (Ife, 2001; Khan & Dominelli, 2000; Midgley, 2000).

Globalisation refers to 'a process of rapidly increasing human interactions within a "one-world" system that transcends previous political, spatial and temporal boundaries' (Midgley, 2001, p. 26). While there may be positive gains associated with globalisation, social work writers have shown, to a large extent, globalisation has led to the marketisation of social services based on business ethics that have eroded a commitment to care; technocratisation that has replaced professionalism to serve the needy in societies; and the deprofessionalisation of social work and loss of professional control over its affairs (Dominelli, 1999; Midgley, 2001; Yuen & Ho, 2007). Further, neoliberal globalism has compromised the ability of most national states to develop appropriate social policies to create full employment owing to increased cuts on social expenditures and the promotion of speculative capitalism (Mishra, 1999). However, other social policy experts see some degree of optimism in the sense that *internationalisation* can be used to regulate speculative capitalism and renew collective responsibility for social welfare across the globe (Deacon et al., 1997; Midgley, 1997). Social work as a profession has a role to lobby international organisations, such as the International Monetary Fund, United Nations, European Commission, and the Commonwealth, among others, for political action to promote social development. For example, the Millennium Development Goals provide an agenda for social action.

Another critical dimension regarding global social work revolves around debates about whether social work should promote remedial, activist, or developmental practices. Generally, the developed countries tend to promote individualistic approaches while the developing countries advocate activism and developmental social work (Gray, 1998; Khinduka, 1971; Midgley 1981, 1997; Nagpaul, 1972). Later studies have revealed that the developmental social work perspective has begun to emerge in both developing and developed countries where community development principles have been used to mobilise local people and promote their involvement in sustainable initiatives for sustainable livelihoods (Hokenstad et al., 1992; Livermore, 1996; Midgley, 1997). Social activism has been popularly applied in regions of the world that have experienced structural oppression leading to the rejection of therapeutic social work as it is associated with maintaining the status quo. For example, in Latin America, social workers have been inspired by the works of Paulo Freire who advocated for conscientisation and empowerment of the poor so they could overthrow oppressive dictatorships in their countries (Jimenez & Alwyn, 1992). In South Africa, liberation theology and radical ideologies have shaped the direction of social work (Mazibuko et al., 1992; Tutu, 1996).

Lastly, global social work is characterised by debates on deep-seated beliefs about values, cultural diversity, and national identity (Goldstein, 1986; Gray, 2005; Gray & Fook, 2004). Advocates for global social work argue there are essential elements of social work that are common across the globe, for example, a unified body of knowledge and identifiable methods of practice, fields of practice, multicultural practice, and antiracist and anti-oppressive practices (Ambrosno et al., 2006; Healy, 2000). However, these perspectives are founded on micro-based cross-cultural models which emphasise rationalism and individualistic approaches that are inappropriate to many non-Western cultures (Hart, 2002; Healy, 2000; Tsang & Yan, 2001). Thus, while it may be useful to promote universal social work values, there is need for a 'commitment to discuss and understand the issues involved. This will also require that more social workers are exposed to these issues and that international social work becomes a more integral part of the profession's discourse' (Midgley, 2001, p. 32). Today many writers believe global social work must embrace the values of other non-Western societies for it to be relevant in diverse cultural contexts. What this actually means remains to be seen.

CONCLUSION: IMPLICATIONS FOR SOCIAL WORK IN DEVELOPING COUNTRIES

Social work as a profession has expanded in the developing countries of Africa and Asia over the last half century. Evidently, the influence of North American and European models of social work is still felt today. However, there is an increasing literature in these global regions to develop culturally relevant social work knowledge and skills to address unique social issues in those societies. It is clear that social work in developing countries must not be regarded as 'the stranger' sidelined in the drive to submit to the order of the hegemonic North. International influences, and political, social, and economic change, shaped the professionalisation of Western social work, while the developing countries were being transformed from agrarian to industrial nations. The past two decades have witnessed the rapid growth of social work, and the development of social welfare programmes in post-communist mainland China and Taiwan (Lin & Wang, 2010; Xiong & Sabin, 2007).

In Africa, there is a need to improve the public image of social work in most countries (South Africa being the exception) where the profession is not recognised and remains underdeveloped (Mwansa, 2011). There is a need for intense debates and commitment to find ways of strengthening the status of the social work profession across the developing countries. As more schools of social work are established, especially in overpopulated countries such as China, India, and Japan, and small societies such as Botswana, there is a need to address issues of accreditation to ensure that professionalism is maintained. International partnerships that promote mutual respect for the exchange of knowledge between countries is the key to achieving the desired professional status (Midgley, 2008). Gray and Fook (2004) suggest a useful framework for developing a universal social work to promote tolerance of diverse cultures, accountability, responsiveness, and connectivity.

REFERENCES

Alfero, L.A. (1973). *New themes in social work education*. New York: International Association of Schools of Social Work.

Ambrosino, R., Hefferman, J., & Shuttlesworth, G. (2005). *Social work and social welfare: An introduction* (5th ed.). Los Angeles, CA: Thomson Brooks/Cole.

Askeland, G.A., & Payne, M. (2006). Social work education's cultural hegemony. *International Social Work*, 49(5), 731–743.

Bar-On, A. (2003). Culture: Social work's new deluge? *Social Work/Maatskaplike Werk*, 39(4), 299–311.

Connell, R. (2007). *Southern theory: The global dynamics of knowledge in social science*. Australia: Allen & Unwin.

Barker, R.L. (2003). *The social work dictionary* (5th ed.). Washington, DC: NASW Press.

Brieland, D., Costin, L.B., & Atherton, C.R. (1985). *Contemporary social work: An introduction to social work and social welfare* (3rd ed.). New York: McGraw-Hill.

CIA World Factbook (2011). Botswana: People. Retrieved February 9, 2011 from http://www.theodora.com/wfbcurrent/botswana/botswana_people.html

Costa, M.D. (1987). Current influence of social work in Brazil: Practice and education. *International Social Work*, 30(2), 115–128.

Deacon, B., Hulse, M., & Stubbs, P. (1997). *Global social policy: International organizations and the future of welfare*. London: Sage.

Dominelli, L. (1999). Neo-liberalism, social exclusion and welfare clients in a global economy. *International Journal of Social Welfare*, 8(1), 14–22.

Edge, W. (1998). Botswana: Developmental state. In W.A. Edge & Lekorwe, M.H. (eds), *Botswana: Politics and society*. Pretoria: van Schaik Publishers, pp. 333–348.

Freire, P. (1970). *The pedagogy of the oppressed*. New York: Herder & Herder.

Goldstein, H. (1986). Education for social work practice: A cognitive, cross-cultural approach. *International Social Work*, 29(2), 149–164.

Gray, M. (ed.) (1998). *Developmental social work in South Africa: Theory and practice*. Cape Town: David Phillip.

Gray, M. (2000). Social work in South Africa: In search of early role models – Interview with Professor Mike Hough. *Social Work/Maatskaplike Werk*, 36(2), 202–206.

Gray, M. (2005). Dilemmas of international social work: Paradoxical processes in indigenisation, imperialism and universalism. *International Journal of Social Welfare*, 14(2), 230–237.

Gray, M. (2006). The progress of social development in South Africa. *International Journal of Social Welfare*, 15(Suppl. 1), S53–64.

Gray, M. (2010). Indigenization in a globalizing world: A response to Yunong and Xiong (2008). *International Social Work*, 53(1), 115–127.

Gray, M., & Allegritti, I. (2002). Cross-cultural practice and the indigenisation of African social work. *Social Work/Maatskaplike Werk*, 38(4), 324–336.

Gray, M., & Allegritti, I. (2003). Towards culturally sensitive social work practice: Re-examining cross-cultural social work. *Social Work/Maatskaplike Werk*, 39(4), 312–325.

Gray, M., & Coates, J. (2008). From 'Indigenization' to cultural relevance. In M. Gray, Coates, J., & Yellow Bird, M. (eds), *Indigenous social work around the world: Towards culturally relevant education and practice*. Aldershot: Ashgate, pp. 1–12.

Gray, M., & Coates, J. (2010). Indigenization and knowledge development: Extending the debate. *International Social Work* [Special Issue on Indigenisation and Globalisation], 53(5), pp. 1–15.

Gray, M., & Fook, J. (2004). The quest for a universal social work: Some issues and implications, *Social Work Education*, 23(5), 625–644.

Gray, M., & Lombard, A. (2008). The post-1994 transformation of social work in South Africa. *International Journal of Social Welfare, 17*(1), 132–145.

Gray, M., & Webb, S.A. (2008). The myth of global social work: Double standards and the local-global divide. *Journal of Progressive Human Services, 19*(1), 61–66.

Gray, M., Coates, J., & Yellow Bird, M. (eds) (2008). *Indigenous social work around the world: Towards culturally relevant education and practice*. Aldershot, Ashgate.

Hare, I. (2004). Defining social work for the 21st century: The International Federation of Social Workers' revised definition of social work. *International Social Work, 47*(3), 407–424.

Hart, M.A. (2002). *Seeking mino-pimatisiwin: An Aboriginal approach to helping*. Halifax, Nova Scotia: Fernwood Publishing.

Healy, K. (2000). *Social work practices: Contemporary perspectives on change*. London: Sage.

Healy, L. (2001). *International social work: Professional action in an interdependent world*. New York: Oxford University Press.

Healy, L.M. (not dated). Introduction: A brief journey through the 80 year history of the International Association of Schools of Social Work. Retrieved July 13, 2011 from http://www.facebook.com/note.php?note_id=191026930924727

Hedenquist, J.A. (1992). *Introduction to social and community development in Botswana*. Gaborone: Ministry of Local Government, Lands & Housing.

Hokenstad, M.C. (1992). *Profiles in international social work*. Washington, DC: NASW Press.

Hokenstad M.C., & Midgley, J. (eds) (1997). *Issues in international social work*. Washington, DC: NASW Press, pp. 74–91.

Hutton, M. (1992). *Social work: An extension of community*. Professorial Inaugural Lecture Series No. 6. Gaborone: University of Botswana.

Hutton, M. (1994). Reshaping the social work curriculum: An African experience. Paper presented at the *Congress of the International Association of Schools of Social Work*. Amsterdam: IASSW.

Hutton, M., & Mwansa, L-K. (eds) (1996). *Social work practice in Africa: social development in a community context*. Gaborone: PrintConsult.

Ife, J. (2001). Local and global practice: Relocating social work as a human rights profession in the new global order. *European Journal of Social Work, 4*(1), 5–15.

International Association of Schools of Social Work (2010). *List of member schools in 2010*. Retrieved July 30, 2011 from http://www.iassw-aiets.org/index.php?option=cpm_content&ask=blogcategory&id=69&lt

Jimenez, M., & Alwyn, N. (1992). Social work in Chile: Support for the struggle for justice in Latin America. In M.C. Hokenstad, Khinduka, S.K., & Midgley, J. (eds), *Profiles in international social work*. Washington, DC: NASW Press, pp. 29–41.

Kendall, K.A. (1973). Dream or nightmare? The future of social work education. *International Social Work, 16*(2), 56–60.

Kendall, K.A. (1995). Foreword. In T.D. Watts, Elliott, D., & Mayads, N. (eds), *International handbook on social work education*. Westport, CT: Greenwood Press, pp. xiii–xvii.

Kendall, K.A. (2000). *Social work education: Its origins in Europe*. Alexandria, VA: Council on Social Work Education.

Khan, P., & Dominelli, L. (2000). The impact of globalization on social work in the UK. *European Journal of Social Work, 3*(2), 95–108.

Khinduka, S.K. (1971). Social work in the third world. *Social Service Review, 45*(2), 62–73.

Lin, W-I., & Wang, K.Y-T. (2010). What does professionalisation mean? Tracing the trajectory of social work education in Taiwan. *Social Work Education, 29*(8), 869–881.

Livermore, M. (1996). Social work, social development and microenterprises: Techniques and issues for implementation. *Journal of Applied Social Sciences, 21*(1), 37–46.

Lucas, T. (1993). *History of social work in Botswana: A social justice and empowerment interpretation*. MSW thesis. Saskatchewan: University of Regina.

Mangaliso, M.P. (2005). Cultural mythology and leadership in South Africa. Symposium Presentation at the Organizational Strategy and Operations Domain, Eastern Academy of Management, *International Managing in a Global Economy*, XI, Cape Town, South Africa, June, pp. 585–588.

Mazibuko, F.N.M., McKendrick, B.W., & Patel, L. (1992). Social work in South Africa. In M.C. Hokenstad, Khinduka, S.K., & Midgley, J. (eds), *Profiles in international social work*. Washington, DC: NASW Press.

Midgley, J. (1981). *Professional imperialism: Social work in the third world*. London: Heinemann.

Midgley, J. (1983). *Professional imperialism: Social work in the third world* (2nd ed.). London: Heinemann.

Midgley, J. (1992). The challenge of international social work. In M.C. Hokenstad, Khinduka, S.K., & Midgley. J. (eds), *Profiles in international social work*. Washington, DC: NASW Press.

Midgley, J. (1997). Social work and international development: promoting a developmental perspective in the profession. In M.C. Hokenstad & J. Midgley (eds), *Issues in international social work: Global challenges for a new century*. Washington, DC: NASW Press.

Midgley, J. (2000). 'Globalisation, capitalism and social welfare', *Canadian Social Work Review, Special Issue, 2*(1), 13–28.

Midgley, J. (2001). Issues in international social work, *Journal of Social Work, 1*(1), 21–35.

Midgley, J. (2008). Promoting reciprocal international social work exchanges: Professional imperialism revisited. In M Gray, Coates, J., & Yellow Bird, M. (eds), *Indigenous social work around the world: Towards culturally relevant education and practice*. Aldershot, Hants: Ashgate, pp. 31–45.

Mupedziswa, R. (1992). Africa at the crossroads: Major challenges for social work education and practice towards the year 2000. *Journal of Social Development in Africa, 7*(2), 19–38.

Mwansa, L-K. (1992). Radical social work practice: The case of Africa. Paper presented at *National Fieldwork Supervisors' Seminar* held by the Department of Social Work, University of Botswana, Ramatea Training Centre, March 27–29.

Mwansa, L-K.J., Lucas, T., & Osei-Hwedie, K. (1998). The practice of social policy in Botswana. *Journal of Social Development in Africa, 13*(2), 55–76.

Mwansa, L-K.J. (2011). Social work education in Africa: Whence and whither? *Social Work Education, 30*(1), 4–16.

Nagpaul, H. (1993). Analysis of social work teaching material from India: The need for indigenous foundations. *International Social Work, 36*(3), 207–220.

National AIDS Coordinating Agency (2008). *Progress Report of the National Response to the UNGASS Declaration of Commitment on HIV/AIDS*. Gaborone: NACA.

Ngwenya, B. (1991). Botswana: Social work education and practice. In N. Hall (ed.), *The social implications of structural adjustment programmes in Africa: Paper presentations and edited proceedings of a workshop* held at the School of Social Work, Harare, Zimbabwe, 23 September–2 October.

Ngwenya, B. (1992). *Social work in Botswana: The agony of irrelevance*. Mimeograph. Gaborone: University of Botswana.

Nimmagadda, J., & Balgopal, P.R. (2000). Indigenisation of social work knowledge: An exploration of the process. *Asia Pacific Journal of Social Work, 10*(2), 4–18.

Osei-Hwedie, K. (1990). Social work and the question of social development in Africa. *Journal of Social Development in Africa, 5*(2), 87–99.

Osei-Hwedie, K. (1994a). Informal social supports and formal provision of social services. *Social Work/Maatskaplike Werk, 30*(2), 149–158.

Osei-Hwedie, K. (1994b). The rationale for using indigenous knowledge in human service provision. Paper presented at the *Conference on Indigenous Knowledge and Practice* at the South African Museum, Cape Town. Organised by the Institute for Indigenous Theory and Practice, Cape Town, November 24.

Osei-Hwedie, K. (1995). The indigenization of social work practice and education in Africa: The dilemma of theory and method. Paper presented at the *Conference of Social Work Educators and Practitioners*, University of Cape Town Waterfront Campus, Cape Town, September 11–13.

Osei-Hwedie, K. (1996a). The rationale for using indigenous knowledge in human service provision. In H. Norman, Snyman, I., & Cohen, M. (eds), *Indigenous knowledge and its uses in Southern Africa*. Pretoria: Human Sciences Research Council, pp. 1–12.

Osei-Hwedie, K. (1996b). *The indigenization of social work practice and education: Vision or vanity?* Professorial inaugural lecture delivered at the University of Botswana, 25 September.

Osei-Hwedie, K. (1997). Southern African regional approaches to indigenizing social work education and practice: The case of Botswana. In D. de Kock, Hall, T., Hayden, W., Katan, J., Kuse, T.T., Lombard, J., Osei-Hwedie, K., Steyn, J.N., Triegaardt, J.D., & Van Zyl, M.A. (eds), *Indigenization in social and community work education*. Pretoria: Human Sciences Research Council.

Osei-Hwedie, K. (2005). Afrocentrism: The challenge of social development. Paper presented at the ASASWEI Conference 2005, *Democracy, Development, Delivery: Mapping the future contributions of the social service professions*. Stellenbosch: Stellenbosch University, South Africa, September 6–7.

Osei-Hwedie, K., Ntseane, D., & Jacques, G. (2006). Searching for appropriateness in social work education in Botswana: The process of developing a masters programme in a developing country. *Journal of Social Work Education, 25*(6), 569–590.

Osei-Hwedie, K., & Rankopo, M.J. (2008). Developing culturally relevant social work education: The case of Botswana. In M. Gray, Coates, J., & Yellow Bird, M. (eds), *Indigenous social work around the world: Towards culturally relevant education and practice*. Aldershot, Hants Ashgate, pp. 203–217.

Parsons, J. (1984). *Botswana: Liberal democracy and the labour reserve in Southern Africa*. Boulder: Westview Press.

Raditlhokwa, L. (1993). Government must revamp welfare services to curb social problems. *The Botswana Gazette*, May 12, p. 9.

Rankopo, M.J. (2004). Three decades of community development in Botswana: Is there social inclusion? In C.J. Finer, & Smyth, P. (eds), *Social policy and the Commonwealth: Prospects for social inclusion*. New York: Palgrave, pp. 68–80.

Rankopo, M.J., & Osei-Hwedie, K. (2011). Globalization and culturally relevant social work: African perspectives on indigenization, *International Social Work*, *54*(1), 137–147.

Rankopo, M.J., Osei-Hwedie, K., & Modie Moroka, T. (2007). Issues in service and volunteerism in Botswana. *Joint Issue of The Social Worker Practitioner-Researcher & Journal of Social Development in Africa*, March 24–38.

Rea, W.F. (1970). Agony on the Zambezi: The First Christian Mission to Southern Africa and its Failure. *Zambezia: Journal of Social Studies in Southern and Central Africa*, *1*(2), 46–53.

Rehklau, C., & Lutz, R. (eds) (2007). *Social work of the south*. Oldenborg: Paulo Freire Publishing House.

Republic of Botswana (1978). *Report of the Community Development Review Committee*. Gaborone: Ministry of Local Government and Lands.

Resnic, R.P. (1976). Conscientisation: An indigenous approach to international social work. *International Social Work*, *19*, 21–29.

Sin, R. (2008). Reconfiguring 'Chineseness' in the international discourse on social work in China. In M. Gray, Coates, J., & Yellow Bird, M. (eds), *Indigenous social work around the world: Towards culturally relevant education and practice*. Aldershot, Hants: Ashgate, pp. 167–176.

Sachs, J. (2005). *The end of poverty: How we can make it happen in our lifetime*. London: Penguin Books.

Tsang, A.K.T., & Yan, M-C. (2001). Chinese corpus, western application: The Chinese strategy of engagement with western social work discourse. *International Social Work*, *44*(4), 433–454.

Tummala, K. (1995). Relevance of home economics knowledge base for social work practice in Botswana. *Journal of Social Development in Africa*, *10*(1), 53–64.

Tutu, D. (1999). *No future without forgiveness*. Oxford: Powell Books.

United Nations (1969). *Proceedings of the International Conference of Ministers responsible for Social Welfare*. New York: United Nations.

United Nations (1971). Social policy and social planning in national development. *International Social Development Review*, *3*, 4–15.

University of Botswana (1985). *Academic Calendar, 1985/86*. Gaborone: University of Botswana.

University of Botswana (1999). *University Calendar 1999/2000 (Semesterisation Begins)*. Gaborone: University of Botswana.

University of Botswana (2009). *Undergraduate academic calendar, 2009/2010*. Gaborone: University of Botswana.

Walton, R.G., & Abo El Nasr, M.M.A. (1988). Indigenisation and authentisation in terms of social work in Egypt. *International Social Work*, *31*(1), 135–144.

Wass, P. (1969). The history of community development in Botswana. *Community Development Review* (original article). Reproduced in *Botswana Notes and Records* (1972), *4*, 81–93.

Webb, S.A. (2003). Local orders and global chaos in social work. *European Journal of Social Work*, *6*(2), 191–204.

Xiong, Y., & Wang, S. (2007). Development of social work education in China in the context of new policy initiatives: Issues and challenges. *Social Work Education*, *26*(6), 560–572.

Yan, M.C., & Cheung, K.W. (2006). The politics of indigenization: A case study of development of Social Work in China. *Journal of Sociology and Social Welfare*, *33*(2), 63–83.

Yuen, A.W.K., & Ho, D.K.L. (2007). Social work education in Hong Kong at crossroads: challenges and opportunities amidst marketization and managerialism. *Social Work Education*, *26*(6), 546–559.

Yuen-Tsang, A.W.K., & Wang, S. (2002). Tensions confronting the development of social work education in China: Challenges and opportunities. *International Social Work*, *45*(3), 375–388.

Yunong, H., & Xiong, Z. (2008). A reflection on the indigenization discourse in social work. *International Social Work*, *51*(5), 611–622.

The Politics of Social Work

Iain Ferguson

In 1988, the British Prime Minister Margaret Thatcher was invited to address the General Assembly of the Church of Scotland in Edinburgh. For her theme, Mrs Thatcher chose the parable of the Good Samaritan, as told by Jesus in the Gospel of Luke (10: 25–37). The parable is well known but, to recap, concerns a Jewish traveller who is beaten, robbed, and left half dead along the road. First a priest and then a Levite come by, but both avoid the man. Finally, a Samaritan comes by. Samaritans and Jews generally despised each other, but the Samaritan helps the injured Jew. Jesus is described as telling the parable in response to a question: 'But who is my neighbour?'

The story of the Good Samaritan has traditionally been seen not only by Christians but universally as a timeless example of the highest form of ethical behaviour, of unconditional care and concern for a stranger and representing, as Terry Eagleton (2009) argues, 'an authentic conjunction of the individual and the universal' (p. 119). In her speech, however, Mrs Thatcher chose to put a novel and distinctly neoliberal spin on Christ's account. In words that outraged her audience and led to uproar in the Assembly, she argued 'No one would have remembered the Good Samaritan if he'd only had good intentions. He had money as well' (Thatcher, 1988). The anger among the assembled clerics was understandable. Introducing the cash nexus into this story of unparalleled altruism undoubtedly distorted and cheapened its original meaning. In addition, Mrs Thatcher's downplaying of the original anti-xenophobic message of the parable fitted only too well with her encouragement of precisely such anti-foreigner feeling among the British people at that time.

In one sense, however, she was making an important point, albeit unintentionally: even in this seemingly most timeless, most universal example of helping, there is a context of political, economic, and social relationships shaping and informing the act of helping and without an awareness of which the nature and significance of the act cannot be fully understood. That understanding of context – political, social, and economic – should also form the starting point for any discussion of the place of social work in society. As Powell (2001) has observed, politics has been in evidence in social work since its infancy in the late 19th century. The very origins of social work as a system of organised helping; the institutional forms it has taken; the ideas and values which have underpinned it; and the activities in which social workers have engaged on a day-to-day basis, have all been profoundly shaped by the dominant political ideologies and concerns of the day.

Despite this, however, discussions on the role of social work – both inside and outside the profession – have often been characterised either by a curious reticence about the relationship between social work and politics or, not infrequently, by a denial of its very existence (see Chapter 17). Instead, it is argued, social work is above all a *practical* activity in which politics, or political explanations of social problems, have no place. Thus, in launching the new social work degree qualification in England and Wales in 2002, the then UK Health Secretary argued:

> Social work is a very practical job. It is about protecting people and changing their lives, not about being able to give a fluent and theoretical explanation of why they got into difficulties in the first place (Jacqui Smith, cited in Sanders, 2002).

A similar disdain for a political understanding of the role of social work had been shown two years previously by her counterpart in Scotland who argued:

> Social work services are not about redressing the major injustices in the world. Their remit is not to battle with the major forces that drive social exclusion. It is to promote social inclusion for each individual within their circumstances (Sam Galbraith, cited in Ferguson, 2008, p. 96).

Within the profession, the argument that social work is primarily a practical–moral activity that should not be 'politicised' was one which was often heard during the 1970s in response to the emergence of radical social work approaches but is one which is still sometimes voiced. In a critique of recent attempts to develop the radical tradition to challenge the impact of neoliberalism within social work, for example, McLaughlin (2008) effectively reverses C. Wright Mills' aphorism concerning the need to connect 'private troubles' to 'public issues' when he argues:

> A useful start would be for social workers, agencies and campaign groups not to extrapolate from their casework to the wider society ... Encouraging such a split between the specifics of practice and wider political intervention could also allow us to find a way of traversing the particular and the universal (McLaughlin, 2008, p. 146; Mills, 1959/1970).

This chapter argues social work *is* a political activity, and any attempts to present it as a purely practical, moral, or technical activity are, in a literal sense, ideological since they conceal and distort not only the role and purpose of social work within capitalist societies but also the origins and nature of the problems experienced by people who use social work services. Accordingly, in the first part of the chapter, through a critique of Whig approaches, which give primacy to the role of progressive ideas in the historical development of social welfare and social work, it is suggested political factors, ranging from ruling-class concerns about social cohesion through to the impact of a variety of social movements, working-class or otherwise, have been much more significant. The point is illustrated using two random examples, one historical (19th-century England) and one contemporary (present-day China). The next part of the chapter addresses the different politics, or ideological frameworks, which have informed the social work profession since its inception, their relationship with the dominant politics within society, and the factors which have shaped that relationship. The final part of the chapter discusses contemporary issues and debates in the politics of social work, with a focus on three recent developments. First, an emerging body of literature and research explores the challenges facing social workers operating in a context of political violence (Ramon, 2008). The potential and possible limitations of this approach to politics and social work are critically assessed. Secondly, the past few years have seen a renewed interest in the place of ethics in social work, including virtue ethics. Some of the factors fuelling this interest are considered and, with reference to the work of Eagleton (2007, 2009; Eagleton & Beaumont, 2009), it is suggested, properly understood, the relationship between ethics and politics in social work should not be seen as an antagonistic one nor one in which either is reducible to the other but rather is concerned with providing different viewpoints on the same issues. Finally, in response to the impact of neoliberalism on social work theory and practice, the past decade has seen the emergence of new critical and radical currents within social work, some of which seek to connect to earlier traditions and to relate these to the changed conditions of the 21st century. These are briefly discussed and their potential to offer a paradigm for a new politics of social work considered.

POLITICS, SOCIAL WELFARE, AND SOCIAL WORK

In a text of the same name published in 1932, British historian Herbert Butterfield criticised what he called the 'Whig interpretation of history' popularised by 19th-century historians, such as Lord McAuley, in which history is seen as a progressive journey away from barbarism and ignorance and towards peace, science, and civilisation (Butterfield, 1932). (The Whigs were the predecessors of the Liberal Party in the British Parliament.) Whig accounts of history tend to share three common characteristics. First, they are *idealist* in seeing change and development within history as occurring through the replacement of one set of ideas by a better one (e.g., slavery by feudalism, feudalism by democracy, and so on). Where such ideas come from, other than out of the heads of 'great men' (women rarely figure in these accounts) and why they emerge at one point in time rather than another are questions seldom posed within this discourse. Second, within this perspective, change is seen as essentially *a top-down process* with progressive ideas succeeding as the result of the actions of governments or far-seeing individuals. Third, as noted above, history is a history of forward movement, of *progress*: the past is essentially a journey towards a present which is the best of all possible worlds. The ideological function is clear: as one recent text put it, 'Whig history constructs a linear narrative to arrange the past according to the expediency of pressing ideological needs in the present' (Annetts et al., 2009, p. 22).

Writing in the aftermath of the mass slaughter of the 1914–1918 war, Butterfield (1932) was clearly in a strong position to tear to shreds any such cosy notions of progress. He was not, however, the first or the last to do so. Marx, for example, while recognising the dynamism of capitalism, was only too well aware of its dark and destructive side (Marx & Engels, 1848/1998) while in the last third of the 20th century, Enlightenment assumptions of historical progress were the primary target of the critique of Michel Foucault and his followers (Foucault & Rabinow, 1991), a critique subsequently developed *ad absurdum* by proponents of postmodernism.

Though not usually described as such, Whig approaches have also been influential within social welfare and social work discourses. In a recent text on social movements which seeks to restore 'the bottom-up element in the contested and contentious politics of state welfare' (Annetts et al., 2009, p. 20), Annetts and his colleagues single out the work of the British postwar academic, T.H. Marshall, and in particular his 1950 essay 'Social class and citizenship', as an exemplar of this approach. In this essay, Marshall (1950) set out his now famous definition of citizenship as involving the progressive capture of three kinds of rights: civil rights, political rights, and social rights, each corresponding to a definite stage of historical evolution. Marshall's essay has been, and continues to be, an extremely influential one in framing discussions of citizenship. What is missing from his account, however, argue Annetts et al. (2009) is any sense of the social forces bringing rights, such as universal franchise, into existence. Rather, Marshall (1950) saw the development of rights as a struggle not between opposing *classes* but rather between opposing *principles*:

> Marshall's Whig history tends to impose an idealist teleology on the history of welfare and downplay material constraints and opportunities. Political reforms therefore appear as the idealist demi-urge of an evolutionary principle of equality rather than an unceasing, now open/now hidden struggle between social groups (Annetts et al., 2009, p. 25).

Thus, for example, rather than seeing the French Revolution of 1789 as providing a huge impetus to the development of bourgeois rights through its sweeping away of feudal social relations, Marshall (1950) referred to it as an 'interruption' (p. 10). By contrast, Annetts et al. (2009) argue, the work of the Marxist historian John Saville, and in particular his 1957 essay 'The Welfare State: An Historical Approach', written partly as a rejoinder to Marshall (1950), rejected any notion of the historical inevitability of progress. Instead, in that essay Saville (1957) argued:

> The Welfare State ... has come about as a result of the interaction of three main factors: the struggle of the working class against their exploitation; the requirements of industrial capitalism (a convenient abstraction) for a more efficient environment in which to operate and in particular the need for a highly productive labour force; and recognition of the property owners of the price that had to be paid for their political security (pp. 5–6).

In several key respects, Saville (1957) offered a richer and more nuanced account than Marshall (1950). First, he recognised the role of *collective* agency. While for Marshall, agency was bound up with the actions of elite institutions, for Saville it concerned the contending sides in the struggle between classes. Change, in other words, came about as a result of pressure from below as well as from above, with reforms often the outcome of a compromise between these social forces. Second, he argued the history of the welfare state was punctuated by *discontinuities*, rather than being a steady march towards progress. While there are many historical examples of such discontinuities, it would be difficult to find a better one than the crisis of global capitalism which erupted in 2007 and which is threatening to throw welfare services in many countries back by more than half a century (Callinicos, 2010). Third, Saville's schema was nonmechanical, nonreductionist, and capable of application to a wide range of different experiences, both historical and geographical, for while almost always present in some form, the mix of the three factors would vary in different situations. Thus, to take a well-known example, the Bismarckian welfare reforms in late 19th-century Germany reflected ruling-class foresight both in seeking to undercut the growth of support for the (Marxist) Social Democratic Party and also addressing the threat posed by rising industrial struggle (Lorenz, 2006). As one contemporary English welfare commentator cited by Gilbert (1966) noted:

> The English progressive will be wise if, in this at any rate, he takes a leaf from the book of Bismarck who dealt with heaviest blow against German socialism not by his laws of oppression ... but by that great system of social insurance which now safeguards the German worker at every point in his career (p. 257).

The political origins of social work: Britain and China

Saville's (1957) analysis is no less relevant to the development of social work. Two examples, one historical and one contemporary, illustrate the point. In his account of the history of social work, Payne (2005a) locates its 19th-century origins in three main sources: the Poor Law, charity organisation, and the settlement movement. While Payne's (2005a) book is a useful source of facts and information, it tends to reflect the kind of Whig approach referred to above. Thus, for example, following what Payne (2005a) describes as the 'growing concern from the 1890s about the British system for dealing with poverty' (p. 39), he continues:

> As ideas of unemployment emerged and socialist thinking became more politically influential and drew attention to the inadequacies of existing provision ..., state responsibility for poverty and unemployment became a logical outcome and the Poor Law was increasingly seen as an inadequate expression of it. The period of 1900–14, therefore, became one of substantial social reform, particularly during the Liberal administrations of 1905–14 ... A Royal Commission on the Reform of the Poor Laws (1909) became the focus of a conflict between COS [Charity Organisation Society] views on the importance of charity organisation, represented by Octavia Hill, and the Fabian priority for more collective social provision, represented by Sydney and Beatrice Webb (pp. 39–40).

All of the elements of a Whig approach are here: the top-down approach to change – change arose from 'growing concern about poverty'; old ideas are replaced by better ones – 'socialist thinking became more politically influential', the Webb's ideas triumph over Hill's; the inevitability of progress – 'state responsibility was .... a logical outcome', and the period 'therefore' became one of reform, reinforced also by the use of the passive tense – ideas about unemployment 'emerge', 'the Poor Law is 'increasingly seen' as inadequate, and so on. What one does not learn from this account is the period from the 1880s until the war of 1914–1918 was frequently one of massive class struggles in Britain and a time of great anxiety for the British ruling class. Among its many concerns was a fear of the 'mob' or 'residuum', the growing army of the poor concentrated in the big cities and especially in the East End of London (Stedman Jones, 1971); the re-occurrence of bread riots in the mid-1880s; the challenge of New Unionism, the unprecedented organisation of unskilled workers into militant trade unions; the threat of growing military competition from Germany, and serious concerns over the physical health of the British working-class; and what became known as 'The Great Unrest', the huge wave of strike action sweeping the country between 1910 and 1914 and ending only with the onset of the First World War. The mood of the middle-classes in the 1880s was well captured by one contemporary commentator who wrote:

> I am deeply convinced that the time is approaching when this seething mass of humanity will shake the social fabric, unless we grapple with it more earnestly than we have done ... The proletariat may strangle us unless we teach it the same virtues which have elevated the other classes of society (Samuel Smith, cited in Charlton, 2000, p. 55).

This was the context in which British social work emerged: a context of growing poverty and inequality, rising class struggle, ruling-class fears and bitter ideological debates in both the working class and the ruling class, all framed by growing imperialist conflict between Britain and Germany especially. Against this background, the Charity Organisation Society's leaders in particular proposed a consciously ideological response, seeing their brand of humanistic individualism as offering an alternative to the socialist ideas then becoming increasingly popular. The demise of that alternative by the time of the World War I, however, and its rejection both by the poor who were its intended beneficiaries, as well as by the more enlightened sections of the ruling class, owed less to the intrinsic merits or deficits of the ideas per se as to the inability of the leadership of the COS to grasp the changing balance of class forces at the end of the 19th century. This left them, according to Stedman Jones (1971), as the defenders 'of what was increasingly becoming to be regarded as an esoteric, sectarian and anachronistic philosophy' (p. 313).

The second example is a contemporary one. The expansion of social work education in China over the last two decades, and especially after 1999, is quite unprecedented in the history of the profession and, with justification, has been described by two Chinese academics as 'phenomenal' (Xiong & Wang, 2007, p. 562). As late as the 1980s, social work education was virtually non-existent within mainland China. By 1999, still only 24 universities and colleges had established social work training programme. By 2001, the number had increased to 36 and in 2003 to 172. By the end of 2006, there were 186 member schools (China Association for Social Work Education, 2006, cited in Xiong & Wang, 2007). By 2008, there were more than 200 schools of social work in China (Yan & Tsang, in Gray et al., 2008). To put this in a global perspective, outside the USA, China probably now has the largest number of schools offering social work training at a university level. A crucial factor in this expansion has been the support of the ruling Chinese Communist Party, which stated in a document published in 2006 'the development of a powerful group of social work professionals is one of the central tasks in the future' (Central Committee of China Communist Party, cited in Xiong & Wang, 2007, p. 561).

This growth of social work education in China has led to a heated debate within the international social work literature over the extent to which 'Western' models of social work are applicable to China or whether 'indigenous' models should be promoted instead (see, e.g., Yunong & Xiong, 2008; Gray, 2008; Gray & Coates, 2010; Gray et al., 2008). Given a long history of Western imperialist involvement in China's affairs, including the notorious Opium Wars of the 19th century when British military power forced the Chinese rulers to agree to the import of opium on a massive scale (Hanes & Sanello, 2004), suspicion of Western cultural influences, including theories of social work and social welfare, is understandable and justified. That said, as critics of the indigenisation thesis have pointed out, a discourse which emphasises localism and 'native' cultural traditions in the current Chinese context can all too easily provide a cover for an authoritarian disregard of human rights and a rejection of more challenging forms of social work. As Sin acidly observes: 'The fantasy of an authentically "culturalist" China serves as an "anti-politics" … while ruling elites join swiftly and smoothly with the rest of the world economically simultaneously clinging to political authoritarianisms' (Sin, in Gray et al., 2008, p. 172). Political rather than cultural factors provide, in fact, the most plausible explanation for the government's promotion of social work and social work education over the past two decades. First, there was the need to address the massive social problems emanating from the decision of the 14th Congress of the Chinese Communist Party in 1992 to inaugurate the construction of a 'socialist market economy' – code for the wholesale privatisation of the majority of state-owned enterprises. One consequence of that decision has been the distribution of income and wealth in Chinese cities went from being the most egalitarian in Asia in the 1970s to the most unequal today (Davis, 2006). Following that shift in policy, the results have been devastating for ordinary workers and peasants. According to the activist network China Labor Net:

> More than 60 million workers in the state and collective sectors were sacked, a scale never seen in history … At the same time, the flourishing private sector led 120 million poor rural residents to leave their land and roam the country as migrant workers in search of employment. The overwhelming number of them ended up working in private enterprises with wages so low that workers are barely able to sustain themselves, and with little social security. The great social transformation of destroying good jobs and creating bad jobs represented great social regression (Au Loong yu & Bai Ruixue, 2010, pp. 27–28).

One explanation, then, for the extraordinary expansion of social work is the need to address the range of social problems produced by the shift from state capitalism to private capitalism. Second, there is the government's stated policy of building a 'harmonious society' (Xiong & Wang, 2007, p. 561). Arguably the current emphasis on such a policy, along with the government's revived interest in neo-Confucianism, reflects concern about growing social unrest arising from the enormous societal changes resulting in, for example, a wave of widely reported strikes involving migrant workers in 2010 (Watts, 2010). The origins of the policy, however, and the perceived role for social work within it, go back almost two decades, to the year 1991. According to Xiong and Wang (2007), it was in that year:

> [U]nder the leadership of the Ministry of Civil Affairs, the China Association of Social Workers was established in the People's Hall in Beijing and the government officially declared that social work as a helping profession was fundamental to the socio-economic development and the social stability of the country (p. 563).

The year is significant. Although the link is not made explicit by Xiong and Wang (2007), it seems official government backing for Chinese social work came only two years after the appearance of the biggest mass movement in China since the 1920s, when thousands of students and workers flooded into Tiananmen Square in Beijing demanding basic democratic rights. That movement was, of course, brutally crushed by the Chinese army on 4 June 1989 (Calhoun, 1997). Twenty years on, however, fear of a repetition continues to inform both the human rights and the industrial relations policies of the Chinese government.

Thus, the award of the Novel Peace Prize in 2010 to long-standing dissident and veteran of the Tiananmen Square protests Liu Xiaobo, while welcomed by human rights groups both in China and throughout the world, was greeted with fury by the Chinese government, which described it as 'obscene' and threatened economic sanctions against Norway which hosts the prize (Garton Ash, 2010).

The sudden embrace of social work by the Chinese Communist Party as a means of promoting social stability so soon after the events of 1989 suggests fear of repetition is likely to have been one factor promoting the growth of social work education in the subsequent years. It is odd, then, there is so little discussion of these events and their continuing influence in the ongoing debates around the indigenisation of social work in China.

SOCIAL WORK POLITICS

The previous section highlighted examples of situations where social work has emerged in response to political concerns or perceived requirements on the part of the State. This section focuses on the *politics* of social work in the sense of the world views or ideologies informing social workers' understanding of the origins of the problems experienced by their clients, their role in addressing these problems, and their relationship with society and the State. In her introduction to an edited collection of papers on the role of social work in the context of political conflict, Ramon (2008) speculates on the reasons why there have been no previous texts on this topic and suggests:

> This may relate to the reticence in social welfare to touch on issues deemed 'political', an attribute that is perceived as unprofessional, unscientific and biased within mainstream welfare ideology, and as a reflection of being 'too lefty' or 'too radical' (p. 3).

Turning these categories on their head would suggest desirable attributes of mainstream welfare approaches would include professionalism (however defined), a scientific approach, a lack of bias, and avoidance of radicalism. Not coincidentally, such attributes are, of course, key elements of the positivist, evidence-based policy approach promoted by Third Way governments over the past decade, an approach which, critics have argued, has sought to transform social work from an ethical profession into a technical occupation, concerned solely with means – 'what works' – rather than ends (Gray & McDonald, 2006). That said, such an avoidance of politics on the part of mainstream social work long pre-dates the arrival of evidence-based practice. As Jordan (1984) noted some time ago:

> Social work has played various roles in contrasting systems of social provision, and has served a number of political ends. Its great virtue – that it is almost infinitely adaptable to social circumstances – also

makes it open to exploitation for any kind of policy objectives (p. 114).

The reasons for such subservience to the goals of the State are not hard to identify. In many countries, social workers, accredited and registered by the state, take their mandate from national government (in the form of statutes prescribing the activities of social workers); are often located within the offices of government, national or local; and are dependent on government for employment and career advancement. An ideology of professionalism shunning 'politics', especially when reinforced by the type of individualist understandings of clients' problems which, in one form or another, have dominated social work for most of its history (Midgley, 2001; Payne, 2005b), might be seen as a price worth paying to allow mainstream social work to survive in even the most hostile of political climates. The problem is, on more than one occasion, that price has been a very high one indeed and paid not by social workers themselves but by the communities they are supposed to serve. Three short examples illustrate this point.

Between 1869 and 1939, over 100,000 children were migrated from the UK to Canada by highly respectable British childcare organisations which believed, no doubt, they were acting in the children's best interests. However, as a long-running campaign led by survivors of this episode and their families has highlighted, although they were described as 'orphans, waifs and strays', around two-thirds had at least one surviving parent and most were from families experiencing extreme poverty. Once they arrived in Canada, the younger children were adopted and the older children committed as indentured labourers. Many experienced horrendous abuse (Institute for Research and Innovation in Social Services, 2008).

A second example concerns the 'Stolen Generations' (or 'Stolen Children') of Australia, Indigenous children removed from their families by the Federal Government between 1869 and 1969. McDonald (2007) writes of mainstream social work's:

> appalling complicity in the dispossession and marginalisation of Australia's indigenous people ... taken from their families and placed in abusive institutions for little reason other than their race ... a history which *centrally implicates* social workers and social welfare organisations (p. 45, original emphasis).

However, the experience of social work in Nazi Germany best illustrates the harmful consequences of an ideology of social work professionalism, which purports to be 'above' politics. In his discussion of this period, Lorenz (2006) notes the use of social workers' diagnostic skills within the regime's eugenicist social programmes to sort out the 'deserving' from the 'unworthy', the latter referring to those with mental illness or learning disabilities who would then be deemed eligible for compulsory sterilisation or admission to institutions:

> Sticking to their professional task with the air of value neutrality and scientific detachment (especially after the 'non-conforming', 'politically active' social workers had been sacked or imprisoned) they did not feel responsible for the consequences of their assessments and may indeed not have been conscious of the full implications their work had in the national context (pp. 34–35).

As Lorenz (2006) rightly argues, the issue here was not simply one of State control or lack of discretion or individualised methods but rather the positivist assumptions and the wider understanding of their role, which informed the practice of these workers:

> [T]he evil of a fascist approach to welfare had not emanated primarily from its collectivism and from the imposition of ideologically determined forms of practice (which social workers usually knew how to get round) but rather from the disjuncture of the political and the professional discourse that prevented the 'ordinary welfare workers' from fully facing up to the consequences of their actions (p. 35).

These are, of course, extreme examples and it is tempting to assume, Whig-style, such things could never happen again. Many would argue, however, the ethical core of social work has been subverted in a different, if less cataclysmic, way over the past two decades by the imposition of a neoliberal business agenda, which has diluted social work's core purpose and commitments (see Garrett, 2009). As Gray and Webb (2009) contend:

> [M]uch of social work is increasingly in the service of calculative reason which represents the colonisation of the professional task and identity of the social worker. Day-to-day practice is increasingly micromanaged, requiring a social work in which professional values are thinned and atomised, with a risk management and performance culture reigning supreme (p. 7).

While the analysis of what Harris (2003) has dubbed the 'social work business' has been mainly undertaken by academics, there is now also a very substantial research literature of workers' views revealing what White (2009) refers to as a 'widespread disquiet that social work has moved from being a bureau-professional service to a service increasingly subject to external regulation and output controls' (p. 135; see Schram, Chapter 4). As an example, the following quotes came from a mixed group of new and experienced frontline workers who were interviewed in 2008:

> We live in a performance framework where outcomes have to be seen to be measured. I think we all know that outcomes are really very, very difficult to measure but nevertheless they are measured, a lot of them are measured in such a meaningless way (Conor, qualified for 30 years, frontline manager in generic social work services).
>
> What we do is the lowest common denominator, it's the minimum that people need to be safe (Kathryn, qualified for 8 months, working in a learning disabilities team).
>
> There simply aren't enough staff to do the job to the level that they're being asked to do it ... we need time to work to a high standard and at the moment we don't have that so we cut corners ... and it seems to me it's been mainly workers ... it's been people in the frontline who have taken the rap when things go wrong (Craig, qualified for 19 years, frontline manager in criminal justice) (pp. 69–71).

While the literature shows many factors contribute to such worker dissatisfaction, including excessive workloads, lack of opportunities to conduct relationship-based work, and the dominance of computer-driven assessment processes, none of these terms really captures the profound sense of anger and disappointment many frontline workers clearly feel. As Ferguson and Lavalette (2004) have argued, a more accurate term is *alienation* in the sense of a loss of control over the work process and a displacement of the values and priorities which brought people into the job in the first place.

The feelings produced by such alienation could have more than one outcome. On the one hand, if internalised, individualised and left unexpressed, they could lead to a range of self-destructive responses, including burnout, mental ill-health, poor work and personal relationships, and, as a last resort, exit from the profession. If, on the other hand, these feelings could be articulated and given collective expression, then they could form the basis both for a challenge to the dominant positivist, neoliberal paradigm and for a new politics of social work, a social work of resistance. In the final section of this chapter, the forms this second response might take are considered.

NEW DIRECTIONS

If social work's dependence on the State, reflected in a narrow ideology of professionalism, has led historically to a tendency to downplay or ignore the political, there are some indications this may be beginning to change. Here three examples are considered.

Social work in the context of contemporary political conflicts

The past decade has seen growing interest in the role of social work in the context of political conflict, for reasons not difficult to understand. Far from ushering in the 'end of history' and the peaceful New World Order some influential commentators had predicted (Fukuyama, 1992), the period since the end of the Cold War and the collapse of communism instead has seen the emergence of new and bloody conflicts across the globe. These include wars in the former Yugoslavia during the 1990s and, since the beginning of the present century, prolonged wars in Iraq and Afghanistan prosecuted under the grand narrative of a 'War on Terror' – the response of a US neoconservative administration and its allies to the attacks on the World Trade Centre in New York on 11 September 2001 by supporters of the Islamicist organisation Al-Qaeda (Callinicos, 2003). In addition, there are, of course, long-running conflicts in areas such as Sri Lanka, or Israel and Palestine pre-dating the 'War on Terror' by several decades.

An emerging development within the profession is concerned with exploring what the social work role should be in such situations and how social workers might relate both to the victims of these struggles and also, in some cases, to the combatants or ex-combatants. It marks a break with the dominant social work tradition in explicitly addressing the political context and in insisting that 'social welfare is also a political project in so far as it is impacted by ideologies and power configurations, and that social workers as members of their respective societies bring with them a personal–political dimension to this issue' (Ramon, 2008, p. 3). As a recent collection of writings on this topic highlights, the challenges, both personal and professional, involved in practising social work *in extremis*, in situations dominated by sharply opposing ideologies, the ongoing experience of domination and oppression, and the memories of often traumatic past events are considerable (Ramon, 2008; see also Lavalette & Ioakimidis, 2011). Nevertheless, valuable lessons about the nature and purpose of social work can be learned from the experience of, for example, colleagues working in Chile under Pinochet's dictatorship, or in the midst of conflict in Kenya, or in post-conflict Yugoslavia.

Insofar as this new development explicitly acknowledges the political nature of social work, it represents a welcome challenge to the dominant ameliorative paradigm. It is, however, necessary to enter a caveat, for unless the theoretical framework informing analysis of such situations is also a *political* one, as opposed to a conventional social work approach which constructs such conflicts as essentially rooted in problems in communication or understanding between different groups, then there is a danger of blurring the issues and obscuring the origins of conflicts. In the collection referred to above, for example, Ramon (2008) argues:

> Conceptually, political conflict is approached in this text as a conflict fought for resolution between social groups, which may differ in size, and where violence is/has been a major feature either in the present or in the past relationships between these groups (p. 5).

Absent here is any acknowledgement of the role of the State or of imperialism, whether British, North American, or Russian, in the genesis and maintenance of many of these conflicts. Yet as the chapters in Ramon (2008) on Bosnia-Herzegovina, Kenya, and Brazil highlight, local States (and in the first example at least, the 'international community') were often heavily implicated in the events taking place. Similarly, as Garrett (2010) has recently argued, portraying the decades-long 'troubles' in Northern Ireland as essentially a conflict between two social groups – or 'tribes' – as the British media habitually does, is hugely misleading since it ignores the central role played over many decades by the British State. Finally, given the oppression of the Palestinian community over many decades by the State of Israel, which has plumbed new depths in recent years in its treatment of the people of Gaza and has been condemned both by the United Nations and by the International Association of Schools of Social Work, it seems even less appropriate to portray this conflict as essentially one between two social groups, one of which happens to be bigger than the other (Pappe, 2004).

Ethics and politics

A second development concerns the changing relationship between ethics and politics in social work. In a review of the terrain of social work ethics, Banks (2008) refers to an 'ethics boom', an upsurge of interest in applied ethics in the social sciences and social welfare, which took off in the 1990s and has continued to the present day. Among the factors which she sees as responsible for this development are concern over the implications of climate change, developments in genetic technologies, and global terrorism, including, one might add, the 'War on Terror' and the implications of practices such as 'extraordinary rendition' and the use of torture in Guantanamo Bay and elsewhere for global ethical standards (Guru, 2010). Of particular importance for social work ethics have been the neoliberal ideas, values, and policies dominating social and economic thought for more than two decades (Ferguson, 2008; Harvey, 2005). First, as seen previously, the thrust of the positivist conceptions underlying government-driven approaches, such as evidence-based policy and practice, has been to undermine social work's (albeit inconsistent) commitment to social justice, prioritising instead technical competence in achieving predetermined goals. Second, there is the increasing use of codes of ethics and codes of conduct as mechanisms for regulation and control of frontline workers. In a critical discussion of this development, Webster (in Gray & Webb, 2010) argued a Code of Conduct 'militates against a lively and expansive ethical environment in social work. By default it pathologises and scapegoats erring individuals without acknowledging the harsh managerial practices, poor supervision or the impossible situations workers often have to confront' (p. 40).

Third, in relation to ethical notions of 'the good society', the individualism associated with neoliberalism has been seen as contributing not only to the breakdown of community (Joseph Rowntree Foundation, 2009) but also to increased levels of unhappiness and poor mental health, fuelling the growth of a 'happiness industry' (Ferguson, 2007; James, 2007; Layard, 2006).

Increasingly, however, the neoliberal offensive is generating resistance, both within social work and more widely. Coming on top of official expectations, social workers would behave in increasingly punitive ways towards oppressed groups, such as asylum seekers and young people. This undermining of ethical standards appears to be having a galvanising effect on many social workers. As argued elsewhere:

> More than any other single factor, it has been the attacks on these core values, and the expectation that social workers will collude with policies that are perceived as harming service users, that has produced the greatest anger and resistance within the profession (Ferguson, 2008, p. 132).

In addition, outwith social work, concerns about climate change, the impact on social relationships of neoliberal individualism, and the negative effects of the stark inequalities market fundamentalist policies have created (Wilkinson & Pickett, 2009) have led to renewed interest in notions of 'the good society' and the question of 'how should we live?' Such interest is reflected in a turn towards virtue ethics, an approach to ethics rooted in the philosophical tradition of Aristotle, Hegel, and Marx. In an argument with particular resonance for social workers, one of the key contemporary exponents of that tradition, Terry Eagleton (2009), argues:

> Ethics and politics are not separate spheres but different viewpoints on the same subject – the former investigating such matters as needs, desires, qualities and values, the latter examining the conventions, forms of power, institutions and social relations within which alone such things are intelligible. It is for this reason that Aristotle regards ethics as a sub-branch of politics (p. 316).

Not surprisingly then, discussions of the application of virtue ethics to social work theory and practice is becoming increasingly common in the professional literature (see, e.g., Banks & Gallagher, 2009; Gray & Lovat,

2007; Webb, 2010a). While also compatible with individualist approaches, the strand of virtue ethics Eagleton (2009) represents is one which seems to hold considerable promise for a social work profession opposing the dominance of corrosive individualism at the level of both theory and practice.

The return of the political?

Finally, there is a range of developments which, in their different ways, arguably represent what Gray and Webb (2009) called 'the return of the political' in social work. First, there are new and ongoing initiatives within the professional literature to develop theoretical and practice frameworks to the left of mainstream approaches. Some of these come from writers associated with the critical social work tradition, which has tended to be strongest in Australia and Canada (Allan et al., 2009; Mullaly, 2007), while others are more concerned to develop the socialist tradition within radical social work (Ferguson & Woodward, 2009; Lavalette & Ferguson, 2007). In addition, recent interventions by individual academics not necessarily associated with either of the above traditions have drawn on the work of a diverse range of critical thinkers, including Antonio Gramsci, Pierre Bourdieu, Alain Badiou, and Canadian social theorist Nancy Fraser in an effort to construct new, critical paradigms (Garrett, 2007, 2008; Gray & Webb, 2009; Webb, 2010b). While some of these engagements are likely to prove more fruitful than others, the fact they are taking place at all is indicative of the widespread desire to challenge the hegemony of neoliberal ideas and approaches.

Second, there is the active and growing involvement of social workers and social work academics across the globe in a wide range of social movements concerned with issues of social justice. These include new social welfare movements challenging the oppression and social exclusion of groups of people who use health and social work services (Beresford & Hasler, 2009); movements in defence of the rights of asylum seekers and those denied citizenship (Briskman et al., 2008; Zorn, 2007); and movements such as the UK Social Work Action Network seeking to combine new, more critical understandings of social work with a campaigning approach across a range of issues, including the media scapegoating of social workers in relation to the deaths of children in care (Ferguson & Lavalette, 2009).

Both of the above developments are mainly located within Western social work, or even more narrowly, social work in the English-speaking world. A positive spin-off of globalisation, however, and the opportunities it provides for the development of international contacts, is an increasing, if belated, awareness of the rich social work traditions in other parts of the world, including countries of the global South. To take the example of Brazil, not only are social workers there much more likely to work in close collaboration with social movements of poor people than their Western counterparts but the theory base from which they work is also an explicitly political one, drawing on the ideas of Marx, Gramsci, and Lukacs [Conselho Federal de Servicio Social (CFDSS), 2006[. Thus, article 13 of the Brazilian social work code of professional ethics places a duty on social workers 'to respect the autonomy of popular movements and of organisations of the working class', while the introduction to the trilingual edition of the social work code of ethics (CFDSS, 2006) is explicit in affirming:

> On the view of Brazilian social workers and their representative entities, the 'advocacy of the profession' does not mean a corporatist bureaucratising and conservative perspective; on the contrary, it represents the protection of the right, pertaining to the users of social services, ... to receive assistance with technical quality supported by a sound ethical assistance (pp. 111–112).

What this development implies is any new politics of social work in the 21st century needs to draw actively on and learn from the traditions and experience of practitioners, academics, service users, and movement activists outside the traditional confines of the English-speaking world, whether they in the global South, the former communist countries or in Indigenous communities across the globe (Gray et al., 2008; McDonald, 2007).

CONCLUSION

If there is one single conclusion to be drawn from this chapter, it is the need for social workers to acknowledge openly the political nature of their profession and to grapple with its consequences. That does not mean social work is *reducible* to politics – it is not. It does mean though, that failure to *consciously* address the political roots and role of social work makes it more likely that, by default, social workers will succumb to political ideologies and agendas inimical to the ethical core of the profession. For that reason, whatever their specific limitations might be, over the past decade the emergence of approaches seeking to challenge a dominant ideology of 'nonpolitical' professionalism is to be welcomed and might be seen as part of social work's political coming of age.

REFERENCES

Allan, J., Briskman, L., & Pease, B. (eds) (2009). *Critical social work: Theories and practices for a socially just world.* Sydney: Allen & Unwin.

Annetts, J., Law, A., McNeish, W., & Mooney, G. (2009). *Understanding social welfare movements.* Bristol: Policy Press.

Au Loong yu & Bai Ruixue (2010). *Contemporary labor resistance in China 1989–2009.* Retrieved August 30, 2010 from China Labor Net www.worldlabour.org/eng

Banks, S. (2008). Critical commentary: Social work ethics. *British Journal of Social Work, 38,* 1238–1249.

Banks, S., & Gallagher, A. (2009). *Ethics in professional life: Virtues for health and social care.* Basingstoke: Palgrave Macmillan.

Beresford, P., & Hasler, F. (2009). *Transforming social care: Changing the future together.* Centre for Citizen Participation: Brunel University Press.

Briskman, L., Latham, S., & Goddard, C. (2008). *Human rights overboard: Seeking asylum in Australia under the Howard Government.* Carlton, Australia: Scribe Publications.

Butterfield, Sir H. (1932). *The Whig Interpretation of History.* Retrieved August 30, 2010 from www.elioh.unifi.it/testi/900/butterfield

Calhoun, C. (1997). *Neither gods nor emperors: Students and the struggle for democracy in China.* Berkeley, CA: University of California Press.

Callinicos, A. (2003). *An anti-capitalist manifesto.* London: Polity.

Callinicos, A. (2010). *Bonfire of illusions: The twin crises of the liberal world.* Cambridge: Polity Press.

Conselho Federal de Servicio Social (CFDSS) (2006). *Social worker code of professional ethics.* Brasilia: CFDSS.

Charlton, J. (2000). Class struggle and the origins of state welfare reform. In G. Mooney & Lavalette, M. (eds), *Class struggle and social welfare.* London: Routledge.

Davis, M. (2006). *Planet of slums.* London: Verso.

Eagleton, T. (2007). *The meaning of life.* Oxford: Oxford University Press

Eagleton, T. (2009). *Trouble with strangers: A study of ethics.* Chichester: Wiley-Blackwell.

Eagleton, T., & Beaumont, M. (2009). *The task of the critic: Terry Eagleton in dialogue.* London: Verso.

Ferguson, I. (2007). Neoliberalism, happiness and well-being. *International Socialism, 117,* 123–143.

Ferguson, I. (2008). *Reclaiming social work: Challenging neoliberalism and promoting social justice.* London: Sage.

Ferguson, I., & Lavalette, M. (2004). Beyond power discourse: Alienation and social work. *British Journal of Social Work, 34*(3), 297–312.

Ferguson, I., & Lavalette, M. (2009). *Social work after Baby P: Issues, debates and alternative perspectives.* Liverpool: Liverpool Hope University.

Ferguson, I., & Woodward, R. (2009). *Radical social work in practice.* Bristol: Policy Press.

Foucault, M., & Rabinow, P. (1991). *The Foucault reader: An introduction to Foucault's thought.* London: Penguin.

Fukuyama, F. (1993). *The end of history and the last man.* London: Penguin.

Garrett, P.M. (2007). The relevance of Bourdieu for social work: Obstacles and omissions. *Journal of Social Work, 7*(3), 355–379.

Garrett, P.M. (2008). Thinking with the Sardinian: Antonio Gramsci and social work. *European Journal of Social Work, 11*(3), 237–250.

Garrett, P.M. (2009). *'Transforming' children's services? Social work, neoliberalism and the 'modern' world.* Maidenhead: McGraw Hill/Open University.

Garrett, P.M. (2010). Recognizing the limitations of the political theory of recognition: Axel Honneth, Nancy Fraser and social work. *British Journal of Social Work, 40*, 1517–1533.

Garton Ash, T. (2010). This Nobel prize was bold and right – but hits China's most sensitive nerve. *The Guardian,* 13 October 2010.

Gilbert, B. (1966). *The evolution of national insurance in Great Britain: The origins of the welfare state.* London: Michael Joseph.

Gray, M. (2008). Some considerations on the debate on social work in China: Who speaks for whom? *International Journal of Social Welfare, 17*(4), 400–406.

Gray, M., Coates, J., & Yellow Bird, M. (eds) (2008). *Indigenous social work around the world: Towards culturally relevant education and practice.* Aldershot: Ashgate.

Gray, M., & Lovat, T. (2007). Horse and carriage: Why Habermas's discourse ethics gives virtue a *praxis* in social work. *Ethics and Social Welfare,* 1(3), 310–328.

Gray, M., & McDonald, C. (2006). Pursuing good practice? The limits of evidence-based practice. *Journal of Social Work,* 6(1), 7–20.

Gray, M., & Webb, S.A. (2009). The return of the political in social work. *International Journal of Social Welfare, 18,* 111–115.

Gray, M., & Coates, J. (2010). 'Indigenization' and knowledge development: Extending the debate. *International Social Work* [Special Issue on Indigenisation and Globalisation], *53*(5), 1–15.

Gray, M., & Webb, S.A. (eds) (2010). *Ethics and value perspectives in social work.* Basingstoke: Palgrave.

Guru, S. (2010). Social work and the *'War on Terror'. British Journal of Social Work, 40*(1), 272–289.

Hanes, W.T. & Sanello, F. (2004). *The Opium Wars.* Naperville, IL: Sourcebooks.

Harris, J. (2003). *The social work business.* London: Sage.

Harvey, D. (2005). *A brief history of neoliberalism.* Oxford: Oxford University Press.

Institute for Research and Innovation in Social Services (IRISS) (2008). *The golden bridge: Child migration from Scotland to Canada 1869–1939,* online exhibition. Retrieved August 31, 2010 from http://www.iriss.ac.uk/goldenbridge

James, O. (2007). *Affluenza.* London: Vermillion.

Jordan, B. (1984). *Invitation to social work.* Oxford: Blackwell.

Joseph Rowntree Foundation (JRF) (2009). *Contemporary social evils.* Bristol: Policy Press.

Lavalette, M., & Ferguson, I. (eds) (2007). *International social work and the radical tradition.* London: Venture Press.

Lavalette, M., & Ioakimidis, V. (2011). Social work in extremis: Lessons for social work internationally. In M. Lavalette (ed.), *Radical social work today: Social work at the crossroads.* Bristol: The Policy Press.

Layard, R. (2006). *Happiness: Lessons from a new science.* London: Penguin.

Lorenz, W. (2006). *Perspectives on European social work.* Opladen: Barbra Budrich.

Marshall, T.H. (1950). Citizenship and social class. In T.H. Marshall & Bottomore, T. (eds) (1992). *Citizenship and social class.* London: Pluto Press.

Marx, K., & Engels, F. (1848/1998). *The communist manifesto.* Oxford: Oxford University Press.

McDonald, C. (2007). Wizards of Oz? The radical tradition in Australian social work (and what we can learn from Aotearoa New Zealand. In M. Lavalette & Ferguson, I. (eds), *International social work and the radical tradition.* Birmingham: Venture Press.

McLaughlin, K. (2008). *Social work, politics and society.* Bristol: Policy Press.

Midgley, J. (2001). Issues in international social work. *Journal of Social Work, 1*(1), 21–35.

Mills, C.W. (1959/1970). *The sociological imagination.* Oxford: Oxford University Press.

Mullaly, B. (2007). *Structural social work: Ideology, theory and practice* (3rd ed.). Don Mills, Ontario: Oxford University Press.

Pappe, I. (2004). *A history of modern Palestine: One land, two peoples.* Cambridge: Cambridge University Press.

Payne, M. (2005a). *The origins of social work: Continuity and change.* Basingstoke: Palgrave Macmillan.

Payne, M. (2005b). *Modern social work theory* (3rd ed.). Basingstoke: Palgrave.

Powell, F. (2001). *The politics of social work.* London: Sage.

Ramon, S. (ed.) (2008). *Social work in the context of political conflict.* Birmingham: Venture Press.

Sanders, C. (2002). Practical bias sparks alarm. *Times Higher Education,* 14 June 2002. Retrieved July 21, 2011 from http://www.timeshighereducation.co.uk/story.asp?storyCode=169747&sectioncode=26

Saville, J. (1957). The welfare state: An historical approach. *The New Reasoner, 3,* 5–25.

Sin, R. (2008). Reconfiguring 'Chineseness' in the international discourse on social work in China. In M. Gray, Coates, J., & Yellow Bird, M. (eds), *Indigenous social work around the world: Towards culturally relevant education and practice.* Aldershot, Hants: Ashgate, pp. 167–176.

Stedman Jones, G. (1971). *Outcast London.* Oxford: Clarendon.

Thatcher, M. (1988). Speech to the General Assembly of the Church of Scotland. Retrieved August 27, 2010 from http://www.margaretthatcher.org/document/107246

Watts, J. (2010). Strikes in China signal end to era of low-cost labour and cheap exports, *The Guardian*, 17 June 2010.

Webb, S.A. (2010a). Virtue ethics. In M. Gray & Webb, S.A. (eds), *Ethics and value perspectives in social work.* Basingstoke: Palgrave, pp. 108–119.

Webb, S.A. (2010). (Re)Assembling the Left: The politics of redistribution and recognition in social work. British Journal of Social Work, *40*(8), 2364–2379.

Webster, P. (2010). Codes of conduct. In M. Gray &. Webb, S.A. (eds), *Ethics and value perspectives in social work.* Basingstoke: Palgrave, pp. 31–40.

White, V. (2009). Quiet challenges? Professional practice in modernised social work. In J. Harris and White, V. (eds), *Modernising social work: Critical considerations.* Bristol: Policy Press.

Wilkinson, R., & Pickett, K. (2009). *The spirit level: Why more equal societies almost always do better.* London: Penguin.

Xiong, Y., & Wang, S. (2007). Development of social work education in China in the context of new policy initiatives: Issues and challenges. *Social Work Education, 26*(6), 560–572.

Yunong, H., & Xiong, Z. (2008). A reflection on the indigenization discourse in social work. *International Social Work, 51*(5), 611–622.

Zorn, J. (2007). Borders, exclusion and resistance: The case of Slovenia. In M. Lavalette & Ferguson, I. (eds), *International social work and the radical tradition.* Birmingham: Venture Press.

Index

INTRODUCTORY NOTE

References such as "178–9" indicate (not necessarily continuous) discussion of a topic across a range of pages. Wherever possible in the case of topics with many references (but not in the case of cited authors), these have either been divided into sub-topics or only the most significant discussions of the topic are listed. Because the entire work is about 'social work' the use of this term (and certain others which occur constantly throughout the book) as an entry point has been restricted. Information will be found under the corresponding detailed topics.

12-Step programmes 590

AASW *see* Australian Association of Social Workers
Abbott, A. 6–7, 11–12, 395, 399, 660, 662, 671–3
ableist attitudes 552, 557–9
Aboriginal communities 619, 711
Abramovitz, M. 35–6, 38, 43–4
accountability 9, 67, 102, 157, 231, 321, 653–5
accreditation 272, 649–50, 731–2, 736
    standards 731–2
accredited programmes 266, 555, 603, 640, 646, 652
accrediting bodies 648, 667–8
accuracy 144–5, 215, 227–30, 471, 488, 493–4
action research, participatory *see* participatory action research
activation 87–8, 253, 285
active crisis states 209, 249–50, 257
activism 46, 99, 101, 103–4, 106, 273, 286
    political 2, 266, 273
    social 99, 266, 286, 735
activities of daily living (ADLs) 181, 532, 535, 541
activity systems 664–5, 669–70, 672
activity theory 662, 664–5, 670–2
    analysis 672–3
actor leaders 669–70
actor stakeholders 665, 671
actuarial approach 208, 228–9, 233
actuarial risk assessment 226, 228, 685
actuarial tools 224, 228–9
acute distress 251, 253, 256, 259
acute stress disorder (ASD) 251
AD *see* Alzheimer's disease
adapted theories 115, 117
Addams, J. 191–2, 202, 266, 330, 375, 389, 399, 456, 550

addiction 64, 75, 150, 579, 584–5, 589, 591 *see also* alcohol; drugs
ADHD *see* attention deficit hyperactivity disorder
Adler, A. 521
ADLs *see* activities of daily living
administration 6, 30, 78, 253, 411, 507, 518
    and codes of ethics 312
administrators 28, 73, 102, 270, 417, 550
adolescents 163–4, 168, 170, 308, 582, 588, 614–16
adolescent substance abuse 170–1, 586, 620
adrenaline 252–3
advanced marginality 58, 61
adversity 69, 101, 255, 525, 539, 616
advocacy 30, 208–9, 264–9, 273–7, 377–8, 456–7, 710–12
    advocates of 277
    class 273, 276
    policy 266, 576–7
    political 267, 539
    research 389, 397–8
    social work research as 397–8
AFDC *see* Aid to Families with Dependent Children
affective equality 346
Africa 22–3, 357, 566, 630, 724–6, 729, 734–6
    sub-Saharan 283, 630
age 22, 56, 117, 122, 531–40, 580–2, 599–601
    of criminal responsibility 606–7
ageing
    in developed countries 533–4
    in developing countries 532–3
    as global phenomenon 532–4
    in a healthy manner 539–43
agency policy 115, 118, 120–2, 305
agent of social change model 267–8

agricultural revolution 22–3
AIC *see* American Immigration Council
AIDS *see* HIV/AIDS
Aid to Families with Dependent Children (AFDC) 38, 69
albinos 550
alcohol 121, 150, 163, 178, 184, 253, 579–92
 community-based interventions 588–91
 dependence 580–1
 individual, group, and family treatment 584–8
 prevalence of abuse 579–81
 prevention programming 581–4
ALFs *see* assisted-living facilities
algorithmisation 684
alienation 526, 572, 619, 748
alliances 197, 238, 332, 337–8, 479, 718
 therapeutic 238–9, 244, 409, 435
 working 687, 689
Altshuler, S.A. 557
Alzheimer's disease (AD) 537–8
American Immigration Council (AIC) 573–4
American Psychological Association (APA) 162–3, 174, 414
analytic risk assessment 225–9
anger 119, 153, 167, 253, 268, 270, 277
Annetts, J. 742–3
anorexia nervosa 163, 620
ANS *see* autonomic nervous system
antecedents 144–6, 148–9, 153, 374
anthropology 11, 23, 389, 455–7
 philosophical 391
antiglobalisation movement 282–3
anti-oppressive practice (AOP) 2, 10, 44, 135, 328–39, 362–4, 599–600
 definition 331
 history 328–31
 limitations 338
 rise 332–5
 theories and practice 331–8
 value orientation 331–2
antiracism 357, 364–5
antiracist practice 363, 365, 599, 618
antiracist social work 193, 361, 363–4
anxiety 77, 119, 146, 154, 240, 435, 521–2
 disorders 239, 435, 554
AOP *see* anti-oppressive practice
applied behaviour analysis 110, 144–5, 147, 149–52, 156–7, 169
appropriateness 179, 271, 311, 445–6, 467, 729
 cultural 732–4
Arabs 715–16
Argyris, C. 213, 218, 394
Aristotle 316, 348, 373, 679, 750
armed conflict 248–9, 567, 614
arousal thresholds 143, 146, 153
Asad, T. 381
ASASWEI *see* Association of South African Social Work Education Institutions

ASD *see* acute stress disorder
Ashby, D. 490–1
Asia 357–8, 565–6, 598, 724–5, 732, 734–5, 745
aspirations 138, 179, 186, 188, 195, 202, 640–1
assessment 131, 134–5, 146–8, 179–80, 182–6, 600–2, 615–16
 family support services 615–17
 initial 116, 212, 616
 methods/techniques/tools 147, 180, 226, 229–31, 241, 415–16, 601–2
 objective 8, 430
 process 113, 184, 616, 748
 risk *see* risk assessment
assets 100, 184, 187, 280, 286, 509, 525
 client 144, 147–8
assimilation 352, 355–8, 360–1, 417, 619
assimilative integration 208–9, 237–8, 241–4
assisted-living facilities (ALFs) 541
assistive technologies 540, 557, 681
Association of South African Social Work Education Institutions (ASASWEI) 729, 731
asylum seekers 121, 279, 377, 500, 564–5, 567–70, 750–1
 refused 500
attachments 200, 342, 349, 579, 590, 653
attention deficit hyperactivity disorder (ADHD) 167, 554
Australia 304, 356–60, 377, 503–4, 573–4, 597–8, 647–52
 multiculturalism 358–9
 New South Wales 266
 Queensland 648–9, 652
 White Australia policy 358
Australian Association of Social Workers (AASW) 304, 648–50
authentisation 732–3
autonomic nervous system (ANS) 252
autonomy 17, 74, 316, 319, 342, 345, 374
 professional 286, 417, 477, 613, 621, 640, 677

baby boomers 533–5, 543
Bachelor of Social Work (BSW) 266, 414, 472, 648, 652, 728, 731
Bailey, R. 28, 333, 476, 696–8, 718
Baker, J. 346
balance 3, 12, 56, 89, 374–5, 378, 521
 of power 37, 56
Baldry, E. 382–3
Baldwin, M. 389, 468–73, 476, 478, 508
Bangladesh 568
Banks, S. 192, 201, 300–1, 316, 318, 321–3, 347, 372, 374, 376, 750
Bannerji, H. 356, 358, 360
Barlow, J. 90, 430, 618
Barnardo's 139, 637
Barr, H. 662, 664, 670
Barry, K. 54, 187, 231
basic behavioural principles 144, 155–6

BASW *see* British Association of Social Workers
BBC (British Broadcasting Corporation) 282, 569–70
BDI *see* Beck Depression Inventory
Beck Depression Inventory (BDI) 410, 428, 431
Beckett, A.E. 519
Beckett, C. 321
before-and-after research designs 426–7, 436
behavioural family therapy 110, 166–8, 171
behavioural methods, cognitive *see* cognitive behavioural methods
behavioural models 144–5, 237
behavioural perspectives 110, 117, 143–57, 162
  future 157
behavioural practice 110, 144, 147–8, 155–6
  hallmarks 143–8
  varieties 148–52
behavioural principles 146, 150, 152, 167
  basic 144, 155–6
behavioural therapy, cognitive *see* cognitive behavioural therapy
behavioural treatment, family 168, 170–1
behaviour analysis, applied 110, 144–5, 147, 149–52, 156–7, 169
behaviourism
  and evidence-based practice (EBP) 417
  radical 149, 152, 157
behaviours
  concurrence-seeking 217–20
  health-promoting 542, 581
  offending 600–1, 603–5, 608
  pro-social 167, 169, 582
Beinecke, R.H. 527
being-in-common 281
Belgium 87, 170, 606
Bell, E.L. 243
benevolence 413, 708, 713
Bentham, J. 373–4
Berg, I.K. 165–6, 310
Berg, J. 310
Bernstein, J. 35, 42, 585
Berthoud, R. 615
best available evidence 410, 437, 519
best practices, and evidence-based practice (EBP) 416–17
Beutler, I.E. 238
bias 409–10, 433, 440, 442–3, 449–50, 460–1, 618
  confirmation 212, 252
Biestek, F. 301, 309, 347
Big Society 10, 282, 285–6, 476, 637
bioethics 319
biological parents 163, 165, 169
biological psychiatry 157
biomedical and psychosocial integrated treatment 584–5
biopsychosocial distress 250
biopsychosocial sequelae 252–6
birth families 225, 229–30, 232
Blacks 38, 40, 358, 598, 716

Blond, P. 286
Blundo, R. 180, 182
Boaz, A. 399, 483, 486, 490–1
Bologna Process 646–7
Bonanno, G.A. 255
bootstrap capitalism 101
Bornstein, D. 654
Botswana 726–32
  University of 726, 728–9, 731
boundaries, of social work 10–13
boundary issues 182, 310
Bourdieu, P. 61, 75, 203, 509, 634
Bowles, S.M. 34–5
Bowles, W. 318, 320–1, 373
boys 116, 122, 248–9, 256, 342, 443 *see also* children
Bracken, P. 526
Bradbury, H. 397, 467–70, 475–6
Brandon, R.N. 660, 674
Braye, S. 121, 334, 484, 491, 493–4, 696
breast cancer 162–3, 165
Brent, D. 164
Breslau, N. 249
bridging social capital 329
Britain (*see also* England and Wales) 9–10, 33–4, 52, 357–9, 363, 503, 566, 571, 614, 617–18, 640–1, 698, 743–4
  Coalition Government 285–6, 479, 672
  future of social work 632–7
British Association of Social Workers (BASW) 287, 301, 303–4, 633, 702
British Broadcasting Corporation *see* BBC
Bronfenbrenner, U. 129–32, 136, 168, 258, 524
  ecology of human development 130–1
Brooks-Harris, J.E 237–8, 241, 245
Brun, C. 188
Brydon-Miller, M. 476
BSW *see* Bachelor of Social Work
budgets 43, 271, 336, 451, 639, 654, 670
bulimia nervosa 163
bureaucracy 9, 58, 75, 118, 218, 275–6
  street-level 16, 61, 67–79, 686
business model 73–4, 78, 534, 680
Butler, J. 333, 539
Butler, R. 539
Butler, S. 536
Butterfield, Sir H. 742
bystander effect 215–16, 218

CAF *see* Common Assessment Framework
Cameron, David 479, 503, 633, 635–6
Campbell, T. 281
Campbell Collaboration 412, 485, 489–93
Canada 304, 337, 356–7, 359–60, 411, 462, 572–3
  development of social work 710–11
  First Nations 335, 462
  multiculturalism 359–60
Canada, G. 654
Canadian Association of Social Workers (CASW) 304

capabilities approach 85, 101, 185, 381, 653
capability 19, 52, 76, 84, 185, 381–2, 652–3
   and social work education 652–3
capital accumulation 62, 634
   crisis of 37
   capitalism 8, 10, 54, 57–8, 61, 194, 283
      bootstrap 101
      global 279, 282, 476, 478–9, 743
capitalist societies 27, 67, 105, 193–4, 351, 741
Caplan, G. 250, 256
care 115–19, 177–80, 303–4, 534–43, 633–8, 661–4, 666–9
   community 280, 347, 451, 590, 666
   coordination 541–2
   definitions and conceptualisation 85–6
   feminist ethics of 341–53
   health *see* health care
   informal 85, 525
   inpatient 177, 185, 187
   kinship 412, 430
   long-term 350, 535, 538, 540–2
   management 230, 666, 697, 702
   medical 43, 117, 259, 536, 638
   as moral and political practice 343–5
   palliative 319, 473, 663
   power and diversity 345–6
   psychiatric 180, 524 *see also* mental health
   social *see* social care
careers 90–1, 185, 663, 743
caregivers 86, 156, 182, 543, 566, 588
   family 538–9, 542–3
caregiving 86, 90, 343, 346, 349
carer involvement/participation 487, 527, 669
carers 88, 116, 121, 232, 345, 665–6, 668–9
Carlton, T. 518
Carroll, K.M. 586, 588
caseloads 70, 267, 273, 276, 576
case management 71–2, 75–6, 78, 176, 178–9, 181, 187–8
   role of risk assessment 230–1
   strengths-based 179, 181–2, 184, 187
   systems (CMS) 678, 681–3, 684, 686
case managers 68–9, 71–9, 177, 179–80, 182, 185–6, 188
casework 7, 69, 202, 226, 287, 330, 450
caseworkers 76–7, 139, 228, 266, 271
cash assistance 36, 69–71, 75, 78
CASW *see* Canadian Association of Social Workers
categorisation 81–2, 506, 684
CBPR *see* community-based participatory research
CBT *see* cognitive behavioural therapy
CCRCs *see* continuing care retirement communities
central nervous system (CNS) 252
Centre for Reviews and Dissemination 435–6, 462
Chamberlain, R. 176–7
change 95, 146–51, 201–2, 275–7, 424–6, 583–6, 605–6
   agents 1, 209, 273–6
   progressive social 98–9, 105–6, 194

Charitable Organization Society (COS) 69, 267, 330, 374–5, 696, 744
charities 33, 121, 266, 286, 431, 559–60, 743–4
Chelimsky, E. 403–4
Chenoweth, L. 320–1, 556, 649, 652
child abuse 121, 287, 412, 420, 430, 434, 616–17
child and family social work 503–13
   information categorisation 505–7
   organisational responses to need 505–8
   panoptical modernisation 506
   preventive regulation 505, 507, 509, 511
   procedural managerialism 507
   risk fixation 505
   towards a sociological understanding of child welfare 508–10
childcare 28, 43, 76, 89, 103, 133, 199
child development 344, 652, 670
childhood 91, 133, 199, 240, 242, 503, 510
child maltreatment 131–4, 430 *see also* child abuse
   ecological determinants 132–4
child neglect 122, 136, 636
child protection 8–9, 228–9, 232–3, 512, 606–7, 621–2, 666–7
   plans 116, 211, 216–17, 633
   services 225, 230, 287, 501, 504, 622, 636
childrearing 23, 88, 91, 352, 504
children 87–91, 164–71, 216–20, 350–1, 473–6, 503–9, 613–23 *see also* child and family social work
   collaborative inquiry 473–4
   disabled 500, 558, 618
   ecological frameworks for work with 130–1
   needs 214, 504, 511–12, 695
   young 68, 87–8, 121, 139, 431, 474, 615
children's services 214, 217, 506, 510, 613, 634–6, 667–9
children's spaces 510–11
child welfare 178, 229–30, 454, 531, 555, 617, 641
   towards a sociological understanding of 508–10
China 40, 335, 403, 533, 713–14, 725, 743–6
Chinese Communist Party 745–6
Chodorow, N. 342
Chowns, G. 468, 470, 473–4, 476, 478
chronic diseases/illness 500, 531, 533, 535–42, 732
chronic distress 253
chrono-system 130–1
church 59, 137, 181, 290, 572
churn, policy 665, 670
CISD *see* critical incident stress debriefing
CISM *see* critical incident stress management
citizenship, democratic 341, 343–4
civic integration 356–8
civil rights 3, 34, 36, 41, 267–8, 559–60, 698–9
   movement 38, 270, 550, 560
class advocacy 273, 276
client assets 144, 147–8
client-directed psychotherapy 244
client rights 309
client self-determination *see* self-determination
climate change 283, 403, 464, 571, 627, 750

clinical expertise 408–9, 415
clinical practice 110, 164, 366, 408, 413–14, 518–19, 527
clinical psychology 396, 414
Clinton, Bill 38, 71
Cloward, R. 52, 58–60, 64–5, 375
cluster randomised controlled intervention research designs 429
CMS *see* case management systems
CNS *see* central nervous system
co-construction of identities 367
codes of ethics 192, 296, 299–313, 317, 319, 322–4, 342
   challenges addressed currently 309–12
   contemporary 302–6
   evolution of ethical standards 300–2
   future challenges 312–13
   multiple uses 306–7
   as risk-management tool 307–9
cognitive behavioural methods 110, 151–2, 239, 587, 603–4
cognitive behavioural therapy (CBT) 151, 164, 170, 412, 430, 586–8
cognitive disabilities 552, 554
cognitive heuristics 208, 325
cognitive therapy (CT) 416, 428–30, 435, 520
collaborative inquiry 470, 473–4, 478
collective identities 202, 377, 379, 547
colour blind approach 38, 243, 360–2, 368, 599
combined family models 168–71
Common Assessment Framework (CAFs) 506, 602, 667, 687–8
common language 358, 662, 688, 694
communication, privileged 302, 309–10
communitarianism, moral 285–6
community
   changing nature 284–6
   meaning 280–2
community activism 285–6
community-based continuity of care practices 590–1
community-based participatory research (CBPR) 456, 458
community-based treatments for offenders 589
community care 280, 347, 451, 590, 666
community education 280, 374
community empowerment 101, 280, 456
community leaders 133–4, 259, 469, 582
community practice 209, 279–90, 411
   case study 288–90
   changing nature of community 284–6
   definition 288
   impact of neoliberal globalisation on local communities 282–4
   meaning of community 280–2
community punishment 598
community reinforcement approaches 588
community resources 147, 181, 581, 588, 622
community social work (CSW) 279, 286–9
   case study 288–90

compatibility 456, 467–8, 478, 663
computer-assisted practice 683
concurrence-seeking behaviour 217–20
confidentiality 302, 304, 308–10, 312, 319, 457, 473
confirmation bias 212, 252
conflicts of interest 9, 299, 310–12, 319, 398
confounding factors 430, 433, 437
Confucius 316, 373, 378
consent, informed 148, 154, 302, 304, 308–10, 312, 319
constitutive power of language 196, 198, 200
constructive controversy 217–20
constructive critical social work 194, 196, 203
consultation 221, 307, 310–11, 321, 667, 694, 709
context 256–8, 440–1, 443–5, 450–1, 486–9, 682–4, 711–14
   and evaluation research 441–9
   social work in 499–623
   systematic reviews 483–4, 486
contingencies 145–7, 149, 151, 153–5, 157, 208, 519
   see also contingency management
contingency management 146, 155, 588
   myths and misconceptions 152–5
continuing care retirement communities (CCRCs) 541
continuing professional development (CPD) 125, 664, 669
Corcoran, J. 110, 156, 166
core groups 215–17, 219–20, 471
corrective emotional experiences 237–8, 244
COS *see* Charitable Organization Society
cost effectiveness 17, 105
Council on Social Work Education (CSWE) 274, 295, 414, 555, 648–52, 661, 711
Courtney, M 269
court work missionaries 597
CPD *see* continuing professional development
criminal justice 121, 150, 184, 188, 411–12, 597–608, 609
   effective practice approaches 602–4
   evidence-based practice (EBP) 602
   evidence base problems 604–5
   orthodoxy in question 604–8
   relationship-based practice 605–6
   risk-based approaches 600–2
   sentencing options 599–600
   system 150, 184, 188, 499, 512, 597–601, 605–9
criminogenic need 602–3, 605
crisis intervention 202, 208, 248–59
   biopsychosocial sequelae 252–6
   signs and symptoms 251–2
   stressful life events and active crises 250–1
crisis states, active 209, 249–50, 257
critical incident stress debriefing (CISD) 257
critical incident stress management (CISM) 257
critical perspectives 110–11, 191–202
critical social science theories, modernist 194–5
critical social theory 193–4, 202, 504, 508, 510, 512–13

critical social work 10, 111, 191–8, 200–3, 273, 335, 351
  case study 199–200
  constructive 194, 196, 203
  definition 192–9
  early beginnings 192–3
  early theoretical influences 193–4
  modernist critical social science theories 194–5
  postmodern and post-structural theories 195–9
  practice 191, 193, 195, 197–8, 200–3, 751
  prospects for survival 200–1
  strengths and weaknesses 201–3
  theory 195, 202–3
cross-cultural understanding 712, 715
CSW *see* community social work
CSWE *see* Council on Social Work Education
CT *see* cognitive therapy
cues 143, 151, 183, 226, 228–9
cultural and social diversity 309
cultural appropriateness 732–4
cultural competence 309, 356–7, 360, 362–7, 500
cultural contexts 212, 381, 523, 526, 732
  diverse 322, 735
  local 712, 733
cultural differences 29, 151, 153, 317, 359, 367, 373
cultural diversity 355–9, 365, 731, 735
cultural groups 309, 356, 359–61, 364–6, 619
cultural inferiority approach 360–1
cultural injustice 335, 339
culturally appropriate social work 472–3, 732
cultural norms 117, 357, 665
cultural practices 143, 212, 337, 339, 472, 517, 679
cultural relevance 724, 729–30, 732–3
cultural sensitivity 321, 357, 360–3, 368
cultural values 146, 241–2, 360, 534, 677
culture 241–3, 337–8, 361–7, 380–1, 555–8, 671–2, 715–17
  deaf 553, 558, 560
  dominant 242–3, 295, 334
  and family support services 618–19
  of listening to adults and children 134–9
  performance 218, 628, 748
  professional 655, 689
Cunning, S 367
curiosity 392–3
curriculum 387, 472–3, 650, 707–8, 711–15, 725, 728–31
  development 318, 666, 729
  review 728–9
customs 356–7, 359, 363, 547
cycle of reflection 320

Daly, M. 16, 82–3, 85, 90, 490, 608
Danseco, E. 367
Darwinism, social 516, 549
Datta Gupta, N. 90
daughters 162, 164, 168, 249, 342, 550 *see also* children

daycare 90, 117, 471–2
DBT *see* dialectical behaviour therapy
deaf culture 553, 558, 560
deafness 552–3, 558
death 8, 211, 215, 255, 580–1, 633, 636
debriefing 257–8, 430
decentralisation 541, 701
decision making
  ad hocery of 216–17
  assumptions about 213–14
  ethical 316–25
  group 212, 214, 219–20
  modes of 684
  and risk assessment 224–33
  as social process 214–15
deduction 684–5
Deegan, P. 180
defensive practice 208, 225, 232–3
defensive routines 213, 215
dehumanisation 152, 180, 448
delinquency 157, 168, 170, 225, 443, 582, 608
dementia 430, 535, 537–9, 542
democracy 27, 46, 64, 266, 280, 343, 359
  liberal 375
  social 59, 346, 505, 633
democratic citizenship 341, 343–4
democratic participation 101, 104
democratisation 513, 700–2
demographics 138–9, 531–2, 569
deontology 373–5
dependence 11, 78, 342, 534, 633, 652, 658
  alcohol 580–1
depression 164, 244–5, 412, 416, 428, 520–2, 537–8
  postpartum 412, 458
deprivation 94–5, 98, 100, 133, 249
deregulation 37, 61, 282–3
descriptive analysis 144–5, 150
desistance 605–7
devaluation 524, 550–1, 558–9, 561
developing countries 96–7, 531–2, 552–3, 657–8, 712–14, 718–19, 723–36
  Botswana 726–32
  history of social work in Africa and Asia 725–6
  internationalisation, globalisation, and universalisation 734–5
  theoretical definitions and concepts of cultural appropriateness 732–4
developmental disabilities 157, 416, 552–3
developmental psychopathology 524–5
deviant identities 503, 510
devolved problem solving 512
diabetes 535–6
diagnosis 179–80, 182, 236, 251, 277, 395, 517
  social 7, 165
dialectical behaviour therapy (DBT) 152, 245
dialogical justice 347–8, 352
dialogical spaces 218–20
dialogue 28–9, 31, 122, 124, 218, 243, 323–5

dignity 29–30, 84, 256, 264, 304–6, 374–5, 551–2
disability 333, 345–8, 431–2, 500, 534–7, 539–42, 547–61
   cognitive disabilities 552, 554
   communities 557–8
   competence 557–8
   deafness 552–3, 558
   definitions 547–8
   developmental disabilities 157, 416, 552–3
   as diversity 556
   groupings 552–4
   health-related disabilities 554–5
   hearing impairments 552–3, 558
   historical perspectives 548–52
   intellectual disabilities 551, 553, 556
   learning disabilities 397, 427, 547, 554, 747–8
   mental health disabilities 552–4, 558, 560
   mobility disabilities 552
   rights 197, 551, 556, 559–61
     movements 332, 336, 525, 548, 550, 552, 699–701
   social model of 555, 558, 561, 700
   and social work 555–6
     future 556–61
   visual disabilities/impairments 547, 552–3, 560
disability-competent social work practice 558–61
disabled children 500, 558, 618
disabled persons 224, 248, 378–9, 549–53, 555–9, 561, 702
   in social work profession 555–6, 561
disabled social workers 555–6, 561
disadvantaged communities 139, 285
   development of capacity to meet own needs 138–9
disadvantaged groups 193, 285–6, 402, 560, 618
disciplinary power 74, 78, 508
discourse analysis 520, 522–3
discretion 16, 68, 72–8, 118, 683–4, 686, 688–9
   frontline 16, 68, 72, 77
   myth of 686
   and new welfare case management 68, 75–8
discrimination 101–2, 122, 154, 332–3, 358, 551–2, 699–700
   racial 360, 716, 726
dishonesty 311
distress 209, 240, 250–3, 256–7, 515–17, 522–4, 526
   acute 251, 253, 256, 259
   biopsychosocial 250
   chronic 253
   post-traumatic 250–1, 254
diversity 13, 197, 296–7, 355–7, 359–61, 365–8, 555–6
   across the globe 356
   approaches to multiculturalism 356–65
   cultural 355–9, 365, 731, 735
   cultural competence 309, 356–7, 360, 362–7, 500
   cultural sensitivity approach 361–3
   disability as 556
   and feminist ethics of care 345–6
   and qualitative social work research 461–2
   and social work practice 355–68
   from working across to working through difference 365–7
Dixon-Woods, M. 462, 484, 489–90, 492
documentation 76, 273–4, 308, 311, 518, 683, 686–7
Dodo Bird effect 446
Doherty, P. 208
Dolan, R.T. 351, 511, 620
Dolgoff, R. 301, 320, 322
domain knowledge, reflexive practice 216–17
Domanski, M.D. 266
domestic violence 199–200, 377, 383, 412, 420, 504, 526
dominance 60, 192, 342, 455–6, 507, 708–9, 719
dominant culture 242–3, 295, 334
dominant groups 21, 364, 716–17
dominant languages 364, 724
dominant social groups 330, 335
dominant values 24, 27, 29
domination 10, 19, 23–4, 26–30, 364, 689, 717–18
Dominelli, L. 2, 34, 43, 118, 296, 321, 328–38, 363–4, 457, 474, 503, 615, 618, 647, 698, 711, 717, 734
double-loop learning 218–19
downsizing 37–8, 42, 277
Dreyfus, H.L. & S.E. 123–4, 207
drinking *see* alcohol
drug and alcohol interventions 579–92
drug courts 589
drugs 163, 238, 462, 499, 518, 579–92, 618
   community-based interventions 588–91
   individual, group, and family treatment 584–8
   prevalence of abuse 579–81
   prevention programming 581–4
dual-processing treatment 587
dual relationships 308, 310–11
due diligence 232
dynamic risk factors 434, 601, 605
dynamics 15–16, 19–20, 26, 29, 90, 119, 664
   of oppression 331–2, 337–8

Eagleton, T. 742
early intervention 507, 518, 607–8, 615, 620, 635
   parent-mediated 431
eating disorders 163–4
Eayrs, C. 620
EBMWG *see* Evidence-based Medicine Working Group
EBP *see* evidence-based practice
EBT *see* evidence-based treatment
ecological determinants of parenting behaviour and child maltreatment 132–4
ecological frameworks for work with children and families 130–1
ecological perspective 110, 129–40, 525
ecological systems 163, 524–5, 619
ecological theory 110, 129–31, 139, 651, 656
ecology of human development 130–1
eco-maps 136–7
economic change 426, 714, 727, 735

economic crisis 33, 37–8, 44, 46, 287, 402, 631
  global 9, 16, 631–2
economic development 17, 95, 98, 103, 105, 376–7
  policies 98–9, 106
economic growth 17, 34–6, 41, 44–5, 94–5,
    105–6, 637–8
economic inequalities 286, 335, 339, 470
economic justice 648, 653
economic liberalism 53, 55–6
economic participation 17, 99, 102, 106
economic policies 45, 94–5, 283, 285
economic power 42, 402–3
economic rights 34, 376, 378, 380, 648
economics 7–8, 11, 97, 116–17, 361, 379, 451
  neoclassical 83
  supply-side 33, 37, 45
economic security 36, 41, 539
economic surplus 22–3, 54
economic systems 19, 27
economy 9, 34, 38, 45, 55, 67, 714–15
  global 37, 64, 87, 283, 569
  local 573–4
  political 8, 16, 35, 55–6, 58, 63, 65
ECP *see* empirical clinical practice
Edley, N. 522
education
  professional *see* social work education
  tertiary 649, 668–9
effectiveness 187–8, 387–8, 424–7, 430–7, 602, 604,
    618–21
  cost 17, 105
  of interventions 388, 402, 428, 432–5, 487, 605
  long-term 364, 617, 698
efficacy 245, 400, 402, 409, 477, 484, 586
ego 416, 521
  psychology 267, 651
Ehrenreich, J. 53–5, 64–5, 151, 184
Eisler, R M. 163
elder care *see* older people
electronic turn 629, 677–8
elites 35, 44, 272, 638, 682, 729
Elliott, D. 500, 576, 631, 635
embeddedness, social 605, 679
emotional experiences 239, 270
  corrective 237–8, 244
emotional neutrality 270
emotional support 135, 137–8, 256, 538
emotions 85, 119, 124, 184, 219, 226, 515–16
empathic understanding 252, 256–7
empathy 6, 153, 238, 242, 244, 342, 462
empirical clinical practice (ECP) 388, 413–15
empirical evidence 224, 245, 398, 444, 490, 493, 501
empirically supported treatments (ESTs)
    388, 414–17, 419
empirical research 143, 146, 156, 224, 320–2,
    417, 419
employees 57, 77, 299, 303, 305, 527, 565
employers 36, 40, 57, 73, 303, 667–70, 672–3

employment 71, 87–91, 94–5, 120–2, 131–2,
    431–2, 575
  creation 97, 102–3
empowering and transformative practice 264–77
  compatibility of social work values with
    transformational practice 269–71
  models for transformational practice 271–3
    elite theory model 272
    group theory model 271–2
    incremental model 272–3
    institutional model 271
    process model 271
    rational model 272
  prescriptions for action 276–7
  social workers as change agents and
    transformers 273–6
empowerment 10, 52, 101, 331, 335–6, 459, 560
  community 101, 280, 456
Engeström, Y. 664–7, 670, 672
England and Wales (*see also* Britain) 121, 214, 231,
    330, 506–7, 509, 597–600, 602, 607, 741
environment
  living 534–5, 541, 677
  physical 146, 254, 331, 338, 540–1, 549, 730
environmental circumstances 131, 149, 156, 252
environmental factors 132, 138, 146, 148, 150,
    157, 252
epistemology 65, 424, 454–5, 461, 485, 708
  extended 469–70, 472
  modernist 342
Epstein, W. 650
equality 17, 21, 270–1, 335–6, 352, 693–4, 703
  affective 346
  gender 16, 86, 88–91
equal worth 352, 557
Esping-Andersen, G. 34, 58–60, 65, 709
Esposito, R. 7, 281–2
ESTs *see* empirically supported treatments
ethical choices 299, 347, 684
ethical codes *see* codes of ethics
ethical decision making 316–25
  common understandings of critical elements 324
  historical overview 318–23
  models 296, 318–22, 324
  protocols 301, 313
ethical dilemmas 43, 301, 312–13, 317–23, 505, 677
ethical practice 86, 148, 197, 303–4, 306, 312, 317
ethical principles 2, 9, 11, 305–6, 317, 320, 322
ethical responsibilities 304–5, 309, 317, 319, 364, 509
ethical standards 296, 299–313, 317, 322, 689, 750
  evolution 300–2
ethical theory 301, 305, 320, 322, 324, 344, 348–9
ethics
  of care 346–9
    feminist *see* feminist ethics of care
    reformulated 351–2
  codes of *see* codes of ethics
  education 320–1, 323

and politics 750–1
  virtue 319, 321, 347–8, 351, 742, 750–1
ethnic identities 357–8, 363
ethnicity 122, 199, 231, 245, 285, 346, 555–7
  and family support services 618–19
ethnic minorities 122, 334, 364, 377, 551, 553, 555
ethnography 75, 389, 455–6, 460
EU *see* European Union
Europe 86–90, 328–9, 357–8, 555–6, 565–6, 569–70, 708–9
  Western 33–4, 87–8, 357–8, 581
European Union (EU) 87–8, 358, 619, 646
evaluation 144, 257, 272–3, 425–6, 440–5, 449–50, 618–20
  and codes of ethics 312
  research 388, 401, 432, 437, 440–52, 493
    context and science issues 441–9
    and social work 449–52
evaluative research *see* evaluation, research
everyday practice 28, 123, 140, 373, 685–6, 689
evidence 117–20, 408–10, 415–19, 484–5, 490–2, 517–19, 614–17
  hierarchies of 388, 430, 435–6, 463, 485, 489
  standards of appraisal 174–5
Evidence-based Medicine Working Group (EBMWG) 408
evidence-based practice (EBP) 388–9, 400–1, 408–20, 482–4, 486–8, 518–19, 657
  and behaviourism 417
  and best practices 416–17
  controversies 418–19
  and criminal justice 602
  critics 410–11, 417
  current status 419–20
  and managerialism 417–18
  and medical models 418
  model 408–9, 413, 417
  and practice guidelines/treatment manuals 415–16
  precursors to 413–15
evidence-based treatment (EBT) 237, 415, 419, 586, 589
exo-system 130–1, 524
experiential knowledge 469, 518, 522, 528
experimental research designs 388, 428, 483, 489, 491
experiments 31, 56–7, 388, 410, 456
  field 650, 656–7
expertise 2–3, 9, 30, 102, 216, 227–8, 289
  clinical 408–9, 415
  professional 3, 54, 330, 647, 662
experts 54, 85, 123, 125, 181, 227, 273–4
expert systems 681–3
explanatory knowledge 394–5, 400, 469
exploitation 19, 22–30, 98, 101–2, 192, 306, 312
  sexual 567
exposure to feared situations 151–2
extended epistemology 469–70, 472
extended family members 136, 539, 617

external resources 103, 184, 259
external validity 410, 430, 432–3, 435, 437
extrinsic qualities 483, 488, 490–1

facilitators 478, 486, 663
facilities 288–9, 364, 484, 518
  nursing 535, 537, 540–1, 552, 557
factual knowledge 114, 120–2, 124–5
  domain 115, 120–2
fairness 258, 349–50, 359, 378, 398
families 86–90, 130–9, 161–2, 165–71, 349–51, 587–92, 613–19
  birth 225, 229–30, 232
  ecological frameworks for work with 130–1
  multigenerational 534, 538, 542
  poor 43, 99, 103–4, 637
family behavioural treatment 168, 170–1
family caregivers 538–9, 542–3
family centres 443
Family Group Conferences (FGCs) 350–1, 617
family interventions 110, 119, 162–4, 171, 576, 582
family members 89, 148, 162, 164, 166, 254–5, 588
  extended 136, 539, 617
family models, combined 168–71
family perspectives 161–71, 173, 175
family reunion 571–2
family social work *see* child and family social work
family support network (FSN) 587
family support services 139, 350, 499, 501, 613–23
  comparative contexts 614–15
  culture and ethnicity 618–19
  effectiveness 619–21
  methods of support 617–18
  models of assessment 615–17
  and social work 621–2
family systems
  perspectives 163–5
  therapy 163–5
family systems models 110, 163
family therapy 110, 118, 161–5, 412, 616, 620
  behavioural 110, 166–8, 171
  functional 168–70
  Maudsley model 164
  multidimensional 168, 170, 587–8
  narrative 165
  structural 163–5, 168
  systemic 164
Farbing, C.A. 589
fathers 69, 87–8, 137, 254–5, 345, 550, 620 *see also* parents
  biological 163
Fawcett, B. 196, 428, 499–500, 516, 519–20, 526, 528
feared situations, exposure to 151–2
Featherstone, B. 296, 318, 342–3, 347, 349, 351, 617
feedback 2, 144, 148, 155, 228, 473, 701
feminism 96, 119, 192–3, 197, 273, 286, 341–53

feminist ethics of care 341–53
  care, power and diversity 345–6
  care as moral and political practice 343–5
  contribution of reformulated ethics of care 351–2
  everyday lives, identities, and practices 349–51
  gendered moral frameworks 341–3
Ferguson, I. 43, 67, 192, 195–8, 225, 476–8, 630, 741, 748, 750
feudalism 8, 27, 742–3
FFT *see* functional family therapy
FGCs *see* Family Group Conferences
field experiments 650, 656–7
Findhelp Information Services 680
Finsbury 288–90
First Nations of Canada 335, 462
fixed identities 197, 353
Flexner, A. 3, 647, 655
Florida 73–4, 573
food 8, 24, 43, 56, 100, 376, 569–70
Fook, J. 12, 191, 193, 195–6, 198, 202, 455, 457, 476, 707, 735–6
forced labour 567
forced migration 565–70
Fordism 60
formalisation 678, 683–6, 689
  modes of 689
  process and consequences 685
formal knowledge 11, 208, 221, 224
Forrester, D. 125, 388, 443, 446, 450
fostercare 169, 199, 225, 728
Foucault, M. 52–4, 62–5, 73–4, 78, 196, 316, 329, 444, 506, 508, 510, 549, 742
frail adults 541–2
France 59, 87, 170, 302, 323, 357–8, 570–1
Frankenberg, R. 362, 717–18
Frankfurt School 194
Franklin, A.J. 245
Fraser, M.W. 118, 156, 401, 425, 431, 456
Fraser, N. 334, 351–2
fraud 311
fraudulent billing 306–7
Freeman, A. 156
free markets 33–4, 55, 57, 283
Freire, P. 733, 735
Freud, S. 456, 521
Frideres, J.S. 477
Friedman, M. 97, 237
frontline discretion 16, 68, 72, 77
frontline workers 68, 72, 75–7, 609, 748, 750
FSN *see* family support network
functional ability 424, 531, 534–5, 540
functional analysis 144–5, 586
functional family therapy (FFT) 168–70
functional limitations 535–6, 541, 547, 551
functions of social work 4, 6–8, 678
future challenges 13, 312, 627–752
futures of social work 631–41

Gambrill, E. 11, 110, 143, 147, 156, 229, 401, 411, 650
Garbarino, J. 133
Garfield, S.L. 238
Garfinkel, H. 686
Garland, E. 586, 598–9, 609
Garrett, P.M. 2, 34, 38, 43, 334–5, 506, 509–10, 628, 632–8, 667, 678, 683, 688, 748–9, 751
GASOW *see* Ghanaian Association of Social Workers
gay men 213, 334, 536–8, 553, 555, 560–1, 618
GCIM *see* Global Commission on International Migration
gender 16, 198–200, 333, 342, 345–7, 363–4, 534–6
  blindness 44, 193
  definition and conceptualisation 81–2
  equality 16, 86, 88–91
  overview of welfare state approach 86–9
  perspective 82, 85–6
  and physical well-being in older people 536
  relations 17, 81–2, 87, 347
  towards a progressive policy agenda 89–92
  and welfare 81–92
gendered moral frameworks 341–3
General Health Questionnaire (GHQ) 431
generalisability 162, 443–5, 456, 486
generalisable knowledge 425, 441, 444–5
general responsivity 603
General Social Care Council (GSCC) 118, 225, 303, 634, 667–8
Gergen, K. & M. 468
geriatric care *see* older people
Germany 34, 37, 59, 357–8, 571–2, 682, 743–4
  Nazi 550, 747
Ghana 472–3, 550–1, 726, 729
Ghanaian Association of Social Workers (GASOW) 472–3
GHQ *see* General Health Questionnaire
Gibbons, J. 135–6, 323
Gibbons, M. 11
Giddens, A. 113, 225, 508
Gilgun, J. 456, 524
Gilligan, C. 86, 341–3, 345
Gillingham, P. 228, 687
girls 248–9, 341–2, 550 *see also* children
global capitalism 279, 282, 476, 478–9, 743
Global Commission on International Migration (GCIM) 564–6
global economic crisis 9, 16, 631–2
global economy 37, 64, 87, 283, 569
global injustice 15, 19, 25, 27
globalisation 2, 40, 282–3, 569, 613, 713–14, 734
  era of 715–16
global justice 19, 21, 28, 31, 715
  meanings 20–2
global North 375, 377, 381, 569, 571, 573, 576
global South 94, 96, 103–4, 381, 568–9, 712, 751–2
Glucksmann, M. 91
goal and case planning 184–7, 188
Goffman, E. 221, 444

Goldberg, T. 451–2
Goldfried, M. 237–8, 240, 244
Goldsmith, S. 653–5
Good Samaritan parable 740
Gordon, C. 52–3, 62–4, 69
Gould, N. 118, 455, 457, 462, 476
governance 5–7, 21–2, 24, 26, 51–2, 56, 73–4
  modern 54–6
  poverty 16, 68, 71, 73–4
  welfare *see* welfare governance
governmentality 16, 55, 62–3, 65, 73, 486–7, 509–10
  and welfare governance 62–4
government policies 9, 56, 102, 285, 424, 426, 693
Gramsci, A. 31, 79, 509, 632, 751
grandchildren 538–9
grandparents 350, 536, 539, 615, 617
Gray, M. 2–3, 12, 52, 113, 118–19, 188, 196–7, 266, 273, 285–6, 289–90, 295, 317, 321, 323, 329, 335, 341, 344, 347–8, 352, 411, 418–19, 468, 476, 478, 486, 519, 574, 608, 615, 619, 621, 627, 657, 685, 708, 711–12, 719, 723–6, 730, 732–6, 745, 748, 750–2
Great Depression 16, 33, 45, 69, 533
Great Recession 44, 46, 537
Great Society 37, 268
Gredig, D. 387, 394, 401
Greencavage, L.M. 238
green shoots of encouragement 504, 510, 512
grounded theory 389, 455–6, 459–60, 462
group decision making 212, 214, 219–20
GSCC *see* General Social Care Council
Guba, E.G. 393
guest workers 357, 565
guidance 121, 132, 150, 256, 306, 490–1, 731

Habermas, J. 5, 194, 509, 512
habitual residence 566–7
habitus 509, 628, 634, 641, 679
Hamilton Project 45
Hammersley, M. 392, 418–19, 484–6, 492
happiness 84
Harden, A. 490
hardship 43, 256, 334, 638
Harlem Children's Zone 654
harmony 280, 522, 548, 730
harm reduction 581, 583
Harris, J. 417, 680, 686, 748
Harvey, D. 33, 37, 42, 58, 60, 251, 639, 750
Haug, E. 708, 712, 714
Haynes, K.S. 209, 266–7, 269–71
health 42–4, 200–3, 538–42, 661–2, 666, 668–9, 671–3
healthcare 28, 43, 120, 137, 264, 269–70, 412
  reform 264, 500, 535, 540
health inequalities 117, 122
health professions 122, 219–20, 318, 377, 662–3, 668

Health Professions Council 634, 667–8
health-promoting behaviours 542, 581
health-related disabilities 554–5
health services 43, 319, 540, 663, 727
health visitors 116, 124, 211, 217–18, 350
Healy, K. 110–11, 191–8, 201–2, 317, 322, 375, 378–9, 381, 469, 474, 477–8, 708–9, 711–12, 715, 719, 724, 734–5
Hean, S. 662, 664, 672
hearing impairments 552–3, 558
Heath, C. 686–7
Heawood, S. 637
hegemonic power 331–3, 718
hegemony 51, 283, 455, 464, 509, 639–40, 716–17
HEIs *see* higher education institutions
Hekman, S. 341–2
helpers 154, 178–9, 188, 215, 431
helping professions 150, 157, 652, 746
Henggeler, S.W. 168
Heron, J. 469–70, 476, 714
heuristics 64, 323, 325
  cognitive 208, 325
  moral 212–13, 220
hierarchies of evidence 388, 430, 435–6, 463, 485, 489
higher education 255, 402, 572, 574–5, 646–8, 662–3, 665
  institutions (HEIs) 663–6, 668–70, 672–3
high-risk areas 133, 139, 232
historical institutionalism 58–60
HIV/AIDS 299, 462, 539, 552, 554–5, 663, 699
Hoff, L.A. 257
Hokenstad, M.G. 707, 712, 715, 734–5
holistic approach 131, 318, 452, 663
Holland, S. 349, 411, 462
hollowing out 60–2
Hollway, W. 344–5, 351
home economics 728
homelessness 399, 420, 459, 531, 581, 715
homicides 231, 248, 581
Honneth, A. 334, 351–2
Hood, C. 5, 232
Hooyman, N. 500
hospitals 136, 163, 211, 229–30, 516–17, 540–3, 638–9
host countries/societies 357–8, 565, 570–3, 577
housing 28, 33, 35, 43, 95, 120–2, 124
Houston, S. 2, 194, 334–5, 348, 351–2, 499, 507, 509, 525
Howard, M.O. 416, 419
Hudson, B. 662, 671, 673–4
Hugman, R. 297, 299, 317, 321, 323, 347, 373, 377, 379, 381–2
human agency 95, 105, 185, 335, 374–5
human capital investments 102–3
human nature 19, 28, 30, 213, 316
  and socially just communities 22–3

human rights 268–9, 296–7, 306, 317, 331, 335–6, 567
　definitions 376
　and social justice 372–84
　　origins of social work's core values 373–6
　　problems of integration 380–2
　　questions for theory and practice 383
human service agencies 184, 274, 304, 584
human services 3, 15, 179, 181, 187–8, 316, 678
Human Services Information Technology Applications (HUSITA) 678
human trafficking 248, 566–8, 571
hunger 56
Husain, S.A. 249, 255
HUSITA *see* Human Services Information Technology Applications
Hutton, M. 729–30
Huxley, P.J. 527
hybrid practitioners 672–4

IASC *see* Inter-Agency Standing Committee
IASSW *see* International Association of Schools of Social Work
IASWs *see* initial assessment social workers
ICIDH *see* International Classification of Impairments, Disabilities, and Handicaps
ICSW *see* International Council on Social Welfare
id 521
identities 195–8, 200, 332–4, 338, 349–50, 361–3, 670–2
　co-construction 367
　collective 202, 377, 379, 547
　deviant 503, 510
　ethnic 357–8, 363
　fixed 197, 353
identity politics 332–4, 351–2
ideologies 25–7, 53, 702–3, 710–11, 717, 746–7, 749
　political 9, 630, 741, 752
　socialist 102, 329, 332
IDPs *see* internally displaced persons
IFSW *see* International Federation of Social Workers
IIS *see* integrated information systems
illness 35, 135–6, 181, 183, 186, 517–18, 539
immigrant groups 569–70, 573–5
immigrants 44, 53–4, 355, 358, 499–500, 564–77, 710–11
　global migrants 565–8
　global migration data 566
　high profile of immigration 564–5
　impact on host countries 573–4
　integration in host countries 571–3
　politicisation of human tragedy 570–1
　role of social work 576
　unaccompanied children 566–7, 571
　unauthorised 573–4
　undocumented 567–8, 574
　unequal burden on Global South 568–70
　voluntary 565, 569, 571, 575
　and welfare 574–6

immigration 356–60, 564, 571, 573, 575–6, 716
　see also immigrants
impairments 253, 310, 312, 517, 547–8, 551, 553–4
　see also disability
　cognitive 535
　hearing 552–3, 558
impartiality 270–1
imperialism 95, 655, 711, 713, 717–19, 749
　professional 713, 732
incentives 43, 56–7, 72–4, 76–7, 103–4, 147
　market 15, 59
inclusion 1, 192, 274, 325, 356, 485, 489–90
　social 285, 337, 345, 366, 396, 475, 491
income redistribution 36, 90
incomes 33, 35–6, 40–5, 90–1, 103–4, 121–2, 283
　retirement 43, 535, 575
incompetence 311–12, 662
independence 95, 255, 342, 345, 353, 482, 726–7
India 357, 381, 403, 462, 538, 565, 725
indigenisation 712–13, 724, 729, 732–3, 746
individualism 27, 33, 284, 750–1
　neoliberal 209, 290, 750
　rampant 279, 285
individualist enterprise strategy 95, 100–1
Individual Responsibility Plans (IRPs) 71–2
inequalities 26, 29–30, 46, 282–3, 338–9, 346, 377–9
　see also equality
　economic 286, 335, 339, 470
　health 117, 122
　social 83, 338, 711, 715
　structural 134, 181, 209, 290, 331, 337, 362
inequality gap 35, 38–9, 43, 45
informal care 85, 535
informal social networks 110, 133
　promotion 135–8
information categorisation 505–7
information technology *see* new technologies
informatisation 678, 682, 689
informed consent 148, 154, 302, 304, 308–10, 312, 319
initial assessment 116, 212, 616
initial assessment social workers (IASWs) 212–13
injustice 22–3, 25–6, 28, 30–1, 249, 282–3, 339
　cultural 335, 339
　global 15, 19, 25, 27
innate capacities 20–2, 30
innovation 61, 74, 110, 177, 328, 654–5, 677
　and social work education 653–5
　technological 677, 679, 681, 688
inpatient care 177, 185, 187
inputs 216, 219, 336, 450, 658, 680
insiders 75, 478
institutionalism, historical 58–60
institutional racism 44, 615
instrumental rationality 4–5
integrated information systems (IIS) 681
integrated services 628–9, 663

integration 4, 114, 132, 237, 373, 408–9, 570–3
  assimilative 208–9, 237–8, 241–4
  civic 356–8
  psychotherapeutic 208, 237–8
  social 185, 360, 500
  technical 237–9
  theoretical 238–41
integrative psychotherapy 208, 236–45
  common factors in psychotherapy 238
  history 237–8
intellectual disabilities 551, 553, 556
interaction
  patterns 146, 155, 163, 165–6
  social 138, 165, 281, 338, 351, 363, 522
Inter-Agency Standing Committee (IASC) 258
interdependence 98, 331, 344–5, 353, 381, 540, 556–7
interdisciplinarity 660–1
internally displaced persons (IDPs) 565, 567–8
internal validity 388, 432–3, 461, 490
International Association of Schools of Social Work (IASSW) 301, 372, 375–6, 475, 709–10, 724, 731
International Classification of Impairments, Disabilities, and Handicaps (ICIDH) 548
International Council on Social Welfare (ICSW) 709
international development 484, 708–9, 714
international exchanges 630, 707–8, 711, 715, 715–18
International Federation of Social Workers (IFSW) 301, 306, 317, 375–6, 475, 694, 709–10
internationalisation 707, 711, 713, 719, 723, 734
International Monetary Fund 34, 96, 282, 472, 714, 735
international recognition 730–1
International Refugee Organization (IRO) 570
international social work 372, 401, 630, 707–19, 734–5
  definition 711–14
  development of social work in Canada as example 710–11
  discourse 711–12, 714, 718, 723
  globalisation and international development 714–15
  international exchanges and collaborations from a critical standpoint 715–18
  literature 717, 719, 745
  organisations 378, 475, 694
  profession's internationalising agenda 708–10
internet 313, 402, 459, 677–8
interpersonal relationships 43, 240, 244, 276
interprofessional education (IPE) 318, 489, 491, 660–3, 665–74
interprofessionalism 629, 672
interprofessionality 673–4
interprofessional learning 660, 664–5, 670–4
interprofessional practice 489, 629, 660–74
  activity theory 664–5
  definitions and discourse 662–3
  and employers 668
  higher education institution stakeholders 669–71
  non-higher education institution stakeholders 665–9
  pedagogic research base 663–4
  and policy makers 666–7
  power in 671–2
  and regulators 667–8
  and service users and carers 668–9
interrupted time series research designs 427–8, 436
intervention groups 427, 429, 433–4
interventionist knowledge 394–5, 400–1
intervention research (IR) 388, 401, 424–37
  before-and-after designs 426–7, 436
  and challenges for social work 430
  cluster randomised controlled intervention designs 429
  developments 425–6
  experimental designs 428
  hierarchy of study designs 436
  longitudinal designs 427
  mediating factors 430, 434–6
  non-randomised controlled intervention designs 427
  observational designs 426–7
  outcome measures 431–5
  parenting programs 167, 427, 430, 430–1, 463
  randomised controlled intervention studies 428–9, 433
  research design types 426–30
  sub-group analysis 435
  waiting list control groups 429–30
interviews 119, 134, 139, 147, 149, 187, 458–9
  research 74, 447, 670
intrinsic qualities 483, 488, 490
intuition 114–15, 124, 226–7, 272, 408, 505
intuitive reasoning 119, 226–7, 229
intuitive risk assessment 225–9
intuitive skills 226–7
investments 17, 95, 103, 299, 460, 494, 537
  human capital 102–3
IPE *see* interprofessional education
IR *see* intervention research
Ireland 9, 87, 89, 302, 346, 728
  future of social work 637–41
IRO *see* International Refugee Organization
IRPs *see* Individual Responsibility Plans
isolation 121, 270, 288, 382, 476, 526, 671
  social 121–2, 136, 254, 445, 537, 619
Israel 302, 411, 456, 459, 462, 570, 749
IT *see* new technologies
Italy 9, 31, 59, 302, 533, 570, 572
iterative approaches 493–4
Ivey, A. 245

James, R.K. 250, 257–8, 356, 750
Japan 37, 245, 284, 302, 532–3, 551, 724
JAR *see* Joint Area Review
Jeffery, D. 365, 710–11
Jessop, B. 60–1, 64–5
Johnson, D. & R. 220
Johnson, W.R. 589
Joint Area Review (JAR) 633–4

Jones, C. 375, 698
Jones, J. 468, 470, 478
Jones, K. 191, 202–3
Jones, R. 121, 620
Jordan, B. 279, 286–8, 379–80, 383, 462, 697, 709, 746
judgement, professional 208, 212–13, 232–3, 447–8, 486, 494, 505
Jung, C.G. 521
justice 83–4, 295, 343–4, 347, 378–81, 599–600, 606
 criminal *see* criminal justice
 dialogical 347–8, 352
 economic 648, 653
 ethic of 342–3, 349
 global 19–21, 28, 31, 715
 juvenile *see* juvenile justice
 restorative 608
 systems 598, 606–8
just societies 21, 104
juvenile justice 168, 170, 583, 597–608
 rights-based approaches 608
 social work in 606–8
juvenile probation service 426

Kahneman, D. 212, 227–8
Kant, I. 347, 373–4
Kaplan, E.A. 257, 717
Karger, H. 628–9
Katz, I. 614
Kendall, K. 328, 375, 605, 708–9, 723–6, 733
Kenya 547, 654, 749
Keynesian welfare state 34, 51–2, 60–1, 65, 67
kinship care 412, 430
Kirk, S. 396, 400, 413, 540
Kishthardt, W. 188
Klein, G. 227–8
Klein, M. 521
Klein, N. 283
Knapp, M. 432, 660, 674
knotworking 670
knowledge 113–16, 119–25, 154–7, 207–8, 212–19, 391–6, 467–74
 base 1–2, 9, 11, 109, 114, 118, 221
 creation 114–15, 123–4, 393, 396, 470
 development 11, 454–5, 464, 468, 470, 476, 487
 experiential 469, 518, 522, 528
 expert 124, 335, 528
 explanatory 394–5, 400, 469
 factual 114, 120–2, 124–5
 formal 11, 208, 221, 224
 generalisable 425, 441, 444–5
 interventionist 394–5, 400–1
 local 334, 730, 732–3
 modes of 684
 practice 109, 114–15, 122–5, 685
 production 11, 392–3, 456, 493–4, 724
 professional 395, 448, 470, 519, 657, 678
 for reflexive practice 211–21

 reviews 663–4
 and science 391–2
 scientific 12, 394, 399–401, 404, 477
 and skills framework 113–25
 tacit 114–15, 124
 theoretical 115–19, 123–5
knowledge-for-action 394
knowledge-for-understanding 394
Kopp, W. 654
Kotz, D. 34, 46
Kreitzer, L. 468, 472–3, 478
Kunkel, J. 153, 155

labelling 147, 333, 684–5, 688
labour 15, 41–2, 55–9, 85, 87, 91, 569
 markets 37, 57, 82, 87, 90, 572, 598
Labour Party 633, 635 *see also* New Labour
laissez-faire 33, 45, 53, 55, 63, 573
Lakatos, I. 392–3
Lampedusa 569–70
Langan, M. 696, 698–700
language 2–4, 152, 198, 225, 363–4, 461, 558
 common 358, 662, 688, 694
 constitutive power 196, 198, 200
Latinos 38, 40, 536–8, 631
Latour, B. 679, 683–4
Lavalette, M. 697–8, 703, 748
lawsuits 302, 307, 310–11
Layard, R. 84, 432, 750
leaders 69, 71, 258, 280, 552, 633, 650
 actor 669–70
 community 133–4, 259, 469, 582
leadership 101, 359, 402, 531, 540–1, 582, 729
learning disabilities 397, 427, 547, 554, 747–8
learning organisations 219, 664, 680
Lee, K.K. 431
Lee, P. 700
legislation 36, 70–1, 102, 120–2, 270–2, 274–6, 589
Leonard, P. 192, 195–6, 333, 618
lesbians 213, 534, 536–7, 551, 553, 555, 558
Lesser, J.G. 208, 241
Lewis, J. 85, 87–8, 91, 97
Lewis, S. 605
Lewy, L. 673–4
liberal democracy 375
liberalism 54, 63, 379
 economic 53, 55–6
 market 55, 57, 96, 105
 social 99
liberation 28–31, 33, 269, 372, 475, 636, 694–5
liberty 25, 27, 29, 31, 77, 374, 379–80
licensing 299–300, 302, 305–7
life expectancy 43, 504, 533–4, 536, 538, 552, 555
life-worlds 394, 402, 500, 509, 512, 684
Lindemann, E. 256
Lipsey, M.W. 604
Lipsky, M. 70, 75, 77–8, 299–300, 686
Lister, R. 88, 91, 352

litigation *see* lawsuits
Littell, J.H. 168, 170, 174, 412, 483, 485
living environments 534–5, 541, 677
local authorities 120–1, 212–13, 216–17, 288, 350, 449, 668
local communities 31, 43, 75, 139, 176, 282, 288–9
local knowledges 334, 730, 732–3
local residents 139, 287–8, 290
Loewenberg, F. 320, 322
lone parents *see* single parents
longitudinal research designs 427
Longmore, P. 549, 556, 558
Longoria, R. 364
long-term care 350, 535, 538, 540–2
long-term effectiveness 364, 617, 698
Lorenz, W. 328, 399, 564, 661, 671, 673–4, 713, 743, 747
Lovett, L. 319
loyalties 59–60, 243
Lucas, T. 729
Luff, P. 686–7
Lundy, C 373, 376–7, 382
Lynch, K. 346, 348, 352
Lyons, M. 346
Lyons, P. 229
Lyons, V. 714

Macdonald, G. 156, 169, 411, 430, 485, 489
Macias, C. 187
Mackelprang, R.W. 547, 549–50, 552, 554–5, 557–8
MacLure, M. 484–5
macro-system 130–1, 524
madness 444, 515–16, 526, 549 *see also* mental health
mainstream society 285, 360–1, 699
malpractice 302, 307–9
Malthus 56–7
managed pluralism 99, 102
management 24, 61, 72, 225–6, 230–1, 686–7, 695–6
　case *see* case management
　contingency 146, 152, 155, 588
　information systems (MIS) 657, 681
　new public 72–4, 117, 650, 695, 701
　performance 5, 67–8, 73–4, 506, 650, 688
　poverty 67, 75, 78
　risk *see* risk management
managerialism 9, 117–18, 280, 417, 477, 486, 695–8
　marketised 701–2
　procedural 507
managers 13, 69, 71–4, 76–8, 116, 186, 687–8
　case *see* case managers
marginalisation 192, 285, 360–6, 471, 552, 556, 558
marginalised communities/groups 75, 282, 285–6, 468, 474–6, 478, 555
marital therapy 412, 416, 430, 615
market forces 42, 45, 61, 477, 614
market incentives 15, 59
marketisation 40, 96, 479, 629, 677, 698, 701
marketised managerialism 701–2

market liberalism 55, 57, 96, 105
markets 33–5, 53, 57–61, 64–5, 67, 85, 89–90
　free 33–4, 55, 57, 283
　labour 37, 57, 82, 87, 90, 572, 598
　self-regulating 55–6, 58
　stock 45–6, 631
market saturation 648–9
Marlatt, G.A. 586
Marshall, T.H. 33, 648, 742–3
Martinez-Brawley, E. 718
Maruna, S. 603, 605
Marx, K. 193–4, 456, 742, 750–1
Marxists 105, 193, 195, 332, 347, 696, 743
Maslow, A.H. 20, 25, 522
Master of Social Work (MSW) 265–6, 414, 649, 652, 728
material resources 25, 83, 257, 378, 380, 382
Mattaini, M.A. 147, 150, 156
Matto, H.C. 500, 579, 583, 587
maturation 309, 312, 420, 537, 605–6
Maudsley, H. 516
Maudsley model of family therapy 164
MBCT *see* mindfulness-based cognitive therapy
McAuliffe, D. 296, 317, 320–1
McDonald, C. 192, 194, 201–3, 590, 646, 747, 752
McDonaldization 697
McLaughlin, H. 398
McLaughlin, K. 634, 741
McNay, L. 10, 351–2
MCT *see* multicultural counselling and therapy
MDFT *see* multidimensional family therapy
Meadows, G. 523–4, 526, 530
meanings 281, 478, 505–6, 512–13, 683–4, 693–4, 711–12
media 44, 102, 211, 282, 302, 376, 679–80
mediating factors 430, 434–6
medical care 43, 117, 259, 536, 638
medical models 116, 445, 526, 549–51, 579
　and evidence-based practice (EBP) 418
medical records 686
Medicare 137, 268, 537, 542
medication 157, 167, 174, 177–8, 185, 240, 518
　compliance 185–6, 588
　life-prolonging 552
mental disorders *see* mental illness
mental distress *see* distress
mental health 180, 245, 258, 319, 431–2, 499–500, 515–29
　clinical perspectives 517–20
　context of mental health social work 526–7
　definition 516–17
　disabilities 552–4, 558, 560
　historical overview 515–17
　psychological perspectives 520–2
　service-user, consumer, and survivor perspectives 525–6
　and social constructionism 523–5
　social perspectives 522–3

mental health (*Cont.*)
  survivors 194, 197, 522
  terminology and medicalisation 515–17
  way forward 527–9
mental illness 121, 177–81, 198, 517–18, 522, 524, 615–16 *see also* mental health
  persistent 176, 179, 184, 432
mental well-being, older people 537–8
meso-system 130–1. 168, 524
MET *see* motivational enhancement therapy
meta-analysis 162, 167, 174, 409–10, 483, 492–3, 620
methodological rigour 491, 519, 621
methodologies 11, 110, 207, 331, 397–9, 442, 485
  qualitative 396, 455, 490
MI *see* motivational interviewing
Mickelson, J.S. 268, 270–1
microenterprises 96, 98–9, 103–5, 290
microfinance 98, 100, 103–4
micro-politics 683, 703
micro-systems 130–1, 168, 524
middle class 35–6, 38–9, 60, 197, 365, 744
Midgley, J. 2, 17, 95, 97–103, 377, 655, 708, 710, 712–15, 723–5, 730, 732, 734–6, 747
migrants *see* immigrants
migration 345, 402, 564–5, 568–9, 571, 573, 577 *see also* immigration
  forced 565–70
  impact on host countries 573–4
Migration Integration Policy Index (MIPEX) 572–3
Millennium Development Goals 97, 106, 735
Miller, N.W. 237
Miller, P. 320
mindfulness-based cognitive therapy (MBCT) 245
mindfulness-based relapse prevention 586–7
mindfulness training 586
Mini-Mental State Examination (MMSE) 431
minorities 104, 254, 309, 360, 535, 559, 561
  ethnic 334, 551, 553, 555
Minuchin, S. 163, 165
MIPEX *see* Migration Integration Policy Index
MIS *see* management, information systems
misconduct 300, 304, 306–7, 311–12
misrepresentation 311, 461
missionaries 54, 708, 725, 727
  court work 597
mixed methods 389, 454, 462–3
MMSE *see* Mini-Mental State Examination
mobility disabilities 552
modernisation 336–7, 506, 732
  panoptical 505–6
modernist critical social science theories 194–5
modernist epistemology 342
modernity 4, 6–8, 12, 508, 639
Modood, T. 363, 366, 615
money 43, 55, 82, 90, 162, 179, 336
moral communitarianism 285–6
moral dilemmas 318, 324, 348, 688–9

moral frameworks, gendered 341–3
moral heuristics 212–13, 220
morality 90, 221, 300, 303, 312, 342, 344
moral philosophy 316–17, 320–1, 324, 341–2, 352
moral theory 296, 341–2
Morris, J. 333
Morris, K. 296, 350
Moss, P. 510–11
mothers 87–90, 162–3, 165–6, 211–12, 216–20, 254–6, 342 *see also* parents
motivation 26, 74, 147, 166, 211, 240, 565–6
motivational enhancement therapy (MET) 447, 586–7
motivational interviewing (MI) 444, 446, 585–6. 589, 592
MST *see* multisystemic treatment
MSW *see* Master of Social Work
MT *see* multimodal therapy
multicultural counselling and therapy (MCT) 241–3, 362
multiculturalism 241, 296, 355–60, 363, 365–8, 716
  from above 359–60
  approaches to 356–65
  Australia 358–9
  from below 356–9
  Canada 359–60
  colour blind approach 38, 243, 360–2, 368, 599
  cultural competence 309, 356–7, 360, 362–7, 500
  cultural inferiority approach 360–1
  cultural sensitivity approach 361–3
  philosophy of 296, 355–6
  USA 358
  Western Europe 357–8
multicultural theory 242–4
multidimensional family therapy (MDFT) 168, 170, 587–8
multigenerational families/households 534, 538, 542
multimethod research 389, 449, 464
multimodal therapy (MT) 237, 245
multisystemic treatment (MST) 168–9
multi-voicedness 665, 667, 672
Muncie, J. 606–8
Munro, E. 8–9, 114, 118–19, 124, 208, 215, 218, 228–9, 232, 325, 507, 634–5, 694–5
munus 281
Mupediziswa, R 733
murder 27, 43, 212, 254 *see also* homicides
Mwansa, L.K. 712–13, 723–7, 733, 736
Myrdal, G. 98
myths 149, 152, 275, 277, 388, 486, 524
  popular 569, 574–5

naloxone 585
naltrexone 585
Nancy, J.L. 280–1
narrative family therapy 165
narrative reviews 485–6, 493
NASW *see* National Association of Social Workers

National Association of Social Workers 69, 207, 236, 264, 301, 364, 531
National Association of Social Workers (NASW) 161, 236, 264–6, 274, 301, 307, 555
　Code of Ethics 171, 269, 301, 304–5
national identity 297, 356–60, 366, 368, 735
National Institute on Drug Abuse (NIDA) 168, 582, 589
nationalism 709–10
nationality 346, 566–7, 572
National Social Work Qualification Board (NSWQB) 640
nation-states 8, 12, 328, 506–7, 564, 572, 716
naturalism 56–7
nature and role of social work 3–6
Nazi Germany 550, 747
neglect 121, 231, 254, 344–5, 349–50, 412, 448
negotiation 266, 281, 322, 404, 448, 527–8, 633
neighbourhoods 130, 133, 139, 146–7, 287–90, 540–1, 582–3
neighbours 116, 134, 136, 185, 258, 288, 425
neoclassical economics 83
neoliberal globalisation 285, 569, 718, 723
　impact on local communities 282–4
neoliberal individualism 209, 290, 750
neoliberalism 15–16, 33–4, 37–8, 41–5, 67, 200–3, 503–5
　explicit critique 346, 353
　future 44–6
　impact 38–42
　implications for social work 42–4
　and new public management 200–1
neoliberal paternalism 68, 72, 79
neoliberal welfare state 42
　theorisation 33–46
Netherlands 87, 90, 170, 284, 526, 550, 580–1
networks 28, 138, 280, 285, 397, 516, 540
　social 103, 110, 133–6, 138, 346, 572, 579
　support 118, 135–6, 139, 539, 587
neutrality 29, 270, 335
　emotional 270
　political 28–9, 269
　value 28–9, 747
New Deal 35–7, 95, 267
New Deal for Communities 279
New Labour 279, 285–6, 336–7, 345, 637, 663, 666
new organisational culture 73–4
new public management 72–4, 117, 650, 695, 701
New Public Management (NPM) 72–4, 117, 191–2, 196, 200–2, 448, 650–1
　and neoliberalism 200–1
　and performance anxiety 72–3
New South Wales 266
new technologies 284, 629, 677–89, 713, 724
　actors, functions and attributions 680–1
　basic process of formalisation 683–6
　documental character of social work 686–7
　empirical studies of impact 687–9

expert systems 681–3
formalisation, discretion and documentation processes 683
social work in the digital age 677–80
New Technology 678
NGOs see nongovernmental organisations
Ngwenya, B. 728–9
Nichols, M. 161–3
NIDA see National Institute on Drug Abuse
nongovernmental organisations (NGOs) 2, 97, 101, 104, 257–8, 380, 655–6
nonpolitical professionalism 630, 752
non-randomised controlled intervention research designs 427
Norcross, J.C. 237–8, 244
Nordic countries 33, 88, 90, 375, 401, 504, 572
normalisation 61, 509–10, 519, 553, 733
normative preferences, and social development strategies 100–2
norms 77, 82, 88, 91, 356–8, 583, 732–3
　cultural 117, 357, 665
　social 82, 360, 582–3, 592, 619
Northern Ireland 411, 428, 640, 663, 749
Norway 88, 282, 302, 357, 571–2, 746
NPM see New Public Management
NSWQB see National Social Work Qualification Board
nurses 211, 300, 302, 319, 377, 410, 543
Nursing and Midwifery Council 667–8
nursing facilities 535, 537, 540–1, 552, 557
Nussbaum, M. 84, 376, 381–2, 652–3
Nutley, S. 484–6, 491
nutrition 33, 94, 97, 103, 218

Oakley, A. 443, 484, 486
OASys see Offender Assessment System
obesity 43, 253, 535
objective assessments 8, 430
objectivity 269–70, 342, 393, 485, 516
obligations 6, 86–7, 90, 265, 270, 281, 296
observation 22, 113, 119, 144–7, 149, 392–3, 459
observers 42, 76, 146, 474, 608, 684
obsessive compulsive disorder (OCD) 239–40, 244, 554
occupational therapy 666, 669
occupations 25, 285, 403, 471, 509, 566, 666
OCD see obsessive compulsive disorder
Offender Assessment System (OASys) 602
offenders 231, 589, 597–8, 600, 602–5, 609
offending behaviour 600–1, 603–5, 608
older people 531–43
　ageing as global phenomenon 532–4
　ageing in a healthy manner 539–43
　community-based initiatives 540–1
　definitions 532
　long-term care living environments 541
　mental well-being 537–8
　models of care coordination 541–3

older people (*Cont.*)
  physical well-being 534–7
    by age and functional ability 534–6
    by gender 536
    by race 536
    by sexual orientation 536–7
    by social class 537
  social well-being 538–9
Oliver, M. 333, 699–700, 702–3
omissions 249, 308
O'Neill, O. 376, 379
online counselling 680–1
operant conditioning 152, 167, 520
oppressed groups/communities 195, 197–8, 448–9, 551, 750
oppression 22–6, 28, 30–1, 154, 197, 332–5, 361–5
  dynamics of 331–2, 337–8
  in practice *see* anti-oppressive practice (AOP)
  social 192–4, 199
oppressive relationships 362, 364, 367
optimism 31, 176, 180, 183, 202, 352, 456
Orford, J. 446–7
organisational context 74, 78, 200, 225, 280, 470, 499
organisational culture 76, 180, 218, 403, 541, 677, 679
  new 73–4
Orme, J.G. 347–9, 352
Orszag, P.R. 45
Osei-Hwedie, K. 723, 727, 729–34
Ostermann, R. 183
others
  needs of 350, 379, 382
  perspective of 166, 433
outcome measures 169, 175, 410, 428, 430–4, 437, 617–18
  intervention research 431–5
  proxy 432–4
  psychometric 431–2
outcomes 144–9, 430–4, 436, 440–3, 449–51, 525–7, 673–4
  and participatory action research (PAR) 476
outsiders 202, 478, 525, 564
overt social control 196, 201
ownership 239, 359, 380, 469, 473, 672

PACE *see* Program of All-Inclusive Care of the Elderly
Padgett, D.K. 388, 454–8, 460, 463
Paiva, F.J.X. 97, 101
Pakistan 568
Palestine 570, 749
palliative care 319, 473, 663
Pandey, R. 98
panoptical modernisation 505–6
PAR *see* participatory action research
parental self-esteem 434
parent education 615, 618
parenting 129, 133, 164, 211, 618, 637
  behaviour 131–2
    ecological determinants 132–4

capacity 131–2
programs, intervention research (IR) 167, 427, 430–1, 463
parent-mediated early intervention 431
parents 132–3, 139, 144–6, 162–71, 350, 587–8, 615–20
  biological 163, 165, 169
  single 117, 164, 534, 614, 619
parent training 166–8
parole 599–600
partiality 51, 342, 349
participation 96, 102–5, 401–2, 467, 475, 477–8, 629–30
  democratic 101, 104
  economic 17, 99, 102, 106
  service-user 475–6, 629
participatory action research (PAR) 389, 456, 467–79
  and critical reflection 476–8
  definition 467–8
  examples 470–4
  focus on participatory action 469
  nature and use in practice 470–4
  nature of knowledge created 469–70
  participatory world view 468–9
  process and outcomes 476
  service-user involvement 475
  social work as form of 478–9
  suitability for social work 474–8
partnerships 103, 201, 324, 489, 618, 666, 668–72
Parton, N. 116, 118, 124, 231, 399, 505–8, 613–14, 684–5
Pascall, G. 91
paternalism
  neoliberal 68, 72, 79
  professional 57, 67, 309
pathology 176, 182, 184, 186, 361, 523, 547
Paton, D. 258, 707
patriarchy 194–5, 383
pauperism 53, 56–7, 300
Pawson, R. 114, 123, 441–2, 482, 486–94
payments 69, 88–90, 122, 573
  direct 700, 703
Payne, M. 3, 374, 380, 521, 743, 747
PEARLS *see* Program to Encourage Active, Rewarding Lives for Seniors
Peck, J. 52, 61–2
Peckover, S. 679, 684, 688
peers 146, 170–1, 242, 318, 412, 559, 582
peer support 526–7, 584
perceptions 7, 20, 134–5, 162–3, 250, 431–2, 617
  subjective 20, 431, 469
performance anxiety, and New Public Management (NPM) 72–3
performance culture 218, 628, 748
performance management 5, 67–8, 73–4, 506, 650, 688
performance pressures 16, 72, 74, 76–8
Perkonigg, A. 254
Perry, P. 717

persecution 524, 567
persistent mental illnesses 176, 179, 184, 432
personality 132–3, 237, 242, 255, 431, 513, 521
personal social services 90, 330, 332, 334, 336, 650
personhood 335, 505, 520
person-in-environment 110, 178, 184, 236, 252, 543, 665
pessimism 31, 180, 599
Petrie, P. 510–11
Petticrew, M. 436, 483, 485
Petzold, H.G. 392
PGs *see* practice, guidelines
pharmacotherapy 430, 585, 592
phenomenology 134, 139, 418, 462
philanthropy 286, 329, 635, 696, 698, 708, 725
philosophical anthropology 391
philosophy 52, 56, 148–9, 156–7, 655–6, 700, 732–3
  Marxist 193
  moral 316–17, 320–1, 324, 341–2, 352
  of multiculturalism 355–6
  political 27, 83, 279–80
  social 27, 194, 197, 373, 648
physical disabilities 150, 432, 535, 550, 556
physical environment 146, 254, 331, 338, 540–1, 549, 730
physical well-being 84
  older people 534–7
Piaget, J. 392
Pickett, K. 43
Pilgrim, D. 516
Pinkerton, J. 614
Piven, F.F. 15, 58–60, 64–5, 375
placement(s) 181, 199, 216–17, 350, 542, 670
Plath, D. 410–11
Plato 316, 373, 378, 548
pluralism 237, 618, 652–3
  managed 99, 102
plurality 346–7, 349, 653
Pockett, R. 318, 661
Polanyi, K. 51–2, 55–9, 64–5, 124
police 69, 211–13, 282, 288, 584
policy advocacy 266, 576–7
policy churn 665, 670
polio 552, 558, 560
political action 31, 209, 266, 269, 277, 312, 398
political activism 2, 266, 273
political context 9, 16, 51, 140, 343, 357, 486
political economy 8, 16, 35, 55–6, 58, 63, 65
political functions 35–6, 38, 42, 58
political ideologies 9, 630, 741, 752
political neutrality 28–9, 269
political origins of social work 743–6
political philosophy 27, 83, 279–80
political rights 7, 21–2, 24–5, 27, 34, 306, 376–8
political science 11, 56, 59, 83, 296, 341, 378–9
political stability 36–7, 42, 45, 404
politicians 3, 64, 102, 302, 378, 417, 556
politicisation 565, 570–1, 577

politics 8, 10, 16, 265–6, 376–7, 486, 636–7
  and ethics 750–1
  of identity *see* identity politics
  of recognition 333–5, 339
  of redistribution 332–4, 336–7
  of social work 630, 740–52
    new directions 748–52
    return of the political 751–2
Polk, D.A. 257
polygamy 727
poor families 43, 99, 103–4, 637
Poor Laws 51, 56, 58, 743–4
Popay, J. 485–6, 489–90, 492–3
Popple, K. 209, 280, 283, 285–8
popular myths 569, 574–5
population 54, 98–100, 532–3, 566, 570–1, 574–5, 648
  growth 35, 38, 532, 573
  migrant 564–5, 567
Portugal 9, 245, 302, 572, 714
positive change skills 154
positive reinforcement 150, 167–9
positivism 149, 389, 413, 418–19, 469, 485–6, 491–3
post-Fordism 60–1
postmodernism 105, 197, 202, 413, 418, 485, 655–6
postpartum depression 412, 458
post-positivism 389, 454
postpsychiatry 526–7
post-theorists 198
post-traumatic distress 250–1, 254
post-traumatic stress disorder (PTSD) 249, 251–5, 257, 428–30, 516, 576, 587
poverty 37–9, 55–6, 94–8, 100–1, 121–2, 379–80, 475–6
  governance 16, 68, 71, 73–4
  management 67, 75, 78
  rates 39, 43, 537, 541, 574
Powell, F. 740
power 63–4, 195–7, 227, 333–4, 361–4, 473–4, 671–4
  balance of 37, 56
  differentials 397, 469, 473, 477, 662, 671
  disciplinary 74, 78, 508
  economic 42, 402–3
  hegemonic 331–3, 718
  imbalances 522, 524, 528, 665
  in interprofessional practice 671–2
  professional 161, 196, 334
  redistribution of 335, 701
  relations 82, 87, 89, 195–7, 333–5, 339, 671
  relationships 475–6, 478
practice
  contexts 109, 114, 119, 123, 171, 196–7, 201–2
  everyday 28, 123, 140, 373, 685–6, 689
  guidelines (PGs) 121, 143, 388, 415–16, 463, 475
  integration with theory 113–25
  knowledge 109, 114–15, 122–5, 685
  perspectives 110, 113–25, 710
  wisdom 124–5, 176, 208, 487, 507, 510

practitioner impairment 311–12
predictions 220, 224, 227, 230–1, 401, 685
prescriptive psychotherapy 238–9
pre-sentence reports (PSR) 600–2
prevention programming 581–3
preventive family support 507, 615, 617
preventive regulation 505, 507, 509, 511
prison 42, 248, 396, 524, 589, 598–9
prisoners 302, 589, 599
privacy 301–2, 309–10, 316, 685
private property 33, 56, 329
private sector 37, 41, 60, 69, 90, 285, 633–4
privatisation 38, 43, 72, 268, 283, 477, 638
privileged communication 302, 309–10
privileges 10, 26, 30, 99, 101, 167–8, 717–18
probabilities 31, 224, 226–30, 323
probation 162, 420, 597–602, 604–6, 609
    clients 598–9
    officers 597–9, 605–6
    services 170, 396, 426, 599, 602, 605
problem solving 3, 124, 207–8, 250–1, 256, 264, 269
    process 274, 395, 478
process model 271, 320, 411, 416–20
Prochaska, J.O 584
productivity 23, 36–7, 41–3, 45, 432, 549
professional action 394–5, 399, 402, 683, 685
professional associations 3, 70, 300, 303–4, 388, 709
professional autonomy 286, 417, 477, 613, 621, 640, 677
professional cultures 655, 689
professional development 265, 277, 472, 669, 708
    continuing 125, 664, 669
professional discretion *see* discretion
professional education *see* social work education
professional ethics *see* codes of ethics; ethics
professional expertise 3, 54, 330, 647, 662
professional identity 3, 11, 662, 671–2
professional imperialism 713, 732
professionalisation 657, 707, 726, 735
professionalism 30, 265, 270, 273, 335, 377, 746–8
    nonpolitical 630, 752
professional judgement 208, 212–13, 232–3, 447–8, 485, 494, 505
professional knowledge 395, 448, 470, 519, 657, 678
professional paternalism 309
professional power 161, 196, 334
professional qualifications *see* qualifications
professional task 218, 396, 683, 685, 688, 747–8
profitability 37, 73, 633
profits 27, 34, 36–7, 41, 44, 154, 209
Program of All-Inclusive Care of the Elderly (PACE) 542
Program to Encourage Active, Rewarding Lives for Seniors (PEARLS) 542
Progressive Era 266–7
progressive social change 98–9, 105–6, 194
progressivism 53–4

property 56, 130, 288, 364, 551, 604, 653
    private 33, 56, 329
propriety 488, 491, 494, 507, 657
pro-social behaviours 167, 169, 582
prosperity 42, 45, 264, 653
protective factors 255, 259, 435, 525, 582–3, 605, 616
protocols 232, 244, 412, 414, 460, 506, 566–7
    ethical decision-making 301, 313
providers 31, 70, 82, 311, 425, 479, 535–6
proxy outcome measures 432–4
PSR *see* pre-sentence reports
psychiatric care 180, 524 *see also* mental health
psychiatric diagnoses 148, 251–2, 517
psychiatrists 11, 161–2, 169, 299, 377, 554
psychiatry 7, 416, 516, 526
    biological 157
psychoanalysis 7, 237, 517, 521, 651
psychoanalytic theory 237, 244, 344, 656
psychodynamic approaches 117–18, 193, 239, 241–2, 244, 520–1, 671
psychological well-being 84, 121, 132, 540
psychologists 11, 300, 410, 509, 651
psychology 7, 11, 115–17, 149, 319, 415–16, 483–4
    clinical 396, 414
    ego 267, 651
psychometric outcome measures 431–2
psychopathology 255, 526
    developmental 524–5
psychosis 516, 518, 523–4
psychosocial interventions 415, 424, 431–2, 435, 445, 451, 542
psychotherapeutic integration 208, 237–8
    forms 238–44
psychotherapy 163–4, 208, 236–8, 241–2, 245, 256–7, 418
    client-directed 244
    common factors in 238
    forms of psychotherapeutic integration 238–44
    integration 237–8, 241, 245
        in the international sphere 244–5
        research on 245
    integrative *see* integrative psychotherapy
    prescriptive 238–9
    transtheoretical 245
PTSD *see* post-traumatic stress disorder
public management 192, 200, 279
    new 72–4, 117, 650, 695, 701
public policy, U-turn 37–8, 41, 44
public protection 306, 598, 602, 609
public sector 9, 54, 73, 90, 290, 336, 636–7
    workers 479, 639–40
public services 64, 285–6, 336, 479, 527, 635, 640
public utility model 648, 655
punishment 148, 150, 167, 248, 378, 599
    community 598
purposivity 488, 491–2
Putman, R. 284–5
Putnam, R. 103, 134

QDA *see* qualitative data, analysis
qualifications 51, 303, 432, 451, 572, 575, 646–7
qualitative data 426, 460, 618
  analysis (QDA) 460
qualitative inquiry *see* qualitative social work research
qualitative methodologies 396, 455, 490
qualitative methods 134, 400, 426, 454–64 *see also* qualitative social work research
qualitative social work research 162, 387, 389, 419, 454–64, 485, 489–90
  current practices 459–63
  diversity in a global context 461–2
  future 463–4
  historic evolution 455–9
  micro-, meso-, and macro-levels 458
  mixed methods 463
  rigour 460–1
  special ethical concerns 457–8
  standards for assessing quality 461
  and systematic reviews 462–3
  in value-based professional advocacy work 458–9
quality 20–1, 23–4, 461, 463, 482–5, 487–8, 490–4
  criteria 483, 488, 490–1
  extrinsic 483, 488, 490–1
  intrinsic 483, 488, 490
  standards for assessing 461
quality standards 402, 490, 492
quantitative research 457, 463, 484–5, 489–90, 492, 687
quasi-experimental research designs 388, 426–7
Queensland 648–9, 652
quotas 67, 72

race 36, 245, 333, 345–6, 360–4, 367, 715–18
racial discrimination 360, 716, 726
racial identity development 241, 243
racial superiority 716–17
racism 241–3, 358, 360–1, 363, 365–6, 559, 715–19
  see also antiracist practice; antiracist social work
  institutional 44, 615
radical behaviourism 149, 152, 157
radicalisation 732–3
radical social work 28–30, 116, 193, 332–4, 476, 696–703, 741
Raditlhokwa, L. 729
Rafferty, J. 678, 680
Ramon, S. 741, 746, 749
rampant individualism 279, 285
random assignment 410, 436
randomisation 168, 428–9, 436, 442
randomised clinical trials 245, 455, 462
randomised controlled intervention research designs 428–9
  ethical challenges 433–4
randomised controlled trials (RCTs) 409–10, 419, 436, 441–7, 451–2, 484–5, 489
Rankopo, J. 727, 732
Rapp, R. 176–9, 181–2, 184–8

Rashid, T. 183
rationality 4–6, 57, 62, 507, 528
  instrumental 4–5
  substantive 4–5
rationing 78, 319, 702
Rawls, J. 379
Razack, N. 630, 712, 715–18
RCTs *see* randomised controlled trials
Reagan, Ronald 38, 41, 67, 73
Reaganomics 33, 37, 268
realist synthesis 486, 493
Reamer, F. 295–6, 300–4, 306–7, 309–12, 320–1, 323
recessions 41–2, 97, 106, 535, 628, 632, 646–7
recidivism 416, 589, 599, 602
reciprocity 6, 86, 134, 138, 281, 316, 713
recognition 226–7, 241–2, 334–5, 347–8, 351–3, 359–60, 605–6
  ethics of 2, 335
  international 730–1
  politics of 333–5, 339
re-conceptualisation 679, 732–3
reconstruction 61, 255, 375, 684
recording 114, 131, 135, 218, 304, 311, 459–60
recovery coaches 590
recovery model 74–5
redistribution 10, 17, 328–9, 334–5, 339, 351–2, 379–80
  ethics of 328, 335
  income 36, 90
  politics of 332–4, 336–7
  of power 335, 701
  of resources 21, 35, 271
redistribution-recognition interaction 335
Reeser, L.C. 320
referral 116, 211–13, 256–7, 311, 505, 604, 688
reflective family support 510–11
reflexive practice 211–21, 364
  assumptions about decision making 213–14
  bystander effect 215–16, 218
  concurrence-seeking behaviour 217–20
  constructive controversy 217–20
  creation of safer organisations 218–20
  decision making as social process 214–15
  domain knowledge and ad hocery of decision making 216–17
reflexivity 114, 123, 212, 322, 389, 418, 486
reforms 56–7, 87, 117–20, 267–8, 635, 695, 743–4
  social 55, 95, 157, 265–7, 399, 710, 744
refugees 121, 338, 377, 461, 499–500, 564–77
refused asylum seekers 500
regulation 4–5, 8–9, 15–16, 51–4, 60, 62, 64–5
  in the abstract 52–3
  logic of 4–5
  preventive 505, 507, 509, 511
regulators 665, 667–8, 672
rehabilitation 541, 584, 589, 599, 603, 606, 609
Reichert, E. 377
Reid, W. 396, 400, 413–14, 418, 450–2, 455

reinforcement 149–50, 155, 167, 171, 238, 696
   negative 146, 167
   positive 150, 167–9
reinforcers 144, 153, 155, 588
Reisch, M. 193, 267, 273, 378–80, 458
rejection 133, 145, 212, 389, 392, 408, 744–5
relapse 227, 584, 586–7, 591
relational frame theory (RFT) 152
relationship-based practice 510–12, 605–6
relationships 161, 221, 264, 269, 305, 372, 381
   close 147, 162, 375, 380
   dual 308, 310–11
   interpersonal 43, 240, 244, 276
   oppressive 362, 364, 367
   power 475–6, 478
   social 55, 132, 195, 316, 378–9, 382, 432
   therapeutic 152, 182, 237, 239, 242, 367, 680
relatives 28, 91, 136, 138–9, 258, 311
relevance, cultural 724, 729–30, 732–3
religion 22, 26, 285, 296, 346, 363–4, 515–16 see also church
replicability 174, 412, 414, 483
reporting 138, 266, 311, 321, 375, 435, 443
representation 41, 151, 271, 333–4, 378, 490, 710
   politics of 333–4
repression 26, 237, 521
reproduction 22, 24, 334, 337, 397, 500
Republic of Ireland see Ireland
reputational risk 232
research
   advocacy 389, 397–8
   capacity 650, 656–7
   and codes of ethics 312
   interviews 74, 447, 670
   multimethod 389, 449, 464
   processes 393, 401, 467–8, 470, 473–4, 476, 478
   quantitative 457, 463, 484–5, 489–90, 492, 687
   synthesis 389, 492–3
   users 397, 490, 492, 495
residence 133, 256, 285, 565
   habitual 566–7
residential schools 329, 711
residential treatment 169–70, 412
residents 133, 145–6, 280, 288–90, 429, 535, 541
   local 139, 287–8, 290
resilience 145, 243, 254–6, 258–9, 289, 331, 345
   factors 230–1, 251
resistance 26, 28, 31, 78, 332–3, 418, 479
resource acquisition model 176, 178
resource allocation 46, 98, 134, 188, 312, 319, 700
resources 21–6, 82–4, 98–100, 178–9, 181, 271–3, 620–2
   community 147, 181, 581, 588, 622
   external 103, 184, 259
   material 25, 83, 257, 378, 380, 382
   redistribution of 21, 35, 271
   scarce 403, 476, 620
   social 179, 181, 254, 336–7, 364, 378

respondents 138, 145, 249, 266, 307, 535
responsibilities 20–2, 24–5, 89–91, 378–9, 559, 569–70, 673–4
   ethical 304–5, 309, 317, 319, 364, 509
   personal 215, 323, 380
responsiveness 86, 321, 343, 600, 736
responsivity
   general 603
   specific 603
restorative justice 608
retirement 420, 575, 729
   incomes 43, 535, 575
retrenchment 38, 41, 43, 61, 96, 479, 621–2
revenues 28, 35, 38, 282
RFT see relational frame theory
rhetoric 44, 267, 336, 365, 475, 484, 598
Ricardo, D. 56–7
Richmond, M. 7, 69, 165, 400
Ridzi, F. 72, 75–6
Riessman, C.K. 455–6, 462
rights
   disability 197, 551, 556, 559–61
   economic 34, 376, 378, 380, 648
   political 7, 21–2, 24–5, 27, 34, 306, 376–8
rigour 389, 397, 427, 433, 436, 463, 488–9
   methodological 491, 519, 621
   qualitative social work research 460–1
risk assessment 208, 322, 499, 501, 519, 600–2, 604
   see also risk management
   accuracy of risk prediction 229–30
   actuarial 226, 228, 685
   analytic v intuitive 225–9
   and decision making 224–33
   role within case management 230–1
   unrealistic expectations 231–2
risk aversion 233, 609
risk factors 224, 226, 231, 254, 434–5, 601, 607–8
   dynamic 434, 601, 605
risk management 7, 9, 199–201, 225, 230, 232, 505
   and codes of ethics 307–9
   creation of fair culture for 232–3
   rise 225
risk-need-responsivity (RNR) 602–3
risk prediction 229
   accuracy 229–30
risk society 225, 231, 233, 505, 508
Ritter, J. 266
rituals 242, 244, 650, 710
RNR see risk-need-responsivity
Roberts, E. 700
Roberts, H. 485
Robinson, G. 601
Robinson, J. 503
Rogers, A. 516
Rogers, B. 96
Rogers, C.R. 521
role blurring 671, 673
role models 75, 504, 553, 559

Romm, N. 398
Ronen, T. 156
Roper, C. 527
Rothman, J. 320, 425–6
routinisation 684–5
Rubin, R.E. 45
Ruch, G. 117, 512
rule of law 282, 374
Russia 302, 403, 570

Saadawi, Nawal El 714
Sackett, D.L. 408–9, 519
safeguards 129, 424, 631, 639, 743
safer organisations, creation 218–20
safety 5–6, 56, 110, 124, 132, 135, 199
Safran, J.D. 237
Saini, M. 462
Saleebey, D. 183–4, 652
samples 133, 139, 228, 230, 341, 429, 436
sample size 414, 435
sanctions 26, 43, 67, 71–2, 74, 76, 307
Satisfaction With Life (SWL) 431
Saville, J. 743
Sayce, L. 525
Scandinavia *see* Nordic countries
scapegoating 233, 513, 616, 751
Schilling, R.F. 425
schizophrenia 156, 179, 185, 445, 517, 554
Schön, D. 123, 218, 455, 476
school attendance 104, 431, 607
schools of social work 277, 364, 467, 651–2, 655–6, 709, 724
Schram, S.F. 16, 44, 71–2, 748
Schultz, T.W. 103
Schumpeterian workfare state 60–1
Schwandt, T. 491
science 156–7, 302, 374, 391–5, 404, 417–18, 516
and knowledge 391–2
Science and Technology Studies (STS) 677, 679
scientific knowledge 12, 394, 399–401, 404, 477
scientific research 392–4
Scotland 213, 411, 444, 602, 640, 740–1
Scourfield, P. 633
SCRs *see* Serious Case Reviews
scrutiny 87, 177, 218, 289, 318, 454, 483
Searson, L. 367
security 4–6, 8, 20, 51, 53, 63, 505
economic 36, 41, 539
logic of 4–8
Seedhouse, D. 319
Seers, D. 98
Segal, U.A. 342, 500, 565
self 7, 86, 115, 149, 151, 255, 509
self-actualisation 20, 269, 350, 521–2
self-awareness 324, 362, 364, 455, 558
self-determination 199, 274, 309, 332, 345, 556–7, 651–2
self-determined life-conduct 394

self-disclosure 243–4, 311
self-efficacy 152, 239–40, 255–6, 542, 587
self-esteem 64, 122, 255, 474, 516, 525, 557
low 520, 554
parental 434
self-harm 225, 310, 430, 526, 618
self-help 43, 64, 424, 476, 588, 615, 699
self-identity 20, 334, 557, 606
self-interest 27, 33, 44, 295, 299, 319, 569
selfishness 21, 26–7, 29, 183, 353
self-knowledge 114–15, 124–5
self-reflection 521, 558
self-regulating market 55–6, 58
self-regulation 5, 52, 586
capacities 585, 587
self-reports 144, 146–7, 149, 230
self-sufficiency 69–70, 77, 87, 329, 346, 556
self-wounds, tacit 239–40
semiotisation 684
Sen, A. 84, 98, 101, 652–3
sensitivity 342, 457, 462, 484, 491
cultural 321, 357, 360–3, 368
sentencing 598–601, 608
SEPI *see* Society for the Exploration of Psychotherapy Integration
Serious Case Reviews (SCRs) 211, 213, 215
service delivery 201, 286–7, 310–11, 334, 336, 362, 364
service-user groups 3, 389, 499, 629, 699
service-user involvement 2, 475, 488, 616, 693–704
competing strands of social work 696–8
emergence 693–4
emergence of service-user movements 699–701
historical ambiguity of social work 695–6
social work reform 694–5
state-led involvement 701–2
service-user movements 286, 448, 500, 628, 696, 702–4
emergence 699–701
service-user organisations 700–1, 703
service users 121–5, 194–201, 230–3, 335–9, 398–403, 447–9, 693–704
Sesink, W. 684
Settlement Grants Programme (SGP) 573
Settlement House movement 192, 266, 374, 379, 725
settlement movement 192–3, 267, 330, 375, 743
SEU *see* Social Exclusion Unit
Sevenhuijsen, S. 86, 89, 345
sex 22, 162, 296, 381, 444, 555
sexism 25, 44, 192, 270, 551, 558
sexual abuse 163, 165, 168, 199, 254–5, 412, 522
sexual exploitation 567
sexuality 346, 348, 381, 516, 521, 523
sexual orientation 122, 363, 500, 531, 534, 547, 555
and physical well-being in older people 536–7
SGP *see* Settlement Grants Programme
Shalev, A.Y. 254
Shardlow, S. 303–4

shared experiences 281, 557
shared lack 209, 279, 281–2, 290
Sharland, E. 11, 389, 482, 489, 491, 661–4, 666, 674
Shaw, I. 400, 457, 487–8, 491, 686
Sheehan Disability Scale 428
Sheldon, B. 156, 483
shelter 7, 181, 248–9, 255, 259, 376, 570
Sheppard, M. 114, 122–5, 449, 456
Sherraden, M. 104
Shlonsky, A. 229, 462, 617
Shoesmith, S. 211, 220
Shohat, E. 717
Shulman, L.S. 12
Shyne, A.W. 450, 452
Sidler, N. 395
Simon, H. 226
Simon, J. 598–9, 609
Simpson, L.C. 689
Simpson, M. 553
Sin, R. 734, 745
single-loop learning 218
single parents 117, 164, 534, 614, 618–19
  unsupported 121–2
single-payer system 264–5
SIR *see* Social Intervention Research
situated learning 664
situatedness of social work 8–10
skilled nursing facilities (SNFs) 535, 537, 540–1
skills 114–15, 119–22, 144–8, 154–6, 273–7, 316–18, 666–7
  base 114, 119, 125, 510
  development 115, 124–5, 619
  framework 113–15
Skinner, B.F. 149, 151, 456
Skolbekken, J.-A. 520
slavery 23, 26, 183, 373, 522, 551, 742
slogans 150, 225, 484, 556
SLT *see* social learning theory
slums 329, 712, 728
smoking 410, 535–6, 585
SNFs *see* skilled nursing facilities
social action 82, 265–8, 287, 312, 346, 616, 679
social activism 99, 266, 286, 735
social capital 99, 103, 134, 254, 279–80, 284–6, 329
  bridging 329
  decline in 284–5
social care 11, 303–4, 484–5, 633–5, 661–2, 666, 668–9
  knowledges 482–3, 488
  workers 303–4, 634
social change 16, 28, 38, 98–9, 268–9, 335–6, 487–8
  agent of 267–8
  progressive 98–9, 105–6, 194
social class 21, 117, 269, 346, 504, 534
  and physical well-being in older people 537
social cohesion 46, 285, 741

social construction 338, 367, 513, 524, 718
  of deviant identities 503
  of reality 237
  of whiteness 718
social constructionism 344, 364, 368, 468, 510, 522–5
social context 6, 20, 171, 499, 524, 583, 628
social control 24, 26, 44, 77, 192, 195–6, 361
  overt 196, 201
social Darwinism 516, 549
social democracy 59, 346, 505, 633
social development 3, 15, 17, 19, 28–9, 714–15, 729–30
  approach 94–5, 98, 106, 576
  features and principles 97–100
  historical evolution 95–7
  interventions 95, 100, 102–5
  limitations and prospects 105–6
  strategies 100–2
  and welfare 94–106
social diagnosis 7, 165
social diversity 309
social divisions 83, 85, 286, 331, 333, 622
social efficiency 650
social embeddedness 605, 679
social entrepreneurship 654
social environment 19, 55, 111, 184–6, 267, 336, 506
social evolution 21–3, 28, 95, 149
social exclusion 6, 122, 365, 395, 520, 616, 681
Social Exclusion Unit (SEU) 279, 285
social groups 24–6, 82, 334, 566, 743, 749
  dominant 330, 335
social inclusion 285, 337, 345, 366, 396, 475, 491
social inequalities 83, 338, 711, 715
social injustice 19, 22–4, 27, 188, 324, 333, 523
  emergence and spread 24–7
social institutions 20–1, 31, 82, 88, 270, 344, 531
social integration 185, 360, 500
social interaction 138, 165, 281, 338, 351, 363, 522
Social Intervention Research (SIR) 425, 431, 436–7
socialisation 20, 22, 24, 26, 254, 583, 664
social isolation 121–2, 136, 254, 445, 537, 619
socialist ideologies 102, 329, 332
social justice 1–2, 19–21, 23–4, 27–9, 192, 269–70, 296–7
  definitions 378
  and human rights 372–84
    origins of social work's core values 373–6
    problems of integration 380–2
    questions for theory and practice 383
  meanings 20–2
  model of social work 28–31
social learning theory (SLT) 151–2, 237, 417, 586
social liberalism 99
social life 8, 23, 86, 200, 280, 383, 508–9
socially constructed categories, deconstruction 337–8
socially just communities, and human nature 22–3
social models 3, 500, 551–2, 555, 558, 561, 702–3

social movements 28, 30–1, 34–5, 193–4, 332–4, 741–2, 751
social networks 103, 110, 133–6, 138, 346, 572, 579
social norms 82, 360, 582–3, 592, 619
social oppression 192–4, 199
social order 5–6, 29, 38, 59–60, 193, 195, 477
social pedagogy 3, 399–400, 511, 616, 708
social philosophy 27, 194, 197, 373, 648
social policy systems 19, 23, 90
  universal dimensions 23–4
social practices 62, 82, 146, 344, 381, 511, 688
social processes 12, 178, 185, 196, 214, 220, 346
social reform 55, 95, 157, 265–7, 399, 710, 744
social relations 20, 23, 59, 329, 331–5, 337, 339
social relationships 55, 132, 195, 316, 378–9, 382, 432
social resources 179, 181, 254, 336–7, 364, 378
social sciences 2, 4, 54, 483–4, 488, 716, 725
social security 28, 38, 82, 87, 120, 268, 574–5
social services 43, 70, 95–6, 179–80, 288–9, 653–4, 696–7
  personal 90, 330, 332, 334, 336, 650
social structures 30, 82, 337, 377, 379–80, 382, 615
Social Structures of Accumulation (SSA) 34–5, 37
social support 6, 83, 121, 135–6, 187, 254–6, 351
  networks 3, 208, 586
social systems 170, 192, 241, 254, 269, 356, 475
social totality 193, 195
social transformation 192, 194, 202, 273, 745
social welfare 17, 63–5, 97, 105–6, 411–12, 714–15, 741–2
social well-being 84, 94, 106, 431, 504, 531
  older people 538–9
social work *see Introductory Note and detailed entries*
Social Work Action Network (SWAN) 477, 698, 703
social work education 220, 268–9, 472, 646–58, 723–6, 728–33, 744–5
  and capability 652–3
  future for 655–7
  growth/expansion 648, 744–6
  and innovation 653–5
  welfare state legacy 647–8
social work research
  as advocacy 397–8
  agenda 387, 391–404, 682
  approaches to 391–7
  on changes in the life-world and conditions of life of citizens and service users 402
  cluster randomised controlled intervention designs 429
  distinctive features 395–7
  experimental designs 428
  futures 401–4
  kinds and quality 486–94
  knowledge and science 391–2
  on large-scale social problems 402
  non-randomised controlled intervention designs 427
  observational designs 426–7
  over time 398–9
  on professional action and social work professionals 402–3
  qualitative *see* qualitative social work research
  randomised controlled intervention designs 428–9, 433
  research in and on social work 394–5
  scientific research 392–4
  on social work organisations within social policy 403
  utilisation 399–401
social work roles 3, 171, 200, 267, 286–7, 448, 539
Social Work Task Force (SWTF) 121, 233, 635
social worlds 117, 398, 444, 505, 508, 510, 687
Society for the Exploration of Psychotherapy Integration (SEPI) 237
sociology 11, 97, 115–17, 389, 396, 513, 725–6
Socrates 316, 373
software 218, 460, 679–80, 682–5, 688
  design 682, 689
Solas, J. 379–80, 383
soldiers 253–4, 550, 560, 566
Solesbury, W. 484, 486, 490
solidarity 10, 26–7, 101, 284, 346, 475, 560
solution-focused therapy 110, 165–6
Somerville, P. 284–5
Sommerfeld, P 387, 395
South Africa 266, 282, 411, 598, 630, 726–7, 729–31
sovereignty 51, 63, 613
Soviet Union 96, 570, 598
spaces 30, 62, 65, 83, 249, 333, 367
  children's 510–11
  dialogical 218–20
Spain 9, 302, 569, 580
Spandler, H. 518
Specht, H. 269
specialisms 2, 40, 194, 214, 216, 233, 451
specific responsivity 603
Speenhamland laws 55, 57–8
Spender, D. 333, 335
spina bifida 552, 554, 558
spirituality 245, 335, 615
Spivak, G.C. 719
spouses 132, 156, 249, 538
SRs *see* systematic reviews
SSA *see* Social Structures of Accumulation
stability 36–7, 42, 45, 132, 404, 504, 537
staffing patterns 74–5
stakeholders 389, 401–2, 471, 618, 639, 657–8, 687
  actor 665, 671
  employer 668, 670
  external 667, 669
standardisation 506, 647, 685, 687, 697
standards 74, 94–5, 103–6, 232, 305–10, 312–13, 461–2
  ethical *see* ethical standards
  quality 402, 490, 492
Stannard, R. 187
statecraft 53–4, 61, 63
stateless persons 568

state regulation theory 55, 60–2, 65
status quo 27–9, 31, 270–1, 380, 470, 649, 654–5
Staub-Bernasconi, S. 377
Stedman Jones, G. 329, 696, 744
stepfathers 162–3, 165–6, 168, 199
stereotyping 91, 277, 552–3, 558, 560, 700
Stern Report 571
Steuart, Sir J. 52–3
Steyaert, J. 678, 680
stigma 59, 178, 185, 444, 508, 699–700
stigmatisation 43, 145, 181, 335, 519, 698
stock markets 45–6, 631
Stoesz, D. 101, 628–9, 647–51, 655–6, 709
strangers 23–4, 86, 329, 344, 550, 648, 740
Strauss, A.L. 455
street-level bureaucracy 16, 61, 67–79, 686
strengths assessments 182–4, 186, 188
strengths-based case management 179, 181–2, 184, 187
strengths-based practice 177, 180, 182, 184–5
strengths model 176–7, 179–82, 187–8
 assumptions and principles 178–82
 effectiveness 187–8
strengths perspective 110, 176–88, 476, 651
 historical overview 177–82
 key elements of strengths-based helping process 182–8
stress 43, 45, 100, 122, 135–6, 168, 251
 acute *see* acute stress disorder (ASD)
 post-traumatic *see* post-traumatic stress disorder (PTSD)
stressors 241, 249–52, 523
Striker, G. 238, 241, 244–5
Stroman, D.E. 553
structural adjustment programmes 34, 96–7, 282, 714
structural family therapy 163–5, 168
structural inequalities 134, 181, 209, 290, 331, 337, 362
structural violence 21
STS *see* Science and Technology Studies
subjective judgements 69, 75
subjective perceptions 20, 431, 469
subjectivity 62, 64, 281, 345, 717
sub-Saharan Africa 283, 630
substance abuse 121, 164–5, 168, 171, 312, 539, 587–90 *see also* drugs
substantive rationality 4–5
substitution strategy 337–8
subsumption, logic of 684–5
suicides 231, 248, 254, 257, 557, 581, 618
Sullivan, P. 110
Sullivan, W.P. 181–2, 184
Sundar, P. 296–7, 355–6, 367
superego 521
supervision 77, 119, 125, 169, 310–11, 411, 599
supervisors 28, 76, 144, 169, 305, 311, 559
supply-side economics 33, 37, 45
support

emotional 135, 137–8, 256, 538
 networks 118, 135–6, 139, 539, 587
Sure Start 10, 499, 614
surveillance 42, 68–9, 506, 508, 608, 634, 681
survival 22, 59, 63, 94, 149, 533, 565
survivor perspectives 525
survivors 198, 200, 397, 525, 699, 747
 mental health 194, 197, 522
sustainability 106, 591, 627–8
Sutton, C. 520–1, 617
SWAN *see* Social Work Action Network
Sweden 34, 88, 284, 302, 411, 507, 571–2
Switzerland 170, 245, 302, 403, 533, 572
SWL *see* Satisfaction With Life
SWTF *see* Social Work Task Force
symptomatology 187, 591
synthesis 425, 462–3, 483, 485, 490, 492–3
 process 493–4
 realist 486, 493
 research 389, 492–3
systematic reviews (SRs) 167–8, 174, 388–90, 412–13, 418–19, 445, 482–95
 characteristics, context, and contest 483–6
 kinds and quality of social work research 486–94
 and qualitative social work research 462–3
 ways forward 494–5
systemic family therapy 164
Szasz, T. 157, 524

tacit knowledge 114–15, 124
tacit self-wounds 239–40
Taiwan 725–6, 735
Tajfel, H. 671
TANF *see* Temporary Assistance for Needy Families
Tanzania 550, 726, 728
TAPUPAS framework 482–3, 488, 490–3
taxes 37–9, 42, 45, 82, 87, 336, 573
taxpayers 336, 657–8
Taylor, B.J. 2, 388, 424, 432, 434, 436, 463, 482, 484
Taylor, I. 629, 666, 669–70, 672, 700
Taylor, J. 184
TCs *see* therapeutic communities
teacher education 668–9
teachers 129, 145–6, 150, 168, 341, 408, 667–8
team managers 216–17, 219
technical eclecticism *see* technical integration
technical integration 237–9
technicization 679
technological innovation 677, 679, 681, 688
technologies, new *see* new technologies
teenage parents 117, 412
Temporary Assistance for Needy Families (TANF) 71
temporary labour migrants 565
termination of services 309, 311
terminology 251, 265, 269, 397, 419, 426, 701–2
Terranova, T. 10
territories 10–13, 22, 62, 712, 725, 727
terror, war on 359, 715, 749–50

terrorism 21, 356, 428–9
terrorists 337, 571
tertiary education 649, 668–9
Texas 565, 574, 648
textbooks 323, 398, 455, 462–3, 731
thematic development 389, 459–60
theoretical integration 238–41
theoretical knowledge 123–5
 domain 115–19
theory and practice integration 113–25
therapeutic alliances 238–9, 244, 409, 435
therapeutic communities (TCs) 584, 589
therapeutic relationships 152, 182, 237, 239, 242, 367, 680
therapists 69, 164, 169–70, 237–40, 244, 447, 588
 primary 182, 187
third-generation rights 376–7
Thomas, E.J. 425–6
Thomas, P. 526
threats 37, 78, 200, 250, 254, 358, 743–4
 perceived 250, 360
thresholds 120, 211, 216, 432, 454, 616, 619
 arousal 143, 146, 153
Thyer, B.A. 149, 152, 156, 388, 401, 410–11, 413–14, 416, 483, 485–6, 490
Tilda Goldberg Centre 452
Tilley, N. 441
timeliness 483, 488, 591
timepiece metaphor 52
TIP see Treatment Improvement Protocol
TP see transtheoretical psychotherapy
transformation, social 192, 194, 202, 273, 745
transformational/transformative practice see empowering and transformative practice
transformers 209, 273–6
transtheoretical psychotherapy (TP) 245
treatment fostercare 168–9, 412
Treatment Improvement Protocol (TIP) 586–7
Trevithick, P. 2, 109, 114, 117, 119–20, 125, 317
Tronto, J.C. 86, 342–5, 348
truth 113, 181, 197, 201–2, 342, 344, 392–3
Tsang, A.K. 713, 734–5
Tunisia 569–70, 726
Turkey 282, 302
Turner, W. 171, 430

UKATT see United Kingdom Alcohol Treatment Trial
UN see United Nations
unaccompanied children 566–7, 571
underclass 636–7
underlying causes 153
UNDESA see United Nations (UN), Department of Economic and Social Affairs
UNDP see United Nations (UN), Development Programme
unemployment 27–8, 37, 58, 289–90, 616–17, 638–9, 744

UNESCO see United Nations (UN), Educational, Scientific, and Cultural Organization
unethical conduct 300, 302, 305–6
UNGIFT see United Nations (UN), Global Initiative to Fight Human Trafficking
UNHCR see United Nations (UN), High Commissioner for Refugees
UNICEF see United Nations (UN), Children's Fund
United Kingdom see Britain
United Kingdom Alcohol Treatment Trial (UKATT) 446–7
United Nations (UN) 96–7, 375, 532–3, 548, 551–2, 708–10, 724
 Children's Fund (UNICEF) 96, 375, 709
 Department of Economic and Social Affairs (UNDESA) 565–7
 Development Programme (UNDP) 283, 552
 Educational, Scientific, and Cultural Organization (UNESCO) 710
 Global Initiative to Fight Human Trafficking (UNGIFT) 567
 High Commissioner for Refugees (UNHCR) 565–70
 Office on Drugs and Crime (UNODC) 567–8, 580
 Relief and Rehabilitation Administration (UNRRA) 709
 Relief and Works Agency (UNRWA) 567–8, 570–1
 World Food Programme (UNWFP) 283
United States 33–5, 266–8, 300–2, 304–5, 356–60, 533–4, 572–5
 Census Bureau 35–6, 38–40, 43, 533–4, 536–7, 631
 Council on Social Work Education 555, 711
 economy 33, 40, 631
 households 36, 39, 45, 575
 multiculturalism 358
 Texas 565, 574, 648
 welfare state 34–5, 52, 647
Universal Declaration of Human Rights 34, 297, 306, 375, 569
universalisation 723, 734
universalism 98–9, 342
universality 212, 707, 714
unjust societies 21, 27, 361, 363
UNODC see United Nations (UN), Office on Drugs and Crime
unpaid work 90–1, 599
UNRRA see United Nations (UN), Relief and Rehabilitation Administration
UNRWA see United Nations (UN), Relief and Works Agency
unsupported single parents 121–2
UNWFP see United Nations (UN), World Food Programme
USA see United States
user involvement 398, 693–4, 699–703
user research 397–8
users 123, 331, 394–5, 397–8, 525–6, 669, 674
utilitarianism 373, 375
utility 83, 123, 176, 178, 182, 188, 488–92

validation 323, 334, 469, 472
validity 105, 408, 410, 418, 420, 432, 478
  external 410, 430, 432–3, 435, 437
  internal 388, 432–3, 461, 490
value dimensions 21, 24, 317, 321
value neutrality 28–9, 747
values
  cultural 146, 241–2, 360, 534, 677
  dominant 24, 27, 29
VanderWaal, C.J. 589
van Rooyen, C. 468–9, 478
Vanstone, M. 597–8
Varela, F.J. 219, 221
Venn, C. 10
Verba, S. 266
victims 30, 215, 230–1, 252, 258, 567–8, 608–9
  of human trafficking 566–8, 571
video 460, 472–4, 559
Vietnam 37, 268
violence 27, 63, 104, 209, 227, 229, 249
  domestic 199–200, 377, 383, 412, 420, 504, 526
  structural 21
virtue ethics 319, 321, 347–8, 351, 742, 750–1
visas 567–8
visual disabilities/impairments 547, 552–3, 560
voluntarism 52, 64, 286, 539
voluntary migrants 566, 569, 571, 575
voluntary professional associations 300, 303–4
voluntary social work associations 302, 306
volunteering 275–6, 285
volunteers 186, 212–13, 259, 284, 403, 413, 540
vouchers 268, 588
vulnerability 6–9, 45, 58, 130, 145, 346, 518–20
vulnerable adults 5, 660
vulnerable children 635–6
vulnerable groups 99, 102, 139

Wachtel, P.L. 241, 244
Wacquant, L.J.D. 58, 61, 68, 598, 609
wages 36, 41–2, 44, 57, 62, 103, 633
waiting list control groups 429–30
Waldron, H.B. 171
Wales *see* England and wales
Walker, S. 501, 511, 614–16, 618–19, 621
Wang, S. 744–6
Ward, D. 602–3, 605–6
Warner, A.G. 413
Warner, J. 518–19
war on terror 359, 715, 749–50
Wass, P. 728
watch mechanism 52, 55
watchmender 54, 65
water 249, 254–5, 376, 565, 570–1
wealth 10, 13, 21–2, 44–6, 56, 63, 283
  transfer of 16, 46
Webb, S.A. 2–3, 5–6, 8, 10, 225, 267, 280–2, 307, 325, 328–30, 335, 339, 345, 347–8, 351–2, 366–7, 411, 416–17, 445, 448, 486,

505, 508, 519, 601, 609, 682–4, 688, 707–8, 719, 724, 733, 744, 751
Weber, M. 4–5
Weedon, C. 717
Weizsäcker, C.F. 392
welfare
  definition and conceptualisation 82–5
  and gender 81–92
  and immigrants 574–6
  reform 38, 65, 67, 70–4, 76–7, 629, 695
  and social development 94–106
  systems 72–3, 99, 332, 352, 575, 606, 608
welfare benefits 60, 124, 574, 639
welfare case management 72–3, 78
  historical perspective 68–71
  new 71–2
  and discretion 68, 75–8
welfare governance 15–16, 67
  beginnings 53–4
  and governmentality 62–4
  historical institutionalism 58–60
  modalities 51–65
  Polanyi's great transformation 55–8
  regulation in the abstract 52–3
  state regulation theory 55, 60–2, 65
welfare professionals 16, 68–9, 71, 73, 75, 77, 79
  and street-level bureaucrats 67–79
welfare state 15, 33–8, 40, 59–61, 82–3, 647–8, 743
  and 20th century economic crises 34–8
  Keynesian 34, 51–2, 60–1, 65, 67
  neoliberal *see* neoliberal welfare state
  overview of approach to gender, welfare and care 86–9
welfare-to-work programmes 42, 70, 74, 76–8, 285, 629
welfarism 15, 19–31, 51, 62, 599
well-being 19–20, 81–6, 91–2, 98–101, 134–6, 250, 349–50
  of children 9, 131, 214, 412
  mental *see* mental well-being
  physical *see* physical well-being
  psychological 84, 121, 132, 540
  social *see* social well-being
Western Europe 33–4, 87–8, 357–8, 581
Wetherell, M. 522
Whaley, A. 364
wheelchairs 548, 552, 558, 560
Whig approaches 741–4
White, S. 2, 208, 634
White Australia policy 358
white middle class 35–6, 60
whiteness 717–18
  social construction of 718
Whitmore, E. 462, 717
Whittaker, J.K. 136
WHO *see* World Health Organisation
wholeness 183, 208, 236

wicked problems 486, 492
Wilkinson, R. 43, 85
Williams, F. 341, 343, 345–6, 348–50, 698
Wintersteen, R. 176, 178–9, 187
Witkin, S.L. 403, 414, 418
Wodarski, J. 156
Wolfe, B.E. 239
Wolfensberger, W. 553
women 81–2, 85–92, 332–4, 341–2, 352, 377, 536–8
　see also gender
　pregnant 337, 580, 727
Wood, A. 161–2, 165, 171
work-based learning 668
workfare 60–1, 650
workforce 53, 288, 634, 640, 667–8
　children's 214, 663, 667, 669
working alliances 687, 689
working class 743–4, 751

workplace 31, 303, 395, 634, 670, 698
World Bank 34, 96–7, 101, 282–3, 547, 657, 714
World Health Organisation (WHO) 248, 375, 523, 532, 548, 581, 661
Wright Mills, C. 109, 741
Wronka, J. 376–7

xenophobia 366, 402, 564, 614, 638
Xiong, Y. 733, 744–6

Yeatman, A. 198, 650
YJB *see* Youth Justice Board
young children 68, 87–8, 121, 139, 431, 474, 615
youth justice 600, 606–8
Youth Justice Board (YJB) 600

Zambia 726
Zimbabwe 726

HV 40 .S24 2012

The Sage handbook of social work